القرآن الكريم

THE HOLY QUR'AN

Arabic Text with
English Translation
Abdullah Yusuf Ali
with a Brief Index of Subjects

Revised Modern English Edition
Dr. S.M. Bleher

IDCI
Islamic Dawah Centre International

First edition printed 2023

ISBN 978-1-910432-06-8

English Translation Revised by Dr. Sahib Mustaqim Bleher

Although initially produced in the early parts of the last century, Pickthall's translation remains a favourite with many English readers of the Qur'an. To improve the readability of the text, the translation has been carefully adapted by Dr S.M. Bleher, replacing some of the more archaic terms with those in current usage without generally altering the flow and register of the original work.

Utmost care has been taken to produce this present print without any typographical errors. However, we do request readers to please inform us if any errors are found so that future reprints can be corrected.

Published by:
IDCI - Islamic Dawah Centre International
Birmingham, UK
Tel: 0121 327 2277 | Web: www.idci.co.uk
Registered Charity No. 1092139

Typeset and cover design by IBS Bookstores, India
Printed by Mega Print in Türkiye

About The Translator

On April 4, 1872 A.C. 1289 A.H., 'Abdullah Yusuf 'Ali was born in a family of the Sunni Bohra community in Surat, India. His father, a merchant, was a very religious man who made sure that his son learned the Qur'an before anything else. Upon the completion of young 'Abdullah's committing the entire Qur'an to memory, his father celebrated the occasion with a grand banquet, thus showing to his son the importance of his achievement and the importance of the Qur'an. In addition to studying contemporary knowledge at school, 'Abdullah continued to receive lessons in Arabic language and never ceased in his studies of the Qur'an. He was a superior student who excelled in academic achievement and won the much coveted Indian Civil Service Award, a prestigious honour resulting from the extremely competitive entrance examinations for high positions in the Indian Civil Service which wealthy families would aspire for their sons to receive. 'Abdullah was easily able to absorb English Literature and was considered to be among the best of his fellow countrymen in writing English. Many of the most well-known scholarly magazines in India published his works and expressed their appreciation for his beautiful literary style. Later 'Abdullah left India for Europe and visited many European capitals and eventually resided in London for a considerable period of time. While in London, he was exposed to many translations of the Qur'an and continued to have a tremendous interest in it and its studies. He then began to closely study the Qur'an giving special attention to its various interpretations, both old and new. After studying what was written about the Qur'an in both European and Eastern languages, he returned to India and took up new residence in Lahore where he became the Dean of the Islamic College. He then began his monumental work of translating and commenting on the Qur'an which after many years of work was completed on his 65th birthday. 'Abdullah Yusuf 'Ali later died in London on December 10. 1953 A.C.1372 A.H.

Table of Contents

Editor's Introduction

The Qur'an is no ordinary book. To Muslims it is the eternal word of God (Allah), dictated to the prophet Muhammad - peace be with him - via the angel Gabriel (*Jibreel*). Originally revealed in Arabic, its style is unrivalled, its language eloquent, its meaning deep. It is beyond any translation to render all this richness of expression in another language. Yet, the Qur'an is primarily a book of guidance and must, therefore, be accessible to those who seek the truth contained in it. Whilst a translation cannot be an authoritative replacement of the original, it can make the meaning of its verses available to a non-Arabic speaking readership.

The verses (*Ayahs*) of the Qur'an were revealed throughout the 23 years of prophet Muhammad's prophethood, often in connection with events of the time. They were then memorised, recorded in writing, collected and arranged into chapters (*Surahs*). Within those verses we find narratives describing the creation of the world from earliest times or recounting the missions of earlier prophets, we come across general exhortation to belief and righteous conduct, we are given the tools and principles for reflection and sound judgement in a multitude of life's situations, and we receive detailed rulings on important aspects of criminal and civil law. Thus the Qur'an is not only a text of inspiration but also the foundation of the legal and social structure of Islamic society.

The text of the Qur'an has not changed since the days the prophet Muhammad - peace be with him - received this revelation, yet its content retains its relevance, validity and dynamics and continues to inspire believers of every generation as well as challenge the status quo of human society. The convincing observations of the Qur'an which, after all, are a communication from our Maker, are a powerful call to action and a rebuttal of complacency. They appeal to both the mind and the heart of the reader or listener, they call for justice and compassion, they decry and defy falsehood, pretence and oppression. They represent an uncomfortable truth for those who would like to banish the courage of one's conviction and do not want us to use our intellect and power of reflection to guide us along our path in life.

Although produced nearly a century ago, Yusuf Ali's translation of the meaning of the Holy Qur'an has not lost its power of conveyance. In spite of the difficulties of finding suitable equivalents between the expressions of a Semitic language like Arabic and a Roman language like English, the translator has taken every care to produce a fluent and rich representation of the message of the Qur'an whilst retaining as much of its poetry and eloquence as possible. His first translation was published side by side with the Arabic text and with an extensive commentary. This edition is based on the revised text produced by the Young Muslims (YM) in which some of the more archaic terms have been replaced by modern equivalents. This text was then checked and carefully revised once more by Dr Sahib Mustaqim Bleher on behalf of IDCI.

سُورَةُ الفَاتِحَةِ

Surah 1: **Al-Fatihah** (The Opening)

1. In the name of Allah,
Most Gracious, Most Merciful.

بِسْمِ ٱللَّهِ ٱلرَّحْمَٰنِ ٱلرَّحِيمِ ﴿١﴾

2. Praise be to Allah the Cherisher and Sustainer of the Worlds;

ٱلْحَمْدُ لِلَّهِ رَبِّ ٱلْعَٰلَمِينَ ﴿٢﴾

3. Most Gracious, Most Merciful;

ٱلرَّحْمَٰنِ ٱلرَّحِيمِ ﴿٣﴾

4. Master of the Day of Judgement.

مَٰلِكِ يَوْمِ ٱلدِّينِ ﴿٤﴾

5. You do we worship, and Your aid we seek.

إِيَّاكَ نَعْبُدُ وَإِيَّاكَ نَسْتَعِينُ ﴿٥﴾

6. Show us the straight way,

ٱهْدِنَا ٱلصِّرَٰطَ ٱلْمُسْتَقِيمَ ﴿٦﴾

7. The way of those on whom You have bestowed Your Grace, those whose (portion) is not wrath, and who go not astray.

صِرَٰطَ ٱلَّذِينَ أَنْعَمْتَ عَلَيْهِمْ غَيْرِ ٱلْمَغْضُوبِ
عَلَيْهِمْ وَلَا ٱلضَّآلِّينَ ﴿٧﴾

سُورَةُ البَقَرَةِ

Surah 2: **Al-Baqarah** (The Heifer)

In the name of Allah,
Most Gracious, Most Merciful.

بِسْمِ ٱللَّهِ ٱلرَّحْمَٰنِ ٱلرَّحِيمِ

1. *Alif Lam Mim.*

الٓمٓ ﴿١﴾

2. This is the book; in it is guidance sure, without doubt, to those who fear Allah;

ذَٰلِكَ ٱلْكِتَٰبُ لَا رَيْبَ ۛ فِيهِ ۛ هُدًى لِّلْمُتَّقِينَ ﴿٢﴾

3. Who believe in the unseen, are steadfast in prayer, and spend out of what We have provided for them;

ٱلَّذِينَ يُؤْمِنُونَ بِٱلْغَيْبِ وَيُقِيمُونَ ٱلصَّلَوٰةَ وَمِمَّا رَزَقْنَٰهُمْ
يُنفِقُونَ ﴿٣﴾

4. And who believe in the revelation sent to you, and sent before your time, and (in their hearts) have the assurance of the Hereafter.

وَٱلَّذِينَ يُؤْمِنُونَ بِمَآ أُنزِلَ إِلَيْكَ وَمَآ أُنزِلَ مِن قَبْلِكَ
وَبِٱلْءَاخِرَةِ هُمْ يُوقِنُونَ ﴿٤﴾

5. They are on (true) guidance from their Lord, and it is these who will prosper.

أُوْلَٰٓئِكَ عَلَىٰ هُدًى مِّن رَّبِّهِمْۖ وَأُوْلَٰٓئِكَ هُمُ
ٱلْمُفْلِحُونَ ﴿٥﴾

6. As to those who reject faith, it is the same to them whether you warn them or do not warn them; they will not believe.

إِنَّ ٱلَّذِينَ كَفَرُواْ سَوَآءٌ عَلَيْهِمْ ءَأَنذَرْتَهُمْ أَمْ لَمْ
تُنذِرْهُمْ لَا يُؤْمِنُونَ ﴿٦﴾

7. Allah has set a seal on their hearts and on their hearing, and on their eyes is a veil; great is the penalty they (incur).

خَتَمَ ٱللَّهُ عَلَىٰ قُلُوبِهِمْ وَعَلَىٰ سَمْعِهِمْۖ وَعَلَىٰٓ
أَبْصَٰرِهِمْ غِشَٰوَةٌۖ وَلَهُمْ عَذَابٌ عَظِيمٌ ﴿٧﴾

8. Of the people there are some who say: "We believe in Allah and the last day"; but they do not (really) believe.

وَمِنَ ٱلنَّاسِ مَن يَقُولُ ءَامَنَّا بِٱللَّهِ وَبِٱلْيَوْمِ
ٱلْءَاخِرِ وَمَا هُم بِمُؤْمِنِينَ ﴿٨﴾

9. They would like to deceive Allah and those who believe, but they only deceive themselves and realise (it) not!

يُخَٰدِعُونَ ٱللَّهَ وَٱلَّذِينَ ءَامَنُواْ وَمَا يَخْدَعُونَ
إِلَّآ أَنفُسَهُمْ وَمَا يَشْعُرُونَ ﴿٩﴾

10. In their hearts is a disease; and Allah has increased their disease; and grievous is the penalty they (incur), because they are false (to themselves).

فِي قُلُوبِهِم مَّرَضٌ فَزَادَهُمُ ٱللَّهُ مَرَضًاۖ وَلَهُمْ
عَذَابٌ أَلِيمٌۢ بِمَا كَانُواْ يَكْذِبُونَ ﴿١٠﴾

11. When it is said to them: "Make not mischief on the earth," they say: "Why, we only want to make peace!"

وَإِذَا قِيلَ لَهُمْ لَا تُفْسِدُواْ فِي ٱلْأَرْضِ قَالُوٓاْ إِنَّمَا نَحْنُ
مُصْلِحُونَ ﴿١١﴾

12. Certainly, they are the ones who make mischief, but they realise (it) not.

أَلَآ إِنَّهُمْ هُمُ ٱلْمُفْسِدُونَ وَلَٰكِن لَّا يَشْعُرُونَ ﴿١٢﴾

13. When it is said to them: "Believe as the others believe:" they say: "Shall we believe as the fools believe?" - Nay, certainly they are the fools, but they do not know.

وَإِذَا قِيلَ لَهُمْ ءَامِنُواْ كَمَآ ءَامَنَ ٱلنَّاسُ قَالُوٓاْ
أَنُؤْمِنُ كَمَآ ءَامَنَ ٱلسُّفَهَآءُۗ أَلَآ إِنَّهُمْ هُمُ ٱلسُّفَهَآءُ
وَلَٰكِن لَّا يَعْلَمُونَ ﴿١٣﴾

14. When they meet those who believe, they say: "We believe"; but when they are alone with their evil ones, they say: "We are really with you, we (were) only jesting."

وَإِذَا لَقُوا۟ ٱلَّذِينَ ءَامَنُوا۟ قَالُوٓا۟ ءَامَنَّا وَإِذَا خَلَوْا۟ إِلَىٰ
شَيَٰطِينِهِمْ قَالُوٓا۟ إِنَّا مَعَكُمْ إِنَّمَا نَحْنُ مُسْتَهْزِءُونَ ١٤

15. Allah will throw back their mockery on them, and give them rope in their trespasses; so they will wander like blind ones (to and fro).

ٱللَّهُ يَسْتَهْزِئُ بِهِمْ وَيَمُدُّهُمْ فِى طُغْيَٰنِهِمْ
يَعْمَهُونَ ١٥

16. These are they who have bartered guidance for error: but their traffic is profitless, and they have lost true direction.

أُو۟لَٰٓئِكَ ٱلَّذِينَ ٱشْتَرَوُا۟ ٱلضَّلَٰلَةَ بِٱلْهُدَىٰ فَمَا
رَبِحَت تِّجَٰرَتُهُمْ وَمَا كَانُوا۟ مُهْتَدِينَ ١٦

17. Their similitude is that of a man who kindled a fire; when it lighted all round him, Allah took away their light and left them in utter darkness, so they could not see.

مَثَلُهُمْ كَمَثَلِ ٱلَّذِى ٱسْتَوْقَدَ نَارًا فَلَمَّآ أَضَآءَتْ
مَا حَوْلَهُۥ ذَهَبَ ٱللَّهُ بِنُورِهِمْ وَتَرَكَهُمْ فِى ظُلُمَٰتٍ
لَّا يُبْصِرُونَ ١٧

18. Deaf, dumb and blind, they will not return (to the path).

صُمٌّۢ بُكْمٌ عُمْىٌ فَهُمْ لَا يَرْجِعُونَ ١٨

19. Or (another similitude) is that of a rain-laden cloud from the sky: in it are zones of darkness, and thunder and lightning, they press their fingers in their ears to keep out the stunning thunderclap, the while they are in terror of death. But Allah is ever round the rejecters of faith!

أَوْ كَصَيِّبٍ مِّنَ ٱلسَّمَآءِ فِيهِ ظُلُمَٰتٌ وَرَعْدٌ وَبَرْقٌ
يَجْعَلُونَ أَصَٰبِعَهُمْ فِىٓ ءَاذَانِهِم مِّنَ ٱلصَّوَٰعِقِ
حَذَرَ ٱلْمَوْتِ ۚ وَٱللَّهُ مُحِيطٌۢ بِٱلْكَٰفِرِينَ ١٩

20. The lightning all but snatches away their sight; every time the light (helps) them, they walk in it, and when the darkness grows on them, they stand still. And if Allah willed, He could take away their faculty of hearing and seeing; for Allah has power over all things.

يَكَادُ ٱلْبَرْقُ يَخْطَفُ أَبْصَٰرَهُمْ ۖ كُلَّمَآ أَضَآءَ لَهُم
مَّشَوْا۟ فِيهِ وَإِذَآ أَظْلَمَ عَلَيْهِمْ قَامُوا۟ ۚ وَلَوْ شَآءَ ٱللَّهُ
لَذَهَبَ بِسَمْعِهِمْ وَأَبْصَٰرِهِمْ ۚ إِنَّ ٱللَّهَ عَلَىٰ كُلِّ
شَىْءٍ قَدِيرٌ ٢٠

21. O you people! Adore your Guardian-Lord, Who created you and those who came before you, that you may become righteous,

يَٰٓأَيُّهَا ٱلنَّاسُ ٱعۡبُدُواْ رَبَّكُمُ ٱلَّذِى خَلَقَكُمۡ
وَٱلَّذِينَ مِن قَبۡلِكُمۡ لَعَلَّكُمۡ تَتَّقُونَ ٢١

22. Who has made the earth your couch, and the heaven your canopy; and sent down rain from the heaven; and brought out with it fruits for your sustenance; then set not up rivals to Allah when you know (the truth).

ٱلَّذِى جَعَلَ لَكُمُ ٱلۡأَرۡضَ فِرَٰشٗا وَٱلسَّمَآءَ بِنَآءٗ
وَأَنزَلَ مِنَ ٱلسَّمَآءِ مَآءٗ فَأَخۡرَجَ بِهِۦ مِنَ ٱلثَّمَرَٰتِ
رِزۡقٗا لَّكُمۡۖ فَلَا تَجۡعَلُواْ لِلَّهِ أَندَادٗا وَأَنتُمۡ
تَعۡلَمُونَ ٢٢

23. And if you are in doubt as to what We have revealed from time to time to Our servant, then produce a Surah like it; and call your witnesses or helpers (if there are any) besides Allah, if your (doubts) are true.

وَإِن كُنتُمۡ فِى رَيۡبٖ مِّمَّا نَزَّلۡنَا عَلَىٰ عَبۡدِنَا فَأۡتُواْ
بِسُورَةٖ مِّن مِّثۡلِهِۦ وَٱدۡعُواْ شُهَدَآءَكُم مِّن
دُونِ ٱللَّهِ إِن كُنتُمۡ صَٰدِقِينَ ٢٣

24. But if you cannot - and certainly you cannot - then fear the fire whose fuel is men and stones - which is prepared for those who reject faith.

فَإِن لَّمۡ تَفۡعَلُواْ وَلَن تَفۡعَلُواْ فَٱتَّقُواْ ٱلنَّارَ ٱلَّتِى
وَقُودُهَا ٱلنَّاسُ وَٱلۡحِجَارَةُۖ أُعِدَّتۡ لِلۡكَٰفِرِينَ ٢٤

25. But give glad tidings to those who believe and work righteousness, that their portion is gardens, beneath which rivers flow. Every time they are fed with fruits from it, they say: "Why, this is what we were fed with before," for they are given things in similitude; and they have in it companions pure (and holy); and they remain in it (forever).

وَبَشِّرِ ٱلَّذِينَ ءَامَنُواْ وَعَمِلُواْ ٱلصَّٰلِحَٰتِ أَنَّ
لَهُمۡ جَنَّٰتٖ تَجۡرِى مِن تَحۡتِهَا ٱلۡأَنۡهَٰرُۖ كُلَّمَا
رُزِقُواْ مِنۡهَا مِن ثَمَرَةٖ رِّزۡقٗا قَالُواْ هَٰذَا ٱلَّذِى
رُزِقۡنَا مِن قَبۡلُۖ وَأُتُواْ بِهِۦ مُتَشَٰبِهٗاۖ وَلَهُمۡ فِيهَآ
أَزۡوَٰجٞ مُّطَهَّرَةٞۖ وَهُمۡ فِيهَا خَٰلِدُونَ ٢٥

26. Allah disdains not to use the similitude of things, lowest as well as highest. Those who believe know that it is truth from their Lord; but those who reject faith say: "What means Allah by this similitude?" By it He causes many to

ربع الحزب ١
۞إِنَّ ٱللَّهَ لَا يَسۡتَحۡيِۦٓ أَن يَضۡرِبَ مَثَلٗا مَّا بَعُوضَةٗ
فَمَا فَوۡقَهَاۚ فَأَمَّا ٱلَّذِينَ ءَامَنُواْ فَيَعۡلَمُونَ أَنَّهُ
ٱلۡحَقُّ مِن رَّبِّهِمۡۖ وَأَمَّا ٱلَّذِينَ كَفَرُواْ فَيَقُولُونَ
مَاذَآ أَرَادَ ٱللَّهُ بِهَٰذَا مَثَلٗاۘ يُضِلُّ بِهِۦ كَثِيرٗا

stray, and many He leads into the right path; but He causes not to stray, except those who forsake (the path) -

وَيَهۡدِي بِهِۦ كَثِيرٗاۚ وَمَا يُضِلُّ بِهِۦٓ إِلَّا
ٱلۡفَٰسِقِينَ ٢٦

27. Those who break Allah's covenant after it is ratified, and who break what Allah has ordered to be joined, and do mischief on earth: these cause loss (only) to themselves.

ٱلَّذِينَ يَنقُضُونَ عَهۡدَ ٱللَّهِ مِنۢ بَعۡدِ مِيثَٰقِهِۦ
وَيَقۡطَعُونَ مَآ أَمَرَ ٱللَّهُ بِهِۦٓ أَن يُوصَلَ وَيُفۡسِدُونَ
فِي ٱلۡأَرۡضِۚ أُوْلَٰٓئِكَ هُمُ ٱلۡخَٰسِرُونَ ٢٧

28. How can you reject the faith in Allah? - Seeing that you were without life, and He gave you life; then will He cause you to die, and will again bring you to life; and again to Him will you return.

كَيۡفَ تَكۡفُرُونَ بِٱللَّهِ وَكُنتُمۡ أَمۡوَٰتٗا
فَأَحۡيَٰكُمۡۖ ثُمَّ يُمِيتُكُمۡ ثُمَّ يُحۡيِيكُمۡ ثُمَّ إِلَيۡهِ
تُرۡجَعُونَ ٢٨

29. It is He who has created for you all things that are on earth; then He turned to the heaven and made them into seven firmaments. And of all things He has perfect knowledge.

هُوَ ٱلَّذِي خَلَقَ لَكُم مَّا فِي ٱلۡأَرۡضِ جَمِيعٗا
ثُمَّ ٱسۡتَوَىٰٓ إِلَى ٱلسَّمَآءِ فَسَوَّىٰهُنَّ سَبۡعَ
سَمَٰوَٰتٖۚ وَهُوَ بِكُلِّ شَيۡءٍ عَلِيمٞ ٢٩

30. Behold, your Lord said to the angels: "I will create a vicegerent on earth." They said: "Will You place in it one who will make mischief in it and shed blood? - Whilst we do celebrate Your praises and glorify Your holy (name)?" He said: "I know what you know not."

وَإِذۡ قَالَ رَبُّكَ لِلۡمَلَٰٓئِكَةِ إِنِّي جَاعِلٞ فِي ٱلۡأَرۡضِ
خَلِيفَةٗۖ قَالُوٓاْ أَتَجۡعَلُ فِيهَا مَن يُفۡسِدُ فِيهَا وَ
يَسۡفِكُ ٱلدِّمَآءَ وَنَحۡنُ نُسَبِّحُ بِحَمۡدِكَ وَنُقَدِّسُ
لَكَۖ قَالَ إِنِّيٓ أَعۡلَمُ مَا لَا تَعۡلَمُونَ ٣٠

31. And He taught Adam the names of all things; then He placed them before the angels, and said: "Tell Me the names of these if you are right."

وَعَلَّمَ ءَادَمَ ٱلۡأَسۡمَآءَ كُلَّهَا ثُمَّ عَرَضَهُمۡ عَلَى
ٱلۡمَلَٰٓئِكَةِ فَقَالَ أَنۢبِـُٔونِي بِأَسۡمَآءِ هَٰٓؤُلَآءِ
إِن كُنتُمۡ صَٰدِقِينَ ٣١

32. They said: "Glory to You: of knowledge we have none, save what You have taught us: in truth it is You who are perfect in knowledge and wisdom."

قَالُواْ سُبۡحَٰنَكَ لَا عِلۡمَ لَنَآ إِلَّا مَا عَلَّمۡتَنَآۖ إِنَّكَ أَنتَ
ٱلۡعَلِيمُ ٱلۡحَكِيمُ ٣٢

33. He said: "O Adam! Tell them their names." When he had told them their names, Allah said: "Did I not tell you that I know the secrets of heaven and earth, and I know what you reveal and what you conceal?"

قَالَ يَـٰٓـَٔادَمُ أَنۢبِئْهُم بِأَسْمَآئِهِمْ ۖ فَلَمَّآ أَنۢبَأَهُم
بِأَسْمَآئِهِمْ قَالَ أَلَمْ أَقُل لَّكُمْ إِنِّىٓ أَعْلَمُ غَيْبَ
ٱلسَّمَـٰوَٰتِ وَٱلْأَرْضِ وَأَعْلَمُ مَا تُبْدُونَ وَمَا كُنتُمْ
تَكْتُمُونَ ﴿٣٣﴾

34. And behold, We said to the angels: "Bow down to Adam," and they bowed down: not so Iblis, he refused and was haughty, he was of those who reject faith.

وَإِذْ قُلْنَا لِلْمَلَـٰٓئِكَةِ ٱسْجُدُوا۟ لِـَٔادَمَ فَسَجَدُوٓا۟ إِلَّآ
إِبْلِيسَ أَبَىٰ وَٱسْتَكْبَرَ وَكَانَ مِنَ ٱلْكَـٰفِرِينَ ﴿٣٤﴾

35. And We said: "O Adam! Dwell you and your wife in the garden; and eat of the bountiful things in it as (where and when) you will; but approach not this tree, or you shall run into harm and transgression."

وَقُلْنَا يَـٰٓـَٔادَمُ ٱسْكُنْ أَنتَ وَزَوْجُكَ ٱلْجَنَّةَ وَكُلَا
مِنْهَا رَغَدًا حَيْثُ شِئْتُمَا وَلَا تَقْرَبَا هَـٰذِهِ ٱلشَّجَرَةَ
فَتَكُونَا مِنَ ٱلظَّـٰلِمِينَ ﴿٣٥﴾

36. Then did Satan make them slip from the (garden), and get them out of the state (of felicity) in which they had been. And We said: "Get you down, all (you people), with enmity between yourselves. On earth will be your dwelling place and your means of livelihood - for a time."

فَأَزَلَّهُمَا ٱلشَّيْطَـٰنُ عَنْهَا فَأَخْرَجَهُمَا مِمَّا كَانَا فِيهِ ۖ
وَقُلْنَا ٱهْبِطُوا۟ بَعْضُكُمْ لِبَعْضٍ عَدُوٌّ ۖ وَلَكُمْ فِى
ٱلْأَرْضِ مُسْتَقَرٌّ وَمَتَـٰعٌ إِلَىٰ حِينٍ ﴿٣٦﴾

37. Then learnt Adam from his Lord words of inspiration, and his Lord turned toward him; for He is Oft-Returning, Most Merciful.

فَتَلَقَّىٰٓ ءَادَمُ مِن رَّبِّهِۦ كَلِمَـٰتٍ فَتَابَ عَلَيْهِ ۚ إِنَّهُۥ
هُوَ ٱلتَّوَّابُ ٱلرَّحِيمُ ﴿٣٧﴾

38. We said: "Get you down all from here: and if, as is sure, there comes to you guidance from Me, whosoever follows My guidance, on them shall be no fear, nor shall they grieve.

قُلْنَا ٱهْبِطُوا۟ مِنْهَا جَمِيعًا ۖ فَإِمَّا يَأْتِيَنَّكُم مِّنِّى هُدًى
فَمَن تَبِعَ هُدَاىَ فَلَا خَوْفٌ عَلَيْهِمْ وَلَا هُمْ
يَحْزَنُونَ ﴿٣٨﴾

39. "But those who reject faith and belie Our signs, they shall be companions of the fire; they shall remain in it."

وَٱلَّذِينَ كَفَرُواْ وَكَذَّبُواْ بِـَٔايَٰتِنَآ أُوْلَٰٓئِكَ أَصۡحَٰبُ
ٱلنَّارِۖ هُمۡ فِيهَا خَٰلِدُونَ ٣٩

40. O Children of Israel call to mind the (special) favour which I bestowed upon you, and fulfil your covenant with Me as I fulfil My covenant with you, and fear none but Me.

يَٰبَنِيٓ إِسۡرَٰٓءِيلَ ٱذۡكُرُواْ نِعۡمَتِيَ ٱلَّتِيٓ أَنۡعَمۡتُ عَلَيۡكُمۡ
وَأَوۡفُواْ بِعَهۡدِيٓ أُوفِ بِعَهۡدِكُمۡ وَإِيَّٰيَ فَٱرۡهَبُونِ ٤٠

41. And believe in what I reveal, confirming the revelation which is with you, and be not the first to reject faith in it, nor sell My signs for a small price; and fear Me, and Me alone.

وَءَامِنُواْ بِمَآ أَنزَلۡتُ مُصَدِّقٗا لِّمَا مَعَكُمۡ وَلَا تَكُونُوٓاْ
أَوَّلَ كَافِرِۭ بِهِۦۖ وَلَا تَشۡتَرُواْ بِـَٔايَٰتِي ثَمَنٗا قَلِيلٗا
وَإِيَّٰيَ فَٱتَّقُونِ ٤١

42. And cover not truth with falsehood, nor conceal the truth when you know (what it is).

وَلَا تَلۡبِسُواْ ٱلۡحَقَّ بِٱلۡبَٰطِلِ وَتَكۡتُمُواْ ٱلۡحَقَّ وَأَنتُمۡ
تَعۡلَمُونَ ٤٢

43. And be steadfast in prayer; practice regular charity; and bow down your heads with those who bow down (in worship).

وَأَقِيمُواْ ٱلصَّلَوٰةَ وَءَاتُواْ ٱلزَّكَوٰةَ وَٱرۡكَعُواْ
مَعَ ٱلرَّٰكِعِينَ ٤٣

44. Do you enjoin right conduct on the people, and forget (to practice it) yourselves? And yet you study the scripture? Will you not understand?

نصف الحزب ١
۞أَتَأۡمُرُونَ ٱلنَّاسَ بِٱلۡبِرِّ وَتَنسَوۡنَ أَنفُسَكُمۡ وَ
أَنتُمۡ تَتۡلُونَ ٱلۡكِتَٰبَۚ أَفَلَا تَعۡقِلُونَ ٤٤

45. Nay, seek (Allah's) help with patient perseverance and prayer: it is indeed hard, except to those who bring a humble spirit -

وَٱسۡتَعِينُواْ بِٱلصَّبۡرِ وَٱلصَّلَوٰةِۚ وَإِنَّهَا لَكَبِيرَةٌ إِلَّا عَلَى
ٱلۡخَٰشِعِينَ ٤٥

46. Who bear in mind the certainty that they are to meet their Lord, and that they are to return to Him.

ٱلَّذِينَ يَظُنُّونَ أَنَّهُم مُّلَٰقُواْ رَبِّهِمۡ وَأَنَّهُمۡ إِلَيۡهِ
رَٰجِعُونَ ٤٦

47. O Children of Israel! Call to mind the (special) favour which I bestowed upon You, and that I preferred you to all others (for My message).

يَٰبَنِيٓ إِسۡرَٰٓءِيلَ ٱذۡكُرُواْ نِعۡمَتِيَ ٱلَّتِيٓ أَنۡعَمۡتُ عَلَيۡكُمۡ
وَأَنِّي فَضَّلۡتُكُمۡ عَلَى ٱلۡعَٰلَمِينَ ٤٧

48. Then guard yourselves against a day when one soul shall not benefit another nor shall intercession be accepted for her, nor shall compensation be taken from her, nor shall anyone be helped (from outside).

وَٱتَّقُوا۟ يَوْمًا لَّا تَجْزِى نَفْسٌ عَن نَّفْسٍ شَيْـًٔا وَلَا
يُقْبَلُ مِنْهَا شَفَـٰعَةٌ وَلَا يُؤْخَذُ مِنْهَا عَدْلٌ وَلَا هُمْ
يُنصَرُونَ ﴿٤٨﴾

49. And remember, We delivered you from the people of Pharaoh: they set you hard tasks and punishments, slaughtered your sons and let your womenfolk live; in it was a tremendous trial from your Lord.

وَإِذْ نَجَّيْنَـٰكُم مِّنْ ءَالِ فِرْعَوْنَ يَسُومُونَكُمْ
سُوٓءَ ٱلْعَذَابِ يُذَبِّحُونَ أَبْنَآءَكُمْ وَيَسْتَحْيُونَ
نِسَآءَكُمْ ۚ وَفِى ذَٰلِكُم بَلَآءٌ مِّن رَّبِّكُمْ عَظِيمٌ ﴿٤٩﴾

50. And remember We divided the sea for you and saved you and drowned Pharaoh's people within your very sight.

وَإِذْ فَرَقْنَا بِكُمُ ٱلْبَحْرَ فَأَنجَيْنَـٰكُمْ وَأَغْرَقْنَآ ءَالَ
فِرْعَوْنَ وَأَنتُمْ تَنظُرُونَ ﴿٥٠﴾

51. And remember We appointed forty nights for Moses, and in his absence you took the calf (for worship), and you did grievous wrong.

وَإِذْ وَٰعَدْنَا مُوسَىٰٓ أَرْبَعِينَ لَيْلَةً ثُمَّ ٱتَّخَذْتُمُ
ٱلْعِجْلَ مِنۢ بَعْدِهِۦ وَأَنتُمْ ظَـٰلِمُونَ ﴿٥١﴾

52. Even then We did forgive you, there was a chance for you to be grateful.

ثُمَّ عَفَوْنَا عَنكُم مِّنۢ بَعْدِ ذَٰلِكَ لَعَلَّكُمْ
تَشْكُرُونَ ﴿٥٢﴾

53. And remember We gave Moses the scripture and the criterion (between right and wrong), there was a chance for you to be guided aright.

وَإِذْ ءَاتَيْنَا مُوسَى ٱلْكِتَـٰبَ وَٱلْفُرْقَانَ لَعَلَّكُمْ
تَهْتَدُونَ ﴿٥٣﴾

54. And remember Moses said to his people: "O my people! You have indeed wronged yourselves by your worship of the calf: so turn (in repentance) to your Maker, and slay yourselves (the wrong-doers); that will be better for you in the sight of your Maker." Then He turned towards you (in forgiveness): for He is Oft-Returning, Most Merciful.

وَإِذْ قَالَ مُوسَىٰ لِقَوْمِهِۦ يَـٰقَوْمِ إِنَّكُمْ ظَلَمْتُمْ أَنفُسَكُم
بِٱتِّخَاذِكُمُ ٱلْعِجْلَ فَتُوبُوٓا۟ إِلَىٰ بَارِئِكُمْ فَٱقْتُلُوٓا۟
أَنفُسَكُمْ ذَٰلِكُمْ خَيْرٌ لَّكُمْ عِندَ بَارِئِكُمْ
فَتَابَ عَلَيْكُمْ ۚ إِنَّهُۥ هُوَ ٱلتَّوَّابُ ٱلرَّحِيمُ ﴿٥٤﴾

55. And remember you said: "O Moses! We shall never believe in you until we see Allah manifestly," but you were dazed by thunder and lightning even as you looked on.

وَإِذْ قُلْتُمْ يَٰمُوسَىٰ لَن نُّؤْمِنَ لَكَ حَتَّىٰ نَرَى ٱللَّهَ
جَهْرَةً فَأَخَذَتْكُمُ ٱلصَّٰعِقَةُ وَأَنتُمْ تَنظُرُونَ ﴿٥٥﴾

56. Then We raised you up after your death; you had the chance to be grateful.

ثُمَّ بَعَثْنَٰكُم مِّنۢ بَعْدِ مَوْتِكُمْ لَعَلَّكُمْ تَشْكُرُونَ ﴿٥٦﴾

57. And We gave you the shade of clouds and sent down to you manna and quails, saying: "Eat of the good things We have provided for you:" (but they rebelled); to Us they did no harm, but they harmed their own souls.

وَظَلَّلْنَا عَلَيْكُمُ ٱلْغَمَامَ وَأَنزَلْنَا عَلَيْكُمُ ٱلْمَنَّ
وَٱلسَّلْوَىٰ ۖ كُلُوا۟ مِن طَيِّبَٰتِ مَا رَزَقْنَٰكُمْ ۚ وَمَا
ظَلَمُونَا وَلَٰكِن كَانُوٓا۟ أَنفُسَهُمْ يَظْلِمُونَ ﴿٥٧﴾

58. And remember We said: "Enter this town, and eat of the plenty in it as you wish; but enter the gate with humility, in posture and in words, and We shall forgive you your faults and increase (the portion of) those who do good."

وَإِذْ قُلْنَا ٱدْخُلُوا۟ هَٰذِهِ ٱلْقَرْيَةَ فَكُلُوا۟ مِنْهَا
حَيْثُ شِئْتُمْ رَغَدًا وَٱدْخُلُوا۟ ٱلْبَابَ سُجَّدًا
وَقُولُوا۟ حِطَّةٌ نَّغْفِرْ لَكُمْ خَطَٰيَٰكُمْ ۚ
وَسَنَزِيدُ ٱلْمُحْسِنِينَ ﴿٥٨﴾

59. But the transgressors changed the word from that which had been given them; so We sent on the transgressors a plague from heaven, for that they infringed (Our command) repeatedly.

فَبَدَّلَ ٱلَّذِينَ ظَلَمُوا۟ قَوْلًا غَيْرَ ٱلَّذِى قِيلَ لَهُمْ
فَأَنزَلْنَا عَلَى ٱلَّذِينَ ظَلَمُوا۟ رِجْزًا مِّنَ ٱلسَّمَآءِ بِمَا
كَانُوا۟ يَفْسُقُونَ ﴿٥٩﴾

60. And remember Moses prayed for water for his people; We said: "Strike the rock with your staff." Then gushed out from it twelve springs. Each group knew its own place for water. So eat and drink of the sustenance provided by Allah. And do no evil nor mischief on the (face of the) earth.

ثلاثة أرباع الحزب ١

۞ وَإِذِ ٱسْتَسْقَىٰ مُوسَىٰ لِقَوْمِهِۦ فَقُلْنَا ٱضْرِب
بِّعَصَاكَ ٱلْحَجَرَ ۖ فَٱنفَجَرَتْ مِنْهُ ٱثْنَتَا عَشْرَةَ
عَيْنًا ۖ قَدْ عَلِمَ كُلُّ أُنَاسٍ مَّشْرَبَهُمْ ۖ كُلُوا۟ وَٱشْرَبُوا۟
مِن رِّزْقِ ٱللَّهِ وَلَا تَعْثَوْا۟ فِى ٱلْأَرْضِ مُفْسِدِينَ ﴿٦٠﴾

61. And remember you said: "O Moses! We cannot endure one kind of food (always); so ask your Lord for us to produce for us of what the earth grows - its pot-herbs, and cucumbers, its garlic, lentils, and onions." He said: "Will you exchange the better for the worse? Go you down to any town, and you shall find what you want!" They were covered with humiliation and misery; they drew on themselves the wrath of Allah. This because they went on rejecting the signs of Allah and slaying His prophets without just cause. This because they rebelled and went on transgressing.

وَإِذْ قُلْتُمْ يَٰمُوسَىٰ لَن نَّصْبِرَ عَلَىٰ طَعَامٍ وَٰحِدٍ
فَٱدْعُ لَنَا رَبَّكَ يُخْرِجْ لَنَا مِمَّا تُنۢبِتُ ٱلْأَرْضُ
مِنۢ بَقْلِهَا وَقِثَّآئِهَا وَفُومِهَا وَعَدَسِهَا وَبَصَلِهَاۖ
قَالَ أَتَسْتَبْدِلُونَ ٱلَّذِى هُوَ أَدْنَىٰ بِٱلَّذِى هُوَ
خَيْرٌۚ ٱهْبِطُوا۟ مِصْرًا فَإِنَّ لَكُم مَّا سَأَلْتُمْۗ وَضُرِبَتْ
عَلَيْهِمُ ٱلذِّلَّةُ وَٱلْمَسْكَنَةُ وَبَآءُو بِغَضَبٍ مِّنَ
ٱللَّهِۗ ذَٰلِكَ بِأَنَّهُمْ كَانُوا۟ يَكْفُرُونَ بِـَٔايَٰتِ ٱللَّهِ
وَيَقْتُلُونَ ٱلنَّبِيِّـۧنَ بِغَيْرِ ٱلْحَقِّۗ ذَٰلِكَ بِمَا عَصَوا۟
وَّكَانُوا۟ يَعْتَدُونَ ﴿٦١﴾

62. Those who believe (in the Qur'an), and those who follow the Jewish (scriptures), and the Christians and the Sabians - any who believe in Allah and the last day, and work righteousness, shall have their reward with their Lord; on them shall be no fear, nor shall they grieve.

إِنَّ ٱلَّذِينَ ءَامَنُوا۟ وَٱلَّذِينَ هَادُوا۟ وَٱلنَّصَٰرَىٰ
وَٱلصَّٰبِـِٔينَ مَنْ ءَامَنَ بِٱللَّهِ وَٱلْيَوْمِ ٱلْءَاخِرِ وَعَمِلَ
صَٰلِحًا فَلَهُمْ أَجْرُهُمْ عِندَ رَبِّهِمْ وَلَا خَوْفٌ عَلَيْهِمْ
وَلَا هُمْ يَحْزَنُونَ ﴿٦٢﴾

63. And remember We took your covenant and We raised above you (the towering height) of mount (Sinai) (saying): "Hold firmly to what We have given you and bring (ever) to remembrance what is in it: perhaps you may fear Allah."

وَإِذْ أَخَذْنَا مِيثَٰقَكُمْ وَرَفَعْنَا فَوْقَكُمُ ٱلطُّورَ
خُذُوا۟ مَآ ءَاتَيْنَٰكُم بِقُوَّةٍ وَٱذْكُرُوا۟ مَا فِيهِ
لَعَلَّكُمْ تَتَّقُونَ ﴿٦٣﴾

64. But you turned back after that; had it not been for the grace and mercy of Allah to you, you had surely been among the lost.

ثُمَّ تَوَلَّيْتُم مِّنۢ بَعْدِ ذَٰلِكَۖ فَلَوْلَا فَضْلُ ٱللَّهِ عَلَيْكُمْ
وَرَحْمَتُهُۥ لَكُنتُم مِّنَ ٱلْخَٰسِرِينَ ﴿٦٤﴾

65. And well you knew those amongst you who transgressed in the matter of the Sabbath; We said to them: "Be you apes, despised and rejected."

وَلَقَدْ عَلِمْتُمُ ٱلَّذِينَ ٱعْتَدَوْا۟ مِنكُمْ فِى ٱلسَّبْتِ
فَقُلْنَا لَهُمْ كُونُوا۟ قِرَدَةً خَٰسِـِٔينَ ﴿٦٥﴾

66. So We made it an example to their own time and to their posterity, and a lesson to those who fear Allah.

فَجَعَلْنَٰهَا نَكَٰلًا لِّمَا بَيْنَ يَدَيْهَا وَمَا خَلْفَهَا وَ
مَوْعِظَةً لِّلْمُتَّقِينَ ٦٦

67. And remember Moses said to his people: "Allah commands that you sacrifice a heifer." They said: "Do you make a laughing-stock of us?" He said: "Allah save me from being an ignorant (fool)!"

وَإِذْ قَالَ مُوسَىٰ لِقَوْمِهِۦٓ إِنَّ ٱللَّهَ يَأْمُرُكُمْ أَن
تَذْبَحُوا۟ بَقَرَةً ۖ قَالُوٓا۟ أَتَتَّخِذُنَا هُزُوًا ۖ قَالَ أَعُوذُ
بِٱللَّهِ أَنْ أَكُونَ مِنَ ٱلْجَٰهِلِينَ ٦٧

68. They said: "Ask on our behalf your Lord to make plain to us what (heifer) it is!" He said: "He says: the heifer should be neither too old nor too young, but of medium age: now do what you are commanded!"

قَالُوا۟ ٱدْعُ لَنَا رَبَّكَ يُبَيِّن لَّنَا مَا هِىَ ۚ قَالَ إِنَّهُۥ يَقُولُ
إِنَّهَا بَقَرَةٌ لَّا فَارِضٌ وَلَا بِكْرٌ عَوَانٌۢ بَيْنَ
ذَٰلِكَ ۖ فَٱفْعَلُوا۟ مَا تُؤْمَرُونَ ٦٨

69. They said: "Ask on our behalf your Lord to make plain to us her colour." He said: "He says: a fawn-coloured heifer, pure and rich in tone, the admiration of onlookers!"

قَالُوا۟ ٱدْعُ لَنَا رَبَّكَ يُبَيِّن لَّنَا مَا لَوْنُهَا ۚ قَالَ إِنَّهُۥ
يَقُولُ إِنَّهَا بَقَرَةٌ صَفْرَآءُ فَاقِعٌ لَّوْنُهَا تَسُرُّ
ٱلنَّٰظِرِينَ ٦٩

70. They said "Ask on our behalf your Lord to make plain to us what she is: to us are all heifers alike: we wish indeed for guidance if Allah wills."

قَالُوا۟ ٱدْعُ لَنَا رَبَّكَ يُبَيِّن لَّنَا مَا هِىَ إِنَّ ٱلْبَقَرَ تَشَٰبَهَ
عَلَيْنَا وَإِنَّآ إِن شَآءَ ٱللَّهُ لَمُهْتَدُونَ ٧٠

71. He said: "He says: a heifer not trained to till the soil or water the fields; sound and without blemish." They said: "Now have you brought the truth." Then they offered her in sacrifice but not with goodwill.

قَالَ إِنَّهُۥ يَقُولُ إِنَّهَا بَقَرَةٌ لَّا ذَلُولٌ تُثِيرُ ٱلْأَرْضَ
وَلَا تَسْقِى ٱلْحَرْثَ مُسَلَّمَةٌ لَّا شِيَةَ فِيهَا ۚ قَالُوا۟
ٱلْـَٰٔنَ جِئْتَ بِٱلْحَقِّ ۚ فَذَبَحُوهَا وَمَا كَادُوا۟
يَفْعَلُونَ ٧١

72. Remember you slew a man and fell into a dispute among yourselves as to the crime: but Allah was to bring out what you did hide.

وَإِذْ قَتَلْتُمْ نَفْسًا فَٱدَّٰرَْٔتُمْ فِيهَا ۖ وَٱللَّهُ مُخْرِجٌ مَّا
كُنتُمْ تَكْتُمُونَ ٧٢

73. So We said: "Strike the (body) with a piece of the (heifer)." Thus Allah brings the dead to life and shows you His signs: perhaps you may understand.

فَقُلْنَا ٱضْرِبُوهُ بِبَعْضِهَا ۚ كَذَٰلِكَ يُحْىِ ٱللَّهُ ٱلْمَوْتَىٰ
وَيُرِيكُمْ ءَايَٰتِهِۦ لَعَلَّكُمْ تَعْقِلُونَ ٧٣

74. From then on were your hearts hardened: they became like a rock and even worse in hardness. For among rocks there are some from which rivers gush out; others there are which when split apart send out water; and others which sink for fear of Allah. And Allah is not unmindful of what you do.

ثُمَّ قَسَتْ قُلُوبُكُم مِّنۢ بَعْدِ ذَٰلِكَ فَهِىَ كَٱلْحِجَارَةِ
أَوْ أَشَدُّ قَسْوَةً ۚ وَإِنَّ مِنَ ٱلْحِجَارَةِ لَمَا يَتَفَجَّرُ مِنْهُ
ٱلْأَنْهَٰرُ ۚ وَإِنَّ مِنْهَا لَمَا يَشَّقَّقُ فَيَخْرُجُ مِنْهُ ٱلْمَآءُ ۚ
وَإِنَّ مِنْهَا لَمَا يَهْبِطُ مِنْ خَشْيَةِ ٱللَّهِ ۗ وَمَا ٱللَّهُ بِغَٰفِلٍ
عَمَّا تَعْمَلُونَ ٧٤

75. Can you (O you men of faith) entertain the hope that they will believe in you? - Seeing that a party of them heard the word of Allah, and perverted it knowingly after they understood it.

الحزب ٢ ۞ أَفَتَطْمَعُونَ أَن يُؤْمِنُوا۟ لَكُمْ وَقَدْ كَانَ فَرِيقٌ
مِّنْهُمْ يَسْمَعُونَ كَلَٰمَ ٱللَّهِ ثُمَّ يُحَرِّفُونَهُۥ مِنۢ
بَعْدِ مَا عَقَلُوهُ وَهُمْ يَعْلَمُونَ ٧٥

76. See! When they meet the men of faith, they say: "We believe": but when they meet each other in private, they say: "Shall you tell them what Allah has revealed to you, that they may engage you in argument about it before your Lord?" - Do you not understand (their aim)?

وَإِذَا لَقُوا۟ ٱلَّذِينَ ءَامَنُوا۟ قَالُوٓا۟ ءَامَنَّا وَإِذَا خَلَا
بَعْضُهُمْ إِلَىٰ بَعْضٍ قَالُوٓا۟ أَتُحَدِّثُونَهُم بِمَا فَتَحَ
ٱللَّهُ عَلَيْكُمْ لِيُحَآجُّوكُم بِهِۦ عِندَ رَبِّكُمْ ۚ أَفَلَا
تَعْقِلُونَ ٧٦

77. Do they not know that Allah knows what they conceal and what they reveal?

أَوَلَا يَعْلَمُونَ أَنَّ ٱللَّهَ يَعْلَمُ مَا يُسِرُّونَ وَمَا
يُعْلِنُونَ ٧٧

78. And there are among them illiterates, who know not the Book, but (see in it their own) desires, and they do nothing but conjecture.

وَمِنْهُمْ أُمِّيُّونَ لَا يَعْلَمُونَ ٱلْكِتَٰبَ إِلَّآ
أَمَانِىَّ وَإِنْ هُمْ إِلَّا يَظُنُّونَ ٧٨

79. Then woe to those who write the Book

فَوَيْلٌ لِّلَّذِينَ يَكْتُبُونَ ٱلْكِتَٰبَ بِأَيْدِيهِمْ ثُمَّ

with their own hands, and then say: "This is from Allah," to trade with it for a miserable price! - Woe to them for what their hands do write, and for the gain they make by it.

يَقُولُونَ هَٰذَا مِنْ عِندِ ٱللَّهِ لِيَشْتَرُوا۟ بِهِۦ ثَمَنًا
قَلِيلًا ۖ فَوَيْلٌ لَّهُم مِّمَّا كَتَبَتْ أَيْدِيهِمْ وَوَيْلٌ
لَّهُم مِّمَّا يَكْسِبُونَ ٧٩

80. And they say: "The fire shall not touch us but for a few numbered days;" Say: "Have you taken a promise from Allah, for He never breaks His promise? Or is it that you say of Allah what you do not know?"

وَقَالُوا۟ لَن تَمَسَّنَا ٱلنَّارُ إِلَّآ أَيَّامًا مَّعْدُودَةً ۚ
قُلْ أَتَّخَذْتُمْ عِندَ ٱللَّهِ عَهْدًا فَلَن يُخْلِفَ ٱللَّهُ
عَهْدَهُۥٓ ۖ أَمْ تَقُولُونَ عَلَى ٱللَّهِ مَا لَا تَعْلَمُونَ ٨٠

81. Nay, those who seek gain in evil, and are surrounded by their sins - they are companions of the fire: in it shall they remain (forever).

بَلَىٰ ۚ مَن كَسَبَ سَيِّئَةً وَأَحَٰطَتْ بِهِۦ خَطِيٓـَٔتُهُۥ
فَأُو۟لَٰٓئِكَ أَصْحَٰبُ ٱلنَّارِ ۖ هُمْ فِيهَا خَٰلِدُونَ ٨١

82. But those who have faith and work righteousness, they are companions of the garden: in it shall they remain (forever).

وَٱلَّذِينَ ءَامَنُوا۟ وَعَمِلُوا۟ ٱلصَّٰلِحَٰتِ أُو۟لَٰٓئِكَ
أَصْحَٰبُ ٱلْجَنَّةِ ۖ هُمْ فِيهَا خَٰلِدُونَ ٨٢

83. And remember We took a covenant from the children of Israel (to this effect): worship none but Allah; treat with kindness your parents and relations, and orphans and those in need; speak fair to the people; be steadfast in prayer; and practice regular charity. Then did you turn back except a few among you, and you backslide (even now).

وَإِذْ أَخَذْنَا مِيثَٰقَ بَنِىٓ إِسْرَٰٓءِيلَ لَا تَعْبُدُونَ
إِلَّا ٱللَّهَ وَبِٱلْوَٰلِدَيْنِ إِحْسَانًا وَذِى ٱلْقُرْبَىٰ
وَٱلْيَتَٰمَىٰ وَٱلْمَسَٰكِينِ وَقُولُوا۟ لِلنَّاسِ
حُسْنًا وَأَقِيمُوا۟ ٱلصَّلَوٰةَ وَءَاتُوا۟ ٱلزَّكَوٰةَ
ثُمَّ تَوَلَّيْتُمْ إِلَّا قَلِيلًا مِّنكُمْ وَأَنتُم
مُّعْرِضُونَ ٨٣

84. And remember We took your covenant (to this effect): shed no blood amongst you, nor turn out your own people from your homes: and this you solemnly ratified, and to this you can bear witness.

وَإِذْ أَخَذْنَا مِيثَٰقَكُمْ لَا تَسْفِكُونَ دِمَآءَكُمْ وَلَا
تُخْرِجُونَ أَنفُسَكُم مِّن دِيَٰرِكُمْ ثُمَّ أَقْرَرْتُمْ
وَأَنتُمْ تَشْهَدُونَ ٨٤

85. After this it is you, the same people, who slay among yourselves, and banish a party of you from their homes; assist (their enemies) against them, in guilt and transgression; and if they come to you as captives, you ransom them, though it was not lawful for you to banish them. Then is it only a part of the book that you believe in, and do you reject the rest? But what is the reward for those among you who behave like this but disgrace in this life? - and on the day of judgement they shall be consigned to the most grievous penalty. For Allah is not unmindful of what you do.

ثُمَّ أَنتُمْ هَٰٓؤُلَآءِ تَقْتُلُونَ أَنفُسَكُمْ وَتُخْرِجُونَ
فَرِيقًا مِّنكُم مِّن دِيَٰرِهِمْ تَظَٰهَرُونَ عَلَيْهِم
بِٱلْإِثْمِ وَٱلْعُدْوَٰنِ وَإِن يَأْتُوكُمْ أُسَٰرَىٰ
تُفَٰدُوهُمْ وَهُوَ مُحَرَّمٌ عَلَيْكُمْ إِخْرَاجُهُمْ ۚ
أَفَتُؤْمِنُونَ بِبَعْضِ ٱلْكِتَٰبِ وَتَكْفُرُونَ بِبَعْضٍ ۚ
فَمَا جَزَآءُ مَن يَفْعَلُ ذَٰلِكَ مِنكُمْ إِلَّا خِزْىٌ فِى
ٱلْحَيَوٰةِ ٱلدُّنْيَا ۖ وَيَوْمَ ٱلْقِيَٰمَةِ يُرَدُّونَ إِلَىٰٓ
أَشَدِّ ٱلْعَذَابِ ۗ وَمَا ٱللَّهُ بِغَٰفِلٍ عَمَّا تَعْمَلُونَ ﴿٨٥﴾

86. These are the people who buy the life of this world at the price of the hereafter: their penalty shall not be lightened nor shall they be helped.

أُو۟لَٰٓئِكَ ٱلَّذِينَ ٱشْتَرَوُا۟ ٱلْحَيَوٰةَ ٱلدُّنْيَا بِٱلْءَاخِرَةِ ۖ
فَلَا يُخَفَّفُ عَنْهُمُ ٱلْعَذَابُ وَلَا هُمْ يُنصَرُونَ ﴿٨٦﴾

87. We gave Moses the book and followed him up with a succession of messengers; We gave Jesus, the son of Mary, clear (signs) and strengthened him with the Holy Spirit. Is it that whenever there comes to you a messenger with what you yourselves desire not, you are puffed up with pride? - Some you called imposters, and others you slay!

وَلَقَدْ ءَاتَيْنَا مُوسَى ٱلْكِتَٰبَ وَقَفَّيْنَا مِنۢ
بَعْدِهِۦ بِٱلرُّسُلِ ۖ وَءَاتَيْنَا عِيسَى ٱبْنَ مَرْيَمَ
ٱلْبَيِّنَٰتِ وَأَيَّدْنَٰهُ بِرُوحِ ٱلْقُدُسِ ۗ أَفَكُلَّمَا جَآءَكُمْ
رَسُولٌۢ بِمَا لَا تَهْوَىٰٓ أَنفُسُكُمُ ٱسْتَكْبَرْتُمْ فَفَرِيقًا
كَذَّبْتُمْ وَفَرِيقًا تَقْتُلُونَ ﴿٨٧﴾

88. They say, "Our hearts are the wrappings (which preserve Allah's Word: we need no more)." Nay, Allah's curse is on them for their blasphemy: little is it they believe.

وَقَالُوا۟ قُلُوبُنَا غُلْفٌۢ ۚ بَل لَّعَنَهُمُ ٱللَّهُ بِكُفْرِهِمْ
فَقَلِيلًا مَّا يُؤْمِنُونَ ﴿٨٨﴾

89. And when there comes to them a Book from Allah, confirming what is with them - although from of old they had prayed for victory against those without faith - when

وَلَمَّا جَآءَهُمْ كِتَٰبٌ مِّنْ عِندِ ٱللَّهِ مُصَدِّقٌ لِّمَا
مَعَهُمْ وَكَانُوا۟ مِن قَبْلُ يَسْتَفْتِحُونَ عَلَى

there comes to them that which they (should) have recognised. They refused to believe in it but the curse of Allah is on those without faith.

ٱلَّذِينَ كَفَرُوا۟ فَلَمَّا جَآءَهُم مَّا عَرَفُوا۟ كَفَرُوا۟
بِهِۦ ۚ فَلَعْنَةُ ٱللَّهِ عَلَى ٱلْكَٰفِرِينَ ﴿٨٩﴾

90. Miserable is the price for which they have sold their souls, in that they deny (the revelation) which Allah has sent down, in insolent envy that Allah of His grace should send it to any of His servants He pleases: thus have they drawn on themselves wrath upon wrath, and humiliating is the punishment of those who reject faith.

بِئْسَمَا ٱشْتَرَوْا۟ بِهِۦٓ أَنفُسَهُمْ أَن يَكْفُرُوا۟ بِمَآ
أَنزَلَ ٱللَّهُ بَغْيًا أَن يُنَزِّلَ ٱللَّهُ مِن فَضْلِهِۦ عَلَىٰ مَن
يَشَآءُ مِنْ عِبَادِهِۦ ۖ فَبَآءُو بِغَضَبٍ عَلَىٰ غَضَبٍ ۚ
وَلِلْكَٰفِرِينَ عَذَابٌ مُّهِينٌ ﴿٩٠﴾

91. When it is said to them, "Believe in what Allah has sent down," they say, "We believe in what was sent down to us;" yet they reject all besides, even if it be the truth confirming what is with them. Say: "Why then have you slain the prophets of Allah in times gone by, if you did indeed believe?"

وَإِذَا قِيلَ لَهُمْ ءَامِنُوا۟ بِمَآ أَنزَلَ ٱللَّهُ قَالُوا۟ نُؤْمِنُ
بِمَآ أُنزِلَ عَلَيْنَا وَيَكْفُرُونَ بِمَا وَرَآءَهُۥ وَهُوَ
ٱلْحَقُّ مُصَدِّقًا لِّمَا مَعَهُمْ ۗ قُلْ فَلِمَ تَقْتُلُونَ
أَنۢبِيَآءَ ٱللَّهِ مِن قَبْلُ إِن كُنتُم مُّؤْمِنِينَ ﴿٩١﴾

92. There came to you Moses with clear (signs); yet you worshipped the calf (even) after that, and you did behave wrongfully.

۞ وَلَقَدْ جَآءَكُم مُّوسَىٰ بِٱلْبَيِّنَٰتِ ثُمَّ (ربع الحزب ٢)
ٱتَّخَذْتُمُ ٱلْعِجْلَ مِنۢ بَعْدِهِۦ وَأَنتُمْ
ظَٰلِمُونَ ﴿٩٢﴾

93. And remember We took your covenant and We raised above you (the towering height) of Mount (Sinai): (saying): "Hold firmly to what We have given you, and listen (to the Law)": they said: "We hear and we disobey", and they had to drink into their hearts (of the taint) of the calf because of their faithlessness. Say: "Vile indeed are the behests of your faith if you have any faith!"

وَإِذْ أَخَذْنَا مِيثَٰقَكُمْ وَرَفَعْنَا فَوْقَكُمُ
ٱلطُّورَ خُذُوا۟ مَآ ءَاتَيْنَٰكُم بِقُوَّةٍ وَٱسْمَعُوا۟ ۖ
قَالُوا۟ سَمِعْنَا وَعَصَيْنَا وَأُشْرِبُوا۟ فِى قُلُوبِهِمُ
ٱلْعِجْلَ بِكُفْرِهِمْ ۚ قُلْ بِئْسَمَا يَأْمُرُكُم
بِهِۦٓ إِيمَٰنُكُمْ إِن كُنتُم مُّؤْمِنِينَ ﴿٩٣﴾

94. Say: "If the last home, with Allah, be for you specially, and not for anyone else, then seek you for death, if you are sincere."

قُلْ إِن كَانَتْ لَكُمُ ٱلدَّارُ ٱلْءَاخِرَةُ عِندَ ٱللَّهِ
خَالِصَةً مِّن دُونِ ٱلنَّاسِ فَتَمَنَّوُا۟ ٱلْمَوْتَ إِن
كُنتُمْ صَٰدِقِينَ ﴿٩٤﴾

95. But they will never seek for death, on account of the (sins) which their hands have sent on before them. And Allah is well acquainted with the wrongdoers.

وَلَن يَتَمَنَّوْهُ أَبَدًۢا بِمَا قَدَّمَتْ أَيْدِيهِمْ ۗ وَٱللَّهُ
عَلِيمٌۢ بِٱلظَّٰلِمِينَ ﴿٩٥﴾

96. You will indeed find them, of all people, most greedy of life - even more than the idolaters: each one of them wishes he could be given a life of a thousand years: but the grant of such life will not save him from (due) punishment. For Allah sees well all that they do.

وَلَتَجِدَنَّهُمْ أَحْرَصَ ٱلنَّاسِ عَلَىٰ حَيَوٰةٍ وَمِنَ ٱلَّذِينَ
أَشْرَكُوا۟ ۚ يَوَدُّ أَحَدُهُمْ لَوْ يُعَمَّرُ أَلْفَ سَنَةٍ وَمَا
هُوَ بِمُزَحْزِحِهِۦ مِنَ ٱلْعَذَابِ أَن يُعَمَّرَ ۗ وَٱللَّهُ
بَصِيرٌۢ بِمَا يَعْمَلُونَ ﴿٩٦﴾

97. Say: Whoever is an enemy to Gabriel - for he brings down the (revelation) to your heart by Allah's Will, a confirmation of what went before. And guidance and glad tidings for those who believe -

قُلْ مَن كَانَ عَدُوًّا لِّجِبْرِيلَ فَإِنَّهُۥ نَزَّلَهُۥ
عَلَىٰ قَلْبِكَ بِإِذْنِ ٱللَّهِ مُصَدِّقًا لِّمَا بَيْنَ
يَدَيْهِ وَهُدًى وَبُشْرَىٰ لِلْمُؤْمِنِينَ ﴿٩٧﴾

98. Whoever is an enemy to Allah and His angels and messengers, to Gabriel and Michael - Allah is an enemy to those who reject faith.

مَن كَانَ عَدُوًّا لِّلَّهِ وَمَلَٰٓئِكَتِهِۦ وَرُسُلِهِۦ
وَجِبْرِيلَ وَمِيكَىٰلَ فَإِنَّ ٱللَّهَ عَدُوٌّ لِّلْكَٰفِرِينَ ﴿٩٨﴾

99. We have sent down to you manifest signs (*ayat*); and none reject them but those who are perverse.

وَلَقَدْ أَنزَلْنَآ إِلَيْكَ ءَايَٰتٍۭ بَيِّنَٰتٍ ۖ وَمَا يَكْفُرُ
بِهَآ إِلَّا ٱلْفَٰسِقُونَ ﴿٩٩﴾

100. Is it not (the case) that every time they make a covenant, some party among them throw it aside? - Nay, most of them are faithless.

أَوَكُلَّمَا عَٰهَدُوا۟ عَهْدًا نَّبَذَهُۥ فَرِيقٌ مِّنْهُم ۚ
بَلْ أَكْثَرُهُمْ لَا يُؤْمِنُونَ ﴿١٠٠﴾

101. And when came to them a messenger from Allah, confirming what was with them, a party of the People of the Book

وَلَمَّا جَآءَهُمْ رَسُولٌ مِّنْ عِندِ ٱللَّهِ مُصَدِّقٌ لِّمَا
مَعَهُمْ نَبَذَ فَرِيقٌ مِّنَ ٱلَّذِينَ أُوتُوا۟

threw away the book of Allah behind their backs. As if (it had been something) they did not know!

ٱلْكِتَـٰبَ كِتَـٰبَ ٱللَّهِ وَرَآءَ ظُهُورِهِمْ
كَأَنَّهُمْ لَا يَعْلَمُونَ ١٠١

102. They followed what the evil ones gave out (falsely) against the power of Solomon: the blasphemers were not Solomon, but the evil ones, teaching men magic, and such things as came down at Babylon to the angels Harut and Marut. But neither of these taught anyone (such things) without saying: "We are only for trial; so do not blaspheme." They learned from them the means to sow discord between man and wife. But they could not thus harm anyone except by Allah's permission. And they learned what harmed them, not what profited them. And they knew that the buyers of (magic) would have no share in the happiness of the hereafter. And vile was the price for which they did sell their souls, if they but knew!

وَٱتَّبَعُوا۟ مَا تَتْلُوا۟ ٱلشَّيَـٰطِينُ عَلَىٰ مُلْكِ سُلَيْمَـٰنَ ۖ
وَمَا كَفَرَ سُلَيْمَـٰنُ وَلَـٰكِنَّ ٱلشَّيَـٰطِينَ
كَفَرُوا۟ يُعَلِّمُونَ ٱلنَّاسَ ٱلسِّحْرَ وَمَآ أُنزِلَ
عَلَى ٱلْمَلَكَيْنِ بِبَابِلَ هَـٰرُوتَ وَمَـٰرُوتَ ۚ وَمَا
يُعَلِّمَانِ مِنْ أَحَدٍ حَتَّىٰ يَقُولَآ إِنَّمَا نَحْنُ فِتْنَةٌ
فَلَا تَكْفُرْ ۖ فَيَتَعَلَّمُونَ مِنْهُمَا مَا يُفَرِّقُونَ
بِهِۦ بَيْنَ ٱلْمَرْءِ وَزَوْجِهِۦ ۚ وَمَا هُم بِضَآرِّينَ بِهِۦ
مِنْ أَحَدٍ إِلَّا بِإِذْنِ ٱللَّهِ ۚ وَيَتَعَلَّمُونَ مَا يَضُرُّهُمْ
وَلَا يَنفَعُهُمْ ۚ وَلَقَدْ عَلِمُوا۟ لَمَنِ ٱشْتَرَىٰهُ مَا لَهُۥ
فِى ٱلْـَٔاخِرَةِ مِنْ خَلَـٰقٍ ۚ وَلَبِئْسَ مَا شَرَوْا۟ بِهِۦٓ
أَنفُسَهُمْ ۚ لَوْ كَانُوا۟ يَعْلَمُونَ ١٠٢

103. If they had kept their faith and guarded themselves from evil, far better had been the reward from their Lord, if they but knew!

وَلَوْ أَنَّهُمْ ءَامَنُوا۟ وَٱتَّقَوْا۟ لَمَثُوبَةٌ مِّنْ عِندِ ٱللَّهِ
خَيْرٌ ۖ لَّوْ كَانُوا۟ يَعْلَمُونَ ١٠٣

104. O you of faith! Say not (to the prophet) words of ambiguous import, but words of respect; and listen (to him): to those without faith is a grievous punishment.

يَـٰٓأَيُّهَا ٱلَّذِينَ ءَامَنُوا۟ لَا تَقُولُوا۟ رَٰعِنَا وَقُولُوا۟
ٱنظُرْنَا وَٱسْمَعُوا۟ ۗ وَلِلْكَـٰفِرِينَ عَذَابٌ
أَلِيمٌ ١٠٤

105. It is never the wish of those without faith among the People of the Book, nor of the pagans, that anything good should come down to you from your Lord. But Allah will choose for His special mercy

مَّا يَوَدُّ ٱلَّذِينَ كَفَرُوا۟ مِنْ أَهْلِ ٱلْكِتَـٰبِ
وَلَا ٱلْمُشْرِكِينَ أَن يُنَزَّلَ عَلَيْكُم مِّنْ خَيْرٍ
مِّن رَّبِّكُمْ ۗ وَٱللَّهُ يَخْتَصُّ بِرَحْمَتِهِۦ مَن

whom He will - for Allah is Lord of grace abounding.

يَشَآءُۚ وَٱللَّهُ ذُو ٱلۡفَضۡلِ ٱلۡعَظِيمِ ١٠٥

106. None of Our revelations do We abrogate or cause to be forgotten, but We substitute something better or similar: do you not know that Allah has power over all things?

نصف الحزب ٢

۞ مَا نَنسَخۡ مِنۡ ءَايَةٍ أَوۡ نُنسِهَا نَأۡتِ بِخَيۡرٖ مِّنۡهَآ
أَوۡ مِثۡلِهَآۗ أَلَمۡ تَعۡلَمۡ أَنَّ ٱللَّهَ عَلَىٰ كُلِّ شَيۡءٖ
قَدِيرٌ ١٠٦

107. Do you not know that to Allah belongs the dominion of the heavens and the earth? And besides Him you have neither patron nor helper.

أَلَمۡ تَعۡلَمۡ أَنَّ ٱللَّهَ لَهُۥ مُلۡكُ ٱلسَّمَٰوَٰتِ وَٱلۡأَرۡضِۗ
وَمَا لَكُم مِّن دُونِ ٱللَّهِ مِن وَلِيّٖ وَلَا نَصِيرٍ ١٠٧

108. Would you question your messenger as Moses was questioned of old? But whoever changes from faith to unbelief, has strayed without doubt from the even way.

أَمۡ تُرِيدُونَ أَن تَسۡـَٔلُواْ رَسُولَكُمۡ كَمَا سُئِلَ
مُوسَىٰ مِن قَبۡلُۗ وَمَن يَتَبَدَّلِ ٱلۡكُفۡرَ بِٱلۡإِيمَٰنِ
فَقَدۡ ضَلَّ سَوَآءَ ٱلسَّبِيلِ ١٠٨

109. Quite a number of the People of the Book wish they could turn you (people) back to infidelity after you have believed. From selfish envy, after the truth has become manifest to them: but forgive and overlook, till Allah accomplishes His purpose: for Allah has power over all things.

وَدَّ كَثِيرٞ مِّنۡ أَهۡلِ ٱلۡكِتَٰبِ لَوۡ يَرُدُّونَكُم
مِّنۢ بَعۡدِ إِيمَٰنِكُمۡ كُفَّارًا حَسَدٗا مِّنۡ عِندِ
أَنفُسِهِم مِّنۢ بَعۡدِ مَا تَبَيَّنَ لَهُمُ ٱلۡحَقُّۖ فَٱعۡفُواْ
وَٱصۡفَحُواْ حَتَّىٰ يَأۡتِيَ ٱللَّهُ بِأَمۡرِهِۦٓۗ إِنَّ ٱللَّهَ عَلَىٰ
كُلِّ شَيۡءٖ قَدِيرٞ ١٠٩

110. And be steadfast in prayer and regular in charity: and whatever good you send for your souls before you, you shall find it with Allah: for Allah sees well all that you do.

وَأَقِيمُواْ ٱلصَّلَوٰةَ وَءَاتُواْ ٱلزَّكَوٰةَۚ وَمَا تُقَدِّمُواْ
لِأَنفُسِكُم مِّنۡ خَيۡرٖ تَجِدُوهُ عِندَ ٱللَّهِۗ إِنَّ ٱللَّهَ
بِمَا تَعۡمَلُونَ بَصِيرٞ ١١٠

111. And they say: "None shall enter paradise unless he be a Jew or a Christian." Those are their (vain) desires. Say: "Produce your proof if you are truthful."

وَقَالُواْ لَن يَدۡخُلَ ٱلۡجَنَّةَ إِلَّا مَن كَانَ هُودًا
أَوۡ نَصَٰرَىٰۗ تِلۡكَ أَمَانِيُّهُمۡۗ قُلۡ هَاتُواْ بُرۡهَٰنَكُمۡ
إِن كُنتُمۡ صَٰدِقِينَ ١١١

112. Nay - whoever submits his whole self to Allah and is a doer of good - he will get his reward with his Lord; on such shall be no fear, nor shall they grieve.

بَلَىٰۚ مَنۡ أَسۡلَمَ وَجۡهَهُۥ لِلَّهِ وَهُوَ مُحۡسِنٞ فَلَهُۥٓ
أَجۡرُهُۥ عِندَ رَبِّهِۦ وَلَا خَوۡفٌ عَلَيۡهِمۡ وَلَا هُمۡ
يَحۡزَنُونَ ١١٢

113. The Jews say: "The Christians have nothing (to stand) upon"; and the Christians say: "The Jews have nothing (to stand) upon." Yet they (profess to) study the (same) book. Similar to their word is what those say who know not; but Allah will judge between them in their quarrel on the day of judgement.

وَقَالَتِ ٱلۡيَهُودُ لَيۡسَتِ ٱلنَّصَٰرَىٰ عَلَىٰ شَيۡءٖ وَقَالَتِ
ٱلنَّصَٰرَىٰ لَيۡسَتِ ٱلۡيَهُودُ عَلَىٰ شَيۡءٖ وَهُمۡ يَتۡلُونَ
ٱلۡكِتَٰبَۗ كَذَٰلِكَ قَالَ ٱلَّذِينَ لَا يَعۡلَمُونَ مِثۡلَ
قَوۡلِهِمۡۚ فَٱللَّهُ يَحۡكُمُ بَيۡنَهُمۡ يَوۡمَ ٱلۡقِيَٰمَةِ فِيمَا
كَانُواْ فِيهِ يَخۡتَلِفُونَ ١١٣

114. And who is more unjust than he who forbids that in places for the worship of Allah His name should be celebrated? - Whose zeal is (in fact) to ruin them? It was not fitting that such should themselves enter them except in fear. For them there is nothing but disgrace in this world, and in the world to come, an exceeding torment.

وَمَنۡ أَظۡلَمُ مِمَّن مَّنَعَ مَسَٰجِدَ ٱللَّهِ أَن يُذۡكَرَ فِيهَا
ٱسۡمُهُۥ وَسَعَىٰ فِي خَرَابِهَآۚ أُوْلَٰٓئِكَ مَا كَانَ لَهُمۡ
أَن يَدۡخُلُوهَآ إِلَّا خَآئِفِينَۚ لَهُمۡ فِي ٱلدُّنۡيَا خِزۡيٞ
وَلَهُمۡ فِي ٱلۡأٓخِرَةِ عَذَابٌ عَظِيمٞ ١١٤

115. To Allah belong the east and the west: whichever way you turn, there is Allah's countenance. For Allah is All-Embracing, All-Knowing.

وَلِلَّهِ ٱلۡمَشۡرِقُ وَٱلۡمَغۡرِبُۚ فَأَيۡنَمَا تُوَلُّواْ فَثَمَّ وَجۡهُ
ٱللَّهِۚ إِنَّ ٱللَّهَ وَٰسِعٌ عَلِيمٞ ١١٥

116. They say: "Allah has begotten a son": Glory be to Him - Nay, to Him belongs all that is in the heavens and on earth: everything renders worship to Him.

وَقَالُواْ ٱتَّخَذَ ٱللَّهُ وَلَدٗاۗ سُبۡحَٰنَهُۥۖ بَل لَّهُۥ مَا فِي
ٱلسَّمَٰوَٰتِ وَٱلۡأَرۡضِۖ كُلّٞ لَّهُۥ قَٰنِتُونَ ١١٦

117. To Him is due the primal origin of the heavens and the earth: when He decrees a matter, He says to it: "Be," and it is.

بَدِيعُ ٱلسَّمَٰوَٰتِ وَٱلۡأَرۡضِۖ وَإِذَا قَضَىٰٓ أَمۡرٗا فَإِنَّمَا
يَقُولُ لَهُۥ كُن فَيَكُونُ ١١٧

118. Say those without knowledge: "Why speaks not Allah to us? Or why comes not to us a sign?" So said the people before them words of similar import. Their hearts are alike. We have indeed made clear the signs to any people who hold firmly to faith (in their hearts).

وَقَالَ ٱلَّذِينَ لَا يَعۡلَمُونَ لَوۡلَا يُكَلِّمُنَا ٱللَّهُ
أَوۡ تَأۡتِينَآ ءَايَةٞۗ كَذَٰلِكَ قَالَ ٱلَّذِينَ مِن
قَبۡلِهِم مِّثۡلَ قَوۡلِهِمۡۘ تَشَٰبَهَتۡ قُلُوبُهُمۡۗ
قَدۡ بَيَّنَّا ٱلۡأٓيَٰتِ لِقَوۡمٖ يُوقِنُونَ ١١٨

119. Verily, We have sent you in truth as a bearer of glad tidings and a warner: But of you no question shall be asked of the companions of the blazing fire.

إِنَّآ أَرۡسَلۡنَٰكَ بِٱلۡحَقِّ بَشِيرٗا وَنَذِيرٗاۖ وَلَا تُسۡـَٔلُ
عَنۡ أَصۡحَٰبِ ٱلۡجَحِيمِ ١١٩

120. Never will the Jews or the Christians be satisfied with you unless you follow their form of religion. Say: "The guidance of Allah - that is the (only) guidance." Were you to follow their desires after the knowledge which has reached you, then would you find neither protector nor helper against Allah.

وَلَن تَرۡضَىٰ عَنكَ ٱلۡيَهُودُ وَلَا ٱلنَّصَٰرَىٰ حَتَّىٰ تَتَّبِعَ
مِلَّتَهُمۡۗ قُلۡ إِنَّ هُدَى ٱللَّهِ هُوَ ٱلۡهُدَىٰۗ وَلَئِنِ ٱتَّبَعۡتَ
أَهۡوَآءَهُم بَعۡدَ ٱلَّذِي جَآءَكَ مِنَ ٱلۡعِلۡمِ مَا لَكَ مِنَ
ٱللَّهِ مِن وَلِيّٖ وَلَا نَصِيرٍ ١٢٠

121. Those to whom We have sent the book study it as it should be studied: they are the ones that believe in it: those who reject faith in it - the loss is their own.

ٱلَّذِينَ ءَاتَيۡنَٰهُمُ ٱلۡكِتَٰبَ يَتۡلُونَهُۥ حَقَّ تِلَاوَتِهِۦٓ
أُوْلَٰٓئِكَ يُؤۡمِنُونَ بِهِۦۗ وَمَن يَكۡفُرۡ بِهِۦ فَأُوْلَٰٓئِكَ هُمُ
ٱلۡخَٰسِرُونَ ١٢١

122. O Children of Israel! Call to mind the special favour which I bestowed upon you, and that I preferred you to all others (for My message).

يَٰبَنِيٓ إِسۡرَٰٓءِيلَ ٱذۡكُرُواْ نِعۡمَتِيَ ٱلَّتِيٓ أَنۡعَمۡتُ عَلَيۡكُمۡ
وَأَنِّي فَضَّلۡتُكُمۡ عَلَى ٱلۡعَٰلَمِينَ ١٢٢

123. Then guard yourselves against a day when one soul shall not benefit another. Nor shall compensation be accepted from her nor shall intercession profit her nor shall anyone be helped (from outside).

وَٱتَّقُواْ يَوۡمٗا لَّا تَجۡزِي نَفۡسٌ عَن نَّفۡسٖ شَيۡـٔٗا وَلَا يُقۡبَلُ
مِنۡهَا عَدۡلٞ وَلَا تَنفَعُهَا شَفَٰعَةٞ وَلَا هُمۡ يُنصَرُونَ ١٢٣

ثلاثة أرباع الحزب ٢

124. And remember that Abraham was tried by his Lord with certain commands, which he fulfilled: He said: "I will make you an Imam to the nations." He pleaded: "And also (Imams) from my offspring!" He answered: "But My promise is not within the reach of evildoers."

۞ وَإِذِ ٱبۡتَلَىٰٓ إِبۡرَٰهِـۧمَ رَبُّهُۥ بِكَلِمَٰتٖ فَأَتَمَّهُنَّۖ قَالَ إِنِّي
جَاعِلُكَ لِلنَّاسِ إِمَامٗاۖ قَالَ وَمِن ذُرِّيَّتِيۖ قَالَ
لَا يَنَالُ عَهۡدِي ٱلظَّٰلِمِينَ ١٢٤

125. Remember We made the House a place of assembly for men and a place of safety; and take you the station of Abraham as a place of prayer; and We covenanted with Abraham and Ishmael, that they should sanctify My House for those who go around it, or use it as a retreat, or bow, or prostrate themselves (in it in prayer).

وَإِذۡ جَعَلۡنَا ٱلۡبَيۡتَ مَثَابَةٗ لِّلنَّاسِ وَأَمۡنٗا وَٱتَّخِذُواْ مِن
مَّقَامِ إِبۡرَٰهِـۧمَ مُصَلّٗىۖ وَعَهِدۡنَآ إِلَىٰٓ إِبۡرَٰهِـۧمَ
وَإِسۡمَٰعِيلَ أَن طَهِّرَا بَيۡتِيَ لِلطَّآئِفِينَ وَٱلۡعَٰكِفِينَ
وَٱلرُّكَّعِ ٱلسُّجُودِ ١٢٥

126. And remember Abraham said: "My Lord, make this a city of peace, and feed its people with fruits - such of them as believe in Allah and the last day." He said: "(Yea), and such as reject faith - for a while will I grant them their pleasure, but will soon drive them to the torment of fire - an evil destination (indeed)!"

وَإِذۡ قَالَ إِبۡرَٰهِـۧمُ رَبِّ ٱجۡعَلۡ هَٰذَا بَلَدًا ءَامِنٗا وَٱرۡزُقۡ
أَهۡلَهُۥ مِنَ ٱلثَّمَرَٰتِ مَنۡ ءَامَنَ مِنۡهُم بِٱللَّهِ وَٱلۡيَوۡمِ
ٱلۡأٓخِرِۚ قَالَ وَمَن كَفَرَ فَأُمَتِّعُهُۥ قَلِيلٗا ثُمَّ أَضۡطَرُّهُۥٓ
إِلَىٰ عَذَابِ ٱلنَّارِۖ وَبِئۡسَ ٱلۡمَصِيرُ ١٢٦

127. And remember Abraham and Ishmael raised the foundations of the House (with this prayer): "Our Lord! Accept (this service) from us: for You are the All-Hearing, the All-Knowing.

وَإِذۡ يَرۡفَعُ إِبۡرَٰهِـۧمُ ٱلۡقَوَاعِدَ مِنَ ٱلۡبَيۡتِ وَإِسۡمَٰعِيلُ
رَبَّنَا تَقَبَّلۡ مِنَّآۖ إِنَّكَ أَنتَ ٱلسَّمِيعُ ٱلۡعَلِيمُ ١٢٧

128. "Our Lord! Make of us Muslims, bowing to Your (will), and of our progeny a people Muslim, bowing to Your (will); and show us our places for the celebration of (due) rites; and turn to us (in mercy); for You are the Oft-Returning, Most Merciful.

رَبَّنَا وَٱجۡعَلۡنَا مُسۡلِمَيۡنِ لَكَ وَمِن ذُرِّيَّتِنَآ أُمَّةٗ
مُّسۡلِمَةٗ لَّكَ وَأَرِنَا مَنَاسِكَنَا وَتُبۡ عَلَيۡنَآۖ إِنَّكَ أَنتَ
ٱلتَّوَّابُ ٱلرَّحِيمُ ١٢٨

129. "Our Lord! Send amongst them a messenger of their own, who shall

رَبَّنَا وَٱبۡعَثۡ فِيهِمۡ رَسُولٗا مِّنۡهُمۡ يَتۡلُواْ عَلَيۡهِمۡ

rehearse Your signs to them and instruct them in scripture and wisdom, and sanctify them: for You are the Exalted in Might, the Wise."

ءَايَـٰتِكَ وَيُعَلِّمُهُمُ ٱلْكِتَـٰبَ وَٱلْحِكْمَةَ
وَيُزَكِّيهِمْ ۚ إِنَّكَ أَنتَ ٱلْعَزِيزُ ٱلْحَكِيمُ ﴿١٢٩﴾

130. And who turns away from the religion of Abraham but such as debase their souls with folly? Him We chose and rendered pure in this world: and he will be in the hereafter in the ranks of the righteous.

وَمَن يَرْغَبُ عَن مِّلَّةِ إِبْرَٰهِـۧمَ إِلَّا مَن سَفِهَ نَفْسَهُۥ ۚ
وَلَقَدِ ٱصْطَفَيْنَـٰهُ فِى ٱلدُّنْيَا ۖ وَإِنَّهُۥ فِى ٱلْـَٔاخِرَةِ
لَمِنَ ٱلصَّـٰلِحِينَ ﴿١٣٠﴾

131. See! His Lord said to him: "Bow (your will) to Me": He said: "I bow (my will) to the Lord and Cherisher of the Universe."

إِذْ قَالَ لَهُۥ رَبُّهُۥٓ أَسْلِمْ ۖ قَالَ أَسْلَمْتُ لِرَبِّ
ٱلْعَـٰلَمِينَ ﴿١٣١﴾

132. And this was the legacy that Abraham left to his sons, and so did Jacob; "O my sons! Allah has chosen the faith for you; then die not except in the state of submission (to Allah).

وَوَصَّىٰ بِهَآ إِبْرَٰهِـۧمُ بَنِيهِ وَيَعْقُوبُ يَـٰبَنِىَّ إِنَّ
ٱللَّهَ ٱصْطَفَىٰ لَكُمُ ٱلدِّينَ فَلَا تَمُوتُنَّ إِلَّا
وَأَنتُم مُّسْلِمُونَ ﴿١٣٢﴾

133. Were you witnesses when Death appeared before Jacob? See, he said to his sons: "What will you worship after me?" They said: "We shall worship your God and the God of your fathers, - of Abraham, Ishmael, and Isaac - the One (True) God: to Him we bow (in Islam)."

أَمْ كُنتُمْ شُهَدَآءَ إِذْ حَضَرَ يَعْقُوبَ ٱلْمَوْتُ إِذْ قَالَ
لِبَنِيهِ مَا تَعْبُدُونَ مِنۢ بَعْدِى ۖ قَالُوا۟ نَعْبُدُ
إِلَـٰهَكَ وَإِلَـٰهَ ءَابَآئِكَ إِبْرَٰهِـۧمَ وَإِسْمَـٰعِيلَ
وَإِسْحَـٰقَ إِلَـٰهًا وَٰحِدًا وَنَحْنُ لَهُۥ مُسْلِمُونَ ﴿١٣٣﴾

134. That was a people that has passed away. They shall reap the fruit of what they did, and you of what you do! Of their merits there is no question in your case!

تِلْكَ أُمَّةٌ قَدْ خَلَتْ ۖ لَهَا مَا كَسَبَتْ وَلَكُم مَّا
كَسَبْتُمْ ۖ وَلَا تُسْـَٔلُونَ عَمَّا كَانُوا۟ يَعْمَلُونَ ﴿١٣٤﴾

135. They say: "Become Jews or Christians if you would be guided (to salvation)." Say you: "Nay! (I would rather) the religion of Abraham, the true, and he joined not gods with Allah."

وَقَالُوا۟ كُونُوا۟ هُودًا أَوْ نَصَـٰرَىٰ تَهْتَدُوا۟ ۗ قُلْ بَلْ
مِلَّةَ إِبْرَٰهِـۧمَ حَنِيفًا ۖ وَمَا كَانَ مِنَ ٱلْمُشْرِكِينَ ﴿١٣٥﴾

136. Say you: "We believe in Allah, and the revelation given to us, and to Abraham, Ishmael, Isaac, Jacob, and the tribes, and that given to Moses and Jesus, and that given to (all) prophets from their Lord: We make no difference between one and another of them: and we bow to Allah (in Islam)."

قُولُوٓا۟ ءَامَنَّا بِٱللَّهِ وَمَآ أُنزِلَ إِلَيْنَا وَمَآ أُنزِلَ إِلَىٰٓ
إِبْرَٰهِـۧمَ وَإِسْمَـٰعِيلَ وَإِسْحَـٰقَ وَيَعْقُوبَ وَٱلْأَسْبَاطِ
وَمَآ أُوتِىَ مُوسَىٰ وَعِيسَىٰ وَمَآ أُوتِىَ ٱلنَّبِيُّونَ مِن
رَّبِّهِمْ لَا نُفَرِّقُ بَيْنَ أَحَدٍ مِّنْهُمْ وَنَحْنُ لَهُۥ
مُسْلِمُونَ ١٣٦

137. So if they believe as you believe, they are indeed on the right path; but if they turn back, it is they who are in schism; but Allah will suffice you as against them, and He is the All-Hearing, the All-Knowing.

فَإِنْ ءَامَنُوا۟ بِمِثْلِ مَآ ءَامَنتُم بِهِۦ فَقَدِ ٱهْتَدَوا۟ ۖ
وَّإِن تَوَلَّوْا۟ فَإِنَّمَا هُمْ فِى شِقَاقٍ ۖ فَسَيَكْفِيكَهُمُ
ٱللَّهُ ۚ وَهُوَ ٱلسَّمِيعُ ٱلْعَلِيمُ ١٣٧

138. (Our religion is) the baptism of Allah: and who can baptize better than Allah? And it is He Whom we worship.

صِبْغَةَ ٱللَّهِ ۖ وَمَنْ أَحْسَنُ مِنَ ٱللَّهِ صِبْغَةً ۖ
وَنَحْنُ لَهُۥ عَـٰبِدُونَ ١٣٨

139. Say: Will you dispute with us about Allah, seeing that He is our Lord and your Lord; that we are responsible for our doings and you for yours; and that we are sincere (in our faith) in Him?

قُلْ أَتُحَآجُّونَنَا فِى ٱللَّهِ وَهُوَ رَبُّنَا وَرَبُّكُمْ وَلَنَآ
أَعْمَـٰلُنَا وَلَكُمْ أَعْمَـٰلُكُمْ وَنَحْنُ لَهُۥ
مُخْلِصُونَ ١٣٩

140. Or do you say that Abraham, Ishmael, Isaac, Jacob and the tribes were Jews or Christians? Say: Do you know better than Allah? Ah! Who is more unjust than those who conceal the testimony they have from Allah? But Allah is not unmindful of what you do!

أَمْ تَقُولُونَ إِنَّ إِبْرَٰهِـۧمَ وَإِسْمَـٰعِيلَ وَإِسْحَـٰقَ
وَيَعْقُوبَ وَٱلْأَسْبَاطَ كَانُوا۟ هُودًا أَوْ نَصَـٰرَىٰ ۗ
قُلْ ءَأَنتُمْ أَعْلَمُ أَمِ ٱللَّهُ ۗ وَمَنْ أَظْلَمُ مِمَّن كَتَمَ
شَهَـٰدَةً عِندَهُۥ مِنَ ٱللَّهِ ۗ وَمَا ٱللَّهُ بِغَـٰفِلٍ عَمَّا
تَعْمَلُونَ ١٤٠

141. That was a people that have passed away. They shall reap the fruit of what they did and you of what you do! Of their merits there is no question in your case.

تِلْكَ أُمَّةٌ قَدْ خَلَتْ ۖ لَهَا مَا كَسَبَتْ وَلَكُم مَّا
كَسَبْتُمْ ۖ وَلَا تُسْـَٔلُونَ عَمَّا كَانُوا۟ يَعْمَلُونَ ١٤١

الجزء ٢ الحزب ٣

❊ **142.** The fools among the people will say: "What has turned them from the *Qiblah* to which they were used?" Say: To Allah belong east and west: He guides whom He will to a way that is straight.

❊ سَيَقُولُ ٱلسُّفَهَآءُ مِنَ ٱلنَّاسِ مَا وَلَّىٰهُمْ عَن قِبْلَتِهِمُ
ٱلَّتِى كَانُوا۟ عَلَيْهَا ۚ قُل لِّلَّهِ ٱلْمَشْرِقُ وَٱلْمَغْرِبُ ۚ يَهْدِى
مَن يَشَآءُ إِلَىٰ صِرَٰطٍ مُّسْتَقِيمٍ ١٤٢

143. Thus have We made of you an Ummah justly balanced, that you might be witnesses over the nations, and the messenger a witness over yourselves; and We appointed the *Qiblah* to which you were used, only to test those who followed the messenger from those who would turn on their heels (from the faith). Indeed it was (a change) momentous, except to those guided by Allah. And never would Allah make your faith of no effect. For Allah is to all people most surely full of kindness, Most Merciful.

وَكَذَٰلِكَ جَعَلْنَٰكُمْ أُمَّةً وَسَطًا لِّتَكُونُوا۟
شُهَدَآءَ عَلَى ٱلنَّاسِ وَيَكُونَ ٱلرَّسُولُ عَلَيْكُمْ
شَهِيدًا ۗ وَمَا جَعَلْنَا ٱلْقِبْلَةَ ٱلَّتِى كُنتَ عَلَيْهَآ إِلَّا
لِنَعْلَمَ مَن يَتَّبِعُ ٱلرَّسُولَ مِمَّن يَنقَلِبُ عَلَىٰ عَقِبَيْهِ ۚ
وَإِن كَانَتْ لَكَبِيرَةً إِلَّا عَلَى ٱلَّذِينَ هَدَى ٱللَّهُ ۗ
وَمَا كَانَ ٱللَّهُ لِيُضِيعَ إِيمَٰنَكُمْ ۚ إِنَّ ٱللَّهَ
بِٱلنَّاسِ لَرَءُوفٌ رَّحِيمٌ ١٤٣

144. We see the turning of your face (for guidance) to the heavens: now shall We turn you to a *Qiblah* that shall please you. Turn then your face in the direction of the Sacred Mosque: wherever you are, turn your faces in that direction. The People of the Book know well that that is the truth from their Lord, nor is Allah unmindful of what they do.

قَدْ نَرَىٰ تَقَلُّبَ وَجْهِكَ فِى ٱلسَّمَآءِ ۖ فَلَنُوَلِّيَنَّكَ قِبْلَةً
تَرْضَىٰهَا ۚ فَوَلِّ وَجْهَكَ شَطْرَ ٱلْمَسْجِدِ ٱلْحَرَامِ ۚ
وَحَيْثُ مَا كُنتُمْ فَوَلُّوا۟ وُجُوهَكُمْ شَطْرَهُۥ ۗ وَإِنَّ
ٱلَّذِينَ أُوتُوا۟ ٱلْكِتَٰبَ لَيَعْلَمُونَ أَنَّهُ ٱلْحَقُّ مِن
رَّبِّهِمْ ۗ وَمَا ٱللَّهُ بِغَٰفِلٍ عَمَّا يَعْمَلُونَ ١٤٤

145. Even if you were to bring to the People of the Book all the signs (together), they would not follow your *Qiblah*; nor are you going to follow their *Qiblah*; nor indeed will they follow each other's *Qiblah*. If you, after the knowledge has reached you, were to follow their (vain) desires - then would you indeed be (clearly) in the wrong.

وَلَئِنْ أَتَيْتَ ٱلَّذِينَ أُوتُوا۟ ٱلْكِتَٰبَ بِكُلِّ ءَايَةٍ
مَّا تَبِعُوا۟ قِبْلَتَكَ ۚ وَمَآ أَنتَ بِتَابِعٍ قِبْلَتَهُمْ ۚ وَمَا
بَعْضُهُم بِتَابِعٍ قِبْلَةَ بَعْضٍ ۚ وَلَئِنِ ٱتَّبَعْتَ
أَهْوَآءَهُم مِّنۢ بَعْدِ مَا جَآءَكَ مِنَ ٱلْعِلْمِ ۙ إِنَّكَ
إِذًا لَّمِنَ ٱلظَّٰلِمِينَ ١٤٥

❊ Part-2

146. The People of the Book know this as they know their own sons; but some of them conceal the truth which they themselves know.

ٱلَّذِينَ ءَاتَيۡنَٰهُمُ ٱلۡكِتَٰبَ يَعۡرِفُونَهُۥ كَمَا يَعۡرِفُونَ
أَبۡنَآءَهُمۡۖ وَإِنَّ فَرِيقٗا مِّنۡهُمۡ لَيَكۡتُمُونَ ٱلۡحَقَّ
وَهُمۡ يَعۡلَمُونَ ١٤٦

147. The truth is from your Lord so be not at all in doubt.

ٱلۡحَقُّ مِن رَّبِّكَ فَلَا تَكُونَنَّ مِنَ ٱلۡمُمۡتَرِينَ ١٤٧

148. To each is a goal to which Allah turns him; then strive together (as in a race) towards all that is good. Wheresoever you are, Allah will bring you together. For Allah has power over all things.

وَلِكُلّٖ وِجۡهَةٌ هُوَ مُوَلِّيهَاۖ فَٱسۡتَبِقُواْ ٱلۡخَيۡرَٰتِۚ
أَيۡنَ مَا تَكُونُواْ يَأۡتِ بِكُمُ ٱللَّهُ جَمِيعًاۚ إِنَّ ٱللَّهَ عَلَىٰ
كُلِّ شَيۡءٖ قَدِيرٞ ١٤٨

149. From wheresoever you start out turn your face in the direction of the Sacred Mosque; that is indeed the truth from your Lord. And Allah is not unmindful of what you do.

وَمِنۡ حَيۡثُ خَرَجۡتَ فَوَلِّ وَجۡهَكَ شَطۡرَ ٱلۡمَسۡجِدِ
ٱلۡحَرَامِۖ وَإِنَّهُۥ لَلۡحَقُّ مِن رَّبِّكَۗ وَمَا ٱللَّهُ بِغَٰفِلٍ عَمَّا
تَعۡمَلُونَ ١٤٩

150. So from wheresoever you start out, turn your face in the direction of the Sacred Mosque; And wheresoever you are, turn your face there: that there be no ground of dispute against you among the people, except those of them that are bent on wickedness; so fear them not, but fear Me; and that I may complete My favours on you, and you may (consent to) be guided;

وَمِنۡ حَيۡثُ خَرَجۡتَ فَوَلِّ وَجۡهَكَ شَطۡرَ ٱلۡمَسۡجِدِ
ٱلۡحَرَامِۚ وَحَيۡثُ مَا كُنتُمۡ فَوَلُّواْ وُجُوهَكُمۡ
شَطۡرَهُۥ لِئَلَّا يَكُونَ لِلنَّاسِ عَلَيۡكُمۡ حُجَّةٌ إِلَّا ٱلَّذِينَ
ظَلَمُواْ مِنۡهُمۡ فَلَا تَخۡشَوۡهُمۡ وَٱخۡشَوۡنِي وَلِأُتِمَّ
نِعۡمَتِي عَلَيۡكُمۡ وَلَعَلَّكُمۡ تَهۡتَدُونَ ١٥٠

151. A similar (favour have you already received) in that We have sent among you a messenger of your own, rehearsing to you Our Signs, and purifying you, and instructing you in scripture and wisdom, and in new knowledge.

كَمَآ أَرۡسَلۡنَا فِيكُمۡ رَسُولٗا مِّنكُمۡ يَتۡلُواْ عَلَيۡكُمۡ
ءَايَٰتِنَا وَيُزَكِّيكُمۡ وَيُعَلِّمُكُمُ ٱلۡكِتَٰبَ
وَٱلۡحِكۡمَةَ وَيُعَلِّمُكُم مَّا لَمۡ تَكُونُواْ تَعۡلَمُونَ ١٥١

152. Then do you remember Me; I will remember you. Be grateful to Me, and reject not faith.

فَٱذۡكُرُونِيٓ أَذۡكُرۡكُمۡ وَٱشۡكُرُواْ لِي وَلَا
تَكۡفُرُونِ ١٥٢

153. O you who believe! Seek help with patient perseverance and prayer: for Allah is with those who patiently persevere.

يَٰٓأَيُّهَا ٱلَّذِينَ ءَامَنُواْ ٱسۡتَعِينُواْ بِٱلصَّبۡرِ
وَٱلصَّلَوٰةِۚ إِنَّ ٱللَّهَ مَعَ ٱلصَّٰبِرِينَ ١٥٣

154. And say not of those who are slain in the way of Allah: "They are dead." Nay, they are living, though you perceive (it) not.

وَلَا تَقُولُواْ لِمَن يُقۡتَلُ فِي سَبِيلِ ٱللَّهِ أَمۡوَٰتُۢۚ بَلۡ
أَحۡيَآءٞ وَلَٰكِن لَّا تَشۡعُرُونَ ١٥٤

155. Be sure We shall test you with something of fear and hunger, some loss in goods or lives or the fruits (of your toil), but give glad tidings to those who patiently persevere -

وَلَنَبۡلُوَنَّكُم بِشَيۡءٖ مِّنَ ٱلۡخَوۡفِ وَٱلۡجُوعِ وَنَقۡصٖ
مِّنَ ٱلۡأَمۡوَٰلِ وَٱلۡأَنفُسِ وَٱلثَّمَرَٰتِۗ وَبَشِّرِ
ٱلصَّٰبِرِينَ ١٥٥

156. Who say, when afflicted with calamity: "To Allah we belong, and to Him is our return" -

ٱلَّذِينَ إِذَآ أَصَٰبَتۡهُم مُّصِيبَةٞ قَالُوٓاْ إِنَّا لِلَّهِ وَإِنَّآ
إِلَيۡهِ رَٰجِعُونَ ١٥٦

157. They are those on whom (descend) blessings from their Lord, and mercy, and they are the ones that receive guidance.

أُوْلَٰٓئِكَ عَلَيۡهِمۡ صَلَوَٰتٞ مِّن رَّبِّهِمۡ وَرَحۡمَةٞۖ
وَأُوْلَٰٓئِكَ هُمُ ٱلۡمُهۡتَدُونَ ١٥٧

158. Behold! as-Safa and al-Marwah are among the symbols of Allah. So if those who visit the House in the season or at other times, should go around them, it is no sin in them. And if anyone obeys his own impulse to good - be sure that Allah is He Who recognises and knows.

۞إِنَّ ٱلصَّفَا وَٱلۡمَرۡوَةَ مِن شَعَآئِرِ ٱللَّهِۖ فَمَنۡ حَجَّ ربع الحزب ٣
ٱلۡبَيۡتَ أَوِ ٱعۡتَمَرَ فَلَا جُنَاحَ عَلَيۡهِ أَن يَطَّوَّفَ بِهِمَاۚ
وَمَن تَطَوَّعَ خَيۡرٗا فَإِنَّ ٱللَّهَ شَاكِرٌ عَلِيمٌ ١٥٨

159. Those who conceal the clear (signs) We have sent down, and the guidance, after We have made it clear for the people in the Book - on them shall be Allah's curse, and the curse of those entitled to curse -

إِنَّ ٱلَّذِينَ يَكۡتُمُونَ مَآ أَنزَلۡنَا مِنَ ٱلۡبَيِّنَٰتِ
وَٱلۡهُدَىٰ مِنۢ بَعۡدِ مَا بَيَّنَّٰهُ لِلنَّاسِ فِي ٱلۡكِتَٰبِ
أُوْلَٰٓئِكَ يَلۡعَنُهُمُ ٱللَّهُ وَيَلۡعَنُهُمُ ٱللَّٰعِنُونَ ١٥٩

160. Except those who repent and make amends and openly declare (the truth): to them I turn; for I am Oft-Returning, Most Merciful.

إِلَّا ٱلَّذِينَ تَابُواْ وَأَصۡلَحُواْ وَبَيَّنُواْ فَأُوْلَٰٓئِكَ أَتُوبُ
عَلَيۡهِمۡ وَأَنَا ٱلتَّوَّابُ ٱلرَّحِيمُ ١٦٠

161. Those who reject faith, and die rejecting - on them is Allah's curse, and the curse of angels, and of all mankind;

إِنَّ ٱلَّذِينَ كَفَرُواْ وَمَاتُواْ وَهُمْ كُفَّارٌ أُوْلَٰٓئِكَ
عَلَيْهِمْ لَعْنَةُ ٱللَّهِ وَٱلْمَلَٰٓئِكَةِ وَٱلنَّاسِ أَجْمَعِينَ ١٦١

162. They will remain in it: Their penalty will not be lightened, nor will respite be their (lot).

خَٰلِدِينَ فِيهَا لَا يُخَفَّفُ عَنْهُمُ ٱلْعَذَابُ وَلَا هُمْ
يُنظَرُونَ ١٦٢

163. And your God is One God: there is no god but He, Most Gracious, Most Merciful.

وَإِلَٰهُكُمْ إِلَٰهٌ وَٰحِدٌ لَّآ إِلَٰهَ إِلَّا هُوَ ٱلرَّحْمَٰنُ
ٱلرَّحِيمُ ١٦٣

164. See! In the creation of the heavens and the earth; in the alternation of the night and the day; in the sailing of the ships through the ocean for the profit of mankind; in the rain which Allah sends down from the skies, and the life which He gives with it to an earth that is dead; in the beasts of all kinds that He scatters through the earth; in the change of the winds, and the clouds which they trail like their slaves between the sky and the earth - (here) indeed are signs for a people that are wise.

إِنَّ فِي خَلْقِ ٱلسَّمَٰوَٰتِ وَٱلْأَرْضِ وَٱخْتِلَٰفِ ٱلَّيْلِ
وَٱلنَّهَارِ وَٱلْفُلْكِ ٱلَّتِي تَجْرِي فِي ٱلْبَحْرِ بِمَا يَنفَعُ
ٱلنَّاسَ وَمَآ أَنزَلَ ٱللَّهُ مِنَ ٱلسَّمَآءِ مِن مَّآءٍ فَأَحْيَا
بِهِ ٱلْأَرْضَ بَعْدَ مَوْتِهَا وَبَثَّ فِيهَا مِن كُلِّ دَآبَّةٍ
وَتَصْرِيفِ ٱلرِّيَٰحِ وَٱلسَّحَابِ ٱلْمُسَخَّرِ بَيْنَ
ٱلسَّمَآءِ وَٱلْأَرْضِ لَأٓيَٰتٍ لِّقَوْمٍ يَعْقِلُونَ ١٦٤

165. Yet there are men who take (for worship) others besides Allah, as equal (with Allah): they love them as they should love Allah. But those of faith are overflowing in their love for Allah. If only the unrighteous could see, they would see the punishment: that to Allah belongs all power, and Allah will strongly enforce the punishment.

وَمِنَ ٱلنَّاسِ مَن يَتَّخِذُ مِن دُونِ ٱللَّهِ أَندَادًا
يُحِبُّونَهُمْ كَحُبِّ ٱللَّهِ وَٱلَّذِينَ ءَامَنُوٓاْ أَشَدُّ حُبًّا لِّلَّهِ
وَلَوْ يَرَى ٱلَّذِينَ ظَلَمُوٓاْ إِذْ يَرَوْنَ ٱلْعَذَابَ
أَنَّ ٱلْقُوَّةَ لِلَّهِ جَمِيعًا وَأَنَّ ٱللَّهَ شَدِيدُ ٱلْعَذَابِ ١٦٥

166. Then would those who are followed clear themselves of those who follow (them): they would see the penalty, and all relations between them would be cut off.

إِذْ تَبَرَّأَ ٱلَّذِينَ ٱتُّبِعُواْ مِنَ ٱلَّذِينَ ٱتَّبَعُواْ وَرَأَوُاْ
ٱلْعَذَابَ وَتَقَطَّعَتْ بِهِمُ ٱلْأَسْبَابُ ١٦٦

167. And those who followed would say: "If only we had one more chance, we would clear ourselves of them, as they have cleared themselves of us." Thus will Allah show them (the fruits of) their deeds as (nothing but) regrets. Nor will there be a way for them out of the fire.

وَقَالَ ٱلَّذِينَ ٱتَّبَعُوا۟ لَوْ أَنَّ لَنَا كَرَّةً فَنَتَبَرَّأَ
مِنْهُمْ كَمَا تَبَرَّءُوا۟ مِنَّا ۗ كَذَٰلِكَ يُرِيهِمُ ٱللَّهُ
أَعْمَٰلَهُمْ حَسَرَٰتٍ عَلَيْهِمْ ۖ وَمَا هُم بِخَٰرِجِينَ مِنَ
ٱلنَّارِ ﴿١٦٧﴾

168. O you people! Eat of what is on earth, lawful and good; and do not follow the footsteps of the evil one, for he is to you an avowed enemy.

يَٰٓأَيُّهَا ٱلنَّاسُ كُلُوا۟ مِمَّا فِى ٱلْأَرْضِ حَلَٰلًا طَيِّبًا
وَلَا تَتَّبِعُوا۟ خُطُوَٰتِ ٱلشَّيْطَٰنِ ۚ إِنَّهُۥ لَكُمْ عَدُوٌّ
مُّبِينٌ ﴿١٦٨﴾

169. For he commands you what is evil and shameful, and that you should say of Allah that of which you have no knowledge.

إِنَّمَا يَأْمُرُكُم بِٱلسُّوٓءِ وَٱلْفَحْشَآءِ وَأَن تَقُولُوا۟
عَلَى ٱللَّهِ مَا لَا تَعْلَمُونَ ﴿١٦٩﴾

170. When it is said to them: "Follow what Allah has revealed:" they say: "Nay! We shall follow the ways of our fathers:" What! Even though their fathers were void of wisdom and guidance?

وَإِذَا قِيلَ لَهُمُ ٱتَّبِعُوا۟ مَآ أَنزَلَ ٱللَّهُ قَالُوا۟ بَلْ نَتَّبِعُ
مَآ أَلْفَيْنَا عَلَيْهِ ءَابَآءَنَآ ۗ أَوَلَوْ كَانَ ءَابَآؤُهُمْ
لَا يَعْقِلُونَ شَيْـًٔا وَلَا يَهْتَدُونَ ﴿١٧٠﴾

171. The parable of those who reject faith is as if one were to shout like a goat-herd, to things that listen to nothing but calls and cries: deaf, dumb and blind, they are void of wisdom.

وَمَثَلُ ٱلَّذِينَ كَفَرُوا۟ كَمَثَلِ ٱلَّذِى يَنْعِقُ بِمَا لَا
يَسْمَعُ إِلَّا دُعَآءً وَنِدَآءً ۚ صُمٌّۢ بُكْمٌ عُمْىٌ فَهُمْ لَا
يَعْقِلُونَ ﴿١٧١﴾

172. O you who believe! Eat of the good things that We have provided for you and be grateful to Allah, if it is Him you worship.

يَٰٓأَيُّهَا ٱلَّذِينَ ءَامَنُوا۟ كُلُوا۟ مِن طَيِّبَٰتِ
مَا رَزَقْنَٰكُمْ وَٱشْكُرُوا۟ لِلَّهِ إِن كُنتُمْ إِيَّاهُ
تَعْبُدُونَ ﴿١٧٢﴾

173. He has only forbidden you dead meat, and blood, and the flesh of swine, and that on which any other name has been invoked besides that of Allah. But if one is forced by

إِنَّمَا حَرَّمَ عَلَيْكُمُ ٱلْمَيْتَةَ وَٱلدَّمَ وَلَحْمَ
ٱلْخِنزِيرِ وَمَآ أُهِلَّ بِهِۦ لِغَيْرِ ٱللَّهِ ۖ فَمَنِ ٱضْطُرَّ غَيْرَ

necessity, without wilful disobedience, nor transgressing due limits - then is he guiltless. For Allah is Oft-Forgiving, Most Merciful.

بَاغٍ وَلَا عَادٍ فَلَآ إِثْمَ عَلَيْهِ ۚ إِنَّ ٱللَّهَ غَفُورٌ
رَّحِيمٌ ﴿١٧٣﴾

174. Those who conceal Allah's revelations in the Book, and purchase for them a miserable profit - they swallow into themselves nothing but fire; Allah will not address them on the day of resurrection, nor purify them; grievous will be their penalty.

إِنَّ ٱلَّذِينَ يَكْتُمُونَ مَآ أَنزَلَ ٱللَّهُ مِنَ ٱلْكِتَٰبِ
وَيَشْتَرُونَ بِهِۦ ثَمَنًا قَلِيلًا ۙ أُو۟لَٰٓئِكَ مَا يَأْكُلُونَ فِى
بُطُونِهِمْ إِلَّا ٱلنَّارَ وَلَا يُكَلِّمُهُمُ ٱللَّهُ يَوْمَ
ٱلْقِيَٰمَةِ وَلَا يُزَكِّيهِمْ وَلَهُمْ عَذَابٌ أَلِيمٌ ﴿١٧٤﴾

175. They are the ones who buy error in place of guidance and torment in place of forgiveness. Ah! What boldness (they show) for the fire!

أُو۟لَٰٓئِكَ ٱلَّذِينَ ٱشْتَرَوُا۟ ٱلضَّلَٰلَةَ بِٱلْهُدَىٰ
وَٱلْعَذَابَ بِٱلْمَغْفِرَةِ ۚ فَمَآ أَصْبَرَهُمْ عَلَى
ٱلنَّارِ ﴿١٧٥﴾

176. (Their doom is) because Allah sent down the book in truth but those who seek causes of dispute in the book are in a schism far (from the purpose).

ذَٰلِكَ بِأَنَّ ٱللَّهَ نَزَّلَ ٱلْكِتَٰبَ بِٱلْحَقِّ ۗ وَإِنَّ ٱلَّذِينَ
ٱخْتَلَفُوا۟ فِى ٱلْكِتَٰبِ لَفِى شِقَاقٍۭ بَعِيدٍ ﴿١٧٦﴾

177. It is not righteousness that you turn your faces toward east or west; but it is righteousness to believe in Allah and the last day, and the angels, and the book, and the prophets; to spend of your substance, out of love for Him, for your relatives, for orphans, for the needy, for the wayfarer, for those who ask, and for the ransom of slaves; to be steadfast in prayer, and practice regular charity, to fulfil the contracts which you have made; and to be firm and patient, in pain (or suffering) and adversity, and throughout all periods of panic. Such are the people of truth, the God-fearing.

نصف الحزب ٣
۞ لَّيْسَ ٱلْبِرَّ أَن تُوَلُّوا۟ وُجُوهَكُمْ قِبَلَ ٱلْمَشْرِقِ
وَٱلْمَغْرِبِ وَلَٰكِنَّ ٱلْبِرَّ مَنْ ءَامَنَ بِٱللَّهِ وَٱلْيَوْمِ
ٱلْءَاخِرِ وَٱلْمَلَٰٓئِكَةِ وَٱلْكِتَٰبِ وَٱلنَّبِيِّۦنَ وَءَاتَى
ٱلْمَالَ عَلَىٰ حُبِّهِۦ ذَوِى ٱلْقُرْبَىٰ وَٱلْيَتَٰمَىٰ وَٱلْمَسَٰكِينَ وَٱبْنَ
ٱلسَّبِيلِ وَٱلسَّآئِلِينَ وَفِى ٱلرِّقَابِ وَأَقَامَ ٱلصَّلَوٰةَ
وَءَاتَى ٱلزَّكَوٰةَ وَٱلْمُوفُونَ بِعَهْدِهِمْ إِذَا عَٰهَدُوا۟ ۖ
وَٱلصَّٰبِرِينَ فِى ٱلْبَأْسَآءِ وَٱلضَّرَّآءِ وَحِينَ ٱلْبَأْسِ ۗ
أُو۟لَٰٓئِكَ ٱلَّذِينَ صَدَقُوا۟ ۖ وَأُو۟لَٰٓئِكَ هُمُ ٱلْمُتَّقُونَ ﴿١٧٧﴾

178. O you who believe! The law of equality is prescribed to you in cases of murder: the free for the free, the slave for the slave, the woman for the woman. But if any remission is made by the brother of the slain, then grant any reasonable demand, and compensate him with handsome gratitude. This is a concession and a mercy from your Lord. After this, whoever exceeds the limits shall be in grave penalty.

يَٰٓأَيُّهَا ٱلَّذِينَ ءَامَنُوا۟ كُتِبَ عَلَيْكُمُ ٱلْقِصَاصُ فِى
ٱلْقَتْلَى ۖ ٱلْحُرُّ بِٱلْحُرِّ وَٱلْعَبْدُ بِٱلْعَبْدِ وَٱلْأُنثَىٰ بِٱلْأُنثَىٰ ۚ
فَمَنْ عُفِىَ لَهُۥ مِنْ أَخِيهِ شَىْءٌ فَٱتِّبَاعٌۢ بِٱلْمَعْرُوفِ
وَأَدَآءٌ إِلَيْهِ بِإِحْسَٰنٍ ۗ ذَٰلِكَ تَخْفِيفٌ مِّن رَّبِّكُمْ
وَرَحْمَةٌ ۗ فَمَنِ ٱعْتَدَىٰ بَعْدَ ذَٰلِكَ فَلَهُۥ عَذَابٌ
أَلِيمٌ ﴿١٧٨﴾

179. In the law of equality there is (saving of) life to you, O you men of understanding; that you may restrain yourselves.

وَلَكُمْ فِى ٱلْقِصَاصِ حَيَوٰةٌ يَٰٓأُو۟لِى ٱلْأَلْبَٰبِ لَعَلَّكُمْ
تَتَّقُونَ ﴿١٧٩﴾

180. It is prescribed, when death approaches any of you, if he leave any goods, that he make a bequest to parents and near relatives, according to reasonable usage; this is due from the God-fearing.

كُتِبَ عَلَيْكُمْ إِذَا حَضَرَ أَحَدَكُمُ ٱلْمَوْتُ إِن تَرَكَ
خَيْرًا ٱلْوَصِيَّةُ لِلْوَٰلِدَيْنِ وَٱلْأَقْرَبِينَ بِٱلْمَعْرُوفِ ۖ
حَقًّا عَلَى ٱلْمُتَّقِينَ ﴿١٨٠﴾

181. If anyone changes the bequest after hearing it, the guilt shall be on those who make the change. For Allah hears and knows (all things).

فَمَنۢ بَدَّلَهُۥ بَعْدَ مَا سَمِعَهُۥ فَإِنَّمَآ إِثْمُهُۥ عَلَى ٱلَّذِينَ
يُبَدِّلُونَهُۥٓ ۚ إِنَّ ٱللَّهَ سَمِيعٌ عَلِيمٌ ﴿١٨١﴾

182. But if anyone fears partiality or wrongdoing on the part of the testator, and makes peace between (the parties concerned), there is no wrong in him: for Allah is Oft-Forgiving, Most Merciful.

فَمَنْ خَافَ مِن مُّوصٍ جَنَفًا أَوْ إِثْمًا فَأَصْلَحَ بَيْنَهُمْ
فَلَآ إِثْمَ عَلَيْهِ ۚ إِنَّ ٱللَّهَ غَفُورٌ رَّحِيمٌ ﴿١٨٢﴾

183. O you who believe! Fasting is prescribed to you as it was prescribed to those before you, that you may (learn) self-restraint -

يَٰٓأَيُّهَا ٱلَّذِينَ ءَامَنُوا۟ كُتِبَ عَلَيْكُمُ ٱلصِّيَامُ
كَمَا كُتِبَ عَلَى ٱلَّذِينَ مِن قَبْلِكُمْ لَعَلَّكُمْ
تَتَّقُونَ ﴿١٨٣﴾

184. (Fasting) for a fixed number of days; but if any of you is ill, or on a journey, the prescribed number (should be made up) from days later. For those who can do it (with hardship), is a ransom, the feeding of one that is needy. But he that will give more, of his own free will - it is better for him. And it is better for you that you fast, if you only knew.

أَيَّامًا مَّعۡدُودَٰتٖۚ فَمَن كَانَ مِنكُم
مَّرِيضًا أَوۡ عَلَىٰ سَفَرٖ فَعِدَّةٞ مِّنۡ أَيَّامٍ أُخَرَۚ وَعَلَى
ٱلَّذِينَ يُطِيقُونَهُۥ فِدۡيَةٞ طَعَامُ مِسۡكِينٖۖ فَمَن
تَطَوَّعَ خَيۡرٗا فَهُوَ خَيۡرٞ لَّهُۥۚ وَأَن تَصُومُواْ خَيۡرٞ لَّكُمۡ
إِن كُنتُمۡ تَعۡلَمُونَ ﴿١٨٤﴾

185. Ramadan is the (month) in which was sent down the Qur'an, as a guide to mankind, also clear (signs) for guidance and judgement (between right and wrong). So every one of you who is present (at his home) during that month should spend it in fasting, but if any one is ill, or on a journey, the prescribed period (should be made up) by days later. Allah intends every facility for you; He does not want to put you to difficulties. (He wants you) to complete the prescribed period, and to glorify Him in that He has guided you; and perhaps you shall be grateful.

شَهۡرُ رَمَضَانَ ٱلَّذِيٓ أُنزِلَ فِيهِ ٱلۡقُرۡءَانُ هُدٗى
لِّلنَّاسِ وَبَيِّنَٰتٖ مِّنَ ٱلۡهُدَىٰ وَٱلۡفُرۡقَانِۚ فَمَن
شَهِدَ مِنكُمُ ٱلشَّهۡرَ فَلۡيَصُمۡهُۖ وَمَن
كَانَ مَرِيضًا أَوۡ عَلَىٰ سَفَرٖ فَعِدَّةٞ مِّنۡ أَيَّامٍ
أُخَرَۗ يُرِيدُ ٱللَّهُ بِكُمُ ٱلۡيُسۡرَ وَلَا يُرِيدُ بِكُمُ
ٱلۡعُسۡرَ وَلِتُكۡمِلُواْ ٱلۡعِدَّةَ وَلِتُكَبِّرُواْ ٱللَّهَ
عَلَىٰ مَا هَدَىٰكُمۡ وَلَعَلَّكُمۡ تَشۡكُرُونَ ﴿١٨٥﴾

186. When my servants ask you concerning Me, I am indeed close (to them): I listen to the prayer of every suppliant when he calls on Me: let them also, with a will, listen to My call, and believe in Me: that they may walk in the right way.

وَإِذَا سَأَلَكَ عِبَادِي عَنِّي فَإِنِّي قَرِيبٌۖ أُجِيبُ
دَعۡوَةَ ٱلدَّاعِ إِذَا دَعَانِۖ فَلۡيَسۡتَجِيبُواْ لِي
وَلۡيُؤۡمِنُواْ بِي لَعَلَّهُمۡ يَرۡشُدُونَ ﴿١٨٦﴾

187. Permitted to you, on the night of the fasts, is the approach to your wives. They are your garments and you are their garments. Allah knows what you used to do secretly among yourselves; but He turned to you and forgave you; so now associate with them, and seek what

أُحِلَّ لَكُمۡ لَيۡلَةَ ٱلصِّيَامِ ٱلرَّفَثُ إِلَىٰ
نِسَآئِكُمۡۚ هُنَّ لِبَاسٞ لَّكُمۡ وَأَنتُمۡ لِبَاسٞ
لَّهُنَّۗ عَلِمَ ٱللَّهُ أَنَّكُمۡ كُنتُمۡ تَخۡتَانُونَ أَنفُسَكُمۡ
فَتَابَ عَلَيۡكُمۡ وَعَفَا عَنكُمۡۖ فَٱلۡـَٰٔنَ بَٰشِرُوهُنَّ

Allah has ordained for you, and eat and drink, until the white thread of dawn appear to you distinct from its black thread; then complete your fast till the night appears; but do not associate with your wives while you are in retreat in the mosques. Those are limits (set by) Allah: come not near to it. Thus does Allah make clear His signs to men: that they may learn self-restraint.

وَابْتَغُوا مَا كَتَبَ اللَّهُ لَكُمْ ۚ وَكُلُوا وَاشْرَبُوا
حَتَّىٰ يَتَبَيَّنَ لَكُمُ الْخَيْطُ الْأَبْيَضُ مِنَ الْخَيْطِ
الْأَسْوَدِ مِنَ الْفَجْرِ ۖ ثُمَّ أَتِمُّوا الصِّيَامَ إِلَى اللَّيْلِ ۚ
وَلَا تُبَاشِرُوهُنَّ وَأَنْتُمْ عَاكِفُونَ فِي الْمَسَاجِدِ ۗ تِلْكَ
حُدُودُ اللَّهِ فَلَا تَقْرَبُوهَا ۗ كَذَٰلِكَ يُبَيِّنُ اللَّهُ آيَاتِهِ
لِلنَّاسِ لَعَلَّهُمْ يَتَّقُونَ ﴿١٨٧﴾

188. And do not eat up your property among yourselves for vanities, nor use it as bait for the judges, with intent that you may eat up wrongfully and knowingly a little of (other) people's property.

وَلَا تَأْكُلُوا أَمْوَالَكُمْ بَيْنَكُمْ بِالْبَاطِلِ
وَتُدْلُوا بِهَا إِلَى الْحُكَّامِ لِتَأْكُلُوا فَرِيقًا
مِنْ أَمْوَالِ النَّاسِ بِالْإِثْمِ وَأَنْتُمْ تَعْلَمُونَ ﴿١٨٨﴾

189. They ask you concerning the new moons. Say: they are but signs to mark fixed periods of time in (the affairs of) men, and for pilgrimage. It is no virtue if you enter your houses from the back: it is virtue if you fear Allah. Enter houses through the proper doors: and fear Allah: that you may prosper.

ثلاثة أرباع الحزب ٣ ۞ يَسْأَلُونَكَ عَنِ الْأَهِلَّةِ ۖ قُلْ هِيَ مَوَاقِيتُ لِلنَّاسِ
وَالْحَجِّ ۗ وَلَيْسَ الْبِرُّ بِأَنْ تَأْتُوا الْبُيُوتَ مِنْ
ظُهُورِهَا وَلَٰكِنَّ الْبِرَّ مَنِ اتَّقَىٰ ۗ وَأْتُوا
الْبُيُوتَ مِنْ أَبْوَابِهَا ۚ وَاتَّقُوا اللَّهَ
لَعَلَّكُمْ تُفْلِحُونَ ﴿١٨٩﴾

190. Fight in the cause of Allah those who fight you, but do not transgress limits; for Allah loves not transgressors.

وَقَاتِلُوا فِي سَبِيلِ اللَّهِ الَّذِينَ يُقَاتِلُونَكُمْ
وَلَا تَعْتَدُوا ۚ إِنَّ اللَّهَ لَا يُحِبُّ الْمُعْتَدِينَ ﴿١٩٠﴾

191. And slay them wherever you catch them, and turn them out from where they have turned you out; for tumult and oppression are worse than slaughter; but fight them not at the Sacred Mosque, unless they (first) fight you there; but if they fight you, slay them. Such is the reward of those who suppress faith.

وَاقْتُلُوهُمْ حَيْثُ ثَقِفْتُمُوهُمْ وَأَخْرِجُوهُمْ مِنْ حَيْثُ
أَخْرَجُوكُمْ ۚ وَالْفِتْنَةُ أَشَدُّ مِنَ الْقَتْلِ ۚ وَلَا تُقَاتِلُوهُمْ
عِنْدَ الْمَسْجِدِ الْحَرَامِ حَتَّىٰ يُقَاتِلُوكُمْ فِيهِ ۖ فَإِنْ قَاتَلُوكُمْ
فَاقْتُلُوهُمْ ۗ كَذَٰلِكَ جَزَاءُ الْكَافِرِينَ ﴿١٩١﴾

192. But if they cease, Allah is Oft-Forgiving, Most Merciful.

فَإِنِ ٱنتَهَوۡاْ فَإِنَّ ٱللَّهَ غَفُورٞ رَّحِيمٞ ١٩٢

193. And fight them on until there is no more tumult or oppression, and there prevail justice and faith in Allah; but if they cease, let there be no hostility except to those who practice oppression.

وَقَٰتِلُوهُمۡ حَتَّىٰ لَا تَكُونَ فِتۡنَةٞ وَيَكُونَ ٱلدِّينُ لِلَّهِۖ فَإِنِ
ٱنتَهَوۡاْ فَلَا عُدۡوَٰنَ إِلَّا عَلَى ٱلظَّٰلِمِينَ ١٩٣

194. The prohibited month - for the prohibited month, and so for all things prohibited - there is the law of equality. If then anyone transgresses the prohibition against you, transgress you likewise against him. But fear Allah, and know that Allah is with those who restrain themselves.

ٱلشَّهۡرُ ٱلۡحَرَامُ بِٱلشَّهۡرِ ٱلۡحَرَامِ وَٱلۡحُرُمَٰتُ قِصَاصٞۚ فَمَنِ
ٱعۡتَدَىٰ عَلَيۡكُمۡ فَٱعۡتَدُواْ عَلَيۡهِ بِمِثۡلِ مَا ٱعۡتَدَىٰ
عَلَيۡكُمۡۚ وَٱتَّقُواْ ٱللَّهَ وَٱعۡلَمُوٓاْ أَنَّ ٱللَّهَ مَعَ ٱلۡمُتَّقِينَ ١٩٤

195. And spend of your substance in the cause of Allah, and make not your own hands contribute to (your) destruction; but do good; for Allah loves those who do good.

وَأَنفِقُواْ فِي سَبِيلِ ٱللَّهِ وَلَا تُلۡقُواْ بِأَيۡدِيكُمۡ إِلَى ٱلتَّهۡلُكَةِ
وَأَحۡسِنُوٓاْۚ إِنَّ ٱللَّهَ يُحِبُّ ٱلۡمُحۡسِنِينَ ١٩٥

196. And complete the Hajj or Umrah in the service of Allah, but if you are prevented (from completing it), send an offering for sacrifice, such as you may find, and do not shave your heads until the offering reaches the place of sacrifice. And if any of you is ill, or has an ailment in his scalp, (necessitating shaving), (he should) in compensation either fast, or feed the poor, or offer sacrifice; and when you are in peaceful conditions (again), if anyone wishes to continue the Umrah on to the Hajj, he must make an offering such as he can afford, but if he cannot afford it, he should fast three days during the Hajj and seven days on his return, making ten days in all. This is for those whose household is not in (the precincts of) the Sacred Mosque, and fear Allah, and know that Allah is strict in punishment.

وَأَتِمُّواْ ٱلۡحَجَّ وَٱلۡعُمۡرَةَ لِلَّهِۚ فَإِنۡ أُحۡصِرۡتُمۡ فَمَا ٱسۡتَيۡسَرَ
مِنَ ٱلۡهَدۡيِۖ وَلَا تَحۡلِقُواْ رُءُوسَكُمۡ حَتَّىٰ يَبۡلُغَ ٱلۡهَدۡيُ مَحِلَّهُۥۚ
فَمَن كَانَ مِنكُم مَّرِيضًا أَوۡ بِهِۦٓ أَذٗى مِّن رَّأۡسِهِۦ فَفِدۡيَةٞ
مِّن صِيَامٍ أَوۡ صَدَقَةٍ أَوۡ نُسُكٖۚ فَإِذَآ أَمِنتُمۡ فَمَن تَمَتَّعَ
بِٱلۡعُمۡرَةِ إِلَى ٱلۡحَجِّ فَمَا ٱسۡتَيۡسَرَ مِنَ ٱلۡهَدۡيِۚ فَمَن لَّمۡ يَجِدۡ
فَصِيَامُ ثَلَٰثَةِ أَيَّامٖ فِي ٱلۡحَجِّ وَسَبۡعَةٍ إِذَا رَجَعۡتُمۡۗ تِلۡكَ
عَشَرَةٞ كَامِلَةٞۗ ذَٰلِكَ لِمَن لَّمۡ يَكُنۡ أَهۡلُهُۥ حَاضِرِي ٱلۡمَسۡجِدِ
ٱلۡحَرَامِۚ وَٱتَّقُواْ ٱللَّهَ وَٱعۡلَمُوٓاْ أَنَّ ٱللَّهَ شَدِيدُ ٱلۡعِقَابِ ١٩٦

197. For Hajj are the months well-known. If anyone undertakes that duty in them, let there be no obscenity, nor wickedness, nor wrangling in the Hajj and whatever good you do, (be sure) Allah knows it. And take a provision (with you) for the journey, but the best of provisions is right conduct. So fear Me, O you that are wise.

ٱلْحَجُّ أَشْهُرٌ مَّعْلُومَٰتٌ ۚ فَمَن فَرَضَ فِيهِنَّ
ٱلْحَجَّ فَلَا رَفَثَ وَلَا فُسُوقَ وَلَا جِدَالَ فِى
ٱلْحَجِّ ۗ وَمَا تَفْعَلُوا۟ مِنْ خَيْرٍ يَعْلَمْهُ ٱللَّهُ ۗ
وَتَزَوَّدُوا۟ فَإِنَّ خَيْرَ ٱلزَّادِ ٱلتَّقْوَىٰ ۖ وَٱتَّقُونِ
يَٰٓأُو۟لِى ٱلْأَلْبَٰبِ ﴿١٩٧﴾

198. It is no crime in you if you seek of the bounty of your Lord (during pilgrimage). Then when you pour down from (mount) Arafat, celebrate the praises of Allah at the Sacred Monument, and celebrate His praises as He has directed you, even though, before this, you went astray.

لَيْسَ عَلَيْكُمْ جُنَاحٌ أَن تَبْتَغُوا۟ فَضْلًا
مِّن رَّبِّكُمْ ۚ فَإِذَآ أَفَضْتُم مِّنْ عَرَفَٰتٍ
فَٱذْكُرُوا۟ ٱللَّهَ عِندَ ٱلْمَشْعَرِ ٱلْحَرَامِ ۖ
وَٱذْكُرُوهُ كَمَا هَدَىٰكُمْ وَإِن كُنتُم
مِّن قَبْلِهِۦ لَمِنَ ٱلضَّآلِّينَ ﴿١٩٨﴾

199. Then pass on at a quick pace from the place from where it is usual for the multitude to do so, and ask for Allah's forgiveness. For Allah is Oft-Forgiving, Most Merciful.

ثُمَّ أَفِيضُوا۟ مِنْ حَيْثُ أَفَاضَ ٱلنَّاسُ
وَٱسْتَغْفِرُوا۟ ٱللَّهَ ۚ إِنَّ ٱللَّهَ غَفُورٌ رَّحِيمٌ ﴿١٩٩﴾

200. So when you have accomplished your holy rites, celebrate the praises of Allah, as you used to celebrate the praises of your fathers - yea, with far more heart and soul. There are men who say: "Our Lord! Give us (Your bounties) in this world!" But they will have no portion in the hereafter.

فَإِذَا قَضَيْتُم مَّنَٰسِكَكُمْ فَٱذْكُرُوا۟ ٱللَّهَ
كَذِكْرِكُمْ ءَابَآءَكُمْ أَوْ أَشَدَّ ذِكْرًا ۗ
فَمِنَ ٱلنَّاسِ مَن يَقُولُ رَبَّنَآ ءَاتِنَا فِى
ٱلدُّنْيَا وَمَا لَهُۥ فِى ٱلْءَاخِرَةِ مِنْ خَلَٰقٍ ﴿٢٠٠﴾

201. And there are men who say: "Our Lord! Give us good in this world and good in the hereafter, and defend us from the torment of the fire!"

وَمِنْهُم مَّن يَقُولُ رَبَّنَآ ءَاتِنَا فِى ٱلدُّنْيَا
حَسَنَةً وَفِى ٱلْءَاخِرَةِ حَسَنَةً وَقِنَا عَذَابَ
ٱلنَّارِ ﴿٢٠١﴾

أُوْلَٰٓئِكَ لَهُمۡ نَصِيبٞ مِّمَّا كَسَبُواْۚ وَٱللَّهُ
سَرِيعُ ٱلۡحِسَابِ ﴿٢٠٢﴾

202. To these will be allotted what they have earned; and Allah is quick in account.

الحزب ٤

۞وَٱذۡكُرُواْ ٱللَّهَ فِيٓ أَيَّامٖ مَّعۡدُودَٰتٖۚ فَمَن
تَعَجَّلَ فِي يَوۡمَيۡنِ فَلَآ إِثۡمَ عَلَيۡهِ وَمَن تَأَخَّرَ
فَلَآ إِثۡمَ عَلَيۡهِۖ لِمَنِ ٱتَّقَىٰۗ وَٱتَّقُواْ ٱللَّهَ وَٱعۡلَمُوٓاْ
أَنَّكُمۡ إِلَيۡهِ تُحۡشَرُونَ ﴿٢٠٣﴾

203. Celebrate the praises of Allah during the appointed days. But if anyone hastens to leave in two days, there is no blame on him, and if anyone stays on, there is no blame on him, if his aim is to do right. Then fear Allah, and know that you will surely be gathered to Him.

وَمِنَ ٱلنَّاسِ مَن يُعۡجِبُكَ قَوۡلُهُۥ فِي ٱلۡحَيَوٰةِ
ٱلدُّنۡيَا وَيُشۡهِدُ ٱللَّهَ عَلَىٰ مَا فِي قَلۡبِهِۦ وَهُوَ
أَلَدُّ ٱلۡخِصَامِ ﴿٢٠٤﴾

204. There is the type of man whose speech about this world's life may dazzle you, and he calls Allah to witness about what is in his heart; yet is he the most contentious of enemies.

وَإِذَا تَوَلَّىٰ سَعَىٰ فِي ٱلۡأَرۡضِ لِيُفۡسِدَ فِيهَا
وَيُهۡلِكَ ٱلۡحَرۡثَ وَٱلنَّسۡلَۚ وَٱللَّهُ لَا يُحِبُّ
ٱلۡفَسَادَ ﴿٢٠٥﴾

205. When he turns his back, his aim everywhere is to spread mischief through the earth and destroy crops and cattle. But Allah loves not mischief.

وَإِذَا قِيلَ لَهُ ٱتَّقِ ٱللَّهَ أَخَذَتۡهُ ٱلۡعِزَّةُ بِٱلۡإِثۡمِۚ
فَحَسۡبُهُۥ جَهَنَّمُۖ وَلَبِئۡسَ ٱلۡمِهَادُ ﴿٢٠٦﴾

206. When it is said to him, "Fear Allah," he is led by arrogance to (more) crime. Enough for him is hell - an evil bed indeed (to lie on)!

وَمِنَ ٱلنَّاسِ مَن يَشۡرِي نَفۡسَهُ ٱبۡتِغَآءَ
مَرۡضَاتِ ٱللَّهِۚ وَٱللَّهُ رَءُوفُۢ بِٱلۡعِبَادِ ﴿٢٠٧﴾

207. And there is the type of man who gives his life to earn the pleasure of Allah; and Allah is full of kindness to (His) devotees.

يَٰٓأَيُّهَا ٱلَّذِينَ ءَامَنُواْ ٱدۡخُلُواْ فِي ٱلسِّلۡمِ
كَآفَّةٗ وَلَا تَتَّبِعُواْ خُطُوَٰتِ ٱلشَّيۡطَٰنِۚ إِنَّهُۥ
لَكُمۡ عَدُوّٞ مُّبِينٞ ﴿٢٠٨﴾

208. O you who believe! Enter into Islam wholeheartedly; and follow not the footsteps of the evil one; for he is to you an avowed enemy.

209. If you backslide after the clear (signs) have come to you, then know that Allah is Exalted in Power, Wise.

فَإِن زَلَلۡتُم مِّنۢ بَعۡدِ مَا جَآءَتۡكُمُ ٱلۡبَيِّنَٰتُ
فَٱعۡلَمُوٓاْ أَنَّ ٱللَّهَ عَزِيزٌ حَكِيمٌ ٢٠٩

210. Will they wait until Allah comes to them in canopies of clouds, with angels (in His train) and the question is (thus) settled? But to Allah do all questions go back (for decision).

هَلۡ يَنظُرُونَ إِلَّآ أَن يَأۡتِيَهُمُ ٱللَّهُ فِي ظُلَلٖ مِّنَ
ٱلۡغَمَامِ وَٱلۡمَلَٰٓئِكَةُ وَقُضِيَ ٱلۡأَمۡرُۚ وَإِلَى ٱللَّهِ
تُرۡجَعُ ٱلۡأُمُورُ ٢١٠

211. Ask the Children of Israel how many clear (signs) We have sent them. But if anyone, after Allah's favour has come to him, substitutes (something else), Allah is strict in punishment.

سَلۡ بَنِيٓ إِسۡرَٰٓءِيلَ كَمۡ ءَاتَيۡنَٰهُم مِّنۡ ءَايَةِۭ بَيِّنَةٖۗ وَمَن
يُبَدِّلۡ نِعۡمَةَ ٱللَّهِ مِنۢ بَعۡدِ مَا جَآءَتۡهُ فَإِنَّ ٱللَّهَ
شَدِيدُ ٱلۡعِقَابِ ٢١١

212. The life of this world is alluring to those who reject faith, and they mock those who believe. But the righteous will be above them on the day of resurrection; for Allah bestows His abundance without measure on whom He will.

زُيِّنَ لِلَّذِينَ كَفَرُواْ ٱلۡحَيَوٰةُ ٱلدُّنۡيَا وَيَسۡخَرُونَ مِنَ
ٱلَّذِينَ ءَامَنُواْۘ وَٱلَّذِينَ ٱتَّقَوۡاْ فَوۡقَهُمۡ يَوۡمَ ٱلۡقِيَٰمَةِۗ
وَٱللَّهُ يَرۡزُقُ مَن يَشَآءُ بِغَيۡرِ حِسَابٖ ٢١٢

213. Mankind was one single nation, and Allah sent prophets with glad tidings and warnings; and with them He sent the book in truth, to judge between people in matters in which they differed; but the People of the Book, after the clear signs came to them, did not differ among themselves, except through selfish rebellion. Allah by His grace guided the believers to the truth, in which they differed. For Allah guides whom He will to a path that is straight.

كَانَ ٱلنَّاسُ أُمَّةٗ وَٰحِدَةٗ فَبَعَثَ ٱللَّهُ ٱلنَّبِيِّـۧنَ
مُبَشِّرِينَ وَمُنذِرِينَ وَأَنزَلَ مَعَهُمُ ٱلۡكِتَٰبَ بِٱلۡحَقِّ
لِيَحۡكُمَ بَيۡنَ ٱلنَّاسِ فِيمَا ٱخۡتَلَفُواْ فِيهِۚ وَمَا ٱخۡتَلَفَ
فِيهِ إِلَّا ٱلَّذِينَ أُوتُوهُ مِنۢ بَعۡدِ مَا جَآءَتۡهُمُ ٱلۡبَيِّنَٰتُ
بَغۡيَۢا بَيۡنَهُمۡۖ فَهَدَى ٱللَّهُ ٱلَّذِينَ ءَامَنُواْ لِمَا
ٱخۡتَلَفُواْ فِيهِ مِنَ ٱلۡحَقِّ بِإِذۡنِهِۦۗ وَٱللَّهُ يَهۡدِي
مَن يَشَآءُ إِلَىٰ صِرَٰطٖ مُّسۡتَقِيمٍ ٢١٣

214. Or do you think that you shall enter the garden (of bliss) without such (trials) as came to those who passed away before you? They encountered suffering and adversity, and were so shaken in spirit that even the messenger and those of faith who were with him cried: "When (will come) the help of Allah?" Ah! Verily, the help of Allah is (always) near!

أَمْ حَسِبْتُمْ أَن تَدْخُلُوا۟ ٱلْجَنَّةَ وَلَمَّا يَأْتِكُم مَّثَلُ
ٱلَّذِينَ خَلَوْا۟ مِن قَبْلِكُم ۖ مَّسَّتْهُمُ ٱلْبَأْسَآءُ وَٱلضَّرَّآءُ
وَزُلْزِلُوا۟ حَتَّىٰ يَقُولَ ٱلرَّسُولُ وَٱلَّذِينَ ءَامَنُوا۟ مَعَهُۥ
مَتَىٰ نَصْرُ ٱللَّهِ ۗ أَلَآ إِنَّ نَصْرَ ٱللَّهِ قَرِيبٌ ﴿٢١٤﴾

215. They ask you what they should spend (in charity). Say: Whatever you spend that is good, is for parents and relations and orphans and those in want and for wayfarers. And whatever you do that is good - Allah knows it well.

يَسْـَٔلُونَكَ مَاذَا يُنفِقُونَ ۖ قُلْ مَآ أَنفَقْتُم مِّنْ خَيْرٍ
فَلِلْوَٰلِدَيْنِ وَٱلْأَقْرَبِينَ وَٱلْيَتَٰمَىٰ وَٱلْمَسَٰكِينِ وَٱبْنِ
ٱلسَّبِيلِ ۗ وَمَا تَفْعَلُوا۟ مِنْ خَيْرٍ فَإِنَّ ٱللَّهَ بِهِۦ
عَلِيمٌ ﴿٢١٥﴾

216. Fighting is prescribed for you, and you dislike it. But it is possible that you dislike a thing which is good for you, and that you love a thing which is bad for you. But Allah knows, and you know not.

كُتِبَ عَلَيْكُمُ ٱلْقِتَالُ وَهُوَ كُرْهٌ لَّكُمْ ۖ وَعَسَىٰٓ
أَن تَكْرَهُوا۟ شَيْـًٔا وَهُوَ خَيْرٌ لَّكُمْ ۖ وَعَسَىٰٓ أَن
تُحِبُّوا۟ شَيْـًٔا وَهُوَ شَرٌّ لَّكُمْ ۗ وَٱللَّهُ يَعْلَمُ
وَأَنتُمْ لَا تَعْلَمُونَ ﴿٢١٦﴾

217. They ask you concerning fighting in the prohibited month. Say: "Fighting in it is a grave (offence); but graver is it in the sight of Allah to prevent access to the path of Allah, to deny Him, to prevent access to the Sacred Mosque, and drive out its members." Tumult and oppression are worse than slaughter. Nor will they cease fighting you until they turn you back from your faith if they can. And if any of you turn back from their faith and die in unbelief, their works will bear no fruit in this life and in the hereafter; they will be companions of the fire and will remain in it.

يَسْـَٔلُونَكَ عَنِ ٱلشَّهْرِ ٱلْحَرَامِ قِتَالٍ فِيهِ ۖ قُلْ قِتَالٌ فِيهِ
كَبِيرٌ ۖ وَصَدٌّ عَن سَبِيلِ ٱللَّهِ وَكُفْرٌۢ بِهِۦ
وَٱلْمَسْجِدِ ٱلْحَرَامِ وَإِخْرَاجُ أَهْلِهِۦ مِنْهُ أَكْبَرُ
عِندَ ٱللَّهِ ۚ وَٱلْفِتْنَةُ أَكْبَرُ مِنَ ٱلْقَتْلِ ۗ وَلَا يَزَالُونَ
يُقَٰتِلُونَكُمْ حَتَّىٰ يَرُدُّوكُمْ عَن دِينِكُمْ إِنِ
ٱسْتَطَٰعُوا۟ ۚ وَمَن يَرْتَدِدْ مِنكُمْ عَن دِينِهِۦ
فَيَمُتْ وَهُوَ كَافِرٌ فَأُو۟لَٰٓئِكَ حَبِطَتْ أَعْمَٰلُهُمْ
فِى ٱلدُّنْيَا وَٱلْءَاخِرَةِ ۖ وَأُو۟لَٰٓئِكَ أَصْحَٰبُ ٱلنَّارِ ۖ
هُمْ فِيهَا خَٰلِدُونَ ﴿٢١٧﴾

218. Those who believed and those who suffered exile and fought (and strove and struggled) in the path of Allah - they have the hope of the mercy of Allah: and Allah is Oft-Forgiving, Most Merciful.

إِنَّ ٱلَّذِينَ ءَامَنُوا۟ وَٱلَّذِينَ هَاجَرُوا۟ وَجَٰهَدُوا۟
فِى سَبِيلِ ٱللَّهِ أُو۟لَٰٓئِكَ يَرْجُونَ رَحْمَتَ ٱللَّهِ ۚ وَٱللَّهُ
غَفُورٌ رَّحِيمٌ ﴿٢١٨﴾

219. They ask you concerning wine and gambling. Say: "In them is great sin, and some profit for men; but the sin is greater than the profit." They ask you how much they are to spend; say: "What is beyond your needs." Thus does Allah make clear to you His signs: in order that you may consider -

ربع الحزب ٤

۞ يَسْـَٔلُونَكَ عَنِ ٱلْخَمْرِ وَٱلْمَيْسِرِ ۖ قُلْ فِيهِمَآ إِثْمٌ
كَبِيرٌ وَمَنَٰفِعُ لِلنَّاسِ وَإِثْمُهُمَآ أَكْبَرُ مِن
نَّفْعِهِمَا ۗ وَيَسْـَٔلُونَكَ مَاذَا يُنفِقُونَ ۖ قُلِ ٱلْعَفْوَ ۗ
كَذَٰلِكَ يُبَيِّنُ ٱللَّهُ لَكُمُ ٱلْـَٔايَٰتِ لَعَلَّكُمْ
تَتَفَكَّرُونَ ﴿٢١٩﴾

220. (Their bearings) on this life and the hereafter. They ask you concerning orphans. Say: "The best thing to do is what is for their good; if you mix their affairs with yours, they are your brothers; but Allah knows the man who means mischief from the man who means good. And if Allah had wished, He could have put you into difficulties: He is indeed Exalted in Power, Wise."

فِى ٱلدُّنْيَا وَٱلْـَٔاخِرَةِ ۗ وَيَسْـَٔلُونَكَ عَنِ ٱلْيَتَٰمَىٰ ۖ قُلْ
إِصْلَاحٌ لَّهُمْ خَيْرٌ ۖ وَإِن تُخَالِطُوهُمْ
فَإِخْوَٰنُكُمْ ۚ وَٱللَّهُ يَعْلَمُ ٱلْمُفْسِدَ مِنَ ٱلْمُصْلِحِ ۚ
وَلَوْ شَآءَ ٱللَّهُ لَأَعْنَتَكُمْ ۚ إِنَّ ٱللَّهَ عَزِيزٌ
حَكِيمٌ ﴿٢٢٠﴾

221. Do not marry unbelieving women until they believe: a slave woman who believes is better than an unbelieving woman, even though she allure you. Nor marry (your girls) to unbelievers until they believe: a man slave who believes is better than an unbeliever even though he allure you. Unbelievers do (but) invite you to the fire. But Allah invites by His grace to the garden (of bliss) and forgiveness, and makes His signs clear to mankind: that they may receive admonition.

وَلَا تَنكِحُوا۟ ٱلْمُشْرِكَٰتِ حَتَّىٰ يُؤْمِنَّ ۚ وَلَأَمَةٌ
مُّؤْمِنَةٌ خَيْرٌ مِّن مُّشْرِكَةٍ وَلَوْ أَعْجَبَتْكُمْ ۗ وَلَا
تُنكِحُوا۟ ٱلْمُشْرِكِينَ حَتَّىٰ يُؤْمِنُوا۟ ۚ وَلَعَبْدٌ مُّؤْمِنٌ خَيْرٌ
مِّن مُّشْرِكٍ وَلَوْ أَعْجَبَكُمْ ۗ أُو۟لَٰٓئِكَ يَدْعُونَ إِلَى
ٱلنَّارِ ۖ وَٱللَّهُ يَدْعُوٓا۟ إِلَى ٱلْجَنَّةِ وَٱلْمَغْفِرَةِ بِإِذْنِهِۦ ۖ
وَيُبَيِّنُ ءَايَٰتِهِۦ لِلنَّاسِ لَعَلَّهُمْ يَتَذَكَّرُونَ ﴿٢٢١﴾

222. They ask you concerning women's courses. Say: They are a hurt and a pollution: so keep away from women in their courses, and do not approach them until they are clean. But when they have purified themselves, you may approach them in any manner, time, or place ordained for you by Allah. For Allah loves those who turn to Him constantly and He loves those who keep themselves pure and clean.

وَيَسْـَٔلُونَكَ عَنِ ٱلْمَحِيضِ ۖ قُلْ هُوَ أَذًى فَٱعْتَزِلُوا۟
ٱلنِّسَآءَ فِى ٱلْمَحِيضِ ۖ وَلَا تَقْرَبُوهُنَّ حَتَّىٰ يَطْهُرْنَ ۖ
فَإِذَا تَطَهَّرْنَ فَأْتُوهُنَّ مِنْ حَيْثُ أَمَرَكُمُ ٱللَّهُ ۚ إِنَّ
ٱللَّهَ يُحِبُّ ٱلتَّوَّٰبِينَ وَيُحِبُّ ٱلْمُتَطَهِّرِينَ ﴿٢٢٢﴾

223. Your wives are as a tilth to you so approach your tilth when or how you will; but do some good act for your souls beforehand; and fear Allah, and know that you are to meet Him (in the hereafter), and give (these) good tidings to those who believe.

نِسَآؤُكُمْ حَرْثٌ لَّكُمْ فَأْتُوا۟ حَرْثَكُمْ أَنَّىٰ شِئْتُمْ ۖ
وَقَدِّمُوا۟ لِأَنفُسِكُمْ ۚ وَٱتَّقُوا۟ ٱللَّهَ وَٱعْلَمُوٓا۟
أَنَّكُم مُّلَٰقُوهُ ۗ وَبَشِّرِ ٱلْمُؤْمِنِينَ ﴿٢٢٣﴾

224. And make not Allah's (name) an excuse in your oaths against doing good, or acting rightly, or making peace between persons; for Allah is One who hears and knows all things.

وَلَا تَجْعَلُوا۟ ٱللَّهَ عُرْضَةً لِّأَيْمَٰنِكُمْ أَن تَبَرُّوا۟
وَتَتَّقُوا۟ وَتُصْلِحُوا۟ بَيْنَ ٱلنَّاسِ ۗ وَٱللَّهُ سَمِيعٌ
عَلِيمٌ ﴿٢٢٤﴾

225. Allah will not call you to account for thoughtlessness in your oaths, but for the intention in your hearts, and He is Oft-Forgiving, Most Forbearing.

لَّا يُؤَاخِذُكُمُ ٱللَّهُ بِٱللَّغْوِ فِىٓ أَيْمَٰنِكُمْ وَلَٰكِن يُؤَاخِذُكُم
بِمَا كَسَبَتْ قُلُوبُكُمْ ۗ وَٱللَّهُ غَفُورٌ حَلِيمٌ ﴿٢٢٥﴾

226. For those who take an oath for abstention from their wives, a waiting for four months is ordained; if then they return, Allah is Oft-Forgiving, Most Merciful.

لِّلَّذِينَ يُؤْلُونَ مِن نِّسَآئِهِمْ تَرَبُّصُ أَرْبَعَةِ أَشْهُرٍ ۖ فَإِن
فَآءُو فَإِنَّ ٱللَّهَ غَفُورٌ رَّحِيمٌ ﴿٢٢٦﴾

227. But if their intention is firm for divorce, Allah hears and knows all things.

وَإِنْ عَزَمُوا۟ ٱلطَّلَٰقَ فَإِنَّ ٱللَّهَ سَمِيعٌ عَلِيمٌ ﴿٢٢٧﴾

228. Divorced women shall wait concerning themselves for three monthly periods. Nor is it lawful for them to hide what Allah has created in their wombs, if they have faith in Allah and the last day. And their husbands have the better right to take them back in that period, if they wish for reconciliation. And women shall have rights similar to the rights against them, according to what is equitable; but men have a degree (of advantage) over them. And Allah is Exalted in Power, Wise.

وَٱلْمُطَلَّقَٰتُ يَتَرَبَّصْنَ بِأَنفُسِهِنَّ ثَلَٰثَةَ قُرُوٓءٍ ۚ وَلَا يَحِلُّ
لَهُنَّ أَن يَكْتُمْنَ مَا خَلَقَ ٱللَّهُ فِىٓ أَرْحَامِهِنَّ إِن كُنَّ
يُؤْمِنَّ بِٱللَّهِ وَٱلْيَوْمِ ٱلْـَٔاخِرِ ۚ وَبُعُولَتُهُنَّ أَحَقُّ بِرَدِّهِنَّ
فِى ذَٰلِكَ إِنْ أَرَادُوٓا۟ إِصْلَٰحًا ۚ وَلَهُنَّ مِثْلُ ٱلَّذِى
عَلَيْهِنَّ بِٱلْمَعْرُوفِ ۚ وَلِلرِّجَالِ عَلَيْهِنَّ دَرَجَةٌ ۗ وَٱللَّهُ
عَزِيزٌ حَكِيمٌ ﴿٢٢٨﴾

229. A divorce is only permissible twice: after that, the parties should either hold together on equitable terms, or separate with kindness. It is not lawful for you, (men), to take back any of your gifts (from your wives), except when both parties fear that they would be unable to keep the limits ordained by Allah. If you (judges) do indeed fear that they would be unable to keep the limits ordained by Allah, there is no blame on either of them if she gives something for her freedom. These are the limits ordained by Allah; so do not transgress them. If any do transgress the limits ordained by Allah, such persons wrong (themselves as well as others).

ٱلطَّلَٰقُ مَرَّتَانِ ۖ فَإِمْسَاكٌۢ بِمَعْرُوفٍ أَوْ تَسْرِيحٌۢ بِإِحْسَٰنٍ ۗ
وَلَا يَحِلُّ لَكُمْ أَن تَأْخُذُوا۟ مِمَّآ ءَاتَيْتُمُوهُنَّ شَيْـًٔا إِلَّآ
أَن يَخَافَآ أَلَّا يُقِيمَا حُدُودَ ٱللَّهِ ۖ فَإِنْ خِفْتُمْ أَلَّا
يُقِيمَا حُدُودَ ٱللَّهِ فَلَا جُنَاحَ عَلَيْهِمَا فِيمَا ٱفْتَدَتْ بِهِۦ ۗ
تِلْكَ حُدُودُ ٱللَّهِ فَلَا تَعْتَدُوهَا ۚ وَمَن يَتَعَدَّ حُدُودَ ٱللَّهِ
فَأُو۟لَٰٓئِكَ هُمُ ٱلظَّٰلِمُونَ ﴿٢٢٩﴾

230. So if a husband divorces his wife (irrevocably), he cannot, after that, remarry her until after she has married another husband and he has divorced her. In that case there is no blame on either of them if they reunite, provided they feel that they can keep the limits ordained by Allah. Such are the limits ordained by Allah, which He makes plain to those who understand.

فَإِن طَلَّقَهَا فَلَا تَحِلُّ لَهُۥ مِنۢ بَعْدُ حَتَّىٰ تَنكِحَ زَوْجًا غَيْرَهُۥ ۗ
فَإِن طَلَّقَهَا فَلَا جُنَاحَ عَلَيْهِمَآ أَن يَتَرَاجَعَآ إِن
ظَنَّآ أَن يُقِيمَا حُدُودَ ٱللَّهِ ۗ وَتِلْكَ حُدُودُ ٱللَّهِ يُبَيِّنُهَا
لِقَوْمٍ يَعْلَمُونَ ﴿٢٣٠﴾

231. When you divorce women, and they fulfil the term of their (Iddah), either take them back on equitable terms or set them free on equitable terms; but do not take them back to injure them, (or) to take undue advantage; if anyone does that, he wrongs his own soul. Do not treat Allah's signs as a jest, but solemnly rehearse Allah's favours on you, and the fact that He sent down to you the book and wisdom, for your instruction. And fear Allah, and know that Allah is well-acquainted with all things.

وَإِذَا طَلَّقْتُمُ ٱلنِّسَآءَ فَبَلَغْنَ أَجَلَهُنَّ فَأَمْسِكُوهُنَّ
بِمَعْرُوفٍ أَوْ سَرِّحُوهُنَّ بِمَعْرُوفٍ وَلَا تُمْسِكُوهُنَّ
ضِرَارًا لِّتَعْتَدُوا۟ ۚ وَمَن يَفْعَلْ ذَٰلِكَ فَقَدْ ظَلَمَ نَفْسَهُۥ ۚ
وَلَا تَتَّخِذُوٓا۟ ءَايَٰتِ ٱللَّهِ هُزُوًا ۚ وَٱذْكُرُوا۟ نِعْمَتَ ٱللَّهِ
عَلَيْكُمْ وَمَآ أَنزَلَ عَلَيْكُم مِّنَ ٱلْكِتَٰبِ وَٱلْحِكْمَةِ يَعِظُكُم
بِهِۦ ۚ وَٱتَّقُوا۟ ٱللَّهَ وَٱعْلَمُوٓا۟ أَنَّ ٱللَّهَ بِكُلِّ شَىْءٍ عَلِيمٌ ﴿٢٣١﴾

232. When you divorce women, and they fulfil the term of their (Iddah), do not prevent them from marrying their (former) husbands, if they mutually agree on equitable terms. This instruction is for all amongst you, who believe in Allah and the last day. That is (the course making for) most virtue and purity amongst you. And Allah knows, and you know not.

وَإِذَا طَلَّقْتُمُ ٱلنِّسَآءَ فَبَلَغْنَ أَجَلَهُنَّ فَلَا
تَعْضُلُوهُنَّ أَن يَنكِحْنَ أَزْوَٰجَهُنَّ إِذَا تَرَٰضَوْا۟ بَيْنَهُم
بِٱلْمَعْرُوفِ ۗ ذَٰلِكَ يُوعَظُ بِهِۦ مَن كَانَ مِنكُمْ يُؤْمِنُ بِٱللَّهِ
وَٱلْيَوْمِ ٱلْءَاخِرِ ۗ ذَٰلِكُمْ أَزْكَىٰ لَكُمْ وَأَطْهَرُ ۗ وَٱللَّهُ يَعْلَمُ
وَأَنتُمْ لَا تَعْلَمُونَ ﴿٢٣٢﴾

233. The mothers shall give suck to their offspring for two whole years, if the father desires to complete the term. But he shall bear the cost of their food and clothing on equitable terms. No soul shall have a burden laid on it greater than it can bear. No mother shall be treated unfairly on account of her child, nor a father on account of his child, and the heir shall be chargeable in the same way. If they both decide on weaning, by mutual consent, and after due consultation, there is no blame on them. If you decide on a foster-mother for your offspring there is no blame on you, provided you pay (the

نصف الحزب ٤
۞ وَٱلْوَٰلِدَٰتُ يُرْضِعْنَ أَوْلَٰدَهُنَّ حَوْلَيْنِ كَامِلَيْنِ ۖ لِمَنْ
أَرَادَ أَن يُتِمَّ ٱلرَّضَاعَةَ ۚ وَعَلَى ٱلْمَوْلُودِ لَهُۥ رِزْقُهُنَّ
وَكِسْوَتُهُنَّ بِٱلْمَعْرُوفِ ۚ لَا تُكَلَّفُ نَفْسٌ إِلَّا وُسْعَهَا ۚ
لَا تُضَآرَّ وَٰلِدَةٌۢ بِوَلَدِهَا وَلَا مَوْلُودٌ لَّهُۥ بِوَلَدِهِۦ ۚ وَعَلَى
ٱلْوَارِثِ مِثْلُ ذَٰلِكَ ۗ فَإِنْ أَرَادَا فِصَالًا عَن تَرَاضٍ
مِّنْهُمَا وَتَشَاوُرٍ فَلَا جُنَاحَ عَلَيْهِمَا ۗ وَإِنْ أَرَدتُّمْ أَن
تَسْتَرْضِعُوٓا۟ أَوْلَٰدَكُمْ فَلَا جُنَاحَ عَلَيْكُمْ إِذَا سَلَّمْتُم

mother) what you offered on equitable terms. But fear Allah and know that Allah sees well what you do.

مَّآ ءَاتَيْتُم بِٱلْمَعْرُوفِ ۗ وَٱتَّقُوا۟ ٱللَّهَ وَٱعْلَمُوٓا۟ أَنَّ ٱللَّهَ بِمَا
تَعْمَلُونَ بَصِيرٌ ﴿٢٣٣﴾

234. If any of you die and leave widows behind, they shall wait concerning themselves four months and ten days: when they have fulfilled their term, there is no blame on you if they dispose of themselves in a just and reasonable manner. And Allah is well acquainted with what you do.

وَٱلَّذِينَ يُتَوَفَّوْنَ مِنكُمْ وَيَذَرُونَ أَزْوَٰجًا يَتَرَبَّصْنَ
بِأَنفُسِهِنَّ أَرْبَعَةَ أَشْهُرٍ وَعَشْرًا ۖ فَإِذَا بَلَغْنَ أَجَلَهُنَّ
فَلَا جُنَاحَ عَلَيْكُمْ فِيمَا فَعَلْنَ فِىٓ أَنفُسِهِنَّ
بِٱلْمَعْرُوفِ ۗ وَٱللَّهُ بِمَا تَعْمَلُونَ خَبِيرٌ ﴿٢٣٤﴾

235. There is no blame on you if you make an offer of betrothal or hold it in your hearts. Allah knows that you cherish them in your hearts: but do not make a secret contract with them except in terms honourable, nor resolve on the tie of marriage till the term prescribed is fulfilled. And know that Allah knows what is in your hearts, and take heed of Him; and know that Allah is Oft-Forgiving, Most Forbearing.

وَلَا جُنَاحَ عَلَيْكُمْ فِيمَا عَرَّضْتُم بِهِۦ مِنْ خِطْبَةِ
ٱلنِّسَآءِ أَوْ أَكْنَنتُمْ فِىٓ أَنفُسِكُمْ ۚ عَلِمَ ٱللَّهُ أَنَّكُمْ
سَتَذْكُرُونَهُنَّ وَلَٰكِن لَّا تُوَاعِدُوهُنَّ
سِرًّا إِلَّآ أَن تَقُولُوا۟ قَوْلًا مَّعْرُوفًا ۚ وَلَا تَعْزِمُوا۟
عُقْدَةَ ٱلنِّكَاحِ حَتَّىٰ يَبْلُغَ ٱلْكِتَٰبُ أَجَلَهُۥ ۚ
وَٱعْلَمُوٓا۟ أَنَّ ٱللَّهَ يَعْلَمُ مَا فِىٓ أَنفُسِكُمْ فَٱحْذَرُوهُ ۚ
وَٱعْلَمُوٓا۟ أَنَّ ٱللَّهَ غَفُورٌ حَلِيمٌ ﴿٢٣٥﴾

236. There is no blame on you if you divorce women before consummation or the fixation of their dower; but bestow on them (a suitable gift), the wealthy according to his means, and the poor according to his means - a gift of a reasonable amount is due from those who wish to do the right thing.

لَّا جُنَاحَ عَلَيْكُمْ إِن طَلَّقْتُمُ ٱلنِّسَآءَ مَا لَمْ تَمَسُّوهُنَّ
أَوْ تَفْرِضُوا۟ لَهُنَّ فَرِيضَةً ۚ وَمَتِّعُوهُنَّ عَلَى
ٱلْمُوسِعِ قَدَرُهُۥ وَعَلَى ٱلْمُقْتِرِ قَدَرُهُۥ مَتَٰعًۢا
بِٱلْمَعْرُوفِ ۖ حَقًّا عَلَى ٱلْمُحْسِنِينَ ﴿٢٣٦﴾

237. And if you divorce them before consummation, but after the fixation of a

وَإِن طَلَّقْتُمُوهُنَّ مِن قَبْلِ أَن تَمَسُّوهُنَّ وَقَدْ

dower for them, then the half of the dower (is due to them), unless they remit it or (the man's half) is remitted by him in whose hands is the marriage tie; and the remission (of the man's half) is the nearest to righteousness and do not forget liberality between yourselves. For Allah sees well all that you do.

فَرَضۡتُمۡ لَهُنَّ فَرِيضَةٗ فَنِصۡفُ مَا فَرَضۡتُمۡ إِلَّآ
أَن يَعۡفُونَ أَوۡ يَعۡفُوَاْ ٱلَّذِي بِيَدِهِۦ عُقۡدَةُ ٱلنِّكَاحِۚ
وَأَن تَعۡفُوٓاْ أَقۡرَبُ لِلتَّقۡوَىٰۚ وَلَا تَنسَوُاْ ٱلۡفَضۡلَ بَيۡنَكُمۡۚ
إِنَّ ٱللَّهَ بِمَا تَعۡمَلُونَ بَصِيرٌ ٢٣٧

238. Guard strictly your (habit) of prayers, especially the middle prayer; and stand before Allah in a devout (frame of mind).

حَٰفِظُواْ عَلَى ٱلصَّلَوَٰتِ وَٱلصَّلَوٰةِ ٱلۡوُسۡطَىٰ
وَقُومُواْ لِلَّهِ قَٰنِتِينَ ٢٣٨

239. If you fear (an enemy), pray on foot, or riding, (as may be most convenient), but when you are in security, celebrate Allah's praises in the manner He has taught you, which you knew not (before).

فَإِنۡ خِفۡتُمۡ فَرِجَالًا أَوۡ رُكۡبَانٗاۖ فَإِذَآ أَمِنتُمۡ
فَٱذۡكُرُواْ ٱللَّهَ كَمَا عَلَّمَكُم مَّا لَمۡ تَكُونُواْ
تَعۡلَمُونَ ٢٣٩

240. Those of you who die and leave widows should bequeath for their widows a year's maintenance and residence; but if they leave (the residence), there is no blame on you for what they do with themselves, provided it is reasonable. And Allah is Exalted in Power, Wise.

وَٱلَّذِينَ يُتَوَفَّوۡنَ مِنكُمۡ وَيَذَرُونَ
أَزۡوَٰجٗا وَصِيَّةٗ لِّأَزۡوَٰجِهِم مَّتَٰعًا إِلَى ٱلۡحَوۡلِ
غَيۡرَ إِخۡرَاجٖۚ فَإِنۡ خَرَجۡنَ فَلَا جُنَاحَ عَلَيۡكُمۡ
فِي مَا فَعَلۡنَ فِيٓ أَنفُسِهِنَّ مِن مَّعۡرُوفٖۗ وَٱللَّهُ
عَزِيزٌ حَكِيمٞ ٢٤٠

241. For divorced women maintenance (should be provided) on a reasonable (scale). This is a duty on the righteous.

وَلِلۡمُطَلَّقَٰتِ مَتَٰعُۢ بِٱلۡمَعۡرُوفِۖ حَقًّا عَلَى
ٱلۡمُتَّقِينَ ٢٤١

242. Thus does Allah make clear His signs to you: in order that you may understand.

كَذَٰلِكَ يُبَيِّنُ ٱللَّهُ لَكُمۡ ءَايَٰتِهِۦ
لَعَلَّكُمۡ تَعۡقِلُونَ ٢٤٢

243. Did you not turn your vision to those who abandoned their homes, though they

ثلاثة أرباع الحزب ٤
۞ أَلَمۡ تَرَ إِلَى ٱلَّذِينَ خَرَجُواْ مِن دِيَٰرِهِمۡ وَهُمۡ

أُلُوفٌ حَذَرَ ٱلْمَوْتِ فَقَالَ لَهُمُ ٱللَّهُ مُوتُوا۟ ثُمَّ
أَحْيَـٰهُمْ ۚ إِنَّ ٱللَّهَ لَذُو فَضْلٍ عَلَى ٱلنَّاسِ
وَلَـٰكِنَّ أَكْثَرَ ٱلنَّاسِ لَا يَشْكُرُونَ ﴿٢٤٣﴾

were thousands (in number), for fear of death? Allah said to them: "Die": Then He restored them to life. For Allah is full of bounty to mankind, but most of them are ungrateful.

وَقَـٰتِلُوا۟ فِى سَبِيلِ ٱللَّهِ وَٱعْلَمُوٓا۟ أَنَّ ٱللَّهَ سَمِيعٌ
عَلِيمٌ ﴿٢٤٤﴾

244. Then fight in the cause of Allah, and know that Allah hears and knows all things.

مَّن ذَا ٱلَّذِى يُقْرِضُ ٱللَّهَ قَرْضًا حَسَنًا فَيُضَـٰعِفَهُۥ
لَهُۥٓ أَضْعَافًا كَثِيرَةً ۚ وَٱللَّهُ يَقْبِضُ وَيَبْصُۜطُ
وَإِلَيْهِ تُرْجَعُونَ ﴿٢٤٥﴾

245. Who is he that will loan to Allah a beautiful loan, which Allah will double to his credit and multiply many times? It is Allah that gives (you) want or plenty, and to Him shall be your return.

أَلَمْ تَرَ إِلَى ٱلْمَلَإِ مِنۢ بَنِىٓ إِسْرَٰٓءِيلَ مِنۢ بَعْدِ
مُوسَىٰٓ إِذْ قَالُوا۟ لِنَبِىٍّ لَّهُمُ ٱبْعَثْ لَنَا مَلِكًا
نُّقَـٰتِلْ فِى سَبِيلِ ٱللَّهِ ۖ قَالَ هَلْ عَسَيْتُمْ إِن كُتِبَ
عَلَيْكُمُ ٱلْقِتَالُ أَلَّا تُقَـٰتِلُوا۟ ۖ قَالُوا۟ وَمَا لَنَآ
أَلَّا نُقَـٰتِلَ فِى سَبِيلِ ٱللَّهِ وَقَدْ أُخْرِجْنَا مِن
دِيَـٰرِنَا وَأَبْنَآئِنَا ۖ فَلَمَّا كُتِبَ عَلَيْهِمُ ٱلْقِتَالُ
تَوَلَّوْا۟ إِلَّا قَلِيلًا مِّنْهُمْ ۗ وَٱللَّهُ عَلِيمٌۢ
بِٱلظَّـٰلِمِينَ ﴿٢٤٦﴾

246. Have you not turned your vision to the chiefs of the Children of Israel after (the time of) Moses? They said to a prophet (that was) among them: "Appoint for us a king, that we may fight in the cause of Allah." He said: "Is it not possible, if you were commanded to fight, that you will not fight?" They said: "How could we refuse to fight in the cause of Allah, seeing that we were turned out of our homes and our families?" But when they were commanded to fight, they turned back, except a small band among them. But Allah has full knowledge of those who do wrong.

وَقَالَ لَهُمْ نَبِيُّهُمْ إِنَّ ٱللَّهَ قَدْ بَعَثَ لَكُمْ
طَالُوتَ مَلِكًا ۚ قَالُوٓا۟ أَنَّىٰ يَكُونُ لَهُ
ٱلْمُلْكُ عَلَيْنَا وَنَحْنُ أَحَقُّ بِٱلْمُلْكِ مِنْهُ

247. Their Prophet said to them: "Allah has appointed Saul (Talut) as king over you." They said: "How can he exercise authority over us when we are better fitted than he to exercise authority, and he is not even gifted with wealth in abundance?" He said: "Allah has chosen him above you, and has gifted him abundantly with knowledge and bodily prowess: Allah grants His authority to whom He pleases. Allah is All-Embracing, and He knows all things."

وَلَمْ يُؤْتَ سَعَةً مِّنَ ٱلْمَالِ ۚ قَالَ إِنَّ ٱللَّهَ
ٱصْطَفَىٰهُ عَلَيْكُمْ وَزَادَهُۥ بَسْطَةً فِى
ٱلْعِلْمِ وَٱلْجِسْمِ ۖ وَٱللَّهُ يُؤْتِى مُلْكَهُۥ مَن
يَشَآءُ ۚ وَٱللَّهُ وَٰسِعٌ عَلِيمٌ ٢٤٧

248. And (further) their Prophet said to them: "A sign of his authority is that there shall come to you the ark of the covenant, with (an assurance) in it of security from your Lord, and the relics left by the family of Moses and the family of Aaron, carried by angels. In this is a symbol for you if you indeed have faith."

وَقَالَ لَهُمْ نَبِيُّهُمْ إِنَّ ءَايَةَ مُلْكِهِۦٓ أَن
يَأْتِيَكُمُ ٱلتَّابُوتُ فِيهِ سَكِينَةٌ مِّن
رَّبِّكُمْ وَبَقِيَّةٌ مِّمَّا تَرَكَ ءَالُ مُوسَىٰ
وَءَالُ هَٰرُونَ تَحْمِلُهُ ٱلْمَلَٰٓئِكَةُ ۚ إِنَّ فِى
ذَٰلِكَ لَءَايَةً لَّكُمْ إِن كُنتُم مُّؤْمِنِينَ ٢٤٨

249. When Saul (Talut) set out with the armies, he said: "Allah will test you at the stream; if any drinks of its water, he goes not with my army; only those who taste not of it go with me; a mere sip out of the hand is excused." But they all drank of it, except a few. When they crossed the river - he and the faithful ones with him, they said: "This day we cannot cope with Goliath and his forces." But those who were convinced that they must meet Allah, said: "How often, by Allah's Will, has a small force conquered a big one? Allah is with those who steadfastly persevere."

فَلَمَّا فَصَلَ طَالُوتُ بِٱلْجُنُودِ قَالَ إِنَّ ٱللَّهَ
مُبْتَلِيكُم بِنَهَرٍ فَمَن شَرِبَ مِنْهُ فَلَيْسَ مِنِّى
وَمَن لَّمْ يَطْعَمْهُ فَإِنَّهُۥ مِنِّىٓ إِلَّا مَنِ ٱغْتَرَفَ
غُرْفَةًۢ بِيَدِهِۦ ۚ فَشَرِبُوا۟ مِنْهُ إِلَّا قَلِيلًا مِّنْهُمْ ۚ
فَلَمَّا جَاوَزَهُۥ هُوَ وَٱلَّذِينَ ءَامَنُوا۟ مَعَهُۥ قَالُوا۟
لَا طَاقَةَ لَنَا ٱلْيَوْمَ بِجَالُوتَ وَجُنُودِهِۦ ۚ
قَالَ ٱلَّذِينَ يَظُنُّونَ أَنَّهُم مُّلَٰقُوا۟ ٱللَّهِ كَم
مِّن فِئَةٍ قَلِيلَةٍ غَلَبَتْ فِئَةً كَثِيرَةًۢ
بِإِذْنِ ٱللَّهِ ۗ وَٱللَّهُ مَعَ ٱلصَّٰبِرِينَ ٢٤٩

250. When they advanced to meet Goliath and his forces, they prayed: "Our Lord! Pour out constancy on us and make our steps firm: help us against those that reject faith."

وَلَمَّا بَرَزُوا۟ لِجَالُوتَ وَجُنُودِهِۦ قَالُوا۟ رَبَّنَآ
أَفْرِغْ عَلَيْنَا صَبْرًا وَثَبِّتْ أَقْدَامَنَا
وَٱنصُرْنَا عَلَى ٱلْقَوْمِ ٱلْكَٰفِرِينَ ٢٥٠

251. By Allah's Will, they routed them: and David slew Goliath: and Allah gave him power and wisdom and taught him whatever (else) He willed. And did not Allah check one set of people by means of another, the earth would indeed be full of mischief: but Allah is full of bounty to all the worlds.

فَهَزَمُوهُم بِإِذْنِ ٱللَّهِ وَقَتَلَ دَاوُۥدُ
جَالُوتَ وَءَاتَىٰهُ ٱللَّهُ ٱلْمُلْكَ وَٱلْحِكْمَةَ
وَعَلَّمَهُۥ مِمَّا يَشَآءُ ۗ وَلَوْلَا دَفْعُ ٱللَّهِ ٱلنَّاسَ
بَعْضَهُم بِبَعْضٍ لَّفَسَدَتِ ٱلْأَرْضُ وَلَٰكِنَّ
ٱللَّهَ ذُو فَضْلٍ عَلَى ٱلْعَٰلَمِينَ ﴿٢٥١﴾

252. These are the signs of Allah: We rehearse them to you in truth: verily you are one of the messengers.

تِلْكَ ءَايَٰتُ ٱللَّهِ نَتْلُوهَا عَلَيْكَ بِٱلْحَقِّ ۚ
وَإِنَّكَ لَمِنَ ٱلْمُرْسَلِينَ ﴿٢٥٢﴾

✻**253.** Those messengers We endowed with gifts, some above others: to one of them Allah spoke; others He raised to degrees (of honour); to Jesus, the son of Mary, We gave clear (signs), and strengthened him with the Holy Spirit. If Allah had so willed, succeeding generations would not have fought among each other, after clear (signs) had come to them but they (chose) to wrangle, some believing and others rejecting. If Allah had so willed, they would not have fought each other; but Allah fulfils His plan.

الجزء ٣ الحزب ٥

✻ تِلْكَ ٱلرُّسُلُ فَضَّلْنَا بَعْضَهُمْ عَلَىٰ بَعْضٍ مِّنْهُم
مَّن كَلَّمَ ٱللَّهُ ۖ وَرَفَعَ بَعْضَهُمْ دَرَجَٰتٍ ۚ وَءَاتَيْنَا
عِيسَى ٱبْنَ مَرْيَمَ ٱلْبَيِّنَٰتِ وَأَيَّدْنَٰهُ بِرُوحِ
ٱلْقُدُسِ ۗ وَلَوْ شَآءَ ٱللَّهُ مَا ٱقْتَتَلَ ٱلَّذِينَ مِنۢ
بَعْدِهِم مِّنۢ بَعْدِ مَا جَآءَتْهُمُ ٱلْبَيِّنَٰتُ وَلَٰكِنِ
ٱخْتَلَفُوا۟ فَمِنْهُم مَّنْ ءَامَنَ وَمِنْهُم مَّن كَفَرَ ۚ وَلَوْ
شَآءَ ٱللَّهُ مَا ٱقْتَتَلُوا۟ وَلَٰكِنَّ ٱللَّهَ يَفْعَلُ مَا يُرِيدُ ﴿٢٥٣﴾

254. O you who believe! Spend out of (the bounties) We have provided for you, before the day comes when no bargaining (will benefit), nor friendship nor intercession. Those who reject faith - they are the wrongdoers.

يَٰٓأَيُّهَا ٱلَّذِينَ ءَامَنُوٓا۟ أَنفِقُوا۟ مِمَّا رَزَقْنَٰكُم مِّن
قَبْلِ أَن يَأْتِىَ يَوْمٌ لَّا بَيْعٌ فِيهِ وَلَا خُلَّةٌ وَلَا
شَفَٰعَةٌ ۗ وَٱلْكَٰفِرُونَ هُمُ ٱلظَّٰلِمُونَ ﴿٢٥٤﴾

255. Allah! There is no god but He - the Living, the Self-subsisting, Eternal. No slumber can seize Him nor sleep. His are all things in the heavens and on earth. Who is

ٱللَّهُ لَآ إِلَٰهَ إِلَّا هُوَ ٱلْحَىُّ ٱلْقَيُّومُ ۚ لَا تَأْخُذُهُۥ سِنَةٌ
وَلَا نَوْمٌ ۚ لَّهُۥ مَا فِى ٱلسَّمَٰوَٰتِ وَمَا فِى ٱلْأَرْضِ ۗ مَن

✻ Part-3

there who can intercede in His presence except as He permits? He knows what (appears to his creatures as) before or after or behind them. Nor shall they encompass anything of His knowledge except as He wills. His Throne does extend over the heavens and the earth, and He feels no fatigue in guarding and preserving them. For He is the Most High, the Supreme (in glory).

ذَا ٱلَّذِي يَشۡفَعُ عِندَهُۥٓ إِلَّا بِإِذۡنِهِۦۚ يَعۡلَمُ مَا بَيۡنَ
أَيۡدِيهِمۡ وَمَا خَلۡفَهُمۡۖ وَلَا يُحِيطُونَ بِشَيۡءٖ مِّنۡ عِلۡمِهِۦٓ
إِلَّا بِمَا شَآءَۚ وَسِعَ كُرۡسِيُّهُ ٱلسَّمَٰوَٰتِ وَٱلۡأَرۡضَۖ وَلَا
يَـُٔودُهُۥ حِفۡظُهُمَاۚ وَهُوَ ٱلۡعَلِيُّ ٱلۡعَظِيمُ ٢٥٥

256. Let there be no compulsion in religion: Truth stands out clear from error: whoever rejects evil and believes in Allah has grasped the most trustworthy handhold, that never breaks. And Allah hears and knows all things.

لَآ إِكۡرَاهَ فِي ٱلدِّينِۖ قَد تَّبَيَّنَ ٱلرُّشۡدُ مِنَ ٱلۡغَيِّۚ فَمَن
يَكۡفُرۡ بِٱلطَّٰغُوتِ وَيُؤۡمِنۢ بِٱللَّهِ فَقَدِ ٱسۡتَمۡسَكَ
بِٱلۡعُرۡوَةِ ٱلۡوُثۡقَىٰ لَا ٱنفِصَامَ لَهَاۗ وَٱللَّهُ
سَمِيعٌ عَلِيمٌ ٢٥٦

257. Allah is the Protector of those who have faith; from the depths of darkness He will lead them out into light. Of those who reject faith the patrons are the evil Ones; from light they will lead them out into the depths of darkness. They will be companions of the fire, to dwell in it (forever).

ٱللَّهُ وَلِيُّ ٱلَّذِينَ ءَامَنُواْ يُخۡرِجُهُم مِّنَ ٱلظُّلُمَٰتِ
إِلَى ٱلنُّورِۖ وَٱلَّذِينَ كَفَرُوٓاْ أَوۡلِيَآؤُهُمُ
ٱلطَّٰغُوتُ يُخۡرِجُونَهُم مِّنَ ٱلنُّورِ إِلَى ٱلظُّلُمَٰتِۗ
أُوْلَٰٓئِكَ أَصۡحَٰبُ ٱلنَّارِۖ هُمۡ فِيهَا
خَٰلِدُونَ ٢٥٧

258. Have you not turned your vision to one who disputed with Abraham about his Lord, because Allah had granted him power? Abraham said: "My Lord is He Who gives life and death." He said: "I give life and death." Said Abraham: "But it is Allah that causes the sun to rise from the east: do you then cause it to rise from the west?" Thus was he confounded who (in arrogance) rejected faith. Nor does Allah

أَلَمۡ تَرَ إِلَى ٱلَّذِي حَآجَّ إِبۡرَٰهِـۧمَ فِي رَبِّهِۦٓ أَنۡ
ءَاتَىٰهُ ٱللَّهُ ٱلۡمُلۡكَ إِذۡ قَالَ إِبۡرَٰهِـۧمُ رَبِّيَ ٱلَّذِي
يُحۡيِۦ وَيُمِيتُ قَالَ أَنَا۠ أُحۡيِۦ وَأُمِيتُۖ قَالَ إِبۡرَٰهِـۧمُ
فَإِنَّ ٱللَّهَ يَأۡتِي بِٱلشَّمۡسِ مِنَ ٱلۡمَشۡرِقِ فَأۡتِ بِهَا
مِنَ ٱلۡمَغۡرِبِ فَبُهِتَ ٱلَّذِي كَفَرَۗ وَٱللَّهُ لَا

give guidance to a people unjust.

يَهْدِي الْقَوْمَ الظَّالِمِينَ ﴿٢٥٨﴾

259. Or (take) the similitude of one who passed by a hamlet, all in ruins to its roofs. He said: "Oh! How shall Allah bring it (ever) to life, after (this) its death?" But Allah caused him to die for a hundred years, then raised him up (again). He said: "How long did you stay (thus)?" He said: "(Perhaps) a day or part of a day." He said: "Nay, you have stayed thus a hundred years; but look at your food and your drink; they show no signs of age; and look at your donkey; and that We may make of you a sign to the people, look further at the bones, how We bring them together and clothe them with flesh. When this was shown clearly to him, he said: "I know that Allah has power over all things."

أَوْ كَالَّذِي مَرَّ عَلَىٰ قَرْيَةٍ وَهِيَ خَاوِيَةٌ عَلَىٰ
عُرُوشِهَا قَالَ أَنَّىٰ يُحْيِي هَٰذِهِ اللَّهُ بَعْدَ مَوْتِهَا ۖ
فَأَمَاتَهُ اللَّهُ مِائَةَ عَامٍ ثُمَّ بَعَثَهُ ۖ قَالَ كَمْ
لَبِثْتَ ۖ قَالَ لَبِثْتُ يَوْمًا أَوْ بَعْضَ يَوْمٍ ۖ قَالَ بَل
لَّبِثْتَ مِائَةَ عَامٍ فَانظُرْ إِلَىٰ طَعَامِكَ وَشَرَابِكَ
لَمْ يَتَسَنَّهْ ۖ وَانظُرْ إِلَىٰ حِمَارِكَ وَلِنَجْعَلَكَ آيَةً
لِّلنَّاسِ ۖ وَانظُرْ إِلَى الْعِظَامِ كَيْفَ نُنشِزُهَا ثُمَّ
نَكْسُوهَا لَحْمًا ۚ فَلَمَّا تَبَيَّنَ لَهُ قَالَ أَعْلَمُ
أَنَّ اللَّهَ عَلَىٰ كُلِّ شَيْءٍ قَدِيرٌ ﴿٢٥٩﴾

260. See! Abraham said: "My Lord! Show me how You give life to the dead. He said: "Do you not then believe?" He said: "Yea! But to satisfy my own understanding." He said: "Take four birds; tame them to turn to you; put a portion of them on every hill, and call to them; they will come to you, (flying) with speed. Then know that Allah is Exalted in Power, Wise."

وَإِذْ قَالَ إِبْرَاهِيمُ رَبِّ أَرِنِي كَيْفَ تُحْيِي الْمَوْتَىٰ ۖ
قَالَ أَوَلَمْ تُؤْمِن ۖ قَالَ بَلَىٰ وَلَٰكِن لِّيَطْمَئِنَّ قَلْبِي ۖ قَالَ
فَخُذْ أَرْبَعَةً مِّنَ الطَّيْرِ فَصُرْهُنَّ إِلَيْكَ ثُمَّ
اجْعَلْ عَلَىٰ كُلِّ جَبَلٍ مِّنْهُنَّ جُزْءًا ثُمَّ ادْعُهُنَّ
يَأْتِينَكَ سَعْيًا ۚ وَاعْلَمْ أَنَّ اللَّهَ عَزِيزٌ حَكِيمٌ ﴿٢٦٠﴾

261. The parable of those who spend their substance in the way of Allah is that of a grain of corn: it grows seven ears, and each ear has a hundred grains. Allah gives manifold increase to whom He pleases: and Allah cares for all and He knows all things.

مَّثَلُ الَّذِينَ يُنفِقُونَ أَمْوَالَهُمْ فِي سَبِيلِ اللَّهِ كَمَثَلِ
حَبَّةٍ أَنبَتَتْ سَبْعَ سَنَابِلَ فِي كُلِّ سُنبُلَةٍ
مِّائَةُ حَبَّةٍ ۗ وَاللَّهُ يُضَاعِفُ لِمَن يَشَاءُ ۗ وَاللَّهُ
وَاسِعٌ عَلِيمٌ ﴿٢٦١﴾

262. Those who spend their substance in the cause of Allah, and follow not up their gifts with reminders of their generosity or with injury - for them their reward is with their Lord; on them shall be no fear, nor shall they grieve.

ٱلَّذِينَ يُنفِقُونَ أَمْوَٰلَهُمْ فِى سَبِيلِ ٱللَّهِ ثُمَّ لَا
يُتْبِعُونَ مَآ أَنفَقُوا۟ مَنًّا وَلَآ أَذًى لَّهُمْ أَجْرُهُمْ
عِندَ رَبِّهِمْ وَلَا خَوْفٌ عَلَيْهِمْ وَلَا هُمْ يَحْزَنُونَ ٢٦٢

ربع الحزب ٥

263. Kind words and the covering of faults are better than charity followed by injury. Allah is free of all wants, and He is most forbearing.

۞ قَوْلٌ مَّعْرُوفٌ وَمَغْفِرَةٌ خَيْرٌ مِّن صَدَقَةٍ
يَتْبَعُهَآ أَذًى ۗ وَٱللَّهُ غَنِىٌّ حَلِيمٌ ٢٦٣

264. O you who believe! Cancel not your charity by reminders of your generosity or by injury - like those who spend their substance to be seen of men, but believe neither in Allah nor in the last day. They are in parable like a hard barren rock, on which is a little soil; on it falls heavy rain, which leaves it (just) a bare stone. They will be able to do nothing with anything they have earned. And Allah guides not those who reject faith.

يَٰٓأَيُّهَا ٱلَّذِينَ ءَامَنُوا۟ لَا تُبْطِلُوا۟ صَدَقَٰتِكُم
بِٱلْمَنِّ وَٱلْأَذَىٰ كَٱلَّذِى يُنفِقُ مَالَهُۥ رِئَآءَ ٱلنَّاسِ
وَلَا يُؤْمِنُ بِٱللَّهِ وَٱلْيَوْمِ ٱلْءَاخِرِ ۖ فَمَثَلُهُۥ كَمَثَلِ
صَفْوَانٍ عَلَيْهِ تُرَابٌ فَأَصَابَهُۥ وَابِلٌ فَتَرَكَهُۥ صَلْدًا ۖ
لَّا يَقْدِرُونَ عَلَىٰ شَىْءٍ مِّمَّا كَسَبُوا۟ ۗ وَٱللَّهُ
لَا يَهْدِى ٱلْقَوْمَ ٱلْكَٰفِرِينَ ٢٦٤

265. And the likeness of those who spend their substance, seeking to please Allah and to strengthen their souls, is as a garden, high and fertile; heavy rain falls on it but makes it yield a double increase of harvest, and if it receives not heavy rain, light moisture suffices it. Allah sees well whatever you do.

وَمَثَلُ ٱلَّذِينَ يُنفِقُونَ أَمْوَٰلَهُمُ ٱبْتِغَآءَ
مَرْضَاتِ ٱللَّهِ وَتَثْبِيتًا مِّنْ أَنفُسِهِمْ كَمَثَلِ
جَنَّةٍۭ بِرَبْوَةٍ أَصَابَهَا وَابِلٌ فَـَٔاتَتْ أُكُلَهَا
ضِعْفَيْنِ فَإِن لَّمْ يُصِبْهَا وَابِلٌ فَطَلٌّ ۗ وَٱللَّهُ
بِمَا تَعْمَلُونَ بَصِيرٌ ٢٦٥

266. Do any of you wish that he should have a garden with date palms and vines and streams flowing underneath, and all kinds of fruit, while he is stricken with old age, and his children are not strong

أَيَوَدُّ أَحَدُكُمْ أَن تَكُونَ لَهُۥ جَنَّةٌ مِّن نَّخِيلٍ
وَأَعْنَابٍ تَجْرِى مِن تَحْتِهَا ٱلْأَنْهَٰرُ لَهُۥ فِيهَا
مِن كُلِّ ٱلثَّمَرَٰتِ وَأَصَابَهُ ٱلْكِبَرُ وَلَهُۥ

(enough to look after themselves) - that it should be caught in a whirlwind, with fire in it, and be burnt up? Thus does Allah make clear to you (His) signs: that you may consider.

ذُرِّيَّةٌ ضُعَفَآءُ فَأَصَابَهَآ إِعْصَارٌ فِيهِ نَارٌ
فَٱحْتَرَقَتْ ۗ كَذَٰلِكَ يُبَيِّنُ ٱللَّهُ لَكُمُ ٱلْءَايَٰتِ
لَعَلَّكُمْ تَتَفَكَّرُونَ ٢٦٦

267. O you who believe! Give of the good things which you have (honourably) earned, and of the fruits of the earth which We have produced for you, and do not even aim at getting anything which is bad, in order that out of it you may give away something, when you yourselves would not receive it except with closed eyes. And know that Allah is free of all wants, and worthy of all praise.

يَٰٓأَيُّهَا ٱلَّذِينَ ءَامَنُوٓا۟ أَنفِقُوا۟ مِن طَيِّبَٰتِ
مَا كَسَبْتُمْ وَمِمَّآ أَخْرَجْنَا لَكُم مِّنَ ٱلْأَرْضِ ۖ
وَلَا تَيَمَّمُوا۟ ٱلْخَبِيثَ مِنْهُ تُنفِقُونَ وَلَسْتُم
بِـَٔاخِذِيهِ إِلَّآ أَن تُغْمِضُوا۟ فِيهِ ۚ وَٱعْلَمُوٓا۟ أَنَّ ٱللَّهَ
غَنِىٌّ حَمِيدٌ ٢٦٧

268. The evil one threatens you with poverty and bids you to conduct unseemly. Allah promises you His forgiveness and bounties. And Allah cares for all and He knows all things.

ٱلشَّيْطَٰنُ يَعِدُكُمُ ٱلْفَقْرَ وَيَأْمُرُكُم بِٱلْفَحْشَآءِ ۖ
وَٱللَّهُ يَعِدُكُم مَّغْفِرَةً مِّنْهُ وَفَضْلًا ۗ وَٱللَّهُ
وَٰسِعٌ عَلِيمٌ ٢٦٨

269. He grants wisdom to whom He pleases; and he to whom wisdom is granted receives indeed a benefit overflowing; but none will grasp the message but men of understanding.

يُؤْتِى ٱلْحِكْمَةَ مَن يَشَآءُ ۚ وَمَن يُؤْتَ
ٱلْحِكْمَةَ فَقَدْ أُوتِىَ خَيْرًا كَثِيرًا ۗ وَمَا
يَذَّكَّرُ إِلَّآ أُو۟لُوا۟ ٱلْأَلْبَٰبِ ٢٦٩

270. And whatever you spend in charity or devotion, be sure Allah knows it all. But the wrongdoers have no helpers.

وَمَآ أَنفَقْتُم مِّن نَّفَقَةٍ أَوْ نَذَرْتُم مِّن نَّذْرٍ
فَإِنَّ ٱللَّهَ يَعْلَمُهُۥ ۗ وَمَا لِلظَّٰلِمِينَ مِنْ
أَنصَارٍ ٢٧٠

271. If you disclose (acts of) charity, even so it is well, but if you conceal them, and make them reach those (really) in need, that is best for you: it will remove from you

إِن تُبْدُوا۟ ٱلصَّدَقَٰتِ فَنِعِمَّا هِىَ ۖ وَإِن
تُخْفُوهَا وَتُؤْتُوهَا ٱلْفُقَرَآءَ فَهُوَ خَيْرٌ

some of your (stains of) evil. And Allah is well acquainted with what you do.

لَّكُمْۚ وَيُكَفِّرُ عَنكُم مِّن سَيِّـَٔاتِكُمْۗ
وَٱللَّهُ بِمَا تَعْمَلُونَ خَبِيرٌ ٢٧١

272. It is not required of you (O messenger), to set them on the right path, but Allah sets on the right path whom He pleases. Whatever of good you give benefits your own souls, and you shall only do so seeking the "Face" of Allah. Whatever good you give, shall be rendered back to you, and you shall not be dealt with unjustly.

نصف الحزب ٥
۞ لَّيْسَ عَلَيْكَ هُدَىٰهُمْ وَلَٰكِنَّ ٱللَّهَ يَهْدِى
مَن يَشَآءُۗ وَمَا تُنفِقُوا۟ مِنْ خَيْرٍ فَلِأَنفُسِكُمْۚ
وَمَا تُنفِقُونَ إِلَّا ٱبْتِغَآءَ وَجْهِ ٱللَّهِۚ
وَمَا تُنفِقُوا۟ مِنْ خَيْرٍ يُوَفَّ إِلَيْكُمْ وَأَنتُمْ
لَا تُظْلَمُونَ ٢٧٢

273. (Charity is) for those in need, who in Allah's cause are restricted (from travel) and cannot move about in the land, seeking (for trade or work): The ignorant man thinks, because of their modesty, that they are free from want. You shall know them by their (unfailing) mark: they beg not importunately from all and sundry, and whatever of good you give, be assured Allah knows it well.

لِلْفُقَرَآءِ ٱلَّذِينَ أُحْصِرُوا۟ فِى سَبِيلِ ٱللَّهِ
لَا يَسْتَطِيعُونَ ضَرْبًا فِى ٱلْأَرْضِ يَحْسَبُهُمُ
ٱلْجَاهِلُ أَغْنِيَآءَ مِنَ ٱلتَّعَفُّفِ تَعْرِفُهُم
بِسِيمَٰهُمْ لَا يَسْـَٔلُونَ ٱلنَّاسَ إِلْحَافًاۗ
وَمَا تُنفِقُوا۟ مِنْ خَيْرٍ فَإِنَّ ٱللَّهَ بِهِۦ عَلِيمٌ ٢٧٣

274. Those who (in charity) spend of their goods by night and by day, in secret and in public, have their reward with their Lord; on them shall be no fear, nor shall they grieve.

ٱلَّذِينَ يُنفِقُونَ أَمْوَٰلَهُم بِٱلَّيْلِ وَٱلنَّهَارِ
سِرًّا وَعَلَانِيَةً فَلَهُمْ أَجْرُهُمْ عِندَ رَبِّهِمْ
وَلَا خَوْفٌ عَلَيْهِمْ وَلَا هُمْ يَحْزَنُونَ ٢٧٤

275. Those who devour usury will not stand except as one whom the evil one by his touch has driven to madness. That is because they say: "Trade is like usury," but Allah has permitted trade and forbidden usury. Those who after receiving direction from their Lord, desist, shall be pardoned for the past; their case is for Allah (to judge), but those who repeat (the offence)

ٱلَّذِينَ يَأْكُلُونَ ٱلرِّبَوٰا۟ لَا يَقُومُونَ إِلَّا كَمَا
يَقُومُ ٱلَّذِى يَتَخَبَّطُهُ ٱلشَّيْطَٰنُ مِنَ ٱلْمَسِّۚ ذَٰلِكَ
بِأَنَّهُمْ قَالُوٓا۟ إِنَّمَا ٱلْبَيْعُ مِثْلُ ٱلرِّبَوٰا۟ۗ وَأَحَلَّ ٱللَّهُ
ٱلْبَيْعَ وَحَرَّمَ ٱلرِّبَوٰا۟ۚ فَمَن جَآءَهُۥ مَوْعِظَةٌ مِّن
رَّبِّهِۦ فَٱنتَهَىٰ فَلَهُۥ مَا سَلَفَ وَأَمْرُهُۥٓ إِلَى ٱللَّهِۖ وَمَنْ عَادَ

are companions of the fire: they will remain in it (forever).

فَأُوْلَٰٓئِكَ أَصۡحَٰبُ ٱلنَّارِۖ هُمۡ فِيهَا خَٰلِدُونَ ٢٧٥

276. Allah will deprive usury of all blessing, but will give increase for deeds of charity; for He loves not creatures ungrateful and wicked.

يَمۡحَقُ ٱللَّهُ ٱلرِّبَوٰاْ وَيُرۡبِي ٱلصَّدَقَٰتِۗ وَٱللَّهُ
لَا يُحِبُّ كُلَّ كَفَّارٍ أَثِيمٍ ٢٧٦

277. Those who believe, and do deeds of righteousness, and establish regular prayers and regular charity, will have their reward with their Lord: on them shall be no fear, nor shall they grieve.

إِنَّ ٱلَّذِينَ ءَامَنُواْ وَعَمِلُواْ ٱلصَّٰلِحَٰتِ وَأَقَامُواْ
ٱلصَّلَوٰةَ وَءَاتَوُاْ ٱلزَّكَوٰةَ لَهُمۡ أَجۡرُهُمۡ عِندَ
رَبِّهِمۡ وَلَا خَوۡفٌ عَلَيۡهِمۡ وَلَا هُمۡ يَحۡزَنُونَ ٢٧٧

278. O you who believe! Fear Allah, and give up what remains of your demand for usury, if you are indeed believers.

يَٰٓأَيُّهَا ٱلَّذِينَ ءَامَنُواْ ٱتَّقُواْ ٱللَّهَ وَذَرُواْ مَا بَقِيَ
مِنَ ٱلرِّبَوٰٓاْ إِن كُنتُم مُّؤۡمِنِينَ ٢٧٨

279. If you do it not, take notice of war from Allah and His messenger: but if you turn back, you shall have your capital sums; deal not unjustly, and you shall not be dealt with unjustly.

فَإِن لَّمۡ تَفۡعَلُواْ فَأۡذَنُواْ بِحَرۡبٖ مِّنَ ٱللَّهِ وَرَسُولِهِۦۖ
وَإِن تُبۡتُمۡ فَلَكُمۡ رُءُوسُ أَمۡوَٰلِكُمۡ لَا تَظۡلِمُونَ
وَلَا تُظۡلَمُونَ ٢٧٩

280. If the debtor is in a difficulty, grant him time till it is easy for him to repay. But if you remit it by way of charity, that is best for you if you only knew.

وَإِن كَانَ ذُو عُسۡرَةٖ فَنَظِرَةٌ إِلَىٰ مَيۡسَرَةٖۚ وَأَن
تَصَدَّقُواْ خَيۡرٞ لَّكُمۡ إِن كُنتُمۡ تَعۡلَمُونَ ٢٨٠

281. And fear the Day when you shall be brought back to Allah. Then shall every soul be paid what it earned, and none shall be dealt with unjustly.

وَٱتَّقُواْ يَوۡمٗا تُرۡجَعُونَ فِيهِ إِلَى ٱللَّهِۖ ثُمَّ تُوَفَّىٰ كُلُّ
نَفۡسٖ مَّا كَسَبَتۡ وَهُمۡ لَا يُظۡلَمُونَ ٢٨١

282. O you who believe! When you deal with each other, in transactions involving future obligations in a fixed period of time,

يَٰٓأَيُّهَا ٱلَّذِينَ ءَامَنُوٓاْ إِذَا تَدَايَنتُم بِدَيۡنٍ إِلَىٰٓ
أَجَلٖ مُّسَمّٗى فَٱكۡتُبُوهُۚ وَلۡيَكۡتُب بَّيۡنَكُمۡ

reduce them to writing. Let a scribe write down faithfully as between the parties; let not the scribe refuse to write: as Allah has taught him, so let him write. Let him who incurs the liability dictate, but let him fear his Lord Allah, and not diminish anything of what he owes. If the party liable is mentally deficient, or weak, or unable himself to dictate, let his guardian dictate faithfully. And get two witnesses, out of your own men, and if there are not two men, then a man and two women, such as you choose, for witnesses, so that if one of them errs, the other can remind her. The witnesses should not refuse when they are called on (for evidence). Disdain not to reduce to writing (your contract) for a future period, whether it be small or big: it is more just in the sight of Allah, more suitable as evidence, and more convenient to prevent doubts among yourselves. But if it be a transaction which you carry out on the spot among yourselves there is no blame on you if you reduce it not to writing. But take witnesses whenever you make a commercial contract; and let neither scribe nor witness suffer harm. If you do (such harm), it would be wickedness in you. So fear Allah; for it is Allah that teaches you. And Allah is well acquainted with all things.

كَاتِبُۢ بِٱلۡعَدۡلِۚ وَلَا يَأۡبَ كَاتِبٌ أَن يَكۡتُبَ
كَمَا عَلَّمَهُ ٱللَّهُۚ فَلۡيَكۡتُبۡ وَلۡيُمۡلِلِ ٱلَّذِي عَلَيۡهِ
ٱلۡحَقُّ وَلۡيَتَّقِ ٱللَّهَ رَبَّهُۥ وَلَا يَبۡخَسۡ مِنۡهُ شَيۡـٔٗاۚ
فَإِن كَانَ ٱلَّذِي عَلَيۡهِ ٱلۡحَقُّ سَفِيهًا أَوۡ ضَعِيفًا
أَوۡ لَا يَسۡتَطِيعُ أَن يُمِلَّ هُوَ فَلۡيُمۡلِلۡ وَلِيُّهُۥ بِٱلۡعَدۡلِۚ
وَٱسۡتَشۡهِدُواْ شَهِيدَيۡنِ مِن رِّجَالِكُمۡۖ فَإِن لَّمۡ
يَكُونَا رَجُلَيۡنِ فَرَجُلٞ وَٱمۡرَأَتَانِ مِمَّن تَرۡضَوۡنَ
مِنَ ٱلشُّهَدَآءِ أَن تَضِلَّ إِحۡدَىٰهُمَا فَتُذَكِّرَ
إِحۡدَىٰهُمَا ٱلۡأُخۡرَىٰۚ وَلَا يَأۡبَ ٱلشُّهَدَآءُ إِذَا مَا
دُعُواْۚ وَلَا تَسۡـَٔمُوٓاْ أَن تَكۡتُبُوهُ صَغِيرًا أَوۡ كَبِيرًا
إِلَىٰٓ أَجَلِهِۦۚ ذَٰلِكُمۡ أَقۡسَطُ عِندَ ٱللَّهِ وَأَقۡوَمُ
لِلشَّهَٰدَةِ وَأَدۡنَىٰٓ أَلَّا تَرۡتَابُوٓاْ إِلَّآ أَن تَكُونَ تِجَٰرَةً
حَاضِرَةٗ تُدِيرُونَهَا بَيۡنَكُمۡ فَلَيۡسَ عَلَيۡكُمۡ
جُنَاحٌ أَلَّا تَكۡتُبُوهَاۗ وَأَشۡهِدُوٓاْ إِذَا تَبَايَعۡتُمۡۚ
وَلَا يُضَآرَّ كَاتِبٞ وَلَا شَهِيدٞۚ وَإِن تَفۡعَلُواْ
فَإِنَّهُۥ فُسُوقُۢ بِكُمۡۗ وَٱتَّقُواْ ٱللَّهَۖ
وَيُعَلِّمُكُمُ ٱللَّهُۗ وَٱللَّهُ بِكُلِّ شَيۡءٍ
عَلِيمٞ ٢٨٢

283. If you are on a journey, and cannot find a scribe, a pledge with possession (may serve the purpose). And if one of you deposits a thing on trust with another, let

ثلاثة أرباع الحزب ٥

۞ وَإِن كُنتُمۡ عَلَىٰ سَفَرٖ وَلَمۡ تَجِدُواْ كَاتِبٗا فَرِهَٰنٞ
مَّقۡبُوضَةٞۖ فَإِنۡ أَمِنَ بَعۡضُكُم بَعۡضٗا فَلۡيُؤَدِّ ٱلَّذِي

the trustee (faithfully) discharge his trust, and let him fear his Lord. Conceal not evidence; for whoever conceals it, his heart is tainted with sin. And Allah knows all that you do.

ٱؤْتُمِنَ أَمَٰنَتَهُۥ وَلْيَتَّقِ ٱللَّهَ رَبَّهُۥ ۗ وَلَا تَكْتُمُوا۟
ٱلشَّهَٰدَةَ ۚ وَمَن يَكْتُمْهَا فَإِنَّهُۥٓ ءَاثِمٌ قَلْبُهُۥ ۗ
وَٱللَّهُ بِمَا تَعْمَلُونَ عَلِيمٌ ﴿٢٨٣﴾

284. To Allah belongs all that is in the heavens and on earth. Whether you show what is in your minds or conceal it, Allah calls you to account for it. He forgives whom He pleases, and punishes whom He pleases. For Allah has power over all things.

لِّلَّهِ مَا فِى ٱلسَّمَٰوَٰتِ وَمَا فِى ٱلْأَرْضِ ۗ وَإِن تُبْدُوا۟
مَا فِىٓ أَنفُسِكُمْ أَوْ تُخْفُوهُ يُحَاسِبْكُم بِهِ
ٱللَّهُ ۖ فَيَغْفِرُ لِمَن يَشَآءُ وَيُعَذِّبُ مَن يَشَآءُ ۗ وَٱللَّهُ
عَلَىٰ كُلِّ شَىْءٍ قَدِيرٌ ﴿٢٨٤﴾

285. The messenger believes in what has been revealed to him from his Lord, as do the men of faith. Each one (of them) believes in Allah, His angels, His books, and His messengers. "We make no distinction (they say) between one and another of His messengers." And they say: "We hear, and we obey: (We seek) Your forgiveness, Our Lord, and to You is the end of all journeys."

ءَامَنَ ٱلرَّسُولُ بِمَآ أُنزِلَ إِلَيْهِ مِن رَّبِّهِۦ وَٱلْمُؤْمِنُونَ ۚ
كُلٌّ ءَامَنَ بِٱللَّهِ وَمَلَٰٓئِكَتِهِۦ وَكُتُبِهِۦ
وَرُسُلِهِۦ لَا نُفَرِّقُ بَيْنَ أَحَدٍ مِّن رُّسُلِهِۦ ۚ وَقَالُوا۟
سَمِعْنَا وَأَطَعْنَا ۖ غُفْرَانَكَ رَبَّنَا وَإِلَيْكَ ٱلْمَصِيرُ ﴿٢٨٥﴾

286. On no soul does Allah place a burden greater than it can bear. It gets every good that it earns, and it suffers every ill that it earns. (Pray): "Our Lord! Condemn us not if we forget or fall into error; our Lord! Lay not on us a burden like that which You did lay on those before us; Our Lord! Lay not on us a burden greater than we have strength to bear. Blot out our sins, and grant us forgiveness. Have mercy on us. You are our Protector; help us against those who stand against faith."

لَا يُكَلِّفُ ٱللَّهُ نَفْسًا إِلَّا وُسْعَهَا ۚ لَهَا مَا كَسَبَتْ
وَعَلَيْهَا مَا ٱكْتَسَبَتْ ۗ رَبَّنَا لَا تُؤَاخِذْنَآ إِن
نَّسِينَآ أَوْ أَخْطَأْنَا ۚ رَبَّنَا وَلَا تَحْمِلْ عَلَيْنَآ
إِصْرًا كَمَا حَمَلْتَهُۥ عَلَى ٱلَّذِينَ مِن قَبْلِنَا ۚ
رَبَّنَا وَلَا تُحَمِّلْنَا مَا لَا طَاقَةَ لَنَا بِهِۦ ۖ وَٱعْفُ
عَنَّا وَٱغْفِرْ لَنَا وَٱرْحَمْنَآ ۚ أَنتَ مَوْلَىٰنَا
فَٱنصُرْنَا عَلَى ٱلْقَوْمِ ٱلْكَٰفِرِينَ ﴿٢٨٦﴾

سُورَةُ آلِ عِمۡرَانَ

Surah 3: ***Al-'Imran*** **(The Family of 'Imran)**

In the name of Allah,
Most Gracious, Most Merciful.

بِسۡمِ ٱللَّهِ ٱلرَّحۡمَٰنِ ٱلرَّحِيمِ

1. *Alif Lam Mim.*

الٓمٓ ١

2. Allah! There is no god but He - the Living, the Self-Subsisting, Eternal.

ٱللَّهُ لَآ إِلَٰهَ إِلَّا هُوَ ٱلۡحَيُّ ٱلۡقَيُّومُ ٢

3. It is He Who sent down to you (step by step), in truth, the book, confirming what went before it; and He sent down the Law (of Moses) and the Gospel (of Jesus).

نَزَّلَ عَلَيۡكَ ٱلۡكِتَٰبَ بِٱلۡحَقِّ مُصَدِّقٗا لِّمَا بَيۡنَ يَدَيۡهِ
وَأَنزَلَ ٱلتَّوۡرَىٰةَ وَٱلۡإِنجِيلَ ٣

4. Before this, as a guide to mankind, and He sent down the criterion (of judgement between right and wrong). Then those who reject faith in the signs of Allah will suffer the severest penalty, and Allah is Exalted in Might, Lord of Retribution.

مِن قَبۡلُ هُدٗى لِّلنَّاسِ وَأَنزَلَ ٱلۡفُرۡقَانَۗ إِنَّ ٱلَّذِينَ
كَفَرُواْ بِـَٔايَٰتِ ٱللَّهِ لَهُمۡ عَذَابٞ شَدِيدٞۗ وَٱللَّهُ عَزِيزٞ
ذُو ٱنتِقَامٍ ٤

5. From Allah, verily nothing is hidden on earth or in the heavens.

إِنَّ ٱللَّهَ لَا يَخۡفَىٰ عَلَيۡهِ شَيۡءٞ فِي ٱلۡأَرۡضِ وَلَا فِي
ٱلسَّمَآءِ ٥

6. He it is Who shapes you in the wombs as He pleases. There is no god but He, the Exalted in Might, the Wise.

هُوَ ٱلَّذِي يُصَوِّرُكُمۡ فِي ٱلۡأَرۡحَامِ كَيۡفَ يَشَآءُۚ لَآ إِلَٰهَ
إِلَّا هُوَ ٱلۡعَزِيزُ ٱلۡحَكِيمُ ٦

7. He it is Who has sent down to you the book; in it are verses basic or fundamental (of established meaning); they are the foundation of the book: others are not of well-established meaning. But those in whose hearts is perversity follow the part of it that is not of well-established

هُوَ ٱلَّذِيٓ أَنزَلَ عَلَيۡكَ ٱلۡكِتَٰبَ مِنۡهُ ءَايَٰتٞ
مُّحۡكَمَٰتٌ هُنَّ أُمُّ ٱلۡكِتَٰبِ وَأُخَرُ مُتَشَٰبِهَٰتٞۖ
فَأَمَّا ٱلَّذِينَ فِي قُلُوبِهِمۡ زَيۡغٞ فَيَتَّبِعُونَ مَا تَشَٰبَهَ مِنۡهُ

meaning. Seeking discord, and searching for its hidden meanings, but no one knows its true meanings except Allah. And those who are firmly grounded in knowledge say: "We believe in the book; the whole of it is from our Lord:" and none will grasp the message except men of understanding.

ٱبْتِغَآءَ ٱلْفِتْنَةِ وَٱبْتِغَآءَ تَأْوِيلِهِۦ ۗ وَمَا يَعْلَمُ تَأْوِيلَهُۥٓ
إِلَّا ٱللَّهُ ۗ وَٱلرَّٰسِخُونَ فِى ٱلْعِلْمِ يَقُولُونَ ءَامَنَّا بِهِۦ
كُلٌّ مِّنْ عِندِ رَبِّنَا ۗ وَمَا يَذَّكَّرُ إِلَّآ أُو۟لُوا۟ ٱلْأَلْبَٰبِ ٧

8. "Our Lord!" (they say), "let not our hearts deviate now after You have guided us, but grant us mercy from Your own Presence; for You are the Grantor of Bounties without measure.

رَبَّنَا لَا تُزِغْ قُلُوبَنَا بَعْدَ إِذْ هَدَيْتَنَا وَهَبْ لَنَا مِن
لَّدُنكَ رَحْمَةً ۚ إِنَّكَ أَنتَ ٱلْوَهَّابُ ٨

9. "Our Lord! You are He that will gather mankind together against a day about which there is no doubt; for Allah never fails in His promise."

رَبَّنَآ إِنَّكَ جَامِعُ ٱلنَّاسِ لِيَوْمٍ لَّا رَيْبَ فِيهِ ۚ إِنَّ ٱللَّهَ لَا
يُخْلِفُ ٱلْمِيعَادَ ٩

10. Those who reject faith, neither their possessions nor their (numerous) progeny will benefit them anything against Allah; they are themselves but fuel for the fire.

إِنَّ ٱلَّذِينَ كَفَرُوا۟ لَن تُغْنِىَ عَنْهُمْ أَمْوَٰلُهُمْ وَلَآ
أَوْلَٰدُهُم مِّنَ ٱللَّهِ شَيْـًٔا ۖ وَأُو۟لَٰٓئِكَ هُمْ وَقُودُ ٱلنَّارِ ١٠

11. (Their plight will be) no better than that of the people of Pharaoh, and their predecessors: they denied Our signs, and Allah called them to account for their sins. For Allah is strict in punishment.

كَدَأْبِ ءَالِ فِرْعَوْنَ وَٱلَّذِينَ مِن قَبْلِهِمْ ۚ
كَذَّبُوا۟ بِـَٔايَٰتِنَا فَأَخَذَهُمُ ٱللَّهُ بِذُنُوبِهِمْ ۗ وَٱللَّهُ
شَدِيدُ ٱلْعِقَابِ ١١

12. Say to those who reject faith: "Soon will you be vanquished and gathered together to hell - an evil bed indeed (to lie on)!"

قُل لِّلَّذِينَ كَفَرُوا۟ سَتُغْلَبُونَ وَتُحْشَرُونَ
إِلَىٰ جَهَنَّمَ ۚ وَبِئْسَ ٱلْمِهَادُ ١٢

13. "There has already been for you a sign in the two armies that met (in combat): one was fighting in the cause of Allah, the other resisting Allah; these saw with their own eyes twice their number. But Allah

قَدْ كَانَ لَكُمْ ءَايَةٌ فِى فِئَتَيْنِ ٱلْتَقَتَا ۖ فِئَةٌ
تُقَٰتِلُ فِى سَبِيلِ ٱللَّهِ وَأُخْرَىٰ كَافِرَةٌ يَرَوْنَهُم

does support with His aid whom He pleases. In this is a warning for such as have eyes to see."

مِّثْلَيْهِمْ رَأْيَ ٱلْعَيْنِ ۚ وَٱللَّهُ يُؤَيِّدُ بِنَصْرِهِۦ مَن
يَشَآءُ ۗ إِنَّ فِى ذَٰلِكَ لَعِبْرَةً لِّأُو۟لِى ٱلْأَبْصَٰرِ ﴿١٣﴾

14. Fair in the eyes of men is the love of things they covet: women and sons; heaped-up hoards of gold and silver; horses branded (for blood and excellence); and (wealth of) cattle and well-tilled land. Such are the possessions of this world's life; but in nearness to Allah is the best of the goals (to return to).

زُيِّنَ لِلنَّاسِ حُبُّ ٱلشَّهَوَٰتِ مِنَ ٱلنِّسَآءِ
وَٱلْبَنِينَ وَٱلْقَنَٰطِيرِ ٱلْمُقَنطَرَةِ مِنَ ٱلذَّهَبِ
وَٱلْفِضَّةِ وَٱلْخَيْلِ ٱلْمُسَوَّمَةِ وَٱلْأَنْعَٰمِ
وَٱلْحَرْثِ ۗ ذَٰلِكَ مَتَٰعُ ٱلْحَيَوٰةِ ٱلدُّنْيَا ۖ وَٱللَّهُ عِندَهُۥ
حُسْنُ ٱلْمَـَٔابِ ﴿١٤﴾

15. Say: Shall I give you glad tidings of things far better than those? For the righteous are gardens in nearness to their Lord, with rivers flowing beneath; in it is their eternal home; with companions pure (and holy) and the good pleasure of Allah. For in Allah's sight are (all) His servants -

الحزب ٦
۞ قُلْ أَؤُنَبِّئُكُم بِخَيْرٍ مِّن ذَٰلِكُمْ ۖ لِلَّذِينَ
ٱتَّقَوْا۟ عِندَ رَبِّهِمْ جَنَّٰتٌ تَجْرِى مِن تَحْتِهَا
ٱلْأَنْهَٰرُ خَٰلِدِينَ فِيهَا وَأَزْوَٰجٌ مُّطَهَّرَةٌ
وَرِضْوَٰنٌ مِّنَ ٱللَّهِ ۗ وَٱللَّهُ بَصِيرٌۢ بِٱلْعِبَادِ ﴿١٥﴾

16. (Namely), those who say: "Our Lord! We have indeed believed: forgive us, then, our sins, and save us from the agony of the fire" -

ٱلَّذِينَ يَقُولُونَ رَبَّنَآ إِنَّنَآ ءَامَنَّا فَٱغْفِرْ لَنَا
ذُنُوبَنَا وَقِنَا عَذَابَ ٱلنَّارِ ﴿١٦﴾

17. Those who show patience, firmness and self-control; who are true (in word and deed); who worship devoutly; who spend (in the way of Allah); and who pray for forgiveness in the early hours of the morning.

ٱلصَّٰبِرِينَ وَٱلصَّٰدِقِينَ وَٱلْقَٰنِتِينَ وَٱلْمُنفِقِينَ
وَٱلْمُسْتَغْفِرِينَ بِٱلْأَسْحَارِ ﴿١٧﴾

18. There is no god but He: that is the witness of Allah, His angels, and those endued with knowledge, standing firm on justice. There is no god but He, the Exalted in Power, the Wise.

شَهِدَ ٱللَّهُ أَنَّهُۥ لَآ إِلَٰهَ إِلَّا هُوَ وَٱلْمَلَٰٓئِكَةُ
وَأُو۟لُوا۟ ٱلْعِلْمِ قَآئِمًۢا بِٱلْقِسْطِ ۚ لَآ إِلَٰهَ إِلَّا هُوَ
ٱلْعَزِيزُ ٱلْحَكِيمُ ﴿١٨﴾

19. The religion before Allah is Islam (submission to His will): nor did the People of the Book dissent from it except through envy of each other, after knowledge had come to them. But if any deny the signs of Allah, Allah is swift in calling to account.

إِنَّ ٱلدِّينَ عِندَ ٱللَّهِ ٱلْإِسْلَٰمُ ۗ وَمَا ٱخْتَلَفَ
ٱلَّذِينَ أُوتُوا۟ ٱلْكِتَٰبَ إِلَّا مِنۢ بَعْدِ مَا جَآءَهُمُ
ٱلْعِلْمُ بَغْيًۢا بَيْنَهُمْ ۗ وَمَن يَكْفُرْ بِـَٔايَٰتِ ٱللَّهِ
فَإِنَّ ٱللَّهَ سَرِيعُ ٱلْحِسَابِ ﴿١٩﴾

20. So if they dispute with you, say: "I have submitted my whole self to Allah and so have those who follow me." And say to the People of the Book and to those who are unlearned: "Do you (also) submit yourselves?" If they do, they are in right guidance, but if they turn back, your duty is to convey the Message; and in Allah's sight are (all) His servants.

فَإِنْ حَآجُّوكَ فَقُلْ أَسْلَمْتُ وَجْهِىَ لِلَّهِ وَمَنِ
ٱتَّبَعَنِ ۗ وَقُل لِّلَّذِينَ أُوتُوا۟ ٱلْكِتَٰبَ وَٱلْأُمِّيِّۦنَ
ءَأَسْلَمْتُمْ ۚ فَإِنْ أَسْلَمُوا۟ فَقَدِ ٱهْتَدَوا۟ ۖ وَّإِن تَوَلَّوْا۟
فَإِنَّمَا عَلَيْكَ ٱلْبَلَٰغُ ۗ وَٱللَّهُ بَصِيرٌۢ بِٱلْعِبَادِ ﴿٢٠﴾

21. As to those who deny the signs of Allah, and in defiance of right, slay the prophets, and slay those who teach just dealing with mankind, announce to them a grievous penalty.

إِنَّ ٱلَّذِينَ يَكْفُرُونَ بِـَٔايَٰتِ ٱللَّهِ وَيَقْتُلُونَ
ٱلنَّبِيِّـۧنَ بِغَيْرِ حَقٍّ وَيَقْتُلُونَ ٱلَّذِينَ يَأْمُرُونَ
بِٱلْقِسْطِ مِنَ ٱلنَّاسِ فَبَشِّرْهُم بِعَذَابٍ أَلِيمٍ ﴿٢١﴾

22. They are those whose works will bear no fruit in this world and in the hereafter, nor will they have anyone to help.

أُو۟لَٰٓئِكَ ٱلَّذِينَ حَبِطَتْ أَعْمَٰلُهُمْ فِى ٱلدُّنْيَا
وَٱلْءَاخِرَةِ وَمَا لَهُم مِّن نَّٰصِرِينَ ﴿٢٢﴾

23. Have you not turned your vision to those who have been given a portion of the book? They are invited to the book of Allah, to settle their dispute, but a party of them turn back and decline (the arbitration).

أَلَمْ تَرَ إِلَى ٱلَّذِينَ أُوتُوا۟ نَصِيبًا مِّنَ ٱلْكِتَٰبِ يُدْعَوْنَ
إِلَىٰ كِتَٰبِ ٱللَّهِ لِيَحْكُمَ بَيْنَهُمْ ثُمَّ يَتَوَلَّىٰ فَرِيقٌ مِّنْهُمْ
وَهُم مُّعْرِضُونَ ﴿٢٣﴾

24. This because they say: "The fire shall not touch us but for a few numbered days"; for their forgeries deceive them as to their own religion.

ذَٰلِكَ بِأَنَّهُمْ قَالُوا۟ لَن تَمَسَّنَا ٱلنَّارُ إِلَّآ أَيَّامًا
مَّعْدُودَٰتٍ ۖ وَغَرَّهُمْ فِى دِينِهِم مَّا كَانُوا۟
يَفْتَرُونَ ﴿٢٤﴾

25. But how (will they fare) when We gather them together against a day about which there is no doubt, and each soul will be paid out just what it has earned, without (favour or) injustice?

فَكَيْفَ إِذَا جَمَعْنَٰهُمْ لِيَوْمٍ لَّا رَيْبَ فِيهِ وَوُفِّيَتْ
كُلُّ نَفْسٍ مَّا كَسَبَتْ وَهُمْ لَا يُظْلَمُونَ ﴿٢٥﴾

26. Say: "O Allah! Lord of power (and rule), You give power to whom You please, and You strip off power from whom You please: You endue with honour whom You please, and You bring low whom You please: in Your Hand is all good. Verily, over all things You have power.

قُلِ ٱللَّهُمَّ مَٰلِكَ ٱلْمُلْكِ تُؤْتِى ٱلْمُلْكَ مَن تَشَآءُ
وَتَنزِعُ ٱلْمُلْكَ مِمَّن تَشَآءُ وَتُعِزُّ مَن تَشَآءُ وَتُذِلُّ
مَن تَشَآءُ ۖ بِيَدِكَ ٱلْخَيْرُ ۖ إِنَّكَ عَلَىٰ كُلِّ شَىْءٍ قَدِيرٌ ﴿٢٦﴾

27. "You cause the night to gain on the day, and You cause the day to gain on the night; You bring the living out of the dead, and You bring the dead out of the living; and You give sustenance to whom You please, without measure."

تُولِجُ ٱلَّيْلَ فِى ٱلنَّهَارِ وَتُولِجُ ٱلنَّهَارَ فِى ٱلَّيْلِ ۖ
وَتُخْرِجُ ٱلْحَىَّ مِنَ ٱلْمَيِّتِ وَتُخْرِجُ ٱلْمَيِّتَ مِنَ ٱلْحَىِّ ۖ
وَتَرْزُقُ مَن تَشَآءُ بِغَيْرِ حِسَابٍ ﴿٢٧﴾

28. Let not the believers take for friends or helpers unbelievers rather than believers; if any do that, in nothing will there be help from Allah: except by way of precaution, that you may guard yourselves from them. But Allah cautions you (to remember) Himself; for the final goal is to Allah.

لَّا يَتَّخِذِ ٱلْمُؤْمِنُونَ ٱلْكَٰفِرِينَ أَوْلِيَآءَ مِن دُونِ
ٱلْمُؤْمِنِينَ ۖ وَمَن يَفْعَلْ ذَٰلِكَ فَلَيْسَ مِنَ ٱللَّهِ فِى شَىْءٍ
إِلَّآ أَن تَتَّقُوا۟ مِنْهُمْ تُقَىٰةً ۗ وَيُحَذِّرُكُمُ ٱللَّهُ
نَفْسَهُۥ ۗ وَإِلَى ٱللَّهِ ٱلْمَصِيرُ ﴿٢٨﴾

29. Say: "Whether you hide what is in your hearts or reveal it, Allah knows it all: He knows what is in the heavens, and what is on earth. And Allah has power over all things.

قُلْ إِن تُخْفُوا۟ مَا فِى صُدُورِكُمْ أَوْ تُبْدُوهُ
يَعْلَمْهُ ٱللَّهُ ۗ وَيَعْلَمُ مَا فِى ٱلسَّمَٰوَٰتِ وَمَا فِى ٱلْأَرْضِ ۗ
وَٱللَّهُ عَلَىٰ كُلِّ شَىْءٍ قَدِيرٌ ﴿٢٩﴾

30. "On the day when every soul will be confronted with all the good it has done, and all the evil it has done, it will wish there were a great distance between it and

يَوْمَ تَجِدُ كُلُّ نَفْسٍ مَّا عَمِلَتْ مِنْ خَيْرٍ مُّحْضَرًا
وَمَا عَمِلَتْ مِن سُوٓءٍ تَوَدُّ لَوْ أَنَّ بَيْنَهَا وَبَيْنَهُۥٓ أَمَدًۢا

its evil. But Allah cautions you (to remember) Himself. And Allah is full of kindness to those that serve Him.

بَعِيدًا ۗ وَيُحَذِّرُكُمُ ٱللَّهُ نَفْسَهُۥ ۗ وَٱللَّهُ رَءُوفٌۢ
بِٱلْعِبَادِ ﴿٣٠﴾

31. Say: "If you do love Allah, follow me: Allah will love you and forgive you your sins; for Allah is Oft-Forgiving, Most Merciful."

قُلْ إِن كُنتُمْ تُحِبُّونَ ٱللَّهَ فَٱتَّبِعُونِى يُحْبِبْكُمُ ٱللَّهُ
وَيَغْفِرْ لَكُمْ ذُنُوبَكُمْ ۗ وَٱللَّهُ غَفُورٌ رَّحِيمٌ ﴿٣١﴾

32. Say: "Obey Allah and His messenger": but if they turn back, Allah loves not those who reject faith.

قُلْ أَطِيعُوا۟ ٱللَّهَ وَٱلرَّسُولَ ۖ فَإِن تَوَلَّوْا۟ فَإِنَّ ٱللَّهَ لَا يُحِبُّ
ٱلْكَٰفِرِينَ ﴿٣٢﴾

33. Allah did choose Adam and Noah, the family of Abraham, and the family of Imran above all people -

ربع الحزب ٦ ۞ إِنَّ ٱللَّهَ ٱصْطَفَىٰٓ ءَادَمَ وَنُوحًا وَءَالَ إِبْرَٰهِيمَ وَءَالَ
عِمْرَٰنَ عَلَى ٱلْعَٰلَمِينَ ﴿٣٣﴾

34. Offspring, one of the other; and Allah hears and knows all things.

ذُرِّيَّةًۢ بَعْضُهَا مِنۢ بَعْضٍ ۗ وَٱللَّهُ سَمِيعٌ عَلِيمٌ ﴿٣٤﴾

35. See! A woman of Imran said: "O my Lord! I do dedicate to You what is in my womb for Your special service: so accept this of me: for You hear and know all things."

إِذْ قَالَتِ ٱمْرَأَتُ عِمْرَٰنَ رَبِّ إِنِّى نَذَرْتُ لَكَ مَا فِى
بَطْنِى مُحَرَّرًا فَتَقَبَّلْ مِنِّىٓ ۖ إِنَّكَ أَنتَ ٱلسَّمِيعُ
ٱلْعَلِيمُ ﴿٣٥﴾

36. When she was delivered, she said: "O my Lord! See! I am delivered of a female child!" - And Allah knew best what she brought out - "and no wise is the male like the female. I have named her Mary, and I commend her and her offspring to Your protection from the evil one, the rejected."

فَلَمَّا وَضَعَتْهَا قَالَتْ رَبِّ إِنِّى وَضَعْتُهَآ أُنثَىٰ وَٱللَّهُ أَعْلَمُ
بِمَا وَضَعَتْ وَلَيْسَ ٱلذَّكَرُ كَٱلْأُنثَىٰ ۖ وَإِنِّى سَمَّيْتُهَا
مَرْيَمَ وَإِنِّىٓ أُعِيذُهَا بِكَ وَذُرِّيَّتَهَا مِنَ ٱلشَّيْطَٰنِ
ٱلرَّجِيمِ ﴿٣٦﴾

37. Right graciously did her Lord accept her: He made her grow in purity and beauty; to the care of Zakariya was she assigned. Every time that he entered (her) chamber to

فَتَقَبَّلَهَا رَبُّهَا بِقَبُولٍ حَسَنٍ وَأَنۢبَتَهَا نَبَاتًا
حَسَنًا وَكَفَّلَهَا زَكَرِيَّا ۖ كُلَّمَا دَخَلَ عَلَيْهَا زَكَرِيَّا

see her, he found her supplied with sustenance. He said: "O Mary! From where (comes) this to you?" She said: "From Allah: for Allah provides sustenance to whom He pleases, without measure."

ٱلْمِحْرَابَ وَجَدَ عِندَهَا رِزْقًا ۖ قَالَ يَٰمَرْيَمُ أَنَّىٰ لَكِ
هَٰذَا ۖ قَالَتْ هُوَ مِنْ عِندِ ٱللَّهِ ۖ إِنَّ ٱللَّهَ يَرْزُقُ مَن يَشَآءُ
بِغَيْرِ حِسَابٍ ﴿٣٧﴾

38. There did Zakariya pray to his Lord, saying: "O my Lord! Grant to me from You a progeny that is pure: for You are He that hears prayer!"

هُنَالِكَ دَعَا زَكَرِيَّا رَبَّهُۥ ۖ قَالَ رَبِّ هَبْ لِى مِن
لَّدُنكَ ذُرِّيَّةً طَيِّبَةً ۖ إِنَّكَ سَمِيعُ ٱلدُّعَآءِ ﴿٣٨﴾

39. While he was standing in prayer in the chamber, the angels called to him: "Allah does give you glad tidings of Yahya, witnessing the truth of a Word from Allah, and (besides) noble, chaste, and a Prophet - of the (goodly) company of the righteous."

فَنَادَتْهُ ٱلْمَلَٰٓئِكَةُ وَهُوَ قَآئِمٌ يُصَلِّى فِى ٱلْمِحْرَابِ
أَنَّ ٱللَّهَ يُبَشِّرُكَ بِيَحْيَىٰ مُصَدِّقًۢا بِكَلِمَةٍ مِّنَ ٱللَّهِ
وَسَيِّدًا وَحَصُورًا وَنَبِيًّا مِّنَ ٱلصَّٰلِحِينَ ﴿٣٩﴾

40. He said: "O my Lord! How shall I have a son, seeing I am very old, and my wife is barren?" "Thus," was the answer, "does Allah accomplish what He wills."

قَالَ رَبِّ أَنَّىٰ يَكُونُ لِى غُلَٰمٌ وَقَدْ بَلَغَنِىَ ٱلْكِبَرُ
وَٱمْرَأَتِى عَاقِرٌ ۖ قَالَ كَذَٰلِكَ ٱللَّهُ يَفْعَلُ
مَا يَشَآءُ ﴿٤٠﴾

41. He said: "O my Lord! Give me a sign!" "Your sign," was the answer, "Shall be that you shall speak to no man for three days but with signals. Then celebrate the praises of your Lord again and again, and glorify Him in the evening and in the morning."

قَالَ رَبِّ ٱجْعَل لِّىٓ ءَايَةً ۖ قَالَ ءَايَتُكَ أَلَّا تُكَلِّمَ
ٱلنَّاسَ ثَلَٰثَةَ أَيَّامٍ إِلَّا رَمْزًا ۗ وَٱذْكُر رَّبَّكَ كَثِيرًا
وَسَبِّحْ بِٱلْعَشِىِّ وَٱلْإِبْكَٰرِ ﴿٤١﴾

42. See! The angels said: "O Mary! Allah has chosen you and purified you - chosen you above the women of all nations."

وَإِذْ قَالَتِ ٱلْمَلَٰٓئِكَةُ يَٰمَرْيَمُ إِنَّ ٱللَّهَ ٱصْطَفَىٰكِ
وَطَهَّرَكِ وَٱصْطَفَىٰكِ عَلَىٰ نِسَآءِ ٱلْعَٰلَمِينَ ﴿٤٢﴾

43. "O Mary! Worship your Lord devoutly: prostrate yourself, and bow down (in prayer) with those who bow down."

يَٰمَرْيَمُ ٱقْنُتِى لِرَبِّكِ وَٱسْجُدِى وَٱرْكَعِى مَعَ
ٱلرَّٰكِعِينَ ﴿٤٣﴾

44. This is part of the tidings of the things unseen, which We reveal to you (O prophet!) by inspiration: you were not with them when they cast lots with arrows, as to which of them should be charged with the care of Mary: nor were you with them when they disputed (the point).

ذَٰلِكَ مِنْ أَنۢبَآءِ ٱلْغَيْبِ نُوحِيهِ إِلَيْكَ ۚ وَمَا كُنتَ
لَدَيْهِمْ إِذْ يُلْقُونَ أَقْلَٰمَهُمْ أَيُّهُمْ يَكْفُلُ مَرْيَمَ
وَمَا كُنتَ لَدَيْهِمْ إِذْ يَخْتَصِمُونَ ﴿٤٤﴾

45. See! The angels said: "O Mary! Allah gives you glad tidings of a word from Him: his name will be Messiah Jesus, the son of Mary, held in honour in this world and the hereafter and of (the company of) those nearest to Allah;"

إِذْ قَالَتِ ٱلْمَلَٰٓئِكَةُ يَٰمَرْيَمُ إِنَّ ٱللَّهَ يُبَشِّرُكِ
بِكَلِمَةٍ مِّنْهُ ٱسْمُهُ ٱلْمَسِيحُ عِيسَى ٱبْنُ مَرْيَمَ
وَجِيهًا فِى ٱلدُّنْيَا وَٱلْـَٔاخِرَةِ وَمِنَ ٱلْمُقَرَّبِينَ ﴿٤٥﴾

46. "He shall speak to the people in childhood and in maturity. And he shall be (of the company) of the righteous."

وَيُكَلِّمُ ٱلنَّاسَ فِى ٱلْمَهْدِ وَكَهْلًا وَمِنَ
ٱلصَّٰلِحِينَ ﴿٤٦﴾

47. She said: "O my Lord! How shall I have a son when no man has touched me?" He said: "Even so: Allah creates what He wills: when He has decreed a plan, He but says to it, 'Be,' and it is!"

قَالَتْ رَبِّ أَنَّىٰ يَكُونُ لِى وَلَدٌ وَلَمْ يَمْسَسْنِى بَشَرٌ ۖ
قَالَ كَذَٰلِكِ ٱللَّهُ يَخْلُقُ مَا يَشَآءُ ۚ إِذَا قَضَىٰٓ أَمْرًا
فَإِنَّمَا يَقُولُ لَهُۥ كُن فَيَكُونُ ﴿٤٧﴾

48. "And Allah will teach him the book and wisdom, the Law and the Gospel,"

وَيُعَلِّمُهُ ٱلْكِتَٰبَ وَٱلْحِكْمَةَ وَٱلتَّوْرَىٰةَ
وَٱلْإِنجِيلَ ﴿٤٨﴾

49. "And (appoint him) a messenger to the Children of Israel, (with this message): "I have come to you, with a sign from your Lord, in that I make for you out of clay, as it were, the figure of a bird, and breathe into it, and it becomes a bird by Allah's permission: and I heal those born blind, and the lepers, and I revive the dead, by Allah's permission; and I declare to you what you eat, and what you store in your

وَرَسُولًا إِلَىٰ بَنِىٓ إِسْرَٰٓءِيلَ أَنِّى قَدْ جِئْتُكُم
بِـَٔايَةٍ مِّن رَّبِّكُمْ أَنِّىٓ أَخْلُقُ لَكُم مِّنَ ٱلطِّينِ
كَهَيْـَٔةِ ٱلطَّيْرِ فَأَنفُخُ فِيهِ فَيَكُونُ طَيْرًۢا بِإِذْنِ
ٱللَّهِ ۖ وَأُبْرِئُ ٱلْأَكْمَهَ وَٱلْأَبْرَصَ وَأُحْىِ ٱلْمَوْتَىٰ
بِإِذْنِ ٱللَّهِ ۖ وَأُنَبِّئُكُم بِمَا تَأْكُلُونَ وَمَا تَدَّخِرُونَ

houses. Surely in it is a sign for you if you did believe;"

فِى بُيُوتِكُمْۚ إِنَّ فِى ذَٰلِكَ لَءَايَةً لَّكُمْ إِن كُنتُم
مُّؤْمِنِينَ ﴿٤٩﴾

50. "(I have come to you), to attest the Law which was before me. And to make lawful to you part of what was (before) forbidden to you; I have come to you with a sign from your Lord. So fear Allah and obey me."

وَمُصَدِّقًا لِّمَا بَيْنَ يَدَىَّ مِنَ ٱلتَّوْرَىٰةِ وَلِأُحِلَّ
لَكُم بَعْضَ ٱلَّذِى حُرِّمَ عَلَيْكُمْۚ وَجِئْتُكُم
بِـَٔايَةٍ مِّن رَّبِّكُمْ فَٱتَّقُوا۟ ٱللَّهَ وَأَطِيعُونِ ﴿٥٠﴾

51. "It is Allah who is my Lord and your Lord; then worship Him. This is a way that is straight."

إِنَّ ٱللَّهَ رَبِّى وَرَبُّكُمْ فَٱعْبُدُوهُۗ هَٰذَا صِرَٰطٌ
مُّسْتَقِيمٌ ﴿٥١﴾

52. When Jesus found unbelief on their part he said: "Who will be my helpers to (the work of) Allah?" Said the disciples: "We are Allah's helpers: we believe in Allah, and do you bear witness that we are Muslims."

نصف الحزب ٦

۞ فَلَمَّآ أَحَسَّ عِيسَىٰ مِنْهُمُ ٱلْكُفْرَ قَالَ مَنْ
أَنصَارِىٓ إِلَى ٱللَّهِۖ قَالَ ٱلْحَوَارِيُّونَ نَحْنُ أَنصَارُ
ٱللَّهِ ءَامَنَّا بِٱللَّهِ وَٱشْهَدْ بِأَنَّا مُسْلِمُونَ ﴿٥٢﴾

53. "Our Lord! We believe in what you have revealed, and we follow the messenger; then write us down among those who bear witness."

رَبَّنَآ ءَامَنَّا بِمَآ أَنزَلْتَ وَٱتَّبَعْنَا ٱلرَّسُولَ
فَٱكْتُبْنَا مَعَ ٱلشَّٰهِدِينَ ﴿٥٣﴾

54. And (the unbelievers) plotted and planned, and Allah too planned, and the best of planners is Allah.

وَمَكَرُوا۟ وَمَكَرَ ٱللَّهُۖ وَٱللَّهُ خَيْرُ ٱلْمَٰكِرِينَ ﴿٥٤﴾

55. See! Allah said: "O Jesus! I will take you and raise you to Myself and clear you (of the falsehoods) of those who blaspheme; I will make those who follow you superior to those who reject faith, to the day of resurrection: then shall you all return to Me, and I will judge between you of the matters in which you dispute."

إِذْ قَالَ ٱللَّهُ يَٰعِيسَىٰٓ إِنِّى مُتَوَفِّيكَ وَرَافِعُكَ إِلَىَّ
وَمُطَهِّرُكَ مِنَ ٱلَّذِينَ كَفَرُوا۟ وَجَاعِلُ ٱلَّذِينَ
ٱتَّبَعُوكَ فَوْقَ ٱلَّذِينَ كَفَرُوٓا۟ إِلَىٰ يَوْمِ ٱلْقِيَٰمَةِۖ
ثُمَّ إِلَىَّ مَرْجِعُكُمْ فَأَحْكُمُ بَيْنَكُمْ فِيمَا
كُنتُمْ فِيهِ تَخْتَلِفُونَ ﴿٥٥﴾

56. "As to those who reject faith, I will punish them with terrible agony in this world and in the hereafter, nor will they have anyone to help."

فَأَمَّا ٱلَّذِينَ كَفَرُواْ فَأُعَذِّبُهُمۡ عَذَابٗا شَدِيدٗا فِي
ٱلدُّنۡيَا وَٱلۡأٓخِرَةِ وَمَا لَهُم مِّن نَّٰصِرِينَ ٥٦

57. "As to those who believe and work righteousness, Allah will pay them (in full) their reward: but Allah loves not those who do wrong."

وَأَمَّا ٱلَّذِينَ ءَامَنُواْ وَعَمِلُواْ ٱلصَّٰلِحَٰتِ
فَيُوَفِّيهِمۡ أُجُورَهُمۡۗ وَٱللَّهُ لَا يُحِبُّ ٱلظَّٰلِمِينَ ٥٧

58. "This is what We rehearse to you of the signs and the message of wisdom."

ذَٰلِكَ نَتۡلُوهُ عَلَيۡكَ مِنَ ٱلۡأٓيَٰتِ وَٱلذِّكۡرِ
ٱلۡحَكِيمِ ٥٨

59. The similitude of Jesus before Allah is as that of Adam; He created him from dust, then said to him: "Be": and he was.

إِنَّ مَثَلَ عِيسَىٰ عِندَ ٱللَّهِ كَمَثَلِ ءَادَمَۖ
خَلَقَهُۥ مِن تُرَابٖ ثُمَّ قَالَ لَهُۥ كُن فَيَكُونُ ٥٩

60. The truth (comes) from Allah alone; so be not of those who doubt.

ٱلۡحَقُّ مِن رَّبِّكَ فَلَا تَكُن مِّنَ ٱلۡمُمۡتَرِينَ ٦٠

61. If anyone disputes in this matter with you, now after (full) knowledge has come to you, say: "Come! Let us gather together - our sons and your sons, our women and your women, ourselves and yourselves: then let us earnestly pray, and invoke the curse of Allah on those who lie!"

فَمَنۡ حَآجَّكَ فِيهِ مِنۢ بَعۡدِ مَا جَآءَكَ مِنَ ٱلۡعِلۡمِ فَقُلۡ
تَعَالَوۡاْ نَدۡعُ أَبۡنَآءَنَا وَأَبۡنَآءَكُمۡ وَنِسَآءَنَا
وَنِسَآءَكُمۡ وَأَنفُسَنَا وَأَنفُسَكُمۡ ثُمَّ نَبۡتَهِلۡ
فَنَجۡعَل لَّعۡنَتَ ٱللَّهِ عَلَى ٱلۡكَٰذِبِينَ ٦١

62. This is the true account: there is no god except Allah; and Allah - He is indeed the Exalted in Power, the Wise.

إِنَّ هَٰذَا لَهُوَ ٱلۡقَصَصُ ٱلۡحَقُّۚ وَمَا مِنۡ إِلَٰهٍ إِلَّا ٱللَّهُۚ
وَإِنَّ ٱللَّهَ لَهُوَ ٱلۡعَزِيزُ ٱلۡحَكِيمُ ٦٢

63. But if they turn back, Allah has full knowledge of those who do mischief.

فَإِن تَوَلَّوۡاْ فَإِنَّ ٱللَّهَ عَلِيمُۢ بِٱلۡمُفۡسِدِينَ ٦٣

64. Say: "O People of the Book! Come to common terms as between us and you: that we worship none but Allah; that we associate

قُلۡ يَٰٓأَهۡلَ ٱلۡكِتَٰبِ تَعَالَوۡاْ إِلَىٰ كَلِمَةٖ سَوَآءِۭ
بَيۡنَنَا وَبَيۡنَكُمۡ أَلَّا نَعۡبُدَ إِلَّا ٱللَّهَ وَلَا نُشۡرِكَ بِهِۦ

no partners with Him; that we erect not, from among ourselves, lords and patrons other than Allah." If then they turn back, say you: "Bear witness that we (at least) are Muslims (bowing to Allah's Will)."

شَيْـًٔا وَلَا يَتَّخِذَ بَعْضُنَا بَعْضًا أَرْبَابًا مِّن دُونِ ٱللَّهِ ۚ
فَإِن تَوَلَّوْا۟ فَقُولُوا۟ ٱشْهَدُوا۟ بِأَنَّا مُسْلِمُونَ ٦٤

65. You People of the Book! Why dispute you about Abraham, when the Law and the Gospel were not revealed till after him? Have you no understanding?

يَـٰٓأَهْلَ ٱلْكِتَـٰبِ لِمَ تُحَآجُّونَ فِىٓ إِبْرَٰهِيمَ وَمَآ
أُنزِلَتِ ٱلتَّوْرَىٰةُ وَٱلْإِنجِيلُ إِلَّا مِنۢ بَعْدِهِۦٓ ۚ أَفَلَا
تَعْقِلُونَ ٦٥

66. Ah! You are those who fell to disputing (even) in matters of which you had some knowledge! But why dispute you in matters of which you have no knowledge? It is Allah Who knows, and you who know not!

هَـٰٓأَنتُمْ هَـٰٓؤُلَآءِ حَـٰجَجْتُمْ فِيمَا لَكُم بِهِۦ
عِلْمٌ فَلِمَ تُحَآجُّونَ فِيمَا لَيْسَ لَكُم بِهِۦ عِلْمٌ ۚ
وَٱللَّهُ يَعْلَمُ وَأَنتُمْ لَا تَعْلَمُونَ ٦٦

67. Abraham was not a Jew nor yet a Christian; but he was true in faith, and bowed his will to Allah's, (which is Islam), and he joined not gods with Allah.

مَا كَانَ إِبْرَٰهِيمُ يَهُودِيًّا وَلَا نَصْرَانِيًّا وَلَـٰكِن
كَانَ حَنِيفًا مُّسْلِمًا وَمَا كَانَ مِنَ ٱلْمُشْرِكِينَ ٦٧

68. Without doubt, among men, the nearest relation to Abraham are those who follow him, as are also this prophet and those who believe; and Allah is the protector of those who have faith.

إِنَّ أَوْلَى ٱلنَّاسِ بِإِبْرَٰهِيمَ لَلَّذِينَ ٱتَّبَعُوهُ وَهَـٰذَا
ٱلنَّبِىُّ وَٱلَّذِينَ ءَامَنُوا۟ ۗ وَٱللَّهُ وَلِىُّ ٱلْمُؤْمِنِينَ ٦٨

69. It is the wish of a section of the People of the Book to lead you astray. But they shall lead astray (not you), but themselves, and they do not perceive!

وَدَّت طَّآئِفَةٌ مِّنْ أَهْلِ ٱلْكِتَـٰبِ لَوْ يُضِلُّونَكُمْ وَمَا
يُضِلُّونَ إِلَّآ أَنفُسَهُمْ وَمَا يَشْعُرُونَ ٦٩

70. You People of the Book! Why reject you the signs of Allah, of which you are (yourselves) witnesses?

يَـٰٓأَهْلَ ٱلْكِتَـٰبِ لِمَ تَكْفُرُونَ بِـَٔايَـٰتِ ٱللَّهِ
وَأَنتُمْ تَشْهَدُونَ ٧٠

71. You People of the Book! Why do you clothe truth with falsehood, and conceal the truth, while you have knowledge?

يَٰٓأَهۡلَ ٱلۡكِتَٰبِ لِمَ تَلۡبِسُونَ ٱلۡحَقَّ بِٱلۡبَٰطِلِ
وَتَكۡتُمُونَ ٱلۡحَقَّ وَأَنتُمۡ تَعۡلَمُونَ ٧١

72. A section of the People of the Book say: "Believe in the morning what is revealed to the believers, but reject it at the end of the day; perhaps they may (themselves) turn back;

وَقَالَت طَّآئِفَةٞ مِّنۡ أَهۡلِ ٱلۡكِتَٰبِ ءَامِنُواْ بِٱلَّذِيٓ
أُنزِلَ عَلَى ٱلَّذِينَ ءَامَنُواْ وَجۡهَ ٱلنَّهَارِ وَٱكۡفُرُوٓاْ
ءَاخِرَهُۥ لَعَلَّهُمۡ يَرۡجِعُونَ ٧٢

73. "And believe no one unless he follows your religion." Say: "True guidance is the guidance of Allah; (fear you) lest a revelation be sent to someone (else) like that which was sent to you. Or that those (receiving such revelation) should engage you in argument before your Lord?" Say: "All bounties are in the Hand of Allah: He grants them to whom He pleases: and Allah cares for all, and He knows all things."

وَلَا تُؤۡمِنُوٓاْ إِلَّا لِمَن تَبِعَ دِينَكُمۡ قُلۡ إِنَّ ٱلۡهُدَىٰ
هُدَى ٱللَّهِ أَن يُؤۡتَىٰٓ أَحَدٞ مِّثۡلَ مَآ أُوتِيتُمۡ أَوۡ يُحَآجُّوكُمۡ
عِندَ رَبِّكُمۡۗ قُلۡ إِنَّ ٱلۡفَضۡلَ بِيَدِ ٱللَّهِ يُؤۡتِيهِ مَن
يَشَآءُۗ وَٱللَّهُ وَٰسِعٌ عَلِيمٞ ٧٣

74. For His Mercy He specially chooses whom He pleases; for Allah is the Lord of bounties unbounded.

يَخۡتَصُّ بِرَحۡمَتِهِۦ مَن يَشَآءُۗ وَٱللَّهُ ذُو ٱلۡفَضۡلِ
ٱلۡعَظِيمِ ٧٤

75. Among the People of the Book are some who, if entrusted with a hoard of gold, will (readily) pay it back; others who, if entrusted with a single silver coin, will not repay it unless you constantly stood demanding, because they say, "There is no call on us (to keep faith) with these ignorant (pagans)." But they tell a lie against Allah and (well) they know it.

ثلاثة أرباع الحزب ٦ ۞ وَمِنۡ أَهۡلِ ٱلۡكِتَٰبِ مَنۡ إِن تَأۡمَنۡهُ بِقِنطَارٖ
يُؤَدِّهِۦٓ إِلَيۡكَ وَمِنۡهُم مَّنۡ إِن تَأۡمَنۡهُ بِدِينَارٖ لَّا
يُؤَدِّهِۦٓ إِلَيۡكَ إِلَّا مَا دُمۡتَ عَلَيۡهِ قَآئِمٗاۗ ذَٰلِكَ
بِأَنَّهُمۡ قَالُواْ لَيۡسَ عَلَيۡنَا فِي ٱلۡأُمِّيِّـۧنَ سَبِيلٞ
وَيَقُولُونَ عَلَى ٱللَّهِ ٱلۡكَذِبَ وَهُمۡ يَعۡلَمُونَ ٧٥

76. Nay - those that keep their promised faith and act aright - verily Allah loves those who act aright.

بَلَىٰۚ مَنۡ أَوۡفَىٰ بِعَهۡدِهِۦ وَٱتَّقَىٰ فَإِنَّ ٱللَّهَ يُحِبُّ
ٱلۡمُتَّقِينَ ٧٦

77. As for those who sell the faith they owe to Allah and their own promised word for a small price, they shall have no portion in the hereafter: nor will Allah (deign to) speak to them or look at them on the day of judgement, nor will He cleanse them (of sin): they shall have a grievous penalty.

إِنَّ ٱلَّذِينَ يَشۡتَرُونَ بِعَهۡدِ ٱللَّهِ وَأَيۡمَٰنِهِمۡ ثَمَنٗا
قَلِيلًا أُوْلَٰٓئِكَ لَا خَلَٰقَ لَهُمۡ فِي ٱلۡأٓخِرَةِ وَلَا
يُكَلِّمُهُمُ ٱللَّهُ وَلَا يَنظُرُ إِلَيۡهِمۡ يَوۡمَ ٱلۡقِيَٰمَةِ وَلَا
يُزَكِّيهِمۡ وَلَهُمۡ عَذَابٌ أَلِيمٞ ٧٧

78. There is among them a section who distort the book with their tongues: (as they read) you would think it is a part of the book, but it is no part of the book; and they say, "That is from Allah," but it is not from Allah: it is they who tell a lie against Allah, and (well) they know it!

وَإِنَّ مِنۡهُمۡ لَفَرِيقٗا يَلۡوُۥنَ أَلۡسِنَتَهُم بِٱلۡكِتَٰبِ
لِتَحۡسَبُوهُ مِنَ ٱلۡكِتَٰبِ وَمَا هُوَ مِنَ ٱلۡكِتَٰبِ
وَيَقُولُونَ هُوَ مِنۡ عِندِ ٱللَّهِ وَمَا هُوَ مِنۡ عِندِ ٱللَّهِ
وَيَقُولُونَ عَلَى ٱللَّهِ ٱلۡكَذِبَ وَهُمۡ يَعۡلَمُونَ ٧٨

79. It is not (possible) that a man, to whom is given the book and wisdom, and the prophetic office, should say to people: "Be you my worshippers rather than Allah's: on the contrary (he would say): "Be you worshippers of Him Who is truly the Cherisher of all: for you have taught the book and you have studied it earnestly."

مَا كَانَ لِبَشَرٍ أَن يُؤۡتِيَهُ ٱللَّهُ ٱلۡكِتَٰبَ وَٱلۡحُكۡمَ
وَٱلنُّبُوَّةَ ثُمَّ يَقُولَ لِلنَّاسِ كُونُواْ عِبَادٗا لِّي مِن
دُونِ ٱللَّهِ وَلَٰكِن كُونُواْ رَبَّٰنِيِّـۧنَ بِمَا كُنتُمۡ
تُعَلِّمُونَ ٱلۡكِتَٰبَ وَبِمَا كُنتُمۡ تَدۡرُسُونَ ٧٩

80. Nor would he instruct you to take angels and prophets for Lords and patrons. What! Would he invite you to unbelief after you have bowed your will (to Allah in Islam)?

وَلَا يَأۡمُرَكُمۡ أَن تَتَّخِذُواْ ٱلۡمَلَٰٓئِكَةَ وَٱلنَّبِيِّـۧنَ
أَرۡبَابًاۗ أَيَأۡمُرُكُم بِٱلۡكُفۡرِ بَعۡدَ إِذۡ أَنتُم مُّسۡلِمُونَ ٨٠

81. See! Allah took the covenant of the prophets, saying: "I give you a book and wisdom; then comes to you a messenger, confirming what is with you; do you believe in him and render him help?" Allah said: "Do you agree, and take this My covenant as binding on you?" They said: "We agree." He said: "Then bear

وَإِذۡ أَخَذَ ٱللَّهُ مِيثَٰقَ ٱلنَّبِيِّـۧنَ لَمَآ ءَاتَيۡتُكُم مِّن
كِتَٰبٖ وَحِكۡمَةٖ ثُمَّ جَآءَكُمۡ رَسُولٞ مُّصَدِّقٞ
لِّمَا مَعَكُمۡ لَتُؤۡمِنُنَّ بِهِۦ وَلَتَنصُرُنَّهُۥۚ قَالَ
ءَأَقۡرَرۡتُمۡ وَأَخَذۡتُمۡ عَلَىٰ ذَٰلِكُمۡ إِصۡرِيۖ قَالُوٓاْ

witness, and I am with you among the witnesses."

أَقۡرَرۡنَاۚ قَالَ فَٱشۡهَدُواْ وَأَنَا۠ مَعَكُم مِّنَ
ٱلشَّٰهِدِينَ ﴿٨١﴾

82. If any turn back after this, they are perverted transgressors.

فَمَن تَوَلَّىٰ بَعۡدَ ذَٰلِكَ فَأُوْلَٰٓئِكَ هُمُ
ٱلۡفَٰسِقُونَ ﴿٨٢﴾

83. Do they seek for other than the religion of Allah? - While all creatures in the heavens and on earth have, willing or unwilling, bowed to His Will (accepted Islam), and to Him shall they all be brought back.

أَفَغَيۡرَ دِينِ ٱللَّهِ يَبۡغُونَ وَلَهُۥٓ أَسۡلَمَ مَن فِي
ٱلسَّمَٰوَٰتِ وَٱلۡأَرۡضِ طَوۡعٗا وَكَرۡهٗا وَإِلَيۡهِ
يُرۡجَعُونَ ﴿٨٣﴾

84. Say: "We believe in Allah, and in what has been revealed to us and what was revealed to Abraham, Ishmael; Isaac, Jacob, and the tribes, and in (the Books) given to Moses, Jesus, and the prophets, from their Lord: we make no distinction between one and another among them, and to Allah do we bow our will (in Islam)."

قُلۡ ءَامَنَّا بِٱللَّهِ وَمَآ أُنزِلَ عَلَيۡنَا وَمَآ أُنزِلَ عَلَىٰٓ
إِبۡرَٰهِيمَ وَإِسۡمَٰعِيلَ وَإِسۡحَٰقَ وَيَعۡقُوبَ
وَٱلۡأَسۡبَاطِ وَمَآ أُوتِيَ مُوسَىٰ وَعِيسَىٰ وَٱلنَّبِيُّونَ
مِن رَّبِّهِمۡ لَا نُفَرِّقُ بَيۡنَ أَحَدٖ مِّنۡهُمۡ وَنَحۡنُ لَهُۥ
مُسۡلِمُونَ ﴿٨٤﴾

85. If anyone desires a religion other than Islam (submission to Allah), never will it be accepted of him; and in the hereafter he will be in the ranks of those who have lost (all spiritual good).

وَمَن يَبۡتَغِ غَيۡرَ ٱلۡإِسۡلَٰمِ دِينٗا فَلَن يُقۡبَلَ مِنۡهُ
وَهُوَ فِي ٱلۡأٓخِرَةِ مِنَ ٱلۡخَٰسِرِينَ ﴿٨٥﴾

86. How shall Allah guide those who reject faith after they accepted it and bore witness that the messenger was true and that clear signs had come to them? But Allah guides not a people unjust.

كَيۡفَ يَهۡدِي ٱللَّهُ قَوۡمٗا كَفَرُواْ بَعۡدَ
إِيمَٰنِهِمۡ وَشَهِدُوٓاْ أَنَّ ٱلرَّسُولَ حَقّٞ وَجَآءَهُمُ
ٱلۡبَيِّنَٰتُۚ وَٱللَّهُ لَا يَهۡدِي ٱلۡقَوۡمَ ٱلظَّٰلِمِينَ ﴿٨٦﴾

87. Of such the reward is that on them (rests) the curse of Allah, of His angels, and of all mankind -

أُوْلَٰٓئِكَ جَزَآؤُهُمۡ أَنَّ عَلَيۡهِمۡ لَعۡنَةَ ٱللَّهِ
وَٱلۡمَلَٰٓئِكَةِ وَٱلنَّاسِ أَجۡمَعِينَ ﴿٨٧﴾

88. In that will they dwell; nor will their penalty be lightened, nor respite be their (lot);

خَٰلِدِينَ فِيهَا لَا يُخَفَّفُ عَنۡهُمُ ٱلۡعَذَابُ وَلَا هُمۡ
يُنظَرُونَ ٨٨

89. Except for those that repent (even) after that, and make amends; for verily Allah is Oft-Forgiving, Most Merciful.

إِلَّا ٱلَّذِينَ تَابُواْ مِنۢ بَعۡدِ ذَٰلِكَ وَأَصۡلَحُواْ فَإِنَّ
ٱللَّهَ غَفُورٞ رَّحِيمٌ ٨٩

90. But those who reject faith after they accepted it, and then go on adding to their defiance of faith - never will their repentance be accepted; for they are those who have (of set purpose) gone astray.

إِنَّ ٱلَّذِينَ كَفَرُواْ بَعۡدَ إِيمَٰنِهِمۡ ثُمَّ ٱزۡدَادُواْ
كُفۡرٗا لَّن تُقۡبَلَ تَوۡبَتُهُمۡ وَأُوْلَٰٓئِكَ هُمُ
ٱلضَّآلُّونَ ٩٠

91. As to those who reject faith, and die rejecting - never would be accepted from any such as much gold as the earth contains, though they should offer it for ransom. For such is (in store) a penalty grievous, and they will find no helpers.

إِنَّ ٱلَّذِينَ كَفَرُواْ وَمَاتُواْ وَهُمۡ كُفَّارٞ فَلَن
يُقۡبَلَ مِنۡ أَحَدِهِم مِّلۡءُ ٱلۡأَرۡضِ ذَهَبٗا وَلَوِ
ٱفۡتَدَىٰ بِهِۦٓۗ أُوْلَٰٓئِكَ لَهُمۡ عَذَابٌ أَلِيمٞ وَمَا لَهُم مِّن
نَّٰصِرِينَ ٩١

92. By no means shall you attain righteousness unless you give (freely) of that which you love; and whatever you give, truly Allah knows it well.

لَن تَنَالُواْ ٱلۡبِرَّ حَتَّىٰ تُنفِقُواْ مِمَّا تُحِبُّونَۚ وَمَا تُنفِقُواْ
مِن شَيۡءٖ فَإِنَّ ٱللَّهَ بِهِۦ عَلِيمٞ ٩٢

❊ **93.** All food was lawful to the Children of Israel, except what Israel made unlawful for itself, before the Law (of Moses) was revealed. Say: "Bring you the Law and study it, if you be men of truth."

الجزء ٤ الحزب ٧

❊ كُلُّ ٱلطَّعَامِ كَانَ حِلّٗا لِّبَنِيٓ إِسۡرَٰٓءِيلَ
إِلَّا مَا حَرَّمَ إِسۡرَٰٓءِيلُ عَلَىٰ نَفۡسِهِۦ مِن قَبۡلِ أَن تُنَزَّلَ
ٱلتَّوۡرَىٰةُۚ قُلۡ فَأۡتُواْ بِٱلتَّوۡرَىٰةِ فَٱتۡلُوهَآ إِن كُنتُمۡ
صَٰدِقِينَ ٩٣

94. If any, after this, invent a lie and attribute it to Allah, they are indeed unjust wrongdoers.

فَمَنِ ٱفۡتَرَىٰ عَلَى ٱللَّهِ ٱلۡكَذِبَ مِنۢ بَعۡدِ ذَٰلِكَ
فَأُوْلَٰٓئِكَ هُمُ ٱلظَّٰلِمُونَ ٩٤

❊ Part-4

95. Say: "Allah speaks the truth: follow the religion of Abraham, the sane in faith; he was not of the pagans."

قُلْ صَدَقَ ٱللَّهُ ۗ فَٱتَّبِعُوا۟ مِلَّةَ إِبْرَٰهِيمَ حَنِيفًا ۖ وَمَا
كَانَ مِنَ ٱلْمُشْرِكِينَ ﴿٩٥﴾

96. The first House (of worship) appointed for men was that at Bakkah; full of blessing and of guidance for all kinds of beings:

إِنَّ أَوَّلَ بَيْتٍ وُضِعَ لِلنَّاسِ لَلَّذِى بِبَكَّةَ مُبَارَكًا
وَهُدًى لِّلْعَٰلَمِينَ ﴿٩٦﴾

97. In it are signs manifest; (for example) the Station of Abraham; whoever enters it attains security; pilgrimage to it is a duty men owe to Allah - those who can afford the journey; but if any deny faith, Allah stands not in need of any of His creatures.

فِيهِ ءَايَٰتٌۢ بَيِّنَٰتٌ مَّقَامُ إِبْرَٰهِيمَ ۖ وَمَن دَخَلَهُۥ
كَانَ ءَامِنًا ۗ وَلِلَّهِ عَلَى ٱلنَّاسِ حِجُّ ٱلْبَيْتِ مَنِ ٱسْتَطَاعَ
إِلَيْهِ سَبِيلًا ۚ وَمَن كَفَرَ فَإِنَّ ٱللَّهَ غَنِىٌّ عَنِ ٱلْعَٰلَمِينَ ﴿٩٧﴾

98. Say: "O People of the Book! Why reject you the signs of Allah, when Allah is Himself witness to all you do?"

قُلْ يَٰٓأَهْلَ ٱلْكِتَٰبِ لِمَ تَكْفُرُونَ بِـَٔايَٰتِ ٱللَّهِ وَٱللَّهُ
شَهِيدٌ عَلَىٰ مَا تَعْمَلُونَ ﴿٩٨﴾

99. Say: "O you People of the Book! Why obstruct you those who believe, from the path of Allah, seeking to make it crooked, while you were yourselves witnesses (to Allah's covenant)? But Allah is not unmindful of all that you do."

قُلْ يَٰٓأَهْلَ ٱلْكِتَٰبِ لِمَ تَصُدُّونَ عَن سَبِيلِ ٱللَّهِ
مَنْ ءَامَنَ تَبْغُونَهَا عِوَجًا وَأَنتُمْ شُهَدَآءُ ۗ وَمَا ٱللَّهُ
بِغَٰفِلٍ عَمَّا تَعْمَلُونَ ﴿٩٩﴾

100. O you who believe! If you listen to a faction among the People of the Book, they would (indeed) render you apostates after you have believed!

يَٰٓأَيُّهَا ٱلَّذِينَ ءَامَنُوٓا۟ إِن تُطِيعُوا۟ فَرِيقًا مِّنَ ٱلَّذِينَ
أُوتُوا۟ ٱلْكِتَٰبَ يَرُدُّوكُم بَعْدَ إِيمَٰنِكُمْ كَٰفِرِينَ ﴿١٠٠﴾

101. And how would you deny faith while to you are rehearsed the signs of Allah, and among you lives the messenger? Whoever holds firmly to Allah will be shown a way that is straight.

وَكَيْفَ تَكْفُرُونَ وَأَنتُمْ تُتْلَىٰ عَلَيْكُمْ ءَايَٰتُ ٱللَّهِ
وَفِيكُمْ رَسُولُهُۥ ۗ وَمَن يَعْتَصِم بِٱللَّهِ فَقَدْ هُدِىَ
إِلَىٰ صِرَٰطٍ مُّسْتَقِيمٍ ﴿١٠١﴾

102. O you who believe! Fear Allah as He should be feared, and die not except in a state of Islam.

يَٰٓأَيُّهَا ٱلَّذِينَ ءَامَنُوا۟ ٱتَّقُوا۟ ٱللَّهَ حَقَّ تُقَاتِهِۦ وَلَا
تَمُوتُنَّ إِلَّا وَأَنتُم مُّسْلِمُونَ ﴿١٠٢﴾

103. And hold fast, all together by the rope which Allah (stretches out for you), and be not divided among yourselves; and remember with gratitude Allah's favour on you; for you were enemies and He joined your hearts in love, so that by His grace, you became brothers; and you were on the brink of the pit of fire, and He saved you from it. Thus does Allah make His signs clear to you: that you may be guided.

وَٱعْتَصِمُوا۟ بِحَبْلِ ٱللَّهِ جَمِيعًا وَلَا تَفَرَّقُوا۟ ۚ وَٱذْكُرُوا۟
نِعْمَتَ ٱللَّهِ عَلَيْكُمْ إِذْ كُنتُمْ أَعْدَآءً فَأَلَّفَ
بَيْنَ قُلُوبِكُمْ فَأَصْبَحْتُم بِنِعْمَتِهِۦٓ إِخْوَٰنًا
وَكُنتُمْ عَلَىٰ شَفَا حُفْرَةٍ مِّنَ ٱلنَّارِ فَأَنقَذَكُم
مِّنْهَا ۗ كَذَٰلِكَ يُبَيِّنُ ٱللَّهُ لَكُمْ ءَايَٰتِهِۦ لَعَلَّكُمْ
تَهْتَدُونَ ﴿١٠٣﴾

104. Let there arise out of you a band of people inviting to all that is good, enjoining what is right, and forbidding what is wrong: they are the ones to attain felicity.

وَلْتَكُن مِّنكُمْ أُمَّةٌ يَدْعُونَ إِلَى ٱلْخَيْرِ وَيَأْمُرُونَ
بِٱلْمَعْرُوفِ وَيَنْهَوْنَ عَنِ ٱلْمُنكَرِ ۚ وَأُو۟لَٰٓئِكَ هُمُ
ٱلْمُفْلِحُونَ ﴿١٠٤﴾

105. Be not like those who are divided amongst themselves and fall into disputations after receiving clear signs: for them is a dreadful penalty -

وَلَا تَكُونُوا۟ كَٱلَّذِينَ تَفَرَّقُوا۟ وَٱخْتَلَفُوا۟ مِنۢ بَعْدِ
مَا جَآءَهُمُ ٱلْبَيِّنَٰتُ ۚ وَأُو۟لَٰٓئِكَ لَهُمْ عَذَابٌ عَظِيمٌ ﴿١٠٥﴾

106. On the day when some faces will be (lit up with) white, and some faces will be (in the gloom of) black: to those whose faces will be black, (will be said): "Did you reject faith after accepting it? Taste then the penalty for rejecting faith."

يَوْمَ تَبْيَضُّ وُجُوهٌ وَتَسْوَدُّ وُجُوهٌ ۚ فَأَمَّا ٱلَّذِينَ
ٱسْوَدَّتْ وُجُوهُهُمْ أَكَفَرْتُم بَعْدَ إِيمَٰنِكُمْ
فَذُوقُوا۟ ٱلْعَذَابَ بِمَا كُنتُمْ تَكْفُرُونَ ﴿١٠٦﴾

107. But those whose faces will be (lit with) white - they will be in (the Light of) Allah's Mercy; in it to dwell (forever).

وَأَمَّا ٱلَّذِينَ ٱبْيَضَّتْ وُجُوهُهُمْ فَفِى رَحْمَةِ ٱللَّهِ ۖ
هُمْ فِيهَا خَٰلِدُونَ ﴿١٠٧﴾

108. These are the signs of Allah: We rehearse them to you in truth; and Allah means no injustice to any of His creatures.

تِلْكَ ءَايَٰتُ ٱللَّهِ نَتْلُوهَا عَلَيْكَ بِٱلْحَقِّ ۗ وَمَا ٱللَّهُ
يُرِيدُ ظُلْمًا لِّلْعَٰلَمِينَ ﴿١٠٨﴾

109. To Allah belongs all that is in the heavens and on earth; to Him do all questions go back (for decision).

وَلِلَّهِ مَا فِي ٱلسَّمَٰوَٰتِ وَمَا فِي ٱلْأَرْضِ ۚ وَإِلَى ٱللَّهِ
تُرْجَعُ ٱلْأُمُورُ ﴿١٠٩﴾

110. You are the best of peoples, evolved for mankind, enjoining what is right, forbidding what is wrong, and believing in Allah. If only the People of the Book had faith, it were best for them: among them are some who have faith, but most of them are perverted transgressors.

كُنتُمْ خَيْرَ أُمَّةٍ أُخْرِجَتْ لِلنَّاسِ تَأْمُرُونَ
بِٱلْمَعْرُوفِ وَتَنْهَوْنَ عَنِ ٱلْمُنكَرِ وَ
تُؤْمِنُونَ بِٱللَّهِ ۗ وَلَوْ ءَامَنَ أَهْلُ ٱلْكِتَٰبِ لَكَانَ
خَيْرًا لَّهُم ۚ مِّنْهُمُ ٱلْمُؤْمِنُونَ وَأَكْثَرُهُمُ
ٱلْفَٰسِقُونَ ﴿١١٠﴾

111. They will do you no harm, barring a trifling annoyance; if they come out to fight you, they will show you their backs, and no help shall they get.

لَن يَضُرُّوكُمْ إِلَّآ أَذًى ۖ وَإِن يُقَٰتِلُوكُمْ
يُوَلُّوكُمُ ٱلْأَدْبَارَ ثُمَّ لَا يُنصَرُونَ ﴿١١١﴾

112. Shame is pitched over them (like a tent) wherever they are found, except when under a covenant (of protection) from Allah and from men; they draw on themselves wrath from Allah, and pitched over them is (the tent of) destitution. This because they rejected the signs of Allah, and slew the prophets in defiance of right; this because they rebelled and transgressed beyond bounds.

ضُرِبَتْ عَلَيْهِمُ ٱلذِّلَّةُ أَيْنَ مَا ثُقِفُوٓا۟ إِلَّا بِحَبْلٍ
مِّنَ ٱللَّهِ وَحَبْلٍ مِّنَ ٱلنَّاسِ وَبَآءُو بِغَضَبٍ مِّنَ
ٱللَّهِ وَضُرِبَتْ عَلَيْهِمُ ٱلْمَسْكَنَةُ ۚ ذَٰلِكَ بِأَنَّهُمْ
كَانُوا۟ يَكْفُرُونَ بِـَٔايَٰتِ ٱللَّهِ وَيَقْتُلُونَ
ٱلْأَنۢبِيَآءَ بِغَيْرِ حَقٍّ ۚ ذَٰلِكَ بِمَا عَصَوا۟ وَّكَانُوا۟
يَعْتَدُونَ ﴿١١٢﴾

113. Not all of them are alike: of the People of the Book are a portion that stand (for the right); they rehearse the signs of Allah all night long, and they prostrate themselves in adoration.

ربع الحزب ٧
۞ لَيْسُوا۟ سَوَآءً ۗ مِّنْ أَهْلِ ٱلْكِتَٰبِ أُمَّةٌ قَآئِمَةٌ
يَتْلُونَ ءَايَٰتِ ٱللَّهِ ءَانَآءَ ٱلَّيْلِ وَهُمْ
يَسْجُدُونَ ﴿١١٣﴾

114. They believe in Allah and the last day; they enjoin what is right, and forbid what is wrong; and they hasten (in

يُؤْمِنُونَ بِٱللَّهِ وَٱلْيَوْمِ ٱلْءَاخِرِ وَيَأْمُرُونَ
بِٱلْمَعْرُوفِ وَيَنْهَوْنَ عَنِ ٱلْمُنكَرِ وَيُسَٰرِعُونَ

emulation) in (all) good works: they are in the ranks of the righteous.

فِي ٱلۡخَيۡرَٰتِۖ وَأُوْلَٰٓئِكَ مِنَ ٱلصَّٰلِحِينَ ١١٤

115. Of the good that they do, nothing will be rejected of them; for Allah knows well those that do right.

وَمَا يَفۡعَلُواْ مِنۡ خَيۡرٖ فَلَن يُكۡفَرُوهُۗ وَٱللَّهُ عَلِيمُۢ
بِٱلۡمُتَّقِينَ ١١٥

116. Those who reject faith - neither their possessions nor their (numerous) progeny will benefit them anything against Allah: they will be companions of the fire - dwelling in it (forever).

إِنَّ ٱلَّذِينَ كَفَرُواْ لَن تُغۡنِيَ عَنۡهُمۡ أَمۡوَٰلُهُمۡ وَلَآ
أَوۡلَٰدُهُم مِّنَ ٱللَّهِ شَيۡـٔٗاۖ وَأُوْلَٰٓئِكَ أَصۡحَٰبُ ٱلنَّارِۖ
هُمۡ فِيهَا خَٰلِدُونَ ١١٦

117. What they spend in the life of this (material) world may be likened to a wind which brings a nipping frost: it strikes and destroys the harvest of men who have wronged their own souls; it is not Allah that has wronged them, but they wrong themselves.

مَثَلُ مَا يُنفِقُونَ فِي هَٰذِهِ ٱلۡحَيَوٰةِ ٱلدُّنۡيَا كَمَثَلِ
رِيحٖ فِيهَا صِرٌّ أَصَابَتۡ حَرۡثَ قَوۡمٖ ظَلَمُوٓاْ أَنفُسَهُمۡ
فَأَهۡلَكَتۡهُۚ وَمَا ظَلَمَهُمُ ٱللَّهُ وَلَٰكِنۡ أَنفُسَهُمۡ
يَظۡلِمُونَ ١١٧

118. O you who believe! Take not into your intimacy those outside your ranks: they will not fail to corrupt you. They only desire your ruin: rank hatred has already appeared from their mouths: what their hearts conceal is far worse. We have made plain to you the signs, if you have wisdom.

يَٰٓأَيُّهَا ٱلَّذِينَ ءَامَنُواْ لَا تَتَّخِذُواْ بِطَانَةٗ مِّن
دُونِكُمۡ لَا يَأۡلُونَكُمۡ خَبَالٗا وَدُّواْ مَا عَنِتُّمۡ قَدۡ
بَدَتِ ٱلۡبَغۡضَآءُ مِنۡ أَفۡوَٰهِهِمۡ وَمَا تُخۡفِي
صُدُورُهُمۡ أَكۡبَرُۚ قَدۡ بَيَّنَّا لَكُمُ ٱلۡأٓيَٰتِۖ إِن كُنتُمۡ
تَعۡقِلُونَ ١١٨

119. Ah! You are those who love them, but they love you not - though you believe in the whole of the book, when they meet you, they say, "We believe": but when they are alone, they bite off the very tips of their fingers at you in their rage. Say: "Perish in your rage; Allah knows well all the secrets of the heart."

هَٰٓأَنتُمۡ أُوْلَآءِ تُحِبُّونَهُمۡ وَلَا يُحِبُّونَكُمۡ وَتُؤۡمِنُونَ
بِٱلۡكِتَٰبِ كُلِّهِۦ وَإِذَا لَقُوكُمۡ قَالُوٓاْ ءَامَنَّا وَإِذَا
خَلَوۡاْ عَضُّواْ عَلَيۡكُمُ ٱلۡأَنَامِلَ مِنَ ٱلۡغَيۡظِۚ قُلۡ
مُوتُواْ بِغَيۡظِكُمۡۗ إِنَّ ٱللَّهَ عَلِيمُۢ بِذَاتِ ٱلصُّدُورِ ١١٩

120. If anything that is good befalls you, it grieves them; but if some misfortune overtakes you, they rejoice at it. But if you are constant and do right, not the least harm will their cunning do to you; for Allah encompasses round about all that they do.

إِن تَمۡسَسۡكُمۡ حَسَنَةٞ تَسُؤۡهُمۡ وَإِن تُصِبۡكُمۡ
سَيِّئَةٞ يَفۡرَحُواْ بِهَاۖ وَإِن تَصۡبِرُواْ وَتَتَّقُواْ لَا يَضُرُّكُمۡ
كَيۡدُهُمۡ شَيۡـًٔاۗ إِنَّ ٱللَّهَ بِمَا يَعۡمَلُونَ مُحِيطٞ ١٢٠

121. Remember that morning you did leave the household (early) to post the faithful at their stations for battle; and Allah hears and knows all things:

وَإِذۡ غَدَوۡتَ مِنۡ أَهۡلِكَ تُبَوِّئُ ٱلۡمُؤۡمِنِينَ مَقَٰعِدَ
لِلۡقِتَالِۗ وَٱللَّهُ سَمِيعٌ عَلِيمٌ ١٢١

122. Remember two of your parties meditated cowardice; but Allah was their protector, and in Allah should the faithful (ever) put their trust.

إِذۡ هَمَّت طَّآئِفَتَانِ مِنكُمۡ أَن تَفۡشَلَا وَٱللَّهُ
وَلِيُّهُمَاۗ وَعَلَى ٱللَّهِ فَلۡيَتَوَكَّلِ ٱلۡمُؤۡمِنُونَ ١٢٢

123. Allah had helped you at Badr, when you were a contemptible little force; then fear Allah; thus may you show your gratitude.

وَلَقَدۡ نَصَرَكُمُ ٱللَّهُ بِبَدۡرٖ وَأَنتُمۡ أَذِلَّةٞۖ فَٱتَّقُواْ ٱللَّهَ
لَعَلَّكُمۡ تَشۡكُرُونَ ١٢٣

124. Remember you said to the faithful: "Is it not enough for you that Allah should help you with three thousand angels (specially) sent down?

إِذۡ تَقُولُ لِلۡمُؤۡمِنِينَ أَلَن يَكۡفِيَكُمۡ أَن يُمِدَّكُمۡ
رَبُّكُم بِثَلَٰثَةِ ءَالَٰفٖ مِّنَ ٱلۡمَلَٰٓئِكَةِ مُنزَلِينَ ١٢٤

125. "Yea - if you remain firm, and act aright, even if the enemy should rush here on you in hot haste, your Lord would help you with five thousand angels making a terrific onslaught."

بَلَىٰٓۚ إِن تَصۡبِرُواْ وَتَتَّقُواْ وَيَأۡتُوكُم مِّن فَوۡرِهِمۡ
هَٰذَا يُمۡدِدۡكُمۡ رَبُّكُم بِخَمۡسَةِ ءَالَٰفٖ مِّنَ ٱلۡمَلَٰٓئِكَةِ
مُسَوِّمِينَ ١٢٥

126. Allah made it but a message of hope for you, and an assurance to your hearts: (in any case) there is no help except from Allah, the Exalted, the Wise.

وَمَا جَعَلَهُ ٱللَّهُ إِلَّا بُشۡرَىٰ لَكُمۡ وَلِتَطۡمَئِنَّ
قُلُوبُكُم بِهِۦۗ وَمَا ٱلنَّصۡرُ إِلَّا مِنۡ عِندِ ٱللَّهِ
ٱلۡعَزِيزِ ٱلۡحَكِيمِ ١٢٦

127. That He might cut off a fringe of the unbelievers or expose them to infamy, and

لِيَقۡطَعَ طَرَفٗا مِّنَ ٱلَّذِينَ كَفَرُوٓاْ أَوۡ يَكۡبِتَهُمۡ

فَيَنقَلِبُواْ خَآئِبِينَ ١٢٧

they should then be turned back, frustrated of their purpose.

لَيْسَ لَكَ مِنَ ٱلْأَمْرِ شَيْءٌ أَوْ يَتُوبَ عَلَيْهِمْ
أَوْ يُعَذِّبَهُمْ فَإِنَّهُمْ ظَٰلِمُونَ ١٢٨

128. Not for you (but for Allah), is the decision: whether He turn in mercy to them, or punish them; for they are indeed wrongdoers.

وَلِلَّهِ مَا فِي ٱلسَّمَٰوَٰتِ وَمَا فِي ٱلْأَرْضِ يَغْفِرُ لِمَن
يَشَآءُ وَيُعَذِّبُ مَن يَشَآءُ وَٱللَّهُ غَفُورٌ
رَّحِيمٌ ١٢٩

129. To Allah belongs all that is in the heavens and on earth. He forgives whom He pleases and punishes whom He pleases; but Allah is Oft-Forgiving, Most Merciful.

يَٰٓأَيُّهَا ٱلَّذِينَ ءَامَنُواْ لَا تَأْكُلُواْ ٱلرِّبَوٰٓاْ
أَضْعَٰفًا مُّضَٰعَفَةً وَٱتَّقُواْ ٱللَّهَ لَعَلَّكُمْ
تُفْلِحُونَ ١٣٠

130. O you who believe! Devour not usury, doubled and multiplied; but fear Allah; that you may (really) prosper.

وَٱتَّقُواْ ٱلنَّارَ ٱلَّتِيٓ أُعِدَّتْ لِلْكَٰفِرِينَ ١٣١

131. Fear the fire, which is prepared for those who reject faith;

وَأَطِيعُواْ ٱللَّهَ وَٱلرَّسُولَ لَعَلَّكُمْ تُرْحَمُونَ ١٣٢

132. And obey Allah and the messenger; that you may obtain mercy.

نصف الحزب ٧
* وَسَارِعُوٓاْ إِلَىٰ مَغْفِرَةٍ مِّن رَّبِّكُمْ وَجَنَّةٍ
عَرْضُهَا ٱلسَّمَٰوَٰتُ وَٱلْأَرْضُ أُعِدَّتْ لِلْمُتَّقِينَ ١٣٣

133. Be quick in the race for forgiveness from your Lord, and for a garden whose width is that (of the whole) of the heavens and of the earth, prepared for the righteous -

ٱلَّذِينَ يُنفِقُونَ فِي ٱلسَّرَّآءِ وَٱلضَّرَّآءِ
وَٱلْكَٰظِمِينَ ٱلْغَيْظَ وَٱلْعَافِينَ عَنِ ٱلنَّاسِ
وَٱللَّهُ يُحِبُّ ٱلْمُحْسِنِينَ ١٣٤

134. Those who spend (freely), whether in prosperity, or in adversity; who restrain anger, and pardon (all) men - for Allah loves those who do good -

وَٱلَّذِينَ إِذَا فَعَلُواْ فَٰحِشَةً أَوْ ظَلَمُوٓاْ أَنفُسَهُمْ
ذَكَرُواْ ٱللَّهَ فَٱسْتَغْفَرُواْ لِذُنُوبِهِمْ وَمَن

135. And those who, having done something to be ashamed of, or wronged their own souls, earnestly bring Allah to mind, and ask for forgiveness for their sins - and who can forgive sins except Allah? - And are never obstinate in persisting knowingly in (the wrong) they have done.

يَغْفِرُ ٱلذُّنُوبَ إِلَّا ٱللَّهُ وَلَمْ يُصِرُّوا۟ عَلَىٰ مَا
فَعَلُوا۟ وَهُمْ يَعْلَمُونَ ﴿١٣٥﴾

136. For such the reward is forgiveness from their Lord, and gardens with rivers flowing underneath - an eternal dwelling: how excellent a recompense for those who work (and strive)!

أُو۟لَـٰٓئِكَ جَزَآؤُهُم مَّغْفِرَةٌ مِّن رَّبِّهِمْ وَجَنَّـٰتٌ
تَجْرِى مِن تَحْتِهَا ٱلْأَنْهَـٰرُ خَـٰلِدِينَ فِيهَا ۚ وَنِعْمَ
أَجْرُ ٱلْعَـٰمِلِينَ ﴿١٣٦﴾

137. Many were the ways of life that have passed away before you: travel through the earth, and see what was the end of those who rejected truth.

قَدْ خَلَتْ مِن قَبْلِكُمْ سُنَنٌ فَسِيرُوا۟
فِى ٱلْأَرْضِ فَٱنظُرُوا۟ كَيْفَ كَانَ عَـٰقِبَةُ
ٱلْمُكَذِّبِينَ ﴿١٣٧﴾

138. Here is a plain statement to men, a guidance and instruction to those who fear Allah!

هَـٰذَا بَيَانٌ لِّلنَّاسِ وَهُدًى وَمَوْعِظَةٌ
لِّلْمُتَّقِينَ ﴿١٣٨﴾

139. So lose not heart, nor fall into despair: for you must gain mastery if you are true in faith.

وَلَا تَهِنُوا۟ وَلَا تَحْزَنُوا۟ وَأَنتُمُ ٱلْأَعْلَوْنَ إِن كُنتُم
مُّؤْمِنِينَ ﴿١٣٩﴾

140. If a wound has touched you, be sure a similar wound has touched the others. Such days (of varying fortunes) We give to men and men by turns: that Allah may know those that believe, and that He may take to Himself from your ranks martyr-witnesses (to truth). And Allah loves not those that do wrong.

إِن يَمْسَسْكُمْ قَرْحٌ فَقَدْ مَسَّ ٱلْقَوْمَ قَرْحٌ مِّثْلُهُۥ ۚ
وَتِلْكَ ٱلْأَيَّامُ نُدَاوِلُهَا بَيْنَ ٱلنَّاسِ وَلِيَعْلَمَ
ٱللَّهُ ٱلَّذِينَ ءَامَنُوا۟ وَيَتَّخِذَ مِنكُمْ شُهَدَآءَ ۗ
وَٱللَّهُ لَا يُحِبُّ ٱلظَّـٰلِمِينَ ﴿١٤٠﴾

141. Allah's object also is to purge those that are true in faith and to deprive of blessing those that resist faith.

وَلِيُمَحِّصَ ٱللَّهُ ٱلَّذِينَ ءَامَنُوا۟ وَيَمْحَقَ
ٱلْكَـٰفِرِينَ ﴿١٤١﴾

142. Did you think that you would enter heaven without Allah testing those of you

أَمْ حَسِبْتُمْ أَن تَدْخُلُوا۟ ٱلْجَنَّةَ وَلَمَّا يَعْلَمِ ٱللَّهُ

who fought hard (in His cause) and remained steadfast?

ٱلَّذِينَ جَٰهَدُواْ مِنكُمۡ وَيَعۡلَمَ ٱلصَّٰبِرِينَ ١٤٢

143. You did indeed wish for death before you met it: now you have seen it with your own eyes, (and you flinch!)

وَلَقَدۡ كُنتُمۡ تَمَنَّوۡنَ ٱلۡمَوۡتَ مِن قَبۡلِ أَن تَلۡقَوۡهُ
فَقَدۡ رَأَيۡتُمُوهُ وَأَنتُمۡ تَنظُرُونَ ١٤٣

144. Muhammad is no more than a messenger: many were the messengers that passed away before him. If he died or were slain, will you then turn back on your heels? If any did turn back on his heels, not the least harm will he do to Allah; but Allah (on the other hand) will swiftly reward those who (serve Him) with gratitude.

وَمَا مُحَمَّدٌ إِلَّا رَسُولٞ قَدۡ خَلَتۡ مِن قَبۡلِهِ ٱلرُّسُلُۚ
أَفَإِيْن مَّاتَ أَوۡ قُتِلَ ٱنقَلَبۡتُمۡ عَلَىٰٓ أَعۡقَٰبِكُمۡۚ وَمَن
يَنقَلِبۡ عَلَىٰ عَقِبَيۡهِ فَلَن يَضُرَّ ٱللَّهَ شَيۡـٔٗاۗ
وَسَيَجۡزِي ٱللَّهُ ٱلشَّٰكِرِينَ ١٤٤

145. Nor can a soul die except by Allah's permission, the term being fixed as by writing. If any do desire a reward in this life, We shall give it to him; and if any do desire a reward in the hereafter, We shall give it to him. And swiftly shall We reward those that (serve Us with) gratitude.

وَمَا كَانَ لِنَفۡسٍ أَن تَمُوتَ إِلَّا بِإِذۡنِ ٱللَّهِ
كِتَٰبٗا مُّؤَجَّلٗاۗ وَمَن يُرِدۡ ثَوَابَ ٱلدُّنۡيَا نُؤۡتِهِۦ
مِنۡهَا وَمَن يُرِدۡ ثَوَابَ ٱلۡأٓخِرَةِ نُؤۡتِهِۦ مِنۡهَاۚ
وَسَنَجۡزِي ٱلشَّٰكِرِينَ ١٤٥

146. How many of the prophets fought (in Allah's way), and with them (fought) large bands of godly men? But they never lost heart if they met with disaster in Allah's way, nor did they weaken (in will) nor give in. And Allah loves those who are firm and steadfast.

وَكَأَيِّن مِّن نَّبِيّٖ قَٰتَلَ مَعَهُۥ رِبِّيُّونَ كَثِيرٞ فَمَا
وَهَنُواْ لِمَآ أَصَابَهُمۡ فِي سَبِيلِ ٱللَّهِ وَمَا ضَعُفُواْ وَمَا
ٱسۡتَكَانُواْۗ وَٱللَّهُ يُحِبُّ ٱلصَّٰبِرِينَ ١٤٦

147. All that they said was: "Our Lord! Forgive us our sins and anything we may have done that transgressed our duty: establish our feet firmly, and help us against those that resist faith."

وَمَا كَانَ قَوۡلَهُمۡ إِلَّآ أَن قَالُواْ رَبَّنَا ٱغۡفِرۡ لَنَا ذُنُوبَنَا
وَإِسۡرَافَنَا فِيٓ أَمۡرِنَا وَثَبِّتۡ أَقۡدَامَنَا وَٱنصُرۡنَا عَلَى
ٱلۡقَوۡمِ ٱلۡكَٰفِرِينَ ١٤٧

148. And Allah gave them a reward in this world, and the excellent reward of the hereafter. For Allah loves those who do good.

فَـَٔاتَىٰهُمُ ٱللَّهُ ثَوَابَ ٱلدُّنْيَا وَحُسْنَ ثَوَابِ
ٱلْـَٔاخِرَةِ ۗ وَٱللَّهُ يُحِبُّ ٱلْمُحْسِنِينَ ﴿١٤٨﴾

149. O you who believe! If you obey the unbelievers, they will drive you back on your heels, and you will turn back (from faith) to your own loss.

يَـٰٓأَيُّهَا ٱلَّذِينَ ءَامَنُوٓا۟ إِن تُطِيعُوا۟ ٱلَّذِينَ
كَفَرُوا۟ يَرُدُّوكُمْ عَلَىٰٓ أَعْقَـٰبِكُمْ
فَتَنقَلِبُوا۟ خَـٰسِرِينَ ﴿١٤٩﴾

150. Nay, Allah is your protector, and He is the best of helpers.

بَلِ ٱللَّهُ مَوْلَىٰكُمْ ۖ وَهُوَ خَيْرُ ٱلنَّـٰصِرِينَ ﴿١٥٠﴾

151. Soon shall We cast terror into the hearts of the unbelievers, for that they joined companions with Allah, for which He had sent no authority; their abode will be the fire; and evil is the home of the wrongdoers!

سَنُلْقِى فِى قُلُوبِ ٱلَّذِينَ كَفَرُوا۟ ٱلرُّعْبَ بِمَآ
أَشْرَكُوا۟ بِٱللَّهِ مَا لَمْ يُنَزِّلْ بِهِۦ سُلْطَـٰنًا ۖ
وَمَأْوَىٰهُمُ ٱلنَّارُ ۚ وَبِئْسَ مَثْوَى
ٱلظَّـٰلِمِينَ ﴿١٥١﴾

152. Allah did indeed fulfil His promise to you when you, with His permission, were about to annihilate your enemy- until you flinched and fell to disputing about the order, and disobeyed it after He brought you in sight (of the booty) which you covet. Among you are some that hanker after this world and some that desire the hereafter. Then did He divert you from your foes in order to test you. But He forgave you: for Allah is full of grace to those who believe.

وَلَقَدْ صَدَقَكُمُ ٱللَّهُ وَعْدَهُۥٓ إِذْ
تَحُسُّونَهُم بِإِذْنِهِۦ ۖ حَتَّىٰٓ إِذَا فَشِلْتُمْ
وَتَنَـٰزَعْتُمْ فِى ٱلْأَمْرِ وَعَصَيْتُم مِّنۢ بَعْدِ مَآ
أَرَىٰكُم مَّا تُحِبُّونَ ۚ مِنكُم مَّن يُرِيدُ
ٱلدُّنْيَا وَمِنكُم مَّن يُرِيدُ ٱلْـَٔاخِرَةَ ۚ ثُمَّ
صَرَفَكُمْ عَنْهُمْ لِيَبْتَلِيَكُمْ ۖ وَلَقَدْ عَفَا
عَنكُمْ ۗ وَٱللَّهُ ذُو فَضْلٍ عَلَى ٱلْمُؤْمِنِينَ ﴿١٥٢﴾

153. See! You were climbing up the high ground, without even casting a side glance at anyone, and the messenger in your rear was calling you back. There did Allah give you one distress after another by way of

ثلاثة أرباع الحزب ٧

۞ إِذْ تُصْعِدُونَ وَلَا تَلْوُۥنَ عَلَىٰٓ
أَحَدٍ وَٱلرَّسُولُ يَدْعُوكُمْ فِىٓ أُخْرَىٰكُمْ
فَأَثَـٰبَكُمْ غَمًّۢا بِغَمٍّ لِّكَيْلَا تَحْزَنُوا۟

requital, to teach you not to grieve for (the booty) that had escaped you and for (the ill) that had befallen you. For Allah is well aware of all that you do.

عَلَىٰ مَا فَاتَكُمْ وَلَا مَآ أَصَٰبَكُمْ ۗ
وَٱللَّهُ خَبِيرٌۢ بِمَا تَعْمَلُونَ ﴿١٥٣﴾

154. After (the excitement) of the distress He sent down calm on a band of you overcome with slumber, while another band was stirred to anxiety by their own feelings, moved by wrong suspicions of Allah - suspicions due to ignorance. They said: "What affair is this of ours?" Say you: "Indeed, this affair is wholly Allah's." They hide in their minds what they dare not reveal to you. They say (to themselves): "If we had had anything to do with this affair, we should not have been in the slaughter here." Say: "Even if you had remained in your homes, those for whom death was decreed would certainly have gone out to the place of their death"; but (all this was) that Allah might test what is in your breasts and purge what is in your hearts. For Allah knows well the secrets of your hearts.

ثُمَّ أَنزَلَ عَلَيْكُم مِّنۢ بَعْدِ ٱلْغَمِّ أَمَنَةً نُّعَاسًا
يَغْشَىٰ طَآئِفَةً مِّنكُمْ ۖ وَطَآئِفَةٌ قَدْ أَهَمَّتْهُمْ
أَنفُسُهُمْ يَظُنُّونَ بِٱللَّهِ غَيْرَ ٱلْحَقِّ ظَنَّ ٱلْجَٰهِلِيَّةِ ۖ
يَقُولُونَ هَل لَّنَا مِنَ ٱلْأَمْرِ مِن شَىْءٍ ۗ قُلْ إِنَّ
ٱلْأَمْرَ كُلَّهُۥ لِلَّهِ ۗ يُخْفُونَ فِىٓ أَنفُسِهِم مَّا لَا يُبْدُونَ
لَكَ ۖ يَقُولُونَ لَوْ كَانَ لَنَا مِنَ ٱلْأَمْرِ شَىْءٌ مَّا قُتِلْنَا
هَٰهُنَا ۗ قُل لَّوْ كُنتُمْ فِى بُيُوتِكُمْ لَبَرَزَ ٱلَّذِينَ كُتِبَ
عَلَيْهِمُ ٱلْقَتْلُ إِلَىٰ مَضَاجِعِهِمْ ۖ وَلِيَبْتَلِىَ ٱللَّهُ مَا فِى
صُدُورِكُمْ وَلِيُمَحِّصَ مَا فِى قُلُوبِكُمْ ۗ وَٱللَّهُ
عَلِيمٌۢ بِذَاتِ ٱلصُّدُورِ ﴿١٥٤﴾

155. Those of you who turned back on the day the two hosts met - it was Satan who caused them to fail, because of some (evil) they had done. But Allah has blotted out (their fault): for Allah is Oft-Forgiving, Most Forbearing.

إِنَّ ٱلَّذِينَ تَوَلَّوْا۟ مِنكُمْ يَوْمَ ٱلْتَقَى ٱلْجَمْعَانِ
إِنَّمَا ٱسْتَزَلَّهُمُ ٱلشَّيْطَٰنُ بِبَعْضِ مَا كَسَبُوا۟ ۖ
وَلَقَدْ عَفَا ٱللَّهُ عَنْهُمْ ۗ إِنَّ ٱللَّهَ غَفُورٌ حَلِيمٌ ﴿١٥٥﴾

156. O you who believe! Be not like the unbelievers, who say of their brothers, when they are travelling through the earth or engaged in fighting: "If they had stayed with us, they would not have died or been slain." This that Allah may make it a cause

يَٰٓأَيُّهَا ٱلَّذِينَ ءَامَنُوا۟ لَا تَكُونُوا۟ كَٱلَّذِينَ كَفَرُوا۟ وَقَالُوا۟
لِإِخْوَٰنِهِمْ إِذَا ضَرَبُوا۟ فِى ٱلْأَرْضِ أَوْ كَانُوا۟ غُزًّى
لَّوْ كَانُوا۟ عِندَنَا مَا مَاتُوا۟ وَمَا قُتِلُوا۟ لِيَجْعَلَ ٱللَّهُ

of sighs and regrets in their hearts. It is Allah that gives life and death, and Allah sees well all that you do.

ذَٰلِكَ حَسْرَةً فِي قُلُوبِهِمْ ۗ وَاللَّهُ يُحْيِي وَيُمِيتُ ۗ
وَاللَّهُ بِمَا تَعْمَلُونَ بَصِيرٌ ﴿١٥٦﴾

157. And if you are slain, or die, in the way of Allah, forgiveness and mercy from Allah are far better than all they could amass.

وَلَئِن قُتِلْتُمْ فِي سَبِيلِ اللَّهِ أَوْ مُتُّمْ لَمَغْفِرَةٌ مِّنَ
اللَّهِ وَرَحْمَةٌ خَيْرٌ مِّمَّا يَجْمَعُونَ ﴿١٥٧﴾

158. And if you die, or are slain, it is to Allah that you are brought together.

وَلَئِن مُّتُّمْ أَوْ قُتِلْتُمْ لَإِلَى اللَّهِ تُحْشَرُونَ ﴿١٥٨﴾

159. It is part of the mercy of Allah that you do deal gently with them. Were you severe or harsh-hearted they would have broken away from you; so pass over (their faults) and ask for (Allah's) forgiveness for them; and consult them in affairs (of moment). Then when you have taken a decision, put your trust in Allah. For Allah loves those who put their trust (in Him).

فَبِمَا رَحْمَةٍ مِّنَ اللَّهِ لِنتَ لَهُمْ ۖ وَلَوْ كُنتَ فَظًّا غَلِيظَ
الْقَلْبِ لَانفَضُّوا مِنْ حَوْلِكَ ۖ فَاعْفُ عَنْهُمْ
وَاسْتَغْفِرْ لَهُمْ وَشَاوِرْهُمْ فِي الْأَمْرِ ۖ فَإِذَا عَزَمْتَ
فَتَوَكَّلْ عَلَى اللَّهِ ۚ إِنَّ اللَّهَ يُحِبُّ الْمُتَوَكِّلِينَ ﴿١٥٩﴾

160. If Allah helps you, none can overcome you: if He forsakes you, who is there, after that, that can help you? In Allah then, let believers put their trust.

إِن يَنصُرْكُمُ اللَّهُ فَلَا غَالِبَ لَكُمْ ۖ وَإِن يَخْذُلْكُمْ
فَمَن ذَا الَّذِي يَنصُرُكُم مِّن بَعْدِهِ ۗ وَعَلَى اللَّهِ
فَلْيَتَوَكَّلِ الْمُؤْمِنُونَ ﴿١٦٠﴾

161. No prophet could (ever) be false to his trust. If any person is so false, He shall, on the day of judgement, restore what he misappropriated; then shall every soul receive its due, whatever it earned - and none shall be dealt with unjustly.

وَمَا كَانَ لِنَبِيٍّ أَن يَغُلَّ ۚ وَمَن يَغْلُلْ يَأْتِ بِمَا غَلَّ
يَوْمَ الْقِيَامَةِ ۚ ثُمَّ تُوَفَّىٰ كُلُّ نَفْسٍ مَّا كَسَبَتْ
وَهُمْ لَا يُظْلَمُونَ ﴿١٦١﴾

162. Is the man who follows the good pleasure of Allah like the man who draws on himself the wrath of Allah, and whose abode is in hell? A woeful refuge!

أَفَمَنِ اتَّبَعَ رِضْوَانَ اللَّهِ كَمَن بَاءَ بِسَخَطٍ مِّنَ اللَّهِ
وَمَأْوَاهُ جَهَنَّمُ ۚ وَبِئْسَ الْمَصِيرُ ﴿١٦٢﴾

163. They are in varying grades in the sight of Allah; and Allah sees well all that they do.

هُمْ دَرَجَٰتٌ عِندَ ٱللَّهِ ۗ وَٱللَّهُ بَصِيرٌۢ بِمَا يَعْمَلُونَ ١٦٣

164. Allah did confer a great favour on the believers when He sent among them a messenger from among themselves, rehearsing to them the signs of Allah, sanctifying them, and instructing them in Scripture and wisdom, while before that they had been in manifest error.

لَقَدْ مَنَّ ٱللَّهُ عَلَى ٱلْمُؤْمِنِينَ إِذْ بَعَثَ فِيهِمْ رَسُولًا
مِّنْ أَنفُسِهِمْ يَتْلُوا۟ عَلَيْهِمْ ءَايَٰتِهِۦ وَيُزَكِّيهِمْ
وَيُعَلِّمُهُمُ ٱلْكِتَٰبَ وَٱلْحِكْمَةَ وَإِن كَانُوا۟
مِن قَبْلُ لَفِى ضَلَٰلٍ مُّبِينٍ ١٦٤

165. What! When a single disaster strikes you, although you struck (your enemies) with one twice as great, do you say? - "From where is this?" Say (to them): "It is from yourselves: for Allah has power over all things."

أَوَلَمَّآ أَصَٰبَتْكُم مُّصِيبَةٌ قَدْ أَصَبْتُم مِّثْلَيْهَا
قُلْتُمْ أَنَّىٰ هَٰذَا ۖ قُلْ هُوَ مِنْ عِندِ أَنفُسِكُمْ ۗ
إِنَّ ٱللَّهَ عَلَىٰ كُلِّ شَىْءٍ قَدِيرٌ ١٦٥

166. What you suffered on the day the two armies met, was with the permission of Allah, in order that He might test the believers.

وَمَآ أَصَٰبَكُمْ يَوْمَ ٱلْتَقَى ٱلْجَمْعَانِ فَبِإِذْنِ ٱللَّهِ
وَلِيَعْلَمَ ٱلْمُؤْمِنِينَ ١٦٦

167. And the hypocrites also. These were told: "Come, fight in the way of Allah, or (at least) drive (the foe from your city)." They say: "had we known there would be a fight, we should certainly have followed you. They were that day nearer to unbelief than to Faith, saying with their lips what was not in their hearts. But Allah has full knowledge of all they conceal.

وَلِيَعْلَمَ ٱلَّذِينَ نَافَقُوا۟ ۚ وَقِيلَ لَهُمْ تَعَالَوْا۟ قَٰتِلُوا۟ فِى
سَبِيلِ ٱللَّهِ أَوِ ٱدْفَعُوا۟ ۖ قَالُوا۟ لَوْ نَعْلَمُ قِتَالًا
لَّٱتَّبَعْنَٰكُمْ ۗ هُمْ لِلْكُفْرِ يَوْمَئِذٍ أَقْرَبُ مِنْهُمْ
لِلْإِيمَٰنِ ۚ يَقُولُونَ بِأَفْوَٰهِهِم مَّا لَيْسَ فِى قُلُوبِهِمْ ۗ
وَٱللَّهُ أَعْلَمُ بِمَا يَكْتُمُونَ ١٦٧

168. (They are) the ones that say, (of their brothers slain), while they themselves sit (at ease): "If only they had listened to us, they would not have been slain." Say: "Avert death from your own selves, if you speak the truth."

ٱلَّذِينَ قَالُوا۟ لِإِخْوَٰنِهِمْ وَقَعَدُوا۟ لَوْ أَطَاعُونَا مَا قُتِلُوا۟ ۗ
قُلْ فَٱدْرَءُوا۟ عَنْ أَنفُسِكُمُ ٱلْمَوْتَ إِن كُنتُمْ
صَٰدِقِينَ ١٦٨

169. Think not of those who are slain in Allah's way as dead. Nay, they live, finding their sustenance in the presence of their Lord.

وَلَا تَحۡسَبَنَّ ٱلَّذِينَ قُتِلُواْ فِي سَبِيلِ ٱللَّهِ أَمۡوَٰتَۢاۚ بَلۡ
أَحۡيَآءٌ عِندَ رَبِّهِمۡ يُرۡزَقُونَ ١٦٩

170. They rejoice in the bounty provided by Allah: and with regard to those left behind, who have not yet joined them (in their bliss), the (martyrs) glory in the fact that on them is no fear, nor have they (cause to) grieve.

فَرِحِينَ بِمَآ ءَاتَىٰهُمُ ٱللَّهُ مِن فَضۡلِهِۦ وَيَسۡتَبۡشِرُونَ
بِٱلَّذِينَ لَمۡ يَلۡحَقُواْ بِهِم مِّنۡ خَلۡفِهِمۡ أَلَّا خَوۡفٌ
عَلَيۡهِمۡ وَلَا هُمۡ يَحۡزَنُونَ ١٧٠

171. They glory in the grace and the bounty from Allah, and in the fact that Allah suffers not the reward of the faithful to be lost (in the least).

الحزب ٨ ۞ يَسۡتَبۡشِرُونَ بِنِعۡمَةٖ مِّنَ ٱللَّهِ وَفَضۡلٖ وَأَنَّ
ٱللَّهَ لَا يُضِيعُ أَجۡرَ ٱلۡمُؤۡمِنِينَ ١٧١

172. Of those who answered the call of Allah and the messenger, even after being wounded, those who do right and refrain from wrong have a great reward -

ٱلَّذِينَ ٱسۡتَجَابُواْ لِلَّهِ وَٱلرَّسُولِ مِنۢ بَعۡدِ مَآ أَصَابَهُمُ
ٱلۡقَرۡحُۚ لِلَّذِينَ أَحۡسَنُواْ مِنۡهُمۡ وَٱتَّقَوۡاْ أَجۡرٌ
عَظِيمٌ ١٧٢

173. Men said to them: "A great army is gathering against you, so fear them": but it (only) increased their faith. They said: "For us Allah suffices and He is the best disposer of affairs."

ٱلَّذِينَ قَالَ لَهُمُ ٱلنَّاسُ إِنَّ ٱلنَّاسَ قَدۡ جَمَعُواْ لَكُمۡ
فَٱخۡشَوۡهُمۡ فَزَادَهُمۡ إِيمَٰنٗا وَقَالُواْ حَسۡبُنَا ٱللَّهُ
وَنِعۡمَ ٱلۡوَكِيلُ ١٧٣

174. And they returned with grace and bounty from Allah: no harm ever touched them; for they followed the good pleasure of Allah: and Allah is the Lord of bounties unbounded.

فَٱنقَلَبُواْ بِنِعۡمَةٖ مِّنَ ٱللَّهِ وَفَضۡلٖ لَّمۡ يَمۡسَسۡهُمۡ
سُوٓءٞ وَٱتَّبَعُواْ رِضۡوَٰنَ ٱللَّهِۗ وَٱللَّهُ ذُو فَضۡلٍ عَظِيمٍ ١٧٤

175. It is only the evil one that suggests to you the fear of his supporters: be you not afraid of them, but fear Me, if you have faith.

إِنَّمَا ذَٰلِكُمُ ٱلشَّيۡطَٰنُ يُخَوِّفُ أَوۡلِيَآءَهُۥ فَلَا تَخَافُوهُمۡ
وَخَافُونِ إِن كُنتُم مُّؤۡمِنِينَ ١٧٥

176. Let not those grieve you who rush headlong into unbelief: not the least harm will they do to Allah: Allah's plan is that He will give them no portion in the hereafter, but a severe punishment.

وَلَا يَحْزُنكَ ٱلَّذِينَ يُسَٰرِعُونَ فِى ٱلْكُفْرِ ۚ إِنَّهُمْ لَن
يَضُرُّوا۟ ٱللَّهَ شَيْـًٔا ۗ يُرِيدُ ٱللَّهُ أَلَّا يَجْعَلَ لَهُمْ حَظًّا فِى
ٱلْءَاخِرَةِ ۖ وَلَهُمْ عَذَابٌ عَظِيمٌ ﴿١٧٦﴾

177. Those who purchase unbelief at the price of faith - not the least harm will they do to Allah, but they will have a grievous punishment.

إِنَّ ٱلَّذِينَ ٱشْتَرَوُا۟ ٱلْكُفْرَ بِٱلْإِيمَٰنِ لَن يَضُرُّوا۟ ٱللَّهَ
شَيْـًٔا ۖ وَلَهُمْ عَذَابٌ أَلِيمٌ ﴿١٧٧﴾

178. Let not the unbelievers think that Our respite to them is good for themselves: We grant them respite that they may grow in their iniquity: but they will have a shameful punishment.

وَلَا يَحْسَبَنَّ ٱلَّذِينَ كَفَرُوٓا۟ أَنَّمَا نُمْلِى لَهُمْ خَيْرٌ
لِّأَنفُسِهِمْ ۚ إِنَّمَا نُمْلِى لَهُمْ لِيَزْدَادُوٓا۟ إِثْمًا ۖ وَلَهُمْ
عَذَابٌ مُّهِينٌ ﴿١٧٨﴾

179. Allah will not leave the believers in the state in which you are now, until He separates what is evil from what is good. Nor will Allah disclose to you the secrets of the unseen. But He chooses of His messengers (for the purpose) whom He pleases. So believe in Allah and His messengers: and if you believe and do right, you have a reward without measure.

مَّا كَانَ ٱللَّهُ لِيَذَرَ ٱلْمُؤْمِنِينَ عَلَىٰ مَآ أَنتُمْ عَلَيْهِ حَتَّىٰ
يَمِيزَ ٱلْخَبِيثَ مِنَ ٱلطَّيِّبِ ۗ وَمَا كَانَ ٱللَّهُ لِيُطْلِعَكُمْ
عَلَى ٱلْغَيْبِ وَلَٰكِنَّ ٱللَّهَ يَجْتَبِى مِن رُّسُلِهِۦ مَن يَشَآءُ ۖ
فَـَٔامِنُوا۟ بِٱللَّهِ وَرُسُلِهِۦ ۚ وَإِن تُؤْمِنُوا۟ وَتَتَّقُوا۟ فَلَكُمْ
أَجْرٌ عَظِيمٌ ﴿١٧٩﴾

180. And let not those who covetously withhold of the gifts which Allah has given them of His grace, think that it is good for them: nay, it will be the worse for them: soon shall the things which they covetously withheld be tied to their necks like a twisted collar, on the day of judgement. To Allah belongs the heritage of the heavens and the earth; and Allah is well acquainted with all that you do.

وَلَا يَحْسَبَنَّ ٱلَّذِينَ يَبْخَلُونَ بِمَآ ءَاتَىٰهُمُ ٱللَّهُ مِن
فَضْلِهِۦ هُوَ خَيْرًا لَّهُم ۖ بَلْ هُوَ شَرٌّ لَّهُمْ ۖ سَيُطَوَّقُونَ
مَا بَخِلُوا۟ بِهِۦ يَوْمَ ٱلْقِيَٰمَةِ ۗ وَلِلَّهِ مِيرَٰثُ ٱلسَّمَٰوَٰتِ
وَٱلْأَرْضِ ۗ وَٱللَّهُ بِمَا تَعْمَلُونَ خَبِيرٌ ﴿١٨٠﴾

181. Allah has heard the taunt of those who say: "Truly Allah is needy and we are rich!" -

لَّقَدْ سَمِعَ ٱللَّهُ قَوْلَ ٱلَّذِينَ قَالُوٓا۟ إِنَّ ٱللَّهَ فَقِيرٌ

وَنَحْنُ أَغْنِيَآءُ سَنَكْتُبُ مَا قَالُواْ وَقَتْلَهُمُ
ٱلْأَنۢبِيَآءَ بِغَيْرِ حَقٍّ وَنَقُولُ ذُوقُواْ عَذَابَ
ٱلْحَرِيقِ ١٨١

We shall certainly record their word and (their act) of slaying the prophets in defiance of right, and We shall say: "Taste you the penalty of the scorching fire!

ذَٰلِكَ بِمَا قَدَّمَتْ أَيْدِيكُمْ وَأَنَّ ٱللَّهَ لَيْسَ
بِظَلَّامٍ لِّلْعَبِيدِ ١٨٢

182. "This is because of the (unrighteous deeds) which your hands sent on before you: for Allah never harms those who serve Him."

ٱلَّذِينَ قَالُوٓاْ إِنَّ ٱللَّهَ عَهِدَ إِلَيْنَآ أَلَّا نُؤْمِنَ
لِرَسُولٍ حَتَّىٰ يَأْتِيَنَا بِقُرْبَانٍ تَأْكُلُهُ ٱلنَّارُ ۗ
قُلْ قَدْ جَآءَكُمْ رُسُلٌ مِّن قَبْلِى بِٱلْبَيِّنَٰتِ
وَبِٱلَّذِى قُلْتُمْ فَلِمَ قَتَلْتُمُوهُمْ إِن كُنتُمْ
صَٰدِقِينَ ١٨٣

183. They (also) said: "Allah took our promise not to believe in a messenger unless He showed us a sacrifice consumed by fire (from heaven)." Say: "There came to you messengers before me with clear signs and even with what you ask for: why then did you slay them, if you speak the truth?"

فَإِن كَذَّبُوكَ فَقَدْ كُذِّبَ رُسُلٌ مِّن قَبْلِكَ
جَآءُو بِٱلْبَيِّنَٰتِ وَٱلزُّبُرِ وَٱلْكِتَٰبِ ٱلْمُنِيرِ ١٨٤

184. Then if they reject you, so were rejected messengers before you, who came with clear signs, scriptures and the book of enlightenment.

كُلُّ نَفْسٍ ذَآئِقَةُ ٱلْمَوْتِ ۗ وَإِنَّمَا تُوَفَّوْنَ
أُجُورَكُمْ يَوْمَ ٱلْقِيَٰمَةِ ۖ فَمَن زُحْزِحَ عَنِ ٱلنَّارِ
وَأُدْخِلَ ٱلْجَنَّةَ فَقَدْ فَازَ ۗ وَمَا ٱلْحَيَوٰةُ
ٱلدُّنْيَآ إِلَّا مَتَٰعُ ٱلْغُرُورِ ١٨٥

185. Every soul shall have a taste of death: and only on the day of judgement shall you be paid your full recompense. Only he who is saved far from the fire and admitted to the garden will have attained the object (of life): for the life of this world is but goods and chattels of deception.

ربع الحزب ٨
۞ لَتُبْلَوُنَّ فِىٓ أَمْوَٰلِكُمْ وَأَنفُسِكُمْ
وَلَتَسْمَعُنَّ مِنَ ٱلَّذِينَ أُوتُواْ ٱلْكِتَٰبَ مِن

186. You shall certainly be tried and tested in your possessions and in your personal selves; and you shall certainly hear much that will grieve you from those who received the book before you and from those who worship many gods. But if you persevere patiently, and guard against evil - then that will be a determining factor in all affairs.

قَبْلِكُمْ وَمِنَ ٱلَّذِينَ أَشْرَكُوٓا۟ أَذًى كَثِيرًا ۚ وَإِن
تَصْبِرُوا۟ وَتَتَّقُوا۟ فَإِنَّ ذَٰلِكَ مِنْ عَزْمِ ٱلْأُمُورِ ﴿١٨٦﴾

187. And remember Allah took a covenant from the People of the Book to make it known and clear to mankind, and not to hide it; but they threw it away behind their backs, and purchased with it some miserable gain! And vile was the bargain they made!

وَإِذْ أَخَذَ ٱللَّهُ مِيثَٰقَ ٱلَّذِينَ أُوتُوا۟ ٱلْكِتَٰبَ لَتُبَيِّنُنَّهُۥ
لِلنَّاسِ وَلَا تَكْتُمُونَهُۥ فَنَبَذُوهُ وَرَآءَ ظُهُورِهِمْ
وَٱشْتَرَوْا۟ بِهِۦ ثَمَنًا قَلِيلًا ۖ فَبِئْسَ مَا يَشْتَرُونَ ﴿١٨٧﴾

188. Think not that those who exult in what they have brought about, and love to be praised for what they have not done - think not that they can escape the penalty. For them is a penalty grievous indeed.

لَا تَحْسَبَنَّ ٱلَّذِينَ يَفْرَحُونَ بِمَآ أَتَوا۟ وَّيُحِبُّونَ أَن
يُحْمَدُوا۟ بِمَا لَمْ يَفْعَلُوا۟ فَلَا تَحْسَبَنَّهُم
بِمَفَازَةٍ مِّنَ ٱلْعَذَابِ ۖ وَلَهُمْ عَذَابٌ أَلِيمٌ ﴿١٨٨﴾

189. To Allah belongs the dominion of the heavens and the earth; and Allah has power over all things.

وَلِلَّهِ مُلْكُ ٱلسَّمَٰوَٰتِ وَٱلْأَرْضِ ۗ وَٱللَّهُ عَلَىٰ
كُلِّ شَىْءٍ قَدِيرٌ ﴿١٨٩﴾

190. See! In the creation of the heavens and the earth and the alternation of night and day - there are indeed signs for men of understanding -

إِنَّ فِى خَلْقِ ٱلسَّمَٰوَٰتِ وَٱلْأَرْضِ وَٱخْتِلَٰفِ ٱلَّيْلِ
وَٱلنَّهَارِ لَءَايَٰتٍ لِّأُو۟لِى ٱلْأَلْبَٰبِ ﴿١٩٠﴾

191. Men who celebrate the praises of Allah, standing, sitting, and lying down on their sides, and contemplate the (wonders of) creation in the heavens and the earth, (with the thought): "Our Lord! Not for nothing have You created (all) this! Glory to You! Give us salvation from the penalty of the fire."

ٱلَّذِينَ يَذْكُرُونَ ٱللَّهَ قِيَٰمًا وَقُعُودًا وَعَلَىٰ
جُنُوبِهِمْ وَيَتَفَكَّرُونَ فِى خَلْقِ ٱلسَّمَٰوَٰتِ
وَٱلْأَرْضِ رَبَّنَا مَا خَلَقْتَ هَٰذَا بَٰطِلًا سُبْحَٰنَكَ
فَقِنَا عَذَابَ ٱلنَّارِ ﴿١٩١﴾

192. "Our Lord! Any whom You do admit to the fire, truly You cover with shame, and never will wrongdoers find any helpers!"

رَبَّنَآ إِنَّكَ مَن تُدْخِلِ ٱلنَّارَ فَقَدْ أَخْزَيْتَهُۥ ۖ وَمَا
لِلظَّٰلِمِينَ مِنْ أَنصَارٍ ﴿١٩٢﴾

193. "Our Lord! We have heard the call of one calling (us) to faith, 'Believe you in the Lord', and we have believed. Our Lord! Forgive us our sins, blot out from us our iniquities, and take to Yourself our souls in the company of the righteous."

رَّبَّنَآ إِنَّنَا سَمِعۡنَا مُنَادِيٗا يُنَادِي لِلۡإِيمَٰنِ أَنۡ
ءَامِنُواْ بِرَبِّكُمۡ فَـَٔامَنَّاۚ رَبَّنَا فَٱغۡفِرۡ لَنَا ذُنُوبَنَا
وَكَفِّرۡ عَنَّا سَيِّـَٔاتِنَا وَتَوَفَّنَا مَعَ ٱلۡأَبۡرَارِ ١٩٣

194. "Our Lord! Grant us what You did promise to us through Your messengers and save us from shame on the day of judgement: for You never break Your promise."

رَبَّنَا وَءَاتِنَا مَا وَعَدتَّنَا عَلَىٰ رُسُلِكَ وَلَا تُخۡزِنَا
يَوۡمَ ٱلۡقِيَٰمَةِۗ إِنَّكَ لَا تُخۡلِفُ ٱلۡمِيعَادَ ١٩٤

195. And their Lord has accepted of them, and answered them: "Never will I suffer to be lost the work of any of you, be he male or female: you are members, one of another; those who have left their homes or been driven out from it, and suffered harm in My cause or fought or been slain - verily I will blot out from them their iniquities, and admit them into gardens with rivers flowing beneath - a reward from the presence of Allah and from His presence is the best of rewards."

فَٱسۡتَجَابَ لَهُمۡ رَبُّهُمۡ أَنِّي لَآ أُضِيعُ عَمَلَ
عَٰمِلٖ مِّنكُم مِّن ذَكَرٍ أَوۡ أُنثَىٰۖ بَعۡضُكُم مِّنۢ بَعۡضٖۖ
فَٱلَّذِينَ هَاجَرُواْ وَأُخۡرِجُواْ مِن دِيَٰرِهِمۡ وَأُوذُواْ
فِي سَبِيلِي وَقَٰتَلُواْ وَقُتِلُواْ لَأُكَفِّرَنَّ عَنۡهُمۡ
سَيِّـَٔاتِهِمۡ وَلَأُدۡخِلَنَّهُمۡ جَنَّٰتٖ تَجۡرِي مِن
تَحۡتِهَا ٱلۡأَنۡهَٰرُ ثَوَابٗا مِّنۡ عِندِ ٱللَّهِۚ وَٱللَّهُ عِندَهُۥ
حُسۡنُ ٱلثَّوَابِ ١٩٥

196. Let not the strutting about of the unbelievers through the land deceive you:

لَا يَغُرَّنَّكَ تَقَلُّبُ ٱلَّذِينَ كَفَرُواْ فِي ٱلۡبِلَٰدِ ١٩٦

197. Little is it for enjoyment; their ultimate abode is hell: what an evil bed (to lie on)!

مَتَٰعٞ قَلِيلٞ ثُمَّ مَأۡوَىٰهُمۡ جَهَنَّمُۖ وَبِئۡسَ ٱلۡمِهَادُ ١٩٧

198. On the other hand, for those who fear their Lord, are gardens, with rivers flowing beneath, in it are they to dwell (for ever) - a gift from the presence of Allah and that which is in the presence of Allah is the best (bliss) for the righteous.

لَٰكِنِ ٱلَّذِينَ ٱتَّقَوۡاْ رَبَّهُمۡ لَهُمۡ جَنَّٰتٞ تَجۡرِي
مِن تَحۡتِهَا ٱلۡأَنۡهَٰرُ خَٰلِدِينَ فِيهَا نُزُلٗا مِّنۡ عِندِ
ٱللَّهِۗ وَمَا عِندَ ٱللَّهِ خَيۡرٞ لِّلۡأَبۡرَارِ ١٩٨

199. And there are, certainly, among the People of the Book, those who believe in Allah, in the revelation to you, and in the revelation to them, bowing in humility to Allah: they will not sell the signs of Allah for a miserable gain! For them is a reward with their Lord, and Allah is swift in account.

وَإِنَّ مِنْ أَهْلِ ٱلْكِتَـٰبِ لَمَن يُؤْمِنُ بِٱللَّهِ
وَمَآ أُنزِلَ إِلَيْكُمْ وَمَآ أُنزِلَ إِلَيْهِمْ خَـٰشِعِينَ
لِلَّهِ لَا يَشْتَرُونَ بِـَٔايَـٰتِ ٱللَّهِ ثَمَنًا قَلِيلًا ۗ
أُو۟لَـٰٓئِكَ لَهُمْ أَجْرُهُمْ عِندَ رَبِّهِمْ ۗ إِنَّ ٱللَّهَ
سَرِيعُ ٱلْحِسَابِ ﴿١٩٩﴾

200. O you who believe! Persevere in patience and constancy: vie in such perseverance; strengthen each other; and fear Allah; that you may prosper.

يَـٰٓأَيُّهَا ٱلَّذِينَ ءَامَنُوا۟ ٱصْبِرُوا۟ وَصَابِرُوا۟
وَرَابِطُوا۟ وَٱتَّقُوا۟ ٱللَّهَ لَعَلَّكُمْ تُفْلِحُونَ ﴿٢٠٠﴾

سُورَةُ النِّسَاءِ

Surah 4: *An-Nisa* (The Women)

In the name of Allah,
Most Gracious, Most Merciful.

بِسْمِ ٱللَّهِ ٱلرَّحْمَـٰنِ ٱلرَّحِيمِ

1. O mankind! Reverence your Guardian-Lord, Who created you from a single person, created of like nature, his mate and from them both scattered (like seeds) countless men and women- Fear Allah through Whom you demand your mutual (rights), and (respect) the wombs (that bore you): for Allah ever watches over you.

نصف الحزب ٨
يَـٰٓأَيُّهَا ٱلنَّاسُ ٱتَّقُوا۟ رَبَّكُمُ ٱلَّذِى خَلَقَكُم مِّن نَّفْسٍ وَٰحِدَةٍ
وَخَلَقَ مِنْهَا زَوْجَهَا وَبَثَّ مِنْهُمَا رِجَالًا كَثِيرًا وَنِسَآءً ۚ
وَٱتَّقُوا۟ ٱللَّهَ ٱلَّذِى تَسَآءَلُونَ بِهِۦ وَٱلْأَرْحَامَ ۚ إِنَّ ٱللَّهَ كَانَ
عَلَيْكُمْ رَقِيبًا ﴿١﴾

2. To orphans restore their property (when they reach their age), nor substitute (your) worthless things for (their) good ones; and devour not their substance (by mixing it up) with your own. For this is indeed a great sin.

وَءَاتُوا۟ ٱلْيَتَـٰمَىٰٓ أَمْوَٰلَهُمْ ۖ وَلَا تَتَبَدَّلُوا۟ ٱلْخَبِيثَ بِٱلطَّيِّبِ ۖ
وَلَا تَأْكُلُوٓا۟ أَمْوَٰلَهُمْ إِلَىٰٓ أَمْوَٰلِكُمْ ۚ إِنَّهُۥ كَانَ حُوبًا
كَبِيرًا ﴿٢﴾

3. If you fear that you shall not be able to deal justly with the orphans, marry women of your choice, two or three or four; but if you fear that you shall not be able to deal justly (with them) then only one, or (a captive) that your right hands possess. That will be more suitable, to prevent you from doing injustice.

وَإِنْ خِفْتُمْ أَلَّا تُقْسِطُوا۟ فِى ٱلْيَتَٰمَىٰ فَٱنكِحُوا۟ مَا طَابَ
لَكُم مِّنَ ٱلنِّسَآءِ مَثْنَىٰ وَثُلَٰثَ وَرُبَٰعَ ۖ فَإِنْ خِفْتُمْ أَلَّا
تَعْدِلُوا۟ فَوَٰحِدَةً أَوْ مَا مَلَكَتْ أَيْمَٰنُكُمْ ۚ ذَٰلِكَ أَدْنَىٰٓ أَلَّا
تَعُولُوا۟ ﴿٣﴾

4. And give the women (on marriage) their dower as a free gift; but if they, of their own good pleasure, remit any part of it to you, take it and enjoy it with right good cheer.

وَءَاتُوا۟ ٱلنِّسَآءَ صَدُقَٰتِهِنَّ نِحْلَةً ۚ فَإِن طِبْنَ لَكُمْ عَن
شَىْءٍ مِّنْهُ نَفْسًا فَكُلُوهُ هَنِيٓـًٔا مَّرِيٓـًٔا ﴿٤﴾

5. To those weak of understanding make not over your property, which Allah has made a means of support for you, but feed and clothe them with it, and speak to them words of kindness and justice.

وَلَا تُؤْتُوا۟ ٱلسُّفَهَآءَ أَمْوَٰلَكُمُ ٱلَّتِى جَعَلَ ٱللَّهُ لَكُمْ
قِيَٰمًا وَٱرْزُقُوهُمْ فِيهَا وَٱكْسُوهُمْ وَقُولُوا۟ لَهُمْ قَوْلًا
مَّعْرُوفًا ﴿٥﴾

6. Make trial of orphans until they reach the age of marriage; if then you find sound judgement in them release their property to them; but consume it not wastefully nor in haste against their growing up. If the guardian is well-off, let him claim no remuneration, but if he is poor, let him have for himself what is just and reasonable. When you release their property to them, take witnesses in their presence: but all-sufficient is Allah in taking account.

وَٱبْتَلُوا۟ ٱلْيَتَٰمَىٰ حَتَّىٰٓ إِذَا بَلَغُوا۟ ٱلنِّكَاحَ فَإِنْ ءَانَسْتُم
مِّنْهُمْ رُشْدًا فَٱدْفَعُوٓا۟ إِلَيْهِمْ أَمْوَٰلَهُمْ ۖ وَلَا تَأْكُلُوهَآ
إِسْرَافًا وَبِدَارًا أَن يَكْبَرُوا۟ ۚ وَمَن كَانَ غَنِيًّا فَلْيَسْتَعْفِفْ ۖ
وَمَن كَانَ فَقِيرًا فَلْيَأْكُلْ بِٱلْمَعْرُوفِ ۚ فَإِذَا دَفَعْتُمْ
إِلَيْهِمْ أَمْوَٰلَهُمْ فَأَشْهِدُوا۟ عَلَيْهِمْ ۚ وَكَفَىٰ بِٱللَّهِ
حَسِيبًا ﴿٦﴾

7. From what is left by parents and those nearest related there is a share for men and a share for women, whether the property be small or large - a determinate share.

لِّلرِّجَالِ نَصِيبٌ مِّمَّا تَرَكَ ٱلْوَٰلِدَانِ وَٱلْأَقْرَبُونَ
وَلِلنِّسَآءِ نَصِيبٌ مِّمَّا تَرَكَ ٱلْوَٰلِدَانِ وَٱلْأَقْرَبُونَ مِمَّا
قَلَّ مِنْهُ أَوْ كَثُرَ ۚ نَصِيبًا مَّفْرُوضًا ﴿٧﴾

8. But if at the time of division other relatives, or orphans, or poor are present,

وَإِذَا حَضَرَ ٱلْقِسْمَةَ أُو۟لُوا۟ ٱلْقُرْبَىٰ وَٱلْيَتَٰمَىٰ

feed them out of the (property) and speak to them words of kindness and justice.

وَٱلْمَسَـٰكِينُ فَٱرْزُقُوهُم مِّنْهُ وَقُولُوا۟ لَهُمْ
قَوْلًا مَّعْرُوفًا ﴿٨﴾

9. Let those (disposing of an estate) have the same fear in their minds as they would have for their own if they had left a helpless family behind: let them fear Allah and speak words of appropriate (comfort).

وَلْيَخْشَ ٱلَّذِينَ لَوْ تَرَكُوا۟ مِنْ خَلْفِهِمْ ذُرِّيَّةً
ضِعَـٰفًا خَافُوا۟ عَلَيْهِمْ فَلْيَتَّقُوا۟ ٱللَّهَ وَلْيَقُولُوا۟
قَوْلًا سَدِيدًا ﴿٩﴾

10. Those who unjustly eat up the property of orphans, eat up a fire into their own bodies: they will soon be enduring a blazing fire!

إِنَّ ٱلَّذِينَ يَأْكُلُونَ أَمْوَٰلَ ٱلْيَتَـٰمَىٰ ظُلْمًا
إِنَّمَا يَأْكُلُونَ فِى بُطُونِهِمْ نَارًا ۖ وَسَيَصْلَوْنَ
سَعِيرًا ﴿١٠﴾

11. Allah (thus) directs you as regards your children's (inheritance): to the male, a portion equal to that of two females: if only daughters, two or more, their share is two-thirds of the inheritance; if only one, her share is a half. For parents, a sixth share of the inheritance to each, if the deceased left children; if no children and the parents are the (only) heirs, the mother has a third; if the deceased left brothers (or sisters) the mother has a sixth. (The distribution in all cases is) after the payment of legacies and debts. You know not whether your parents or your children are nearest to you in benefit. These are settled portions ordained by Allah and Allah is All-Knowing, All-Wise.

يُوصِيكُمُ ٱللَّهُ فِىٓ أَوْلَـٰدِكُمْ ۖ لِلذَّكَرِ مِثْلُ حَظِّ
ٱلْأُنثَيَيْنِ ۚ فَإِن كُنَّ نِسَآءً فَوْقَ ٱثْنَتَيْنِ فَلَهُنَّ
ثُلُثَا مَا تَرَكَ ۖ وَإِن كَانَتْ وَٰحِدَةً فَلَهَا ٱلنِّصْفُ ۚ
وَلِأَبَوَيْهِ لِكُلِّ وَٰحِدٍ مِّنْهُمَا ٱلسُّدُسُ مِمَّا تَرَكَ
إِن كَانَ لَهُۥ وَلَدٌ ۚ فَإِن لَّمْ يَكُن لَّهُۥ وَلَدٌ وَوَرِثَهُۥٓ أَبَوَاهُ
فَلِأُمِّهِ ٱلثُّلُثُ ۚ فَإِن كَانَ لَهُۥٓ إِخْوَةٌ فَلِأُمِّهِ ٱلسُّدُسُ ۚ
مِنۢ بَعْدِ وَصِيَّةٍ يُوصِى بِهَآ أَوْ دَيْنٍ ۗ ءَابَآؤُكُمْ
وَأَبْنَآؤُكُمْ لَا تَدْرُونَ أَيُّهُمْ أَقْرَبُ لَكُمْ نَفْعًا ۚ
فَرِيضَةً مِّنَ ٱللَّهِ ۗ إِنَّ ٱللَّهَ كَانَ عَلِيمًا حَكِيمًا ﴿١١﴾

12. In what your wives leave, your share is a half, if they leave no child; but if they leave a child you get a fourth; after payment of legacies and debts. In what you leave their share is a fourth if you leave no child; but if you leave a child they get an eighth; after payment of legacies and debts. If the man or woman whose

ثلاثة أرباع الحزب ٨

۞ وَلَكُمْ نِصْفُ مَا تَرَكَ أَزْوَٰجُكُمْ إِن
لَّمْ يَكُن لَّهُنَّ وَلَدٌ ۚ فَإِن كَانَ لَهُنَّ وَلَدٌ
فَلَكُمُ ٱلرُّبُعُ مِمَّا تَرَكْنَ ۚ مِنۢ بَعْدِ وَصِيَّةٍ
يُوصِينَ بِهَآ أَوْ دَيْنٍ ۚ وَلَهُنَّ ٱلرُّبُعُ مِمَّا

inheritance is in question has left neither ascendants nor descendants, but has left a brother or a sister, each one of the two gets a sixth; but if more than two, they share in a third; after payment of legacies and debts; so that no loss is caused (to anyone). Thus is it ordained by Allah, and Allah is All-Knowing, Most Forbearing.

تَرَكْتُمْ إِن لَّمْ يَكُن لَّكُمْ وَلَدٌ فَإِن
كَانَ لَكُمْ وَلَدٌ فَلَهُنَّ ٱلثُّمُنُ مِمَّا
تَرَكْتُم مِّنۢ بَعْدِ وَصِيَّةٍ تُوصُونَ بِهَآ
أَوْ دَيْنٍ ۗ وَإِن كَانَ رَجُلٌ يُورَثُ كَلَٰلَةً
أَوِ ٱمْرَأَةٌ وَلَهُۥٓ أَخٌ أَوْ أُخْتٌ فَلِكُلِّ وَٰحِدٍ مِّنْهُمَا
ٱلسُّدُسُ ۚ فَإِن كَانُوٓا۟ أَكْثَرَ مِن ذَٰلِكَ فَهُمْ
شُرَكَآءُ فِى ٱلثُّلُثِ ۚ مِنۢ بَعْدِ وَصِيَّةٍ
يُوصَىٰ بِهَآ أَوْ دَيْنٍ غَيْرَ مُضَآرٍّ ۚ وَصِيَّةً
مِّنَ ٱللَّهِ ۗ وَٱللَّهُ عَلِيمٌ حَلِيمٌ ﴿١٢﴾

13. Those are limits set by Allah: those who obey Allah and His messenger will be admitted to gardens with rivers flowing beneath, to remain in it (forever) and that will be the supreme achievement.

تِلْكَ حُدُودُ ٱللَّهِ ۚ وَمَن يُطِعِ ٱللَّهَ وَرَسُولَهُۥ
يُدْخِلْهُ جَنَّٰتٍ تَجْرِى مِن تَحْتِهَا
ٱلْأَنْهَٰرُ خَٰلِدِينَ فِيهَا ۚ وَذَٰلِكَ ٱلْفَوْزُ
ٱلْعَظِيمُ ﴿١٣﴾

14. But those who disobey Allah and His messenger and transgress His limits will be admitted to a fire to remain in it: and they shall have a humiliating punishment.

وَمَن يَعْصِ ٱللَّهَ وَرَسُولَهُۥ وَيَتَعَدَّ
حُدُودَهُۥ يُدْخِلْهُ نَارًا خَٰلِدًا فِيهَا وَلَهُۥ
عَذَابٌ مُّهِينٌ ﴿١٤﴾

15. If any of your women are guilty of lewdness, take the evidence of four (reliable) witnesses from amongst you against them; and if they testify, confine them to houses until death do claim them, or Allah ordain for them some (other) way.

وَٱلَّٰتِى يَأْتِينَ ٱلْفَٰحِشَةَ مِن نِّسَآئِكُمْ
فَٱسْتَشْهِدُوا۟ عَلَيْهِنَّ أَرْبَعَةً مِّنكُمْ ۖ فَإِن شَهِدُوا۟
فَأَمْسِكُوهُنَّ فِى ٱلْبُيُوتِ حَتَّىٰ يَتَوَفَّىٰهُنَّ
ٱلْمَوْتُ أَوْ يَجْعَلَ ٱللَّهُ لَهُنَّ سَبِيلًا ﴿١٥﴾

16. If two men among you are guilty of lewdness, punish them both. If they repent and amend, leave them alone; for Allah is Oft-Returning, Most Merciful.

وَٱلَّذَانِ يَأۡتِيَٰنِهَا مِنكُمۡ فَـَٔاذُوهُمَاۖ فَإِن
تَابَا وَأَصۡلَحَا فَأَعۡرِضُواْ عَنۡهُمَآۗ إِنَّ ٱللَّهَ كَانَ
تَوَّابٗا رَّحِيمًا ١٦

17. Allah accepts the repentance of those who do evil in ignorance and repent soon afterwards; to them will Allah turn in mercy; for Allah is full of knowledge and wisdom.

إِنَّمَا ٱلتَّوۡبَةُ عَلَى ٱللَّهِ لِلَّذِينَ يَعۡمَلُونَ
ٱلسُّوٓءَ بِجَهَٰلَةٖ ثُمَّ يَتُوبُونَ مِن قَرِيبٖ فَأُوْلَٰٓئِكَ
يَتُوبُ ٱللَّهُ عَلَيۡهِمۡۗ وَكَانَ ٱللَّهُ عَلِيمًا حَكِيمٗا ١٧

18. Of no effect is the repentance of those who continue to do evil, until death faces one of them, and he says "Now have I repented indeed"; nor of those who die rejecting faith: for them have We prepared a punishment most grievous.

وَلَيۡسَتِ ٱلتَّوۡبَةُ لِلَّذِينَ يَعۡمَلُونَ ٱلسَّيِّـَٔاتِ
حَتَّىٰٓ إِذَا حَضَرَ أَحَدَهُمُ ٱلۡمَوۡتُ قَالَ إِنِّي تُبۡتُ
ٱلۡـَٰٔنَ وَلَا ٱلَّذِينَ يَمُوتُونَ وَهُمۡ كُفَّارٌۚ
أُوْلَٰٓئِكَ أَعۡتَدۡنَا لَهُمۡ عَذَابًا أَلِيمٗا ١٨

19. O you who believe! You are forbidden to inherit women against their will. Nor should you treat them with harshness, that you may take away part of the dower you have given them, except where they have been guilty of open lewdness; on the contrary live with them on a footing of kindness and equity. If you take a dislike to them it may be that you dislike a thing and Allah brings about through it a great deal of good.

يَٰٓأَيُّهَا ٱلَّذِينَ ءَامَنُواْ لَا يَحِلُّ لَكُمۡ أَن تَرِثُواْ
ٱلنِّسَآءَ كَرۡهٗاۖ وَلَا تَعۡضُلُوهُنَّ لِتَذۡهَبُواْ بِبَعۡضِ
مَآ ءَاتَيۡتُمُوهُنَّ إِلَّآ أَن يَأۡتِينَ بِفَٰحِشَةٖ مُّبَيِّنَةٖۚ
وَعَاشِرُوهُنَّ بِٱلۡمَعۡرُوفِۚ فَإِن كَرِهۡتُمُوهُنَّ
فَعَسَىٰٓ أَن تَكۡرَهُواْ شَيۡـٔٗا وَيَجۡعَلَ ٱللَّهُ فِيهِ
خَيۡرٗا كَثِيرٗا ١٩

20. But if you decide to take one wife in place of another, even if you had given the latter a whole treasure for dower, take not the least bit of it back: would you take it by slander and a manifest wrong?

وَإِنۡ أَرَدتُّمُ ٱسۡتِبۡدَالَ زَوۡجٖ مَّكَانَ زَوۡجٖ
وَءَاتَيۡتُمۡ إِحۡدَىٰهُنَّ قِنطَارٗا فَلَا تَأۡخُذُواْ مِنۡهُ
شَيۡـًٔاۚ أَتَأۡخُذُونَهُۥ بُهۡتَٰنٗا وَإِثۡمٗا مُّبِينٗا ٢٠

21. And how could you take it when you have gone in to each other, and they have taken from you a solemn covenant?

وَكَيْفَ تَأْخُذُونَهُۥ وَقَدْ أَفْضَىٰ بَعْضُكُمْ إِلَىٰ
بَعْضٍ وَأَخَذْنَ مِنكُم مِّيثَٰقًا غَلِيظًا ﴿٢١﴾

22. And marry not women whom your fathers married - except what is past - it was shameful and odious, an abominable custom indeed.

وَلَا تَنكِحُوا۟ مَا نَكَحَ ءَابَآؤُكُم مِّنَ
ٱلنِّسَآءِ إِلَّا مَا قَدْ سَلَفَ ۚ إِنَّهُۥ كَانَ فَٰحِشَةً
وَمَقْتًا وَسَآءَ سَبِيلًا ﴿٢٢﴾

23. Prohibited to you (for marriage) are: your mothers, daughters, sisters; father's sisters, mother's sisters; brother's daughters, sister's daughters; foster-mothers (who suckled you), foster-sisters; your wives' mothers; your step-daughters under your guardianship, born of your wives to whom you have gone in, no prohibition if you have not gone in; (those who have been) wives of your sons proceeding from your loins; and two sisters in wedlock at one and the same time, except for what is past; for Allah is Oft-Forgiving, Most Merciful.

حُرِّمَتْ عَلَيْكُمْ أُمَّهَٰتُكُمْ وَبَنَاتُكُمْ
وَأَخَوَٰتُكُمْ وَعَمَّٰتُكُمْ وَخَٰلَٰتُكُمْ
وَبَنَاتُ ٱلْأَخِ وَبَنَاتُ ٱلْأُخْتِ وَأُمَّهَٰتُكُمُ
ٱلَّٰتِىٓ أَرْضَعْنَكُمْ وَأَخَوَٰتُكُم مِّنَ ٱلرَّضَٰعَةِ
وَأُمَّهَٰتُ نِسَآئِكُمْ وَرَبَٰٓئِبُكُمُ ٱلَّٰتِى
فِى حُجُورِكُم مِّن نِّسَآئِكُمُ ٱلَّٰتِى دَخَلْتُم
بِهِنَّ فَإِن لَّمْ تَكُونُوا۟ دَخَلْتُم بِهِنَّ فَلَا
جُنَاحَ عَلَيْكُمْ وَحَلَٰٓئِلُ أَبْنَآئِكُمُ
ٱلَّذِينَ مِنْ أَصْلَٰبِكُمْ وَأَن تَجْمَعُوا۟ بَيْنَ
ٱلْأُخْتَيْنِ إِلَّا مَا قَدْ سَلَفَ ۗ إِنَّ ٱللَّهَ كَانَ
غَفُورًا رَّحِيمًا ﴿٢٣﴾

✼ **24.** Also (prohibited are) women already married, except those whom your right hands possess; thus has Allah ordained (prohibitions) against you: except for these, all others are lawful, provided you seek (them in marriage) with gifts from your property - desiring chastity, not lust. Seeing that you derive benefit from them, give them their dowers (at least) as prescribed; but if, after a dower is

الجزء ٥ الحزب ٩

✼ وَٱلْمُحْصَنَٰتُ مِنَ ٱلنِّسَآءِ إِلَّا مَا مَلَكَتْ
أَيْمَٰنُكُمْ ۖ كِتَٰبَ ٱللَّهِ عَلَيْكُمْ ۚ وَأُحِلَّ لَكُم مَّا وَرَآءَ
ذَٰلِكُمْ أَن تَبْتَغُوا۟ بِأَمْوَٰلِكُم مُّحْصِنِينَ غَيْرَ
مُسَٰفِحِينَ ۚ فَمَا ٱسْتَمْتَعْتُم بِهِۦ مِنْهُنَّ فَـَٔاتُوهُنَّ
أُجُورَهُنَّ فَرِيضَةً ۚ وَلَا جُنَاحَ عَلَيْكُمْ فِيمَا

✼ Part-5

تَرَٰضَيۡتُم بِهِۦ مِنۢ بَعۡدِ ٱلۡفَرِيضَةِۚ إِنَّ ٱللَّهَ
كَانَ عَلِيمًا حَكِيمٗا ٢٤

prescribed, you agree mutually (to vary it) there is no blame on you and Allah is All-Knowing, All-Wise.

وَمَن لَّمۡ يَسۡتَطِعۡ مِنكُمۡ طَوۡلًا أَن يَنكِحَ
ٱلۡمُحۡصَنَٰتِ ٱلۡمُؤۡمِنَٰتِ فَمِن مَّا مَلَكَتۡ
أَيۡمَٰنُكُم مِّن فَتَيَٰتِكُمُ ٱلۡمُؤۡمِنَٰتِۚ وَٱللَّهُ أَعۡلَمُ
بِإِيمَٰنِكُمۚ بَعۡضُكُم مِّنۢ بَعۡضٖۚ فَٱنكِحُوهُنَّ
بِإِذۡنِ أَهۡلِهِنَّ وَءَاتُوهُنَّ أُجُورَهُنَّ بِٱلۡمَعۡرُوفِ
مُحۡصَنَٰتٍ غَيۡرَ مُسَٰفِحَٰتٖ وَلَا مُتَّخِذَٰتِ
أَخۡدَانٖۚ فَإِذَآ أُحۡصِنَّ فَإِنۡ أَتَيۡنَ بِفَٰحِشَةٖ
فَعَلَيۡهِنَّ نِصۡفُ مَا عَلَى ٱلۡمُحۡصَنَٰتِ مِنَ
ٱلۡعَذَابِۚ ذَٰلِكَ لِمَنۡ خَشِيَ ٱلۡعَنَتَ مِنكُمۡۚ وَأَن
تَصۡبِرُواْ خَيۡرٞ لَّكُمۡۗ وَٱللَّهُ غَفُورٞ رَّحِيمٞ ٢٥

25. If any of you have not the means with which to wed free believing women, they may wed believing girls from among those whom your right hands possess: and Allah has full knowledge about your faith. You are one from another: wed them with the permission of their owners, and give them their dowers, according to what is reasonable: they should be chaste, not lustful, nor taking illicit lovers; when they are taken in wedlock, if they fall into shame, their punishment is half that for free women. This (permission) is for those among you who fear sin; but it is better for you that you practice self-restraint: and Allah is Oft-Forgiving, Most Merciful.

يُرِيدُ ٱللَّهُ لِيُبَيِّنَ لَكُمۡ وَيَهۡدِيَكُمۡ سُنَنَ
ٱلَّذِينَ مِن قَبۡلِكُمۡ وَيَتُوبَ عَلَيۡكُمۡۗ وَٱللَّهُ
عَلِيمٌ حَكِيمٞ ٢٦

26. Allah does wish to make clear to you and to show you the ordinances of those before you; and (He does wish to) turn to you (in mercy): and Allah is All-Knowing, All-Wise.

وَٱللَّهُ يُرِيدُ أَن يَتُوبَ عَلَيۡكُمۡ وَيُرِيدُ ٱلَّذِينَ
يَتَّبِعُونَ ٱلشَّهَوَٰتِ أَن تَمِيلُواْ مَيۡلًا عَظِيمٗا ٢٧

27. Allah does wish to turn to you, but the wish of those who follow their lusts is that you should turn away (from Him)- far, far away.

يُرِيدُ ٱللَّهُ أَن يُخَفِّفَ عَنكُمۡۚ وَخُلِقَ ٱلۡإِنسَٰنُ
ضَعِيفٗا ٢٨

28. Allah does wish to lighten your (difficulties): for man was created weak (in flesh).

يَٰٓأَيُّهَا ٱلَّذِينَ ءَامَنُواْ لَا تَأۡكُلُوٓاْ أَمۡوَٰلَكُم

29. O you who believe! Eat not up your property among yourselves in vanities; but let there be amongst you traffic and trade by mutual good will; nor kill (or destroy) yourselves; for verily Allah has been to you Most Merciful!

بَيْنَكُم بِٱلْبَٰطِلِ إِلَّآ أَن تَكُونَ تِجَٰرَةً عَن
تَرَاضٍ مِّنكُمْ ۚ وَلَا تَقْتُلُوٓا۟ أَنفُسَكُمْ ۚ إِنَّ
ٱللَّهَ كَانَ بِكُمْ رَحِيمًا ﴿٢٩﴾

30. If any do that in rancour and injustice - soon shall We cast them into the fire; and easy it is for Allah.

وَمَن يَفْعَلْ ذَٰلِكَ عُدْوَٰنًا وَظُلْمًا فَسَوْفَ نُصْلِيهِ
نَارًا ۚ وَكَانَ ذَٰلِكَ عَلَى ٱللَّهِ يَسِيرًا ﴿٣٠﴾

31. If you (but) eschew the most heinous of the things which you are forbidden to do, We shall expel out of you all the evil in you, and admit you to a gate of great honour.

إِن تَجْتَنِبُوا۟ كَبَآئِرَ مَا تُنْهَوْنَ عَنْهُ نُكَفِّرْ
عَنكُمْ سَيِّـَٔاتِكُمْ وَنُدْخِلْكُم مُّدْخَلًا
كَرِيمًا ﴿٣١﴾

32. And in no way covet those things in which Allah has bestowed His gifts more freely on some of you than on others; to men is allotted what they earn, and to women what they earn; but ask Allah of His bounty: for Allah has full knowledge of all things.

وَلَا تَتَمَنَّوْا۟ مَا فَضَّلَ ٱللَّهُ بِهِۦ بَعْضَكُمْ عَلَىٰ بَعْضٍ ۚ
لِّلرِّجَالِ نَصِيبٌ مِّمَّا ٱكْتَسَبُوا۟ ۖ وَلِلنِّسَآءِ
نَصِيبٌ مِّمَّا ٱكْتَسَبْنَ ۚ وَسْـَٔلُوا۟ ٱللَّهَ مِن فَضْلِهِۦٓ ۗ
إِنَّ ٱللَّهَ كَانَ بِكُلِّ شَىْءٍ عَلِيمًا ﴿٣٢﴾

33. To (benefit) every one, We have appointed sharers and heirs to property left by parents and relatives. To those, also, to whom your right hand was pledged, give their due portion: for truly Allah is witness to all things.

وَلِكُلٍّ جَعَلْنَا مَوَٰلِىَ مِمَّا تَرَكَ ٱلْوَٰلِدَانِ
وَٱلْأَقْرَبُونَ ۚ وَٱلَّذِينَ عَقَدَتْ أَيْمَٰنُكُمْ
فَـَٔاتُوهُمْ نَصِيبَهُمْ ۚ إِنَّ ٱللَّهَ كَانَ عَلَىٰ
كُلِّ شَىْءٍ شَهِيدًا ﴿٣٣﴾

34. Men are the protectors and maintainers of women, because Allah has given the one more (strength) than the other, and because they support them from their means. Therefore, the righteous women are devoutly obedient, and guard in (the husband's) absence what Allah would have them guard. As to those women on whose

ٱلرِّجَالُ قَوَّٰمُونَ عَلَى ٱلنِّسَآءِ بِمَا فَضَّلَ ٱللَّهُ
بَعْضَهُمْ عَلَىٰ بَعْضٍ وَبِمَآ أَنفَقُوا۟ مِنْ أَمْوَٰلِهِمْ ۚ
فَٱلصَّٰلِحَٰتُ قَٰنِتَٰتٌ حَٰفِظَٰتٌ لِّلْغَيْبِ بِمَا
حَفِظَ ٱللَّهُ ۚ وَٱلَّٰتِى تَخَافُونَ نُشُوزَهُنَّ

part you fear disloyalty and ill-conduct, admonish them (first), (next), refuse to share their beds, (and last) beat them (lightly); but if they return to obedience, seek not against them means (of annoyance): for Allah is Most High, Great (above you all).

فَعِظُوهُنَّ وَٱهْجُرُوهُنَّ فِى ٱلْمَضَاجِعِ
وَٱضْرِبُوهُنَّ ۖ فَإِنْ أَطَعْنَكُمْ فَلَا تَبْغُوا۟ عَلَيْهِنَّ
سَبِيلًا ۗ إِنَّ ٱللَّهَ كَانَ عَلِيًّا كَبِيرًا ﴿٣٤﴾

35. If you fear a breach between them both, appoint (two) arbiters, one from his family, and the other from hers; if they wish for peace, Allah will cause their reconciliation: for Allah has full knowledge, and is acquainted with all things.

وَإِنْ خِفْتُمْ شِقَاقَ بَيْنِهِمَا فَٱبْعَثُوا۟ حَكَمًا مِّنْ
أَهْلِهِۦ وَحَكَمًا مِّنْ أَهْلِهَآ إِن يُرِيدَآ
إِصْلَٰحًا يُوَفِّقِ ٱللَّهُ بَيْنَهُمَآ ۗ إِنَّ ٱللَّهَ كَانَ
عَلِيمًا خَبِيرًا ﴿٣٥﴾

36. Serve Allah, and join not any partners with Him; and do good - to parents, relatives, orphans, those in need, neighbours who are near, neighbours who are strangers, the companion by your side, the wayfarer (you meet), and what your right hands possess: for Allah loves not the arrogant, the vainglorious -

ربع الحزب ٩ ۞ وَٱعْبُدُوا۟ ٱللَّهَ وَلَا تُشْرِكُوا۟ بِهِۦ شَيْـًٔا ۖ
وَبِٱلْوَٰلِدَيْنِ إِحْسَٰنًا وَبِذِى ٱلْقُرْبَىٰ وَٱلْيَتَٰمَىٰ
وَٱلْمَسَٰكِينِ وَٱلْجَارِ ذِى ٱلْقُرْبَىٰ وَٱلْجَارِ
ٱلْجُنُبِ وَٱلصَّاحِبِ بِٱلْجَنۢبِ وَٱبْنِ ٱلسَّبِيلِ وَمَا
مَلَكَتْ أَيْمَٰنُكُمْ ۗ إِنَّ ٱللَّهَ لَا يُحِبُّ
مَن كَانَ مُخْتَالًا فَخُورًا ﴿٣٦﴾

37. (Nor) those who are niggardly, or enjoin niggardliness on others, or hide the bounties which Allah has bestowed on them; for We have prepared, for those who resist faith, a punishment that steeps them in contempt -

ٱلَّذِينَ يَبْخَلُونَ وَيَأْمُرُونَ ٱلنَّاسَ بِٱلْبُخْلِ
وَيَكْتُمُونَ مَآ ءَاتَىٰهُمُ ٱللَّهُ مِن فَضْلِهِۦ ۗ
وَأَعْتَدْنَا لِلْكَٰفِرِينَ عَذَابًا مُّهِينًا ﴿٣٧﴾

38. Nor those who spend of their substance, to be seen of men, but have no faith in Allah and the last day: if any take the evil one for their intimate, what a dreadful intimate he is!

وَٱلَّذِينَ يُنفِقُونَ أَمْوَٰلَهُمْ رِئَآءَ ٱلنَّاسِ وَلَا
يُؤْمِنُونَ بِٱللَّهِ وَلَا بِٱلْيَوْمِ ٱلْءَاخِرِ ۗ وَمَن يَكُنِ
ٱلشَّيْطَٰنُ لَهُۥ قَرِينًا فَسَآءَ قَرِينًا ﴿٣٨﴾

39. And what burden were it on them if they had faith in Allah and in the last day, and they spent out of what Allah has given them for sustenance? For Allah has full knowledge of them.

وَمَاذَا عَلَيْهِمْ لَوْ ءَامَنُوا۟ بِٱللَّهِ وَٱلْيَوْمِ ٱلْـَٔاخِرِ وَأَنفَقُوا۟
مِمَّا رَزَقَهُمُ ٱللَّهُ ۚ وَكَانَ ٱللَّهُ بِهِمْ عَلِيمًا ﴿٣٩﴾

40. Allah is never unjust in the least degree: if there is any good (done), He doubles it, and gives from His own presence a great reward.

إِنَّ ٱللَّهَ لَا يَظْلِمُ مِثْقَالَ ذَرَّةٍ ۖ وَإِن تَكُ حَسَنَةً
يُضَٰعِفْهَا وَيُؤْتِ مِن لَّدُنْهُ أَجْرًا عَظِيمًا ﴿٤٠﴾

41. How then if We brought from each people a witness, and We brought you as a witness against these people!

فَكَيْفَ إِذَا جِئْنَا مِن كُلِّ أُمَّةٍۭ بِشَهِيدٍ وَجِئْنَا
بِكَ عَلَىٰ هَٰٓؤُلَآءِ شَهِيدًا ﴿٤١﴾

42. On that day those who reject faith and disobey the messenger will wish that the earth were made one with them; but never will they hide a single fact from Allah!

يَوْمَئِذٍ يَوَدُّ ٱلَّذِينَ كَفَرُوا۟ وَعَصَوُا۟ ٱلرَّسُولَ
لَوْ تُسَوَّىٰ بِهِمُ ٱلْأَرْضُ وَلَا يَكْتُمُونَ ٱللَّهَ حَدِيثًا ﴿٤٢﴾

43. O you who believe! Approach not prayers with a mind befogged, until you can understand all that you say - nor in a state of ceremonial impurity (except when travelling on the road), until after washing your whole body. If you are ill, or on a journey, or one of you comes from offices of nature, or you have been in contact with women, and you find no water, then take for yourselves clean sand or earth, and rub with it your faces and hands. For Allah does blot out sins and forgive again and again.

يَٰٓأَيُّهَا ٱلَّذِينَ ءَامَنُوا۟ لَا تَقْرَبُوا۟ ٱلصَّلَوٰةَ وَأَنتُمْ
سُكَٰرَىٰ حَتَّىٰ تَعْلَمُوا۟ مَا تَقُولُونَ وَلَا جُنُبًا
إِلَّا عَابِرِى سَبِيلٍ حَتَّىٰ تَغْتَسِلُوا۟ ۚ وَإِن كُنتُم مَّرْضَىٰٓ
أَوْ عَلَىٰ سَفَرٍ أَوْ جَآءَ أَحَدٌ مِّنكُم مِّنَ ٱلْغَآئِطِ
أَوْ لَٰمَسْتُمُ ٱلنِّسَآءَ فَلَمْ تَجِدُوا۟ مَآءً فَتَيَمَّمُوا۟
صَعِيدًا طَيِّبًا فَٱمْسَحُوا۟ بِوُجُوهِكُمْ وَأَيْدِيكُمْ ۗ
إِنَّ ٱللَّهَ كَانَ عَفُوًّا غَفُورًا ﴿٤٣﴾

44. (O Muhammad!) Have you not turned your vision to those who were given a portion of the book? They traffic in error, and wish that you should lose the right path.

أَلَمْ تَرَ إِلَى ٱلَّذِينَ أُوتُوا۟ نَصِيبًا مِّنَ ٱلْكِتَٰبِ يَشْتَرُونَ
ٱلضَّلَٰلَةَ وَيُرِيدُونَ أَن تَضِلُّوا۟ ٱلسَّبِيلَ ﴿٤٤﴾

45. But Allah has full knowledge of your enemies: Allah is enough for a protector, and Allah is enough for a helper.

وَٱللَّهُ أَعۡلَمُ بِأَعۡدَآئِكُمۡۚ وَكَفَىٰ بِٱللَّهِ وَلِيّٗا وَكَفَىٰ بِٱللَّهِ
نَصِيرٗا ٤٥

46. Of the Jews there are those who displace words from their (right) places, and say: "We hear and we disobey"; and "Hear, may you not hear"; and *"Ra'ina,"* with a twist of their tongues and a slander to faith. If only they had said: "We hear and we obey"; and "Do hear"; and "Do look at us"; it would have been better for them, and more proper; but Allah has cursed them for their unbelief; and but few of them will believe.

مِّنَ ٱلَّذِينَ هَادُواْ يُحَرِّفُونَ ٱلۡكَلِمَ عَن مَّوَاضِعِهِۦ
وَيَقُولُونَ سَمِعۡنَا وَعَصَيۡنَا وَٱسۡمَعۡ غَيۡرَ مُسۡمَعٖ
وَرَٰعِنَا لَيَّۢا بِأَلۡسِنَتِهِمۡ وَطَعۡنٗا فِي ٱلدِّينِۚ وَلَوۡ أَنَّهُمۡ
قَالُواْ سَمِعۡنَا وَأَطَعۡنَا وَٱسۡمَعۡ وَٱنظُرۡنَا لَكَانَ خَيۡرٗا
لَّهُمۡ وَأَقۡوَمَ وَلَٰكِن لَّعَنَهُمُ ٱللَّهُ بِكُفۡرِهِمۡ فَلَا يُؤۡمِنُونَ
إِلَّا قَلِيلٗا ٤٦

47. O you People of the Book! Believe in what We have (now) revealed, confirming what was (already) with you, before We change the face and fame of some (of you) beyond all recognition, and turn them hindwards, or curse them as We cursed the Sabbath-breakers, for the decision of Allah must be carried out.

يَٰٓأَيُّهَا ٱلَّذِينَ أُوتُواْ ٱلۡكِتَٰبَ ءَامِنُواْ بِمَا نَزَّلۡنَا
مُصَدِّقٗا لِّمَا مَعَكُم مِّن قَبۡلِ أَن نَّطۡمِسَ وُجُوهٗا
فَنَرُدَّهَا عَلَىٰٓ أَدۡبَارِهَآ أَوۡ نَلۡعَنَهُمۡ كَمَا لَعَنَّآ
أَصۡحَٰبَ ٱلسَّبۡتِۚ وَكَانَ أَمۡرُ ٱللَّهِ مَفۡعُولًا ٤٧

48. Allah forgives not that partners should be set up with Him; but He forgives anything else, to whom He pleases; to set up partners with Allah is to devise a sin most heinous indeed.

إِنَّ ٱللَّهَ لَا يَغۡفِرُ أَن يُشۡرَكَ بِهِۦ وَيَغۡفِرُ مَا دُونَ ذَٰلِكَ
لِمَن يَشَآءُۚ وَمَن يُشۡرِكۡ بِٱللَّهِ فَقَدِ ٱفۡتَرَىٰٓ إِثۡمًا
عَظِيمًا ٤٨

49. Have you not turned your vision to those who claim sanctity for themselves? Nay - but Allah does sanctify whom He pleases. But never will they fail to receive justice in the least little thing.

أَلَمۡ تَرَ إِلَى ٱلَّذِينَ يُزَكُّونَ أَنفُسَهُمۚ بَلِ ٱللَّهُ يُزَكِّي مَن
يَشَآءُ وَلَا يُظۡلَمُونَ فَتِيلًا ٤٩

50. See! How they invent a lie against Allah! But that by itself is a manifest sin!

ٱنظُرۡ كَيۡفَ يَفۡتَرُونَ عَلَى ٱللَّهِ ٱلۡكَذِبَۖ وَكَفَىٰ بِهِۦٓ
إِثۡمٗا مُّبِينًا ٥٠

51. Have you not turned your vision to those who were given a portion of the book? They believe in sorcery and evil, and say to the unbelievers that they are better guided in the (right) way than the believers!

أَلَمْ تَرَ إِلَى ٱلَّذِينَ أُوتُوا۟ نَصِيبًا مِّنَ ٱلْكِتَٰبِ
يُؤْمِنُونَ بِٱلْجِبْتِ وَٱلطَّٰغُوتِ وَيَقُولُونَ لِلَّذِينَ
كَفَرُوا۟ هَٰٓؤُلَآءِ أَهْدَىٰ مِنَ ٱلَّذِينَ ءَامَنُوا۟
سَبِيلًا ﴿٥١﴾

52. They are (men) whom Allah has cursed: and those whom Allah has cursed, you will find, have no one to help.

أُو۟لَٰٓئِكَ ٱلَّذِينَ لَعَنَهُمُ ٱللَّهُ ۖ وَمَن يَلْعَنِ ٱللَّهُ فَلَن تَجِدَ لَهُۥ
نَصِيرًا ﴿٥٢﴾

53. Have they a share in dominion or power? See, they give not a farthing to their fellow-men?

أَمْ لَهُمْ نَصِيبٌ مِّنَ ٱلْمُلْكِ فَإِذًا لَّا يُؤْتُونَ ٱلنَّاسَ
نَقِيرًا ﴿٥٣﴾

54. Or do they envy mankind for what Allah has given them of His bounty? But We had already given the people of Abraham the book and wisdom, and conferred upon them a great kingdom.

أَمْ يَحْسُدُونَ ٱلنَّاسَ عَلَىٰ مَآ ءَاتَىٰهُمُ ٱللَّهُ مِن فَضْلِهِۦ ۖ
فَقَدْ ءَاتَيْنَآ ءَالَ إِبْرَٰهِيمَ ٱلْكِتَٰبَ وَٱلْحِكْمَةَ
وَءَاتَيْنَٰهُم مُّلْكًا عَظِيمًا ﴿٥٤﴾

55. Some of them believed, and some of them averted their faces from him; and enough is hell for a burning fire.

فَمِنْهُم مَّنْ ءَامَنَ بِهِۦ وَمِنْهُم مَّن صَدَّ عَنْهُ ۚ وَكَفَىٰ بِجَهَنَّمَ
سَعِيرًا ﴿٥٥﴾

56. Those who reject Our signs, We shall soon cast into the fire; as often as their skins are roasted through, We shall change them for fresh skins, that they may taste the penalty; for Allah is Exalted in Power, Wise.

إِنَّ ٱلَّذِينَ كَفَرُوا۟ بِـَٔايَٰتِنَا سَوْفَ نُصْلِيهِمْ نَارًا كُلَّمَا
نَضِجَتْ جُلُودُهُم بَدَّلْنَٰهُمْ جُلُودًا غَيْرَهَا لِيَذُوقُوا۟
ٱلْعَذَابَ ۗ إِنَّ ٱللَّهَ كَانَ عَزِيزًا حَكِيمًا ﴿٥٦﴾

57. But those who believe and do deeds of righteousness, We shall soon admit to gardens, with rivers flowing beneath - their eternal home; in it shall they have companions pure and holy; We shall admit them to shades, cool and ever deepening.

وَٱلَّذِينَ ءَامَنُوا۟ وَعَمِلُوا۟ ٱلصَّٰلِحَٰتِ سَنُدْخِلُهُمْ جَنَّٰتٍ
تَجْرِى مِن تَحْتِهَا ٱلْأَنْهَٰرُ خَٰلِدِينَ فِيهَآ أَبَدًا ۖ لَّهُمْ
فِيهَآ أَزْوَٰجٌ مُّطَهَّرَةٌ ۖ وَنُدْخِلُهُمْ ظِلًّا ظَلِيلًا ﴿٥٧﴾

نصف الحزب ٩

58. Allah does command you to render back your trusts to those to whom they are due; and when you judge between man and man, that you judge with justice; verily how excellent is the teaching which He gives you! For Allah is He Who hears and sees all things.

۞إِنَّ ٱللَّهَ يَأۡمُرُكُمۡ أَن تُؤَدُّواْ ٱلۡأَمَٰنَٰتِ إِلَىٰٓ أَهۡلِهَا
وَإِذَا حَكَمۡتُم بَيۡنَ ٱلنَّاسِ أَن تَحۡكُمُواْ بِٱلۡعَدۡلِۚ إِنَّ
ٱللَّهَ نِعِمَّا يَعِظُكُم بِهِۦٓۗ إِنَّ ٱللَّهَ كَانَ سَمِيعَۢا بَصِيرٗا ٥٨

59. O you who believe! Obey Allah, and obey the messenger, and those charged with authority among you. If you differ in anything among yourselves, refer it to Allah and His messenger, if you do believe in Allah and the last day; that is best, and most suitable for final determination.

يَٰٓأَيُّهَا ٱلَّذِينَ ءَامَنُوٓاْ أَطِيعُواْ ٱللَّهَ وَأَطِيعُواْ ٱلرَّسُولَ وَأُوْلِي
ٱلۡأَمۡرِ مِنكُمۡۖ فَإِن تَنَٰزَعۡتُمۡ فِي شَيۡءٖ فَرُدُّوهُ إِلَى ٱللَّهِ
وَٱلرَّسُولِ إِن كُنتُمۡ تُؤۡمِنُونَ بِٱللَّهِ وَٱلۡيَوۡمِ ٱلۡأٓخِرِۚ ذَٰلِكَ
خَيۡرٞ وَأَحۡسَنُ تَأۡوِيلًا ٥٩

60. Have you not turned your vision to those who declare that they believe in the revelations that have come to you and to those before you? Their (real) wish is to resort together for judgement (in their disputes) to the evil one, though they were ordered to reject him. But Satan's wish is to lead them astray, far away (from the right).

أَلَمۡ تَرَ إِلَى ٱلَّذِينَ يَزۡعُمُونَ أَنَّهُمۡ ءَامَنُواْ بِمَآ أُنزِلَ
إِلَيۡكَ وَمَآ أُنزِلَ مِن قَبۡلِكَ يُرِيدُونَ أَن يَتَحَاكَمُوٓاْ
إِلَى ٱلطَّٰغُوتِ وَقَدۡ أُمِرُوٓاْ أَن يَكۡفُرُواْ بِهِۦۖ وَيُرِيدُ
ٱلشَّيۡطَٰنُ أَن يُضِلَّهُمۡ ضَلَٰلَۢا بَعِيدٗا ٦٠

61. When it is said to them: "Come to what Allah has revealed, and to the messenger"; you see the hypocrites avert their faces from you in disgust.

وَإِذَا قِيلَ لَهُمۡ تَعَالَوۡاْ إِلَىٰ مَآ أَنزَلَ ٱللَّهُ وَإِلَى ٱلرَّسُولِ
رَأَيۡتَ ٱلۡمُنَٰفِقِينَ يَصُدُّونَ عَنكَ صُدُودٗا ٦١

62. How then, when they are seized by misfortune, because of the deeds which their hands have sent forward? Then they come to you, swearing by Allah: "We meant no more than goodwill and conciliation!"

فَكَيۡفَ إِذَآ أَصَٰبَتۡهُم مُّصِيبَةُۢ بِمَا
قَدَّمَتۡ أَيۡدِيهِمۡ ثُمَّ جَآءُوكَ يَحۡلِفُونَ بِٱللَّهِ إِنۡ
أَرَدۡنَآ إِلَّآ إِحۡسَٰنٗا وَتَوۡفِيقًا ٦٢

63. Those men - Allah knows what is in their hearts; so keep clear of them, but admonish them, and speak to them a word to reach their very souls.

أُوْلَٰٓئِكَ ٱلَّذِينَ يَعۡلَمُ ٱللَّهُ مَا فِي قُلُوبِهِمۡ
فَأَعۡرِضۡ عَنۡهُمۡ وَعِظۡهُمۡ وَقُل لَّهُمۡ فِيٓ
أَنفُسِهِمۡ قَوۡلَۢا بَلِيغٗا ٦٣

وَمَآ أَرْسَلْنَا مِن رَّسُولٍ إِلَّا لِيُطَاعَ بِإِذْنِ ٱللَّهِ ۚ وَلَوْ أَنَّهُمْ إِذ ظَّلَمُوٓا۟ أَنفُسَهُمْ جَآءُوكَ فَٱسْتَغْفَرُوا۟ ٱللَّهَ وَٱسْتَغْفَرَ لَهُمُ ٱلرَّسُولُ لَوَجَدُوا۟ ٱللَّهَ تَوَّابًا رَّحِيمًا ﴿٦٤﴾

64. We sent not a messenger, but to be obeyed, in accordance with the will of Allah. If they had only, when they were unjust to themselves, come to you and asked Allah's forgiveness, and the messenger had asked forgiveness for them, they would have found Allah indeed Oft-Returning, Most Merciful.

فَلَا وَرَبِّكَ لَا يُؤْمِنُونَ حَتَّىٰ يُحَكِّمُوكَ فِيمَا شَجَرَ بَيْنَهُمْ ثُمَّ لَا يَجِدُوا۟ فِىٓ أَنفُسِهِمْ حَرَجًا مِّمَّا قَضَيْتَ وَيُسَلِّمُوا۟ تَسْلِيمًا ﴿٦٥﴾

65. But no, by your Lord, they can have no (real) faith, until they make you judge in all disputes between them, and find in their souls no resistance against your decisions, but accept them with the fullest conviction.

وَلَوْ أَنَّا كَتَبْنَا عَلَيْهِمْ أَنِ ٱقْتُلُوٓا۟ أَنفُسَكُمْ أَوِ ٱخْرُجُوا۟ مِن دِيَٰرِكُم مَّا فَعَلُوهُ إِلَّا قَلِيلٌ مِّنْهُمْ ۖ وَلَوْ أَنَّهُمْ فَعَلُوا۟ مَا يُوعَظُونَ بِهِۦ لَكَانَ خَيْرًا لَّهُمْ وَأَشَدَّ تَثْبِيتًا ﴿٦٦﴾

66. If We had ordered them to sacrifice their lives or to leave their homes, very few of them would have done it; but if they had done what they were (actually) told, it would have been best for them, and would have gone farthest to strengthen their (faith).

وَإِذًا لَّءَاتَيْنَٰهُم مِّن لَّدُنَّآ أَجْرًا عَظِيمًا ﴿٦٧﴾

67. And We should then have given them from Our presence a great reward;

وَلَهَدَيْنَٰهُمْ صِرَٰطًا مُّسْتَقِيمًا ﴿٦٨﴾

68. And We should have shown them the straight way.

وَمَن يُطِعِ ٱللَّهَ وَٱلرَّسُولَ فَأُو۟لَٰٓئِكَ مَعَ ٱلَّذِينَ أَنْعَمَ ٱللَّهُ عَلَيْهِم مِّنَ ٱلنَّبِيِّۦنَ وَٱلصِّدِّيقِينَ وَٱلشُّهَدَآءِ وَٱلصَّٰلِحِينَ ۚ وَحَسُنَ أُو۟لَٰٓئِكَ رَفِيقًا ﴿٦٩﴾

69. All who obey Allah and the messenger are in the company of those on whom is the grace of Allah - of the prophets (who teach), the sincere (lovers of truth), the witnesses (who testify), and the righteous (who do good): Ah! What a beautiful fellowship!

ذَٰلِكَ ٱلْفَضْلُ مِنَ ٱللَّهِ ۚ وَكَفَىٰ بِٱللَّهِ عَلِيمًا ﴿٧٠﴾

70. Such is the bounty from Allah: and sufficient is it that Allah knows all.

71. O you who believe! Take your precautions, and either go out in parties or go out all together.

يَٰٓأَيُّهَا ٱلَّذِينَ ءَامَنُواْ خُذُواْ حِذْرَكُمْ
فَٱنفِرُواْ ثُبَاتٍ أَوِ ٱنفِرُواْ جَمِيعًا ﴿٧١﴾

72. There are certainly among you men who would stay behind; if a misfortune befalls you, they say: "Allah did favour us in that we were not present among them."

وَإِنَّ مِنكُمْ لَمَن لَّيُبَطِّئَنَّ فَإِنْ أَصَٰبَتْكُم مُّصِيبَةٌ
قَالَ قَدْ أَنْعَمَ ٱللَّهُ عَلَيَّ إِذْ لَمْ أَكُن مَّعَهُمْ
شَهِيدًا ﴿٧٢﴾

73. But if good fortune comes to you from Allah, they would be sure to say - as if there had never been ties of affection between you and them - "Oh! I wish I had been with them; a fine thing should I then have made of it!"

وَلَئِنْ أَصَٰبَكُمْ فَضْلٌ مِّنَ ٱللَّهِ لَيَقُولَنَّ كَأَن لَّمْ تَكُنۢ
بَيْنَكُمْ وَبَيْنَهُۥ مَوَدَّةٌ يَٰلَيْتَنِى كُنتُ مَعَهُمْ
فَأَفُوزَ فَوْزًا عَظِيمًا ﴿٧٣﴾

74. Let those fight in the cause of Allah who sell the life of this world for the hereafter. To him who fights in the cause of Allah - whether he is slain or gets victory - soon shall We give him a reward of great (value).

۞ فَلْيُقَٰتِلْ فِى سَبِيلِ ٱللَّهِ ٱلَّذِينَ يَشْرُونَ ثلاثة أرباع الحزب ٩
ٱلْحَيَوٰةَ ٱلدُّنْيَا بِٱلْءَاخِرَةِ وَمَن يُقَٰتِلْ فِى سَبِيلِ
ٱللَّهِ فَيُقْتَلْ أَوْ يَغْلِبْ فَسَوْفَ نُؤْتِيهِ أَجْرًا
عَظِيمًا ﴿٧٤﴾

75. And why should you not fight in the cause of Allah and of those who, being weak, are ill-treated (and oppressed)? - Men, women, and children, whose call is: "Our Lord! Rescue us from this town, whose people are oppressors; and raise for us from You one who will protect; and raise for us from You one who will help!"

وَمَا لَكُمْ لَا تُقَٰتِلُونَ فِى سَبِيلِ ٱللَّهِ وَٱلْمُسْتَضْعَفِينَ
مِنَ ٱلرِّجَالِ وَٱلنِّسَآءِ وَٱلْوِلْدَٰنِ ٱلَّذِينَ يَقُولُونَ رَبَّنَآ
أَخْرِجْنَا مِنْ هَٰذِهِ ٱلْقَرْيَةِ ٱلظَّالِمِ أَهْلُهَا وَٱجْعَل لَّنَا
مِن لَّدُنكَ وَلِيًّا وَٱجْعَل لَّنَا مِن لَّدُنكَ نَصِيرًا ﴿٧٥﴾

76. Those who believe fight in the cause of Allah, and those who reject faith fight in the cause of evil: so fight you against the friends of Satan: feeble indeed is the cunning of Satan.

ٱلَّذِينَ ءَامَنُواْ يُقَٰتِلُونَ فِى سَبِيلِ ٱللَّهِ ۖ وَٱلَّذِينَ كَفَرُواْ
يُقَٰتِلُونَ فِى سَبِيلِ ٱلطَّٰغُوتِ فَقَٰتِلُوٓاْ أَوْلِيَآءَ
ٱلشَّيْطَٰنِ ۖ إِنَّ كَيْدَ ٱلشَّيْطَٰنِ كَانَ ضَعِيفًا ﴿٧٦﴾

77. Have you not turned your vision to those who were told to hold back their hands (from fight) but establish regular prayers and spend in regular charity? When (at length) the order for fighting was issued to them, behold! A section of them feared men as - or even more than - they should have feared Allah: they say: "Our Lord! Why have You ordered us to fight? Would You not grant us respite to our (natural) term, near (enough)?" Say: "Short is the enjoyment of this world: the hereafter is the best for those who do right; never will you be dealt with unjustly in the very least!"

أَلَمْ تَرَ إِلَى ٱلَّذِينَ قِيلَ لَهُمْ كُفُّوٓا۟ أَيْدِيَكُمْ وَأَقِيمُوا۟
ٱلصَّلَوٰةَ وَءَاتُوا۟ ٱلزَّكَوٰةَ فَلَمَّا كُتِبَ عَلَيْهِمُ ٱلْقِتَالُ
إِذَا فَرِيقٌ مِّنْهُمْ يَخْشَوْنَ ٱلنَّاسَ كَخَشْيَةِ ٱللَّهِ أَوْ أَشَدَّ
خَشْيَةً ۚ وَقَالُوا۟ رَبَّنَا لِمَ كَتَبْتَ عَلَيْنَا ٱلْقِتَالَ لَوْلَآ
أَخَّرْتَنَآ إِلَىٰٓ أَجَلٍ قَرِيبٍ ۗ قُلْ مَتَٰعُ ٱلدُّنْيَا قَلِيلٌ
وَٱلْـَٔاخِرَةُ خَيْرٌ لِّمَنِ ٱتَّقَىٰ وَلَا تُظْلَمُونَ فَتِيلًا ٧٧

78. "Wherever you are, death will find you out, even if you are in towers built up strong and high!" If some good befalls them, they say, "This is from Allah"; but if evil, they say, "this is from you" (O Prophet). Say: "All things are from Allah." But what has come to these people, that they fail to understand a single fact?

أَيْنَمَا تَكُونُوا۟ يُدْرِككُّمُ ٱلْمَوْتُ وَلَوْ كُنتُمْ فِى بُرُوجٍ
مُّشَيَّدَةٍ ۗ وَإِن تُصِبْهُمْ حَسَنَةٌ يَقُولُوا۟ هَٰذِهِۦ مِنْ عِندِ
ٱللَّهِ ۖ وَإِن تُصِبْهُمْ سَيِّئَةٌ يَقُولُوا۟ هَٰذِهِۦ مِنْ عِندِكَ ۚ قُلْ
كُلٌّ مِّنْ عِندِ ٱللَّهِ ۖ فَمَالِ هَٰٓؤُلَآءِ ٱلْقَوْمِ لَا يَكَادُونَ يَفْقَهُونَ
حَدِيثًا ٧٨

79. Whatever good, (O man!) happens to you, is from Allah; but whatever evil happens to you, is from your (own) soul. And We have sent you as a messenger to (instruct) mankind. And enough is Allah for a witness.

مَّآ أَصَابَكَ مِنْ حَسَنَةٍ فَمِنَ ٱللَّهِ ۖ وَمَآ أَصَابَكَ مِن سَيِّئَةٍ
فَمِن نَّفْسِكَ ۚ وَأَرْسَلْنَٰكَ لِلنَّاسِ رَسُولًا ۚ وَكَفَىٰ بِٱللَّهِ
شَهِيدًا ٧٩

80. He who obeys the messenger, obeys Allah: but if any turn away, We have not sent you to watch over their (evil deeds).

مَّن يُطِعِ ٱلرَّسُولَ فَقَدْ أَطَاعَ ٱللَّهَ ۖ وَمَن تَوَلَّىٰ فَمَآ
أَرْسَلْنَٰكَ عَلَيْهِمْ حَفِيظًا ٨٠

81. They have "obedience" on their lips; but when they leave you, a section of them meditate all night on things very different from what you tell them. But Allah records

وَيَقُولُونَ طَاعَةٌ فَإِذَا بَرَزُوا۟ مِنْ عِندِكَ بَيَّتَ
طَآئِفَةٌ مِّنْهُمْ غَيْرَ ٱلَّذِى تَقُولُ ۖ وَٱللَّهُ يَكْتُبُ

their nightly (plots): so keep clear of them and put your trust in Allah, and enough is Allah as a disposer of affairs.

مَا يُبَيِّتُونَ ۖ فَأَعْرِضْ عَنْهُمْ وَتَوَكَّلْ عَلَى ٱللَّهِ ۚ
وَكَفَىٰ بِٱللَّهِ وَكِيلًا ﴿٨١﴾

82. Do they not consider the Qur'an (with care)? Had it been from other than Allah, they would surely have found in it much discrepancy.

أَفَلَا يَتَدَبَّرُونَ ٱلْقُرْءَانَ ۚ وَلَوْ كَانَ مِنْ عِندِ
غَيْرِ ٱللَّهِ لَوَجَدُوا۟ فِيهِ ٱخْتِلَٰفًا كَثِيرًا ﴿٨٢﴾

83. When there comes to them some matter touching (public) safety or fear, they divulge it. If they had only referred it to the messenger or to those charged with authority among them, the proper investigators would have tested it from them (direct). Were it not for the grace and mercy of Allah to you, all but a few of you would have followed Satan.

وَإِذَا جَآءَهُمْ أَمْرٌ مِّنَ ٱلْأَمْنِ أَوِ ٱلْخَوْفِ أَذَاعُوا۟ بِهِۦ ۖ
وَلَوْ رَدُّوهُ إِلَى ٱلرَّسُولِ وَإِلَىٰٓ أُو۟لِى ٱلْأَمْرِ مِنْهُمْ لَعَلِمَهُ
ٱلَّذِينَ يَسْتَنۢبِطُونَهُۥ مِنْهُمْ ۗ وَلَوْلَا فَضْلُ ٱللَّهِ
عَلَيْكُمْ وَرَحْمَتُهُۥ لَٱتَّبَعْتُمُ ٱلشَّيْطَٰنَ
إِلَّا قَلِيلًا ﴿٨٣﴾

84. Then fight in Allah's cause - you are held responsible only for yourself - and rouse the believers. It may be that Allah will restrain the fury of the unbelievers: for Allah is the strongest in might and in punishment.

فَقَٰتِلْ فِى سَبِيلِ ٱللَّهِ لَا تُكَلَّفُ إِلَّا نَفْسَكَ ۚ وَحَرِّضِ
ٱلْمُؤْمِنِينَ ۖ عَسَى ٱللَّهُ أَن يَكُفَّ بَأْسَ ٱلَّذِينَ
كَفَرُوا۟ ۚ وَٱللَّهُ أَشَدُّ بَأْسًا وَأَشَدُّ تَنكِيلًا ﴿٨٤﴾

85. Whoever recommends and helps a good cause becomes a partner in it; and whoever recommends and helps an evil cause, shares in its burden; and Allah has power over all things.

مَّن يَشْفَعْ شَفَٰعَةً حَسَنَةً يَكُن لَّهُۥ نَصِيبٌ
مِّنْهَا ۖ وَمَن يَشْفَعْ شَفَٰعَةً سَيِّئَةً يَكُن لَّهُۥ كِفْلٌ
مِّنْهَا ۗ وَكَانَ ٱللَّهُ عَلَىٰ كُلِّ شَىْءٍ مُّقِيتًا ﴿٨٥﴾

86. When a (courteous) greeting is offered you, meet it with a greeting still more courteous, (at least) of equal courtesy. Allah takes careful account of all things.

وَإِذَا حُيِّيتُم بِتَحِيَّةٍ فَحَيُّوا۟ بِأَحْسَنَ مِنْهَآ
أَوْ رُدُّوهَآ ۗ إِنَّ ٱللَّهَ كَانَ عَلَىٰ كُلِّ شَىْءٍ حَسِيبًا ﴿٨٦﴾

87. Allah! There is no god but He; certainly He will gather you together against the day of judgement, about which there is no doubt. And whose word can be truer than Allah's?

ٱللَّهُ لَآ إِلَٰهَ إِلَّا هُوَ ۚ لَيَجْمَعَنَّكُمْ إِلَىٰ يَوْمِ ٱلْقِيَٰمَةِ
لَا رَيْبَ فِيهِ ۗ وَمَنْ أَصْدَقُ مِنَ ٱللَّهِ حَدِيثًا ﴿٨٧﴾

الحزب ١٠

88. Why should you be divided into two parties about the hypocrites? Allah has upset them for their (evil) deeds. Would you guide those whom Allah has thrown out of the way? For those whom Allah has thrown out of the way, never shall you find the way.

۞ فَمَا لَكُمْ فِي ٱلْمُنَٰفِقِينَ فِئَتَيْنِ وَٱللَّهُ أَرْكَسَهُم
بِمَا كَسَبُوٓا۟ ۚ أَتُرِيدُونَ أَن تَهْدُوا۟ مَنْ أَضَلَّ ٱللَّهُ ۖ
وَمَن يُضْلِلِ ٱللَّهُ فَلَن تَجِدَ لَهُۥ سَبِيلًا ﴿٨٨﴾

89. They but wish that you should reject faith, as they do, and thus be on the same footing (as they); but take not friends from their ranks until they flee in the way of Allah (from what is forbidden). But if they turn renegades, seize them and slay them wherever you find them; And (in any case) take no friends or helpers from their ranks -

وَدُّوا۟ لَوْ تَكْفُرُونَ كَمَا كَفَرُوا۟ فَتَكُونُونَ سَوَآءً ۖ فَلَا
تَتَّخِذُوا۟ مِنْهُمْ أَوْلِيَآءَ حَتَّىٰ يُهَاجِرُوا۟ فِي سَبِيلِ
ٱللَّهِ ۚ فَإِن تَوَلَّوْا۟ فَخُذُوهُمْ وَٱقْتُلُوهُمْ حَيْثُ
وَجَدتُّمُوهُمْ ۖ وَلَا تَتَّخِذُوا۟ مِنْهُمْ وَلِيًّا وَلَا نَصِيرًا ﴿٨٩﴾

90. Except those who join a group between whom and you there is a treaty (of peace), or those who approach you with hearts restraining them from fighting you as well as fighting their own people. If Allah had pleased, He could have given them power over you, and they would have fought you; therefore if they withdraw from you but fight you not and (instead) send you (guarantees of) peace, then Allah has opened no way for you (to war against them).

إِلَّا ٱلَّذِينَ يَصِلُونَ إِلَىٰ قَوْمٍۭ بَيْنَكُمْ وَبَيْنَهُم مِّيثَٰقٌ
أَوْ جَآءُوكُمْ حَصِرَتْ صُدُورُهُمْ أَن يُقَٰتِلُوكُمْ
أَوْ يُقَٰتِلُوا۟ قَوْمَهُمْ ۚ وَلَوْ شَآءَ ٱللَّهُ لَسَلَّطَهُمْ عَلَيْكُمْ
فَلَقَٰتَلُوكُمْ ۚ فَإِنِ ٱعْتَزَلُوكُمْ فَلَمْ يُقَٰتِلُوكُمْ وَأَلْقَوْا۟
إِلَيْكُمُ ٱلسَّلَمَ فَمَا جَعَلَ ٱللَّهُ لَكُمْ عَلَيْهِمْ سَبِيلًا ﴿٩٠﴾

91. Others you will find that wish to gain your confidence as well as that of their people; every time they are sent back to temptation, they succumb to it; if they withdraw not from you nor give you (guarantees) of peace besides restraining their hands, seize them and slay them wherever you get them; in their case We have provided you with a clear argument against them.

سَتَجِدُونَ ءَاخَرِينَ يُرِيدُونَ أَن يَأْمَنُوكُمْ وَيَأْمَنُوا۟
قَوْمَهُمْ كُلَّ مَا رُدُّوٓا۟ إِلَى ٱلْفِتْنَةِ أُرْكِسُوا۟ فِيهَا ۚ فَإِن
لَّمْ يَعْتَزِلُوكُمْ وَيُلْقُوٓا۟ إِلَيْكُمُ ٱلسَّلَمَ وَيَكُفُّوٓا۟
أَيْدِيَهُمْ فَخُذُوهُمْ وَٱقْتُلُوهُمْ حَيْثُ ثَقِفْتُمُوهُمْ ۚ
وَأُو۟لَٰٓئِكُمْ جَعَلْنَا لَكُمْ عَلَيْهِمْ سُلْطَٰنًا مُّبِينًا ﴿٩١﴾

92. Never should a believer kill a believer; but (if it so happens) by mistake,

وَمَا كَانَ لِمُؤْمِنٍ أَن يَقْتُلَ مُؤْمِنًا إِلَّا خَطَـًٔا ۚ

(compensation is due); if one (so) kills a believer, it is ordained that he should free a believing slave and pay compensation to the deceased's family, unless they remit it freely. If the deceased belonged to a people at war with you, and he was a believer, the freeing of a believing slave (is enough). If he belonged to a people with whom you have a treaty of mutual alliance, compensation should be paid to his family, and a believing slave be freed. For those who find this beyond their means, (is prescribed) a fast for two months running: by way of repentance to Allah: for Allah has all knowledge and all wisdom.

وَمَن قَتَلَ مُؤْمِنًا خَطَـًٔا فَتَحْرِيرُ رَقَبَةٍ مُّؤْمِنَةٍ
وَدِيَةٌ مُّسَلَّمَةٌ إِلَىٰٓ أَهْلِهِۦٓ إِلَّآ أَن يَصَّدَّقُوا۟ ۚ
فَإِن كَانَ مِن قَوْمٍ عَدُوٍّ لَّكُمْ وَهُوَ مُؤْمِنٌ
فَتَحْرِيرُ رَقَبَةٍ مُّؤْمِنَةٍ ۖ وَإِن كَانَ مِن قَوْمٍۭ
بَيْنَكُمْ وَبَيْنَهُم مِّيثَٰقٌ فَدِيَةٌ مُّسَلَّمَةٌ إِلَىٰٓ
أَهْلِهِۦ وَتَحْرِيرُ رَقَبَةٍ مُّؤْمِنَةٍ ۖ فَمَن لَّمْ يَجِدْ
فَصِيَامُ شَهْرَيْنِ مُتَتَابِعَيْنِ تَوْبَةً مِّنَ
ٱللَّهِ ۗ وَكَانَ ٱللَّهُ عَلِيمًا حَكِيمًا ﴿٩٢﴾

93. If a man kills a believer intentionally, his recompense is hell, to remain in it (for ever); and the wrath and the curse of Allah are upon him, and a dreadful penalty is prepared for him.

وَمَن يَقْتُلْ مُؤْمِنًا مُّتَعَمِّدًا فَجَزَآؤُهُۥ
جَهَنَّمُ خَٰلِدًا فِيهَا وَغَضِبَ ٱللَّهُ عَلَيْهِ
وَلَعَنَهُۥ وَأَعَدَّ لَهُۥ عَذَابًا عَظِيمًا ﴿٩٣﴾

94. O you who believe! When you go abroad in the cause of Allah, investigate carefully, and say not to anyone who offers you a salutation: "You are not a believer!" coveting the perishable goods of this life; with Allah are profits and spoils abundant. Even thus were you yourselves before, till Allah conferred on you His favours; therefore carefully investigate. For Allah is well aware of all that you do.

يَٰٓأَيُّهَا ٱلَّذِينَ ءَامَنُوٓا۟ إِذَا ضَرَبْتُمْ فِى سَبِيلِ
ٱللَّهِ فَتَبَيَّنُوا۟ وَلَا تَقُولُوا۟ لِمَنْ أَلْقَىٰٓ إِلَيْكُمُ
ٱلسَّلَٰمَ لَسْتَ مُؤْمِنًا تَبْتَغُونَ عَرَضَ
ٱلْحَيَوٰةِ ٱلدُّنْيَا فَعِندَ ٱللَّهِ مَغَانِمُ كَثِيرَةٌ ۚ
كَذَٰلِكَ كُنتُم مِّن قَبْلُ فَمَنَّ ٱللَّهُ
عَلَيْكُمْ فَتَبَيَّنُوٓا۟ ۚ إِنَّ ٱللَّهَ كَانَ بِمَا
تَعْمَلُونَ خَبِيرًا ﴿٩٤﴾

95. Not equal are those believers who sit (at home) and receive no hurt, and those who strive and fight in the cause of Allah with their goods and their persons. Allah has granted a grade higher to those who strive and fight with their goods and persons than to those who sit (at home). To all (in faith) has Allah promised good: but those who strive and fight has He distinguished above those who sit (at home) by a special reward -

لَّا يَسْتَوِي الْقَاعِدُونَ مِنَ الْمُؤْمِنِينَ غَيْرُ أُولِي الضَّرَرِ
وَالْمُجَاهِدُونَ فِي سَبِيلِ اللَّهِ بِأَمْوَالِهِمْ وَأَنفُسِهِمْ ۚ فَضَّلَ
اللَّهُ الْمُجَاهِدِينَ بِأَمْوَالِهِمْ وَأَنفُسِهِمْ عَلَى الْقَاعِدِينَ دَرَجَةً ۚ
وَكُلًّا وَعَدَ اللَّهُ الْحُسْنَىٰ ۚ وَفَضَّلَ اللَّهُ الْمُجَاهِدِينَ عَلَى
الْقَاعِدِينَ أَجْرًا عَظِيمًا ﴿٩٥﴾

96. Ranks specially bestowed by Him and forgiveness and mercy, for Allah is Oft-Forgiving, Most Merciful.

دَرَجَاتٍ مِّنْهُ وَمَغْفِرَةً وَرَحْمَةً ۚ وَكَانَ اللَّهُ غَفُورًا
رَّحِيمًا ﴿٩٦﴾

97. When angels take the souls of those who die in sin against their souls, they say: "In what (plight) were you?" They reply: "Weak and oppressed were we in the earth." They say: "Was not the earth of Allah spacious enough for you to move yourselves away (from evil)?" Such men will find their abode in hell - what an evil refuge! -

إِنَّ الَّذِينَ تَوَفَّاهُمُ الْمَلَائِكَةُ ظَالِمِي أَنفُسِهِمْ قَالُوا
فِيمَ كُنتُمْ ۖ قَالُوا كُنَّا مُسْتَضْعَفِينَ فِي الْأَرْضِ ۚ قَالُوا أَلَمْ
تَكُنْ أَرْضُ اللَّهِ وَاسِعَةً فَتُهَاجِرُوا فِيهَا ۚ فَأُولَٰئِكَ
مَأْوَاهُمْ جَهَنَّمُ ۖ وَسَاءَتْ مَصِيرًا ﴿٩٧﴾

98. Except those who are (really) weak and oppressed - men, women and children who have no means in their power, nor (a guide-post) to direct their way.

إِلَّا الْمُسْتَضْعَفِينَ مِنَ الرِّجَالِ وَالنِّسَاءِ وَالْوِلْدَانِ
لَا يَسْتَطِيعُونَ حِيلَةً وَلَا يَهْتَدُونَ سَبِيلًا ﴿٩٨﴾

99. For these, there is hope that Allah will forgive: for Allah does blot out (sins) and forgive again and again.

فَأُولَٰئِكَ عَسَى اللَّهُ أَن يَعْفُوَ عَنْهُمْ ۚ وَكَانَ اللَّهُ عَفُوًّا
غَفُورًا ﴿٩٩﴾

100. He who forsakes his home in the cause of Allah, finds in the earth many a refuge, wide and spacious; should he die as a refugee from home for Allah and His messenger, his reward becomes due and

۞ وَمَن يُهَاجِرْ فِي سَبِيلِ اللَّهِ يَجِدْ فِي الْأَرْضِ مُرَاغَمًا ربع الحزب ١٠
كَثِيرًا وَسَعَةً ۚ وَمَن يَخْرُجْ مِن بَيْتِهِ مُهَاجِرًا إِلَى اللَّهِ
وَرَسُولِهِ ثُمَّ يُدْرِكْهُ الْمَوْتُ فَقَدْ وَقَعَ أَجْرُهُ عَلَى اللَّهِ ۗ

sure with Allah; and Allah is Oft-Forgiving, Most Merciful.

وَكَانَ ٱللَّهُ غَفُورًا رَّحِيمًا ﴿١٠٠﴾

101. When you travel through the earth, there is no blame on you if you shorten your prayers, for fear the unbelievers may attack you: for the unbelievers are to you open enemies.

وَإِذَا ضَرَبْتُمْ فِي ٱلْأَرْضِ فَلَيْسَ عَلَيْكُمْ جُنَاحٌ أَن
تَقْصُرُوا۟ مِنَ ٱلصَّلَوٰةِ إِنْ خِفْتُمْ أَن يَفْتِنَكُمُ ٱلَّذِينَ
كَفَرُوٓا۟ ۚ إِنَّ ٱلْكَٰفِرِينَ كَانُوا۟ لَكُمْ عَدُوًّا مُّبِينًا ﴿١٠١﴾

102. When you (O messenger) are with them, and stand to lead them in prayer, let one party of them stand up (in prayer) with you, taking their arms with them; when they finish their prostrations, let them take their positions in the rear. And let the other party come up which has not yet prayed - and let them pray with you, taking all precautions, and bearing arms; the unbelievers wish, if you were negligent of your arms and your baggage, to assault you in a single rush. But there is no blame on you if you put away your arms because of the inconvenience of rain or because you are ill; but take (every) precaution for yourselves. For the unbelievers Allah has prepared a humiliating punishment.

وَإِذَا كُنتَ فِيهِمْ فَأَقَمْتَ لَهُمُ ٱلصَّلَوٰةَ فَلْتَقُمْ
طَآئِفَةٌ مِّنْهُم مَّعَكَ وَلْيَأْخُذُوٓا۟ أَسْلِحَتَهُمْ فَإِذَا
سَجَدُوا۟ فَلْيَكُونُوا۟ مِن وَرَآئِكُمْ وَلْتَأْتِ طَآئِفَةٌ
أُخْرَىٰ لَمْ يُصَلُّوا۟ فَلْيُصَلُّوا۟ مَعَكَ وَلْيَأْخُذُوا۟
حِذْرَهُمْ وَأَسْلِحَتَهُمْ ۗ وَدَّ ٱلَّذِينَ كَفَرُوا۟
لَوْ تَغْفُلُونَ عَنْ أَسْلِحَتِكُمْ وَأَمْتِعَتِكُمْ فَيَمِيلُونَ
عَلَيْكُم مَّيْلَةً وَٰحِدَةً ۚ وَلَا جُنَاحَ عَلَيْكُمْ إِن كَانَ
بِكُمْ أَذًى مِّن مَّطَرٍ أَوْ كُنتُم مَّرْضَىٰٓ أَن تَضَعُوٓا۟
أَسْلِحَتَكُمْ ۖ وَخُذُوا۟ حِذْرَكُمْ ۗ إِنَّ ٱللَّهَ أَعَدَّ
لِلْكَٰفِرِينَ عَذَابًا مُّهِينًا ﴿١٠٢﴾

103. When you pass (congregational) prayers, celebrate Allah's praises, standing, sitting down, or lying down on your sides; but when you are free from danger, set up regular prayers; for such prayers are enjoined on believers at stated times.

فَإِذَا قَضَيْتُمُ ٱلصَّلَوٰةَ فَٱذْكُرُوا۟ ٱللَّهَ قِيَٰمًا
وَقُعُودًا وَعَلَىٰ جُنُوبِكُمْ ۚ فَإِذَا ٱطْمَأْنَنتُمْ
فَأَقِيمُوا۟ ٱلصَّلَوٰةَ ۚ إِنَّ ٱلصَّلَوٰةَ كَانَتْ عَلَى ٱلْمُؤْمِنِينَ
كِتَٰبًا مَّوْقُوتًا ﴿١٠٣﴾

104. And slacken not in following up the

وَلَا تَهِنُوا۟ فِي ٱبْتِغَآءِ ٱلْقَوْمِ ۖ إِن تَكُونُوا۟ تَأْلَمُونَ

enemy; if you are suffering hardships, they are suffering similar hardships; but you have hope from Allah, while they have none. And Allah is full of knowledge and wisdom.

فَإِنَّهُمْ يَأْلَمُونَ كَمَا تَأْلَمُونَ ۖ وَتَرْجُونَ
مِنَ ٱللَّهِ مَا لَا يَرْجُونَ ۗ وَكَانَ ٱللَّهُ عَلِيمًا
حَكِيمًا ﴿١٠٤﴾

105. We have sent down to you the book in truth, that you might judge between men, as guided by Allah: so be not (used) as an advocate by those who betray their trust;

إِنَّآ أَنزَلْنَآ إِلَيْكَ ٱلْكِتَٰبَ بِٱلْحَقِّ لِتَحْكُمَ بَيْنَ
ٱلنَّاسِ بِمَآ أَرَىٰكَ ٱللَّهُ ۚ وَلَا تَكُن لِّلْخَآئِنِينَ
خَصِيمًا ﴿١٠٥﴾

106. But seek the forgiveness of Allah; for Allah is Oft-Forgiving, Most Merciful.

وَٱسْتَغْفِرِ ٱللَّهَ ۖ إِنَّ ٱللَّهَ كَانَ غَفُورًا رَّحِيمًا ﴿١٠٦﴾

107. Contend not on behalf of such as betray their own souls: for Allah loves not one given to perfidy and crime;

وَلَا تُجَٰدِلْ عَنِ ٱلَّذِينَ يَخْتَانُونَ أَنفُسَهُمْ ۚ إِنَّ
ٱللَّهَ لَا يُحِبُّ مَن كَانَ خَوَّانًا أَثِيمًا ﴿١٠٧﴾

108. They may hide (their crimes) from men, but they cannot hide (them) from Allah, seeing that He is in their midst when they plot by night, in words that He cannot approve; and Allah does encompass all that they do.

يَسْتَخْفُونَ مِنَ ٱلنَّاسِ وَلَا يَسْتَخْفُونَ مِنَ ٱللَّهِ
وَهُوَ مَعَهُمْ إِذْ يُبَيِّتُونَ مَا لَا يَرْضَىٰ مِنَ ٱلْقَوْلِ ۚ
وَكَانَ ٱللَّهُ بِمَا يَعْمَلُونَ مُحِيطًا ﴿١٠٨﴾

109. Ah! These are the sort of men on whose behalf you may contend in this world; but who will contend with Allah on their behalf on the day of judgement, or who will carry their affairs through?

هَٰٓأَنتُمْ هَٰٓؤُلَآءِ جَٰدَلْتُمْ عَنْهُمْ فِى ٱلْحَيَوٰةِ
ٱلدُّنْيَا فَمَن يُجَٰدِلُ ٱللَّهَ عَنْهُمْ يَوْمَ ٱلْقِيَٰمَةِ أَم
مَّن يَكُونُ عَلَيْهِمْ وَكِيلًا ﴿١٠٩﴾

110. If anyone does evil or wrongs his own soul but afterwards seeks Allah's forgiveness, he will find Allah Oft-Forgiving, Most Merciful.

وَمَن يَعْمَلْ سُوٓءًا أَوْ يَظْلِمْ نَفْسَهُۥ ثُمَّ يَسْتَغْفِرِ
ٱللَّهَ يَجِدِ ٱللَّهَ غَفُورًا رَّحِيمًا ﴿١١٠﴾

111. And if anyone earns sin, he earns it

وَمَن يَكْسِبْ إِثْمًا فَإِنَّمَا يَكْسِبُهُۥ عَلَىٰ نَفْسِهِۦ ۚ

against his own soul: for Allah is full of knowledge and wisdom.

وَكَانَ ٱللَّهُ عَلِيمًا حَكِيمًا ١١١

112. But if anyone earns a fault or a sin and throws it on to one that is innocent, he carries (on himself) (both) a falsehood and a flagrant sin.

وَمَن يَكْسِبْ خَطِيٓـَٔةً أَوْ إِثْمًا ثُمَّ يَرْمِ بِهِۦ
بَرِيٓـًٔا فَقَدِ ٱحْتَمَلَ بُهْتَٰنًا وَإِثْمًا مُّبِينًا ١١٢

113. But for the grace of Allah to you and His mercy, a party of them would certainly have plotted to lead you astray. But (in fact) they will only lead their own souls astray, and to you they can do no harm in the least. For Allah has sent down to you the book and wisdom and taught you what you knew not (before); and great is the grace of Allah to you.

وَلَوْلَا فَضْلُ ٱللَّهِ عَلَيْكَ وَرَحْمَتُهُۥ لَهَمَّت طَّآئِفَةٌ
مِّنْهُمْ أَن يُضِلُّوكَ وَمَا يُضِلُّونَ إِلَّآ أَنفُسَهُمْ ۖ
وَمَا يَضُرُّونَكَ مِن شَىْءٍ ۚ وَأَنزَلَ ٱللَّهُ عَلَيْكَ
ٱلْكِتَٰبَ وَٱلْحِكْمَةَ وَعَلَّمَكَ مَا لَمْ تَكُن تَعْلَمُ ۚ
وَكَانَ فَضْلُ ٱللَّهِ عَلَيْكَ عَظِيمًا ١١٣

114. In most of their secret talks there is no good: but if one exhorts to a deed of charity or justice or conciliation between men, (secrecy is permissible): to him who does this, seeking the good pleasure of Allah, We shall soon give a reward of the highest (value).

نصف الحزب ١٠

۞ لَّا خَيْرَ فِى كَثِيرٍ مِّن نَّجْوَىٰهُمْ إِلَّا مَنْ أَمَرَ
بِصَدَقَةٍ أَوْ مَعْرُوفٍ أَوْ إِصْلَٰحٍۭ بَيْنَ ٱلنَّاسِ ۚ
وَمَن يَفْعَلْ ذَٰلِكَ ٱبْتِغَآءَ مَرْضَاتِ ٱللَّهِ فَسَوْفَ
نُؤْتِيهِ أَجْرًا عَظِيمًا ١١٤

115. If anyone contends with the messenger even after guidance has been plainly conveyed to him, and follows a path other than that becoming to men of faith, We shall leave him in the path he has chosen, and land him in hell - what an evil refuge!

وَمَن يُشَاقِقِ ٱلرَّسُولَ مِنۢ بَعْدِ مَا تَبَيَّنَ لَهُ
ٱلْهُدَىٰ وَيَتَّبِعْ غَيْرَ سَبِيلِ ٱلْمُؤْمِنِينَ نُوَلِّهِۦ
مَا تَوَلَّىٰ وَنُصْلِهِۦ جَهَنَّمَ ۖ وَسَآءَتْ مَصِيرًا ١١٥

116. Allah forgives not (the sin of) joining other gods with Him; but He forgives whom He pleases, other sins than this; one who joins other gods with Allah, has strayed far, far away (from the right).

إِنَّ ٱللَّهَ لَا يَغْفِرُ أَن يُشْرَكَ بِهِۦ وَيَغْفِرُ مَا دُونَ
ذَٰلِكَ لِمَن يَشَآءُ ۚ وَمَن يُشْرِكْ بِٱللَّهِ فَقَدْ
ضَلَّ ضَلَٰلًۢا بَعِيدًا ١١٦

117. (The pagans), leaving Him, call but upon female deities; they call but upon Satan the persistent rebel!

إِن يَدْعُونَ مِن دُونِهِۦٓ إِلَّآ إِنَٰثًا وَإِن يَدْعُونَ
إِلَّا شَيْطَٰنًا مَّرِيدًا ١١٧

118. Allah did curse him, but he said: "I will take of Your servants a portion marked off;

لَّعَنَهُ ٱللَّهُ وَقَالَ لَأَتَّخِذَنَّ مِنْ عِبَادِكَ نَصِيبًا
مَّفْرُوضًا ١١٨

119. I will mislead them, and I will create in them false desires; I will order them to slit the ears of cattle, and to deface the (fair) nature created by Allah." Whoever, forsaking Allah, takes Satan for a friend, has of a surety suffered a loss that is manifest.

وَلَأُضِلَّنَّهُمْ وَلَأُمَنِّيَنَّهُمْ وَلَءَامُرَنَّهُمْ فَلَيُبَتِّكُنَّ
ءَاذَانَ ٱلْأَنْعَٰمِ وَلَءَامُرَنَّهُمْ فَلَيُغَيِّرُنَّ خَلْقَ
ٱللَّهِ ۚ وَمَن يَتَّخِذِ ٱلشَّيْطَٰنَ وَلِيًّا مِّن دُونِ ٱللَّهِ
فَقَدْ خَسِرَ خُسْرَانًا مُّبِينًا ١١٩

120. Satan makes them promises, and creates in them false desires; but Satan's promises are nothing but deception.

يَعِدُهُمْ وَيُمَنِّيهِمْ ۖ وَمَا يَعِدُهُمُ ٱلشَّيْطَٰنُ
إِلَّا غُرُورًا ١٢٠

121. They (his dupes) will have their dwelling in hell, and from it they will find no way of escape.

أُو۟لَٰٓئِكَ مَأْوَىٰهُمْ جَهَنَّمُ وَلَا يَجِدُونَ
عَنْهَا مَحِيصًا ١٢١

122. But those who believe and do deeds of righteousness - We shall soon admit them to gardens, with rivers flowing beneath to dwell in it, for ever. Allah's promise is the truth, and whose word can be truer than Allah's?

وَٱلَّذِينَ ءَامَنُوا۟ وَعَمِلُوا۟ ٱلصَّٰلِحَٰتِ سَنُدْخِلُهُمْ
جَنَّٰتٍ تَجْرِى مِن تَحْتِهَا ٱلْأَنْهَٰرُ خَٰلِدِينَ فِيهَآ
أَبَدًا ۖ وَعْدَ ٱللَّهِ حَقًّا ۚ وَمَنْ أَصْدَقُ مِنَ ٱللَّهِ قِيلًا ١٢٢

123. Not your desires, nor those of the People of the Book (can prevail): whoever works evil, will be requited accordingly. Nor will he find, besides Allah, any protector or helper.

لَّيْسَ بِأَمَانِيِّكُمْ وَلَآ أَمَانِىِّ أَهْلِ ٱلْكِتَٰبِ ۗ
مَن يَعْمَلْ سُوٓءًا يُجْزَ بِهِۦ وَلَا يَجِدْ لَهُۥ مِن
دُونِ ٱللَّهِ وَلِيًّا وَلَا نَصِيرًا ١٢٣

124. If any do deeds of righteousness - be they male or female - and have faith, they will enter heaven, and not the least injustice will be done to them.

وَمَن يَعْمَلْ مِنَ ٱلصَّٰلِحَٰتِ مِن ذَكَرٍ أَوْ
أُنثَىٰ وَهُوَ مُؤْمِنٌ فَأُو۟لَٰٓئِكَ يَدْخُلُونَ ٱلْجَنَّةَ
وَلَا يُظْلَمُونَ نَقِيرًا ﴿١٢٤﴾

125. Who can be better in religion than one who submits his whole self to Allah, does good, and follows the way of Abraham the true in faith? For Allah did take Abraham for a friend.

وَمَنْ أَحْسَنُ دِينًا مِّمَّنْ أَسْلَمَ وَجْهَهُۥ لِلَّهِ وَهُوَ
مُحْسِنٌ وَٱتَّبَعَ مِلَّةَ إِبْرَٰهِيمَ حَنِيفًا ۗ وَٱتَّخَذَ
ٱللَّهُ إِبْرَٰهِيمَ خَلِيلًا ﴿١٢٥﴾

126. But to Allah belong all things in the heavens and on earth; and He it is that encompasses all things.

وَلِلَّهِ مَا فِى ٱلسَّمَٰوَٰتِ وَمَا فِى ٱلْأَرْضِ ۚ وَكَانَ
ٱللَّهُ بِكُلِّ شَىْءٍ مُّحِيطًا ﴿١٢٦﴾

127. They ask your instruction concerning the women. Say: Allah does instruct you about them; and (remember) what has been rehearsed to you in the book, concerning the orphans of women to whom you give not the portions prescribed, and yet whom you desire to marry, as also concerning the children who are weak and oppressed; that you stand firm for justice to orphans. There is not a good deed which you do, but Allah is well-acquainted with it.

وَيَسْتَفْتُونَكَ فِى ٱلنِّسَآءِ ۖ قُلِ ٱللَّهُ يُفْتِيكُمْ
فِيهِنَّ وَمَا يُتْلَىٰ عَلَيْكُمْ فِى ٱلْكِتَٰبِ فِى يَتَٰمَى
ٱلنِّسَآءِ ٱلَّٰتِى لَا تُؤْتُونَهُنَّ مَا كُتِبَ لَهُنَّ
وَتَرْغَبُونَ أَن تَنكِحُوهُنَّ وَٱلْمُسْتَضْعَفِينَ مِنَ
ٱلْوِلْدَٰنِ وَأَن تَقُومُوا۟ لِلْيَتَٰمَىٰ بِٱلْقِسْطِ ۚ وَمَا تَفْعَلُوا۟
مِنْ خَيْرٍ فَإِنَّ ٱللَّهَ كَانَ بِهِۦ عَلِيمًا ﴿١٢٧﴾

128. If a wife fears cruelty or desertion on her husband's part, there is no blame on them if they arrange an amicable settlement between themselves; and such settlement is best; even though men's souls are swayed by greed. But if you do good and practice self-restraint, Allah is well-acquainted with all that you do.

وَإِنِ ٱمْرَأَةٌ خَافَتْ مِنۢ بَعْلِهَا نُشُوزًا أَوْ إِعْرَاضًا
فَلَا جُنَاحَ عَلَيْهِمَآ أَن يُصْلِحَا بَيْنَهُمَا
صُلْحًا ۚ وَٱلصُّلْحُ خَيْرٌ ۗ وَأُحْضِرَتِ ٱلْأَنفُسُ
ٱلشُّحَّ ۚ وَإِن تُحْسِنُوا۟ وَتَتَّقُوا۟ فَإِنَّ ٱللَّهَ كَانَ بِمَا
تَعْمَلُونَ خَبِيرًا ﴿١٢٨﴾

129. You are never able to be fair and just as between women, even if it is your ardent desire; but turn not away (from a woman) altogether, so as to leave her (as it were) hanging (in the air). If you come to a friendly understanding, and practice self-restraint, Allah is Oft-Forgiving, Most Merciful.

وَلَن تَسْتَطِيعُوٓا۟ أَن تَعْدِلُوا۟ بَيْنَ ٱلنِّسَآءِ وَلَوْ حَرَصْتُمْ ۖ
فَلَا تَمِيلُوا۟ كُلَّ ٱلْمَيْلِ فَتَذَرُوهَا كَٱلْمُعَلَّقَةِ ۚ
وَإِن تُصْلِحُوا۟ وَتَتَّقُوا۟ فَإِنَّ ٱللَّهَ كَانَ غَفُورًا
رَّحِيمًا ﴿١٢٩﴾

130. But if they disagree (and must part), Allah will provide abundance for all from His all-reaching bounty: for Allah is He that cares for all and is Wise.

وَإِن يَتَفَرَّقَا يُغْنِ ٱللَّهُ كُلًّا مِّن سَعَتِهِۦ ۚ وَكَانَ
ٱللَّهُ وَٰسِعًا حَكِيمًا ﴿١٣٠﴾

131. To Allah belong all things in the heavens and on earth. Verily We have directed the People of the Book before you, and you (O Muslims) to fear Allah. But if you deny Him, to Allah belong all things in the heavens and on earth, and Allah is free of all wants, worthy of all praise.

وَلِلَّهِ مَا فِى ٱلسَّمَٰوَٰتِ وَمَا فِى ٱلْأَرْضِ ۗ وَلَقَدْ
وَصَّيْنَا ٱلَّذِينَ أُوتُوا۟ ٱلْكِتَٰبَ مِن قَبْلِكُمْ
وَإِيَّاكُمْ أَنِ ٱتَّقُوا۟ ٱللَّهَ ۚ وَإِن تَكْفُرُوا۟ فَإِنَّ لِلَّهِ
مَا فِى ٱلسَّمَٰوَٰتِ وَمَا فِى ٱلْأَرْضِ ۚ وَكَانَ ٱللَّهُ غَنِيًّا
حَمِيدًا ﴿١٣١﴾

132. Yea, to Allah belong all things in the heavens and on earth, and enough is Allah to carry through all affairs.

وَلِلَّهِ مَا فِى ٱلسَّمَٰوَٰتِ وَمَا فِى ٱلْأَرْضِ ۚ وَكَفَىٰ بِٱللَّهِ
وَكِيلًا ﴿١٣٢﴾

133. If it were His Will, He could destroy you, O mankind, and create another race; for He has power to do this.

إِن يَشَأْ يُذْهِبْكُمْ أَيُّهَا ٱلنَّاسُ وَيَأْتِ بِـَٔاخَرِينَ ۚ
وَكَانَ ٱللَّهُ عَلَىٰ ذَٰلِكَ قَدِيرًا ﴿١٣٣﴾

134. If anyone desires a reward in this life, in Allah's (gift) is the reward (both) of this life and of the hereafter; for Allah is He that hears and sees (all things).

مَّن كَانَ يُرِيدُ ثَوَابَ ٱلدُّنْيَا فَعِندَ ٱللَّهِ ثَوَابُ ٱلدُّنْيَا
وَٱلْـَٔاخِرَةِ ۚ وَكَانَ ٱللَّهُ سَمِيعًۢا بَصِيرًا ﴿١٣٤﴾

135. O you who believe! Stand out firmly for justice, as witnesses to Allah, even as against yourselves, or your parents, or

ثلاثة أرباع الحزب ١٠
۞ يَٰٓأَيُّهَا ٱلَّذِينَ ءَامَنُوا۟ كُونُوا۟ قَوَّٰمِينَ بِٱلْقِسْطِ
شُهَدَآءَ لِلَّهِ وَلَوْ عَلَىٰٓ أَنفُسِكُمْ أَوِ ٱلْوَٰلِدَيْنِ

your relatives, and whether it be (against) rich or poor: for Allah can best protect both. Follow not the lusts (of your hearts), lest you swerve, and if you distort (justice), or decline to do justice, verily Allah is well-acquainted with all that you do.

وَٱلْأَقْرَبِينَ ۚ إِن يَكُنْ غَنِيًّا أَوْ فَقِيرًا فَٱللَّهُ أَوْلَىٰ
بِهِمَا ۖ فَلَا تَتَّبِعُوا۟ ٱلْهَوَىٰٓ أَن تَعْدِلُوا۟ ۚ وَإِن تَلْوُۥٓا۟
أَوْ تُعْرِضُوا۟ فَإِنَّ ٱللَّهَ كَانَ بِمَا تَعْمَلُونَ
خَبِيرًا ﴿١٣٥﴾

136. O you who believe! Believe in Allah and His messenger, and the scripture which He has sent to His messenger and the scripture which He sent to those before (him). And who denies Allah, His angels, His Books, His messengers, and the day of judgement, has gone far, far astray.

يَٰٓأَيُّهَا ٱلَّذِينَ ءَامَنُوٓا۟ ءَامِنُوا۟ بِٱللَّهِ وَرَسُولِهِۦ
وَٱلْكِتَٰبِ ٱلَّذِى نَزَّلَ عَلَىٰ رَسُولِهِۦ وَٱلْكِتَٰبِ
ٱلَّذِىٓ أَنزَلَ مِن قَبْلُ ۚ وَمَن يَكْفُرْ بِٱللَّهِ
وَمَلَٰٓئِكَتِهِۦ وَكُتُبِهِۦ وَرُسُلِهِۦ وَٱلْيَوْمِ ٱلْءَاخِرِ فَقَدْ
ضَلَّ ضَلَٰلًۢا بَعِيدًا ﴿١٣٦﴾

137. Those who believe, then reject faith, then believe (again) and (again) reject faith, and go on increasing in unbelief - Allah will not forgive them nor guide them on the way.

إِنَّ ٱلَّذِينَ ءَامَنُوا۟ ثُمَّ كَفَرُوا۟ ثُمَّ ءَامَنُوا۟ ثُمَّ كَفَرُوا۟
ثُمَّ ٱزْدَادُوا۟ كُفْرًا لَّمْ يَكُنِ ٱللَّهُ لِيَغْفِرَ لَهُمْ وَلَا
لِيَهْدِيَهُمْ سَبِيلًۢا ﴿١٣٧﴾

138. To the hypocrites give the glad tidings that there is for them (but) a grievous penalty-

بَشِّرِ ٱلْمُنَٰفِقِينَ بِأَنَّ لَهُمْ عَذَابًا أَلِيمًا ﴿١٣٨﴾

139. Yea, to those who take for friends unbelievers rather than believers; is it honour they seek among them? Nay - all honour is with Allah.

ٱلَّذِينَ يَتَّخِذُونَ ٱلْكَٰفِرِينَ أَوْلِيَآءَ مِن دُونِ
ٱلْمُؤْمِنِينَ ۚ أَيَبْتَغُونَ عِندَهُمُ ٱلْعِزَّةَ فَإِنَّ ٱلْعِزَّةَ
لِلَّهِ جَمِيعًا ﴿١٣٩﴾

140. Already has He sent you word in the book, that when you hear the signs of Allah held in defiance and ridicule, you are not to sit with them unless they turn to a different theme; if you did, you would be like them.

وَقَدْ نَزَّلَ عَلَيْكُمْ فِى ٱلْكِتَٰبِ أَنْ إِذَا سَمِعْتُمْ ءَايَٰتِ
ٱللَّهِ يُكْفَرُ بِهَا وَيُسْتَهْزَأُ بِهَا فَلَا تَقْعُدُوا۟ مَعَهُمْ حَتَّىٰ
يَخُوضُوا۟ فِى حَدِيثٍ غَيْرِهِۦٓ ۚ إِنَّكُمْ إِذًا مِّثْلُهُمْ ۗ إِنَّ ٱللَّهَ

For Allah will collect the hypocrites and those who defy faith - all in hell -

جَامِعُ ٱلْمُنَٰفِقِينَ وَٱلْكَٰفِرِينَ فِي جَهَنَّمَ
جَمِيعًا ﴿١٤٠﴾

141. (These are) the ones who wait and watch about you: if you do gain a victory from Allah, they say: "Were we not with you?" - but if the unbelievers gain a success, they say (to them): "Did we not gain an advantage over you, and did we not guard you from the believers?" But Allah will judge between you on the day of judgement. And never will Allah grant to the unbelievers a way (to triumph) over the believers.

ٱلَّذِينَ يَتَرَبَّصُونَ بِكُمْ فَإِن كَانَ لَكُمْ فَتْحٌ مِّنَ
ٱللَّهِ قَالُوٓاْ أَلَمْ نَكُن مَّعَكُمْ وَإِن كَانَ لِلْكَٰفِرِينَ
نَصِيبٌ قَالُوٓاْ أَلَمْ نَسْتَحْوِذْ عَلَيْكُمْ وَنَمْنَعْكُم مِّنَ
ٱلْمُؤْمِنِينَ ۚ فَٱللَّهُ يَحْكُمُ بَيْنَكُمْ يَوْمَ ٱلْقِيَٰمَةِ ۗ وَلَن
يَجْعَلَ ٱللَّهُ لِلْكَٰفِرِينَ عَلَى ٱلْمُؤْمِنِينَ سَبِيلًا ﴿١٤١﴾

142. The hypocrites - they think they are over-reaching Allah but He will over-reach them; when they stand up to prayer, they stand without earnestness, to be seen of men, but little do they hold Allah in remembrance.

إِنَّ ٱلْمُنَٰفِقِينَ يُخَٰدِعُونَ ٱللَّهَ وَهُوَ خَٰدِعُهُمْ وَإِذَا
قَامُوٓاْ إِلَى ٱلصَّلَوٰةِ قَامُواْ كُسَالَىٰ يُرَآءُونَ ٱلنَّاسَ
وَلَا يَذْكُرُونَ ٱللَّهَ إِلَّا قَلِيلًا ﴿١٤٢﴾

143. (They are) distracted in mind even in the midst of it - being (sincerely) for neither one group nor for another. Whom Allah leaves straying - never will you find for him the way.

مُّذَبْذَبِينَ بَيْنَ ذَٰلِكَ لَآ إِلَىٰ هَٰٓؤُلَآءِ وَلَآ إِلَىٰ هَٰٓؤُلَآءِ ۚ
وَمَن يُضْلِلِ ٱللَّهُ فَلَن تَجِدَ لَهُۥ سَبِيلًا ﴿١٤٣﴾

144. O you who believe! Take not for friends unbelievers rather than believers; do you wish to offer Allah an open proof against yourselves?

يَٰٓأَيُّهَا ٱلَّذِينَ ءَامَنُواْ لَا تَتَّخِذُواْ ٱلْكَٰفِرِينَ أَوْلِيَآءَ
مِن دُونِ ٱلْمُؤْمِنِينَ ۚ أَتُرِيدُونَ أَن تَجْعَلُواْ لِلَّهِ
عَلَيْكُمْ سُلْطَٰنًا مُّبِينًا ﴿١٤٤﴾

145. The hypocrites will be in the lowest depths of the fire; no helper will you find for them -

إِنَّ ٱلْمُنَٰفِقِينَ فِي ٱلدَّرْكِ ٱلْأَسْفَلِ مِنَ ٱلنَّارِ وَلَن
تَجِدَ لَهُمْ نَصِيرًا ﴿١٤٥﴾

146. Except for those who repent, mend (their life), hold fast to Allah, and purify their religion as in Allah's sight; if so they will be (numbered) with the believers. And soon will Allah grant to the believers a reward of immense value.

إِلَّا ٱلَّذِينَ تَابُوا۟ وَأَصْلَحُوا۟ وَٱعْتَصَمُوا۟ بِٱللَّهِ
وَأَخْلَصُوا۟ دِينَهُمْ لِلَّهِ فَأُو۟لَٰٓئِكَ مَعَ ٱلْمُؤْمِنِينَ ۖ
وَسَوْفَ يُؤْتِ ٱللَّهُ ٱلْمُؤْمِنِينَ أَجْرًا عَظِيمًا ﴿١٤٦﴾

147. What can Allah gain by your punishment, if you are grateful and you believe? Nay, it is Allah that recognises (all good), and knows all things.

مَّا يَفْعَلُ ٱللَّهُ بِعَذَابِكُمْ إِن شَكَرْتُمْ
وَءَامَنتُمْ ۚ وَكَانَ ٱللَّهُ شَاكِرًا عَلِيمًا ﴿١٤٧﴾

الجزء ٦ الحزب ١١

✻ **148.** Allah loves not that evil should be noised abroad in public speech, except where injustice has been done; for Allah is He Who hears and knows all things.

✻ لَّا يُحِبُّ ٱللَّهُ ٱلْجَهْرَ بِٱلسُّوٓءِ مِنَ ٱلْقَوْلِ إِلَّا مَن
ظُلِمَ ۚ وَكَانَ ٱللَّهُ سَمِيعًا عَلِيمًا ﴿١٤٨﴾

149. Whether you publish a good deed or conceal it or cover evil with pardon, verily Allah does blot out (sins) and has power (in the judgement of values).

إِن تُبْدُوا۟ خَيْرًا أَوْ تُخْفُوهُ أَوْ تَعْفُوا۟ عَن سُوٓءٍ فَإِنَّ
ٱللَّهَ كَانَ عَفُوًّا قَدِيرًا ﴿١٤٩﴾

150. Those who deny Allah and His messengers, and (those who) wish to separate Allah from His messengers, saying: "We believe in some but reject others"; and (those who) wish to take a course midway -

إِنَّ ٱلَّذِينَ يَكْفُرُونَ بِٱللَّهِ وَرُسُلِهِۦ وَيُرِيدُونَ أَن
يُفَرِّقُوا۟ بَيْنَ ٱللَّهِ وَرُسُلِهِۦ وَيَقُولُونَ نُؤْمِنُ بِبَعْضٍ
وَنَكْفُرُ بِبَعْضٍ وَيُرِيدُونَ أَن يَتَّخِذُوا۟
بَيْنَ ذَٰلِكَ سَبِيلًا ﴿١٥٠﴾

151. They are in truth (equally) unbelievers; and We have prepared for unbelievers a humiliating punishment.

أُو۟لَٰٓئِكَ هُمُ ٱلْكَٰفِرُونَ حَقًّا ۚ وَأَعْتَدْنَا لِلْكَٰفِرِينَ
عَذَابًا مُّهِينًا ﴿١٥١﴾

152. To those who believe in Allah and His messengers and make no distinction between any of the messengers, We shall soon give their (due) rewards: for Allah is Oft-Forgiving, Most Merciful.

وَٱلَّذِينَ ءَامَنُوا۟ بِٱللَّهِ وَرُسُلِهِۦ وَلَمْ يُفَرِّقُوا۟ بَيْنَ
أَحَدٍ مِّنْهُمْ أُو۟لَٰٓئِكَ سَوْفَ يُؤْتِيهِمْ أُجُورَهُمْ ۗ
وَكَانَ ٱللَّهُ غَفُورًا رَّحِيمًا ﴿١٥٢﴾

✻ Part-6

153. The People of the Book ask you to cause a book to descend to them from heaven; indeed they asked Moses for an even greater (miracle), for they said: "Show us Allah in public," but they were dazed for their presumption, by thunder and lightning. Yet they worshipped the calf even after clear signs had come to them; even so We forgave them; and gave Moses manifest proofs of authority.

يَسْـَٔلُكَ أَهْلُ ٱلْكِتَٰبِ أَن تُنَزِّلَ عَلَيْهِمْ كِتَٰبًا مِّنَ
ٱلسَّمَآءِ ۚ فَقَدْ سَأَلُوا۟ مُوسَىٰٓ أَكْبَرَ مِن ذَٰلِكَ
فَقَالُوٓا۟ أَرِنَا ٱللَّهَ جَهْرَةً فَأَخَذَتْهُمُ ٱلصَّٰعِقَةُ بِظُلْمِهِمْ ۚ
ثُمَّ ٱتَّخَذُوا۟ ٱلْعِجْلَ مِنۢ بَعْدِ مَا جَآءَتْهُمُ ٱلْبَيِّنَٰتُ
فَعَفَوْنَا عَن ذَٰلِكَ ۚ وَءَاتَيْنَا مُوسَىٰ سُلْطَٰنًا
مُّبِينًا ﴿١٥٣﴾

154. And for their covenant We raised over them (the towering height) of mount (Sinai); and (on another occasion) We said: "Enter the gate with humility"; and (once again) We commanded them: "Transgress not in the matter of the Sabbath." And We took from them a solemn covenant.

وَرَفَعْنَا فَوْقَهُمُ ٱلطُّورَ بِمِيثَٰقِهِمْ وَقُلْنَا لَهُمُ
ٱدْخُلُوا۟ ٱلْبَابَ سُجَّدًا وَقُلْنَا لَهُمْ لَا تَعْدُوا۟ فِى
ٱلسَّبْتِ وَأَخَذْنَا مِنْهُم مِّيثَٰقًا غَلِيظًا ﴿١٥٤﴾

155. (They have incurred divine displeasure); in that they broke their covenant; that they rejected the signs of Allah; that they slew the messengers in defiance of right; that they said, "Our hearts are the wrappings (which preserve Allah's Word; we need no more)" - nay, Allah has set the seal on their hearts for their blasphemy, and little is it they believe -

فَبِمَا نَقْضِهِم مِّيثَٰقَهُمْ وَكُفْرِهِم بِـَٔايَٰتِ ٱللَّهِ
وَقَتْلِهِمُ ٱلْأَنۢبِيَآءَ بِغَيْرِ حَقٍّ وَقَوْلِهِمْ قُلُوبُنَا غُلْفٌۢ ۚ بَلْ
طَبَعَ ٱللَّهُ عَلَيْهَا بِكُفْرِهِمْ فَلَا يُؤْمِنُونَ إِلَّا قَلِيلًا ﴿١٥٥﴾

156. That they rejected faith: that they uttered against Mary a grave false charge;

وَبِكُفْرِهِمْ وَقَوْلِهِمْ عَلَىٰ مَرْيَمَ بُهْتَٰنًا عَظِيمًا ﴿١٥٦﴾

157. That they said (in boast), "We killed the Messiah Jesus the son of Mary, the messenger of Allah" - but they killed him not, nor crucified him, but so it was made to appear to them, and those who differ in it are full of doubts, with no (certain) knowledge, but only conjecture to follow, for certainly they killed him not -

وَقَوْلِهِمْ إِنَّا قَتَلْنَا ٱلْمَسِيحَ عِيسَى ٱبْنَ مَرْيَمَ رَسُولَ
ٱللَّهِ وَمَا قَتَلُوهُ وَمَا صَلَبُوهُ وَلَٰكِن شُبِّهَ لَهُمْ ۚ
وَإِنَّ ٱلَّذِينَ ٱخْتَلَفُوا۟ فِيهِ لَفِى شَكٍّ مِّنْهُ ۚ مَا لَهُم بِهِۦ
مِنْ عِلْمٍ إِلَّا ٱتِّبَاعَ ٱلظَّنِّ ۚ وَمَا قَتَلُوهُ يَقِينًۢا ﴿١٥٧﴾

158. Nay, Allah raised him up to Himself; and Allah is Exalted in Power, Wise -

بَل رَّفَعَهُ ٱللَّهُ إِلَيۡهِۚ وَكَانَ ٱللَّهُ عَزِيزًا حَكِيمًا ١٥٨

159. And there is none of the People of the Book but must believe in him before his death; and on the day of judgement he will be a witness against them -

وَإِن مِّنۡ أَهۡلِ ٱلۡكِتَٰبِ إِلَّا لَيُؤۡمِنَنَّ بِهِۦ قَبۡلَ
مَوۡتِهِۦۖ وَيَوۡمَ ٱلۡقِيَٰمَةِ يَكُونُ عَلَيۡهِمۡ شَهِيدٗا ١٥٩

160. For the iniquity of the Jews We made unlawful for them certain (foods) good and wholesome which had been lawful for them - in that they hindered many from Allah's way -

فَبِظُلۡمٖ مِّنَ ٱلَّذِينَ هَادُواْ حَرَّمۡنَا عَلَيۡهِمۡ طَيِّبَٰتٍ
أُحِلَّتۡ لَهُمۡ وَبِصَدِّهِمۡ عَن سَبِيلِ ٱللَّهِ كَثِيرٗا ١٦٠

161. That they took usury, though they were forbidden; and that they devoured men's substance wrongfully - We have prepared for those among them who reject faith a grievous punishment.

وَأَخۡذِهِمُ ٱلرِّبَوٰاْ وَقَدۡ نُهُواْ عَنۡهُ وَأَكۡلِهِمۡ أَمۡوَٰلَ
ٱلنَّاسِ بِٱلۡبَٰطِلِۚ وَأَعۡتَدۡنَا لِلۡكَٰفِرِينَ مِنۡهُمۡ عَذَابًا
أَلِيمٗا ١٦١

162. But those among them who are well-grounded in knowledge, and the believers, believe in what has been revealed to you and what was revealed before you; and (especially) those who establish regular prayer and practice regular charity and believe in Allah and in the last day: to them shall We soon give a great reward.

لَّٰكِنِ ٱلرَّٰسِخُونَ فِي ٱلۡعِلۡمِ مِنۡهُمۡ وَٱلۡمُؤۡمِنُونَ يُؤۡمِنُونَ
بِمَآ أُنزِلَ إِلَيۡكَ وَمَآ أُنزِلَ مِن قَبۡلِكَۚ وَٱلۡمُقِيمِينَ
ٱلصَّلَوٰةَۚ وَٱلۡمُؤۡتُونَ ٱلزَّكَوٰةَ وَٱلۡمُؤۡمِنُونَ بِٱللَّهِ
وَٱلۡيَوۡمِ ٱلۡأٓخِرِ أُوْلَٰٓئِكَ سَنُؤۡتِيهِمۡ أَجۡرًا عَظِيمًا ١٦٢

163. We have sent you inspiration, as We sent it to Noah and the messengers after him; We sent inspiration to Abraham, Ishmael, Isaac, Jacob and the Tribes, to Jesus, Job, Jonah, Aaron, and Solomon, and to David We gave the Psalms.

۞إِنَّآ أَوۡحَيۡنَآ إِلَيۡكَ كَمَآ أَوۡحَيۡنَآ إِلَىٰ نُوحٖ وَٱلنَّبِيِّـۧنَ ربع الحزب ١١
مِنۢ بَعۡدِهِۦۚ وَأَوۡحَيۡنَآ إِلَىٰٓ إِبۡرَٰهِيمَ وَإِسۡمَٰعِيلَ
وَإِسۡحَٰقَ وَيَعۡقُوبَ وَٱلۡأَسۡبَاطِ وَعِيسَىٰ
وَأَيُّوبَ وَيُونُسَ وَهَٰرُونَ وَسُلَيۡمَٰنَۚ وَءَاتَيۡنَا
دَاوُۥدَ زَبُورٗا ١٦٣

164. Of some messengers We have already told you the story; of others We have not - and to Moses Allah spoke direct.

وَرُسُلٗا قَدۡ قَصَصۡنَٰهُمۡ عَلَيۡكَ مِن قَبۡلُ وَرُسُلٗا لَّمۡ
نَقۡصُصۡهُمۡ عَلَيۡكَۚ وَكَلَّمَ ٱللَّهُ مُوسَىٰ تَكۡلِيمٗا ١٦٤

165. Messengers who gave good news as well as warning, that mankind, after (the coming) of the messengers, should have no plea against Allah: for Allah is Exalted in Power, Wise.

رُّسُلًا مُّبَشِّرِينَ وَمُنذِرِينَ لِئَلَّا يَكُونَ لِلنَّاسِ
عَلَى ٱللَّهِ حُجَّةُۢ بَعْدَ ٱلرُّسُلِ ۚ وَكَانَ ٱللَّهُ عَزِيزًا
حَكِيمًا ١٦٥

166. But Allah bears witness that what He has sent to you, He has sent from His (own) knowledge, and the angels bear witness; but enough is Allah for a Witness.

لَّٰكِنِ ٱللَّهُ يَشْهَدُ بِمَآ أَنزَلَ إِلَيْكَ ۖ أَنزَلَهُۥ بِعِلْمِهِۦ ۖ
وَٱلْمَلَٰٓئِكَةُ يَشْهَدُونَ ۚ وَكَفَىٰ بِٱللَّهِ شَهِيدًا ١٦٦

167. Those who reject faith and keep off (men) from the way of Allah, have verily strayed far, far away from the path.

إِنَّ ٱلَّذِينَ كَفَرُوا۟ وَصَدُّوا۟ عَن سَبِيلِ ٱللَّهِ قَدْ
ضَلُّوا۟ ضَلَٰلًۢا بَعِيدًا ١٦٧

168. Those who reject faith and do wrong - Allah will not forgive them nor guide them to any way -

إِنَّ ٱلَّذِينَ كَفَرُوا۟ وَظَلَمُوا۟ لَمْ يَكُنِ ٱللَّهُ لِيَغْفِرَ
لَهُمْ وَلَا لِيَهْدِيَهُمْ طَرِيقًا ١٦٨

169. Except the way of hell, to dwell in it for ever. And this to Allah is easy.

إِلَّا طَرِيقَ جَهَنَّمَ خَٰلِدِينَ فِيهَآ أَبَدًا ۚ وَكَانَ
ذَٰلِكَ عَلَى ٱللَّهِ يَسِيرًا ١٦٩

170. O mankind! The messenger has come to you in truth from Allah: believe in him; it is best for you. But if you reject faith, to Allah belong all things in the heavens and on earth: and Allah is All-Knowing, All-Wise.

يَٰٓأَيُّهَا ٱلنَّاسُ قَدْ جَآءَكُمُ ٱلرَّسُولُ بِٱلْحَقِّ مِن رَّبِّكُمْ
فَـَٔامِنُوا۟ خَيْرًا لَّكُمْ ۚ وَإِن تَكْفُرُوا۟ فَإِنَّ لِلَّهِ
مَا فِى ٱلسَّمَٰوَٰتِ وَٱلْأَرْضِ ۚ وَكَانَ ٱللَّهُ عَلِيمًا
حَكِيمًا ١٧٠

171. O People of the Book! Commit no excesses in your religion; nor say of Allah anything but truth. The Messiah Jesus the son of Mary was (no more than) a messenger of Allah, and His word which He bestowed on Mary, and a Spirit proceeding from Him: so believe in Allah and His messengers. Say not "trinity"; desist; it will be better for you: for Allah is

يَٰٓأَهْلَ ٱلْكِتَٰبِ لَا تَغْلُوا۟ فِى دِينِكُمْ وَلَا
تَقُولُوا۟ عَلَى ٱللَّهِ إِلَّا ٱلْحَقَّ ۚ إِنَّمَا ٱلْمَسِيحُ عِيسَى
ٱبْنُ مَرْيَمَ رَسُولُ ٱللَّهِ وَكَلِمَتُهُۥٓ أَلْقَىٰهَآ إِلَىٰ
مَرْيَمَ وَرُوحٌ مِّنْهُ ۖ فَـَٔامِنُوا۟ بِٱللَّهِ وَرُسُلِهِۦ ۖ وَلَا
تَقُولُوا۟ ثَلَٰثَةٌ ۚ ٱنتَهُوا۟ خَيْرًا لَّكُمْ ۚ إِنَّمَا ٱللَّهُ

One God; glory be to Him: (for Exalted is He) above having a son. To Him belong all things in the heavens and on earth. And enough is Allah as a Disposer of affairs.

إِلَٰهٌ وَٰحِدٌ سُبْحَٰنَهُۥٓ أَن يَكُونَ لَهُۥ وَلَدٌ لَّهُۥ مَا فِى
ٱلسَّمَٰوَٰتِ وَمَا فِى ٱلْأَرْضِ وَكَفَىٰ بِٱللَّهِ وَكِيلًا ١٧١

172. The Messiah disdains not to serve and worship Allah, nor do the angels, those nearest (to Allah): those who disdain His worship and are arrogant - He will gather them all together to Himself to (answer).

لَّن يَسْتَنكِفَ ٱلْمَسِيحُ أَن يَكُونَ عَبْدًا لِّلَّهِ وَلَا
ٱلْمَلَٰٓئِكَةُ ٱلْمُقَرَّبُونَ وَمَن يَسْتَنكِفْ عَنْ عِبَادَتِهِۦ
وَيَسْتَكْبِرْ فَسَيَحْشُرُهُمْ إِلَيْهِ جَمِيعًا ١٧٢

173. But those who believe and do deeds of righteousness, He will give their (due) rewards - and more, out of His bounty; but those who are disdainful and arrogant, He will punish with a grievous penalty; nor will they find besides Allah, any to protect or help them.

فَأَمَّا ٱلَّذِينَ ءَامَنُوا۟ وَعَمِلُوا۟ ٱلصَّٰلِحَٰتِ فَيُوَفِّيهِمْ
أُجُورَهُمْ وَيَزِيدُهُم مِّن فَضْلِهِۦ وَأَمَّا ٱلَّذِينَ
ٱسْتَنكَفُوا۟ وَٱسْتَكْبَرُوا۟ فَيُعَذِّبُهُمْ عَذَابًا
أَلِيمًا وَلَا يَجِدُونَ لَهُم مِّن دُونِ ٱللَّهِ وَلِيًّا وَلَا
نَصِيرًا ١٧٣

174. O mankind! Verily there has come to you a convincing proof from your Lord: for We have sent to you a light (that is) manifest.

يَٰٓأَيُّهَا ٱلنَّاسُ قَدْ جَآءَكُم بُرْهَٰنٌ مِّن رَّبِّكُمْ وَأَنزَلْنَآ
إِلَيْكُمْ نُورًا مُّبِينًا ١٧٤

175. Then those who believe in Allah, and hold fast to Him - soon will He admit them to mercy and grace from Himself, and guide them to Himself by a straight way.

فَأَمَّا ٱلَّذِينَ ءَامَنُوا۟ بِٱللَّهِ وَٱعْتَصَمُوا۟ بِهِۦ
فَسَيُدْخِلُهُمْ فِى رَحْمَةٍ مِّنْهُ وَفَضْلٍ وَيَهْدِيهِمْ
إِلَيْهِ صِرَٰطًا مُّسْتَقِيمًا ١٧٥

176. They ask you for a legal decision. Say: Allah directs (thus) about those who leave no descendants or ascendants as heirs. If it is a man that dies, leaving a sister but no child, she shall have half the inheritance; if (such a deceased was) a woman, who left no child, her brother takes her inheritance; if there are two sisters, they shall have two-thirds of the inheritance (between them): if there are brothers and sisters, (they

يَسْتَفْتُونَكَ قُلِ ٱللَّهُ يُفْتِيكُمْ فِى ٱلْكَلَٰلَةِ إِنِ
ٱمْرُؤٌا۟ هَلَكَ لَيْسَ لَهُۥ وَلَدٌ وَلَهُۥٓ أُخْتٌ فَلَهَا نِصْفُ
مَا تَرَكَ وَهُوَ يَرِثُهَآ إِن لَّمْ يَكُن لَّهَا وَلَدٌ فَإِن كَانَتَا
ٱثْنَتَيْنِ فَلَهُمَا ٱلثُّلُثَانِ مِمَّا تَرَكَ وَإِن كَانُوٓا۟
إِخْوَةً رِّجَالًا وَنِسَآءً فَلِلذَّكَرِ مِثْلُ حَظِّ ٱلْأُنثَيَيْنِ

share) the male having twice the share of the female. Thus does Allah make clear to you (His law) lest you err. And Allah has knowledge of all things.

يُبَيِّنُ ٱللَّهُ لَكُمْ أَن تَضِلُّوا۟ ۗ وَٱللَّهُ بِكُلِّ شَىْءٍ
عَلِيمٌۢ ﴿١٧٦﴾

سُورَةُ المَائِدَةِ

Surah 5: **Al-Ma'idah** (The Table Spread)

In the name of Allah,
Most Gracious, Most Merciful.

بِسْمِ ٱللَّهِ ٱلرَّحْمَٰنِ ٱلرَّحِيمِ

1. O you who believe! Fulfil (all) obligations. Lawful to you (for food) are all beasts of cattle with the exceptions named; but animals of the chase are forbidden while you are in the sacred precincts or in pilgrims garb: For Allah does command according to His will and plan.

نصف الحزب ١١ يَٰٓأَيُّهَا ٱلَّذِينَ ءَامَنُوٓا۟ أَوْفُوا۟ بِٱلْعُقُودِ ۚ أُحِلَّتْ لَكُم
بَهِيمَةُ ٱلْأَنْعَٰمِ إِلَّا مَا يُتْلَىٰ عَلَيْكُمْ غَيْرَ مُحِلِّى
ٱلصَّيْدِ وَأَنتُمْ حُرُمٌ ۗ إِنَّ ٱللَّهَ يَحْكُمُ مَا يُرِيدُ ﴿١﴾

2. O you who believe! Violate not the sanctity of the symbols of Allah, nor of the sacred month, nor of the animals brought for sacrifice, nor the garlands that mark out such animals, nor the people resorting to the Sacred House, seeking of the bounty and good pleasure of their Lord. But when you are clear of the sacred precincts and of pilgrim garb, you may hunt and let not the hatred of some people in (once) shutting you out of the Sacred Mosque lead you to transgression (and hostility on your part). Help you one another in righteousness and piety, but help you not one another in sin and rancour; fear Allah; for Allah is strict in punishment.

يَٰٓأَيُّهَا ٱلَّذِينَ ءَامَنُوا۟ لَا تُحِلُّوا۟ شَعَٰٓئِرَ ٱللَّهِ وَلَا
ٱلشَّهْرَ ٱلْحَرَامَ وَلَا ٱلْهَدْىَ وَلَا ٱلْقَلَٰٓئِدَ وَلَآ ءَآمِّينَ
ٱلْبَيْتَ ٱلْحَرَامَ يَبْتَغُونَ فَضْلًا مِّن رَّبِّهِمْ وَرِضْوَٰنًا ۚ
وَإِذَا حَلَلْتُمْ فَٱصْطَادُوا۟ ۚ وَلَا يَجْرِمَنَّكُمْ شَنَـَٔانُ قَوْمٍ أَن
صَدُّوكُمْ عَنِ ٱلْمَسْجِدِ ٱلْحَرَامِ أَن تَعْتَدُوا۟ ۘ وَتَعَاوَنُوا۟
عَلَى ٱلْبِرِّ وَٱلتَّقْوَىٰ ۖ وَلَا تَعَاوَنُوا۟ عَلَى ٱلْإِثْمِ
وَٱلْعُدْوَٰنِ ۚ وَٱتَّقُوا۟ ٱللَّهَ ۖ إِنَّ ٱللَّهَ شَدِيدُ
ٱلْعِقَابِ ﴿٢﴾

3. Forbidden to you (for food) are: dead meat, blood, the flesh of swine, and that on which has been invoked the name of other

حُرِّمَتْ عَلَيْكُمُ ٱلْمَيْتَةُ وَٱلدَّمُ وَلَحْمُ ٱلْخِنزِيرِ وَمَآ أُهِلَّ
لِغَيْرِ ٱللَّهِ بِهِۦ وَٱلْمُنْخَنِقَةُ وَٱلْمَوْقُوذَةُ وَٱلْمُتَرَدِّيَةُ

than Allah; that which has been killed by strangling, or by a violent blow, or by a headlong fall, or by being gored to death; that which has been (partly) eaten by a wild animal; unless you are able to slaughter it (in due form); that which is sacrificed on stone (altars); (forbidden) also is the division (of meat) by raffling with arrows: that is impiety. This day have those who reject faith given up all hope of your religion: yet fear them not but fear Me. This day have I perfected your religion for you, completed My favour upon you, and have chosen for you Islam as your religion. But if any is forced by hunger, with no inclination to transgression, Allah is indeed Oft-Forgiving, Most Merciful.

وَٱلنَّطِيحَةُ وَمَآ أَكَلَ ٱلسَّبُعُ إِلَّا مَا ذَكَّيۡتُمۡ
وَمَا ذُبِحَ عَلَى ٱلنُّصُبِ وَأَن تَسۡتَقۡسِمُواْ بِٱلۡأَزۡلَٰمِۚ ذَٰلِكُمۡ
فِسۡقٌۗ ٱلۡيَوۡمَ يَئِسَ ٱلَّذِينَ كَفَرُواْ مِن دِينِكُمۡ فَلَا
تَخۡشَوۡهُمۡ وَٱخۡشَوۡنِۚ ٱلۡيَوۡمَ أَكۡمَلۡتُ لَكُمۡ دِينَكُمۡ
وَأَتۡمَمۡتُ عَلَيۡكُمۡ نِعۡمَتِي وَرَضِيتُ لَكُمُ ٱلۡإِسۡلَٰمَ
دِينٗاۚ فَمَنِ ٱضۡطُرَّ فِي مَخۡمَصَةٍ غَيۡرَ مُتَجَانِفٖ
لِّإِثۡمٖ فَإِنَّ ٱللَّهَ غَفُورٞ رَّحِيمٞ ٣

4. They ask you what is lawful to them (as food). Say: Lawful to you are (all) things good and pure: and what you have taught your trained hunting animals (to catch) in the manner directed to you by Allah; eat what they catch for you, but pronounce the name of Allah over it; and fear Allah; for Allah is swift in taking account.

يَسۡـَٔلُونَكَ مَاذَآ أُحِلَّ لَهُمۡۖ قُلۡ أُحِلَّ لَكُمُ ٱلطَّيِّبَٰتُ
وَمَا عَلَّمۡتُم مِّنَ ٱلۡجَوَارِحِ مُكَلِّبِينَ تُعَلِّمُونَهُنَّ مِمَّا
عَلَّمَكُمُ ٱللَّهُۖ فَكُلُواْ مِمَّآ أَمۡسَكۡنَ عَلَيۡكُمۡ وَٱذۡكُرُواْ ٱسۡمَ ٱللَّهِ
عَلَيۡهِۖ وَٱتَّقُواْ ٱللَّهَۚ إِنَّ ٱللَّهَ سَرِيعُ ٱلۡحِسَابِ ٤

5. This day are (all) things good and pure made lawful to you. The food of the People of the Book is lawful to you and yours is lawful to them. (Lawful to you in marriage) are (not only) chaste women who are believers, but chaste women among the People of the Book, revealed before your time - when you give them their due dowers, and desire chastity, not lewdness, nor secret intrigues. If anyone rejects faith, fruitless is his work and in the hereafter he will be in the ranks of those who have lost (all spiritual good).

ٱلۡيَوۡمَ أُحِلَّ لَكُمُ ٱلطَّيِّبَٰتُۖ وَطَعَامُ ٱلَّذِينَ أُوتُواْ ٱلۡكِتَٰبَ
حِلّٞ لَّكُمۡ وَطَعَامُكُمۡ حِلّٞ لَّهُمۡۖ وَٱلۡمُحۡصَنَٰتُ مِنَ
ٱلۡمُؤۡمِنَٰتِ وَٱلۡمُحۡصَنَٰتُ مِنَ ٱلَّذِينَ أُوتُواْ ٱلۡكِتَٰبَ
مِن قَبۡلِكُمۡ إِذَآ ءَاتَيۡتُمُوهُنَّ أُجُورَهُنَّ مُحۡصِنِينَ
غَيۡرَ مُسَٰفِحِينَ وَلَا مُتَّخِذِيٓ أَخۡدَانٖۗ وَمَن يَكۡفُرۡ
بِٱلۡإِيمَٰنِ فَقَدۡ حَبِطَ عَمَلُهُۥ وَهُوَ فِي ٱلۡأٓخِرَةِ مِنَ
ٱلۡخَٰسِرِينَ ٥

6. O you who believe! When you prepare for prayer, wash your faces, and your hands (and arms) to the elbows; rub your heads (with water); and (wash) your feet to the ankles. If you are in a state of ceremonial impurity, bathe your whole body. But if you are ill, or on a journey, or one of you comes from offices of nature, or you have been in contact with women, and you find no water, then take for yourselves clean sand or earth, and rub with it your faces and hands. Allah does not wish to place you in a difficulty, but to make you clean, and to complete His favour to you, that you may be grateful.

يَٰٓأَيُّهَا ٱلَّذِينَ ءَامَنُوٓاْ إِذَا قُمْتُمْ إِلَى ٱلصَّلَوٰةِ
فَٱغْسِلُواْ وُجُوهَكُمْ وَأَيْدِيَكُمْ إِلَى ٱلْمَرَافِقِ
وَٱمْسَحُواْ بِرُءُوسِكُمْ وَأَرْجُلَكُمْ إِلَى ٱلْكَعْبَيْنِۚ
وَإِن كُنتُمْ جُنُبًا فَٱطَّهَّرُواْۚ وَإِن كُنتُم مَّرْضَىٰٓ
أَوْ عَلَىٰ سَفَرٍ أَوْ جَآءَ أَحَدٌ مِّنكُم مِّنَ ٱلْغَآئِطِ
أَوْ لَٰمَسْتُمُ ٱلنِّسَآءَ فَلَمْ تَجِدُواْ مَآءً فَتَيَمَّمُواْ صَعِيدًا
طَيِّبًا فَٱمْسَحُواْ بِوُجُوهِكُمْ وَأَيْدِيكُم مِّنْهُۚ
مَا يُرِيدُ ٱللَّهُ لِيَجْعَلَ عَلَيْكُم مِّنْ حَرَجٍ وَلَٰكِن
يُرِيدُ لِيُطَهِّرَكُمْ وَلِيُتِمَّ نِعْمَتَهُۥ عَلَيْكُمْ
لَعَلَّكُمْ تَشْكُرُونَ ﴿٦﴾

7. And call in remembrance the favour of Allah to you, and His covenant, which He ratified with you, when you said: "We hear and we obey"; and fear Allah, for Allah knows well the secrets of your hearts.

وَٱذْكُرُواْ نِعْمَةَ ٱللَّهِ عَلَيْكُمْ وَمِيثَٰقَهُ ٱلَّذِى
وَاثَقَكُم بِهِۦٓ إِذْ قُلْتُمْ سَمِعْنَا وَأَطَعْنَاۖ وَٱتَّقُواْ
ٱللَّهَۚ إِنَّ ٱللَّهَ عَلِيمٌۢ بِذَاتِ ٱلصُّدُورِ ﴿٧﴾

8. O you who believe! Stand out firmly for Allah, as witnesses to fair dealing, and let not the hatred of others to you make you swerve to wrong and depart from justice. Be just: that is next to Piety: and fear Allah. For Allah is well-acquainted with all that you do.

يَٰٓأَيُّهَا ٱلَّذِينَ ءَامَنُواْ كُونُواْ قَوَّٰمِينَ لِلَّهِ شُهَدَآءَ
بِٱلْقِسْطِۖ وَلَا يَجْرِمَنَّكُمْ شَنَـَٔانُ قَوْمٍ عَلَىٰٓ
أَلَّا تَعْدِلُواْۚ ٱعْدِلُواْ هُوَ أَقْرَبُ لِلتَّقْوَىٰۖ وَٱتَّقُواْ
ٱللَّهَۚ إِنَّ ٱللَّهَ خَبِيرٌۢ بِمَا تَعْمَلُونَ ﴿٨﴾

9. To those who believe and do deeds of righteousness has Allah promised forgiveness and a great reward.

وَعَدَ ٱللَّهُ ٱلَّذِينَ ءَامَنُواْ وَعَمِلُواْ ٱلصَّٰلِحَٰتِ
لَهُم مَّغْفِرَةٌ وَأَجْرٌ عَظِيمٌ ﴿٩﴾

10. Those who reject faith and deny our signs will be companions of hellfire.

وَٱلَّذِينَ كَفَرُواْ وَكَذَّبُواْ بِـَٔايَٰتِنَآ أُوْلَٰٓئِكَ
أَصْحَٰبُ ٱلْجَحِيمِ ﴿١٠﴾

11. O you who believe! Call in remembrance the favour of Allah to you when certain men formed the design to stretch out their hands against you, but (Allah) held back their hands from you: so fear Allah. And on Allah let believers put (all) their trust.

يَٰٓأَيُّهَا ٱلَّذِينَ ءَامَنُواْ ٱذۡكُرُواْ نِعۡمَتَ ٱللَّهِ
عَلَيۡكُمۡ إِذۡ هَمَّ قَوۡمٌ أَن يَبۡسُطُوٓاْ إِلَيۡكُمۡ
أَيۡدِيَهُمۡ فَكَفَّ أَيۡدِيَهُمۡ عَنكُمۡۖ وَٱتَّقُواْ ٱللَّهَۚ وَعَلَى
ٱللَّهِ فَلۡيَتَوَكَّلِ ٱلۡمُؤۡمِنُونَ ١١

ثلاثة أرباع الحزب ١١

12. Allah did before take a covenant from the Children of Israel, and We appointed twelve captains among them. And Allah said: "I am with you: if you (but) establish regular prayers, practice regular charity, believe in My messengers, honour and assist them, and loan to Allah a beautiful loan, verily I will wipe out from you your evils, and admit you to gardens with rivers flowing beneath; but if any of you, after this, resists faith, he has truly wandered from the path of rectitude."

۞وَلَقَدۡ أَخَذَ ٱللَّهُ مِيثَٰقَ بَنِيٓ إِسۡرَٰٓءِيلَ وَبَعَثۡنَا
مِنۡهُمُ ٱثۡنَيۡ عَشَرَ نَقِيبٗاۖ وَقَالَ ٱللَّهُ إِنِّي
مَعَكُمۡۖ لَئِنۡ أَقَمۡتُمُ ٱلصَّلَوٰةَ وَءَاتَيۡتُمُ
ٱلزَّكَوٰةَ وَءَامَنتُم بِرُسُلِي وَعَزَّرۡتُمُوهُمۡ
وَأَقۡرَضۡتُمُ ٱللَّهَ قَرۡضًا حَسَنٗا لَّأُكَفِّرَنَّ
عَنكُمۡ سَيِّـَٔاتِكُمۡ وَلَأُدۡخِلَنَّكُمۡ جَنَّٰتٖ تَجۡرِي
مِن تَحۡتِهَا ٱلۡأَنۡهَٰرُۚ فَمَن كَفَرَ بَعۡدَ ذَٰلِكَ
مِنكُمۡ فَقَدۡ ضَلَّ سَوَآءَ ٱلسَّبِيلِ ١٢

13. But because of their breach of their covenant, We cursed them, and made their hearts grow hard: they change the words from their (right) places and forget a good part of the message that was sent them, nor will you cease to find them - barring a few - ever bent on (new) deceits: but forgive them and overlook (their misdeeds): for Allah loves those who are kind.

فَبِمَا نَقۡضِهِم مِّيثَٰقَهُمۡ لَعَنَّٰهُمۡ وَجَعَلۡنَا
قُلُوبَهُمۡ قَٰسِيَةٗۖ يُحَرِّفُونَ ٱلۡكَلِمَ عَن
مَّوَاضِعِهِۦ وَنَسُواْ حَظّٗا مِّمَّا ذُكِّرُواْ بِهِۦۚ
وَلَا تَزَالُ تَطَّلِعُ عَلَىٰ خَآئِنَةٖ مِّنۡهُمۡ إِلَّا قَلِيلٗا
مِّنۡهُمۡۖ فَٱعۡفُ عَنۡهُمۡ وَٱصۡفَحۡۚ إِنَّ ٱللَّهَ يُحِبُّ
ٱلۡمُحۡسِنِينَ ١٣

14. From those, too, who call themselves Christians, We did take a covenant, but they forgot a good part of the message that was sent them: so We estranged them, with enmity and hatred between the one and the other, to the day of judgement. And soon will Allah show them what it is they have done.

وَمِنَ ٱلَّذِينَ قَالُوٓاْ إِنَّا نَصَٰرَىٰٓ أَخَذۡنَا مِيثَٰقَهُمۡ
فَنَسُواْ حَظّٗا مِّمَّا ذُكِّرُواْ بِهِۦ فَأَغۡرَيۡنَا
بَيۡنَهُمُ ٱلۡعَدَاوَةَ وَٱلۡبَغۡضَآءَ إِلَىٰ يَوۡمِ
ٱلۡقِيَٰمَةِۚ وَسَوۡفَ يُنَبِّئُهُمُ ٱللَّهُ بِمَا كَانُواْ
يَصۡنَعُونَ ١٤

15. O People of the Book! There has come to you Our messenger, revealing to you much that you used to hide in the Book, and passing over much (that is now unnecessary): There has come to you from Allah a (new) light and a perspicuous book -

يَٰٓأَهۡلَ ٱلۡكِتَٰبِ قَدۡ جَآءَكُمۡ رَسُولُنَا
يُبَيِّنُ لَكُمۡ كَثِيرٗا مِّمَّا كُنتُمۡ تُخۡفُونَ
مِنَ ٱلۡكِتَٰبِ وَيَعۡفُواْ عَن كَثِيرٖۚ قَدۡ جَآءَكُم
مِّنَ ٱللَّهِ نُورٞ وَكِتَٰبٞ مُّبِينٞ ١٥

16. With which Allah guides all who seek His good pleasure to ways of peace and safety, and leads them out of darkness, by His Will, to the light - guides them to a path that is straight.

يَهۡدِي بِهِ ٱللَّهُ مَنِ ٱتَّبَعَ رِضۡوَٰنَهُۥ سُبُلَ
ٱلسَّلَٰمِ وَيُخۡرِجُهُم مِّنَ ٱلظُّلُمَٰتِ إِلَى ٱلنُّورِ
بِإِذۡنِهِۦ وَيَهۡدِيهِمۡ إِلَىٰ صِرَٰطٖ مُّسۡتَقِيمٖ ١٦

17. In blasphemy indeed are those that say that Allah is the Messiah the son of Mary. Say: "Who then has the least power against Allah, if His Will were to destroy the Messiah the son of Mary, his mother, and all - everyone that is on the earth? For to Allah belongs the dominion of the heavens and the earth, and all that is between. He creates what He pleases. For Allah has power over all things."

لَّقَدۡ كَفَرَ ٱلَّذِينَ قَالُوٓاْ إِنَّ ٱللَّهَ هُوَ ٱلۡمَسِيحُ
ٱبۡنُ مَرۡيَمَۚ قُلۡ فَمَن يَمۡلِكُ مِنَ ٱللَّهِ شَيۡـًٔا
إِنۡ أَرَادَ أَن يُهۡلِكَ ٱلۡمَسِيحَ ٱبۡنَ مَرۡيَمَ
وَأُمَّهُۥ وَمَن فِي ٱلۡأَرۡضِ جَمِيعٗاۗ وَلِلَّهِ
مُلۡكُ ٱلسَّمَٰوَٰتِ وَٱلۡأَرۡضِ وَمَا بَيۡنَهُمَاۚ يَخۡلُقُ
مَا يَشَآءُۚ وَٱللَّهُ عَلَىٰ كُلِّ شَيۡءٖ قَدِيرٞ ١٧

18. (Both) the Jews and the Christians say: "We are sons of Allah, and His beloved." Say: "Why then does He punish you for your sins? Nay, you are but men, - of the men He has created; He forgives whom He pleases. And He punishes whom He pleases; and to Allah belongs the dominion of the heavens and the earth and all that is between: and to Him is the final goal (of all)."

وَقَالَتِ ٱلۡيَهُودُ وَٱلنَّصَٰرَىٰ نَحۡنُ أَبۡنَٰٓؤُاْ ٱللَّهِ
وَأَحِبَّٰٓؤُهُۥۚ قُلۡ فَلِمَ يُعَذِّبُكُم بِذُنُوبِكُمۖ بَلۡ أَنتُم
بَشَرٞ مِّمَّنۡ خَلَقَۚ يَغۡفِرُ لِمَن يَشَآءُ وَيُعَذِّبُ مَن
يَشَآءُۚ وَلِلَّهِ مُلۡكُ ٱلسَّمَٰوَٰتِ وَٱلۡأَرۡضِ وَمَا
بَيۡنَهُمَاۖ وَإِلَيۡهِ ٱلۡمَصِيرُ ١٨

19. O People of the Book! Now has come to you, making (things) clear to you, Our messenger, after the break in (the series of) Our messengers, lest you should say: "There came to us no bringer of glad tidings and no warner (from evil)"; but now has come to you

يَٰٓأَهۡلَ ٱلۡكِتَٰبِ قَدۡ جَآءَكُمۡ رَسُولُنَا يُبَيِّنُ لَكُمۡ
عَلَىٰ فَتۡرَةٖ مِّنَ ٱلرُّسُلِ أَن تَقُولُواْ مَا جَآءَنَا مِنۢ
بَشِيرٖ وَلَا نَذِيرٖۖ فَقَدۡ جَآءَكُم بَشِيرٞ وَنَذِيرٞۗ وَٱللَّهُ

عَلَىٰ كُلِّ شَيْءٍ قَدِيرٌ ١٩

a bringer of glad tidings and a warner (from evil). And Allah has power over all things.

وَإِذْ قَالَ مُوسَىٰ لِقَوْمِهِۦ يَٰقَوْمِ ٱذْكُرُوا۟ نِعْمَةَ
ٱللَّهِ عَلَيْكُمْ إِذْ جَعَلَ فِيكُمْ أَنۢبِيَآءَ وَجَعَلَكُم
مُّلُوكًا وَءَاتَىٰكُم مَّا لَمْ يُؤْتِ أَحَدًا مِّنَ ٱلْعَٰلَمِينَ ٢٠

20. Remember Moses said to his people: "O my People! Call in remembrance the favour of Allah to you, when He produced prophets among you, made you kings, and gave you what He had not given to any other among the peoples.

يَٰقَوْمِ ٱدْخُلُوا۟ ٱلْأَرْضَ ٱلْمُقَدَّسَةَ ٱلَّتِى كَتَبَ
ٱللَّهُ لَكُمْ وَلَا تَرْتَدُّوا۟ عَلَىٰٓ أَدْبَارِكُمْ فَتَنقَلِبُوا۟
خَٰسِرِينَ ٢١

21. "O my people! Enter the holy land which Allah has assigned to you, and turn not back ignominiously, for then will you be overthrown to your own ruin."

قَالُوا۟ يَٰمُوسَىٰٓ إِنَّ فِيهَا قَوْمًا جَبَّارِينَ وَإِنَّا لَن
نَّدْخُلَهَا حَتَّىٰ يَخْرُجُوا۟ مِنْهَا فَإِن يَخْرُجُوا۟ مِنْهَا فَإِنَّا
دَٰخِلُونَ ٢٢

22. They said: "O Moses! In this land are a people of exceeding strength; never shall we enter it until they leave it; if (once) they leave, then shall we enter."

قَالَ رَجُلَانِ مِنَ ٱلَّذِينَ يَخَافُونَ أَنْعَمَ ٱللَّهُ عَلَيْهِمَا
ٱدْخُلُوا۟ عَلَيْهِمُ ٱلْبَابَ فَإِذَا دَخَلْتُمُوهُ فَإِنَّكُمْ غَٰلِبُونَ ۚ
وَعَلَى ٱللَّهِ فَتَوَكَّلُوٓا۟ إِن كُنتُم مُّؤْمِنِينَ ٢٣

23. (But) among (their) God-fearing men were two on whom Allah had bestowed His grace; they said: "Assault them at the (proper) gate; when once you are in, victory will be yours; but on Allah put your trust if you have faith."

قَالُوا۟ يَٰمُوسَىٰٓ إِنَّا لَن نَّدْخُلَهَآ أَبَدًا مَّا دَامُوا۟ فِيهَا
فَٱذْهَبْ أَنتَ وَرَبُّكَ فَقَٰتِلَآ إِنَّا هَٰهُنَا
قَٰعِدُونَ ٢٤

24. They said: "O Moses! While they remain there, never shall We be able to enter, to the end of time. Go you, and your Lord, and fight you two, while we sit here (and watch)."

قَالَ رَبِّ إِنِّى لَآ أَمْلِكُ إِلَّا نَفْسِى وَأَخِى ۖ فَٱفْرُقْ
بَيْنَنَا وَبَيْنَ ٱلْقَوْمِ ٱلْفَٰسِقِينَ ٢٥

25. He said: "O my Lord! I have power only over myself and my brother; so separate us from this rebellious people!"

26. Allah said: "Therefore, will the land be out of their reach for forty years; in distraction will they wander through the land; but sorrow you not over these rebellious people.

قَالَ فَإِنَّهَا مُحَرَّمَةٌ عَلَيْهِمْ ۛ أَرْبَعِينَ سَنَةً ۛ
يَتِيهُونَ فِى ٱلْأَرْضِ ۚ فَلَا تَأْسَ عَلَى ٱلْقَوْمِ
ٱلْفَٰسِقِينَ ﴿٢٦﴾

27. Recite to them the truth of the story of the two sons of Adam. See! They each presented a sacrifice (to Allah): it was accepted from one, but not from the other. Said the latter: "Be sure I will slay you." "Surely," said the former, "Allah does accept of the sacrifice of those who are righteous.

۞ وَٱتْلُ عَلَيْهِمْ نَبَأَ ٱبْنَىْ ءَادَمَ بِٱلْحَقِّ إِذْ قَرَّبَا قُرْبَانًا الحزب ١٢
فَتُقُبِّلَ مِنْ أَحَدِهِمَا وَلَمْ يُتَقَبَّلْ مِنَ ٱلْءَاخَرِ
قَالَ لَأَقْتُلَنَّكَ ۖ قَالَ إِنَّمَا يَتَقَبَّلُ ٱللَّهُ مِنَ
ٱلْمُتَّقِينَ ﴿٢٧﴾

28. "If you do stretch your hand against me, to slay me, it is not for me to stretch my hand against you to slay you: for I do fear Allah, the Cherisher of the Worlds.

لَئِنۢ بَسَطتَ إِلَىَّ يَدَكَ لِتَقْتُلَنِى مَآ أَنَا۠ بِبَاسِطٍ يَدِىَ
إِلَيْكَ لِأَقْتُلَكَ ۖ إِنِّىٓ أَخَافُ ٱللَّهَ رَبَّ ٱلْعَٰلَمِينَ ﴿٢٨﴾

29. "For me, I intend to let you draw on yourself my sin as well as yours, for you will be among the companions of the fire, and that is the reward of those who do wrong."

إِنِّىٓ أُرِيدُ أَن تَبُوٓأَ بِإِثْمِى وَإِثْمِكَ فَتَكُونَ مِنْ
أَصْحَٰبِ ٱلنَّارِ ۚ وَذَٰلِكَ جَزَٰٓؤُا۟ ٱلظَّٰلِمِينَ ﴿٢٩﴾

30. The (selfish) soul of the other led him to the murder of his brother: he murdered him and became (himself) one of the lost ones.

فَطَوَّعَتْ لَهُۥ نَفْسُهُۥ قَتْلَ أَخِيهِ فَقَتَلَهُۥ
فَأَصْبَحَ مِنَ ٱلْخَٰسِرِينَ ﴿٣٠﴾

31. Then Allah sent a raven, who scratched the ground to show him how to hide the shame of his brother. "Woe is me!" said he; "Was I not even able to be as this raven, and to hide the shame of my brother?" Then he became full of regrets -

فَبَعَثَ ٱللَّهُ غُرَابًا يَبْحَثُ فِى ٱلْأَرْضِ لِيُرِيَهُۥ
كَيْفَ يُوَٰرِى سَوْءَةَ أَخِيهِ ۚ قَالَ يَٰوَيْلَتَىٰٓ
أَعَجَزْتُ أَنْ أَكُونَ مِثْلَ هَٰذَا ٱلْغُرَابِ فَأُوَٰرِىَ
سَوْءَةَ أَخِى ۖ فَأَصْبَحَ مِنَ ٱلنَّٰدِمِينَ ﴿٣١﴾

32. On that account: We ordained for the Children of Israel that if anyone slew a person - unless it be for murder or for spreading

مِنْ أَجْلِ ذَٰلِكَ كَتَبْنَا عَلَىٰ بَنِىٓ إِسْرَٰٓءِيلَ أَنَّهُۥ
مَن قَتَلَ نَفْسًۢا بِغَيْرِ نَفْسٍ أَوْ فَسَادٍ فِى ٱلْأَرْضِ

mischief in the land - it would be as if he slew the whole people; and if anyone saved a life, it would be as if he saved the life of the whole people. Then although there came to them Our messengers with clear signs, yet, even after that, many of them continued to commit excesses in the land.

فَكَأَنَّمَا قَتَلَ ٱلنَّاسَ جَمِيعًا وَمَنْ أَحْيَاهَا
فَكَأَنَّمَآ أَحْيَا ٱلنَّاسَ جَمِيعًاۚ وَلَقَدْ جَآءَتْهُمْ
رُسُلُنَا بِٱلْبَيِّنَٰتِ ثُمَّ إِنَّ كَثِيرًا مِّنْهُم بَعْدَ
ذَٰلِكَ فِى ٱلْأَرْضِ لَمُسْرِفُونَ ٣٢

33. The punishment of those who wage war against Allah and His messenger, and strive with might and main for mischief through the land is: execution, or crucifixion, or the cutting off of hands and feet from opposite sides, or exile from the land: that is their disgrace in this world, and a heavy punishment is theirs in the hereafter;

إِنَّمَا جَزَٰٓؤُا۟ ٱلَّذِينَ يُحَارِبُونَ ٱللَّهَ وَرَسُولَهُۥ
وَيَسْعَوْنَ فِى ٱلْأَرْضِ فَسَادًا أَن يُقَتَّلُوٓا۟
أَوْ يُصَلَّبُوٓا۟ أَوْ تُقَطَّعَ أَيْدِيهِمْ وَأَرْجُلُهُم مِّنْ
خِلَٰفٍ أَوْ يُنفَوْا۟ مِنَ ٱلْأَرْضِۚ ذَٰلِكَ لَهُمْ خِزْىٌ
فِى ٱلدُّنْيَاۖ وَلَهُمْ فِى ٱلْءَاخِرَةِ عَذَابٌ عَظِيمٌ ٣٣

34. Except for those who repent before they fall into your power: in that case, know that Allah is Oft-Forgiving, Most Merciful.

إِلَّا ٱلَّذِينَ تَابُوا۟ مِن قَبْلِ أَن تَقْدِرُوا۟ عَلَيْهِمْۖ
فَٱعْلَمُوٓا۟ أَنَّ ٱللَّهَ غَفُورٌ رَّحِيمٌ ٣٤

35. O you who believe! Do your duty to Allah, seek the means of approach to Him, and strive (with might and main) in His cause; that you may prosper.

يَٰٓأَيُّهَا ٱلَّذِينَ ءَامَنُوا۟ ٱتَّقُوا۟ ٱللَّهَ وَٱبْتَغُوٓا۟ إِلَيْهِ
ٱلْوَسِيلَةَ وَجَٰهِدُوا۟ فِى سَبِيلِهِۦ لَعَلَّكُمْ
تُفْلِحُونَ ٣٥

36. As to those who reject faith - if they had everything on earth, and twice repeated, to give as ransom for the penalty of the day of judgement, it would never be accepted of them. Theirs will be a grievous penalty.

إِنَّ ٱلَّذِينَ كَفَرُوا۟ لَوْ أَنَّ لَهُم مَّا فِى ٱلْأَرْضِ جَمِيعًا
وَمِثْلَهُۥ مَعَهُۥ لِيَفْتَدُوا۟ بِهِۦ مِنْ عَذَابِ يَوْمِ
ٱلْقِيَٰمَةِ مَا تُقُبِّلَ مِنْهُمْۖ وَلَهُمْ عَذَابٌ أَلِيمٌ ٣٦

37. Their wish will be to get out of the fire, but never will they get out from it: their penalty will be one that endures.

يُرِيدُونَ أَن يَخْرُجُوا۟ مِنَ ٱلنَّارِ وَمَا هُم
بِخَٰرِجِينَ مِنْهَاۖ وَلَهُمْ عَذَابٌ مُّقِيمٌ ٣٧

38. As to the thief, male or female, cut off his or her hands; a punishment by way of example, from Allah, for their crime; and Allah is Exalted in Power, full of wisdom.

وَٱلسَّارِقُ وَٱلسَّارِقَةُ فَٱقْطَعُوٓا۟ أَيْدِيَهُمَا جَزَآءًۢ
بِمَا كَسَبَا نَكَـٰلًا مِّنَ ٱللَّهِ ۗ وَٱللَّهُ عَزِيزٌ
حَكِيمٌ ﴿٣٨﴾

39. But if the thief repents after his crime, and amends his conduct, Allah turns to him in forgiveness; for Allah is Oft-Forgiving, Most Merciful.

فَمَن تَابَ مِنۢ بَعْدِ ظُلْمِهِۦ وَأَصْلَحَ فَإِنَّ ٱللَّهَ
يَتُوبُ عَلَيْهِ ۗ إِنَّ ٱللَّهَ غَفُورٌ رَّحِيمٌ ﴿٣٩﴾

40. Do you not know that to Allah (alone) belongs the dominion of the heavens and the earth? He punishes whom He pleases, and He forgives whom He pleases: and Allah has power over all things.

أَلَمْ تَعْلَمْ أَنَّ ٱللَّهَ لَهُۥ مُلْكُ ٱلسَّمَـٰوَٰتِ وَٱلْأَرْضِ
يُعَذِّبُ مَن يَشَآءُ وَيَغْفِرُ لِمَن يَشَآءُ ۗ وَٱللَّهُ عَلَىٰ
كُلِّ شَىْءٍ قَدِيرٌ ﴿٤٠﴾

41. O messenger! Let not those grieve you, who race each other into unbelief: (whether it be) among those who say "We believe" with their lips but whose hearts have no faith, or it be among the Jews; men who will listen to any lie, will listen even to others who have never so much as come to you. They change the words from their (right) times and places; they say, "If you are given this, take it, but if not, beware!" If anyone's trial is intended by Allah, you have no authority in the least for him against Allah. For such - it is not Allah's Will to purify their hearts. For them there is disgrace in this world, and in the hereafter a heavy punishment.

۞ يَـٰٓأَيُّهَا ٱلرَّسُولُ لَا يَحْزُنكَ ٱلَّذِينَ يُسَـٰرِعُونَ (ربع الحزب ١٢)
فِى ٱلْكُفْرِ مِنَ ٱلَّذِينَ قَالُوٓا۟ ءَامَنَّا بِأَفْوَٰهِهِمْ
وَلَمْ تُؤْمِن قُلُوبُهُمْ ۛ وَمِنَ ٱلَّذِينَ هَادُوا۟ ۛ سَمَّـٰعُونَ
لِلْكَذِبِ سَمَّـٰعُونَ لِقَوْمٍ ءَاخَرِينَ لَمْ يَأْتُوكَ ۖ
يُحَرِّفُونَ ٱلْكَلِمَ مِنۢ بَعْدِ مَوَاضِعِهِۦ ۖ يَقُولُونَ
إِنْ أُوتِيتُمْ هَـٰذَا فَخُذُوهُ وَإِن لَّمْ تُؤْتَوْهُ
فَٱحْذَرُوا۟ ۚ وَمَن يُرِدِ ٱللَّهُ فِتْنَتَهُۥ فَلَن تَمْلِكَ لَهُۥ
مِنَ ٱللَّهِ شَيْـًٔا ۚ أُو۟لَـٰٓئِكَ ٱلَّذِينَ لَمْ يُرِدِ ٱللَّهُ أَن
يُطَهِّرَ قُلُوبَهُمْ ۚ لَهُمْ فِى ٱلدُّنْيَا خِزْىٌ ۖ وَلَهُمْ فِى
ٱلْـَٔاخِرَةِ عَذَابٌ عَظِيمٌ ﴿٤١﴾

42. (They are fond of) listening to falsehood, of devouring anything forbidden. If they do come to you, either judge between them, or decline to interfere. If you decline, they cannot hurt

سَمَّـٰعُونَ لِلْكَذِبِ أَكَّـٰلُونَ لِلسُّحْتِ ۚ
فَإِن جَآءُوكَ فَٱحْكُم بَيْنَهُمْ أَوْ أَعْرِضْ
عَنْهُمْ ۖ وَإِن تُعْرِضْ عَنْهُمْ فَلَن يَضُرُّوكَ شَيْـًٔا ۖ

وَإِنْ حَكَمْتَ فَاحْكُم بَيْنَهُم بِالْقِسْطِ ۚ
إِنَّ اللَّهَ يُحِبُّ الْمُقْسِطِينَ ﴿٤٢﴾

you in the least. If you judge, judge in equity between them. For Allah loves those who judge in equity.

وَكَيْفَ يُحَكِّمُونَكَ وَعِندَهُمُ التَّوْرَاةُ
فِيهَا حُكْمُ اللَّهِ ثُمَّ يَتَوَلَّوْنَ مِن بَعْدِ ذَٰلِكَ ۚ وَمَا
أُولَٰئِكَ بِالْمُؤْمِنِينَ ﴿٤٣﴾

43. But why do they come to you for decision, when they have (their own) law before them? - In it is the (plain) command of Allah; yet even after that, they would turn away. For they are not (really) people of faith.

إِنَّا أَنزَلْنَا التَّوْرَاةَ فِيهَا هُدًى وَنُورٌ ۚ يَحْكُمُ
بِهَا النَّبِيُّونَ الَّذِينَ أَسْلَمُوا لِلَّذِينَ هَادُوا
وَالرَّبَّانِيُّونَ وَالْأَحْبَارُ بِمَا اسْتُحْفِظُوا مِن
كِتَابِ اللَّهِ وَكَانُوا عَلَيْهِ شُهَدَاءَ ۚ فَلَا
تَخْشَوُا النَّاسَ وَاخْشَوْنِ وَلَا تَشْتَرُوا بِآيَاتِي
ثَمَنًا قَلِيلًا ۚ وَمَن لَّمْ يَحْكُم بِمَا أَنزَلَ اللَّهُ
فَأُولَٰئِكَ هُمُ الْكَافِرُونَ ﴿٤٤﴾

44. It was We who revealed the law (to Moses): in it was guidance and light. By its standard have been judged the Jews, by the prophets who bowed (as in Islam) to Allah's will, by the rabbis and the doctors of law; for to them was entrusted the protection of Allah's Book, and they were witnesses to it; therefore fear not men, but fear Me, and sell not My signs for a miserable price. If any do fail to judge by (the light of) what Allah has revealed, they are (no better than) unbelievers.

وَكَتَبْنَا عَلَيْهِمْ فِيهَا أَنَّ النَّفْسَ بِالنَّفْسِ
وَالْعَيْنَ بِالْعَيْنِ وَالْأَنفَ بِالْأَنفِ وَالْأُذُنَ بِالْأُذُنِ
وَالسِّنَّ بِالسِّنِّ وَالْجُرُوحَ قِصَاصٌ ۚ فَمَن
تَصَدَّقَ بِهِ فَهُوَ كَفَّارَةٌ لَّهُ ۚ وَمَن لَّمْ يَحْكُم
بِمَا أَنزَلَ اللَّهُ فَأُولَٰئِكَ هُمُ الظَّالِمُونَ ﴿٤٥﴾

45. We ordained in it for them: "Life for life, eye for eye, nose for nose, ear for ear, tooth for tooth, and wounds equal for equal." But if anyone remits the retaliation by way of charity, it is an act of atonement for himself. And if any fail to judge by what Allah has revealed, they are (no better than) wrongdoers.

وَقَفَّيْنَا عَلَىٰ آثَارِهِم بِعِيسَى ابْنِ مَرْيَمَ مُصَدِّقًا
لِّمَا بَيْنَ يَدَيْهِ مِنَ التَّوْرَاةِ ۖ وَآتَيْنَاهُ الْإِنجِيلَ فِيهِ
هُدًى وَنُورٌ وَمُصَدِّقًا لِّمَا بَيْنَ يَدَيْهِ مِنَ التَّوْرَاةِ
وَهُدًى وَمَوْعِظَةً لِّلْمُتَّقِينَ ﴿٤٦﴾

46. And in their footsteps We sent Jesus the son of Mary, confirming the law that had come before him; We sent him the Gospel; in it was guidance and light, and confirmation of the law that had come before him: a guidance and an admonition to those who fear Allah.

47. Let the People of the Gospel judge by what Allah has revealed in it. If any do fail to judge by (the light of) what Allah has revealed, they are (no better than) those who rebel.

وَلْيَحْكُمْ أَهْلُ ٱلْإِنجِيلِ بِمَآ أَنزَلَ ٱللَّهُ فِيهِ ۚ وَمَن
لَّمْ يَحْكُم بِمَآ أَنزَلَ ٱللَّهُ فَأُو۟لَٰٓئِكَ هُمُ
ٱلْفَٰسِقُونَ ﴿٤٧﴾

48. To you We sent the Scripture in truth, confirming the scripture that came before it, and guarding it in safety: so judge between them by what Allah has revealed, and follow not their vain desires, diverging from the truth that has come to you. To each among you have We prescribed a law and an open way. If Allah had so willed, He would have made you a single People, but (His plan is) to test you in what He has given you; so strive as in a race in all virtues. The goal of you all is to Allah; it is He that will show you the truth of the matters in which you dispute;

وَأَنزَلْنَآ إِلَيْكَ ٱلْكِتَٰبَ بِٱلْحَقِّ مُصَدِّقًا لِّمَا بَيْنَ
يَدَيْهِ مِنَ ٱلْكِتَٰبِ وَمُهَيْمِنًا عَلَيْهِ ۖ فَٱحْكُم
بَيْنَهُم بِمَآ أَنزَلَ ٱللَّهُ ۖ وَلَا تَتَّبِعْ أَهْوَآءَهُمْ عَمَّا جَآءَكَ
مِنَ ٱلْحَقِّ ۚ لِكُلٍّ جَعَلْنَا مِنكُمْ شِرْعَةً وَمِنْهَاجًا ۚ
وَلَوْ شَآءَ ٱللَّهُ لَجَعَلَكُمْ أُمَّةً وَٰحِدَةً وَلَٰكِن
لِّيَبْلُوَكُمْ فِى مَآ ءَاتَىٰكُمْ ۖ فَٱسْتَبِقُوا۟ ٱلْخَيْرَٰتِ ۚ
إِلَى ٱللَّهِ مَرْجِعُكُمْ جَمِيعًا فَيُنَبِّئُكُم بِمَا كُنتُمْ
فِيهِ تَخْتَلِفُونَ ﴿٤٨﴾

49. And this (He commands): judge you between them by what Allah has revealed, and follow not their vain desires, but beware of them lest they deceive you from any of that (teaching) which Allah has sent down to you. And if they turn away, be assured that for some of their crimes it is Allah's purpose to punish them. And truly most men are rebellious.

وَأَنِ ٱحْكُم بَيْنَهُم بِمَآ أَنزَلَ ٱللَّهُ وَلَا تَتَّبِعْ
أَهْوَآءَهُمْ وَٱحْذَرْهُمْ أَن يَفْتِنُوكَ عَنۢ بَعْضِ مَآ أَنزَلَ
ٱللَّهُ إِلَيْكَ ۖ فَإِن تَوَلَّوْا۟ فَٱعْلَمْ أَنَّمَا يُرِيدُ ٱللَّهُ أَن يُصِيبَهُم
بِبَعْضِ ذُنُوبِهِمْ ۗ وَإِنَّ كَثِيرًا مِّنَ ٱلنَّاسِ لَفَٰسِقُونَ ﴿٤٩﴾

50. Do they then seek after a judgement of (the Days of) Ignorance? But who, for a people whose faith is assured, can give better judgement than Allah?

أَفَحُكْمَ ٱلْجَٰهِلِيَّةِ يَبْغُونَ ۚ وَمَنْ أَحْسَنُ مِنَ ٱللَّهِ
حُكْمًا لِّقَوْمٍ يُوقِنُونَ ﴿٥٠﴾

51. O you who believe! Take not the Jews and the Christians for your friends and protectors: they are but friends and protectors to each other. And he amongst you

نصف الحزب ١٢ ۞ يَٰٓأَيُّهَا ٱلَّذِينَ ءَامَنُوا۟ لَا تَتَّخِذُوا۟ ٱلْيَهُودَ وَٱلنَّصَٰرَىٰٓ
أَوْلِيَآءَ ۘ بَعْضُهُمْ أَوْلِيَآءُ بَعْضٍ ۚ وَمَن يَتَوَلَّهُم مِّنكُمْ فَإِنَّهُۥ

that turns to them (for friendship) is of them. Verily Allah guides not a people unjust.

مِنْهُمْ ۗ إِنَّ ٱللَّهَ لَا يَهْدِى ٱلْقَوْمَ ٱلظَّٰلِمِينَ ﴿٥١﴾

52. Those in whose heart is a disease - you see how eagerly they run about amongst them, saying: "We do fear lest a change of fortune bring us disaster." Ah! Perhaps Allah will give (you) victory, or a decision from Him. Then will they repent of the thoughts which they secretly harboured in their hearts.

فَتَرَى ٱلَّذِينَ فِى قُلُوبِهِم مَّرَضٌ يُسَٰرِعُونَ فِيهِمْ يَقُولُونَ
نَخْشَىٰٓ أَن تُصِيبَنَا دَآئِرَةٌ ۚ فَعَسَى ٱللَّهُ أَن يَأْتِىَ بِٱلْفَتْحِ
أَوْ أَمْرٍ مِّنْ عِندِهِۦ فَيُصْبِحُوا۟ عَلَىٰ مَآ أَسَرُّوا۟ فِىٓ أَنفُسِهِمْ
نَٰدِمِينَ ﴿٥٢﴾

53. And those who believe will say: "Are these the men who swore their strongest oaths by Allah, that they were with you?" All that they do will be in vain, and they will fall into (nothing but) ruin.

وَيَقُولُ ٱلَّذِينَ ءَامَنُوٓا۟ أَهَٰٓؤُلَآءِ ٱلَّذِينَ أَقْسَمُوا۟ بِٱللَّهِ
جَهْدَ أَيْمَٰنِهِمْ ۙ إِنَّهُمْ لَمَعَكُمْ ۚ حَبِطَتْ أَعْمَٰلُهُمْ
فَأَصْبَحُوا۟ خَٰسِرِينَ ﴿٥٣﴾

54. O you who believe! If any from among you turn back from his faith, soon will Allah produce a people whom He will love as they will love Him - lowly with the believers, mighty against the rejecters, fighting in the way of Allah, and never afraid of the reproaches of such as find fault. That is the grace of Allah, which He will bestow on whom He pleases: and Allah encompasses all, and He knows all things.

يَٰٓأَيُّهَا ٱلَّذِينَ ءَامَنُوا۟ مَن يَرْتَدَّ مِنكُمْ عَن دِينِهِۦ
فَسَوْفَ يَأْتِى ٱللَّهُ بِقَوْمٍ يُحِبُّهُمْ وَيُحِبُّونَهُۥٓ أَذِلَّةٍ
عَلَى ٱلْمُؤْمِنِينَ أَعِزَّةٍ عَلَى ٱلْكَٰفِرِينَ يُجَٰهِدُونَ فِى
سَبِيلِ ٱللَّهِ وَلَا يَخَافُونَ لَوْمَةَ لَآئِمٍ ۚ ذَٰلِكَ فَضْلُ ٱللَّهِ
يُؤْتِيهِ مَن يَشَآءُ ۚ وَٱللَّهُ وَٰسِعٌ عَلِيمٌ ﴿٥٤﴾

55. Your (real) friends are (no less than) Allah, His messenger, and the (fellowship of) believers - those who establish regular prayers and regular charity, and they bow down humbly (in worship).

إِنَّمَا وَلِيُّكُمُ ٱللَّهُ وَرَسُولُهُۥ وَٱلَّذِينَ ءَامَنُوا۟ ٱلَّذِينَ يُقِيمُونَ
ٱلصَّلَوٰةَ وَيُؤْتُونَ ٱلزَّكَوٰةَ وَهُمْ رَٰكِعُونَ ﴿٥٥﴾

56. As to those who turn (for friendship) to Allah, His messenger, and the (fellowship of) believers, it is the party of Allah that must certainly triumph.

وَمَن يَتَوَلَّ ٱللَّهَ وَرَسُولَهُۥ وَٱلَّذِينَ ءَامَنُوا۟ فَإِنَّ حِزْبَ ٱللَّهِ
هُمُ ٱلْغَٰلِبُونَ ﴿٥٦﴾

57. O you who believe! Take not for friends and protectors those who take your religion for a mockery or sport - whether among those who received the scripture before you, or among those who reject faith; but fear you Allah, if you have faith (indeed).

يَٰٓأَيُّهَا ٱلَّذِينَ ءَامَنُوا۟ لَا تَتَّخِذُوا۟ ٱلَّذِينَ ٱتَّخَذُوا۟
دِينَكُمْ هُزُوًا وَلَعِبًا مِّنَ ٱلَّذِينَ أُوتُوا۟ ٱلْكِتَٰبَ مِن
قَبْلِكُمْ وَٱلْكُفَّارَ أَوْلِيَآءَ ۚ وَٱتَّقُوا۟ ٱللَّهَ إِن كُنتُم مُّؤْمِنِينَ ﴿٥٧﴾

58. When you proclaim your call to prayer, they take it (but) as mockery and sport; that is because they are a people without understanding.

وَإِذَا نَادَيْتُمْ إِلَى ٱلصَّلَوٰةِ ٱتَّخَذُوهَا هُزُوًا وَلَعِبًا ۚ ذَٰلِكَ
بِأَنَّهُمْ قَوْمٌ لَّا يَعْقِلُونَ ﴿٥٨﴾

59. Say: "O People of the Book! Do you disapprove of us for no other reason than that we believe in Allah, and the revelation that has come to us and that which came before (us), and (perhaps) that most of you are rebellious and disobedient?"

قُلْ يَٰٓأَهْلَ ٱلْكِتَٰبِ هَلْ تَنقِمُونَ مِنَّآ إِلَّآ أَنْ ءَامَنَّا
بِٱللَّهِ وَمَآ أُنزِلَ إِلَيْنَا وَمَآ أُنزِلَ مِن قَبْلُ وَأَنَّ أَكْثَرَكُمْ
فَٰسِقُونَ ﴿٥٩﴾

60. Say: "Shall I point out to you something much worse than this, (as judged) by the treatment it received from Allah? Those who incurred the curse of Allah and His wrath, those of whom some He transformed into apes and swine, those who worshipped evil - these are (many times) worse in rank, and far more astray from the even path!"

قُلْ هَلْ أُنَبِّئُكُم بِشَرٍّ مِّن ذَٰلِكَ مَثُوبَةً عِندَ ٱللَّهِ ۚ مَن لَّعَنَهُ ٱللَّهُ
وَغَضِبَ عَلَيْهِ وَجَعَلَ مِنْهُمُ ٱلْقِرَدَةَ وَٱلْخَنَازِيرَ وَعَبَدَ
ٱلطَّٰغُوتَ ۚ أُو۟لَٰٓئِكَ شَرٌّ مَّكَانًا وَأَضَلُّ عَن سَوَآءِ
ٱلسَّبِيلِ ﴿٦٠﴾

61. When they come to you, they say: "We believe"; but in fact they enter with a mind against faith, and they go out with the same. But Allah knows fully all that they hide.

وَإِذَا جَآءُوكُمْ قَالُوٓا۟ ءَامَنَّا وَقَد دَّخَلُوا۟ بِٱلْكُفْرِ وَهُمْ
قَدْ خَرَجُوا۟ بِهِۦ ۚ وَٱللَّهُ أَعْلَمُ بِمَا كَانُوا۟ يَكْتُمُونَ ﴿٦١﴾

62. Many of them do you see, racing each other in sin and transgression and their eating of things forbidden; evil indeed are the things that they do.

وَتَرَىٰ كَثِيرًا مِّنْهُمْ يُسَٰرِعُونَ فِى ٱلْإِثْمِ وَٱلْعُدْوَٰنِ
وَأَكْلِهِمُ ٱلسُّحْتَ ۚ لَبِئْسَ مَا كَانُوا۟ يَعْمَلُونَ ﴿٦٢﴾

63. Why do not the rabbis and the doctors of law forbid them from their (habit of) uttering sinful words and eating things forbidden? Evil indeed are their works.

لَوْلَا يَنْهَىٰهُمُ ٱلرَّبَّٰنِيُّونَ وَٱلْأَحْبَارُ عَن قَوْلِهِمُ
ٱلْإِثْمَ وَأَكْلِهِمُ ٱلسُّحْتَ ۚ لَبِئْسَ مَا كَانُوا۟ يَصْنَعُونَ ﴿٦٣﴾

64. The Jews say: "Allah's hand is tied up." Be their hands tied up and be they accursed for the (blasphemy) they utter. Nay, both His hands are widely outstretched: He gives and spends (of His bounty) as He pleases. But the revelation that comes to you from Allah increases in most of them their obstinate rebellion and blasphemy. Amongst them We have placed enmity and hatred till the day of judgement. Every time they kindle the fire of war Allah does extinguish it; but they (ever) strive to do mischief on earth. And Allah loves not those who do mischief.

وَقَالَتِ ٱلْيَهُودُ يَدُ ٱللَّهِ مَغْلُولَةٌ ۚ غُلَّتْ أَيْدِيهِمْ وَلُعِنُوا۟
بِمَا قَالُوا۟ ۘ بَلْ يَدَاهُ مَبْسُوطَتَانِ يُنفِقُ كَيْفَ يَشَآءُ ۚ
وَلَيَزِيدَنَّ كَثِيرًا مِّنْهُم مَّآ أُنزِلَ إِلَيْكَ مِن رَّبِّكَ طُغْيَـٰنًا
وَكُفْرًا ۚ وَأَلْقَيْنَا بَيْنَهُمُ ٱلْعَدَٰوَةَ وَٱلْبَغْضَآءَ إِلَىٰ يَوْمِ
ٱلْقِيَـٰمَةِ ۚ كُلَّمَآ أَوْقَدُوا۟ نَارًا لِّلْحَرْبِ أَطْفَأَهَا ٱللَّهُ ۚ
وَيَسْعَوْنَ فِى ٱلْأَرْضِ فَسَادًا ۚ وَٱللَّهُ لَا يُحِبُّ
ٱلْمُفْسِدِينَ ﴿٦٤﴾

65. If only the People of the Book had believed and been righteous, We should indeed have blotted out their iniquities and admitted them to gardens of bliss.

وَلَوْ أَنَّ أَهْلَ ٱلْكِتَـٰبِ ءَامَنُوا۟ وَٱتَّقَوْا۟
لَكَفَّرْنَا عَنْهُمْ سَيِّـَٔاتِهِمْ وَلَأَدْخَلْنَـٰهُمْ
جَنَّـٰتِ ٱلنَّعِيمِ ﴿٦٥﴾

66. If only they had stood fast by the law, the Gospel, and all the revelation that was sent to them from their Lord, they would have enjoyed happiness from every side. There is from among them a party of the right course; but many of them follow a course that is evil.

وَلَوْ أَنَّهُمْ أَقَامُوا۟ ٱلتَّوْرَىٰةَ وَٱلْإِنجِيلَ وَمَآ أُنزِلَ
إِلَيْهِم مِّن رَّبِّهِمْ لَأَكَلُوا۟ مِن فَوْقِهِمْ وَمِن
تَحْتِ أَرْجُلِهِم ۚ مِّنْهُمْ أُمَّةٌ مُّقْتَصِدَةٌ ۖ
وَكَثِيرٌ مِّنْهُمْ سَآءَ مَا يَعْمَلُونَ ﴿٦٦﴾

67. O messenger! Proclaim (the Message) which has been sent to you from your Lord. If you did not, you would not have fulfilled and proclaimed His mission: and Allah will defend you from men (who mean mischief). For Allah guides not those who reject faith.

ثلاثة أرباع الحزب ١٢

۞ يَـٰٓأَيُّهَا ٱلرَّسُولُ بَلِّغْ مَآ أُنزِلَ إِلَيْكَ مِن رَّبِّكَ ۖ
وَإِن لَّمْ تَفْعَلْ فَمَا بَلَّغْتَ رِسَالَتَهُۥ ۚ وَٱللَّهُ
يَعْصِمُكَ مِنَ ٱلنَّاسِ ۗ إِنَّ ٱللَّهَ لَا يَهْدِى ٱلْقَوْمَ
ٱلْكَـٰفِرِينَ ﴿٦٧﴾

68. Say: "O People of the Book! You have no ground to stand upon unless you stand fast by the law, the Gospel, and all the revelation that has come to you from your Lord." It is the revelation that comes to you

قُلْ يَـٰٓأَهْلَ ٱلْكِتَـٰبِ لَسْتُمْ عَلَىٰ شَىْءٍ حَتَّىٰ تُقِيمُوا۟
ٱلتَّوْرَىٰةَ وَٱلْإِنجِيلَ وَمَآ أُنزِلَ إِلَيْكُم مِّن رَّبِّكُمْ ۗ

from your Lord, that increases in most of them their obstinate rebellion and blasphemy. But sorrow you not over (these) people without faith.

وَلَيَزِيدَنَّ كَثِيرًا مِّنْهُم مَّآ أُنزِلَ إِلَيْكَ مِن رَّبِّكَ
طُغْيَٰنًا وَكُفْرًا فَلَا تَأْسَ عَلَى ٱلْقَوْمِ ٱلْكَٰفِرِينَ ﴿٦٨﴾

69. Those who believe (in the Qur'an), those who follow the Jewish (Scriptures) and the Sabians and the Christians - any who believe in Allah and the last day, and work righteousness - on them shall be no fear, nor shall they grieve.

إِنَّ ٱلَّذِينَ ءَامَنُوا۟ وَٱلَّذِينَ هَادُوا۟ وَٱلصَّٰبِـُٔونَ
وَٱلنَّصَٰرَىٰ مَنْ ءَامَنَ بِٱللَّهِ وَٱلْيَوْمِ ٱلْءَاخِرِ وَعَمِلَ
صَٰلِحًا فَلَا خَوْفٌ عَلَيْهِمْ وَلَا هُمْ يَحْزَنُونَ ﴿٦٩﴾

70. We took the covenant of the Children of Israel and sent them messengers. Every time there came to them a messenger with what they themselves desired not - some (of these) they called imposters and some they slay.

لَقَدْ أَخَذْنَا مِيثَٰقَ بَنِىٓ إِسْرَٰٓءِيلَ وَأَرْسَلْنَآ إِلَيْهِمْ رُسُلًا
كُلَّمَا جَآءَهُمْ رَسُولٌۢ بِمَا لَا تَهْوَىٰٓ أَنفُسُهُمْ فَرِيقًا
كَذَّبُوا۟ وَفَرِيقًا يَقْتُلُونَ ﴿٧٠﴾

71. They thought there would be no trial (or punishment); so they became blind and deaf; yet Allah (in mercy) turned to them; yet again many of them became blind and deaf. But Allah sees well all that they do.

وَحَسِبُوٓا۟ أَلَّا تَكُونَ فِتْنَةٌ فَعَمُوا۟ وَصَمُّوا۟ ثُمَّ تَابَ ٱللَّهُ
عَلَيْهِمْ ثُمَّ عَمُوا۟ وَصَمُّوا۟ كَثِيرٌ مِّنْهُمْ ۚ وَٱللَّهُ
بَصِيرٌۢ بِمَا يَعْمَلُونَ ﴿٧١﴾

72. They do blaspheme who say: "Allah is the Messiah the son of Mary." But said the Messiah: "O Children of Israel! Worship Allah, my Lord and your Lord." Whoever joins other gods with Allah - Allah will forbid him the garden, and the fire will be his abode. There will for the wrongdoers be no one to help.

لَقَدْ كَفَرَ ٱلَّذِينَ قَالُوٓا۟ إِنَّ ٱللَّهَ هُوَ ٱلْمَسِيحُ ٱبْنُ مَرْيَمَ ۖ
وَقَالَ ٱلْمَسِيحُ يَٰبَنِىٓ إِسْرَٰٓءِيلَ ٱعْبُدُوا۟ ٱللَّهَ رَبِّى
وَرَبَّكُمْ ۖ إِنَّهُۥ مَن يُشْرِكْ بِٱللَّهِ فَقَدْ حَرَّمَ ٱللَّهُ
عَلَيْهِ ٱلْجَنَّةَ وَمَأْوَىٰهُ ٱلنَّارُ ۖ وَمَا لِلظَّٰلِمِينَ
مِنْ أَنصَارٍ ﴿٧٢﴾

73. They do blaspheme who say: Allah is one of three in a trinity; for there is no god except One God. If they desist not from their word (of blasphemy), verily a grievous penalty will befall the blasphemers among them.

لَّقَدْ كَفَرَ ٱلَّذِينَ قَالُوٓا۟ إِنَّ ٱللَّهَ ثَالِثُ ثَلَٰثَةٍ ۘ
وَمَا مِنْ إِلَٰهٍ إِلَّآ إِلَٰهٌ وَٰحِدٌ ۚ وَإِن لَّمْ يَنتَهُوا۟
عَمَّا يَقُولُونَ لَيَمَسَّنَّ ٱلَّذِينَ كَفَرُوا۟ مِنْهُمْ
عَذَابٌ أَلِيمٌ ﴿٧٣﴾

74. Why turn they not to Allah and seek His forgiveness? For Allah is Oft-Forgiving, Most Merciful.

أَفَلَا يَتُوبُونَ إِلَى ٱللَّهِ وَيَسْتَغْفِرُونَهُۥ ۚ وَٱللَّهُ غَفُورٌ
رَّحِيمٌ ٧٤

75. The Messiah, the son of Mary, was no more than a messenger; many were the messengers that passed away before him. His mother was a woman of truth. They had both to eat their (daily) food. See how Allah does make His signs clear to them; yet see in what ways they are deluded away from the truth!

مَّا ٱلْمَسِيحُ ٱبْنُ مَرْيَمَ إِلَّا رَسُولٌ قَدْ خَلَتْ مِن قَبْلِهِ
ٱلرُّسُلُ وَأُمُّهُۥ صِدِّيقَةٌ ۖ كَانَا يَأْكُلَانِ ٱلطَّعَامَ ۗ ٱنظُرْ
كَيْفَ نُبَيِّنُ لَهُمُ ٱلْـَٔايَـٰتِ ثُمَّ ٱنظُرْ أَنَّىٰ يُؤْفَكُونَ ٧٥

76. Say: "Will you worship, besides Allah, something which has no power either to harm or benefit you? But Allah - He it is that hears and knows all things."

قُلْ أَتَعْبُدُونَ مِن دُونِ ٱللَّهِ مَا لَا يَمْلِكُ لَكُمْ
ضَرًّا وَلَا نَفْعًا ۚ وَٱللَّهُ هُوَ ٱلسَّمِيعُ ٱلْعَلِيمُ ٧٦

77. Say: "O People of the Book! Exceed not in your religion the bounds (of what is proper), trespassing beyond the truth, nor follow the vain desires of people who went wrong in times gone by - who misled many, and strayed (themselves) from the even way.

قُلْ يَـٰٓأَهْلَ ٱلْكِتَـٰبِ لَا تَغْلُوا۟ فِى دِينِكُمْ غَيْرَ ٱلْحَقِّ وَلَا
تَتَّبِعُوٓا۟ أَهْوَآءَ قَوْمٍ قَدْ ضَلُّوا۟ مِن قَبْلُ وَأَضَلُّوا۟ كَثِيرًا
وَضَلُّوا۟ عَن سَوَآءِ ٱلسَّبِيلِ ٧٧

78. Curses were pronounced on those among the Children of Israel who rejected faith, by the tongue of David and of Jesus, the son of Mary, because they disobeyed and persisted in excesses.

لُعِنَ ٱلَّذِينَ كَفَرُوا۟ مِنۢ بَنِىٓ إِسْرَٰٓءِيلَ
عَلَىٰ لِسَانِ دَاوُۥدَ وَعِيسَى ٱبْنِ مَرْيَمَ ۚ ذَٰلِكَ
بِمَا عَصَوا۟ وَّكَانُوا۟ يَعْتَدُونَ ٧٨

79. Nor did they (usually) forbid one another the iniquities which they committed: evil indeed were the deeds which they did.

كَانُوا۟ لَا يَتَنَاهَوْنَ عَن مُّنكَرٍ فَعَلُوهُ ۚ
لَبِئْسَ مَا كَانُوا۟ يَفْعَلُونَ ٧٩

80. You see many of them turning in friendship to the unbelievers. Evil indeed are (the works) which their souls have sent before them (with the result), that Allah's wrath is on them, and in torment will they remain.

تَرَىٰ كَثِيرًا مِّنْهُمْ يَتَوَلَّوْنَ ٱلَّذِينَ كَفَرُوا۟ ۚ
لَبِئْسَ مَا قَدَّمَتْ لَهُمْ أَنفُسُهُمْ أَن سَخِطَ
ٱللَّهُ عَلَيْهِمْ وَفِى ٱلْعَذَابِ هُمْ خَـٰلِدُونَ ٨٠

81. If only they had believed in Allah, in the prophet, and in what has been revealed to him, never would they have taken them for friends and protectors, but most of them are rebellious wrongdoers.

وَلَوْ كَانُوا۟ يُؤْمِنُونَ بِٱللَّهِ وَٱلنَّبِىِّ وَمَآ أُنزِلَ
إِلَيْهِ مَا ٱتَّخَذُوهُمْ أَوْلِيَآءَ وَلَٰكِنَّ
كَثِيرًا مِّنْهُمْ فَٰسِقُونَ ﴿٨١﴾

الجزء ٧ الحزب ١٣

✻**82.** Strongest among men in enmity to the believers will you find the Jews and pagans; and nearest among them in love to the believers will you find those who say, "We are Christians"; because amongst these are men devoted to learning and men who have renounced the world, and they are not arrogant.

✻ لَتَجِدَنَّ أَشَدَّ ٱلنَّاسِ عَدَٰوَةً لِّلَّذِينَ
ءَامَنُوا۟ ٱلْيَهُودَ وَٱلَّذِينَ أَشْرَكُوا۟ ۖ وَلَتَجِدَنَّ
أَقْرَبَهُم مَّوَدَّةً لِّلَّذِينَ ءَامَنُوا۟ ٱلَّذِينَ قَالُوٓا۟
إِنَّا نَصَٰرَىٰ ۚ ذَٰلِكَ بِأَنَّ مِنْهُمْ قِسِّيسِينَ
وَرُهْبَانًا وَأَنَّهُمْ لَا يَسْتَكْبِرُونَ ﴿٨٢﴾

83. And when they listen to the revelation received by the messenger, you will see their eyes overflowing with tears, for they recognise the truth: they pray: "Our Lord! We believe; write us down among the witnesses."

وَإِذَا سَمِعُوا۟ مَآ أُنزِلَ إِلَى ٱلرَّسُولِ تَرَىٰٓ
أَعْيُنَهُمْ تَفِيضُ مِنَ ٱلدَّمْعِ مِمَّا عَرَفُوا۟
مِنَ ٱلْحَقِّ ۖ يَقُولُونَ رَبَّنَآ ءَامَنَّا فَٱكْتُبْنَا مَعَ
ٱلشَّٰهِدِينَ ﴿٨٣﴾

84. "What cause can we have not to believe in Allah and the truth which has come to us, seeing that we long for our Lord to admit us to the company of the righteous?"

وَمَا لَنَا لَا نُؤْمِنُ بِٱللَّهِ وَمَا جَآءَنَا مِنَ ٱلْحَقِّ وَنَطْمَعُ
أَن يُدْخِلَنَا رَبُّنَا مَعَ ٱلْقَوْمِ ٱلصَّٰلِحِينَ ﴿٨٤﴾

85. And for this their prayer, has Allah rewarded them with gardens, with rivers flowing underneath-their eternal home. Such is the recompense of those who do good.

فَأَثَٰبَهُمُ ٱللَّهُ بِمَا قَالُوا۟ جَنَّٰتٍ تَجْرِى مِن تَحْتِهَا
ٱلْأَنْهَٰرُ خَٰلِدِينَ فِيهَا ۚ وَذَٰلِكَ جَزَآءُ
ٱلْمُحْسِنِينَ ﴿٨٥﴾

86. But those who reject faith and belie Our signs - they shall be companions of hellfire.

وَٱلَّذِينَ كَفَرُوا۟ وَكَذَّبُوا۟ بِـَٔايَٰتِنَآ أُو۟لَٰٓئِكَ
أَصْحَٰبُ ٱلْجَحِيمِ ﴿٨٦﴾

✻ Part-7

87. O you who believe! Make not unlawful the good things which Allah has made lawful for you, but commit no excess: for Allah loves not those given to excess.

يَٰٓأَيُّهَا ٱلَّذِينَ ءَامَنُوا۟ لَا تُحَرِّمُوا۟ طَيِّبَٰتِ مَآ أَحَلَّ
ٱللَّهُ لَكُمْ وَلَا تَعْتَدُوٓا۟ ۚ إِنَّ ٱللَّهَ لَا يُحِبُّ
ٱلْمُعْتَدِينَ ﴿٨٧﴾

88. Eat of the things which Allah has provided for you, lawful and good: but fear Allah, in Whom you believe.

وَكُلُوا۟ مِمَّا رَزَقَكُمُ ٱللَّهُ حَلَٰلًا طَيِّبًا ۚ
وَٱتَّقُوا۟ ٱللَّهَ ٱلَّذِىٓ أَنتُم بِهِۦ مُؤْمِنُونَ ﴿٨٨﴾

89. Allah will not call you to account for what is futile in your oaths, but He will call you to account for your deliberate oaths: for expiation, feed ten needy persons, on a scale of the average for the food of your families; or clothe them; or give a slave his freedom. If that is beyond your means, fast for three days. That is the expiation for the oaths you have sworn. But keep to your oaths. Thus does Allah make clear to you His signs, that you may be grateful.

لَا يُؤَاخِذُكُمُ ٱللَّهُ بِٱللَّغْوِ فِىٓ أَيْمَٰنِكُمْ وَلَٰكِن
يُؤَاخِذُكُم بِمَا عَقَّدتُّمُ ٱلْأَيْمَٰنَ ۖ فَكَفَّٰرَتُهُۥٓ
إِطْعَامُ عَشَرَةِ مَسَٰكِينَ مِنْ أَوْسَطِ مَا تُطْعِمُونَ
أَهْلِيكُمْ أَوْ كِسْوَتُهُمْ أَوْ تَحْرِيرُ رَقَبَةٍ ۖ فَمَن لَّمْ يَجِدْ
فَصِيَامُ ثَلَٰثَةِ أَيَّامٍ ۚ ذَٰلِكَ كَفَّٰرَةُ أَيْمَٰنِكُمْ إِذَا
حَلَفْتُمْ ۚ وَٱحْفَظُوٓا۟ أَيْمَٰنَكُمْ ۚ كَذَٰلِكَ يُبَيِّنُ ٱللَّهُ لَكُمْ
ءَايَٰتِهِۦ لَعَلَّكُمْ تَشْكُرُونَ ﴿٨٩﴾

90. O you who believe! Intoxicants and gambling, sacrificing to stones, and (divination by) arrows, are an abomination of Satan's handiwork; eschew such (abomination), that you may prosper.

يَٰٓأَيُّهَا ٱلَّذِينَ ءَامَنُوٓا۟ إِنَّمَا ٱلْخَمْرُ وَٱلْمَيْسِرُ وَ
ٱلْأَنصَابُ وَٱلْأَزْلَٰمُ رِجْسٌ مِّنْ عَمَلِ ٱلشَّيْطَٰنِ
فَٱجْتَنِبُوهُ لَعَلَّكُمْ تُفْلِحُونَ ﴿٩٠﴾

91. Satan's plan is (but) to excite enmity and hatred between you, with intoxicants and gambling, and hinder you from the remembrance of Allah, and from prayer: will you not then abstain?

إِنَّمَا يُرِيدُ ٱلشَّيْطَٰنُ أَن يُوقِعَ بَيْنَكُمُ ٱلْعَدَٰوَةَ
وَٱلْبَغْضَآءَ فِى ٱلْخَمْرِ وَٱلْمَيْسِرِ وَيَصُدَّكُمْ عَن
ذِكْرِ ٱللَّهِ وَعَنِ ٱلصَّلَوٰةِ ۖ فَهَلْ أَنتُم
مُّنتَهُونَ ﴿٩١﴾

92. Obey Allah, and obey the messenger and beware (of evil): if you do turn back, know you that it is Our messenger's duty to proclaim (the Message) in the clearest manner.

وَأَطِيعُوا۟ ٱللَّهَ وَأَطِيعُوا۟ ٱلرَّسُولَ وَٱحْذَرُوا۟ ۚ فَإِن
تَوَلَّيْتُمْ فَٱعْلَمُوٓا۟ أَنَّمَا عَلَىٰ رَسُولِنَا ٱلْبَلَٰغُ
ٱلْمُبِينُ ﴿٩٢﴾

93. On those who believe and do deeds of righteousness there is no blame for what they ate (in the past), when they guard themselves from evil, and believe, and do deeds of righteousness - (or) again, guard themselves from evil and believe - (or) again, guard themselves from evil and do good. For Allah loves those who do good.

لَيْسَ عَلَى ٱلَّذِينَ ءَامَنُوا۟ وَعَمِلُوا۟ ٱلصَّٰلِحَٰتِ جُنَاحٌ
فِيمَا طَعِمُوٓا۟ إِذَا مَا ٱتَّقَوا۟ وَّءَامَنُوا۟ وَعَمِلُوا۟
ٱلصَّٰلِحَٰتِ ثُمَّ ٱتَّقَوا۟ وَّءَامَنُوا۟ ثُمَّ ٱتَّقَوا۟
وَّأَحْسَنُوا۟ ۗ وَٱللَّهُ يُحِبُّ ٱلْمُحْسِنِينَ ﴿٩٣﴾

94. O you who believe! Allah does but make a trial of you in a little matter of game well within reach of your hands and your lances, that He may test who fears Him unseen: any who transgress thereafter, will have a grievous penalty.

يَٰٓأَيُّهَا ٱلَّذِينَ ءَامَنُوا۟ لَيَبْلُوَنَّكُمُ ٱللَّهُ بِشَىْءٍ مِّنَ
ٱلصَّيْدِ تَنَالُهُۥٓ أَيْدِيكُمْ وَرِمَاحُكُمْ لِيَعْلَمَ ٱللَّهُ مَن
يَخَافُهُۥ بِٱلْغَيْبِ ۚ فَمَنِ ٱعْتَدَىٰ بَعْدَ ذَٰلِكَ فَلَهُۥ
عَذَابٌ أَلِيمٌ ﴿٩٤﴾

95. O you who believe! Kill not game while in the sacred precincts or in pilgrim garb. If any of you does so intentionally, the compensation is an offering, brought to the Ka'bah, of a domestic animal equivalent to the one he killed, as adjudged by two just men among you; or by way of atonement, the feeding of the needy; or its equivalent in fasts: that he may taste of the penalty of his deed. Allah forgives what is past: for repetition Allah will exact from him the penalty. For Allah is Exalted, and Lord of Retribution.

يَٰٓأَيُّهَا ٱلَّذِينَ ءَامَنُوا۟ لَا تَقْتُلُوا۟ ٱلصَّيْدَ وَأَنتُمْ
حُرُمٌ ۚ وَمَن قَتَلَهُۥ مِنكُم مُّتَعَمِّدًا فَجَزَآءٌ مِّثْلُ
مَا قَتَلَ مِنَ ٱلنَّعَمِ يَحْكُمُ بِهِۦ ذَوَا عَدْلٍ مِّنكُمْ هَدْيًۢا
بَٰلِغَ ٱلْكَعْبَةِ أَوْ كَفَّٰرَةٌ طَعَامُ مَسَٰكِينَ أَوْ عَدْلُ
ذَٰلِكَ صِيَامًا لِّيَذُوقَ وَبَالَ أَمْرِهِۦ ۗ عَفَا ٱللَّهُ
عَمَّا سَلَفَ ۚ وَمَنْ عَادَ فَيَنتَقِمُ ٱللَّهُ مِنْهُ ۗ وَٱللَّهُ
عَزِيزٌ ذُو ٱنتِقَامٍ ﴿٩٥﴾

96. Lawful to you is the pursuit of water-game and its use for food - for the benefit of yourselves and those who travel; but forbidden is the pursuit of land-game - as long as you are in the sacred precincts or in pilgrim garb. And fear Allah, to whom you shall be gathered back.

أُحِلَّ لَكُمْ صَيْدُ ٱلْبَحْرِ وَطَعَامُهُۥ مَتَٰعًا لَّكُمْ
وَلِلسَّيَّارَةِ ۖ وَحُرِّمَ عَلَيْكُمْ صَيْدُ ٱلْبَرِّ مَا دُمْتُمْ
حُرُمًا ۗ وَٱتَّقُوا۟ ٱللَّهَ ٱلَّذِىٓ إِلَيْهِ تُحْشَرُونَ ﴿٩٦﴾

97. Allah made the Ka'bah, the Sacred House, an asylum of security for men, as also the sacred months, the animals for offerings,

ربع الحزب ١٣ ۞ جَعَلَ ٱللَّهُ ٱلْكَعْبَةَ ٱلْبَيْتَ ٱلْحَرَامَ قِيَٰمًا
لِّلنَّاسِ وَٱلشَّهْرَ ٱلْحَرَامَ وَٱلْهَدْىَ وَٱلْقَلَٰٓئِدَ ۚ ذَٰلِكَ

and the garlands that mark them: that you may know that Allah has knowledge of what is in the heavens and on earth and that Allah is well acquainted with all things.

لِتَعۡلَمُوٓاْ أَنَّ ٱللَّهَ يَعۡلَمُ مَا فِي ٱلسَّمَٰوَٰتِ وَمَا فِي
ٱلۡأَرۡضِ وَأَنَّ ٱللَّهَ بِكُلِّ شَيۡءٍ عَلِيمٌ ٩٧

98. Know you that Allah is strict in punishment and that Allah is Oft-Forgiving, Most Merciful.

ٱعۡلَمُوٓاْ أَنَّ ٱللَّهَ شَدِيدُ ٱلۡعِقَابِ وَأَنَّ ٱللَّهَ
غَفُورٞ رَّحِيمٞ ٩٨

99. The messenger's duty is but to proclaim (the message). But Allah knows all that you reveal and all that you conceal.

مَّا عَلَى ٱلرَّسُولِ إِلَّا ٱلۡبَلَٰغُۗ وَٱللَّهُ يَعۡلَمُ مَا تُبۡدُونَ
وَمَا تَكۡتُمُونَ ٩٩

100. Say: "Not equal are things that are bad and things that are good, even though the abundance of the bad may dazzle you; so fear Allah, O you that understand! That (so) you may prosper."

قُل لَّا يَسۡتَوِي ٱلۡخَبِيثُ وَٱلطَّيِّبُ وَلَوۡ أَعۡجَبَكَ
كَثۡرَةُ ٱلۡخَبِيثِۚ فَٱتَّقُواْ ٱللَّهَ يَٰٓأُوْلِي ٱلۡأَلۡبَٰبِ
لَعَلَّكُمۡ تُفۡلِحُونَ ١٠٠

101. O you who believe! Ask not questions about things which, if made plain to you, may cause you trouble. But if you ask about things when the Qur'an is being revealed, they will be made plain to you, Allah will forgive those: for Allah is Oft-Forgiving, Most Forbearing.

يَٰٓأَيُّهَا ٱلَّذِينَ ءَامَنُواْ لَا تَسۡـَٔلُواْ عَنۡ أَشۡيَآءَ إِن
تُبۡدَ لَكُمۡ تَسُؤۡكُمۡ وَإِن تَسۡـَٔلُواْ عَنۡهَا حِينَ يُنَزَّلُ
ٱلۡقُرۡءَانُ تُبۡدَ لَكُمۡ عَفَا ٱللَّهُ عَنۡهَاۗ وَٱللَّهُ
غَفُورٌ حَلِيمٞ ١٠١

102. Some people before you did ask such questions, and on that account lost their faith.

قَدۡ سَأَلَهَا قَوۡمٞ مِّن قَبۡلِكُمۡ ثُمَّ أَصۡبَحُواْ بِهَا
كَٰفِرِينَ ١٠٢

103. It was not Allah Who instituted (superstitions like those of) a slit-ear she-camel, or a she-camel let loose for free pasture, or idol sacrifices for twin-births in animals, or stallion-camels freed from work: it is blasphemers who invent a lie against Allah; but most of them lack wisdom.

مَا جَعَلَ ٱللَّهُ مِنۢ بَحِيرَةٖ وَلَا سَآئِبَةٖ وَلَا وَصِيلَةٖ
وَلَا حَامٖ وَلَٰكِنَّ ٱلَّذِينَ كَفَرُواْ يَفۡتَرُونَ عَلَى ٱللَّهِ
ٱلۡكَذِبَۖ وَأَكۡثَرُهُمۡ لَا يَعۡقِلُونَ ١٠٣

104. When it is said to them: "Come to what Allah has revealed; come to the messenger"; they say: "Enough for us are the ways we found our fathers following." What! Even though their fathers were void of knowledge and guidance?

وَإِذَا قِيلَ لَهُمْ تَعَالَوْا إِلَىٰ مَا أَنزَلَ اللَّهُ وَإِلَى الرَّسُولِ
قَالُوا حَسْبُنَا مَا وَجَدْنَا عَلَيْهِ آبَاءَنَا ۚ أَوَلَوْ كَانَ
آبَاؤُهُمْ لَا يَعْلَمُونَ شَيْئًا وَلَا يَهْتَدُونَ ﴿١٠٤﴾

105. O you who believe! Guard your own souls: if you follow (right) guidance, no hurt can come to you from those who stray. The goal of you all is to Allah: it is He that will show you the truth of all that you do.

يَا أَيُّهَا الَّذِينَ آمَنُوا عَلَيْكُمْ أَنفُسَكُمْ ۖ لَا يَضُرُّكُم
مَّن ضَلَّ إِذَا اهْتَدَيْتُمْ ۚ إِلَى اللَّهِ مَرْجِعُكُمْ جَمِيعًا
فَيُنَبِّئُكُم بِمَا كُنتُمْ تَعْمَلُونَ ﴿١٠٥﴾

106. O you who believe! When death approaches any of you, (take) witnesses among yourselves when making bequests - two just men of your own (brotherhood) or others from outside if you are journeying through the earth, and the chance of death befalls you (thus). If you doubt (their truth), detain them both after prayer, and let them both swear by Allah: "We wish not in this for any worldly gain, even though the (beneficiary) be our near relation: we shall hide not the evidence before Allah: if we do, then see! The sin be upon us!"

يَا أَيُّهَا الَّذِينَ آمَنُوا شَهَادَةُ بَيْنِكُمْ إِذَا حَضَرَ
أَحَدَكُمُ الْمَوْتُ حِينَ الْوَصِيَّةِ اثْنَانِ ذَوَا عَدْلٍ
مِّنكُمْ أَوْ آخَرَانِ مِنْ غَيْرِكُمْ إِنْ أَنتُمْ ضَرَبْتُمْ فِي
الْأَرْضِ فَأَصَابَتْكُم مُّصِيبَةُ الْمَوْتِ ۚ تَحْبِسُونَهُمَا
مِن بَعْدِ الصَّلَاةِ فَيُقْسِمَانِ بِاللَّهِ إِنِ ارْتَبْتُمْ
لَا نَشْتَرِي بِهِ ثَمَنًا وَلَوْ كَانَ ذَا قُرْبَىٰ ۙ وَلَا نَكْتُمُ
شَهَادَةَ اللَّهِ إِنَّا إِذًا لَّمِنَ الْآثِمِينَ ﴿١٠٦﴾

107. But if it gets known that these two were guilty of the sin (of perjury), let two others stand up in their places - nearest in relation from among those who claim a lawful right: let them swear by Allah; "We affirm that our witness is truer than that of those two, and that we have not trespassed (beyond the truth): if we did, see! The wrong will be upon us!"

فَإِنْ عُثِرَ عَلَىٰ أَنَّهُمَا اسْتَحَقَّا إِثْمًا فَآخَرَانِ يَقُومَانِ
مَقَامَهُمَا مِنَ الَّذِينَ اسْتَحَقَّ عَلَيْهِمُ الْأَوْلَيَانِ
فَيُقْسِمَانِ بِاللَّهِ لَشَهَادَتُنَا أَحَقُّ مِن شَهَادَتِهِمَا
وَمَا اعْتَدَيْنَا إِنَّا إِذًا لَّمِنَ الظَّالِمِينَ ﴿١٠٧﴾

108. That is most suitable: that they may give the evidence in its true nature and shape, or else they would fear that other oaths would be taken after their oaths. But

ذَٰلِكَ أَدْنَىٰ أَن يَأْتُوا بِالشَّهَادَةِ عَلَىٰ وَجْهِهَا
أَوْ يَخَافُوا أَن تُرَدَّ أَيْمَانٌ بَعْدَ أَيْمَانِهِمْ ۗ وَاتَّقُوا اللَّهَ

fear Allah, and listen (to His counsel): for Allah guides not a rebellious people.

وَٱسۡمَعُواْۗ وَٱللَّهُ لَا يَهۡدِي ٱلۡقَوۡمَ ٱلۡفَٰسِقِينَ ١٠٨

109. One day will Allah gather the messengers together, and ask: "What was the response you received (from men to your teaching)?" They will say: "We have no knowledge: it is You who knows in full all that is hidden."

نصف الحزب ١٣

۞يَوۡمَ يَجۡمَعُ ٱللَّهُ ٱلرُّسُلَ فَيَقُولُ مَاذَآ أُجِبۡتُمۡۖ
قَالُواْ لَا عِلۡمَ لَنَآۖ إِنَّكَ أَنتَ عَلَّٰمُ ٱلۡغُيُوبِ ١٠٩

110. Then will Allah say: "O Jesus the son of Mary! Recount My favour to you and to your mother. See! I strengthened you with the holy spirit, so that you did speak to the people in childhood and in maturity. See! I taught you the book and wisdom, the law and the Gospel. And see! You make out of clay, as it were, the figure of a bird, by My permission, and you breathe into it, and it becomes a bird by My permission, and you heal those born blind, and the lepers, by My permission. And see! You bring forth the dead by My permission. And see! I did restrain the Children of Israel from (violence to) you when you did show them the clear signs, and the unbelievers among them said: 'This is nothing but evident magic.'"

إِذۡ قَالَ ٱللَّهُ يَٰعِيسَى ٱبۡنَ مَرۡيَمَ ٱذۡكُرۡ نِعۡمَتِي
عَلَيۡكَ وَعَلَىٰ وَٰلِدَتِكَ إِذۡ أَيَّدتُّكَ بِرُوحِ
ٱلۡقُدُسِ تُكَلِّمُ ٱلنَّاسَ فِي ٱلۡمَهۡدِ وَكَهۡلٗاۖ
وَإِذۡ عَلَّمۡتُكَ ٱلۡكِتَٰبَ وَٱلۡحِكۡمَةَ وَٱلتَّوۡرَىٰةَ
وَٱلۡإِنجِيلَۖ وَإِذۡ تَخۡلُقُ مِنَ ٱلطِّينِ كَهَيۡـَٔةِ ٱلطَّيۡرِ
بِإِذۡنِي فَتَنفُخُ فِيهَا فَتَكُونُ طَيۡرَۢا بِإِذۡنِيۖ
وَتُبۡرِئُ ٱلۡأَكۡمَهَ وَٱلۡأَبۡرَصَ بِإِذۡنِيۖ وَإِذۡ تُخۡرِجُ
ٱلۡمَوۡتَىٰ بِإِذۡنِيۖ وَإِذۡ كَفَفۡتُ بَنِيٓ إِسۡرَٰٓءِيلَ
عَنكَ إِذۡ جِئۡتَهُم بِٱلۡبَيِّنَٰتِ فَقَالَ ٱلَّذِينَ
كَفَرُواْ مِنۡهُمۡ إِنۡ هَٰذَآ إِلَّا سِحۡرٞ مُّبِينٞ ١١٠

111. "And see! I inspired the disciples to have faith in Me and My messenger; they said, 'We have faith, and do you bear witness that we bow to Allah as Muslims'."

وَإِذۡ أَوۡحَيۡتُ إِلَى ٱلۡحَوَارِيِّـۧنَ أَنۡ ءَامِنُواْ بِي
وَبِرَسُولِي قَالُوٓاْ ءَامَنَّا وَٱشۡهَدۡ بِأَنَّنَا
مُسۡلِمُونَ ١١١

112. See! The disciples said: "O Jesus the son of Mary! Can your Lord send down to us a table set (with viands) from heaven?" Said Jesus: "Fear Allah, if you have faith."

إِذۡ قَالَ ٱلۡحَوَارِيُّونَ يَٰعِيسَى ٱبۡنَ مَرۡيَمَ هَلۡ
يَسۡتَطِيعُ رَبُّكَ أَن يُنَزِّلَ عَلَيۡنَا مَآئِدَةٗ مِّنَ
ٱلسَّمَآءِۖ قَالَ ٱتَّقُواْ ٱللَّهَ إِن كُنتُم مُّؤۡمِنِينَ ١١٢

113. They said: "We only wish to eat of it and satisfy our hearts, and to know that you have indeed told us the truth; and that we ourselves may be witnesses to the miracle."

قَالُواْ نُرِيدُ أَن نَّأۡكُلَ مِنۡهَا وَتَطۡمَئِنَّ قُلُوبُنَا
وَنَعۡلَمَ أَن قَدۡ صَدَقۡتَنَا وَنَكُونَ عَلَيۡهَا مِنَ
ٱلشَّٰهِدِينَ ١١٣

114. Said Jesus the son of Mary: "O Allah our Lord! Send us from heaven a table set (with viands) that there may be for us - for the first and the last of us - a solemn festival and a sign from You; and provide for our sustenance, for You are the best Sustainer (of our needs)."

قَالَ عِيسَى ٱبۡنُ مَرۡيَمَ ٱللَّهُمَّ رَبَّنَآ أَنزِلۡ عَلَيۡنَا مَآئِدَةٗ
مِّنَ ٱلسَّمَآءِ تَكُونُ لَنَا عِيدٗا لِّأَوَّلِنَا وَءَاخِرِنَا وَءَايَةٗ
مِّنكَۖ وَٱرۡزُقۡنَا وَأَنتَ خَيۡرُ ٱلرَّٰزِقِينَ ١١٤

115. Allah said: "I will send it down to you: but if any of you after that resists faith, I will punish him with a penalty such as I have not inflicted on anyone among all the peoples."

قَالَ ٱللَّهُ إِنِّي مُنَزِّلُهَا عَلَيۡكُمۡۖ فَمَن يَكۡفُرۡ بَعۡدُ مِنكُمۡ
فَإِنِّيٓ أُعَذِّبُهُۥ عَذَابٗا لَّآ أُعَذِّبُهُۥٓ أَحَدٗا مِّنَ
ٱلۡعَٰلَمِينَ ١١٥

116. And see! Allah will say: "O Jesus the son of Mary! Did you say to men, 'Worship me and my mother as gods in derogation of Allah'?" He will say: "Glory to You! Never could I say what I had no right (to say). Had I said such a thing, You would indeed have known it. You know what is in my heart, though I know not what is in Yours. For You know in full all that is hidden."

وَإِذۡ قَالَ ٱللَّهُ يَٰعِيسَى ٱبۡنَ مَرۡيَمَ ءَأَنتَ قُلۡتَ لِلنَّاسِ
ٱتَّخِذُونِي وَأُمِّيَ إِلَٰهَيۡنِ مِن دُونِ ٱللَّهِۖ قَالَ
سُبۡحَٰنَكَ مَا يَكُونُ لِيٓ أَنۡ أَقُولَ مَا لَيۡسَ لِي بِحَقٍّۚ إِن
كُنتُ قُلۡتُهُۥ فَقَدۡ عَلِمۡتَهُۥۚ تَعۡلَمُ مَا فِي نَفۡسِي وَلَآ
أَعۡلَمُ مَا فِي نَفۡسِكَۚ إِنَّكَ أَنتَ عَلَّٰمُ ٱلۡغُيُوبِ ١١٦

117. "Never said I to them anything except what You did command me to say: 'Worship Allah, my Lord and your Lord'; and I was a witness over them whilst I dwelt amongst them; when You did take me up You were the Watcher over them, and You are a Witness to all things."

مَا قُلۡتُ لَهُمۡ إِلَّا مَآ أَمَرۡتَنِي بِهِۦٓ أَنِ ٱعۡبُدُواْ ٱللَّهَ رَبِّي
وَرَبَّكُمۡۚ وَكُنتُ عَلَيۡهِمۡ شَهِيدٗا مَّا دُمۡتُ فِيهِمۡۖ
فَلَمَّا تَوَفَّيۡتَنِي كُنتَ أَنتَ ٱلرَّقِيبَ عَلَيۡهِمۡۚ وَأَنتَ عَلَىٰ كُلِّ
شَيۡءٖ شَهِيدٌ ١١٧

118. "If You do punish them, they are Your servants: if You do forgive them, You are the Exalted in Power, the Wise."

إِن تُعَذِّبۡهُمۡ فَإِنَّهُمۡ عِبَادُكَۖ وَإِن تَغۡفِرۡ لَهُمۡ فَإِنَّكَ
أَنتَ ٱلۡعَزِيزُ ٱلۡحَكِيمُ ١١٨

119. Allah will say: "This is a day on which the truthful will profit from their truth: theirs are gardens, with rivers flowing beneath - their eternal home; Allah well-pleased with them, and they with Allah; that is the great salvation (the fulfilment of all desires)."

قَالَ ٱللَّهُ هَٰذَا يَوْمُ يَنفَعُ ٱلصَّٰدِقِينَ صِدْقُهُمْ ۚ لَهُمْ جَنَّٰتٌ تَجْرِى مِن تَحْتِهَا ٱلْأَنْهَٰرُ خَٰلِدِينَ فِيهَآ أَبَدًا ۚ رَّضِىَ ٱللَّهُ عَنْهُمْ وَرَضُوا۟ عَنْهُ ۚ ذَٰلِكَ ٱلْفَوْزُ ٱلْعَظِيمُ ﴿١١٩﴾

120. To Allah does belong the dominion of the heavens and the earth, and all that is in it, and it is He Who has power over all things.

لِلَّهِ مُلْكُ ٱلسَّمَٰوَٰتِ وَٱلْأَرْضِ وَمَا فِيهِنَّ ۚ وَهُوَ عَلَىٰ كُلِّ شَىْءٍ قَدِيرٌۢ ﴿١٢٠﴾

سُورَةُ الأَنْعَامِ

Surah 6: ***Al-An'am*** **(The Cattle)**

In the name of Allah,
Most Gracious, Most Merciful.

بِسْمِ ٱللَّهِ ٱلرَّحْمَٰنِ ٱلرَّحِيمِ

1. Praise be to Allah, Who created the heavens and the earth, and made the darkness and the light. Yet those who reject faith hold (others) as equal with their guardian-Lord.

ٱلْحَمْدُ لِلَّهِ ٱلَّذِى خَلَقَ ٱلسَّمَٰوَٰتِ وَٱلْأَرْضَ وَجَعَلَ ٱلظُّلُمَٰتِ وَٱلنُّورَ ۖ ثُمَّ ٱلَّذِينَ كَفَرُوا۟ بِرَبِّهِمْ يَعْدِلُونَ ﴿١﴾

2. He it is Who created you from clay, and then decreed a stated term (for you). And there is in His presence another determined term; yet you doubt within yourselves!

هُوَ ٱلَّذِى خَلَقَكُم مِّن طِينٍ ثُمَّ قَضَىٰٓ أَجَلًا ۖ وَأَجَلٌ مُّسَمًّى عِندَهُۥ ۖ ثُمَّ أَنتُمْ تَمْتَرُونَ ﴿٢﴾

3. And He is Allah in the heavens and on earth. He knows what you hide, and what you reveal, and He knows the (recompense) which you earn (by your deeds).

وَهُوَ ٱللَّهُ فِى ٱلسَّمَٰوَٰتِ وَفِى ٱلْأَرْضِ ۖ يَعْلَمُ سِرَّكُمْ وَجَهْرَكُمْ وَيَعْلَمُ مَا تَكْسِبُونَ ﴿٣﴾

4. But never did a single one of the signs of their Lord reach them, but they turned away from it.

وَمَا تَأْتِيهِم مِّنْ ءَايَةٍ مِّنْ ءَايَٰتِ رَبِّهِمْ إِلَّا كَانُوا۟ عَنْهَا مُعْرِضِينَ ﴿٤﴾

5. And now they reject the truth when it reaches them; but soon shall learn the

فَقَدْ كَذَّبُوا۟ بِٱلْحَقِّ لَمَّا جَآءَهُمْ ۖ فَسَوْفَ يَأْتِيهِمْ أَنۢبَٰٓؤُا۟

reality of what they used to mock at.

مَا كَانُوا۟ بِهِۦ يَسْتَهْزِءُونَ ٥

6. Do they not see how many of those before them We did destroy? - Generations We had established on the earth, in strength such as We have not given to you - for whom We poured out rain from the skies in abundance, and gave (fertile) streams flowing beneath their (feet): yet for their sins We destroyed them, and raised in their wake fresh generations (to succeed them).

أَلَمْ يَرَوْا۟ كَمْ أَهْلَكْنَا مِن قَبْلِهِم مِّن قَرْنٍ مَّكَّنَّـٰهُمْ
فِى ٱلْأَرْضِ مَا لَمْ نُمَكِّن لَّكُمْ وَأَرْسَلْنَا ٱلسَّمَآءَ عَلَيْهِم
مِّدْرَارًا وَجَعَلْنَا ٱلْأَنْهَـٰرَ تَجْرِى مِن تَحْتِهِمْ فَأَهْلَكْنَـٰهُم
بِذُنُوبِهِمْ وَأَنشَأْنَا مِنۢ بَعْدِهِمْ قَرْنًا ءَاخَرِينَ ٦

7. If We had sent to you a written (Message) on parchment, so that they could touch it with their hands, the unbelievers would have been sure to say: "This is nothing but obvious magic!"

وَلَوْ نَزَّلْنَا عَلَيْكَ كِتَـٰبًا فِى قِرْطَاسٍ فَلَمَسُوهُ بِأَيْدِيهِمْ
لَقَالَ ٱلَّذِينَ كَفَرُوٓا۟ إِنْ هَـٰذَآ إِلَّا سِحْرٌ مُّبِينٌ ٧

8. They say: "Why is not an angel sent down to him?" If We did send down an angel, the matter would be settled at once, and no respite would be granted them.

وَقَالُوا۟ لَوْلَآ أُنزِلَ عَلَيْهِ مَلَكٌ ۖ وَلَوْ أَنزَلْنَا مَلَكًا لَّقُضِىَ
ٱلْأَمْرُ ثُمَّ لَا يُنظَرُونَ ٨

9. If We had made it an angel, We should have sent him as a man, and We should certainly have caused them confusion in a matter which they have already covered with confusion.

وَلَوْ جَعَلْنَـٰهُ مَلَكًا لَّجَعَلْنَـٰهُ رَجُلًا وَلَلَبَسْنَا
عَلَيْهِم مَّا يَلْبِسُونَ ٩

10. Mocked were (many) messengers before you; but their scoffers were hemmed in by the thing that they mocked.

وَلَقَدِ ٱسْتُهْزِئَ بِرُسُلٍ مِّن قَبْلِكَ فَحَاقَ بِٱلَّذِينَ
سَخِرُوا۟ مِنْهُم مَّا كَانُوا۟ بِهِۦ يَسْتَهْزِءُونَ ١٠

11. Say: "Travel through the earth and see what was the end of those who rejected truth."

قُلْ سِيرُوا۟ فِى ٱلْأَرْضِ ثُمَّ ٱنظُرُوا۟ كَيْفَ كَانَ
عَـٰقِبَةُ ٱلْمُكَذِّبِينَ ١١

12. Say: "To whom belongs all that is in the heavens and on earth?" Say: "To Allah. He

قُل لِّمَن مَّا فِى ٱلسَّمَـٰوَٰتِ وَٱلْأَرْضِ ۖ قُل لِّلَّهِ

has inscribed for Himself (the rule of) mercy. That He will gather you together for the day of judgement, there is no doubt whatever. It is they who have lost their own souls, that will not believe.

كَتَبَ عَلَىٰ نَفْسِهِ ٱلرَّحْمَةَ ۚ لَيَجْمَعَنَّكُمْ
إِلَىٰ يَوْمِ ٱلْقِيَٰمَةِ لَا رَيْبَ فِيهِ ۚ ٱلَّذِينَ خَسِرُوٓا۟
أَنفُسَهُمْ فَهُمْ لَا يُؤْمِنُونَ ﴿١٢﴾

13. "To Him belongs all that dwells (or lurks) in the night and the day. For He is the One Who hears and knows all things."

ثلاثة أرباع الحزب ١٣
۞ وَلَهُۥ مَا سَكَنَ فِى ٱلَّيْلِ وَٱلنَّهَارِ ۚ وَهُوَ
ٱلسَّمِيعُ ٱلْعَلِيمُ ﴿١٣﴾

14. Say: "Shall I take for my protector any other than Allah, the Maker of the heavens and the earth? And He it is that feeds but is not fed." Say: "Nay! But I am commanded to be the first of those who bow to Allah (in Islam), and be not you of the company of those who join gods with Allah."

قُلْ أَغَيْرَ ٱللَّهِ أَتَّخِذُ وَلِيًّا فَاطِرِ ٱلسَّمَٰوَٰتِ
وَٱلْأَرْضِ وَهُوَ يُطْعِمُ وَلَا يُطْعَمُ ۗ قُلْ إِنِّىٓ أُمِرْتُ
أَنْ أَكُونَ أَوَّلَ مَنْ أَسْلَمَ ۖ وَلَا تَكُونَنَّ مِنَ
ٱلْمُشْرِكِينَ ﴿١٤﴾

15. Say: "I would, if I disobeyed my Lord, indeed have fear of the penalty of a mighty day."

قُلْ إِنِّىٓ أَخَافُ إِنْ عَصَيْتُ رَبِّى عَذَابَ يَوْمٍ
عَظِيمٍ ﴿١٥﴾

16. "On that day, if the penalty is averted from any, it is due to Allah's mercy; and that would be (salvation), the obvious fulfilment of all desire."

مَّن يُصْرَفْ عَنْهُ يَوْمَئِذٍ فَقَدْ رَحِمَهُۥ ۚ وَذَٰلِكَ ٱلْفَوْزُ
ٱلْمُبِينُ ﴿١٦﴾

17. "If Allah touches you with affliction, none can remove it but He; and if He touches you with happiness (there is none that can impair it); He has power over all things."

وَإِن يَمْسَسْكَ ٱللَّهُ بِضُرٍّ فَلَا كَاشِفَ لَهُۥٓ إِلَّا هُوَ ۖ
وَإِن يَمْسَسْكَ بِخَيْرٍ فَهُوَ عَلَىٰ كُلِّ شَىْءٍ
قَدِيرٌ ﴿١٧﴾

18. "He is the Irresistible, (watching) from above over His worshippers; and He is the Wise, acquainted with all things."

وَهُوَ ٱلْقَاهِرُ فَوْقَ عِبَادِهِۦ ۚ وَهُوَ ٱلْحَكِيمُ
ٱلْخَبِيرُ ﴿١٨﴾

19. Say: "What thing is most weighty in evidence?" Say: "Allah is Witness between

قُلْ أَىُّ شَىْءٍ أَكْبَرُ شَهَٰدَةً ۖ قُلِ ٱللَّهُ ۖ شَهِيدٌۢ بَيْنِى وَبَيْنَكُمْ ۚ

me and you; this Qur'an has been revealed to me by inspiration. That I may warn you and all whom it reaches. Can you possibly bear witness that besides Allah there is another God?" Say: "Nay! I cannot bear witness!" Say: "But in truth He is the One God, and I truly am innocent of (your blasphemy of) joining others with Him."

وَأُوحِيَ إِلَيَّ هَٰذَا ٱلْقُرْءَانُ لِأُنذِرَكُم بِهِۦ وَمَنۢ بَلَغَۚ أَئِنَّكُمْ
لَتَشْهَدُونَ أَنَّ مَعَ ٱللَّهِ ءَالِهَةً أُخْرَىٰۚ قُل لَّآ أَشْهَدُۚ قُلْ
إِنَّمَا هُوَ إِلَٰهٌ وَٰحِدٌ وَإِنَّنِى بَرِىٓءٌ مِّمَّا تُشْرِكُونَ ١٩

20. Those to whom We have given the book know this as they know their own sons. Those who have lost their own souls refuse therefore to believe.

ٱلَّذِينَ ءَاتَيْنَٰهُمُ ٱلْكِتَٰبَ يَعْرِفُونَهُۥ كَمَا يَعْرِفُونَ أَبْنَآءَهُمُ
ٱلَّذِينَ خَسِرُوٓا۟ أَنفُسَهُمْ فَهُمْ لَا يُؤْمِنُونَ ٢٠

21. Who does more wrong than he who invents a lie against Allah or rejects His signs? But verily the wrongdoers never shall prosper.

وَمَنْ أَظْلَمُ مِمَّنِ ٱفْتَرَىٰ عَلَى ٱللَّهِ كَذِبًا أَوْ كَذَّبَ بِـَٔايَٰتِهِۦٓۚ
إِنَّهُۥ لَا يُفْلِحُ ٱلظَّٰلِمُونَ ٢١

22. One day shall We gather them all together: We shall say to those who ascribed partners (to Us): "Where are the partners whom you (invented and) talked about?"

وَيَوْمَ نَحْشُرُهُمْ جَمِيعًا ثُمَّ نَقُولُ لِلَّذِينَ أَشْرَكُوٓا۟ أَيْنَ
شُرَكَآؤُكُمُ ٱلَّذِينَ كُنتُمْ تَزْعُمُونَ ٢٢

23. There will then be (left) no subterfuge for them but to say: "By Allah Our Lord, we were not those who joined gods with Allah."

ثُمَّ لَمْ تَكُن فِتْنَتُهُمْ إِلَّآ أَن قَالُوا۟ وَٱللَّهِ رَبِّنَا مَا كُنَّا
مُشْرِكِينَ ٢٣

24. See! How they lie against their own souls! But the (lie) which they invented will leave them in the lurch.

ٱنظُرْ كَيْفَ كَذَبُوا۟ عَلَىٰٓ أَنفُسِهِمْۚ وَضَلَّ عَنْهُم مَّا كَانُوا۟
يَفْتَرُونَ ٢٤

25. Of them there are some who (pretend to) listen to you; but We have thrown veils on their hearts, so they understand it not, and deafness in their ears; if they saw every one of the signs, they will not believe in them; in so much that when they come to you, they (but) dispute with you; the unbelievers say: "These are nothing but tales of the ancients."

وَمِنْهُم مَّن يَسْتَمِعُ إِلَيْكَۖ وَجَعَلْنَا عَلَىٰ قُلُوبِهِمْ أَكِنَّةً
أَن يَفْقَهُوهُ وَفِىٓ ءَاذَانِهِمْ وَقْرًاۚ وَإِن يَرَوْا۟ كُلَّ
ءَايَةٍ لَّا يُؤْمِنُوا۟ بِهَاۚ حَتَّىٰٓ إِذَا جَآءُوكَ يُجَٰدِلُونَكَ يَقُولُ
ٱلَّذِينَ كَفَرُوٓا۟ إِنْ هَٰذَآ إِلَّآ أَسَٰطِيرُ ٱلْأَوَّلِينَ ٢٥

26. Others they keep away from it, and themselves they keep away; but they only destroy their own souls, and they perceive it not.

وَهُمْ يَنْهَوْنَ عَنْهُ وَيَنْـَٔوْنَ عَنْهُ ۖ وَإِن يُهْلِكُونَ إِلَّآ
أَنفُسَهُمْ وَمَا يَشْعُرُونَ ﴿٢٦﴾

27. If you could but see when they are confronted with the fire! They will say: "Would that we were but sent back! Then would we not reject the signs of our Lord, but would be amongst those who believe!"

وَلَوْ تَرَىٰٓ إِذْ وُقِفُوا۟ عَلَى ٱلنَّارِ فَقَالُوا۟ يَٰلَيْتَنَا نُرَدُّ وَلَا
نُكَذِّبَ بِـَٔايَٰتِ رَبِّنَا وَنَكُونَ مِنَ ٱلْمُؤْمِنِينَ ﴿٢٧﴾

28. Yea, in their own (eyes) will become manifest what before they concealed. But if they were returned, they would certainly relapse to the things they were forbidden, for they are indeed liars.

بَلْ بَدَا لَهُم مَّا كَانُوا۟ يُخْفُونَ مِن قَبْلُ ۖ وَلَوْ رُدُّوا۟ لَعَادُوا۟
لِمَا نُهُوا۟ عَنْهُ وَإِنَّهُمْ لَكَٰذِبُونَ ﴿٢٨﴾

29. And they (sometimes) say: "There is nothing except our life on this earth, and never shall we be raised up again."

وَقَالُوٓا۟ إِنْ هِىَ إِلَّا حَيَاتُنَا ٱلدُّنْيَا وَمَا نَحْنُ
بِمَبْعُوثِينَ ﴿٢٩﴾

30. If you could but see when they are confronted with their Lord! He will say: "Is not this the truth?" They will say: "Yea, by our Lord!" He will say: "Taste you then the penalty, because you rejected faith."

وَلَوْ تَرَىٰٓ إِذْ وُقِفُوا۟ عَلَىٰ رَبِّهِمْ ۚ قَالَ أَلَيْسَ هَٰذَا
بِٱلْحَقِّ ۚ قَالُوا۟ بَلَىٰ وَرَبِّنَا ۚ قَالَ فَذُوقُوا۟ ٱلْعَذَابَ بِمَا
كُنتُمْ تَكْفُرُونَ ﴿٣٠﴾

31. Lost indeed are they who treat it as a falsehood that they must meet Allah - until on a sudden the hour is on them, and they say: "Ah! Woe to us that we took no thought of it"; for they bear their burdens on their backs, and evil indeed are the burdens that they bear.

قَدْ خَسِرَ ٱلَّذِينَ كَذَّبُوا۟ بِلِقَآءِ ٱللَّهِ ۖ حَتَّىٰٓ إِذَا جَآءَتْهُمُ
ٱلسَّاعَةُ بَغْتَةً قَالُوا۟ يَٰحَسْرَتَنَا عَلَىٰ مَا فَرَّطْنَا فِيهَا
وَهُمْ يَحْمِلُونَ أَوْزَارَهُمْ عَلَىٰ ظُهُورِهِمْ ۚ أَلَا سَآءَ
مَا يَزِرُونَ ﴿٣١﴾

32. What is the life of this world but play and amusement? But best is the home in the hereafter, for those who are righteous. Will you not then understand?

وَمَا ٱلْحَيَوٰةُ ٱلدُّنْيَآ إِلَّا لَعِبٌ وَلَهْوٌ ۖ وَلَلدَّارُ
ٱلْءَاخِرَةُ خَيْرٌ لِّلَّذِينَ يَتَّقُونَ ۗ أَفَلَا تَعْقِلُونَ ﴿٣٢﴾

33. We know indeed the grief which their words do cause you; it is not you (O Muhammad) they reject; it is the signs of Allah, which the wicked condemn.

قَدۡ نَعۡلَمُ إِنَّهُۥ لَيَحۡزُنُكَ ٱلَّذِي يَقُولُونَۖ فَإِنَّهُمۡ
لَا يُكَذِّبُونَكَ وَلَٰكِنَّ ٱلظَّٰلِمِينَ بِـَٔايَٰتِ ٱللَّهِ
يَجۡحَدُونَ ٣٣

34. Rejected were the messengers before you; with patience and constancy they bore their rejection and their wrongs, until Our aid did reach them; there is none that can alter the words (and decrees) of Allah. Already have you received some account of those messengers.

وَلَقَدۡ كُذِّبَتۡ رُسُلٞ مِّن قَبۡلِكَ فَصَبَرُواْ عَلَىٰ مَا
كُذِّبُواْ وَأُوذُواْ حَتَّىٰٓ أَتَىٰهُمۡ نَصۡرُنَاۚ وَلَا مُبَدِّلَ
لِكَلِمَٰتِ ٱللَّهِۚ وَلَقَدۡ جَآءَكَ مِن نَّبَإِيْ ٱلۡمُرۡسَلِينَ ٣٤

35. If their spurning is hard on your mind, yet if you were able to seek a tunnel in the ground or a ladder to the skies and bring them a sign - (what good?). If it were Allah's Will, He could gather them together to true guidance: so be not you amongst those who are swayed by ignorance (and impatience)!

وَإِن كَانَ كَبُرَ عَلَيۡكَ إِعۡرَاضُهُمۡ فَإِنِ ٱسۡتَطَعۡتَ
أَن تَبۡتَغِيَ نَفَقٗا فِي ٱلۡأَرۡضِ أَوۡ سُلَّمٗا فِي ٱلسَّمَآءِ
فَتَأۡتِيَهُم بِـَٔايَةٖۚ وَلَوۡ شَآءَ ٱللَّهُ لَجَمَعَهُمۡ عَلَى
ٱلۡهُدَىٰۚ فَلَا تَكُونَنَّ مِنَ ٱلۡجَٰهِلِينَ ٣٥

36. Those who listen (in truth), be sure, will accept; as to the dead, Allah will raise them up; then will they be returned to Him.

الحزب ١٤ * إِنَّمَا يَسۡتَجِيبُ ٱلَّذِينَ يَسۡمَعُونَۘ وَٱلۡمَوۡتَىٰ يَبۡعَثُهُمُ
ٱللَّهُ ثُمَّ إِلَيۡهِ يُرۡجَعُونَ ٣٦

37. They say: "Why is not a sign sent down to him from his Lord?" Say: "Allah has certainly power to send down a sign; but most of them understand not."

وَقَالُواْ لَوۡلَا نُزِّلَ عَلَيۡهِ ءَايَةٞ مِّن رَّبِّهِۦۚ قُلۡ إِنَّ ٱللَّهَ قَادِرٌ
عَلَىٰٓ أَن يُنَزِّلَ ءَايَةٗ وَلَٰكِنَّ أَكۡثَرَهُمۡ لَا يَعۡلَمُونَ ٣٧

38. There is not an animal (that lives) on the earth, nor a being that flies on its wings, but (forms part of) communities like you. Nothing have We omitted from the book, and they (all) shall be gathered to their Lord in the end.

وَمَا مِن دَآبَّةٖ فِي ٱلۡأَرۡضِ وَلَا طَٰٓئِرٖ يَطِيرُ بِجَنَاحَيۡهِ
إِلَّآ أُمَمٌ أَمۡثَالُكُمۚ مَّا فَرَّطۡنَا فِي ٱلۡكِتَٰبِ مِن شَيۡءٖۚ
ثُمَّ إِلَىٰ رَبِّهِمۡ يُحۡشَرُونَ ٣٨

39. Those who reject Our signs are deaf and dumb - in the midst of darkness profound:

وَٱلَّذِينَ كَذَّبُواْ بِـَٔايَٰتِنَا صُمّٞ وَبُكۡمٞ فِي ٱلظُّلُمَٰتِۗ

whom Allah wills, He leaves to wander; whom He wills, He places on the way that is straight.

مَن يَشَإِ ٱللَّهُ يُضْلِلْهُ وَمَن يَشَأْ يَجْعَلْهُ عَلَىٰ
صِرَٰطٍ مُّسْتَقِيمٍ ٣٩

40. Say: "Think you to yourselves, if there come upon you the wrath of Allah, or the hour (that you dread), would you then call upon other than Allah? - (Reply) if you are truthful!"

قُلْ أَرَءَيْتَكُمْ إِنْ أَتَىٰكُمْ عَذَابُ ٱللَّهِ أَوْ أَتَتْكُمُ
ٱلسَّاعَةُ أَغَيْرَ ٱللَّهِ تَدْعُونَ إِن كُنتُمْ صَٰدِقِينَ ٤٠

41. "Nay - On Him would you call, and if it be His Will, He would remove (the distress) which occasioned your call upon Him, and you would forget (the false gods) which you join with Him!"

بَلْ إِيَّاهُ تَدْعُونَ فَيَكْشِفُ مَا تَدْعُونَ إِلَيْهِ إِن شَآءَ
وَتَنسَوْنَ مَا تُشْرِكُونَ ٤١

42. Before you We sent (messengers) to many nations, and We afflicted the nations with suffering and adversity, that they might learn humility.

وَلَقَدْ أَرْسَلْنَآ إِلَىٰٓ أُمَمٍ مِّن قَبْلِكَ فَأَخَذْنَٰهُم
بِٱلْبَأْسَآءِ وَٱلضَّرَّآءِ لَعَلَّهُمْ يَتَضَرَّعُونَ ٤٢

43. When the suffering reached them from Us, why then did they not learn humility? On the contrary, their hearts became hardened, and Satan made their (sinful) acts seem alluring to them.

فَلَوْلَآ إِذْ جَآءَهُم بَأْسُنَا تَضَرَّعُوا۟ وَلَٰكِن قَسَتْ
قُلُوبُهُمْ وَزَيَّنَ لَهُمُ ٱلشَّيْطَٰنُ مَا كَانُوا۟
يَعْمَلُونَ ٤٣

44. But when they forget the warning they had received, We opened to them the gates of all (good) things, until, in the midst of their enjoyment of Our gifts, on a sudden, We called them to account, when they were plunged in despair!

فَلَمَّا نَسُوا۟ مَا ذُكِّرُوا۟ بِهِۦ فَتَحْنَا عَلَيْهِمْ أَبْوَٰبَ
كُلِّ شَىْءٍ حَتَّىٰٓ إِذَا فَرِحُوا۟ بِمَآ أُوتُوٓا۟ أَخَذْنَٰهُم
بَغْتَةً فَإِذَا هُم مُّبْلِسُونَ ٤٤

45. Of the wrongdoers the last remnant was cut off. Praise be to Allah, the Cherisher of the Worlds.

فَقُطِعَ دَابِرُ ٱلْقَوْمِ ٱلَّذِينَ ظَلَمُوا۟ ۚ وَٱلْحَمْدُ لِلَّهِ رَبِّ
ٱلْعَٰلَمِينَ ٤٥

46. Say: "Think you, if Allah took away your hearing and your sight, and sealed up your hearts, who - a god other than Allah - could restore them to you?" See how We

قُلْ أَرَءَيْتُمْ إِنْ أَخَذَ ٱللَّهُ سَمْعَكُمْ وَأَبْصَٰرَكُمْ وَخَتَمَ
عَلَىٰ قُلُوبِكُم مَّنْ إِلَٰهٌ غَيْرُ ٱللَّهِ يَأْتِيكُم بِهِ ۗ ٱنظُرْ

explain the signs by various (symbols); Yet they turn aside.

كَيْفَ نُصَرِّفُ ٱلْءَايَٰتِ ثُمَّ هُمْ يَصْدِفُونَ ﴿٤٦﴾

47. Say: "Think you, if the punishment of Allah comes to you, whether suddenly or openly, will any be destroyed except those who do wrong?"

قُلْ أَرَءَيْتَكُمْ إِنْ أَتَىٰكُمْ عَذَابُ ٱللَّهِ بَغْتَةً
أَوْ جَهْرَةً هَلْ يُهْلَكُ إِلَّا ٱلْقَوْمُ ٱلظَّٰلِمُونَ ﴿٤٧﴾

48. We send the messengers only to give good news and to warn: so those who believe and mend (their lives) - upon them shall be no fear, nor shall they grieve.

وَمَا نُرْسِلُ ٱلْمُرْسَلِينَ إِلَّا مُبَشِّرِينَ وَمُنذِرِينَ ۖ فَمَنْ
ءَامَنَ وَأَصْلَحَ فَلَا خَوْفٌ عَلَيْهِمْ وَلَا هُمْ يَحْزَنُونَ ﴿٤٨﴾

49. But those who reject Our signs - them shall punishment touch, for that they ceased not from transgressing.

وَٱلَّذِينَ كَذَّبُوا۟ بِـَٔايَٰتِنَا يَمَسُّهُمُ ٱلْعَذَابُ بِمَا كَانُوا۟
يَفْسُقُونَ ﴿٤٩﴾

50. Say: "I tell you not that with me are the Treasures of Allah, nor do I know what is hidden, nor do I tell you I am an angel. I but follow what is revealed to me." Say: "Can the blind be held equal to the seeing?" Will you then not consider?

قُل لَّآ أَقُولُ لَكُمْ عِندِى خَزَآئِنُ ٱللَّهِ وَلَآ أَعْلَمُ
ٱلْغَيْبَ وَلَآ أَقُولُ لَكُمْ إِنِّى مَلَكٌ ۖ إِنْ أَتَّبِعُ إِلَّا
مَا يُوحَىٰٓ إِلَىَّ ۚ قُلْ هَلْ يَسْتَوِى ٱلْأَعْمَىٰ وَٱلْبَصِيرُ ۚ
أَفَلَا تَتَفَكَّرُونَ ﴿٥٠﴾

51. Give the warning to those in whose (hearts) is the fear that they will be brought (to judgement) before their Lord: except for Him they will have no protector nor intercessor; that they may guard (against evil).

وَأَنذِرْ بِهِ ٱلَّذِينَ يَخَافُونَ أَن يُحْشَرُوٓا۟ إِلَىٰ رَبِّهِمْ ۙ
لَيْسَ لَهُم مِّن دُونِهِۦ وَلِىٌّ وَلَا شَفِيعٌ لَّعَلَّهُمْ
يَتَّقُونَ ﴿٥١﴾

52. Send not away those who call on their Lord morning and evening, seeking His Face. In nothing are you accountable for them, and in nothing are they accountable for you, that you should turn them away, and thus be (one) of the unjust.

وَلَا تَطْرُدِ ٱلَّذِينَ يَدْعُونَ رَبَّهُم بِٱلْغَدَوٰةِ وَٱلْعَشِىِّ
يُرِيدُونَ وَجْهَهُۥ ۖ مَا عَلَيْكَ مِنْ حِسَابِهِم مِّن
شَىْءٍ وَمَا مِنْ حِسَابِكَ عَلَيْهِم مِّن شَىْءٍ فَتَطْرُدَهُمْ
فَتَكُونَ مِنَ ٱلظَّٰلِمِينَ ﴿٥٢﴾

53. Thus did We try some of them by comparison with others, that they should say: "Is it these then that Allah has favoured from amongst us?" Does not Allah know best those who are grateful?

وَكَذَٰلِكَ فَتَنَّا بَعْضَهُم بِبَعْضٍ لِّيَقُولُوٓا۟ أَهَٰٓؤُلَآءِ
مَنَّ ٱللَّهُ عَلَيْهِم مِّنۢ بَيْنِنَآ ۗ أَلَيْسَ ٱللَّهُ بِأَعْلَمَ
بِٱلشَّٰكِرِينَ ﴿٥٣﴾

54. When those come to you who believe in Our signs, say: "Peace be on you"; your Lord has inscribed for Himself (the rule of) mercy: verily, if any of you did evil in ignorance, and thereafter repented, and amended (his conduct), He is Oft-Forgiving, Most Merciful."

وَإِذَا جَآءَكَ ٱلَّذِينَ يُؤْمِنُونَ بِـَٔايَٰتِنَا فَقُلْ سَلَٰمٌ
عَلَيْكُمْ ۖ كَتَبَ رَبُّكُمْ عَلَىٰ نَفْسِهِ ٱلرَّحْمَةَ ۖ أَنَّهُۥ
مَنْ عَمِلَ مِنكُمْ سُوٓءًۢا بِجَهَٰلَةٍ ثُمَّ تَابَ مِنۢ
بَعْدِهِۦ وَأَصْلَحَ فَأَنَّهُۥ غَفُورٌ رَّحِيمٌ ﴿٥٤﴾

55. Thus do We explain the signs in detail: that the way of the sinners may be shown up.

وَكَذَٰلِكَ نُفَصِّلُ ٱلْءَايَٰتِ وَلِتَسْتَبِينَ سَبِيلُ
ٱلْمُجْرِمِينَ ﴿٥٥﴾

56. Say: "I am forbidden to worship those - other than Allah - whom you call upon." Say: "I will not follow your vain desires; if I did, I would stray from the path, and be not of the company of those who receive guidance."

قُلْ إِنِّى نُهِيتُ أَنْ أَعْبُدَ ٱلَّذِينَ تَدْعُونَ مِن دُونِ
ٱللَّهِ ۚ قُل لَّآ أَتَّبِعُ أَهْوَآءَكُمْ ۙ قَدْ ضَلَلْتُ إِذًا وَمَآ
أَنَا۠ مِنَ ٱلْمُهْتَدِينَ ﴿٥٦﴾

57. Say: "For me, I (work) on a clear sign from my Lord, but you reject Him. What you would see hastened, is not in my power. The command rests with none but Allah: He declares the truth, and He is the best of judges."

قُلْ إِنِّى عَلَىٰ بَيِّنَةٍ مِّن رَّبِّى وَكَذَّبْتُم بِهِۦ ۚ
مَا عِندِى مَا تَسْتَعْجِلُونَ بِهِۦٓ ۚ إِنِ ٱلْحُكْمُ
إِلَّا لِلَّهِ ۖ يَقُصُّ ٱلْحَقَّ ۖ وَهُوَ خَيْرُ ٱلْفَٰصِلِينَ ﴿٥٧﴾

58. Say: "If what you would see hastened were in my power, the matter would be settled at once between you and me. But Allah knows best those who do wrong."

قُل لَّوْ أَنَّ عِندِى مَا تَسْتَعْجِلُونَ بِهِۦ لَقُضِىَ ٱلْأَمْرُ
بَيْنِى وَبَيْنَكُمْ ۗ وَٱللَّهُ أَعْلَمُ بِٱلظَّٰلِمِينَ ﴿٥٨﴾

59. With Him are the keys of the unseen, the treasures that none knows but He. He knows whatever there is on the earth and in the sea. Not a leaf does fall but with His knowledge;

۞ وَعِندَهُۥ مَفَاتِحُ ٱلْغَيْبِ لَا يَعْلَمُهَآ إِلَّا هُوَ ۚ ربع الحزب ١٤
وَيَعْلَمُ مَا فِى ٱلْبَرِّ وَٱلْبَحْرِ ۚ وَمَا تَسْقُطُ مِن وَرَقَةٍ

there is not a grain in the darkness (or depths) of the earth, nor anything fresh or dry (green or withered), but is (inscribed) in a record clear (to those who can read).

إِلَّا يَعْلَمُهَا وَلَا حَبَّةٍ فِي ظُلُمَٰتِ ٱلْأَرْضِ وَلَا رَطْبٍ
وَلَا يَابِسٍ إِلَّا فِي كِتَٰبٍ مُّبِينٍ ٥٩

60. It is He Who does take your souls by night, and has knowledge of all that you have done by day; by day does He raise you up again; that a term appointed be fulfilled; in the end to Him will be your return; then will He show you the truth of all that you did.

وَهُوَ ٱلَّذِي يَتَوَفَّىٰكُم بِٱلَّيْلِ وَيَعْلَمُ مَا جَرَحْتُم
بِٱلنَّهَارِ ثُمَّ يَبْعَثُكُمْ فِيهِ لِيُقْضَىٰٓ أَجَلٌ مُّسَمًّى ۖ
ثُمَّ إِلَيْهِ مَرْجِعُكُمْ ثُمَّ يُنَبِّئُكُم بِمَا كُنتُمْ تَعْمَلُونَ ٦٠

61. He is the Irresistible, (watching) from above over His worshippers, and He sets guardians over you. At length, when death approaches one of you, Our angels take his soul, and they never fail in their duty.

وَهُوَ ٱلْقَاهِرُ فَوْقَ عِبَادِهِۦ ۖ وَيُرْسِلُ عَلَيْكُمْ
حَفَظَةً حَتَّىٰٓ إِذَا جَآءَ أَحَدَكُمُ ٱلْمَوْتُ تَوَفَّتْهُ
رُسُلُنَا وَهُمْ لَا يُفَرِّطُونَ ٦١

62. Then are men returned to Allah, their true protector, surely His is the command, and He is the swiftest in taking account.

ثُمَّ رُدُّوٓا۟ إِلَى ٱللَّهِ مَوْلَىٰهُمُ ٱلْحَقِّ ۚ أَلَا لَهُ ٱلْحُكْمُ
وَهُوَ أَسْرَعُ ٱلْحَٰسِبِينَ ٦٢

63. Say; "Who is it that delivers you from the dark recesses of land and sea, when you call upon Him in humility and in the secrecy of the heart: 'if He only delivers us from these (dangers), (we vow) we shall truly show our gratitude'?"

قُلْ مَن يُنَجِّيكُم مِّن ظُلُمَٰتِ ٱلْبَرِّ وَٱلْبَحْرِ تَدْعُونَهُۥ
تَضَرُّعًا وَخُفْيَةً لَّئِنْ أَنجَىٰنَا مِنْ هَٰذِهِۦ لَنَكُونَنَّ مِنَ
ٱلشَّٰكِرِينَ ٦٣

64. Say: "It is Allah that delivers you from these and all (other) distresses: and yet you worship false gods!"

قُلِ ٱللَّهُ يُنَجِّيكُم مِّنْهَا وَمِن كُلِّ كَرْبٍ ثُمَّ أَنتُمْ تُشْرِكُونَ ٦٤

65. Say: "He has power to send calamities on you, from above and below, or to cover you with confusion in party strife, giving you a taste of mutual vengeance - each from the other." See how We explain the signs by various (symbols); that they may understand.

قُلْ هُوَ ٱلْقَادِرُ عَلَىٰٓ أَن يَبْعَثَ عَلَيْكُمْ عَذَابًا مِّن فَوْقِكُمْ
أَوْ مِن تَحْتِ أَرْجُلِكُمْ أَوْ يَلْبِسَكُمْ شِيَعًا وَيُذِيقَ
بَعْضَكُم بَأْسَ بَعْضٍ ۗ ٱنظُرْ كَيْفَ نُصَرِّفُ ٱلْءَايَٰتِ
لَعَلَّهُمْ يَفْقَهُونَ ٦٥

66. But your people reject this, though it is the truth. Say: "Not mine is the responsibility for arranging your affairs;

وَكَذَّبَ بِهِۦ قَوْمُكَ وَهُوَ ٱلْحَقُّ ۚ قُل لَّسْتُ عَلَيْكُم
بِوَكِيلٍ ﴿٦٦﴾

67. For every Message is a limit of time, and soon shall you know it."

لِّكُلِّ نَبَإٍ مُّسْتَقَرٌّ ۚ وَسَوْفَ تَعْلَمُونَ ﴿٦٧﴾

68. When you see men engaged in vain discourse about Our signs, turn away from them unless they turn to a different theme. If Satan ever makes you forget, then after recollection, sit not you in the company of those who do wrong.

وَإِذَا رَأَيْتَ ٱلَّذِينَ يَخُوضُونَ فِىٓ ءَايَٰتِنَا فَأَعْرِضْ عَنْهُمْ
حَتَّىٰ يَخُوضُوا۟ فِى حَدِيثٍ غَيْرِهِۦ ۚ وَإِمَّا يُنسِيَنَّكَ
ٱلشَّيْطَٰنُ فَلَا تَقْعُدْ بَعْدَ ٱلذِّكْرَىٰ مَعَ ٱلْقَوْمِ
ٱلظَّٰلِمِينَ ﴿٦٨﴾

69. On their account no responsibility falls on the righteous, but (their duty) is to remind them, that they may (learn to) fear Allah.

وَمَا عَلَى ٱلَّذِينَ يَتَّقُونَ مِنْ حِسَابِهِم مِّن شَىْءٍ
وَلَٰكِن ذِكْرَىٰ لَعَلَّهُمْ يَتَّقُونَ ﴿٦٩﴾

70. Leave alone those who take their religion to be mere play and amusement, and are deceived by the life of this world. But proclaim (to them) this (truth): that every soul delivers itself to ruin by its own acts; it will find for itself no protector or intercessor except Allah; if it offered every ransom, (or reparation), none will be accepted; such is (the end of) those who deliver themselves to ruin by their own acts: they will have for drink (only) boiling water, and for punishment, one most grievous; for they persisted in rejecting Allah.

وَذَرِ ٱلَّذِينَ ٱتَّخَذُوا۟ دِينَهُمْ لَعِبًا وَلَهْوًا
وَغَرَّتْهُمُ ٱلْحَيَوٰةُ ٱلدُّنْيَا ۚ وَذَكِّرْ بِهِۦٓ أَن
تُبْسَلَ نَفْسٌۢ بِمَا كَسَبَتْ لَيْسَ لَهَا مِن
دُونِ ٱللَّهِ وَلِىٌّ وَلَا شَفِيعٌ وَإِن تَعْدِلْ كُلَّ عَدْلٍ
لَّا يُؤْخَذْ مِنْهَآ ۗ أُو۟لَٰٓئِكَ ٱلَّذِينَ أُبْسِلُوا۟ بِمَا
كَسَبُوا۟ ۖ لَهُمْ شَرَابٌ مِّنْ حَمِيمٍ وَعَذَابٌ
أَلِيمٌۢ بِمَا كَانُوا۟ يَكْفُرُونَ ﴿٧٠﴾

71. Say: "Shall we indeed call on others besides Allah - things that can do us neither good nor harm - and turn on our heels after receiving guidance from Allah - like one whom the evil ones have made into a fool, wandering bewildered through the earth, his friends calling 'Come to us,' (vainly) guiding him to the path?" Say:

قُلْ أَنَدْعُوا۟ مِن دُونِ ٱللَّهِ مَا لَا يَنفَعُنَا وَلَا يَضُرُّنَا
وَنُرَدُّ عَلَىٰٓ أَعْقَابِنَا بَعْدَ إِذْ هَدَىٰنَا ٱللَّهُ كَٱلَّذِى
ٱسْتَهْوَتْهُ ٱلشَّيَٰطِينُ فِى ٱلْأَرْضِ حَيْرَانَ لَهُۥٓ
أَصْحَٰبٌ يَدْعُونَهُۥٓ إِلَى ٱلْهُدَى ٱئْتِنَا ۗ قُلْ إِنَّ

"Allah's guidance is the (only) guidance, and we have been directed to submit ourselves to the Lord of the Worlds -

هُدَى ٱللَّهِ هُوَ ٱلْهُدَىٰ ۖ وَأُمِرْنَا لِنُسْلِمَ لِرَبِّ
ٱلْعَٰلَمِينَ ﴿٧١﴾

72. To establish regular prayers and to fear Allah: for it is to Him that we shall be gathered together."

وَأَنْ أَقِيمُوا۟ ٱلصَّلَوٰةَ وَٱتَّقُوهُ ۚ وَهُوَ ٱلَّذِىٓ إِلَيْهِ
تُحْشَرُونَ ﴿٧٢﴾

73. It is He Who created the heavens and the earth in true (proportions): the day He says, "Be," see! It is. His word is the truth. His will be the dominion the day the trumpet will be blown. He knows the unseen as well as that which is open. For He is the Wise, well-acquainted (with all things).

وَهُوَ ٱلَّذِى خَلَقَ ٱلسَّمَٰوَٰتِ وَٱلْأَرْضَ بِٱلْحَقِّ ۖ
وَيَوْمَ يَقُولُ كُن فَيَكُونُ ۚ قَوْلُهُ ٱلْحَقُّ ۚ وَلَهُ ٱلْمُلْكُ
يَوْمَ يُنفَخُ فِى ٱلصُّورِ ۚ عَٰلِمُ ٱلْغَيْبِ وَٱلشَّهَٰدَةِ ۚ
وَهُوَ ٱلْحَكِيمُ ٱلْخَبِيرُ ﴿٧٣﴾

74. Abraham said to his father Azar: "Do you take idols for gods? For I see you and your people in manifest error."

۞ وَإِذْ قَالَ إِبْرَٰهِيمُ لِأَبِيهِ ءَازَرَ أَتَتَّخِذُ أَصْنَامًا نصف حزب ١٤
ءَالِهَةً ۖ إِنِّىٓ أَرَىٰكَ وَقَوْمَكَ فِى ضَلَٰلٍ مُّبِينٍ ﴿٧٤﴾

75. So also did We show Abraham the power and the laws of the heavens and the earth, that he might (with understanding) have certitude.

وَكَذَٰلِكَ نُرِىٓ إِبْرَٰهِيمَ مَلَكُوتَ ٱلسَّمَٰوَٰتِ
وَٱلْأَرْضِ وَلِيَكُونَ مِنَ ٱلْمُوقِنِينَ ﴿٧٥﴾

76. When the night covered him over, he saw a star: he said: "This is my Lord." But when it set, he said: "I love not those that set."

فَلَمَّا جَنَّ عَلَيْهِ ٱلَّيْلُ رَءَا كَوْكَبًا ۖ قَالَ هَٰذَا رَبِّى ۖ
فَلَمَّآ أَفَلَ قَالَ لَآ أُحِبُّ ٱلْءَافِلِينَ ﴿٧٦﴾

77. When he saw the moon rising in splendour, he said: "This is my Lord." But when the moon set, he said: "Unless my Lord guide me, I shall surely be among those who go astray."

فَلَمَّا رَءَا ٱلْقَمَرَ بَازِغًا قَالَ هَٰذَا رَبِّى ۖ فَلَمَّآ أَفَلَ قَالَ
لَئِن لَّمْ يَهْدِنِى رَبِّى لَأَكُونَنَّ مِنَ ٱلْقَوْمِ
ٱلضَّآلِّينَ ﴿٧٧﴾

78. When he saw the sun rising in splendour, he said: "This is my Lord; this is the greatest (of all)." But when the sun set, he said: "O my people! I am indeed free from your (guilt) of giving partners to Allah."

فَلَمَّا رَءَا ٱلشَّمْسَ بَازِغَةً قَالَ هَٰذَا رَبِّى هَٰذَآ
أَكْبَرُ ۖ فَلَمَّآ أَفَلَتْ قَالَ يَٰقَوْمِ إِنِّى بَرِىٓءٌ مِّمَّا
تُشْرِكُونَ ﴿٧٨﴾

79. "For me, I have set my face, firmly and truly, towards Him Who created the heavens and the earth, and never shall I give partners to Allah."

إِنِّي وَجَّهْتُ وَجْهِيَ لِلَّذِي فَطَرَ ٱلسَّمَٰوَٰتِ
وَٱلْأَرْضَ حَنِيفًا ۖ وَمَآ أَنَا۠ مِنَ ٱلْمُشْرِكِينَ ﴿٧٩﴾

80. His people disputed with him. He said: "(Come) you to dispute with me, about Allah, when He (Himself) has guided me? I fear not (the beings) you associate with Allah: unless my Lord wills, (nothing can happen). My Lord comprehends in His knowledge all things: will you not (yourselves) be admonished?"

وَحَآجَّهُۥ قَوْمُهُۥ ۚ قَالَ أَتُحَٰٓجُّوٓنِّى فِى ٱللَّهِ وَقَدْ هَدَىٰنِ ۚ
وَلَآ أَخَافُ مَا تُشْرِكُونَ بِهِۦٓ إِلَّآ أَن يَشَآءَ رَبِّى
شَيْـًٔا ۗ وَسِعَ رَبِّى كُلَّ شَىْءٍ عِلْمًا ۗ أَفَلَا
تَتَذَكَّرُونَ ﴿٨٠﴾

81. "How should I fear (the beings) you associate with Allah, when you fear not to give partners to Allah without any authority having been given to you? Which of (us) two parties has more right to security? (Tell me) if you know."

وَكَيْفَ أَخَافُ مَآ أَشْرَكْتُمْ وَلَا تَخَافُونَ أَنَّكُمْ
أَشْرَكْتُم بِٱللَّهِ مَا لَمْ يُنَزِّلْ بِهِۦ عَلَيْكُمْ سُلْطَٰنًا ۚ
فَأَىُّ ٱلْفَرِيقَيْنِ أَحَقُّ بِٱلْأَمْنِ ۖ إِن كُنتُمْ
تَعْلَمُونَ ﴿٨١﴾

82. "It is those who believe and confuse not their beliefs with wrong - that are (truly) in security, for they are on (right) guidance."

ٱلَّذِينَ ءَامَنُوا۟ وَلَمْ يَلْبِسُوٓا۟ إِيمَٰنَهُم بِظُلْمٍ أُو۟لَٰٓئِكَ
لَهُمُ ٱلْأَمْنُ وَهُم مُّهْتَدُونَ ﴿٨٢﴾

83. That was the reasoning about Us, which We gave to Abraham (to use) against his people; We raise whom We will, degree after degree; for your Lord is full of wisdom and knowledge.

وَتِلْكَ حُجَّتُنَآ ءَاتَيْنَٰهَآ إِبْرَٰهِيمَ عَلَىٰ قَوْمِهِۦ ۚ
نَرْفَعُ دَرَجَٰتٍ مَّن نَّشَآءُ ۗ إِنَّ رَبَّكَ حَكِيمٌ
عَلِيمٌ ﴿٨٣﴾

84. We gave him Isaac and Jacob; all (three) We guided; and before him, We guided Noah, and among his progeny, David, Solomon, Job, Joseph, Moses, and Aaron: thus do We reward those who do good:

وَوَهَبْنَا لَهُۥٓ إِسْحَٰقَ وَيَعْقُوبَ ۚ كُلًّا هَدَيْنَا ۚ
وَنُوحًا هَدَيْنَا مِن قَبْلُ ۖ وَمِن ذُرِّيَّتِهِۦ دَاوُۥدَ
وَسُلَيْمَٰنَ وَأَيُّوبَ وَيُوسُفَ وَمُوسَىٰ وَهَٰرُونَ ۚ
وَكَذَٰلِكَ نَجْزِى ٱلْمُحْسِنِينَ ﴿٨٤﴾

85. And Zakariya and Yahya, and Jesus and Elias: all in the ranks of the righteous:

وَزَكَرِيَّا وَيَحْيَىٰ وَعِيسَىٰ وَإِلْيَاسَ ۖ كُلٌّ مِّنَ
ٱلصَّٰلِحِينَ ﴿٨٥﴾

86. And Ishmael and Elisha, and Jonah, and Lot: and to all We gave favour above the nations:

وَإِسْمَٰعِيلَ وَٱلْيَسَعَ وَيُونُسَ وَلُوطًا ۚ وَكُلًّا
فَضَّلْنَا عَلَى ٱلْعَٰلَمِينَ ﴿٨٦﴾

87. (To them) and to their fathers, and progeny and brothers: We chose them, And We guided them to a straight way.

وَمِنْ ءَابَآئِهِمْ وَذُرِّيَّٰتِهِمْ وَإِخْوَٰنِهِمْ ۖ وَٱجْتَبَيْنَٰهُمْ
وَهَدَيْنَٰهُمْ إِلَىٰ صِرَٰطٍ مُّسْتَقِيمٍ ﴿٨٧﴾

88. This is the guidance of Allah: He gives that guidance to whom He pleases of His worshippers. If they were to join other gods with Him, all that they did would be vain for them.

ذَٰلِكَ هُدَى ٱللَّهِ يَهْدِى بِهِۦ مَن يَشَآءُ مِنْ عِبَادِهِۦ ۚ
وَلَوْ أَشْرَكُوا۟ لَحَبِطَ عَنْهُم مَّا كَانُوا۟ يَعْمَلُونَ ﴿٨٨﴾

89. These were the men to whom We gave the book, and authority, and prophethood: if these (their descendants) reject them, see! We shall entrust their charge to a new people who reject them not.

أُو۟لَٰٓئِكَ ٱلَّذِينَ ءَاتَيْنَٰهُمُ ٱلْكِتَٰبَ وَٱلْحُكْمَ
وَٱلنُّبُوَّةَ ۚ فَإِن يَكْفُرْ بِهَا هَٰٓؤُلَآءِ فَقَدْ وَكَّلْنَا بِهَا
قَوْمًا لَّيْسُوا۟ بِهَا بِكَٰفِرِينَ ﴿٨٩﴾

90. Those were the (prophets) who received Allah's guidance: copy the guidance they received; Say: "No reward for this do I ask of you: this is no less than a message for the nations."

أُو۟لَٰٓئِكَ ٱلَّذِينَ هَدَى ٱللَّهُ ۖ فَبِهُدَىٰهُمُ ٱقْتَدِهْ ۗ قُل
لَّآ أَسْـَٔلُكُمْ عَلَيْهِ أَجْرًا ۖ إِنْ هُوَ إِلَّا ذِكْرَىٰ
لِلْعَٰلَمِينَ ﴿٩٠﴾

91. No just estimate of Allah do they make when they say: "Nothing does Allah send down to man (by way of revelation)": Say: "Who then sent down the book which Moses brought? - A light and guidance to man: but you make it into (separate) sheets for show, while you conceal much (of its contents); in it were you taught that which you knew not - neither you nor your fathers." Say: "Allah (sent it down)": then leave them to plunge in vain discourse and trifling.

وَمَا قَدَرُوا۟ ٱللَّهَ حَقَّ قَدْرِهِۦٓ إِذْ قَالُوا۟ مَآ أَنزَلَ ٱللَّهُ عَلَىٰ
بَشَرٍ مِّن شَىْءٍ ۗ قُلْ مَنْ أَنزَلَ ٱلْكِتَٰبَ ٱلَّذِى جَآءَ
بِهِۦ مُوسَىٰ نُورًا وَهُدًى لِّلنَّاسِ ۖ تَجْعَلُونَهُۥ قَرَاطِيسَ
تُبْدُونَهَا وَتُخْفُونَ كَثِيرًا ۖ وَعُلِّمْتُم مَّا لَمْ تَعْلَمُوٓا۟ أَنتُمْ
وَلَآ ءَابَآؤُكُمْ ۖ قُلِ ٱللَّهُ ۖ ثُمَّ ذَرْهُمْ فِى خَوْضِهِمْ
يَلْعَبُونَ ﴿٩١﴾

92. And this is a book which We have sent down, bringing blessings, and confirming (the revelations) which came before it; that you may warn the mother of cities and all around her. Those who believe in the hereafter, believe in this (book), and they are constant in guarding their prayers.

وَهَٰذَا كِتَٰبٌ أَنزَلْنَٰهُ مُبَارَكٌ مُّصَدِّقُ ٱلَّذِى بَيْنَ
يَدَيْهِ وَلِتُنذِرَ أُمَّ ٱلْقُرَىٰ وَمَنْ حَوْلَهَا ۚ وَٱلَّذِينَ
يُؤْمِنُونَ بِٱلْءَاخِرَةِ يُؤْمِنُونَ بِهِۦ ۖ وَهُمْ عَلَىٰ صَلَاتِهِمْ
يُحَافِظُونَ ﴿٩٢﴾

93. Who can be more wicked than one who invents a lie against Allah, or said, "I have received inspiration," when he has received none, or (again) who says, "I can reveal the like of what Allah has revealed?" If you could but see how the wicked (do fare) in the flood of confusion at death! - the angels stretch forth their hands, (saying), "Yield up your souls: this day shall you receive your reward - a penalty of shame, for that you used to tell lies against Allah, and scornfully to reject of His signs!"

وَمَنْ أَظْلَمُ مِمَّنِ ٱفْتَرَىٰ عَلَى ٱللَّهِ كَذِبًا أَوْ قَالَ أُوحِىَ
إِلَىَّ وَلَمْ يُوحَ إِلَيْهِ شَىْءٌ وَمَن قَالَ سَأُنزِلُ مِثْلَ مَآ
أَنزَلَ ٱللَّهُ ۗ وَلَوْ تَرَىٰٓ إِذِ ٱلظَّٰلِمُونَ فِى غَمَرَٰتِ ٱلْمَوْتِ
وَٱلْمَلَٰٓئِكَةُ بَاسِطُوٓا۟ أَيْدِيهِمْ أَخْرِجُوٓا۟ أَنفُسَكُمُ ۖ ٱلْيَوْمَ
تُجْزَوْنَ عَذَابَ ٱلْهُونِ بِمَا كُنتُمْ تَقُولُونَ عَلَى ٱللَّهِ
غَيْرَ ٱلْحَقِّ وَكُنتُمْ عَنْ ءَايَٰتِهِۦ تَسْتَكْبِرُونَ ﴿٩٣﴾

94. "And see! You come to Us bare and alone as We created you for the first time: You have left behind you all (the favours) which We bestowed on you: We see not with you your intercessors whom you thought to be partners in your affairs: so now all relations between you have been cut off, and your (pet) fancies have left you in the lurch!"

وَلَقَدْ جِئْتُمُونَا فُرَٰدَىٰ كَمَا خَلَقْنَٰكُمْ أَوَّلَ مَرَّةٍ
وَتَرَكْتُم مَّا خَوَّلْنَٰكُمْ وَرَآءَ ظُهُورِكُمْ ۖ وَمَا نَرَىٰ
مَعَكُمْ شُفَعَآءَكُمُ ٱلَّذِينَ زَعَمْتُمْ أَنَّهُمْ فِيكُمْ
شُرَكَٰٓؤُا۟ ۚ لَقَد تَّقَطَّعَ بَيْنَكُمْ وَضَلَّ عَنكُم مَّا كُنتُمْ
تَزْعُمُونَ ﴿٩٤﴾

95. It is Allah Who causes the seed-grain and the date-stone to split and sprout. He causes the living to issue from the dead, and He is the One to cause the dead to issue from the living. That is Allah; then how are you deluded away from the truth?

۞ إِنَّ ٱللَّهَ فَالِقُ ٱلْحَبِّ وَٱلنَّوَىٰ ۖ يُخْرِجُ ٱلْحَىَّ مِنَ ٱلْمَيِّتِ (ثلاثة أرباع الحزب ١٤)
وَمُخْرِجُ ٱلْمَيِّتِ مِنَ ٱلْحَىِّ ۚ ذَٰلِكُمُ ٱللَّهُ ۖ فَأَنَّىٰ
تُؤْفَكُونَ ﴿٩٥﴾

96. He it is that cleaves the daybreak (from the dark): He makes the night for rest and tranquillity, and the sun and moon for the

فَالِقُ ٱلْإِصْبَاحِ وَجَعَلَ ٱلَّيْلَ سَكَنًا وَٱلشَّمْسَ

reckoning (of time): such is the judgement and ordering of (Him), the Exalted in Power, the Omniscient.

وَٱلْقَمَرَ حُسْبَانًا ۚ ذَٰلِكَ تَقْدِيرُ ٱلْعَزِيزِ ٱلْعَلِيمِ ﴿٩٦﴾

97. It is He Who makes the stars (as beacons) for you, that you may guide yourselves, with their help, through the dark spaces of land and sea: We detail Our signs for people who know.

وَهُوَ ٱلَّذِى جَعَلَ لَكُمُ ٱلنُّجُومَ لِتَهْتَدُوا۟ بِهَا فِى
ظُلُمَٰتِ ٱلْبَرِّ وَٱلْبَحْرِ ۗ قَدْ فَصَّلْنَا ٱلْءَايَٰتِ لِقَوْمٍ
يَعْلَمُونَ ﴿٩٧﴾

98. It is He Who has produced you from a single person; here is a place of sojourn and a place of departure; We detail Our signs for people who understand.

وَهُوَ ٱلَّذِىٓ أَنشَأَكُم مِّن نَّفْسٍ وَٰحِدَةٍ فَمُسْتَقَرٌّ
وَمُسْتَوْدَعٌ ۗ قَدْ فَصَّلْنَا ٱلْءَايَٰتِ لِقَوْمٍ يَفْقَهُونَ ﴿٩٨﴾

99. It is He Who sends down rain from the skies; with it We produce vegetation of all kinds: from some We produce green (crops), out of which We produce grain, heaped up (at harvest); out of the date-palm and its sheaths (or spathes) (come) clusters of dates hanging low and near; and (then there are) gardens of grapes, and olives, and pomegranates, each similar (in kind) yet different (in variety); when they begin to bear fruit, feast your eyes with the fruit and the ripeness of it. See! In these things there are signs for people who believe.

وَهُوَ ٱلَّذِىٓ أَنزَلَ مِنَ ٱلسَّمَآءِ مَآءً فَأَخْرَجْنَا بِهِۦ
نَبَاتَ كُلِّ شَىْءٍ فَأَخْرَجْنَا مِنْهُ خَضِرًا نُّخْرِجُ مِنْهُ
حَبًّا مُّتَرَاكِبًا وَمِنَ ٱلنَّخْلِ مِن طَلْعِهَا قِنْوَانٌ دَانِيَةٌ
وَجَنَّٰتٍ مِّنْ أَعْنَابٍ وَٱلزَّيْتُونَ وَٱلرُّمَّانَ مُشْتَبِهًا
وَغَيْرَ مُتَشَٰبِهٍ ۗ ٱنظُرُوٓا۟ إِلَىٰ ثَمَرِهِۦٓ إِذَآ أَثْمَرَ وَيَنْعِهِۦٓ ۚ
إِنَّ فِى ذَٰلِكُمْ لَءَايَٰتٍ لِّقَوْمٍ يُؤْمِنُونَ ﴿٩٩﴾

100. Yet they make the Jinns equals with Allah, though Allah did create the Jinns; and they falsely, having no knowledge, attribute to Him sons and daughters. Praise and glory be to Him! (For He is) above what they attribute to Him!

وَجَعَلُوا۟ لِلَّهِ شُرَكَآءَ ٱلْجِنَّ وَخَلَقَهُمْ ۖ وَخَرَقُوا۟ لَهُۥ
بَنِينَ وَبَنَٰتٍۭ بِغَيْرِ عِلْمٍ ۚ سُبْحَٰنَهُۥ وَتَعَٰلَىٰ عَمَّا
يَصِفُونَ ﴿١٠٠﴾

101. To Him is due the primal origin of the heavens and the earth: how can He have a son when He has no consort? He created all things, and He has full knowledge of all things.

بَدِيعُ ٱلسَّمَٰوَٰتِ وَٱلْأَرْضِ ۖ أَنَّىٰ يَكُونُ لَهُۥ وَلَدٌ وَلَمْ
تَكُن لَّهُۥ صَٰحِبَةٌ ۖ وَخَلَقَ كُلَّ شَىْءٍ ۖ وَهُوَ بِكُلِّ
شَىْءٍ عَلِيمٌ ﴿١٠١﴾

102. That is Allah, your Lord! There is no god but He, the Creator of all things; then worship you Him; and He has power to dispose of all affairs.

ذَٰلِكُمُ ٱللَّهُ رَبُّكُمْ ۖ لَآ إِلَٰهَ إِلَّا هُوَ ۖ خَٰلِقُ كُلِّ شَىْءٍ
فَٱعْبُدُوهُ ۚ وَهُوَ عَلَىٰ كُلِّ شَىْءٍ وَكِيلٌ ١٠٢

103. No vision can grasp Him. But His grasp is over all vision: He is above all comprehension, yet is acquainted with all things.

لَّا تُدْرِكُهُ ٱلْأَبْصَٰرُ وَهُوَ يُدْرِكُ ٱلْأَبْصَٰرَ ۖ وَهُوَ
ٱللَّطِيفُ ٱلْخَبِيرُ ١٠٣

104. "Now have come to you, from your Lord, proofs (to open your eyes): if any will see, it will be for (the good of) his own soul; if any will be blind, it will be to his own (harm): I am not (here) to watch over your doings."

قَدْ جَآءَكُم بَصَآئِرُ مِن رَّبِّكُمْ ۖ فَمَنْ أَبْصَرَ
فَلِنَفْسِهِۦ ۖ وَمَنْ عَمِىَ فَعَلَيْهَا ۚ وَمَآ أَنَا۠ عَلَيْكُم
بِحَفِيظٍ ١٠٤

105. Thus do We explain the signs by various (symbols): that they may say, "You have taught (us) diligently," and that We may make the matter clear to those who know.

وَكَذَٰلِكَ نُصَرِّفُ ٱلْءَايَٰتِ وَلِيَقُولُوا۟ دَرَسْتَ
وَلِنُبَيِّنَهُۥ لِقَوْمٍ يَعْلَمُونَ ١٠٥

106. Follow what you are taught by inspiration from your Lord; there is no god but He; and turn aside from those who join gods with Allah.

ٱتَّبِعْ مَآ أُوحِىَ إِلَيْكَ مِن رَّبِّكَ ۖ لَآ إِلَٰهَ إِلَّا هُوَ ۖ
وَأَعْرِضْ عَنِ ٱلْمُشْرِكِينَ ١٠٦

107. If it had been Allah's plan, they would not have taken false gods; but We made you not one to watch over their doings, nor are you set over them to dispose of their affairs.

وَلَوْ شَآءَ ٱللَّهُ مَآ أَشْرَكُوا۟ ۗ وَمَا جَعَلْنَٰكَ عَلَيْهِمْ
حَفِيظًا ۖ وَمَآ أَنتَ عَلَيْهِم بِوَكِيلٍ ١٠٧

108. Revile not you those whom they call upon besides Allah, lest they out of spite revile Allah in their ignorance. Thus have We made alluring to each people its own doings. In the end will they return to their Lord, and We shall then tell them the truth of all that they did.

وَلَا تَسُبُّوا۟ ٱلَّذِينَ يَدْعُونَ مِن دُونِ ٱللَّهِ فَيَسُبُّوا۟
ٱللَّهَ عَدْوًۢا بِغَيْرِ عِلْمٍ ۗ كَذَٰلِكَ زَيَّنَّا لِكُلِّ أُمَّةٍ عَمَلَهُمْ ثُمَّ
إِلَىٰ رَبِّهِم مَّرْجِعُهُمْ فَيُنَبِّئُهُم بِمَا كَانُوا۟ يَعْمَلُونَ ١٠٨

109. They swear their strongest oaths by Allah, that if a (special) sign came to them, by it they would believe. Say: "Certainly (all) signs are in the power of Allah; but what will

وَأَقْسَمُوا۟ بِٱللَّهِ جَهْدَ أَيْمَٰنِهِمْ لَئِن جَآءَتْهُمْ ءَايَةٌ
لَّيُؤْمِنُنَّ بِهَا ۚ قُلْ إِنَّمَا ٱلْءَايَٰتُ عِندَ ٱللَّهِ ۖ وَمَا

make you (Muslims) realise that even if (special) signs came, they will not believe?"

يُشْعِرُكُمْ أَنَّهَآ إِذَا جَآءَتْ لَا يُؤْمِنُونَ ﴿١٠٩﴾

110. We (too) shall turn to (confusion) their hearts and their eyes, even as they refused to believe in this in the first instance: We shall leave them in their trespasses, to wander in distraction.

وَنُقَلِّبُ أَفْـِٔدَتَهُمْ وَأَبْصَٰرَهُمْ كَمَا لَمْ يُؤْمِنُوا۟ بِهِۦٓ
أَوَّلَ مَرَّةٍ وَنَذَرُهُمْ فِى طُغْيَٰنِهِمْ يَعْمَهُونَ ﴿١١٠﴾

✻ **111.** Even if We did send to them angels, and the dead did speak to them, and We gathered together all things before their very eyes, they are not the ones to believe, unless it is in Allah's plan: but most of them ignore (the truth).

الجزء ٨ الحزب ١٥

✻ وَلَوْ أَنَّنَا نَزَّلْنَآ إِلَيْهِمُ ٱلْمَلَٰٓئِكَةَ وَكَلَّمَهُمُ ٱلْمَوْتَىٰ
وَحَشَرْنَا عَلَيْهِمْ كُلَّ شَىْءٍ قُبُلًا مَّا كَانُوا۟ لِيُؤْمِنُوٓا۟
إِلَّآ أَن يَشَآءَ ٱللَّهُ وَلَٰكِنَّ أَكْثَرَهُمْ يَجْهَلُونَ ﴿١١١﴾

112. Likewise did We make for every messenger an enemy - evil ones among men and Jinns, inspiring each other with flowery discourses by way of deception. If your Lord had so planned, they would not have done it: so leave them and their inventions alone.

وَكَذَٰلِكَ جَعَلْنَا لِكُلِّ نَبِىٍّ عَدُوًّا شَيَٰطِينَ
ٱلْإِنسِ وَٱلْجِنِّ يُوحِى بَعْضُهُمْ إِلَىٰ بَعْضٍ
زُخْرُفَ ٱلْقَوْلِ غُرُورًا ۚ وَلَوْ شَآءَ رَبُّكَ مَا فَعَلُوهُ ۖ
فَذَرْهُمْ وَمَا يَفْتَرُونَ ﴿١١٢﴾

113. To such (deceit) let the hearts of those incline, who have no faith in the hereafter: let them delight in it, and let them earn from it what they may.

وَلِتَصْغَىٰٓ إِلَيْهِ أَفْـِٔدَةُ ٱلَّذِينَ لَا يُؤْمِنُونَ بِٱلْـَٔاخِرَةِ
وَلِيَرْضَوْهُ وَلِيَقْتَرِفُوا۟ مَا هُم مُّقْتَرِفُونَ ﴿١١٣﴾

114. Say: "Shall I seek for judge other than Allah? - When He it is Who has sent to you the book, explained in detail." They know full well, to whom We have given the book, that it has been sent down from your Lord in truth. Never be then of those who doubt.

أَفَغَيْرَ ٱللَّهِ أَبْتَغِى حَكَمًا وَهُوَ ٱلَّذِىٓ أَنزَلَ
إِلَيْكُمُ ٱلْكِتَٰبَ مُفَصَّلًا ۚ وَٱلَّذِينَ ءَاتَيْنَٰهُمُ
ٱلْكِتَٰبَ يَعْلَمُونَ أَنَّهُۥ مُنَزَّلٌ مِّن رَّبِّكَ بِٱلْحَقِّ ۖ
فَلَا تَكُونَنَّ مِنَ ٱلْمُمْتَرِينَ ﴿١١٤﴾

115. The word of your Lord does find its fulfilment in truth and in justice: none can change His words: for He is the one Who hears and knows all.

وَتَمَّتْ كَلِمَتُ رَبِّكَ صِدْقًا وَعَدْلًا ۚ لَّا مُبَدِّلَ
لِكَلِمَٰتِهِۦ ۚ وَهُوَ ٱلسَّمِيعُ ٱلْعَلِيمُ ﴿١١٥﴾

✻ Part-8

116. Were you to follow the common run of those on earth, they will lead you away from the way of Allah. They follow nothing but conjecture; they do nothing but lie.

وَإِن تُطِعْ أَكْثَرَ مَن فِى ٱلْأَرْضِ يُضِلُّوكَ عَن سَبِيلِ ٱللَّهِ ۚ إِن يَتَّبِعُونَ إِلَّا ٱلظَّنَّ وَإِنْ هُمْ إِلَّا يَخْرُصُونَ ﴿١١٦﴾

117. Your Lord knows best who strays from His way. He knows best who they are that receive His guidance.

إِنَّ رَبَّكَ هُوَ أَعْلَمُ مَن يَضِلُّ عَن سَبِيلِهِۦ ۖ وَهُوَ أَعْلَمُ بِٱلْمُهْتَدِينَ ﴿١١٧﴾

118. So eat of (meats) on which Allah's name has been pronounced, if you have faith in His signs.

فَكُلُوا۟ مِمَّا ذُكِرَ ٱسْمُ ٱللَّهِ عَلَيْهِ إِن كُنتُم بِـَٔايَٰتِهِۦ مُؤْمِنِينَ ﴿١١٨﴾

119. Why should you not eat of (meats) on which Allah's name has been pronounced, when He has explained to you in detail what is forbidden to you - except under compulsion of necessity? But many do mislead (men) by their appetites unchecked by knowledge. Your Lord knows best those who transgress.

وَمَا لَكُمْ أَلَّا تَأْكُلُوا۟ مِمَّا ذُكِرَ ٱسْمُ ٱللَّهِ عَلَيْهِ وَقَدْ فَصَّلَ لَكُم مَّا حَرَّمَ عَلَيْكُمْ إِلَّا مَا ٱضْطُرِرْتُمْ إِلَيْهِ ۗ وَإِنَّ كَثِيرًا لَّيُضِلُّونَ بِأَهْوَآئِهِم بِغَيْرِ عِلْمٍ ۗ إِنَّ رَبَّكَ هُوَ أَعْلَمُ بِٱلْمُعْتَدِينَ ﴿١١٩﴾

120. Eschew all sin, open or secret: those who earn sin will get due recompense for their "earnings."

وَذَرُوا۟ ظَٰهِرَ ٱلْإِثْمِ وَبَاطِنَهُۥٓ ۚ إِنَّ ٱلَّذِينَ يَكْسِبُونَ ٱلْإِثْمَ سَيُجْزَوْنَ بِمَا كَانُوا۟ يَقْتَرِفُونَ ﴿١٢٠﴾

121. Eat not of (meats) on which Allah's name has not been pronounced: that would be impiety. But the evil ones ever inspire their friends to contend with you; if you were to obey them, you would indeed be pagans.

وَلَا تَأْكُلُوا۟ مِمَّا لَمْ يُذْكَرِ ٱسْمُ ٱللَّهِ عَلَيْهِ وَإِنَّهُۥ لَفِسْقٌ ۗ وَإِنَّ ٱلشَّيَٰطِينَ لَيُوحُونَ إِلَىٰٓ أَوْلِيَآئِهِمْ لِيُجَٰدِلُوكُمْ ۖ وَإِنْ أَطَعْتُمُوهُمْ إِنَّكُمْ لَمُشْرِكُونَ ﴿١٢١﴾

122. Can he who was dead, to whom We gave life, and a light by which he can walk amongst men, be like him who is in the depths of darkness, from which he can never come out? Thus to those without faith their own deeds seem pleasing.

أَوَمَن كَانَ مَيْتًا فَأَحْيَيْنَٰهُ وَجَعَلْنَا لَهُۥ نُورًا يَمْشِى بِهِۦ فِى ٱلنَّاسِ كَمَن مَّثَلُهُۥ فِى ٱلظُّلُمَٰتِ لَيْسَ بِخَارِجٍ مِّنْهَا ۚ كَذَٰلِكَ زُيِّنَ لِلْكَٰفِرِينَ مَا كَانُوا۟ يَعْمَلُونَ ﴿١٢٢﴾

123. Thus have We placed leaders in every town, its wicked men, to plot (and burrow) in it: but they only plot against their own souls, and they perceive it not.

وَكَذَٰلِكَ جَعَلْنَا فِي كُلِّ قَرْيَةٍ أَكَٰبِرَ
مُجْرِمِيهَا لِيَمْكُرُوا۟ فِيهَا ۖ وَمَا يَمْكُرُونَ
إِلَّا بِأَنفُسِهِمْ وَمَا يَشْعُرُونَ ﴿١٢٣﴾

124. When there comes to them a sign (from Allah), they say: "We shall not believe until we receive one (exactly) like those received by Allah's messengers." Allah knows best where (and how) to carry out His mission. Soon will the wicked be overtaken by humiliation before Allah, and a severe punishment, for all their plots.

وَإِذَا جَآءَتْهُمْ ءَايَةٌ قَالُوا۟ لَن نُّؤْمِنَ حَتَّىٰ نُؤْتَىٰ مِثْلَ
مَآ أُوتِىَ رُسُلُ ٱللَّهِ ۘ ٱللَّهُ أَعْلَمُ حَيْثُ يَجْعَلُ رِسَالَتَهُۥ ۗ
سَيُصِيبُ ٱلَّذِينَ أَجْرَمُوا۟ صَغَارٌ عِندَ ٱللَّهِ وَعَذَابٌ
شَدِيدٌۢ بِمَا كَانُوا۟ يَمْكُرُونَ ﴿١٢٤﴾

125. Those whom Allah (in His plan) wills to guide - He opens their breast to Islam; those whom He wills to leave straying - He makes their breast close and constricted, as if they had to climb up to the skies; thus does Allah (heap) the penalty on those who refuse to believe.

فَمَن يُرِدِ ٱللَّهُ أَن يَهْدِيَهُۥ يَشْرَحْ صَدْرَهُۥ
لِلْإِسْلَٰمِ ۖ وَمَن يُرِدْ أَن يُضِلَّهُۥ يَجْعَلْ صَدْرَهُۥ
ضَيِّقًا حَرَجًا كَأَنَّمَا يَصَّعَّدُ فِى ٱلسَّمَآءِ ۚ
كَذَٰلِكَ يَجْعَلُ ٱللَّهُ ٱلرِّجْسَ عَلَى ٱلَّذِينَ
لَا يُؤْمِنُونَ ﴿١٢٥﴾

126. This is the way of your Lord, leading straight: We have detailed the signs for those who receive admonition.

وَهَٰذَا صِرَٰطُ رَبِّكَ مُسْتَقِيمًا ۗ قَدْ فَصَّلْنَا
ٱلْءَايَٰتِ لِقَوْمٍ يَذَّكَّرُونَ ﴿١٢٦﴾

127. For them will be a home of peace in the presence of their Lord: He will be their Friend, because they practised (righteousness).

ربع الحزب ١٥ * لَهُمْ دَارُ ٱلسَّلَٰمِ عِندَ رَبِّهِمْ ۖ وَهُوَ وَلِيُّهُم بِمَا
كَانُوا۟ يَعْمَلُونَ ﴿١٢٧﴾

128. One day will He gather them all together, (and say): "O you assembly of Jinns! Much (toll) did you take of men." Their friends amongst men will say: "Our Lord! We made profit from each other: but (alas!) we reached our term - which You did appoint for us." He will say: "The fire be your dwelling-place: you will dwell in it

وَيَوْمَ يَحْشُرُهُمْ جَمِيعًا يَٰمَعْشَرَ ٱلْجِنِّ قَدِ
ٱسْتَكْثَرْتُم مِّنَ ٱلْإِنسِ ۖ وَقَالَ أَوْلِيَآؤُهُم
مِّنَ ٱلْإِنسِ رَبَّنَا ٱسْتَمْتَعَ بَعْضُنَا بِبَعْضٍ وَبَلَغْنَآ
أَجَلَنَا ٱلَّذِىٓ أَجَّلْتَ لَنَا ۚ قَالَ ٱلنَّارُ مَثْوَىٰكُمْ

forever, except as Allah wills." For your Lord is full of wisdom and knowledge.

خَٰلِدِينَ فِيهَآ إِلَّا مَا شَآءَ ٱللَّهُۗ إِنَّ رَبَّكَ حَكِيمٌ
عَلِيمٌ ١٢٨

129. Thus do We make the wrongdoers turn to each other, because of what they earn.

وَكَذَٰلِكَ نُوَلِّي بَعْضَ ٱلظَّٰلِمِينَ بَعْضَۢا بِمَا كَانُواْ
يَكْسِبُونَ ١٢٩

130. O you assembly of Jinns and men! Came there not to you messengers from amongst you, setting forth to you My signs, and warning you of the meeting of this day of yours?" They will say: "We bear witness against ourselves." It was the life of this world that deceived them. So against themselves will they bear witness that they rejected faith.

يَٰمَعْشَرَ ٱلْجِنِّ وَٱلْإِنسِ أَلَمْ يَأْتِكُمْ رُسُلٌ
مِّنكُمْ يَقُصُّونَ عَلَيْكُمْ ءَايَٰتِي
وَيُنذِرُونَكُمْ لِقَآءَ يَوْمِكُمْ هَٰذَاۚ قَالُواْ شَهِدْنَا
عَلَىٰٓ أَنفُسِنَاۖ وَغَرَّتْهُمُ ٱلْحَيَوٰةُ ٱلدُّنْيَا وَشَهِدُواْ
عَلَىٰٓ أَنفُسِهِمْ أَنَّهُمْ كَانُواْ كَٰفِرِينَ ١٣٠

131. (The messengers were sent) thus, for your Lord would not destroy, for their wrongdoing, men's habitations whilst their occupants were unwarned.

ذَٰلِكَ أَن لَّمْ يَكُن رَّبُّكَ مُهْلِكَ ٱلْقُرَىٰ
بِظُلْمٍ وَأَهْلُهَا غَٰفِلُونَ ١٣١

132. To all are degrees (or ranks) according to their deeds: for your Lord is not unmindful of anything that they do.

وَلِكُلٍّ دَرَجَٰتٌ مِّمَّا عَمِلُواْۚ وَمَا رَبُّكَ
بِغَٰفِلٍ عَمَّا يَعْمَلُونَ ١٣٢

133. Your Lord is Self-sufficient, full of mercy: if it were His will, He could destroy you, and in your place appoint whom He will as your successors, even as He raised you up from the posterity of other people.

وَرَبُّكَ ٱلْغَنِيُّ ذُو ٱلرَّحْمَةِۚ إِن يَشَأْ
يُذْهِبْكُمْ وَيَسْتَخْلِفْ مِنۢ بَعْدِكُم
مَّا يَشَآءُ كَمَآ أَنشَأَكُم مِّن ذُرِّيَّةِ قَوْمٍ
ءَاخَرِينَ ١٣٣

134. All that has been promised to you will come to pass; nor can you frustrate it (in the least bit).

إِنَّ مَا تُوعَدُونَ لَأٓتٍۖ وَمَآ أَنتُم بِمُعْجِزِينَ ١٣٤

135. Say: "O my people! Do whatever you can; I will do (my part); soon will you

قُلْ يَٰقَوْمِ ٱعْمَلُواْ عَلَىٰ مَكَانَتِكُمْ إِنِّي عَامِلٌۖ

know who it is whose end will be (best) in the hereafter: Certain it is that the wrongdoers will not prosper."

فَسَوْفَ تَعْلَمُونَ مَن تَكُونُ لَهُۥ عَٰقِبَةُ ٱلدَّارِۗ
إِنَّهُۥ لَا يُفْلِحُ ٱلظَّٰلِمُونَ ﴿١٣٥﴾

136. Out of what Allah has produced in abundance in tilth and in cattle, they assigned Him a share: They say, according to their fancies: "This is for Allah, and this - for our 'partners'"! But the share of their 'partners' reaches not Allah, whilst the share of Allah reaches their 'partners'! Evil (and unjust) is their assignment!

وَجَعَلُوا۟ لِلَّهِ مِمَّا ذَرَأَ مِنَ ٱلْحَرْثِ وَٱلْأَنْعَٰمِ
نَصِيبًا فَقَالُوا۟ هَٰذَا لِلَّهِ بِزَعْمِهِمْ وَهَٰذَا
لِشُرَكَآئِنَاۖ فَمَا كَانَ لِشُرَكَآئِهِمْ فَلَا
يَصِلُ إِلَى ٱللَّهِۖ وَمَا كَانَ لِلَّهِ فَهُوَ يَصِلُ
إِلَىٰ شُرَكَآئِهِمْۗ سَآءَ مَا يَحْكُمُونَ ﴿١٣٦﴾

137. Even so, in the eyes of most of the pagans their "partners" made alluring the slaughter of their children, in order to lead them to their own destruction, and cause confusion in their religion. If Allah had willed, they would not have done so: but leave alone them and their inventions.

وَكَذَٰلِكَ زَيَّنَ لِكَثِيرٍ مِّنَ ٱلْمُشْرِكِينَ
قَتْلَ أَوْلَٰدِهِمْ شُرَكَآؤُهُمْ لِيُرْدُوهُمْ
وَلِيَلْبِسُوا۟ عَلَيْهِمْ دِينَهُمْۖ وَلَوْ شَآءَ ٱللَّهُ
مَا فَعَلُوهُۖ فَذَرْهُمْ وَمَا يَفْتَرُونَ ﴿١٣٧﴾

138. And they say that such and such cattle and crops are taboo, and none should eat of them except those whom - so they say - We wish; further, there are cattle forbidden to yoke or burden, and cattle on which, (at slaughter), the name of Allah is not pronounced - inventions against Allah's name: soon will He repay them for their inventions.

وَقَالُوا۟ هَٰذِهِۦٓ أَنْعَٰمٌ وَحَرْثٌ حِجْرٌ لَّا يَطْعَمُهَآ إِلَّا
مَن نَّشَآءُ بِزَعْمِهِمْ وَأَنْعَٰمٌ حُرِّمَتْ ظُهُورُهَا
وَأَنْعَٰمٌ لَّا يَذْكُرُونَ ٱسْمَ ٱللَّهِ عَلَيْهَا ٱفْتِرَآءً
عَلَيْهِۚ سَيَجْزِيهِم بِمَا كَانُوا۟ يَفْتَرُونَ ﴿١٣٨﴾

139. They say: "What is in the wombs of such and such cattle is specially reserved (for food) for our men, and forbidden to our women; but if it is stillborn, then all have shares in it. For their (false) attribution (of superstitions to Allah), He will soon punish them: for He is full of wisdom and knowledge.

وَقَالُوا۟ مَا فِى بُطُونِ هَٰذِهِ ٱلْأَنْعَٰمِ خَالِصَةٌ
لِّذُكُورِنَا وَمُحَرَّمٌ عَلَىٰٓ أَزْوَٰجِنَاۖ وَإِن
يَكُن مَّيْتَةً فَهُمْ فِيهِ شُرَكَآءُۚ سَيَجْزِيهِمْ
وَصْفَهُمْۚ إِنَّهُۥ حَكِيمٌ عَلِيمٌ ﴿١٣٩﴾

140. Lost are those who slay their children, from folly, without knowledge, and forbid food which Allah has provided for them, inventing (lies) against Allah. They have indeed gone astray and heeded no guidance.

قَدْ خَسِرَ ٱلَّذِينَ قَتَلُوٓا۟ أَوْلَـٰدَهُمْ سَفَهًۢا بِغَيْرِ
عِلْمٍ وَحَرَّمُوا۟ مَا رَزَقَهُمُ ٱللَّهُ ٱفْتِرَآءً عَلَى ٱللَّهِ ۚ
قَدْ ضَلُّوا۟ وَمَا كَانُوا۟ مُهْتَدِينَ ﴿١٤٠﴾

141. It is He Who produces gardens, with trellises and without, and dates, and tilth with produce of all kinds, and olives and pomegranates, similar (in kind) and different (in variety): eat of their fruit in their season, but render the dues that are proper on the day that the harvest is gathered. But waste not by excess: for Allah loves not the wasters.

۞ وَهُوَ ٱلَّذِىٓ أَنشَأَ جَنَّـٰتٍ مَّعْرُوشَـٰتٍ وَغَيْرَ نصف الحزب ١٥
مَعْرُوشَـٰتٍ وَٱلنَّخْلَ وَٱلزَّرْعَ مُخْتَلِفًا أُكُلُهُۥ
وَٱلزَّيْتُونَ وَٱلرُّمَّانَ مُتَشَـٰبِهًا وَغَيْرَ مُتَشَـٰبِهٍ ۚ
كُلُوا۟ مِن ثَمَرِهِۦٓ إِذَآ أَثْمَرَ وَءَاتُوا۟ حَقَّهُۥ يَوْمَ
حَصَادِهِۦ ۖ وَلَا تُسْرِفُوٓا۟ ۚ إِنَّهُۥ لَا يُحِبُّ
ٱلْمُسْرِفِينَ ﴿١٤١﴾

142. Of the cattle are some for burden and some for meat: eat what Allah has provided for you, and follow not the footsteps of Satan; for he is to you an avowed enemy.

وَمِنَ ٱلْأَنْعَـٰمِ حَمُولَةً وَفَرْشًا ۚ كُلُوا۟ مِمَّا
رَزَقَكُمُ ٱللَّهُ وَلَا تَتَّبِعُوا۟ خُطُوَٰتِ ٱلشَّيْطَـٰنِ ۚ
إِنَّهُۥ لَكُمْ عَدُوٌّ مُّبِينٌ ﴿١٤٢﴾

143. (Take) eight (head of cattle) in (four) pairs: of sheep a pair, and of goats a pair; say, has He forbidden the two males, or the two females, or (the young) which the wombs of the two females enclose? Tell me with knowledge if you are truthful.

ثَمَـٰنِيَةَ أَزْوَٰجٍ ۖ مِّنَ ٱلضَّأْنِ ٱثْنَيْنِ وَمِنَ
ٱلْمَعْزِ ٱثْنَيْنِ ۗ قُلْ ءَآلذَّكَرَيْنِ حَرَّمَ أَمِ
ٱلْأُنثَيَيْنِ أَمَّا ٱشْتَمَلَتْ عَلَيْهِ أَرْحَامُ ٱلْأُنثَيَيْنِ ۖ
نَبِّـُٔونِى بِعِلْمٍ إِن كُنتُمْ صَـٰدِقِينَ ﴿١٤٣﴾

144. Of camels a pair, and of oxen a pair; say, has He forbidden the two males, or the two females, or (the young) which the wombs of the two females enclose? - Were you present when Allah ordered you such a thing? But who does more wrong than one who invents a lie against Allah, to lead

وَمِنَ ٱلْإِبِلِ ٱثْنَيْنِ وَمِنَ ٱلْبَقَرِ ٱثْنَيْنِ ۗ قُلْ
ءَآلذَّكَرَيْنِ حَرَّمَ أَمِ ٱلْأُنثَيَيْنِ أَمَّا ٱشْتَمَلَتْ
عَلَيْهِ أَرْحَامُ ٱلْأُنثَيَيْنِ ۖ أَمْ كُنتُمْ شُهَدَآءَ
إِذْ وَصَّىٰكُمُ ٱللَّهُ بِهَـٰذَا ۚ فَمَنْ أَظْلَمُ مِمَّنِ

astray men without knowledge? For Allah guides not people who do wrong.

افْتَرَىٰ عَلَى اللَّهِ كَذِبًا لِّيُضِلَّ النَّاسَ بِغَيْرِ
عِلْمٍ ۗ إِنَّ اللَّهَ لَا يَهْدِي الْقَوْمَ الظَّالِمِينَ ﴿١٤٤﴾

145. Say: "I find not in the message received by me by inspiration any (meat) forbidden to be eaten by one who wishes to eat it, unless it be dead meat, or blood poured out, or the flesh of swine - for it is an abomination - or what is impious, (meat) on which a name has been invoked other than Allah's." But (even so), if a person is forced by necessity, without wilful disobedience, nor transgressing due limits - your Lord is Oft-Forgiving, Most Merciful.

قُل لَّا أَجِدُ فِي مَا أُوحِيَ إِلَيَّ مُحَرَّمًا عَلَىٰ طَاعِمٍ
يَطْعَمُهُ إِلَّا أَن يَكُونَ مَيْتَةً أَوْ دَمًا مَّسْفُوحًا
أَوْ لَحْمَ خِنزِيرٍ فَإِنَّهُ رِجْسٌ أَوْ فِسْقًا أُهِلَّ
لِغَيْرِ اللَّهِ بِهِ ۚ فَمَنِ اضْطُرَّ غَيْرَ بَاغٍ وَلَا عَادٍ
فَإِنَّ رَبَّكَ غَفُورٌ رَّحِيمٌ ﴿١٤٥﴾

146. For those who followed the Jewish law, We forbade every (animal) with undivided hoof, and We forbade them the fat of the ox and the sheep, except what adheres to their backs or their entrails, or is mixed up with a bone; this in recompense for their wilful disobedience: for We are True (in Our ordinances).

وَعَلَى الَّذِينَ هَادُوا حَرَّمْنَا كُلَّ ذِي ظُفُرٍ ۖ
وَمِنَ الْبَقَرِ وَالْغَنَمِ حَرَّمْنَا عَلَيْهِمْ شُحُومَهُمَا
إِلَّا مَا حَمَلَتْ ظُهُورُهُمَا أَوِ الْحَوَايَا أَوْ مَا اخْتَلَطَ
بِعَظْمٍ ۚ ذَٰلِكَ جَزَيْنَاهُم بِبَغْيِهِمْ ۖ وَإِنَّا
لَصَادِقُونَ ﴿١٤٦﴾

147. If they accuse you (O Muhammad) of falsehood, say: "Your Lord is full of mercy, All-Embracing;" but from people in guilt never will His wrath be turned back.

فَإِن كَذَّبُوكَ فَقُل رَّبُّكُمْ ذُو رَحْمَةٍ وَاسِعَةٍ
وَلَا يُرَدُّ بَأْسُهُ عَنِ الْقَوْمِ الْمُجْرِمِينَ ﴿١٤٧﴾

148. Those who give partners to Allah will say: "If Allah had wished, we should not have given partners to Him, nor would our fathers; nor should we have had any taboos." So did their ancestors argue falsely, until they tasted of Our wrath. Say: "Have you any (certain) knowledge? If so, produce it before us. You follow nothing but conjecture: You do nothing but lie."

سَيَقُولُ الَّذِينَ أَشْرَكُوا لَوْ شَاءَ اللَّهُ مَا
أَشْرَكْنَا وَلَا آبَاؤُنَا وَلَا حَرَّمْنَا مِن شَيْءٍ ۚ
كَذَٰلِكَ كَذَّبَ الَّذِينَ مِن قَبْلِهِمْ حَتَّىٰ
ذَاقُوا بَأْسَنَا ۗ قُلْ هَلْ عِندَكُم مِّنْ عِلْمٍ
فَتُخْرِجُوهُ لَنَا ۖ إِن تَتَّبِعُونَ إِلَّا الظَّنَّ وَإِنْ أَنتُمْ
إِلَّا تَخْرُصُونَ ﴿١٤٨﴾

149. Say: "With Allah is the argument that reaches home: if it had been His will, He could indeed have guided you all."

قُلْ فَلِلَّهِ ٱلْحُجَّةُ ٱلْبَٰلِغَةُ ۖ فَلَوْ شَآءَ لَهَدَىٰكُمْ
أَجْمَعِينَ ﴿١٤٩﴾

150. Say: "Bring forward your witnesses to prove that Allah did forbid so and so." If they bring such witnesses, be not you amongst them: nor follow you the vain desires of such as treat Our signs as falsehoods, and such as believe not in the hereafter: for they hold others as equal with their Guardian-Lord.

قُلْ هَلُمَّ شُهَدَآءَكُمُ ٱلَّذِينَ يَشْهَدُونَ أَنَّ ٱللَّهَ
حَرَّمَ هَٰذَا ۖ فَإِن شَهِدُوا۟ فَلَا تَشْهَدْ مَعَهُمْ ۚ وَلَا
تَتَّبِعْ أَهْوَآءَ ٱلَّذِينَ كَذَّبُوا۟ بِـَٔايَٰتِنَا وَٱلَّذِينَ
لَا يُؤْمِنُونَ بِٱلْءَاخِرَةِ وَهُم بِرَبِّهِمْ يَعْدِلُونَ ﴿١٥٠﴾

151. Say: "Come, I will rehearse what Allah has (really) prohibited you from: join not anything as equal with Him; be good to your parents; kill not your children on a plea of want - We provide sustenance for you and for them - come not near to shameful deeds, whether open or secret; take not life, which Allah has made sacred, except by way of justice and law: thus does He command you, that you may learn wisdom.

۞ قُلْ تَعَالَوْا۟ أَتْلُ مَا حَرَّمَ رَبُّكُمْ عَلَيْكُمْ ۖ ثلاثة أرباع الحزب ١٥
أَلَّا تُشْرِكُوا۟ بِهِۦ شَيْـًٔا ۖ وَبِٱلْوَٰلِدَيْنِ إِحْسَٰنًا ۖ
وَلَا تَقْتُلُوٓا۟ أَوْلَٰدَكُم مِّنْ إِمْلَٰقٍ ۖ نَّحْنُ
نَرْزُقُكُمْ وَإِيَّاهُمْ ۖ وَلَا تَقْرَبُوا۟ ٱلْفَوَٰحِشَ
مَا ظَهَرَ مِنْهَا وَمَا بَطَنَ ۖ وَلَا تَقْتُلُوا۟ ٱلنَّفْسَ ٱلَّتِى
حَرَّمَ ٱللَّهُ إِلَّا بِٱلْحَقِّ ۚ ذَٰلِكُمْ وَصَّىٰكُم بِهِۦ
لَعَلَّكُمْ تَعْقِلُونَ ﴿١٥١﴾

152. And come not near to the orphan's property, except to improve it until he attain the age of full strength; And give measure and weight with (full) justice - no burden do We place on any soul, but that which it can bear - whenever you speak, speak justly, even if a near relative is concerned; and fulfil the covenant of Allah: thus does He command you, that you may remember.

وَلَا تَقْرَبُوا۟ مَالَ ٱلْيَتِيمِ إِلَّا بِٱلَّتِى هِىَ أَحْسَنُ حَتَّىٰ
يَبْلُغَ أَشُدَّهُۥ ۖ وَأَوْفُوا۟ ٱلْكَيْلَ وَٱلْمِيزَانَ بِٱلْقِسْطِ ۖ
لَا نُكَلِّفُ نَفْسًا إِلَّا وُسْعَهَا ۖ وَإِذَا قُلْتُمْ فَٱعْدِلُوا۟
وَلَوْ كَانَ ذَا قُرْبَىٰ ۖ وَبِعَهْدِ ٱللَّهِ أَوْفُوا۟ ۚ ذَٰلِكُمْ
وَصَّىٰكُم بِهِۦ لَعَلَّكُمْ تَذَكَّرُونَ ﴿١٥٢﴾

153. Verily, this is My way leading straight: follow it: follow not (other) paths: they will scatter you about from His (great)

وَأَنَّ هَٰذَا صِرَٰطِى مُسْتَقِيمًا فَٱتَّبِعُوهُ ۖ وَلَا
تَتَّبِعُوا۟ ٱلسُّبُلَ فَتَفَرَّقَ بِكُمْ عَن سَبِيلِهِۦ ۚ ذَٰلِكُمْ

path; thus does He command you that you may be righteous.

وَصَّىٰكُم بِهِۦ لَعَلَّكُمْ تَتَّقُونَ ﴿١٥٣﴾

154. Moreover, We gave Moses the book, completing (Our favour) to those who would do right, and explaining all things in detail - and a guide and a mercy, that they might believe in the meeting with their Lord.

ثُمَّ ءَاتَيْنَا مُوسَى ٱلْكِتَٰبَ تَمَامًا عَلَى ٱلَّذِىٓ
أَحْسَنَ وَتَفْصِيلًا لِّكُلِّ شَىْءٍ وَهُدًى وَرَحْمَةً
لَّعَلَّهُم بِلِقَآءِ رَبِّهِمْ يُؤْمِنُونَ ﴿١٥٤﴾

155. And this is a book, which We have revealed as a blessing: so follow it and be righteous, that you may receive mercy;

وَهَٰذَا كِتَٰبٌ أَنزَلْنَٰهُ مُبَارَكٌ فَٱتَّبِعُوهُ وَٱتَّقُوا۟
لَعَلَّكُمْ تُرْحَمُونَ ﴿١٥٥﴾

156. Lest you should say: "The book was sent down to two Peoples before us, and for our part, we remained unacquainted with all that they learned by assiduous study";

أَن تَقُولُوٓا۟ إِنَّمَآ أُنزِلَ ٱلْكِتَٰبُ عَلَىٰ طَآئِفَتَيْنِ مِن
قَبْلِنَا وَإِن كُنَّا عَن دِرَاسَتِهِمْ لَغَٰفِلِينَ ﴿١٥٦﴾

157. Or lest you should say: "If the book had only been sent down to us, we should have followed its guidance better than they." Now then has come to you a clear (sign) from your Lord - and a guide and a mercy: then who could do more wrong than one who rejects Allah's signs, and turns away from it? In good time shall We repay those who turn away from Our signs, with a dreadful penalty, for their turning away.

أَوْ تَقُولُوا۟ لَوْ أَنَّآ أُنزِلَ عَلَيْنَا ٱلْكِتَٰبُ لَكُنَّآ
أَهْدَىٰ مِنْهُمْ ۚ فَقَدْ جَآءَكُم بَيِّنَةٌ مِّن رَّبِّكُمْ
وَهُدًى وَرَحْمَةٌ ۚ فَمَنْ أَظْلَمُ مِمَّن كَذَّبَ بِـَٔايَٰتِ ٱللَّهِ
وَصَدَفَ عَنْهَا ۗ سَنَجْزِى ٱلَّذِينَ يَصْدِفُونَ عَنْ ءَايَٰتِنَا
سُوٓءَ ٱلْعَذَابِ بِمَا كَانُوا۟ يَصْدِفُونَ ﴿١٥٧﴾

158. Are they waiting to see if the angels come to them, or your Lord (Himself), or certain of the signs of your Lord! The day that certain of the signs of your Lord do come, no good will it do to a soul to believe in them then, if it believed not before, nor earned righteousness through its faith. Say: "Wait you: we too are waiting."

هَلْ يَنظُرُونَ إِلَّآ أَن تَأْتِيَهُمُ ٱلْمَلَٰٓئِكَةُ أَوْ يَأْتِىَ رَبُّكَ
أَوْ يَأْتِىَ بَعْضُ ءَايَٰتِ رَبِّكَ ۗ يَوْمَ يَأْتِى بَعْضُ ءَايَٰتِ رَبِّكَ
لَا يَنفَعُ نَفْسًا إِيمَٰنُهَا لَمْ تَكُنْ ءَامَنَتْ مِن قَبْلُ
أَوْ كَسَبَتْ فِىٓ إِيمَٰنِهَا خَيْرًا ۗ قُلِ ٱنتَظِرُوٓا۟
إِنَّا مُنتَظِرُونَ ﴿١٥٨﴾

159. As for those who divide their religion and break up into sects, you have no part in them in the least; their affair is with Allah: He will in the end tell them the truth of all that they did.

إِنَّ ٱلَّذِينَ فَرَّقُواْ دِينَهُمۡ وَكَانُواْ شِيَعٗا لَّسۡتَ مِنۡهُمۡ
فِي شَيۡءٍۚ إِنَّمَآ أَمۡرُهُمۡ إِلَى ٱللَّهِ ثُمَّ يُنَبِّئُهُم بِمَا كَانُواْ
يَفۡعَلُونَ ١٥٩

160. He that does good shall have ten times as much to his credit; he that does evil shall only be recompensed according to his evil; no wrong shall be done to (any of) them.

مَن جَآءَ بِٱلۡحَسَنَةِ فَلَهُۥ عَشۡرُ أَمۡثَالِهَاۖ وَمَن جَآءَ
بِٱلسَّيِّئَةِ فَلَا يُجۡزَىٰٓ إِلَّا مِثۡلَهَا وَهُمۡ لَا يُظۡلَمُونَ ١٦٠

161. Say: "Verily, my Lord has guided me to a way that is straight - a religion of right - the path (trod) by Abraham the true in faith, and he (certainly) joined not gods with Allah."

قُلۡ إِنَّنِي هَدَىٰنِي رَبِّيٓ إِلَىٰ صِرَٰطٖ مُّسۡتَقِيمٖ دِينٗا قِيَمٗا
مِّلَّةَ إِبۡرَٰهِيمَ حَنِيفٗاۚ وَمَا كَانَ مِنَ ٱلۡمُشۡرِكِينَ ١٦١

162. Say: "Truly, my prayer and my service of sacrifice, my life and my death, are (all) for Allah, the Cherisher of the Worlds;

قُلۡ إِنَّ صَلَاتِي وَنُسُكِي وَمَحۡيَايَ وَمَمَاتِي لِلَّهِ رَبِّ
ٱلۡعَٰلَمِينَ ١٦٢

163. No partner has He: this am I commanded, and I am the first of those who bow to His Will.

لَا شَرِيكَ لَهُۥۖ وَبِذَٰلِكَ أُمِرۡتُ وَأَنَا۠ أَوَّلُ ٱلۡمُسۡلِمِينَ ١٦٣

164. Say: "Shall I seek for (my) Cherisher other than Allah, when He is the Cherisher of all things (that exist)? Every soul draws the meed of its acts on none but itself: no bearer of burdens can bear the burden of another. Your goal in the end is towards Allah: He will tell you the truth of the things in which you disputed."

قُلۡ أَغَيۡرَ ٱللَّهِ أَبۡغِي رَبّٗا وَهُوَ رَبُّ كُلِّ شَيۡءٖۚ وَلَا تَكۡسِبُ
كُلُّ نَفۡسٍ إِلَّا عَلَيۡهَاۚ وَلَا تَزِرُ وَازِرَةٞ وِزۡرَ أُخۡرَىٰۚ ثُمَّ
إِلَىٰ رَبِّكُم مَّرۡجِعُكُمۡ فَيُنَبِّئُكُم بِمَا كُنتُمۡ فِيهِ
تَخۡتَلِفُونَ ١٦٤

165. It is He Who has made you (His) agents, inheritors of the earth: He has raised you in ranks, some above others; that He may try you in the gifts He has given you: for your Lord is quick in punishment; yet He is indeed Oft-Forgiving, Most Merciful.

وَهُوَ ٱلَّذِي جَعَلَكُمۡ خَلَٰٓئِفَ ٱلۡأَرۡضِ وَرَفَعَ بَعۡضَكُمۡ
فَوۡقَ بَعۡضٖ دَرَجَٰتٖ لِّيَبۡلُوَكُمۡ فِي مَآ ءَاتَىٰكُمۡۗ إِنَّ رَبَّكَ
سَرِيعُ ٱلۡعِقَابِ وَإِنَّهُۥ لَغَفُورٞ رَّحِيمُۢ ١٦٥

سُورَةُ الأَعْرَافِ

Surah 7: ***Al-A'raf*** **(The Heights)**

In the name of Allah,
Most Gracious, Most Merciful.

بِسۡمِ ٱللَّهِ ٱلرَّحۡمَٰنِ ٱلرَّحِيمِ

الحزب ١٦

1. *Alif Lam Mim Sad.*

الٓمٓصٓ ﴿١﴾

2. A book revealed to you - so let your heart be oppressed no more by any difficulty on that account - that with it you might warn (the erring) and teach the believers.

كِتَٰبٌ أُنزِلَ إِلَيۡكَ فَلَا يَكُن فِي صَدۡرِكَ حَرَجٞ مِّنۡهُ
لِتُنذِرَ بِهِۦ وَذِكۡرَىٰ لِلۡمُؤۡمِنِينَ ﴿٢﴾

3. Follow (O men!) the revelation given to you from your Lord, and follow not, as friends or protectors, other than Him. Little it is you remember of admonition.

ٱتَّبِعُواْ مَآ أُنزِلَ إِلَيۡكُم مِّن رَّبِّكُمۡ وَلَا تَتَّبِعُواْ مِن
دُونِهِۦٓ أَوۡلِيَآءَۗ قَلِيلٗا مَّا تَذَكَّرُونَ ﴿٣﴾

4. How many towns have We destroyed (for their sins)? Our punishment took them on a sudden by night or while they slept for their afternoon rest.

وَكَم مِّن قَرۡيَةٍ أَهۡلَكۡنَٰهَا فَجَآءَهَا بَأۡسُنَا بَيَٰتًا
أَوۡ هُمۡ قَآئِلُونَ ﴿٤﴾

5. When (thus) Our punishment took them, no call did they utter but this: "Indeed we did wrong."

فَمَا كَانَ دَعۡوَىٰهُمۡ إِذۡ جَآءَهُم بَأۡسُنَآ إِلَّآ أَن قَالُوٓاْ
إِنَّا كُنَّا ظَٰلِمِينَ ﴿٥﴾

6. Then shall We question those to whom Our Message was sent and those by whom We sent it.

فَلَنَسۡـَٔلَنَّ ٱلَّذِينَ أُرۡسِلَ إِلَيۡهِمۡ وَلَنَسۡـَٔلَنَّ
ٱلۡمُرۡسَلِينَ ﴿٦﴾

7. And verily We shall recount their whole story with knowledge, for We were never absent (at any time or place).

فَلَنَقُصَّنَّ عَلَيۡهِم بِعِلۡمٖۖ وَمَا كُنَّا غَآئِبِينَ ﴿٧﴾

8. The balance that day will be true (to a nicety); those whose scale (of good) will be heavy, will prosper;

وَٱلۡوَزۡنُ يَوۡمَئِذٍ ٱلۡحَقُّۚ فَمَن ثَقُلَتۡ مَوَٰزِينُهُۥ
فَأُوْلَٰٓئِكَ هُمُ ٱلۡمُفۡلِحُونَ ﴿٨﴾

9. Those whose scale will be light, will find their souls in perdition, for that they wrongfully treated Our signs.

وَمَنْ خَفَّتْ مَوَٰزِينُهُۥ فَأُو۟لَٰٓئِكَ ٱلَّذِينَ خَسِرُوٓا۟
أَنفُسَهُم بِمَا كَانُوا۟ بِـَٔايَٰتِنَا يَظْلِمُونَ ٩

10. It is We who have placed you with authority on earth, and provided you in it with means for the fulfilment of your life; small are the thanks that you give!

وَلَقَدْ مَكَّنَّٰكُمْ فِى ٱلْأَرْضِ وَجَعَلْنَا لَكُمْ فِيهَا
مَعَٰيِشَ ۗ قَلِيلًا مَّا تَشْكُرُونَ ١٠

11. It is We who created you and gave you shape; then We asked the angels to bow down to Adam, and they bowed down; not so Iblis; he refused to be of those who bow down.

وَلَقَدْ خَلَقْنَٰكُمْ ثُمَّ صَوَّرْنَٰكُمْ ثُمَّ قُلْنَا
لِلْمَلَٰٓئِكَةِ ٱسْجُدُوا۟ لِءَادَمَ فَسَجَدُوٓا۟ إِلَّآ إِبْلِيسَ
لَمْ يَكُن مِّنَ ٱلسَّٰجِدِينَ ١١

12. (Allah) said: "What prevented you from bowing down when I commanded you?" He said: "I am better than he: You did create me from fire, and him from clay."

قَالَ مَا مَنَعَكَ أَلَّا تَسْجُدَ إِذْ أَمَرْتُكَ ۖ قَالَ أَنَا۠ خَيْرٌ مِّنْهُ
خَلَقْتَنِى مِن نَّارٍ وَخَلَقْتَهُۥ مِن طِينٍ ١٢

13. (Allah) said: "Get you down from this; it is not for you to be arrogant here; get out, for you are of the meanest (of creatures)."

قَالَ فَٱهْبِطْ مِنْهَا فَمَا يَكُونُ لَكَ أَن تَتَكَبَّرَ فِيهَا
فَٱخْرُجْ إِنَّكَ مِنَ ٱلصَّٰغِرِينَ ١٣

14. He said: "Give me respite till the day they are raised up."

قَالَ أَنظِرْنِىٓ إِلَىٰ يَوْمِ يُبْعَثُونَ ١٤

15. (Allah) said: "Be you among those who have respite."

قَالَ إِنَّكَ مِنَ ٱلْمُنظَرِينَ ١٥

16. He said: "Because You have thrown me out of the way, I will lie in wait for them on Your straight way."

قَالَ فَبِمَآ أَغْوَيْتَنِى لَأَقْعُدَنَّ لَهُمْ صِرَٰطَكَ
ٱلْمُسْتَقِيمَ ١٦

17. "Then will I assault them from before them and behind them, from their right and their left; nor will You find, in most of them, gratitude (for Your mercies)."

ثُمَّ لَءَاتِيَنَّهُم مِّنۢ بَيْنِ أَيْدِيهِمْ وَمِنْ خَلْفِهِمْ وَعَنْ أَيْمَٰنِهِمْ
وَعَن شَمَآئِلِهِمْ ۖ وَلَا تَجِدُ أَكْثَرَهُمْ شَٰكِرِينَ ١٧

18. (Allah) said: "Get out from this,

قَالَ ٱخْرُجْ مِنْهَا مَذْءُومًا مَّدْحُورًا ۖ لَّمَن تَبِعَكَ مِنْهُمْ

disgraced and expelled. If any of them follow you - hell will I fill with you all.

لَأَمۡلَأَنَّ جَهَنَّمَ مِنكُمۡ أَجۡمَعِينَ ١٨

19. O Adam! Dwell you and your wife in the garden, and enjoy (its good things) as you wish; but approach not this tree, or you run into harmand transgression."

وَيَٰٓـَٔادَمُ ٱسۡكُنۡ أَنتَ وَزَوۡجُكَ ٱلۡجَنَّةَ فَكُلَا مِنۡ حَيۡثُ
شِئۡتُمَا وَلَا تَقۡرَبَا هَٰذِهِ ٱلشَّجَرَةَ فَتَكُونَا مِنَ ٱلظَّٰلِمِينَ ١٩

20. Then began Satan to whisper suggestions to them, in order to reveal to them their shame that was hidden from them (before); he said: "Your Lord only forbade you this tree, lest you should become angels or such beings as live for ever."

فَوَسۡوَسَ لَهُمَا ٱلشَّيۡطَٰنُ لِيُبۡدِيَ لَهُمَا مَا وُۥرِيَ عَنۡهُمَا
مِن سَوۡءَٰتِهِمَا وَقَالَ مَا نَهَىٰكُمَا رَبُّكُمَا عَنۡ هَٰذِهِ
ٱلشَّجَرَةِ إِلَّآ أَن تَكُونَا مَلَكَيۡنِ أَوۡ تَكُونَا مِنَ
ٱلۡخَٰلِدِينَ ٢٠

21. And he swore to them both, that he was their sincere adviser.

وَقَاسَمَهُمَآ إِنِّي لَكُمَا لَمِنَ ٱلنَّٰصِحِينَ ٢١

22. So by deceit he brought about their fall: when they tasted of the tree, their shame became manifest to them, and they began to sew together the leaves of the garden over their bodies. And their Lord called to them: "Did I not forbid you that tree, and tell you that Satan was an avowed enemy to you?"

فَدَلَّىٰهُمَا بِغُرُورٖۚ فَلَمَّا ذَاقَا ٱلشَّجَرَةَ بَدَتۡ لَهُمَا
سَوۡءَٰتُهُمَا وَطَفِقَا يَخۡصِفَانِ عَلَيۡهِمَا مِن وَرَقِ ٱلۡجَنَّةِۖ
وَنَادَىٰهُمَا رَبُّهُمَآ أَلَمۡ أَنۡهَكُمَا عَن تِلۡكُمَا ٱلشَّجَرَةِ وَأَقُل
لَّكُمَآ إِنَّ ٱلشَّيۡطَٰنَ لَكُمَا عَدُوّٞ مُّبِينٞ ٢٢

23. They said: "Our Lord! We have wronged our own souls; if You forgive us not and bestow not upon us Your mercy, we shall certainly be lost."

قَالَا رَبَّنَا ظَلَمۡنَآ أَنفُسَنَا وَإِن لَّمۡ تَغۡفِرۡ لَنَا وَتَرۡحَمۡنَا
لَنَكُونَنَّ مِنَ ٱلۡخَٰسِرِينَ ٢٣

24. (Allah) said: "Get you down, with enmity between yourselves. On earth will be your dwelling-place and your means of livelihood - for a time."

قَالَ ٱهۡبِطُواْ بَعۡضُكُمۡ لِبَعۡضٍ عَدُوّٞۖ وَلَكُمۡ
فِي ٱلۡأَرۡضِ مُسۡتَقَرّٞ وَمَتَٰعٌ إِلَىٰ حِينٖ ٢٤

25. He said: "In it shall you live, and in it shall you die; but from it shall you be taken out (at last).

قَالَ فِيهَا تَحۡيَوۡنَ وَفِيهَا تَمُوتُونَ وَمِنۡهَا تُخۡرَجُونَ ٢٥

26. O you Children of Adam! We have bestowed garment upon you to cover your shame, as well as to be an adornment to you. But the garment of righteousness - that is the best. Such are among the signs of Allah, that they may receive admonition!

يَٰبَنِيٓ ءَادَمَ قَدۡ أَنزَلۡنَا عَلَيۡكُمۡ لِبَاسٗا يُوَٰرِي سَوۡءَٰتِكُمۡ وَرِيشٗاۖ وَلِبَاسُ ٱلتَّقۡوَىٰ ذَٰلِكَ خَيۡرٞۚ ذَٰلِكَ مِنۡ ءَايَٰتِ ٱللَّهِ لَعَلَّهُمۡ يَذَّكَّرُونَ ٢٦

27. O you Children of Adam! Let not Satan seduce you, in the same manner as he got your parents out of the garden, stripping them of their garment, to expose their shame; for he and his tribe watch you from a position where you cannot see them; We made the evil ones friends (only) to those without faith.

يَٰبَنِيٓ ءَادَمَ لَا يَفۡتِنَنَّكُمُ ٱلشَّيۡطَٰنُ كَمَآ أَخۡرَجَ أَبَوَيۡكُم مِّنَ ٱلۡجَنَّةِ يَنزِعُ عَنۡهُمَا لِبَاسَهُمَا لِيُرِيَهُمَا سَوۡءَٰتِهِمَآۚ إِنَّهُۥ يَرَىٰكُمۡ هُوَ وَقَبِيلُهُۥ مِنۡ حَيۡثُ لَا تَرَوۡنَهُمۡۗ إِنَّا جَعَلۡنَا ٱلشَّيَٰطِينَ أَوۡلِيَآءَ لِلَّذِينَ لَا يُؤۡمِنُونَ ٢٧

28. When they do anything that is shameful, they say: "We found our fathers doing so"; and "Allah commanded us thus"; say: "Nay, Allah never commands what is shameful: Do you say of Allah what you know not?"

وَإِذَا فَعَلُواْ فَٰحِشَةٗ قَالُواْ وَجَدۡنَا عَلَيۡهَآ ءَابَآءَنَا وَٱللَّهُ أَمَرَنَا بِهَاۗ قُلۡ إِنَّ ٱللَّهَ لَا يَأۡمُرُ بِٱلۡفَحۡشَآءِۖ أَتَقُولُونَ عَلَى ٱللَّهِ مَا لَا تَعۡلَمُونَ ٢٨

29. Say: "My Lord has commanded justice; and that you set your whole selves (to Him) at every time and place of prayer, and call upon Him, making your devotion sincere as in His sight; such as He created you in the beginning, so shall you return."

قُلۡ أَمَرَ رَبِّي بِٱلۡقِسۡطِۖ وَأَقِيمُواْ وُجُوهَكُمۡ عِندَ كُلِّ مَسۡجِدٖ وَٱدۡعُوهُ مُخۡلِصِينَ لَهُ ٱلدِّينَۚ كَمَا بَدَأَكُمۡ تَعُودُونَ ٢٩

30. Some He has guided: others have (by their choice) deserved the loss of their way; in that they took the evil ones, in preference to Allah, for their friends and protectors, and think that they receive guidance.

فَرِيقًا هَدَىٰ وَفَرِيقًا حَقَّ عَلَيۡهِمُ ٱلضَّلَٰلَةُۚ إِنَّهُمُ ٱتَّخَذُواْ ٱلشَّيَٰطِينَ أَوۡلِيَآءَ مِن دُونِ ٱللَّهِ وَيَحۡسَبُونَ أَنَّهُم مُّهۡتَدُونَ ٣٠

31. O Children of Adam! Wear your beautiful apparel at every time and place of prayer; eat and drink; but waste not by excess, for Allah loves not the wasters.

۞ يَٰبَنِيٓ ءَادَمَ خُذُواْ زِينَتَكُمۡ عِندَ كُلِّ مَسۡجِدٖ وَكُلُواْ وَٱشۡرَبُواْ وَلَا تُسۡرِفُوٓاْۚ إِنَّهُۥ لَا يُحِبُّ ٱلۡمُسۡرِفِينَ ٣١ ربع الحزب ١٦

32. Say: "Who has forbidden the beautiful (gifts) of Allah, which He has produced for His servants, and the things, clean and pure, (which He has provided) for sustenance? Say: They are in the life of this world, for those who believe, (and) purely for them on the day of judgement. Thus do We explain the signs in detail for those who understand."

قُلْ مَنْ حَرَّمَ زِينَةَ ٱللَّهِ ٱلَّتِيٓ أَخْرَجَ لِعِبَادِهِۦ
وَٱلطَّيِّبَٰتِ مِنَ ٱلرِّزْقِۚ قُلْ هِيَ لِلَّذِينَ ءَامَنُواْ فِي ٱلْحَيَوٰةِ
ٱلدُّنْيَا خَالِصَةٗ يَوْمَ ٱلْقِيَٰمَةِۗ كَذَٰلِكَ نُفَصِّلُ ٱلْأٓيَٰتِ
لِقَوْمٖ يَعْلَمُونَ ٣٢

33. Say: "The things that my Lord has indeed forbidden are: shameful deeds, whether open or secret; sins and trespasses against truth or reason; assigning of partners to Allah, for which He has given no authority; and saying things about Allah of which you have no knowledge."

قُلْ إِنَّمَا حَرَّمَ رَبِّيَ ٱلْفَوَٰحِشَ مَا ظَهَرَ مِنْهَا وَمَا بَطَنَ
وَٱلْإِثْمَ وَٱلْبَغْيَ بِغَيْرِ ٱلْحَقِّ وَأَن تُشْرِكُواْ بِٱللَّهِ
مَا لَمْ يُنَزِّلْ بِهِۦ سُلْطَٰنٗا وَأَن تَقُولُواْ عَلَى ٱللَّهِ مَا لَا
تَعْلَمُونَ ٣٣

34. To every People is a term appointed: when their term is reached, not an hour can they cause delay, nor (an hour) can they advance (it in anticipation).

وَلِكُلِّ أُمَّةٍ أَجَلٞۖ فَإِذَا جَآءَ أَجَلُهُمْ لَا يَسْتَـْٔخِرُونَ
سَاعَةٗ وَلَا يَسْتَقْدِمُونَ ٣٤

35. O you Children of Adam! Whenever there come to you messengers from amongst you, rehearsing My signs to you - those who are righteous and mend (their lives) - on them shall be no fear nor shall they grieve.

يَٰبَنِيٓ ءَادَمَ إِمَّا يَأْتِيَنَّكُمْ رُسُلٞ مِّنكُمْ يَقُصُّونَ عَلَيْكُمْ
ءَايَٰتِي فَمَنِ ٱتَّقَىٰ وَأَصْلَحَ فَلَا خَوْفٌ عَلَيْهِمْ وَلَا هُمْ
يَحْزَنُونَ ٣٥

36. But those who reject Our signs and treat them with arrogance - they are companions of the fire, to dwell in it (for ever).

وَٱلَّذِينَ كَذَّبُواْ بِـَٔايَٰتِنَا وَٱسْتَكْبَرُواْ عَنْهَآ أُوْلَٰٓئِكَ
أَصْحَٰبُ ٱلنَّارِۖ هُمْ فِيهَا خَٰلِدُونَ ٣٦

37. Who is more unjust than one who invents a lie against Allah or rejects His signs? For such, their portion appointed must reach them from the book (of decrees); until, when Our messengers (of death) arrive and take their souls, they say: "Where are the things that you used to invoke besides Allah?" They will reply,

فَمَنْ أَظْلَمُ مِمَّنِ ٱفْتَرَىٰ عَلَى ٱللَّهِ كَذِبًا أَوْ كَذَّبَ
بِـَٔايَٰتِهِۦٓۚ أُوْلَٰٓئِكَ يَنَالُهُمْ نَصِيبُهُم مِّنَ ٱلْكِتَٰبِۖ حَتَّىٰٓ
إِذَا جَآءَتْهُمْ رُسُلُنَا يَتَوَفَّوْنَهُمْ قَالُوٓاْ أَيْنَ مَا كُنتُمْ
تَدْعُونَ مِن دُونِ ٱللَّهِۖ قَالُواْ ضَلُّواْ عَنَّا وَشَهِدُواْ عَلَىٰٓ

"they have left us in the lurch," and they will bear witness against themselves, that they had rejected Allah.

أَنفُسِهِمْ أَنَّهُمْ كَانُوا كَافِرِينَ ﴿٣٧﴾

38. He will say: "Enter you in the company of the peoples who passed away before you - men and Jinns - into the fire. Every time a new people enters, it curses its sister-people (that went before), until they follow each other all into the fire. Says the last about the first: "Our Lord! It is these that misled us: so give them a double penalty in the fire." He will say: "Doubled for all": but this You do not understand.

قَالَ ادْخُلُوا فِي أُمَمٍ قَدْ خَلَتْ مِن قَبْلِكُم مِّنَ الْجِنِّ
وَالْإِنسِ فِي النَّارِ ۖ كُلَّمَا دَخَلَتْ أُمَّةٌ لَّعَنَتْ أُخْتَهَا ۖ
حَتَّىٰ إِذَا ادَّارَكُوا فِيهَا جَمِيعًا قَالَتْ أُخْرَاهُمْ
لِأُولَاهُمْ رَبَّنَا هَٰؤُلَاءِ أَضَلُّونَا فَآتِهِمْ عَذَابًا ضِعْفًا
مِّنَ النَّارِ ۖ قَالَ لِكُلٍّ ضِعْفٌ وَلَٰكِن لَّا تَعْلَمُونَ ﴿٣٨﴾

39. Then the first will say to the last: "See then! No advantage have you over us; so taste you of the penalty for all that you did!"

وَقَالَتْ أُولَاهُمْ لِأُخْرَاهُمْ فَمَا كَانَ لَكُمْ عَلَيْنَا
مِن فَضْلٍ فَذُوقُوا الْعَذَابَ بِمَا كُنتُمْ تَكْسِبُونَ ﴿٣٩﴾

40. To those who reject Our signs and treat them with arrogance, no opening will there be of the gates of heaven, nor will they enter the garden, until the camel can pass through the eye of the needle: such is Our reward for those in sin.

إِنَّ الَّذِينَ كَذَّبُوا بِآيَاتِنَا وَاسْتَكْبَرُوا عَنْهَا
لَا تُفَتَّحُ لَهُمْ أَبْوَابُ السَّمَاءِ وَلَا يَدْخُلُونَ الْجَنَّةَ
حَتَّىٰ يَلِجَ الْجَمَلُ فِي سَمِّ الْخِيَاطِ ۚ وَكَذَٰلِكَ نَجْزِي
الْمُجْرِمِينَ ﴿٤٠﴾

41. For them there is hell, as a couch (below) and folds and folds of covering above: such is Our requital of those who do wrong.

لَهُم مِّن جَهَنَّمَ مِهَادٌ وَمِن فَوْقِهِمْ غَوَاشٍ ۚ وَكَذَٰلِكَ
نَجْزِي الظَّالِمِينَ ﴿٤١﴾

42. But those who believe and work righteousness - no burden do We place on any soul, but that which it can bear - they will be companions of the garden, in it to dwell (for ever).

وَالَّذِينَ آمَنُوا وَعَمِلُوا الصَّالِحَاتِ لَا نُكَلِّفُ نَفْسًا
إِلَّا وُسْعَهَا أُولَٰئِكَ أَصْحَابُ الْجَنَّةِ ۖ هُمْ فِيهَا
خَالِدُونَ ﴿٤٢﴾

43. And We shall remove from their hearts any lurking sense of injury - beneath them will be rivers flowing - and they shall say: "Praise be to Allah, Who has guided us to this

وَنَزَعْنَا مَا فِي صُدُورِهِم مِّنْ غِلٍّ تَجْرِي مِن تَحْتِهِمُ
الْأَنْهَارُ ۖ وَقَالُوا الْحَمْدُ لِلَّهِ الَّذِي هَدَانَا لِهَٰذَا وَمَا كُنَّا

(felicity); never could we have found guidance, had it not been for the guidance of Allah; indeed it was the truth that the messengers of our Lord brought to us." And they shall hear the call: "See! The garden before you! You have been made its inheritors for your deeds (of righteousness)."

لِنَهْتَدِيَ لَوْلَآ أَنْ هَدَىٰنَا ٱللَّهُ ۖ لَقَدْ جَآءَتْ رُسُلُ
رَبِّنَا بِٱلْحَقِّ ۖ وَنُودُوٓا۟ أَن تِلْكُمُ ٱلْجَنَّةُ أُورِثْتُمُوهَا
بِمَا كُنتُمْ تَعْمَلُونَ ﴿٤٣﴾

44. The companions of the garden will call out to the companions of the fire: "We have indeed found the promises of our Lord to us true; have you also found your Lord's promises true?" They shall say, "Yes"; but a Caller shall proclaim between them: "The curse of Allah is on the wrongdoers -

وَنَادَىٰٓ أَصْحَـٰبُ ٱلْجَنَّةِ أَصْحَـٰبَ ٱلنَّارِ أَن قَدْ وَجَدْنَا
مَا وَعَدَنَا رَبُّنَا حَقًّا فَهَلْ وَجَدتُّم مَّا وَعَدَ رَبُّكُمْ حَقًّا ۖ
قَالُوا۟ نَعَمْ ۚ فَأَذَّنَ مُؤَذِّنٌۢ بَيْنَهُمْ أَن لَّعْنَةُ ٱللَّهِ عَلَى
ٱلظَّـٰلِمِينَ ﴿٤٤﴾

45. Those who would hinder (men) from the path of Allah and would seek in it something crooked; they were those who denied the hereafter."

ٱلَّذِينَ يَصُدُّونَ عَن سَبِيلِ ٱللَّهِ وَيَبْغُونَهَا عِوَجًا وَهُم
بِٱلْـَٔاخِرَةِ كَـٰفِرُونَ ﴿٤٥﴾

46. Between them shall be a veil, and on the heights will be men who would know everyone by his marks: they will call out to the companions of the garden, "Peace on you": they will not have entered, but they will have an assurance (of it.)

وَبَيْنَهُمَا حِجَابٌ ۚ وَعَلَى ٱلْأَعْرَافِ رِجَالٌ يَعْرِفُونَ
كُلًّۢا بِسِيمَىٰهُمْ ۚ وَنَادَوْا۟ أَصْحَـٰبَ ٱلْجَنَّةِ أَن سَلَـٰمٌ
عَلَيْكُمْ ۚ لَمْ يَدْخُلُوهَا وَهُمْ يَطْمَعُونَ ﴿٤٦﴾

47. When their eyes shall be turned towards the companions of the fire, they will say: "Our Lord! Send us not to the company of the wrongdoers."

نصف الحزب ١٦ ۞ وَإِذَا صُرِفَتْ أَبْصَـٰرُهُمْ تِلْقَآءَ أَصْحَـٰبِ ٱلنَّارِ قَالُوا۟
رَبَّنَا لَا تَجْعَلْنَا مَعَ ٱلْقَوْمِ ٱلظَّـٰلِمِينَ ﴿٤٧﴾

48. The men on the heights will call to certain men whom they will know from their marks, saying: "Of what profit to you were you hoards and your arrogant ways?"

وَنَادَىٰٓ أَصْحَـٰبُ ٱلْأَعْرَافِ رِجَالًا يَعْرِفُونَهُم بِسِيمَىٰهُمْ
قَالُوا۟ مَآ أَغْنَىٰ عَنكُمْ جَمْعُكُمْ وَمَا كُنتُمْ تَسْتَكْبِرُونَ ﴿٤٨﴾

49. "See! Are these not the men whom you swore that Allah with His mercy would never bless? Enter you the garden: no fear shall be on you, nor shall you grieve."

أَهَـٰٓؤُلَآءِ ٱلَّذِينَ أَقْسَمْتُمْ لَا يَنَالُهُمُ ٱللَّهُ بِرَحْمَةٍ ۚ
ٱدْخُلُوا۟ ٱلْجَنَّةَ لَا خَوْفٌ عَلَيْكُمْ وَلَآ أَنتُمْ تَحْزَنُونَ ﴿٤٩﴾

50. The companions of the fire will call to the companions of the garden; "Pour down to us water or anything that Allah does provide for your sustenance." They will say: "Both these things has Allah forbidden to those who rejected Him -

وَنَادَىٰٓ أَصۡحَٰبُ ٱلنَّارِ أَصۡحَٰبَ ٱلۡجَنَّةِ أَنۡ أَفِيضُواْ عَلَيۡنَا
مِنَ ٱلۡمَآءِ أَوۡ مِمَّا رَزَقَكُمُ ٱللَّهُۚ قَالُوٓاْ إِنَّ ٱللَّهَ
حَرَّمَهُمَا عَلَى ٱلۡكَٰفِرِينَ ٥٠

51. Such as took their religion to be mere amusement and play, and were deceived by the life of the world." That day shall We forget them as they forgot the meeting of this day of theirs, and as they used to reject Our signs.

ٱلَّذِينَ ٱتَّخَذُواْ دِينَهُمۡ لَهۡوٗا وَلَعِبٗا وَغَرَّتۡهُمُ ٱلۡحَيَوٰةُ
ٱلدُّنۡيَاۚ فَٱلۡيَوۡمَ نَنسَىٰهُمۡ كَمَا نَسُواْ لِقَآءَ يَوۡمِهِمۡ
هَٰذَا وَمَا كَانُواْ بِـَٔايَٰتِنَا يَجۡحَدُونَ ٥١

52. For We had certainly sent to them a book, based on knowledge, which We explained in detail - a guide and a mercy to all who believe.

وَلَقَدۡ جِئۡنَٰهُم بِكِتَٰبٖ فَصَّلۡنَٰهُ عَلَىٰ عِلۡمٍ هُدٗى
وَرَحۡمَةٗ لِّقَوۡمٖ يُؤۡمِنُونَ ٥٢

53. Do they just wait for the final fulfilment of the event? On the day the event is finally fulfilled, those who disregarded it before will say: "The messengers of our Lord did indeed bring true (tidings). Have we no intercessors now to intercede on our behalf? Or could we be sent back? Then should we behave differently from our behaviour in the past." In fact, they will have lost their souls, and the things they invented will leave them in the lurch.

هَلۡ يَنظُرُونَ إِلَّا تَأۡوِيلَهُۥۚ يَوۡمَ يَأۡتِي تَأۡوِيلُهُۥ يَقُولُ
ٱلَّذِينَ نَسُوهُ مِن قَبۡلُ قَدۡ جَآءَتۡ رُسُلُ رَبِّنَا بِٱلۡحَقِّ
فَهَل لَّنَا مِن شُفَعَآءَ فَيَشۡفَعُواْ لَنَآ أَوۡ نُرَدُّ فَنَعۡمَلَ
غَيۡرَ ٱلَّذِي كُنَّا نَعۡمَلُۚ قَدۡ خَسِرُوٓاْ أَنفُسَهُمۡ
وَضَلَّ عَنۡهُم مَّا كَانُواْ يَفۡتَرُونَ ٥٣

54. Your Guardian-Lord is Allah, Who created the heavens and the earth in six Days, and is firmly established on the throne (of authority); He draws the night as a veil over the day, each seeking the other in rapid succession; He created the sun, the moon, and the stars (all) governed by laws under His command. Is it not His to create and to govern? Blessed be Allah, the Cherisher and Sustainer of the Worlds!

إِنَّ رَبَّكُمُ ٱللَّهُ ٱلَّذِي خَلَقَ ٱلسَّمَٰوَٰتِ وَٱلۡأَرۡضَ فِي
سِتَّةِ أَيَّامٖ ثُمَّ ٱسۡتَوَىٰ عَلَى ٱلۡعَرۡشِۖ يُغۡشِي ٱلَّيۡلَ
ٱلنَّهَارَ يَطۡلُبُهُۥ حَثِيثٗا وَٱلشَّمۡسَ وَٱلۡقَمَرَ
وَٱلنُّجُومَ مُسَخَّرَٰتِۭ بِأَمۡرِهِۦٓۗ أَلَا لَهُ ٱلۡخَلۡقُ
وَٱلۡأَمۡرُۗ تَبَارَكَ ٱللَّهُ رَبُّ ٱلۡعَٰلَمِينَ ٥٤

55. Call on your Lord with humility and in private: for Allah loves not those who trespass beyond bounds.

ٱدۡعُواْ رَبَّكُمۡ تَضَرُّعٗا وَخُفۡيَةًۚ إِنَّهُۥ لَا يُحِبُّ
ٱلۡمُعۡتَدِينَ ٥٥

56. Do no mischief on the earth, after it has been set in order, but call on Him with fear and longing (in your hearts): for the mercy of Allah is (always) near to those who do good.

وَلَا تُفۡسِدُواْ فِي ٱلۡأَرۡضِ بَعۡدَ إِصۡلَٰحِهَا وَٱدۡعُوهُ خَوۡفٗا
وَطَمَعًاۚ إِنَّ رَحۡمَتَ ٱللَّهِ قَرِيبٞ مِّنَ ٱلۡمُحۡسِنِينَ ٥٦

57. It is He Who sends the winds like heralds of glad tidings, going before His mercy; when they have carried the heavy-laden clouds, We drive them to a land that is dead, make rain to descend on it, and produce every kind of harvest with it; thus shall We raise up the dead; perhaps you may remember.

وَهُوَ ٱلَّذِي يُرۡسِلُ ٱلرِّيَٰحَ بُشۡرَۢا بَيۡنَ يَدَيۡ رَحۡمَتِهِۦۖ
حَتَّىٰٓ إِذَآ أَقَلَّتۡ سَحَابٗا ثِقَالٗا سُقۡنَٰهُ لِبَلَدٖ مَّيِّتٖ
فَأَنزَلۡنَا بِهِ ٱلۡمَآءَ فَأَخۡرَجۡنَا بِهِۦ مِن كُلِّ ٱلثَّمَرَٰتِۚ
كَذَٰلِكَ نُخۡرِجُ ٱلۡمَوۡتَىٰ لَعَلَّكُمۡ تَذَكَّرُونَ ٥٧

58. From the land that is clean and good, by the will of its Cherisher, springs up produce, (rich) after its kind; but from the land that is bad, spring up nothing but that which is niggardly; thus do We explain the signs by various (symbols) to those who are grateful.

وَٱلۡبَلَدُ ٱلطَّيِّبُ يَخۡرُجُ نَبَاتُهُۥ بِإِذۡنِ رَبِّهِۦۖ وَٱلَّذِي
خَبُثَ لَا يَخۡرُجُ إِلَّا نَكِدٗاۚ كَذَٰلِكَ نُصَرِّفُ ٱلۡأٓيَٰتِ
لِقَوۡمٖ يَشۡكُرُونَ ٥٨

59. We sent Noah to his people. He said: "O my people! Worship Allah! You have no other god but Him. I fear for you the punishment of a dreadful day!"

لَقَدۡ أَرۡسَلۡنَا نُوحًا إِلَىٰ قَوۡمِهِۦ فَقَالَ يَٰقَوۡمِ ٱعۡبُدُواْ
ٱللَّهَ مَا لَكُم مِّنۡ إِلَٰهٍ غَيۡرُهُۥٓ إِنِّيٓ أَخَافُ عَلَيۡكُمۡ
عَذَابَ يَوۡمٍ عَظِيمٖ ٥٩

60. The leaders of his people said: "Ah! We see you evidently wandering (in mind)."

قَالَ ٱلۡمَلَأُ مِن قَوۡمِهِۦٓ إِنَّا لَنَرَىٰكَ فِي ضَلَٰلٖ مُّبِينٖ ٦٠

61. He said: "O my people! No wandering is there in my (mind): on the contrary, I am a messenger from the Lord and Cherisher of the Worlds!"

قَالَ يَٰقَوۡمِ لَيۡسَ بِي ضَلَٰلَةٞ وَلَٰكِنِّي رَسُولٞ مِّن
رَّبِّ ٱلۡعَٰلَمِينَ ٦١

62. "I but fulfil towards you the duties of my Lord's mission: sincere is my advice to

أُبَلِّغُكُمۡ رِسَٰلَٰتِ رَبِّي وَأَنصَحُ لَكُمۡ وَأَعۡلَمُ

you, and I know from Allah something that you know not."

مِنَ ٱللَّهِ مَا لَا تَعۡلَمُونَ ٦٢

63. "Do you wonder that there has come to you a message from your Lord, through a man of your own people, to warn you - so that you may fear Allah and perhaps receive His mercy?"

أَوَعَجِبۡتُمۡ أَن جَآءَكُمۡ ذِكۡرٞ مِّن رَّبِّكُمۡ عَلَىٰ
رَجُلٖ مِّنكُمۡ لِيُنذِرَكُمۡ وَلِتَتَّقُواْ وَلَعَلَّكُمۡ
تُرۡحَمُونَ ٦٣

64. But they rejected him, and We delivered him, and those with him in the Ark; But We overwhelmed in the flood those who rejected Our signs. They were indeed a blind people!

فَكَذَّبُوهُ فَأَنجَيۡنَٰهُ وَٱلَّذِينَ مَعَهُۥ فِي ٱلۡفُلۡكِ وَأَغۡرَقۡنَا
ٱلَّذِينَ كَذَّبُواْ بِـَٔايَٰتِنَآۚ إِنَّهُمۡ كَانُواْ قَوۡمًا عَمِينَ ٦٤

65. To the 'Ad people, (We sent) Hud, one of their (own) brothers: he said: "O my people! Worship Allah! You have no other god but Him. Will you not fear (Allah)?"

ثلاثة أرباع الحزب ١٦ ۞وَإِلَىٰ عَادٍ أَخَاهُمۡ هُودٗاۚ قَالَ يَٰقَوۡمِ ٱعۡبُدُواْ ٱللَّهَ
مَا لَكُم مِّنۡ إِلَٰهٍ غَيۡرُهُۥٓۚ أَفَلَا تَتَّقُونَ ٦٥

66. The leaders of the unbelievers among his people said: "Ah! We see you are an imbecile!" And "We think you are a liar!"

قَالَ ٱلۡمَلَأُ ٱلَّذِينَ كَفَرُواْ مِن قَوۡمِهِۦٓ إِنَّا لَنَرَىٰكَ فِي
سَفَاهَةٖ وَإِنَّا لَنَظُنُّكَ مِنَ ٱلۡكَٰذِبِينَ ٦٦

67. He said: "O my people! I am no imbecile, but (I am) a messenger from the Lord and Cherisher of the Worlds!"

قَالَ يَٰقَوۡمِ لَيۡسَ بِي سَفَاهَةٞ وَلَٰكِنِّي رَسُولٞ مِّن رَّبِّ
ٱلۡعَٰلَمِينَ ٦٧

68. "I but fulfil towards you the duties of my Lord's mission: I am to you a sincere and trustworthy adviser."

أُبَلِّغُكُمۡ رِسَٰلَٰتِ رَبِّي وَأَنَا۠ لَكُمۡ نَاصِحٌ أَمِينٌ ٦٨

69. "Do you wonder that there has come to you a message from your Lord through a man of your own people, to warn you? Call in remembrance that He made you inheritors after the people of Noah, and gave you a stature tall among the nations. Call in remembrance the benefits (you have received) from Allah; so that you may prosper."

أَوَعَجِبۡتُمۡ أَن جَآءَكُمۡ ذِكۡرٞ مِّن رَّبِّكُمۡ عَلَىٰ رَجُلٖ
مِّنكُمۡ لِيُنذِرَكُمۡۚ وَٱذۡكُرُوٓاْ إِذۡ جَعَلَكُمۡ
خُلَفَآءَ مِنۢ بَعۡدِ قَوۡمِ نُوحٖ وَزَادَكُمۡ فِي ٱلۡخَلۡقِ
بَصۜۡطَةٗۖ فَٱذۡكُرُوٓاْ ءَالَآءَ ٱللَّهِ لَعَلَّكُمۡ تُفۡلِحُونَ ٦٩

70. They said: "Do you come to us, that we may worship Allah alone, and give up the cult of our fathers? Bring us what you threaten us with, if so be that you tell the truth!"

قَالُوٓا۟ أَجِئْتَنَا لِنَعْبُدَ ٱللَّهَ وَحْدَهُۥ وَنَذَرَ مَا كَانَ
يَعْبُدُ ءَابَآؤُنَا فَأْتِنَا بِمَا تَعِدُنَآ إِن كُنتَ مِنَ
ٱلصَّٰدِقِينَ ﴿٧٠﴾

71. He said: "Punishment and wrath have already come upon you from your Lord; dispute you with me over names which you have devised - you and your fathers - without authority from Allah? Then wait: I am amongst you, also waiting."

قَالَ قَدْ وَقَعَ عَلَيْكُم مِّن رَّبِّكُمْ رِجْسٌ
وَغَضَبٌ ۖ أَتُجَٰدِلُونَنِى فِىٓ أَسْمَآءٍ سَمَّيْتُمُوهَآ
أَنتُمْ وَءَابَآؤُكُم مَّا نَزَّلَ ٱللَّهُ بِهَا مِن سُلْطَٰنٍ ۚ
فَٱنتَظِرُوٓا۟ إِنِّى مَعَكُم مِّنَ ٱلْمُنتَظِرِينَ ﴿٧١﴾

72. We saved him and those who adhered to him, by Our mercy and We cut off the roots of those who rejected Our signs and did not believe.

فَأَنجَيْنَٰهُ وَٱلَّذِينَ مَعَهُۥ بِرَحْمَةٍ مِّنَّا وَقَطَعْنَا
دَابِرَ ٱلَّذِينَ كَذَّبُوا۟ بِـَٔايَٰتِنَا ۖ وَمَا كَانُوا۟ مُؤْمِنِينَ ﴿٧٢﴾

73. To the Thamud people (We sent) Salih, one of their own brothers: he said: "O my people! Worship Allah; you have no other god but Him. Now has come to you a clear (sign) from your Lord! This she-camel of Allah is a sign to you: so leave her to graze in Allah's earth, and let her come to no harm, or you shall be seized with a grievous punishment."

وَإِلَىٰ ثَمُودَ أَخَاهُمْ صَٰلِحًا ۗ قَالَ يَٰقَوْمِ ٱعْبُدُوا۟
ٱللَّهَ مَا لَكُم مِّنْ إِلَٰهٍ غَيْرُهُۥ ۖ قَدْ جَآءَتْكُم
بَيِّنَةٌ مِّن رَّبِّكُمْ ۖ هَٰذِهِۦ نَاقَةُ ٱللَّهِ لَكُمْ ءَايَةً ۖ
فَذَرُوهَا تَأْكُلْ فِىٓ أَرْضِ ٱللَّهِ ۖ وَلَا تَمَسُّوهَا
بِسُوٓءٍ فَيَأْخُذَكُمْ عَذَابٌ أَلِيمٌ ﴿٧٣﴾

74. "And remember how He made you inheritors after the 'Ad people and gave you habitations in the land: you build for yourselves palaces and castles in (open) plains, and carve out homes in the mountains; so bring to remembrance the benefits (you have received) from Allah, and refrain from evil and mischief on the earth."

وَٱذْكُرُوٓا۟ إِذْ جَعَلَكُمْ خُلَفَآءَ مِنۢ بَعْدِ عَادٍ
وَبَوَّأَكُمْ فِى ٱلْأَرْضِ تَتَّخِذُونَ مِن سُهُولِهَا
قُصُورًا وَتَنْحِتُونَ ٱلْجِبَالَ بُيُوتًا ۖ فَٱذْكُرُوٓا۟
ءَالَآءَ ٱللَّهِ وَلَا تَعْثَوْا۟ فِى ٱلْأَرْضِ مُفْسِدِينَ ﴿٧٤﴾

75. The leaders of the arrogant party among his people said to those who were

قَالَ ٱلْمَلَأُ ٱلَّذِينَ ٱسْتَكْبَرُوا۟ مِن قَوْمِهِۦ لِلَّذِينَ

reckoned powerless- those among them who believed: "Do you know that Salih is a messenger from his Lord?" They said: "We do indeed believe in the revelation which has been sent through him."

ٱسْتُضْعِفُوا۟ لِمَنْ ءَامَنَ مِنْهُمْ أَتَعْلَمُونَ أَنَّ
صَٰلِحًا مُّرْسَلٌ مِّن رَّبِّهِۦ ۚ قَالُوٓا۟ إِنَّا بِمَآ
أُرْسِلَ بِهِۦ مُؤْمِنُونَ ﴿٧٥﴾

76. The arrogant party said: "For our part, we reject what you believe in."

قَالَ ٱلَّذِينَ ٱسْتَكْبَرُوٓا۟ إِنَّا بِٱلَّذِىٓ
ءَامَنتُم بِهِۦ كَٰفِرُونَ ﴿٧٦﴾

77. Then they hamstrung the she-camel, and insolently defied the order of their Lord, saying: "O Salih! Bring about your threats, if you are a messenger (of Allah)!"

فَعَقَرُوا۟ ٱلنَّاقَةَ وَعَتَوْا۟ عَنْ أَمْرِ رَبِّهِمْ وَقَالُوا۟
يَٰصَٰلِحُ ٱئْتِنَا بِمَا تَعِدُنَآ إِن كُنتَ مِنَ
ٱلْمُرْسَلِينَ ﴿٧٧﴾

78. So the earthquake took them unawares, and they lay prostrate in their homes in the morning!

فَأَخَذَتْهُمُ ٱلرَّجْفَةُ فَأَصْبَحُوا۟ فِى دَارِهِمْ
جَٰثِمِينَ ﴿٧٨﴾

79. So Salih left them, saying: "O my people! I did indeed convey to you the message for which I was sent by my Lord: I gave you good counsel, but you love not good counsellors!"

فَتَوَلَّىٰ عَنْهُمْ وَقَالَ يَٰقَوْمِ لَقَدْ أَبْلَغْتُكُمْ
رِسَالَةَ رَبِّى وَنَصَحْتُ لَكُمْ وَلَٰكِن لَّا تُحِبُّونَ
ٱلنَّٰصِحِينَ ﴿٧٩﴾

80. We also (sent) Lot: he said to his people: "Do you commit lewdness such as no people in creation (ever) committed before you?"

وَلُوطًا إِذْ قَالَ لِقَوْمِهِۦٓ أَتَأْتُونَ ٱلْفَٰحِشَةَ
مَا سَبَقَكُم بِهَا مِنْ أَحَدٍ مِّنَ ٱلْعَٰلَمِينَ ﴿٨٠﴾

81. "For you practice your lusts on men in preference to women: you are indeed a people transgressing beyond bounds."

إِنَّكُمْ لَتَأْتُونَ ٱلرِّجَالَ شَهْوَةً مِّن دُونِ
ٱلنِّسَآءِ ۚ بَلْ أَنتُمْ قَوْمٌ مُّسْرِفُونَ ﴿٨١﴾

82. And his people gave no answer but this: they said, "Drive them out of your city: these are indeed men who want to be clean and pure!"

وَمَا كَانَ جَوَابَ قَوْمِهِۦٓ إِلَّآ أَن قَالُوٓا۟ أَخْرِجُوهُم
مِّن قَرْيَتِكُمْ ۖ إِنَّهُمْ أُنَاسٌ يَتَطَهَّرُونَ ﴿٨٢﴾

83. But We saved him and his family, except his wife: she was of those who lagged behind.

فَأَنجَيْنَـٰهُ وَأَهْلَهُۥٓ إِلَّا ٱمْرَأَتَهُۥ كَانَتْ
مِنَ ٱلْغَـٰبِرِينَ ﴿٨٣﴾

84. And We rained down on them a shower (of brimstone): then see what was the end of those who indulged in sin and crime!

وَأَمْطَرْنَا عَلَيْهِم مَّطَرًا ۖ فَٱنظُرْ كَيْفَ كَانَ
عَـٰقِبَةُ ٱلْمُجْرِمِينَ ﴿٨٤﴾

85. To the Madyan people We sent Shu'ayb, one of their own brothers: he said: "O my people! Worship Allah; You have no other god but Him. Now has come to you a clear (sign) from your Lord! Give just measure and weight, nor withhold from the people the things that are their due; and do no mischief on the earth after it has been set in order: that will be best for you, if you have faith."

وَإِلَىٰ مَدْيَنَ أَخَاهُمْ شُعَيْبًا ۗ قَالَ يَـٰقَوْمِ ٱعْبُدُوا۟
ٱللَّهَ مَا لَكُم مِّنْ إِلَـٰهٍ غَيْرُهُۥ ۖ قَدْ جَآءَتْكُم بَيِّنَةٌ
مِّن رَّبِّكُمْ ۖ فَأَوْفُوا۟ ٱلْكَيْلَ وَٱلْمِيزَانَ وَلَا
تَبْخَسُوا۟ ٱلنَّاسَ أَشْيَآءَهُمْ وَلَا تُفْسِدُوا۟
فِى ٱلْأَرْضِ بَعْدَ إِصْلَـٰحِهَا ۚ ذَٰلِكُمْ خَيْرٌ
لَّكُمْ إِن كُنتُم مُّؤْمِنِينَ ﴿٨٥﴾

86. "And squat not on every road, breathing threats, hindering from the path of Allah those who believe in Him, and seeking in it something crooked; but remember how you were little, and He gave you increase. And hold in your mind's eye what was the end of those who did mischief."

وَلَا تَقْعُدُوا۟ بِكُلِّ صِرَٰطٍ تُوعِدُونَ
وَتَصُدُّونَ عَن سَبِيلِ ٱللَّهِ مَنْ ءَامَنَ بِهِۦ
وَتَبْغُونَهَا عِوَجًا ۚ وَٱذْكُرُوٓا۟ إِذْ كُنتُمْ قَلِيلًا
فَكَثَّرَكُمْ ۖ وَٱنظُرُوا۟ كَيْفَ كَانَ عَـٰقِبَةُ
ٱلْمُفْسِدِينَ ﴿٨٦﴾

87. "And if there is a party among you who believes in the message with which I have been sent, and a party which does not believe, hold yourselves in patience until Allah does decide between us: for He is the best to decide."

وَإِن كَانَ طَآئِفَةٌ مِّنكُمْ ءَامَنُوا۟ بِٱلَّذِىٓ
أُرْسِلْتُ بِهِۦ وَطَآئِفَةٌ لَّمْ يُؤْمِنُوا۟ فَٱصْبِرُوا۟ حَتَّىٰ
يَحْكُمَ ٱللَّهُ بَيْنَنَا ۚ وَهُوَ خَيْرُ ٱلْحَـٰكِمِينَ ﴿٨٧﴾

✻**88.** The leaders, the arrogant party among his people, said: "O Shu'ayb! We shall certainly drive you out of our city - (you)

✻قَالَ ٱلْمَلَأُ ٱلَّذِينَ ٱسْتَكْبَرُوا۟ مِن قَوْمِهِۦ لَنُخْرِجَنَّكَ
يَـٰشُعَيْبُ وَٱلَّذِينَ ءَامَنُوا۟ مَعَكَ مِن قَرْيَتِنَآ أَوْ لَتَعُودُنَّ

الجزء ٩ الحزب ١٧

✻ Part-9

and those who believe with you; or else you (you and they) shall have to return to our ways and religion." He said: "What! Even though we do detest (them)?"

فِي مِلَّتِنَا ۚ قَالَ أَوَلَوْ كُنَّا كَارِهِينَ ﴿٨٨﴾

89. "We should indeed invent a lie against Allah, if we returned to your ways after Allah has rescued us from it; nor could we by any manner of means return to it unless it be as in the will and plan of Allah, Our Lord. Our Lord can reach out to the utmost recesses of things by His knowledge. In Allah is our trust. Our Lord! Decide You between us and our people in truth, for You are the best to decide."

قَدِ افْتَرَيْنَا عَلَى اللَّهِ كَذِبًا إِنْ عُدْنَا فِي مِلَّتِكُم بَعْدَ
إِذْ نَجَّانَا اللَّهُ مِنْهَا ۚ وَمَا يَكُونُ لَنَا أَن نَّعُودَ فِيهَا إِلَّا
أَن يَشَاءَ اللَّهُ رَبُّنَا ۚ وَسِعَ رَبُّنَا كُلَّ شَيْءٍ عِلْمًا ۚ عَلَى
اللَّهِ تَوَكَّلْنَا ۚ رَبَّنَا افْتَحْ بَيْنَنَا وَبَيْنَ قَوْمِنَا بِالْحَقِّ
وَأَنتَ خَيْرُ الْفَاتِحِينَ ﴿٨٩﴾

90. The leaders, the unbelievers among his people, said: "If you follow Shu'ayb, be sure then you are ruined!"

وَقَالَ الْمَلَأُ الَّذِينَ كَفَرُوا مِن قَوْمِهِ لَئِنِ اتَّبَعْتُمْ
شُعَيْبًا إِنَّكُمْ إِذًا لَّخَاسِرُونَ ﴿٩٠﴾

91. But the earthquake took them unawares, and they lay prostrate in their homes before the morning!

فَأَخَذَتْهُمُ الرَّجْفَةُ فَأَصْبَحُوا فِي دَارِهِمْ جَاثِمِينَ ﴿٩١﴾

92. The men who rejected Shu'ayb became as if they had never been in the homes where they had flourished: the men who rejected Shu'ayb - it was they who were ruined!

الَّذِينَ كَذَّبُوا شُعَيْبًا كَأَن لَّمْ يَغْنَوْا فِيهَا ۚ الَّذِينَ كَذَّبُوا
شُعَيْبًا كَانُوا هُمُ الْخَاسِرِينَ ﴿٩٢﴾

93. So Shu'ayb left them, saying: "O my people! I did indeed convey to you the messages for which I was sent by my Lord: I gave you good counsel, but how shall I lament over a people who refuse to believe!"

فَتَوَلَّىٰ عَنْهُمْ وَقَالَ يَا قَوْمِ لَقَدْ أَبْلَغْتُكُمْ رِسَالَاتِ
رَبِّي وَنَصَحْتُ لَكُمْ ۖ فَكَيْفَ آسَىٰ عَلَىٰ قَوْمٍ
كَافِرِينَ ﴿٩٣﴾

94. Whenever We sent a prophet to a town, We took up its people in suffering and adversity, in order that they might learn humility.

وَمَا أَرْسَلْنَا فِي قَرْيَةٍ مِّن نَّبِيٍّ إِلَّا أَخَذْنَا أَهْلَهَا
بِالْبَأْسَاءِ وَالضَّرَّاءِ لَعَلَّهُمْ يَضَّرَّعُونَ ﴿٩٤﴾

95. Then We changed their suffering into prosperity, until they grew and multiplied, and began to say: "Our fathers (too) were touched by suffering and affluence." See! We called them to account of a sudden, while they realised not (their peril).

ثُمَّ بَدَّلْنَا مَكَانَ ٱلسَّيِّئَةِ ٱلْحَسَنَةَ حَتَّىٰ
عَفَوا۟ وَّقَالُوا۟ قَدْ مَسَّ ءَابَآءَنَا ٱلضَّرَّآءُ وَٱلسَّرَّآءُ
فَأَخَذْنَٰهُم بَغْتَةً وَهُمْ لَا يَشْعُرُونَ ﴿٩٥﴾

96. If the people of the towns had but believed and feared Allah, We should indeed have opened out to them (all kinds of) blessings from heaven and earth; but they rejected (the truth), and We brought them to book for their misdeeds.

وَلَوْ أَنَّ أَهْلَ ٱلْقُرَىٰٓ ءَامَنُوا۟ وَٱتَّقَوْا۟ لَفَتَحْنَا عَلَيْهِم
بَرَكَٰتٍ مِّنَ ٱلسَّمَآءِ وَٱلْأَرْضِ وَلَٰكِن كَذَّبُوا۟
فَأَخَذْنَٰهُم بِمَا كَانُوا۟ يَكْسِبُونَ ﴿٩٦﴾

97. Did the people of the towns feel secure against the coming of Our wrath by night while they were asleep?

أَفَأَمِنَ أَهْلُ ٱلْقُرَىٰٓ أَن يَأْتِيَهُم بَأْسُنَا بَيَٰتًا
وَهُمْ نَآئِمُونَ ﴿٩٧﴾

98. Or else did they feel secure against its coming in broad daylight while they played about (carefree)?

أَوَأَمِنَ أَهْلُ ٱلْقُرَىٰٓ أَن يَأْتِيَهُم بَأْسُنَا ضُحًى
وَهُمْ يَلْعَبُونَ ﴿٩٨﴾

99. Did they then feel secure against the plan of Allah? - But no one can feel secure from the plan of Allah, except those (doomed) to ruin!

أَفَأَمِنُوا۟ مَكْرَ ٱللَّهِ ۚ فَلَا يَأْمَنُ مَكْرَ ٱللَّهِ
إِلَّا ٱلْقَوْمُ ٱلْخَٰسِرُونَ ﴿٩٩﴾

100. To those who inherit the earth in succession to its (previous) possessors, is it not a guiding (lesson) that, if We so willed, We could punish them (too) for their sins, and seal up their hearts so that they could not hear?

أَوَلَمْ يَهْدِ لِلَّذِينَ يَرِثُونَ ٱلْأَرْضَ مِنۢ بَعْدِ أَهْلِهَآ
أَن لَّوْ نَشَآءُ أَصَبْنَٰهُم بِذُنُوبِهِمْ ۚ وَنَطْبَعُ عَلَىٰ
قُلُوبِهِمْ فَهُمْ لَا يَسْمَعُونَ ﴿١٠٠﴾

101. Such were the towns whose story We (thus) relate to you: there came indeed to them their messengers with clear (signs); but they would not believe what they had rejected before. Thus does Allah seal up the hearts of those who reject faith.

تِلْكَ ٱلْقُرَىٰ نَقُصُّ عَلَيْكَ مِنْ أَنۢبَآئِهَا ۚ وَلَقَدْ
جَآءَتْهُمْ رُسُلُهُم بِٱلْبَيِّنَٰتِ فَمَا كَانُوا۟ لِيُؤْمِنُوا۟
بِمَا كَذَّبُوا۟ مِن قَبْلُ ۚ كَذَٰلِكَ يَطْبَعُ ٱللَّهُ عَلَىٰ قُلُوبِ
ٱلْكَٰفِرِينَ ﴿١٠١﴾

102. Most of them We found not men (true) to their covenant; but most of them We found rebellious and disobedient.

وَمَا وَجَدْنَا لِأَكْثَرِهِم مِّنْ عَهْدٍ ۖ وَإِن وَجَدْنَآ
أَكْثَرَهُمْ لَفَٰسِقِينَ ﴿١٠٢﴾

103. Then after them We sent Moses with Our signs to Pharaoh and his chiefs, but they wrongfully rejected them: so see what was the end of those who made mischief.

ثُمَّ بَعَثْنَا مِنۢ بَعْدِهِم مُّوسَىٰ بِـَٔايَٰتِنَآ إِلَىٰ فِرْعَوْنَ
وَمَلَإِي۟هِۦ فَظَلَمُوا۟ بِهَا ۖ فَٱنظُرْ كَيْفَ كَانَ
عَٰقِبَةُ ٱلْمُفْسِدِينَ ﴿١٠٣﴾

104. Moses said: "O Pharaoh! I am a messenger from the Lord of the Worlds -

وَقَالَ مُوسَىٰ يَٰفِرْعَوْنُ إِنِّى رَسُولٌ مِّن رَّبِّ
ٱلْعَٰلَمِينَ ﴿١٠٤﴾

105. One for whom it is right to say nothing but truth about Allah. Now have I come to you (people), from your Lord, with a clear (sign): so let the Children of Israel depart along with me."

حَقِيقٌ عَلَىٰٓ أَن لَّآ أَقُولَ عَلَى ٱللَّهِ إِلَّا ٱلْحَقَّ ۚ قَدْ
جِئْتُكُم بِبَيِّنَةٍ مِّن رَّبِّكُمْ فَأَرْسِلْ مَعِىَ بَنِىٓ
إِسْرَٰٓءِيلَ ﴿١٠٥﴾

106. (Pharaoh) said: "If indeed you have come with a sign, show it now - if you tell the truth."

قَالَ إِن كُنتَ جِئْتَ بِـَٔايَةٍ فَأْتِ بِهَآ إِن كُنتَ
مِنَ ٱلصَّٰدِقِينَ ﴿١٠٦﴾

107. Then (Moses) threw his rod and see! It was a serpent, plain (for all to see)!

فَأَلْقَىٰ عَصَاهُ فَإِذَا هِىَ ثُعْبَانٌ مُّبِينٌ ﴿١٠٧﴾

108. And he drew out his hand, and see! It was white to all onlookers!

وَنَزَعَ يَدَهُۥ فَإِذَا هِىَ بَيْضَآءُ لِلنَّٰظِرِينَ ﴿١٠٨﴾

109. Said the Chiefs of the people of Pharaoh: "This is indeed a sorcerer well-versed."

قَالَ ٱلْمَلَأُ مِن قَوْمِ فِرْعَوْنَ إِنَّ هَٰذَا لَسَٰحِرٌ
عَلِيمٌ ﴿١٠٩﴾

110. "His plan is to get you out of your land: then what is it you counsel?"

يُرِيدُ أَن يُخْرِجَكُم مِّنْ أَرْضِكُمْ ۖ فَمَاذَا تَأْمُرُونَ ﴿١١٠﴾

111. They said: "Keep him and his brother in suspense (for a while); and send to the cities men to collect -

قَالُوٓا۟ أَرْجِهْ وَأَخَاهُ وَأَرْسِلْ فِى ٱلْمَدَآئِنِ حَٰشِرِينَ ﴿١١١﴾

112. And bring up to you all (our) sorcerers well-versed."

يَأْتُوكَ بِكُلِّ سَٰحِرٍ عَلِيمٍ ﴿١١٢﴾

113. So there came the sorcerers to Pharaoh: they said, "Of course, we shall have a (suitable) reward if we win!"

وَجَآءَ ٱلسَّحَرَةُ فِرْعَوْنَ قَالُوٓاْ إِنَّ لَنَا لَأَجْرًا إِن
كُنَّا نَحْنُ ٱلْغَٰلِبِينَ ﴿١١٣﴾

114. He said: "Yea, (and more) - for you shall in that case be (raised to posts) nearest (to my person)."

قَالَ نَعَمْ وَإِنَّكُمْ لَمِنَ ٱلْمُقَرَّبِينَ ﴿١١٤﴾

115. They said: "O Moses! Will you throw (first), or shall we have the (first) throw?"

قَالُواْ يَٰمُوسَىٰٓ إِمَّآ أَن تُلْقِيَ وَإِمَّآ أَن نَّكُونَ
نَحْنُ ٱلْمُلْقِينَ ﴿١١٥﴾

116. Said Moses: "Throw you (first)." So when they threw, they bewitched the eyes of the people, and struck terror into them; for they showed a great (feat of) magic.

قَالَ أَلْقُواْ ۖ فَلَمَّآ أَلْقَوْاْ سَحَرُوٓاْ أَعْيُنَ ٱلنَّاسِ
وَٱسْتَرْهَبُوهُمْ وَجَآءُو بِسِحْرٍ عَظِيمٍ ﴿١١٦﴾

117. We put it into Moses's mind by inspiration: "Throw (now) your rod"; and see! It swallowed up straightaway all the falsehoods which they faked!

ربع حزب ١٧ ۞ وَأَوْحَيْنَآ إِلَىٰ مُوسَىٰٓ أَنْ أَلْقِ عَصَاكَ ۖ فَإِذَا هِيَ تَلْقَفُ
مَا يَأْفِكُونَ ﴿١١٧﴾

118. Thus truth was confirmed. And all that they did was made of no effect.

فَوَقَعَ ٱلْحَقُّ وَبَطَلَ مَا كَانُواْ يَعْمَلُونَ ﴿١١٨﴾

119. So the (great ones) were vanquished there and then, and were made to look small.

فَغُلِبُواْ هُنَالِكَ وَٱنقَلَبُواْ صَٰغِرِينَ ﴿١١٩﴾

120. But the sorcerers fell down prostrate in adoration.

وَأُلْقِيَ ٱلسَّحَرَةُ سَٰجِدِينَ ﴿١٢٠﴾

121. Saying: "We believe in the Lord of the Worlds."

قَالُوٓاْ ءَامَنَّا بِرَبِّ ٱلْعَٰلَمِينَ ﴿١٢١﴾

122. "The Lord of Moses and Aaron."

رَبِّ مُوسَىٰ وَهَٰرُونَ ﴿١٢٢﴾

123. Said Pharaoh: "Believe you in Him before I give you permission? Surely this is

قَالَ فِرْعَوْنُ ءَامَنتُم بِهِۦ قَبْلَ أَنْ ءَاذَنَ لَكُمْ ۖ

a trick which you have planned in the city to drive out its people; but soon shall you know (the consequences)."

إِنَّ هَٰذَا لَمَكْرٌ مَّكَرْتُمُوهُ فِي ٱلْمَدِينَةِ لِتُخْرِجُوا۟
مِنْهَآ أَهْلَهَا ۖ فَسَوْفَ تَعْلَمُونَ ﴿١٢٣﴾

124. "Be sure I will cut off your hands and your feet on opposite sides, and I will cause you all to die on the cross."

لَأُقَطِّعَنَّ أَيْدِيَكُمْ وَأَرْجُلَكُم مِّنْ خِلَٰفٍ
ثُمَّ لَأُصَلِّبَنَّكُمْ أَجْمَعِينَ ﴿١٢٤﴾

125. They said: "For us, we are but sent back to our Lord:

قَالُوٓا۟ إِنَّآ إِلَىٰ رَبِّنَا مُنقَلِبُونَ ﴿١٢٥﴾

126. But you do wreak your vengeance on us simply because we believed in the signs of our Lord when they reached us! Our Lord! Pour out on us patience and constancy, and tak.e our souls to you as Muslims (who bow to Your will)!"

وَمَا تَنقِمُ مِنَّآ إِلَّآ أَنْ ءَامَنَّا بِـَٔايَٰتِ رَبِّنَا لَمَّا
جَآءَتْنَا ۚ رَبَّنَآ أَفْرِغْ عَلَيْنَا صَبْرًا وَتَوَفَّنَا مُسْلِمِينَ ﴿١٢٦﴾

127. Said the chiefs of Pharaoh's people: "Will you leave Moses and his people, to spread mischief in the land, and to abandon you and your gods?" He said: "Their male children will we slay; (only) their females will we save alive; and we have over them (power) irresistible."

وَقَالَ ٱلْمَلَأُ مِن قَوْمِ فِرْعَوْنَ أَتَذَرُ مُوسَىٰ وَقَوْمَهُۥ
لِيُفْسِدُوا۟ فِى ٱلْأَرْضِ وَيَذَرَكَ وَءَالِهَتَكَ ۚ قَالَ
سَنُقَتِّلُ أَبْنَآءَهُمْ وَنَسْتَحْىِۦ نِسَآءَهُمْ وَإِنَّا
فَوْقَهُمْ قَٰهِرُونَ ﴿١٢٧﴾

128. Said Moses to his people: "Pray for help from Allah and (wait) in patience and constancy: for the earth is Allah's, to give as a heritage to such of His servants as He pleases; and the end is (best) for the righteous."

قَالَ مُوسَىٰ لِقَوْمِهِ ٱسْتَعِينُوا۟ بِٱللَّهِ وَٱصْبِرُوٓا۟ ۖ
إِنَّ ٱلْأَرْضَ لِلَّهِ يُورِثُهَا مَن يَشَآءُ مِنْ عِبَادِهِۦ ۖ
وَٱلْعَٰقِبَةُ لِلْمُتَّقِينَ ﴿١٢٨﴾

129. They said: "We have had (nothing but) trouble, both before and after you came to us." He said: "It may be that your Lord will destroy your enemy and make you inheritors in the earth; that so He may try you by your deeds."

قَالُوٓا۟ أُوذِينَا مِن قَبْلِ أَن تَأْتِيَنَا وَمِنۢ بَعْدِ
مَا جِئْتَنَا ۚ قَالَ عَسَىٰ رَبُّكُمْ أَن يُهْلِكَ عَدُوَّكُمْ
وَيَسْتَخْلِفَكُمْ فِى ٱلْأَرْضِ فَيَنظُرَ كَيْفَ
تَعْمَلُونَ ﴿١٢٩﴾

130. We punished the people of Pharaoh with years (of drought) and shortness of crops; that they might receive admonition.

وَلَقَدْ أَخَذْنَآ ءَالَ فِرْعَوْنَ بِٱلسِّنِينَ وَنَقْصٍ
مِّنَ ٱلثَّمَرَٰتِ لَعَلَّهُمْ يَذَّكَّرُونَ ﴿١٣٠﴾

131. But when good (times) came, they said, "This is due to us"; when gripped by calamity, they ascribed it to evil omens connected with Moses and those with him! See! In truth, the omens of evil are theirs in Allah's sight, but most of them do not understand!

فَإِذَا جَآءَتْهُمُ ٱلْحَسَنَةُ قَالُوا۟ لَنَا هَٰذِهِۦ ۖ وَإِن تُصِبْهُمْ
سَيِّئَةٌ يَطَّيَّرُوا۟ بِمُوسَىٰ وَمَن مَّعَهُۥٓ ۗ أَلَآ إِنَّمَا
طَٰٓئِرُهُمْ عِندَ ٱللَّهِ وَلَٰكِنَّ أَكْثَرَهُمْ لَا
يَعْلَمُونَ ﴿١٣١﴾

132. They said (to Moses): "Whatever be the signs you bring, to work with it the sorcery on us, we shall never believe in you."

وَقَالُوا۟ مَهْمَا تَأْتِنَا بِهِۦ مِنْ ءَايَةٍ لِّتَسْحَرَنَا بِهَا فَمَا
نَحْنُ لَكَ بِمُؤْمِنِينَ ﴿١٣٢﴾

133. So We sent (plagues) on them wholesale death, locusts, lice, frogs, and blood: signs openly self-explained; but they were steeped in arrogance, a people given to sin.

فَأَرْسَلْنَا عَلَيْهِمُ ٱلطُّوفَانَ وَٱلْجَرَادَ وَٱلْقُمَّلَ
وَٱلضَّفَادِعَ وَٱلدَّمَ ءَايَٰتٍ مُّفَصَّلَٰتٍ فَٱسْتَكْبَرُوا۟
وَكَانُوا۟ قَوْمًا مُّجْرِمِينَ ﴿١٣٣﴾

134. Every time the penalty fell on them, they said: "O Moses! On our behalf call on your Lord in virtue of His promise to you; if you will remove the penalty from us, we shall truly believe in you, and we shall send away the Children of Israel with you."

وَلَمَّا وَقَعَ عَلَيْهِمُ ٱلرِّجْزُ قَالُوا۟ يَٰمُوسَى ٱدْعُ لَنَا رَبَّكَ
بِمَا عَهِدَ عِندَكَ ۖ لَئِن كَشَفْتَ عَنَّا ٱلرِّجْزَ
لَنُؤْمِنَنَّ لَكَ وَلَنُرْسِلَنَّ مَعَكَ بَنِىٓ إِسْرَٰٓءِيلَ ﴿١٣٤﴾

135. But every time We removed the penalty from them according to a fixed term which they had to fulfil - See! They broke their word!

فَلَمَّا كَشَفْنَا عَنْهُمُ ٱلرِّجْزَ إِلَىٰٓ أَجَلٍ هُم
بَٰلِغُوهُ إِذَا هُمْ يَنكُثُونَ ﴿١٣٥﴾

136. So We exacted retribution from them: We drowned them in the sea, because they rejected Our signs, and failed to take warning from them.

فَٱنتَقَمْنَا مِنْهُمْ فَأَغْرَقْنَٰهُمْ فِى ٱلْيَمِّ بِأَنَّهُمْ كَذَّبُوا۟
بِـَٔايَٰتِنَا وَكَانُوا۟ عَنْهَا غَٰفِلِينَ ﴿١٣٦﴾

137. And We made a people, considered weak (and of no account), inheritors of lands in both east and west - lands upon which We sent down Our blessings. The fair promise of your Lord was fulfilled for the Children of Israel, because they had patience and constancy, and We levelled to the ground the great works and fine buildings which Pharaoh and his people erected (with such pride).

وَأَوْرَثْنَا ٱلْقَوْمَ ٱلَّذِينَ كَانُوا۟ يُسْتَضْعَفُونَ
مَشَٰرِقَ ٱلْأَرْضِ وَمَغَٰرِبَهَا ٱلَّتِى بَٰرَكْنَا فِيهَا ۖ وَتَمَّتْ
كَلِمَتُ رَبِّكَ ٱلْحُسْنَىٰ عَلَىٰ بَنِىٓ إِسْرَٰٓءِيلَ بِمَا
صَبَرُوا۟ ۖ وَدَمَّرْنَا مَا كَانَ يَصْنَعُ فِرْعَوْنُ وَقَوْمُهُۥ
وَمَا كَانُوا۟ يَعْرِشُونَ ﴿١٣٧﴾

138. We took the Children of Israel (with safety) across the sea. They came upon a people devoted entirely to some idols they had. They said: "O Moses! Fashion for us a god like the gods they have." He said: "Surely you are a people without knowledge."

وَجَٰوَزْنَا بِبَنِىٓ إِسْرَٰٓءِيلَ ٱلْبَحْرَ فَأَتَوْا۟ عَلَىٰ قَوْمٍ
يَعْكُفُونَ عَلَىٰٓ أَصْنَامٍ لَّهُمْ ۚ قَالُوا۟ يَٰمُوسَى
ٱجْعَل لَّنَآ إِلَٰهًا كَمَا لَهُمْ ءَالِهَةٌ ۚ قَالَ
إِنَّكُمْ قَوْمٌ تَجْهَلُونَ ﴿١٣٨﴾

139. "As to these folk - the cult they are in is (but) a fragment of a ruin, and vain is the (worship) which they practice."

إِنَّ هَٰٓؤُلَآءِ مُتَبَّرٌ مَّا هُمْ فِيهِ وَبَٰطِلٌ مَّا كَانُوا۟
يَعْمَلُونَ ﴿١٣٩﴾

140. He said: "Shall I seek for you a god other than the (true) God, when it is Allah who has endowed you with gifts above the nations?"

قَالَ أَغَيْرَ ٱللَّهِ أَبْغِيكُمْ إِلَٰهًا وَهُوَ فَضَّلَكُمْ عَلَى
ٱلْعَٰلَمِينَ ﴿١٤٠﴾

141. And remember We rescued you from Pharaoh's people, who afflicted you with the worst of penalties, who slew your male children and saved alive your females: in that was a momentous trial from your Lord.

وَإِذْ أَنجَيْنَٰكُم مِّنْ ءَالِ فِرْعَوْنَ يَسُومُونَكُمْ سُوٓءَ
ٱلْعَذَابِ يُقَتِّلُونَ أَبْنَآءَكُمْ وَيَسْتَحْيُونَ
نِسَآءَكُمْ ۚ وَفِى ذَٰلِكُم بَلَآءٌ مِّن رَّبِّكُمْ
عَظِيمٌ ﴿١٤١﴾

142. We appointed for Moses thirty nights, and completed (the period) with ten (more): thus was completed the term (of communion) with his Lord, forty nights. And Moses had charged his brother Aaron (before he went up): "Act for me amongst

نصف الحزب ١٧
۞ وَوَٰعَدْنَا مُوسَىٰ ثَلَٰثِينَ لَيْلَةً وَأَتْمَمْنَٰهَا بِعَشْرٍ
فَتَمَّ مِيقَٰتُ رَبِّهِۦٓ أَرْبَعِينَ لَيْلَةً ۚ وَقَالَ مُوسَىٰ
لِأَخِيهِ هَٰرُونَ ٱخْلُفْنِى فِى قَوْمِى وَأَصْلِحْ وَلَا

my people; do right, and follow not the way of those who do mischief."

تَتَّبِعْ سَبِيلَ ٱلْمُفْسِدِينَ ﴿١٤٢﴾

143. When Moses came to the place appointed by Us, and his Lord addressed him, He said: "O my Lord! Show (Yourself) to me, that I may look upon You." Allah said: "By no means can you see Me (direct); but look upon the Mount; if it remain in its place, then shall you see Me." When his Lord manifested His glory on the Mount, He made it as dust, and Moses fell down in a swoon. When he recovered his senses he said: "Glory be to You! To You I turn in repentance, and I am the first to believe."

وَلَمَّا جَآءَ مُوسَىٰ لِمِيقَـٰتِنَا وَكَلَّمَهُۥ رَبُّهُۥ قَالَ رَبِّ
أَرِنِىٓ أَنظُرْ إِلَيْكَ ۚ قَالَ لَن تَرَىٰنِى وَلَـٰكِنِ
ٱنظُرْ إِلَى ٱلْجَبَلِ فَإِنِ ٱسْتَقَرَّ مَكَانَهُۥ فَسَوْفَ
تَرَىٰنِى ۚ فَلَمَّا تَجَلَّىٰ رَبُّهُۥ لِلْجَبَلِ جَعَلَهُۥ دَكًّا وَخَرَّ
مُوسَىٰ صَعِقًا ۚ فَلَمَّآ أَفَاقَ قَالَ سُبْحَـٰنَكَ تُبْتُ
إِلَيْكَ وَأَنَا۠ أَوَّلُ ٱلْمُؤْمِنِينَ ﴿١٤٣﴾

144. (Allah) said: "O Moses! I have chosen you above (other) men, by the mission I (have given you) and the words I (have spoken to you): Take then the (revelation) which I give you, and be of those Who give thanks."

قَالَ يَـٰمُوسَىٰٓ إِنِّى ٱصْطَفَيْتُكَ عَلَى ٱلنَّاسِ
بِرِسَـٰلَـٰتِى وَبِكَلَـٰمِى فَخُذْ مَآ ءَاتَيْتُكَ وَكُن مِّنَ
ٱلشَّـٰكِرِينَ ﴿١٤٤﴾

145. And We ordained laws for him in the tablets in all matters, both commanding and explaining all things, (and said): "Take and hold these with firmness, and enjoin your people to hold fast by the best in the precepts: soon shall I show you the homes of the wicked - (how they lie desolate)."

وَكَتَبْنَا لَهُۥ فِى ٱلْأَلْوَاحِ مِن كُلِّ شَىْءٍ
مَّوْعِظَةً وَتَفْصِيلًا لِّكُلِّ شَىْءٍ فَخُذْهَا بِقُوَّةٍ
وَأْمُرْ قَوْمَكَ يَأْخُذُوا۟ بِأَحْسَنِهَا ۚ سَأُو۟رِيكُمْ
دَارَ ٱلْفَـٰسِقِينَ ﴿١٤٥﴾

146. Those who behave arrogantly on the earth in defiance of right - them will I turn away from My signs, they will not believe in them; and if they see the way of right conduct, they will not adopt it as the way; but if they see the way of error, that is the way they will adopt; for they have rejected Our signs, and failed to take warning from them.

سَأَصْرِفُ عَنْ ءَايَـٰتِىَ ٱلَّذِينَ يَتَكَبَّرُونَ فِى ٱلْأَرْضِ
بِغَيْرِ ٱلْحَقِّ وَإِن يَرَوْا۟ كُلَّ ءَايَةٍ لَّا يُؤْمِنُوا۟ بِهَا
وَإِن يَرَوْا۟ سَبِيلَ ٱلرُّشْدِ لَا يَتَّخِذُوهُ سَبِيلًا وَإِن
يَرَوْا۟ سَبِيلَ ٱلْغَىِّ يَتَّخِذُوهُ سَبِيلًا ۚ ذَٰلِكَ بِأَنَّهُمْ
كَذَّبُوا۟ بِـَٔايَـٰتِنَا وَكَانُوا۟ عَنْهَا غَـٰفِلِينَ ﴿١٤٦﴾

147. Those who reject Our signs and the meeting in the hereafter - vain are their deeds: can they expect to be rewarded except as they have wrought?

وَٱلَّذِينَ كَذَّبُواْ بِـَٔايَٰتِنَا وَلِقَآءِ ٱلۡأٓخِرَةِ حَبِطَتۡ
أَعۡمَٰلُهُمۡۚ هَلۡ يُجۡزَوۡنَ إِلَّا مَا كَانُواْ يَعۡمَلُونَ ١٤٧

148. The people of Moses made, in his absence, out of their ornaments, the image of a calf, (for worship); it seemed to low: did they not see that it could neither speak to them, nor show them the way? They took it for worship and they did wrong.

وَٱتَّخَذَ قَوۡمُ مُوسَىٰ مِنۢ بَعۡدِهِۦ مِنۡ حُلِيِّهِمۡ عِجۡلٗا
جَسَدٗا لَّهُۥ خُوَارٌۚ أَلَمۡ يَرَوۡاْ أَنَّهُۥ لَا يُكَلِّمُهُمۡ
وَلَا يَهۡدِيهِمۡ سَبِيلًاۘ ٱتَّخَذُوهُ وَكَانُواْ
ظَٰلِمِينَ ١٤٨

149. When they repented, and saw that they had erred, they said: "If our Lord have not mercy upon us and forgive us, we shall indeed be of those who perish."

وَلَمَّا سُقِطَ فِيٓ أَيۡدِيهِمۡ وَرَأَوۡاْ أَنَّهُمۡ قَدۡ ضَلُّواْ
قَالُواْ لَئِن لَّمۡ يَرۡحَمۡنَا رَبُّنَا وَيَغۡفِرۡ لَنَا لَنَكُونَنَّ
مِنَ ٱلۡخَٰسِرِينَ ١٤٩

150. When Moses came back to his people, angry and grieved, he said: "Evil it is that you have done in my place in my absence; did you make haste to bring on the judgement of your Lord?" He put down the tablets, seized his brother by (the hair of) his head, and dragged him to him. Aaron said: "Son of my mother! The people did indeed reckon me as nothing, and went near to slaying me! Make not the enemies rejoice over my misfortune, nor count you me amongst the people of sin."

وَلَمَّا رَجَعَ مُوسَىٰٓ إِلَىٰ قَوۡمِهِۦ غَضۡبَٰنَ أَسِفٗا قَالَ بِئۡسَمَا
خَلَفۡتُمُونِي مِنۢ بَعۡدِيٓۖ أَعَجِلۡتُمۡ أَمۡرَ رَبِّكُمۡۖ وَأَلۡقَى
ٱلۡأَلۡوَاحَ وَأَخَذَ بِرَأۡسِ أَخِيهِ يَجُرُّهُۥٓ إِلَيۡهِۚ قَالَ ٱبۡنَ أُمَّ
إِنَّ ٱلۡقَوۡمَ ٱسۡتَضۡعَفُونِي وَكَادُواْ يَقۡتُلُونَنِي فَلَا
تُشۡمِتۡ بِيَ ٱلۡأَعۡدَآءَ وَلَا تَجۡعَلۡنِي مَعَ ٱلۡقَوۡمِ
ٱلظَّٰلِمِينَ ١٥٠

151. Moses prayed: "O my Lord! Forgive me and my brother! Admit us to Your mercy! For You are the Most Merciful of those who show mercy!"

قَالَ رَبِّ ٱغۡفِرۡ لِي وَلِأَخِي وَأَدۡخِلۡنَا فِي رَحۡمَتِكَۖ
وَأَنتَ أَرۡحَمُ ٱلرَّٰحِمِينَ ١٥١

152. Those who took the calf (for worship) will indeed be overwhelmed with wrath from their Lord, and with

إِنَّ ٱلَّذِينَ ٱتَّخَذُواْ ٱلۡعِجۡلَ سَيَنَالُهُمۡ غَضَبٞ مِّن
رَّبِّهِمۡ وَذِلَّةٞ فِي ٱلۡحَيَوٰةِ ٱلدُّنۡيَاۚ وَكَذَٰلِكَ نَجۡزِي

shame in this life; thus do We recompense those who invent (falsehoods).

ٱلْمُفْتَرِينَ ١٥٢

153. But those who do wrong but repent afterwards and (truly) believe - verily Your Lord is afterwards Oft-Forgiving, Most Merciful.

وَٱلَّذِينَ عَمِلُوا۟ ٱلسَّيِّـَٔاتِ ثُمَّ تَابُوا۟ مِنۢ بَعْدِهَا
وَءَامَنُوٓا۟ إِنَّ رَبَّكَ مِنۢ بَعْدِهَا لَغَفُورٌ رَّحِيمٌ ١٥٣

154. When the anger of Moses was appeased, he took up the tablets: in the writing on them was guidance and mercy for such as fear their Lord.

وَلَمَّا سَكَتَ عَن مُّوسَى ٱلْغَضَبُ أَخَذَ ٱلْأَلْوَاحَ ۖ وَفِى
نُسْخَتِهَا هُدًى وَرَحْمَةٌ لِّلَّذِينَ هُمْ لِرَبِّهِمْ يَرْهَبُونَ ١٥٤

155. And Moses chose seventy of his people for Our place of meeting; when they were seized with violent quaking, he prayed; "O my Lord! If it had been Your will You could have destroyed, long before, both them and me; would You destroy us for the deeds of the foolish ones among us? This is no more than Your trial; by it You cause whom You will to stray and You lead whom You will into the right path. You are our protector: so forgive us and give us Your mercy; for You are the best of those who forgive."

وَٱخْتَارَ مُوسَىٰ قَوْمَهُۥ سَبْعِينَ رَجُلًا لِّمِيقَٰتِنَا ۖ
فَلَمَّآ أَخَذَتْهُمُ ٱلرَّجْفَةُ قَالَ رَبِّ لَوْ شِئْتَ
أَهْلَكْتَهُم مِّن قَبْلُ وَإِيَّٰىَ ۖ أَتُهْلِكُنَا بِمَا فَعَلَ
ٱلسُّفَهَآءُ مِنَّآ ۖ إِنْ هِىَ إِلَّا فِتْنَتُكَ تُضِلُّ بِهَا مَن
تَشَآءُ وَتَهْدِى مَن تَشَآءُ ۖ أَنتَ وَلِيُّنَا فَٱغْفِرْ لَنَا
وَٱرْحَمْنَا ۖ وَأَنتَ خَيْرُ ٱلْغَٰفِرِينَ ١٥٥

156. "And ordain for us that which is good, in this life and in the hereafter: for we have turned to You." He said: "With My punishment I visit whom I will; but My mercy extends to all things. That (mercy) I shall ordain for those who do right, and practice regular charity, and those who believe in Our signs -

ثلاثة أرباع الحزب ١٧

۞ وَٱكْتُبْ لَنَا فِى هَٰذِهِ ٱلدُّنْيَا حَسَنَةً وَفِى
ٱلْءَاخِرَةِ إِنَّا هُدْنَآ إِلَيْكَ ۚ قَالَ عَذَابِىٓ أُصِيبُ
بِهِۦ مَنْ أَشَآءُ ۖ وَرَحْمَتِى وَسِعَتْ كُلَّ شَىْءٍ ۚ
فَسَأَكْتُبُهَا لِلَّذِينَ يَتَّقُونَ وَيُؤْتُونَ
ٱلزَّكَوٰةَ وَٱلَّذِينَ هُم بِـَٔايَٰتِنَا يُؤْمِنُونَ ١٥٦

157. Those who follow the messenger, the unlettered prophet, whom they find mentioned in their own (scriptures) - in the law and the Gospel - for he commands them what is just and forbids them what is

ٱلَّذِينَ يَتَّبِعُونَ ٱلرَّسُولَ ٱلنَّبِىَّ ٱلْأُمِّىَّ ٱلَّذِى
يَجِدُونَهُۥ مَكْتُوبًا عِندَهُمْ فِى ٱلتَّوْرَىٰةِ
وَٱلْإِنجِيلِ يَأْمُرُهُم بِٱلْمَعْرُوفِ وَيَنْهَىٰهُمْ

evil; he allows them as lawful what is good (and pure) and prohibits them from what is bad (and impure); he releases them from their heavy burdens and from the yokes that are upon them. So it is those who believe in him, honour him, help him, and follow the light which is sent down with him - it is they who will prosper."

عَنِ الْمُنكَرِ وَيُحِلُّ لَهُمُ الطَّيِّبَاتِ وَيُحَرِّمُ
عَلَيْهِمُ الْخَبَائِثَ وَيَضَعُ عَنْهُمْ إِصْرَهُمْ
وَالْأَغْلَالَ الَّتِي كَانَتْ عَلَيْهِمْ ۚ فَالَّذِينَ آمَنُوا
بِهِ وَعَزَّرُوهُ وَنَصَرُوهُ وَاتَّبَعُوا النُّورَ الَّذِي
أُنزِلَ مَعَهُ ۙ أُولَٰئِكَ هُمُ الْمُفْلِحُونَ ﴿١٥٧﴾

158. Say: "O men! I am sent to you all, as the messenger of Allah, to Whom belongs the dominion of the heavens and the earth; there is no god but He; it is He that gives both life and death. So believe in Allah and His messenger, the unlettered prophet, who believes in Allah and His words: follow him (so) that you may be guided."

قُلْ يَا أَيُّهَا النَّاسُ إِنِّي رَسُولُ اللَّهِ إِلَيْكُمْ
جَمِيعًا الَّذِي لَهُ مُلْكُ السَّمَاوَاتِ وَالْأَرْضِ ۖ
لَا إِلَٰهَ إِلَّا هُوَ يُحْيِي وَيُمِيتُ ۖ فَآمِنُوا بِاللَّهِ وَرَسُولِهِ
النَّبِيِّ الْأُمِّيِّ الَّذِي يُؤْمِنُ بِاللَّهِ وَكَلِمَاتِهِ
وَاتَّبِعُوهُ لَعَلَّكُمْ تَهْتَدُونَ ﴿١٥٨﴾

159. Of the people of Moses there is a section who guide and do justice in the light of truth.

وَمِن قَوْمِ مُوسَىٰ أُمَّةٌ يَهْدُونَ بِالْحَقِّ
وَبِهِ يَعْدِلُونَ ﴿١٥٩﴾

160. We divided them into twelve tribes or nations. We directed Moses by inspiration, when his (thirsty) people asked him for water: "Strike the rock with your staff": out of it there gushed forth twelve springs; each group knew its own place for water. We gave them the shade of clouds, and sent down to them manna and quails, (saying): "Eat of the good things We have provided for you"; (but they rebelled); to Us they did no harm, but they harmed their own souls.

وَقَطَّعْنَاهُمُ اثْنَتَيْ عَشْرَةَ أَسْبَاطًا أُمَمًا ۚ
وَأَوْحَيْنَا إِلَىٰ مُوسَىٰ إِذِ اسْتَسْقَاهُ قَوْمُهُ أَنِ
اضْرِب بِّعَصَاكَ الْحَجَرَ ۖ فَانبَجَسَتْ مِنْهُ اثْنَتَا
عَشْرَةَ عَيْنًا ۖ قَدْ عَلِمَ كُلُّ أُنَاسٍ مَّشْرَبَهُمْ ۚ
وَظَلَّلْنَا عَلَيْهِمُ الْغَمَامَ وَأَنزَلْنَا عَلَيْهِمُ الْمَنَّ
وَالسَّلْوَىٰ ۖ كُلُوا مِن طَيِّبَاتِ مَا رَزَقْنَاكُمْ ۚ
وَمَا ظَلَمُونَا وَلَٰكِن كَانُوا أَنفُسَهُمْ
يَظْلِمُونَ ﴿١٦٠﴾

161. And remember it was said to them: "Dwell in this town and eat in it as you wish, but say the word of humility and enter the gate in a posture of humility; We shall forgive you your faults; We shall increase (the portion of) those who do good."

وَإِذْ قِيلَ لَهُمُ ٱسْكُنُوا۟ هَٰذِهِ ٱلْقَرْيَةَ وَكُلُوا۟ مِنْهَا حَيْثُ شِئْتُمْ وَقُولُوا۟ حِطَّةٌ وَٱدْخُلُوا۟ ٱلْبَابَ سُجَّدًا نَّغْفِرْ لَكُمْ خَطِيٓـَٰٔتِكُمْ ۚ سَنَزِيدُ ٱلْمُحْسِنِينَ ﴿١٦١﴾

162. But the transgressors among them changed the word from that which had been given them; so We sent on them a plague from heaven for that they repeatedly transgressed.

فَبَدَّلَ ٱلَّذِينَ ظَلَمُوا۟ مِنْهُمْ قَوْلًا غَيْرَ ٱلَّذِى قِيلَ لَهُمْ فَأَرْسَلْنَا عَلَيْهِمْ رِجْزًا مِّنَ ٱلسَّمَآءِ بِمَا كَانُوا۟ يَظْلِمُونَ ﴿١٦٢﴾

163. Ask them concerning the town standing close by the sea. See! They transgressed in the matter of the Sabbath. For on the day of their Sabbath their fish did come to them openly holding up their heads, but on the day they had no Sabbath, they came not: thus did We make a trial of them, for they were given to transgression.

وَسْـَٔلْهُمْ عَنِ ٱلْقَرْيَةِ ٱلَّتِى كَانَتْ حَاضِرَةَ ٱلْبَحْرِ إِذْ يَعْدُونَ فِى ٱلسَّبْتِ إِذْ تَأْتِيهِمْ حِيتَانُهُمْ يَوْمَ سَبْتِهِمْ شُرَّعًا وَيَوْمَ لَا يَسْبِتُونَ لَا تَأْتِيهِمْ ۚ كَذَٰلِكَ نَبْلُوهُم بِمَا كَانُوا۟ يَفْسُقُونَ ﴿١٦٣﴾

164. When some of them said: "Why do you preach to a people whom Allah will destroy or visit with a terrible punishment?" - Said the preachers: "To discharge our duty to your Lord, and perhaps they may fear Him."

وَإِذْ قَالَتْ أُمَّةٌ مِّنْهُمْ لِمَ تَعِظُونَ قَوْمًا ٱللَّهُ مُهْلِكُهُمْ أَوْ مُعَذِّبُهُمْ عَذَابًا شَدِيدًا ۖ قَالُوا۟ مَعْذِرَةً إِلَىٰ رَبِّكُمْ وَلَعَلَّهُمْ يَتَّقُونَ ﴿١٦٤﴾

165. When they disregarded the warnings that had been given them, We rescued those who forbade evil; but We visited the wrongdoers with a grievous punishment, because they were given to transgression.

فَلَمَّا نَسُوا۟ مَا ذُكِّرُوا۟ بِهِۦٓ أَنجَيْنَا ٱلَّذِينَ يَنْهَوْنَ عَنِ ٱلسُّوٓءِ وَأَخَذْنَا ٱلَّذِينَ ظَلَمُوا۟ بِعَذَابٍۭ بَـِٔيسٍۭ بِمَا كَانُوا۟ يَفْسُقُونَ ﴿١٦٥﴾

166. When in their insolence they transgressed (all) prohibitions, We said to them: "Be you apes, despised and rejected."

فَلَمَّا عَتَوْا۟ عَن مَّا نُهُوا۟ عَنْهُ قُلْنَا لَهُمْ كُونُوا۟ قِرَدَةً خَـٰسِـِٔينَ ﴿١٦٦﴾

167. See! Your Lord did declare that He would send against them to the day of judgement, those who would afflict them with grievous penalty. Your Lord is quick in retribution, but He is also Oft-Forgiving, Most Merciful.

وَإِذْ تَأَذَّنَ رَبُّكَ لَيَبْعَثَنَّ عَلَيْهِمْ إِلَىٰ يَوْمِ ٱلْقِيَٰمَةِ
مَن يَسُومُهُمْ سُوٓءَ ٱلْعَذَابِ ۗ إِنَّ رَبَّكَ لَسَرِيعُ
ٱلْعِقَابِ وَإِنَّهُۥ لَغَفُورٌ رَّحِيمٌ ١٦٧

168. We broke them up into sections on this earth. There are among them some that are the righteous, and some that are the opposite. We have tried them with both prosperity and adversity: in order that they might turn (to Us).

وَقَطَّعْنَٰهُمْ فِى ٱلْأَرْضِ أُمَمًا ۖ مِّنْهُمُ ٱلصَّٰلِحُونَ
وَمِنْهُمْ دُونَ ذَٰلِكَ ۖ وَبَلَوْنَٰهُم بِٱلْحَسَنَٰتِ
وَٱلسَّيِّـَٔاتِ لَعَلَّهُمْ يَرْجِعُونَ ١٦٨

169. After them succeeded an (evil) generation; they inherited the book, but they chose (for themselves) the vanities of this world, saying (for excuse): "(Everything) will be forgiven us." (Even so), if similar vanities came their way, they would (again) seize them. Was not the covenant of the book taken from them, that they would not ascribe to Allah anything but the truth? And they study what is in the book. But best for the righteous is the home in the hereafter: will you not understand?

فَخَلَفَ مِنۢ بَعْدِهِمْ خَلْفٌ وَرِثُوا۟ ٱلْكِتَٰبَ
يَأْخُذُونَ عَرَضَ هَٰذَا ٱلْأَدْنَىٰ وَيَقُولُونَ
سَيُغْفَرُ لَنَا وَإِن يَأْتِهِمْ عَرَضٌ مِّثْلُهُۥ يَأْخُذُوهُ ۚ أَلَمْ
يُؤْخَذْ عَلَيْهِم مِّيثَٰقُ ٱلْكِتَٰبِ أَن لَّا يَقُولُوا۟ عَلَى ٱللَّهِ
إِلَّا ٱلْحَقَّ وَدَرَسُوا۟ مَا فِيهِ ۗ وَٱلدَّارُ ٱلْءَاخِرَةُ خَيْرٌ
لِّلَّذِينَ يَتَّقُونَ ۗ أَفَلَا تَعْقِلُونَ ١٦٩

170. As to those who hold fast by the book and establish regular prayer - never shall We suffer the reward of the righteous to perish.

وَٱلَّذِينَ يُمَسِّكُونَ بِٱلْكِتَٰبِ وَأَقَامُوا۟ ٱلصَّلَوٰةَ
إِنَّا لَا نُضِيعُ أَجْرَ ٱلْمُصْلِحِينَ ١٧٠

171. When We shook the Mount over them, as if it had been a canopy, and they thought it was going to fall on them (We said): "Hold firmly to what We have given you, and bring (ever) to remembrance what is in it; perhaps you may fear Allah."

الحزب ١٨ ۞ وَإِذْ نَتَقْنَا ٱلْجَبَلَ فَوْقَهُمْ كَأَنَّهُۥ ظُلَّةٌ وَظَنُّوٓا۟ أَنَّهُۥ
وَاقِعٌۢ بِهِمْ خُذُوا۟ مَآ ءَاتَيْنَٰكُم بِقُوَّةٍ وَٱذْكُرُوا۟ مَا فِيهِ
لَعَلَّكُمْ تَتَّقُونَ ١٧١

172. When your Lord brought out from the Children of Adam from their loins their

وَإِذْ أَخَذَ رَبُّكَ مِنۢ بَنِىٓ ءَادَمَ مِن ظُهُورِهِمْ ذُرِّيَّتَهُمْ

descendants, and made them testify concerning themselves (saying): "Am I not your Lord (who cherishes and sustains you)?" They said: "Yea! We do testify!" (This), lest you should say on the day of judgement: "Of this we were never mindful."

وَأَشْهَدَهُمْ عَلَىٰٓ أَنفُسِهِمْ أَلَسْتُ بِرَبِّكُمْ ۖ قَالُوا۟ بَلَىٰ ۛ
شَهِدْنَآ ۛ أَن تَقُولُوا۟ يَوْمَ ٱلْقِيَـٰمَةِ إِنَّا كُنَّا عَنْ
هَـٰذَا غَـٰفِلِينَ ﴿١٧٢﴾

173. Or lest you should say: "Our fathers before us may have taken false gods, but we are (their) descendants after them: will You then destroy us because of the deeds of men who were futile?"

أَوْ تَقُولُوٓا۟ إِنَّمَآ أَشْرَكَ ءَابَآؤُنَا مِن قَبْلُ وَكُنَّا
ذُرِّيَّةً مِّنۢ بَعْدِهِمْ ۖ أَفَتُهْلِكُنَا بِمَا فَعَلَ
ٱلْمُبْطِلُونَ ﴿١٧٣﴾

174. Thus do We explain the signs in detail! And perhaps they may turn (to Us).

وَكَذَٰلِكَ نُفَصِّلُ ٱلْـَٔايَـٰتِ وَلَعَلَّهُمْ يَرْجِعُونَ ﴿١٧٤﴾

175. Relate to them the story of the man to whom We sent Our signs, but he passed them by: so Satan followed him up, and he went astray.

وَٱتْلُ عَلَيْهِمْ نَبَأَ ٱلَّذِىٓ ءَاتَيْنَـٰهُ ءَايَـٰتِنَا فَٱنسَلَخَ
مِنْهَا فَأَتْبَعَهُ ٱلشَّيْطَـٰنُ فَكَانَ مِنَ ٱلْغَاوِينَ ﴿١٧٥﴾

176. If it had been Our Will, We should have elevated him with Our signs; but he inclined to the earth, and followed his own vain desires. His similitude is that of a dog: if you attack him, he lolls out his tongue, or if you leave him alone, he (still) lolls out his tongue. That is the similitude of those who reject Our signs; so relate the story; perhaps they may reflect.

وَلَوْ شِئْنَا لَرَفَعْنَـٰهُ بِهَا وَلَـٰكِنَّهُۥٓ أَخْلَدَ إِلَى
ٱلْأَرْضِ وَٱتَّبَعَ هَوَىٰهُ ۚ فَمَثَلُهُۥ كَمَثَلِ ٱلْكَلْبِ
إِن تَحْمِلْ عَلَيْهِ يَلْهَثْ أَوْ تَتْرُكْهُ يَلْهَث ۚ ذَّٰلِكَ
مَثَلُ ٱلْقَوْمِ ٱلَّذِينَ كَذَّبُوا۟ بِـَٔايَـٰتِنَا ۚ فَٱقْصُصِ
ٱلْقَصَصَ لَعَلَّهُمْ يَتَفَكَّرُونَ ﴿١٧٦﴾

177. Evil as an example are people who reject Our signs and wrong their own souls.

سَآءَ مَثَلًا ٱلْقَوْمُ ٱلَّذِينَ كَذَّبُوا۟ بِـَٔايَـٰتِنَا وَأَنفُسَهُمْ
كَانُوا۟ يَظْلِمُونَ ﴿١٧٧﴾

178. Whom Allah does guide - he is on the right path: whom He rejects from His guidance - such are the persons who perish.

مَن يَهْدِ ٱللَّهُ فَهُوَ ٱلْمُهْتَدِى ۖ وَمَن يُضْلِلْ
فَأُو۟لَـٰٓئِكَ هُمُ ٱلْخَـٰسِرُونَ ﴿١٧٨﴾

179. Many are the Jinns and men We have made for hell: They have hearts with which

وَلَقَدْ ذَرَأْنَا لِجَهَنَّمَ كَثِيرًا مِّنَ ٱلْجِنِّ وَٱلْإِنسِ ۖ لَهُمْ قُلُوبٌ

they understand not, eyes with which they see not, and ears with which they hear not. They are like cattle - nay more misguided: for they are heedless (of warning).

لَا يَفْقَهُونَ بِهَا وَلَهُمْ أَعْيُنٌ لَّا يُبْصِرُونَ بِهَا وَلَهُمْ
ءَاذَانٌ لَّا يَسْمَعُونَ بِهَآ أُوْلَٰٓئِكَ كَٱلْأَنْعَٰمِ بَلْ هُمْ
أَضَلُّ أُوْلَٰٓئِكَ هُمُ ٱلْغَٰفِلُونَ ١٧٩

180. The most beautiful names belong to Allah: so call on Him by them; but shun such men as use profanity in His names: for what they do, they will soon be requited.

وَلِلَّهِ ٱلْأَسْمَآءُ ٱلْحُسْنَىٰ فَٱدْعُوهُ بِهَا وَذَرُواْ ٱلَّذِينَ
يُلْحِدُونَ فِىٓ أَسْمَٰٓئِهِۦ سَيُجْزَوْنَ مَا كَانُواْ يَعْمَلُونَ ١٨٠

181. Of those We have created are people who direct (others) with truth, and dispense justice with it.

وَمِمَّنْ خَلَقْنَآ أُمَّةٌ يَهْدُونَ بِٱلْحَقِّ وَبِهِۦ يَعْدِلُونَ ١٨١

182. Those who reject Our signs, We shall gradually visit with punishment, in ways they perceive not.

وَٱلَّذِينَ كَذَّبُواْ بِـَٔايَٰتِنَا سَنَسْتَدْرِجُهُم مِّنْ حَيْثُ
لَا يَعْلَمُونَ ١٨٢

183. Respite will I grant to them: for My scheme is strong (and unfailing).

وَأُمْلِى لَهُمْ إِنَّ كَيْدِى مَتِينٌ ١٨٣

184. Do they not reflect? Their companion is not seized with madness: he is but a perspicuous warner.

أَوَلَمْ يَتَفَكَّرُواْ مَا بِصَاحِبِهِم مِّن جِنَّةٍ إِنْ هُوَ إِلَّا
نَذِيرٌ مُّبِينٌ ١٨٤

185. Do they see nothing in the government of the heavens and the earth and all that Allah has created? (Do they not see) that it may well be that their term is near drawing to an end? In what message after this will they then believe?

أَوَلَمْ يَنظُرُواْ فِى مَلَكُوتِ ٱلسَّمَٰوَٰتِ وَٱلْأَرْضِ وَمَا
خَلَقَ ٱللَّهُ مِن شَىْءٍ وَأَنْ عَسَىٰٓ أَن يَكُونَ قَدِ ٱقْتَرَبَ
أَجَلُهُمْ فَبِأَىِّ حَدِيثٍ بَعْدَهُۥ يُؤْمِنُونَ ١٨٥

186. To such as Allah rejects from His guidance, there can be no guide; He will leave them in their trespasses, wandering in distraction.

مَن يُضْلِلِ ٱللَّهُ فَلَا هَادِىَ لَهُۥ وَيَذَرُهُمْ فِى
طُغْيَٰنِهِمْ يَعْمَهُونَ ١٨٦

187. They ask you about the (final) hour - when will be its appointed time? Say: "The

يَسْـَٔلُونَكَ عَنِ ٱلسَّاعَةِ أَيَّانَ مُرْسَىٰهَا قُلْ إِنَّمَا عِلْمُهَا

knowledge of it is with my Lord (alone): none but He can reveal as to when it will occur. Heavy were its burdens through the heavens and the earth. Only all of a sudden will it come to you." They ask you as if you were eager in search of it: Say: "The knowledge of it is with Allah (alone), but most men know not."

عِندَ رَبِّي ۖ لَا يُجَلِّيهَا لِوَقْتِهَآ إِلَّا هُوَ ۚ ثَقُلَتْ فِي
ٱلسَّمَـٰوَٰتِ وَٱلْأَرْضِ ۚ لَا تَأْتِيكُمْ إِلَّا بَغْتَةً ۗ يَسْـَٔلُونَكَ
كَأَنَّكَ حَفِىٌّ عَنْهَا ۖ قُلْ إِنَّمَا عِلْمُهَا عِندَ ٱللَّهِ وَلَـٰكِنَّ
أَكْثَرَ ٱلنَّاسِ لَا يَعْلَمُونَ ﴿١٨٧﴾

188. Say: "I have no power over any good or harm to myself except as Allah wills. If I had knowledge of the unseen, I should have multiplied all good, and no evil should have touched me: I am but a warner, and a bringer of glad tidings to those who have faith."

قُل لَّآ أَمْلِكُ لِنَفْسِى نَفْعًا وَلَا ضَرًّا إِلَّا مَا شَآءَ ٱللَّهُ ۚ
وَلَوْ كُنتُ أَعْلَمُ ٱلْغَيْبَ لَٱسْتَكْثَرْتُ مِنَ ٱلْخَيْرِ
وَمَا مَسَّنِىَ ٱلسُّوٓءُ ۚ إِنْ أَنَا۠ إِلَّا نَذِيرٌ وَبَشِيرٌ لِّقَوْمٍ
يُؤْمِنُونَ ﴿١٨٨﴾

189. It is He Who created you from a single person, and made his mate of like nature, in order that he might dwell with her (in love). When they are united, she bears a light burden and carries it about (unnoticed). When she grows heavy, they both pray to Allah their Lord, (saying): "If You give us a goodly child, we vow we shall (ever) be grateful."

ربع الحزب ١٨ ۞ هُوَ ٱلَّذِى خَلَقَكُم مِّن نَّفْسٍ وَٰحِدَةٍ وَجَعَلَ مِنْهَا
زَوْجَهَا لِيَسْكُنَ إِلَيْهَا ۖ فَلَمَّا تَغَشَّىٰهَا حَمَلَتْ
حَمْلًا خَفِيفًا فَمَرَّتْ بِهِۦ ۖ فَلَمَّآ أَثْقَلَت دَّعَوَا ٱللَّهَ
رَبَّهُمَا لَئِنْ ءَاتَيْتَنَا صَـٰلِحًا لَّنَكُونَنَّ مِنَ
ٱلشَّـٰكِرِينَ ﴿١٨٩﴾

190. But when He gives them a goodly child, they ascribe to others a share in the gift they have received: but Allah is exalted high above the partners they ascribe to Him.

فَلَمَّآ ءَاتَىٰهُمَا صَـٰلِحًا جَعَلَا لَهُۥ شُرَكَآءَ فِيمَآ
ءَاتَىٰهُمَا ۚ فَتَعَـٰلَى ٱللَّهُ عَمَّا يُشْرِكُونَ ﴿١٩٠﴾

191. Do they indeed ascribe to Him as partners things that can create nothing, but are themselves created?

أَيُشْرِكُونَ مَا لَا يَخْلُقُ شَيْـًٔا وَهُمْ يُخْلَقُونَ ﴿١٩١﴾

192. No aid can they give them, nor can they aid themselves!

وَلَا يَسْتَطِيعُونَ لَهُمْ نَصْرًا وَلَآ أَنفُسَهُمْ
يَنصُرُونَ ﴿١٩٢﴾

193. If you call them to guidance, they will not obey: for you it is the same whether you call them or you hold your peace!

وَإِن تَدْعُوهُمْ إِلَى ٱلْهُدَىٰ لَا يَتَّبِعُوكُمْ ۚ سَوَآءٌ عَلَيْكُمْ
أَدَعَوْتُمُوهُمْ أَمْ أَنتُمْ صَٰمِتُونَ ﴿١٩٣﴾

194. Verily those whom you call upon besides Allah are servants like to you: call upon them, and let them listen to your prayer, if you are (indeed) truthful!

إِنَّ ٱلَّذِينَ تَدْعُونَ مِن دُونِ ٱللَّهِ عِبَادٌ أَمْثَالُكُمْ ۖ
فَٱدْعُوهُمْ فَلْيَسْتَجِيبُوا۟ لَكُمْ إِن كُنتُمْ
صَٰدِقِينَ ﴿١٩٤﴾

195. Have they feet to walk with? Or hands to lay hold with? Or eyes to see with? Or ears to hear with? Say: "Call your 'god-partners', scheme (your worst) against me, and give me no respite!"

أَلَهُمْ أَرْجُلٌ يَمْشُونَ بِهَآ ۖ أَمْ لَهُمْ أَيْدٍ يَبْطِشُونَ
بِهَآ ۖ أَمْ لَهُمْ أَعْيُنٌ يُبْصِرُونَ بِهَآ ۖ أَمْ لَهُمْ ءَاذَانٌ
يَسْمَعُونَ بِهَا ۗ قُلِ ٱدْعُوا۟ شُرَكَآءَكُمْ ثُمَّ
كِيدُونِ فَلَا تُنظِرُونِ ﴿١٩٥﴾

196. "For my protector is Allah, Who revealed the book (from time to time), and He will choose and befriend the righteous."

إِنَّ وَلِـِّۧىَ ٱللَّهُ ٱلَّذِى نَزَّلَ ٱلْكِتَٰبَ ۖ وَهُوَ يَتَوَلَّى
ٱلصَّٰلِحِينَ ﴿١٩٦﴾

197. "But those you call upon besides Him, are unable to help you, and indeed to help themselves."

وَٱلَّذِينَ تَدْعُونَ مِن دُونِهِۦ لَا يَسْتَطِيعُونَ
نَصْرَكُمْ وَلَآ أَنفُسَهُمْ يَنصُرُونَ ﴿١٩٧﴾

198. If you (Muslims) call them to guidance, they hear not. You (O Muhammad) will see them looking at you, but they see not.

وَإِن تَدْعُوهُمْ إِلَى ٱلْهُدَىٰ لَا يَسْمَعُوا۟ ۖ وَتَرَىٰهُمْ
يَنظُرُونَ إِلَيْكَ وَهُمْ لَا يُبْصِرُونَ ﴿١٩٨﴾

199. Hold to forgiveness; command what is right; but turn away from the ignorant.

خُذِ ٱلْعَفْوَ وَأْمُرْ بِٱلْعُرْفِ وَأَعْرِضْ عَنِ
ٱلْجَٰهِلِينَ ﴿١٩٩﴾

200. If a suggestion from Satan assail your (mind), seek refuge with Allah; for He hears and knows (all things).

وَإِمَّا يَنزَغَنَّكَ مِنَ ٱلشَّيْطَٰنِ نَزْغٌ فَٱسْتَعِذْ بِٱللَّهِ ۚ
إِنَّهُۥ سَمِيعٌ عَلِيمٌ ﴿٢٠٠﴾

201. Those who fear Allah, when a thought of evil from Satan assaults them, bring Allah to remembrance, when they see (aright)!

إِنَّ ٱلَّذِينَ ٱتَّقَوۡاْ إِذَا مَسَّهُمۡ طَٰٓئِفٞ مِّنَ
ٱلشَّيۡطَٰنِ تَذَكَّرُواْ فَإِذَا هُم مُّبۡصِرُونَ ٢٠١

202. But their brothers (the evil ones) plunge them deeper into error, and never relax (their efforts).

وَإِخۡوَٰنُهُمۡ يَمُدُّونَهُمۡ فِي ٱلۡغَيِّ ثُمَّ لَا يُقۡصِرُونَ ٢٠٢

203. If you bring them not a revelation, they say: "Why have you not got it together?" Say: "I but follow what is revealed to me from my Lord: This is (nothing but) lights from your Lord, and guidance and mercy, for any who have faith."

وَإِذَا لَمۡ تَأۡتِهِم بِـَٔايَةٖ قَالُواْ لَوۡلَا ٱجۡتَبَيۡتَهَاۚ قُلۡ
إِنَّمَآ أَتَّبِعُ مَا يُوحَىٰٓ إِلَيَّ مِن رَّبِّيۚ هَٰذَا بَصَآئِرُ مِن
رَّبِّكُمۡ وَهُدٗى وَرَحۡمَةٞ لِّقَوۡمٖ يُؤۡمِنُونَ ٢٠٣

204. When the Qur'an is read, listen to it with attention, and hold your peace; that you may receive mercy.

وَإِذَا قُرِئَ ٱلۡقُرۡءَانُ فَٱسۡتَمِعُواْ لَهُۥ وَأَنصِتُواْ
لَعَلَّكُمۡ تُرۡحَمُونَ ٢٠٤

205. And do you (O reader!) Bring your Lord to remembrance in your (very) soul, with humility and in reverence, without loudness in words, in the mornings and evenings; and be not you of those who are unheedful.

وَٱذۡكُر رَّبَّكَ فِي نَفۡسِكَ تَضَرُّعٗا وَخِيفَةٗ وَدُونَ
ٱلۡجَهۡرِ مِنَ ٱلۡقَوۡلِ بِٱلۡغُدُوِّ وَٱلۡأٓصَالِ وَلَا تَكُن
مِّنَ ٱلۡغَٰفِلِينَ ٢٠٥

206. Those who are near to your Lord, disdain not to do Him worship: They celebrate His praises, and bow down before Him.

إِنَّ ٱلَّذِينَ عِندَ رَبِّكَ لَا يَسۡتَكۡبِرُونَ عَنۡ عِبَادَتِهِۦ
سجدة وَيُسَبِّحُونَهُۥ وَلَهُۥ يَسۡجُدُونَ ۩ ٢٠٦

سُورَةُ الأَنفَالِ

Surah 8: **Al-Anfal** (The Spoils of War)

In the name of Allah, Most Gracious, Most Merciful.

بِسْمِ ٱللَّهِ ٱلرَّحْمَٰنِ ٱلرَّحِيمِ

1. They ask you (O Muhammad) concerning (things taken as) spoils of war. Say: "(Such) spoils are at the disposal of Allah and the messenger: so fear Allah, and keep straight the relations between yourselves: obey Allah and His messenger, if you do believe."

نصف الحزب ١٨ يَسْـَٔلُونَكَ عَنِ ٱلْأَنفَالِ ۖ قُلِ ٱلْأَنفَالُ لِلَّهِ وَٱلرَّسُولِ ۖ
فَٱتَّقُوا۟ ٱللَّهَ وَأَصْلِحُوا۟ ذَاتَ بَيْنِكُمْ ۖ وَأَطِيعُوا۟
ٱللَّهَ وَرَسُولَهُۥٓ إِن كُنتُم مُّؤْمِنِينَ ١

2. For, believers are those who, when Allah is mentioned, feel a tremor in their hearts, and when they hear His signs rehearsed, find their faith strengthened, and put (all) their trust in their Lord.

إِنَّمَا ٱلْمُؤْمِنُونَ ٱلَّذِينَ إِذَا ذُكِرَ ٱللَّهُ وَجِلَتْ
قُلُوبُهُمْ وَإِذَا تُلِيَتْ عَلَيْهِمْ ءَايَٰتُهُۥ زَادَتْهُمْ إِيمَٰنًا
وَعَلَىٰ رَبِّهِمْ يَتَوَكَّلُونَ ٢

3. Who establish regular prayers and spend (freely) out of the gifts We have given them for sustenance:

ٱلَّذِينَ يُقِيمُونَ ٱلصَّلَوٰةَ وَمِمَّا رَزَقْنَٰهُمْ
يُنفِقُونَ ٣

4. Such in truth are the believers: they have grades of dignity with their Lord, and forgiveness, and generous sustenance.

أُو۟لَٰٓئِكَ هُمُ ٱلْمُؤْمِنُونَ حَقًّا ۚ لَّهُمْ دَرَجَٰتٌ عِندَ
رَبِّهِمْ وَمَغْفِرَةٌ وَرِزْقٌ كَرِيمٌ ٤

5. Just as your Lord ordered you (O Muhammad) out of your house in truth, even though a party among the believers disliked it.

كَمَآ أَخْرَجَكَ رَبُّكَ مِنۢ بَيْتِكَ بِٱلْحَقِّ وَإِنَّ فَرِيقًا
مِّنَ ٱلْمُؤْمِنِينَ لَكَٰرِهُونَ ٥

6. Disputing with you concerning the truth after it was made manifest, as if they were being driven to death and they (actually) saw it.

يُجَٰدِلُونَكَ فِى ٱلْحَقِّ بَعْدَ مَا تَبَيَّنَ كَأَنَّمَا يُسَاقُونَ
إِلَى ٱلْمَوْتِ وَهُمْ يَنظُرُونَ ٦

7. See! Allah promised you one of the two (enemy) parties, that it should be yours: you wished that the one unarmed should be yours, but Allah willed to justify the truth according to His words, and to cut off the roots of the unbelievers -

وَإِذْ يَعِدُكُمُ ٱللَّهُ إِحْدَى ٱلطَّآئِفَتَيْنِ أَنَّهَا لَكُمْ
وَتَوَدُّونَ أَنَّ غَيْرَ ذَاتِ ٱلشَّوْكَةِ تَكُونُ لَكُمْ وَيُرِيدُ
ٱللَّهُ أَن يُحِقَّ ٱلْحَقَّ بِكَلِمَٰتِهِۦ وَيَقْطَعَ دَابِرَ
ٱلْكَٰفِرِينَ ﴿٧﴾

8. That He might justify truth and prove falsehood false, distasteful though it be to those in guilt.

لِيُحِقَّ ٱلْحَقَّ وَيُبْطِلَ ٱلْبَٰطِلَ وَلَوْ كَرِهَ
ٱلْمُجْرِمُونَ ﴿٨﴾

9. Remember you implored the assistance of your Lord, and He answered you: "I will assist you with a thousand of the angels, ranks on ranks."

إِذْ تَسْتَغِيثُونَ رَبَّكُمْ فَٱسْتَجَابَ لَكُمْ أَنِّي
مُمِدُّكُم بِأَلْفٍ مِّنَ ٱلْمَلَٰٓئِكَةِ مُرْدِفِينَ ﴿٩﴾

10. Allah made it but a message of hope, and an assurance to your hearts: (in any case) there is no help except from Allah; and Allah is Exalted in Power, Wise.

وَمَا جَعَلَهُ ٱللَّهُ إِلَّا بُشْرَىٰ وَلِتَطْمَئِنَّ بِهِۦ قُلُوبُكُمْ
وَمَا ٱلنَّصْرُ إِلَّا مِنْ عِندِ ٱللَّهِ إِنَّ ٱللَّهَ عَزِيزٌ حَكِيمٌ ﴿١٠﴾

11. Remember He covered you with a sort of drowsiness, to give you calm as from Himself, and He caused rain to descend on you from heaven, to clean you with it, to remove from you the stain of Satan, to strengthen your hearts, and to plant your feet firmly with it.

إِذْ يُغَشِّيكُمُ ٱلنُّعَاسَ أَمَنَةً مِّنْهُ وَيُنَزِّلُ
عَلَيْكُم مِّنَ ٱلسَّمَآءِ مَآءً لِّيُطَهِّرَكُم بِهِۦ
وَيُذْهِبَ عَنكُمْ رِجْزَ ٱلشَّيْطَٰنِ وَلِيَرْبِطَ عَلَىٰ
قُلُوبِكُمْ وَيُثَبِّتَ بِهِ ٱلْأَقْدَامَ ﴿١١﴾

12. Remember your Lord inspired the angels (with the message): "I am with you; give firmness to the believers; I will instil terror into the hearts of the unbelievers: strike you above their necks and strike all their finger tips off them."

إِذْ يُوحِي رَبُّكَ إِلَى ٱلْمَلَٰٓئِكَةِ أَنِّي مَعَكُمْ فَثَبِّتُوا۟
ٱلَّذِينَ ءَامَنُوا۟ سَأُلْقِي فِي قُلُوبِ ٱلَّذِينَ كَفَرُوا۟
ٱلرُّعْبَ فَٱضْرِبُوا۟ فَوْقَ ٱلْأَعْنَاقِ وَٱضْرِبُوا۟ مِنْهُمْ
كُلَّ بَنَانٍ ﴿١٢﴾

13. This because they contended against Allah and His messenger: if any contend

ذَٰلِكَ بِأَنَّهُمْ شَآقُّوا۟ ٱللَّهَ وَرَسُولَهُۥ وَمَن يُشَاقِقِ

ٱللَّهَ وَرَسُولَهُۥ فَإِنَّ ٱللَّهَ شَدِيدُ ٱلْعِقَابِ ١٣

against Allah and His messenger, Allah is strict in punishment.

ذَٰلِكُمْ فَذُوقُوهُ وَأَنَّ لِلْكَٰفِرِينَ عَذَابَ
ٱلنَّارِ ١٤

14. Thus (will it be said): "Taste you then of the (punishment): for those who resist Allah, is the penalty of the fire."

يَٰٓأَيُّهَا ٱلَّذِينَ ءَامَنُوٓا۟ إِذَا لَقِيتُمُ ٱلَّذِينَ كَفَرُوا۟
زَحْفًا فَلَا تُوَلُّوهُمُ ٱلْأَدْبَارَ ١٥

15. O you who believe! When you meet the unbelievers in hostile array, never turn your backs to them.

وَمَن يُوَلِّهِمْ يَوْمَئِذٍ دُبُرَهُۥٓ إِلَّا مُتَحَرِّفًا لِّقِتَالٍ
أَوْ مُتَحَيِّزًا إِلَىٰ فِئَةٍ فَقَدْ بَآءَ بِغَضَبٍ مِّنَ ٱللَّهِ
وَمَأْوَىٰهُ جَهَنَّمُ ۖ وَبِئْسَ ٱلْمَصِيرُ ١٦

16. If any do turn his back to them on such a day - unless it be in a stratagem of war, or to retreat to a troop (of his own)- he draws on himself the wrath of Allah, and his abode is hell - an evil refuge (indeed)!

فَلَمْ تَقْتُلُوهُمْ وَلَٰكِنَّ ٱللَّهَ قَتَلَهُمْ ۚ وَمَا رَمَيْتَ
إِذْ رَمَيْتَ وَلَٰكِنَّ ٱللَّهَ رَمَىٰ ۚ وَلِيُبْلِىَ ٱلْمُؤْمِنِينَ
مِنْهُ بَلَآءً حَسَنًا ۚ إِنَّ ٱللَّهَ سَمِيعٌ عَلِيمٌ ١٧

17. It is not you (O believers) who slew them; it was Allah; when you (O Muhammad) threw (a handful of dust), it was not your act, but Allah's; in order that He might test the believers by a gracious trial from Himself: for Allah is He Who hears and knows (all things).

ذَٰلِكُمْ وَأَنَّ ٱللَّهَ مُوهِنُ كَيْدِ ٱلْكَٰفِرِينَ ١٨

18. That, and also because Allah is He Who makes feeble the plans and stratagems of the unbelievers.

إِن تَسْتَفْتِحُوا۟ فَقَدْ جَآءَكُمُ ٱلْفَتْحُ ۖ وَإِن
تَنتَهُوا۟ فَهُوَ خَيْرٌ لَّكُمْ ۖ وَإِن تَعُودُوا۟ نَعُدْ وَلَن
تُغْنِىَ عَنكُمْ فِئَتُكُمْ شَيْـًٔا وَلَوْ كَثُرَتْ وَأَنَّ
ٱللَّهَ مَعَ ٱلْمُؤْمِنِينَ ١٩

19. (O unbelievers!) If you prayed for victory and judgement, now has the judgement come to you: if you desist (from wrong), it will be best for you: if you return (to the attack), so shall We. Not the least good will your forces be to you even if they were multiplied; for verily Allah is with those who believe!

يَٰٓأَيُّهَا ٱلَّذِينَ ءَامَنُوٓا۟ أَطِيعُوا۟ ٱللَّهَ وَرَسُولَهُۥ وَلَا
تَوَلَّوْا۟ عَنْهُ وَأَنتُمْ تَسْمَعُونَ ٢٠

20. O you who believe! Obey Allah and His messenger, and turn not away from him when you hear (him speak).

21. Nor be like those who say, "we hear," but listen not;

وَلَا تَكُونُوا۟ كَٱلَّذِينَ قَالُوا۟ سَمِعْنَا وَهُمْ لَا يَسْمَعُونَ ﴿٢١﴾

22. For the worst of beasts in the sight of Allah are the deaf and the dumb - those who understand not.

ثلاثة أرباع الحزب ١٨

۞ إِنَّ شَرَّ ٱلدَّوَآبِّ عِندَ ٱللَّهِ ٱلصُّمُّ ٱلْبُكْمُ
ٱلَّذِينَ لَا يَعْقِلُونَ ﴿٢٢﴾

23. If Allah had found in them any good, He would indeed have made them listen; (as it is), if He had made them listen, they would but have turned back and declined (faith).

وَلَوْ عَلِمَ ٱللَّهُ فِيهِمْ خَيْرًا لَّأَسْمَعَهُمْ ۖ وَلَوْ أَسْمَعَهُمْ
لَتَوَلَّوا۟ وَّهُم مُّعْرِضُونَ ﴿٢٣﴾

24. O you who believe! Give your response to Allah and His messenger, when He calls you to that which will give you life; and know that Allah comes in between a man and his heart, and that it is He to whom You shall (all) be gathered.

يَٰٓأَيُّهَا ٱلَّذِينَ ءَامَنُوا۟ ٱسْتَجِيبُوا۟ لِلَّهِ وَلِلرَّسُولِ
إِذَا دَعَاكُمْ لِمَا يُحْيِيكُمْ ۖ وَٱعْلَمُوٓا۟ أَنَّ ٱللَّهَ يَحُولُ
بَيْنَ ٱلْمَرْءِ وَقَلْبِهِۦ وَأَنَّهُۥٓ إِلَيْهِ تُحْشَرُونَ ﴿٢٤﴾

25. And fear tumult or oppression, which affects not in particular (only) those of you who do wrong: and know that Allah is strict in punishment.

وَٱتَّقُوا۟ فِتْنَةً لَّا تُصِيبَنَّ ٱلَّذِينَ ظَلَمُوا۟ مِنكُمْ
خَآصَّةً ۖ وَٱعْلَمُوٓا۟ أَنَّ ٱللَّهَ شَدِيدُ ٱلْعِقَابِ ﴿٢٥﴾

26. Call to mind when you were a small (band), despised through the land, and afraid that men might despoil and kidnap you; but He provided a safe asylum for you, strengthened you with His aid, and gave you good things for sustenance: that you might be grateful.

وَٱذْكُرُوٓا۟ إِذْ أَنتُمْ قَلِيلٌ مُّسْتَضْعَفُونَ فِى ٱلْأَرْضِ
تَخَافُونَ أَن يَتَخَطَّفَكُمُ ٱلنَّاسُ فَـَٔاوَىٰكُمْ وَأَيَّدَكُم
بِنَصْرِهِۦ وَرَزَقَكُم مِّنَ ٱلطَّيِّبَٰتِ لَعَلَّكُمْ
تَشْكُرُونَ ﴿٢٦﴾

27. O you who believe! Betray not the trust of Allah and the messenger, nor misappropriate knowingly things entrusted to you.

يَٰٓأَيُّهَا ٱلَّذِينَ ءَامَنُوا۟ لَا تَخُونُوا۟ ٱللَّهَ وَٱلرَّسُولَ وَتَخُونُوٓا۟
أَمَٰنَٰتِكُمْ وَأَنتُمْ تَعْلَمُونَ ﴿٢٧﴾

28. And know you that your possessions and your progeny are but a trial; and that it is Allah with whom lies your highest reward.

وَٱعْلَمُوٓا۟ أَنَّمَآ أَمْوَٰلُكُمْ وَأَوْلَٰدُكُمْ فِتْنَةٌ
وَأَنَّ ٱللَّهَ عِندَهُۥٓ أَجْرٌ عَظِيمٌ ﴿٢٨﴾

29. O you who believe! If you fear Allah, He will grant you a criterion (to judge between right and wrong), remove from you (all) evil (that may afflict) you, and forgive you; for Allah is the Lord of grace unbounded.

يَٰٓأَيُّهَا ٱلَّذِينَ ءَامَنُوٓاْ إِن تَتَّقُواْ ٱللَّهَ يَجۡعَل
لَّكُمۡ فُرۡقَانٗا وَيُكَفِّرۡ عَنكُمۡ سَيِّـَٔاتِكُمۡ
وَيَغۡفِرۡ لَكُمۡۗ وَٱللَّهُ ذُو ٱلۡفَضۡلِ ٱلۡعَظِيمِ ٢٩

30. Remember how the unbelievers plotted against you (O Muhammad), to keep you in bonds, or slay you, or get you out (of your home). They plot and plan, and Allah too plans, but the best of planners is Allah.

وَإِذۡ يَمۡكُرُ بِكَ ٱلَّذِينَ كَفَرُواْ لِيُثۡبِتُوكَ
أَوۡ يَقۡتُلُوكَ أَوۡ يُخۡرِجُوكَۚ وَيَمۡكُرُونَ وَيَمۡكُرُ ٱللَّهُۖ
وَٱللَّهُ خَيۡرُ ٱلۡمَٰكِرِينَ ٣٠

31. When Our signs are rehearsed to them, they say: "We have heard this (before); if we wished, we could say (words) like these; these are nothing but tales of the ancients."

وَإِذَا تُتۡلَىٰ عَلَيۡهِمۡ ءَايَٰتُنَا قَالُواْ قَدۡ سَمِعۡنَا لَوۡ نَشَآءُ
لَقُلۡنَا مِثۡلَ هَٰذَآ إِنۡ هَٰذَآ إِلَّآ أَسَٰطِيرُ ٱلۡأَوَّلِينَ ٣١

32. Remember how they said: "O Allah! If this is indeed the truth from You, rain down on us a shower of stones from the sky, or send us a grievous penalty."

وَإِذۡ قَالُواْ ٱللَّهُمَّ إِن كَانَ هَٰذَا هُوَ ٱلۡحَقَّ مِنۡ عِندِكَ
فَأَمۡطِرۡ عَلَيۡنَا حِجَارَةٗ مِّنَ ٱلسَّمَآءِ أَوِ ٱئۡتِنَا
بِعَذَابٍ أَلِيمٖ ٣٢

33. But Allah was not going to send them a penalty whilst you were amongst them; nor was He going to send it whilst they could ask for pardon.

وَمَا كَانَ ٱللَّهُ لِيُعَذِّبَهُمۡ وَأَنتَ فِيهِمۡۚ وَمَا كَانَ ٱللَّهُ
مُعَذِّبَهُمۡ وَهُمۡ يَسۡتَغۡفِرُونَ ٣٣

34. But what plea have they that Allah should not punish them, when they keep out (men) from the Sacred Mosque - and they are not its guardians? No men can be its guardians except the righteous; but most of them do not understand.

وَمَا لَهُمۡ أَلَّا يُعَذِّبَهُمُ ٱللَّهُ وَهُمۡ يَصُدُّونَ عَنِ
ٱلۡمَسۡجِدِ ٱلۡحَرَامِ وَمَا كَانُوٓاْ أَوۡلِيَآءَهُۥٓۚ إِنۡ أَوۡلِيَآؤُهُۥٓ
إِلَّا ٱلۡمُتَّقُونَ وَلَٰكِنَّ أَكۡثَرَهُمۡ لَا يَعۡلَمُونَ ٣٤

35. Their prayer at the House (of Allah) is nothing but whistling and clapping of hands: (its only answer can be), "Taste you the penalty because you blasphemed."

وَمَا كَانَ صَلَاتُهُمۡ عِندَ ٱلۡبَيۡتِ إِلَّا مُكَآءٗ
وَتَصۡدِيَةٗۚ فَذُوقُواْ ٱلۡعَذَابَ بِمَا كُنتُمۡ
تَكۡفُرُونَ ٣٥

36. The unbelievers spend their wealth to hinder (men) from the path of Allah, and so will they continue to spend; but in the end they will have (only) regrets and sighs; at length they will be overcome: and the unbelievers will be gathered together to hell -

إِنَّ ٱلَّذِينَ كَفَرُواْ يُنفِقُونَ أَمْوَٰلَهُمْ لِيَصُدُّواْ
عَن سَبِيلِ ٱللَّهِۚ فَسَيُنفِقُونَهَا ثُمَّ تَكُونُ عَلَيْهِمْ
حَسْرَةً ثُمَّ يُغْلَبُونَۗ وَٱلَّذِينَ كَفَرُوٓاْ إِلَىٰ جَهَنَّمَ
يُحْشَرُونَ ٣٦

37. In order that Allah may separate the impure from the pure, put the impure, one on another, heap them together, and cast them into hell. They will be the ones to have lost.

لِيَمِيزَ ٱللَّهُ ٱلْخَبِيثَ مِنَ ٱلطَّيِّبِ وَيَجْعَلَ ٱلْخَبِيثَ
بَعْضَهُۥ عَلَىٰ بَعْضٍ فَيَرْكُمَهُۥ جَمِيعًا فَيَجْعَلَهُۥ
فِي جَهَنَّمَۚ أُوْلَٰٓئِكَ هُمُ ٱلْخَٰسِرُونَ ٣٧

38. Say to the unbelievers, if (now) they desist (from unbelief), their past would be forgiven them; but if they persist, the punishment of those before them is already (a matter of warning for them).

قُل لِّلَّذِينَ كَفَرُوٓاْ إِن يَنتَهُواْ يُغْفَرْ لَهُم
مَّا قَدْ سَلَفَ وَإِن يَعُودُواْ فَقَدْ مَضَتْ سُنَّتُ
ٱلْأَوَّلِينَ ٣٨

39. And fight them on until there is no more tumult or oppression, and there prevail justice and faith in Allah altogether and everywhere; but if they cease, verily Allah does see all that they do.

وَقَٰتِلُوهُمْ حَتَّىٰ لَا تَكُونَ فِتْنَةٌ وَيَكُونَ
ٱلدِّينُ كُلُّهُۥ لِلَّهِۚ فَإِنِ ٱنتَهَوْاْ فَإِنَّ ٱللَّهَ بِمَا
يَعْمَلُونَ بَصِيرٌ ٣٩

40. If they refuse, be sure that Allah is your protector - the best to protect and the best to help.

وَإِن تَوَلَّوْاْ فَٱعْلَمُوٓاْ أَنَّ ٱللَّهَ مَوْلَىٰكُمْۚ نِعْمَ
ٱلْمَوْلَىٰ وَنِعْمَ ٱلنَّصِيرُ ٤٠

✻**41.** And know that out of all the booty that you may acquire (in war), a fifth share is assigned to Allah and to the messenger, and to near relatives, orphans, the needy, and the wayfarer - if you do believe in Allah and in the revelation We sent down to Our servant on the day of testing - the day of the meeting of the two forces. For Allah has power over all things.

۞ وَٱعْلَمُوٓاْ أَنَّمَا غَنِمْتُم مِّن شَيْءٍ فَأَنَّ لِلَّهِ خُمُسَهُۥ الجزء ١٠ الحزب ١٩
وَلِلرَّسُولِ وَلِذِي ٱلْقُرْبَىٰ وَٱلْيَتَٰمَىٰ وَٱلْمَسَٰكِينِ
وَٱبْنِ ٱلسَّبِيلِ إِن كُنتُمْ ءَامَنتُم بِٱللَّهِ وَمَآ أَنزَلْنَا
عَلَىٰ عَبْدِنَا يَوْمَ ٱلْفُرْقَانِ يَوْمَ ٱلْتَقَى ٱلْجَمْعَانِۗ
وَٱللَّهُ عَلَىٰ كُلِّ شَيْءٍ قَدِيرٌ ٤١

✻ Part-10

42. Remember you were on the near side of the valley, and they on the far side, and the caravan on lower ground than you. Even if you had made a mutual appointment to meet, you would certainly have failed in the appointment: but (thus you met), that Allah might accomplish a matter already enacted; that those who died might die after a clear sign (had been given), and those who lived might live after a clear sign (had been given). And verily Allah is He Who hears and knows (all things).

إِذْ أَنتُم بِٱلْعُدْوَةِ ٱلدُّنْيَا وَهُم بِٱلْعُدْوَةِ ٱلْقُصْوَىٰ
وَٱلرَّكْبُ أَسْفَلَ مِنكُمْ ۚ وَلَوْ تَوَاعَدتُّمْ
لَٱخْتَلَفْتُمْ فِى ٱلْمِيعَـٰدِ ۙ وَلَـٰكِن لِّيَقْضِىَ ٱللَّهُ
أَمْرًا كَانَ مَفْعُولًا لِّيَهْلِكَ مَنْ هَلَكَ عَنۢ
بَيِّنَةٍ وَيَحْيَىٰ مَنْ حَىَّ عَنۢ بَيِّنَةٍ ۗ وَإِنَّ ٱللَّهَ
لَسَمِيعٌ عَلِيمٌ ﴿٤٢﴾

43. Remember in your dream Allah showed them to you (O Muhammad) as few; if He had shown them to you as many, you would surely have been discouraged, and you would surely have disputed in (your) decision; but Allah saved (you): for He knows well the (secrets) of (all) hearts.

إِذْ يُرِيكَهُمُ ٱللَّهُ فِى مَنَامِكَ قَلِيلًا ۖ وَلَوْ
أَرَىٰكَهُمْ كَثِيرًا لَّفَشِلْتُمْ وَلَتَنَـٰزَعْتُمْ فِى
ٱلْأَمْرِ وَلَـٰكِنَّ ٱللَّهَ سَلَّمَ ۗ إِنَّهُۥ عَلِيمٌۢ بِذَاتِ
ٱلصُّدُورِ ﴿٤٣﴾

44. And remember when you met, He showed them to you as few in your eyes, and He made you appear as contemptible in their eyes; That Allah might accomplish a matter already enacted: for to Allah do all questions go back (for decision).

وَإِذْ يُرِيكُمُوهُمْ إِذِ ٱلْتَقَيْتُمْ فِىٓ أَعْيُنِكُمْ قَلِيلًا
وَيُقَلِّلُكُمْ فِىٓ أَعْيُنِهِمْ لِيَقْضِىَ ٱللَّهُ أَمْرًا كَانَ
مَفْعُولًا ۗ وَإِلَى ٱللَّهِ تُرْجَعُ ٱلْأُمُورُ ﴿٤٤﴾

45. O you who believe! When you meet a force, be firm, and call Allah in remembrance much (and often); that you may prosper.

يَـٰٓأَيُّهَا ٱلَّذِينَ ءَامَنُوٓا۟ إِذَا لَقِيتُمْ فِئَةً فَٱثْبُتُوا۟
وَٱذْكُرُوا۟ ٱللَّهَ كَثِيرًا لَّعَلَّكُمْ تُفْلِحُونَ ﴿٤٥﴾

46. And obey Allah and His messenger; and fall into no disputes, lest you lose heart and your power depart; and be patient and persevering: for Allah is with those who patiently persevere.

وَأَطِيعُوا۟ ٱللَّهَ وَرَسُولَهُۥ وَلَا تَنَـٰزَعُوا۟ فَتَفْشَلُوا۟
وَتَذْهَبَ رِيحُكُمْ ۖ وَٱصْبِرُوٓا۟ ۚ إِنَّ ٱللَّهَ مَعَ
ٱلصَّـٰبِرِينَ ﴿٤٦﴾

47. And be not like those who started from their homes insolently and to be seen of men,

وَلَا تَكُونُوا۟ كَٱلَّذِينَ خَرَجُوا۟ مِن دِيَـٰرِهِم بَطَرًا وَرِئَآءَ

and to hinder (men) from the path of Allah; for Allah encompasses all that they do.

ٱلنَّاسِ وَيَصُدُّونَ عَن سَبِيلِ ٱللَّهِ ۚ وَٱللَّهُ بِمَا
يَعْمَلُونَ مُحِيطٌ ﴿٤٧﴾

48. Remember Satan made their (sinful) acts seem alluring to them, and said: "No one among men can overcome you this day, while I am near to you"; but when the two forces came in sight of each other, he turned on his heels, and said: "I am clear of you; I see what you see not; I fear Allah; for Allah is strict in punishment."

وَإِذْ زَيَّنَ لَهُمُ ٱلشَّيْطَٰنُ أَعْمَٰلَهُمْ وَقَالَ لَا غَالِبَ
لَكُمُ ٱلْيَوْمَ مِنَ ٱلنَّاسِ وَإِنِّى جَارٌ لَّكُمْ ۖ فَلَمَّا
تَرَآءَتِ ٱلْفِئَتَانِ نَكَصَ عَلَىٰ عَقِبَيْهِ وَقَالَ إِنِّى
بَرِىٓءٌ مِّنكُمْ إِنِّىٓ أَرَىٰ مَا لَا تَرَوْنَ إِنِّىٓ
أَخَافُ ٱللَّهَ ۚ وَٱللَّهُ شَدِيدُ ٱلْعِقَابِ ﴿٤٨﴾

49. The hypocrites say, and those in whose hearts is a disease: "These people - their religion has misled them." But if any trust in Allah, behold! Allah is Exalted in Might, Wise.

إِذْ يَقُولُ ٱلْمُنَٰفِقُونَ وَٱلَّذِينَ فِى قُلُوبِهِم مَّرَضٌ
غَرَّ هَٰٓؤُلَآءِ دِينُهُمْ ۗ وَمَن يَتَوَكَّلْ عَلَى ٱللَّهِ
فَإِنَّ ٱللَّهَ عَزِيزٌ حَكِيمٌ ﴿٤٩﴾

50. If you could see, when the angels take the souls of the unbelievers (at death), (how) they strike their faces and their backs, (saying): "Taste the penalty of the blazing fire -

وَلَوْ تَرَىٰٓ إِذْ يَتَوَفَّى ٱلَّذِينَ كَفَرُوا۟ ٱلْمَلَٰٓئِكَةُ
يَضْرِبُونَ وُجُوهَهُمْ وَأَدْبَٰرَهُمْ وَذُوقُوا۟ عَذَابَ
ٱلْحَرِيقِ ﴿٥٠﴾

51. Because of (the deeds) which your (own) hands sent before: for Allah is never unjust to His servants:

ذَٰلِكَ بِمَا قَدَّمَتْ أَيْدِيكُمْ وَأَنَّ ٱللَّهَ لَيْسَ
بِظَلَّٰمٍ لِّلْعَبِيدِ ﴿٥١﴾

52. (Deeds) after the manner of the people of Pharaoh and of those before them: they rejected the signs of Allah and Allah punished them for their crimes: for Allah is Strong, and Strict in punishment:

كَدَأْبِ ءَالِ فِرْعَوْنَ وَٱلَّذِينَ مِن قَبْلِهِمْ ۚ
كَفَرُوا۟ بِـَٔايَٰتِ ٱللَّهِ فَأَخَذَهُمُ ٱللَّهُ بِذُنُوبِهِمْ ۗ
إِنَّ ٱللَّهَ قَوِىٌّ شَدِيدُ ٱلْعِقَابِ ﴿٥٢﴾

53. Because Allah will never change the grace which He has bestowed on a people

ذَٰلِكَ بِأَنَّ ٱللَّهَ لَمْ يَكُ مُغَيِّرًا نِّعْمَةً أَنْعَمَهَا عَلَىٰ

قَوۡمٍ حَتَّىٰ يُغَيِّرُواْ مَا بِأَنفُسِهِمۡ وَأَنَّ ٱللَّهَ سَمِيعٌ
عَلِيمٞ ﴿٥٣﴾

until they change what is in their (own) souls: and verily Allah is He Who hears and knows (all things)."

كَدَأۡبِ ءَالِ فِرۡعَوۡنَ وَٱلَّذِينَ مِن قَبۡلِهِمۡۚ كَذَّبُواْ
بِـَٔايَٰتِ رَبِّهِمۡ فَأَهۡلَكۡنَٰهُم بِذُنُوبِهِمۡ وَأَغۡرَقۡنَآ
ءَالَ فِرۡعَوۡنَۚ وَكُلّٞ كَانُواْ ظَٰلِمِينَ ﴿٥٤﴾

54. "(Deeds) after the manner of the people of Pharaoh and those before them": they treated as false the signs of their Lord; so We destroyed them for their crimes, and We drowned the People of Pharaoh: for they were all oppressors and wrongdoers.

إِنَّ شَرَّ ٱلدَّوَآبِّ عِندَ ٱللَّهِ ٱلَّذِينَ كَفَرُواْ فَهُمۡ
لَا يُؤۡمِنُونَ ﴿٥٥﴾

55. For the worst of beasts in the sight of Allah are those who reject Him; They will not believe.

ٱلَّذِينَ عَٰهَدتَّ مِنۡهُمۡ ثُمَّ يَنقُضُونَ عَهۡدَهُمۡ فِي
كُلِّ مَرَّةٖ وَهُمۡ لَا يَتَّقُونَ ﴿٥٦﴾

56. They are those with whom you did make a covenant, but they break their covenant every time, and they have not the fear (of Allah).

فَإِمَّا تَثۡقَفَنَّهُمۡ فِي ٱلۡحَرۡبِ فَشَرِّدۡ بِهِم مَّنۡ خَلۡفَهُمۡ
لَعَلَّهُمۡ يَذَّكَّرُونَ ﴿٥٧﴾

57. If you gain the mastery over them in war, disperse, with them, those who follow them, that they may remember.

وَإِمَّا تَخَافَنَّ مِن قَوۡمٍ خِيَانَةٗ فَٱنۢبِذۡ إِلَيۡهِمۡ عَلَىٰ
سَوَآءٍۚ إِنَّ ٱللَّهَ لَا يُحِبُّ ٱلۡخَآئِنِينَ ﴿٥٨﴾

58. If you fear treachery from any group, throw back (their covenant) to them, (so as to be) on equal terms: for Allah loves not the treacherous.

وَلَا يَحۡسَبَنَّ ٱلَّذِينَ كَفَرُواْ سَبَقُوٓاْۚ إِنَّهُمۡ
لَا يُعۡجِزُونَ ﴿٥٩﴾

59. Let not the unbelievers think that they can get the better (of the Godly): they will never frustrate (them).

وَأَعِدُّواْ لَهُم مَّا ٱسۡتَطَعۡتُم مِّن قُوَّةٖ وَمِن رِّبَاطِ
ٱلۡخَيۡلِ تُرۡهِبُونَ بِهِۦ عَدُوَّ ٱللَّهِ وَعَدُوَّكُمۡ
وَءَاخَرِينَ مِن دُونِهِمۡ لَا تَعۡلَمُونَهُمُ ٱللَّهُ يَعۡلَمُهُمۡۚ

60. Against them make ready your strength to the utmost of your power, including steeds of war, to strike terror into (the hearts of) the enemies of Allah and your enemies, and others besides, whom you may not know, but whom Allah does know.

Whatever you shall spend in the cause of Allah, shall be repaid to you, and you shall not be treated unjustly.

وَمَا تُنفِقُوا۟ مِن شَىْءٍ فِى سَبِيلِ ٱللَّهِ يُوَفَّ إِلَيْكُمْ
وَأَنتُمْ لَا تُظْلَمُونَ ﴿٦٠﴾

61. But if the enemy incline towards peace, do you (also) incline towards peace, and trust in Allah: for He is the One that hears and knows (all things).

ربع الحزب ١٩ ۞ وَإِن جَنَحُوا۟ لِلسَّلْمِ فَٱجْنَحْ لَهَا وَتَوَكَّلْ عَلَى ٱللَّهِ ۚ
إِنَّهُۥ هُوَ ٱلسَّمِيعُ ٱلْعَلِيمُ ﴿٦١﴾

62. Should they intend to deceive you - verily Allah suffices you: He it is that has strengthened you with His aid and with (the company of) the believers;

وَإِن يُرِيدُوٓا۟ أَن يَخْدَعُوكَ فَإِنَّ حَسْبَكَ ٱللَّهُ ۚ
هُوَ ٱلَّذِىٓ أَيَّدَكَ بِنَصْرِهِۦ وَبِٱلْمُؤْمِنِينَ ﴿٦٢﴾

63. And (moreover) He has put affection between their hearts: not if you had spent all that is in the earth, could you have produced that affection, but Allah has done it: for He is Exalted in might, Wise.

وَأَلَّفَ بَيْنَ قُلُوبِهِمْ ۚ لَوْ أَنفَقْتَ مَا فِى ٱلْأَرْضِ
جَمِيعًا مَّآ أَلَّفْتَ بَيْنَ قُلُوبِهِمْ وَلَٰكِنَّ ٱللَّهَ
أَلَّفَ بَيْنَهُمْ ۚ إِنَّهُۥ عَزِيزٌ حَكِيمٌ ﴿٦٣﴾

64. O Prophet! Sufficient to you is Allah - (to you) and to those who follow you among the believers.

يَٰٓأَيُّهَا ٱلنَّبِىُّ حَسْبُكَ ٱللَّهُ وَمَنِ ٱتَّبَعَكَ مِنَ
ٱلْمُؤْمِنِينَ ﴿٦٤﴾

65. O Prophet! Rouse the believers to the fight. If there are twenty amongst you, patient and persevering, they will vanquish two hundred; if a hundred, they will vanquish a thousand of the unbelievers; for these are a people without understanding.

يَٰٓأَيُّهَا ٱلنَّبِىُّ حَرِّضِ ٱلْمُؤْمِنِينَ عَلَى ٱلْقِتَالِ ۚ إِن
يَكُن مِّنكُمْ عِشْرُونَ صَٰبِرُونَ يَغْلِبُوا۟ مِا۟ئَتَيْنِ ۚ
وَإِن يَكُن مِّنكُم مِّا۟ئَةٌ يَغْلِبُوٓا۟ أَلْفًا مِّنَ
ٱلَّذِينَ كَفَرُوا۟ بِأَنَّهُمْ قَوْمٌ لَّا يَفْقَهُونَ ﴿٦٥﴾

66. For the present, Allah has lightened your (task) for He knows that there is a weak spot in you: but (even so), if there are a hundred of you, patient and persevering, they will vanquish two hundred, and if a thousand, they will vanquish two thousand, with the leave of Allah; for Allah is with those who patiently persevere.

ٱلْـَٰٔنَ خَفَّفَ ٱللَّهُ عَنكُمْ وَعَلِمَ أَنَّ فِيكُمْ ضَعْفًا ۚ
فَإِن يَكُن مِّنكُم مِّا۟ئَةٌ صَابِرَةٌ يَغْلِبُوا۟ مِا۟ئَتَيْنِ ۚ
وَإِن يَكُن مِّنكُمْ أَلْفٌ يَغْلِبُوٓا۟ أَلْفَيْنِ بِإِذْنِ
ٱللَّهِ ۗ وَٱللَّهُ مَعَ ٱلصَّٰبِرِينَ ﴿٦٦﴾

67. It is not fitting for a prophet that he should have prisoners of war until he has thoroughly subdued the land. You look for the temporal goods of this world; but Allah looks to the hereafter; and Allah is Exalted in might, Wise.

مَا كَانَ لِنَبِيٍّ أَن يَكُونَ لَهُۥٓ أَسْرَىٰ حَتَّىٰ يُثْخِنَ
فِى ٱلْأَرْضِ ۚ تُرِيدُونَ عَرَضَ ٱلدُّنْيَا وَٱللَّهُ يُرِيدُ
ٱلْـَٔاخِرَةَ ۗ وَٱللَّهُ عَزِيزٌ حَكِيمٌ ﴿٦٧﴾

68. Had it not been for a previous ordainment from Allah, a severe penalty would have reached you for the (ransom) that you took.

لَّوْلَا كِتَـٰبٌ مِّنَ ٱللَّهِ سَبَقَ لَمَسَّكُمْ فِيمَآ أَخَذْتُمْ
عَذَابٌ عَظِيمٌ ﴿٦٨﴾

69. But (now) enjoy what you took in war, lawful and good; but fear Allah; for Allah is Oft-Forgiving, Most Merciful.

فَكُلُوا۟ مِمَّا غَنِمْتُمْ حَلَـٰلًا طَيِّبًا ۚ وَٱتَّقُوا۟ ٱللَّهَ ۚ إِنَّ ٱللَّهَ
غَفُورٌ رَّحِيمٌ ﴿٦٩﴾

70. O Prophet! Say to those who are captives in your hands: "If Allah finds any good in your hearts, He will give you something better than what has been taken from you, and He will forgive you; for Allah is Oft-Forgiving, Most Merciful."

يَـٰٓأَيُّهَا ٱلنَّبِىُّ قُل لِّمَن فِىٓ أَيْدِيكُم مِّنَ ٱلْأَسْرَىٰٓ إِن
يَعْلَمِ ٱللَّهُ فِى قُلُوبِكُمْ خَيْرًا يُؤْتِكُمْ خَيْرًا مِّمَّآ أُخِذَ
مِنكُمْ وَيَغْفِرْ لَكُمْ ۗ وَٱللَّهُ غَفُورٌ رَّحِيمٌ ﴿٧٠﴾

71. But if they have treacherous designs against you, (O messenger!), they have already been in treason against Allah, and so has He given (you) power over them. And Allah is He Who has (full) knowledge and wisdom.

وَإِن يُرِيدُوا۟ خِيَانَتَكَ فَقَدْ خَانُوا۟ ٱللَّهَ مِن قَبْلُ
فَأَمْكَنَ مِنْهُمْ ۗ وَٱللَّهُ عَلِيمٌ حَكِيمٌ ﴿٧١﴾

72. Those who believed, and adopted exile, and fought for the faith, with their property and their persons, in the cause of Allah, as well as those who gave (them) asylum and aid - these are (all) friends and protectors, one of another. As to those who believed but came not into exile; you owe no duty of protection to them until they come into exile; but if they seek your aid in religion, it is your duty to help them, except

إِنَّ ٱلَّذِينَ ءَامَنُوا۟ وَهَاجَرُوا۟ وَجَـٰهَدُوا۟ بِأَمْوَٰلِهِمْ
وَأَنفُسِهِمْ فِى سَبِيلِ ٱللَّهِ وَٱلَّذِينَ ءَاوَوا۟ وَّنَصَرُوٓا۟
أُو۟لَـٰٓئِكَ بَعْضُهُمْ أَوْلِيَآءُ بَعْضٍ ۚ وَٱلَّذِينَ ءَامَنُوا۟ وَلَمْ
يُهَاجِرُوا۟ مَا لَكُم مِّن وَلَـٰيَتِهِم مِّن شَىْءٍ حَتَّىٰ يُهَاجِرُوا۟ ۚ
وَإِنِ ٱسْتَنصَرُوكُمْ فِى ٱلدِّينِ فَعَلَيْكُمُ ٱلنَّصْرُ

against a people with whom you have a treaty of mutual alliance. And (remember) Allah sees all that you do.

إِلَّا عَلَىٰ قَوْمٍ بَيْنَكُمْ وَبَيْنَهُم مِّيثَٰقٌ ۗ وَٱللَّهُ بِمَا تَعْمَلُونَ بَصِيرٌ ﴿٧٢﴾

73. The unbelievers are protectors, one of another: unless you do this, (protect each other), there would be tumult and oppression on earth, and great mischief.

وَٱلَّذِينَ كَفَرُوا۟ بَعْضُهُمْ أَوْلِيَآءُ بَعْضٍ ۚ إِلَّا تَفْعَلُوهُ تَكُن فِتْنَةٌ فِى ٱلْأَرْضِ وَفَسَادٌ كَبِيرٌ ﴿٧٣﴾

74. Those who believe, and adopt exile, and fight for the faith, in the cause of Allah, as well as those who give (them) asylum and aid - these are (all) in very truth the believers: for them is the forgiveness of sins and a provision most generous.

وَٱلَّذِينَ ءَامَنُوا۟ وَهَاجَرُوا۟ وَجَٰهَدُوا۟ فِى سَبِيلِ ٱللَّهِ وَٱلَّذِينَ ءَاوَوا۟ وَّنَصَرُوٓا۟ أُو۟لَٰٓئِكَ هُمُ ٱلْمُؤْمِنُونَ حَقًّا ۚ لَّهُم مَّغْفِرَةٌ وَرِزْقٌ كَرِيمٌ ﴿٧٤﴾

75. And those who accept faith subsequently, and adopt exile, and fight for the faith in your company - they are of you. But relations by blood have prior rights against each other in the book of Allah. Verily Allah is well-acquainted with all things.

وَٱلَّذِينَ ءَامَنُوا۟ مِنۢ بَعْدُ وَهَاجَرُوا۟ وَجَٰهَدُوا۟ مَعَكُمْ فَأُو۟لَٰٓئِكَ مِنكُمْ ۚ وَأُو۟لُوا۟ ٱلْأَرْحَامِ بَعْضُهُمْ أَوْلَىٰ بِبَعْضٍ فِى كِتَٰبِ ٱللَّهِ ۗ إِنَّ ٱللَّهَ بِكُلِّ شَىْءٍ عَلِيمٌۢ ﴿٧٥﴾

سُورَةُ التَّوْبَةِ

*Surah 9: **At-Taubah*** (The Repentance)

1. A (declaration) of immunity from Allah and His messenger, to those of the pagans with whom you have contracted mutual alliances -

نصف حزب ١٩ بَرَآءَةٌ مِّنَ ٱللَّهِ وَرَسُولِهِۦٓ إِلَى ٱلَّذِينَ عَٰهَدتُّم مِّنَ ٱلْمُشْرِكِينَ ﴿١﴾

2. Go you, then, for four months, backwards and forwards, (as you will), throughout the land, but know you that you cannot frustrate Allah (by your falsehood) but that Allah will cover with shame those who reject Him.

فَسِيحُوا۟ فِى ٱلْأَرْضِ أَرْبَعَةَ أَشْهُرٍ وَٱعْلَمُوٓا۟ أَنَّكُمْ غَيْرُ مُعْجِزِى ٱللَّهِ ۙ وَأَنَّ ٱللَّهَ مُخْزِى ٱلْكَٰفِرِينَ ﴿٢﴾

3. And an announcement from Allah and His messenger, to the people (assembled) on the day of the great pilgrimage - that Allah and His messenger dissolve (treaty) obligations with the pagans. If, then, you repent, it were best for you; but if you turn away, know you that you cannot frustrate Allah. And proclaim a grievous penalty to those who reject faith.

وَأَذَٰنٌ مِّنَ ٱللَّهِ وَرَسُولِهِۦٓ إِلَى ٱلنَّاسِ يَوْمَ ٱلْحَجِّ
ٱلْأَكْبَرِ أَنَّ ٱللَّهَ بَرِىٓءٌ مِّنَ ٱلْمُشْرِكِينَ وَرَسُولُهُۥ ۚ
فَإِن تُبْتُمْ فَهُوَ خَيْرٌ لَّكُمْ ۖ وَإِن تَوَلَّيْتُمْ فَٱعْلَمُوٓا۟
أَنَّكُمْ غَيْرُ مُعْجِزِى ٱللَّهِ ۗ وَبَشِّرِ ٱلَّذِينَ كَفَرُوا۟
بِعَذَابٍ أَلِيمٍ ٣

4. (But the treaties are) not dissolved with those pagans with whom You have entered into alliance and who have not subsequently failed you in anything, nor aided anyone against you. So fulfil your engagements with them to the end of their term: for Allah loves the righteous.

إِلَّا ٱلَّذِينَ عَٰهَدتُّم مِّنَ ٱلْمُشْرِكِينَ ثُمَّ لَمْ يَنقُصُوكُمْ
شَيْـًٔا وَلَمْ يُظَٰهِرُوا۟ عَلَيْكُمْ أَحَدًا فَأَتِمُّوٓا۟ إِلَيْهِمْ
عَهْدَهُمْ إِلَىٰ مُدَّتِهِمْ ۚ إِنَّ ٱللَّهَ يُحِبُّ ٱلْمُتَّقِينَ ٤

5. But when the forbidden months are past, then fight and slay the pagans wherever you find them, and seize them, beleaguer them, and lie in wait for them, in every stratagem (of war); but if they repent, and establish regular prayers and practice regular charity, then open the way for them: for Allah is Oft-Forgiving, Most Merciful.

فَإِذَا ٱنسَلَخَ ٱلْأَشْهُرُ ٱلْحُرُمُ فَٱقْتُلُوا۟ ٱلْمُشْرِكِينَ
حَيْثُ وَجَدتُّمُوهُمْ وَخُذُوهُمْ وَٱحْصُرُوهُمْ وَٱقْعُدُوا۟
لَهُمْ كُلَّ مَرْصَدٍ ۚ فَإِن تَابُوا۟ وَأَقَامُوا۟ ٱلصَّلَوٰةَ وَءَاتَوُا۟
ٱلزَّكَوٰةَ فَخَلُّوا۟ سَبِيلَهُمْ ۚ إِنَّ ٱللَّهَ غَفُورٌ رَّحِيمٌ ٥

6. If one amongst the pagans ask you for asylum, grant it to him, so that he may hear the word of Allah; and then escort him to where he can be secure. That is because they are men without knowledge.

وَإِنْ أَحَدٌ مِّنَ ٱلْمُشْرِكِينَ ٱسْتَجَارَكَ فَأَجِرْهُ
حَتَّىٰ يَسْمَعَ كَلَٰمَ ٱللَّهِ ثُمَّ أَبْلِغْهُ مَأْمَنَهُۥ ۚ ذَٰلِكَ
بِأَنَّهُمْ قَوْمٌ لَّا يَعْلَمُونَ ٦

7. How can there be a league, before Allah and His messenger, with the pagans, except those with whom you made a treaty near the Sacred Mosque? As long as these stand true to you, stand you true to them: For Allah does love the righteous.

كَيْفَ يَكُونُ لِلْمُشْرِكِينَ عَهْدٌ عِندَ ٱللَّهِ وَعِندَ
رَسُولِهِۦٓ إِلَّا ٱلَّذِينَ عَٰهَدتُّمْ عِندَ ٱلْمَسْجِدِ
ٱلْحَرَامِ ۖ فَمَا ٱسْتَقَٰمُوا۟ لَكُمْ فَٱسْتَقِيمُوا۟ لَهُمْ ۚ
إِنَّ ٱللَّهَ يُحِبُّ ٱلْمُتَّقِينَ ٧

8. How (can there be such a league), seeing that if they get an advantage over you, they respect not in you the ties either of relationship or of covenant? With (fair words from) their mouths they entice you, but their hearts are averse from you; and most of them are rebellious and wicked.

كَيْفَ وَإِن يَظْهَرُوا۟ عَلَيْكُمْ لَا يَرْقُبُوا۟
فِيكُمْ إِلًّا وَلَا ذِمَّةً ۚ يُرْضُونَكُم بِأَفْوَٰهِهِمْ
وَتَأْبَىٰ قُلُوبُهُمْ وَأَكْثَرُهُمْ فَٰسِقُونَ ٨

9. The signs of Allah have they sold for a miserable price, and (many) have they hindered from His Way: evil indeed are the deeds they have done.

ٱشْتَرَوْا۟ بِـَٔايَٰتِ ٱللَّهِ ثَمَنًا قَلِيلًا فَصَدُّوا۟ عَن
سَبِيلِهِۦٓ ۚ إِنَّهُمْ سَآءَ مَا كَانُوا۟ يَعْمَلُونَ ٩

10. In a believer they respect not the ties either of relationship or of covenant! It is they who have transgressed all bounds.

لَا يَرْقُبُونَ فِى مُؤْمِنٍ إِلًّا وَلَا ذِمَّةً ۚ وَأُو۟لَٰٓئِكَ
هُمُ ٱلْمُعْتَدُونَ ١٠

11. But (even so), if they repent, establish regular prayers, and practice regular charity - they are your brothers in faith: (thus) do We explain the signs in detail, for those who understand.

فَإِن تَابُوا۟ وَأَقَامُوا۟ ٱلصَّلَوٰةَ وَءَاتَوُا۟ ٱلزَّكَوٰةَ
فَإِخْوَٰنُكُمْ فِى ٱلدِّينِ ۗ وَنُفَصِّلُ ٱلْءَايَٰتِ
لِقَوْمٍ يَعْلَمُونَ ١١

12. But if they violate their oaths after their covenant, and taunt you for your faith - fight you the chiefs of unfaith: for their oaths are nothing to them: that thus they may be restrained.

وَإِن نَّكَثُوٓا۟ أَيْمَٰنَهُم مِّنۢ بَعْدِ عَهْدِهِمْ
وَطَعَنُوا۟ فِى دِينِكُمْ فَقَٰتِلُوٓا۟ أَئِمَّةَ ٱلْكُفْرِ ۙ
إِنَّهُمْ لَآ أَيْمَٰنَ لَهُمْ لَعَلَّهُمْ يَنتَهُونَ ١٢

13. Will you not fight people who violated their oaths, plotted to expel the messenger, and took the aggressive by being the first (to assault) you? Do you fear them? Nay, it is Allah whom you should more justly fear, if you believe!

أَلَا تُقَٰتِلُونَ قَوْمًا نَّكَثُوٓا۟ أَيْمَٰنَهُمْ
وَهَمُّوا۟ بِإِخْرَاجِ ٱلرَّسُولِ وَهُم بَدَءُوكُمْ
أَوَّلَ مَرَّةٍ ۚ أَتَخْشَوْنَهُمْ ۚ فَٱللَّهُ أَحَقُّ أَن تَخْشَوْهُ
إِن كُنتُم مُّؤْمِنِينَ ١٣

14. Fight them, and Allah will punish them by your hands; cover them with shame; help you (to victory) over them, heal the breasts of believers,

قَٰتِلُوهُمْ يُعَذِّبْهُمُ ٱللَّهُ بِأَيْدِيكُمْ وَيُخْزِهِمْ
وَيَنصُرْكُمْ عَلَيْهِمْ وَيَشْفِ صُدُورَ قَوْمٍ مُّؤْمِنِينَ ١٤

15. And still the indignation of their hearts. For Allah will turn (in mercy) to whom He will; and Allah is All-Knowing, All-Wise.

وَيُذْهِبْ غَيْظَ قُلُوبِهِمْ ۗ وَيَتُوبُ ٱللَّهُ عَلَىٰ مَن
يَشَآءُ ۗ وَٱللَّهُ عَلِيمٌ حَكِيمٌ ﴿١٥﴾

16. Or do you think that you shall be abandoned, as though Allah did not know those among you who strive with might and main, and take none for friends and protectors except Allah, His messenger, and the (community of) believers? But Allah is well-acquainted with (all) that you do.

أَمْ حَسِبْتُمْ أَن تُتْرَكُوا۟ وَلَمَّا يَعْلَمِ ٱللَّهُ ٱلَّذِينَ جَٰهَدُوا۟
مِنكُمْ وَلَمْ يَتَّخِذُوا۟ مِن دُونِ ٱللَّهِ وَلَا رَسُولِهِۦ
وَلَا ٱلْمُؤْمِنِينَ وَلِيجَةً ۚ وَٱللَّهُ خَبِيرٌۢ بِمَا تَعْمَلُونَ ﴿١٦﴾

17. It is not for such as join gods with Allah, to visit or maintain the mosques of Allah while they witness against their own souls to infidelity. The works of such bear no fruit: in fire shall they dwell.

مَا كَانَ لِلْمُشْرِكِينَ أَن يَعْمُرُوا۟ مَسَٰجِدَ ٱللَّهِ شَٰهِدِينَ
عَلَىٰٓ أَنفُسِهِم بِٱلْكُفْرِ ۚ أُو۟لَٰٓئِكَ حَبِطَتْ
أَعْمَٰلُهُمْ وَفِى ٱلنَّارِ هُمْ خَٰلِدُونَ ﴿١٧﴾

18. The mosques of Allah shall be visited and maintained by such as believe in Allah and the last day, establish regular prayers, and practice regular charity, and fear none (at all) except Allah. It is they who are expected to be on true guidance.

إِنَّمَا يَعْمُرُ مَسَٰجِدَ ٱللَّهِ مَنْ ءَامَنَ بِٱللَّهِ وَٱلْيَوْمِ
ٱلْءَاخِرِ وَأَقَامَ ٱلصَّلَوٰةَ وَءَاتَى ٱلزَّكَوٰةَ وَلَمْ يَخْشَ إِلَّا
ٱللَّهَ ۖ فَعَسَىٰٓ أُو۟لَٰٓئِكَ أَن يَكُونُوا۟ مِنَ ٱلْمُهْتَدِينَ ﴿١٨﴾

19. Do you make the giving of drink to pilgrims, or the maintenance of the Sacred Mosque, equal to (the pious service of) those who believe in Allah and the last day, and strive with might and main in the cause of Allah? They are not comparable in the sight of Allah: and Allah guides not those who do wrong.

ثلاثة أرباع الحزب ١٩
۞ أَجَعَلْتُمْ سِقَايَةَ ٱلْحَآجِّ وَعِمَارَةَ ٱلْمَسْجِدِ
ٱلْحَرَامِ كَمَنْ ءَامَنَ بِٱللَّهِ وَٱلْيَوْمِ ٱلْءَاخِرِ وَجَٰهَدَ
فِى سَبِيلِ ٱللَّهِ ۚ لَا يَسْتَوُۥنَ عِندَ ٱللَّهِ ۗ وَٱللَّهُ لَا يَهْدِى
ٱلْقَوْمَ ٱلظَّٰلِمِينَ ﴿١٩﴾

20. Those who believe, and suffer exile and strive with might and main, in Allah's cause, with their goods and their persons, have the highest rank in the sight of Allah: They are the people who will achieve (salvation).

ٱلَّذِينَ ءَامَنُوا۟ وَهَاجَرُوا۟ وَجَٰهَدُوا۟ فِى سَبِيلِ ٱللَّهِ
بِأَمْوَٰلِهِمْ وَأَنفُسِهِمْ أَعْظَمُ دَرَجَةً عِندَ ٱللَّهِ ۚ
وَأُو۟لَٰٓئِكَ هُمُ ٱلْفَآئِزُونَ ﴿٢٠﴾

21. Their Lord does give them glad tidings of a mercy from Himself, of His good pleasure, and of gardens for them, in which are delights that endure:

يُبَشِّرُهُمْ رَبُّهُم بِرَحْمَةٍ مِّنْهُ وَرِضْوَٰنٍ وَجَنَّٰتٍ
لَّهُمْ فِيهَا نَعِيمٌ مُّقِيمٌ ٢١

22. They will dwell in it forever. Verily in Allah's presence is a reward, the greatest (of all).

خَٰلِدِينَ فِيهَآ أَبَدًا ۚ إِنَّ ٱللَّهَ عِندَهُۥٓ أَجْرٌ
عَظِيمٌ ٢٢

23. O you who believe! Take not for protectors your fathers and your brothers, if they love infidelity above faith: if any of you do so, they do wrong.

يَٰٓأَيُّهَا ٱلَّذِينَ ءَامَنُوا۟ لَا تَتَّخِذُوٓا۟ ءَابَآءَكُمْ
وَإِخْوَٰنَكُمْ أَوْلِيَآءَ إِنِ ٱسْتَحَبُّوا۟ ٱلْكُفْرَ
عَلَى ٱلْإِيمَٰنِ ۚ وَمَن يَتَوَلَّهُم مِّنكُمْ فَأُو۟لَٰٓئِكَ هُمُ
ٱلظَّٰلِمُونَ ٢٣

24. Say: If it be that your fathers, your sons, your brothers, your mates, or your relations; the wealth that you have gained; the commerce in which you fear a decline; or the dwellings in which you delight - are dearer to you than Allah, or His messenger, or the striving in His cause - then wait until Allah brings about His decision: and Allah guides not the rebellious.

قُلْ إِن كَانَ ءَابَآؤُكُمْ وَأَبْنَآؤُكُمْ وَإِخْوَٰنُكُمْ
وَأَزْوَٰجُكُمْ وَعَشِيرَتُكُمْ وَأَمْوَٰلٌ ٱقْتَرَفْتُمُوهَا
وَتِجَٰرَةٌ تَخْشَوْنَ كَسَادَهَا وَمَسَٰكِنُ
تَرْضَوْنَهَآ أَحَبَّ إِلَيْكُم مِّنَ ٱللَّهِ وَرَسُولِهِۦ
وَجِهَادٍ فِى سَبِيلِهِۦ فَتَرَبَّصُوا۟ حَتَّىٰ يَأْتِىَ ٱللَّهُ
بِأَمْرِهِۦ ۗ وَٱللَّهُ لَا يَهْدِى ٱلْقَوْمَ ٱلْفَٰسِقِينَ ٢٤

25. Assuredly Allah did help you in many battlefields and on the day of Hunayn: See! Your great numbers elated you, but they availed you nothing; the land, for all that it is wide, did constrain you, and you turned back in retreat.

لَقَدْ نَصَرَكُمُ ٱللَّهُ فِى مَوَاطِنَ كَثِيرَةٍ ۙ وَيَوْمَ
حُنَيْنٍ ۙ إِذْ أَعْجَبَتْكُمْ كَثْرَتُكُمْ فَلَمْ تُغْنِ
عَنكُمْ شَيْـًٔا وَضَاقَتْ عَلَيْكُمُ ٱلْأَرْضُ بِمَا
رَحُبَتْ ثُمَّ وَلَّيْتُم مُّدْبِرِينَ ٢٥

26. But Allah did pour His calm on the messenger and on the believers, and sent down forces which you saw not; He

ثُمَّ أَنزَلَ ٱللَّهُ سَكِينَتَهُۥ عَلَىٰ رَسُولِهِۦ وَعَلَى
ٱلْمُؤْمِنِينَ وَأَنزَلَ جُنُودًا لَّمْ تَرَوْهَا وَعَذَّبَ

punished the unbelievers: thus does He reward those without faith.

ٱلَّذِينَ كَفَرُوا۟ ۚ وَذَٰلِكَ جَزَآءُ ٱلْكَٰفِرِينَ ٢٦

27. Again will Allah, after this, turn (in mercy) to whom He will: for Allah is Oft-Forgiving, Most Merciful.

ثُمَّ يَتُوبُ ٱللَّهُ مِنۢ بَعْدِ ذَٰلِكَ عَلَىٰ مَن
يَشَآءُ ۗ وَٱللَّهُ غَفُورٌ رَّحِيمٌ ٢٧

28. O you who believe! Truly the pagans are unclean; so let them not, after this year of theirs, approach the Sacred Mosque. And if you fear poverty, soon will Allah enrich you, if He wills, out of His bounty, for Allah is All-Knowing, All-Wise.

يَٰٓأَيُّهَا ٱلَّذِينَ ءَامَنُوٓا۟ إِنَّمَا ٱلْمُشْرِكُونَ نَجَسٌ
فَلَا يَقْرَبُوا۟ ٱلْمَسْجِدَ ٱلْحَرَامَ بَعْدَ عَامِهِمْ
هَٰذَا ۚ وَإِنْ خِفْتُمْ عَيْلَةً فَسَوْفَ يُغْنِيكُمُ ٱللَّهُ
مِن فَضْلِهِۦٓ إِن شَآءَ ۚ إِنَّ ٱللَّهَ عَلِيمٌ حَكِيمٌ ٢٨

29. Fight those who believe not in Allah nor the last day, nor hold that forbidden which has been forbidden by Allah and His messenger, nor acknowledge the religion of truth, (even if they are) of the People of the Book, until they pay the *Jizyah* with willing submission, and feel themselves subdued.

قَٰتِلُوا۟ ٱلَّذِينَ لَا يُؤْمِنُونَ بِٱللَّهِ وَلَا بِٱلْيَوْمِ
ٱلْءَاخِرِ وَلَا يُحَرِّمُونَ مَا حَرَّمَ ٱللَّهُ وَرَسُولُهُۥ
وَلَا يَدِينُونَ دِينَ ٱلْحَقِّ مِنَ ٱلَّذِينَ أُوتُوا۟ ٱلْكِتَٰبَ
حَتَّىٰ يُعْطُوا۟ ٱلْجِزْيَةَ عَن يَدٍ وَهُمْ صَٰغِرُونَ ٢٩

30. The Jews call 'Uzayr a son of God, and the Christians call the Messiah the son of God. That is a saying from their mouths; (in this) they but imitate what the unbelievers of old used to say. Allah's curse be on them: how they are deluded away from the truth!

وَقَالَتِ ٱلْيَهُودُ عُزَيْرٌ ٱبْنُ ٱللَّهِ وَقَالَتِ
ٱلنَّصَٰرَى ٱلْمَسِيحُ ٱبْنُ ٱللَّهِ ۖ ذَٰلِكَ قَوْلُهُم
بِأَفْوَٰهِهِمْ ۖ يُضَٰهِـُٔونَ قَوْلَ ٱلَّذِينَ كَفَرُوا۟
مِن قَبْلُ ۚ قَٰتَلَهُمُ ٱللَّهُ ۚ أَنَّىٰ يُؤْفَكُونَ ٣٠

31. They take their priests and their anchorites to be their lords in derogation of Allah, and (they take as their Lord) the Messiah the son of Mary; Yet they were commanded to worship but One God: there is no god but He. Praise and glory to Him: (far is He) from having the partners they associate (with Him).

ٱتَّخَذُوٓا۟ أَحْبَارَهُمْ وَرُهْبَٰنَهُمْ أَرْبَابًا مِّن
دُونِ ٱللَّهِ وَٱلْمَسِيحَ ٱبْنَ مَرْيَمَ وَمَآ أُمِرُوٓا۟
إِلَّا لِيَعْبُدُوٓا۟ إِلَٰهًا وَٰحِدًا ۖ لَّآ إِلَٰهَ إِلَّا
هُوَ ۚ سُبْحَٰنَهُۥ عَمَّا يُشْرِكُونَ ٣١

32. They would like to extinguish Allah's light with their mouths, but Allah will not allow but that His light should be perfected, even though the unbelievers may detest (it).

يُرِيدُونَ أَن يُطْفِـُٔوا۟ نُورَ ٱللَّهِ بِأَفْوَٰهِهِمْ وَيَأْبَى
ٱللَّهُ إِلَّآ أَن يُتِمَّ نُورَهُۥ وَلَوْ كَرِهَ ٱلْكَٰفِرُونَ ﴿٣٢﴾

33. It is He Who has sent His messenger with guidance and religion of truth, to proclaim it over all religion, even though the pagans may detest (it).

هُوَ ٱلَّذِىٓ أَرْسَلَ رَسُولَهُۥ بِٱلْهُدَىٰ وَدِينِ
ٱلْحَقِّ لِيُظْهِرَهُۥ عَلَى ٱلدِّينِ كُلِّهِۦ وَلَوْ كَرِهَ
ٱلْمُشْرِكُونَ ﴿٣٣﴾

34. O you who believe! There are indeed many among the priests and anchorites, who in falsehood devour the substance of men and hinder (them) from the way of Allah. And there are those who bury gold and silver and spend it not in the way of Allah: announce to them a most grievous penalty -

حِزْب ٢٠ ۞ يَٰٓأَيُّهَا ٱلَّذِينَ ءَامَنُوٓا۟ إِنَّ كَثِيرًا مِّنَ ٱلْأَحْبَارِ
وَٱلرُّهْبَانِ لَيَأْكُلُونَ أَمْوَٰلَ ٱلنَّاسِ بِٱلْبَٰطِلِ
وَيَصُدُّونَ عَن سَبِيلِ ٱللَّهِ ۗ وَٱلَّذِينَ يَكْنِزُونَ
ٱلذَّهَبَ وَٱلْفِضَّةَ وَلَا يُنفِقُونَهَا فِى سَبِيلِ
ٱللَّهِ فَبَشِّرْهُم بِعَذَابٍ أَلِيمٍ ﴿٣٤﴾

35. On the day when heat will be produced out of that (wealth) in the fire of hell, and with it will be branded their foreheads, their flanks, and their backs - "This is the (treasure) which you buried for yourselves: taste you, then, the (treasures) you buried!"

يَوْمَ يُحْمَىٰ عَلَيْهَا فِى نَارِ جَهَنَّمَ فَتُكْوَىٰ بِهَا
جِبَاهُهُمْ وَجُنُوبُهُمْ وَظُهُورُهُمْ ۖ هَٰذَا مَا
كَنَزْتُمْ لِأَنفُسِكُمْ فَذُوقُوا۟ مَا كُنتُمْ
تَكْنِزُونَ ﴿٣٥﴾

36. The number of months in the sight of Allah is twelve (in a year) - so ordained by Him the day He created the heavens and the earth; of them four are sacred; that is the straight usage. So wrong not yourselves in it, and fight the pagans all together as they fight you all together. But know that Allah is with those who restrain themselves.

إِنَّ عِدَّةَ ٱلشُّهُورِ عِندَ ٱللَّهِ ٱثْنَا عَشَرَ شَهْرًا فِى
كِتَٰبِ ٱللَّهِ يَوْمَ خَلَقَ ٱلسَّمَٰوَٰتِ وَٱلْأَرْضَ مِنْهَآ
أَرْبَعَةٌ حُرُمٌ ۚ ذَٰلِكَ ٱلدِّينُ ٱلْقَيِّمُ ۚ فَلَا تَظْلِمُوا۟
فِيهِنَّ أَنفُسَكُمْ ۚ وَقَٰتِلُوا۟ ٱلْمُشْرِكِينَ
كَآفَّةً كَمَا يُقَٰتِلُونَكُمْ كَآفَّةً ۚ وَٱعْلَمُوٓا۟
أَنَّ ٱللَّهَ مَعَ ٱلْمُتَّقِينَ ﴿٣٦﴾

37. Verily the transposing (of a prohibited month) is an addition to unbelief: the unbelievers are led to wrong thereby; for they make it lawful one year, and forbidden another year, in order to adjust the number of months forbidden by Allah and make such forbidden ones lawful. The evil of their course seems pleasing to them. But Allah guides not those who reject faith.

إِنَّمَا ٱلنَّسِىٓءُ زِيَادَةٌ فِى ٱلْكُفْرِ ۖ يُضَلُّ بِهِ ٱلَّذِينَ
كَفَرُوا۟ يُحِلُّونَهُۥ عَامًا وَيُحَرِّمُونَهُۥ عَامًا
لِّيُوَاطِـُٔوا۟ عِدَّةَ مَا حَرَّمَ ٱللَّهُ فَيُحِلُّوا۟ مَا حَرَّمَ
ٱللَّهُ ۚ زُيِّنَ لَهُمْ سُوٓءُ أَعْمَٰلِهِمْ ۗ وَٱللَّهُ لَا يَهْدِى
ٱلْقَوْمَ ٱلْكَٰفِرِينَ ﴿٣٧﴾

38. O you who believe! What is the matter with you, that, when you are asked to go out in the cause of Allah, you cling heavily to the earth? Do you prefer the life of this world to the hereafter? But little is the comfort of this life, as compared with the hereafter.

يَٰٓأَيُّهَا ٱلَّذِينَ ءَامَنُوا۟ مَا لَكُمْ إِذَا قِيلَ
لَكُمُ ٱنفِرُوا۟ فِى سَبِيلِ ٱللَّهِ ٱثَّاقَلْتُمْ إِلَى
ٱلْأَرْضِ ۚ أَرَضِيتُم بِٱلْحَيَوٰةِ ٱلدُّنْيَا مِنَ ٱلْءَاخِرَةِ ۚ
فَمَا مَتَٰعُ ٱلْحَيَوٰةِ ٱلدُّنْيَا فِى ٱلْءَاخِرَةِ إِلَّا قَلِيلٌ ﴿٣٨﴾

39. Unless you go out, He will punish you with a grievous penalty, and put others in your place; but Him you would not harm in the least. For Allah has power over all things.

إِلَّا تَنفِرُوا۟ يُعَذِّبْكُمْ عَذَابًا أَلِيمًا
وَيَسْتَبْدِلْ قَوْمًا غَيْرَكُمْ وَلَا تَضُرُّوهُ
شَيْـًٔا ۗ وَٱللَّهُ عَلَىٰ كُلِّ شَىْءٍ قَدِيرٌ ﴿٣٩﴾

40. If you help not (your leader) (it is no matter): for Allah did indeed help him, when the unbelievers drove him out; he had no more than one companion; they two were in the Cave, and he said to his companion, "Have no fear for Allah is with us"; then Allah sent down His peace upon him, and strengthened him with forces which you saw not, and humbled to the depths the word of the unbelievers. But the word of Allah is exalted to the heights: for Allah is Exalted in Might, Wise.

إِلَّا تَنصُرُوهُ فَقَدْ نَصَرَهُ ٱللَّهُ إِذْ أَخْرَجَهُ
ٱلَّذِينَ كَفَرُوا۟ ثَانِىَ ٱثْنَيْنِ إِذْ هُمَا فِى ٱلْغَارِ
إِذْ يَقُولُ لِصَٰحِبِهِۦ لَا تَحْزَنْ إِنَّ ٱللَّهَ مَعَنَا ۖ
فَأَنزَلَ ٱللَّهُ سَكِينَتَهُۥ عَلَيْهِ وَأَيَّدَهُۥ بِجُنُودٍ
لَّمْ تَرَوْهَا وَجَعَلَ كَلِمَةَ ٱلَّذِينَ كَفَرُوا۟
ٱلسُّفْلَىٰ ۗ وَكَلِمَةُ ٱللَّهِ هِىَ ٱلْعُلْيَا ۗ وَٱللَّهُ
عَزِيزٌ حَكِيمٌ ﴿٤٠﴾

41. Go you out, (whether equipped) lightly or heavily, and strive and struggle,

ٱنفِرُوا۟ خِفَافًا وَثِقَالًا وَجَٰهِدُوا۟ بِأَمْوَٰلِكُمْ

with your goods and your persons, in the cause of Allah. That is best for you, if you (but) knew.

وَأَنفُسِكُمْ فِي سَبِيلِ ٱللَّهِ ذَٰلِكُمْ خَيْرٌ لَّكُمْ إِن
كُنتُمْ تَعْلَمُونَ ﴿٤١﴾

42. If there had been immediate gain (in sight), and the journey easy, they would (all) without doubt have followed you, but the distance was long, (and weighed) on them. They would indeed swear by Allah, "If we only could we should certainly have come out with you": they would destroy their own souls; for Allah does know that they are certainly lying.

لَوْ كَانَ عَرَضًا قَرِيبًا وَسَفَرًا قَاصِدًا لَّٱتَّبَعُوكَ
وَلَٰكِنۢ بَعُدَتْ عَلَيْهِمُ ٱلشُّقَّةُ وَسَيَحْلِفُونَ
بِٱللَّهِ لَوِ ٱسْتَطَعْنَا لَخَرَجْنَا مَعَكُمْ يُهْلِكُونَ
أَنفُسَهُمْ وَٱللَّهُ يَعْلَمُ إِنَّهُمْ لَكَٰذِبُونَ ﴿٤٢﴾

43. Allah give you grace! Why did you grant them exemption until those who told the truth were seen by you in a clear light, and you had proved the liars?

عَفَا ٱللَّهُ عَنكَ لِمَ أَذِنتَ لَهُمْ حَتَّىٰ يَتَبَيَّنَ لَكَ
ٱلَّذِينَ صَدَقُوا۟ وَتَعْلَمَ ٱلْكَٰذِبِينَ ﴿٤٣﴾

44. Those who believe in Allah and the last day ask you for no exemption from fighting with their goods and persons. And Allah knows well those who do their duty.

لَا يَسْتَـْٔذِنُكَ ٱلَّذِينَ يُؤْمِنُونَ بِٱللَّهِ وَٱلْيَوْمِ ٱلْـَٔاخِرِ
أَن يُجَٰهِدُوا۟ بِأَمْوَٰلِهِمْ وَأَنفُسِهِمْ ۗ وَٱللَّهُ عَلِيمٌۢ
بِٱلْمُتَّقِينَ ﴿٤٤﴾

45. Only those ask you for exemption who believe not in Allah and the last day, and whose hearts are in doubt, so that they are tossed in their doubts to and fro.

إِنَّمَا يَسْتَـْٔذِنُكَ ٱلَّذِينَ لَا يُؤْمِنُونَ بِٱللَّهِ وَٱلْيَوْمِ
ٱلْـَٔاخِرِ وَٱرْتَابَتْ قُلُوبُهُمْ فَهُمْ فِي رَيْبِهِمْ
يَتَرَدَّدُونَ ﴿٤٥﴾

46. If they had intended to come out, they would certainly have made some preparation for it; but Allah was averse to their being sent out; so He made them lag behind, and they were told, "sit you among those who sit (inactive)."

۞ وَلَوْ أَرَادُوا۟ ٱلْخُرُوجَ لَأَعَدُّوا۟ لَهُۥ عُدَّةً وَلَٰكِن كَرِهَ (ربع حزب ٢٠)
ٱللَّهُ ٱنۢبِعَاثَهُمْ فَثَبَّطَهُمْ وَقِيلَ ٱقْعُدُوا۟ مَعَ
ٱلْقَٰعِدِينَ ﴿٤٦﴾

47. If they had come out with you, they would not have added to your (strength) but only (made for) disorder, hurrying to and fro in your midst and sowing sedition among you,

لَوْ خَرَجُوا۟ فِيكُم مَّا زَادُوكُمْ إِلَّا خَبَالًا وَلَأَوْضَعُوا۟
خِلَٰلَكُمْ يَبْغُونَكُمُ ٱلْفِتْنَةَ وَفِيكُمْ سَمَّٰعُونَ

and there would have been some among you who would have listened to them. But Allah knows well those who do wrong.

لَهُمۡۗ وَٱللَّهُ عَلِيمُۢ بِٱلظَّٰلِمِينَ ٤٧

48. Indeed they had plotted sedition before, and upset matters for you - until the truth arrived, and the decree of Allah became manifest, much to their disgust.

لَقَدِ ٱبۡتَغَوُاْ ٱلۡفِتۡنَةَ مِن قَبۡلُ وَقَلَّبُواْ لَكَ
ٱلۡأُمُورَ حَتَّىٰ جَآءَ ٱلۡحَقُّ وَظَهَرَ أَمۡرُ ٱللَّهِ
وَهُمۡ كَٰرِهُونَ ٤٨

49. Among them is (many) a man who says: "Grant me exemption and draw me not into trial." Have they not fallen into trial already? And indeed hell surrounds the unbelievers (on all sides).

وَمِنۡهُم مَّن يَقُولُ ٱئۡذَن لِّي وَلَا تَفۡتِنِّيٓۚ أَلَا
فِي ٱلۡفِتۡنَةِ سَقَطُواْۗ وَإِنَّ جَهَنَّمَ لَمُحِيطَةُۢ
بِٱلۡكَٰفِرِينَ ٤٩

50. If good befalls you, it grieves them; but if a misfortune befalls you, they say, "We took indeed our precautions beforehand," and they turn away rejoicing.

إِن تُصِبۡكَ حَسَنَةٞ تَسُؤۡهُمۡۖ وَإِن تُصِبۡكَ
مُصِيبَةٞ يَقُولُواْ قَدۡ أَخَذۡنَآ أَمۡرَنَا مِن قَبۡلُ
وَيَتَوَلَّواْ وَّهُمۡ فَرِحُونَ ٥٠

51. Say: "Nothing will happen to us except what Allah has decreed for us; He is our protector": and on Allah let the believers put their trust.

قُل لَّن يُصِيبَنَآ إِلَّا مَا كَتَبَ ٱللَّهُ لَنَا هُوَ
مَوۡلَىٰنَاۚ وَعَلَى ٱللَّهِ فَلۡيَتَوَكَّلِ ٱلۡمُؤۡمِنُونَ ٥١

52. Say: "Can you expect for us (any fate) other than one of two glorious things - (martyrdom or victory)? But we can expect for you either that Allah will send His punishment from Himself, or by our hands. So wait (expectant); we too will wait with you."

قُلۡ هَلۡ تَرَبَّصُونَ بِنَآ إِلَّآ إِحۡدَى ٱلۡحُسۡنَيَيۡنِۖ وَنَحۡنُ
نَتَرَبَّصُ بِكُمۡ أَن يُصِيبَكُمُ ٱللَّهُ بِعَذَابٖ مِّنۡ
عِندِهِۦٓ أَوۡ بِأَيۡدِينَاۖ فَتَرَبَّصُوٓاْ إِنَّا مَعَكُم
مُّتَرَبِّصُونَ ٥٢

53. Say: "Spend (for the cause) willingly or unwillingly; not from you will it be accepted; for you are indeed a people rebellious and wicked."

قُلۡ أَنفِقُواْ طَوۡعًا أَوۡ كَرۡهٗا لَّن يُتَقَبَّلَ مِنكُمۡ
إِنَّكُمۡ كُنتُمۡ قَوۡمٗا فَٰسِقِينَ ٥٣

54. The only reasons why their contributions are not accepted are: that they reject Allah and His messenger; that they come to prayer without earnestness; and that they offer contributions unwillingly.

وَمَا مَنَعَهُمْ أَن تُقْبَلَ مِنْهُمْ نَفَقَٰتُهُمْ إِلَّآ
أَنَّهُمْ كَفَرُوا۟ بِٱللَّهِ وَبِرَسُولِهِۦ وَلَا يَأْتُونَ
ٱلصَّلَوٰةَ إِلَّا وَهُمْ كُسَالَىٰ وَلَا
يُنفِقُونَ إِلَّا وَهُمْ كَٰرِهُونَ ٥٤

55. Let not their wealth nor their (following in) sons dazzle you (O Muhammad): in reality Allah's plan is to punish them with these things in this life, and that their souls may perish in their (very) denial of Allah.

فَلَا تُعْجِبْكَ أَمْوَٰلُهُمْ وَلَآ أَوْلَٰدُهُمْ ۚ إِنَّمَا يُرِيدُ ٱللَّهُ
لِيُعَذِّبَهُم بِهَا فِى ٱلْحَيَوٰةِ ٱلدُّنْيَا وَتَزْهَقَ
أَنفُسُهُمْ وَهُمْ كَٰفِرُونَ ٥٥

56. They swear by Allah that they are indeed of you; but they are not of you; yet they are afraid (to appear in their true colours).

وَيَحْلِفُونَ بِٱللَّهِ إِنَّهُمْ لَمِنكُمْ وَمَا هُم مِّنكُمْ
وَلَٰكِنَّهُمْ قَوْمٌ يَفْرَقُونَ ٥٦

57. If they could find a place to flee to, or caves or a place of concealment, they would turn straightway to it, with an obstinate rush.

لَوْ يَجِدُونَ مَلْجَـًٔا أَوْ مَغَٰرَٰتٍ أَوْ مُدَّخَلًا لَّوَلَّوْا۟
إِلَيْهِ وَهُمْ يَجْمَحُونَ ٥٧

58. And among them are men who slander you in the matter of (the distribution of) the alms. If they are given part of it, they are pleased, but if not, see! They are indignant!

وَمِنْهُم مَّن يَلْمِزُكَ فِى ٱلصَّدَقَٰتِ فَإِنْ أُعْطُوا۟
مِنْهَا رَضُوا۟ وَإِن لَّمْ يُعْطَوْا۟ مِنْهَآ إِذَا هُمْ
يَسْخَطُونَ ٥٨

59. If only they had been content with what Allah and His messenger gave them, and had said, "Sufficient to us is Allah! Allah and His messenger will soon give us of His bounty: to Allah do we turn our hopes!" (That would have been the right course).

وَلَوْ أَنَّهُمْ رَضُوا۟ مَآ ءَاتَىٰهُمُ ٱللَّهُ وَرَسُولُهُۥ وَقَالُوا۟
حَسْبُنَا ٱللَّهُ سَيُؤْتِينَا ٱللَّهُ مِن فَضْلِهِۦ
وَرَسُولُهُۥٓ إِنَّآ إِلَى ٱللَّهِ رَٰغِبُونَ ٥٩

60. Alms are for the poor and the needy, and those employed to administer the

۞ إِنَّمَا ٱلصَّدَقَٰتُ لِلْفُقَرَآءِ وَٱلْمَسَٰكِينِ وَٱلْعَٰمِلِينَ

(funds); for those whose hearts have been (recently) reconciled (to the truth); for those in bondage and in debt; in the cause of Allah; and for the wayfarer: (thus is it) ordained by Allah, and Allah is full of knowledge and wisdom.

عَلَيْهَا وَٱلْمُؤَلَّفَةِ قُلُوبُهُمْ وَفِي ٱلرِّقَابِ
وَٱلْغَٰرِمِينَ وَفِي سَبِيلِ ٱللَّهِ وَٱبْنِ ٱلسَّبِيلِۖ
فَرِيضَةً مِّنَ ٱللَّهِۗ وَٱللَّهُ عَلِيمٌ حَكِيمٌ ﴿٦٠﴾

61. Among them are men who molest the prophet and say, "He is (all) ear." Say, "He listens to what is best for you; he believes in Allah, has faith in the believers and is a mercy to those of you who believe." But those who molest the messenger will have a grievous penalty.

وَمِنْهُمُ ٱلَّذِينَ يُؤْذُونَ ٱلنَّبِيَّ وَيَقُولُونَ هُوَ
أُذُنٌۚ قُلْ أُذُنُ خَيْرٍ لَّكُمْ يُؤْمِنُ بِٱللَّهِ وَيُؤْمِنُ
لِلْمُؤْمِنِينَ وَرَحْمَةٌ لِّلَّذِينَ ءَامَنُوا۟ مِنكُمْۚ
وَٱلَّذِينَ يُؤْذُونَ رَسُولَ ٱللَّهِ لَهُمْ عَذَابٌ أَلِيمٌ ﴿٦١﴾

62. To you they swear by Allah. In order to please you: but it is more fitting that they should please Allah and His messenger if they are believers.

يَحْلِفُونَ بِٱللَّهِ لَكُمْ لِيُرْضُوكُمْ وَٱللَّهُ وَرَسُولُهُۥٓ
أَحَقُّ أَن يُرْضُوهُ إِن كَانُوا۟ مُؤْمِنِينَ ﴿٦٢﴾

63. Do they not know that for those who oppose Allah and His messenger, is the fire of hell? - in which they shall dwell. That is the supreme disgrace.

أَلَمْ يَعْلَمُوٓا۟ أَنَّهُۥ مَن يُحَادِدِ ٱللَّهَ وَرَسُولَهُۥ فَأَنَّ
لَهُۥ نَارَ جَهَنَّمَ خَٰلِدًا فِيهَاۚ ذَٰلِكَ ٱلْخِزْىُ
ٱلْعَظِيمُ ﴿٦٣﴾

64. The hypocrites are afraid lest a Surah should be sent down about them, showing them, what is (really passing) in their hearts. Say: "Mock you! But verily Allah will bring to light all that you fear (should be revealed)."

يَحْذَرُ ٱلْمُنَٰفِقُونَ أَن تُنَزَّلَ عَلَيْهِمْ سُورَةٌ
تُنَبِّئُهُم بِمَا فِى قُلُوبِهِمْۚ قُلِ ٱسْتَهْزِءُوٓا۟ إِنَّ ٱللَّهَ
مُخْرِجٌ مَّا تَحْذَرُونَ ﴿٦٤﴾

65. If you do question them, they declare (with emphasis): "We were only talking idly and in play." Say: "Was it at Allah, and His signs, and His messenger, that you were mocking?"

وَلَئِن سَأَلْتَهُمْ لَيَقُولُنَّ إِنَّمَا كُنَّا نَخُوضُ
وَنَلْعَبُۚ قُلْ أَبِٱللَّهِ وَءَايَٰتِهِۦ وَرَسُولِهِۦ كُنتُمْ
تَسْتَهْزِءُونَ ﴿٦٥﴾

66. Make you no excuses: you have rejected faith after you had accepted it. If We pardon some of you, We will punish others amongst you, for that they are in sin.

لَا تَعْتَذِرُوا۟ قَدْ كَفَرْتُم بَعْدَ إِيمَـٰنِكُمْ ۚ إِن نَّعْفُ
عَن طَآئِفَةٍ مِّنكُمْ نُعَذِّبْ طَآئِفَةًۢ بِأَنَّهُمْ كَانُوا۟
مُجْرِمِينَ ﴿٦٦﴾

67. The hypocrites, men and women, (have an understanding) with each other: they enjoin evil, and forbid what is just, and are close with their hands. They have forgotten Allah; so He has forgotten them. Verily the hypocrites are rebellious and perverse.

ٱلْمُنَـٰفِقُونَ وَٱلْمُنَـٰفِقَـٰتُ بَعْضُهُم مِّنۢ بَعْضٍ ۚ
يَأْمُرُونَ بِٱلْمُنكَرِ وَيَنْهَوْنَ عَنِ ٱلْمَعْرُوفِ
وَيَقْبِضُونَ أَيْدِيَهُمْ ۚ نَسُوا۟ ٱللَّهَ فَنَسِيَهُمْ ۗ إِنَّ
ٱلْمُنَـٰفِقِينَ هُمُ ٱلْفَـٰسِقُونَ ﴿٦٧﴾

68. Allah has promised the hypocrites men and women, and the rejecters of faith, the fire of hell; in it shall they dwell; sufficient is it for them: for them is the curse of Allah, and an enduring punishment -

وَعَدَ ٱللَّهُ ٱلْمُنَـٰفِقِينَ وَٱلْمُنَـٰفِقَـٰتِ وَٱلْكُفَّارَ
نَارَ جَهَنَّمَ خَـٰلِدِينَ فِيهَا ۚ هِىَ حَسْبُهُمْ ۚ
وَلَعَنَهُمُ ٱللَّهُ ۖ وَلَهُمْ عَذَابٌ مُّقِيمٌ ﴿٦٨﴾

69. As in the case of those before you: they were mightier than you in power and more flourishing in wealth and children. They had their enjoyment of their portion; and you have of yours, as did those before you; and you indulge in idle talk as they did. They! - Their works are fruitless in this world and in the hereafter, and they will lose (all spiritual good).

كَٱلَّذِينَ مِن قَبْلِكُمْ كَانُوٓا۟ أَشَدَّ مِنكُمْ قُوَّةً
وَأَكْثَرَ أَمْوَٰلًا وَأَوْلَـٰدًا فَٱسْتَمْتَعُوا۟ بِخَلَـٰقِهِمْ
فَٱسْتَمْتَعْتُم بِخَلَـٰقِكُمْ كَمَا ٱسْتَمْتَعَ ٱلَّذِينَ
مِن قَبْلِكُم بِخَلَـٰقِهِمْ وَخُضْتُمْ كَٱلَّذِى خَاضُوٓا۟ ۚ
أُو۟لَـٰٓئِكَ حَبِطَتْ أَعْمَـٰلُهُمْ فِى ٱلدُّنْيَا وَٱلْـَٔاخِرَةِ ۖ
وَأُو۟لَـٰٓئِكَ هُمُ ٱلْخَـٰسِرُونَ ﴿٦٩﴾

70. Has not the story reached them of those before them? - The people of Noah, and 'Ad, and Thamud; the people of Abraham, the men of Madyan, and the cities overthrown. To them came their messengers with clear signs. It is not Allah who wrongs them, but they wrong their own souls.

أَلَمْ يَأْتِهِمْ نَبَأُ ٱلَّذِينَ مِن قَبْلِهِمْ قَوْمِ نُوحٍ وَعَادٍ
وَثَمُودَ وَقَوْمِ إِبْرَٰهِيمَ وَأَصْحَـٰبِ مَدْيَنَ
وَٱلْمُؤْتَفِكَـٰتِ ۚ أَتَتْهُمْ رُسُلُهُم بِٱلْبَيِّنَـٰتِ ۖ فَمَا
كَانَ ٱللَّهُ لِيَظْلِمَهُمْ وَلَـٰكِن كَانُوٓا۟
أَنفُسَهُمْ يَظْلِمُونَ ﴿٧٠﴾

71. The believers, men and women, are protectors, one of another: they enjoin what is just, and forbid what is evil: they observe regular prayers, practice regular charity, and obey Allah and His messenger. On them will Allah pour His mercy: for Allah is Exalted in Power, Wise.

وَٱلْمُؤْمِنُونَ وَٱلْمُؤْمِنَٰتُ بَعْضُهُمْ أَوْلِيَآءُ بَعْضٍ ۚ
يَأْمُرُونَ بِٱلْمَعْرُوفِ وَيَنْهَوْنَ عَنِ ٱلْمُنكَرِ
وَيُقِيمُونَ ٱلصَّلَوٰةَ وَيُؤْتُونَ ٱلزَّكَوٰةَ
وَيُطِيعُونَ ٱللَّهَ وَرَسُولَهُۥٓ ۚ أُو۟لَٰٓئِكَ سَيَرْحَمُهُمُ
ٱللَّهُ ۗ إِنَّ ٱللَّهَ عَزِيزٌ حَكِيمٌ ﴿٧١﴾

72. Allah has promised to believers - men and women - gardens under which rivers flow, to dwell in it, and beautiful mansions in gardens of everlasting bliss. But the greatest bliss is the good pleasure of Allah: that is the supreme felicity.

وَعَدَ ٱللَّهُ ٱلْمُؤْمِنِينَ وَٱلْمُؤْمِنَٰتِ جَنَّٰتٍ تَجْرِى
مِن تَحْتِهَا ٱلْأَنْهَٰرُ خَٰلِدِينَ فِيهَا وَمَسَٰكِنَ
طَيِّبَةً فِى جَنَّٰتِ عَدْنٍ ۚ وَرِضْوَٰنٌ مِّنَ ٱللَّهِ أَكْبَرُ ۚ
ذَٰلِكَ هُوَ ٱلْفَوْزُ ٱلْعَظِيمُ ﴿٧٢﴾

73. O Prophet! Strive hard against the unbelievers and the hypocrites, and be firm against them. Their abode is hell - an evil refuge indeed.

يَٰٓأَيُّهَا ٱلنَّبِىُّ جَٰهِدِ ٱلْكُفَّارَ وَٱلْمُنَٰفِقِينَ وَٱغْلُظْ
عَلَيْهِمْ ۚ وَمَأْوَىٰهُمْ جَهَنَّمُ ۖ وَبِئْسَ ٱلْمَصِيرُ ﴿٧٣﴾

74. They swear by Allah that they said nothing (evil), but indeed they uttered blasphemy, and they did it after accepting Islam; and they meditated a plot which they were unable to carry out; this revenge of theirs was (their) only return for the bounty with which Allah and His messenger had enriched them! If they repent, it will be best for them; but if they turn back (to their evil ways), Allah will punish them with a grievous penalty in this life and in the hereafter: they shall have none on earth to protect or help them.

يَحْلِفُونَ بِٱللَّهِ مَا قَالُوا۟ وَلَقَدْ قَالُوا۟ كَلِمَةَ ٱلْكُفْرِ
وَكَفَرُوا۟ بَعْدَ إِسْلَٰمِهِمْ وَهَمُّوا۟ بِمَا لَمْ يَنَالُوا۟ ۚ وَمَا
نَقَمُوٓا۟ إِلَّآ أَنْ أَغْنَىٰهُمُ ٱللَّهُ وَرَسُولُهُۥ مِن
فَضْلِهِۦ ۚ فَإِن يَتُوبُوا۟ يَكُ خَيْرًا لَّهُمْ ۖ وَإِن يَتَوَلَّوْا۟
يُعَذِّبْهُمُ ٱللَّهُ عَذَابًا أَلِيمًا فِى ٱلدُّنْيَا وَٱلْءَاخِرَةِ ۚ
وَمَا لَهُمْ فِى ٱلْأَرْضِ مِن وَلِىٍّ وَلَا نَصِيرٍ ﴿٧٤﴾

75. Amongst them are men who made a covenant with Allah, that if He bestowed on them of His bounty, they would give (largely) in charity, and be truly amongst those who are righteous.

ثلاثة أرباع الحزب ٢٠ ۞ وَمِنْهُم مَّنْ عَٰهَدَ ٱللَّهَ لَئِنْ ءَاتَىٰنَا مِن فَضْلِهِۦ
لَنَصَّدَّقَنَّ وَلَنَكُونَنَّ مِنَ ٱلصَّٰلِحِينَ ﴿٧٥﴾

76. But when He did bestow of His bounty, they became covetous, and turned back (from their covenant), averse (from its fulfilment).

فَلَمَّآ ءَاتَىٰهُم مِّن فَضْلِهِۦ بَخِلُوا۟ بِهِۦ وَتَوَلَّوا۟
وَّهُم مُّعْرِضُونَ ٧٦

77. So He has put as a consequence hypocrisy into their hearts, (to last) till the day on which they shall meet Him: because they broke their covenant with Allah, and because they lied (again and again).

فَأَعْقَبَهُمْ نِفَاقًا فِى قُلُوبِهِمْ إِلَىٰ يَوْمِ يَلْقَوْنَهُۥ بِمَآ
أَخْلَفُوا۟ ٱللَّهَ مَا وَعَدُوهُ وَبِمَا كَانُوا۟ يَكْذِبُونَ ٧٧

78. Do they not know that Allah does know their secret (thoughts) and their secret counsels, and that Allah knows well all things unseen?

أَلَمْ يَعْلَمُوٓا۟ أَنَّ ٱللَّهَ يَعْلَمُ سِرَّهُمْ وَنَجْوَىٰهُمْ
وَأَنَّ ٱللَّهَ عَلَّٰمُ ٱلْغُيُوبِ ٧٨

79. Those who slander such of the believers as give themselves freely to (deeds of) charity, as well as such as can find nothing to give except the fruits of their labour - and throw ridicule on them - Allah will throw back their ridicule on them; and they shall have a grievous penalty.

ٱلَّذِينَ يَلْمِزُونَ ٱلْمُطَّوِّعِينَ مِنَ ٱلْمُؤْمِنِينَ
فِى ٱلصَّدَقَٰتِ وَٱلَّذِينَ لَا يَجِدُونَ إِلَّا جُهْدَهُمْ
فَيَسْخَرُونَ مِنْهُمْ سَخِرَ ٱللَّهُ مِنْهُمْ وَلَهُمْ
عَذَابٌ أَلِيمٌ ٧٩

80. Whether you ask for their forgiveness, or not, (their sin is unforgivable); if you ask seventy times for their forgiveness, Allah will not forgive them; because they have rejected Allah and His messenger; and Allah guides not those who are perversely rebellious.

ٱسْتَغْفِرْ لَهُمْ أَوْ لَا تَسْتَغْفِرْ لَهُمْ إِن تَسْتَغْفِرْ لَهُمْ
سَبْعِينَ مَرَّةً فَلَن يَغْفِرَ ٱللَّهُ لَهُمْ ۚ ذَٰلِكَ بِأَنَّهُمْ
كَفَرُوا۟ بِٱللَّهِ وَرَسُولِهِۦ ۗ وَٱللَّهُ لَا يَهْدِى ٱلْقَوْمَ
ٱلْفَٰسِقِينَ ٨٠

81. Those who were left behind (in the Tabuk expedition) rejoiced in their inaction behind the back of the messenger of Allah; they hated to strive and fight, with their goods and their persons, in the cause of Allah; they said, "Do not go out in the heat." Say, "The fire of hell is fiercer in heat." If only they could understand!

فَرِحَ ٱلْمُخَلَّفُونَ بِمَقْعَدِهِمْ خِلَٰفَ رَسُولِ ٱللَّهِ وَكَرِهُوٓا۟
أَن يُجَٰهِدُوا۟ بِأَمْوَٰلِهِمْ وَأَنفُسِهِمْ فِى سَبِيلِ ٱللَّهِ
وَقَالُوا۟ لَا تَنفِرُوا۟ فِى ٱلْحَرِّ ۗ قُلْ نَارُ جَهَنَّمَ أَشَدُّ حَرًّا ۚ
لَّوْ كَانُوا۟ يَفْقَهُونَ ٨١

82. Let them laugh a little; much will they weep: a recompense for the (evil) that they do.

فَلْيَضْحَكُوا۟ قَلِيلًا وَلْيَبْكُوا۟ كَثِيرًا جَزَآءًۢ بِمَا كَانُوا۟
يَكْسِبُونَ ﴿٨٢﴾

83. If then, Allah brings you back to any of them, and they ask your permission to come out (with you), say: "Never shall you come out with me, nor fight an enemy with me; for you preferred to sit inactive on the first occasion; then sit you (now) with those who lag behind."

فَإِن رَّجَعَكَ ٱللَّهُ إِلَىٰ طَآئِفَةٍ مِّنْهُمْ فَٱسْتَـْٔذَنُوكَ
لِلْخُرُوجِ فَقُل لَّن تَخْرُجُوا۟ مَعِىَ أَبَدًا وَلَن تُقَـٰتِلُوا۟
مَعِىَ عَدُوًّا ۖ إِنَّكُمْ رَضِيتُم بِٱلْقُعُودِ أَوَّلَ مَرَّةٍ
فَٱقْعُدُوا۟ مَعَ ٱلْخَـٰلِفِينَ ﴿٨٣﴾

84. Nor do you (O Muhammad) ever pray for any of them that dies, nor stand at his grave: for they rejected Allah and His messenger, and died in a state of perverse rebellion.

وَلَا تُصَلِّ عَلَىٰٓ أَحَدٍ مِّنْهُم مَّاتَ أَبَدًا وَلَا تَقُمْ عَلَىٰ
قَبْرِهِۦٓ ۖ إِنَّهُمْ كَفَرُوا۟ بِٱللَّهِ وَرَسُولِهِۦ وَمَاتُوا۟ وَهُمْ
فَـٰسِقُونَ ﴿٨٤﴾

85. Nor let their wealth nor their (following in) sons dazzle you (O Muhammad): Allah's Plan is to punish them with these things in this world, and that their souls may perish in their (very) denial of Allah.

وَلَا تُعْجِبْكَ أَمْوَٰلُهُمْ وَأَوْلَـٰدُهُمْ ۚ إِنَّمَا يُرِيدُ ٱللَّهُ أَن
يُعَذِّبَهُم بِهَا فِى ٱلدُّنْيَا وَتَزْهَقَ أَنفُسُهُمْ وَهُمْ
كَـٰفِرُونَ ﴿٨٥﴾

86. When a Surah comes down, enjoining them to believe in Allah and to strive and fight along with His messenger, those with wealth and influence among them ask you for exemption, and say: "Leave us (behind); we would be with those who sit (at home)."

وَإِذَآ أُنزِلَتْ سُورَةٌ أَنْ ءَامِنُوا۟ بِٱللَّهِ وَجَـٰهِدُوا۟ مَعَ
رَسُولِهِ ٱسْتَـْٔذَنَكَ أُو۟لُوا۟ ٱلطَّوْلِ مِنْهُمْ وَقَالُوا۟ ذَرْنَا
نَكُن مَّعَ ٱلْقَـٰعِدِينَ ﴿٨٦﴾

87. They prefer to be with (the women), who remain behind (at home): their hearts are sealed and so they understand not.

رَضُوا۟ بِأَن يَكُونُوا۟ مَعَ ٱلْخَوَالِفِ وَطُبِعَ عَلَىٰ
قُلُوبِهِمْ فَهُمْ لَا يَفْقَهُونَ ﴿٨٧﴾

88. But the messenger, and those who believe with him, strive and fight with their wealth and their persons: for them are (all) good things; and it is they who will prosper.

لَـٰكِنِ ٱلرَّسُولُ وَٱلَّذِينَ ءَامَنُوا۟ مَعَهُۥ جَـٰهَدُوا۟
بِأَمْوَٰلِهِمْ وَأَنفُسِهِمْ ۚ وَأُو۟لَـٰٓئِكَ لَهُمُ ٱلْخَيْرَٰتُ ۖ
وَأُو۟لَـٰٓئِكَ هُمُ ٱلْمُفْلِحُونَ ﴿٨٨﴾

89. Allah has prepared for them gardens under which rivers flow, to dwell in it: that is the supreme felicity.

أَعَدَّ ٱللَّهُ لَهُمْ جَنَّٰتٍ تَجْرِى مِن تَحْتِهَا ٱلْأَنْهَٰرُ
خَٰلِدِينَ فِيهَا ۚ ذَٰلِكَ ٱلْفَوْزُ ٱلْعَظِيمُ ﴿٨٩﴾

90. And there were, among the desert Arabs (also), men who made excuses and came to claim exemption; and those who were false to Allah and His messenger (merely) sat inactive. Soon will a grievous penalty seize the unbelievers among them.

وَجَآءَ ٱلْمُعَذِّرُونَ مِنَ ٱلْأَعْرَابِ لِيُؤْذَنَ لَهُمْ
وَقَعَدَ ٱلَّذِينَ كَذَبُوا۟ ٱللَّهَ وَرَسُولَهُۥ ۚ سَيُصِيبُ
ٱلَّذِينَ كَفَرُوا۟ مِنْهُمْ عَذَابٌ أَلِيمٌ ﴿٩٠﴾

91. There is no blame on those who are infirm, or ill, or who find no resources to spend (on the cause), if they are sincere (in duty) to Allah and His messenger; no ground (of complaint) can there be against such as do right; and Allah is Oft-Forgiving, Most Merciful.

لَّيْسَ عَلَى ٱلضُّعَفَآءِ وَلَا عَلَى ٱلْمَرْضَىٰ وَلَا عَلَى ٱلَّذِينَ
لَا يَجِدُونَ مَا يُنفِقُونَ حَرَجٌ إِذَا نَصَحُوا۟ لِلَّهِ
وَرَسُولِهِۦ ۚ مَا عَلَى ٱلْمُحْسِنِينَ مِن سَبِيلٍ ۚ
وَٱللَّهُ غَفُورٌ رَّحِيمٌ ﴿٩١﴾

92. Nor (is there blame) on those who came to you to be provided with mounts, and when you said, "I can find no mounts for you," they turned back, their eyes streaming with tears of grief that they had no resources with which to provide the expenses.

وَلَا عَلَى ٱلَّذِينَ إِذَا مَآ أَتَوْكَ لِتَحْمِلَهُمْ قُلْتَ
لَآ أَجِدُ مَآ أَحْمِلُكُمْ عَلَيْهِ تَوَلَّوا۟ وَّأَعْيُنُهُمْ
تَفِيضُ مِنَ ٱلدَّمْعِ حَزَنًا أَلَّا يَجِدُوا۟ مَا يُنفِقُونَ ﴿٩٢﴾

*93. The ground (of complaint) is against such as claim exemption while they are rich. They prefer to stay with the (women) who remain behind: Allah has sealed their hearts; so they know not (what they miss).

*إِنَّمَا ٱلسَّبِيلُ عَلَى ٱلَّذِينَ يَسْتَـْٔذِنُونَكَ وَهُمْ الجزء ١١ الحزب ٢١
أَغْنِيَآءُ ۚ رَضُوا۟ بِأَن يَكُونُوا۟ مَعَ ٱلْخَوَالِفِ وَطَبَعَ
ٱللَّهُ عَلَىٰ قُلُوبِهِمْ فَهُمْ لَا يَعْلَمُونَ ﴿٩٣﴾

94. They will present their excuses to you when you return to them. Say you: "Present no excuses: we shall not believe you: Allah has already informed us of the true state of matters concerning you; it is your actions that Allah and His messenger will observe; in the end will you

يَعْتَذِرُونَ إِلَيْكُمْ إِذَا رَجَعْتُمْ إِلَيْهِمْ ۚ قُل
لَّا تَعْتَذِرُوا۟ لَن نُّؤْمِنَ لَكُمْ قَدْ نَبَّأَنَا ٱللَّهُ مِنْ
أَخْبَارِكُمْ ۚ وَسَيَرَى ٱللَّهُ عَمَلَكُمْ وَرَسُولُهُۥ

* Part-11

be brought back to Him who knows what is hidden and what is open: then will He show you the truth of all that you did."

ثُمَّ تُرَدُّونَ إِلَىٰ عَٰلِمِ ٱلْغَيْبِ وَٱلشَّهَٰدَةِ فَيُنَبِّئُكُم بِمَا
كُنتُمْ تَعْمَلُونَ ﴿٩٤﴾

95. They will swear to you by Allah, when you return to them, that you may leave them alone. So leave them alone: for they are an abomination, and hell is their dwelling place - a fitting recompense for the (evil) that they did.

سَيَحْلِفُونَ بِٱللَّهِ لَكُمْ إِذَا ٱنقَلَبْتُمْ إِلَيْهِمْ
لِتُعْرِضُوا۟ عَنْهُمْ ۖ فَأَعْرِضُوا۟ عَنْهُمْ ۖ إِنَّهُمْ رِجْسٌ ۖ
وَمَأْوَىٰهُمْ جَهَنَّمُ جَزَآءًۢ بِمَا كَانُوا۟
يَكْسِبُونَ ﴿٩٥﴾

96. They will swear to you, that you may be pleased with them. But if you are pleased with them, Allah is not pleased with those who disobey.

يَحْلِفُونَ لَكُمْ لِتَرْضَوْا۟ عَنْهُمْ ۖ فَإِن تَرْضَوْا۟
عَنْهُمْ فَإِنَّ ٱللَّهَ لَا يَرْضَىٰ عَنِ ٱلْقَوْمِ ٱلْفَٰسِقِينَ ﴿٩٦﴾

97. The Arabs of the desert are the worst in unbelief and hypocrisy, and most fitted to be in ignorance of the command which Allah has sent down to His messenger: but Allah is All-Knowing, All-Wise.

ٱلْأَعْرَابُ أَشَدُّ كُفْرًا وَنِفَاقًا وَأَجْدَرُ أَلَّا يَعْلَمُوا۟
حُدُودَ مَآ أَنزَلَ ٱللَّهُ عَلَىٰ رَسُولِهِۦ ۗ وَٱللَّهُ عَلِيمٌ
حَكِيمٌ ﴿٩٧﴾

98. Some of the desert Arabs look upon their payments as a fine, and watch for disasters for you: on them be the disaster of evil; for Allah is He that hears and knows (all things).

وَمِنَ ٱلْأَعْرَابِ مَن يَتَّخِذُ مَا يُنفِقُ مَغْرَمًا
وَيَتَرَبَّصُ بِكُمُ ٱلدَّوَآئِرَ ۚ عَلَيْهِمْ دَآئِرَةُ ٱلسَّوْءِ ۗ
وَٱللَّهُ سَمِيعٌ عَلِيمٌ ﴿٩٨﴾

99. But some of the desert Arabs believe in Allah and the last day, and look on their payments as pious gifts bringing them nearer to Allah and obtaining the prayers of the messenger. Yes, indeed they bring them nearer (to Him); soon will Allah admit them to His mercy: for Allah is Oft-Forgiving, Most Merciful.

وَمِنَ ٱلْأَعْرَابِ مَن يُؤْمِنُ بِٱللَّهِ وَٱلْيَوْمِ ٱلْءَاخِرِ
وَيَتَّخِذُ مَا يُنفِقُ قُرُبَٰتٍ عِندَ ٱللَّهِ وَصَلَوَٰتِ
ٱلرَّسُولِ ۚ أَلَآ إِنَّهَا قُرْبَةٌ لَّهُمْ ۚ سَيُدْخِلُهُمُ ٱللَّهُ
فِى رَحْمَتِهِۦٓ ۗ إِنَّ ٱللَّهَ غَفُورٌ رَّحِيمٌ ﴿٩٩﴾

100. The vanguard (of Islam) - the first of those who forsook (their homes) and of those who gave them aid, and (also) those who follow them in (all) good deeds - well-pleased is Allah with them, as are they with Him: for them has He prepared gardens under which rivers flow, to dwell in it for ever: that is the supreme felicity.

وَٱلسَّٰبِقُونَ ٱلْأَوَّلُونَ مِنَ ٱلْمُهَٰجِرِينَ وَٱلْأَنصَارِ
وَٱلَّذِينَ ٱتَّبَعُوهُم بِإِحْسَٰنٍ رَّضِيَ ٱللَّهُ عَنْهُمْ
وَرَضُوا۟ عَنْهُ وَأَعَدَّ لَهُمْ جَنَّٰتٍ تَجْرِى تَحْتَهَا
ٱلْأَنْهَٰرُ خَٰلِدِينَ فِيهَآ أَبَدًا ۚ ذَٰلِكَ ٱلْفَوْزُ
ٱلْعَظِيمُ ﴿١٠٠﴾

101. Certain of the desert Arabs round about you are hypocrites, as well as (desert Arabs) among the Madinah folk: they are obstinate in hypocrisy; you do not know them; We know them; twice shall We punish them: and in addition shall they be sent to a grievous penalty.

وَمِمَّنْ حَوْلَكُم مِّنَ ٱلْأَعْرَابِ مُنَٰفِقُونَ ۖ وَمِنْ
أَهْلِ ٱلْمَدِينَةِ مَرَدُوا۟ عَلَى ٱلنِّفَاقِ لَا تَعْلَمُهُمْ ۖ
نَحْنُ نَعْلَمُهُمْ ۚ سَنُعَذِّبُهُم مَّرَّتَيْنِ ثُمَّ يُرَدُّونَ
إِلَىٰ عَذَابٍ عَظِيمٍ ﴿١٠١﴾

102. Others (there are who) have acknowledged their wrongdoings: they have mixed an act that was good with another that was evil. Perhaps Allah will turn to them (in mercy): for Allah is Oft-Forgiving, Most Merciful.

وَءَاخَرُونَ ٱعْتَرَفُوا۟ بِذُنُوبِهِمْ خَلَطُوا۟ عَمَلًا صَٰلِحًا
وَءَاخَرَ سَيِّئًا عَسَى ٱللَّهُ أَن يَتُوبَ عَلَيْهِمْ ۚ إِنَّ ٱللَّهَ
غَفُورٌ رَّحِيمٌ ﴿١٠٢﴾

103. Of their goods take alms, so that you might purify and sanctify them; and pray on their behalf, verily your prayers are a source of security for them: and Allah is One who hears and knows.

خُذْ مِنْ أَمْوَٰلِهِمْ صَدَقَةً تُطَهِّرُهُمْ وَتُزَكِّيهِم بِهَا وَصَلِّ
عَلَيْهِمْ ۖ إِنَّ صَلَوٰتَكَ سَكَنٌ لَّهُمْ ۗ وَٱللَّهُ سَمِيعٌ عَلِيمٌ ﴿١٠٣﴾

104. Do they not know that Allah does accept repentance from His supporters and receives their gifts of charity, and that Allah is verily He, the Oft-Returning, Most Merciful?

أَلَمْ يَعْلَمُوٓا۟ أَنَّ ٱللَّهَ هُوَ يَقْبَلُ ٱلتَّوْبَةَ عَنْ عِبَادِهِۦ
وَيَأْخُذُ ٱلصَّدَقَٰتِ وَأَنَّ ٱللَّهَ هُوَ ٱلتَّوَّابُ ٱلرَّحِيمُ ﴿١٠٤﴾

105. And say: "Work (righteousness): soon will Allah observe your work, and His messenger, and the believers: soon will you be brought back to the Knower of what

وَقُلِ ٱعْمَلُوا۟ فَسَيَرَى ٱللَّهُ عَمَلَكُمْ وَرَسُولُهُۥ
وَٱلْمُؤْمِنُونَ ۖ وَسَتُرَدُّونَ إِلَىٰ عَٰلِمِ ٱلْغَيْبِ وَٱلشَّهَٰدَةِ

is hidden and what is open: then will He show you the truth of all that you did."

فَيُنَبِّئُكُم بِمَا كُنتُمْ تَعْمَلُونَ ١٠٥

106. There are (yet) others, held in suspense for the command of Allah, whether He will punish them, or turn in mercy to them: and Allah is All-Knowing, Wise.

وَءَاخَرُونَ مُرْجَوْنَ لِأَمْرِ ٱللَّهِ إِمَّا يُعَذِّبُهُمْ وَإِمَّا
يَتُوبُ عَلَيْهِمْ ۗ وَٱللَّهُ عَلِيمٌ حَكِيمٌ ١٠٦

107. And there are those who put up a mosque by way of mischief and infidelity - to disunite the believers - and in preparation for one who warred against Allah and His messenger before. They will indeed swear that their intention is nothing but good; but Allah does declare that they are certainly liars.

وَٱلَّذِينَ ٱتَّخَذُوا۟ مَسْجِدًا ضِرَارًا وَكُفْرًا
وَتَفْرِيقًۢا بَيْنَ ٱلْمُؤْمِنِينَ وَإِرْصَادًا لِّمَنْ حَارَبَ
ٱللَّهَ وَرَسُولَهُۥ مِن قَبْلُ ۚ وَلَيَحْلِفُنَّ إِنْ أَرَدْنَآ إِلَّا
ٱلْحُسْنَىٰ ۖ وَٱللَّهُ يَشْهَدُ إِنَّهُمْ لَكَٰذِبُونَ ١٠٧

108. Never stand you up in it. There is a mosque whose foundation was laid from the first day on piety; it is more worthy of you standing up (for prayer) in it. In it are men who love to be purified; and Allah loves those who make themselves pure.

لَا تَقُمْ فِيهِ أَبَدًا ۚ لَّمَسْجِدٌ أُسِّسَ عَلَى ٱلتَّقْوَىٰ مِنْ أَوَّلِ
يَوْمٍ أَحَقُّ أَن تَقُومَ فِيهِ ۚ فِيهِ رِجَالٌ يُحِبُّونَ أَن
يَتَطَهَّرُوا۟ ۚ وَٱللَّهُ يُحِبُّ ٱلْمُطَّهِّرِينَ ١٠٨

109. Which then is best? - he that lays his foundation on piety to Allah and His good pleasure? - or he that lays his foundation on an undermined sand cliff ready to crumble to pieces? And it does crumble to pieces with him, into the fire of hell. And Allah guides not people that do wrong.

أَفَمَنْ أَسَّسَ بُنْيَٰنَهُۥ عَلَىٰ تَقْوَىٰ مِنَ ٱللَّهِ وَرِضْوَٰنٍ
خَيْرٌ أَم مَّنْ أَسَّسَ بُنْيَٰنَهُۥ عَلَىٰ شَفَا جُرُفٍ هَارٍ
فَٱنْهَارَ بِهِۦ فِى نَارِ جَهَنَّمَ ۗ وَٱللَّهُ لَا يَهْدِى ٱلْقَوْمَ
ٱلظَّٰلِمِينَ ١٠٩

110. The foundation of those who so build is never free from suspicion and shakiness in their hearts, until their hearts are cut to pieces. And Allah is All-Knowing, Wise.

لَا يَزَالُ بُنْيَٰنُهُمُ ٱلَّذِى بَنَوْا۟ رِيبَةً فِى قُلُوبِهِمْ إِلَّآ
أَن تَقَطَّعَ قُلُوبُهُمْ ۗ وَٱللَّهُ عَلِيمٌ حَكِيمٌ ١١٠

111. Allah has purchased of the believers their persons and their goods; for theirs (in return) is the garden (of paradise): they fight in His cause, and slay and are slain: a

ربع الحزب ٢١
۞ إِنَّ ٱللَّهَ ٱشْتَرَىٰ مِنَ ٱلْمُؤْمِنِينَ أَنفُسَهُمْ
وَأَمْوَٰلَهُم بِأَنَّ لَهُمُ ٱلْجَنَّةَ ۚ يُقَٰتِلُونَ فِى سَبِيلِ

ٱللَّهِ فَيَقۡتُلُونَ وَيُقۡتَلُونَۖ وَعۡدًا عَلَيۡهِ حَقّٗا
فِي ٱلتَّوۡرَىٰةِ وَٱلۡإِنجِيلِ وَٱلۡقُرۡءَانِۚ وَمَنۡ أَوۡفَىٰ
بِعَهۡدِهِۦ مِنَ ٱللَّهِۚ فَٱسۡتَبۡشِرُواْ بِبَيۡعِكُمُ ٱلَّذِي
بَايَعۡتُم بِهِۦۚ وَذَٰلِكَ هُوَ ٱلۡفَوۡزُ ٱلۡعَظِيمُ ١١١

promise binding on Him in truth, through the law, the Gospel, and the Qur'an: and who is more faithful to his covenant than Allah? Then rejoice in the bargain which you have concluded: that is the achievement supreme.

ٱلتَّٰٓئِبُونَ ٱلۡعَٰبِدُونَ ٱلۡحَٰمِدُونَ
ٱلسَّٰٓئِحُونَ ٱلرَّٰكِعُونَ ٱلسَّٰجِدُونَ
ٱلۡأٓمِرُونَ بِٱلۡمَعۡرُوفِ وَٱلنَّاهُونَ عَنِ
ٱلۡمُنكَرِ وَٱلۡحَٰفِظُونَ لِحُدُودِ ٱللَّهِۗ
وَبَشِّرِ ٱلۡمُؤۡمِنِينَ ١١٢

112. Those that turn (to Allah) in repentance; that serve Him, and praise Him; that wander in devotion to the cause of Allah; that bow down and prostrate themselves in prayer; that enjoin good and forbid evil; and observe the limits set by Allah - (these do rejoice). So proclaim the glad tidings to the believers.

مَا كَانَ لِلنَّبِيِّ وَٱلَّذِينَ ءَامَنُوٓاْ أَن يَسۡتَغۡفِرُواْ
لِلۡمُشۡرِكِينَ وَلَوۡ كَانُوٓاْ أُوْلِي قُرۡبَىٰ مِنۢ بَعۡدِ
مَا تَبَيَّنَ لَهُمۡ أَنَّهُمۡ أَصۡحَٰبُ ٱلۡجَحِيمِ ١١٣

113. It is not fitting, for the prophet and those who believe that they should pray for forgiveness for pagans, even though they be of kin, after it is clear to them that they are companions of the fire.

وَمَا كَانَ ٱسۡتِغۡفَارُ إِبۡرَٰهِيمَ لِأَبِيهِ إِلَّا عَن
مَّوۡعِدَةٖ وَعَدَهَآ إِيَّاهُ فَلَمَّا تَبَيَّنَ لَهُۥٓ أَنَّهُۥ عَدُوّٞ
لِّلَّهِ تَبَرَّأَ مِنۡهُۚ إِنَّ إِبۡرَٰهِيمَ لَأَوَّٰهٌ حَلِيمٞ ١١٤

114. And Abraham prayed for his father's forgiveness only because of a promise he had made to him. But when it became clear to him that he was an enemy to Allah, he dissociated himself from him: for Abraham was most tender-hearted, forbearing.

وَمَا كَانَ ٱللَّهُ لِيُضِلَّ قَوۡمَۢا بَعۡدَ إِذۡ هَدَىٰهُمۡ
حَتَّىٰ يُبَيِّنَ لَهُم مَّا يَتَّقُونَۚ إِنَّ ٱللَّهَ بِكُلِّ شَيۡءٍ
عَلِيمٌ ١١٥

115. And Allah will not mislead a people after He has guided them, in order that He may make clear to them what to fear (and avoid) - for Allah has knowledge of all things.

إِنَّ ٱللَّهَ لَهُۥ مُلۡكُ ٱلسَّمَٰوَٰتِ وَٱلۡأَرۡضِۖ يُحۡيِۦ
وَيُمِيتُۚ وَمَا لَكُم مِّن دُونِ ٱللَّهِ مِن وَلِيّٖ وَلَا
نَصِيرٖ ١١٦

116. To Allah belongs the dominion of the heavens and the earth. He gives life and He takes it. Except for Him you have no protector nor helper.

117. Allah turned with favour to the prophet, the Muhajirs, and the Ansar - who followed him in a time of distress, after that the hearts of a part of them had nearly swerved (from duty); but He turned to them (also); for He is to them Most Kind, Most Merciful.

لَّقَد تَّابَ ٱللَّهُ عَلَى ٱلنَّبِيِّ وَٱلْمُهَٰجِرِينَ وَٱلْأَنصَارِ
ٱلَّذِينَ ٱتَّبَعُوهُ فِي سَاعَةِ ٱلْعُسْرَةِ مِنۢ بَعْدِ مَا
كَادَ يَزِيغُ قُلُوبُ فَرِيقٖ مِّنْهُمْ ثُمَّ تَابَ عَلَيْهِمْۚ
إِنَّهُۥ بِهِمْ رَءُوفٞ رَّحِيمٞ ١١٧

118. (He turned in mercy also) to the three who were left behind; (they felt guilty) to such a degree that the earth seemed constrained to them, for all its spaciousness, and their (very) souls seemed straitened to them - and they perceived that there is no fleeing from Allah (and no refuge) but to Himself. Then He turned to them, that they might repent: for Allah is Oft-Returning, Most Merciful.

وَعَلَى ٱلثَّلَٰثَةِ ٱلَّذِينَ خُلِّفُواْ حَتَّىٰٓ إِذَا ضَاقَتْ
عَلَيْهِمُ ٱلْأَرْضُ بِمَا رَحُبَتْ وَضَاقَتْ عَلَيْهِمْ
أَنفُسُهُمْ وَظَنُّوٓاْ أَن لَّا مَلْجَأَ مِنَ ٱللَّهِ إِلَّآ إِلَيْهِ
ثُمَّ تَابَ عَلَيْهِمْ لِيَتُوبُوٓاْۚ إِنَّ ٱللَّهَ هُوَ ٱلتَّوَّابُ
ٱلرَّحِيمُ ١١٨

119. O you who believe! Fear Allah and be with those who are true (in word and deed).

يَٰٓأَيُّهَا ٱلَّذِينَ ءَامَنُواْ ٱتَّقُواْ ٱللَّهَ وَكُونُواْ مَعَ
ٱلصَّٰدِقِينَ ١١٩

120. It was not fitting for the people of Madinah and the Bedouin Arabs of the neighbourhood, to refuse to follow Allah's messenger, nor to prefer their own lives to his; because nothing could they suffer or do, but was reckoned to their credit as a deed of righteousness - whether they suffered thirst, or fatigue or hunger, in the cause of Allah, or trod paths to raise the ire of the unbelievers, or received any injury whatever from an enemy: for Allah suffers not the reward to be lost of those who do good -

مَا كَانَ لِأَهْلِ ٱلْمَدِينَةِ وَمَنْ حَوْلَهُم مِّنَ
ٱلْأَعْرَابِ أَن يَتَخَلَّفُواْ عَن رَّسُولِ ٱللَّهِ وَلَا
يَرْغَبُواْ بِأَنفُسِهِمْ عَن نَّفْسِهِۦۚ ذَٰلِكَ بِأَنَّهُمْ
لَا يُصِيبُهُمْ ظَمَأٞ وَلَا نَصَبٞ وَلَا مَخْمَصَةٞ فِي
سَبِيلِ ٱللَّهِ وَلَا يَطَـُٔونَ مَوْطِئٗا يَغِيظُ ٱلْكُفَّارَ
وَلَا يَنَالُونَ مِنْ عَدُوّٖ نَّيْلًا إِلَّا كُتِبَ لَهُم بِهِۦ
عَمَلٞ صَٰلِحٌۚ إِنَّ ٱللَّهَ لَا يُضِيعُ أَجْرَ ٱلْمُحْسِنِينَ ١٢٠

121. Nor could they spend anything (for the cause) - small or great - nor cut across a valley, but the deed is inscribed to their

وَلَا يُنفِقُونَ نَفَقَةٗ صَغِيرَةٗ وَلَا كَبِيرَةٗ وَلَا
يَقْطَعُونَ وَادِيًا إِلَّا كُتِبَ لَهُمْ لِيَجْزِيَهُمُ ٱللَّهُ

credit; that Allah might repay their deed with the best (possible reward).

أَحۡسَنَ مَا كَانُواْ يَعۡمَلُونَ ١٢١

نصف الحزب ٢١

122. Nor should the believers all go forth together: if a contingent from every expedition remained behind, they could devote themselves to studies in religion, and admonish the people when they return to them - that thus they (may learn) to guard themselves (against evil).

۞وَمَا كَانَ ٱلۡمُؤۡمِنُونَ لِيَنفِرُواْ كَآفَّةٗۚ
فَلَوۡلَا نَفَرَ مِن كُلِّ فِرۡقَةٖ مِّنۡهُمۡ طَآئِفَةٞ لِّيَتَفَقَّهُواْ
فِي ٱلدِّينِ وَلِيُنذِرُواْ قَوۡمَهُمۡ إِذَا رَجَعُوٓاْ إِلَيۡهِمۡ
لَعَلَّهُمۡ يَحۡذَرُونَ ١٢٢

123. O you who believe! Fight the unbelievers who surround you, and let them find firmness in you; and know that Allah is with those who fear Him.

يَٰٓأَيُّهَا ٱلَّذِينَ ءَامَنُواْ قَٰتِلُواْ ٱلَّذِينَ يَلُونَكُم مِّنَ
ٱلۡكُفَّارِ وَلۡيَجِدُواْ فِيكُمۡ غِلۡظَةٗۚ وَٱعۡلَمُوٓاْ
أَنَّ ٱللَّهَ مَعَ ٱلۡمُتَّقِينَ ١٢٣

124. Whenever there comes down a Surah, some of them say: "Which of you has had his faith increased by it?" Yea, those who believe - their faith is increased, and they do rejoice.

وَإِذَا مَآ أُنزِلَتۡ سُورَةٞ فَمِنۡهُم مَّن يَقُولُ أَيُّكُمۡ
زَادَتۡهُ هَٰذِهِۦٓ إِيمَٰنٗاۚ فَأَمَّا ٱلَّذِينَ ءَامَنُواْ
فَزَادَتۡهُمۡ إِيمَٰنٗا وَهُمۡ يَسۡتَبۡشِرُونَ ١٢٤

125. But those in whose hearts is a disease - it will add doubt to their doubt, and they will die in a state of unbelief.

وَأَمَّا ٱلَّذِينَ فِي قُلُوبِهِم مَّرَضٞ فَزَادَتۡهُمۡ رِجۡسًا إِلَىٰ
رِجۡسِهِمۡ وَمَاتُواْ وَهُمۡ كَٰفِرُونَ ١٢٥

126. Do they not see that they are tried every year once or twice? Yet they turn not in repentance, and they take no heed.

أَوَلَا يَرَوۡنَ أَنَّهُمۡ يُفۡتَنُونَ فِي كُلِّ عَامٖ
مَّرَّةً أَوۡ مَرَّتَيۡنِ ثُمَّ لَا يَتُوبُونَ وَلَا هُمۡ
يَذَّكَّرُونَ ١٢٦

127. Whenever there comes down a Surah, they look at each other, (saying) "Does anyone see you?" Then they turn aside: Allah has turned their hearts (from the light); for they are a people that understand not.

وَإِذَا مَآ أُنزِلَتۡ سُورَةٞ نَّظَرَ بَعۡضُهُمۡ إِلَىٰ بَعۡضٍ
هَلۡ يَرَىٰكُم مِّنۡ أَحَدٖ ثُمَّ ٱنصَرَفُواْۚ صَرَفَ
ٱللَّهُ قُلُوبَهُم بِأَنَّهُمۡ قَوۡمٞ لَّا يَفۡقَهُونَ ١٢٧

128. Now has come to you a messenger from amongst yourselves; it grieves him that you should perish; ardently anxious is he over you; to the believers is he most kind and merciful.

لَقَدْ جَآءَكُمْ رَسُولٌ مِّنْ أَنفُسِكُمْ عَزِيزٌ
عَلَيْهِ مَا عَنِتُّمْ حَرِيصٌ عَلَيْكُم
بِٱلْمُؤْمِنِينَ رَءُوفٌ رَّحِيمٌ ١٢٨

129. But if they turn away say: "Allah suffices me: There is no god but He: On Him is my trust - He is the Lord of the throne (of glory) supreme!

فَإِن تَوَلَّوْا۟ فَقُلْ حَسْبِىَ ٱللَّهُ لَآ إِلَٰهَ إِلَّا هُوَ ۖ عَلَيْهِ
تَوَكَّلْتُ ۖ وَهُوَ رَبُّ ٱلْعَرْشِ ٱلْعَظِيمِ ١٢٩

سُورَةُ يُونُسَ

Surah 10: ***Yunus*** **(Jonah)**

In the name of Allah,
Most Gracious, Most Merciful.

بِسْمِ ٱللَّهِ ٱلرَّحْمَٰنِ ٱلرَّحِيمِ

1. *Alif Lam Ra*. These are the Ayat of the book of wisdom.

الٓر ۚ تِلْكَ ءَايَٰتُ ٱلْكِتَٰبِ ٱلْحَكِيمِ ١

2. It is a matter of wonderment to men that We have sent Our inspiration to a man from among themselves - that he should warn mankind (of their danger), and give the good news to the believers that they have before their Lord the lofty rank of truth. (But) say the unbelievers: "This is indeed an evident sorcerer!"

أَكَانَ لِلنَّاسِ عَجَبًا أَنْ أَوْحَيْنَآ إِلَىٰ رَجُلٍ مِّنْهُمْ أَنْ
أَنذِرِ ٱلنَّاسَ وَبَشِّرِ ٱلَّذِينَ ءَامَنُوٓا۟ أَنَّ لَهُمْ قَدَمَ
صِدْقٍ عِندَ رَبِّهِمْ ۗ قَالَ ٱلْكَٰفِرُونَ إِنَّ هَٰذَا
لَسَٰحِرٌ مُّبِينٌ ٢

3. Verily your Lord is Allah, Who created the heavens and the earth in six Days, and He established Himself on the throne (of authority), regulating and governing all things. No intercessor (can plead with Him) except after His leave (has been obtained). This is Allah your Lord; Him therefore serve you: will you not receive admonition?

إِنَّ رَبَّكُمُ ٱللَّهُ ٱلَّذِى خَلَقَ ٱلسَّمَٰوَٰتِ وَٱلْأَرْضَ فِى
سِتَّةِ أَيَّامٍ ثُمَّ ٱسْتَوَىٰ عَلَى ٱلْعَرْشِ ۖ يُدَبِّرُ ٱلْأَمْرَ ۖ
مَا مِن شَفِيعٍ إِلَّا مِنۢ بَعْدِ إِذْنِهِۦ ۚ ذَٰلِكُمُ ٱللَّهُ رَبُّكُمْ
فَٱعْبُدُوهُ ۚ أَفَلَا تَذَكَّرُونَ ٣

4. To Him will be your return - of all of you. The promise of Allah is true and sure. It is He Who begins the process of creation, and repeats it, that He may reward with justice those who believe and work righteousness; but those who reject Him will have draughts of boiling fluids, and a penalty grievous, because they did reject Him.

إِلَيۡهِ مَرۡجِعُكُمۡ جَمِيعٗاۖ وَعۡدَ ٱللَّهِ حَقًّاۚ إِنَّهُۥ يَبۡدَؤُاْ
ٱلۡخَلۡقَ ثُمَّ يُعِيدُهُۥ لِيَجۡزِيَ ٱلَّذِينَ ءَامَنُواْ وَعَمِلُواْ
ٱلصَّٰلِحَٰتِ بِٱلۡقِسۡطِۚ وَٱلَّذِينَ كَفَرُواْ لَهُمۡ شَرَابٞ
مِّنۡ حَمِيمٖ وَعَذَابٌ أَلِيمُۢ بِمَا كَانُواْ يَكۡفُرُونَ ٤

5. It is He Who made the sun to be a shining glory and the moon to be a light (of beauty), and measured out stages for it: that you might know the number of years and the count (of time). No way did Allah create this but in truth and righteousness. (Thus) does He explain His signs in detail, for those who understand.

هُوَ ٱلَّذِي جَعَلَ ٱلشَّمۡسَ ضِيَآءٗ وَٱلۡقَمَرَ نُورٗا وَقَدَّرَهُۥ
مَنَازِلَ لِتَعۡلَمُواْ عَدَدَ ٱلسِّنِينَ وَٱلۡحِسَابَۚ
مَا خَلَقَ ٱللَّهُ ذَٰلِكَ إِلَّا بِٱلۡحَقِّۚ يُفَصِّلُ ٱلۡأٓيَٰتِ
لِقَوۡمٖ يَعۡلَمُونَ ٥

6. Verily, in the alternation of the night and the day, and in all that Allah has created, in the heavens and the earth, are signs for those who fear Him.

إِنَّ فِي ٱخۡتِلَٰفِ ٱلَّيۡلِ وَٱلنَّهَارِ وَمَا خَلَقَ ٱللَّهُ فِي
ٱلسَّمَٰوَٰتِ وَٱلۡأَرۡضِ لَأٓيَٰتٖ لِّقَوۡمٖ يَتَّقُونَ ٦

7. Those who rest not their hope on their meeting with Us, but are pleased and satisfied with the life of the present, and those who heed not Our signs -

إِنَّ ٱلَّذِينَ لَا يَرۡجُونَ لِقَآءَنَا وَرَضُواْ بِٱلۡحَيَوٰةِ ٱلدُّنۡيَا
وَٱطۡمَأَنُّواْ بِهَا وَٱلَّذِينَ هُمۡ عَنۡ ءَايَٰتِنَا غَٰفِلُونَ ٧

8. Their abode is the fire, because of the (evil) they earned.

أُوْلَٰٓئِكَ مَأۡوَىٰهُمُ ٱلنَّارُ بِمَا كَانُواْ يَكۡسِبُونَ ٨

9. Those who believe, and work righteousness - their Lord will guide them because of their faith: beneath them will flow rivers in gardens of bliss.

إِنَّ ٱلَّذِينَ ءَامَنُواْ وَعَمِلُواْ ٱلصَّٰلِحَٰتِ يَهۡدِيهِمۡ
رَبُّهُم بِإِيمَٰنِهِمۡۖ تَجۡرِي مِن تَحۡتِهِمُ ٱلۡأَنۡهَٰرُ فِي
جَنَّٰتِ ٱلنَّعِيمِ ٩

10. (This will be) their call in it: "Glory to You, O Allah!" and "Peace" will be their greeting in it! And the close of their call

دَعۡوَىٰهُمۡ فِيهَا سُبۡحَٰنَكَ ٱللَّهُمَّ وَتَحِيَّتُهُمۡ
فِيهَا سَلَٰمٞۚ وَءَاخِرُ دَعۡوَىٰهُمۡ أَنِ ٱلۡحَمۡدُ لِلَّهِ

will be: "Praise be to Allah, the Cherisher and Sustainer of the Worlds!"

رَبِّ ٱلۡعَٰلَمِينَ ١٠

11. If Allah were to hasten for men the ill (they have earned) as they would fain hasten on the good - then would their respite be settled at once. But We leave those who rest not their hope of their meeting with Us, in their trespasses, wandering in distraction to and fro.

ثلاثة أرباع الحزب ٢١

۞ وَلَوۡ يُعَجِّلُ ٱللَّهُ لِلنَّاسِ ٱلشَّرَّ ٱسۡتِعۡجَالَهُم
بِٱلۡخَيۡرِ لَقُضِيَ إِلَيۡهِمۡ أَجَلُهُمۡۖ فَنَذَرُ ٱلَّذِينَ
لَا يَرۡجُونَ لِقَآءَنَا فِي طُغۡيَٰنِهِمۡ يَعۡمَهُونَ ١١

12. When trouble touches a man, he calls to Us (in all postures) - lying down on his side, or sitting, or standing. But when We have solved his trouble, he passes on his way as if he had never called to Us for a trouble that touched him! Thus do the deeds of transgressors seem fair in their eyes!

وَإِذَا مَسَّ ٱلۡإِنسَٰنَ ٱلضُّرُّ دَعَانَا لِجَنۢبِهِۦٓ أَوۡ قَاعِدًا
أَوۡ قَآئِمٗا فَلَمَّا كَشَفۡنَا عَنۡهُ ضُرَّهُۥ مَرَّ كَأَن لَّمۡ
يَدۡعُنَآ إِلَىٰ ضُرّٖ مَّسَّهُۥۚ كَذَٰلِكَ زُيِّنَ لِلۡمُسۡرِفِينَ
مَا كَانُواْ يَعۡمَلُونَ ١٢

13. Generations before you We destroyed when they did wrong: their messengers came to them with clear signs, but they would not believe! Thus do We requite those who sin!

وَلَقَدۡ أَهۡلَكۡنَا ٱلۡقُرُونَ مِن قَبۡلِكُمۡ لَمَّا ظَلَمُواْ
وَجَآءَتۡهُمۡ رُسُلُهُم بِٱلۡبَيِّنَٰتِ وَمَا كَانُواْ لِيُؤۡمِنُواْۚ
كَذَٰلِكَ نَجۡزِي ٱلۡقَوۡمَ ٱلۡمُجۡرِمِينَ ١٣

14. Then We made you heirs in the land after them, to see how you would behave!

ثُمَّ جَعَلۡنَٰكُمۡ خَلَٰٓئِفَ فِي ٱلۡأَرۡضِ مِنۢ بَعۡدِهِمۡ
لِنَنظُرَ كَيۡفَ تَعۡمَلُونَ ١٤

15. But when Our clear signs are rehearsed to them, those who rest not their hope on their meeting with Us, say: "Bring us a reading other than this, or change this." Say: "It is not for me, of my own accord, to change it: I follow nothing but what is revealed to me: if I were to disobey my Lord, I should myself fear the penalty of a great day (to come)."

وَإِذَا تُتۡلَىٰ عَلَيۡهِمۡ ءَايَاتُنَا بَيِّنَٰتٖ قَالَ ٱلَّذِينَ
لَا يَرۡجُونَ لِقَآءَنَا ٱئۡتِ بِقُرۡءَانٍ غَيۡرِ هَٰذَآ أَوۡ
بَدِّلۡهُۚ قُلۡ مَا يَكُونُ لِيٓ أَنۡ أُبَدِّلَهُۥ مِن تِلۡقَآيِٕ
نَفۡسِيٓۖ إِنۡ أَتَّبِعُ إِلَّا مَا يُوحَىٰٓ إِلَيَّۖ إِنِّيٓ أَخَافُ إِنۡ
عَصَيۡتُ رَبِّي عَذَابَ يَوۡمٍ عَظِيمٖ ١٥

16. Say: "If Allah had so willed, I should not have rehearsed it to you, or would He have made it known to you. A whole lifetime before this have I stayed amongst you: will you not then understand?"

قُل لَّوۡ شَآءَ ٱللَّهُ مَا تَلَوۡتُهُۥ عَلَيۡكُمۡ وَلَآ
أَدۡرَىٰكُم بِهِۦۖ فَقَدۡ لَبِثۡتُ فِيكُمۡ عُمُرٗا
مِّن قَبۡلِهِۦٓۚ أَفَلَا تَعۡقِلُونَ ١٦

17. Who does more wrong than such as forge a lie against Allah, or deny His signs? But never will prosper those who sin.

فَمَنۡ أَظۡلَمُ مِمَّنِ ٱفۡتَرَىٰ عَلَى ٱللَّهِ كَذِبًا أَوۡ كَذَّبَ
بِـَٔايَٰتِهِۦٓۚ إِنَّهُۥ لَا يُفۡلِحُ ٱلۡمُجۡرِمُونَ ١٧

18. They serve, besides Allah, things that hurt them not nor profit them, and they say: "These are our intercessors with Allah." Say: "Do you indeed inform Allah of something He knows not, in the heavens or on earth? - Glory to Him! And far is He above the partners they ascribe (to Him)!"

وَيَعۡبُدُونَ مِن دُونِ ٱللَّهِ مَا لَا يَضُرُّهُمۡ وَلَا
يَنفَعُهُمۡ وَيَقُولُونَ هَٰٓؤُلَآءِ شُفَعَٰٓؤُنَا عِندَ ٱللَّهِۚ
قُلۡ أَتُنَبِّـُٔونَ ٱللَّهَ بِمَا لَا يَعۡلَمُ فِي ٱلسَّمَٰوَٰتِ
وَلَا فِي ٱلۡأَرۡضِۚ سُبۡحَٰنَهُۥ وَتَعَٰلَىٰ عَمَّا
يُشۡرِكُونَ ١٨

19. Mankind was but one nation, but differed (later). Had it not been for a word that went before from your Lord, their differences would have been settled between them.

وَمَا كَانَ ٱلنَّاسُ إِلَّآ أُمَّةٗ وَٰحِدَةٗ فَٱخۡتَلَفُواْۚ
وَلَوۡلَا كَلِمَةٞ سَبَقَتۡ مِن رَّبِّكَ لَقُضِيَ بَيۡنَهُمۡ
فِيمَا فِيهِ يَخۡتَلِفُونَ ١٩

20. They say: "Why is not a sign sent down to him from his Lord?" Say: "The unseen is only for Allah (to know). Then wait you: I too will wait with you."

وَيَقُولُونَ لَوۡلَآ أُنزِلَ عَلَيۡهِ ءَايَةٞ مِّن رَّبِّهِۦۖ
فَقُلۡ إِنَّمَا ٱلۡغَيۡبُ لِلَّهِ فَٱنتَظِرُوٓاْ إِنِّي مَعَكُم
مِّنَ ٱلۡمُنتَظِرِينَ ٢٠

21. When We make mankind taste of some mercy after adversity has touched them, see! They take to plotting against Our signs! Say: "Swifter to plan is Allah!" Verily Our messengers record all the plots that you make!

وَإِذَآ أَذَقۡنَا ٱلنَّاسَ رَحۡمَةٗ مِّنۢ بَعۡدِ ضَرَّآءَ مَسَّتۡهُمۡ إِذَا
لَهُم مَّكۡرٞ فِيٓ ءَايَاتِنَاۚ قُلِ ٱللَّهُ أَسۡرَعُ مَكۡرًاۚ إِنَّ رُسُلَنَا
يَكۡتُبُونَ مَا تَمۡكُرُونَ ٢١

22. He it is Who enables you to traverse through land and sea; so that you even board ships - they sail with them with a favourable wind, and they rejoice thereat; then comes a stormy wind and the waves come to them from all sides, and they think they are being overwhelmed; they call to Allah, sincerely offering (their) duty to Him, saying "If You do deliver us from this, we shall truly show our gratitude!"

هُوَ ٱلَّذِى يُسَيِّرُكُمْ فِى ٱلْبَرِّ وَٱلْبَحْرِ ۖ حَتَّىٰٓ إِذَا كُنتُمْ فِى
ٱلْفُلْكِ وَجَرَيْنَ بِهِم بِرِيحٍ طَيِّبَةٍ وَفَرِحُوا۟ بِهَا
جَآءَتْهَا رِيحٌ عَاصِفٌ وَجَآءَهُمُ ٱلْمَوْجُ مِن كُلِّ
مَكَانٍ وَظَنُّوٓا۟ أَنَّهُمْ أُحِيطَ بِهِمْ ۙ دَعَوُا۟ ٱللَّهَ
مُخْلِصِينَ لَهُ ٱلدِّينَ لَئِنْ أَنجَيْتَنَا مِنْ هَٰذِهِۦ لَنَكُونَنَّ
مِنَ ٱلشَّٰكِرِينَ ﴿٢٢﴾

23. But when He delivers them, see! They transgress insolently through the earth in defiance of right! O mankind! Your insolence is against your own souls - an enjoyment of the life of the present; in the end, to Us is your return, and We shall show you the truth of all that you did.

فَلَمَّآ أَنجَىٰهُمْ إِذَا هُمْ يَبْغُونَ فِى ٱلْأَرْضِ بِغَيْرِ ٱلْحَقِّ ۗ
يَٰٓأَيُّهَا ٱلنَّاسُ إِنَّمَا بَغْيُكُمْ عَلَىٰٓ أَنفُسِكُم ۖ مَّتَٰعَ
ٱلْحَيَوٰةِ ٱلدُّنْيَا ۖ ثُمَّ إِلَيْنَا مَرْجِعُكُمْ فَنُنَبِّئُكُم
بِمَا كُنتُمْ تَعْمَلُونَ ﴿٢٣﴾

24. The likeness of the life of the present is as the rain which We send down from the skies; by its mingling arises the produce of the earth - which provides food for men and animals; (it grows) till the earth is clad with its golden ornaments and is decked out (in beauty); the people to whom it belongs think they have all powers of disposal over it; there reaches it Our command by night or by day, and We make it like a harvest clean-mown, as if it had not flourished only the day before! Thus do We explain the signs in detail for those who reflect.

إِنَّمَا مَثَلُ ٱلْحَيَوٰةِ ٱلدُّنْيَا كَمَآءٍ أَنزَلْنَٰهُ مِنَ ٱلسَّمَآءِ
فَٱخْتَلَطَ بِهِۦ نَبَاتُ ٱلْأَرْضِ مِمَّا يَأْكُلُ ٱلنَّاسُ
وَٱلْأَنْعَٰمُ حَتَّىٰٓ إِذَآ أَخَذَتِ ٱلْأَرْضُ زُخْرُفَهَا
وَٱزَّيَّنَتْ وَظَنَّ أَهْلُهَآ أَنَّهُمْ قَٰدِرُونَ عَلَيْهَآ أَتَىٰهَآ
أَمْرُنَا لَيْلًا أَوْ نَهَارًا فَجَعَلْنَٰهَا حَصِيدًا كَأَن لَّمْ تَغْنَ
بِٱلْأَمْسِ ۚ كَذَٰلِكَ نُفَصِّلُ ٱلْءَايَٰتِ لِقَوْمٍ يَتَفَكَّرُونَ ﴿٢٤﴾

25. But Allah does call to the home of Peace: He does guide whom He pleases to a way that is straight.

وَٱللَّهُ يَدْعُوٓا۟ إِلَىٰ دَارِ ٱلسَّلَٰمِ وَيَهْدِى مَن يَشَآءُ
إِلَىٰ صِرَٰطٍ مُّسْتَقِيمٍ ﴿٢٥﴾

26. To those who do right is a goodly (reward) - yea, more (than in measure)!

الحزب ٢٢ * لِّلَّذِينَ أَحْسَنُوا۟ ٱلْحُسْنَىٰ وَزِيَادَةٌ ۖ وَلَا يَرْهَقُ

No darkness nor shame shall cover their faces! They are companions of the garden; they will remain in it (forever)!

وُجُوهَهُمْ قَتَرٌ وَلَا ذِلَّةٌ ۚ أُولَٰئِكَ أَصْحَابُ الْجَنَّةِ ۖ هُمْ
فِيهَا خَالِدُونَ ﴿٢٦﴾

27. But those who have earned evil will have a reward of like evil; disgrace will cover their (faces); no defender will they have from (the wrath of) Allah; their faces will be covered, as it were, with pieces from the depth of the darkness of night; they are companions of the fire; they will remain in it (forever)!

وَالَّذِينَ كَسَبُوا السَّيِّئَاتِ جَزَاءُ سَيِّئَةٍ بِمِثْلِهَا
وَتَرْهَقُهُمْ ذِلَّةٌ ۖ مَا لَهُمْ مِنَ اللَّهِ مِنْ عَاصِمٍ ۖ كَأَنَّمَا
أُغْشِيَتْ وُجُوهُهُمْ قِطَعًا مِنَ اللَّيْلِ مُظْلِمًا ۚ أُولَٰئِكَ
أَصْحَابُ النَّارِ ۖ هُمْ فِيهَا خَالِدُونَ ﴿٢٧﴾

28. One day shall We gather them all together. Then shall We say to those who joined gods (with Us): "To your place! You and those you joined as 'partners.'" We shall separate them, and their 'partners' shall say: "It was not us that you worshipped!"

وَيَوْمَ نَحْشُرُهُمْ جَمِيعًا ثُمَّ نَقُولُ لِلَّذِينَ أَشْرَكُوا مَكَانَكُمْ
أَنْتُمْ وَشُرَكَاؤُكُمْ ۚ فَزَيَّلْنَا بَيْنَهُمْ ۖ وَقَالَ شُرَكَاؤُهُمْ مَا
كُنْتُمْ إِيَّانَا تَعْبُدُونَ ﴿٢٨﴾

29. "Enough is Allah for a witness between us and you: we certainly knew nothing of your worship of us!"

فَكَفَىٰ بِاللَّهِ شَهِيدًا بَيْنَنَا وَبَيْنَكُمْ إِنْ كُنَّا عَنْ
عِبَادَتِكُمْ لَغَافِلِينَ ﴿٢٩﴾

30. There will every soul prove (the fruits of) the deeds it sent before: they will be brought back to Allah their rightful Lord, and their invented falsehoods will leave them in the lurch.

هُنَالِكَ تَبْلُو كُلُّ نَفْسٍ مَا أَسْلَفَتْ ۚ وَرُدُّوا إِلَى
اللَّهِ مَوْلَاهُمُ الْحَقِّ ۖ وَضَلَّ عَنْهُمْ مَا كَانُوا يَفْتَرُونَ ﴿٣٠﴾

31. Say: "Who is it that sustains you (in life) from the sky and from the earth? Or who is it that has power over hearing and sight? And who is it that brings out the living from the dead and the dead from the living? And who is it that rules and regulates all affairs?" They will soon say, "Allah." Say, "Will you not then show piety (to Him)?"

قُلْ مَنْ يَرْزُقُكُمْ مِنَ السَّمَاءِ وَالْأَرْضِ أَمَّنْ يَمْلِكُ
السَّمْعَ وَالْأَبْصَارَ وَمَنْ يُخْرِجُ الْحَيَّ مِنَ الْمَيِّتِ
وَيُخْرِجُ الْمَيِّتَ مِنَ الْحَيِّ وَمَنْ يُدَبِّرُ الْأَمْرَ ۚ
فَسَيَقُولُونَ اللَّهُ ۚ فَقُلْ أَفَلَا تَتَّقُونَ ﴿٣١﴾

32. Such is Allah, your real Cherisher and Sustainer: apart from truth, what (remains) but error? How then are you turned away?

فَذَٰلِكُمُ ٱللَّهُ رَبُّكُمُ ٱلْحَقُّ ۖ فَمَاذَا بَعْدَ ٱلْحَقِّ إِلَّا
ٱلضَّلَٰلُ ۖ فَأَنَّىٰ تُصْرَفُونَ ﴿٣٢﴾

33. Thus is the word of your Lord proved true against those who rebel; verily they will not believe.

كَذَٰلِكَ حَقَّتْ كَلِمَتُ رَبِّكَ عَلَى ٱلَّذِينَ فَسَقُوٓا۟
أَنَّهُمْ لَا يُؤْمِنُونَ ﴿٣٣﴾

34. Say: "Of your 'partners', can any originate creation and repeat it?" Say: "It is Allah Who originates creation and repeats it: then how are you deluded away (from the truth)?"

قُلْ هَلْ مِن شُرَكَآئِكُم مَّن يَبْدَؤُا۟ ٱلْخَلْقَ ثُمَّ يُعِيدُهُۥ ۚ
قُلِ ٱللَّهُ يَبْدَؤُا۟ ٱلْخَلْقَ ثُمَّ يُعِيدُهُۥ ۖ فَأَنَّىٰ تُؤْفَكُونَ ﴿٣٤﴾

35. Say: "Of your 'partners' is there any that can give any guidance towards truth?" Say: "It is Allah Who gives guidance towards truth. Is then He Who gives guidance to truth more worthy to be followed, or he who finds not guidance (himself) unless he is guided? What then is the matter with you? How do you judge?"

قُلْ هَلْ مِن شُرَكَآئِكُم مَّن يَهْدِىٓ إِلَى ٱلْحَقِّ ۚ قُلِ ٱللَّهُ يَهْدِى
لِلْحَقِّ ۗ أَفَمَن يَهْدِىٓ إِلَى ٱلْحَقِّ أَحَقُّ أَن يُتَّبَعَ أَمَّن
لَّا يَهِدِّىٓ إِلَّآ أَن يُهْدَىٰ ۖ فَمَا لَكُمْ كَيْفَ تَحْكُمُونَ ﴿٣٥﴾

36. But most of them follow nothing but fancy: truly fancy can be of no benefit against truth. Verily Allah is well aware of all that they do.

وَمَا يَتَّبِعُ أَكْثَرُهُمْ إِلَّا ظَنًّا ۚ إِنَّ ٱلظَّنَّ لَا يُغْنِى مِنَ
ٱلْحَقِّ شَيْـًٔا ۚ إِنَّ ٱللَّهَ عَلِيمٌۢ بِمَا يَفْعَلُونَ ﴿٣٦﴾

37. This Qur'an is not such as can be produced by other than Allah; on the contrary, it is a confirmation of (revelations) that went before it, and a fuller explanation of the book - in which there is no doubt - from the Lord of the Worlds.

وَمَا كَانَ هَٰذَا ٱلْقُرْءَانُ أَن يُفْتَرَىٰ مِن دُونِ ٱللَّهِ
وَلَٰكِن تَصْدِيقَ ٱلَّذِى بَيْنَ يَدَيْهِ وَتَفْصِيلَ ٱلْكِتَٰبِ
لَا رَيْبَ فِيهِ مِن رَّبِّ ٱلْعَٰلَمِينَ ﴿٣٧﴾

38. Or do they say "He forged it"? Say: "Bring then a Surah like it, and call (to your aid) anyone you can, besides Allah, if it be you speak the truth!"

أَمْ يَقُولُونَ ٱفْتَرَىٰهُ ۖ قُلْ فَأْتُوا۟ بِسُورَةٍ مِّثْلِهِۦ وَٱدْعُوا۟
مَنِ ٱسْتَطَعْتُم مِّن دُونِ ٱللَّهِ إِن كُنتُمْ صَٰدِقِينَ ﴿٣٨﴾

39. Nay, they charge with falsehood that whose knowledge they cannot encompass, even before the elucidation of it has reached them; thus did those before them make charges of falsehood; but see what was the end of those who did wrong!

بَلۡ كَذَّبُواْ بِمَا لَمۡ يُحِيطُواْ بِعِلۡمِهِۦ وَلَمَّا يَأۡتِهِمۡ تَأۡوِيلُهُۥۚ
كَذَٰلِكَ كَذَّبَ ٱلَّذِينَ مِن قَبۡلِهِمۡۖ فَٱنظُرۡ كَيۡفَ كَانَ
عَٰقِبَةُ ٱلظَّٰلِمِينَ ٣٩

40. Of them there are some who believe in it, and some who do not: and your Lord knows best those who are out for mischief.

وَمِنۡهُم مَّن يُؤۡمِنُ بِهِۦ وَمِنۡهُم مَّن لَّا يُؤۡمِنُ بِهِۦۚ
وَرَبُّكَ أَعۡلَمُ بِٱلۡمُفۡسِدِينَ ٤٠

41. If they charge you with falsehood, say: "My work to me, and yours to you! You are free from responsibility for what I do, and I for what you do!"

وَإِن كَذَّبُوكَ فَقُل لِّي عَمَلِي وَلَكُمۡ عَمَلُكُمۡۖ أَنتُم
بَرِيٓـُٔونَ مِمَّآ أَعۡمَلُ وَأَنَا۠ بَرِيٓءٞ مِّمَّا تَعۡمَلُونَ ٤١

42. Among them are some who (pretend to) listen to you: but can you make the deaf to hear - even though they are without understanding?

وَمِنۡهُم مَّن يَسۡتَمِعُونَ إِلَيۡكَۚ أَفَأَنتَ تُسۡمِعُ ٱلصُّمَّ
وَلَوۡ كَانُواْ لَا يَعۡقِلُونَ ٤٢

43. And among them are some who look at you: but can you guide the blind - even though they will not see?

وَمِنۡهُم مَّن يَنظُرُ إِلَيۡكَۚ أَفَأَنتَ تَهۡدِي ٱلۡعُمۡيَ وَلَوۡ كَانُواْ
لَا يُبۡصِرُونَ ٤٣

44. Verily Allah will not deal unjustly with man in anything: it is man that wrongs his own soul.

إِنَّ ٱللَّهَ لَا يَظۡلِمُ ٱلنَّاسَ شَيۡـٔٗا وَلَٰكِنَّ ٱلنَّاسَ
أَنفُسَهُمۡ يَظۡلِمُونَ ٤٤

45. One day He will gather them together; (it will be) as if they had stayed but an hour of a day; they will recognise each other: surely those will be lost who denied the meeting with Allah and refused to receive true guidance.

وَيَوۡمَ يَحۡشُرُهُمۡ كَأَن لَّمۡ يَلۡبَثُوٓاْ إِلَّا سَاعَةٗ مِّنَ ٱلنَّهَارِ
يَتَعَارَفُونَ بَيۡنَهُمۡۚ قَدۡ خَسِرَ ٱلَّذِينَ كَذَّبُواْ بِلِقَآءِ ٱللَّهِ
وَمَا كَانُواْ مُهۡتَدِينَ ٤٥

46. Whether We show you (realised in your lifetime) some part of what We promise them - or We take your soul (to Our mercy) (before that) - in any case, to Us is their return: ultimately Allah is witness to all that they do.

وَإِمَّا نُرِيَنَّكَ بَعۡضَ ٱلَّذِي نَعِدُهُمۡ أَوۡ نَتَوَفَّيَنَّكَ
فَإِلَيۡنَا مَرۡجِعُهُمۡ ثُمَّ ٱللَّهُ شَهِيدٌ عَلَىٰ مَا يَفۡعَلُونَ ٤٦

47. To every people (was sent) a messenger: when their messenger comes (before them), the matter will be judged between them with justice, and they will not be wronged.

وَلِكُلِّ أُمَّةٍ رَّسُولٌ ۖ فَإِذَا جَآءَ رَسُولُهُمْ قُضِىَ
بَيْنَهُم بِٱلْقِسْطِ وَهُمْ لَا يُظْلَمُونَ ﴿٤٧﴾

48. They say: "When will this promise come to pass - if you speak the truth?"

وَيَقُولُونَ مَتَىٰ هَٰذَا ٱلْوَعْدُ إِن كُنتُمْ صَٰدِقِينَ ﴿٤٨﴾

49. Say: "I have no power over any harm or profit to myself except as Allah Wills. To every people is a term appointed: when their term is reached not an hour can they cause delay, nor (an hour) can they advance (it in anticipation)."

قُل لَّآ أَمْلِكُ لِنَفْسِى ضَرًّا وَلَا نَفْعًا إِلَّا مَا شَآءَ ٱللَّهُ ۗ
لِكُلِّ أُمَّةٍ أَجَلٌ ۚ إِذَا جَآءَ أَجَلُهُمْ فَلَا يَسْتَـْٔخِرُونَ سَاعَةً
وَلَا يَسْتَقْدِمُونَ ﴿٤٩﴾

50. Say: "Do you see - if His punishment should come to you by night or by day, what portion of it would the sinners wish to hasten?"

قُلْ أَرَءَيْتُمْ إِنْ أَتَىٰكُمْ عَذَابُهُۥ بَيَٰتًا أَوْ نَهَارًا مَّاذَا
يَسْتَعْجِلُ مِنْهُ ٱلْمُجْرِمُونَ ﴿٥٠﴾

51. "Would you then believe in it at last, when it actually comes to pass?" (It will then be said): 'Ah! Now? And you wanted (before) to hasten it on!'

أَثُمَّ إِذَا مَا وَقَعَ ءَامَنتُم بِهِۦٓ ۚ ءَآلْـَٰٔنَ وَقَدْ كُنتُم بِهِۦ
تَسْتَعْجِلُونَ ﴿٥١﴾

52. "At length will be said to the wrongdoers: 'Taste you the enduring punishment! You get but the recompense of what you earned!'"

ثُمَّ قِيلَ لِلَّذِينَ ظَلَمُوا۟ ذُوقُوا۟ عَذَابَ ٱلْخُلْدِ هَلْ
تُجْزَوْنَ إِلَّا بِمَا كُنتُمْ تَكْسِبُونَ ﴿٥٢﴾

53. They seek to be informed by you: "Is that true?" Say: "Aye! By my Lord! It is the very truth! And you cannot frustrate it!"

ربع الحزب ٤٢ ۞ وَيَسْتَنۢبِـُٔونَكَ أَحَقٌّ هُوَ ۖ قُلْ إِى وَرَبِّىٓ إِنَّهُۥ
لَحَقٌّ ۖ وَمَآ أَنتُم بِمُعْجِزِينَ ﴿٥٣﴾

54. Every soul that has sinned, if it possessed all that is on earth, would like to give it in ransom: they would declare (their) repentance when they see the penalty: but the judgement between them will be with justice, and no wrong will be done to them.

وَلَوْ أَنَّ لِكُلِّ نَفْسٍ ظَلَمَتْ مَا فِى ٱلْأَرْضِ لَٱفْتَدَتْ
بِهِۦ ۗ وَأَسَرُّوا۟ ٱلنَّدَامَةَ لَمَّا رَأَوُا۟ ٱلْعَذَابَ ۖ وَقُضِىَ
بَيْنَهُم بِٱلْقِسْطِ ۚ وَهُمْ لَا يُظْلَمُونَ ﴿٥٤﴾

55. Is it not (the case) that to Allah belongs whatever is in the heavens and on earth? Is it not (the case) that Allah's promise is assuredly true? Yet most of them understand not.

أَلَآ إِنَّ لِلَّهِ مَا فِي ٱلسَّمَٰوَٰتِ وَٱلۡأَرۡضِۗ أَلَآ إِنَّ وَعۡدَ
ٱللَّهِ حَقّٞ وَلَٰكِنَّ أَكۡثَرَهُمۡ لَا يَعۡلَمُونَ ٥٥

56. It is He Who gives life and who takes it, and to Him shall you all be brought back.

هُوَ يُحۡيِۦ وَيُمِيتُ وَإِلَيۡهِ تُرۡجَعُونَ ٥٦

57. O mankind! There has come to you a direction from your Lord and a healing for the (diseases) in your hearts - and for those who believe, a guidance and a mercy.

يَٰٓأَيُّهَا ٱلنَّاسُ قَدۡ جَآءَتۡكُم مَّوۡعِظَةٞ مِّن رَّبِّكُمۡ
وَشِفَآءٞ لِّمَا فِي ٱلصُّدُورِ وَهُدٗى وَرَحۡمَةٞ
لِّلۡمُؤۡمِنِينَ ٥٧

58. Say: "In the bounty of Allah, and in His mercy - in that let them rejoice": that is better than the (wealth) they hoard.

قُلۡ بِفَضۡلِ ٱللَّهِ وَبِرَحۡمَتِهِۦ فَبِذَٰلِكَ فَلۡيَفۡرَحُواْ
هُوَ خَيۡرٞ مِّمَّا يَجۡمَعُونَ ٥٨

59. Say: "See you what things Allah has sent down to you for sustenance? Yet you hold forbidden some things of it and (some things) lawful." Say: "Has Allah indeed permitted you, or do you invent (things) to attribute to Allah?"

قُلۡ أَرَءَيۡتُم مَّآ أَنزَلَ ٱللَّهُ لَكُم مِّن رِّزۡقٖ فَجَعَلۡتُم
مِّنۡهُ حَرَامٗا وَحَلَٰلٗا قُلۡ ءَآللَّهُ أَذِنَ لَكُمۡۖ أَمۡ عَلَى
ٱللَّهِ تَفۡتَرُونَ ٥٩

60. And what think those who invent lies against Allah, of the day of judgement? Verily Allah is full of bounty to mankind, but most of them are ungrateful.

وَمَا ظَنُّ ٱلَّذِينَ يَفۡتَرُونَ عَلَى ٱللَّهِ ٱلۡكَذِبَ يَوۡمَ
ٱلۡقِيَٰمَةِۗ إِنَّ ٱللَّهَ لَذُو فَضۡلٍ عَلَى ٱلنَّاسِ وَلَٰكِنَّ
أَكۡثَرَهُمۡ لَا يَشۡكُرُونَ ٦٠

61. In whatever business you may be, and whatever portion you may be reciting from the Qur'an - and whatever deed you (mankind) may be doing - We are Witnesses of it when you are deeply engrossed in it. Nor is hidden from your Lord (so much as) the weight of an atom on the earth or in heaven. And not the least and not the greatest of these things but are recorded in a clear record.

وَمَا تَكُونُ فِي شَأۡنٖ وَمَا تَتۡلُواْ مِنۡهُ مِن قُرۡءَانٖ
وَلَا تَعۡمَلُونَ مِنۡ عَمَلٍ إِلَّا كُنَّا عَلَيۡكُمۡ شُهُودًا
إِذۡ تُفِيضُونَ فِيهِۚ وَمَا يَعۡزُبُ عَن رَّبِّكَ مِن مِّثۡقَالِ
ذَرَّةٖ فِي ٱلۡأَرۡضِ وَلَا فِي ٱلسَّمَآءِ وَلَآ أَصۡغَرَ مِن
ذَٰلِكَ وَلَآ أَكۡبَرَ إِلَّا فِي كِتَٰبٖ مُّبِينٍ ٦١

62. See! Verily on the friends of Allah there is no fear, nor shall they grieve;

أَلَآ إِنَّ أَوۡلِيَآءَ ٱللَّهِ لَا خَوۡفٌ عَلَيۡهِمۡ وَلَا هُمۡ يَحۡزَنُونَ ٦٢

63. Those who believe and (constantly) guard against evil -

ٱلَّذِينَ ءَامَنُواْ وَكَانُواْ يَتَّقُونَ ٦٣

64. For them are glad tidings, in the life of the present and in the hereafter: no change can there be in the words of Allah. This is indeed the supreme felicity.

لَهُمُ ٱلۡبُشۡرَىٰ فِي ٱلۡحَيَوٰةِ ٱلدُّنۡيَا وَفِي ٱلۡأٓخِرَةِۚ
لَا تَبۡدِيلَ لِكَلِمَٰتِ ٱللَّهِۚ ذَٰلِكَ هُوَ ٱلۡفَوۡزُ
ٱلۡعَظِيمُ ٦٤

65. Let not their speech grieve you: for all power and honour belong to Allah: it is He Who hears and knows (all things).

وَلَا يَحۡزُنكَ قَوۡلُهُمۡۘ إِنَّ ٱلۡعِزَّةَ لِلَّهِ جَمِيعًاۚ هُوَ
ٱلسَّمِيعُ ٱلۡعَلِيمُ ٦٥

66. See! Verily to Allah belong all creatures, in the heavens and on earth. What do they follow who worship as His 'partners' other than Allah? They follow nothing but fancy, and they do nothing but lie.

أَلَآ إِنَّ لِلَّهِ مَن فِي ٱلسَّمَٰوَٰتِ وَمَن فِي ٱلۡأَرۡضِۗ
وَمَا يَتَّبِعُ ٱلَّذِينَ يَدۡعُونَ مِن دُونِ ٱللَّهِ شُرَكَآءَۚ
إِن يَتَّبِعُونَ إِلَّا ٱلظَّنَّ وَإِنۡ هُمۡ إِلَّا يَخۡرُصُونَ ٦٦

67. He it is that has made you the night that you may rest in it, and the day to make things visible (to you). Verily in this are signs for those who listen (to His message).

هُوَ ٱلَّذِي جَعَلَ لَكُمُ ٱلَّيۡلَ لِتَسۡكُنُواْ فِيهِ
وَٱلنَّهَارَ مُبۡصِرًاۚ إِنَّ فِي ذَٰلِكَ لَأٓيَٰتٖ لِّقَوۡمٖ
يَسۡمَعُونَ ٦٧

68. They say "Allah has begotten a son!" - Glory be to Him! He is self- sufficient! His are all things in the heavens and on earth! No authority have you for this! Do you say about Allah what you do not know?

قَالُواْ ٱتَّخَذَ ٱللَّهُ وَلَدٗاۗ سُبۡحَٰنَهُۥۖ هُوَ ٱلۡغَنِيُّۖ
لَهُۥ مَا فِي ٱلسَّمَٰوَٰتِ وَمَا فِي ٱلۡأَرۡضِۚ إِنۡ
عِندَكُم مِّن سُلۡطَٰنِۭ بِهَٰذَآۚ أَتَقُولُونَ
عَلَى ٱللَّهِ مَا لَا تَعۡلَمُونَ ٦٨

69. Say: "Those who invent a lie against Allah will never prosper."

قُلۡ إِنَّ ٱلَّذِينَ يَفۡتَرُونَ عَلَى ٱللَّهِ ٱلۡكَذِبَ
لَا يُفۡلِحُونَ ٦٩

70. A little enjoyment in this world! - And then, to Us will be their return. Then shall We make them taste the severest penalty for their blasphemies.

مَتَٰعٌ فِي ٱلدُّنۡيَا ثُمَّ إِلَيۡنَا مَرۡجِعُهُمۡ ثُمَّ نُذِيقُهُمُ
ٱلۡعَذَابَ ٱلشَّدِيدَ بِمَا كَانُواْ يَكۡفُرُونَ ٧٠

71. Relate to them the story of Noah. See! He said to his people: "O my people, if it be hard on your (mind) that I should stay (with you) and commemorate the signs of Allah - yet I put my trust in Allah. Get you then an agreement about your plan and among your partners, so your plan be not to you dark and dubious. Then pass your sentence on me, and give me no respite.

نصف الحزب ٢٢

۞وَٱتۡلُ عَلَيۡهِمۡ نَبَأَ نُوحٍ إِذۡ قَالَ لِقَوۡمِهِۦ يَٰقَوۡمِ إِن كَانَ
كَبُرَ عَلَيۡكُم مَّقَامِي وَتَذۡكِيرِي بِـَٔايَٰتِ ٱللَّهِ فَعَلَى ٱللَّهِ
تَوَكَّلۡتُ فَأَجۡمِعُوٓاْ أَمۡرَكُمۡ وَشُرَكَآءَكُمۡ ثُمَّ لَا يَكُنۡ
أَمۡرُكُمۡ عَلَيۡكُمۡ غُمَّةٗ ثُمَّ ٱقۡضُوٓاْ إِلَيَّ وَلَا تُنظِرُونِ ٧١

72. "But if you turn back, (consider): no reward have I asked of you: my reward is only due from Allah, and I have been commanded to be of those who submit to Allah's will (in Islam)."

فَإِن تَوَلَّيۡتُمۡ فَمَا سَأَلۡتُكُم مِّنۡ أَجۡرٍۖ إِنۡ أَجۡرِيَ إِلَّا
عَلَى ٱللَّهِۖ وَأُمِرۡتُ أَنۡ أَكُونَ مِنَ ٱلۡمُسۡلِمِينَ ٧٢

73. They rejected him, but We delivered him, and those with him in the ark, and We made them inherit (the earth) while We overwhelmed in the flood those who rejected Our signs. Then see what was the end of those who were warned (but heeded not)!

فَكَذَّبُوهُ فَنَجَّيۡنَٰهُ وَمَن مَّعَهُۥ فِي ٱلۡفُلۡكِ وَجَعَلۡنَٰهُمۡ
خَلَٰٓئِفَ وَأَغۡرَقۡنَا ٱلَّذِينَ كَذَّبُواْ بِـَٔايَٰتِنَاۖ فَٱنظُرۡ كَيۡفَ
كَانَ عَٰقِبَةُ ٱلۡمُنذَرِينَ ٧٣

74. Then after him We sent (many) messengers to their peoples: they brought them clear signs, but they would not believe what they had already rejected beforehand. Thus do We seal the hearts of the transgressors.

ثُمَّ بَعَثۡنَا مِنۢ بَعۡدِهِۦ رُسُلًا إِلَىٰ قَوۡمِهِمۡ فَجَآءُوهُم
بِٱلۡبَيِّنَٰتِ فَمَا كَانُواْ لِيُؤۡمِنُواْ بِمَا كَذَّبُواْ بِهِۦ مِن قَبۡلُۚ
كَذَٰلِكَ نَطۡبَعُ عَلَىٰ قُلُوبِ ٱلۡمُعۡتَدِينَ ٧٤

75. Then after them sent We Moses and Aaron to Pharaoh and his chiefs with Our signs. But they were arrogant: they were a people in sin.

ثُمَّ بَعَثۡنَا مِنۢ بَعۡدِهِم مُّوسَىٰ وَهَٰرُونَ إِلَىٰ فِرۡعَوۡنَ
وَمَلَإِيْهِۦ بِـَٔايَٰتِنَا فَٱسۡتَكۡبَرُواْ وَكَانُواْ قَوۡمٗا
مُّجۡرِمِينَ ٧٥

76. When the truth did come to them from Us, they said: "This is indeed evident sorcery!"

فَلَمَّا جَآءَهُمُ ٱلْحَقُّ مِنْ عِندِنَا قَالُوٓا۟ إِنَّ هَٰذَا لَسِحْرٌ
مُّبِينٌ ٧٦

77. Said Moses: "Do you say (this) about the truth when it has (actually) reached you? Is sorcery (like) this? But sorcerers will not prosper."

قَالَ مُوسَىٰٓ أَتَقُولُونَ لِلْحَقِّ لَمَّا جَآءَكُمْ ۖ أَسِحْرٌ هَٰذَا
وَلَا يُفْلِحُ ٱلسَّٰحِرُونَ ٧٧

78. They said: "Have you come to us to turn us away from the ways We found our fathers following - in order that you and your brother may have greatness in the land? But we shall not believe in you!"

قَالُوٓا۟ أَجِئْتَنَا لِتَلْفِتَنَا عَمَّا وَجَدْنَا عَلَيْهِ ءَابَآءَنَا
وَتَكُونَ لَكُمَا ٱلْكِبْرِيَآءُ فِى ٱلْأَرْضِ وَمَا نَحْنُ لَكُمَا
بِمُؤْمِنِينَ ٧٨

79. Said Pharaoh: "Bring me every sorcerer well-versed."

وَقَالَ فِرْعَوْنُ ٱئْتُونِى بِكُلِّ سَٰحِرٍ عَلِيمٍ ٧٩

80. When the sorcerers came, Moses said to them: "Throw you what you (wish) to throw!"

فَلَمَّا جَآءَ ٱلسَّحَرَةُ قَالَ لَهُم مُّوسَىٰٓ أَلْقُوا۟ مَآ أَنتُم
مُّلْقُونَ ٨٠

81. When they had had their throw, Moses said: "What you have brought is sorcery: Allah will surely make it of no effect: for Allah prospers not the work of those who make mischief."

فَلَمَّآ أَلْقَوْا۟ قَالَ مُوسَىٰ مَا جِئْتُم بِهِ ٱلسِّحْرُ ۖ إِنَّ ٱللَّهَ
سَيُبْطِلُهُۥٓ ۖ إِنَّ ٱللَّهَ لَا يُصْلِحُ عَمَلَ ٱلْمُفْسِدِينَ ٨١

82. "And Allah by His words does prove and establish His truth, however much the sinners may hate it!"

وَيُحِقُّ ٱللَّهُ ٱلْحَقَّ بِكَلِمَٰتِهِۦ وَلَوْ كَرِهَ ٱلْمُجْرِمُونَ ٨٢

83. But none believed in Moses except some children of his people, because of the fear of Pharaoh and his chiefs, lest they should persecute them; and certainly Pharaoh was mighty on the earth and one who transgressed all bounds.

فَمَآ ءَامَنَ لِمُوسَىٰٓ إِلَّا ذُرِّيَّةٌ مِّن قَوْمِهِۦ عَلَىٰ خَوْفٍ
مِّن فِرْعَوْنَ وَمَلَإِي۟هِمْ أَن يَفْتِنَهُمْ ۚ وَإِنَّ فِرْعَوْنَ
لَعَالٍ فِى ٱلْأَرْضِ وَإِنَّهُۥ لَمِنَ ٱلْمُسْرِفِينَ ٨٣

84. Moses said: "O my people! If you do (really) believe in Allah, then in Him put

وَقَالَ مُوسَىٰ يَٰقَوْمِ إِن كُنتُمْ ءَامَنتُم بِٱللَّهِ فَعَلَيْهِ

your trust, if you submit (your will to His)."

تَوَكَّلُوٓاْ إِن كُنتُم مُّسۡلِمِينَ ٨٤

85. They said: "In Allah do we put our trust. Our Lord! Make us not a trial for those who practice oppression;

فَقَالُواْ عَلَى ٱللَّهِ تَوَكَّلۡنَا رَبَّنَا لَا تَجۡعَلۡنَا فِتۡنَةٗ لِّلۡقَوۡمِ
ٱلظَّٰلِمِينَ ٨٥

86. And deliver us by Your mercy from those who reject (You)."

وَنَجِّنَا بِرَحۡمَتِكَ مِنَ ٱلۡقَوۡمِ ٱلۡكَٰفِرِينَ ٨٦

87. We inspired Moses and his brother with this message: "Provide dwellings for your people in Egypt, make your dwellings into places of worship, and establish regular prayers: and give glad tidings to those who believe!"

وَأَوۡحَيۡنَآ إِلَىٰ مُوسَىٰ وَأَخِيهِ أَن تَبَوَّءَا لِقَوۡمِكُمَا
بِمِصۡرَ بُيُوتٗا وَٱجۡعَلُواْ بُيُوتَكُمۡ قِبۡلَةٗ وَأَقِيمُواْ
ٱلصَّلَوٰةَۗ وَبَشِّرِ ٱلۡمُؤۡمِنِينَ ٨٧

88. Moses prayed: "Our Lord! You have indeed bestowed on Pharaoh and his chiefs splendour and wealth in the life of the present, and so, our Lord, they mislead (men) from Your path. Deface, our Lord, the features of their wealth, and send hardness to their hearts, so they will not believe until they see the grievous penalty."

وَقَالَ مُوسَىٰ رَبَّنَآ إِنَّكَ ءَاتَيۡتَ فِرۡعَوۡنَ وَمَلَأَهُۥ
زِينَةٗ وَأَمۡوَٰلٗا فِي ٱلۡحَيَوٰةِ ٱلدُّنۡيَا رَبَّنَا لِيُضِلُّواْ عَن
سَبِيلِكَۖ رَبَّنَا ٱطۡمِسۡ عَلَىٰٓ أَمۡوَٰلِهِمۡ وَٱشۡدُدۡ عَلَىٰ
قُلُوبِهِمۡ فَلَا يُؤۡمِنُواْ حَتَّىٰ يَرَوُاْ ٱلۡعَذَابَ ٱلۡأَلِيمَ ٨٨

89. Allah said: "Accepted is your prayer (O Moses and Aaron)! So stand you straight, and follow not the path of those who know not."

قَالَ قَدۡ أُجِيبَت دَّعۡوَتُكُمَا فَٱسۡتَقِيمَا وَلَا
تَتَّبِعَآنِّ سَبِيلَ ٱلَّذِينَ لَا يَعۡلَمُونَ ٨٩

90. We took the Children of Israel across the sea: Pharaoh and his forces followed them in insolence and spite. At length, when overwhelmed with the flood, he said: "I believe that there is no god except Him Whom the Children of Israel believe in: I am of those who submit (to Allah in Islam)."

ثلاثة أرباع الحزب ٢٢

۞ وَجَٰوَزۡنَا بِبَنِيٓ إِسۡرَٰٓءِيلَ ٱلۡبَحۡرَ فَأَتۡبَعَهُمۡ فِرۡعَوۡنُ
وَجُنُودُهُۥ بَغۡيٗا وَعَدۡوًاۖ حَتَّىٰٓ إِذَآ أَدۡرَكَهُ ٱلۡغَرَقُ
قَالَ ءَامَنتُ أَنَّهُۥ لَآ إِلَٰهَ إِلَّا ٱلَّذِيٓ ءَامَنَتۡ بِهِۦ
بَنُوٓاْ إِسۡرَٰٓءِيلَ وَأَنَا۠ مِنَ ٱلۡمُسۡلِمِينَ ٩٠

91. (It was said to him): "Ah now! - But a little while before, were you in rebellion! - And you did mischief (and violence)!"

ءَآلۡـَٰٔنَ وَقَدۡ عَصَيۡتَ قَبۡلُ وَكُنتَ مِنَ
ٱلۡمُفۡسِدِينَ ٩١

92. "This day shall We save you in your body, that you may be a sign to those who come after you! But verily, many among mankind are heedless of Our signs!"

فَٱلۡيَوۡمَ نُنَجِّيكَ بِبَدَنِكَ لِتَكُونَ لِمَنۡ خَلۡفَكَ ءَايَةٗۚ
وَإِنَّ كَثِيرٗا مِّنَ ٱلنَّاسِ عَنۡ ءَايَٰتِنَا لَغَٰفِلُونَ ٩٢

93. We settled the Children of Israel in a beautiful dwelling-place, and provided for them sustenance of the best; it was after knowledge had been granted to them, that they fell into schisms. Verily Allah will judge between them as to the schisms amongst them on the day of judgement.

وَلَقَدۡ بَوَّأۡنَا بَنِيٓ إِسۡرَٰٓءِيلَ مُبَوَّأَ صِدۡقٖ وَرَزَقۡنَٰهُم
مِّنَ ٱلطَّيِّبَٰتِ فَمَا ٱخۡتَلَفُواْ حَتَّىٰ جَآءَهُمُ ٱلۡعِلۡمُۚ
إِنَّ رَبَّكَ يَقۡضِي بَيۡنَهُمۡ يَوۡمَ ٱلۡقِيَٰمَةِ فِيمَا كَانُواْ فِيهِ
يَخۡتَلِفُونَ ٩٣

94. If you are in doubt as to what We have revealed to you, then ask those who have been reading the book from before you; the truth has indeed come to you from your Lord: so be in no way of those in doubt.

فَإِن كُنتَ فِي شَكّٖ مِّمَّآ أَنزَلۡنَآ إِلَيۡكَ فَسۡـَٔلِ ٱلَّذِينَ
يَقۡرَءُونَ ٱلۡكِتَٰبَ مِن قَبۡلِكَۚ لَقَدۡ جَآءَكَ ٱلۡحَقُّ
مِن رَّبِّكَ فَلَا تَكُونَنَّ مِنَ ٱلۡمُمۡتَرِينَ ٩٤

95. Nor be of those who reject the signs of Allah, or you shall be of those who perish.

وَلَا تَكُونَنَّ مِنَ ٱلَّذِينَ كَذَّبُواْ بِـَٔايَٰتِ ٱللَّهِ فَتَكُونَ
مِنَ ٱلۡخَٰسِرِينَ ٩٥

96. Those against whom the word of your Lord has been verified would not believe -

إِنَّ ٱلَّذِينَ حَقَّتۡ عَلَيۡهِمۡ كَلِمَتُ رَبِّكَ لَا
يُؤۡمِنُونَ ٩٦

97. Even if every sign was brought to them - until they see (for themselves) the grievous penalty.

وَلَوۡ جَآءَتۡهُمۡ كُلُّ ءَايَةٍ حَتَّىٰ يَرَوُاْ ٱلۡعَذَابَ
ٱلۡأَلِيمَ ٩٧

98. Why was there not a single township (among those We warned), which believed - so its faith should have profited it - except the people of Yunus? When they believed, We removed from them the penalty of disgrace in the life of the present, and permitted them to enjoy (their life) for a while.

فَلَوۡلَا كَانَتۡ قَرۡيَةٌ ءَامَنَتۡ فَنَفَعَهَآ إِيمَٰنُهَآ إِلَّا
قَوۡمَ يُونُسَ لَمَّآ ءَامَنُواْ كَشَفۡنَا عَنۡهُمۡ عَذَابَ
ٱلۡخِزۡيِ فِي ٱلۡحَيَوٰةِ ٱلدُّنۡيَا وَمَتَّعۡنَٰهُمۡ إِلَىٰ حِينٖ ٩٨

99. If it had been the Lord's will, they would all have believed - all who are on earth! Will you then compel mankind, against their will, to believe!

وَلَوْ شَآءَ رَبُّكَ لَءَامَنَ مَن فِى ٱلْأَرْضِ كُلُّهُمْ جَمِيعًا ۚ
أَفَأَنتَ تُكْرِهُ ٱلنَّاسَ حَتَّىٰ يَكُونُوا۟ مُؤْمِنِينَ ﴿٩٩﴾

100. No soul can believe, except by the will of Allah, and He will place doubt (or obscurity) on those who will not understand.

وَمَا كَانَ لِنَفْسٍ أَن تُؤْمِنَ إِلَّا بِإِذْنِ ٱللَّهِ ۚ وَيَجْعَلُ
ٱلرِّجْسَ عَلَى ٱلَّذِينَ لَا يَعْقِلُونَ ﴿١٠٠﴾

101. Say: "See all that is in the heavens and on earth"; but neither signs nor warners profit those who believe not.

قُلِ ٱنظُرُوا۟ مَاذَا فِى ٱلسَّمَٰوَٰتِ وَٱلْأَرْضِ ۚ وَمَا
تُغْنِى ٱلْءَايَٰتُ وَٱلنُّذُرُ عَن قَوْمٍ لَّا يُؤْمِنُونَ ﴿١٠١﴾

102. Do they then expect (anything) but (what happened in) the days of the men who passed away before them? Say: "Wait you then: for I, too, will wait with you."

فَهَلْ يَنتَظِرُونَ إِلَّا مِثْلَ أَيَّامِ ٱلَّذِينَ خَلَوْا۟ مِن
قَبْلِهِمْ ۚ قُلْ فَٱنتَظِرُوٓا۟ إِنِّى مَعَكُم مِّنَ
ٱلْمُنتَظِرِينَ ﴿١٠٢﴾

103. In the end We deliver Our messengers and those who believe: thus is it fitting on Our part that We should deliver those who believe!

ثُمَّ نُنَجِّى رُسُلَنَا وَٱلَّذِينَ ءَامَنُوا۟ ۚ كَذَٰلِكَ حَقًّا
عَلَيْنَا نُنجِ ٱلْمُؤْمِنِينَ ﴿١٠٣﴾

104. Say: "O you men! If you are in doubt as to my religion, (see!) I worship not what you worship other than Allah! But I worship Allah - Who will take your souls (at death): I am commanded to be (in the ranks) of the believers."

قُلْ يَٰٓأَيُّهَا ٱلنَّاسُ إِن كُنتُمْ فِى شَكٍّ مِّن دِينِى فَلَآ
أَعْبُدُ ٱلَّذِينَ تَعْبُدُونَ مِن دُونِ ٱللَّهِ وَلَٰكِنْ أَعْبُدُ
ٱللَّهَ ٱلَّذِى يَتَوَفَّىٰكُمْ ۖ وَأُمِرْتُ أَنْ أَكُونَ مِنَ
ٱلْمُؤْمِنِينَ ﴿١٠٤﴾

105. And further (thus): "Set your face towards religion with true piety, and never in any way be of the unbelievers;

وَأَنْ أَقِمْ وَجْهَكَ لِلدِّينِ حَنِيفًا وَلَا تَكُونَنَّ مِنَ
ٱلْمُشْرِكِينَ ﴿١٠٥﴾

106. Nor call on any, other than Allah - such will neither profit you nor hurt you: if

وَلَا تَدْعُ مِن دُونِ ٱللَّهِ مَا لَا يَنفَعُكَ وَلَا يَضُرُّكَ ۖ

you do, see! You shall certainly be of those who do wrong."

فَإِن فَعَلْتَ فَإِنَّكَ إِذًا مِّنَ ٱلظَّٰلِمِينَ ١٠٦

107. If Allah touches you with hurt, there is none who can remove it but He: if He designs some benefit for you, there is none who can keep back His favour: He causes it to reach whomsoever of His servants He pleases. And He is the Oft-Forgiving, Most Merciful.

وَإِن يَمْسَسْكَ ٱللَّهُ بِضُرٍّ فَلَا كَاشِفَ لَهُۥٓ إِلَّا هُوَ ۖ
وَإِن يُرِدْكَ بِخَيْرٍ فَلَا رَآدَّ لِفَضْلِهِۦ ۚ يُصِيبُ بِهِۦ
مَن يَشَآءُ مِنْ عِبَادِهِۦ ۚ وَهُوَ ٱلْغَفُورُ ٱلرَّحِيمُ ١٠٧

108. Say: "O you men! Now truth has reached you from your Lord! Those who receive guidance, do so for the good of their own souls; those who stray, do so to their own loss: and I am not (set) over you to arrange your affairs."

قُلْ يَٰٓأَيُّهَا ٱلنَّاسُ قَدْ جَآءَكُمُ ٱلْحَقُّ مِن رَّبِّكُمْ ۖ
فَمَنِ ٱهْتَدَىٰ فَإِنَّمَا يَهْتَدِى لِنَفْسِهِۦ ۖ وَمَن ضَلَّ
فَإِنَّمَا يَضِلُّ عَلَيْهَا ۖ وَمَآ أَنَا۠ عَلَيْكُم بِوَكِيلٍ ١٠٨

109. Follow you the inspiration sent to you, and be patient and constant, till Allah does decide: for He is the best to decide.

وَٱتَّبِعْ مَا يُوحَىٰٓ إِلَيْكَ وَٱصْبِرْ حَتَّىٰ يَحْكُمَ ٱللَّهُ ۚ
وَهُوَ خَيْرُ ٱلْحَٰكِمِينَ ١٠٩

سُورَةُ هُودٍ

Surah 11: **Hud**

In the name of Allah,
Most Gracious, Most Merciful.

بِسْمِ ٱللَّهِ ٱلرَّحْمَٰنِ ٱلرَّحِيمِ

1. *Alif Lam Ra.* (This is) a book with verses basic or fundamental (of established meaning) - further explained in detail - from One Who is Wise and Well-Acquainted (with all things):

الٓر ۚ كِتَٰبٌ أُحْكِمَتْ ءَايَٰتُهُۥ ثُمَّ فُصِّلَتْ مِن لَّدُنْ
حَكِيمٍ خَبِيرٍ ١

2. (It teaches) that you should worship none but Allah. (Say:) "Verily I am (sent) to you from Him to warn and to bring glad tidings:"

أَلَّا تَعْبُدُوٓا۟ إِلَّا ٱللَّهَ ۚ إِنَّنِى لَكُم مِّنْهُ نَذِيرٌ وَبَشِيرٌ ٢

3. ("And to preach thus), 'Seek you the forgiveness of your Lord, and turn to Him in repentance; that He may grant you enjoyment, good (and true), for a term appointed, and bestow His abounding grace on all who abound in merit! But if you turn away, then I fear for you the penalty of a great day:

وَأَنِ ٱسْتَغْفِرُوا۟ رَبَّكُمْ ثُمَّ تُوبُوٓا۟ إِلَيْهِ يُمَتِّعْكُم مَّتَـٰعًا
حَسَنًا إِلَىٰٓ أَجَلٍ مُّسَمًّى وَيُؤْتِ كُلَّ ذِى فَضْلٍ
فَضْلَهُۥ ۖ وَإِن تَوَلَّوْا۟ فَإِنِّىٓ أَخَافُ عَلَيْكُمْ عَذَابَ يَوْمٍ
كَبِيرٍ ۝٣

4. 'To Allah is your return and He has power over all things.'"

إِلَى ٱللَّهِ مَرْجِعُكُمْ ۖ وَهُوَ عَلَىٰ كُلِّ شَىْءٍ قَدِيرٌ ۝٤

5. See! They fold up their hearts, that they may lie hidden from Him! Ah! Even when they cover themselves with their garments, He knows what they conceal and what they reveal: for He knows well the (inmost secrets) of the hearts.

أَلَآ إِنَّهُمْ يَثْنُونَ صُدُورَهُمْ لِيَسْتَخْفُوا۟ مِنْهُ ۚ أَلَا
حِينَ يَسْتَغْشُونَ ثِيَابَهُمْ يَعْلَمُ مَا يُسِرُّونَ وَمَا
يُعْلِنُونَ ۚ إِنَّهُۥ عَلِيمٌۢ بِذَاتِ ٱلصُّدُورِ ۝٥

✻**6.** There is no moving creature on earth but its sustenance depends on Allah; He knows the time and place of its temporary deposit: all is in a clear record.

✻ وَمَا مِن دَآبَّةٍ فِى ٱلْأَرْضِ إِلَّا عَلَى ٱللَّهِ رِزْقُهَا
وَيَعْلَمُ مُسْتَقَرَّهَا وَمُسْتَوْدَعَهَا ۚ كُلٌّ فِى
كِتَـٰبٍ مُّبِينٍ ۝٦

7. He it is Who created the heavens and the earth in six days - and His throne was over the waters - that He might try you, which of you is best in conduct. But if you were to say to them, "You shall indeed be raised up after death," the unbelievers would be sure to say, "This is nothing but obvious sorcery!"

وَهُوَ ٱلَّذِى خَلَقَ ٱلسَّمَـٰوَٰتِ وَٱلْأَرْضَ فِى سِتَّةِ
أَيَّامٍ وَكَانَ عَرْشُهُۥ عَلَى ٱلْمَآءِ لِيَبْلُوَكُمْ أَيُّكُمْ
أَحْسَنُ عَمَلًا ۗ وَلَئِن قُلْتَ إِنَّكُم مَّبْعُوثُونَ مِنۢ
بَعْدِ ٱلْمَوْتِ لَيَقُولَنَّ ٱلَّذِينَ كَفَرُوٓا۟ إِنْ هَـٰذَآ إِلَّا
سِحْرٌ مُّبِينٌ ۝٧

8. If We delay the penalty for them for a definite term, they are sure to say, "What keeps it back?" Ah! On the day it (actually) reaches them, nothing will turn it away from them, and they will be completely encircled by that which they used to mock at!

وَلَئِنْ أَخَّرْنَا عَنْهُمُ ٱلْعَذَابَ إِلَىٰٓ أُمَّةٍ مَّعْدُودَةٍ
لَّيَقُولُنَّ مَا يَحْبِسُهُۥٓ ۗ أَلَا يَوْمَ يَأْتِيهِمْ لَيْسَ مَصْرُوفًا
عَنْهُمْ وَحَاقَ بِهِم مَّا كَانُوا۟ بِهِۦ يَسْتَهْزِءُونَ ۝٨

✻ Part-12

9. If We give man a taste of mercy from Ourselves, and then withdraw it from him, See! He is in despair and (falls into) blasphemy.

وَلَئِنۡ أَذَقۡنَا ٱلۡإِنسَٰنَ مِنَّا رَحۡمَةٗ ثُمَّ نَزَعۡنَٰهَا
مِنۡهُ إِنَّهُۥ لَيَـُٔوسٞ كَفُورٞ ٩

10. But if We give him a taste of (Our) favours after adversity has touched him, he is sure to say, "All with evil has departed from me"; see! He falls into exultation and pride.

وَلَئِنۡ أَذَقۡنَٰهُ نَعۡمَآءَ بَعۡدَ ضَرَّآءَ مَسَّتۡهُ
لَيَقُولَنَّ ذَهَبَ ٱلسَّيِّـَٔاتُ عَنِّيٓۚ إِنَّهُۥ لَفَرِحٞ
فَخُورٌ ١٠

11. Not so do those who show patience and constancy, and work righteousness; for them is forgiveness (of sins) and a great reward.

إِلَّا ٱلَّذِينَ صَبَرُواْ وَعَمِلُواْ ٱلصَّٰلِحَٰتِ أُوْلَٰٓئِكَ
لَهُم مَّغۡفِرَةٞ وَأَجۡرٞ كَبِيرٞ ١١

12. Perhaps you may (feel the inclination) to give up a part of what is revealed to you, and your heart feels straitened lest they say, "Why is not a treasure sent down to him, or why does not an angel come down with him?" But you are there only to warn! It is Allah that arranges all affairs!

فَلَعَلَّكَ تَارِكُۢ بَعۡضَ مَا يُوحَىٰٓ إِلَيۡكَ وَضَآئِقُۢ بِهِۦ
صَدۡرُكَ أَن يَقُولُواْ لَوۡلَآ أُنزِلَ عَلَيۡهِ كَنزٌ أَوۡ جَآءَ
مَعَهُۥ مَلَكٌۚ إِنَّمَآ أَنتَ نَذِيرٞۚ وَٱللَّهُ عَلَىٰ كُلِّ شَيۡءٖ
وَكِيلٌ ١٢

13. Or they may say, "He forged it." Say "Bring you then ten Surahs forged, like it, and call (to your aid) whomsoever you can, other than Allah! If you speak the truth!"

أَمۡ يَقُولُونَ ٱفۡتَرَىٰهُۖ قُلۡ فَأۡتُواْ بِعَشۡرِ سُوَرٖ مِّثۡلِهِۦ
مُفۡتَرَيَٰتٖ وَٱدۡعُواْ مَنِ ٱسۡتَطَعۡتُم مِّن دُونِ ٱللَّهِ إِن
كُنتُمۡ صَٰدِقِينَ ١٣

14. "If then they (your false gods) answer not your (call), know you that this revelation is sent down (replete) with the knowledge of Allah, and that there is no god but He! Will you even then submit (to Islam)?"

فَإِلَّمۡ يَسۡتَجِيبُواْ لَكُمۡ فَٱعۡلَمُوٓاْ أَنَّمَآ أُنزِلَ بِعِلۡمِ
ٱللَّهِ وَأَن لَّآ إِلَٰهَ إِلَّا هُوَۖ فَهَلۡ أَنتُم مُّسۡلِمُونَ ١٤

15. Those who desire the life of the present and its glitter - to them We shall pay (the price of) their deeds in it - without diminution.

مَن كَانَ يُرِيدُ ٱلۡحَيَوٰةَ ٱلدُّنۡيَا وَزِينَتَهَا نُوَفِّ إِلَيۡهِمۡ
أَعۡمَٰلَهُمۡ فِيهَا وَهُمۡ فِيهَا لَا يُبۡخَسُونَ ١٥

16. They are those for whom there is nothing in the hereafter but the fire: vain are the designs they frame in it, and of no effect are the deeds that they do!

أُوْلَٰٓئِكَ ٱلَّذِينَ لَيۡسَ لَهُمۡ فِي ٱلۡأٓخِرَةِ إِلَّا ٱلنَّارُۖ
وَحَبِطَ مَا صَنَعُواْ فِيهَا وَبَٰطِلٞ مَّا كَانُواْ يَعۡمَلُونَ ١٦

17. Can they be (like) those who accept a clear (sign) from their Lord, and whom a witness from Himself does teach, as did the book of Moses before it - a guide and a mercy? They believe in it; but those of the sects that reject it - the fire will be their promised meeting place. Be not then in doubt about it; for it is the truth from your Lord; yet many among men do not believe!

أَفَمَن كَانَ عَلَىٰ بَيِّنَةٖ مِّن رَّبِّهِۦ وَيَتۡلُوهُ شَاهِدٞ مِّنۡهُ
وَمِن قَبۡلِهِۦ كِتَٰبُ مُوسَىٰٓ إِمَامٗا وَرَحۡمَةًۚ أُوْلَٰٓئِكَ
يُؤۡمِنُونَ بِهِۦۚ وَمَن يَكۡفُرۡ بِهِۦ مِنَ ٱلۡأَحۡزَابِ فَٱلنَّارُ
مَوۡعِدُهُۥۚ فَلَا تَكُ فِي مِرۡيَةٖ مِّنۡهُۚ إِنَّهُ ٱلۡحَقُّ مِن رَّبِّكَ
وَلَٰكِنَّ أَكۡثَرَ ٱلنَّاسِ لَا يُؤۡمِنُونَ ١٧

18. Who does more wrong than those who invent a lie against Allah? They will be turned back to the presence of their Lord, and the witnesses will say, "These are the ones who lied against their Lord! See! The curse of Allah is on those who do wrong! -

وَمَنۡ أَظۡلَمُ مِمَّنِ ٱفۡتَرَىٰ عَلَى ٱللَّهِ كَذِبًاۚ أُوْلَٰٓئِكَ
يُعۡرَضُونَ عَلَىٰ رَبِّهِمۡ وَيَقُولُ ٱلۡأَشۡهَٰدُ هَٰٓؤُلَآءِ
ٱلَّذِينَ كَذَبُواْ عَلَىٰ رَبِّهِمۡۚ أَلَا لَعۡنَةُ ٱللَّهِ عَلَى
ٱلظَّٰلِمِينَ ١٨

19. Those who would hinder (men) from the path of Allah and would seek in it something crooked: these were they who denied the hereafter!"

ٱلَّذِينَ يَصُدُّونَ عَن سَبِيلِ ٱللَّهِ وَيَبۡغُونَهَا عِوَجٗا
وَهُم بِٱلۡأٓخِرَةِ هُمۡ كَٰفِرُونَ ١٩

20. They will in no way frustrate (His design) on earth, nor have they protectors besides Allah! Their penalty will be doubled! They lost the power to hear, and they did not see!

أُوْلَٰٓئِكَ لَمۡ يَكُونُواْ مُعۡجِزِينَ فِي ٱلۡأَرۡضِ وَمَا كَانَ
لَهُم مِّن دُونِ ٱللَّهِ مِنۡ أَوۡلِيَآءَۘ يُضَٰعَفُ لَهُمُ ٱلۡعَذَابُۚ
مَا كَانُواْ يَسۡتَطِيعُونَ ٱلسَّمۡعَ وَمَا كَانُواْ يُبۡصِرُونَ ٢٠

21. They are the ones who have lost their own souls; and the (fancies) they invented have left them in the lurch!

أُوْلَٰٓئِكَ ٱلَّذِينَ خَسِرُوٓاْ أَنفُسَهُمۡ وَضَلَّ عَنۡهُم
مَّا كَانُواْ يَفۡتَرُونَ ٢١

22. Without a doubt, these are the very ones who will lose most in the hereafter!

لَا جَرَمَ أَنَّهُمۡ فِي ٱلۡأٓخِرَةِ هُمُ ٱلۡأَخۡسَرُونَ ٢٢

23. But those who believe and work righteousness, and humble themselves before their Lord - they will be companions of the garden, to dwell in it for ever!

إِنَّ ٱلَّذِينَ ءَامَنُواْ وَعَمِلُواْ ٱلصَّٰلِحَٰتِ وَأَخْبَتُوٓاْ
إِلَىٰ رَبِّهِمْ أُوْلَٰٓئِكَ أَصْحَٰبُ ٱلْجَنَّةِ ۖ هُمْ فِيهَا
خَٰلِدُونَ ﴿٢٣﴾

24. These two kinds (of men) may be compared to the blind and deaf, and those who can see and hear well. Are they equal when compared? Will you not then take heed?

ربع الحزب ٢٣
۞ مَثَلُ ٱلْفَرِيقَيْنِ كَٱلْأَعْمَىٰ وَٱلْأَصَمِّ وَٱلْبَصِيرِ
وَٱلسَّمِيعِ ۚ هَلْ يَسْتَوِيَانِ مَثَلًا ۚ أَفَلَا تَذَكَّرُونَ ﴿٢٤﴾

25. We sent Noah to his People (with a mission): "I have come to you with a clear Warning:

وَلَقَدْ أَرْسَلْنَا نُوحًا إِلَىٰ قَوْمِهِۦٓ إِنِّى لَكُمْ نَذِيرٌ
مُّبِينٌ ﴿٢٥﴾

26. That you serve none but Allah: verily I do fear for you the penalty of a grievous day."

أَن لَّا تَعْبُدُوٓاْ إِلَّا ٱللَّهَ ۖ إِنِّىٓ أَخَافُ عَلَيْكُمْ عَذَابَ يَوْمٍ
أَلِيمٍ ﴿٢٦﴾

27. But the chiefs of the unbelievers among his people said: "We see (in) you nothing but a man like ourselves: nor do we see that any follow you but the meanest among us, in judgement immature: nor do we see in you (all) any merit above us: in fact we think you are liars!"

فَقَالَ ٱلْمَلَأُ ٱلَّذِينَ كَفَرُواْ مِن قَوْمِهِۦ مَا نَرَىٰكَ إِلَّا
بَشَرًا مِّثْلَنَا وَمَا نَرَىٰكَ ٱتَّبَعَكَ إِلَّا ٱلَّذِينَ هُمْ أَرَاذِلُنَا
بَادِىَ ٱلرَّأْىِ وَمَا نَرَىٰ لَكُمْ عَلَيْنَا مِن فَضْلٍۭ
بَلْ نَظُنُّكُمْ كَٰذِبِينَ ﴿٢٧﴾

28. He said: "O my people! See you if (it be that) I have a clear sign from my Lord, and that He has sent mercy to me from His own presence, but that the mercy has been obscured from your sight? Shall we compel you to accept it when you are averse to it?

قَالَ يَٰقَوْمِ أَرَءَيْتُمْ إِن كُنتُ عَلَىٰ بَيِّنَةٍ مِّن رَّبِّى وَءَاتَىٰنِى
رَحْمَةً مِّنْ عِندِهِۦ فَعُمِّيَتْ عَلَيْكُمْ أَنُلْزِمُكُمُوهَا
وَأَنتُمْ لَهَا كَٰرِهُونَ ﴿٢٨﴾

29. And O my people! I ask you for no wealth in return: my reward is from none but Allah: but I will not drive away (in contempt) those who believe: for verily they are to meet their Lord, and you, I see, are the ignorant ones!

وَيَٰقَوْمِ لَآ أَسْـَٔلُكُمْ عَلَيْهِ مَالًا ۖ إِنْ أَجْرِىَ إِلَّا عَلَى
ٱللَّهِ ۚ وَمَآ أَنَا۠ بِطَارِدِ ٱلَّذِينَ ءَامَنُوٓاْ ۚ إِنَّهُم مُّلَٰقُواْ
رَبِّهِمْ وَلَٰكِنِّىٓ أَرَىٰكُمْ قَوْمًا تَجْهَلُونَ ﴿٢٩﴾

30. And O my people! Who would help me against Allah if I drove them away? Will you not then take heed?

وَيَٰقَوۡمِ مَن يَنصُرُنِي مِنَ ٱللَّهِ إِن طَرَدتُّهُمۡۚ أَفَلَا
تَذَكَّرُونَ ٣٠

31. I tell you not that with me are the treasures of Allah, nor do I know what is hidden, nor claim I to be an angel. Nor yet do I say, of those whom your eyes do despise that Allah will not grant them (all) that is good: Allah knows best what is in their souls: I should, if I did, indeed be a wrongdoer."

وَلَآ أَقُولُ لَكُمۡ عِندِي خَزَآئِنُ ٱللَّهِ وَلَآ أَعۡلَمُ
ٱلۡغَيۡبَ وَلَآ أَقُولُ إِنِّي مَلَكٞ وَلَآ أَقُولُ لِلَّذِينَ
تَزۡدَرِيٓ أَعۡيُنُكُمۡ لَن يُؤۡتِيَهُمُ ٱللَّهُ خَيۡرًاۖ ٱللَّهُ أَعۡلَمُ
بِمَا فِيٓ أَنفُسِهِمۡ إِنِّيٓ إِذٗا لَّمِنَ ٱلظَّٰلِمِينَ ٣١

32. They said: "O Noah! You have disputed with us, and (much) have you prolonged the dispute with us: now bring upon us what you threaten us with, if you speak the truth!"

قَالُواْ يَٰنُوحُ قَدۡ جَٰدَلۡتَنَا فَأَكۡثَرۡتَ جِدَٰلَنَا فَأۡتِنَا بِمَا
تَعِدُنَآ إِن كُنتَ مِنَ ٱلصَّٰدِقِينَ ٣٢

33. He said: "Truly, Allah will bring it on you if He wills - and then you will not be able to frustrate it!

قَالَ إِنَّمَا يَأۡتِيكُم بِهِ ٱللَّهُ إِن شَآءَ وَمَآ أَنتُم
بِمُعۡجِزِينَ ٣٣

34. "Of no profit will be my counsel to you, much as I desire to give you (good) counsel, if it be that Allah wills to leave you astray: He is your Lord! And to Him will you return!"

وَلَا يَنفَعُكُمۡ نُصۡحِيٓ إِنۡ أَرَدتُّ أَنۡ أَنصَحَ لَكُمۡ
إِن كَانَ ٱللَّهُ يُرِيدُ أَن يُغۡوِيَكُمۡۚ هُوَ رَبُّكُمۡ وَإِلَيۡهِ
تُرۡجَعُونَ ٣٤

35. Or do they say, "He has forged it?" Say: "If I had forged it, on me were my sin! And I am free of the sins of which you are guilty!"

أَمۡ يَقُولُونَ ٱفۡتَرَىٰهُۖ قُلۡ إِنِ ٱفۡتَرَيۡتُهُۥ فَعَلَيَّ
إِجۡرَامِي وَأَنَا۠ بَرِيٓءٞ مِّمَّا تُجۡرِمُونَ ٣٥

36. It was revealed to Noah: "None of your people will believe except those who have believed already! So grieve no longer over their (evil) deeds.

وَأُوحِيَ إِلَىٰ نُوحٍ أَنَّهُۥ لَن يُؤۡمِنَ مِن قَوۡمِكَ إِلَّا مَن
قَدۡ ءَامَنَ فَلَا تَبۡتَئِسۡ بِمَا كَانُواْ يَفۡعَلُونَ ٣٦

37. But construct an ark under Our eyes and Our inspiration, and address Me no (further) on behalf of those who are in sin: for they are about to be overwhelmed (in the flood)."

وَٱصۡنَعِ ٱلۡفُلۡكَ بِأَعۡيُنِنَا وَوَحۡيِنَا وَلَا تُخَٰطِبۡنِي فِي
ٱلَّذِينَ ظَلَمُوٓاْ إِنَّهُم مُّغۡرَقُونَ ٣٧

38. Forthwith he (started) constructing the ark: every time that the chiefs of his people passed by him, they threw ridicule on him. He said: "If you ridicule us now, we (in our turn) can look down on you with ridicule likewise!

وَيَصْنَعُ ٱلْفُلْكَ وَكُلَّمَا مَرَّ عَلَيْهِ مَلَأٌ مِّن قَوْمِهِۦ
سَخِرُوا۟ مِنْهُ ۚ قَالَ إِن تَسْخَرُوا۟ مِنَّا فَإِنَّا نَسْخَرُ
مِنكُمْ كَمَا تَسْخَرُونَ ٣٨

39. But soon will you know who it is on whom will descend a penalty that will cover them with shame - on whom will be unloosed a penalty lasting:"

فَسَوْفَ تَعْلَمُونَ مَن يَأْتِيهِ عَذَابٌ يُخْزِيهِ وَيَحِلُّ
عَلَيْهِ عَذَابٌ مُّقِيمٌ ٣٩

40. At length, see! There came Our command, and the fountains of the earth gushed forward! We said: "Embark in it, of each kind two, male and female, and your family - except those against whom the word has already gone before - and the believers." But only a few believed with him.

حَتَّىٰٓ إِذَا جَآءَ أَمْرُنَا وَفَارَ ٱلتَّنُّورُ قُلْنَا ٱحْمِلْ فِيهَا
مِن كُلٍّ زَوْجَيْنِ ٱثْنَيْنِ وَأَهْلَكَ إِلَّا مَن سَبَقَ عَلَيْهِ
ٱلْقَوْلُ وَمَنْ ءَامَنَ ۚ وَمَآ ءَامَنَ مَعَهُۥٓ إِلَّا قَلِيلٌ ٤٠

41. So he said: "Embark you on the ark in the name of Allah, whether it move or be at rest! For my Lord is, be sure, Oft-Forgiving, Most Merciful!"

نصف الحزب ٢٣

۞ وَقَالَ ٱرْكَبُوا۟ فِيهَا بِسْمِ ٱللَّهِ مَجْر۪ىٰهَا
وَمُرْسَىٰهَآ ۚ إِنَّ رَبِّى لَغَفُورٌ رَّحِيمٌ ٤١

42. So the Ark floated with them on the waves (towering) like mountains, and Noah called out to his son, who had separated himself (from the rest): "O my son! Embark with us, and be not with the unbelievers!"

وَهِىَ تَجْرِى بِهِمْ فِى مَوْجٍ كَٱلْجِبَالِ وَنَادَىٰ نُوحٌ
ٱبْنَهُۥ وَكَانَ فِى مَعْزِلٍ يَـٰبُنَىَّ ٱرْكَب مَّعَنَا وَلَا تَكُن
مَّعَ ٱلْكَـٰفِرِينَ ٤٢

43. The son replied: "I will betake myself to some mountain: it will save me from the water." Noah said: "This day nothing can save, from the command of Allah, any but those on whom He has mercy!" - and the waves came between them, and the son was among those overwhelmed in the flood.

قَالَ سَـَٔاوِىٓ إِلَىٰ جَبَلٍ يَعْصِمُنِى مِنَ ٱلْمَآءِ ۚ قَالَ
لَا عَاصِمَ ٱلْيَوْمَ مِنْ أَمْرِ ٱللَّهِ إِلَّا مَن رَّحِمَ ۚ وَحَالَ
بَيْنَهُمَا ٱلْمَوْجُ فَكَانَ مِنَ ٱلْمُغْرَقِينَ ٤٣

44. Then the word went out: "O earth! Swallow up your water, and O sky! Withhold (your rain)!" And the water abated, and the matter was ended. The ark rested on mount Judi, and the word went forth: "Away with those who do wrong!"

وَقِيلَ يَٰٓأَرۡضُ ٱبۡلَعِي مَآءَكِ وَيَٰسَمَآءُ أَقۡلِعِي
وَغِيضَ ٱلۡمَآءُ وَقُضِيَ ٱلۡأَمۡرُ وَٱسۡتَوَتۡ عَلَى
ٱلۡجُودِيِّۖ وَقِيلَ بُعۡدٗا لِّلۡقَوۡمِ ٱلظَّٰلِمِينَ ٤٤

45. And Noah called upon his Lord, and said: "O my Lord! Surely my son is of my family! And Your promise is true, and You are the justest of judges!"

وَنَادَىٰ نُوحٞ رَّبَّهُۥ فَقَالَ رَبِّ إِنَّ ٱبۡنِي مِنۡ أَهۡلِي وَإِنَّ
وَعۡدَكَ ٱلۡحَقُّ وَأَنتَ أَحۡكَمُ ٱلۡحَٰكِمِينَ ٤٥

46. He said: "O Noah! He is not of your family: for his conduct is unrighteous. So ask not of Me that of which you have no knowledge! I give you counsel lest you act like the ignorant!"

قَالَ يَٰنُوحُ إِنَّهُۥ لَيۡسَ مِنۡ أَهۡلِكَۖ إِنَّهُۥ عَمَلٌ غَيۡرُ
صَٰلِحٖۖ فَلَا تَسۡـَٔلۡنِ مَا لَيۡسَ لَكَ بِهِۦ عِلۡمٌۖ إِنِّيٓ أَعِظُكَ
أَن تَكُونَ مِنَ ٱلۡجَٰهِلِينَ ٤٦

47. Noah said: "O my Lord! I do seek refuge with You, lest I ask You for that of which I have no knowledge. And unless You forgive me and have mercy on me, I should indeed be lost!"

قَالَ رَبِّ إِنِّيٓ أَعُوذُ بِكَ أَنۡ أَسۡـَٔلَكَ مَا لَيۡسَ لِي بِهِۦ عِلۡمٞۖ
وَإِلَّا تَغۡفِرۡ لِي وَتَرۡحَمۡنِيٓ أَكُن مِّنَ ٱلۡخَٰسِرِينَ ٤٧

48. The word came: "O Noah! Come down (from the ark) with peace from Us, and blessing on you and on some of the peoples (who will spring) from those with you: but (there will be other) peoples to whom We shall grant their pleasures (for a time), but in the end will a grievous penalty reach them from Us."

قِيلَ يَٰنُوحُ ٱهۡبِطۡ بِسَلَٰمٖ مِّنَّا وَبَرَكَٰتٍ عَلَيۡكَ
وَعَلَىٰٓ أُمَمٖ مِّمَّن مَّعَكَۚ وَأُمَمٞ سَنُمَتِّعُهُمۡ ثُمَّ
يَمَسُّهُم مِّنَّا عَذَابٌ أَلِيمٞ ٤٨

49. Such are some of the stories of the unseen, which We have revealed to you: before this, neither you nor your people knew them. So persevere patiently: for the end is for those who are righteous.

تِلۡكَ مِنۡ أَنۢبَآءِ ٱلۡغَيۡبِ نُوحِيهَآ إِلَيۡكَۖ مَا كُنتَ
تَعۡلَمُهَآ أَنتَ وَلَا قَوۡمُكَ مِن قَبۡلِ هَٰذَاۖ فَٱصۡبِرۡۖ إِنَّ
ٱلۡعَٰقِبَةَ لِلۡمُتَّقِينَ ٤٩

50. To the 'Ad people (We sent) Hud, one of their own brothers. He said: "O my people! Worship Allah! You have no other

وَإِلَىٰ عَادٍ أَخَاهُمۡ هُودٗاۚ قَالَ يَٰقَوۡمِ ٱعۡبُدُواْ ٱللَّهَ

god but Him. (Your other gods) you do nothing but invent!"

مَا لَكُم مِّنْ إِلَٰهٍ غَيْرُهُۥٓ ۖ إِنْ أَنتُمْ إِلَّا مُفْتَرُونَ ﴿٥٠﴾

51. "O my people! I ask of you no reward for this (message). My reward is from none but Him Who created me: will you not then understand?

يَٰقَوْمِ لَآ أَسْـَٔلُكُمْ عَلَيْهِ أَجْرًا ۖ إِنْ أَجْرِىَ إِلَّا عَلَى
ٱلَّذِى فَطَرَنِىٓ ۚ أَفَلَا تَعْقِلُونَ ﴿٥١﴾

52. "And O my people! Ask forgiveness of your Lord, and turn to Him (in repentance): He will send you the skies pouring abundant rain, and add strength to your strength: so turn you not back in sin!"

وَيَٰقَوْمِ ٱسْتَغْفِرُوا۟ رَبَّكُمْ ثُمَّ تُوبُوٓا۟ إِلَيْهِ
يُرْسِلِ ٱلسَّمَآءَ عَلَيْكُم مِّدْرَارًا وَيَزِدْكُمْ قُوَّةً
إِلَىٰ قُوَّتِكُمْ وَلَا تَتَوَلَّوْا۟ مُجْرِمِينَ ﴿٥٢﴾

53. They said: "O Hud! No clear (sign) have you brought us, and we are not the ones to desert our gods on your word! Nor shall we believe in you!

قَالُوا۟ يَٰهُودُ مَا جِئْتَنَا بِبَيِّنَةٍ وَمَا نَحْنُ
بِتَارِكِىٓ ءَالِهَتِنَا عَن قَوْلِكَ وَمَا نَحْنُ لَكَ
بِمُؤْمِنِينَ ﴿٥٣﴾

54. "We say nothing but that (perhaps) some of our gods may have seized you with imbecility." He said: "I call Allah to witness, and do you bear witness, that I am free from the sin of ascribing, to Him,

إِن نَّقُولُ إِلَّا ٱعْتَرَىٰكَ بَعْضُ ءَالِهَتِنَا بِسُوٓءٍ ۗ قَالَ إِنِّىٓ
أُشْهِدُ ٱللَّهَ وَٱشْهَدُوٓا۟ أَنِّى بَرِىٓءٌ مِّمَّا تُشْرِكُونَ ﴿٥٤﴾

55. Other gods as partners! So scheme (your worst) against me, all of you, and give me no respite.

مِن دُونِهِۦ ۖ فَكِيدُونِى جَمِيعًا ثُمَّ لَا تُنظِرُونِ ﴿٥٥﴾

56. I put my trust in Allah, my Lord and your Lord! There is not a moving creature, but He has grasp of its forelock. Verily, it is my Lord that is on a straight path.

إِنِّى تَوَكَّلْتُ عَلَى ٱللَّهِ رَبِّى وَرَبِّكُم ۚ مَّا مِن دَآبَّةٍ إِلَّا
هُوَ ءَاخِذٌۢ بِنَاصِيَتِهَآ ۚ إِنَّ رَبِّى عَلَىٰ صِرَٰطٍ مُّسْتَقِيمٍ ﴿٥٦﴾

57. If you turn away - I (at least) have conveyed the message with which I was sent to you. My Lord will make another people to succeed you, and you will not harm Him in the least. For my Lord has care and watch over all things."

فَإِن تَوَلَّوْا۟ فَقَدْ أَبْلَغْتُكُم مَّآ أُرْسِلْتُ بِهِۦٓ إِلَيْكُمْ ۚ
وَيَسْتَخْلِفُ رَبِّى قَوْمًا غَيْرَكُمْ وَلَا تَضُرُّونَهُۥ شَيْـًٔا ۚ
إِنَّ رَبِّى عَلَىٰ كُلِّ شَىْءٍ حَفِيظٌ ﴿٥٧﴾

58. So when Our decree issued, We saved Hud and those who believed with him, by (special) grace from Ourselves: We saved them from a severe penalty.

وَلَمَّا جَآءَ أَمْرُنَا نَجَّيْنَا هُودًا وَٱلَّذِينَ ءَامَنُوا۟ مَعَهُۥ
بِرَحْمَةٍ مِّنَّا وَنَجَّيْنَٰهُم مِّنْ عَذَابٍ غَلِيظٍ ﴿٥٨﴾

59. Such were the 'Ad people: they rejected the signs of their Lord and Cherisher; disobeyed His messengers; and followed the command of every powerful, obstinate transgressor.

وَتِلْكَ عَادٌ ۖ جَحَدُوا۟ بِـَٔايَٰتِ رَبِّهِمْ وَعَصَوْا۟ رُسُلَهُۥ
وَٱتَّبَعُوٓا۟ أَمْرَ كُلِّ جَبَّارٍ عَنِيدٍ ﴿٥٩﴾

60. And they were pursued by a curse in this life - and on the day of judgement. Ah! See! For the 'Ad rejected their Lord and Cherisher! Ah! See! Removed (from sight) were 'Ad, the people of Hud!

وَأُتْبِعُوا۟ فِى هَٰذِهِ ٱلدُّنْيَا لَعْنَةً وَيَوْمَ ٱلْقِيَٰمَةِ ۗ أَلَآ إِنَّ
عَادًا كَفَرُوا۟ رَبَّهُمْ ۗ أَلَا بُعْدًا لِّعَادٍ قَوْمِ هُودٍ ﴿٦٠﴾

61. To the Thamud people (We sent) Salih, one of their own brothers. He said: "O my people! Worship Allah: you have no other god but Him. It is He Who has produced you from the earth and settled you in it: then ask forgiveness of Him, and turn to Him (in repentance): for my Lord is (always) near, ready to answer."

۞ وَإِلَىٰ ثَمُودَ أَخَاهُمْ صَٰلِحًا ۚ قَالَ يَٰقَوْمِ ٱعْبُدُوا۟ ٱللَّهَ ثلاثة أرباع الحزب ٢٣
مَا لَكُم مِّنْ إِلَٰهٍ غَيْرُهُۥ ۖ هُوَ أَنشَأَكُم مِّنَ ٱلْأَرْضِ
وَٱسْتَعْمَرَكُمْ فِيهَا فَٱسْتَغْفِرُوهُ ثُمَّ تُوبُوٓا۟ إِلَيْهِ ۚ إِنَّ رَبِّى
قَرِيبٌ مُّجِيبٌ ﴿٦١﴾

62. They said: "O Salih! You have been of us! - A centre of our hopes so far! Do you (now) forbid us the worship of what our fathers worshipped? But we are really in suspicious (disquieting) doubt as to that to which you invite us."

قَالُوا۟ يَٰصَٰلِحُ قَدْ كُنتَ فِينَا مَرْجُوًّا قَبْلَ هَٰذَآ ۖ أَتَنْهَىٰنَآ
أَن نَّعْبُدَ مَا يَعْبُدُ ءَابَآؤُنَا وَإِنَّنَا لَفِى شَكٍّ مِّمَّا
تَدْعُونَآ إِلَيْهِ مُرِيبٍ ﴿٦٢﴾

63. He said: "O my people! Do you see? - If I have a clear (sign) from my Lord and He has sent mercy to me from Himself - who then can help me against Allah if I were to disobey Him? What then would you add to my (portion) but perdition?

قَالَ يَٰقَوْمِ أَرَءَيْتُمْ إِن كُنتُ عَلَىٰ بَيِّنَةٍ مِّن رَّبِّى
وَءَاتَىٰنِى مِنْهُ رَحْمَةً فَمَن يَنصُرُنِى مِنَ ٱللَّهِ إِنْ
عَصَيْتُهُۥ ۖ فَمَا تَزِيدُونَنِى غَيْرَ تَخْسِيرٍ ﴿٦٣﴾

64. And O my people! This she-camel of Allah is a symbol to you: leave her to feed

وَيَٰقَوْمِ هَٰذِهِۦ نَاقَةُ ٱللَّهِ لَكُمْ ءَايَةً ۖ

on Allah's (free) earth, and inflict no harm on her, or a swift penalty will seize you!"

فَذَرُوهَا تَأْكُلْ فِىٓ أَرْضِ ٱللَّهِ ۖ وَلَا تَمَسُّوهَا بِسُوٓءٍ
فَيَأْخُذَكُمْ عَذَابٌ قَرِيبٌ ﴿٦٤﴾

65. But they did hamstring her. So he said: "Enjoy yourselves in your homes for three days: (then will be your ruin): there a promise not to be belied!"

فَعَقَرُوهَا فَقَالَ تَمَتَّعُوا۟ فِى دَارِكُمْ ثَلَٰثَةَ
أَيَّامٍ ۖ ذَٰلِكَ وَعْدٌ غَيْرُ مَكْذُوبٍ ﴿٦٥﴾

66. When Our decree issued, We saved Salih and those who believed with him, by (special) grace from Ourselves - and from the disgrace of that day. For your Lord - He is the Strong One, and Able to enforce His Will.

فَلَمَّا جَآءَ أَمْرُنَا نَجَّيْنَا صَٰلِحًا وَٱلَّذِينَ ءَامَنُوا۟
مَعَهُۥ بِرَحْمَةٍ مِّنَّا وَمِنْ خِزْىِ يَوْمِئِذٍ ۗ إِنَّ
رَبَّكَ هُوَ ٱلْقَوِىُّ ٱلْعَزِيزُ ﴿٦٦﴾

67. The (mighty) blast overtook the wrongdoers, and they lay prostrate in their homes before the morning -

وَأَخَذَ ٱلَّذِينَ ظَلَمُوا۟ ٱلصَّيْحَةُ فَأَصْبَحُوا۟ فِى
دِيَٰرِهِمْ جَٰثِمِينَ ﴿٦٧﴾

68. As if they had never dwelt and flourished there. Ah! See! For the Thamud rejected their Lord and Cherisher! Ah! See! Removed (from sight) were the Thamud!

كَأَن لَّمْ يَغْنَوْا۟ فِيهَآ ۗ أَلَآ إِنَّ ثَمُودَا۟ كَفَرُوا۟
رَبَّهُمْ ۗ أَلَا بُعْدًا لِّثَمُودَ ﴿٦٨﴾

69. There came Our messengers to Abraham with glad tidings. They said, "Peace!" He answered, "Peace!" And hastened to entertain them with a roasted calf.

وَلَقَدْ جَآءَتْ رُسُلُنَآ إِبْرَٰهِيمَ بِٱلْبُشْرَىٰ قَالُوا۟
سَلَٰمًا ۖ قَالَ سَلَٰمٌ ۖ فَمَا لَبِثَ أَن جَآءَ بِعِجْلٍ حَنِيذٍ ﴿٦٩﴾

70. But when he saw their hands went not towards the (meal), he felt some mistrust of them, and conceived a fear of them. They said: "Fear not: we have been sent against the people of Lot."

فَلَمَّا رَءَآ أَيْدِيَهُمْ لَا تَصِلُ إِلَيْهِ نَكِرَهُمْ
وَأَوْجَسَ مِنْهُمْ خِيفَةً ۚ قَالُوا۟ لَا تَخَفْ إِنَّآ
أُرْسِلْنَآ إِلَىٰ قَوْمِ لُوطٍ ﴿٧٠﴾

71. And his wife was standing (there), and she laughed: but We gave her glad tidings of Isaac, and after him, of Jacob.

وَٱمْرَأَتُهُۥ قَآئِمَةٌ فَضَحِكَتْ فَبَشَّرْنَٰهَا بِإِسْحَٰقَ
وَمِن وَرَآءِ إِسْحَٰقَ يَعْقُوبَ ﴿٧١﴾

72. She said: "Alas for me! Shall I bear a child, seeing I am an old woman, and my husband here is an old man? That would indeed be a wonderful thing!"

قَالَتْ يَٰوَيْلَتَىٰٓ ءَأَلِدُ وَأَنَا۠ عَجُوزٌ وَهَٰذَا بَعْلِى شَيْخًا ۖ
إِنَّ هَٰذَا لَشَىْءٌ عَجِيبٌ ﴿٧٢﴾

73. They said: "Do you wonder at Allah's decree? The grace of Allah and His blessings on you, O you people of the house! For He is indeed worthy of all praise, full of all glory!"

قَالُوٓا۟ أَتَعْجَبِينَ مِنْ أَمْرِ ٱللَّهِ ۖ رَحْمَتُ ٱللَّهِ وَبَرَكَٰتُهُۥ
عَلَيْكُمْ أَهْلَ ٱلْبَيْتِ ۚ إِنَّهُۥ حَمِيدٌ مَّجِيدٌ ﴿٧٣﴾

74. When fear had passed from (the mind of) Abraham and the glad tidings had reached him, he began to plead with Us for Lot's people.

فَلَمَّا ذَهَبَ عَنْ إِبْرَٰهِيمَ ٱلرَّوْعُ وَجَآءَتْهُ ٱلْبُشْرَىٰ
يُجَٰدِلُنَا فِى قَوْمِ لُوطٍ ﴿٧٤﴾

75. For Abraham was, without doubt, forbearing (of faults), compassionate, and given to look to Allah.

إِنَّ إِبْرَٰهِيمَ لَحَلِيمٌ أَوَّٰهٌ مُّنِيبٌ ﴿٧٥﴾

76. O Abraham! Seek not this. The decree of your Lord has gone out: for them there comes a penalty that cannot be turned back!

يَٰٓإِبْرَٰهِيمُ أَعْرِضْ عَنْ هَٰذَآ ۖ إِنَّهُۥ قَدْ جَآءَ أَمْرُ رَبِّكَ ۖ
وَإِنَّهُمْ ءَاتِيهِمْ عَذَابٌ غَيْرُ مَرْدُودٍ ﴿٧٦﴾

77. When Our messengers came to Lot, he was grieved on their account and felt himself powerless (to protect) them. He said: "This is a distressful day."

وَلَمَّا جَآءَتْ رُسُلُنَا لُوطًا سِىٓءَ بِهِمْ وَضَاقَ بِهِمْ
ذَرْعًا وَقَالَ هَٰذَا يَوْمٌ عَصِيبٌ ﴿٧٧﴾

78. And his people came rushing towards him, and they had been long in the habit of practising abominations. He said: "O my people! Here are my daughters: they are purer for you (if you marry)! Now fear Allah, and cover me not with shame about my guests! Is there not among you a single right-minded man?"

وَجَآءَهُۥ قَوْمُهُۥ يُهْرَعُونَ إِلَيْهِ وَمِن قَبْلُ كَانُوا۟
يَعْمَلُونَ ٱلسَّيِّـَٔاتِ ۚ قَالَ يَٰقَوْمِ هَٰٓؤُلَآءِ بَنَاتِى هُنَّ
أَطْهَرُ لَكُمْ ۖ فَٱتَّقُوا۟ ٱللَّهَ وَلَا تُخْزُونِ فِى ضَيْفِىٓ ۖ
أَلَيْسَ مِنكُمْ رَجُلٌ رَّشِيدٌ ﴿٧٨﴾

79. They said: "Well do you know we have no need of your daughters: indeed you know quite well what we want!"

قَالُوا۟ لَقَدْ عَلِمْتَ مَا لَنَا فِى بَنَاتِكَ مِنْ حَقٍّ وَإِنَّكَ
لَتَعْلَمُ مَا نُرِيدُ ﴿٧٩﴾

80. He said: "Would that I had power to suppress you or that I could betake myself to some powerful support."

قَالَ لَوْ أَنَّ لِي بِكُمْ قُوَّةً أَوْ آوِي إِلَىٰ رُكْنٍ شَدِيدٍ ٨٠

81. (The messengers) said, "O Lot! We are messengers from your Lord! By no means shall they reach you! Now travel with your family while yet a part of the night remains, and let not any of you look back; but your wife (will remain behind); to her will happen what happens to the people. Morning is their time appointed: is not the morning near?"

قَالُوا يَا لُوطُ إِنَّا رُسُلُ رَبِّكَ لَنْ يَصِلُوا إِلَيْكَ ۖ
فَأَسْرِ بِأَهْلِكَ بِقِطْعٍ مِنَ اللَّيْلِ وَلَا يَلْتَفِتْ مِنْكُمْ
أَحَدٌ إِلَّا امْرَأَتَكَ ۖ إِنَّهُ مُصِيبُهَا مَا أَصَابَهُمْ ۚ إِنَّ
مَوْعِدَهُمُ الصُّبْحُ ۚ أَلَيْسَ الصُّبْحُ بِقَرِيبٍ ٨١

82. When Our decree issued, We turned (the cities) upside down, and rained down on them brimstones hard as baked clay, spread layer on layer -

فَلَمَّا جَاءَ أَمْرُنَا جَعَلْنَا عَالِيَهَا سَافِلَهَا وَأَمْطَرْنَا
عَلَيْهَا حِجَارَةً مِنْ سِجِّيلٍ مَنْضُودٍ ٨٢

83. Marked as from your Lord: nor are they ever far from those who do wrong!

مُسَوَّمَةً عِنْدَ رَبِّكَ ۖ وَمَا هِيَ مِنَ الظَّالِمِينَ
بِبَعِيدٍ ٨٣

84. To the Madyan people (We sent) Shu'ayb, one of their own brothers: he said: "O my people! Worship Allah: you have no other god but Him. And give not short measure or weight: I see you in prosperity, but I fear for you the penalty of a day that will compass (you) all round."

الحزب ٢٤

۞ وَإِلَىٰ مَدْيَنَ أَخَاهُمْ شُعَيْبًا ۚ قَالَ يَا قَوْمِ اعْبُدُوا
اللَّهَ مَا لَكُمْ مِنْ إِلَٰهٍ غَيْرُهُ ۖ وَلَا تَنْقُصُوا
الْمِكْيَالَ وَالْمِيزَانَ ۚ إِنِّي أَرَاكُمْ بِخَيْرٍ
وَإِنِّي أَخَافُ عَلَيْكُمْ عَذَابَ يَوْمٍ مُحِيطٍ ٨٤

85. "And O my people! Give just measure and weight, nor withhold from the people the things that are their due: commit not evil in the land with intent to do mischief.

وَيَا قَوْمِ أَوْفُوا الْمِكْيَالَ وَالْمِيزَانَ بِالْقِسْطِ ۖ
وَلَا تَبْخَسُوا النَّاسَ أَشْيَاءَهُمْ وَلَا تَعْثَوْا فِي
الْأَرْضِ مُفْسِدِينَ ٨٥

86. That which is left you by Allah is best for you, if you (but) believed! But I am not set over you to keep watch!"

بَقِيَّتُ اللَّهِ خَيْرٌ لَكُمْ إِنْ كُنْتُمْ مُؤْمِنِينَ ۚ
وَمَا أَنَا عَلَيْكُمْ بِحَفِيظٍ ٨٦

87. They said: "O Shu'ayb! Does your (religion of) prayer command you that we leave off the worship which our fathers practised, or that we leave off doing what we like with our property? Truly, you are the one that forbears with faults and is right-minded!"

قَالُوا۟ يَٰشُعَيْبُ أَصَلَوٰتُكَ تَأْمُرُكَ أَن نَّتْرُكَ
مَا يَعْبُدُ ءَابَآؤُنَآ أَوْ أَن نَّفْعَلَ فِىٓ أَمْوَٰلِنَا
مَا نَشَٰٓؤُا۟ ۖ إِنَّكَ لَأَنتَ ٱلْحَلِيمُ ٱلرَّشِيدُ ﴿٨٧﴾

88. He said: "O my people! See you whether I have a clear (sign) from my Lord, and He has given me sustenance (pure and) good as from Himself? I wish not, in opposition to you, to do that which I forbid you to do. I only desire (your) betterment to the best of my power; and my success (in my task) can only come from Allah: in Him I trust, and to Him I look.

قَالَ يَٰقَوْمِ أَرَءَيْتُمْ إِن كُنتُ عَلَىٰ بَيِّنَةٍ مِّن
رَّبِّى وَرَزَقَنِى مِنْهُ رِزْقًا حَسَنًا ۚ وَمَآ أُرِيدُ أَنْ
أُخَالِفَكُمْ إِلَىٰ مَآ أَنْهَىٰكُمْ عَنْهُ ۚ إِنْ أُرِيدُ
إِلَّا ٱلْإِصْلَٰحَ مَا ٱسْتَطَعْتُ ۚ وَمَا تَوْفِيقِىٓ إِلَّا بِٱللَّهِ ۚ
عَلَيْهِ تَوَكَّلْتُ وَإِلَيْهِ أُنِيبُ ﴿٨٨﴾

89. "And O my people! Let not my dissent (from you) cause you to sin, lest you suffer a fate similar to that of the people of Noah or of Hud or of Salih, nor are the people of Lot far off from you!

وَيَٰقَوْمِ لَا يَجْرِمَنَّكُمْ شِقَاقِىٓ أَن يُصِيبَكُم مِّثْلُ
مَآ أَصَابَ قَوْمَ نُوحٍ أَوْ قَوْمَ هُودٍ أَوْ قَوْمَ صَٰلِحٍ ۚ وَمَا
قَوْمُ لُوطٍ مِّنكُم بِبَعِيدٍ ﴿٨٩﴾

90. But ask forgiveness of you Lord, and turn to Him (in repentance): for my Lord is indeed Full of mercy and loving-kindness."

وَٱسْتَغْفِرُوا۟ رَبَّكُمْ ثُمَّ تُوبُوٓا۟ إِلَيْهِ ۚ إِنَّ رَبِّى
رَحِيمٌ وَدُودٌ ﴿٩٠﴾

91. They said: "O Shu'ayb! Much of what you say we do not understand! In fact, among us we see that you have no strength! Were it not for your family, we should certainly have stoned you! For you have among us no great position!"

قَالُوا۟ يَٰشُعَيْبُ مَا نَفْقَهُ كَثِيرًا مِّمَّا تَقُولُ وَإِنَّا
لَنَرَىٰكَ فِينَا ضَعِيفًا ۖ وَلَوْلَا رَهْطُكَ لَرَجَمْنَٰكَ ۖ
وَمَآ أَنتَ عَلَيْنَا بِعَزِيزٍ ﴿٩١﴾

92. He said: "O my people! Is then my family of more consideration with you than Allah? For you cast Him away behind your backs (with contempt). But verily my Lord encompasses on all sides all that you do!

قَالَ يَٰقَوْمِ أَرَهْطِىٓ أَعَزُّ عَلَيْكُم مِّنَ ٱللَّهِ
وَٱتَّخَذْتُمُوهُ وَرَآءَكُمْ ظِهْرِيًّا ۖ إِنَّ رَبِّى بِمَا
تَعْمَلُونَ مُحِيطٌ ﴿٩٢﴾

93. And O my people! Do whatever you can: I will do (my part): soon will you know who it is on whom descends the penalty of disgrace, and who is a liar! And watch you! For I too am watching with you!"

وَيَٰقَوۡمِ ٱعۡمَلُواْ عَلَىٰ مَكَانَتِكُمۡ إِنِّي عَٰمِلٞۖ
سَوۡفَ تَعۡلَمُونَ مَن يَأۡتِيهِ عَذَابٞ يُخۡزِيهِ وَمَنۡ
هُوَ كَٰذِبٞۖ وَٱرۡتَقِبُوٓاْ إِنِّي مَعَكُمۡ رَقِيبٞ ﴿٩٣﴾

94. When Our decree issued, We saved Shu'ayb and those who believed with him, by (special) mercy from Ourselves: but the (mighty) blast did seize the wrongdoers, and they lay prostrate in their homes by the morning -

وَلَمَّا جَآءَ أَمۡرُنَا نَجَّيۡنَا شُعَيۡبٗا وَٱلَّذِينَ ءَامَنُواْ
مَعَهُۥ بِرَحۡمَةٖ مِّنَّا وَأَخَذَتِ ٱلَّذِينَ ظَلَمُواْ
ٱلصَّيۡحَةُ فَأَصۡبَحُواْ فِي دِيَٰرِهِمۡ جَٰثِمِينَ ﴿٩٤﴾

95. As if they had never dwelt and flourished there! Ah! See! How the Madyan were removed (from sight) as were removed the Thamud!

كَأَن لَّمۡ يَغۡنَوۡاْ فِيهَآۗ أَلَا بُعۡدٗا لِّمَدۡيَنَ كَمَا
بَعِدَتۡ ثَمُودُ ﴿٩٥﴾

96. And We sent Moses with Our clear (signs) and an authority manifest,

وَلَقَدۡ أَرۡسَلۡنَا مُوسَىٰ بِـَٔايَٰتِنَا وَسُلۡطَٰنٖ مُّبِينٍ ﴿٩٦﴾

97. To Pharaoh and his chiefs: but they followed the command of Pharaoh, and the command of Pharaoh was no right (guide).

إِلَىٰ فِرۡعَوۡنَ وَمَلَإِيْهِۦ فَٱتَّبَعُوٓاْ أَمۡرَ فِرۡعَوۡنَۖ وَمَآ
أَمۡرُ فِرۡعَوۡنَ بِرَشِيدٖ ﴿٩٧﴾

98. He will go before his people on the day of judgement, and lead them into the fire (as cattle are led to water): but woeful indeed will be the place to which they are led!

يَقۡدُمُ قَوۡمَهُۥ يَوۡمَ ٱلۡقِيَٰمَةِ فَأَوۡرَدَهُمُ ٱلنَّارَۖ
وَبِئۡسَ ٱلۡوِرۡدُ ٱلۡمَوۡرُودُ ﴿٩٨﴾

99. And they are followed by a curse in this (life) and on the day of judgement: and woeful is the gift which shall be given (to them)!

وَأُتۡبِعُواْ فِي هَٰذِهِۦ لَعۡنَةٗ وَيَوۡمَ ٱلۡقِيَٰمَةِۚ بِئۡسَ
ٱلرِّفۡدُ ٱلۡمَرۡفُودُ ﴿٩٩﴾

100. These are some of the stories of communities which We relate to you: of them some are standing, and some have been mown down (by the sickle of time).

ذَٰلِكَ مِنۡ أَنۢبَآءِ ٱلۡقُرَىٰ نَقُصُّهُۥ عَلَيۡكَۖ مِنۡهَا
قَآئِمٞ وَحَصِيدٞ ﴿١٠٠﴾

101. It was not We that wronged them: they wronged their own souls: the deities, other than Allah, whom they invoked, profited them not at all when there issued the decree of your Lord nor did they add anything (to their lot) but perdition!

وَمَا ظَلَمْنَٰهُمْ وَلَٰكِن ظَلَمُوٓا۟ أَنفُسَهُمْ ۖ فَمَآ أَغْنَتْ عَنْهُمْ ءَالِهَتُهُمُ ٱلَّتِى يَدْعُونَ مِن دُونِ ٱللَّهِ مِن شَىْءٍ لَّمَّا جَآءَ أَمْرُ رَبِّكَ ۖ وَمَا زَادُوهُمْ غَيْرَ تَتْبِيبٍ ﴿١٠١﴾

102. Such is the chastisement of your Lord when He chastises communities in the midst of their wrong: grievous, indeed, and severe is His chastisement.

وَكَذَٰلِكَ أَخْذُ رَبِّكَ إِذَآ أَخَذَ ٱلْقُرَىٰ وَهِىَ ظَٰلِمَةٌ ۚ إِنَّ أَخْذَهُۥٓ أَلِيمٌ شَدِيدٌ ﴿١٠٢﴾

103. In that is a sign for those who fear the penalty of the hereafter; that is a day for which mankind will be gathered together; that will be a day of testimony.

إِنَّ فِى ذَٰلِكَ لَءَايَةً لِّمَنْ خَافَ عَذَابَ ٱلْءَاخِرَةِ ۚ ذَٰلِكَ يَوْمٌ مَّجْمُوعٌ لَّهُ ٱلنَّاسُ وَذَٰلِكَ يَوْمٌ مَّشْهُودٌ ﴿١٠٣﴾

104. Nor shall We delay it but for a term appointed.

وَمَا نُؤَخِّرُهُۥٓ إِلَّا لِأَجَلٍ مَّعْدُودٍ ﴿١٠٤﴾

105. The day it arrives, no soul shall speak except by His permission; of those (gathered) some will be wretched and some will be blessed.

يَوْمَ يَأْتِ لَا تَكَلَّمُ نَفْسٌ إِلَّا بِإِذْنِهِۦ ۚ فَمِنْهُمْ شَقِىٌّ وَسَعِيدٌ ﴿١٠٥﴾

106. Those who are wretched shall be in the fire; there will be for them in it (nothing but) the heaving of sighs and sobs;

فَأَمَّا ٱلَّذِينَ شَقُوا۟ فَفِى ٱلنَّارِ لَهُمْ فِيهَا زَفِيرٌ وَشَهِيقٌ ﴿١٠٦﴾

107. They will dwell in it for all the time that the heavens and the earth endure, except as your Lord wills: for your Lord is the (sure) Accomplisher of what He plans.

خَٰلِدِينَ فِيهَا مَا دَامَتِ ٱلسَّمَٰوَٰتُ وَٱلْأَرْضُ إِلَّا مَا شَآءَ رَبُّكَ ۚ إِنَّ رَبَّكَ فَعَّالٌ لِّمَا يُرِيدُ ﴿١٠٧﴾

108. And those who are blessed shall be in the garden; they will dwell in it for all the time that the heavens and the earth endure, except as your Lord wills: a gift without break.

۞ وَأَمَّا ٱلَّذِينَ سُعِدُوا۟ فَفِى ٱلْجَنَّةِ خَٰلِدِينَ فِيهَا مَا دَامَتِ ٱلسَّمَٰوَٰتُ وَٱلْأَرْضُ إِلَّا مَا شَآءَ رَبُّكَ ۖ عَطَآءً غَيْرَ مَجْذُوذٍ ﴿١٠٨﴾ ربع الحزب ٢٤

109. Be not then in doubt as to what these men worship. They worship nothing but what their fathers worshipped before (them): but verily We shall pay them back (in full) their portion without (the least) abatement.

فَلَا تَكُ فِي مِرۡيَةٖ مِّمَّا يَعۡبُدُ هَٰٓؤُلَآءِۚ مَا يَعۡبُدُونَ
إِلَّا كَمَا يَعۡبُدُ ءَابَآؤُهُم مِّن قَبۡلُۚ وَإِنَّا لَمُوَفُّوهُمۡ
نَصِيبَهُمۡ غَيۡرَ مَنقُوصٖ ١٠٩

110. We certainly gave the book to Moses, but differences arose in it; had it not been that a word had gone before from your Lord, the matter would have been decided between them; but they are in suspicious doubt concerning it.

وَلَقَدۡ ءَاتَيۡنَا مُوسَى ٱلۡكِتَٰبَ فَٱخۡتُلِفَ فِيهِۚ
وَلَوۡلَا كَلِمَةٞ سَبَقَتۡ مِن رَّبِّكَ لَقُضِيَ بَيۡنَهُمۡۚ وَإِنَّهُمۡ
لَفِي شَكّٖ مِّنۡهُ مُرِيبٖ ١١٠

111. And of a surety, to all will your Lord pay back (in full the recompense) of their deeds: for He knows well all that they do.

وَإِنَّ كُلّٗا لَّمَّا لَيُوَفِّيَنَّهُمۡ رَبُّكَ أَعۡمَٰلَهُمۡۚ إِنَّهُۥ بِمَا
يَعۡمَلُونَ خَبِيرٞ ١١١

112. Therefore, stand firm (in the straight path) as you are commanded - you and those who with you turn (to Allah); and transgress not (from the path): for He sees well all that you do.

فَٱسۡتَقِمۡ كَمَآ أُمِرۡتَ وَمَن تَابَ مَعَكَ وَلَا تَطۡغَوۡاْۚ
إِنَّهُۥ بِمَا تَعۡمَلُونَ بَصِيرٞ ١١٢

113. And incline not to those who do wrong, or the fire will seize you; and you have no protectors other than Allah, nor shall you be helped.

وَلَا تَرۡكَنُوٓاْ إِلَى ٱلَّذِينَ ظَلَمُواْ فَتَمَسَّكُمُ ٱلنَّارُ
وَمَا لَكُم مِّن دُونِ ٱللَّهِ مِنۡ أَوۡلِيَآءَ ثُمَّ
لَا تُنصَرُونَ ١١٣

114. And establish regular prayers at the two ends of the day and at the approaches of the night; for those things that are good remove those that are evil; be that the word of remembrance to those who remember (their Lord);

وَأَقِمِ ٱلصَّلَوٰةَ طَرَفَيِ ٱلنَّهَارِ وَزُلَفٗا مِّنَ ٱلَّيۡلِۚ
إِنَّ ٱلۡحَسَنَٰتِ يُذۡهِبۡنَ ٱلسَّيِّـَٔاتِۚ ذَٰلِكَ
ذِكۡرَىٰ لِلذَّٰكِرِينَ ١١٤

115. And be steadfast in patience; for verily Allah will not suffer the reward of the righteous to perish.

وَٱصۡبِرۡ فَإِنَّ ٱللَّهَ لَا يُضِيعُ أَجۡرَ ٱلۡمُحۡسِنِينَ ١١٥

116. Why were there not, among the generations before you, persons possessed of balanced good sense, prohibiting (men) from mischief in the earth - except a few among them whom We saved (from harm)? But the wrongdoers pursued the enjoyment of the good things of life which were given them, and persisted in sin.

فَلَوْلَا كَانَ مِنَ ٱلْقُرُونِ مِن قَبْلِكُمْ أُو۟لُوا۟ بَقِيَّةٍ
يَنْهَوْنَ عَنِ ٱلْفَسَادِ فِى ٱلْأَرْضِ إِلَّا قَلِيلًا مِّمَّنْ
أَنجَيْنَا مِنْهُمْ ۗ وَٱتَّبَعَ ٱلَّذِينَ ظَلَمُوا۟ مَآ أُتْرِفُوا۟ فِيهِ
وَكَانُوا۟ مُجْرِمِينَ ﴿١١٦﴾

117. Nor would your Lord be the One to destroy communities for a single wrongdoing if its members were likely to mend.

وَمَا كَانَ رَبُّكَ لِيُهْلِكَ ٱلْقُرَىٰ بِظُلْمٍ وَأَهْلُهَا
مُصْلِحُونَ ﴿١١٧﴾

118. If your Lord had so willed, He could have made mankind one people: but they will not cease to dispute,

وَلَوْ شَآءَ رَبُّكَ لَجَعَلَ ٱلنَّاسَ أُمَّةً وَٰحِدَةً ۖ وَلَا يَزَالُونَ
مُخْتَلِفِينَ ﴿١١٨﴾

119. Except those on whom your Lord has bestowed His mercy: and for this did He create them: and the word of your Lord shall be fulfilled: "I will fill hell with jinns and men all together."

إِلَّا مَن رَّحِمَ رَبُّكَ ۚ وَلِذَٰلِكَ خَلَقَهُمْ ۗ وَتَمَّتْ
كَلِمَةُ رَبِّكَ لَأَمْلَأَنَّ جَهَنَّمَ مِنَ ٱلْجِنَّةِ وَٱلنَّاسِ
أَجْمَعِينَ ﴿١١٩﴾

120. All that We relate to you of the stories of the messengers - with it We make firm your heart: in them there comes to you the truth, as well as an exhortation and a message of remembrance to those who believe.

وَكُلًّا نَّقُصُّ عَلَيْكَ مِنْ أَنۢبَآءِ ٱلرُّسُلِ مَا نُثَبِّتُ بِهِۦ
فُؤَادَكَ ۚ وَجَآءَكَ فِى هَٰذِهِ ٱلْحَقُّ وَمَوْعِظَةٌ وَذِكْرَىٰ
لِلْمُؤْمِنِينَ ﴿١٢٠﴾

121. Say to those who do not believe: "Do whatever you can: we shall do our part;

وَقُل لِّلَّذِينَ لَا يُؤْمِنُونَ ٱعْمَلُوا۟ عَلَىٰ مَكَانَتِكُمْ إِنَّا
عَٰمِلُونَ ﴿١٢١﴾

122. And wait you! We too shall wait."

وَٱنتَظِرُوٓا۟ إِنَّا مُنتَظِرُونَ ﴿١٢٢﴾

123. To Allah do belong the unseen (secrets) of the heavens and the earth, and to Him goes back every affair (for decision): then worship Him, and put your

وَلِلَّهِ غَيْبُ ٱلسَّمَٰوَٰتِ وَٱلْأَرْضِ وَإِلَيْهِ يُرْجَعُ
ٱلْأَمْرُ كُلُّهُۥ فَٱعْبُدْهُ وَتَوَكَّلْ عَلَيْهِ ۚ وَمَا رَبُّكَ

بِغَٰفِلٍ عَمَّا تَعۡمَلُونَ ﴿١٢٣﴾

trust in Him; and your Lord is not unmindful of anything that you do.

سُورَةُ يُوسُفَ

Surah 12: **Yusuf** (Joseph)

بِسۡمِ ٱللَّهِ ٱلرَّحۡمَٰنِ ٱلرَّحِيمِ

In the name of Allah, Most Gracious, Most Merciful.

الٓرۚ تِلۡكَ ءَايَٰتُ ٱلۡكِتَٰبِ ٱلۡمُبِينِ ﴿١﴾

1. *Alif Lam Ra*. These are the symbols (or verses) of the perspicuous book.

إِنَّآ أَنزَلۡنَٰهُ قُرۡءَٰنًا عَرَبِيّٗا لَّعَلَّكُمۡ تَعۡقِلُونَ ﴿٢﴾

2. We have sent it down as an Arabic Qur'an, in order that you may learn wisdom.

نَحۡنُ نَقُصُّ عَلَيۡكَ أَحۡسَنَ ٱلۡقَصَصِ بِمَآ أَوۡحَيۡنَآ
إِلَيۡكَ هَٰذَا ٱلۡقُرۡءَانَ وَإِن كُنتَ مِن قَبۡلِهِۦ لَمِنَ
ٱلۡغَٰفِلِينَ ﴿٣﴾

3. We do relate to you the most beautiful of stories, in that We reveal to you this (portion of the) Qur'an; before this, you too were among those who knew it not.

إِذۡ قَالَ يُوسُفُ لِأَبِيهِ يَٰٓأَبَتِ إِنِّي رَأَيۡتُ أَحَدَ
عَشَرَ كَوۡكَبٗا وَٱلشَّمۡسَ وَٱلۡقَمَرَ رَأَيۡتُهُمۡ لِي
سَٰجِدِينَ ﴿٤﴾

4. See, Joseph said to his father: "O my father! I did see eleven stars and the sun and the moon; I saw them prostrate themselves to me!"

قَالَ يَٰبُنَيَّ لَا تَقۡصُصۡ رُءۡيَاكَ عَلَىٰٓ إِخۡوَتِكَ فَيَكِيدُواْ
لَكَ كَيۡدًاۖ إِنَّ ٱلشَّيۡطَٰنَ لِلۡإِنسَٰنِ عَدُوّٞ مُّبِينٞ ﴿٥﴾

5. Said (the father): "My (dear) little son! Relate not your vision to your brothers, lest they concoct a plot against you; for Satan is to man an avowed enemy!"

وَكَذَٰلِكَ يَجۡتَبِيكَ رَبُّكَ وَيُعَلِّمُكَ مِن تَأۡوِيلِ
ٱلۡأَحَادِيثِ وَيُتِمُّ نِعۡمَتَهُۥ عَلَيۡكَ وَعَلَىٰٓ ءَالِ يَعۡقُوبَ
كَمَآ أَتَمَّهَا عَلَىٰٓ أَبَوَيۡكَ مِن قَبۡلُ إِبۡرَٰهِيمَ وَإِسۡحَٰقَۚ
إِنَّ رَبَّكَ عَلِيمٌ حَكِيمٞ ﴿٦﴾

6. "Thus will your Lord choose you and teach you the interpretation of stories (and events) and perfect His favour to you and to the posterity of Jacob - even as He perfected it to your fathers Abraham and Isaac before! For your Lord is full of knowledge and wisdom."

نصف الحزب ٢٤

7. Verily in Joseph and his brothers are signs (or symbols) for seekers (after truth).

۞ لَّقَدْ كَانَ فِي يُوسُفَ وَإِخْوَتِهِۦٓ ءَايَٰتٌ
لِّلسَّآئِلِينَ ٧

8. They said: "Truly Joseph and his brother are loved more by our father than we; but we are a goodly body! Really our father is obviously wandering (in his mind)!

إِذْ قَالُواْ لَيُوسُفُ وَأَخُوهُ أَحَبُّ إِلَىٰٓ أَبِينَا مِنَّا وَنَحْنُ
عُصْبَةٌ إِنَّ أَبَانَا لَفِي ضَلَٰلٍ مُّبِينٍ ٨

9. Slay you Joseph or cast him out to some (unknown) land, that so the favour of your father may be given to you alone: (There will be time enough) for you to be righteous after that!"

ٱقْتُلُواْ يُوسُفَ أَوِ ٱطْرَحُوهُ أَرْضًا يَخْلُ لَكُمْ وَجْهُ
أَبِيكُمْ وَتَكُونُواْ مِنۢ بَعْدِهِۦ قَوْمًا صَٰلِحِينَ ٩

10. Said one of them: "Slay not Joseph, but if you must do something, throw him down to the bottom of the well: he will be picked up by some caravan of travellers."

قَالَ قَآئِلٌ مِّنْهُمْ لَا تَقْتُلُواْ يُوسُفَ وَأَلْقُوهُ فِي غَيَٰبَتِ
ٱلْجُبِّ يَلْتَقِطْهُ بَعْضُ ٱلسَّيَّارَةِ إِن كُنتُمْ فَٰعِلِينَ ١٠

11. They said: "O our father! Why do you not trust us with Joseph - seeing we are indeed his sincere well-wishers?"

قَالُواْ يَٰٓأَبَانَا مَا لَكَ لَا تَأْمَ۬نَّا عَلَىٰ يُوسُفَ وَإِنَّا لَهُۥ
لَنَٰصِحُونَ ١١

12. "Send him with us tomorrow to enjoy himself and play, and we shall take every care of him."

أَرْسِلْهُ مَعَنَا غَدًا يَرْتَعْ وَيَلْعَبْ وَإِنَّا لَهُۥ لَحَٰفِظُونَ ١٢

13. (Jacob) said: "Really it saddens me that you should take him away: I fear lest the wolf should devour him while you attend not to him."

قَالَ إِنِّي لَيَحْزُنُنِيٓ أَن تَذْهَبُواْ بِهِۦ وَأَخَافُ أَن
يَأْكُلَهُ ٱلذِّئْبُ وَأَنتُمْ عَنْهُ غَٰفِلُونَ ١٣

14. They said: "If the wolf were to devour him while we are (so large) a party, then should we indeed (first) have perished ourselves!"

قَالُواْ لَئِنْ أَكَلَهُ ٱلذِّئْبُ وَنَحْنُ عُصْبَةٌ إِنَّآ
إِذًا لَّخَٰسِرُونَ ١٤

15. So they did take him away, and they all agreed to throw him down to the bottom

فَلَمَّا ذَهَبُواْ بِهِۦ وَأَجْمَعُوٓاْ أَن يَجْعَلُوهُ فِي غَيَٰبَتِ

of the well; and We put into his heart (this message): "Certainly you shall (one day) tell them the truth of this their affair while they know (you) not."

ٱلْجُبِّ ۚ وَأَوْحَيْنَآ إِلَيْهِ لَتُنَبِّئَنَّهُم بِأَمْرِهِمْ هَـٰذَا وَهُمْ
لَا يَشْعُرُونَ ﴿١٥﴾

16. Then they came to their father in the early part of the night, weeping.

وَجَآءُوٓ أَبَاهُمْ عِشَآءً يَبْكُونَ ﴿١٦﴾

17. They said: "O our father! We went racing with one another and left Joseph with our things; and the wolf devoured him. But you will never believe us even though we tell the truth."

قَالُوا۟ يَـٰٓأَبَانَآ إِنَّا ذَهَبْنَا نَسْتَبِقُ وَتَرَكْنَا يُوسُفَ
عِندَ مَتَـٰعِنَا فَأَكَلَهُ ٱلذِّئْبُ ۖ وَمَآ أَنتَ بِمُؤْمِنٍ
لَّنَا وَلَوْ كُنَّا صَـٰدِقِينَ ﴿١٧﴾

18. They stained his shirt with false blood. He said: "Nay, but your minds have made up a tale (that may pass) with you. (For me) patience is most fitting: against that which you assert, it is Allah (alone) whose help can be sought."

وَجَآءُو عَلَىٰ قَمِيصِهِۦ بِدَمٍ كَذِبٍ ۚ قَالَ بَلْ سَوَّلَتْ
لَكُمْ أَنفُسُكُمْ أَمْرًا ۖ فَصَبْرٌ جَمِيلٌ ۖ وَٱللَّهُ
ٱلْمُسْتَعَانُ عَلَىٰ مَا تَصِفُونَ ﴿١٨﴾

19. Then there came a caravan of travellers: they sent their water-carrier (for water), and he let down his bucket (into the well). He said: "Ah there! Good news! Here is a (fine) young man!" So they concealed him as a treasure! But Allah knows well all that they do!

وَجَآءَتْ سَيَّارَةٌ فَأَرْسَلُوا۟ وَارِدَهُمْ فَأَدْلَىٰ دَلْوَهُۥ ۖ
قَالَ يَـٰبُشْرَىٰ هَـٰذَا غُلَـٰمٌ ۚ وَأَسَرُّوهُ بِضَـٰعَةً ۚ وَٱللَّهُ عَلِيمٌۢ
بِمَا يَعْمَلُونَ ﴿١٩﴾

20. The (Brothers) sold him for a miserable price - for a few dirhams counted out: in such low estimation did they hold him!

وَشَرَوْهُ بِثَمَنٍۭ بَخْسٍ دَرَٰهِمَ مَعْدُودَةٍ وَكَانُوا۟
فِيهِ مِنَ ٱلزَّٰهِدِينَ ﴿٢٠﴾

21. The man in Egypt who bought him, said to his wife: "Make his stay (among us) honourable: maybe he will bring us much good, or we shall adopt him as a son." Thus did We establish Joseph in the land, that We might teach him the interpretation of stories (and events). And Allah has full

وَقَالَ ٱلَّذِى ٱشْتَرَىٰهُ مِن مِّصْرَ لِٱمْرَأَتِهِۦٓ
أَكْرِمِى مَثْوَىٰهُ عَسَىٰٓ أَن يَنفَعَنَآ أَوْ نَتَّخِذَهُۥ
وَلَدًا ۚ وَكَذَٰلِكَ مَكَّنَّا لِيُوسُفَ فِى ٱلْأَرْضِ
وَلِنُعَلِّمَهُۥ مِن تَأْوِيلِ ٱلْأَحَادِيثِ ۚ وَٱللَّهُ غَالِبٌ

power and control over His affairs; but most among mankind know it not.

عَلَىٰٓ أَمْرِهِۦ وَلَٰكِنَّ أَكْثَرَ ٱلنَّاسِ لَا يَعْلَمُونَ ﴿٢١﴾

22. When Joseph attained his full manhood, We gave him power and knowledge: thus do We reward those who do right.

وَلَمَّا بَلَغَ أَشُدَّهُۥٓ ءَاتَيْنَٰهُ حُكْمًا وَعِلْمًا ۚ وَكَذَٰلِكَ
نَجْزِى ٱلْمُحْسِنِينَ ﴿٢٢﴾

23. But she in whose house he was, sought to seduce him from his (true) self; she fastened the doors and said: "Now come you (dear one)!" He said: "Allah forbid! Truly (your husband) is my lord! He made my sojourn agreeable! Truly to no good come those who do wrong!"

وَرَٰوَدَتْهُ ٱلَّتِى هُوَ فِى بَيْتِهَا عَن نَّفْسِهِۦ وَغَلَّقَتِ
ٱلْأَبْوَٰبَ وَقَالَتْ هَيْتَ لَكَ ۚ قَالَ مَعَاذَ ٱللَّهِ ۖ إِنَّهُۥ
رَبِّىٓ أَحْسَنَ مَثْوَاىَ ۖ إِنَّهُۥ لَا يُفْلِحُ ٱلظَّٰلِمُونَ ﴿٢٣﴾

24. And (with passion) did she desire him, and he would have desired her, but that he saw the evidence of his Lord; thus (did We order) that We might turn away from him (all) evil and shameful deeds; for he was one of Our servants sincere and purified.

وَلَقَدْ هَمَّتْ بِهِۦ ۖ وَهَمَّ بِهَا لَوْلَآ أَن رَّءَا بُرْهَٰنَ
رَبِّهِۦ ۚ كَذَٰلِكَ لِنَصْرِفَ عَنْهُ ٱلسُّوٓءَ وَٱلْفَحْشَآءَ ۚ
إِنَّهُۥ مِنْ عِبَادِنَا ٱلْمُخْلَصِينَ ﴿٢٤﴾

25. So they both raced each other to the door, and she tore his shirt from the back; they both found her lord near the door. She said: "What is the (fitting) punishment for one who formed an evil design against your wife, but prison or a grievous chastisement?"

وَٱسْتَبَقَا ٱلْبَابَ وَقَدَّتْ قَمِيصَهُۥ مِن دُبُرٍ وَأَلْفَيَا
سَيِّدَهَا لَدَا ٱلْبَابِ ۚ قَالَتْ مَا جَزَآءُ مَنْ أَرَادَ بِأَهْلِكَ
سُوٓءًا إِلَّآ أَن يُسْجَنَ أَوْ عَذَابٌ أَلِيمٌ ﴿٢٥﴾

26. He said: "It was she that sought to seduce me - from my (true) self." And one of her household saw (this) and bore witness, (thus) - "If it be that his shirt is torn from the front, then is her tale true, and he is a liar!"

قَالَ هِىَ رَٰوَدَتْنِى عَن نَّفْسِى ۚ وَشَهِدَ شَاهِدٌ مِّنْ
أَهْلِهَآ إِن كَانَ قَمِيصُهُۥ قُدَّ مِن قُبُلٍ فَصَدَقَتْ
وَهُوَ مِنَ ٱلْكَٰذِبِينَ ﴿٢٦﴾

27. "But if it be that his shirt is torn from the back, then is she the liar, and he is telling the truth!"

وَإِن كَانَ قَمِيصُهُۥ قُدَّ مِن دُبُرٍ فَكَذَبَتْ وَهُوَ مِنَ
ٱلصَّٰدِقِينَ ﴿٢٧﴾

فَلَمَّا رَءَا قَمِيصَهُۥ قُدَّ مِن دُبُرٍ قَالَ إِنَّهُۥ مِن
كَيْدِكُنَّ ۖ إِنَّ كَيْدَكُنَّ عَظِيمٌ ﴿٢٨﴾

28. So when he saw his shirt - that it was torn at the back - (her husband) said: "See! It is a snare of you women! Truly, mighty is your snare!"

يُوسُفُ أَعْرِضْ عَنْ هَٰذَا ۚ وَٱسْتَغْفِرِى لِذَنۢبِكِ ۖ
إِنَّكِ كُنتِ مِنَ ٱلْخَاطِـِٔينَ ﴿٢٩﴾

29. "O Joseph, pass this over! (O wife), ask forgiveness for your sin, for truly you have been at fault!"

ثلاثة أرباع الحزب ٢٤

۞ وَقَالَ نِسْوَةٌ فِى ٱلْمَدِينَةِ ٱمْرَأَتُ ٱلْعَزِيزِ تُرَٰوِدُ
فَتَىٰهَا عَن نَّفْسِهِۦ ۖ قَدْ شَغَفَهَا حُبًّا ۖ إِنَّا لَنَرَىٰهَا فِى
ضَلَٰلٍ مُّبِينٍ ﴿٣٠﴾

30. Ladies said in the city: "The wife of the (great) Aziz is seeking to seduce her slave from his (true) self; truly has he inspired her with violent love; we see she is evidently going astray."

فَلَمَّا سَمِعَتْ بِمَكْرِهِنَّ أَرْسَلَتْ إِلَيْهِنَّ وَأَعْتَدَتْ
لَهُنَّ مُتَّكَـًٔا وَءَاتَتْ كُلَّ وَٰحِدَةٍ مِّنْهُنَّ سِكِّينًا وَقَالَتِ
ٱخْرُجْ عَلَيْهِنَّ ۖ فَلَمَّا رَأَيْنَهُۥٓ أَكْبَرْنَهُۥ وَقَطَّعْنَ أَيْدِيَهُنَّ
وَقُلْنَ حَٰشَ لِلَّهِ مَا هَٰذَا بَشَرًا إِنْ هَٰذَآ إِلَّا مَلَكٌ كَرِيمٌ ﴿٣١﴾

31. When she heard of their malicious talk, she sent for them and prepared a banquet for them: she gave each of them a knife; and she said (to Joseph) "Come out before them. When they saw him, they did extol him, and (in their amazement) cut their hands: they said, "Allah preserve us! No mortal is this! This is none other than a noble angel!"

قَالَتْ فَذَٰلِكُنَّ ٱلَّذِى لُمْتُنَّنِى فِيهِ ۖ وَلَقَدْ رَٰوَدتُّهُۥ عَن
نَّفْسِهِۦ فَٱسْتَعْصَمَ ۖ وَلَئِن لَّمْ يَفْعَلْ مَآ ءَامُرُهُۥ
لَيُسْجَنَنَّ وَلَيَكُونًا مِّنَ ٱلصَّٰغِرِينَ ﴿٣٢﴾

32. She said: "There before you is the man about whom you did blame me! I did seek to seduce him from his (true) self but he did firmly save himself guiltless! And now if he does not my bidding he shall certainly be cast into prison and (what is more) be in the company of the vilest!"

قَالَ رَبِّ ٱلسِّجْنُ أَحَبُّ إِلَىَّ مِمَّا يَدْعُونَنِىٓ إِلَيْهِ ۖ وَإِلَّا تَصْرِفْ
عَنِّى كَيْدَهُنَّ أَصْبُ إِلَيْهِنَّ وَأَكُن مِّنَ ٱلْجَٰهِلِينَ ﴿٣٣﴾

33. He said: "O my Lord! The prison is more to my liking than that to which they invite me: unless you turn away their snare from me, I should (in my youthful folly) feel inclined towards them and join the ranks of the ignorant."

34. So his Lord listened to him (in his prayer) and turned away from him their snare; verily He hears and knows (all things).

فَٱسۡتَجَابَ لَهُۥ رَبُّهُۥ فَصَرَفَ عَنۡهُ كَيۡدَهُنَّۚ إِنَّهُۥ هُوَ
ٱلسَّمِيعُ ٱلۡعَلِيمُ ٣٤

35. Then it occurred to the men after they had seen the signs, (that it was best) to imprison him for a time.

ثُمَّ بَدَا لَهُم مِّنۢ بَعۡدِ مَا رَأَوُاْ ٱلۡأٓيَٰتِ لَيَسۡجُنُنَّهُۥ
حَتَّىٰ حِينٖ ٣٥

36. Now with him there came into the prison two young men. Said one of them: "I see myself (in a dream) pressing wine." Said the other: "I see myself (in a dream) carrying bread on my head, and birds are eating of it." "Tell us," (they said), "the truth and meaning of it: for we see you are one that does good (to all)."

وَدَخَلَ مَعَهُ ٱلسِّجۡنَ فَتَيَانِۖ قَالَ أَحَدُهُمَآ إِنِّيٓ
أَرَىٰنِيٓ أَعۡصِرُ خَمۡرٗاۖ وَقَالَ ٱلۡأٓخَرُ إِنِّيٓ أَرَىٰنِيٓ أَحۡمِلُ
فَوۡقَ رَأۡسِي خُبۡزٗا تَأۡكُلُ ٱلطَّيۡرُ مِنۡهُۖ نَبِّئۡنَا
بِتَأۡوِيلِهِۦٓۖ إِنَّا نَرَىٰكَ مِنَ ٱلۡمُحۡسِنِينَ ٣٦

37. He said: "Before any food comes (in due course) to feed either of you I will surely reveal to you the truth and meaning of this before it befall you: that is part of the (duty) which my Lord has taught me. I have (I assure you) abandoned the ways of a people that believe not in Allah and that (even) deny the hereafter."

قَالَ لَا يَأۡتِيكُمَا طَعَامٞ تُرۡزَقَانِهِۦٓ إِلَّا نَبَّأۡتُكُمَا
بِتَأۡوِيلِهِۦ قَبۡلَ أَن يَأۡتِيَكُمَاۚ ذَٰلِكُمَا مِمَّا عَلَّمَنِي
رَبِّيٓۚ إِنِّي تَرَكۡتُ مِلَّةَ قَوۡمٖ لَّا يُؤۡمِنُونَ بِٱللَّهِ وَهُم
بِٱلۡأٓخِرَةِ هُمۡ كَٰفِرُونَ ٣٧

38. "And I follow the ways of my fathers - Abraham, Isaac and Jacob; and never could we attribute any partners whatever to Allah; that (comes) of the grace of Allah to us and to mankind; yet most men are not grateful.

وَٱتَّبَعۡتُ مِلَّةَ ءَابَآءِيٓ إِبۡرَٰهِيمَ وَإِسۡحَٰقَ وَيَعۡقُوبَۚ
مَا كَانَ لَنَآ أَن نُّشۡرِكَ بِٱللَّهِ مِن شَيۡءٖۚ ذَٰلِكَ مِن
فَضۡلِ ٱللَّهِ عَلَيۡنَا وَعَلَى ٱلنَّاسِ وَلَٰكِنَّ أَكۡثَرَ ٱلنَّاسِ
لَا يَشۡكُرُونَ ٣٨

39. "O my two companions of the prison! (I ask you): are many lords differing among themselves better, or Allah, the One, Supreme and Irresistible?"

يَٰصَٰحِبَيِ ٱلسِّجۡنِ ءَأَرۡبَابٞ مُّتَفَرِّقُونَ خَيۡرٌ أَمِ
ٱللَّهُ ٱلۡوَٰحِدُ ٱلۡقَهَّارُ ٣٩

40. "If not Him, you worship nothing but names which you have named - you and your fathers - for which Allah has sent down no authority; the command is for none but Allah; He has commanded that you worship none but Him: that is the right religion, but most men understand not."

مَا تَعۡبُدُونَ مِن دُونِهِۦٓ إِلَّآ أَسۡمَآءٗ سَمَّيۡتُمُوهَآ
أَنتُمۡ وَءَابَآؤُكُم مَّآ أَنزَلَ ٱللَّهُ بِهَا مِن سُلۡطَٰنٍۚ
إِنِ ٱلۡحُكۡمُ إِلَّا لِلَّهِ أَمَرَ أَلَّا تَعۡبُدُوٓاْ إِلَّآ إِيَّاهُۚ ذَٰلِكَ
ٱلدِّينُ ٱلۡقَيِّمُ وَلَٰكِنَّ أَكۡثَرَ ٱلنَّاسِ لَا يَعۡلَمُونَ ٤٠

41. "O my two companions of the prison! As to one of you, he will pour out the wine for his lord to drink: as for the other, he will hang from the cross, and the birds will eat from off his head. (So) has been decreed that matter of which you two do enquire."

يَٰصَٰحِبَيِ ٱلسِّجۡنِ أَمَّآ أَحَدُكُمَا فَيَسۡقِي رَبَّهُۥ
خَمۡرٗاۖ وَأَمَّا ٱلۡأٓخَرُ فَيُصۡلَبُ فَتَأۡكُلُ ٱلطَّيۡرُ
مِن رَّأۡسِهِۦۚ قُضِيَ ٱلۡأَمۡرُ ٱلَّذِي فِيهِ تَسۡتَفۡتِيَانِ ٤١

42. And of the two, to that one whom he considered about to be saved, he said: "Mention me to your lord." But Satan made him forget to mention him to his lord: and (Joseph) lingered in prison a few (more) years.

وَقَالَ لِلَّذِي ظَنَّ أَنَّهُۥ نَاجٖ مِّنۡهُمَا ٱذۡكُرۡنِي عِندَ
رَبِّكَ فَأَنسَىٰهُ ٱلشَّيۡطَٰنُ ذِكۡرَ رَبِّهِۦ فَلَبِثَ
فِي ٱلسِّجۡنِ بِضۡعَ سِنِينَ ٤٢

43. The king (of Egypt) said: "I do see (in a vision) seven fat cows, whom seven lean ones devour - and seven green ears of corn, and seven (others) withered. O you chiefs! Explain to me my vision, if it be that you can interpret visions."

وَقَالَ ٱلۡمَلِكُ إِنِّيٓ أَرَىٰ سَبۡعَ بَقَرَٰتٖ سِمَانٖ
يَأۡكُلُهُنَّ سَبۡعٌ عِجَافٞ وَسَبۡعَ سُنۢبُلَٰتٍ
خُضۡرٖ وَأُخَرَ يَابِسَٰتٖۖ يَٰٓأَيُّهَا ٱلۡمَلَأُ أَفۡتُونِي فِي
رُءۡيَٰيَ إِن كُنتُمۡ لِلرُّءۡيَا تَعۡبُرُونَ ٤٣

44. They said: "A confused medley of dreams; and we are not skilled in the interpretation of dreams."

قَالُوٓاْ أَضۡغَٰثُ أَحۡلَٰمٖۖ وَمَا نَحۡنُ بِتَأۡوِيلِ ٱلۡأَحۡلَٰمِ
بِعَٰلِمِينَ ٤٤

45. But the man who had been released, one of the two (who had been in prison) and who now remembered him after (so long) a space of time, said: "I will tell you the truth of its interpretation; send you me (therefore)."

وَقَالَ ٱلَّذِي نَجَا مِنۡهُمَا وَٱدَّكَرَ بَعۡدَ أُمَّةٍ أَنَا۠
أُنَبِّئُكُم بِتَأۡوِيلِهِۦ فَأَرۡسِلُونِ ٤٥

46. "O Joseph!" (he said) "O man of truth! Explain to us (the dream) of seven fat cows whom seven lean ones devour, and of seven green ears of corn and (seven) others withered: that I may return to the people and that they may understand."

يُوسُفُ أَيُّهَا ٱلصِّدِّيقُ أَفْتِنَا فِي سَبْعِ بَقَرَٰتٍ
سِمَانٍ يَأْكُلُهُنَّ سَبْعٌ عِجَافٌ وَسَبْعِ
سُنۢبُلَٰتٍ خُضْرٍ وَأُخَرَ يَابِسَٰتٍ لَّعَلِّيٓ أَرْجِعُ إِلَى ٱلنَّاسِ
لَعَلَّهُمْ يَعْلَمُونَ ﴿٤٦﴾

47. (Joseph) said: "For seven years shall you diligently sow as is your habit; and the harvests that you reap, you shall leave them in the ear except a little, of which you shall eat.

قَالَ تَزْرَعُونَ سَبْعَ سِنِينَ دَأَبًا فَمَا حَصَدتُّمْ فَذَرُوهُ
فِي سُنۢبُلِهِۦٓ إِلَّا قَلِيلًا مِّمَّا تَأْكُلُونَ ﴿٤٧﴾

48. Then will come after that (period) seven dreadful (years), which will devour what you shall have laid by in advance for them - (all) except a little which you shall have (specially) guarded.

ثُمَّ يَأْتِي مِنۢ بَعْدِ ذَٰلِكَ سَبْعٌ شِدَادٌ يَأْكُلْنَ مَا قَدَّمْتُمْ
لَهُنَّ إِلَّا قَلِيلًا مِّمَّا تُحْصِنُونَ ﴿٤٨﴾

49. "Then will come after that (period) a year in which the people will have abundant water, and in which they will press (wine and oil)."

ثُمَّ يَأْتِي مِنۢ بَعْدِ ذَٰلِكَ عَامٌ فِيهِ يُغَاثُ ٱلنَّاسُ وَفِيهِ
يَعْصِرُونَ ﴿٤٩﴾

50. So the king said: "Bring you him to me." But when the messenger came to him, (Joseph) said: "Go you back to your lord, and ask him, 'What is the state of mind of the ladies who cut their hands?' For my Lord is certainly well aware of their snare."

وَقَالَ ٱلْمَلِكُ ٱئْتُونِي بِهِۦ ۖ فَلَمَّا جَآءَهُ ٱلرَّسُولُ قَالَ
ٱرْجِعْ إِلَىٰ رَبِّكَ فَسْـَٔلْهُ مَا بَالُ ٱلنِّسْوَةِ ٱلَّٰتِي
قَطَّعْنَ أَيْدِيَهُنَّ ۚ إِنَّ رَبِّي بِكَيْدِهِنَّ عَلِيمٌ ﴿٥٠﴾

51. (The king) said (to the ladies): "What was your affair when you did seek to seduce Joseph from his (true) self?" The ladies said: "Allah preserve us! No evil know we against him!" Said the Aziz's wife: "Now is the truth manifest (to all): it was I who sought to seduce him from his (true) self; he is indeed of those who are (ever) true (and virtuous)."

قَالَ مَا خَطْبُكُنَّ إِذْ رَٰوَدتُّنَّ يُوسُفَ عَن نَّفْسِهِۦ ۚ
قُلْنَ حَٰشَ لِلَّهِ مَا عَلِمْنَا عَلَيْهِ مِن سُوٓءٍ ۚ قَالَتِ ٱمْرَأَتُ
ٱلْعَزِيزِ ٱلْـَٰٔنَ حَصْحَصَ ٱلْحَقُّ أَنَا۠ رَٰوَدتُّهُۥ عَن نَّفْسِهِۦ
وَإِنَّهُۥ لَمِنَ ٱلصَّٰدِقِينَ ﴿٥١﴾

52. "This (say I), in order that he may know that I have never been false to him in his absence, and that Allah will never guide the snare of the false ones."

ذَٰلِكَ لِيَعۡلَمَ أَنِّي لَمۡ أَخُنۡهُ بِٱلۡغَيۡبِ وَأَنَّ ٱللَّهَ لَا يَهۡدِي
كَيۡدَ ٱلۡخَآئِنِينَ ﴿٥٢﴾

✻**53.** "Nor do I absolve my own self (of blame); the (human) soul is certainly prone to evil, unless my Lord do bestow His mercy: but surely certainly my Lord is Oft-Forgiving, Most Merciful."

الجزء ١٣ الحزب ٢٥

✻وَمَآ أُبَرِّئُ نَفۡسِيٓۚ إِنَّ ٱلنَّفۡسَ لَأَمَّارَةُۢ بِٱلسُّوٓءِ إِلَّا
مَا رَحِمَ رَبِّيٓۚ إِنَّ رَبِّي غَفُورٞ رَّحِيمٞ ﴿٥٣﴾

54. So the king said: "Bring him to me; I will take him specially to serve about my own person." Therefore, when he had spoken to him, he said: "Be assured this day, you are, before our own presence, with rank firmly established, and fidelity fully proved!"

وَقَالَ ٱلۡمَلِكُ ٱئۡتُونِي بِهِۦٓ أَسۡتَخۡلِصۡهُ لِنَفۡسِيۖ فَلَمَّا
كَلَّمَهُۥ قَالَ إِنَّكَ ٱلۡيَوۡمَ لَدَيۡنَا مَكِينٌ أَمِينٞ ﴿٥٤﴾

55. (Joseph) said: "Set me over the storehouses of the land: I will indeed guard them, as one that knows (their importance)."

قَالَ ٱجۡعَلۡنِي عَلَىٰ خَزَآئِنِ ٱلۡأَرۡضِۖ إِنِّي حَفِيظٌ عَلِيمٞ ﴿٥٥﴾

56. Thus did We give established power to Joseph in the land, to take possession in it as, when, or where he pleased. We bestow of Our mercy on whom We please, and We suffer not, to be lost, the reward of those who do good.

وَكَذَٰلِكَ مَكَّنَّا لِيُوسُفَ فِي ٱلۡأَرۡضِ يَتَبَوَّأُ مِنۡهَا حَيۡثُ
يَشَآءُۚ نُصِيبُ بِرَحۡمَتِنَا مَن نَّشَآءُۖ وَلَا نُضِيعُ
أَجۡرَ ٱلۡمُحۡسِنِينَ ﴿٥٦﴾

57. But verily the reward of the hereafter is the best, for those who believe, and are constant in righteousness.

وَلَأَجۡرُ ٱلۡأٓخِرَةِ خَيۡرٞ لِّلَّذِينَ ءَامَنُواْ وَكَانُواْ
يَتَّقُونَ ﴿٥٧﴾

58. Then came Joseph's brothers: they entered his presence, and he knew them, but they knew him not.

وَجَآءَ إِخۡوَةُ يُوسُفَ فَدَخَلُواْ عَلَيۡهِ فَعَرَفَهُمۡ
وَهُمۡ لَهُۥ مُنكِرُونَ ﴿٥٨﴾

59. And when he had furnished them with provisions (suitable) for them he said: "Bring to me a brother you have, of the same father as yourselves, (but a different mother); see you not that I pay out full

وَلَمَّا جَهَّزَهُم بِجَهَازِهِمۡ قَالَ ٱئۡتُونِي بِأَخٖ لَّكُم مِّنۡ
أَبِيكُمۡۚ أَلَا تَرَوۡنَ أَنِّيٓ أُوفِي ٱلۡكَيۡلَ وَأَنَا۠ خَيۡرُ

✻ Part-13

ٱلْمُنزِلِينَ ٥٩

measure, and that I do provide the best hospitality?"

فَإِن لَّمْ تَأْتُونِى بِهِۦ فَلَا كَيْلَ لَكُمْ عِندِى وَلَا
تَقْرَبُونِ ٦٠

60. "Now if you bring him not to me, you shall have no measure (of corn) from me, nor shall you (even) come near me."

قَالُوا۟ سَنُرَٰوِدُ عَنْهُ أَبَاهُ وَإِنَّا لَفَٰعِلُونَ ٦١

61. They said: "We shall certainly seek to get our wish about him from his father; indeed we shall do it."

وَقَالَ لِفِتْيَٰنِهِ ٱجْعَلُوا۟ بِضَٰعَتَهُمْ فِى رِحَالِهِمْ لَعَلَّهُمْ
يَعْرِفُونَهَآ إِذَا ٱنقَلَبُوٓا۟ إِلَىٰٓ أَهْلِهِمْ لَعَلَّهُمْ
يَرْجِعُونَ ٦٢

62. And (Joseph) told his servants to put their stock in trade (with which they had bartered) into their saddlebags, so they should know it only when they returned to their people, in order that they might come back.

فَلَمَّا رَجَعُوٓا۟ إِلَىٰٓ أَبِيهِمْ قَالُوا۟ يَٰٓأَبَانَا مُنِعَ مِنَّا
ٱلْكَيْلُ فَأَرْسِلْ مَعَنَآ أَخَانَا نَكْتَلْ وَإِنَّا
لَهُۥ لَحَٰفِظُونَ ٦٣

63. Now when they returned to their father, they said: "O our father! No more measure of grain shall we get (unless we take our brother): so send our brother with us that we may get our measure; and we will indeed take every care of him."

قَالَ هَلْ ءَامَنُكُمْ عَلَيْهِ إِلَّا كَمَآ أَمِنتُكُمْ عَلَىٰٓ
أَخِيهِ مِن قَبْلُ فَٱللَّهُ خَيْرٌ حَٰفِظًا ۖ وَهُوَ أَرْحَمُ
ٱلرَّٰحِمِينَ ٦٤

64. He said: "Shall I trust you with him with any result other than when I trusted you with his brother before? But Allah is the best to take care (of him), and He is the Most Merciful of those who show mercy!"

وَلَمَّا فَتَحُوا۟ مَتَٰعَهُمْ وَجَدُوا۟ بِضَٰعَتَهُمْ رُدَّتْ
إِلَيْهِمْ ۖ قَالُوا۟ يَٰٓأَبَانَا مَا نَبْغِى ۖ هَٰذِهِۦ بِضَٰعَتُنَا
رُدَّتْ إِلَيْنَا ۖ وَنَمِيرُ أَهْلَنَا وَنَحْفَظُ أَخَانَا وَنَزْدَادُ
كَيْلَ بَعِيرٍ ۖ ذَٰلِكَ كَيْلٌ يَسِيرٌ ٦٥

65. Then when they opened their baggage, they found their stock in trade had been returned to them. They said: "O our father! What (more) can we desire? This our stock in trade has been returned to us; so we shall get (more) food for our family; we shall take care of our brother; and add (at the same time) a full camel's load (of grain to our provisions); this is but a small quantity."

66. (Jacob) said: "Never will I send him with you until you swear a solemn oath to me, in Allah's name, that you will be sure to bring him back to me unless you are yourselves hemmed in (and made powerless)." And when they had sworn their solemn oath, he said: "Over all that we say be Allah the Witness and Guardian!"

قَالَ لَنۡ أُرۡسِلَهُۥ مَعَكُمۡ حَتَّىٰ تُؤۡتُونِ مَوۡثِقٗا مِّنَ
ٱللَّهِ لَتَأۡتُنَّنِي بِهِۦٓ إِلَّآ أَن يُحَاطَ بِكُمۡۖ فَلَمَّآ ءَاتَوۡهُ
مَوۡثِقَهُمۡ قَالَ ٱللَّهُ عَلَىٰ مَا نَقُولُ وَكِيلٞ ٦٦

67. Further he said; "O my sons! Enter not all by one gate; enter you by different gates. Not that I can profit you anything against Allah (with my advice); none can command except Allah; on Him do I put my trust and let all that trust put their trust on Him."

وَقَالَ يَٰبَنِيَّ لَا تَدۡخُلُواْ مِنۢ بَابٖ وَٰحِدٖ وَٱدۡخُلُواْ
مِنۡ أَبۡوَٰبٖ مُّتَفَرِّقَةٖۖ وَمَآ أُغۡنِي عَنكُم مِّنَ ٱللَّهِ
مِن شَيۡءٍۖ إِنِ ٱلۡحُكۡمُ إِلَّا لِلَّهِۖ عَلَيۡهِ تَوَكَّلۡتُۖ وَعَلَيۡهِ
فَلۡيَتَوَكَّلِ ٱلۡمُتَوَكِّلُونَ ٦٧

68. And when they entered in the manner their father had enjoined, it did not profit them in the least against (the plan of) Allah; it was but a necessity of Jacob's soul, which he discharged. For he was, by Our instruction, full of knowledge (and experience); but most men know not.

وَلَمَّا دَخَلُواْ مِنۡ حَيۡثُ أَمَرَهُمۡ أَبُوهُم مَّا كَانَ يُغۡنِي
عَنۡهُم مِّنَ ٱللَّهِ مِن شَيۡءٍ إِلَّا حَاجَةٗ فِي نَفۡسِ
يَعۡقُوبَ قَضَىٰهَاۚ وَإِنَّهُۥ لَذُو عِلۡمٖ لِّمَا عَلَّمۡنَٰهُ
وَلَٰكِنَّ أَكۡثَرَ ٱلنَّاسِ لَا يَعۡلَمُونَ ٦٨

69. Now when they came into Joseph's presence he received his (full) brother to stay with him. He said (to him): "See! I am your (own) brother; so grieve not at any of their doings."

وَلَمَّا دَخَلُواْ عَلَىٰ يُوسُفَ ءَاوَىٰٓ إِلَيۡهِ أَخَاهُۖ قَالَ
إِنِّيٓ أَنَا۠ أَخُوكَ فَلَا تَبۡتَئِسۡ بِمَا كَانُواْ يَعۡمَلُونَ ٦٩

70. At length when he had furnished them with provisions (suitable) for them, he put the drinking cup into his brother's saddlebag. Then shouted out a caller: "O you (in) the caravan! See! You are thieves, without doubt!"

فَلَمَّا جَهَّزَهُم بِجَهَازِهِمۡ جَعَلَ ٱلسِّقَايَةَ فِي
رَحۡلِ أَخِيهِ ثُمَّ أَذَّنَ مُؤَذِّنٌ أَيَّتُهَا ٱلۡعِيرُ إِنَّكُمۡ
لَسَٰرِقُونَ ٧٠

71. They said, turning towards them: "What is it that you miss?"

قَالُوا۟ وَأَقْبَلُوا۟ عَلَيْهِم مَّاذَا تَفْقِدُونَ ﴿٧١﴾

72. They said: "We miss the great beaker of the king; for him who produces it is (the reward of) a camel-load; I will be bound by it."

قَالُوا۟ نَفْقِدُ صُوَاعَ ٱلْمَلِكِ وَلِمَن جَآءَ بِهِۦ حِمْلُ
بَعِيرٍ وَأَنَا۠ بِهِۦ زَعِيمٌ ﴿٧٢﴾

73. (The brothers) said: "By Allah! Well you know that we came not to make mischief in the land, and we are no thieves!"

قَالُوا۟ تَٱللَّهِ لَقَدْ عَلِمْتُم مَّا جِئْنَا لِنُفْسِدَ فِى
ٱلْأَرْضِ وَمَا كُنَّا سَٰرِقِينَ ﴿٧٣﴾

74. (The Egyptians) said: "What then shall be the penalty of this, if you are (proved) to have lied?"

قَالُوا۟ فَمَا جَزَٰٓؤُهُۥٓ إِن كُنتُمْ كَٰذِبِينَ ﴿٧٤﴾

75. They said: "The penalty should be that he in whose saddle bag it is found, should be held (as bondman) to atone for the (crime). Thus it is we punish the wrongdoers!"

قَالُوا۟ جَزَٰٓؤُهُۥ مَن وُجِدَ فِى رَحْلِهِۦ فَهُوَ جَزَٰٓؤُهُۥ ۚ
كَذَٰلِكَ نَجْزِى ٱلظَّٰلِمِينَ ﴿٧٥﴾

76. So he began (the search) with their baggage, before (he came to) the baggage of his brother; at length he brought it out of his brother's baggage. Thus did We plan for Joseph. He could not take his brother by the law of the king except that Allah willed it (so). We raise to degrees (of wisdom) whom We please: but over all endued with knowledge is One, the All-Knowing.

فَبَدَأَ بِأَوْعِيَتِهِمْ قَبْلَ وِعَآءِ أَخِيهِ ثُمَّ
ٱسْتَخْرَجَهَا مِن وِعَآءِ أَخِيهِ ۚ كَذَٰلِكَ كِدْنَا
لِيُوسُفَ ۖ مَا كَانَ لِيَأْخُذَ أَخَاهُ فِى دِينِ ٱلْمَلِكِ
إِلَّآ أَن يَشَآءَ ٱللَّهُ ۚ نَرْفَعُ دَرَجَٰتٍ مَّن نَّشَآءُ ۗ
وَفَوْقَ كُلِّ ذِى عِلْمٍ عَلِيمٌ ﴿٧٦﴾

77. They said: "If he steals, there was a brother of his who did steal before (him)." But these things did Joseph keep locked in his heart, revealing not the secrets to them. He (simply) said (to himself): "You are the worse situated; and Allah knows best the truth of what you assert!"

ربع الحزب ٢٥ ۞ قَالُوٓا۟ إِن يَسْرِقْ فَقَدْ سَرَقَ أَخٌ لَّهُۥ مِن
قَبْلُ ۚ فَأَسَرَّهَا يُوسُفُ فِى نَفْسِهِۦ وَلَمْ يُبْدِهَا
لَهُمْ ۚ قَالَ أَنتُمْ شَرٌّ مَّكَانًا ۖ وَٱللَّهُ أَعْلَمُ بِمَا
تَصِفُونَ ﴿٧٧﴾

78. They said: "O exalted one! See! He has a father, aged and venerable, (who will grieve for him); so take one of us in his place; for we see that you are (gracious) in doing good."

قَالُوا۟ يَٰٓأَيُّهَا ٱلْعَزِيزُ إِنَّ لَهُۥٓ أَبًا شَيْخًا كَبِيرًا فَخُذْ
أَحَدَنَا مَكَانَهُۥٓ ۖ إِنَّا نَرَىٰكَ مِنَ ٱلْمُحْسِنِينَ ﴿٧٨﴾

79. He said: "Allah forbid that we take other than him with whom we found our property; indeed (if we did so), we should be acting wrongfully."

قَالَ مَعَاذَ ٱللَّهِ أَن نَّأْخُذَ إِلَّا مَن وَجَدْنَا مَتَٰعَنَا
عِندَهُۥٓ إِنَّآ إِذًا لَّظَٰلِمُونَ ﴿٧٩﴾

80. Now when they saw no hope of his (yielding), they held a conference in private. The leader among them said: "Do you not know that your father did take an oath from you in Allah's name, and how before this, you did fail in your duty with Joseph? Therefore, I will not leave this land until my father permits me, or Allah commands me; and He is the best to command."

فَلَمَّا ٱسْتَيْـَٔسُوا۟ مِنْهُ خَلَصُوا۟ نَجِيًّا ۖ قَالَ
كَبِيرُهُمْ أَلَمْ تَعْلَمُوٓا۟ أَنَّ أَبَاكُمْ قَدْ أَخَذَ
عَلَيْكُم مَّوْثِقًا مِّنَ ٱللَّهِ وَمِن قَبْلُ مَا فَرَّطتُمْ فِى
يُوسُفَ ۖ فَلَنْ أَبْرَحَ ٱلْأَرْضَ حَتَّىٰ يَأْذَنَ لِىٓ أَبِىٓ
أَوْ يَحْكُمَ ٱللَّهُ لِى ۖ وَهُوَ خَيْرُ ٱلْحَٰكِمِينَ ﴿٨٠﴾

81. "Turn you back to your father, and say, 'O our father! See! Your son committed theft: we bear witness only to what we know, and we could not well guard against the unseen!"

ٱرْجِعُوٓا۟ إِلَىٰٓ أَبِيكُمْ فَقُولُوا۟ يَٰٓأَبَانَآ إِنَّ ٱبْنَكَ
سَرَقَ وَمَا شَهِدْنَآ إِلَّا بِمَا عَلِمْنَا وَمَا كُنَّا
لِلْغَيْبِ حَٰفِظِينَ ﴿٨١﴾

82. "'Ask at the town where we have been and the caravan in which we returned, and (you will find) we are indeed telling the truth.'"

وَسْـَٔلِ ٱلْقَرْيَةَ ٱلَّتِى كُنَّا فِيهَا وَٱلْعِيرَ ٱلَّتِىٓ
أَقْبَلْنَا فِيهَا ۖ وَإِنَّا لَصَٰدِقُونَ ﴿٨٢﴾

83. Jacob said: "Nay, but you have yourselves contrived a story (good enough) for you. So patience is most fitting (for me). Maybe Allah will bring them (back) all to me (in the end); for He is indeed full of knowledge and wisdom."

قَالَ بَلْ سَوَّلَتْ لَكُمْ أَنفُسُكُمْ أَمْرًا ۖ فَصَبْرٌ
جَمِيلٌ ۖ عَسَى ٱللَّهُ أَن يَأْتِيَنِى بِهِمْ جَمِيعًا ۚ إِنَّهُۥ
هُوَ ٱلْعَلِيمُ ٱلْحَكِيمُ ﴿٨٣﴾

84. And he turned away from them, and said: "How great is my grief for Joseph!" And his eyes became white with sorrow, and he fell into silent melancholy.

وَتَوَلَّىٰ عَنْهُمْ وَقَالَ يَٰٓأَسَفَىٰ عَلَىٰ يُوسُفَ
وَٱبْيَضَّتْ عَيْنَاهُ مِنَ ٱلْحُزْنِ فَهُوَ كَظِيمٌ ﴿٨٤﴾

85. They said: "By Allah! (Never) will you cease to remember Joseph until you reach the last extremity of illness, or until you die!"

قَالُوا۟ تَٱللَّهِ تَفْتَؤُا۟ تَذْكُرُ يُوسُفَ حَتَّىٰ تَكُونَ
حَرَضًا أَوْ تَكُونَ مِنَ ٱلْهَٰلِكِينَ ﴿٨٥﴾

86. He said: "I only complain of my distraction and anguish to Allah, and I know from Allah that which you know not."

قَالَ إِنَّمَآ أَشْكُوا۟ بَثِّى وَحُزْنِىٓ إِلَى ٱللَّهِ
وَأَعْلَمُ مِنَ ٱللَّهِ مَا لَا تَعْلَمُونَ ﴿٨٦﴾

87. "O my sons! Go you and enquire about Joseph and his brother, and never give up hope of Allah's soothing mercy; truly no one despairs of Allah's soothing mercy, except those who have no faith."

يَٰبَنِىَّ ٱذْهَبُوا۟ فَتَحَسَّسُوا۟ مِن يُوسُفَ وَأَخِيهِ
وَلَا تَا۟يْـَٔسُوا۟ مِن رَّوْحِ ٱللَّهِ ۖ إِنَّهُۥ لَا يَا۟يْـَٔسُ مِن
رَّوْحِ ٱللَّهِ إِلَّا ٱلْقَوْمُ ٱلْكَٰفِرُونَ ﴿٨٧﴾

88. Then, when they came (back) into (Joseph's) presence they said: "O exalted one! Distress has seized us and our family; we have (now) brought but scanty capital: so pay us full measure, (we pray you) and treat it as charity to us; for Allah does reward the charitable."

فَلَمَّا دَخَلُوا۟ عَلَيْهِ قَالُوا۟ يَٰٓأَيُّهَا ٱلْعَزِيزُ مَسَّنَا
وَأَهْلَنَا ٱلضُّرُّ وَجِئْنَا بِبِضَٰعَةٍ مُّزْجَىٰةٍ فَأَوْفِ
لَنَا ٱلْكَيْلَ وَتَصَدَّقْ عَلَيْنَآ ۖ إِنَّ ٱللَّهَ يَجْزِى
ٱلْمُتَصَدِّقِينَ ﴿٨٨﴾

89. He said: "Know you how you dealt with Joseph and his brother, not knowing (what you were doing)?"

قَالَ هَلْ عَلِمْتُم مَّا فَعَلْتُم بِيُوسُفَ وَأَخِيهِ
إِذْ أَنتُمْ جَٰهِلُونَ ﴿٨٩﴾

90. They said: "Are you indeed Joseph?" He said: "I am Joseph, and this is my brother: Allah has indeed been gracious to us (all); see, he that is righteous and patient - never will Allah suffer the reward to be lost, of those who do right."

قَالُوٓا۟ أَءِنَّكَ لَأَنتَ يُوسُفُ ۖ قَالَ أَنَا۠ يُوسُفُ وَهَٰذَآ
أَخِى ۖ قَدْ مَنَّ ٱللَّهُ عَلَيْنَآ ۖ إِنَّهُۥ مَن يَتَّقِ وَيَصْبِرْ
فَإِنَّ ٱللَّهَ لَا يُضِيعُ أَجْرَ ٱلْمُحْسِنِينَ ﴿٩٠﴾

91. They said: "By Allah! Indeed has Allah preferred you above us, and we certainly have been guilty of sin!"

قَالُوا۟ تَٱللَّهِ لَقَدْ ءَاثَرَكَ ٱللَّهُ عَلَيْنَا وَإِن
كُنَّا لَخَـٰطِـِٔينَ ﴿٩١﴾

92. He said: "This day let no reproach be (cast) on you: Allah will forgive you, and He is the Most Merciful of those who show mercy!"

قَالَ لَا تَثْرِيبَ عَلَيْكُمُ ٱلْيَوْمَ ۖ يَغْفِرُ ٱللَّهُ
لَكُمْ ۖ وَهُوَ أَرْحَمُ ٱلرَّٰحِمِينَ ﴿٩٢﴾

93. "Go with this my shirt, and cast it over the face of my father: he will come to see (clearly). Then come you (here) to me together with all your family."

ٱذْهَبُوا۟ بِقَمِيصِى هَـٰذَا فَأَلْقُوهُ عَلَىٰ وَجْهِ أَبِى
يَأْتِ بَصِيرًا وَأْتُونِى بِأَهْلِكُمْ أَجْمَعِينَ ﴿٩٣﴾

94. When the caravan left (Egypt) their father said: "I do indeed scent the presence of Joseph; nay, think me not a senile."

وَلَمَّا فَصَلَتِ ٱلْعِيرُ قَالَ أَبُوهُمْ إِنِّى لَأَجِدُ
رِيحَ يُوسُفَ ۖ لَوْلَآ أَن تُفَنِّدُونِ ﴿٩٤﴾

95. They said: "By Allah! Truly you are in your old wandering mind."

قَالُوا۟ تَٱللَّهِ إِنَّكَ لَفِى ضَلَـٰلِكَ ٱلْقَدِيمِ ﴿٩٥﴾

96. Then when the bearer of the good news came, he cast (the shirt) over his face, and he forthwith regained clear sight. He said: "Did I not say to you, 'I know from Allah that which you know not?'"

فَلَمَّآ أَن جَآءَ ٱلْبَشِيرُ أَلْقَىٰهُ عَلَىٰ وَجْهِهِۦ فَٱرْتَدَّ
بَصِيرًا ۖ قَالَ أَلَمْ أَقُل لَّكُمْ إِنِّىٓ أَعْلَمُ مِنَ ٱللَّهِ مَا
لَا تَعْلَمُونَ ﴿٩٦﴾

97. They said: "O our father! Ask for us forgiveness for our sins, for we were truly at fault."

قَالُوا۟ يَـٰٓأَبَانَا ٱسْتَغْفِرْ لَنَا ذُنُوبَنَآ إِنَّا كُنَّا
خَـٰطِـِٔينَ ﴿٩٧﴾

98. He said: "Soon will I ask my Lord for forgiveness for you; for He is indeed Oft-Forgiving, Most Merciful."

قَالَ سَوْفَ أَسْتَغْفِرُ لَكُمْ رَبِّىٓ ۖ إِنَّهُۥ هُوَ
ٱلْغَفُورُ ٱلرَّحِيمُ ﴿٩٨﴾

99. Then when they entered the presence of Joseph, he provided a home for his parents with himself, and said: "Enter you Egypt (all) in safety if it please Allah."

فَلَمَّا دَخَلُوا۟ عَلَىٰ يُوسُفَ ءَاوَىٰٓ إِلَيْهِ أَبَوَيْهِ وَقَالَ
ٱدْخُلُوا۟ مِصْرَ إِن شَآءَ ٱللَّهُ ءَامِنِينَ ﴿٩٩﴾

100. And he raised his parents high on the throne (of dignity), and they fell down in prostration, (all) before him. He said: "O my father! This is the fulfilment of my vision of old! Allah has made it come true! He was indeed good to me when He took me out of prison and brought you (all here) out of the desert, (even) after Satan had sown enmity between me and my brothers. Verily my Lord understands best the mysteries of all that He plans to do. For verily He is full of knowledge and wisdom."

وَرَفَعَ أَبَوَيۡهِ عَلَى ٱلۡعَرۡشِ وَخَرُّواْ لَهُۥ سُجَّدٗاۖ وَقَالَ
يَٰٓأَبَتِ هَٰذَا تَأۡوِيلُ رُءۡيَٰيَ مِن قَبۡلُ قَدۡ جَعَلَهَا رَبِّي
حَقّٗاۖ وَقَدۡ أَحۡسَنَ بِيٓ إِذۡ أَخۡرَجَنِي مِنَ ٱلسِّجۡنِ
وَجَآءَ بِكُم مِّنَ ٱلۡبَدۡوِ مِنۢ بَعۡدِ أَن نَّزَغَ ٱلشَّيۡطَٰنُ
بَيۡنِي وَبَيۡنَ إِخۡوَتِيٓۚ إِنَّ رَبِّي لَطِيفٞ لِّمَا يَشَآءُۚ
إِنَّهُۥ هُوَ ٱلۡعَلِيمُ ٱلۡحَكِيمُ ١٠٠

101. "O my Lord! You have indeed bestowed on me some power, and taught me something of the interpretation of dreams and events - O You Creator of the heavens and the earth! You are my protector in this world and in the hereafter. Take You my soul (at death) as one submitting to Your Will (as a Muslim), and unite me with the righteous."

۞ رَبِّ قَدۡ ءَاتَيۡتَنِي مِنَ ٱلۡمُلۡكِ وَعَلَّمۡتَنِي مِن
تَأۡوِيلِ ٱلۡأَحَادِيثِۚ فَاطِرَ ٱلسَّمَٰوَٰتِ وَٱلۡأَرۡضِ
أَنتَ وَلِيِّۦ فِي ٱلدُّنۡيَا وَٱلۡأٓخِرَةِۖ تَوَفَّنِي مُسۡلِمٗا
وَأَلۡحِقۡنِي بِٱلصَّٰلِحِينَ ١٠١

102. Such is one of the stories of what happened unseen, which We reveal by inspiration to you; nor were you (present) with them when they concerted their plans together in the process of weaving their plots.

ذَٰلِكَ مِنۡ أَنۢبَآءِ ٱلۡغَيۡبِ نُوحِيهِ إِلَيۡكَۖ وَمَا كُنتَ
لَدَيۡهِمۡ إِذۡ أَجۡمَعُوٓاْ أَمۡرَهُمۡ وَهُمۡ يَمۡكُرُونَ ١٠٢

103. Yet no faith will the greater part of mankind have, however ardently you do desire it.

وَمَآ أَكۡثَرُ ٱلنَّاسِ وَلَوۡ حَرَصۡتَ بِمُؤۡمِنِينَ ١٠٣

104. And no reward do you ask of them for this: it is no less than a Message for all creatures.

وَمَا تَسۡـَٔلُهُمۡ عَلَيۡهِ مِنۡ أَجۡرٍۚ إِنۡ هُوَ إِلَّا ذِكۡرٞ
لِّلۡعَٰلَمِينَ ١٠٤

105. And how many signs in the heavens and the earth do they pass by? Yet they turn (their faces) away from them!

وَكَأَيِّن مِّنۡ ءَايَةٖ فِي ٱلسَّمَٰوَٰتِ وَٱلۡأَرۡضِ يَمُرُّونَ
عَلَيۡهَا وَهُمۡ عَنۡهَا مُعۡرِضُونَ ١٠٥

106. And most of them believe not in Allah without associating (others as partners) with Him!

وَمَا يُؤْمِنُ أَكْثَرُهُم بِٱللَّهِ إِلَّا وَهُم مُّشْرِكُونَ ١٠٦

107. Do they then feel secure from the coming against them of the covering veil of the wrath of Allah - or of the coming against them of the (final) hour all of a sudden while they perceive not?

أَفَأَمِنُوٓا۟ أَن تَأْتِيَهُمْ غَـٰشِيَةٌ مِّنْ عَذَابِ ٱللَّهِ
أَوْ تَأْتِيَهُمُ ٱلسَّاعَةُ بَغْتَةً وَهُمْ لَا يَشْعُرُونَ ١٠٧

108. Say you: "This my way: I do invite to Allah - on evidence clear as the seeing with one's eyes - I and whoever follows me: Glory to Allah! And never will I join gods with Allah!"

قُلْ هَـٰذِهِۦ سَبِيلِىٓ أَدْعُوٓا۟ إِلَى ٱللَّهِ ۚ عَلَىٰ بَصِيرَةٍ
أَنَا۠ وَمَنِ ٱتَّبَعَنِى ۖ وَسُبْحَـٰنَ ٱللَّهِ وَمَآ أَنَا۠ مِنَ
ٱلْمُشْرِكِينَ ١٠٨

109. Nor did We send before you (as messengers) any but men, whom We did inspire - (men) living in human habitations. Do they not travel through the earth, and see what was the end of those before them? But the home of the hereafter is best, for those who do right. Will you not then understand?

وَمَآ أَرْسَلْنَا مِن قَبْلِكَ إِلَّا رِجَالًا نُّوحِىٓ إِلَيْهِم مِّنْ
أَهْلِ ٱلْقُرَىٰٓ ۗ أَفَلَمْ يَسِيرُوا۟ فِى ٱلْأَرْضِ فَيَنظُرُوا۟
كَيْفَ كَانَ عَـٰقِبَةُ ٱلَّذِينَ مِن قَبْلِهِمْ ۗ
وَلَدَارُ ٱلْـَٔاخِرَةِ خَيْرٌ لِّلَّذِينَ ٱتَّقَوْا۟ ۚ أَفَلَا تَعْقِلُونَ ١٠٩

110. (Respite will be granted) until, when the messengers give up hope (of their people) and (come to) think that they were treated as liars, there reaches them Our help, and those whom We will, are delivered into safety. But never will be warded off Our punishment from those who are in sin.

حَتَّىٰٓ إِذَا ٱسْتَيْـَٔسَ ٱلرُّسُلُ وَظَنُّوٓا۟ أَنَّهُمْ قَدْ
كُذِبُوا۟ جَآءَهُمْ نَصْرُنَا فَنُجِّىَ مَن نَّشَآءُ ۖ وَلَا
يُرَدُّ بَأْسُنَا عَنِ ٱلْقَوْمِ ٱلْمُجْرِمِينَ ١١٠

111. There is, in their stories, instruction for men endued with understanding. It is not a tale invented, but a confirmation of what went before it - a detailed exposition of all things, and a guide and a mercy to any such as believe.

لَقَدْ كَانَ فِى قَصَصِهِمْ عِبْرَةٌ لِّأُو۟لِى ٱلْأَلْبَـٰبِ ۗ مَا كَانَ
حَدِيثًا يُفْتَرَىٰ وَلَـٰكِن تَصْدِيقَ ٱلَّذِى بَيْنَ
يَدَيْهِ وَتَفْصِيلَ كُلِّ شَىْءٍ وَهُدًى وَرَحْمَةً
لِّقَوْمٍ يُؤْمِنُونَ ١١١

سُورَةُ الرَّعۡدِ

Surah 13: **Ar-Ra'd (The Thunder)**

In the name of Allah,
Most Gracious, Most Merciful.

بِسۡمِ ٱللَّهِ ٱلرَّحۡمَٰنِ ٱلرَّحِيمِ

1. *Alif Lam Mim Ra'*. These are the signs (or verses) of the book; that which has been revealed to you from your Lord is the truth; but most men believe not.

الٓمٓرۚ تِلۡكَ ءَايَٰتُ ٱلۡكِتَٰبِۗ وَٱلَّذِيٓ أُنزِلَ إِلَيۡكَ مِن
رَّبِّكَ ٱلۡحَقُّ وَلَٰكِنَّ أَكۡثَرَ ٱلنَّاسِ لَا يُؤۡمِنُونَ ١

2. Allah is He Who raised the heavens without any pillars that you can see; then He established Himself on the throne (of authority); He has subjected the sun and the moon (to His law)! Each one runs (its course) for a term appointed. He does regulate affairs explaining the signs in detail, that you may believe with certainty in the meeting with your Lord.

ٱللَّهُ ٱلَّذِي رَفَعَ ٱلسَّمَٰوَٰتِ بِغَيۡرِ عَمَدٖ تَرَوۡنَهَاۖ ثُمَّ
ٱسۡتَوَىٰ عَلَى ٱلۡعَرۡشِۖ وَسَخَّرَ ٱلشَّمۡسَ وَٱلۡقَمَرَۖ كُلّٞ
يَجۡرِي لِأَجَلٖ مُّسَمّٗىۚ يُدَبِّرُ ٱلۡأَمۡرَ يُفَصِّلُ ٱلۡأٓيَٰتِ
لَعَلَّكُم بِلِقَآءِ رَبِّكُمۡ تُوقِنُونَ ٢

3. And it is He Who spread out the earth, and set on it mountains standing firm, and (flowing) rivers; and fruit of every kind He made in pairs, two and two; He draws the night as a veil over the day. See, verily in these things there are signs for those who consider!

وَهُوَ ٱلَّذِي مَدَّ ٱلۡأَرۡضَ وَجَعَلَ فِيهَا رَوَٰسِيَ وَأَنۡهَٰرٗاۖ وَمِن
كُلِّ ٱلثَّمَرَٰتِ جَعَلَ فِيهَا زَوۡجَيۡنِ ٱثۡنَيۡنِۖ يُغۡشِي ٱلَّيۡلَ
ٱلنَّهَارَۚ إِنَّ فِي ذَٰلِكَ لَأٓيَٰتٖ لِّقَوۡمٖ يَتَفَكَّرُونَ ٣

4. And in the earth are tracts (diverse though) neighbouring, and gardens of vines and fields sown with corn, and palm trees - growing out of single roots or otherwise; watered with the same water, yet some of them We make more excellent than others to eat. See, verily in these things there are signs for those who understand!

وَفِي ٱلۡأَرۡضِ قِطَعٞ مُّتَجَٰوِرَٰتٞ وَجَنَّٰتٞ مِّنۡ أَعۡنَٰبٖ
وَزَرۡعٞ وَنَخِيلٞ صِنۡوَانٞ وَغَيۡرُ صِنۡوَانٖ يُسۡقَىٰ بِمَآءٖ
وَٰحِدٖ وَنُفَضِّلُ بَعۡضَهَا عَلَىٰ بَعۡضٖ فِي ٱلۡأُكُلِۚ
إِنَّ فِي ذَٰلِكَ لَأٓيَٰتٖ لِّقَوۡمٖ يَعۡقِلُونَ ٤

ثلاثة أرباع الحزب ٢٥

5. If you do marvel (at their want of faith), strange is their saying: "When we are (actually) dust, shall we indeed then be in a creation renewed?" They are those who deny their Lord! They are those around whose necks will be yokes (of servitude): they will be companions of the fire, to dwell in it (forever)!

۞وَإِن تَعۡجَبۡ فَعَجَبٞ قَوۡلُهُمۡ أَءِذَا كُنَّا تُرَٰبًا
أَءِنَّا لَفِي خَلۡقٖ جَدِيدٍۗ أُوْلَٰٓئِكَ ٱلَّذِينَ
كَفَرُواْ بِرَبِّهِمۡۖ وَأُوْلَٰٓئِكَ ٱلۡأَغۡلَٰلُ فِيٓ
أَعۡنَاقِهِمۡۖ وَأُوْلَٰٓئِكَ أَصۡحَٰبُ ٱلنَّارِۖ هُمۡ فِيهَا
خَٰلِدُونَ ٥

6. They ask you to hasten on the evil in preference to the good; yet have come to pass, before them, (many) exemplary punishments! But verily your Lord is full of forgiveness for mankind for their wrongdoing. And verily your Lord is (also) strict in punishment.

وَيَسۡتَعۡجِلُونَكَ بِٱلسَّيِّئَةِ قَبۡلَ ٱلۡحَسَنَةِ وَقَدۡ
خَلَتۡ مِن قَبۡلِهِمُ ٱلۡمَثُلَٰتُۗ وَإِنَّ رَبَّكَ لَذُو مَغۡفِرَةٖ
لِّلنَّاسِ عَلَىٰ ظُلۡمِهِمۡۖ وَإِنَّ رَبَّكَ لَشَدِيدُ ٱلۡعِقَابِ ٦

7. And the unbelievers say: "Why is not a sign sent down to him from his Lord?" But you are truly a warner, and to every people a guide.

وَيَقُولُ ٱلَّذِينَ كَفَرُواْ لَوۡلَآ أُنزِلَ عَلَيۡهِ ءَايَةٞ مِّن
رَّبِّهِۦٓۗ إِنَّمَآ أَنتَ مُنذِرٞۖ وَلِكُلِّ قَوۡمٍ هَادٍ ٧

8. Allah does know what every female (womb) does bear, by how much the wombs fall short (of their time or number) or do exceed. Every single thing is before His sight, in (due) proportion.

ٱللَّهُ يَعۡلَمُ مَا تَحۡمِلُ كُلُّ أُنثَىٰ وَمَا تَغِيضُ ٱلۡأَرۡحَامُ
وَمَا تَزۡدَادُۚ وَكُلُّ شَيۡءٍ عِندَهُۥ بِمِقۡدَارٍ ٨

9. He knows the unseen and that which is open: He is the Great, the Most High.

عَٰلِمُ ٱلۡغَيۡبِ وَٱلشَّهَٰدَةِ ٱلۡكَبِيرُ ٱلۡمُتَعَالِ ٩

10. It is the same (to Him) whether any of you conceal his speech or declare it openly; whether he lie hidden by night or walk freely by day.

سَوَآءٞ مِّنكُم مَّنۡ أَسَرَّ ٱلۡقَوۡلَ وَمَن جَهَرَ بِهِۦ
وَمَنۡ هُوَ مُسۡتَخۡفِۢ بِٱلَّيۡلِ وَسَارِبُۢ بِٱلنَّهَارِ ١٠

11. For each (such person) there are (angels) in succession, before and behind him; they guard him by command of Allah. Verily

لَهُۥ مُعَقِّبَٰتٞ مِّنۢ بَيۡنِ يَدَيۡهِ وَمِنۡ خَلۡفِهِۦ
يَحۡفَظُونَهُۥ مِنۡ أَمۡرِ ٱللَّهِۗ إِنَّ ٱللَّهَ لَا يُغَيِّرُ مَا بِقَوۡمٍ

never will Allah change the condition of a people until they change it themselves (with their own souls). But when (once) Allah wills a people's punishment, there can be no turning it back, nor will they find besides Him, any to protect.

حَتَّىٰ يُغَيِّرُوا۟ مَا بِأَنفُسِهِمْ ۗ وَإِذَآ أَرَادَ ٱللَّهُ بِقَوْمٍ
سُوٓءًا فَلَا مَرَدَّ لَهُۥ ۚ وَمَا لَهُم مِّن دُونِهِۦ مِن وَالٍ ﴿١١﴾

12. It is He Who does show you the lightning, by way both of fear and of hope; it is He Who does raise up the clouds, heavy with (fertilising) rain!

هُوَ ٱلَّذِى يُرِيكُمُ ٱلْبَرْقَ خَوْفًا وَطَمَعًا وَيُنشِئُ
ٱلسَّحَابَ ٱلثِّقَالَ ﴿١٢﴾

13. Nay, thunder repeats His praises, and so do the angels, with awe; He flings the loud-voiced thunderbolts, and with it He strikes whomsoever He will. Yet these (are the men) who (dare to) dispute about Allah, with the strength of His power (supreme)!

وَيُسَبِّحُ ٱلرَّعْدُ بِحَمْدِهِۦ وَٱلْمَلَٰٓئِكَةُ مِنْ خِيفَتِهِۦ
وَيُرْسِلُ ٱلصَّوَٰعِقَ فَيُصِيبُ بِهَا مَن يَشَآءُ وَهُمْ
يُجَٰدِلُونَ فِى ٱللَّهِ وَهُوَ شَدِيدُ ٱلْمِحَالِ ﴿١٣﴾

14. For Him (alone) is prayer in truth: any others that they call upon besides Him hear them no more than if they were to stretch forth their hands for water to reach their mouths, but it reaches them not: for the prayer of those without faith is nothing but (futile) wandering (in the mind).

لَهُۥ دَعْوَةُ ٱلْحَقِّ ۖ وَٱلَّذِينَ يَدْعُونَ مِن دُونِهِۦ لَا يَسْتَجِيبُونَ
لَهُم بِشَىْءٍ إِلَّا كَبَٰسِطِ كَفَّيْهِ إِلَى ٱلْمَآءِ لِيَبْلُغَ فَاهُ وَمَا هُوَ
بِبَٰلِغِهِۦ ۚ وَمَا دُعَآءُ ٱلْكَٰفِرِينَ إِلَّا فِى ضَلَٰلٍ ﴿١٤﴾

15. Whatever beings there are in the heavens and the earth, do prostrate themselves to Allah (acknowledging subjection) - with goodwill or in spite of themselves; so do their shadows in the mornings and evenings.

وَلِلَّهِ يَسْجُدُ مَن فِى ٱلسَّمَٰوَٰتِ وَٱلْأَرْضِ طَوْعًا وَكَرْهًا سجدة
وَظِلَٰلُهُم بِٱلْغُدُوِّ وَٱلْءَاصَالِ ۩ ﴿١٥﴾

16. Say: "Who is the Lord and Sustainer of the heavens and the earth?" Say: "It is Allah." Say: "Do you then take (for worship) protectors other than Him, such as have no power either for good or for harm to themselves?" Say: "Are the blind equal with those who see? Or the depths of

قُلْ مَن رَّبُّ ٱلسَّمَٰوَٰتِ وَٱلْأَرْضِ قُلِ ٱللَّهُ ۚ قُلْ أَفَٱتَّخَذْتُم
مِّن دُونِهِۦٓ أَوْلِيَآءَ لَا يَمْلِكُونَ لِأَنفُسِهِمْ نَفْعًا وَلَا
ضَرًّا ۚ قُلْ هَلْ يَسْتَوِى ٱلْأَعْمَىٰ وَٱلْبَصِيرُ أَمْ هَلْ تَسْتَوِى

darkness equal with light?" Or do they assign to Allah partners who have created (anything) as He has created, so that the creation seemed to them similar? Say: "Allah is the Creator of all things: He is the One, the Supreme and Irresistible."

ٱلظُّلُمَٰتُ وَٱلنُّورُۗ أَمۡ جَعَلُواْ لِلَّهِ شُرَكَآءَ خَلَقُواْ كَخَلۡقِهِۦ
فَتَشَٰبَهَ ٱلۡخَلۡقُ عَلَيۡهِمۡۚ قُلِ ٱللَّهُ خَٰلِقُ كُلِّ شَيۡءٖ وَهُوَ
ٱلۡوَٰحِدُ ٱلۡقَهَّٰرُ ١٦

17. He sends down water from the skies, and the channels flow, each according to its measure; but the torrent bears away the foam that mounts up to the surface. Even so, from that (ore) which they heat in the fire, to make ornaments or utensils from it, there is a scum likewise. Thus does Allah (by parables) show truth and vanity. For the scum disappears like froth cast out; while that which is for the good of mankind remains on the earth. Thus does Allah set out parables.

أَنزَلَ مِنَ ٱلسَّمَآءِ مَآءٗ فَسَالَتۡ أَوۡدِيَةُۢ بِقَدَرِهَا فَٱحۡتَمَلَ
ٱلسَّيۡلُ زَبَدٗا رَّابِيٗاۖ وَمِمَّا يُوقِدُونَ عَلَيۡهِ فِي ٱلنَّارِ ٱبۡتِغَآءَ
حِلۡيَةٍ أَوۡ مَتَٰعٖ زَبَدٞ مِّثۡلُهُۥۚ كَذَٰلِكَ يَضۡرِبُ ٱللَّهُ ٱلۡحَقَّ
وَٱلۡبَٰطِلَۚ فَأَمَّا ٱلزَّبَدُ فَيَذۡهَبُ جُفَآءٗۖ وَأَمَّا مَا يَنفَعُ
ٱلنَّاسَ فَيَمۡكُثُ فِي ٱلۡأَرۡضِۚ كَذَٰلِكَ يَضۡرِبُ ٱللَّهُ
ٱلۡأَمۡثَالَ ١٧

18. For those who respond to their Lord, are (all) good things. But those who respond not to Him - even if they had all that is in the heavens and on earth, and as much more, (in vain) would they offer it for ransom. For them will the reckoning be terrible; their abode will be hell - what a bed of misery!

لِلَّذِينَ ٱسۡتَجَابُواْ لِرَبِّهِمُ ٱلۡحُسۡنَىٰۚ وَٱلَّذِينَ لَمۡ يَسۡتَجِيبُواْ
لَهُۥ لَوۡ أَنَّ لَهُم مَّا فِي ٱلۡأَرۡضِ جَمِيعٗا وَمِثۡلَهُۥ مَعَهُۥ
لَٱفۡتَدَوۡاْ بِهِۦٓۚ أُوْلَٰٓئِكَ لَهُمۡ سُوٓءُ ٱلۡحِسَابِ وَمَأۡوَىٰهُمۡ
جَهَنَّمُۖ وَبِئۡسَ ٱلۡمِهَادُ ١٨

19. Is then one who does know that that which has been revealed to these from your Lord is the truth, like one who is blind? It is those who are endued with understanding that receive admonition -

الحزب ٣٦ ۞أَفَمَن يَعۡلَمُ أَنَّمَآ أُنزِلَ إِلَيۡكَ مِن رَّبِّكَ ٱلۡحَقُّ كَمَنۡ هُوَ أَعۡمَىٰٓۚ
إِنَّمَا يَتَذَكَّرُ أُوْلُواْ ٱلۡأَلۡبَٰبِ ١٩

20. Those who fulfil the covenant of Allah and fail not in their promised word;

ٱلَّذِينَ يُوفُونَ بِعَهۡدِ ٱللَّهِ وَلَا يَنقُضُونَ ٱلۡمِيثَٰقَ ٢٠

21. Those who join together those things which Allah has commanded to be joined,

وَٱلَّذِينَ يَصِلُونَ مَآ أَمَرَ ٱللَّهُ بِهِۦٓ أَن يُوصَلَ وَيَخۡشَوۡنَ

رَبَّهُمۡ وَيَخَافُونَ سُوٓءَ ٱلۡحِسَابِ ﴿٢١﴾

hold their Lord in awe, and fear the terrible reckoning;

وَٱلَّذِينَ صَبَرُواْ ٱبۡتِغَآءَ وَجۡهِ رَبِّهِمۡ وَأَقَامُواْ ٱلصَّلَوٰةَ
وَأَنفَقُواْ مِمَّا رَزَقۡنَٰهُمۡ سِرّٗا وَعَلَانِيَةٗ وَيَدۡرَءُونَ
بِٱلۡحَسَنَةِ ٱلسَّيِّئَةَ أُوْلَٰٓئِكَ لَهُمۡ عُقۡبَى ٱلدَّارِ ﴿٢٢﴾

22. Those who patiently persevere, seeking the countenance of their Lord; establish regular prayers; spend, out of (the gifts) We have bestowed for their sustenance, secretly and openly; and turn off evil with good: for such there is the final attainment of the (eternal) home -

جَنَّٰتُ عَدۡنٖ يَدۡخُلُونَهَا وَمَن صَلَحَ مِنۡ ءَابَآئِهِمۡ وَأَزۡوَٰجِهِمۡ
وَذُرِّيَّٰتِهِمۡۖ وَٱلۡمَلَٰٓئِكَةُ يَدۡخُلُونَ عَلَيۡهِم مِّن كُلِّ بَابٖ ﴿٢٣﴾

23. Gardens of perpetual bliss; they shall enter there, as well as the righteous among their fathers, their spouses, and their offspring and angels shall enter to them from every gate (with the salutation):

سَلَٰمٌ عَلَيۡكُم بِمَا صَبَرۡتُمۡۚ فَنِعۡمَ عُقۡبَى ٱلدَّارِ ﴿٢٤﴾

24. "Peace to you for that you persevered in patience! Now how excellent is the final home!"

وَٱلَّذِينَ يَنقُضُونَ عَهۡدَ ٱللَّهِ مِنۢ بَعۡدِ مِيثَٰقِهِۦ
وَيَقۡطَعُونَ مَآ أَمَرَ ٱللَّهُ بِهِۦٓ أَن يُوصَلَ وَيُفۡسِدُونَ فِي
ٱلۡأَرۡضِ أُوْلَٰٓئِكَ لَهُمُ ٱللَّعۡنَةُ وَلَهُمۡ سُوٓءُ ٱلدَّارِ ﴿٢٥﴾

25. But those who break the covenant of Allah, after having promised their word to it, and cut apart those things which Allah has commanded to be joined, and work mischief in the land - on them is the curse; for them is the terrible home!

ٱللَّهُ يَبۡسُطُ ٱلرِّزۡقَ لِمَن يَشَآءُ وَيَقۡدِرُۚ وَفَرِحُواْ
بِٱلۡحَيَوٰةِ ٱلدُّنۡيَا وَمَا ٱلۡحَيَوٰةُ ٱلدُّنۡيَا فِي ٱلۡأٓخِرَةِ إِلَّا
مَتَٰعٞ ﴿٢٦﴾

26. Allah does enlarge, or grant by (strict) measure, the sustenance (which He gives) to whom so He pleases. (The worldly) rejoice in the life of this world; but the life of this world is but little comfort in the hereafter.

وَيَقُولُ ٱلَّذِينَ كَفَرُواْ لَوۡلَآ أُنزِلَ عَلَيۡهِ ءَايَةٞ مِّن رَّبِّهِۦۚ
قُلۡ إِنَّ ٱللَّهَ يُضِلُّ مَن يَشَآءُ وَيَهۡدِيٓ إِلَيۡهِ مَنۡ أَنَابَ ﴿٢٧﴾

27. The unbelievers say: "Why is not a sign sent down to him from his Lord?" Say: "Truly Allah leaves, to stray, whom He will; but He guides to Himself those who turn to Him in penitence -

28. Those who believe, and whose hearts find satisfaction in the remembrance of Allah: for without doubt in the remembrance of Allah do hearts find satisfaction.

ٱلَّذِينَ ءَامَنُوا۟ وَتَطْمَئِنُّ قُلُوبُهُم بِذِكْرِ ٱللَّهِ ۗ أَلَا بِذِكْرِ
ٱللَّهِ تَطْمَئِنُّ ٱلْقُلُوبُ ٢٨

29. For those who believe and work righteousness, is (every) blessedness, and a beautiful place of (final) return."

ٱلَّذِينَ ءَامَنُوا۟ وَعَمِلُوا۟ ٱلصَّٰلِحَٰتِ طُوبَىٰ لَهُمْ
وَحُسْنُ مَـَٔابٍ ٢٩

30. Thus have We sent you amongst a people before whom (long since) have (other) peoples (gone and) passed away; in order that you might rehearse to them what We send down to you by inspiration; yet do they reject (Him) the Most Gracious! Say: "He is my Lord! There is no god but He! On Him is my trust, and to Him do I turn!"

كَذَٰلِكَ أَرْسَلْنَٰكَ فِىٓ أُمَّةٍ قَدْ خَلَتْ مِن قَبْلِهَآ
أُمَمٌ لِّتَتْلُوَا۟ عَلَيْهِمُ ٱلَّذِىٓ أَوْحَيْنَآ إِلَيْكَ وَهُمْ
يَكْفُرُونَ بِٱلرَّحْمَٰنِ ۚ قُلْ هُوَ رَبِّى لَآ إِلَٰهَ إِلَّا هُوَ عَلَيْهِ
تَوَكَّلْتُ وَإِلَيْهِ مَتَابِ ٣٠

31. If there were a Qur'an with which mountains were moved, or the earth were cloven asunder, or the dead were made to speak, (this would be the one!) But, truly, the command is with Allah in all things! Do not the believers know, that, had Allah (so) willed, He could have guided all mankind (to the right)? But the unbelievers - never will disaster cease to seize them for their (ill) deeds, or to settle close to their homes, until the promise of Allah come to pass, for, verily, Allah will not fail in His promise.

وَلَوْ أَنَّ قُرْءَانًا سُيِّرَتْ بِهِ ٱلْجِبَالُ أَوْ قُطِّعَتْ بِهِ
ٱلْأَرْضُ أَوْ كُلِّمَ بِهِ ٱلْمَوْتَىٰ ۗ بَل لِّلَّهِ ٱلْأَمْرُ جَمِيعًا ۗ
أَفَلَمْ يَا۟يْـَٔسِ ٱلَّذِينَ ءَامَنُوٓا۟ أَن لَّوْ يَشَآءُ ٱللَّهُ لَهَدَى
ٱلنَّاسَ جَمِيعًا ۗ وَلَا يَزَالُ ٱلَّذِينَ كَفَرُوا۟ تُصِيبُهُم
بِمَا صَنَعُوا۟ قَارِعَةٌ أَوْ تَحُلُّ قَرِيبًا مِّن دَارِهِمْ
حَتَّىٰ يَأْتِىَ وَعْدُ ٱللَّهِ ۚ إِنَّ ٱللَّهَ لَا يُخْلِفُ ٱلْمِيعَادَ ٣١

32. Mocked were (many) messengers before you: but I granted respite to the unbelievers, and finally I punished them; then how (terrible) was My requital!

وَلَقَدِ ٱسْتُهْزِئَ بِرُسُلٍ مِّن قَبْلِكَ فَأَمْلَيْتُ لِلَّذِينَ
كَفَرُوا۟ ثُمَّ أَخَذْتُهُمْ ۖ فَكَيْفَ كَانَ عِقَابِ ٣٢

33. Is then He Who stands over every soul (and knows) all that it does, (like any others)? And yet they ascribe partners to

أَفَمَنْ هُوَ قَآئِمٌ عَلَىٰ كُلِّ نَفْسٍۭ بِمَا كَسَبَتْ ۗ وَجَعَلُوا۟
لِلَّهِ شُرَكَآءَ قُلْ سَمُّوهُمْ ۚ أَمْ تُنَبِّـُٔونَهُۥ بِمَا لَا يَعْلَمُ فِى

ٱلْأَرْضِ أَم بِظَٰهِرٍ مِّنَ ٱلْقَوْلِ ۗ بَلْ زُيِّنَ لِلَّذِينَ
كَفَرُوا۟ مَكْرُهُمْ وَصُدُّوا۟ عَنِ ٱلسَّبِيلِ ۗ وَمَن يُضْلِلِ
ٱللَّهُ فَمَا لَهُۥ مِنْ هَادٍ ﴿٣٣﴾

Allah. Say: "But name them! Is it that you will inform Him of something He knows not on earth, or is it (just) a show of words?" Nay! To those who believe not, their pretence seems pleasing, but they are kept back (thereby) from the path. And those whom Allah leaves to stray, no one can guide.

لَّهُمْ عَذَابٌ فِى ٱلْحَيَوٰةِ ٱلدُّنْيَا ۖ وَلَعَذَابُ ٱلْءَاخِرَةِ أَشَقُّ ۖ
وَمَا لَهُم مِّنَ ٱللَّهِ مِن وَاقٍ ﴿٣٤﴾

34. For them is a penalty in the life of this world, but harder, truly, is the penalty of the hereafter; and defender have they none against Allah.

ربع الحزب ٢٦

۞ مَّثَلُ ٱلْجَنَّةِ ٱلَّتِى وُعِدَ ٱلْمُتَّقُونَ ۖ تَجْرِى مِن تَحْتِهَا
ٱلْأَنْهَٰرُ ۖ أُكُلُهَا دَآئِمٌ وَظِلُّهَا ۚ تِلْكَ عُقْبَى
ٱلَّذِينَ ٱتَّقَوا۟ ۖ وَّعُقْبَى ٱلْكَٰفِرِينَ ٱلنَّارُ ﴿٣٥﴾

35. The parable of the garden which the righteous are promised! - Beneath it flow rivers; perpetual is the enjoyment of it and the shade in it; such is the end of the righteous; and the end of unbelievers is the fire.

وَٱلَّذِينَ ءَاتَيْنَٰهُمُ ٱلْكِتَٰبَ يَفْرَحُونَ بِمَآ أُنزِلَ
إِلَيْكَ ۖ وَمِنَ ٱلْأَحْزَابِ مَن يُنكِرُ بَعْضَهُۥ ۚ قُلْ
إِنَّمَآ أُمِرْتُ أَنْ أَعْبُدَ ٱللَّهَ وَلَآ أُشْرِكَ بِهِۦٓ ۚ إِلَيْهِ أَدْعُوا۟
وَإِلَيْهِ مَـَٔابِ ﴿٣٦﴾

36. Those to whom We have given the book rejoice at what has been revealed to you: but there are among the clans those who reject a part of it. Say: "I am commanded to worship Allah, and not to join partners with Him. To Him do I call, and to Him is my return."

وَكَذَٰلِكَ أَنزَلْنَٰهُ حُكْمًا عَرَبِيًّا ۚ وَلَئِنِ ٱتَّبَعْتَ
أَهْوَآءَهُم بَعْدَمَا جَآءَكَ مِنَ ٱلْعِلْمِ مَا لَكَ مِنَ ٱللَّهِ مِن
وَلِىٍّ وَلَا وَاقٍ ﴿٣٧﴾

37. Thus have We revealed it to be a judgement of authority in Arabic. Were you to follow their (vain) desires after the knowledge which has reached you, then would you find neither protector nor defender against Allah.

وَلَقَدْ أَرْسَلْنَا رُسُلًا مِّن قَبْلِكَ وَجَعَلْنَا لَهُمْ
أَزْوَٰجًا وَذُرِّيَّةً ۚ وَمَا كَانَ لِرَسُولٍ أَن يَأْتِىَ بِـَٔايَةٍ إِلَّا
بِإِذْنِ ٱللَّهِ ۗ لِكُلِّ أَجَلٍ كِتَابٌ ﴿٣٨﴾

38. We did send messengers before you, and appointed for them wives and children; and it was never the part of a messenger to bring a sign except as Allah permitted (or commanded). For each period is a book (revealed).

39. Allah does blot out or confirm what He pleases: with Him is the mother of the book.

يَمْحُوا۟ ٱللَّهُ مَا يَشَآءُ وَيُثْبِتُ ۖ وَعِندَهُۥٓ أُمُّ
ٱلْكِتَـٰبِ ﴿٣٩﴾

40. Whether We shall show you (within your lifetime) part of what We promised them, or take to Ourselves your soul (before it is all accomplished), your duty is to (make the message) reach them; it is Our part to call them to account.

وَإِن مَّا نُرِيَنَّكَ بَعْضَ ٱلَّذِى نَعِدُهُمْ أَوْ نَتَوَفَّيَنَّكَ
فَإِنَّمَا عَلَيْكَ ٱلْبَلَـٰغُ وَعَلَيْنَا ٱلْحِسَابُ ﴿٤٠﴾

41. Do they not see that We gradually reduce the land (in their control) from its outlying borders? (Where) Allah commands, there is none to put back His command: and He is Swift in calling to account.

أَوَلَمْ يَرَوْا۟ أَنَّا نَأْتِى ٱلْأَرْضَ نَنقُصُهَا مِنْ أَطْرَافِهَا ۚ
وَٱللَّهُ يَحْكُمُ لَا مُعَقِّبَ لِحُكْمِهِۦ ۚ وَهُوَ سَرِيعُ
ٱلْحِسَابِ ﴿٤١﴾

42. Those before them did (also) devise plots; but in all things the master-planning is Allah's. He knows the doings of every soul; and soon will the unbelievers know who gets home in the end.

وَقَدْ مَكَرَ ٱلَّذِينَ مِن قَبْلِهِمْ فَلِلَّهِ ٱلْمَكْرُ جَمِيعًا ۖ
يَعْلَمُ مَا تَكْسِبُ كُلُّ نَفْسٍ ۗ وَسَيَعْلَمُ ٱلْكُفَّـٰرُ لِمَنْ
عُقْبَى ٱلدَّارِ ﴿٤٢﴾

43. The unbelievers say: "No messenger are you." Say: "Enough for a witness between me and you is Allah, and such as have knowledge of the book."

وَيَقُولُ ٱلَّذِينَ كَفَرُوا۟ لَسْتَ مُرْسَلًا ۚ قُلْ كَفَىٰ
بِٱللَّهِ شَهِيدًۢا بَيْنِى وَبَيْنَكُمْ وَمَنْ عِندَهُۥ عِلْمُ
ٱلْكِتَـٰبِ ﴿٤٣﴾

سُورَةُ إِبْرَاهِيمَ

Surah 14: ***Ibrahim*** **(Abraham)**

In the name of Allah,
Most Gracious, Most Merciful.

بِسْمِ ٱللَّهِ ٱلرَّحْمَـٰنِ ٱلرَّحِيمِ

1. *Alif Lam Ra.* A book which We have revealed to you, in order that you

الٓر ۚ كِتَـٰبٌ أَنزَلْنَـٰهُ إِلَيْكَ لِتُخْرِجَ ٱلنَّاسَ مِنَ

might lead mankind out of the depths of darkness into light - by the leave of their Lord - to the way of (Him) Exalted in Power, Worthy of all Praise! -

ٱلظُّلُمَٰتِ إِلَى ٱلنُّورِ بِإِذْنِ رَبِّهِمْ إِلَىٰ صِرَٰطِ
ٱلْعَزِيزِ ٱلْحَمِيدِ ﴿١﴾

2. Of Allah, to Whom do belong all things in the heavens and on earth! But alas for the unbelievers, for a terrible penalty (their unfaith will bring them)! -

ٱللَّهِ ٱلَّذِى لَهُۥ مَا فِى ٱلسَّمَٰوَٰتِ وَمَا فِى ٱلْأَرْضِ ۗ
وَوَيْلٌ لِّلْكَٰفِرِينَ مِنْ عَذَابٍ شَدِيدٍ ﴿٢﴾

3. Those who love the life of this world more than the hereafter, who hinder (men) from the path of Allah and seek in it something crooked; they are astray by a long distance.

ٱلَّذِينَ يَسْتَحِبُّونَ ٱلْحَيَوٰةَ ٱلدُّنْيَا عَلَى ٱلْءَاخِرَةِ
وَيَصُدُّونَ عَن سَبِيلِ ٱللَّهِ وَيَبْغُونَهَا عِوَجًا ۚ
أُو۟لَٰٓئِكَ فِى ضَلَٰلٍۭ بَعِيدٍ ﴿٣﴾

4. We sent not a messenger except (to teach) in the language of his (own) people, in order to make (things) clear to them. Now Allah leaves straying those whom He pleases and guides whom He pleases; and He is Exalted in Power, Full of Wisdom.

وَمَآ أَرْسَلْنَا مِن رَّسُولٍ إِلَّا بِلِسَانِ قَوْمِهِۦ
لِيُبَيِّنَ لَهُمْ ۖ فَيُضِلُّ ٱللَّهُ مَن يَشَآءُ وَيَهْدِى
مَن يَشَآءُ ۚ وَهُوَ ٱلْعَزِيزُ ٱلْحَكِيمُ ﴿٤﴾

5. We sent Moses with Our signs (and the command): "Bring out your people from the depths of darkness into light, and teach them to remember the Days of Allah." Verily in this there are signs for such as are firmly patient and constant - grateful and appreciative.

وَلَقَدْ أَرْسَلْنَا مُوسَىٰ بِـَٔايَٰتِنَآ أَنْ أَخْرِجْ
قَوْمَكَ مِنَ ٱلظُّلُمَٰتِ إِلَى ٱلنُّورِ وَذَكِّرْهُم
بِأَيَّىٰمِ ٱللَّهِ ۚ إِنَّ فِى ذَٰلِكَ لَءَايَٰتٍ لِّكُلِّ
صَبَّارٍ شَكُورٍ ﴿٥﴾

6. Remember! Moses said to his people: "Call to mind the favour of Allah to you when He delivered you from the people of Pharaoh; they set you hard tasks and punishments, slaughtered your sons, and let your womenfolk live; in it was a tremendous trial from your Lord."

وَإِذْ قَالَ مُوسَىٰ لِقَوْمِهِ ٱذْكُرُوا۟ نِعْمَةَ ٱللَّهِ
عَلَيْكُمْ إِذْ أَنجَىٰكُم مِّنْ ءَالِ فِرْعَوْنَ
يَسُومُونَكُمْ سُوٓءَ ٱلْعَذَابِ وَيُذَبِّحُونَ
أَبْنَآءَكُمْ وَيَسْتَحْيُونَ نِسَآءَكُمْ ۚ وَفِى
ذَٰلِكُم بَلَآءٌ مِّن رَّبِّكُمْ عَظِيمٌ ﴿٦﴾

7. And remember! Your Lord caused to be declared (publicly): "If you are grateful, I will add more (favours) to you; but if you show ingratitude, truly My punishment is terrible indeed."

وَإِذْ تَأَذَّنَ رَبُّكُمْ لَئِن شَكَرْتُمْ لَأَزِيدَنَّكُمْ ۖ
وَلَئِن كَفَرْتُمْ إِنَّ عَذَابِى لَشَدِيدٌ ﴿٧﴾

8. And Moses said: "If you show ingratitude, you and all on earth together - yet is Allah Free of all wants, Worthy of all praise."

وَقَالَ مُوسَىٰٓ إِن تَكْفُرُوٓا۟ أَنتُمْ وَمَن فِى
ٱلْأَرْضِ جَمِيعًا فَإِنَّ ٱللَّهَ لَغَنِىٌّ حَمِيدٌ ﴿٨﴾

9. Has not the story reached you, (O people!), of those who (went) before you? - Of the people of Noah, and 'Ad, and Thamud? And of those who (came) after them? None knows them but Allah. To them came messengers with clear (signs); but they put their hands up to their mouths, and said: "We do deny (the mission) on which you have been sent, and we are really in suspicious (disquieting) doubt as to that to which you invite us."

أَلَمْ يَأْتِكُمْ نَبَؤُا۟ ٱلَّذِينَ مِن قَبْلِكُمْ قَوْمِ نُوحٍ
وَعَادٍ وَثَمُودَ وَٱلَّذِينَ مِنۢ بَعْدِهِمْ لَا
يَعْلَمُهُمْ إِلَّا ٱللَّهُ ۚ جَآءَتْهُمْ رُسُلُهُم
بِٱلْبَيِّنَٰتِ فَرَدُّوٓا۟ أَيْدِيَهُمْ فِىٓ أَفْوَٰهِهِمْ وَقَالُوٓا۟
إِنَّا كَفَرْنَا بِمَآ أُرْسِلْتُم بِهِۦ وَإِنَّا لَفِى شَكٍّ مِّمَّا
تَدْعُونَنَآ إِلَيْهِ مُرِيبٍ ﴿٩﴾

10. Their messengers said: "Is there a doubt about Allah, the Creator of the heavens and the earth? It is He Who invites you, in order that He may forgive you your sins and give you respite for a term appointed!" They said: "Ah! You are no more than human, like ourselves! You wish to turn us away from the (gods) our fathers used to worship: then bring us some clear authority."

نصف الحزب ٢٦

۞ قَالَتْ رُسُلُهُمْ أَفِى ٱللَّهِ شَكٌّ فَاطِرِ ٱلسَّمَٰوَٰتِ
وَٱلْأَرْضِ ۖ يَدْعُوكُمْ لِيَغْفِرَ لَكُم مِّن ذُنُوبِكُمْ
وَيُؤَخِّرَكُمْ إِلَىٰٓ أَجَلٍ مُّسَمًّى ۚ قَالُوٓا۟ إِنْ أَنتُمْ إِلَّا بَشَرٌ
مِّثْلُنَا تُرِيدُونَ أَن تَصُدُّونَا عَمَّا كَانَ يَعْبُدُ
ءَابَآؤُنَا فَأْتُونَا بِسُلْطَٰنٍ مُّبِينٍ ﴿١٠﴾

11. Their messengers said to them: "True, we are human like yourselves, but Allah does grant His grace to such of His servants as He pleases. It is not for us to bring you an authority except as Allah permits. And on Allah let all men of faith put their trust."

قَالَتْ لَهُمْ رُسُلُهُمْ إِن نَّحْنُ إِلَّا بَشَرٌ مِّثْلُكُمْ
وَلَٰكِنَّ ٱللَّهَ يَمُنُّ عَلَىٰ مَن يَشَآءُ مِنْ عِبَادِهِۦ ۖ وَمَا
كَانَ لَنَآ أَن نَّأْتِيَكُم بِسُلْطَٰنٍ إِلَّا بِإِذْنِ ٱللَّهِ ۚ
وَعَلَى ٱللَّهِ فَلْيَتَوَكَّلِ ٱلْمُؤْمِنُونَ ﴿١١﴾

12. "No reason have we why we should not put our trust on Allah. Indeed He has guided us to the ways we (follow). We shall certainly bear with patience all the hurt you may cause us; for those who put their trust should put their trust on Allah."

وَمَا لَنَآ أَلَّا نَتَوَكَّلَ عَلَى ٱللَّهِ وَقَدۡ هَدَىٰنَا سُبُلَنَاۚ
وَلَنَصۡبِرَنَّ عَلَىٰ مَآ ءَاذَيۡتُمُونَاۚ وَعَلَى ٱللَّهِ
فَلۡيَتَوَكَّلِ ٱلۡمُتَوَكِّلُونَ ١٢

13. And the unbelievers said to their messengers: "Be sure we shall drive you out of our land, or you shall return to our religion." But their Lord inspired (this Message) to them: "Verily We shall cause the wrongdoers to perish!

وَقَالَ ٱلَّذِينَ كَفَرُواْ لِرُسُلِهِمۡ لَنُخۡرِجَنَّكُم مِّنۡ
أَرۡضِنَآ أَوۡ لَتَعُودُنَّ فِي مِلَّتِنَاۖ فَأَوۡحَىٰٓ إِلَيۡهِمۡ
رَبُّهُمۡ لَنُهۡلِكَنَّ ٱلظَّٰلِمِينَ ١٣

14. "And verily We shall cause you to remain in the land, and succeed them. This for such as fear the time when they shall stand before My tribunal - such as fear the punishment denounced."

وَلَنُسۡكِنَنَّكُمُ ٱلۡأَرۡضَ مِنۢ بَعۡدِهِمۡۚ ذَٰلِكَ
لِمَنۡ خَافَ مَقَامِي وَخَافَ وَعِيدِ ١٤

15. But they sought victory and decision (there and then), and frustration was the lot of every powerful obstinate transgressor.

وَٱسۡتَفۡتَحُواْ وَخَابَ كُلُّ جَبَّارٍ عَنِيدٖ ١٥

16. In front of such a one is hell, and he is given for drink, boiling fetid water.

مِّن وَرَآئِهِۦ جَهَنَّمُ وَيُسۡقَىٰ مِن مَّآءٖ صَدِيدٖ ١٦

17. In gulps will he sip it, but never well he be near swallowing it down his throat: death will come to him from every quarter, yet will he not die; and in front of him will be a chastisement unrelenting.

يَتَجَرَّعُهُۥ وَلَا يَكَادُ يُسِيغُهُۥ وَيَأۡتِيهِ ٱلۡمَوۡتُ مِن
كُلِّ مَكَانٖ وَمَا هُوَ بِمَيِّتٖۖ وَمِن وَرَآئِهِۦ
عَذَابٌ غَلِيظٞ ١٧

18. The parable of those who reject their Lord is that their works are as ashes, on which the wind blows furiously on a tempestuous day; no power have they over anything that they have earned; that is the straying far, far (from the goal).

مَّثَلُ ٱلَّذِينَ كَفَرُواْ بِرَبِّهِمۡۖ أَعۡمَٰلُهُمۡ كَرَمَادٍ
ٱشۡتَدَّتۡ بِهِ ٱلرِّيحُ فِي يَوۡمٍ عَاصِفٖۖ لَّا يَقۡدِرُونَ
مِمَّا كَسَبُواْ عَلَىٰ شَيۡءٖۚ ذَٰلِكَ هُوَ ٱلضَّلَٰلُ
ٱلۡبَعِيدُ ١٨

19. Do you not see that Allah created the Heavens and the earth in truth? If He so will, He can remove you and put (in your place) a new Creation?

أَلَمْ تَرَ أَنَّ ٱللَّهَ خَلَقَ ٱلسَّمَٰوَٰتِ وَٱلْأَرْضَ بِٱلْحَقِّ ۚ
إِن يَشَأْ يُذْهِبْكُمْ وَيَأْتِ بِخَلْقٍ جَدِيدٍ ﴿١٩﴾

20. Nor is that for Allah any great matter.

وَمَا ذَٰلِكَ عَلَى ٱللَّهِ بِعَزِيزٍ ﴿٢٠﴾

21. They will all be marshalled before Allah together: then will the weak say to those who were arrogant: "For us, we but followed you; can you then benefit us at all against the wrath of Allah?" They will reply, "If we had received the guidance of Allah, we should have given it to you; to us it makes no difference (now) whether we rage, or bear (these torments) with patience: for ourselves there is no way of escape."

وَبَرَزُوا۟ لِلَّهِ جَمِيعًا فَقَالَ ٱلضُّعَفَٰٓؤُا۟ لِلَّذِينَ
ٱسْتَكْبَرُوٓا۟ إِنَّا كُنَّا لَكُمْ تَبَعًا فَهَلْ أَنتُم مُّغْنُونَ
عَنَّا مِنْ عَذَابِ ٱللَّهِ مِن شَىْءٍ ۚ قَالُوا۟ لَوْ هَدَىٰنَا ٱللَّهُ
لَهَدَيْنَٰكُمْ ۖ سَوَآءٌ عَلَيْنَآ أَجَزِعْنَآ أَمْ صَبَرْنَا
مَا لَنَا مِن مَّحِيصٍ ﴿٢١﴾

22. And Satan will say when the matter is decided: "It was Allah Who gave you a promise of truth; I too promised, but I failed in my promise to you. I had no authority over you except to call you, but you listened to me; then reproach not me, but reproach your own souls. I cannot listen to your cries, nor can you listen to mine. I reject your former act in associating me with Allah. For wrongdoers there must be a grievous penalty."

وَقَالَ ٱلشَّيْطَٰنُ لَمَّا قُضِىَ ٱلْأَمْرُ إِنَّ ٱللَّهَ وَعَدَكُمْ
وَعْدَ ٱلْحَقِّ وَوَعَدتُّكُمْ فَأَخْلَفْتُكُمْ ۖ وَمَا
كَانَ لِىَ عَلَيْكُم مِّن سُلْطَٰنٍ إِلَّآ أَن دَعَوْتُكُمْ
فَٱسْتَجَبْتُمْ لِى ۖ فَلَا تَلُومُونِى وَلُومُوٓا۟ أَنفُسَكُم ۖ
مَّآ أَنَا۠ بِمُصْرِخِكُمْ وَمَآ أَنتُم بِمُصْرِخِىَّ ۖ إِنِّى
كَفَرْتُ بِمَآ أَشْرَكْتُمُونِ مِن قَبْلُ ۗ إِنَّ
ٱلظَّٰلِمِينَ لَهُمْ عَذَابٌ أَلِيمٌ ﴿٢٢﴾

23. But those who believe and work righteousness will be admitted to gardens beneath which rivers flow - to dwell in it for ever with the permission of their Lord; their greeting in it will be: "Peace!"

وَأُدْخِلَ ٱلَّذِينَ ءَامَنُوا۟ وَعَمِلُوا۟ ٱلصَّٰلِحَٰتِ جَنَّٰتٍ
تَجْرِى مِن تَحْتِهَا ٱلْأَنْهَٰرُ خَٰلِدِينَ فِيهَا بِإِذْنِ
رَبِّهِمْ ۖ تَحِيَّتُهُمْ فِيهَا سَلَٰمٌ ﴿٢٣﴾

24. Do you not see how Allah sets out a parable? - A goodly word like a goodly

أَلَمْ تَرَ كَيْفَ ضَرَبَ ٱللَّهُ مَثَلًا كَلِمَةً طَيِّبَةً

tree, whose root is firmly fixed, and its branches (reach) to the heavens -

كَشَجَرَةٍ طَيِّبَةٍ أَصْلُهَا ثَابِتٌ وَفَرْعُهَا فِي
السَّمَاءِ ﴿٢٤﴾

25. It brings out its fruit at all times, by the permission of its Lord. So Allah sets out parables for men, in order that they may receive admonition.

تُؤْتِي أُكُلَهَا كُلَّ حِينٍ بِإِذْنِ رَبِّهَا ۗ وَيَضْرِبُ اللَّهُ
الْأَمْثَالَ لِلنَّاسِ لَعَلَّهُمْ يَتَذَكَّرُونَ ﴿٢٥﴾

26. And the parable of an evil word is that of an evil tree. It is torn up by the root from the surface of the earth; it has no stability.

وَمَثَلُ كَلِمَةٍ خَبِيثَةٍ كَشَجَرَةٍ خَبِيثَةٍ
اجْتُثَّتْ مِنْ فَوْقِ الْأَرْضِ مَا لَهَا مِنْ قَرَارٍ ﴿٢٦﴾

27. Allah will establish in strength those who believe, with the word that stands firm, in this world and in the hereafter; but Allah will leave, to stray, those who do wrong: Allah does what He wills.

يُثَبِّتُ اللَّهُ الَّذِينَ آمَنُوا بِالْقَوْلِ الثَّابِتِ فِي الْحَيَاةِ
الدُّنْيَا وَفِي الْآخِرَةِ ۖ وَيُضِلُّ اللَّهُ الظَّالِمِينَ ۚ
وَيَفْعَلُ اللَّهُ مَا يَشَاءُ ﴿٢٧﴾

28. Have you not turned your vision to those who have changed the favour of Allah into blasphemy and caused their people to descend to the house of perdition -

ثلاثة أرباع الحزب ٢٦

۞ أَلَمْ تَرَ إِلَى الَّذِينَ بَدَّلُوا نِعْمَتَ اللَّهِ كُفْرًا
وَأَحَلُّوا قَوْمَهُمْ دَارَ الْبَوَارِ ﴿٢٨﴾

29. Into hell? They will burn in it - an evil place to stay in!

جَهَنَّمَ يَصْلَوْنَهَا ۖ وَبِئْسَ الْقَرَارُ ﴿٢٩﴾

30. And they set up (idols) as equal to Allah, to mislead (men) from the path! Say: "Enjoy (your brief power)! But verily you are making straightway for hell!"

وَجَعَلُوا لِلَّهِ أَندَادًا لِّيُضِلُّوا عَن سَبِيلِهِ ۗ قُلْ
تَمَتَّعُوا فَإِنَّ مَصِيرَكُمْ إِلَى النَّارِ ﴿٣٠﴾

31. Speak to My servants who have believed, that they may establish regular prayers, and spend (in charity) out of the sustenance We have given them, secretly and openly, before the coming of a day in which there will be neither mutual bargaining nor befriending.

قُل لِّعِبَادِيَ الَّذِينَ آمَنُوا يُقِيمُوا الصَّلَاةَ
وَيُنفِقُوا مِمَّا رَزَقْنَاهُمْ سِرًّا وَعَلَانِيَةً مِّن قَبْلِ أَن
يَأْتِيَ يَوْمٌ لَّا بَيْعٌ فِيهِ وَلَا خِلَالٌ ﴿٣١﴾

32. It is Allah Who has created the heavens and the earth and sends down rain from the skies, and with it brings out fruits with which to feed you; it is He Who has made the ships subject to you, that they may sail through the sea by His command; and the rivers (also) has He made subject to you.

ٱللَّهُ ٱلَّذِى خَلَقَ ٱلسَّمَٰوَٰتِ وَٱلْأَرْضَ وَأَنزَلَ مِنَ
ٱلسَّمَآءِ مَآءً فَأَخْرَجَ بِهِۦ مِنَ ٱلثَّمَرَٰتِ رِزْقًا
لَّكُمْ ۖ وَسَخَّرَ لَكُمُ ٱلْفُلْكَ لِتَجْرِىَ فِى ٱلْبَحْرِ
بِأَمْرِهِۦ ۖ وَسَخَّرَ لَكُمُ ٱلْأَنْهَٰرَ ﴿٣٢﴾

33. And He has made subject to you the sun and the moon, both diligently pursuing their courses; and the night and the day has He (also) made subject you.

وَسَخَّرَ لَكُمُ ٱلشَّمْسَ وَٱلْقَمَرَ دَآئِبَيْنِ ۖ وَسَخَّرَ
لَكُمُ ٱلَّيْلَ وَٱلنَّهَارَ ﴿٣٣﴾

34. And He gives you of all that you ask for. But if you count the favours of Allah, never will you be able to number them; verily, man is given up to injustice and ingratitude.

وَءَاتَىٰكُم مِّن كُلِّ مَا سَأَلْتُمُوهُ ۚ وَإِن تَعُدُّوا۟
نِعْمَتَ ٱللَّهِ لَا تُحْصُوهَآ ۗ إِنَّ ٱلْإِنسَٰنَ لَظَلُومٌ
كَفَّارٌ ﴿٣٤﴾

35. Remember Abraham said: "O my Lord! Make this city one of peace and security and preserve me and my sons from worshipping idols.

وَإِذْ قَالَ إِبْرَٰهِيمُ رَبِّ ٱجْعَلْ هَٰذَا ٱلْبَلَدَ ءَامِنًا
وَٱجْنُبْنِى وَبَنِىَّ أَن نَّعْبُدَ ٱلْأَصْنَامَ ﴿٣٥﴾

36. "O my Lord! They have indeed led astray many among mankind: he then who follows my (ways) is of me, and he that disobeys me - but You are indeed Oft-Forgiving, Most Merciful."

رَبِّ إِنَّهُنَّ أَضْلَلْنَ كَثِيرًا مِّنَ ٱلنَّاسِ ۖ فَمَن تَبِعَنِى
فَإِنَّهُۥ مِنِّى ۖ وَمَنْ عَصَانِى فَإِنَّكَ غَفُورٌ رَّحِيمٌ ﴿٣٦﴾

37. "O our Lord! I have made some of my offspring to dwell in a valley without cultivation, by your Sacred House; in order, O our Lord, that they may establish regular prayer: so fill the hearts of some among men with love towards them, and feed them with fruits; so that they may give thanks."

رَّبَّنَآ إِنِّىٓ أَسْكَنتُ مِن ذُرِّيَّتِى بِوَادٍ غَيْرِ ذِى زَرْعٍ
عِندَ بَيْتِكَ ٱلْمُحَرَّمِ رَبَّنَا لِيُقِيمُوا۟ ٱلصَّلَوٰةَ
فَٱجْعَلْ أَفْـِٔدَةً مِّنَ ٱلنَّاسِ تَهْوِىٓ إِلَيْهِمْ وَٱرْزُقْهُم
مِّنَ ٱلثَّمَرَٰتِ لَعَلَّهُمْ يَشْكُرُونَ ﴿٣٧﴾

38. "O our Lord! Truly You do know what we conceal and what we reveal: for nothing whatever is hidden from Allah, whether on earth or in heaven."

رَبَّنَآ إِنَّكَ تَعْلَمُ مَا نُخْفِى وَمَا نُعْلِنُ ۗ وَمَا يَخْفَىٰ
عَلَى ٱللَّهِ مِن شَىْءٍ فِى ٱلْأَرْضِ وَلَا فِى ٱلسَّمَآءِ ﴿٣٨﴾

39. "Praise be to Allah who has granted to me in old age Ishmael and Isaac: for truly my Lord is He, the Hearer of prayer!"

ٱلْحَمْدُ لِلَّهِ ٱلَّذِى وَهَبَ لِى عَلَى ٱلْكِبَرِ
إِسْمَٰعِيلَ وَإِسْحَٰقَ ۚ إِنَّ رَبِّى لَسَمِيعُ ٱلدُّعَآءِ ﴿٣٩﴾

40. "O my Lord! Make me one who establishes regular prayer, and also (raise such) among my offspring O our Lord! And accept You my prayer."

رَبِّ ٱجْعَلْنِى مُقِيمَ ٱلصَّلَوٰةِ وَمِن ذُرِّيَّتِى ۚ رَبَّنَا
وَتَقَبَّلْ دُعَآءِ ﴿٤٠﴾

41. "O our Lord! Cover (us) with Your forgiveness - me, my parents, and (all) believers, on the day that the reckoning will be established!"

رَبَّنَا ٱغْفِرْ لِى وَلِوَٰلِدَىَّ وَلِلْمُؤْمِنِينَ يَوْمَ
يَقُومُ ٱلْحِسَابُ ﴿٤١﴾

42. Do not think that Allah does not heed the deeds of those who do wrong. He but gives them respite against a day when the eyes will fixedly stare in horror -

وَلَا تَحْسَبَنَّ ٱللَّهَ غَٰفِلًا عَمَّا يَعْمَلُ ٱلظَّٰلِمُونَ ۚ
إِنَّمَا يُؤَخِّرُهُمْ لِيَوْمٍ تَشْخَصُ فِيهِ ٱلْأَبْصَٰرُ ﴿٤٢﴾

43. They are running forward with necks outstretched, their heads uplifted, their gaze returning not towards them, and their hearts a (gaping) void!

مُهْطِعِينَ مُقْنِعِى رُءُوسِهِمْ لَا يَرْتَدُّ إِلَيْهِمْ
طَرْفُهُمْ ۖ وَأَفْـِٔدَتُهُمْ هَوَآءٌ ﴿٤٣﴾

44. So warn mankind of the day when the wrath will reach them; then will the wrongdoers say: "Our Lord! respite us (if only) for a short term; we will answer Your call, and follow the messengers!" "What! Were you not used to swear before that you should suffer no decline?

وَأَنذِرِ ٱلنَّاسَ يَوْمَ يَأْتِيهِمُ ٱلْعَذَابُ فَيَقُولُ
ٱلَّذِينَ ظَلَمُوا۟ رَبَّنَآ أَخِّرْنَآ إِلَىٰٓ أَجَلٍ قَرِيبٍ
نُّجِبْ دَعْوَتَكَ وَنَتَّبِعِ ٱلرُّسُلَ ۗ أَوَلَمْ تَكُونُوٓا۟
أَقْسَمْتُم مِّن قَبْلُ مَا لَكُم مِّن زَوَالٍ ﴿٤٤﴾

45. And you dwelt in the dwellings of men who wronged their own souls; you were clearly shown how We dealt with them; and We put out many parables in your behalf!"

وَسَكَنتُمْ فِى مَسَٰكِنِ ٱلَّذِينَ ظَلَمُوٓا۟ أَنفُسَهُمْ
وَتَبَيَّنَ لَكُمْ كَيْفَ فَعَلْنَا بِهِمْ وَضَرَبْنَا لَكُمُ
ٱلْأَمْثَالَ ﴿٤٥﴾

46. Mighty indeed were the plots which they made, but their plots were (well) within the sight of Allah, even though they were such as to shake the hills!

وَقَدْ مَكَرُوا۟ مَكْرَهُمْ وَعِندَ ٱللَّهِ مَكْرُهُمْ
وَإِن كَانَ مَكْرُهُمْ لِتَزُولَ مِنْهُ ٱلْجِبَالُ ﴿٤٦﴾

47. Never think that Allah would fail His messengers in His promise; for Allah is Exalted in Power - the Lord of Retribution.

فَلَا تَحْسَبَنَّ ٱللَّهَ مُخْلِفَ وَعْدِهِۦ رُسُلَهُۥٓ ۚ
إِنَّ ٱللَّهَ عَزِيزٌ ذُو ٱنتِقَامٍ ﴿٤٧﴾

48. One day the earth will be changed to a different earth, and so will be the heavens, and (men) will be marshalled forward, before Allah, the One, the Irresistible;

يَوْمَ تُبَدَّلُ ٱلْأَرْضُ غَيْرَ ٱلْأَرْضِ وَٱلسَّمَٰوَٰتُ ۖ
وَبَرَزُوا۟ لِلَّهِ ٱلْوَٰحِدِ ٱلْقَهَّارِ ﴿٤٨﴾

49. And you will see the sinners that day bound together in fetters -

وَتَرَى ٱلْمُجْرِمِينَ يَوْمَئِذٍ مُّقَرَّنِينَ فِى ٱلْأَصْفَادِ ﴿٤٩﴾

50. Their garments of liquid pitch, and their faces covered with fire;

سَرَابِيلُهُم مِّن قَطِرَانٍ وَتَغْشَىٰ وُجُوهَهُمُ ٱلنَّارُ ﴿٥٠﴾

51. That Allah may repay each soul according to its due; and verily Allah is Swift in calling to account.

لِيَجْزِىَ ٱللَّهُ كُلَّ نَفْسٍ مَّا كَسَبَتْ ۚ إِنَّ ٱللَّهَ
سَرِيعُ ٱلْحِسَابِ ﴿٥١﴾

52. Here is a message for mankind; let them take warning from it, and let them know that He is (no other than) One God; let men of understanding take heed.

هَٰذَا بَلَٰغٌ لِّلنَّاسِ وَلِيُنذَرُوا۟ بِهِۦ وَلِيَعْلَمُوٓا۟ أَنَّمَا
هُوَ إِلَٰهٌ وَٰحِدٌ وَلِيَذَّكَّرَ أُو۟لُوا۟ ٱلْأَلْبَٰبِ ﴿٥٢﴾

سُورَةُ الحِجْرِ

*Surah 15: **Al-Hijr*** **(The Rocky Tracts)**

In the name of Allah,
Most Gracious, Most Merciful.

بِسْمِ ٱللَّهِ ٱلرَّحْمَٰنِ ٱلرَّحِيمِ

الجزء ١٤ الحزب ٢٧

*1. *Alif Lam Ra*. These are the *Ayat* of revelation - of a Qur'an that makes things clear.

الٓر ۚ تِلْكَ ءَايَٰتُ ٱلْكِتَٰبِ وَقُرْءَانٍ مُّبِينٍ ﴿١﴾

* Part-14

2. Again and again will those who disbelieve wish that they had bowed (to Allah's will) in Islam.

رُّبَمَا يَوَدُّ ٱلَّذِينَ كَفَرُوا۟ لَوْ كَانُوا۟ مُسْلِمِينَ ﴿٢﴾

3. Leave them alone, to enjoy (the good things of this life) and to please themselves; let (false) hope amuse them; soon will knowledge (undeceive them).

ذَرْهُمْ يَأْكُلُوا۟ وَيَتَمَتَّعُوا۟ وَيُلْهِهِمُ ٱلْأَمَلُ ۖ فَسَوْفَ يَعْلَمُونَ ﴿٣﴾

4. Never did We destroy a population that had not a term decreed and assigned beforehand.

وَمَآ أَهْلَكْنَا مِن قَرْيَةٍ إِلَّا وَلَهَا كِتَابٌ مَّعْلُومٌ ﴿٤﴾

5. Neither can a people anticipate its term, nor delay it.

مَّا تَسْبِقُ مِنْ أُمَّةٍ أَجَلَهَا وَمَا يَسْتَـْٔخِرُونَ ﴿٥﴾

6. They say: "O you to whom the message is being revealed! Truly you are mad (or possessed)!"

وَقَالُوا۟ يَـٰٓأَيُّهَا ٱلَّذِى نُزِّلَ عَلَيْهِ ٱلذِّكْرُ إِنَّكَ لَمَجْنُونٌ ﴿٦﴾

7. "Why do you not bring angels to us if it be that you have the truth?"

لَّوْ مَا تَأْتِينَا بِٱلْمَلَـٰٓئِكَةِ إِن كُنتَ مِنَ ٱلصَّـٰدِقِينَ ﴿٧﴾

8. We send not the angels down except for just cause; if they came (to the ungodly), see! No respite would they have!

مَا نُنَزِّلُ ٱلْمَلَـٰٓئِكَةَ إِلَّا بِٱلْحَقِّ وَمَا كَانُوٓا۟ إِذًا مُّنظَرِينَ ﴿٨﴾

9. We have, without doubt, sent down the message; and We will assuredly guard it (from corruption).

إِنَّا نَحْنُ نَزَّلْنَا ٱلذِّكْرَ وَإِنَّا لَهُۥ لَحَـٰفِظُونَ ﴿٩﴾

10. We did send messengers before you amongst the religious sects of old;

وَلَقَدْ أَرْسَلْنَا مِن قَبْلِكَ فِى شِيَعِ ٱلْأَوَّلِينَ ﴿١٠﴾

11. But never came a messenger to them but they mocked him.

وَمَا يَأْتِيهِم مِّن رَّسُولٍ إِلَّا كَانُوا۟ بِهِۦ يَسْتَهْزِءُونَ ﴿١١﴾

12. Even so do We let it creep into the hearts of the sinners -

كَذَٰلِكَ نَسْلُكُهُۥ فِى قُلُوبِ ٱلْمُجْرِمِينَ ﴿١٢﴾

13. That they should not believe in the (message); but the ways of the ancients have passed away.

لَا يُؤْمِنُونَ بِهِۦ وَقَدْ خَلَتْ سُنَّةُ ٱلْأَوَّلِينَ ﴿١٣﴾

14. Even if We opened out to them a gate from heaven, and they were to continue (all day) ascending in it,

وَلَوْ فَتَحْنَا عَلَيْهِم بَابًا مِّنَ ٱلسَّمَآءِ فَظَلُّوا۟ فِيهِ
يَعْرُجُونَ ﴿١٤﴾

15. They would only say: "Our eyes have been intoxicated: nay, we have been bewitched by sorcery."

لَقَالُوٓا۟ إِنَّمَا سُكِّرَتْ أَبْصَٰرُنَا بَلْ نَحْنُ قَوْمٌ
مَّسْحُورُونَ ﴿١٥﴾

16. It is We who have set out the Zodiacal signs in the heavens, and made them fair-seeming to (all) beholders;

وَلَقَدْ جَعَلْنَا فِى ٱلسَّمَآءِ بُرُوجًا وَزَيَّنَّٰهَا
لِلنَّٰظِرِينَ ﴿١٦﴾

17. And (moreover) We have guarded them from every evil spirit accursed;

وَحَفِظْنَٰهَا مِن كُلِّ شَيْطَٰنٍ رَّجِيمٍ ﴿١٧﴾

18. But any that gains a hearing by stealth, is pursued by a flaming fire, bright (to see).

إِلَّا مَنِ ٱسْتَرَقَ ٱلسَّمْعَ فَأَتْبَعَهُۥ شِهَابٌ مُّبِينٌ ﴿١٨﴾

19. And the earth We have spread out (like a carpet); set on it mountains firm and immovable; and produced in it all kinds of things in due balance.

وَٱلْأَرْضَ مَدَدْنَٰهَا وَأَلْقَيْنَا فِيهَا رَوَٰسِىَ وَأَنۢبَتْنَا
فِيهَا مِن كُلِّ شَىْءٍ مَّوْزُونٍ ﴿١٩﴾

20. And We have provided in it means of subsistence - for you and for those for whose sustenance you are not responsible.

وَجَعَلْنَا لَكُمْ فِيهَا مَعَٰيِشَ وَمَن لَّسْتُمْ لَهُۥ
بِرَٰزِقِينَ ﴿٢٠﴾

21. And there is not a thing but its (sources and) treasures (inexhaustible) are with Us; but We only send down of it in due and ascertainable measures.

وَإِن مِّن شَىْءٍ إِلَّا عِندَنَا خَزَآئِنُهُۥ وَمَا نُنَزِّلُهُۥٓ إِلَّا
بِقَدَرٍ مَّعْلُومٍ ﴿٢١﴾

22. And We send the fecundating winds, then cause the rain to descend from the sky, with it providing you with water (in abundance), though you are not the guardians of its stores.

وَأَرْسَلْنَا ٱلرِّيَٰحَ لَوَٰقِحَ فَأَنزَلْنَا مِنَ ٱلسَّمَآءِ مَآءً
فَأَسْقَيْنَٰكُمُوهُ وَمَآ أَنتُمْ لَهُۥ بِخَٰزِنِينَ ﴿٢٢﴾

23. And verily, it is We Who give life, and Who give death; it is We Who remain Inheritors (after all else passes away).

وَإِنَّا لَنَحْنُ نُحْيِۦ وَنُمِيتُ وَنَحْنُ ٱلْوَٰرِثُونَ ٢٣

24. To Us are known those of you who hasten forward, and those who lag behind.

وَلَقَدْ عَلِمْنَا ٱلْمُسْتَقْدِمِينَ مِنكُمْ وَلَقَدْ عَلِمْنَا ٱلْمُسْتَـْٔخِرِينَ ٢٤

25. Assuredly it is your Lord Who will gather them together; for He is Perfect in wisdom and knowledge.

وَإِنَّ رَبَّكَ هُوَ يَحْشُرُهُمْ ۚ إِنَّهُۥ حَكِيمٌ عَلِيمٌ ٢٥

26. We created man from sounding clay, from mud moulded into shape;

وَلَقَدْ خَلَقْنَا ٱلْإِنسَٰنَ مِن صَلْصَٰلٍ مِّنْ حَمَإٍ مَّسْنُونٍ ٢٦

27. And the Jinn race, We had created before, from the fire of a scorching wind.

وَٱلْجَآنَّ خَلَقْنَٰهُ مِن قَبْلُ مِن نَّارِ ٱلسَّمُومِ ٢٧

28. See! Your Lord said to the angels: "I am about to create man from sounding clay from mud moulded into shape;

وَإِذْ قَالَ رَبُّكَ لِلْمَلَٰٓئِكَةِ إِنِّى خَٰلِقٌۢ بَشَرًا مِّن صَلْصَٰلٍ مِّنْ حَمَإٍ مَّسْنُونٍ ٢٨

29. When I have fashioned him (in due proportion) and breathed into him of My spirit, fall you down in obeisance to him."

فَإِذَا سَوَّيْتُهُۥ وَنَفَخْتُ فِيهِ مِن رُّوحِى فَقَعُوا۟ لَهُۥ سَٰجِدِينَ ٢٩

30. So the angels prostrated themselves, all of them together:

فَسَجَدَ ٱلْمَلَٰٓئِكَةُ كُلُّهُمْ أَجْمَعُونَ ٣٠

31. Not so Iblis: he refused to be among those who prostrated themselves.

إِلَّآ إِبْلِيسَ أَبَىٰٓ أَن يَكُونَ مَعَ ٱلسَّٰجِدِينَ ٣١

32. (Allah) said: "O Iblis! What is your reason for not being among those who prostrated themselves?"

قَالَ يَٰٓإِبْلِيسُ مَا لَكَ أَلَّا تَكُونَ مَعَ ٱلسَّٰجِدِينَ ٣٢

33. (Iblis) said: "I am not one to prostrate myself to man, whom You did create from sounding clay, from mud moulded into shape."

قَالَ لَمْ أَكُن لِّأَسْجُدَ لِبَشَرٍ خَلَقْتَهُۥ مِن صَلْصَٰلٍ مِّنْ حَمَإٍ مَّسْنُونٍ ٣٣

34. (Allah) said: "Then get you out from here; for you are rejected, accursed."

قَالَ فَٱخۡرُجۡ مِنۡهَا فَإِنَّكَ رَجِيمٞ ٣٤

35. "And the curse shall be on you till the day of judgement."

وَإِنَّ عَلَيۡكَ ٱللَّعۡنَةَ إِلَىٰ يَوۡمِ ٱلدِّينِ ٣٥

36. (Iblis) said: "O my Lord! Give me then respite till the day the (dead) are raised."

قَالَ رَبِّ فَأَنظِرۡنِيٓ إِلَىٰ يَوۡمِ يُبۡعَثُونَ ٣٦

37. (Allah) said: "Respite is granted you -

قَالَ فَإِنَّكَ مِنَ ٱلۡمُنظَرِينَ ٣٧

38. Till the day of the time appointed."

إِلَىٰ يَوۡمِ ٱلۡوَقۡتِ ٱلۡمَعۡلُومِ ٣٨

39. (Iblis) said: "O my Lord! Because You have put me in the wrong, I will make (wrong) fair-seeming to them on the earth, and I will put them all in the wrong -

قَالَ رَبِّ بِمَآ أَغۡوَيۡتَنِي لَأُزَيِّنَنَّ لَهُمۡ فِي ٱلۡأَرۡضِ
وَلَأُغۡوِيَنَّهُمۡ أَجۡمَعِينَ ٣٩

40. Except Your servants among them, sincere and purified (by Your grace)."

إِلَّا عِبَادَكَ مِنۡهُمُ ٱلۡمُخۡلَصِينَ ٤٠

41. (Allah) said: "This (way of My sincere servants) is indeed a way that leads straight to Me.

قَالَ هَٰذَا صِرَٰطٌ عَلَيَّ مُسۡتَقِيمٌ ٤١

42. For over My servants no authority shall you have, except such as put themselves in the wrong and follow you."

إِنَّ عِبَادِي لَيۡسَ لَكَ عَلَيۡهِمۡ سُلۡطَٰنٌ إِلَّا مَنِ
ٱتَّبَعَكَ مِنَ ٱلۡغَاوِينَ ٤٢

43. And verily, hell is the promised abode for them all!

وَإِنَّ جَهَنَّمَ لَمَوۡعِدُهُمۡ أَجۡمَعِينَ ٤٣

44. To it are seven gates: for each of those gates is a (special) class (of sinners) assigned.

لَهَا سَبۡعَةُ أَبۡوَٰبٖ لِّكُلِّ بَابٖ مِّنۡهُمۡ جُزۡءٞ
مَّقۡسُومٌ ٤٤

45. The righteous (will be) amid gardens and fountains (of clear-flowing water).

إِنَّ ٱلۡمُتَّقِينَ فِي جَنَّٰتٖ وَعُيُونٍ ٤٥

46. (Their greeting will be): "Enter you here in peace and security."

ٱدْخُلُوهَا بِسَلَٰمٍ ءَامِنِينَ ٤٦

47. And We shall remove from their hearts any lurking sense of injury: (they will be) brothers (joyfully) facing each other on thrones (of dignity).

وَنَزَعْنَا مَا فِى صُدُورِهِم مِّنْ غِلٍّ إِخْوَٰنًا عَلَىٰ سُرُرٍ
مُّتَقَٰبِلِينَ ٤٧

48. There, no sense of fatigue shall touch them, nor shall they (ever) be asked to leave.

لَا يَمَسُّهُمْ فِيهَا نَصَبٌ وَمَا هُم مِّنْهَا
بِمُخْرَجِينَ ٤٨

49. Tell My servants that I am indeed the Oft-Forgiving, Most Merciful;

ربع حزب ٢٧ ۞ نَبِّئْ عِبَادِىٓ أَنِّىٓ أَنَا ٱلْغَفُورُ ٱلرَّحِيمُ ٤٩

50. And that My penalty will be indeed the most grievous penalty.

وَأَنَّ عَذَابِى هُوَ ٱلْعَذَابُ ٱلْأَلِيمُ ٥٠

51. Tell them about the guests of Abraham.

وَنَبِّئْهُمْ عَن ضَيْفِ إِبْرَٰهِيمَ ٥١

52. When they entered his presence and said, "Peace!" He said, "We feel afraid of you!"

إِذْ دَخَلُوا۟ عَلَيْهِ فَقَالُوا۟ سَلَٰمًا قَالَ إِنَّا مِنكُمْ
وَجِلُونَ ٥٢

53. They said: "Fear not! We give you glad tidings of a son endowed with wisdom."

قَالُوا۟ لَا تَوْجَلْ إِنَّا نُبَشِّرُكَ بِغُلَٰمٍ عَلِيمٍ ٥٣

54. He said: "Do you give me glad tidings that old age has seized me? Of what then, is your good news?"

قَالَ أَبَشَّرْتُمُونِى عَلَىٰٓ أَن مَّسَّنِىَ ٱلْكِبَرُ فَبِمَ
تُبَشِّرُونَ ٥٤

55. They said: "We give you glad tidings in truth; be not then in despair!"

قَالُوا۟ بَشَّرْنَٰكَ بِٱلْحَقِّ فَلَا تَكُن مِّنَ
ٱلْقَٰنِطِينَ ٥٥

56. He said: "And who despairs of the mercy of his Lord, but such as go astray?"

قَالَ وَمَن يَقْنَطُ مِن رَّحْمَةِ رَبِّهِۦٓ إِلَّا
ٱلضَّآلُّونَ ٥٦

57. (Abraham) said: "What then is the business on which you (have come), O you messengers (of Allah)?"

قَالَ فَمَا خَطْبُكُمْ أَيُّهَا الْمُرْسَلُونَ ٥٧

58. They said: "We have been sent to a people (deep) in sin.

قَالُوا إِنَّا أُرْسِلْنَا إِلَىٰ قَوْمٍ مُجْرِمِينَ ٥٨

59. Excepting the adherents of Lot: them we are certainly (charged) to save (from harm) - all -

إِلَّا آلَ لُوطٍ إِنَّا لَمُنَجُّوهُمْ أَجْمَعِينَ ٥٩

60. Except his wife, who, we have ascertained, will be among those who will lag behind."

إِلَّا امْرَأَتَهُ قَدَّرْنَا إِنَّهَا لَمِنَ الْغَابِرِينَ ٦٠

61. At length, when the messengers arrived among the adherents of Lot,

فَلَمَّا جَاءَ آلَ لُوطٍ الْمُرْسَلُونَ ٦١

62. He said: "You appear to be uncommon folk."

قَالَ إِنَّكُمْ قَوْمٌ مُنْكَرُونَ ٦٢

63. They said: "Yea, we have come to you to accomplish that of which they doubt."

قَالُوا بَلْ جِئْنَاكَ بِمَا كَانُوا فِيهِ يَمْتَرُونَ ٦٣

64. "We have brought to you that which is inevitably due, and assuredly we tell the truth."

وَأَتَيْنَاكَ بِالْحَقِّ وَإِنَّا لَصَادِقُونَ ٦٤

65. "Then travel by night with your household, when a portion of the night (yet remains), and do you bring up the rear; let no one amongst you look back, but pass on where you are ordered."

فَأَسْرِ بِأَهْلِكَ بِقِطْعٍ مِنَ اللَّيْلِ وَاتَّبِعْ أَدْبَارَهُمْ وَلَا
يَلْتَفِتْ مِنْكُمْ أَحَدٌ وَامْضُوا حَيْثُ تُؤْمَرُونَ ٦٥

66. And We made known this decree to him, that the last remnants of those (sinners) should be cut off by the morning.

وَقَضَيْنَا إِلَيْهِ ذَٰلِكَ الْأَمْرَ أَنَّ دَابِرَ هَٰؤُلَاءِ مَقْطُوعٌ
مُصْبِحِينَ ٦٦

67. The inhabitants of the city came in (mad) joy (at news of the young men).

وَجَاءَ أَهْلُ الْمَدِينَةِ يَسْتَبْشِرُونَ ٦٧

68. Lot said: "These are my guests: disgrace me not;

قَالَ إِنَّ هَٰٓؤُلَآءِ ضَيۡفِي فَلَا تَفۡضَحُونِ ٦٨

69. But fear Allah and shame me not."

وَٱتَّقُواْ ٱللَّهَ وَلَا تُخۡزُونِ ٦٩

70. They said: "Did we not forbid you (to speak) for all and sundry?"

قَالُوٓاْ أَوَلَمۡ نَنۡهَكَ عَنِ ٱلۡعَٰلَمِينَ ٧٠

71. He said: "There are my daughters (to marry), if you must act (so)."

قَالَ هَٰٓؤُلَآءِ بَنَاتِيٓ إِن كُنتُمۡ فَٰعِلِينَ ٧١

72. Verily, by your life (O Prophet), in their wild intoxication, they wandered in distraction, to and fro.

لَعَمۡرُكَ إِنَّهُمۡ لَفِي سَكۡرَتِهِمۡ يَعۡمَهُونَ ٧٢

73. But the (mighty) blast overtook them before morning,

فَأَخَذَتۡهُمُ ٱلصَّيۡحَةُ مُشۡرِقِينَ ٧٣

74. And We turned (the cities) upside down, and rained down on them brimstones hard as baked clay.

فَجَعَلۡنَا عَٰلِيَهَا سَافِلَهَا وَأَمۡطَرۡنَا عَلَيۡهِمۡ حِجَارَةٗ
مِّن سِجِّيلٍ ٧٤

75. See! In this are signs for those who by signs do understand.

إِنَّ فِي ذَٰلِكَ لَأٓيَٰتٖ لِّلۡمُتَوَسِّمِينَ ٧٥

76. And the (cities were) right on the highroad.

وَإِنَّهَا لَبِسَبِيلٖ مُّقِيمٍ ٧٦

77. See! In this is a sign for those who believe!

إِنَّ فِي ذَٰلِكَ لَأٓيَةٗ لِّلۡمُؤۡمِنِينَ ٧٧

78. And the companions of the wood were also wrongdoers;

وَإِن كَانَ أَصۡحَٰبُ ٱلۡأَيۡكَةِ لَظَٰلِمِينَ ٧٨

79. So We exacted retribution from them. They were both on an open highway, plain to see.

فَٱنتَقَمۡنَا مِنۡهُمۡ وَإِنَّهُمَا لَبِإِمَامٖ مُّبِينٖ ٧٩

80. The companions of the rocky Tract also rejected the messengers:

وَلَقَدۡ كَذَّبَ أَصۡحَٰبُ ٱلۡحِجۡرِ ٱلۡمُرۡسَلِينَ ٨٠

81. We sent them Our signs, but they persisted in turning away from them.

وَءَاتَيۡنَٰهُمۡ ءَايَٰتِنَا فَكَانُواْ عَنۡهَا مُعۡرِضِينَ ٨١

82. Out of the mountains did they hew (their) edifices, (feeling themselves) secure.

وَكَانُواْ يَنۡحِتُونَ مِنَ ٱلۡجِبَالِ بُيُوتًا ءَامِنِينَ ٨٢

83. But the (mighty) blast seized them of a morning,

فَأَخَذَتۡهُمُ ٱلصَّيۡحَةُ مُصۡبِحِينَ ٨٣

84. And of no benefit to them was all that they did (with such art and care)!

فَمَآ أَغۡنَىٰ عَنۡهُم مَّا كَانُواْ يَكۡسِبُونَ ٨٤

85. We created not the heavens, the earth, and all between them, but for just ends. And the hour is surely coming (when this will be manifest). So overlook (any human faults) with gracious forgiveness.

وَمَا خَلَقۡنَا ٱلسَّمَٰوَٰتِ وَٱلۡأَرۡضَ وَمَا بَيۡنَهُمَآ إِلَّا
بِٱلۡحَقِّۗ وَإِنَّ ٱلسَّاعَةَ لَأٓتِيَةٞۖ فَٱصۡفَحِ ٱلصَّفۡحَ
ٱلۡجَمِيلَ ٨٥

86. For verily it is your Lord Who is the Master-Creator, knowing all things.

إِنَّ رَبَّكَ هُوَ ٱلۡخَلَّٰقُ ٱلۡعَلِيمُ ٨٦

87. And We have bestowed upon you the seven oft-repeated (verses) and the grand Qur'an.

وَلَقَدۡ ءَاتَيۡنَٰكَ سَبۡعٗا مِّنَ ٱلۡمَثَانِي وَٱلۡقُرۡءَانَ
ٱلۡعَظِيمَ ٨٧

88. Strain not your eyes (wistfully) at what We have bestowed on certain classes of them, nor grieve over them; but lower your wing (in gentleness) to the believers.

لَا تَمُدَّنَّ عَيۡنَيۡكَ إِلَىٰ مَا مَتَّعۡنَا بِهِۦٓ أَزۡوَٰجٗا مِّنۡهُمۡ وَلَا
تَحۡزَنۡ عَلَيۡهِمۡ وَٱخۡفِضۡ جَنَاحَكَ لِلۡمُؤۡمِنِينَ ٨٨

89. And say: "I am indeed he that warns openly and without ambiguity" -

وَقُلۡ إِنِّيٓ أَنَا ٱلنَّذِيرُ ٱلۡمُبِينُ ٨٩

90. (Of just such wrath) as We sent down on those who divided (Scripture into arbitrary parts) -

كَمَآ أَنزَلۡنَا عَلَى ٱلۡمُقۡتَسِمِينَ ٩٠

91. (So also on such) as have made the Qur'an into shreds (as they please).

ٱلَّذِينَ جَعَلُواْ ٱلۡقُرۡءَانَ عِضِينَ ٩١

92. Therefore, by your Lord, We will, of a surety, call them to account,

فَوَرَبِّكَ لَنَسْـَٔلَنَّهُمْ أَجْمَعِينَ ﴿٩٢﴾

93. For all their deeds.

عَمَّا كَانُوا۟ يَعْمَلُونَ ﴿٩٣﴾

94. Therefore, explain openly what you are commanded, and turn away from those who join false gods with Allah.

فَٱصْدَعْ بِمَا تُؤْمَرُ وَأَعْرِضْ عَنِ ٱلْمُشْرِكِينَ ﴿٩٤﴾

95. For sufficient are We to you against those who scoff -

إِنَّا كَفَيْنَٰكَ ٱلْمُسْتَهْزِءِينَ ﴿٩٥﴾

96. Those who adopt, with Allah, another god; but soon will they come to know.

ٱلَّذِينَ يَجْعَلُونَ مَعَ ٱللَّهِ إِلَٰهًا ءَاخَرَ ۚ فَسَوْفَ يَعْلَمُونَ ﴿٩٦﴾

97. We do indeed know how your heart is distressed at what they say.

وَلَقَدْ نَعْلَمُ أَنَّكَ يَضِيقُ صَدْرُكَ بِمَا يَقُولُونَ ﴿٩٧﴾

98. But celebrate the praises of your Lord, and be of those who prostrate themselves in adoration.

فَسَبِّحْ بِحَمْدِ رَبِّكَ وَكُن مِّنَ ٱلسَّٰجِدِينَ ﴿٩٨﴾

99. And serve your Lord until there come to you the hour that is certain.

وَٱعْبُدْ رَبَّكَ حَتَّىٰ يَأْتِيَكَ ٱلْيَقِينُ ﴿٩٩﴾

سُورَةُ النَّحْلِ

Surah 16: ***An-Nahl*** **(The Bee)**

In the name of Allah,
Most Gracious, Most Merciful.

بِسْمِ ٱللَّهِ ٱلرَّحْمَٰنِ ٱلرَّحِيمِ

1. (Inevitably) comes (to pass) the command of Allah; seek you not then to hasten it; glory to Him, and far is He above having the partners they ascribe to Him!

أَتَىٰٓ أَمْرُ ٱللَّهِ فَلَا تَسْتَعْجِلُوهُ ۚ سُبْحَٰنَهُۥ وَتَعَٰلَىٰ عَمَّا يُشْرِكُونَ ﴿١﴾

2. He does send down His angels with inspiration of His command, to such of

يُنَزِّلُ ٱلْمَلَٰٓئِكَةَ بِٱلرُّوحِ مِنْ أَمْرِهِۦ عَلَىٰ مَن

His servants as He pleases, (saying): "Warn (man) that there is no god but I; so do your duty to Me."

يَشَآءُ مِنۡ عِبَادِهِۦٓ أَنۡ أَنذِرُوٓاْ أَنَّهُۥ لَآ إِلَٰهَ إِلَّآ أَنَا۠
فَٱتَّقُونِ ٢

3. He has created the heavens and the earth for just ends; far is He above having the partners they ascribe to Him!

خَلَقَ ٱلسَّمَٰوَٰتِ وَٱلۡأَرۡضَ بِٱلۡحَقِّۚ تَعَٰلَىٰ عَمَّا
يُشۡرِكُونَ ٣

4. He has created man from a sperm-drop; and see this same (man) becomes an open disputer!

خَلَقَ ٱلۡإِنسَٰنَ مِن نُّطۡفَةٖ فَإِذَا هُوَ خَصِيمٞ
مُّبِينٞ ٤

5. And cattle He has created for you (men); from them you derive warmth, and numerous benefits, and of their (meat) you eat.

وَٱلۡأَنۡعَٰمَ خَلَقَهَاۖ لَكُمۡ فِيهَا دِفۡءٞ وَمَنَٰفِعُ
وَمِنۡهَا تَأۡكُلُونَ ٥

6. And you have a sense of pride and beauty in them as you drive them home in the evening, and as you lead them out to pasture in the morning.

وَلَكُمۡ فِيهَا جَمَالٌ حِينَ تُرِيحُونَ وَحِينَ
تَسۡرَحُونَ ٦

7. And they carry your heavy loads to lands that you could not (otherwise) reach except with souls distressed; for your Lord is indeed Most Kind, Most Merciful.

وَتَحۡمِلُ أَثۡقَالَكُمۡ إِلَىٰ بَلَدٖ لَّمۡ تَكُونُواْ بَٰلِغِيهِ
إِلَّا بِشِقِّ ٱلۡأَنفُسِۚ إِنَّ رَبَّكُمۡ لَرَءُوفٞ رَّحِيمٞ ٧

8. And (He has created) horses, mules, and donkeys, for you to ride and use for show; and He has created (other) things of what you have no knowledge.

وَٱلۡخَيۡلَ وَٱلۡبِغَالَ وَٱلۡحَمِيرَ لِتَرۡكَبُوهَا وَزِينَةٗۚ
وَيَخۡلُقُ مَا لَا تَعۡلَمُونَ ٨

9. And to Allah leads straight the way, but there are ways that turn aside; if Allah had willed, He could have guided all of you.

وَعَلَى ٱللَّهِ قَصۡدُ ٱلسَّبِيلِ وَمِنۡهَا جَآئِرٞۚ وَلَوۡ شَآءَ
لَهَدَىٰكُمۡ أَجۡمَعِينَ ٩

10. It is He Who sends down rain from the sky. From it you drink, and out of it (grows) the vegetation on which you feed your cattle.

هُوَ ٱلَّذِيٓ أَنزَلَ مِنَ ٱلسَّمَآءِ مَآءٗۖ لَّكُم مِّنۡهُ
شَرَابٞ وَمِنۡهُ شَجَرٞ فِيهِ تُسِيمُونَ ١٠

11. With it He produces for you corn, olives, date palms, grapes, and every kind of fruit; verily in this is a sign for those who give thought.

يُنۢبِتُ لَكُم بِهِ ٱلزَّرۡعَ وَٱلزَّيۡتُونَ وَٱلنَّخِيلَ
وَٱلۡأَعۡنَٰبَ وَمِن كُلِّ ٱلثَّمَرَٰتِۚ إِنَّ فِي ذَٰلِكَ
لَأٓيَةٗ لِّقَوۡمٖ يَتَفَكَّرُونَ ١١

12. He has made subject to you the night and the day; the sun and the moon; and the stars are in subjection by His command; verily in this are signs for men who are wise.

وَسَخَّرَ لَكُمُ ٱلَّيۡلَ وَٱلنَّهَارَ وَٱلشَّمۡسَ
وَٱلۡقَمَرَۖ وَٱلنُّجُومُ مُسَخَّرَٰتُۢ بِأَمۡرِهِۦٓۚ إِنَّ فِي
ذَٰلِكَ لَأٓيَٰتٖ لِّقَوۡمٖ يَعۡقِلُونَ ١٢

13. And the things on this earth which He has multiplied in varying colours (and qualities): verily in this is a sign for men who celebrate the praises of Allah (in gratitude).

وَمَا ذَرَأَ لَكُمۡ فِي ٱلۡأَرۡضِ مُخۡتَلِفًا أَلۡوَٰنُهُۥٓۚ
إِنَّ فِي ذَٰلِكَ لَأٓيَةٗ لِّقَوۡمٖ يَذَّكَّرُونَ ١٣

14. It is He Who has made the sea subject, that you may eat of it flesh that is fresh and tender, and that you may extract from it ornaments to wear, and you see the ships in it that plough the waves, that you may seek (thus) of the bounty of Allah and that you may be grateful.

وَهُوَ ٱلَّذِي سَخَّرَ ٱلۡبَحۡرَ لِتَأۡكُلُواْ مِنۡهُ
لَحۡمٗا طَرِيّٗا وَتَسۡتَخۡرِجُواْ مِنۡهُ حِلۡيَةٗ
تَلۡبَسُونَهَاۖ وَتَرَى ٱلۡفُلۡكَ مَوَاخِرَ فِيهِ وَلِتَبۡتَغُواْ
مِن فَضۡلِهِۦ وَلَعَلَّكُمۡ تَشۡكُرُونَ ١٤

15. And He has set up on the earth mountains standing firm, lest it should shake with you; and rivers and roads; that you may guide yourselves,

وَأَلۡقَىٰ فِي ٱلۡأَرۡضِ رَوَٰسِيَ أَن تَمِيدَ بِكُمۡ
وَأَنۡهَٰرٗا وَسُبُلٗا لَّعَلَّكُمۡ تَهۡتَدُونَ ١٥

16. And marks and signposts; and by the stars (men) guide themselves.

وَعَلَٰمَٰتٖۚ وَبِٱلنَّجۡمِ هُمۡ يَهۡتَدُونَ ١٦

17. Is then He Who creates like one that creates not? Will you not receive admonition?

أَفَمَن يَخۡلُقُ كَمَن لَّا يَخۡلُقُۚ أَفَلَا تَذَكَّرُونَ ١٧

18. If you would count up the favours of Allah, never would you be able to number them; for Allah is Oft-Forgiving, Most Merciful.

وَإِن تَعُدُّواْ نِعۡمَةَ ٱللَّهِ لَا تُحۡصُوهَآۗ إِنَّ ٱللَّهَ
لَغَفُورٞ رَّحِيمٞ ١٨

19. And Allah does know what you conceal, and what you reveal.

وَٱللَّهُ يَعْلَمُ مَا تُسِرُّونَ وَمَا تُعْلِنُونَ ١٩

20. Those whom they invoke besides Allah create nothing and are themselves created.

وَٱلَّذِينَ يَدْعُونَ مِن دُونِ ٱللَّهِ لَا يَخْلُقُونَ شَيْـًٔا
وَهُمْ يُخْلَقُونَ ٢٠

21. (They are things) dead, lifeless; nor do you know when they will be raised up.

أَمْوَٰتٌ غَيْرُ أَحْيَآءٍ ۖ وَمَا يَشْعُرُونَ أَيَّانَ يُبْعَثُونَ ٢١

22. Your God is One God; as to those who believe not in the hereafter, their hearts refuse to know, and they are arrogant.

إِلَٰهُكُمْ إِلَٰهٌ وَٰحِدٌ ۚ فَٱلَّذِينَ لَا يُؤْمِنُونَ بِٱلْـَٔاخِرَةِ
قُلُوبُهُم مُّنكِرَةٌ وَهُم مُّسْتَكْبِرُونَ ٢٢

23. Undoubtedly, Allah does know what they conceal, and what they reveal; verily He loves not the arrogant.

لَا جَرَمَ أَنَّ ٱللَّهَ يَعْلَمُ مَا يُسِرُّونَ وَمَا يُعْلِنُونَ ۚ
إِنَّهُۥ لَا يُحِبُّ ٱلْمُسْتَكْبِرِينَ ٢٣

24. When it is said to them, "What is it that your Lord has revealed?" They say, "Tales of the ancients!"

وَإِذَا قِيلَ لَهُم مَّاذَآ أَنزَلَ رَبُّكُمْ قَالُوٓا۟
أَسَٰطِيرُ ٱلْأَوَّلِينَ ٢٤

25. Let them bear, on the day of judgement, their own burdens in full, and also (something) of the burdens of those without knowledge, whom they misled. Alas, how grievous the burdens they will bear!

لِيَحْمِلُوٓا۟ أَوْزَارَهُمْ كَامِلَةً يَوْمَ ٱلْقِيَٰمَةِ وَمِنْ
أَوْزَارِ ٱلَّذِينَ يُضِلُّونَهُم بِغَيْرِ عِلْمٍ ۗ أَلَا سَآءَ
مَا يَزِرُونَ ٢٥

26. Those before them did also plot (against Allah's way); but Allah took their structures from their foundations, and the roof fell down on them from above; and the wrath seized them from directions they did not perceive.

قَدْ مَكَرَ ٱلَّذِينَ مِن قَبْلِهِمْ فَأَتَى ٱللَّهُ بُنْيَٰنَهُم
مِّنَ ٱلْقَوَاعِدِ فَخَرَّ عَلَيْهِمُ ٱلسَّقْفُ مِن فَوْقِهِمْ
وَأَتَىٰهُمُ ٱلْعَذَابُ مِنْ حَيْثُ لَا يَشْعُرُونَ ٢٦

27. Then, on the day of judgement, He will cover them with shame, and say: "Where are My 'partners' concerning whom you used to dispute (with the godly)?" Those

ثُمَّ يَوْمَ ٱلْقِيَٰمَةِ يُخْزِيهِمْ وَيَقُولُ أَيْنَ شُرَكَآءِىَ
ٱلَّذِينَ كُنتُمْ تُشَٰٓقُّونَ فِيهِمْ ۚ قَالَ ٱلَّذِينَ أُوتُوا۟

endued with knowledge will say: "This day, indeed, are the unbelievers covered with shame and misery -

ٱلْعِلْمَ إِنَّ ٱلْخِزْىَ ٱلْيَوْمَ وَٱلسُّوٓءَ عَلَى ٱلْكَـٰفِرِينَ ٢٧

28. (Namely) those whose lives the angels take in a state of wrongdoing to their own souls. Then would they offer submission (with the pretence), 'We did no evil (knowingly).'" (The angels will reply), "Nay, but verily Allah knows all that you did;

ٱلَّذِينَ تَتَوَفَّىٰهُمُ ٱلْمَلَـٰٓئِكَةُ ظَالِمِىٓ أَنفُسِهِمْ ۖ فَأَلْقَوُا۟
ٱلسَّلَمَ مَا كُنَّا نَعْمَلُ مِن سُوٓءٍۭ ۚ بَلَىٰٓ إِنَّ ٱللَّهَ عَلِيمٌۢ
بِمَا كُنتُمْ تَعْمَلُونَ ٢٨

29. So enter the gates of hell, to dwell in it. Thus evil indeed is the abode of the arrogant."

فَٱدْخُلُوٓا۟ أَبْوَٰبَ جَهَنَّمَ خَـٰلِدِينَ فِيهَا ۖ فَلَبِئْسَ
مَثْوَى ٱلْمُتَكَبِّرِينَ ٢٩

30. To the righteous (when) it is said, "What is it that your Lord has revealed?" They say, "All that is good." To those who do good, there is good in this world, and the home of the hereafter is even better. And excellent indeed is the home of the righteous -

ثلاثة أرباع الحزب ٢٧

۞ وَقِيلَ لِلَّذِينَ ٱتَّقَوْا۟ مَاذَآ أَنزَلَ رَبُّكُمْ ۚ قَالُوا۟ خَيْرًا ۗ
لِّلَّذِينَ أَحْسَنُوا۟ فِى هَـٰذِهِ ٱلدُّنْيَا حَسَنَةٌ ۚ وَلَدَارُ
ٱلْـَٔاخِرَةِ خَيْرٌ ۚ وَلَنِعْمَ دَارُ ٱلْمُتَّقِينَ ٣٠

31. Gardens of eternity which they will enter; beneath them flow (pleasant) rivers; they will have in it all that they wish; thus does Allah reward the righteous -

جَنَّـٰتُ عَدْنٍ يَدْخُلُونَهَا تَجْرِى مِن تَحْتِهَا
ٱلْأَنْهَـٰرُ ۖ لَهُمْ فِيهَا مَا يَشَآءُونَ ۚ كَذَٰلِكَ يَجْزِى
ٱللَّهُ ٱلْمُتَّقِينَ ٣١

32. (Namely) those whose lives the angels take in a state of purity, saying (to them), "Peace be on you; enter you the garden, because of the good which you did (in the world)."

ٱلَّذِينَ تَتَوَفَّىٰهُمُ ٱلْمَلَـٰٓئِكَةُ طَيِّبِينَ ۙ يَقُولُونَ
سَلَـٰمٌ عَلَيْكُمُ ٱدْخُلُوا۟ ٱلْجَنَّةَ بِمَا كُنتُمْ تَعْمَلُونَ ٣٢

33. Do the (ungodly) wait until the angels come to them, or there comes the command of your Lord (for their doom)? So did those who went before them. But Allah wronged them not; nay, they wronged their own souls.

هَلْ يَنظُرُونَ إِلَّآ أَن تَأْتِيَهُمُ ٱلْمَلَـٰٓئِكَةُ أَوْ يَأْتِىَ
أَمْرُ رَبِّكَ ۚ كَذَٰلِكَ فَعَلَ ٱلَّذِينَ مِن قَبْلِهِمْ ۚ وَمَا
ظَلَمَهُمُ ٱللَّهُ وَلَـٰكِن كَانُوٓا۟ أَنفُسَهُمْ يَظْلِمُونَ ٣٣

34. But the evil results of their deeds overtook them, and that very (wrath) at which they had scoffed hemmed them in.

فَأَصَابَهُمْ سَيِّئَاتُ مَا عَمِلُوا وَحَاقَ بِهِم مَّا كَانُوا بِهِ
يَسْتَهْزِءُونَ ﴿٣٤﴾

35. The worshippers of false gods say: "If Allah had so willed, we should not have worshipped any but Him - neither we nor our fathers - nor should we have prescribed prohibitions other than His." So did those who went before them. But what is the mission of messengers but to preach the clear message?

وَقَالَ الَّذِينَ أَشْرَكُوا لَوْ شَاءَ اللَّهُ مَا عَبَدْنَا مِن
دُونِهِ مِن شَيْءٍ نَّحْنُ وَلَا آبَاؤُنَا وَلَا حَرَّمْنَا مِن
دُونِهِ مِن شَيْءٍ ۚ كَذَٰلِكَ فَعَلَ الَّذِينَ مِن قَبْلِهِمْ ۚ فَهَلْ
عَلَى الرُّسُلِ إِلَّا الْبَلَاغُ الْمُبِينُ ﴿٣٥﴾

36. For We assuredly sent amongst every people a messenger, (with the command), "Serve Allah, and eschew evil"; of the people were some whom Allah guided, and some on whom error became inevitably (established). So travel through the earth, and see what was the end of those who denied (the truth).

وَلَقَدْ بَعَثْنَا فِي كُلِّ أُمَّةٍ رَّسُولًا أَنِ اعْبُدُوا
اللَّهَ وَاجْتَنِبُوا الطَّاغُوتَ ۖ فَمِنْهُم مَّنْ هَدَى
اللَّهُ وَمِنْهُم مَّنْ حَقَّتْ عَلَيْهِ الضَّلَالَةُ ۚ فَسِيرُوا فِي
الْأَرْضِ فَانظُرُوا كَيْفَ كَانَ عَاقِبَةُ
الْمُكَذِّبِينَ ﴿٣٦﴾

37. If you are anxious for their guidance, yet Allah guides not such as He leaves to stray. And there is none to help them.

إِن تَحْرِصْ عَلَىٰ هُدَاهُمْ فَإِنَّ اللَّهَ لَا يَهْدِي مَن
يُضِلُّ ۖ وَمَا لَهُم مِّن نَّاصِرِينَ ﴿٣٧﴾

38. They swear their strongest oaths by Allah, that Allah will not raise up those who die; nay, but it is a promise (binding) on Him in truth; but most among mankind realise it not.

وَأَقْسَمُوا بِاللَّهِ جَهْدَ أَيْمَانِهِمْ لَا يَبْعَثُ اللَّهُ مَن
يَمُوتُ ۚ بَلَىٰ وَعْدًا عَلَيْهِ حَقًّا وَلَٰكِنَّ أَكْثَرَ
النَّاسِ لَا يَعْلَمُونَ ﴿٣٨﴾

39. (They must be raised up), in order that He may manifest to them the truth of that in which they differ, and that the rejecters of truth may realise that they had indeed (surrendered to) falsehood.

لِيُبَيِّنَ لَهُمُ الَّذِي يَخْتَلِفُونَ فِيهِ وَلِيَعْلَمَ
الَّذِينَ كَفَرُوا أَنَّهُمْ كَانُوا كَاذِبِينَ ﴿٣٩﴾

40. For to anything which We have willed, We but say the word, "Be", and it is.

إِنَّمَا قَوۡلُنَا لِشَيۡءٍ إِذَآ أَرَدۡنَٰهُ أَن نَّقُولَ لَهُۥ كُن فَيَكُونُ ٤٠

41. To those who leave their homes in the cause of Allah, after suffering oppression - We will assuredly give a goodly home in this world; but truly the reward of the hereafter will be greater if they only realise (this)!

وَٱلَّذِينَ هَٰجَرُواْ فِي ٱللَّهِ مِنۢ بَعۡدِ مَا ظُلِمُواْ
لَنُبَوِّئَنَّهُمۡ فِي ٱلدُّنۡيَا حَسَنَةٗۖ وَلَأَجۡرُ ٱلۡأٓخِرَةِ
أَكۡبَرُۚ لَوۡ كَانُواْ يَعۡلَمُونَ ٤١

42. (They are) those who persevere in patience, and put their trust on their Lord.

ٱلَّذِينَ صَبَرُواْ وَعَلَىٰ رَبِّهِمۡ يَتَوَكَّلُونَ ٤٢

43. And before you also, the messengers We sent were but men, to whom We granted inspiration; if you realise this not, ask of those who possess the message.

وَمَآ أَرۡسَلۡنَا مِن قَبۡلِكَ إِلَّا رِجَالٗا نُّوحِيٓ إِلَيۡهِمۡۖ
فَسۡـَٔلُوٓاْ أَهۡلَ ٱلذِّكۡرِ إِن كُنتُمۡ لَا تَعۡلَمُونَ ٤٣

44. (We sent them) with clear signs and scriptures and We have sent down to you (also, O Muhammad) the message; that you may explain clearly to men what is sent for them, and that they may give thought.

بِٱلۡبَيِّنَٰتِ وَٱلزُّبُرِۗ وَأَنزَلۡنَآ إِلَيۡكَ ٱلذِّكۡرَ لِتُبَيِّنَ
لِلنَّاسِ مَا نُزِّلَ إِلَيۡهِمۡ وَلَعَلَّهُمۡ يَتَفَكَّرُونَ ٤٤

45. Do then those who devise evil (plots) feel secure that Allah will not cause the earth to swallow them up, or that the wrath will not seize them from directions they little perceive? -

أَفَأَمِنَ ٱلَّذِينَ مَكَرُواْ ٱلسَّيِّـَٔاتِ أَن يَخۡسِفَ ٱللَّهُ
بِهِمُ ٱلۡأَرۡضَ أَوۡ يَأۡتِيَهُمُ ٱلۡعَذَابُ مِنۡ حَيۡثُ
لَا يَشۡعُرُونَ ٤٥

46. Or that He may not call them to account in the midst of their goings to and fro, without a chance of their frustrating Him? -

أَوۡ يَأۡخُذَهُمۡ فِي تَقَلُّبِهِمۡ فَمَا هُم بِمُعۡجِزِينَ ٤٦

47. Or that He may not call them to account by a process of slow wastage - for your Lord is indeed full of kindness and mercy.

أَوۡ يَأۡخُذَهُمۡ عَلَىٰ تَخَوُّفٖ فَإِنَّ رَبَّكُمۡ لَرَءُوفٞ
رَّحِيمٌ ٤٧

48. Do they not look at Allah's creation, (even) among (inanimate) things - how their (very) shadows turn round, from the

أَوَلَمۡ يَرَوۡاْ إِلَىٰ مَا خَلَقَ ٱللَّهُ مِن شَيۡءٖ يَتَفَيَّؤُاْ ظِلَٰلُهُۥ

right and the left, prostrating themselves to Allah, and that in the humblest manner?

عَنِ ٱلْيَمِينِ وَٱلشَّمَآئِلِ سُجَّدًا لِّلَّهِ وَهُمْ دَٰخِرُونَ ﴿٤٨﴾

49. And to Allah does obeisance all that is in the heavens and on earth, whether moving (living), creatures or the angels; for none are arrogant (before their Lord).

وَلِلَّهِ يَسْجُدُ مَا فِى ٱلسَّمَٰوَٰتِ وَمَا فِى ٱلْأَرْضِ
مِن دَآبَّةٍ وَٱلْمَلَٰٓئِكَةُ وَهُمْ لَا يَسْتَكْبِرُونَ ﴿٤٩﴾

50. They all revere their Lord, high above them, and they do all that they are commanded.

سَجْدَة
يَخَافُونَ رَبَّهُم مِّن فَوْقِهِمْ وَيَفْعَلُونَ مَا يُؤْمَرُونَ ۩ ﴿٥٠﴾

51. Allah has said: "Take not (for worship) two gods; for He is just One God; then fear Me (and Me alone)."

الحِزْبُ ٢٨
۞ وَقَالَ ٱللَّهُ لَا تَتَّخِذُوٓا۟ إِلَٰهَيْنِ ٱثْنَيْنِ ۖ إِنَّمَا هُوَ
إِلَٰهٌ وَٰحِدٌ ۖ فَإِيَّٰىَ فَٱرْهَبُونِ ﴿٥١﴾

52. To Him belongs whatever is in the heavens and on earth. And to Him is duty due always; then will you fear other than Allah?

وَلَهُۥ مَا فِى ٱلسَّمَٰوَٰتِ وَٱلْأَرْضِ وَلَهُ ٱلدِّينُ وَاصِبًا ۚ أَفَغَيْرَ
ٱللَّهِ تَتَّقُونَ ﴿٥٢﴾

53. And you have no good thing but is from Allah and moreover when you are touched by distress, to Him you call with groans;

وَمَا بِكُم مِّن نِّعْمَةٍ فَمِنَ ٱللَّهِ ۖ ثُمَّ إِذَا مَسَّكُمُ ٱلضُّرُّ
فَإِلَيْهِ تَجْـَٔرُونَ ﴿٥٣﴾

54. Yet, when He removes the distress from you, see! Some of you turn to other gods to join with their Lord -

ثُمَّ إِذَا كَشَفَ ٱلضُّرَّ عَنكُمْ إِذَا فَرِيقٌ مِّنكُم
بِرَبِّهِمْ يُشْرِكُونَ ﴿٥٤﴾

55. (As if) to show their ingratitude for the favours We have bestowed on them! Then enjoy (your brief day); but soon will you know (your folly)!

لِيَكْفُرُوا۟ بِمَآ ءَاتَيْنَٰهُمْ ۚ فَتَمَتَّعُوا۟ ۖ فَسَوْفَ تَعْلَمُونَ ﴿٥٥﴾

56. And they (even) assign, to things they do not know, a portion out of that which We have bestowed for their sustenance! By Allah, you shall certainly be called to account for your false inventions.

وَيَجْعَلُونَ لِمَا لَا يَعْلَمُونَ نَصِيبًا مِّمَّا رَزَقْنَٰهُمْ ۗ تَٱللَّهِ
لَتُسْـَٔلُنَّ عَمَّا كُنتُمْ تَفْتَرُونَ ﴿٥٦﴾

57. And they assign daughters for Allah! - Glory be to Him! - And for themselves (sons - the issue) they desire!

وَيَجۡعَلُونَ لِلَّهِ ٱلۡبَنَٰتِ سُبۡحَٰنَهُۥ وَلَهُم مَّا يَشۡتَهُونَ ٥٧

58. When news is brought to one of them, of (the birth of) a female (child), his face darkens, and he is filled with inward grief!

وَإِذَا بُشِّرَ أَحَدُهُم بِٱلۡأُنثَىٰ ظَلَّ وَجۡهُهُۥ مُسۡوَدّٗا وَهُوَ كَظِيمٞ ٥٨

59. With shame does he hide himself from his people, because of the bad news he has had! Shall he retain it on (sufferance and) contempt, or bury it in the dust? Ah! What an evil (choice) they decide on!

يَتَوَٰرَىٰ مِنَ ٱلۡقَوۡمِ مِن سُوٓءِ مَا بُشِّرَ بِهِۦٓۚ أَيُمۡسِكُهُۥ عَلَىٰ هُونٍ أَمۡ يَدُسُّهُۥ فِي ٱلتُّرَابِۗ أَلَا سَآءَ مَا يَحۡكُمُونَ ٥٩

60. To those who believe not in the hereafter, applies the similitude of evil; to Allah applies the highest similitude; for He is the Exalted in Power, Full of wisdom.

لِلَّذِينَ لَا يُؤۡمِنُونَ بِٱلۡأٓخِرَةِ مَثَلُ ٱلسَّوۡءِۖ وَلِلَّهِ ٱلۡمَثَلُ ٱلۡأَعۡلَىٰۚ وَهُوَ ٱلۡعَزِيزُ ٱلۡحَكِيمُ ٦٠

61. If Allah were to punish men for their wrongdoing, He would not leave, on the (earth), a single living creature; but He gives them respite for a stated term: when their term expires, they would not be able to delay (the punishment) for a single hour, just as they would not be able to anticipate it (for a single hour).

وَلَوۡ يُؤَاخِذُ ٱللَّهُ ٱلنَّاسَ بِظُلۡمِهِم مَّا تَرَكَ عَلَيۡهَا مِن دَآبَّةٖ وَلَٰكِن يُؤَخِّرُهُمۡ إِلَىٰٓ أَجَلٖ مُّسَمّٗىۖ فَإِذَا جَآءَ أَجَلُهُمۡ لَا يَسۡتَـٔۡخِرُونَ سَاعَةٗ وَلَا يَسۡتَقۡدِمُونَ ٦١

62. They attribute to Allah what they hate (for themselves). And their tongues assert the falsehood that all good things are for themselves: without doubt for them is the fire, and they will be the first to be hastened on into it!

وَيَجۡعَلُونَ لِلَّهِ مَا يَكۡرَهُونَۚ وَتَصِفُ أَلۡسِنَتُهُمُ ٱلۡكَذِبَ أَنَّ لَهُمُ ٱلۡحُسۡنَىٰۖ لَا جَرَمَ أَنَّ لَهُمُ ٱلنَّارَ وَأَنَّهُم مُّفۡرَطُونَ ٦٢

63. By Allah, We (also) sent (our prophets) to peoples before you; but Satan made, (to the wicked), their own acts seem alluring: he is also their patron today, but they shall have a most grievous penalty.

تَٱللَّهِ لَقَدۡ أَرۡسَلۡنَآ إِلَىٰٓ أُمَمٖ مِّن قَبۡلِكَ فَزَيَّنَ لَهُمُ ٱلشَّيۡطَٰنُ أَعۡمَٰلَهُمۡ فَهُوَ وَلِيُّهُمُ ٱلۡيَوۡمَ وَلَهُمۡ عَذَابٌ أَلِيمٞ ٦٣

64. And We sent down the book to you for the express purpose, that you should make clear to them those things in which they differ, and that it should be a guide and a mercy to those who believe.

وَمَآ أَنزَلْنَا عَلَيْكَ ٱلْكِتَـٰبَ إِلَّا لِتُبَيِّنَ لَهُمُ ٱلَّذِى
ٱخْتَلَفُوا۟ فِيهِ ۙ وَهُدًى وَرَحْمَةً لِّقَوْمٍ يُؤْمِنُونَ ﴿٦٤﴾

65. And Allah sends down rain from the skies, and gives with it life to the earth after its death: verily in this is a sign for those who listen.

وَٱللَّهُ أَنزَلَ مِنَ ٱلسَّمَآءِ مَآءً فَأَحْيَا بِهِ ٱلْأَرْضَ بَعْدَ
مَوْتِهَآ ۚ إِنَّ فِى ذَٰلِكَ لَـَٔايَةً لِّقَوْمٍ يَسْمَعُونَ ﴿٦٥﴾

66. And verily in cattle (too) will you find an instructive sign. From what is within their bodies, between excretions and blood, We produce for your drink, milk, pure and agreeable to those who drink it.

وَإِنَّ لَكُمْ فِى ٱلْأَنْعَـٰمِ لَعِبْرَةً ۖ نُّسْقِيكُم مِّمَّا فِى بُطُونِهِۦ
مِنۢ بَيْنِ فَرْثٍ وَدَمٍ لَّبَنًا خَالِصًا سَآئِغًا لِّلشَّـٰرِبِينَ ﴿٦٦﴾

67. And from the fruit of the date-palm and the vine, you get out wholesome drink, and food: see, in this also is a sign for those who are wise.

وَمِن ثَمَرَٰتِ ٱلنَّخِيلِ وَٱلْأَعْنَـٰبِ تَتَّخِذُونَ مِنْهُ
سَكَرًا وَرِزْقًا حَسَنًا ۗ إِنَّ فِى ذَٰلِكَ لَـَٔايَةً لِّقَوْمٍ يَعْقِلُونَ ﴿٦٧﴾

68. And your Lord taught the Bee to build its cells in hills, on trees, and in (men's) habitations;

وَأَوْحَىٰ رَبُّكَ إِلَى ٱلنَّحْلِ أَنِ ٱتَّخِذِى مِنَ ٱلْجِبَالِ بُيُوتًا
وَمِنَ ٱلشَّجَرِ وَمِمَّا يَعْرِشُونَ ﴿٦٨﴾

69. Then to eat of all the produce (of the earth), and find with skill the spacious paths of its Lord: there issues from within their bodies a drink of varying colours, in which is healing for men: verily in this is a sign for those who give thought.

ثُمَّ كُلِى مِن كُلِّ ٱلثَّمَرَٰتِ فَٱسْلُكِى سُبُلَ رَبِّكِ ذُلُلًا ۚ
يَخْرُجُ مِنۢ بُطُونِهَا شَرَابٌ مُّخْتَلِفٌ أَلْوَٰنُهُۥ فِيهِ شِفَآءٌ
لِّلنَّاسِ ۗ إِنَّ فِى ذَٰلِكَ لَـَٔايَةً لِّقَوْمٍ يَتَفَكَّرُونَ ﴿٦٩﴾

70. It is Allah who creates you and takes your souls at death; and of you there are some who are sent back to a feeble age, so that they know nothing after having known (much): for Allah is All-Knowing, All-Powerful.

وَٱللَّهُ خَلَقَكُمْ ثُمَّ يَتَوَفَّىٰكُمْ ۚ وَمِنكُم مَّن يُرَدُّ إِلَىٰٓ
أَرْذَلِ ٱلْعُمُرِ لِكَىْ لَا يَعْلَمَ بَعْدَ عِلْمٍ شَيْـًٔا ۚ إِنَّ ٱللَّهَ
عَلِيمٌ قَدِيرٌ ﴿٧٠﴾

71. Allah has bestowed His gifts of sustenance more freely on some of you than on others: those more favoured are not going to throw back their gifts to those whom their right hands possess, so as to be equal in that respect. Will they then deny the favours of Allah?

وَٱللَّهُ فَضَّلَ بَعۡضَكُمۡ عَلَىٰ بَعۡضٖ فِي ٱلرِّزۡقِۚ فَمَا
ٱلَّذِينَ فُضِّلُواْ بِرَآدِّي رِزۡقِهِمۡ عَلَىٰ مَا مَلَكَتۡ
أَيۡمَٰنُهُمۡ فَهُمۡ فِيهِ سَوَآءٌۚ أَفَبِنِعۡمَةِ ٱللَّهِ يَجۡحَدُونَ ٧١

72. And Allah has made for you mates (and companions) of your own nature, and made for you, out of them, sons and daughters and grandchildren. And provided for your sustenance of the best; will they then believe in vain things, and be ungrateful for Allah's favours? -

وَٱللَّهُ جَعَلَ لَكُم مِّنۡ أَنفُسِكُمۡ أَزۡوَٰجٗا وَجَعَلَ
لَكُم مِّنۡ أَزۡوَٰجِكُم بَنِينَ وَحَفَدَةٗ وَرَزَقَكُم
مِّنَ ٱلطَّيِّبَٰتِۚ أَفَبِٱلۡبَٰطِلِ يُؤۡمِنُونَ وَبِنِعۡمَتِ ٱللَّهِ
هُمۡ يَكۡفُرُونَ ٧٢

73. And worship others than Allah - such as have no power of providing them, for sustenance, with anything in heavens or earth, and cannot possibly have such power?

وَيَعۡبُدُونَ مِن دُونِ ٱللَّهِ مَا لَا يَمۡلِكُ لَهُمۡ رِزۡقٗا مِّنَ
ٱلسَّمَٰوَٰتِ وَٱلۡأَرۡضِ شَيۡـٔٗا وَلَا يَسۡتَطِيعُونَ ٧٣

74. Invent not similitudes for Allah; for Allah knows, and you know not.

فَلَا تَضۡرِبُواْ لِلَّهِ ٱلۡأَمۡثَالَۚ إِنَّ ٱللَّهَ يَعۡلَمُ وَأَنتُمۡ لَا
تَعۡلَمُونَ ٧٤

75. Allah sets out the parable (of two men: one) a slave under the dominion of another; he has no power of any sort; and (the other) a man on whom We have bestowed goodly favours from Ourselves. And he spends of it (freely), privately and publicly; are the two equal? (By no means); praise be to Allah. But most of them understand not.

۞ضَرَبَ ٱللَّهُ مَثَلًا عَبۡدٗا مَّمۡلُوكٗا لَّا يَقۡدِرُ ربع الحزب ٢٨
عَلَىٰ شَيۡءٖ وَمَن رَّزَقۡنَٰهُ مِنَّا رِزۡقًا حَسَنٗا فَهُوَ يُنفِقُ
مِنۡهُ سِرّٗا وَجَهۡرًاۖ هَلۡ يَسۡتَوُۥنَۚ ٱلۡحَمۡدُ لِلَّهِۚ
بَلۡ أَكۡثَرُهُمۡ لَا يَعۡلَمُونَ ٧٥

76. Allah sets out (another) parable of two men: one of them dumb, with no power of any sort: a wearisome burden is he to his master; whichever way he directs him, he brings no good: is such a man equal with

وَضَرَبَ ٱللَّهُ مَثَلٗا رَّجُلَيۡنِ أَحَدُهُمَآ أَبۡكَمُ
لَا يَقۡدِرُ عَلَىٰ شَيۡءٖ وَهُوَ كَلٌّ عَلَىٰ مَوۡلَىٰهُ أَيۡنَمَا
يُوَجِّههُّ لَا يَأۡتِ بِخَيۡرٍ هَلۡ يَسۡتَوِي هُوَ وَمَن

one who commands justice, and is on a straight way?

يَأْمُرُ بِالْعَدْلِ وَهُوَ عَلَىٰ صِرَاطٍ مُّسْتَقِيمٍ ٧٦

77. To Allah belongs the mystery of the heavens and the earth. And the decision of the hour (of judgement) is as the twinkling of an eye, or even quicker: for Allah has power over all things.

وَلِلَّهِ غَيْبُ السَّمَاوَاتِ وَالْأَرْضِ ۚ وَمَا أَمْرُ
السَّاعَةِ إِلَّا كَلَمْحِ الْبَصَرِ أَوْ هُوَ أَقْرَبُ ۚ
إِنَّ اللَّهَ عَلَىٰ كُلِّ شَيْءٍ قَدِيرٌ ٧٧

78. It is He Who brought you out from the wombs of your mothers when you knew nothing; and He gave you hearing and sight and intelligence and affection; that you may give thanks (to Allah).

وَاللَّهُ أَخْرَجَكُم مِّن بُطُونِ أُمَّهَاتِكُمْ لَا
تَعْلَمُونَ شَيْئًا وَجَعَلَ لَكُمُ السَّمْعَ
وَالْأَبْصَارَ وَالْأَفْئِدَةَ لَعَلَّكُمْ تَشْكُرُونَ ٧٨

79. Do they not look at the birds, held poised in the midst of (the air and) the sky? Nothing holds them up but (the power of) Allah. Verily in this are signs for those who believe.

أَلَمْ يَرَوْا إِلَى الطَّيْرِ مُسَخَّرَاتٍ فِي جَوِّ السَّمَاءِ
مَا يُمْسِكُهُنَّ إِلَّا اللَّهُ ۗ إِنَّ فِي ذَٰلِكَ لَآيَاتٍ لِّقَوْمٍ
يُؤْمِنُونَ ٧٩

80. It is Allah who made your habitations homes of rest and quiet for you; and made for you, out of the skins of animals, (tents for) dwellings, which you find so light (and handy) when you travel and when you stop (in your travels), and out of their wool, and their soft fibres (between wool and hair), and their hair, rich stuff and articles of convenience (to serve you) for a time.

وَاللَّهُ جَعَلَ لَكُم مِّن بُيُوتِكُمْ سَكَنًا وَجَعَلَ
لَكُم مِّن جُلُودِ الْأَنْعَامِ بُيُوتًا تَسْتَخِفُّونَهَا يَوْمَ
ظَعْنِكُمْ وَيَوْمَ إِقَامَتِكُمْ وَمِنْ أَصْوَافِهَا
وَأَوْبَارِهَا وَأَشْعَارِهَا أَثَاثًا وَمَتَاعًا إِلَىٰ حِينٍ ٨٠

81. It is Allah who made out of the things He created, some things to give you shade; of the hills He made some for your shelter; He made you garments to protect you from heat, and coats of mail to protect you from your (mutual) violence. Thus does He complete His favours on you, that you may bow to His will (in Islam).

وَاللَّهُ جَعَلَ لَكُم مِّمَّا خَلَقَ ظِلَالًا وَجَعَلَ
لَكُم مِّنَ الْجِبَالِ أَكْنَانًا وَجَعَلَ لَكُمْ
سَرَابِيلَ تَقِيكُمُ الْحَرَّ وَسَرَابِيلَ تَقِيكُم
بَأْسَكُمْ ۚ كَذَٰلِكَ يُتِمُّ نِعْمَتَهُ عَلَيْكُمْ
لَعَلَّكُمْ تُسْلِمُونَ ٨١

82. But if they turn away, your duty is only to preach the clear message.

فَإِن تَوَلَّوْاْ فَإِنَّمَا عَلَيْكَ ٱلْبَلَٰغُ ٱلْمُبِينُ ﴿٨٢﴾

83. They recognise the favours of Allah; then they deny them; and most of them are (creatures) ungrateful.

يَعْرِفُونَ نِعْمَتَ ٱللَّهِ ثُمَّ يُنكِرُونَهَا
وَأَكْثَرُهُمُ ٱلْكَٰفِرُونَ ﴿٨٣﴾

84. One day We shall raise from all peoples a witness: then will no excuse be accepted from unbelievers, nor will they receive any favours.

وَيَوْمَ نَبْعَثُ مِن كُلِّ أُمَّةٍ شَهِيدًا ثُمَّ لَا
يُؤْذَنُ لِلَّذِينَ كَفَرُواْ وَلَا هُمْ يُسْتَعْتَبُونَ ﴿٨٤﴾

85. When the wrongdoers (actually) see the penalty, then will it in no way be mitigated, nor will they then receive respite.

وَإِذَا رَءَا ٱلَّذِينَ ظَلَمُواْ ٱلْعَذَابَ فَلَا يُخَفَّفُ عَنْهُمْ
وَلَا هُمْ يُنظَرُونَ ﴿٨٥﴾

86. When those who gave partners to Allah will see their 'partners', they will say: "Our Lord! These are our 'partners', those whom we used to invoke besides You." But they will throw back their word at them (and say): "Indeed you are liars!"

وَإِذَا رَءَا ٱلَّذِينَ أَشْرَكُواْ شُرَكَآءَهُمْ قَالُواْ رَبَّنَا
هَٰٓؤُلَآءِ شُرَكَآؤُنَا ٱلَّذِينَ كُنَّا نَدْعُواْ مِن
دُونِكَۖ فَأَلْقَوْاْ إِلَيْهِمُ ٱلْقَوْلَ إِنَّكُمْ لَكَٰذِبُونَ ﴿٨٦﴾

87. That day shall they (openly) show (their) submission to Allah; and all their inventions shall leave them in the lurch.

وَأَلْقَوْاْ إِلَى ٱللَّهِ يَوْمَئِذٍ ٱلسَّلَمَۖ وَضَلَّ عَنْهُم
مَّا كَانُواْ يَفْتَرُونَ ﴿٨٧﴾

88. Those who reject Allah and hinder (men) from the path of Allah - for them will We add penalty to penalty; for that they used to spread mischief.

ٱلَّذِينَ كَفَرُواْ وَصَدُّواْ عَن سَبِيلِ ٱللَّهِ
زِدْنَٰهُمْ عَذَابًا فَوْقَ ٱلْعَذَابِ بِمَا كَانُواْ
يُفْسِدُونَ ﴿٨٨﴾

89. One day We shall raise from all peoples a witness against them, from amongst themselves: and We shall bring you as a witness against these (your people); and We have sent down to you the book explaining all things, a guide, a mercy, and glad tidings to Muslims.

وَيَوْمَ نَبْعَثُ فِي كُلِّ أُمَّةٍ شَهِيدًا عَلَيْهِم مِّنْ
أَنفُسِهِمْۖ وَجِئْنَا بِكَ شَهِيدًا عَلَىٰ هَٰٓؤُلَآءِۚ
وَنَزَّلْنَا عَلَيْكَ ٱلْكِتَٰبَ تِبْيَٰنًا لِّكُلِّ شَيْءٍ
وَهُدًى وَرَحْمَةً وَبُشْرَىٰ لِلْمُسْلِمِينَ ﴿٨٩﴾

نصف الحزب ٢٨

90. Allah commands justice, the doing of good, and generosity to relatives, and He forbids all shameful deeds, and injustice and rebellion: He instructs you, that you may receive admonition.

۞ إِنَّ ٱللَّهَ يَأْمُرُ بِٱلْعَدْلِ وَٱلْإِحْسَٰنِ وَإِيتَآيِٕ
ذِى ٱلْقُرْبَىٰ وَيَنْهَىٰ عَنِ ٱلْفَحْشَآءِ وَٱلْمُنكَرِ
وَٱلْبَغْىِ ۚ يَعِظُكُمْ لَعَلَّكُمْ تَذَكَّرُونَ ﴿٩٠﴾

91. Fulfil the covenant of Allah when you have entered into it, and break not your oaths after you have confirmed them; indeed you have made Allah your surety; for Allah knows all that you do.

وَأَوْفُوا۟ بِعَهْدِ ٱللَّهِ إِذَا عَٰهَدتُّمْ وَلَا تَنقُضُوا۟
ٱلْأَيْمَٰنَ بَعْدَ تَوْكِيدِهَا وَقَدْ جَعَلْتُمُ ٱللَّهَ
عَلَيْكُمْ كَفِيلًا ۚ إِنَّ ٱللَّهَ يَعْلَمُ مَا تَفْعَلُونَ ﴿٩١﴾

92. And be not like a woman who breaks into untwisted strands the yarn which she has spun after it has become strong. Nor take your oaths to practice deception between yourselves, lest one party should be more numerous than another; for Allah will test you by this; and on the day of judgement He will certainly make clear to you (the truth of) that in which you disagree.

وَلَا تَكُونُوا۟ كَٱلَّتِى نَقَضَتْ غَزْلَهَا مِنۢ بَعْدِ قُوَّةٍ
أَنكَٰثًا تَتَّخِذُونَ أَيْمَٰنَكُمْ دَخَلًۢا بَيْنَكُمْ
أَن تَكُونَ أُمَّةٌ هِىَ أَرْبَىٰ مِنْ أُمَّةٍ ۚ إِنَّمَا يَبْلُوكُمُ ٱللَّهُ
بِهِۦ ۚ وَلَيُبَيِّنَنَّ لَكُمْ يَوْمَ ٱلْقِيَٰمَةِ مَا كُنتُمْ فِيهِ
تَخْتَلِفُونَ ﴿٩٢﴾

93. If Allah so willed, He could make you all one people; but He leaves straying whom He pleases, and He guides whom He pleases; but you shall certainly be called to account for all your actions.

وَلَوْ شَآءَ ٱللَّهُ لَجَعَلَكُمْ أُمَّةً وَٰحِدَةً وَلَٰكِن
يُضِلُّ مَن يَشَآءُ وَيَهْدِى مَن يَشَآءُ ۚ وَلَتُسْـَٔلُنَّ عَمَّا
كُنتُمْ تَعْمَلُونَ ﴿٩٣﴾

94. And take not your oaths, to practice deception between yourselves, with the result that someone's foot may slip after it was firmly planted, and you may have to taste the evil (consequences) of having hindered (men) from the path of Allah, and a mighty wrath descend on you.

وَلَا تَتَّخِذُوٓا۟ أَيْمَٰنَكُمْ دَخَلًۢا بَيْنَكُمْ فَتَزِلَّ
قَدَمٌۢ بَعْدَ ثُبُوتِهَا وَتَذُوقُوا۟ ٱلسُّوٓءَ بِمَا
صَدَدتُّمْ عَن سَبِيلِ ٱللَّهِ ۖ وَلَكُمْ عَذَابٌ عَظِيمٌ ﴿٩٤﴾

95. Nor sell the covenant of Allah for a miserable price: for with Allah is (a prize) far better for you, if you only knew.

وَلَا تَشْتَرُوا۟ بِعَهْدِ ٱللَّهِ ثَمَنًا قَلِيلًا ۚ إِنَّمَا عِندَ ٱللَّهِ
هُوَ خَيْرٌ لَّكُمْ إِن كُنتُمْ تَعْلَمُونَ ﴿٩٥﴾

96. What is with you must vanish; what is with Allah will endure. And We will certainly bestow, on those who patiently persevere, their reward according to the best of their actions.

مَا عِندَكُمۡ يَنفَدُ وَمَا عِندَ ٱللَّهِ بَاقٖۗ وَلَنَجۡزِيَنَّ
ٱلَّذِينَ صَبَرُوٓاْ أَجۡرَهُم بِأَحۡسَنِ مَا كَانُواْ
يَعۡمَلُونَ ٩٦

97. Whoever works righteousness, man or woman, and has faith, verily, to him will We give a new life, a life that is good and pure, and We will bestow on such their reward according to the best of their actions.

مَنۡ عَمِلَ صَٰلِحٗا مِّن ذَكَرٍ أَوۡ أُنثَىٰ وَهُوَ
مُؤۡمِنٞ فَلَنُحۡيِيَنَّهُۥ حَيَوٰةٗ طَيِّبَةٗۖ وَلَنَجۡزِيَنَّهُمۡ
أَجۡرَهُم بِأَحۡسَنِ مَا كَانُواْ يَعۡمَلُونَ ٩٧

98. When you do read the Qur'an, seek Allah's protection from Satan the rejected one.

فَإِذَا قَرَأۡتَ ٱلۡقُرۡءَانَ فَٱسۡتَعِذۡ بِٱللَّهِ مِنَ
ٱلشَّيۡطَٰنِ ٱلرَّجِيمِ ٩٨

99. No authority has he over those who believe and put their trust in their Lord.

إِنَّهُۥ لَيۡسَ لَهُۥ سُلۡطَٰنٌ عَلَى ٱلَّذِينَ ءَامَنُواْ وَعَلَىٰ
رَبِّهِمۡ يَتَوَكَّلُونَ ٩٩

100. His authority is over those only, who take him as patron and who join partners with Allah.

إِنَّمَا سُلۡطَٰنُهُۥ عَلَى ٱلَّذِينَ يَتَوَلَّوۡنَهُۥ وَٱلَّذِينَ هُم
بِهِۦ مُشۡرِكُونَ ١٠٠

101. When We substitute one revelation for another - and Allah knows best what He reveals (in stages) - they say, "You are but a forger": but most of them understand not.

وَإِذَا بَدَّلۡنَآ ءَايَةٗ مَّكَانَ ءَايَةٖ وَٱللَّهُ أَعۡلَمُ
بِمَا يُنَزِّلُ قَالُوٓاْ إِنَّمَآ أَنتَ مُفۡتَرِۢۚ بَلۡ أَكۡثَرُهُمۡ
لَا يَعۡلَمُونَ ١٠١

102. Say, the Holy Spirit has brought the revelation from your Lord in truth, in order to strengthen those who believe, and as a guide and glad tidings to Muslims.

قُلۡ نَزَّلَهُۥ رُوحُ ٱلۡقُدُسِ مِن رَّبِّكَ بِٱلۡحَقِّ لِيُثَبِّتَ
ٱلَّذِينَ ءَامَنُواْ وَهُدٗى وَبُشۡرَىٰ لِلۡمُسۡلِمِينَ ١٠٢

103. We know indeed that they say, "It is a man that teaches him." The tongue of him they wickedly point to is notably foreign, while this is Arabic, pure and clear.

وَلَقَدۡ نَعۡلَمُ أَنَّهُمۡ يَقُولُونَ إِنَّمَا يُعَلِّمُهُۥ
بَشَرٞۗ لِّسَانُ ٱلَّذِي يُلۡحِدُونَ إِلَيۡهِ أَعۡجَمِيّٞ
وَهَٰذَا لِسَانٌ عَرَبِيّٞ مُّبِينٞ ١٠٣

104. Those who believe not in the signs of Allah - Allah will not guide them, and theirs will be a grievous penalty.

إِنَّ ٱلَّذِينَ لَا يُؤْمِنُونَ بِـَٔايَٰتِ ٱللَّهِ لَا يَهْدِيهِمُ
ٱللَّهُ وَلَهُمْ عَذَابٌ أَلِيمٌ ١٠٤

105. It is those who believe not in the signs of Allah, that forge falsehood; it is they who lie!

إِنَّمَا يَفْتَرِى ٱلْكَذِبَ ٱلَّذِينَ لَا يُؤْمِنُونَ
بِـَٔايَٰتِ ٱللَّهِ ۖ وَأُو۟لَٰٓئِكَ هُمُ ٱلْكَٰذِبُونَ ١٠٥

106. Anyone who, after accepting faith in Allah, utters unbelief - except under compulsion, his heart remaining firm in faith - but such as open their breast to unbelief - on them is wrath from Allah, and theirs will be a dreadful penalty.

مَن كَفَرَ بِٱللَّهِ مِنۢ بَعْدِ إِيمَٰنِهِۦٓ إِلَّا مَنْ
أُكْرِهَ وَقَلْبُهُۥ مُطْمَئِنٌّۢ بِٱلْإِيمَٰنِ وَلَٰكِن
مَّن شَرَحَ بِٱلْكُفْرِ صَدْرًا فَعَلَيْهِمْ غَضَبٌ
مِّنَ ٱللَّهِ وَلَهُمْ عَذَابٌ عَظِيمٌ ١٠٦

107. This because they love the life of this world better than the hereafter: and Allah will not guide those who reject faith.

ذَٰلِكَ بِأَنَّهُمُ ٱسْتَحَبُّوا۟ ٱلْحَيَوٰةَ ٱلدُّنْيَا عَلَى
ٱلْءَاخِرَةِ وَأَنَّ ٱللَّهَ لَا يَهْدِى ٱلْقَوْمَ ٱلْكَٰفِرِينَ ١٠٧

108. Those are they whose hearts, ears, and eyes Allah has sealed up and they take no heed.

أُو۟لَٰٓئِكَ ٱلَّذِينَ طَبَعَ ٱللَّهُ عَلَىٰ قُلُوبِهِمْ وَسَمْعِهِمْ
وَأَبْصَٰرِهِمْ ۖ وَأُو۟لَٰٓئِكَ هُمُ ٱلْغَٰفِلُونَ ١٠٨

109. Without doubt, in the hereafter they will perish.

لَا جَرَمَ أَنَّهُمْ فِى ٱلْءَاخِرَةِ هُمُ ٱلْخَٰسِرُونَ ١٠٩

110. But verily your Lord - to those who leave their homes after trials and persecutions - and who after that strive and fight for the faith and patiently persevere - your Lord, after all this is Oft-Forgiving, Most Merciful.

ثُمَّ إِنَّ رَبَّكَ لِلَّذِينَ هَاجَرُوا۟ مِنۢ بَعْدِ
مَا فُتِنُوا۟ ثُمَّ جَٰهَدُوا۟ وَصَبَرُوٓا۟ إِنَّ رَبَّكَ
مِنۢ بَعْدِهَا لَغَفُورٌ رَّحِيمٌ ١١٠

111. One day every soul will come up struggling for itself, and every soul will be recompensed (fully) for all its actions, and none will be unjustly dealt with.

ثلاثة أرباع الحزب ٢٨ ۞ يَوْمَ تَأْتِى كُلُّ نَفْسٍ تُجَٰدِلُ عَن نَّفْسِهَا وَتُوَفَّىٰ
كُلُّ نَفْسٍ مَّا عَمِلَتْ وَهُمْ لَا يُظْلَمُونَ ١١١

112. Allah sets out a parable: a city enjoying security and quiet, abundantly supplied with sustenance from every place: yet was it ungrateful for the favours of Allah: so Allah made it taste of hunger and terror (in extremes) (closing in on it) like a garment (from every side), because of the (evil) which (its people) wrought.

وَضَرَبَ ٱللَّهُ مَثَلًا قَرْيَةً كَانَتْ ءَامِنَةً
مُّطْمَئِنَّةً يَأْتِيهَا رِزْقُهَا رَغَدًا مِّن كُلِّ مَكَانٍ
فَكَفَرَتْ بِأَنْعُمِ ٱللَّهِ فَأَذَٰقَهَا ٱللَّهُ لِبَاسَ
ٱلْجُوعِ وَٱلْخَوْفِ بِمَا كَانُوا۟ يَصْنَعُونَ ﴿١١٢﴾

113. And there came to them a messenger from among themselves, but they falsely rejected him; so the wrath seized them even in the midst of their iniquities.

وَلَقَدْ جَآءَهُمْ رَسُولٌ مِّنْهُمْ فَكَذَّبُوهُ فَأَخَذَهُمُ
ٱلْعَذَابُ وَهُمْ ظَٰلِمُونَ ﴿١١٣﴾

114. So eat of the sustenance which Allah has provided for you, lawful and good; and be grateful for the favours of Allah, if it is He Whom you serve.

فَكُلُوا۟ مِمَّا رَزَقَكُمُ ٱللَّهُ حَلَٰلًا طَيِّبًا
وَٱشْكُرُوا۟ نِعْمَتَ ٱللَّهِ إِن كُنتُمْ إِيَّاهُ
تَعْبُدُونَ ﴿١١٤﴾

115. He has only forbidden you dead meat, and blood, and the flesh of swine, and any (food) over which the name of other than Allah has been invoked. But if one is forced by necessity, without wilful disobedience, nor transgressing due limits - then Allah is Oft-Forgiving, Most Merciful.

إِنَّمَا حَرَّمَ عَلَيْكُمُ ٱلْمَيْتَةَ وَٱلدَّمَ وَلَحْمَ
ٱلْخِنزِيرِ وَمَآ أُهِلَّ لِغَيْرِ ٱللَّهِ بِهِۦ ۖ فَمَنِ ٱضْطُرَّ غَيْرَ
بَاغٍ وَلَا عَادٍ فَإِنَّ ٱللَّهَ غَفُورٌ رَّحِيمٌ ﴿١١٥﴾

116. But say not - for any false thing that your tongues may put out - "This is lawful, and this is forbidden," so as to ascribe false things to Allah. For those who ascribe false things to Allah, will never prosper.

وَلَا تَقُولُوا۟ لِمَا تَصِفُ أَلْسِنَتُكُمُ ٱلْكَذِبَ
هَٰذَا حَلَٰلٌ وَهَٰذَا حَرَامٌ لِّتَفْتَرُوا۟ عَلَى ٱللَّهِ
ٱلْكَذِبَ ۚ إِنَّ ٱلَّذِينَ يَفْتَرُونَ عَلَى ٱللَّهِ ٱلْكَذِبَ
لَا يُفْلِحُونَ ﴿١١٦﴾

117. (In such falsehood) is but a paltry profit; but they will have a most grievous penalty.

مَتَٰعٌ قَلِيلٌ وَلَهُمْ عَذَابٌ أَلِيمٌ ﴿١١٧﴾

118. To the Jews We prohibited such things as We have mentioned to you before; We did them no wrong, but they were used to doing wrong to themselves.

وَعَلَى ٱلَّذِينَ هَادُواْ حَرَّمۡنَا مَا قَصَصۡنَا عَلَيۡكَ مِن قَبۡلُۖ
وَمَا ظَلَمۡنَٰهُمۡ وَلَٰكِن كَانُوٓاْ أَنفُسَهُمۡ يَظۡلِمُونَ ١١٨

119. But verily your Lord - to those who do wrong in ignorance, but who after that repent and make amends - your Lord, after all this, is Oft- Forgiving, Most Merciful.

ثُمَّ إِنَّ رَبَّكَ لِلَّذِينَ عَمِلُواْ ٱلسُّوٓءَ بِجَهَٰلَةٖ ثُمَّ تَابُواْ
مِنۢ بَعۡدِ ذَٰلِكَ وَأَصۡلَحُوٓاْ إِنَّ رَبَّكَ مِنۢ بَعۡدِهَا
لَغَفُورٞ رَّحِيمٌ ١١٩

120. Abraham was indeed a model. Devoutly obedient to Allah, (and) true in faith, and he joined not gods with Allah:

إِنَّ إِبۡرَٰهِيمَ كَانَ أُمَّةٗ قَانِتٗا لِّلَّهِ حَنِيفٗا وَلَمۡ يَكُ
مِنَ ٱلۡمُشۡرِكِينَ ١٢٠

121. He showed his gratitude for the favours of Allah, Who chose him, and guided him to a straight way.

شَاكِرٗا لِّأَنۡعُمِهِۚ ٱجۡتَبَىٰهُ وَهَدَىٰهُ إِلَىٰ صِرَٰطٖ
مُّسۡتَقِيمٖ ١٢١

122. And We gave him good in this world, and he will be, in the hereafter, in the ranks of the righteous.

وَءَاتَيۡنَٰهُ فِي ٱلدُّنۡيَا حَسَنَةٗۖ وَإِنَّهُۥ فِي ٱلۡأٓخِرَةِ لَمِنَ
ٱلصَّٰلِحِينَ ١٢٢

123. So We have taught you the inspired (message), "Follow the ways of Abraham the True in faith, and he joined not gods with Allah."

ثُمَّ أَوۡحَيۡنَآ إِلَيۡكَ أَنِ ٱتَّبِعۡ مِلَّةَ إِبۡرَٰهِيمَ حَنِيفٗاۖ
وَمَا كَانَ مِنَ ٱلۡمُشۡرِكِينَ ١٢٣

124. The Sabbath was only made (strict) to those who disagreed (as to its observance); but Allah will judge between them on the day of judgement, as to their differences.

إِنَّمَا جُعِلَ ٱلسَّبۡتُ عَلَى ٱلَّذِينَ ٱخۡتَلَفُواْ فِيهِۚ وَإِنَّ
رَبَّكَ لَيَحۡكُمُ بَيۡنَهُمۡ يَوۡمَ ٱلۡقِيَٰمَةِ فِيمَا
كَانُواْ فِيهِ يَخۡتَلِفُونَ ١٢٤

125. Invite (all) to the way of your Lord with wisdom and beautiful preaching; and argue with them in ways that are best and most gracious: for your Lord knows best, who have strayed from His path, and who receive guidance.

ٱدۡعُ إِلَىٰ سَبِيلِ رَبِّكَ بِٱلۡحِكۡمَةِ وَٱلۡمَوۡعِظَةِ
ٱلۡحَسَنَةِۖ وَجَٰدِلۡهُم بِٱلَّتِي هِيَ أَحۡسَنُۚ إِنَّ
رَبَّكَ هُوَ أَعۡلَمُ بِمَن ضَلَّ عَن سَبِيلِهِۦ وَهُوَ أَعۡلَمُ
بِٱلۡمُهۡتَدِينَ ١٢٥

126. And if you do catch them out, catch them out no worse than they catch you out; but if you show patience, that is indeed the best (course) for those who are patient.

وَإِنْ عَاقَبْتُمْ فَعَاقِبُوا۟ بِمِثْلِ مَا عُوقِبْتُم بِهِۦ ۖ وَلَئِن صَبَرْتُمْ لَهُوَ خَيْرٌ لِّلصَّـٰبِرِينَ ﴿١٢٦﴾

127. And do you be patient, for your patience is but from Allah; nor grieve over them; and distress not yourself because of their plots.

وَٱصْبِرْ وَمَا صَبْرُكَ إِلَّا بِٱللَّهِ ۚ وَلَا تَحْزَنْ عَلَيْهِمْ وَلَا تَكُ فِى ضَيْقٍ مِّمَّا يَمْكُرُونَ ﴿١٢٧﴾

128. For Allah is with those who restrain themselves, and those who do good.

إِنَّ ٱللَّهَ مَعَ ٱلَّذِينَ ٱتَّقَوا۟ وَّٱلَّذِينَ هُم مُّحْسِنُونَ ﴿١٢٨﴾

سُورَةُ الإِسْرَاءِ

Surah 17: ***Bani Israel*** **(The Children of Israel)**

In the name of Allah,
Most Gracious, Most Merciful.

بِسْمِ ٱللَّهِ ٱلرَّحْمَـٰنِ ٱلرَّحِيمِ

✻ **1.** Glory to (Allah) Who did take His servant for journey by night from the Sacred Mosque to the Farthest Mosque, whose precincts We did bless - in order that We might show him some of Our signs: for He is the One Who hears and sees (all things).

سُبْحَـٰنَ ٱلَّذِىٓ أَسْرَىٰ بِعَبْدِهِۦ لَيْلًا مِّنَ ٱلْمَسْجِدِ ٱلْحَرَامِ إِلَى ٱلْمَسْجِدِ ٱلْأَقْصَا ٱلَّذِى بَـٰرَكْنَا حَوْلَهُۥ لِنُرِيَهُۥ مِنْ ءَايَـٰتِنَآ ۚ إِنَّهُۥ هُوَ ٱلسَّمِيعُ ٱلْبَصِيرُ ﴿١﴾ جزء ١٥ حزب ٢٩

2. We gave Moses the book, and made it a guide to the Children of Israel, (commanding): "Take not other than Me as Disposer of (your) affairs."

وَءَاتَيْنَا مُوسَى ٱلْكِتَـٰبَ وَجَعَلْنَـٰهُ هُدًى لِّبَنِىٓ إِسْرَٰٓءِيلَ أَلَّا تَتَّخِذُوا۟ مِن دُونِى وَكِيلًا ﴿٢﴾

3. O you that are sprung from those whom We carried (in the ark) with Noah! Verily he was a devotee most grateful.

ذُرِّيَّةَ مَنْ حَمَلْنَا مَعَ نُوحٍ ۚ إِنَّهُۥ كَانَ عَبْدًا شَكُورًا ﴿٣﴾

4. And We gave (clear) warning to the Children of Israel in the book, that twice would they do mischief on the earth and be elated with mighty arrogance, (and twice would they be punished)!

وَقَضَيْنَآ إِلَىٰ بَنِىٓ إِسْرَٰٓءِيلَ فِى ٱلْكِتَـٰبِ لَتُفْسِدُنَّ فِى ٱلْأَرْضِ مَرَّتَيْنِ وَلَتَعْلُنَّ عُلُوًّا كَبِيرًا ﴿٤﴾

✻ Part-15

5. When the first of the warnings came to pass, We sent against you Our servants given to terrible warfare. They entered the very inmost parts of your homes; and it was a warning (completely) fulfilled.

فَإِذَا جَآءَ وَعْدُ أُولَىٰهُمَا بَعَثْنَا عَلَيْكُمْ عِبَادًا
لَّنَآ أُو۟لِى بَأْسٍ شَدِيدٍ فَجَاسُوا۟ خِلَـٰلَ ٱلدِّيَارِ ۚ
وَكَانَ وَعْدًا مَّفْعُولًا ﴿٥﴾

6. Then did We grant you the return as against them; We gave you increase in resources and sons, and made you the more numerous in manpower.

ثُمَّ رَدَدْنَا لَكُمُ ٱلْكَرَّةَ عَلَيْهِمْ وَأَمْدَدْنَـٰكُم بِأَمْوَٰلٍ
وَبَنِينَ وَجَعَلْنَـٰكُمْ أَكْثَرَ نَفِيرًا ﴿٦﴾

7. If you did well, you did well for yourselves; if you did evil, (you did it) against yourselves. So when the second of the warnings came to pass, (We permitted your enemies) to disfigure your faces, and to enter your temple as they had entered it before, and to visit with destruction all that fell into their power.

إِنْ أَحْسَنتُمْ أَحْسَنتُمْ لِأَنفُسِكُمْ ۖ وَإِنْ أَسَأْتُمْ
فَلَهَا ۚ فَإِذَا جَآءَ وَعْدُ ٱلْـَٔاخِرَةِ لِيَسُـۥٓـُٔوا۟ وُجُوهَكُمْ
وَلِيَدْخُلُوا۟ ٱلْمَسْجِدَ كَمَا دَخَلُوهُ أَوَّلَ مَرَّةٍ
وَلِيُتَبِّرُوا۟ مَا عَلَوْا۟ تَتْبِيرًا ﴿٧﴾

8. It may be that your Lord may (yet) show mercy to you; but if you revert (to your sins) We shall revert (to Our punishments); and We have made hell a prison for those who reject (all faith).

عَسَىٰ رَبُّكُمْ أَن يَرْحَمَكُمْ ۚ وَإِنْ عُدتُّمْ عُدْنَا ۘ وَجَعَلْنَا
جَهَنَّمَ لِلْكَـٰفِرِينَ حَصِيرًا ﴿٨﴾

9. Verily this Qur'an does guide to that which is most right (or stable), and gives the glad tidings to the believers who work deeds of righteousness, that they shall have a magnificent reward;

إِنَّ هَـٰذَا ٱلْقُرْءَانَ يَهْدِى لِلَّتِى هِىَ أَقْوَمُ وَيُبَشِّرُ
ٱلْمُؤْمِنِينَ ٱلَّذِينَ يَعْمَلُونَ ٱلصَّـٰلِحَـٰتِ أَنَّ لَهُمْ
أَجْرًا كَبِيرًا ﴿٩﴾

10. And to those who believe not in the hereafter, (it announces) that We have prepared for them a penalty grievous (indeed).

وَأَنَّ ٱلَّذِينَ لَا يُؤْمِنُونَ بِٱلْـَٔاخِرَةِ أَعْتَدْنَا لَهُمْ
عَذَابًا أَلِيمًا ﴿١٠﴾

11. The prayer that man should make for good, he makes for evil; for man is given to hasty (deeds).

وَيَدْعُ ٱلْإِنسَـٰنُ بِٱلشَّرِّ دُعَآءَهُۥ بِٱلْخَيْرِ ۖ وَكَانَ
ٱلْإِنسَـٰنُ عَجُولًا ﴿١١﴾

12. We have made the night and the day as two (of Our) signs: the sign of the night have We obscured, while the sign of the day We have made to enlighten you; that you may seek bounty from your Lord, and that you may know the number and count of the years; all things have We explained in detail.

وَجَعَلۡنَا ٱلَّيۡلَ وَٱلنَّهَارَ ءَايَتَيۡنِۖ فَمَحَوۡنَآ ءَايَةَ ٱلَّيۡلِ وَجَعَلۡنَآ ءَايَةَ ٱلنَّهَارِ مُبۡصِرَةٗ لِّتَبۡتَغُواْ فَضۡلٗا مِّن رَّبِّكُمۡ وَلِتَعۡلَمُواْ عَدَدَ ٱلسِّنِينَ وَٱلۡحِسَابَۚ وَكُلَّ شَيۡءٖ فَصَّلۡنَٰهُ تَفۡصِيلٗا ١٢

13. Every man's fate We have fastened on his own neck: on the day of judgement We shall bring out for him a scroll, which he will see spread open.

وَكُلَّ إِنسَٰنٍ أَلۡزَمۡنَٰهُ طَٰٓئِرَهُۥ فِي عُنُقِهِۦۖ وَنُخۡرِجُ لَهُۥ يَوۡمَ ٱلۡقِيَٰمَةِ كِتَٰبٗا يَلۡقَىٰهُ مَنشُورًا ١٣

14. (It will be said to him:) "Read your (own) record: sufficient is your soul this day to make out an account against you."

ٱقۡرَأۡ كِتَٰبَكَ كَفَىٰ بِنَفۡسِكَ ٱلۡيَوۡمَ عَلَيۡكَ حَسِيبٗا ١٤

15. Who receives guidance, receives it for his own benefit; who goes astray, does so to his own loss; no bearer of burdens can bear the burden of another; nor would We visit with Our wrath until We had sent a messenger (to give warning).

مَّنِ ٱهۡتَدَىٰ فَإِنَّمَا يَهۡتَدِي لِنَفۡسِهِۦۖ وَمَن ضَلَّ فَإِنَّمَا يَضِلُّ عَلَيۡهَاۚ وَلَا تَزِرُ وَازِرَةٞ وِزۡرَ أُخۡرَىٰۗ وَمَا كُنَّا مُعَذِّبِينَ حَتَّىٰ نَبۡعَثَ رَسُولٗا ١٥

16. When We decide to destroy a population, We (first) send a definite order to those among them who are given the good things of this life and yet transgress; so that the word is proved true against them; then (it is) We destroy them utterly.

وَإِذَآ أَرَدۡنَآ أَن نُّهۡلِكَ قَرۡيَةً أَمَرۡنَا مُتۡرَفِيهَا فَفَسَقُواْ فِيهَا فَحَقَّ عَلَيۡهَا ٱلۡقَوۡلُ فَدَمَّرۡنَٰهَا تَدۡمِيرٗا ١٦

17. How many generations have We destroyed after Noah? And enough is your Lord to note and see the sins of His servants.

وَكَمۡ أَهۡلَكۡنَا مِنَ ٱلۡقُرُونِ مِنۢ بَعۡدِ نُوحٖۗ وَكَفَىٰ بِرَبِّكَ بِذُنُوبِ عِبَادِهِۦ خَبِيرَۢا بَصِيرٗا ١٧

18. If any do wish for the transitory things (of this life), We readily grant them - such things as We will, to such persons as We will: in the end have We provided hell for them: they will burn in it, disgraced and rejected.

مَّن كَانَ يُرِيدُ ٱلۡعَاجِلَةَ عَجَّلۡنَا لَهُۥ فِيهَا مَا نَشَآءُ لِمَن نُّرِيدُ ثُمَّ جَعَلۡنَا لَهُۥ جَهَنَّمَ يَصۡلَىٰهَا مَذۡمُومٗا مَّدۡحُورٗا ١٨

19. Those who do wish for the (things of) the hereafter, and strive for it with all due striving, and have faith - they are the ones whose striving is acceptable (to Allah).

وَمَنْ أَرَادَ ٱلْـَٔاخِرَةَ وَسَعَىٰ لَهَا سَعْيَهَا وَهُوَ
مُؤْمِنٌ فَأُوْلَٰٓئِكَ كَانَ سَعْيُهُم مَّشْكُورًا ﴿١٩﴾

20. Of the bounties of your Lord We bestow freely on all - these as well as those; the bounties of your Lord are not closed (to anyone).

كُلًّا نُّمِدُّ هَٰٓؤُلَآءِ وَهَٰٓؤُلَآءِ مِنْ عَطَآءِ رَبِّكَ ۚ
وَمَا كَانَ عَطَآءُ رَبِّكَ مَحْظُورًا ﴿٢٠﴾

21. See how We have bestowed more on some than on others but verily the hereafter is more in rank and gradation and more in excellence.

ٱنظُرْ كَيْفَ فَضَّلْنَا بَعْضَهُمْ عَلَىٰ بَعْضٍ ۚ وَلَلْـَٔاخِرَةُ
أَكْبَرُ دَرَجَٰتٍ وَأَكْبَرُ تَفْضِيلًا ﴿٢١﴾

22. Take not with Allah another object of worship; or you (O man!) will sit in disgrace and destitution.

لَّا تَجْعَلْ مَعَ ٱللَّهِ إِلَٰهًا ءَاخَرَ فَتَقْعُدَ مَذْمُومًا مَّخْذُولًا ﴿٢٢﴾

23. Your Lord has decreed that you worship none but Him, and that you be kind to parents. Whether one or both of them attain old age in your life, say not to them a word of contempt, nor repel them, but address them in terms of honour.

ربع الحزب ٢٩ ۞ وَقَضَىٰ رَبُّكَ أَلَّا تَعْبُدُوٓاْ إِلَّآ إِيَّاهُ وَبِٱلْوَٰلِدَيْنِ
إِحْسَٰنًا ۚ إِمَّا يَبْلُغَنَّ عِندَكَ ٱلْكِبَرَ أَحَدُهُمَآ
أَوْ كِلَاهُمَا فَلَا تَقُل لَّهُمَآ أُفٍّ وَلَا تَنْهَرْهُمَا
وَقُل لَّهُمَا قَوْلًا كَرِيمًا ﴿٢٣﴾

24. And, out of kindness, lower to them the wing of humility, and say: "My Lord! Bestow on them Your mercy even as they cherished me in childhood."

وَٱخْفِضْ لَهُمَا جَنَاحَ ٱلذُّلِّ مِنَ ٱلرَّحْمَةِ وَقُل رَّبِّ
ٱرْحَمْهُمَا كَمَا رَبَّيَانِى صَغِيرًا ﴿٢٤﴾

25. Your Lord knows best what is in your hearts; if you do deeds of righteousness, verily He is Most Forgiving to those who turn to Him again and again (in true penitence).

رَّبُّكُمْ أَعْلَمُ بِمَا فِى نُفُوسِكُمْ ۚ إِن تَكُونُواْ صَٰلِحِينَ
فَإِنَّهُۥ كَانَ لِلْأَوَّٰبِينَ غَفُورًا ﴿٢٥﴾

26. And render to the relations their due rights, as (also) to those in want, and to the wayfarer; but squander not (your wealth) in the manner of a spendthrift.

وَءَاتِ ذَا ٱلْقُرْبَىٰ حَقَّهُۥ وَٱلْمِسْكِينَ وَٱبْنَ ٱلسَّبِيلِ
وَلَا تُبَذِّرْ تَبْذِيرًا ﴿٢٦﴾

27. Verily spendthrifts are brothers of the evil ones; and the evil one is to his Lord (Himself) ungrateful.

إِنَّ ٱلْمُبَذِّرِينَ كَانُوٓا۟ إِخْوَٰنَ ٱلشَّيَٰطِينِ ۖ وَكَانَ
ٱلشَّيْطَٰنُ لِرَبِّهِۦ كَفُورًا ﴿٢٧﴾

28. And even if you have to turn away from them in pursuit of the mercy from your Lord which you do expect, yet speak to them a word of easy kindness.

وَإِمَّا تُعْرِضَنَّ عَنْهُمُ ٱبْتِغَآءَ رَحْمَةٍ مِّن رَّبِّكَ تَرْجُوهَا
فَقُل لَّهُمْ قَوْلًا مَّيْسُورًا ﴿٢٨﴾

29. Make not your hand tied (like a niggard's) to your neck, nor stretch it out to its utmost reach, so that you become blameworthy and destitute.

وَلَا تَجْعَلْ يَدَكَ مَغْلُولَةً إِلَىٰ عُنُقِكَ وَلَا تَبْسُطْهَا
كُلَّ ٱلْبَسْطِ فَتَقْعُدَ مَلُومًا مَّحْسُورًا ﴿٢٩﴾

30. Verily your Lord does provide sustenance in abundance for whom He pleases, and He provides in a just measure, for He does know and regard all His servants.

إِنَّ رَبَّكَ يَبْسُطُ ٱلرِّزْقَ لِمَن يَشَآءُ وَيَقْدِرُ ۚ إِنَّهُۥ كَانَ
بِعِبَادِهِۦ خَبِيرًۢا بَصِيرًا ﴿٣٠﴾

31. Kill not your children for fear of want; We shall provide sustenance for them as well as for you. Verily the killing of them is a great sin.

وَلَا تَقْتُلُوٓا۟ أَوْلَٰدَكُمْ خَشْيَةَ إِمْلَٰقٍ ۖ نَّحْنُ نَرْزُقُهُمْ
وَإِيَّاكُمْ ۚ إِنَّ قَتْلَهُمْ كَانَ خِطْـًٔا كَبِيرًا ﴿٣١﴾

32. Nor come near to adultery for it is a shameful (deed) and an evil, opening the road (to other evils).

وَلَا تَقْرَبُوا۟ ٱلزِّنَىٰٓ ۖ إِنَّهُۥ كَانَ فَٰحِشَةً وَسَآءَ
سَبِيلًا ﴿٣٢﴾

33. Nor take life - which Allah has made sacred - except for just cause. And if anyone is slain wrongfully, We have given his heir authority (to demand *Qisas* or to forgive): but let him not exceed bounds in the matter of taking life: for he is helped (by the law).

وَلَا تَقْتُلُوا۟ ٱلنَّفْسَ ٱلَّتِى حَرَّمَ ٱللَّهُ إِلَّا بِٱلْحَقِّ ۗ
وَمَن قُتِلَ مَظْلُومًا فَقَدْ جَعَلْنَا لِوَلِيِّهِۦ سُلْطَٰنًا
فَلَا يُسْرِف فِّى ٱلْقَتْلِ ۖ إِنَّهُۥ كَانَ مَنصُورًا ﴿٣٣﴾

34. Come not near to the orphan's property except to improve it, until he attains the age of full strength; and fulfil (every) engagement, for (every) engagement will be enquired into (on the day of reckoning).

وَلَا تَقْرَبُوا۟ مَالَ ٱلْيَتِيمِ إِلَّا بِٱلَّتِى هِىَ أَحْسَنُ حَتَّىٰ
يَبْلُغَ أَشُدَّهُۥ ۚ وَأَوْفُوا۟ بِٱلْعَهْدِ ۖ إِنَّ ٱلْعَهْدَ كَانَ
مَسْـُٔولًا ﴿٣٤﴾

35. Give full measure when you measure, and weigh with a balance that is straight; that is the most fitting and the most advantageous in the final determination.

وَأَوۡفُواْ ٱلۡكَيۡلَ إِذَا كِلۡتُمۡ وَزِنُواْ بِٱلۡقِسۡطَاسِ ٱلۡمُسۡتَقِيمِۚ
ذَٰلِكَ خَيۡرٞ وَأَحۡسَنُ تَأۡوِيلٗا ﴿٣٥﴾

36. And pursue not that of which you have no knowledge; for every act of hearing, or of seeing, or of (feeling in) the heart, will be enquired into (on the day of reckoning).

وَلَا تَقۡفُ مَا لَيۡسَ لَكَ بِهِۦ عِلۡمٌۚ إِنَّ ٱلسَّمۡعَ وَٱلۡبَصَرَ
وَٱلۡفُؤَادَ كُلُّ أُوْلَٰٓئِكَ كَانَ عَنۡهُ مَسۡـُٔولٗا ﴿٣٦﴾

37. Nor walk on the earth with insolence; for you can not split the earth apart, nor reach the mountains in height.

وَلَا تَمۡشِ فِي ٱلۡأَرۡضِ مَرَحًاۖ إِنَّكَ لَن تَخۡرِقَ ٱلۡأَرۡضَ
وَلَن تَبۡلُغَ ٱلۡجِبَالَ طُولٗا ﴿٣٧﴾

38. Of all such things, the evil is hateful in the sight of your Lord.

كُلُّ ذَٰلِكَ كَانَ سَيِّئُهُۥ عِندَ رَبِّكَ مَكۡرُوهٗا ﴿٣٨﴾

39. These are among the (precepts of) wisdom, which your Lord has revealed to you. Take not, with Allah, another object of worship, lest you should be thrown into hell, blameworthy and rejected.

ذَٰلِكَ مِمَّآ أَوۡحَىٰٓ إِلَيۡكَ رَبُّكَ مِنَ ٱلۡحِكۡمَةِۗ وَلَا تَجۡعَلۡ
مَعَ ٱللَّهِ إِلَٰهًا ءَاخَرَ فَتُلۡقَىٰ فِي جَهَنَّمَ مَلُومٗا
مَّدۡحُورًا ﴿٣٩﴾

40. Has then your Lord, (O pagans!) preferred for you sons, and taken for Himself daughters among the angels? Truly you utter a most dreadful saying!

أَفَأَصۡفَىٰكُمۡ رَبُّكُم بِٱلۡبَنِينَ وَٱتَّخَذَ مِنَ ٱلۡمَلَٰٓئِكَةِ
إِنَٰثًاۚ إِنَّكُمۡ لَتَقُولُونَ قَوۡلًا عَظِيمٗا ﴿٤٠﴾

41. We have explained (things) in various (ways) in this Qur'an, in order that they may receive admonition, but it only increases their flight (from the truth)!

وَلَقَدۡ صَرَّفۡنَا فِي هَٰذَا ٱلۡقُرۡءَانِ لِيَذَّكَّرُواْ وَمَا يَزِيدُهُمۡ
إِلَّا نُفُورٗا ﴿٤١﴾

42. Say: if there had been (other) gods with Him - as they say - see, they would certainly have sought out a way to the Lord of the Throne!

قُل لَّوۡ كَانَ مَعَهُۥٓ ءَالِهَةٞ كَمَا يَقُولُونَ إِذٗا لَّٱبۡتَغَوۡاْ إِلَىٰ ذِي
ٱلۡعَرۡشِ سَبِيلٗا ﴿٤٢﴾

43. Glory to him! He is high above all that they say! - Exalted and Great (beyond measure)!

سُبۡحَٰنَهُۥ وَتَعَٰلَىٰ عَمَّا يَقُولُونَ عُلُوّٗا كَبِيرٗا ﴿٤٣﴾

44. The seven heavens and the earth, and all beings in it, declare His glory: there is not a thing but celebrates His praise; and yet you understand not how they declare His glory! Verily He is Oft-Forbearing, Most Forgiving!

تُسَبِّحُ لَهُ ٱلسَّمَٰوَٰتُ ٱلسَّبْعُ وَٱلْأَرْضُ وَمَن فِيهِنَّ ۚ وَإِن
مِّن شَىْءٍ إِلَّا يُسَبِّحُ بِحَمْدِهِۦ وَلَٰكِن لَّا تَفْقَهُونَ
تَسْبِيحَهُمْ ۗ إِنَّهُۥ كَانَ حَلِيمًا غَفُورًا ﴿٤٤﴾

45. When you do recite the Qur'an, We put, between you and those who believe not in the hereafter, a veil invisible;

وَإِذَا قَرَأْتَ ٱلْقُرْءَانَ جَعَلْنَا بَيْنَكَ وَبَيْنَ ٱلَّذِينَ
لَا يُؤْمِنُونَ بِٱلْـَٔاخِرَةِ حِجَابًا مَّسْتُورًا ﴿٤٥﴾

46. And We put coverings over their hearts (and minds) lest they should understand the Qur'an, and deafness into their ears; when you do commemorate your Lord - and Him alone - in the Qur'an, they turn on their backs, fleeing (from the truth).

وَجَعَلْنَا عَلَىٰ قُلُوبِهِمْ أَكِنَّةً أَن يَفْقَهُوهُ وَفِىٓ ءَاذَانِهِمْ
وَقْرًا ۚ وَإِذَا ذَكَرْتَ رَبَّكَ فِى ٱلْقُرْءَانِ وَحْدَهُۥ وَلَّوْا۟ عَلَىٰٓ
أَدْبَٰرِهِمْ نُفُورًا ﴿٤٦﴾

47. We know best why it is they listen, when they listen to you; and when they meet in private conference, behold, the wicked say, "You follow none other than a man bewitched!"

نَّحْنُ أَعْلَمُ بِمَا يَسْتَمِعُونَ بِهِۦٓ إِذْ يَسْتَمِعُونَ إِلَيْكَ
وَإِذْ هُمْ نَجْوَىٰٓ إِذْ يَقُولُ ٱلظَّٰلِمُونَ إِن تَتَّبِعُونَ إِلَّا
رَجُلًا مَّسْحُورًا ﴿٤٧﴾

48. See what similes they strike for you; but they have gone astray, and never can they find a way.

ٱنظُرْ كَيْفَ ضَرَبُوا۟ لَكَ ٱلْأَمْثَالَ فَضَلُّوا۟ فَلَا
يَسْتَطِيعُونَ سَبِيلًا ﴿٤٨﴾

49. They say: "What! When we are reduced to bones and dust, should we really be raised up (to be) a new creation?"

وَقَالُوٓا۟ أَءِذَا كُنَّا عِظَٰمًا وَرُفَٰتًا أَءِنَّا لَمَبْعُوثُونَ خَلْقًا
جَدِيدًا ﴿٤٩﴾

50. Say: "(Nay!) Be you stones or iron,

۞ قُلْ كُونُوا۟ حِجَارَةً أَوْ حَدِيدًا ﴿٥٠﴾ نصف الحزب ٢٩

51. Or created matter which, in your minds, is hardest (to be raised up) - (yet shall you be raised up)!" Then will they say: "Who will cause us to return?" Say: "He Who created you first!" Then will they wag their heads towards you and say,

أَوْ خَلْقًا مِّمَّا يَكْبُرُ فِى صُدُورِكُمْ ۚ فَسَيَقُولُونَ
مَن يُعِيدُنَا ۖ قُلِ ٱلَّذِى فَطَرَكُمْ أَوَّلَ مَرَّةٍ ۚ فَسَيُنْغِضُونَ
إِلَيْكَ رُءُوسَهُمْ وَيَقُولُونَ مَتَىٰ هُوَ ۖ قُلْ عَسَىٰٓ أَن

"When will that be?" Say, "Maybe it will be quite soon!"

يَكُونَ قَرِيبًا ﴿٥١﴾

52. "It will be on a day when He will call you, and you will answer (His call) with (words of) His praise, and you will think that you stayed but a little while!"

يَوْمَ يَدْعُوكُمْ فَتَسْتَجِيبُونَ بِحَمْدِهِۦ وَتَظُنُّونَ إِن
لَّبِثْتُمْ إِلَّا قَلِيلًا ﴿٥٢﴾

53. Say to My servants that they should (only) say those things that are best; for Satan does sow dissensions among them; for Satan is to man an avowed enemy.

وَقُل لِّعِبَادِى يَقُولُوا۟ ٱلَّتِى هِىَ أَحْسَنُ ۚ إِنَّ ٱلشَّيْطَٰنَ
يَنزَغُ بَيْنَهُمْ ۚ إِنَّ ٱلشَّيْطَٰنَ كَانَ لِلْإِنسَٰنِ عَدُوًّا
مُّبِينًا ﴿٥٣﴾

54. It is your Lord that knows you best; if He please, He grants you mercy, or if He please, punishment; We have not sent you to be a disposer of their affairs for them.

رَّبُّكُمْ أَعْلَمُ بِكُمْ ۖ إِن يَشَأْ يَرْحَمْكُمْ أَوْ إِن يَشَأْ
يُعَذِّبْكُمْ ۚ وَمَآ أَرْسَلْنَٰكَ عَلَيْهِمْ وَكِيلًا ﴿٥٤﴾

55. And it is your Lord that knows best all beings that are in the heavens and on earth; We did bestow on some prophets more (and other) gifts than on others; and We gave to David (the gift of) the Psalms.

وَرَبُّكَ أَعْلَمُ بِمَن فِى ٱلسَّمَٰوَٰتِ وَٱلْأَرْضِ ۗ وَلَقَدْ
فَضَّلْنَا بَعْضَ ٱلنَّبِيِّـۧنَ عَلَىٰ بَعْضٍ ۖ وَءَاتَيْنَا دَاوُۥدَ
زَبُورًا ﴿٥٥﴾

56. Say: "Call on those - besides Him - whom you fancy; they have neither the power to remove your troubles from you nor to change them."

قُلِ ٱدْعُوا۟ ٱلَّذِينَ زَعَمْتُم مِّن دُونِهِۦ فَلَا يَمْلِكُونَ
كَشْفَ ٱلضُّرِّ عَنكُمْ وَلَا تَحْوِيلًا ﴿٥٦﴾

57. Those whom they call upon do desire (for themselves) means of access to their Lord - even those who are nearest; they hope for His mercy and fear His wrath; for the wrath of your Lord is something to take heed of.

أُو۟لَٰٓئِكَ ٱلَّذِينَ يَدْعُونَ يَبْتَغُونَ إِلَىٰ رَبِّهِمُ
ٱلْوَسِيلَةَ أَيُّهُمْ أَقْرَبُ وَيَرْجُونَ رَحْمَتَهُۥ وَيَخَافُونَ
عَذَابَهُۥٓ ۚ إِنَّ عَذَابَ رَبِّكَ كَانَ مَحْذُورًا ﴿٥٧﴾

58. There is not a population but We shall destroy it before the day of judgement or punish it with a dreadful penalty; that is written in the (eternal) record.

وَإِن مِّن قَرْيَةٍ إِلَّا نَحْنُ مُهْلِكُوهَا قَبْلَ يَوْمِ ٱلْقِيَٰمَةِ
أَوْ مُعَذِّبُوهَا عَذَابًا شَدِيدًا ۚ كَانَ ذَٰلِكَ فِى ٱلْكِتَٰبِ
مَسْطُورًا ﴿٥٨﴾

59. And We refrain from sending the signs, only because the men of former generations treated them as false; We sent the she-camel to the Thamud to open their eyes, but they treated her wrongfully; We only send the signs by way of terror (and warning from evil).

وَمَا مَنَعَنَآ أَن نُّرْسِلَ بِٱلْـَٔايَٰتِ إِلَّآ أَن كَذَّبَ
بِهَا ٱلْأَوَّلُونَ ۚ وَءَاتَيْنَا ثَمُودَ ٱلنَّاقَةَ مُبْصِرَةً
فَظَلَمُوا۟ بِهَا ۚ وَمَا نُرْسِلُ بِٱلْـَٔايَٰتِ إِلَّا تَخْوِيفًا ﴿٥٩﴾

60. See! We told you that your Lord does encompass mankind; We granted the vision which We showed you, but as a trial for men - as also the cursed tree (mentioned) in the Qur'an: We put terror (and warning) into them, but it only increases their inordinate transgression!

وَإِذْ قُلْنَا لَكَ إِنَّ رَبَّكَ أَحَاطَ بِٱلنَّاسِ ۚ وَمَا جَعَلْنَا
ٱلرُّءْيَا ٱلَّتِىٓ أَرَيْنَٰكَ إِلَّا فِتْنَةً لِّلنَّاسِ وَٱلشَّجَرَةَ
ٱلْمَلْعُونَةَ فِى ٱلْقُرْءَانِ ۚ وَنُخَوِّفُهُمْ فَمَا يَزِيدُهُمْ
إِلَّا طُغْيَٰنًا كَبِيرًا ﴿٦٠﴾

61. See! We said to the angels: "Bow down to Adam": they bowed down except Iblis: he said, "Shall I bow down to one whom You did create from clay?"

وَإِذْ قُلْنَا لِلْمَلَٰٓئِكَةِ ٱسْجُدُوا۟ لِءَادَمَ فَسَجَدُوٓا۟
إِلَّآ إِبْلِيسَ قَالَ ءَأَسْجُدُ لِمَنْ خَلَقْتَ طِينًا ﴿٦١﴾

62. He said, "See You (O Allah)? This is the one whom You have honoured above me! If You will but respite me to the day of judgement, I will surely bring his descendants under my sway - all but a few!"

قَالَ أَرَءَيْتَكَ هَٰذَا ٱلَّذِى كَرَّمْتَ عَلَىَّ لَئِنْ
أَخَّرْتَنِ إِلَىٰ يَوْمِ ٱلْقِيَٰمَةِ لَأَحْتَنِكَنَّ ذُرِّيَّتَهُۥٓ
إِلَّا قَلِيلًا ﴿٦٢﴾

63. Allah said: "Go your way; if any of them follow you, verily hell will be the recompense of you (all) - an ample recompense."

قَالَ ٱذْهَبْ فَمَن تَبِعَكَ مِنْهُمْ فَإِنَّ جَهَنَّمَ
جَزَآؤُكُمْ جَزَآءً مَّوْفُورًا ﴿٦٣﴾

64. "Lead to destruction those whom you can among them, with your (seductive) voice; make assaults on them with your cavalry and your infantry; mutually share with them wealth and children; and make promises to them. But Satan promises them nothing but deceit."

وَٱسْتَفْزِزْ مَنِ ٱسْتَطَعْتَ مِنْهُم بِصَوْتِكَ
وَأَجْلِبْ عَلَيْهِم بِخَيْلِكَ وَرَجِلِكَ وَشَارِكْهُمْ فِى
ٱلْأَمْوَٰلِ وَٱلْأَوْلَٰدِ وَعِدْهُمْ ۚ وَمَا يَعِدُهُمُ
ٱلشَّيْطَٰنُ إِلَّا غُرُورًا ﴿٦٤﴾

65. "As for My servants, no authority shall you have over them." Enough is your Lord for a Disposer of affairs.

إِنَّ عِبَادِى لَيْسَ لَكَ عَلَيْهِمْ سُلْطَٰنٌ ۚ وَكَفَىٰ
بِرَبِّكَ وَكِيلًا ﴿٦٥﴾

66. Your Lord is He that makes the ship go smoothly for you through the sea, in order that you may seek of His bounty. For He is to you Most Merciful.

رَّبُّكُمُ ٱلَّذِى يُزْجِى لَكُمُ ٱلْفُلْكَ فِى ٱلْبَحْرِ
لِتَبْتَغُوا۟ مِن فَضْلِهِۦٓ ۚ إِنَّهُۥ كَانَ بِكُمْ رَحِيمًا ﴿٦٦﴾

67. When distress seizes you at sea, those that you call upon - besides Himself - leave you in the lurch! But when He brings you back safe to land, you turn away (from Him), Most ungrateful is man!

وَإِذَا مَسَّكُمُ ٱلضُّرُّ فِى ٱلْبَحْرِ ضَلَّ مَن تَدْعُونَ
إِلَّآ إِيَّاهُ ۖ فَلَمَّا نَجَّىٰكُمْ إِلَى ٱلْبَرِّ أَعْرَضْتُمْ ۚ وَكَانَ
ٱلْإِنسَٰنُ كَفُورًا ﴿٦٧﴾

68. Do you then feel secure that He will not cause you to be swallowed up beneath the earth when you are on land, or that He will not send against you a violent tornado (with showers of stones) so that you shall find no one to carry out your affairs for you?

أَفَأَمِنتُمْ أَن يَخْسِفَ بِكُمْ جَانِبَ ٱلْبَرِّ أَوْ يُرْسِلَ
عَلَيْكُمْ حَاصِبًا ثُمَّ لَا تَجِدُوا۟ لَكُمْ وَكِيلًا ﴿٦٨﴾

69. Or do you feel secure that He will not send you back a second time to sea and send against you a heavy gale to drown you because of your ingratitude, so that you find no helper in it against Us?

أَمْ أَمِنتُمْ أَن يُعِيدَكُمْ فِيهِ تَارَةً أُخْرَىٰ فَيُرْسِلَ
عَلَيْكُمْ قَاصِفًا مِّنَ ٱلرِّيحِ فَيُغْرِقَكُم بِمَا كَفَرْتُمْ ثُمَّ
لَا تَجِدُوا۟ لَكُمْ عَلَيْنَا بِهِۦ تَبِيعًا ﴿٦٩﴾

70. We have honoured the sons of Adam; provided them with transport on land and sea; given them for sustenance things good and pure; and conferred on them special favours, above a great part of Our creation.

ثلاثة أرباع الحزب ٢٩ ۞ وَلَقَدْ كَرَّمْنَا بَنِىٓ ءَادَمَ وَحَمَلْنَٰهُمْ فِى ٱلْبَرِّ
وَٱلْبَحْرِ وَرَزَقْنَٰهُم مِّنَ ٱلطَّيِّبَٰتِ وَفَضَّلْنَٰهُمْ
عَلَىٰ كَثِيرٍ مِّمَّنْ خَلَقْنَا تَفْضِيلًا ﴿٧٠﴾

71. One day We shall call together all human beings with their (respective) Imams; those who are given their record in their right hand will read it (with pleasure), and they will not be dealt with unjustly in the least.

يَوْمَ نَدْعُوا۟ كُلَّ أُنَاسٍۭ بِإِمَٰمِهِمْ ۖ فَمَنْ أُوتِىَ
كِتَٰبَهُۥ بِيَمِينِهِۦ فَأُو۟لَٰٓئِكَ يَقْرَءُونَ كِتَٰبَهُمْ وَلَا
يُظْلَمُونَ فَتِيلًا ﴿٧١﴾

72. But those who were blind in this world, will be blind in the hereafter, and most astray from the path.

وَمَن كَانَ فِي هَٰذِهِۦٓ أَعۡمَىٰ فَهُوَ فِي ٱلۡأٓخِرَةِ
أَعۡمَىٰ وَأَضَلُّ سَبِيلٗا ٧٢

73. And their purpose was to tempt you away from that which We had revealed to you, to substitute in Our name something quite different: (in that case), see! They would certainly have made you (their) friend!

وَإِن كَادُواْ لَيَفۡتِنُونَكَ عَنِ ٱلَّذِيٓ أَوۡحَيۡنَآ
إِلَيۡكَ لِتَفۡتَرِيَ عَلَيۡنَا غَيۡرَهُۥۖ وَإِذٗا لَّٱتَّخَذُوكَ
خَلِيلٗا ٧٣

74. And had We not given you strength you would nearly have inclined to them a little.

وَلَوۡلَآ أَن ثَبَّتۡنَٰكَ لَقَدۡ كِدتَّ تَرۡكَنُ إِلَيۡهِمۡ شَيۡـٔٗا
قَلِيلًا ٧٤

75. In that case We should have made you taste an equal portion (of punishment) in this life, and an equal portion in death and moreover you would have found none to help you against Us!

إِذٗا لَّأَذَقۡنَٰكَ ضِعۡفَ ٱلۡحَيَوٰةِ وَضِعۡفَ ٱلۡمَمَاتِ
ثُمَّ لَا تَجِدُ لَكَ عَلَيۡنَا نَصِيرٗا ٧٥

76. Their purpose was to scare you off the land, in order to expel you; but in that case they would not have stayed (in it) after you, except for a little while.

وَإِن كَادُواْ لَيَسۡتَفِزُّونَكَ مِنَ ٱلۡأَرۡضِ لِيُخۡرِجُوكَ
مِنۡهَاۖ وَإِذٗا لَّا يَلۡبَثُونَ خِلَٰفَكَ إِلَّا قَلِيلٗا ٧٦

77. (This was Our) way with the messengers We sent before you; you will find no change in Our ways.

سُنَّةَ مَن قَدۡ أَرۡسَلۡنَا قَبۡلَكَ مِن رُّسُلِنَاۖ وَلَا
تَجِدُ لِسُنَّتِنَا تَحۡوِيلًا ٧٧

78. Establish regular prayers - at the sun's decline till the darkness of the night, and the morning prayer and reading: for the prayer and reading in the morning carry their testimony.

أَقِمِ ٱلصَّلَوٰةَ لِدُلُوكِ ٱلشَّمۡسِ إِلَىٰ غَسَقِ ٱلَّيۡلِ
وَقُرۡءَانَ ٱلۡفَجۡرِۖ إِنَّ قُرۡءَانَ ٱلۡفَجۡرِ كَانَ
مَشۡهُودٗا ٧٨

79. And pray in the small watches of the morning; (it would be) an additional prayer (or spiritual profit) for you: soon will your Lord raise you to a station of praise and glory!

وَمِنَ ٱلَّيۡلِ فَتَهَجَّدۡ بِهِۦ نَافِلَةٗ لَّكَ عَسَىٰٓ أَن
يَبۡعَثَكَ رَبُّكَ مَقَامٗا مَّحۡمُودٗا ٧٩

80. Say: "O my Lord! Let my entry be by the gate of truth and honour, and likewise my exit by the gate of truth and honour; and grant me from Your presence an authority to aid (me)."

وَقُل رَّبِّ أَدْخِلْنِي مُدْخَلَ صِدْقٍ وَأَخْرِجْنِي مُخْرَجَ
صِدْقٍ وَاجْعَل لِّي مِن لَّدُنكَ سُلْطَانًا نَّصِيرًا ﴿٨٠﴾

81. And say: "Truth has (now) arrived, and falsehood perished: for falsehood is (by its nature) bound to perish."

وَقُلْ جَاءَ الْحَقُّ وَزَهَقَ الْبَاطِلُ ۚ إِنَّ الْبَاطِلَ كَانَ
زَهُوقًا ﴿٨١﴾

82. We send down (stage by stage) in the Qur'an that which is a healing and a mercy to those who believe; to the unjust it causes nothing but loss after loss.

وَنُنَزِّلُ مِنَ الْقُرْآنِ مَا هُوَ شِفَاءٌ وَرَحْمَةٌ
لِّلْمُؤْمِنِينَ وَلَا يَزِيدُ الظَّالِمِينَ إِلَّا خَسَارًا ﴿٨٢﴾

83. Yet when We bestow Our favours on man, he turns away and becomes remote on his side (instead of coming to Us), and when evil seizes him he gives himself up to despair!

وَإِذَا أَنْعَمْنَا عَلَى الْإِنسَانِ أَعْرَضَ وَنَأَىٰ بِجَانِبِهِ
وَإِذَا مَسَّهُ الشَّرُّ كَانَ يَئُوسًا ﴿٨٣﴾

84. Say: "Everyone acts according to his own disposition; but your Lord knows best who it is that is best guided on the way."

قُلْ كُلٌّ يَعْمَلُ عَلَىٰ شَاكِلَتِهِ فَرَبُّكُمْ أَعْلَمُ بِمَنْ هُوَ
أَهْدَىٰ سَبِيلًا ﴿٨٤﴾

85. They ask you concerning the spirit (of inspiration). Say: "The spirit (comes) by command of my Lord: of knowledge it is only a little that is communicated to you, (O men!)"

وَيَسْأَلُونَكَ عَنِ الرُّوحِ ۖ قُلِ الرُّوحُ مِنْ أَمْرِ رَبِّي وَمَا
أُوتِيتُم مِّنَ الْعِلْمِ إِلَّا قَلِيلًا ﴿٨٥﴾

86. If it were Our will, We could take away that which We have sent you by inspiration; then would you find none to plead your affair in that matter as against Us -

وَلَئِن شِئْنَا لَنَذْهَبَنَّ بِالَّذِي أَوْحَيْنَا إِلَيْكَ ثُمَّ لَا تَجِدُ
لَكَ بِهِ عَلَيْنَا وَكِيلًا ﴿٨٦﴾

87. Except for mercy from your Lord: for His bounty is to you (indeed) great.

إِلَّا رَحْمَةً مِّن رَّبِّكَ ۚ إِنَّ فَضْلَهُ كَانَ عَلَيْكَ
كَبِيرًا ﴿٨٧﴾

88. Say: "If the whole of mankind and Jinns were to gather together to produce

قُل لَّئِنِ اجْتَمَعَتِ الْإِنسُ وَالْجِنُّ عَلَىٰ أَن يَأْتُوا بِمِثْلِ

the like of this Qur'an, they could not produce the like of it, even if they backed up each other with help and support."

هَٰذَا ٱلْقُرْءَانِ لَا يَأْتُونَ بِمِثْلِهِۦ وَلَوْ كَانَ بَعْضُهُمْ
لِبَعْضٍ ظَهِيرًا ﴿٨٨﴾

89. And We have explained to man, in this Qur'an, every kind of similitude; yet the greater part of men refuse (to receive it) except with ingratitude!

وَلَقَدْ صَرَّفْنَا لِلنَّاسِ فِى هَٰذَا ٱلْقُرْءَانِ مِن كُلِّ مَثَلٍ
فَأَبَىٰٓ أَكْثَرُ ٱلنَّاسِ إِلَّا كُفُورًا ﴿٨٩﴾

90. They say: "We shall not believe in you, until you cause a spring to gush out for us from the earth,

وَقَالُوا۟ لَن نُّؤْمِنَ لَكَ حَتَّىٰ تَفْجُرَ لَنَا مِنَ ٱلْأَرْضِ
يَنۢبُوعًا ﴿٩٠﴾

91. Or (until) you have a garden of date trees and vines, and cause rivers to gush out in their midst, carrying abundant water,

أَوْ تَكُونَ لَكَ جَنَّةٌ مِّن نَّخِيلٍ وَعِنَبٍ فَتُفَجِّرَ
ٱلْأَنْهَٰرَ خِلَٰلَهَا تَفْجِيرًا ﴿٩١﴾

92. Or you cause the sky to fall in pieces, as you say (will happen), against us, or you bring Allah and the angels before (us) face to face;

أَوْ تُسْقِطَ ٱلسَّمَآءَ كَمَا زَعَمْتَ عَلَيْنَا كِسَفًا
أَوْ تَأْتِىَ بِٱللَّهِ وَٱلْمَلَٰٓئِكَةِ قَبِيلًا ﴿٩٢﴾

93. Or you have a house adorned with gold, or you mount a ladder right into the skies. No, we shall not even believe in your mounting until you send down to us a book that we can read." Say: "Glory to my Lord! I am nothing but a man - a messenger?"

أَوْ يَكُونَ لَكَ بَيْتٌ مِّن زُخْرُفٍ أَوْ تَرْقَىٰ فِى ٱلسَّمَآءِ
وَلَن نُّؤْمِنَ لِرُقِيِّكَ حَتَّىٰ تُنَزِّلَ عَلَيْنَا كِتَٰبًا
نَّقْرَؤُهُۥ ۗ قُلْ سُبْحَانَ رَبِّى هَلْ كُنتُ إِلَّا بَشَرًا
رَّسُولًا ﴿٩٣﴾

94. What kept men back from belief when guidance came to them, was nothing but this: they said, "Has Allah sent a man (like us) to be (His) messenger?"

وَمَا مَنَعَ ٱلنَّاسَ أَن يُؤْمِنُوٓا۟ إِذْ جَآءَهُمُ ٱلْهُدَىٰٓ إِلَّآ
أَن قَالُوٓا۟ أَبَعَثَ ٱللَّهُ بَشَرًا رَّسُولًا ﴿٩٤﴾

95. Say, "If there were settled, on earth, angels walking about in peace and quiet, We should certainly have sent them down from the heavens an angel for a messenger."

قُل لَّوْ كَانَ فِى ٱلْأَرْضِ مَلَٰٓئِكَةٌ يَمْشُونَ مُطْمَئِنِّينَ
لَنَزَّلْنَا عَلَيْهِم مِّنَ ٱلسَّمَآءِ مَلَكًا رَّسُولًا ﴿٩٥﴾

96. Say: "Enough is Allah for a witness between me and you; for He is well-acquainted with His servants, and He sees (all things)."

قُلْ كَفَىٰ بِٱللَّهِ شَهِيدًۢا بَيْنِى وَبَيْنَكُمْ ۚ إِنَّهُۥ كَانَ
بِعِبَادِهِۦ خَبِيرًۢا بَصِيرًا ﴿٩٦﴾

97. It is he whom Allah guides, that is on true guidance; but he whom He leaves astray - for such will you find no protector besides Him. On the day of judgement We shall gather them together, prone on their faces, blind, dumb, and deaf; their abode will be hell: every time it shows abatement, We shall increase for them the fierceness of the fire.

وَمَن يَهْدِ ٱللَّهُ فَهُوَ ٱلْمُهْتَدِ ۖ وَمَن يُضْلِلْ فَلَن تَجِدَ
لَهُمْ أَوْلِيَآءَ مِن دُونِهِۦ ۖ وَنَحْشُرُهُمْ يَوْمَ ٱلْقِيَٰمَةِ عَلَىٰ
وُجُوهِهِمْ عُمْيًا وَبُكْمًا وَصُمًّا ۖ مَّأْوَىٰهُمْ جَهَنَّمُ ۖ
كُلَّمَا خَبَتْ زِدْنَٰهُمْ سَعِيرًا ﴿٩٧﴾

98. That is their recompense, because they rejected Our signs, and said, "When we are reduced to bones and broken dust, should we really be raised up (to be) a new creation?"

ذَٰلِكَ جَزَآؤُهُم بِأَنَّهُمْ كَفَرُوا۟ بِـَٔايَٰتِنَا وَقَالُوٓا۟ أَءِذَا كُنَّا
عِظَٰمًا وَرُفَٰتًا أَءِنَّا لَمَبْعُوثُونَ خَلْقًا جَدِيدًا ﴿٩٨﴾

99. Do they not see that Allah, Who created the heavens and the earth, has power to create the like of them (anew)? Only He has decreed a term appointed, of which there is no doubt. But the unjust refuse (to receive it) except with ingratitude.

الحزب ٣٠ ۞ أَوَلَمْ يَرَوْا۟ أَنَّ ٱللَّهَ ٱلَّذِى خَلَقَ ٱلسَّمَٰوَٰتِ وَٱلْأَرْضَ
قَادِرٌ عَلَىٰٓ أَن يَخْلُقَ مِثْلَهُمْ وَجَعَلَ لَهُمْ أَجَلًا
لَّا رَيْبَ فِيهِ فَأَبَى ٱلظَّٰلِمُونَ إِلَّا كُفُورًا ﴿٩٩﴾

100. Say: "If you had control of the treasures of the mercy of my Lord, behold you would keep them back, for fear of spending them; for man is (ever) niggardly!"

قُل لَّوْ أَنتُمْ تَمْلِكُونَ خَزَآئِنَ رَحْمَةِ رَبِّىٓ إِذًا لَّأَمْسَكْتُمْ
خَشْيَةَ ٱلْإِنفَاقِ ۚ وَكَانَ ٱلْإِنسَٰنُ قَتُورًا ﴿١٠٠﴾

101. To Moses We did give nine clear signs: ask the Children of Israel; when he came to them, Pharaoh said to him: "O Moses! I consider you, indeed, to have been worked upon by sorcery!"

وَلَقَدْ ءَاتَيْنَا مُوسَىٰ تِسْعَ ءَايَٰتٍۭ بَيِّنَٰتٍ ۖ فَسْـَٔلْ بَنِىٓ
إِسْرَٰٓءِيلَ إِذْ جَآءَهُمْ فَقَالَ لَهُۥ فِرْعَوْنُ إِنِّى لَأَظُنُّكَ
يَٰمُوسَىٰ مَسْحُورًا ﴿١٠١﴾

102. Moses said, "You know well that these things have been sent down by none but the

قَالَ لَقَدْ عَلِمْتَ مَآ أَنزَلَ هَٰٓؤُلَآءِ إِلَّا رَبُّ ٱلسَّمَٰوَٰتِ

Lord of the heavens and the earth as eye-opening evidence; and I consider you indeed, O Pharaoh, to be one doomed to destruction!"

وَٱلْأَرْضِ بَصَآئِرَ وَإِنِّى لَأَظُنُّكَ يَٰفِرْعَوْنُ
مَثْبُورًا ﴿١٠٢﴾

103. So he resolved to remove them from the face of the earth: but We did drown him and all who were with him.

فَأَرَادَ أَن يَسْتَفِزَّهُم مِّنَ ٱلْأَرْضِ فَأَغْرَقْنَٰهُ
وَمَن مَّعَهُۥ جَمِيعًا ﴿١٠٣﴾

104. And We said thereafter to the Children of Israel, "Dwell securely in the land (of promise)"; but when the second of the warnings came to pass, We gathered you together in a mingled crowd.

وَقُلْنَا مِنۢ بَعْدِهِۦ لِبَنِىٓ إِسْرَٰٓءِيلَ ٱسْكُنُوا۟ ٱلْأَرْضَ فَإِذَا
جَآءَ وَعْدُ ٱلْءَاخِرَةِ جِئْنَا بِكُمْ لَفِيفًا ﴿١٠٤﴾

105. We sent down the (Qur'an) in truth, and in truth has it descended; and We sent you but to give glad tidings and to warn (sinners).

وَبِٱلْحَقِّ أَنزَلْنَٰهُ وَبِٱلْحَقِّ نَزَلَ ۗ وَمَآ أَرْسَلْنَٰكَ إِلَّا مُبَشِّرًا
وَنَذِيرًا ﴿١٠٥﴾

106. (It is) a Qur'an which We have divided (into parts from time to time), in order that you might recite it to men at intervals; We have revealed it by stages.

وَقُرْءَانًا فَرَقْنَٰهُ لِتَقْرَأَهُۥ عَلَى ٱلنَّاسِ عَلَىٰ مُكْثٍ وَنَزَّلْنَٰهُ
تَنزِيلًا ﴿١٠٦﴾

107. Say: "Whether you believe in it or not, it is true that those who were given knowledge beforehand, when it is recited to them, fall down on their faces in humble prostration,

قُلْ ءَامِنُوا۟ بِهِۦٓ أَوْ لَا تُؤْمِنُوٓا۟ ۚ إِنَّ ٱلَّذِينَ أُوتُوا۟ ٱلْعِلْمَ مِن
قَبْلِهِۦٓ إِذَا يُتْلَىٰ عَلَيْهِمْ يَخِرُّونَ لِلْأَذْقَانِ سُجَّدًا ﴿١٠٧﴾

108. And they say: 'Glory to our Lord! Truly has the promise of our Lord been fulfilled!'"

وَيَقُولُونَ سُبْحَٰنَ رَبِّنَآ إِن كَانَ وَعْدُ رَبِّنَا لَمَفْعُولًا ﴿١٠٨﴾

109. They fall down on their faces in tears, and it increases their (earnest) humility.

سجدة وَيَخِرُّونَ لِلْأَذْقَانِ يَبْكُونَ وَيَزِيدُهُمْ خُشُوعًا ۩ ﴿١٠٩﴾

110. Say: "Call upon Allah, or call upon ar-Rahman: by whatever name you call upon Him, (it is well); for to Him belong the most beautiful Names. Neither speak your prayer aloud, nor speak it in a low tone, but seek a middle course between."

قُلِ ٱدْعُوا۟ ٱللَّهَ أَوِ ٱدْعُوا۟ ٱلرَّحْمَٰنَ ۖ أَيًّا مَّا تَدْعُوا۟ فَلَهُ
ٱلْأَسْمَآءُ ٱلْحُسْنَىٰ ۚ وَلَا تَجْهَرْ بِصَلَاتِكَ وَلَا تُخَافِتْ
بِهَا وَٱبْتَغِ بَيْنَ ذَٰلِكَ سَبِيلًا ﴿١١٠﴾

111. Say: "Praise be to Allah, Who begets no son, and has no partner in (His) dominion; nor (needs) He any to protect Him from humiliation; yea, magnify Him for His greatness and glory!"

وَقُلِ ٱلْحَمْدُ لِلَّهِ ٱلَّذِى لَمْ يَتَّخِذْ وَلَدًا وَلَمْ يَكُن لَّهُۥ شَرِيكٌ
فِى ٱلْمُلْكِ وَلَمْ يَكُن لَّهُۥ وَلِىٌّ مِّنَ ٱلذُّلِّ ۖ وَكَبِّرْهُ تَكْبِيرًۢا ﴿١١١﴾

سُورَةُ الكَهْفِ

Surah 18: ***Al-Kahf*** **(The Cave)**

In the name of Allah,
Most Gracious, Most Merciful.

بِسْمِ ٱللَّهِ ٱلرَّحْمَٰنِ ٱلرَّحِيمِ

1. Praise be to Allah, Who has sent to His servant the book, and has allowed in it no crookedness:

سكتة لطيفة من ألف عوجا

ٱلْحَمْدُ لِلَّهِ ٱلَّذِىٓ أَنزَلَ عَلَىٰ عَبْدِهِ ٱلْكِتَٰبَ وَلَمْ
يَجْعَل لَّهُۥ عِوَجَا ۜ ﴿١﴾

2. (He has made it) straight (and clear) in order that He may warn (the godless) of a terrible punishment from Him, and that He may give glad tidings to the believers who work righteous deeds, that they shall have a goodly reward,

قَيِّمًا لِّيُنذِرَ بَأْسًا شَدِيدًا مِّن لَّدُنْهُ وَيُبَشِّرَ
ٱلْمُؤْمِنِينَ ٱلَّذِينَ يَعْمَلُونَ ٱلصَّٰلِحَٰتِ أَنَّ
لَهُمْ أَجْرًا حَسَنًا ﴿٢﴾

3. In which they shall remain forever:

مَّٰكِثِينَ فِيهِ أَبَدًا ﴿٣﴾

4. Further, that He may warn those (also) who say, "Allah has begotten a son":

وَيُنذِرَ ٱلَّذِينَ قَالُوا۟ ٱتَّخَذَ ٱللَّهُ وَلَدًا ﴿٤﴾

5. No knowledge have they of such a thing, nor had their fathers. It is a grievous thing that issues from their mouths as a saying. What they say is nothing but falsehood!

مَّا لَهُم بِهِۦ مِنْ عِلْمٍ وَلَا لِءَابَآئِهِمْ ۚ كَبُرَتْ كَلِمَةً
تَخْرُجُ مِنْ أَفْوَٰهِهِمْ ۚ إِن يَقُولُونَ إِلَّا كَذِبًا ﴿٥﴾

6. You would only, perhaps, fret yourself to death, following after them, in grief, if they believe not in this message.

فَلَعَلَّكَ بَٰخِعٌ نَّفْسَكَ عَلَىٰٓ ءَاثَٰرِهِمْ إِن لَّمْ يُؤْمِنُوا۟
بِهَٰذَا ٱلْحَدِيثِ أَسَفًا ﴿٦﴾

7. That which is on earth We have made but as a glittering show for the earth, in order that We may test them - as to which of them are best in conduct.

إِنَّا جَعَلْنَا مَا عَلَى ٱلْأَرْضِ زِينَةً لَّهَا لِنَبْلُوَهُمْ
أَيُّهُمْ أَحْسَنُ عَمَلًا ﴿٧﴾

8. Verily what is on earth We shall make but as dust and dry soil (without growth or herbage).

وَإِنَّا لَجَٰعِلُونَ مَا عَلَيْهَا صَعِيدًا جُرُزًا ﴿٨﴾

9. Or do you reflect that the companions of the cave and of the inscription were wonders among Our signs?

أَمْ حَسِبْتَ أَنَّ أَصْحَٰبَ ٱلْكَهْفِ وَٱلرَّقِيمِ
كَانُوا۟ مِنْ ءَايَٰتِنَا عَجَبًا ﴿٩﴾

10. See, the youths went to the cave: they said, "Our Lord! Bestow on us mercy from Yourself, and dispose of our affair for us in the right way!"

إِذْ أَوَى ٱلْفِتْيَةُ إِلَى ٱلْكَهْفِ فَقَالُوا۟ رَبَّنَآ ءَاتِنَا
مِن لَّدُنكَ رَحْمَةً وَهَيِّئْ لَنَا مِنْ أَمْرِنَا رَشَدًا ﴿١٠﴾

11. Then We drew (a veil) over their ears, for a number of years, in the cave (so that they heard not).

فَضَرَبْنَا عَلَىٰٓ ءَاذَانِهِمْ فِى ٱلْكَهْفِ سِنِينَ
عَدَدًا ﴿١١﴾

12. Then We roused them, in order to test which of the two parties was best at calculating the term of years they had stayed!

ثُمَّ بَعَثْنَٰهُمْ لِنَعْلَمَ أَىُّ ٱلْحِزْبَيْنِ أَحْصَىٰ لِمَا
لَبِثُوٓا۟ أَمَدًا ﴿١٢﴾

13. We relate to you their story in truth: they were youths who believed in their Lord, and We advanced them in guidance.

نَّحْنُ نَقُصُّ عَلَيْكَ نَبَأَهُم بِٱلْحَقِّ ۚ إِنَّهُمْ فِتْيَةٌ
ءَامَنُوا۟ بِرَبِّهِمْ وَزِدْنَٰهُمْ هُدًى ﴿١٣﴾

14. We gave strength to their hearts: see, they stood up and said: "Our Lord is the Lord of the heavens and of the earth: never shall we call upon any god other than Him: if we did, we should indeed have uttered an enormity!"

وَرَبَطْنَا عَلَىٰ قُلُوبِهِمْ إِذْ قَامُوا۟ فَقَالُوا۟ رَبُّنَا رَبُّ
ٱلسَّمَٰوَٰتِ وَٱلْأَرْضِ لَن نَّدْعُوَا۟ مِن دُونِهِۦٓ إِلَٰهًا ۖ
لَّقَدْ قُلْنَآ إِذًا شَطَطًا ﴿١٤﴾

15. "These our people have taken for worship gods other than Him: why do they not bring forward an authority clear (and convincing) for what they do? Who does

هَٰٓؤُلَآءِ قَوْمُنَا ٱتَّخَذُوا۟ مِن دُونِهِۦٓ ءَالِهَةً ۖ لَّوْلَا
يَأْتُونَ عَلَيْهِم بِسُلْطَٰنٍۭ بَيِّنٍ ۖ فَمَنْ أَظْلَمُ مِمَّنِ

أَفْتَرَىٰ عَلَى ٱللَّهِ كَذِبًا ﴿١٥﴾

more wrong than such as invent a falsehood against Allah?"

وَإِذِ ٱعْتَزَلْتُمُوهُمْ وَمَا يَعْبُدُونَ إِلَّا ٱللَّهَ فَأْوُۥٓا۟
إِلَى ٱلْكَهْفِ يَنشُرْ لَكُمْ رَبُّكُم مِّن رَّحْمَتِهِۦ
وَيُهَيِّئْ لَكُم مِّنْ أَمْرِكُم مِّرْفَقًا ﴿١٦﴾

16. "When you turn away from them and the things they worship other than Allah go to the cave; your Lord will shower His mercies on you and dispose of your affair towards comfort and ease."

ربع الحزب ٣٠
۞ وَتَرَى ٱلشَّمْسَ إِذَا طَلَعَت تَّزَٰوَرُ عَن كَهْفِهِمْ
ذَاتَ ٱلْيَمِينِ وَإِذَا غَرَبَت تَّقْرِضُهُمْ ذَاتَ ٱلشِّمَالِ
وَهُمْ فِى فَجْوَةٍ مِّنْهُ ۚ ذَٰلِكَ مِنْ ءَايَٰتِ ٱللَّهِ ۗ مَن
يَهْدِ ٱللَّهُ فَهُوَ ٱلْمُهْتَدِ ۖ وَمَن يُضْلِلْ فَلَن تَجِدَ لَهُۥ
وَلِيًّا مُّرْشِدًا ﴿١٧﴾

17. You would have seen the sun, when it rose, declining to the right from their cave, and when it set, turning away from them to the left, while they lay in the open space in the midst of the cave. Such are among the signs of Allah: he whom Allah guides is rightly guided; but he whom Allah leaves to stray - for him will you find no protector to lead him to the Right way.

وَتَحْسَبُهُمْ أَيْقَاظًا وَهُمْ رُقُودٌ ۚ وَنُقَلِّبُهُمْ ذَاتَ
ٱلْيَمِينِ وَذَاتَ ٱلشِّمَالِ ۖ وَكَلْبُهُم بَٰسِطٌ ذِرَاعَيْهِ
بِٱلْوَصِيدِ ۚ لَوِ ٱطَّلَعْتَ عَلَيْهِمْ لَوَلَّيْتَ مِنْهُمْ فِرَارًا
وَلَمُلِئْتَ مِنْهُمْ رُعْبًا ﴿١٨﴾

18. You would have deemed them awake, whilst they were asleep, and We turned them on their right and their left sides; their dog stretching forth his two forelegs on the threshold: if you had come up on to them, you would have certainly turned back from them in flight, and would certainly have been filled with terror of them.

وَكَذَٰلِكَ بَعَثْنَٰهُمْ لِيَتَسَآءَلُوا۟ بَيْنَهُمْ ۚ قَالَ
قَآئِلٌ مِّنْهُمْ كَمْ لَبِثْتُمْ ۖ قَالُوا۟ لَبِثْنَا يَوْمًا أَوْ بَعْضَ
يَوْمٍ ۚ قَالُوا۟ رَبُّكُمْ أَعْلَمُ بِمَا لَبِثْتُمْ فَٱبْعَثُوٓا۟
أَحَدَكُم بِوَرِقِكُمْ هَٰذِهِۦٓ إِلَى ٱلْمَدِينَةِ فَلْيَنظُرْ
أَيُّهَآ أَزْكَىٰ طَعَامًا فَلْيَأْتِكُم بِرِزْقٍ مِّنْهُ
وَلْيَتَلَطَّفْ وَلَا يُشْعِرَنَّ بِكُمْ أَحَدًا ﴿١٩﴾

19. Such (being their state), We raised them up (from sleep), that they might question each other. Said one of them, "How long have you stayed (here)?" They said, "We have stayed (perhaps) a day, or part of a day." (At length) they (all) said, "Allah (alone) knows best how long you have stayed here. Now send you then one of you with this money of yours to the town; let him find out which is the best food (to be had) and bring some to you, that (you may) satisfy hunger with it; and let him behave with care and courtesy, and let him not inform anyone about you."

20. "For if they should come upon you, they would stone you or force you to return to their cult, and in that case you would never attain prosperity."

إِنَّهُمْ إِن يَظْهَرُوا۟ عَلَيْكُمْ يَرْجُمُوكُمْ
أَوْ يُعِيدُوكُمْ فِى مِلَّتِهِمْ وَلَن تُفْلِحُوٓا۟ إِذًا
أَبَدًا ٢٠

21. Thus did We make their case known to the people, that they might know that the promise of Allah is true, and that there can be no doubt about the hour of judgement. See, they dispute among themselves as to their affair. (Some) said, "Construct a building over them"; their Lord knows best about them; those who prevailed over their affair said, "Let us surely build a place of worship over them."

وَكَذَٰلِكَ أَعْثَرْنَا عَلَيْهِمْ لِيَعْلَمُوٓا۟ أَنَّ وَعْدَ
ٱللَّهِ حَقٌّ وَأَنَّ ٱلسَّاعَةَ لَا رَيْبَ فِيهَآ إِذْ يَتَنَٰزَعُونَ
بَيْنَهُمْ أَمْرَهُمْ ۖ فَقَالُوا۟ ٱبْنُوا۟ عَلَيْهِم بُنْيَٰنًا ۖ رَّبُّهُمْ
أَعْلَمُ بِهِمْ ۚ قَالَ ٱلَّذِينَ غَلَبُوا۟ عَلَىٰٓ أَمْرِهِمْ لَنَتَّخِذَنَّ
عَلَيْهِم مَّسْجِدًا ٢١

22. (Some) say they were three, the dog being the fourth among them; (others) say they were five, the dog being the sixth - doubtfully guessing at the unknown; (yet others) say they were seven, the dog being the eighth. Say you; "My Lord knows best their number; it is but few that know their (real case)." Enter not, therefore, into controversies concerning them, except on a matter that is clear, nor consult any of them about (the affair of) the sleepers.

سَيَقُولُونَ ثَلَٰثَةٌ رَّابِعُهُمْ كَلْبُهُمْ وَيَقُولُونَ
خَمْسَةٌ سَادِسُهُمْ كَلْبُهُمْ رَجْمًۢا بِٱلْغَيْبِ ۖ
وَيَقُولُونَ سَبْعَةٌ وَثَامِنُهُمْ كَلْبُهُمْ ۚ قُل رَّبِّىٓ أَعْلَمُ
بِعِدَّتِهِم مَّا يَعْلَمُهُمْ إِلَّا قَلِيلٌ ۗ فَلَا تُمَارِ فِيهِمْ
إِلَّا مِرَآءً ظَٰهِرًا وَلَا تَسْتَفْتِ فِيهِم مِّنْهُمْ أَحَدًا ٢٢

23. Nor say of anything, "I shall be sure to do so and so tomorrow" -

وَلَا تَقُولَنَّ لِشَا۟ىْءٍ إِنِّى فَاعِلٌ ذَٰلِكَ غَدًا ٢٣

24. Without adding, "So please Allah!" And call your Lord to mind when you forget, and say, "I hope that my Lord will guide me ever closer (even) than this to the right road."

إِلَّآ أَن يَشَآءَ ٱللَّهُ ۚ وَٱذْكُر رَّبَّكَ إِذَا نَسِيتَ وَقُلْ
عَسَىٰٓ أَن يَهْدِيَنِ رَبِّى لِأَقْرَبَ مِنْ هَٰذَا رَشَدًا ٢٤

25. So they stayed in their cave three hundred years, and (some) add nine (more).

وَلَبِثُوا۟ فِى كَهْفِهِمْ ثَلَٰثَ مِا۟ئَةٍ سِنِينَ وَٱزْدَادُوا۟
تِسْعًا ٢٥

26. Say: "Allah knows best how long they stayed; with Him is (the knowledge of) the secrets of the heavens and the earth: how clearly He sees, how finely He hears (everything)! They have no protector other than Him; nor does He share His command with any person whatsoever.

قُلِ ٱللَّهُ أَعْلَمُ بِمَا لَبِثُوا۟ ۖ لَهُۥ غَيْبُ ٱلسَّمَٰوَٰتِ
وَٱلْأَرْضِ ۖ أَبْصِرْ بِهِۦ وَأَسْمِعْ ۚ مَا لَهُم مِّن دُونِهِۦ
مِن وَلِىٍّ وَلَا يُشْرِكُ فِى حُكْمِهِۦٓ أَحَدًا ﴿٢٦﴾

27. And recite (and teach) what has been revealed to you of the book of your Lord: none can change His words, and none will you find as a refuge other than Him.

وَٱتْلُ مَآ أُوحِىَ إِلَيْكَ مِن كِتَابِ رَبِّكَ ۖ لَا مُبَدِّلَ
لِكَلِمَٰتِهِۦ وَلَن تَجِدَ مِن دُونِهِۦ مُلْتَحَدًا ﴿٢٧﴾

28. And keep your soul content with those who call on their Lord morning and evening, seeking His Face; and let not your eyes pass beyond them seeking the pomp and glitter of this life; nor obey any whose heart We have permitted to neglect the remembrance of Us; one who follows his own desires, whose case has gone beyond all bounds.

وَٱصْبِرْ نَفْسَكَ مَعَ ٱلَّذِينَ يَدْعُونَ رَبَّهُم بِٱلْغَدَوٰةِ
وَٱلْعَشِىِّ يُرِيدُونَ وَجْهَهُۥ ۖ وَلَا تَعْدُ عَيْنَاكَ عَنْهُمْ
تُرِيدُ زِينَةَ ٱلْحَيَوٰةِ ٱلدُّنْيَا ۖ وَلَا تُطِعْ مَنْ أَغْفَلْنَا
قَلْبَهُۥ عَن ذِكْرِنَا وَٱتَّبَعَ هَوَىٰهُ وَكَانَ أَمْرُهُۥ فُرُطًا ﴿٢٨﴾

29. Say, "The truth is from your Lord"; let him who will, believe, and let him who will, reject (it): for the wrongdoers We have prepared a fire whose (smoke and flames), like the wall and roof of a tent, will hem them in: if they implore relief they will be granted water like melted brass that will scald their faces. How dreadful the drink! How uncomfortable a couch to recline on!

وَقُلِ ٱلْحَقُّ مِن رَّبِّكُمْ ۖ فَمَن شَآءَ فَلْيُؤْمِن وَمَن شَآءَ
فَلْيَكْفُرْ ۚ إِنَّآ أَعْتَدْنَا لِلظَّٰلِمِينَ نَارًا أَحَاطَ بِهِمْ
سُرَادِقُهَا ۚ وَإِن يَسْتَغِيثُوا۟ يُغَاثُوا۟ بِمَآءٍ كَٱلْمُهْلِ
يَشْوِى ٱلْوُجُوهَ ۚ بِئْسَ ٱلشَّرَابُ وَسَآءَتْ
مُرْتَفَقًا ﴿٢٩﴾

30. As to those who believe and work righteousness, verily We shall not suffer to perish the reward of any who do a (single) righteous deed.

إِنَّ ٱلَّذِينَ ءَامَنُوا۟ وَعَمِلُوا۟ ٱلصَّٰلِحَٰتِ إِنَّا
لَا نُضِيعُ أَجْرَ مَنْ أَحْسَنَ عَمَلًا ﴿٣٠﴾

31. For them will be Gardens of Eternity; beneath them rivers will flow; they will be adorned in it with bracelets of gold, and

أُو۟لَٰٓئِكَ لَهُمْ جَنَّٰتُ عَدْنٍ تَجْرِى مِن تَحْتِهِمُ ٱلْأَنْهَٰرُ
يُحَلَّوْنَ فِيهَا مِنْ أَسَاوِرَ مِن ذَهَبٍ وَيَلْبَسُونَ ثِيَابًا

they will wear green garments of fine silk and heavy brocade; they will recline in it on raised thrones. How good the recompense! How beautiful a couch to recline on!

خُضْرًا مِّن سُندُسٍ وَإِسْتَبْرَقٍ مُّتَّكِـِٔينَ فِيهَا عَلَى
ٱلْأَرَآئِكِۚ نِعْمَ ٱلثَّوَابُ وَحَسُنَتْ مُرْتَفَقًا ﴿٣١﴾

32. Set out to them the parable of two men: for one of them We provided two gardens of grapevines and surrounded them with date-palms; in between the two We placed cornfields.

نف
زب
٣

۞ وَٱضْرِبْ لَهُم مَّثَلًا رَّجُلَيْنِ جَعَلْنَا لِأَحَدِهِمَا جَنَّتَيْنِ
مِنْ أَعْنَٰبٍ وَحَفَفْنَٰهُمَا بِنَخْلٍ وَجَعَلْنَا بَيْنَهُمَا زَرْعًا ﴿٣٢﴾

33. Each of those gardens brought forth its produce, and failed not in the least in it; in the midst of them We caused a river to flow.

كِلْتَا ٱلْجَنَّتَيْنِ ءَاتَتْ أُكُلَهَا وَلَمْ تَظْلِم مِّنْهُ شَيْـًٔاۚ
وَفَجَّرْنَا خِلَٰلَهُمَا نَهَرًا ﴿٣٣﴾

34. (Abundant) was the produce, this man had; he said to his companion, in the course of a mutual argument: "More wealth have I than you, and more honour and power in (my following of) men."

وَكَانَ لَهُۥ ثَمَرٌ فَقَالَ لِصَٰحِبِهِۦ وَهُوَ يُحَاوِرُهُۥٓ أَنَا۠
أَكْثَرُ مِنكَ مَالًا وَأَعَزُّ نَفَرًا ﴿٣٤﴾

35. He went into his garden in a state (of mind) unjust to his soul: He said, "I think not that this will ever perish."

وَدَخَلَ جَنَّتَهُۥ وَهُوَ ظَالِمٌ لِّنَفْسِهِۦ قَالَ مَآ أَظُنُّ أَن
تَبِيدَ هَٰذِهِۦٓ أَبَدًا ﴿٣٥﴾

36. "Nor do I think that the hour (of judgement) will (ever) come; even if I am brought back to my Lord, I shall surely find (there) something better in exchange."

وَمَآ أَظُنُّ ٱلسَّاعَةَ قَآئِمَةً وَلَئِن رُّدِدتُّ إِلَىٰ رَبِّى
لَأَجِدَنَّ خَيْرًا مِّنْهَا مُنقَلَبًا ﴿٣٦﴾

37. His companion said to him, in the course of the argument with him: "Do you deny Him Who created you out of dust, then out of a sperm-drop, then fashioned you into a man?

قَالَ لَهُۥ صَاحِبُهُۥ وَهُوَ يُحَاوِرُهُۥٓ أَكَفَرْتَ بِٱلَّذِى
خَلَقَكَ مِن تُرَابٍ ثُمَّ مِن نُّطْفَةٍ ثُمَّ سَوَّىٰكَ
رَجُلًا ﴿٣٧﴾

38. But (I think) for my part that He is Allah, my Lord, and none shall I associate with my Lord.

لَّٰكِنَّا۠ هُوَ ٱللَّهُ رَبِّى وَلَآ أُشْرِكُ بِرَبِّىٓ أَحَدًا ﴿٣٨﴾

39. Why did you not, as you went into your garden, say: 'Allah's Will (be done)! There is no power but with Allah!' If you do see me less than you in wealth and sons,

وَلَوْلَآ إِذْ دَخَلْتَ جَنَّتَكَ قُلْتَ مَا شَآءَ ٱللَّهُ لَا قُوَّةَ
إِلَّا بِٱللَّهِ ۚ إِن تَرَنِ أَنَا۠ أَقَلَّ مِنكَ مَالًا وَوَلَدًا ﴿٣٩﴾

40. It may be that my Lord will give me something better than your garden, and that He will send on your garden thunderbolts (by way of reckoning) from heaven, making it (but) slippery sand! -

فَعَسَىٰ رَبِّىٓ أَن يُؤْتِيَنِ خَيْرًا مِّن جَنَّتِكَ وَيُرْسِلَ عَلَيْهَا
حُسْبَانًا مِّنَ ٱلسَّمَآءِ فَتُصْبِحَ صَعِيدًا زَلَقًا ﴿٤٠﴾

41. Or the water of the garden will run off underground so that you will never be able to find it."

أَوْ يُصْبِحَ مَآؤُهَا غَوْرًا فَلَن تَسْتَطِيعَ لَهُۥ طَلَبًا ﴿٤١﴾

42. So his fruits (and enjoyment) were encompassed (with ruin), and he remained twisting and turning his hands over what he had spent on his property, which had (now) tumbled to pieces to its very foundations, and he could only say, "Woe is me! Would I had never ascribed partners to my Lord and Cherisher!"

وَأُحِيطَ بِثَمَرِهِۦ فَأَصْبَحَ يُقَلِّبُ كَفَّيْهِ عَلَىٰ
مَآ أَنفَقَ فِيهَا وَهِىَ خَاوِيَةٌ عَلَىٰ عُرُوشِهَا وَيَقُولُ
يَـٰلَيْتَنِى لَمْ أُشْرِكْ بِرَبِّىٓ أَحَدًا ﴿٤٢﴾

43. Nor had he numbers to help him against Allah, nor was he able to deliver himself.

وَلَمْ تَكُن لَّهُۥ فِئَةٌ يَنصُرُونَهُۥ مِن دُونِ ٱللَّهِ وَمَا كَانَ
مُنتَصِرًا ﴿٤٣﴾

44. There, the (only) protection comes from Allah, the True One. He is the Best to reward, and the Best to give success.

هُنَالِكَ ٱلْوَلَـٰيَةُ لِلَّهِ ٱلْحَقِّ ۚ هُوَ خَيْرٌ ثَوَابًا وَخَيْرٌ عُقْبًا ﴿٤٤﴾

45. Set out to them the similitude of the life of this world; it is like the rain which We send down from the skies; the earth's vegetation absorbs it, but soon it becomes dry stubble, which the winds do scatter: it is (only) Allah Who prevails over all things.

وَٱضْرِبْ لَهُم مَّثَلَ ٱلْحَيَوٰةِ ٱلدُّنْيَا كَمَآءٍ أَنزَلْنَـٰهُ مِنَ
ٱلسَّمَآءِ فَٱخْتَلَطَ بِهِۦ نَبَاتُ ٱلْأَرْضِ فَأَصْبَحَ هَشِيمًا
تَذْرُوهُ ٱلرِّيَـٰحُ ۗ وَكَانَ ٱللَّهُ عَلَىٰ كُلِّ شَىْءٍ مُّقْتَدِرًا ﴿٤٥﴾

46. Wealth and sons are allurements of the life of this world; but the things that endure, good deeds, are best in the sight of your Lord, as rewards, and best as (the foundation for) hopes.

ٱلْمَالُ وَٱلْبَنُونَ زِينَةُ ٱلْحَيَوٰةِ ٱلدُّنْيَا ۖ وَٱلْبَـٰقِيَـٰتُ
ٱلصَّـٰلِحَـٰتُ خَيْرٌ عِندَ رَبِّكَ ثَوَابًا وَخَيْرٌ أَمَلًا ﴿٤٦﴾

47. One day We shall remove the mountains, and you will see the earth as a level stretch, and We shall gather them all together, nor shall We leave out any one of them.

وَيَوْمَ نُسَيِّرُ ٱلْجِبَالَ وَتَرَى ٱلْأَرْضَ بَارِزَةً وَحَشَرْنَـٰهُمْ
فَلَمْ نُغَادِرْ مِنْهُمْ أَحَدًا ﴿٤٧﴾

48. And they will be marshalled before your Lord in ranks, (with the announcement) "Now have you come to Us (bare) as We created you first: aye, you thought We shall not fulfil the appointment made to you to meet (Us)!"

وَعُرِضُوا۟ عَلَىٰ رَبِّكَ صَفًّا لَّقَدْ جِئْتُمُونَا كَمَا خَلَقْنَـٰكُمْ
أَوَّلَ مَرَّةٍۭ ۚ بَلْ زَعَمْتُمْ أَلَّن نَّجْعَلَ لَكُم مَّوْعِدًا ﴿٤٨﴾

49. And the book (of deeds) will be placed (before you); and you will see the sinful in great terror because of what is (recorded) in it; they will say, "Ah! Woe to us! What a book is this! It leaves out nothing small or great, but takes account of it!" They will find all that they did, placed before them, and not one will your Lord treat with injustice.

وَوُضِعَ ٱلْكِتَـٰبُ فَتَرَى ٱلْمُجْرِمِينَ مُشْفِقِينَ مِمَّا
فِيهِ وَيَقُولُونَ يَـٰوَيْلَتَنَا مَالِ هَـٰذَا ٱلْكِتَـٰبِ لَا
يُغَادِرُ صَغِيرَةً وَلَا كَبِيرَةً إِلَّآ أَحْصَىٰهَا ۚ وَوَجَدُوا۟
مَا عَمِلُوا۟ حَاضِرًا ۗ وَلَا يَظْلِمُ رَبُّكَ أَحَدًا ﴿٤٩﴾

50. See! We said to the angels, "Bow down to Adam"; they bowed down except Iblis. He was one of the Jinns, and he broke the command of his Lord. Will you then take him and his progeny as protectors rather than Me? And they are enemies to you! Evil would be the exchange for the wrongdoers!

وَإِذْ قُلْنَا لِلْمَلَـٰٓئِكَةِ ٱسْجُدُوا۟ لِـَٔادَمَ فَسَجَدُوٓا۟ إِلَّآ
إِبْلِيسَ كَانَ مِنَ ٱلْجِنِّ فَفَسَقَ عَنْ أَمْرِ رَبِّهِۦٓ ۗ
أَفَتَتَّخِذُونَهُۥ وَذُرِّيَّتَهُۥٓ أَوْلِيَآءَ مِن دُونِى وَهُمْ
لَكُمْ عَدُوٌّۢ ۚ بِئْسَ لِلظَّـٰلِمِينَ بَدَلًا ﴿٥٠﴾

51. I called them not to witness the creation of the heavens and the earth, nor (even) their own creation; nor is it for Me to take as helpers such as lead (men) astray!

۞ مَّآ أَشْهَدتُّهُمْ خَلْقَ ٱلسَّمَـٰوَٰتِ وَٱلْأَرْضِ وَلَا
خَلْقَ أَنفُسِهِمْ وَمَا كُنتُ مُتَّخِذَ ٱلْمُضِلِّينَ عَضُدًا ﴿٥١﴾

52. One day He will say, "Call on those whom you thought to be My partners," and they will call on them, but they will not listen to them; and We shall make for them a place of common perdition.

وَيَوْمَ يَقُولُ نَادُوا۟ شُرَكَآءِىَ ٱلَّذِينَ زَعَمْتُمْ
فَدَعَوْهُمْ فَلَمْ يَسْتَجِيبُوا۟ لَهُمْ وَجَعَلْنَا بَيْنَهُم
مَّوْبِقًا ﴿٥٢﴾

53. And the sinful shall see the fire and apprehend that they have to fall in it; no means will they find to turn away from it.

وَرَءَا ٱلْمُجْرِمُونَ ٱلنَّارَ فَظَنُّوٓا۟ أَنَّهُم مُّوَاقِعُوهَا وَلَمْ
يَجِدُوا۟ عَنْهَا مَصْرِفًا ﴿٥٣﴾

54. We have explained in detail in this Qur'an, for the benefit of mankind, every kind of similitude; but man is, in most things, contentious.

وَلَقَدْ صَرَّفْنَا فِى هَٰذَا ٱلْقُرْءَانِ لِلنَّاسِ مِن كُلِّ
مَثَلٍ ۚ وَكَانَ ٱلْإِنسَٰنُ أَكْثَرَ شَىْءٍ جَدَلًا ﴿٥٤﴾

55. And what is there to keep back men from believing, now that guidance has come to them, nor from praying for forgiveness from their Lord, but that (they ask that) the ways of the ancients be repeated with them, or the wrath be brought to them face to face?

وَمَا مَنَعَ ٱلنَّاسَ أَن يُؤْمِنُوٓا۟ إِذْ جَآءَهُمُ ٱلْهُدَىٰ
وَيَسْتَغْفِرُوا۟ رَبَّهُمْ إِلَّآ أَن تَأْتِيَهُمْ سُنَّةُ ٱلْأَوَّلِينَ
أَوْ يَأْتِيَهُمُ ٱلْعَذَابُ قُبُلًا ﴿٥٥﴾

56. We only send the messengers to give glad tidings and to give warnings: but the unbelievers dispute with vain argument, in order therewith to weaken the truth, and they treat My signs as a jest, as also the fact that they are warned!

وَمَا نُرْسِلُ ٱلْمُرْسَلِينَ إِلَّا مُبَشِّرِينَ وَمُنذِرِينَ ۚ
وَيُجَٰدِلُ ٱلَّذِينَ كَفَرُوا۟ بِٱلْبَٰطِلِ لِيُدْحِضُوا۟ بِهِ
ٱلْحَقَّ ۖ وَٱتَّخَذُوٓا۟ ءَايَٰتِى وَمَآ أُنذِرُوا۟ هُزُوًا ﴿٥٦﴾

57. And who does more wrong than one who is reminded of the signs of his Lord, but turns away from them, forgetting the (deeds) which his hands have sent before? Verily We have set veils over their hearts lest they should understand this, and over their ears, deafness. If you call them to guidance, even then will they never accept guidance.

وَمَنْ أَظْلَمُ مِمَّن ذُكِّرَ بِـَٔايَٰتِ رَبِّهِۦ فَأَعْرَضَ
عَنْهَا وَنَسِىَ مَا قَدَّمَتْ يَدَاهُ ۚ إِنَّا جَعَلْنَا عَلَىٰ قُلُوبِهِمْ
أَكِنَّةً أَن يَفْقَهُوهُ وَفِىٓ ءَاذَانِهِمْ وَقْرًا ۖ وَإِن
تَدْعُهُمْ إِلَى ٱلْهُدَىٰ فَلَن يَهْتَدُوٓا۟ إِذًا أَبَدًا ﴿٥٧﴾

58. But your Lord is Most Forgiving, full of Mercy. If He were to call them (at once) to account for what they have earned, then surely He would have hastened their punishment: but they have their appointed time, beyond which they will find no refuge.

وَرَبُّكَ ٱلْغَفُورُ ذُو ٱلرَّحْمَةِ ۖ لَوْ يُؤَاخِذُهُم بِمَا
كَسَبُوا۟ لَعَجَّلَ لَهُمُ ٱلْعَذَابَ ۚ بَل لَّهُم مَّوْعِدٌ لَّن
يَجِدُوا۟ مِن دُونِهِۦ مَوْئِلًا ﴿٥٨﴾

59. Such were the populations We destroyed when they committed iniquities; but We fixed an appointed time for their destruction.

وَتِلْكَ ٱلْقُرَىٰٓ أَهْلَكْنَٰهُمْ لَمَّا ظَلَمُوا۟ وَجَعَلْنَا
لِمَهْلِكِهِم مَّوْعِدًا ﴿٥٩﴾

60. See, Moses said to his attendant, "I will not give up (until) I reach the junction of the two seas or (until) I spend years and years in travel."

وَإِذْ قَالَ مُوسَىٰ لِفَتَىٰهُ لَآ أَبْرَحُ حَتَّىٰٓ أَبْلُغَ مَجْمَعَ
ٱلْبَحْرَيْنِ أَوْ أَمْضِىَ حُقُبًا ﴿٦٠﴾

61. But when they reached the junction, they forgot (about) their fish, which took its course through the sea (straight) as in a tunnel.

فَلَمَّا بَلَغَا مَجْمَعَ بَيْنِهِمَا نَسِيَا حُوتَهُمَا فَٱتَّخَذَ
سَبِيلَهُۥ فِى ٱلْبَحْرِ سَرَبًا ﴿٦١﴾

62. When they had passed on (some distance), Moses said to his attendant: "Bring us our early meal; truly we have suffered much fatigue at this (stage of) our journey."

فَلَمَّا جَاوَزَا قَالَ لِفَتَىٰهُ ءَاتِنَا غَدَآءَنَا لَقَدْ لَقِينَا
مِن سَفَرِنَا هَٰذَا نَصَبًا ﴿٦٢﴾

63. He replied: "Did you see (what happened) when we went to the rock? I did indeed forget (about) the fish: none but Satan made me forget to tell (you) about it: it took its course through the sea in a marvellous way!"

قَالَ أَرَءَيْتَ إِذْ أَوَيْنَآ إِلَى ٱلصَّخْرَةِ فَإِنِّى نَسِيتُ ٱلْحُوتَ
وَمَآ أَنسَىٰنِيهُ إِلَّا ٱلشَّيْطَٰنُ أَنْ أَذْكُرَهُۥ ۚ وَٱتَّخَذَ
سَبِيلَهُۥ فِى ٱلْبَحْرِ عَجَبًا ﴿٦٣﴾

64. Moses said: "That was what we were seeking after": so they went back on their footsteps, following (the path they had come).

قَالَ ذَٰلِكَ مَا كُنَّا نَبْغِ ۚ فَٱرْتَدَّا عَلَىٰٓ ءَاثَارِهِمَا
قَصَصًا ﴿٦٤﴾

65. So they found one of Our servants, on whom We had bestowed mercy from Ourselves and whom We had taught knowledge from Our own presence.

فَوَجَدَا عَبْدًا مِّنْ عِبَادِنَآ ءَاتَيْنَٰهُ رَحْمَةً مِّنْ عِندِنَا
وَعَلَّمْنَٰهُ مِن لَّدُنَّا عِلْمًا ﴿٦٥﴾

66. Moses said to him: "May I follow you, on the footing that you teach me something of the (higher) truth which you have been taught?"

قَالَ لَهُۥ مُوسَىٰ هَلۡ أَتَّبِعُكَ عَلَىٰٓ أَن تُعَلِّمَنِ مِمَّا
عُلِّمۡتَ رُشۡدٗا ٦٦

67. (The other) said: "Verily you will not be able to have patience with me!

قَالَ إِنَّكَ لَن تَسۡتَطِيعَ مَعِيَ صَبۡرٗا ٦٧

68. And how can you have patience about things about which your understanding is not complete?"

وَكَيۡفَ تَصۡبِرُ عَلَىٰ مَا لَمۡ تُحِطۡ بِهِۦ خُبۡرٗا ٦٨

69. Moses said: "You will find me, if Allah so wills, (truly) patient: nor shall I disobey you in anything."

قَالَ سَتَجِدُنِيٓ إِن شَآءَ ٱللَّهُ صَابِرٗا وَلَآ أَعۡصِي
لَكَ أَمۡرٗا ٦٩

70. The other said: "If then you would follow me, ask me no questions about anything until I myself speak to you concerning it."

قَالَ فَإِنِ ٱتَّبَعۡتَنِي فَلَا تَسۡـَٔلۡنِي عَن شَيۡءٍ حَتَّىٰٓ أُحۡدِثَ
لَكَ مِنۡهُ ذِكۡرٗا ٧٠

71. So they both proceeded; until, when they were in the boat, he scuttled it. Said Moses: "Have you scuttled it in order to drown those in it? Truly a strange thing have you done!"

فَٱنطَلَقَا حَتَّىٰٓ إِذَا رَكِبَا فِي ٱلسَّفِينَةِ خَرَقَهَاۖ قَالَ
أَخَرَقۡتَهَا لِتُغۡرِقَ أَهۡلَهَا لَقَدۡ جِئۡتَ شَيۡـًٔا إِمۡرٗا ٧١

72. He answered: "Did I not tell you that you can have no patience with me?"

قَالَ أَلَمۡ أَقُلۡ إِنَّكَ لَن تَسۡتَطِيعَ مَعِيَ صَبۡرٗا ٧٢

73. Moses said: "Rebuke me not for forgetting, nor grieve me by raising difficulties in my case."

قَالَ لَا تُؤَاخِذۡنِي بِمَا نَسِيتُ وَلَا تُرۡهِقۡنِي مِنۡ
أَمۡرِي عُسۡرٗا ٧٣

74. Then they proceeded; until, when they met a young man, he slew him. Moses said: "Have you slain an innocent person who had slain none? Truly a foul (unheard-of) thing have you done!"

فَٱنطَلَقَا حَتَّىٰٓ إِذَا لَقِيَا غُلَٰمٗا فَقَتَلَهُۥ قَالَ أَقَتَلۡتَ نَفۡسٗا
زَكِيَّةَۢ بِغَيۡرِ نَفۡسٖ لَّقَدۡ جِئۡتَ شَيۡـٔٗا نُّكۡرٗا ٧٤

الجُزْءُ ١٦ الحِزْبُ ٣١

*75. He answered: "Did I not tell you that you can have no patience with me?"

* قَالَ أَلَمْ أَقُل لَّكَ إِنَّكَ لَن تَسْتَطِيعَ مَعِىَ
صَبْرًا ﴿٧٥﴾

76. (Moses) said: "If ever I ask you about anything after this, keep me not in your company: then would you have received (full) excuse from my side."

قَالَ إِن سَأَلْتُكَ عَن شَىْءٍۭ بَعْدَهَا فَلَا تُصَٰحِبْنِى ۖ
قَدْ بَلَغْتَ مِن لَّدُنِّى عُذْرًا ﴿٧٦﴾

77. Then they proceeded until, when they came to the inhabitants of a town, they asked them for food, but they refused them hospitality. They found there a wall on the point of falling down, but he set it up straight. (Moses) said: "If you had wished, surely you could have exacted some recompense for it!"

فَٱنطَلَقَا حَتَّىٰٓ إِذَآ أَتَيَآ أَهْلَ قَرْيَةٍ ٱسْتَطْعَمَآ أَهْلَهَا
فَأَبَوْا۟ أَن يُضَيِّفُوهُمَا فَوَجَدَا فِيهَا جِدَارًا يُرِيدُ
أَن يَنقَضَّ فَأَقَامَهُۥ ۖ قَالَ لَوْ شِئْتَ لَتَّخَذْتَ
عَلَيْهِ أَجْرًا ﴿٧٧﴾

78. He answered: "This is the parting between me and you; now will I tell you the interpretation of (those things) over which you were unable to hold patience.

قَالَ هَٰذَا فِرَاقُ بَيْنِى وَبَيْنِكَ ۚ سَأُنَبِّئُكَ بِتَأْوِيلِ
مَا لَمْ تَسْتَطِع عَّلَيْهِ صَبْرًا ﴿٧٨﴾

79. As for the boat, it belonged to certain men in dire want; they plied on the water, I but wished to render it unserviceable, for there was after them a certain king who seized on every boat by force.

أَمَّا ٱلسَّفِينَةُ فَكَانَتْ لِمَسَٰكِينَ يَعْمَلُونَ فِى
ٱلْبَحْرِ فَأَرَدتُّ أَنْ أَعِيبَهَا وَكَانَ وَرَآءَهُم مَّلِكٌ يَأْخُذُ
كُلَّ سَفِينَةٍ غَصْبًا ﴿٧٩﴾

80. As for the youth, his parents were people of faith, and we feared that he would grieve them by obstinate rebellion and ingratitude (to Allah and man).

وَأَمَّا ٱلْغُلَٰمُ فَكَانَ أَبَوَاهُ مُؤْمِنَيْنِ فَخَشِينَآ أَن
يُرْهِقَهُمَا طُغْيَٰنًا وَكُفْرًا ﴿٨٠﴾

81. So we desired that their Lord would give them in exchange (a son) better in purity (of conduct) and closer in affection.

فَأَرَدْنَآ أَن يُبْدِلَهُمَا رَبُّهُمَا خَيْرًا مِّنْهُ زَكَوٰةً
وَأَقْرَبَ رُحْمًا ﴿٨١﴾

82. As for the wall, it belonged to two youths, orphans, in the town; there was, beneath it, a

وَأَمَّا ٱلْجِدَارُ فَكَانَ لِغُلَٰمَيْنِ يَتِيمَيْنِ فِى ٱلْمَدِينَةِ

* Part-16

buried treasure, to which they were entitled: their father had been a righteous man: so your Lord desired that they should attain their age of full strength and get out their treasure - a mercy (and favour) from your Lord. I did it not of my own accord. Such is the interpretation of (those things) over which you were unable to hold patience."

وَكَانَ تَحْتَهُۥ كَنزٌ لَّهُمَا وَكَانَ أَبُوهُمَا صَٰلِحًا فَأَرَادَ
رَبُّكَ أَن يَبْلُغَآ أَشُدَّهُمَا وَيَسْتَخْرِجَا كَنزَهُمَا
رَحْمَةً مِّن رَّبِّكَ ۚ وَمَا فَعَلْتُهُۥ عَنْ أَمْرِى ۚ ذَٰلِكَ تَأْوِيلُ
مَا لَمْ تَسْطِع عَّلَيْهِ صَبْرًا ﴿٨٢﴾

83. They ask you concerning Dhu al-Qarnayn. Say, "I will rehearse to you something of his story."

وَيَسْـَٔلُونَكَ عَن ذِى ٱلْقَرْنَيْنِ ۖ قُلْ سَأَتْلُوا۟ عَلَيْكُم مِّنْهُ
ذِكْرًا ﴿٨٣﴾

84. Verily We established his power on earth, and We gave him the ways and the means to all ends.

إِنَّا مَكَّنَّا لَهُۥ فِى ٱلْأَرْضِ وَءَاتَيْنَٰهُ مِن كُلِّ شَىْءٍ سَبَبًا ﴿٨٤﴾

85. One (such) way he followed,

فَأَتْبَعَ سَبَبًا ﴿٨٥﴾

86. Until, when he reached the setting of the sun, He found it set in a spring of murky water: near it he found a people; We said: "O Dhu al-Qarnayn! (you have authority) either to punish them, or to treat them with kindness."

حَتَّىٰٓ إِذَا بَلَغَ مَغْرِبَ ٱلشَّمْسِ وَجَدَهَا تَغْرُبُ فِى عَيْنٍ
حَمِئَةٍ وَوَجَدَ عِندَهَا قَوْمًا ۗ قُلْنَا يَٰذَا ٱلْقَرْنَيْنِ إِمَّآ أَن
تُعَذِّبَ وَإِمَّآ أَن تَتَّخِذَ فِيهِمْ حُسْنًا ﴿٨٦﴾

87. He said: "Whoever does wrong, him shall we punish; then shall he be sent back to his Lord; and He will punish him with a punishment unheard-of (before)."

قَالَ أَمَّا مَن ظَلَمَ فَسَوْفَ نُعَذِّبُهُۥ ثُمَّ يُرَدُّ إِلَىٰ رَبِّهِۦ
فَيُعَذِّبُهُۥ عَذَابًا نُّكْرًا ﴿٨٧﴾

88. "But whoever believes, and works righteousness - he shall have a goodly reward, and easy will be his task as we order it by our command."

وَأَمَّا مَنْ ءَامَنَ وَعَمِلَ صَٰلِحًا فَلَهُۥ جَزَآءً ٱلْحُسْنَىٰ ۖ
وَسَنَقُولُ لَهُۥ مِنْ أَمْرِنَا يُسْرًا ﴿٨٨﴾

89. Then followed he (another) way.

ثُمَّ أَتْبَعَ سَبَبًا ﴿٨٩﴾

90. Until, when he came to the rising of the sun, he found it rising on a people for whom We had provided no covering protection against the sun.

حَتَّىٰٓ إِذَا بَلَغَ مَطۡلِعَ ٱلشَّمۡسِ وَجَدَهَا تَطۡلُعُ عَلَىٰ قَوۡمٖ
لَّمۡ نَجۡعَل لَّهُم مِّن دُونِهَا سِتۡرٗا ﴿٩٠﴾

91. (He left them) as they were; We completely understood what was before him.

كَذَٰلِكَۖ وَقَدۡ أَحَطۡنَا بِمَا لَدَيۡهِ خُبۡرٗا ﴿٩١﴾

92. Then followed he (another) way,

ثُمَّ أَتۡبَعَ سَبَبًا ﴿٩٢﴾

93. Until, when he reached (a tract) between two mountains, he found, beneath them, a people who scarcely understood a word.

حَتَّىٰٓ إِذَا بَلَغَ بَيۡنَ ٱلسَّدَّيۡنِ وَجَدَ مِن دُونِهِمَا قَوۡمٗا
لَّا يَكَادُونَ يَفۡقَهُونَ قَوۡلٗا ﴿٩٣﴾

94. They said: "O Dhu al-Qarnayn! The Gog and Magog (people) do great mischief on earth; shall we then render you tribute in order that you might erect a barrier between us and them?"

قَالُواْ يَٰذَا ٱلۡقَرۡنَيۡنِ إِنَّ يَأۡجُوجَ وَمَأۡجُوجَ مُفۡسِدُونَ
فِي ٱلۡأَرۡضِ فَهَلۡ نَجۡعَلُ لَكَ خَرۡجًا عَلَىٰٓ أَن تَجۡعَلَ
بَيۡنَنَا وَبَيۡنَهُمۡ سَدّٗا ﴿٩٤﴾

95. He said: "(The power) in which my Lord has established me is better (than tribute); help me therefore with strength (and labour); I will erect a strong barrier between you and them;

قَالَ مَا مَكَّنِّي فِيهِ رَبِّي خَيۡرٞ فَأَعِينُونِي بِقُوَّةٍ أَجۡعَلۡ بَيۡنَكُمۡ
وَبَيۡنَهُمۡ رَدۡمًا ﴿٩٥﴾

96. Bring me blocks of iron." At length, when he had filled up the space between the two steep mountainsides, he said, "Blow (with your bellows)." Then when he had made it (red) as fire, he said: "Bring me, that I may pour over it, molten lead."

ءَاتُونِي زُبَرَ ٱلۡحَدِيدِۖ حَتَّىٰٓ إِذَا سَاوَىٰ بَيۡنَ ٱلصَّدَفَيۡنِ قَالَ ٱنفُخُواْۖ
حَتَّىٰٓ إِذَا جَعَلَهُۥ نَارٗا قَالَ ءَاتُونِيٓ أُفۡرِغۡ عَلَيۡهِ قِطۡرٗا ﴿٩٦﴾

97. Thus were they made powerless to scale it or to dig through it.

فَمَا ٱسۡطَٰعُوٓاْ أَن يَظۡهَرُوهُ وَمَا ٱسۡتَطَٰعُواْ لَهُۥ نَقۡبٗا ﴿٩٧﴾

98. He said: "This is a mercy from my Lord; but when the promise of my Lord comes to pass, He will make it into dust; and the promise of My Lord is true."

قَالَ هَٰذَا رَحۡمَةٞ مِّن رَّبِّيۖ فَإِذَا جَآءَ وَعۡدُ رَبِّي جَعَلَهُۥ دَكَّآءَۖ
وَكَانَ وَعۡدُ رَبِّي حَقّٗا ﴿٩٨﴾

ربع الحزب ٣١

99. On that day We shall leave them to surge like waves on one another; the trumpet will be blown, and We shall collect them all together.

۞ وَتَرَكْنَا بَعْضَهُمْ يَوْمَئِذٍ يَمُوجُ فِي بَعْضٍ ۖ وَنُفِخَ فِي الصُّورِ
فَجَمَعْنَاهُمْ جَمْعًا ﴿٩٩﴾

100. And We shall present hell that day for unbelievers to see, all spread out -

وَعَرَضْنَا جَهَنَّمَ يَوْمَئِذٍ لِّلْكَافِرِينَ عَرْضًا ﴿١٠٠﴾

101. (Unbelievers) whose eyes had been under a veil from remembrance of Me, and who had been unable even to hear.

الَّذِينَ كَانَتْ أَعْيُنُهُمْ فِي غِطَاءٍ عَن ذِكْرِي وَكَانُوا
لَا يَسْتَطِيعُونَ سَمْعًا ﴿١٠١﴾

102. Do the unbelievers think that they can take My servants as protectors besides Me? Verily We have prepared hell for the unbelievers for (their) entertainment.

أَفَحَسِبَ الَّذِينَ كَفَرُوا أَن يَتَّخِذُوا عِبَادِي مِن دُونِي
أَوْلِيَاءَ ۚ إِنَّا أَعْتَدْنَا جَهَنَّمَ لِلْكَافِرِينَ نُزُلًا ﴿١٠٢﴾

103. Say: "Shall we tell you of those who lose most in respect of their deeds? -

قُلْ هَلْ نُنَبِّئُكُم بِالْأَخْسَرِينَ أَعْمَالًا ﴿١٠٣﴾

104. Those whose efforts have been wasted in this life. While they thought that they were acquiring good by their works?"

الَّذِينَ ضَلَّ سَعْيُهُمْ فِي الْحَيَاةِ الدُّنْيَا وَهُمْ يَحْسَبُونَ أَنَّهُمْ
يُحْسِنُونَ صُنْعًا ﴿١٠٤﴾

105. They are those who deny the signs of their Lord and the fact of their having to meet Him (in the hereafter): vain will be their works, nor shall We, on the day of judgement, give them any weight.

أُولَٰئِكَ الَّذِينَ كَفَرُوا بِآيَاتِ رَبِّهِمْ وَلِقَائِهِ فَحَبِطَتْ
أَعْمَالُهُمْ فَلَا نُقِيمُ لَهُمْ يَوْمَ الْقِيَامَةِ وَزْنًا ﴿١٠٥﴾

106. That is their reward, hell; because they rejected faith, and took My signs and My messengers by way of jest.

ذَٰلِكَ جَزَاؤُهُمْ جَهَنَّمُ بِمَا كَفَرُوا وَاتَّخَذُوا آيَاتِي وَرُسُلِي
هُزُوًا ﴿١٠٦﴾

107. As to those who believe and work righteous deeds, they have, for their entertainment, the gardens of paradise,

إِنَّ الَّذِينَ آمَنُوا وَعَمِلُوا الصَّالِحَاتِ كَانَتْ لَهُمْ جَنَّاتُ
الْفِرْدَوْسِ نُزُلًا ﴿١٠٧﴾

108. In which they shall dwell (forever): no change will they wish for from themselves.

خَالِدِينَ فِيهَا لَا يَبْغُونَ عَنْهَا حِوَلًا ﴿١٠٨﴾

109. Say: "If the ocean were ink (with which to write out) the words of my Lord, sooner would the ocean be exhausted than would the words of my Lord, even if we added another ocean like it, for its aid."

قُل لَّوۡ كَانَ ٱلۡبَحۡرُ مِدَادٗا لِّكَلِمَٰتِ رَبِّي لَنَفِدَ ٱلۡبَحۡرُ قَبۡلَ
أَن تَنفَدَ كَلِمَٰتُ رَبِّي وَلَوۡ جِئۡنَا بِمِثۡلِهِۦ مَدَدٗا ١٠٩

110. Say: "I am but a man like yourselves, (but) the inspiration has come to me, that your God is one God: whoever expects to meet his Lord, let him work righteousness and in the worship of his Lord, admit no one as partner."

قُلۡ إِنَّمَآ أَنَا۠ بَشَرٞ مِّثۡلُكُمۡ يُوحَىٰٓ إِلَيَّ أَنَّمَآ إِلَٰهُكُمۡ إِلَٰهٞ وَٰحِدٞۖ
فَمَن كَانَ يَرۡجُواْ لِقَآءَ رَبِّهِۦ فَلۡيَعۡمَلۡ عَمَلٗا صَٰلِحٗا وَلَا
يُشۡرِكۡ بِعِبَادَةِ رَبِّهِۦٓ أَحَدَۢا ١١٠

سُورَةُ مَرۡيَمَ

Surah 19: ***Maryam*** **(Mary)**

In the name of Allah,
Most Gracious, Most Merciful.

بِسۡمِ ٱللَّهِ ٱلرَّحۡمَٰنِ ٱلرَّحِيمِ

1. *Kaf, Ha, Ya, Ayn, Sad.*

كٓهيعٓصٓ ١

2. (This is) a recital of the mercy of your Lord to His servant Zakariya.

ذِكۡرُ رَحۡمَتِ رَبِّكَ عَبۡدَهُۥ زَكَرِيَّآ ٢

3. See! He called to his Lord in secret,

إِذۡ نَادَىٰ رَبَّهُۥ نِدَآءً خَفِيّٗا ٣

4. Praying: "O my Lord! Infirm indeed are my bones, and the hair of my head does glisten with grey; but never am I unblessed, O my Lord, in my prayer to You!"

قَالَ رَبِّ إِنِّي وَهَنَ ٱلۡعَظۡمُ مِنِّي وَٱشۡتَعَلَ ٱلرَّأۡسُ
شَيۡبٗا وَلَمۡ أَكُنۢ بِدُعَآئِكَ رَبِّ شَقِيّٗا ٤

5. "Now I fear (what) my relatives (and colleagues) (will do) after me: but my wife is barren: so give me an heir as from Yourself -

وَإِنِّي خِفۡتُ ٱلۡمَوَٰلِيَ مِن وَرَآءِي وَكَانَتِ
ٱمۡرَأَتِي عَاقِرٗا فَهَبۡ لِي مِن لَّدُنكَ وَلِيّٗا ٥

6. (One that) will (truly) represent me and represent the posterity of Jacob; and make him, O my Lord! One with whom You are well-pleased!"

يَرِثُنِي وَيَرِثُ مِنۡ ءَالِ يَعۡقُوبَۖ وَٱجۡعَلۡهُ رَبِّ
رَضِيّٗا ٦

7. (His prayer was answered): "O Zakariya! We give you good news of a son; his name shall be Yahya; on none by that name have We conferred distinction before."

يَٰزَكَرِيَّآ إِنَّا نُبَشِّرُكَ بِغُلَٰمٍ ٱسْمُهُۥ يَحْيَىٰ
لَمْ نَجْعَل لَّهُۥ مِن قَبْلُ سَمِيًّا ٧

8. He said: "O my Lord! How shall I have a son, when my wife is barren and I have grown quite infirm from old age?"

قَالَ رَبِّ أَنَّىٰ يَكُونُ لِى غُلَٰمٌ وَكَانَتِ ٱمْرَأَتِى
عَاقِرًا وَقَدْ بَلَغْتُ مِنَ ٱلْكِبَرِ عِتِيًّا ٨

9. He said: "So (it will be): your Lord said, 'That is easy for Me: I did indeed create you before when you had been nothing!'"

قَالَ كَذَٰلِكَ قَالَ رَبُّكَ هُوَ عَلَىَّ هَيِّنٌ وَقَدْ
خَلَقْتُكَ مِن قَبْلُ وَلَمْ تَكُ شَيْـًٔا ٩

10. (Zakariya) said, "O my Lord! Give me a sign." "Your sign," was the answer, "shall be that you shall speak to no man for three nights, although you are not dumb."

قَالَ رَبِّ ٱجْعَل لِّىٓ ءَايَةً ۚ قَالَ ءَايَتُكَ أَلَّا
تُكَلِّمَ ٱلنَّاسَ ثَلَٰثَ لَيَالٍ سَوِيًّا ١٠

11. So Zakariya came out to his people from his chamber; he told them by signs to celebrate Allah's praises in the morning and in the evening.

فَخَرَجَ عَلَىٰ قَوْمِهِۦ مِنَ ٱلْمِحْرَابِ فَأَوْحَىٰٓ إِلَيْهِمْ أَن
سَبِّحُوا۟ بُكْرَةً وَعَشِيًّا ١١

12. (To his son came the command): "O Yahya! Take hold of the book with might": and We gave him wisdom even as a youth.

يَٰيَحْيَىٰ خُذِ ٱلْكِتَٰبَ بِقُوَّةٍ ۖ وَءَاتَيْنَٰهُ ٱلْحُكْمَ
صَبِيًّا ١٢

13. And pity (for all creatures) as from Us, and purity: he was devout,

وَحَنَانًا مِّن لَّدُنَّا وَزَكَوٰةً ۖ وَكَانَ تَقِيًّا ١٣

14. And kind to his parents, and he was not overbearing or rebellious.

وَبَرًّۢا بِوَٰلِدَيْهِ وَلَمْ يَكُن جَبَّارًا عَصِيًّا ١٤

15. So peace on him the day he was born, the day that he dies, and the day that he will be raised up to life (again)!

وَسَلَٰمٌ عَلَيْهِ يَوْمَ وُلِدَ وَيَوْمَ يَمُوتُ وَيَوْمَ
يُبْعَثُ حَيًّا ١٥

16. Relate in the book (the story of) Mary, when she withdrew from her family to a place in the east.

وَٱذْكُرْ فِى ٱلْكِتَٰبِ مَرْيَمَ إِذِ ٱنتَبَذَتْ مِنْ أَهْلِهَا
مَكَانًا شَرْقِيًّا ١٦

17. She placed a screen (to screen herself) from them: then We sent to her Our angel, and he appeared before her as a man in all respects.

فَٱتَّخَذَتۡ مِن دُونِهِمۡ حِجَابٗا فَأَرۡسَلۡنَآ إِلَيۡهَا
رُوحَنَا فَتَمَثَّلَ لَهَا بَشَرٗا سَوِيّٗا ١٧

18. She said: "I seek refuge from you to (Allah) Most Gracious: (come not near) if you do fear Allah."

قَالَتۡ إِنِّيٓ أَعُوذُ بِٱلرَّحۡمَٰنِ مِنكَ إِن كُنتَ تَقِيّٗا ١٨

19. He said: "Nay, I am only a messenger from your Lord, (to announce) to you the gift of a holy son."

قَالَ إِنَّمَآ أَنَا۠ رَسُولُ رَبِّكِ لِأَهَبَ لَكِ غُلَٰمٗا
زَكِيّٗا ١٩

20. She said: "How shall I have a son, seeing that no man has touched me, and I am not unchaste?"

قَالَتۡ أَنَّىٰ يَكُونُ لِي غُلَٰمٞ وَلَمۡ يَمۡسَسۡنِي بَشَرٞ وَلَمۡ
أَكُ بَغِيّٗا ٢٠

21. He said: "So (it will be); your Lord says, 'That is easy for Me: and (We wish) to appoint him as a Sign to men and a mercy from Us'; it is a matter (so) decreed."

قَالَ كَذَٰلِكِ قَالَ رَبُّكِ هُوَ عَلَيَّ هَيِّنٞۖ
وَلِنَجۡعَلَهُۥٓ ءَايَةٗ لِّلنَّاسِ وَرَحۡمَةٗ مِّنَّاۚ وَكَانَ
أَمۡرٗا مَّقۡضِيّٗا ٢١

22. So she conceived him, and she retired with him to a remote place.

نصف الحزب ٣١ ۞فَحَمَلَتۡهُ فَٱنتَبَذَتۡ بِهِۦ مَكَانٗا قَصِيّٗا ٢٢

23. And the pains of childbirth drove her to the trunk of a palm-tree; she cried (in her anguish): "Ah! Would that I had died before this! Would that I had been a thing forgotten and out of sight!"

فَأَجَآءَهَا ٱلۡمَخَاضُ إِلَىٰ جِذۡعِ ٱلنَّخۡلَةِ قَالَتۡ
يَٰلَيۡتَنِي مِتُّ قَبۡلَ هَٰذَا وَكُنتُ نَسۡيٗا مَّنسِيّٗا ٢٣

24. But (a voice) called to her from beneath the (palm tree): "Grieve not! For your Lord has provided a rivulet beneath you;

فَنَادَىٰهَا مِن تَحۡتِهَآ أَلَّا تَحۡزَنِي قَدۡ جَعَلَ رَبُّكِ
تَحۡتَكِ سَرِيّٗا ٢٤

25. And shake towards yourself the trunk of the palm tree; it will let fall fresh ripe dates upon you.

وَهُزِّيٓ إِلَيۡكِ بِجِذۡعِ ٱلنَّخۡلَةِ تُسَٰقِطۡ عَلَيۡكِ رُطَبٗا
جَنِيّٗا ٢٥

26. So eat and drink and cool (your) eye. And if you do see any man, say, 'I have vowed a fast to (Allah) Most Gracious, and this day will I enter into no talk with any human being.'"

فَكُلِي وَٱشْرَبِي وَقَرِّي عَيْنًا ۖ فَإِمَّا تَرَيِنَّ مِنَ ٱلْبَشَرِ
أَحَدًا فَقُولِىٓ إِنِّى نَذَرْتُ لِلرَّحْمَٰنِ صَوْمًا فَلَنْ أُكَلِّمَ
ٱلْيَوْمَ إِنسِيًّا ﴿٢٦﴾

27. At length she brought the (babe) to her people, carrying him (in her arms). They said: "O Mary! Truly an amazing thing have you brought!

فَأَتَتْ بِهِۦ قَوْمَهَا تَحْمِلُهُۥ ۖ قَالُوا۟ يَٰمَرْيَمُ لَقَدْ جِئْتِ
شَيْـًٔا فَرِيًّا ﴿٢٧﴾

28. O sister of Aaron! Your father was not a man of evil, nor your mother a woman unchaste!"

يَٰٓأُخْتَ هَٰرُونَ مَا كَانَ أَبُوكِ ٱمْرَأَ سَوْءٍ وَمَا
كَانَتْ أُمُّكِ بَغِيًّا ﴿٢٨﴾

29. But she pointed to the babe. They said: "How can we talk to one who is a child in the cradle?"

فَأَشَارَتْ إِلَيْهِ ۖ قَالُوا۟ كَيْفَ نُكَلِّمُ مَن كَانَ فِى
ٱلْمَهْدِ صَبِيًّا ﴿٢٩﴾

30. He said: "I am indeed a servant of Allah; He has given me revelation and made me a prophet;

قَالَ إِنِّى عَبْدُ ٱللَّهِ ءَاتَىٰنِىَ ٱلْكِتَٰبَ وَجَعَلَنِى نَبِيًّا ﴿٣٠﴾

31. And He has made me blessed wheresoever I be, and has enjoined on me prayer and charity as long as I live."

وَجَعَلَنِى مُبَارَكًا أَيْنَ مَا كُنتُ وَأَوْصَٰنِى بِٱلصَّلَوٰةِ
وَٱلزَّكَوٰةِ مَا دُمْتُ حَيًّا ﴿٣١﴾

32. "(He) has made me kind to my mother, and not overbearing or miserable."

وَبَرًّۢا بِوَٰلِدَتِى وَلَمْ يَجْعَلْنِى جَبَّارًا شَقِيًّا ﴿٣٢﴾

33. "So peace is on me the day I was born, the day that I die, and the day that I shall be raised up to life (again)"!

وَٱلسَّلَٰمُ عَلَىَّ يَوْمَ وُلِدتُّ وَيَوْمَ أَمُوتُ وَيَوْمَ
أُبْعَثُ حَيًّا ﴿٣٣﴾

34. Such (was) Jesus the son of Mary; (it is) a statement of truth, about which they (vainly) dispute.

ذَٰلِكَ عِيسَى ٱبْنُ مَرْيَمَ ۖ قَوْلَ ٱلْحَقِّ ٱلَّذِى فِيهِ
يَمْتَرُونَ ﴿٣٤﴾

35. It is not befitting to (the majesty of) Allah that He should beget a son. Glory be to Him! When He determines a matter, He only says to it, "Be," and it is.

مَا كَانَ لِلَّهِ أَن يَتَّخِذَ مِن وَلَدٍ ۖ سُبْحَٰنَهُۥٓ ۚ إِذَا قَضَىٰٓ أَمْرًا
فَإِنَّمَا يَقُولُ لَهُۥ كُن فَيَكُونُ ﴿٣٥﴾

36. Verily Allah is my Lord and your Lord; Him therefore serve you; this is a way that is straight.

وَإِنَّ ٱللَّهَ رَبِّى وَرَبُّكُمْ فَٱعْبُدُوهُ ۚ هَٰذَا صِرَٰطٌ مُّسْتَقِيمٌ ﴿٣٦﴾

37. But the sects differ among themselves and woe to the unbelievers because of the (coming) judgement of a momentous day!

فَٱخْتَلَفَ ٱلْأَحْزَابُ مِنۢ بَيْنِهِمْ ۖ فَوَيْلٌ لِّلَّذِينَ كَفَرُوا۟
مِن مَّشْهَدِ يَوْمٍ عَظِيمٍ ﴿٣٧﴾

38. How plainly will they see and hear, the day that they will appear before Us! But the unjust today are in error manifest!

أَسْمِعْ بِهِمْ وَأَبْصِرْ يَوْمَ يَأْتُونَنَا ۖ لَٰكِنِ ٱلظَّٰلِمُونَ ٱلْيَوْمَ
فِى ضَلَٰلٍ مُّبِينٍ ﴿٣٨﴾

39. But warn them of the day of distress, when the matter will be determined: for (see,) they are negligent and they do not believe!

وَأَنذِرْهُمْ يَوْمَ ٱلْحَسْرَةِ إِذْ قُضِىَ ٱلْأَمْرُ وَهُمْ فِى غَفْلَةٍ
وَهُمْ لَا يُؤْمِنُونَ ﴿٣٩﴾

40. It is We Who will inherit the earth, and all beings thereon: to Us will they all be returned.

إِنَّا نَحْنُ نَرِثُ ٱلْأَرْضَ وَمَنْ عَلَيْهَا وَإِلَيْنَا يُرْجَعُونَ ﴿٤٠﴾

41. (Also) mention in the book (the story of) Abraham: he was a man of truth, a prophet.

وَٱذْكُرْ فِى ٱلْكِتَٰبِ إِبْرَٰهِيمَ ۚ إِنَّهُۥ كَانَ صِدِّيقًا نَّبِيًّا ﴿٤١﴾

42. See, he said to his father: "O my father! Why worship that which hears not and sees not and can profit you nothing?"

إِذْ قَالَ لِأَبِيهِ يَٰٓأَبَتِ لِمَ تَعْبُدُ مَا لَا يَسْمَعُ وَلَا يُبْصِرُ
وَلَا يُغْنِى عَنكَ شَيْـًٔا ﴿٤٢﴾

43. "O my father! To me has come knowledge which has not reached you: so follow me; I will guide you to a way that is even and straight."

يَٰٓأَبَتِ إِنِّى قَدْ جَآءَنِى مِنَ ٱلْعِلْمِ مَا لَمْ يَأْتِكَ فَٱتَّبِعْنِىٓ
أَهْدِكَ صِرَٰطًا سَوِيًّا ﴿٤٣﴾

44. "O my father! Serve not Satan: for Satan is a rebel against (Allah) Most Gracious."

يَٰٓأَبَتِ لَا تَعْبُدِ ٱلشَّيْطَٰنَ ۖ إِنَّ ٱلشَّيْطَٰنَ كَانَ لِلرَّحْمَٰنِ
عَصِيًّا ﴿٤٤﴾

45. "O my father! I fear lest a penalty afflict you from (Allah) Most Gracious, so that you become to Satan a friend."

يَٰٓأَبَتِ إِنِّيٓ أَخَافُ أَن يَمَسَّكَ عَذَابٞ مِّنَ ٱلرَّحۡمَٰنِ
فَتَكُونَ لِلشَّيۡطَٰنِ وَلِيّٗا ٤٥

46. (The father) replied: "Do you hate my gods, O Abraham? If you forbear not, I will indeed stone you; now get away from me for a good long while!"

قَالَ أَرَاغِبٌ أَنتَ عَنۡ ءَالِهَتِي يَٰٓإِبۡرَٰهِيمُۖ لَئِن لَّمۡ
تَنتَهِ لَأَرۡجُمَنَّكَۖ وَٱهۡجُرۡنِي مَلِيّٗا ٤٦

47. Abraham said: "Peace be on you; I will pray to my Lord for your forgiveness: for He is to me Most Gracious."

قَالَ سَلَٰمٌ عَلَيۡكَۖ سَأَسۡتَغۡفِرُ لَكَ رَبِّيٓۖ إِنَّهُۥ كَانَ
بِي حَفِيّٗا ٤٧

48. "And I will turn away from you (all) and from those whom you invoke besides Allah; I will call on my Lord; perhaps, by my prayer to my Lord, I shall be not unblessed!"

وَأَعۡتَزِلُكُمۡ وَمَا تَدۡعُونَ مِن دُونِ ٱللَّهِ وَأَدۡعُواْ رَبِّي
عَسَىٰٓ أَلَّآ أَكُونَ بِدُعَآءِ رَبِّي شَقِيّٗا ٤٨

49. When he had turned away from them and from those whom they worshipped besides Allah, We bestowed on him Isaac and Jacob, and each one of them We made a prophet.

فَلَمَّا ٱعۡتَزَلَهُمۡ وَمَا يَعۡبُدُونَ مِن دُونِ ٱللَّهِ وَهَبۡنَا لَهُۥٓ
إِسۡحَٰقَ وَيَعۡقُوبَۖ وَكُلّٗا جَعَلۡنَا نَبِيّٗا ٤٩

50. And We bestowed of Our mercy on them, and We granted them lofty honour on the tongue of truth.

وَوَهَبۡنَا لَهُم مِّن رَّحۡمَتِنَا وَجَعَلۡنَا لَهُمۡ لِسَانَ
صِدۡقٍ عَلِيّٗا ٥٠

51. Also mention in the book (the story of) Moses: for he was specially chosen, and he was a messenger (and) a prophet.

وَٱذۡكُرۡ فِي ٱلۡكِتَٰبِ مُوسَىٰٓۚ إِنَّهُۥ كَانَ مُخۡلَصٗا وَكَانَ
رَسُولٗا نَّبِيّٗا ٥١

52. And We called him from the right side of mount (Sinai), and made him draw near to Us, for mystic (converse).

وَنَٰدَيۡنَٰهُ مِن جَانِبِ ٱلطُّورِ ٱلۡأَيۡمَنِ وَقَرَّبۡنَٰهُ نَجِيّٗا ٥٢

53. And, out of Our mercy, We gave him his brother Aaron, (also) a prophet.

وَوَهَبۡنَا لَهُۥ مِن رَّحۡمَتِنَآ أَخَاهُ هَٰرُونَ نَبِيّٗا ٥٣

54. Also mention in the book (the story of) Ishmael: He was (strictly) true to what

وَٱذۡكُرۡ فِي ٱلۡكِتَٰبِ إِسۡمَٰعِيلَۚ إِنَّهُۥ كَانَ صَادِقَ ٱلۡوَعۡدِ

he promised, and he was a messenger (and) a prophet.

وَكَانَ رَسُولٗا نَّبِيّٗا ٥٤

55. He used to enjoin on his people prayer and charity, and he was most acceptable in the sight of his Lord.

وَكَانَ يَأۡمُرُ أَهۡلَهُۥ بِٱلصَّلَوٰةِ وَٱلزَّكَوٰةِ وَكَانَ عِندَ رَبِّهِۦ
مَرۡضِيّٗا ٥٥

56. Also mention in the book the case of Idris: he was a man of truth (and sincerity), (and) a prophet:

وَٱذۡكُرۡ فِي ٱلۡكِتَٰبِ إِدۡرِيسَۚ إِنَّهُۥ كَانَ صِدِّيقٗا نَّبِيّٗا ٥٦

57. And We raised him to a lofty station.

وَرَفَعۡنَٰهُ مَكَانًا عَلِيًّا ٥٧

58. Those were some of the prophets on whom Allah did bestow His grace - of the posterity of Adam, and of those whom We carried (in the ark) with Noah, and of the posterity of Abraham and Israel - of those whom We guided and chose; whenever the signs of (Allah) Most Gracious were rehearsed to them, they would fall down in prostrate adoration and in tears.

أُوْلَٰٓئِكَ ٱلَّذِينَ أَنۡعَمَ ٱللَّهُ عَلَيۡهِم مِّنَ ٱلنَّبِيِّـۧنَ مِن ذُرِّيَّةِ
ءَادَمَ وَمِمَّنۡ حَمَلۡنَا مَعَ نُوحٖ وَمِن ذُرِّيَّةِ إِبۡرَٰهِيمَ وَإِسۡرَٰٓءِيلَ
وَمِمَّنۡ هَدَيۡنَا وَٱجۡتَبَيۡنَآۚ إِذَا تُتۡلَىٰ عَلَيۡهِمۡ ءَايَٰتُ ٱلرَّحۡمَٰنِ
سجدة خَرُّواْۤ سُجَّدٗاۤ وَبُكِيّٗا۩ ٥٨

59. But after them there followed a posterity who missed prayers and followed after lusts; soon, then, will they face destruction -

ثلاثة أرباع الحزب ٣١ ۞فَخَلَفَ مِنۢ بَعۡدِهِمۡ خَلۡفٌ أَضَاعُواْ ٱلصَّلَوٰةَ وَٱتَّبَعُواْ
ٱلشَّهَوَٰتِۖ فَسَوۡفَ يَلۡقَوۡنَ غَيًّا ٥٩

60. Except those who repent and believe, and work righteousness; for these will enter the garden and will not be wronged in the least -

إِلَّا مَن تَابَ وَءَامَنَ وَعَمِلَ صَٰلِحٗا فَأُوْلَٰٓئِكَ يَدۡخُلُونَ
ٱلۡجَنَّةَ وَلَا يُظۡلَمُونَ شَيۡـٔٗا ٦٠

61. Gardens of eternity, those which (Allah) Most Gracious has promised to His servants in the unseen; for His promise must (necessarily) come to pass.

جَنَّٰتِ عَدۡنٍ ٱلَّتِي وَعَدَ ٱلرَّحۡمَٰنُ عِبَادَهُۥ بِٱلۡغَيۡبِۚ إِنَّهُۥ
كَانَ وَعۡدُهُۥ مَأۡتِيّٗا ٦١

62. They will not there hear any vain discourse, but only salutations of peace and they will have in it their sustenance, morning and evening.

لَّا يَسۡمَعُونَ فِيهَا لَغۡوًا إِلَّا سَلَٰمٗاۖ وَلَهُمۡ رِزۡقُهُمۡ
فِيهَا بُكۡرَةٗ وَعَشِيّٗا ٦٢

63. Such is the garden which We give as an inheritance to those of Our servants who guard against evil.

تِلْكَ ٱلْجَنَّةُ ٱلَّتِى نُورِثُ مِنْ عِبَادِنَا مَن كَانَ تَقِيًّا ﴿٦٣﴾

64. (The angels say:) "We descend not but by command of your Lord; to Him belongs what is before us, and what is behind us, and what is between; and your Lord never does forget" -

وَمَا نَتَنَزَّلُ إِلَّا بِأَمْرِ رَبِّكَ ۖ لَهُۥ مَا بَيْنَ أَيْدِينَا وَمَا خَلْفَنَا
وَمَا بَيْنَ ذَٰلِكَ ۚ وَمَا كَانَ رَبُّكَ نَسِيًّا ﴿٦٤﴾

65. "Lord of the heavens and of the earth, and of all that is between them; so worship Him, and be constant and patient in His worship; know you of any who is worthy of the same name as He?"

رَّبُّ ٱلسَّمَٰوَٰتِ وَٱلْأَرْضِ وَمَا بَيْنَهُمَا فَٱعْبُدْهُ
وَٱصْطَبِرْ لِعِبَٰدَتِهِۦ ۚ هَلْ تَعْلَمُ لَهُۥ سَمِيًّا ﴿٦٥﴾

66. Man says: "What! When I am dead, shall I then be raised up alive?"

وَيَقُولُ ٱلْإِنسَٰنُ أَءِذَا مَا مِتُّ لَسَوْفَ أُخْرَجُ حَيًّا ﴿٦٦﴾

67. But does not man call to mind that We created him before out of nothing?

أَوَلَا يَذْكُرُ ٱلْإِنسَٰنُ أَنَّا خَلَقْنَٰهُ مِن قَبْلُ
وَلَمْ يَكُ شَيْـًٔا ﴿٦٧﴾

68. So, by your Lord, without doubt, We shall gather them together, and (also) the evil ones (with them); then shall We bring them forth on their knees round about hell;

فَوَرَبِّكَ لَنَحْشُرَنَّهُمْ وَٱلشَّيَٰطِينَ ثُمَّ
لَنُحْضِرَنَّهُمْ حَوْلَ جَهَنَّمَ جِثِيًّا ﴿٦٨﴾

69. Then shall We certainly drag out from every sect all those who were worst in obstinate rebellion against (Allah) Most Gracious.

ثُمَّ لَنَنزِعَنَّ مِن كُلِّ شِيعَةٍ أَيُّهُمْ أَشَدُّ عَلَى
ٱلرَّحْمَٰنِ عِتِيًّا ﴿٦٩﴾

70. And certainly We know best those who are most worthy of being burned in it.

ثُمَّ لَنَحْنُ أَعْلَمُ بِٱلَّذِينَ هُمْ أَوْلَىٰ بِهَا صِلِيًّا ﴿٧٠﴾

71. Not one of you but will pass over it; this is, with your Lord, a decree which must be accomplished.

وَإِن مِّنكُمْ إِلَّا وَارِدُهَا ۚ كَانَ عَلَىٰ رَبِّكَ حَتْمًا
مَّقْضِيًّا ﴿٧١﴾

72. But We shall save those who guarded against evil, and We shall leave the

ثُمَّ نُنَجِّى ٱلَّذِينَ ٱتَّقَوا۟ وَّنَذَرُ ٱلظَّٰلِمِينَ فِيهَا

wrongdoers in it, (humbled) to their knees.

جِثِيًّا ﴿٧٢﴾

73. When Our clear signs are rehearsed to them, the unbelievers say to who believe, "Which of the two sides is best in point of position? Which makes the best show in council?"

وَإِذَا تُتْلَىٰ عَلَيْهِمْ ءَايَٰتُنَا بَيِّنَٰتٍ قَالَ ٱلَّذِينَ كَفَرُوا۟ لِلَّذِينَ
ءَامَنُوٓا۟ أَىُّ ٱلْفَرِيقَيْنِ خَيْرٌ مَّقَامًا وَأَحْسَنُ نَدِيًّا ﴿٧٣﴾

74. But how many (countless) generations before them have We destroyed, who were even better in equipment and in glitter to the eye?

وَكَمْ أَهْلَكْنَا قَبْلَهُم مِّن قَرْنٍ هُمْ أَحْسَنُ أَثَٰثًا
وَرِءْيًا ﴿٧٤﴾

75. Say: "If any men go astray, (Allah) Most Gracious extends (the rope) to them. Until, when they see the warning of Allah (being fulfilled) - either in punishment or in (the approach of) the hour - they will at length realise who is worst in position, and (who) weakest in forces!"

قُلْ مَن كَانَ فِى ٱلضَّلَٰلَةِ فَلْيَمْدُدْ لَهُ ٱلرَّحْمَٰنُ مَدًّا ۚ
حَتَّىٰٓ إِذَا رَأَوْا۟ مَا يُوعَدُونَ إِمَّا ٱلْعَذَابَ وَإِمَّا ٱلسَّاعَةَ
فَسَيَعْلَمُونَ مَنْ هُوَ شَرٌّ مَّكَانًا وَأَضْعَفُ جُندًا ﴿٧٥﴾

76. "And Allah does advance in guidance those who seek guidance; and the things that endure, good deeds, are best in the sight of your Lord, as rewards, and best in respect of (their) eventual returns."

وَيَزِيدُ ٱللَّهُ ٱلَّذِينَ ٱهْتَدَوْا۟ هُدًى ۗ وَٱلْبَٰقِيَٰتُ
ٱلصَّٰلِحَٰتُ خَيْرٌ عِندَ رَبِّكَ ثَوَابًا وَخَيْرٌ مَّرَدًّا ﴿٧٦﴾

77. Have you then seen the (sort of) man who rejects Our signs, yet says: "I shall certainly be given wealth and children?"

أَفَرَءَيْتَ ٱلَّذِى كَفَرَ بِـَٔايَٰتِنَا وَقَالَ لَأُوتَيَنَّ
مَالًا وَوَلَدًا ﴿٧٧﴾

78. Has he penetrated to the unseen, or has he taken a contract with (Allah) Most Gracious?

أَطَّلَعَ ٱلْغَيْبَ أَمِ ٱتَّخَذَ عِندَ ٱلرَّحْمَٰنِ عَهْدًا ﴿٧٨﴾

79. Nay! We shall record what he says, and We shall add and add to his punishment.

كَلَّا ۚ سَنَكْتُبُ مَا يَقُولُ وَنَمُدُّ لَهُۥ مِنَ
ٱلْعَذَابِ مَدًّا ﴿٧٩﴾

80. To Us shall return all that he talks of, and he shall appear before Us bare and alone.

وَنَرِثُهُۥ مَا يَقُولُ وَيَأْتِينَا فَرْدًا ﴿٨٠﴾

81. And they have taken (for worship) gods other than Allah to give them power and glory!

وَٱتَّخَذُوا۟ مِن دُونِ ٱللَّهِ ءَالِهَةً لِّيَكُونُوا۟
لَهُمْ عِزًّا ﴿٨١﴾

82. Instead, they shall reject their worship, and become adversaries against them.

كَلَّا ۚ سَيَكْفُرُونَ بِعِبَادَتِهِمْ وَيَكُونُونَ عَلَيْهِمْ
ضِدًّا ﴿٨٢﴾

83. Do you not see that We have set the evil ones on against the unbelievers, to incite them with fury?

أَلَمْ تَرَ أَنَّآ أَرْسَلْنَا ٱلشَّيَٰطِينَ عَلَى ٱلْكَٰفِرِينَ
تَؤُزُّهُمْ أَزًّا ﴿٨٣﴾

84. So make no haste against them, for We but count out to them a (limited) number (of days).

فَلَا تَعْجَلْ عَلَيْهِمْ ۖ إِنَّمَا نَعُدُّ لَهُمْ عَدًّا ﴿٨٤﴾

85. The day We shall gather the righteous to (Allah) Most Gracious, like a band presented before a king for honours.

يَوْمَ نَحْشُرُ ٱلْمُتَّقِينَ إِلَى ٱلرَّحْمَٰنِ وَفْدًا ﴿٨٥﴾

86. And We shall drive the sinners to hell, like thirsty cattle driven down to water -

وَنَسُوقُ ٱلْمُجْرِمِينَ إِلَىٰ جَهَنَّمَ وِرْدًا ﴿٨٦﴾

87. None shall have the power of intercession, but such a one as has received permission (or promise) from (Allah) Most Gracious.

لَّا يَمْلِكُونَ ٱلشَّفَٰعَةَ إِلَّا مَنِ ٱتَّخَذَ عِندَ ٱلرَّحْمَٰنِ
عَهْدًا ﴿٨٧﴾

88. They say: "(Allah) Most Gracious has begotten a son!"

وَقَالُوا۟ ٱتَّخَذَ ٱلرَّحْمَٰنُ وَلَدًا ﴿٨٨﴾

89. Indeed you have put forward a thing most monstrous!

لَّقَدْ جِئْتُمْ شَيْـًٔا إِدًّا ﴿٨٩﴾

90. As if the skies are ready to burst, the earth to split apart, and the mountains to fall down in utter ruin.

تَكَادُ ٱلسَّمَٰوَٰتُ يَتَفَطَّرْنَ مِنْهُ وَتَنشَقُّ
ٱلْأَرْضُ وَتَخِرُّ ٱلْجِبَالُ هَدًّا ﴿٩٠﴾

91. That they should invoke a son for (Allah) Most Gracious.

أَن دَعَوْا۟ لِلرَّحْمَـٰنِ وَلَدًا ﴿٩١﴾

92. For it is not consonant with the majesty of (Allah) Most Gracious that He should beget a son.

وَمَا يَنۢبَغِى لِلرَّحْمَـٰنِ أَن يَتَّخِذَ وَلَدًا ﴿٩٢﴾

93. Not one of the beings in the heavens and the earth but must come to (Allah) Most Gracious as a servant.

إِن كُلُّ مَن فِى ٱلسَّمَـٰوَٰتِ وَٱلْأَرْضِ إِلَّآ ءَاتِى
ٱلرَّحْمَـٰنِ عَبْدًا ﴿٩٣﴾

94. He does take an account of them (all), and has numbered them (all) exactly.

لَّقَدْ أَحْصَىٰهُمْ وَعَدَّهُمْ عَدًّا ﴿٩٤﴾

95. And every one of them will come to him singly on the day of judgement.

وَكُلُّهُمْ ءَاتِيهِ يَوْمَ ٱلْقِيَـٰمَةِ فَرْدًا ﴿٩٥﴾

96. On those who believe and work deeds of righteousness, will (Allah) Most Gracious bestow love.

إِنَّ ٱلَّذِينَ ءَامَنُوا۟ وَعَمِلُوا۟ ٱلصَّـٰلِحَـٰتِ
سَيَجْعَلُ لَهُمُ ٱلرَّحْمَـٰنُ وُدًّا ﴿٩٦﴾

97. So have We made the (Qur'an) easy in your own tongue, that with it you may give glad tidings to the righteous, and warnings to people given to contention.

فَإِنَّمَا يَسَّرْنَـٰهُ بِلِسَانِكَ لِتُبَشِّرَ بِهِ
ٱلْمُتَّقِينَ وَتُنذِرَ بِهِۦ قَوْمًا لُّدًّا ﴿٩٧﴾

98. But how many (countless) generation before them have We destroyed? Can you find a single one of them (now) or hear (so much as) a whisper of them?

وَكَمْ أَهْلَكْنَا قَبْلَهُم مِّن قَرْنٍ هَلْ تُحِسُّ مِنْهُم
مِّنْ أَحَدٍ أَوْ تَسْمَعُ لَهُمْ رِكْزًۢا ﴿٩٨﴾

سُورَةُ طه

Surah 20: ***Ta-Ha***

In the name of Allah,
Most Gracious, Most Merciful.

بِسْمِ ٱللَّهِ ٱلرَّحْمَـٰنِ ٱلرَّحِيمِ

1. *Ta Ha.*

طه ﴿١﴾ الحزب ٣٢

2. We have not sent down the Qur'an to you to be (an occasion) for your distress,

مَآ أَنزَلۡنَا عَلَيۡكَ ٱلۡقُرۡءَانَ لِتَشۡقَىٰٓ ٢

3. But only as an admonition to those who fear (Allah) -

إِلَّا تَذۡكِرَةٗ لِّمَن يَخۡشَىٰ ٣

4. A revelation from Him Who created the earth and the heavens on high.

تَنزِيلٗا مِّمَّنۡ خَلَقَ ٱلۡأَرۡضَ وَٱلسَّمَٰوَٰتِ ٱلۡعُلَى ٤

5. (Allah) Most Gracious is firmly established on the throne (of authority).

ٱلرَّحۡمَٰنُ عَلَى ٱلۡعَرۡشِ ٱسۡتَوَىٰ ٥

6. To Him belongs what is in the heavens and on earth, and all between them, and all beneath the soil.

لَهُۥ مَا فِي ٱلسَّمَٰوَٰتِ وَمَا فِي ٱلۡأَرۡضِ وَمَا بَيۡنَهُمَا
وَمَا تَحۡتَ ٱلثَّرَىٰ ٦

7. If you pronounce the word aloud, (it is no matter); for verily He knows what is secret and what is yet more hidden.

وَإِن تَجۡهَرۡ بِٱلۡقَوۡلِ فَإِنَّهُۥ يَعۡلَمُ ٱلسِّرَّ وَأَخۡفَى ٧

8. Allah! There is no god but He! To Him belong the most beautiful names.

ٱللَّهُ لَآ إِلَٰهَ إِلَّا هُوَۖ لَهُ ٱلۡأَسۡمَآءُ ٱلۡحُسۡنَىٰ ٨

9. Has the story of Moses reached you?

وَهَلۡ أَتَىٰكَ حَدِيثُ مُوسَىٰٓ ٩

10. See, he saw a fire: so he said to his family, "stay you; I perceive a fire; perhaps I can bring you some burning brand from it, or find some guidance at the fire."

إِذۡ رَءَا نَارٗا فَقَالَ لِأَهۡلِهِ ٱمۡكُثُوٓاْ إِنِّيٓ ءَانَسۡتُ نَارٗا
لَّعَلِّيٓ ءَاتِيكُم مِّنۡهَا بِقَبَسٍ أَوۡ أَجِدُ عَلَى ٱلنَّارِ هُدٗى ١٠

11. But when he came to the fire, a voice was heard: "O Moses!"

فَلَمَّآ أَتَىٰهَا نُودِيَ يَٰمُوسَىٰٓ ١١

12. "Verily I am your Lord! Therefore, (in My presence) put off your shoes; you are in the sacred valley Tuwa."

إِنِّيٓ أَنَا۠ رَبُّكَ فَٱخۡلَعۡ نَعۡلَيۡكَ إِنَّكَ بِٱلۡوَادِ
ٱلۡمُقَدَّسِ طُوٗى ١٢

13. "I have chosen you: listen, then to the inspiration (sent to you)."

وَأَنَا ٱخۡتَرۡتُكَ فَٱسۡتَمِعۡ لِمَا يُوحَىٰٓ ١٣

14. "Verily, I am Allah: there is no god but I; so serve you Me (only), and establish regular prayer for celebrating My praise."

إِنَّنِيٓ أَنَا ٱللَّهُ لَآ إِلَٰهَ إِلَّآ أَنَا۠ فَٱعْبُدْنِي وَأَقِمِ ٱلصَّلَوٰةَ
لِذِكْرِيٓ ١٤

15. "Verily the hour is coming - My design is to keep it hidden - for every soul to receive its reward by the measure of its endeavour."

إِنَّ ٱلسَّاعَةَ ءَاتِيَةٌ أَكَادُ أُخْفِيهَا لِتُجْزَىٰ كُلُّ
نَفْسِۭ بِمَا تَسْعَىٰ ١٥

16. "Therefore, let not such as believe not in it but follow their own lusts, divert you from it, lest you perish!"

فَلَا يَصُدَّنَّكَ عَنْهَا مَن لَّا يُؤْمِنُ بِهَا وَٱتَّبَعَ هَوَىٰهُ
فَتَرْدَىٰ ١٦

17. "And what is that in your right hand, O Moses?"

وَمَا تِلْكَ بِيَمِينِكَ يَٰمُوسَىٰ ١٧

18. He said, "It is my rod; on it I lean; with it I beat down fodder for my flocks; and in it I find other uses."

قَالَ هِيَ عَصَايَ أَتَوَكَّؤُا۟ عَلَيْهَا وَأَهُشُّ بِهَا
عَلَىٰ غَنَمِي وَلِيَ فِيهَا مَـَٔارِبُ أُخْرَىٰ ١٨

19. (Allah) said, "Throw it, O Moses!"

قَالَ أَلْقِهَا يَٰمُوسَىٰ ١٩

20. He threw it, and see! It was a snake, active in motion.

فَأَلْقَىٰهَا فَإِذَا هِيَ حَيَّةٌ تَسْعَىٰ ٢٠

21. (Allah) said, "Seize it and fear not; We shall return it at once to its former condition".

قَالَ خُذْهَا وَلَا تَخَفْ سَنُعِيدُهَا سِيرَتَهَا
ٱلْأُولَىٰ ٢١

22. "Now draw your hand close to your side: it shall come out white (and shining), without harm (or stain) - as another sign -

وَٱضْمُمْ يَدَكَ إِلَىٰ جَنَاحِكَ تَخْرُجْ بَيْضَآءَ مِنْ غَيْرِ
سُوٓءٍ ءَايَةً أُخْرَىٰ ٢٢

23. In order that We may show you (two) of Our greater signs.

لِنُرِيَكَ مِنْ ءَايَٰتِنَا ٱلْكُبْرَى ٢٣

24. Go you to Pharaoh, for he had indeed transgressed all bounds."

ٱذْهَبْ إِلَىٰ فِرْعَوْنَ إِنَّهُۥ طَغَىٰ ٢٤

25. (Moses) said: "O my Lord! Expand me my breast;

قَالَ رَبِّ ٱشۡرَحۡ لِي صَدۡرِي ﴿٢٥﴾

26. Ease my task for me;

وَيَسِّرۡ لِيٓ أَمۡرِي ﴿٢٦﴾

27. And remove the impediment from my speech.

وَٱحۡلُلۡ عُقۡدَةٗ مِّن لِّسَانِي ﴿٢٧﴾

28. So they may understand what I say:

يَفۡقَهُواْ قَوۡلِي ﴿٢٨﴾

29. And give me a minister from my family,

وَٱجۡعَل لِّي وَزِيرٗا مِّنۡ أَهۡلِي ﴿٢٩﴾

30. Aaron, my brother;

هَٰرُونَ أَخِي ﴿٣٠﴾

31. Add to my strength through him,

ٱشۡدُدۡ بِهِۦٓ أَزۡرِي ﴿٣١﴾

32. And make him share my task:

وَأَشۡرِكۡهُ فِيٓ أَمۡرِي ﴿٣٢﴾

33. That we may celebrate Your praise aplenty,

كَيۡ نُسَبِّحَكَ كَثِيرٗا ﴿٣٣﴾

34. And remember You aplenty:

وَنَذۡكُرَكَ كَثِيرًا ﴿٣٤﴾

35. For You are He that (ever) regards us."

إِنَّكَ كُنتَ بِنَا بَصِيرٗا ﴿٣٥﴾

36. (Allah) said: "Granted is your prayer, O Moses!"

قَالَ قَدۡ أُوتِيتَ سُؤۡلَكَ يَٰمُوسَىٰ ﴿٣٦﴾

37. "And indeed We conferred a favour on you another time (before)."

وَلَقَدۡ مَنَنَّا عَلَيۡكَ مَرَّةً أُخۡرَىٰٓ ﴿٣٧﴾

38. "See! We sent to your mother, by inspiration, the message:

إِذۡ أَوۡحَيۡنَآ إِلَىٰٓ أُمِّكَ مَا يُوحَىٰٓ ﴿٣٨﴾

39. 'Throw (the child) into the chest, and throw (the chest) into the river: the river will cast him up on the bank, and he will be

أَنِ ٱقۡذِفِيهِ فِي ٱلتَّابُوتِ فَٱقۡذِفِيهِ فِي ٱلۡيَمِّ فَلۡيُلۡقِهِ ٱلۡيَمُّ

بِٱلسَّاحِلِ يَأْخُذْهُ عَدُوٌّ لِّي وَعَدُوٌّ لَّهُۥۚ وَأَلْقَيْتُ عَلَيْكَ
مَحَبَّةً مِّنِّي وَلِتُصْنَعَ عَلَىٰ عَيْنِيٓ ﴿٣٩﴾

taken up by one who is an enemy to Me and an enemy to him': but I cast (the garment of) love over you from Me and (this) in order that you may be reared under my eye.

إِذْ تَمْشِيٓ أُخْتُكَ فَتَقُولُ هَلْ أَدُلُّكُمْ عَلَىٰ مَن يَكْفُلُهُۥۖ
فَرَجَعْنَٰكَ إِلَىٰٓ أُمِّكَ كَيْ تَقَرَّ عَيْنُهَا وَلَا تَحْزَنَۚ وَقَتَلْتَ
نَفْسًا فَنَجَّيْنَٰكَ مِنَ ٱلْغَمِّ وَفَتَنَّٰكَ فُتُونًاۚ فَلَبِثْتَ
سِنِينَ فِيٓ أَهْلِ مَدْيَنَ ثُمَّ جِئْتَ عَلَىٰ قَدَرٍ يَٰمُوسَىٰ ﴿٤٠﴾

40. See! Your sister goes out and says, 'Shall I show you one who will nurse and rear the (child)?' So We brought you back to your mother, that her eye might be cooled and she should not grieve. Then you slew a man, but We saved you from trouble, and We tried you in various ways. Then you stayed a number of years with the people of Madyan. Then you came here as ordained, O Moses!

وَٱصْطَنَعْتُكَ لِنَفْسِي ﴿٤١﴾

41. And I have prepared you for Myself (for service)"...

ٱذْهَبْ أَنتَ وَأَخُوكَ بِـَٔايَٰتِي وَلَا تَنِيَا فِي ذِكْرِي ﴿٤٢﴾

42. "Go, you and your brother, with My signs, and slacken not, either of you, in keeping Me in remembrance."

ٱذْهَبَآ إِلَىٰ فِرْعَوْنَ إِنَّهُۥ طَغَىٰ ﴿٤٣﴾

43. "Go, both of you, to Pharaoh for he has indeed transgressed all bounds;

فَقُولَا لَهُۥ قَوْلًا لَّيِّنًا لَّعَلَّهُۥ يَتَذَكَّرُ أَوْ يَخْشَىٰ ﴿٤٤﴾

44. But speak to him mildly; perhaps he may take warning or fear (Allah)."

قَالَا رَبَّنَآ إِنَّنَا نَخَافُ أَن يَفْرُطَ عَلَيْنَآ أَوْ أَن يَطْغَىٰ ﴿٤٥﴾

45. They (Moses and Aaron) said: "Our Lord! We fear lest He hasten with insolence against us, or lest he transgress all bounds."

قَالَ لَا تَخَافَآۖ إِنَّنِي مَعَكُمَآ أَسْمَعُ وَأَرَىٰ ﴿٤٦﴾

46. He said: "Fear not: for I am with you: I hear and see (everything)."

فَأْتِيَاهُ فَقُولَآ إِنَّا رَسُولَا رَبِّكَ فَأَرْسِلْ مَعَنَا بَنِيٓ
إِسْرَٰٓءِيلَ وَلَا تُعَذِّبْهُمْۖ قَدْ جِئْنَٰكَ بِـَٔايَةٍ مِّن رَّبِّكَۖ
وَٱلسَّلَٰمُ عَلَىٰ مَنِ ٱتَّبَعَ ٱلْهُدَىٰٓ ﴿٤٧﴾

47. "So go you both to him, and say, 'Verily we are messengers sent by your Lord: send out, therefore the Children of Israel with us and afflict them not: with a sign, indeed, have we come from your Lord! And peace to all who follow guidance!'

48. Verily it has been revealed to us that the penalty (awaits) those who reject and turn away."

إِنَّا قَدْ أُوحِيَ إِلَيْنَآ أَنَّ ٱلْعَذَابَ عَلَىٰ مَن كَذَّبَ
وَتَوَلَّىٰ ﴿٤٨﴾

49. (When this message was delivered), (Pharaoh) said: "Who then, O Moses, is the Lord of you two?"

قَالَ فَمَن رَّبُّكُمَا يَٰمُوسَىٰ ﴿٤٩﴾

50. He said: "Our Lord is He Who gave to each (created) thing its form and nature, and further gave (it) guidance."

قَالَ رَبُّنَا ٱلَّذِىٓ أَعْطَىٰ كُلَّ شَىْءٍ خَلْقَهُۥ ثُمَّ هَدَىٰ ﴿٥٠﴾

51. (Pharaoh) said: "What then is the condition of previous generations?"

قَالَ فَمَا بَالُ ٱلْقُرُونِ ٱلْأُولَىٰ ﴿٥١﴾

52. He replied: "The knowledge of that is with my Lord, duly recorded: my Lord never errs, nor forgets -

قَالَ عِلْمُهَا عِندَ رَبِّى فِى كِتَٰبٍ ۖ لَّا يَضِلُّ رَبِّى وَلَا
يَنسَى ﴿٥٢﴾

53. He Who has made for you the earth like a carpet spread out; has enabled you to go about in it by roads (and channels); and has sent down water from the sky." With it have We produced diverse pairs of plants each separate from the others.

ٱلَّذِى جَعَلَ لَكُمُ ٱلْأَرْضَ مَهْدًا وَسَلَكَ لَكُمْ فِيهَا
سُبُلًا وَأَنزَلَ مِنَ ٱلسَّمَآءِ مَآءً فَأَخْرَجْنَا بِهِۦٓ أَزْوَٰجًا
مِّن نَّبَاتٍ شَتَّىٰ ﴿٥٣﴾

54. Eat (for yourselves) and pasture your cattle: verily, in this are signs, for men endued with understanding.

كُلُوا۟ وَٱرْعَوْا۟ أَنْعَٰمَكُمْ ۗ إِنَّ فِى ذَٰلِكَ لَءَايَٰتٍ لِّأُو۟لِى
ٱلنُّهَىٰ ﴿٥٤﴾

55. From the (earth) did We create you, and into it shall We return you, and from it shall We bring you out once again.

ربع الحزب ٣٢ ۞ مِنْهَا خَلَقْنَٰكُمْ وَفِيهَا نُعِيدُكُمْ وَمِنْهَا نُخْرِجُكُمْ تَارَةً
أُخْرَىٰ ﴿٥٥﴾

56. And We showed Pharaoh all Our signs, but he did reject and refuse.

وَلَقَدْ أَرَيْنَٰهُ ءَايَٰتِنَا كُلَّهَا فَكَذَّبَ وَأَبَىٰ ﴿٥٦﴾

57. He said: "Have you come to drive us out of our land with your magic O Moses?"

قَالَ أَجِئْتَنَا لِتُخْرِجَنَا مِنْ أَرْضِنَا بِسِحْرِكَ
يَٰمُوسَىٰ ﴿٥٧﴾

58. "But we can surely produce magic to match yours! So make an appointment between us and you, which we shall not fail to keep - neither we nor you - in a place where both shall have even chances."

فَلَنَأْتِيَنَّكَ بِسِحْرٍ مِّثْلِهِۦ فَٱجْعَلْ بَيْنَنَا وَبَيْنَكَ
مَوْعِدًا لَّا نُخْلِفُهُۥ نَحْنُ وَلَآ أَنتَ مَكَانًا سُوًى ٥٨

59. Moses said: "Your appointment is the day of the festival, and let the people be assembled when the sun is well up."

قَالَ مَوْعِدُكُمْ يَوْمُ ٱلزِّينَةِ وَأَن يُحْشَرَ ٱلنَّاسُ ضُحًى ٥٩

60. So Pharaoh withdrew; he concerted his plan, and then came (back).

فَتَوَلَّىٰ فِرْعَوْنُ فَجَمَعَ كَيْدَهُۥ ثُمَّ أَتَىٰ ٦٠

61. Moses said to him: "Woe to you! Forge not you a lie against Allah, lest He destroy you (at once) utterly by chastisement; the forger must suffer frustration!"

قَالَ لَهُم مُّوسَىٰ وَيْلَكُمْ لَا تَفْتَرُوا۟ عَلَى ٱللَّهِ كَذِبًا
فَيُسْحِتَكُم بِعَذَابٍ ۖ وَقَدْ خَابَ مَنِ ٱفْتَرَىٰ ٦١

62. So they disputed, one with another, over their affair, but they kept their talk secret.

فَتَنَٰزَعُوٓا۟ أَمْرَهُم بَيْنَهُمْ وَأَسَرُّوا۟ ٱلنَّجْوَىٰ ٦٢

63. They said: "These two are certainly (expert) magicians; their object is to drive you out from your land with their magic, and to do away with your most cherished institutions."

قَالُوٓا۟ إِنْ هَٰذَٰنِ لَسَٰحِرَٰنِ يُرِيدَانِ أَن يُخْرِجَاكُم مِّنْ
أَرْضِكُم بِسِحْرِهِمَا وَيَذْهَبَا بِطَرِيقَتِكُمُ
ٱلْمُثْلَىٰ ٦٣

64. "Therefore, concert your plan. And then assemble in (ordered) ranks; he wins (all along) today who gains the upper hand."

فَأَجْمِعُوا۟ كَيْدَكُمْ ثُمَّ ٱئْتُوا۟ صَفًّا ۚ وَقَدْ أَفْلَحَ ٱلْيَوْمَ مَنِ
ٱسْتَعْلَىٰ ٦٤

65. They said: "O Moses! Whether will you that you throw (first) or that we be the first to throw?"

قَالُوا۟ يَٰمُوسَىٰٓ إِمَّآ أَن تُلْقِىَ وَإِمَّآ أَن نَّكُونَ أَوَّلَ مَنْ أَلْقَىٰ ٦٥

66. He said, "Nay, throw you first!" Then see their ropes and their rods - so it seemed to him on account of their magic - began to be in lively motion!

قَالَ بَلْ أَلْقُوا۟ ۖ فَإِذَا حِبَالُهُمْ وَعِصِيُّهُمْ يُخَيَّلُ إِلَيْهِ مِن
سِحْرِهِمْ أَنَّهَا تَسْعَىٰ ٦٦

67. So Moses conceived in his mind a (sort of) fear.

فَأَوْجَسَ فِي نَفْسِهِۦ خِيفَةً مُّوسَىٰ ﴿٦٧﴾

68. We said, "Fear not! For you have indeed the upper hand:

قُلْنَا لَا تَخَفْ إِنَّكَ أَنتَ ٱلْأَعْلَىٰ ﴿٦٨﴾

69. "Throw that which is in your right hand: quickly will it swallow up that which they have faked. What they have faked is but a magician's trick and the magician thrives not, (no matter) where he goes."

وَأَلْقِ مَا فِي يَمِينِكَ تَلْقَفْ مَا صَنَعُوٓاْۖ إِنَّمَا صَنَعُواْ
كَيْدُ سَٰحِرٍۖ وَلَا يُفْلِحُ ٱلسَّاحِرُ حَيْثُ أَتَىٰ ﴿٦٩﴾

70. So the magicians were thrown down to prostration; they said, "We believe in the Lord of Aaron and Moses."

فَأُلْقِيَ ٱلسَّحَرَةُ سُجَّدًا قَالُوٓاْ ءَامَنَّا بِرَبِّ هَٰرُونَ وَمُوسَىٰ ﴿٧٠﴾

71. (Pharaoh) said: "Do you believe in Him before I give you permission? Surely this must be your leader, who has taught you magic! Be sure I will cut off your hands and feet on opposite sides, and I will have you crucified on trunks of palm trees; so shall you know for certain which of us can give the more severe and the more lasting punishment!"

قَالَ ءَامَنتُمْ لَهُۥ قَبْلَ أَنْ ءَاذَنَ لَكُمْۖ إِنَّهُۥ لَكَبِيرُكُمُ ٱلَّذِي
عَلَّمَكُمُ ٱلسِّحْرَۖ فَلَأُقَطِّعَنَّ أَيْدِيَكُمْ وَأَرْجُلَكُم مِّنْ
خِلَٰفٍ وَلَأُصَلِّبَنَّكُمْ فِي جُذُوعِ ٱلنَّخْلِ وَلَتَعْلَمُنَّ أَيُّنَآ
أَشَدُّ عَذَابًا وَأَبْقَىٰ ﴿٧١﴾

72. They said: "Never shall we regard you as more than the clear signs that have come to us or than Him Who created us! So decree whatever you desire to decree; for you can only decree (touching) the life of this world.

قَالُواْ لَن نُّؤْثِرَكَ عَلَىٰ مَا جَآءَنَا مِنَ ٱلْبَيِّنَٰتِ وَٱلَّذِي
فَطَرَنَاۖ فَٱقْضِ مَآ أَنتَ قَاضٍۖ إِنَّمَا تَقْضِي هَٰذِهِ
ٱلْحَيَوٰةَ ٱلدُّنْيَآ ﴿٧٢﴾

73. For us, we have believed in our Lord; may He forgive us our faults, and the magic to which you did compel us: for Allah is Best and Most Lasting."

إِنَّآ ءَامَنَّا بِرَبِّنَا لِيَغْفِرَ لَنَا خَطَٰيَٰنَا وَمَآ أَكْرَهْتَنَا عَلَيْهِ
مِنَ ٱلسِّحْرِۗ وَٱللَّهُ خَيْرٌ وَأَبْقَىٰٓ ﴿٧٣﴾

74. Verily he who comes to his Lord as a sinner (at judgement) - for him is hell; in it shall he neither die nor live.

إِنَّهُۥ مَن يَأْتِ رَبَّهُۥ مُجْرِمًا فَإِنَّ لَهُۥ جَهَنَّمَ لَا يَمُوتُ فِيهَا
وَلَا يَحْيَىٰ ﴿٧٤﴾

75. But such as comes to Him as believers who have worked righteous deeds - for them are ranks exalted -

وَمَن يَأْتِهِۦ مُؤْمِنًا قَدْ عَمِلَ ٱلصَّٰلِحَٰتِ فَأُو۟لَٰٓئِكَ لَهُمُ
ٱلدَّرَجَٰتُ ٱلْعُلَىٰ ٧٥

76. Gardens of eternity, beneath which flow rivers; they will dwell in it forever; such is the reward of those who purify themselves (from evil).

جَنَّٰتُ عَدْنٍ تَجْرِى مِن تَحْتِهَا ٱلْأَنْهَٰرُ خَٰلِدِينَ فِيهَا ۚ
وَذَٰلِكَ جَزَآءُ مَن تَزَكَّىٰ ٧٦

77. We sent an inspiration to Moses: "Travel by night with my servants, and strike a dry path for them through the sea, without fear of being overtaken (by Pharaoh) and without (any other) fear."

وَلَقَدْ أَوْحَيْنَآ إِلَىٰ مُوسَىٰٓ أَنْ أَسْرِ بِعِبَادِى فَٱضْرِبْ
لَهُمْ طَرِيقًا فِى ٱلْبَحْرِ يَبَسًا لَّا تَخَٰفُ دَرَكًا وَلَا تَخْشَىٰ ٧٧

78. Then Pharaoh pursued them with his forces, but the waters completely overwhelmed them and covered them up.

فَأَتْبَعَهُمْ فِرْعَوْنُ بِجُنُودِهِۦ فَغَشِيَهُم مِّنَ ٱلْيَمِّ
مَا غَشِيَهُمْ ٧٨

79. Pharaoh led his people astray instead of leading them aright.

وَأَضَلَّ فِرْعَوْنُ قَوْمَهُۥ وَمَا هَدَىٰ ٧٩

80. O you Children of Israel! We delivered you from your enemy, and We made a covenant with you on the side of mount (Sinai), and We sent down to you manna and quails:

يَٰبَنِىٓ إِسْرَٰٓءِيلَ قَدْ أَنجَيْنَٰكُم مِّنْ عَدُوِّكُمْ وَوَٰعَدْنَٰكُمْ
جَانِبَ ٱلطُّورِ ٱلْأَيْمَنَ وَنَزَّلْنَا عَلَيْكُمُ ٱلْمَنَّ وَٱلسَّلْوَىٰ ٨٠

81. (Saying): "Eat of the good things We have provided for your sustenance, but commit no excess in it, lest My wrath should justly descend on you: and those on whom descends My wrath do perish indeed!"

كُلُوا۟ مِن طَيِّبَٰتِ مَا رَزَقْنَٰكُمْ وَلَا تَطْغَوْا۟ فِيهِ فَيَحِلَّ
عَلَيْكُمْ غَضَبِى ۖ وَمَن يَحْلِلْ عَلَيْهِ غَضَبِى فَقَدْ هَوَىٰ ٨١

82. "But, without doubt, I am (also) He that forgives again and again, to those who repent, believe, and do right - who, in fine, are ready to receive true guidance."

وَإِنِّى لَغَفَّارٌ لِّمَن تَابَ وَءَامَنَ وَعَمِلَ صَٰلِحًا ثُمَّ
ٱهْتَدَىٰ ٨٢

83. (When Moses was up on the mount Allah said:) "What made you hasten in advance of your people, O Moses?"

نصف الحزب ٣٢ ۞ وَمَآ أَعْجَلَكَ عَن قَوْمِكَ يَٰمُوسَىٰ ٨٣

84. He replied: "See, they are close on my footsteps: I hastened to You, O my Lord, to please You."

قَالَ هُمۡ أُوْلَآءِ عَلَىٰٓ أَثَرِي وَعَجِلۡتُ إِلَيۡكَ رَبِّ
لِتَرۡضَىٰ ﴿٨٤﴾

85. (Allah) said: "We have tested your people in your absence: the Samiri has led them astray."

قَالَ فَإِنَّا قَدۡ فَتَنَّا قَوۡمَكَ مِنۢ بَعۡدِكَ وَأَضَلَّهُمُ
ٱلسَّامِرِيُّ ﴿٨٥﴾

86. So Moses returned to his people in state of indignation and sorrow. He said: "O my people! Did not your Lord make a handsome promise to you? Did then the promise seem to you long (in coming)? Or did you desire that wrath should descend from your Lord on you, and so you broke your promise to me?"

فَرَجَعَ مُوسَىٰٓ إِلَىٰ قَوۡمِهِۦ غَضۡبَٰنَ أَسِفٗاۚ قَالَ يَٰقَوۡمِ
أَلَمۡ يَعِدۡكُمۡ رَبُّكُمۡ وَعۡدًا حَسَنًاۚ أَفَطَالَ عَلَيۡكُمُ ٱلۡعَهۡدُ
أَمۡ أَرَدتُّمۡ أَن يَحِلَّ عَلَيۡكُمۡ غَضَبٞ مِّن رَّبِّكُمۡ
فَأَخۡلَفۡتُم مَّوۡعِدِي ﴿٨٦﴾

87. They said: "We broke not the promise to you, as far as lay in our power: but we were made to carry the weight of the ornaments of the (whole) people, and we threw them (into the fire), and that was what the Samiri suggested."

قَالُواْ مَآ أَخۡلَفۡنَا مَوۡعِدَكَ بِمَلۡكِنَا وَلَٰكِنَّا حُمِّلۡنَآ
أَوۡزَارٗا مِّن زِينَةِ ٱلۡقَوۡمِ فَقَذَفۡنَٰهَا فَكَذَٰلِكَ أَلۡقَى
ٱلسَّامِرِيُّ ﴿٨٧﴾

88. "Then he brought out (of the fire) before the (people) the image of a calf: it seemed to low; so they said: 'This is your god, and the god of Moses, but (Moses) has forgotten!'"

فَأَخۡرَجَ لَهُمۡ عِجۡلٗا جَسَدٗا لَّهُۥ خُوَارٞ فَقَالُواْ هَٰذَآ
إِلَٰهُكُمۡ وَإِلَٰهُ مُوسَىٰ فَنَسِيَ ﴿٨٨﴾

89. Could they not see that it could not return them a word (for answer), and that it had no power either to harm them or to do them good?

أَفَلَا يَرَوۡنَ أَلَّا يَرۡجِعُ إِلَيۡهِمۡ قَوۡلٗا وَلَا يَمۡلِكُ
لَهُمۡ ضَرّٗا وَلَا نَفۡعٗا ﴿٨٩﴾

90. Aaron had already, before this said to them: "O my people! You are being tested in this; for verily your Lord is (Allah) Most Gracious; so follow me and obey my command."

وَلَقَدۡ قَالَ لَهُمۡ هَٰرُونُ مِن قَبۡلُ يَٰقَوۡمِ إِنَّمَا فُتِنتُم
بِهِۦۖ وَإِنَّ رَبَّكُمُ ٱلرَّحۡمَٰنُ فَٱتَّبِعُونِي وَأَطِيعُوٓاْ أَمۡرِي ﴿٩٠﴾

91. They had said: "We will not abandon this cult, but we will devote ourselves to it until Moses returns to us."

قَالُواْ لَن نَّبْرَحَ عَلَيْهِ عَٰكِفِينَ حَتَّىٰ يَرْجِعَ إِلَيْنَا
مُوسَىٰ ٩١

92. (Moses) said: "O Aaron! What kept you back when you saw them going wrong,

قَالَ يَٰهَٰرُونُ مَا مَنَعَكَ إِذْ رَأَيْتَهُمْ ضَلُّوٓاْ ٩٢

93. From following me? Did you then disobey my order?"

أَلَّا تَتَّبِعَنِۖ أَفَعَصَيْتَ أَمْرِي ٩٣

94. (Aaron) replied: "O son of my mother! Seize (me not) by my beard nor by (the hair of) my head! Truly I feared lest you should say, 'You have caused a division among the Children of Israel, and you did not respect my word!'"

قَالَ يَبْنَؤُمَّ لَا تَأْخُذْ بِلِحْيَتِي وَلَا بِرَأْسِيٓۖ إِنِّي خَشِيتُ
أَن تَقُولَ فَرَّقْتَ بَيْنَ بَنِيٓ إِسْرَٰٓءِيلَ وَلَمْ تَرْقُبْ
قَوْلِي ٩٤

95. (Moses) said: "What then is your case O Samiri?"

قَالَ فَمَا خَطْبُكَ يَٰسَٰمِرِيُّ ٩٥

96. He replied: "I saw what they saw not, so I took a handful (of dust) from the footprint of the messenger, and threw it (into the calf); thus did my soul suggest to me."

قَالَ بَصُرْتُ بِمَا لَمْ يَبْصُرُواْ بِهِۦ فَقَبَضْتُ قَبْضَةً
مِّنْ أَثَرِ ٱلرَّسُولِ فَنَبَذْتُهَا وَكَذَٰلِكَ سَوَّلَتْ
لِي نَفْسِي ٩٦

97. (Moses) said: "Go away! But your (punishment) in this life will be that you will say, 'Touch me not'; and moreover (for a future penalty) you have a promise that will not fail; now look at your god, of whom you have become a devoted worshipper; we will certainly (melt) it in a blazing fire and scatter it broadcast in the sea!"

قَالَ فَٱذْهَبْ فَإِنَّ لَكَ فِي ٱلْحَيَوٰةِ أَن تَقُولَ لَا مِسَاسَۖ
وَإِنَّ لَكَ مَوْعِدًا لَّن تُخْلَفَهُۥۖ وَٱنظُرْ إِلَىٰٓ إِلَٰهِكَ
ٱلَّذِي ظَلْتَ عَلَيْهِ عَاكِفًاۖ لَّنُحَرِّقَنَّهُۥ ثُمَّ
لَنَنسِفَنَّهُۥ فِي ٱلْيَمِّ نَسْفًا ٩٧

98. But the God of you all is Allah; there is no god but He: all things He comprehends in His knowledge.

إِنَّمَآ إِلَٰهُكُمُ ٱللَّهُ ٱلَّذِي لَآ إِلَٰهَ إِلَّا هُوَۚ وَسِعَ كُلَّ
شَيْءٍ عِلْمًا ٩٨

99. Thus do We relate to you some stories of what happened before; for We

كَذَٰلِكَ نَقُصُّ عَلَيْكَ مِنْ أَنۢبَآءِ مَا قَدْ سَبَقَۚ وَقَدْ ءَاتَيْنَٰكَ

have sent you a message from Our own presence.

مِن لَّدُنَّا ذِكْرًا ٩٩

100. If any do turn away from it, verily they will bear a burden on the day of judgement;

مَّنْ أَعْرَضَ عَنْهُ فَإِنَّهُۥ يَحْمِلُ يَوْمَ ٱلْقِيَٰمَةِ وِزْرًا ١٠٠

101. They will remain in this (state); and grievous will the burden be to them on that day -

خَٰلِدِينَ فِيهِ ۖ وَسَآءَ لَهُمْ يَوْمَ ٱلْقِيَٰمَةِ حِمْلًا ١٠١

102. The day when the trumpet will be sounded; that day, We shall gather the sinful, blear-eyed (with terror),

يَوْمَ يُنفَخُ فِى ٱلصُّورِ ۚ وَنَحْشُرُ ٱلْمُجْرِمِينَ يَوْمَئِذٍ
زُرْقًا ١٠٢

103. In whispers will they consult each other: "You stayed not longer than ten (days);"

يَتَخَٰفَتُونَ بَيْنَهُمْ إِن لَّبِثْتُمْ إِلَّا عَشْرًا ١٠٣

104. We know best what they will say, when their leader most eminent in conduct will say: "You stayed not longer than a day!"

نَّحْنُ أَعْلَمُ بِمَا يَقُولُونَ إِذْ يَقُولُ أَمْثَلُهُمْ طَرِيقَةً إِن
لَّبِثْتُمْ إِلَّا يَوْمًا ١٠٤

105. They ask you concerning the mountains, say, "My Lord will uproot them and scatter them as dust;"

وَيَسْـَٔلُونَكَ عَنِ ٱلْجِبَالِ فَقُلْ يَنسِفُهَا رَبِّى نَسْفًا ١٠٥

106. "He will leave them as plains smooth and level;

فَيَذَرُهَا قَاعًا صَفْصَفًا ١٠٦

107. Nothing crooked or curved will you see in their place."

لَّا تَرَىٰ فِيهَا عِوَجًا وَلَآ أَمْتًا ١٠٧

108. On that day will they follow the caller (straight); no crookedness (can they show) him; all sounds shall humble themselves in the presence of (Allah) Most Gracious: nothing shall you hear but the tramp of their feet (as they march).

يَوْمَئِذٍ يَتَّبِعُونَ ٱلدَّاعِىَ لَا عِوَجَ لَهُۥ ۖ وَخَشَعَتِ
ٱلْأَصْوَاتُ لِلرَّحْمَٰنِ فَلَا تَسْمَعُ إِلَّا هَمْسًا ١٠٨

109. On that day shall no intercession benefit except for those for whom permission has been granted by (Allah) Most Gracious and whose word is acceptable to Him.

يَوۡمَئِذٖ لَّا تَنفَعُ ٱلشَّفَٰعَةُ إِلَّا مَنۡ أَذِنَ لَهُ ٱلرَّحۡمَٰنُ وَ
رَضِيَ لَهُۥ قَوۡلٗا ١٠٩

110. He knows what (appears to His creatures as) before or after or behind them; but they shall not encompass it with their knowledge.

يَعۡلَمُ مَا بَيۡنَ أَيۡدِيهِمۡ وَمَا خَلۡفَهُمۡ وَلَا يُحِيطُونَ بِهِۦ
عِلۡمٗا ١١٠

111. (All) faces shall be humbled before (Him) - the Living, the Self-Subsisting, Eternal: hopeless indeed will be the man that carries iniquity (on his back).

ثلاثة أرباع الحزب ٣٢ * وَعَنَتِ ٱلۡوُجُوهُ لِلۡحَيِّ ٱلۡقَيُّومِۖ وَقَدۡ خَابَ مَنۡ حَمَلَ
ظُلۡمٗا ١١١

112. But he who works deeds of righteousness, and has faith, will have no fear of harm nor of any curtailment (of what is his due).

وَمَن يَعۡمَلۡ مِنَ ٱلصَّٰلِحَٰتِ وَهُوَ مُؤۡمِنٞ فَلَا يَخَافُ
ظُلۡمٗا وَلَا هَضۡمٗا ١١٢

113. Thus have We sent this down - an Arabic Qur'an - and explained in it in detail some of the warnings, in order that they may fear Allah, or that it may cause their remembrance (of Him).

وَكَذَٰلِكَ أَنزَلۡنَٰهُ قُرۡءَانًا عَرَبِيّٗا وَصَرَّفۡنَا فِيهِ
مِنَ ٱلۡوَعِيدِ لَعَلَّهُمۡ يَتَّقُونَ أَوۡ يُحۡدِثُ لَهُمۡ
ذِكۡرٗا ١١٣

114. High above all is Allah, the King, the Truth! Be not in haste with the Qur'an before its revelation to you is completed, but say, "O my Lord! Advance me in knowledge."

فَتَعَٰلَى ٱللَّهُ ٱلۡمَلِكُ ٱلۡحَقُّۗ وَلَا تَعۡجَلۡ بِٱلۡقُرۡءَانِ
مِن قَبۡلِ أَن يُقۡضَىٰٓ إِلَيۡكَ وَحۡيُهُۥۖ وَقُل رَّبِّ زِدۡنِي
عِلۡمٗا ١١٤

115. We had already, beforehand, taken the covenant of Adam, but he forgot; and We found on his part no firm resolve.

وَلَقَدۡ عَهِدۡنَآ إِلَىٰٓ ءَادَمَ مِن قَبۡلُ فَنَسِيَ وَلَمۡ نَجِدۡ
لَهُۥ عَزۡمٗا ١١٥

116. When We said to the angels, "Prostrate yourselves to Adam", they prostrated themselves but not Iblis; he refused.

وَإِذۡ قُلۡنَا لِلۡمَلَٰٓئِكَةِ ٱسۡجُدُواْ لِأٓدَمَ فَسَجَدُوٓاْ
إِلَّآ إِبۡلِيسَ أَبَىٰ ١١٦

117. Then We said: "O Adam! Verily this is an enemy to you and your wife; so let him not get you both out of the garden, so that you are landed in misery."

فَقُلْنَا يَٰٓـَٔادَمُ إِنَّ هَٰذَا عَدُوٌّ لَّكَ وَلِزَوْجِكَ فَلَا
يُخْرِجَنَّكُمَا مِنَ ٱلْجَنَّةِ فَتَشْقَىٰٓ ﴿١١٧﴾

118. "There is in it (enough provision) for you not to go hungry nor to go naked,"

إِنَّ لَكَ أَلَّا تَجُوعَ فِيهَا وَلَا تَعْرَىٰ ﴿١١٨﴾

119. "Nor to suffer from thirst, nor from the sun's heat."

وَأَنَّكَ لَا تَظْمَؤُا۟ فِيهَا وَلَا تَضْحَىٰ ﴿١١٩﴾

120. But Satan whispered evil to him: he said, "O Adam! Shall I lead you to the tree of eternity and to a kingdom that never decays?"

فَوَسْوَسَ إِلَيْهِ ٱلشَّيْطَٰنُ قَالَ يَٰٓـَٔادَمُ هَلْ أَدُلُّكَ
عَلَىٰ شَجَرَةِ ٱلْخُلْدِ وَمُلْكٍ لَّا يَبْلَىٰ ﴿١٢٠﴾

121. In the result, they both ate of the tree, and so their nakedness appeared to them; they began to sew together, for their covering, leaves from the garden; thus did Adam disobey His Lord, and allow himself to be seduced.

فَأَكَلَا مِنْهَا فَبَدَتْ لَهُمَا سَوْءَٰتُهُمَا وَطَفِقَا
يَخْصِفَانِ عَلَيْهِمَا مِن وَرَقِ ٱلْجَنَّةِ ۚ وَعَصَىٰٓ ءَادَمُ
رَبَّهُۥ فَغَوَىٰ ﴿١٢١﴾

122. But his Lord chose him (for His grace): He turned to him, and gave him guidance.

ثُمَّ ٱجْتَبَٰهُ رَبُّهُۥ فَتَابَ عَلَيْهِ وَهَدَىٰ ﴿١٢٢﴾

123. He said: "Get you down, both of you - all together, from the garden, with enmity one to another: but if, as is sure, there comes to you guidance from Me, whosoever follows My guidance, will not lose his way, nor fall into misery."

قَالَ ٱهْبِطَا مِنْهَا جَمِيعًۢا ۖ بَعْضُكُمْ لِبَعْضٍ عَدُوٌّ ۖ فَإِمَّا
يَأْتِيَنَّكُم مِّنِّى هُدًى فَمَنِ ٱتَّبَعَ هُدَاىَ فَلَا
يَضِلُّ وَلَا يَشْقَىٰ ﴿١٢٣﴾

124. "But whosoever turns away from My message, verily for him is a life narrowed down and We shall raise him up blind on the day of judgement."

وَمَنْ أَعْرَضَ عَن ذِكْرِى فَإِنَّ لَهُۥ مَعِيشَةً ضَنكًا
وَنَحْشُرُهُۥ يَوْمَ ٱلْقِيَٰمَةِ أَعْمَىٰ ﴿١٢٤﴾

125. He will say: "O my Lord! Why have you raised me up blind, while I had sight (before)?"

قَالَ رَبِّ لِمَ حَشَرْتَنِىٓ أَعْمَىٰ وَقَدْ كُنتُ بَصِيرًا ﴿١٢٥﴾

126. (Allah) will say: "Thus did you, when Our signs came to you, disregard them: so will you, this day, be disregarded."

قَالَ كَذَٰلِكَ أَتَتْكَ ءَايَٰتُنَا فَنَسِيتَهَا ۖ وَكَذَٰلِكَ ٱلْيَوْمَ
تُنسَىٰ ١٢٦

127. And thus do We recompense him who transgresses beyond bounds and believes not in the signs of his Lord: and the penalty of the hereafter is far more grievous and more enduring.

وَكَذَٰلِكَ نَجْزِى مَنْ أَسْرَفَ وَلَمْ يُؤْمِنۢ بِـَٔايَٰتِ رَبِّهِۦ ۚ
وَلَعَذَابُ ٱلْءَاخِرَةِ أَشَدُّ وَأَبْقَىٰٓ ١٢٧

128. Is it not a warning to such men (to call to mind) how many generations before them We destroyed, in whose haunts they (now) move? Verily, in this are signs for men endued with understanding,

أَفَلَمْ يَهْدِ لَهُمْ كَمْ أَهْلَكْنَا قَبْلَهُم مِّنَ ٱلْقُرُونِ
يَمْشُونَ فِى مَسَٰكِنِهِمْ ۗ إِنَّ فِى ذَٰلِكَ لَءَايَٰتٍ لِّأُو۟لِى
ٱلنُّهَىٰ ١٢٨

129. Had it not been for a word that went ahead before from your Lord, (their punishment) must necessarily have come; but there is a term appointed (for respite).

وَلَوْلَا كَلِمَةٌ سَبَقَتْ مِن رَّبِّكَ لَكَانَ لِزَامًا وَأَجَلٌ
مُّسَمًّى ١٢٩

130. Therefore, be patient with what they say, and celebrate (constantly) the praises of your Lord before the rising of the sun, and before its setting; yea, celebrate them for part of the hours of the night, and at the sides of the day; that you may have (spiritual) joy.

فَٱصْبِرْ عَلَىٰ مَا يَقُولُونَ وَسَبِّحْ بِحَمْدِ رَبِّكَ قَبْلَ طُلُوعِ
ٱلشَّمْسِ وَقَبْلَ غُرُوبِهَا ۖ وَمِنْ ءَانَآئِ ٱلَّيْلِ فَسَبِّحْ
وَأَطْرَافَ ٱلنَّهَارِ لَعَلَّكَ تَرْضَىٰ ١٣٠

131. Nor strain your eyes in longing for the things We have given for enjoyment to parties of them, the splendour of the life of this world, through which We test them: but the provision of your Lord is better and more enduring.

وَلَا تَمُدَّنَّ عَيْنَيْكَ إِلَىٰ مَا مَتَّعْنَا بِهِۦٓ أَزْوَٰجًا مِّنْهُمْ زَهْرَةَ
ٱلْحَيَوٰةِ ٱلدُّنْيَا لِنَفْتِنَهُمْ فِيهِ ۚ وَرِزْقُ رَبِّكَ خَيْرٌ وَأَبْقَىٰ ١٣١

132. Enjoin prayer on your people, and be constant in it. We ask you not to provide sustenance; We provide it for you. But the (fruit of) the hereafter is for righteousness.

وَأْمُرْ أَهْلَكَ بِٱلصَّلَوٰةِ وَٱصْطَبِرْ عَلَيْهَا ۖ لَا نَسْـَٔلُكَ رِزْقًا ۖ
نَّحْنُ نَرْزُقُكَ ۗ وَٱلْعَٰقِبَةُ لِلتَّقْوَىٰ ١٣٢

133. They say: "Why does he not bring us a sign from His Lord?" Has not a clear sign come to them of all that was in the former books of revelation?

وَقَالُوا۟ لَوْلَا يَأْتِينَا بِـَٔايَةٍ مِّن رَّبِّهِۦٓ ۚ أَوَلَمْ تَأْتِهِم
بَيِّنَةُ مَا فِى ٱلصُّحُفِ ٱلْأُولَىٰ ١٣٣

134. And if We had inflicted on them a penalty before this, they would have said: "Our Lord! If only You had sent us a messenger, we should certainly have followed Your signs before we were humbled and put to shame."

وَلَوْ أَنَّآ أَهْلَكْنَٰهُم بِعَذَابٍ مِّن قَبْلِهِۦ لَقَالُوا۟ رَبَّنَا
لَوْلَآ أَرْسَلْتَ إِلَيْنَا رَسُولًا فَنَتَّبِعَ ءَايَٰتِكَ مِن قَبْلِ
أَن نَّذِلَّ وَنَخْزَىٰ ١٣٤

135. Say: "Each one (of us) is waiting: wait you, therefore, and soon shall you know who it is that is on the straight and even way, and who it is that has received guidance."

قُلْ كُلٌّ مُّتَرَبِّصٌ فَتَرَبَّصُوا۟ ۖ فَسَتَعْلَمُونَ مَنْ أَصْحَٰبُ
ٱلصِّرَٰطِ ٱلسَّوِىِّ وَمَنِ ٱهْتَدَىٰ ١٣٥

سُورَةُ الأَنبِيَاءِ

Surah 21: ***Al-Anbiya*** **(The Prophets)**

In the name of Allah,
Most Gracious, Most Merciful.

بِسْمِ ٱللَّهِ ٱلرَّحْمَٰنِ ٱلرَّحِيمِ

*** 1.** Closer and closer to mankind comes their reckoning: yet they heed not and they turn away.

الجزء ١٧ الحزب ٣٣

ٱقْتَرَبَ لِلنَّاسِ حِسَابُهُمْ وَهُمْ فِى غَفْلَةٍ
مُّعْرِضُونَ ١

2. Never comes (anything) to them of a renewed message from their Lord, but they listen to it as in jest-

مَا يَأْتِيهِم مِّن ذِكْرٍ مِّن رَّبِّهِم مُّحْدَثٍ إِلَّا
ٱسْتَمَعُوهُ وَهُمْ يَلْعَبُونَ ٢

3. Their hearts toying as with trifles. The wrongdoers conceal their private counsels (saying) "Is this (one) more than a man like yourselves? Will you go to witchcraft with your eyes open?"

لَاهِيَةً قُلُوبُهُمْ ۗ وَأَسَرُّوا۟ ٱلنَّجْوَى ٱلَّذِينَ
ظَلَمُوا۟ هَلْ هَٰذَآ إِلَّا بَشَرٌ مِّثْلُكُمْ ۖ أَفَتَأْتُونَ
ٱلسِّحْرَ وَأَنتُمْ تُبْصِرُونَ ٣

* Part-17

4. Say: "My Lord knows (every) word (spoken) in the heavens and the earth: He is the One that hears and knows (all things)."

قَالَ رَبِّي يَعْلَمُ ٱلْقَوْلَ فِي ٱلسَّمَآءِ وَٱلْأَرْضِ ۖ
وَهُوَ ٱلسَّمِيعُ ٱلْعَلِيمُ ٤

5. "Nay," they say, "(these are) medleys of dreams! Nay he forged it! - Nay he is (but) a poet! Let him then bring us a sign like the ones that were sent to (prophets) of old!"

بَلْ قَالُوٓا۟ أَضْغَـٰثُ أَحْلَـٰمٍۭ بَلِ ٱفْتَرَىٰهُ بَلْ هُوَ
شَاعِرٌ فَلْيَأْتِنَا بِـَٔايَةٍ كَمَآ أُرْسِلَ ٱلْأَوَّلُونَ ٥

6. (As to those) before them not one of the populations which We destroyed believed: will these believe?

مَآ ءَامَنَتْ قَبْلَهُم مِّن قَرْيَةٍ أَهْلَكْنَـٰهَآ ۖ أَفَهُمْ
يُؤْمِنُونَ ٦

7. Before you, also, the messengers We sent were but men, to whom We granted inspiration; if you realise this not, ask of those who possess the message.

وَمَآ أَرْسَلْنَا قَبْلَكَ إِلَّا رِجَالًا نُّوحِىٓ إِلَيْهِمْ ۖ فَسْـَٔلُوٓا۟
أَهْلَ ٱلذِّكْرِ إِن كُنتُمْ لَا تَعْلَمُونَ ٧

8. Nor did We give them bodies that ate no food, nor were they exempt from death.

وَمَا جَعَلْنَـٰهُمْ جَسَدًا لَّا يَأْكُلُونَ ٱلطَّعَامَ
وَمَا كَانُوا۟ خَـٰلِدِينَ ٨

9. In the end We fulfilled to them Our promise, and We saved them and those whom We pleased, but We destroyed those who transgressed beyond bounds.

ثُمَّ صَدَقْنَـٰهُمُ ٱلْوَعْدَ فَأَنجَيْنَـٰهُمْ وَمَن نَّشَآءُ
وَأَهْلَكْنَا ٱلْمُسْرِفِينَ ٩

10. We have revealed for you (O men!) a book in which is a message for you; will you not then understand?

لَقَدْ أَنزَلْنَآ إِلَيْكُمْ كِتَـٰبًا فِيهِ ذِكْرُكُمْ ۚ أَفَلَا
تَعْقِلُونَ ١٠

11. How many were the populations We utterly destroyed because of their iniquities, setting up in their places other peoples!

وَكَمْ قَصَمْنَا مِن قَرْيَةٍ كَانَتْ ظَالِمَةً وَأَنشَأْنَا
بَعْدَهَا قَوْمًا ءَاخَرِينَ ١١

12. Yet, when they felt Our punishment (coming), see they (tried to) flee from it.

فَلَمَّآ أَحَسُّوا۟ بَأْسَنَآ إِذَا هُم مِّنْهَا يَرْكُضُونَ ١٢

13. Flee not, but return to the good things of this life which were given you, and to your homes in order that you may be called to account.

لَا تَرْكُضُوا۟ وَٱرْجِعُوٓا۟ إِلَىٰ مَآ أُتْرِفْتُمْ فِيهِ وَمَسَٰكِنِكُمْ
لَعَلَّكُمْ تُسْـَٔلُونَ ﴿١٣﴾

14. They said: "Ah! Woe to us! We were indeed wrongdoers!"

قَالُوا۟ يَٰوَيْلَنَآ إِنَّا كُنَّا ظَٰلِمِينَ ﴿١٤﴾

15. And that call of theirs ceased not, till We made them as a field that is mown, as ashes silent and quenched.

فَمَا زَالَت تِّلْكَ دَعْوَىٰهُمْ حَتَّىٰ جَعَلْنَٰهُمْ حَصِيدًا
خَٰمِدِينَ ﴿١٥﴾

16. Not for (idle) sport did We create the heavens and the earth and all that is between!

وَمَا خَلَقْنَا ٱلسَّمَآءَ وَٱلْأَرْضَ وَمَا بَيْنَهُمَا لَٰعِبِينَ ﴿١٦﴾

17. If it had been Our wish to take (just) a pastime, We should surely have taken it from the things nearest to Us, if We would do (such a thing)!

لَوْ أَرَدْنَآ أَن نَّتَّخِذَ لَهْوًا لَّٱتَّخَذْنَٰهُ مِن لَّدُنَّآ إِن
كُنَّا فَٰعِلِينَ ﴿١٧﴾

18. Nay We hurl the truth against falsehood and it knocks out its brain and behold falsehood does perish! Ah! Woe be to you for the (false) things you ascribe (to Us).

بَلْ نَقْذِفُ بِٱلْحَقِّ عَلَى ٱلْبَٰطِلِ فَيَدْمَغُهُۥ فَإِذَا هُوَ
زَاهِقٌ ۚ وَلَكُمُ ٱلْوَيْلُ مِمَّا تَصِفُونَ ﴿١٨﴾

19. To Him belong all (creatures) in the heavens and on earth; even those who are in His (very) presence are not too proud to serve Him. Nor are they (ever) weary (of His service).

وَلَهُۥ مَن فِى ٱلسَّمَٰوَٰتِ وَٱلْأَرْضِ ۚ وَمَنْ عِندَهُۥ لَا
يَسْتَكْبِرُونَ عَنْ عِبَادَتِهِۦ وَلَا يَسْتَحْسِرُونَ ﴿١٩﴾

20. They celebrate His praises night and day, nor do they ever flag or intermit.

يُسَبِّحُونَ ٱلَّيْلَ وَٱلنَّهَارَ لَا يَفْتُرُونَ ﴿٢٠﴾

21. Or have they taken (for worship) gods from the earth who can raise (the dead)?

أَمِ ٱتَّخَذُوٓا۟ ءَالِهَةً مِّنَ ٱلْأَرْضِ هُمْ يُنشِرُونَ ﴿٢١﴾

22. If there were in the heavens and the earth, other gods besides Allah, there would have been confusion in both! But glory to

لَوْ كَانَ فِيهِمَآ ءَالِهَةٌ إِلَّا ٱللَّهُ لَفَسَدَتَا ۚ فَسُبْحَٰنَ ٱللَّهِ

رَبِّ ٱلْعَرْشِ عَمَّا يَصِفُونَ ﴿٢٢﴾

Allah, the Lord of the throne: (high is He) above what they attribute to Him!

لَا يُسْـَٔلُ عَمَّا يَفْعَلُ وَهُمْ يُسْـَٔلُونَ ﴿٢٣﴾

23. He cannot be questioned for His acts, but they will be questioned (for theirs).

أَمِ ٱتَّخَذُوا۟ مِن دُونِهِۦٓ ءَالِهَةً ۖ قُلْ هَاتُوا۟ بُرْهَـٰنَكُمْ ۖ
هَـٰذَا ذِكْرُ مَن مَّعِىَ وَذِكْرُ مَن قَبْلِى ۗ بَلْ أَكْثَرُهُمْ لَا
يَعْلَمُونَ ٱلْحَقَّ ۖ فَهُم مُّعْرِضُونَ ﴿٢٤﴾

24. Or have they taken for worship (other) gods besides Him? Say, "Bring your convincing proof; this is the message of those with me and the message of those before me." But most of them know not the truth, and so turn away.

وَمَآ أَرْسَلْنَا مِن قَبْلِكَ مِن رَّسُولٍ إِلَّا نُوحِىٓ إِلَيْهِ
أَنَّهُۥ لَآ إِلَـٰهَ إِلَّآ أَنَا۠ فَٱعْبُدُونِ ﴿٢٥﴾

25. Not a messenger did We send before you without this inspiration sent by Us to him: that there is no god but I; therefore worship and serve Me.

وَقَالُوا۟ ٱتَّخَذَ ٱلرَّحْمَـٰنُ وَلَدًا ۗ سُبْحَـٰنَهُۥ ۚ بَلْ عِبَادٌ
مُّكْرَمُونَ ﴿٢٦﴾

26. And they say: "(Allah) Most Gracious has begotten offspring." Glory to Him! They are (but) servants raised to honour.

لَا يَسْبِقُونَهُۥ بِٱلْقَوْلِ وَهُم بِأَمْرِهِۦ يَعْمَلُونَ ﴿٢٧﴾

27. They speak not before He speaks, and they act (in all things) by His command.

يَعْلَمُ مَا بَيْنَ أَيْدِيهِمْ وَمَا خَلْفَهُمْ وَلَا
يَشْفَعُونَ إِلَّا لِمَنِ ٱرْتَضَىٰ وَهُم مِّنْ خَشْيَتِهِۦ
مُشْفِقُونَ ﴿٢٨﴾

28. He knows what is before them, and what is behind them, and they offer no intercession except for those who are acceptable, and they stand in awe and reverence of His (glory).

ربع الحزب ٣٣ ۞ وَمَن يَقُلْ مِنْهُمْ إِنِّىٓ إِلَـٰهٌ مِّن دُونِهِۦ فَذَٰلِكَ
نَجْزِيهِ جَهَنَّمَ ۚ كَذَٰلِكَ نَجْزِى ٱلظَّـٰلِمِينَ ﴿٢٩﴾

29. If any of them should say, "I am a god besides Him", such a god We should reward with hell; thus do We reward those who do wrong.

أَوَلَمْ يَرَ ٱلَّذِينَ كَفَرُوٓا۟ أَنَّ ٱلسَّمَـٰوَٰتِ وَٱلْأَرْضَ
كَانَتَا رَتْقًا فَفَتَقْنَـٰهُمَا ۖ وَجَعَلْنَا مِنَ ٱلْمَآءِ كُلَّ
شَىْءٍ حَىٍّ ۖ أَفَلَا يُؤْمِنُونَ ﴿٣٠﴾

30. Do not the unbelievers see that the heavens and the earth were joined together (as one unit of creation), before We split them apart? We made from water every living thing. Will they not then believe?

31. And We have set on the earth mountains standing firm, lest it should shake with them, and We have made in it broad highways (between mountains) for them to pass through: that they may receive guidance.

وَجَعَلْنَا فِي ٱلْأَرْضِ رَوَٰسِيَ أَن تَمِيدَ بِهِمْ وَ
جَعَلْنَا فِيهَا فِجَاجًا سُبُلًا لَّعَلَّهُمْ يَهْتَدُونَ ٣١

32. And We have made the heavens as a canopy well-guarded: yet do they turn away from the signs which these things (point to)!

وَجَعَلْنَا ٱلسَّمَآءَ سَقْفًا مَّحْفُوظًا ۖ وَهُمْ عَنْ
ءَايَٰتِهَا مُعْرِضُونَ ٣٢

33. It is He Who created the night and the day, and the sun and the moon; all (the celestial bodies) swim along, each in its rounded course.

وَهُوَ ٱلَّذِي خَلَقَ ٱلَّيْلَ وَٱلنَّهَارَ وَٱلشَّمْسَ وَٱلْقَمَرَ ۖ
كُلٌّ فِي فَلَكٍ يَسْبَحُونَ ٣٣

34. We granted not to any man before you permanent life (here); if then you should die, would they live permanently?

وَمَا جَعَلْنَا لِبَشَرٍ مِّن قَبْلِكَ ٱلْخُلْدَ ۖ أَفَإِيْن مِّتَّ
فَهُمُ ٱلْخَٰلِدُونَ ٣٤

35. Every soul shall have a taste of death; and We test you by evil and by good by way of trial; to Us must you return.

كُلُّ نَفْسٍ ذَآئِقَةُ ٱلْمَوْتِ ۗ وَنَبْلُوكُم بِٱلشَّرِّ
وَٱلْخَيْرِ فِتْنَةً ۖ وَإِلَيْنَا تُرْجَعُونَ ٣٥

36. When the unbelievers see you, they treat you not except with ridicule. "Is this," (they say), "the one who talks of your gods?" And they blaspheme at the mention of (Allah) Most Gracious!

وَإِذَا رَءَاكَ ٱلَّذِينَ كَفَرُوٓا۟ إِن يَتَّخِذُونَكَ إِلَّا
هُزُوًا أَهَٰذَا ٱلَّذِي يَذْكُرُ ءَالِهَتَكُمْ وَهُم
بِذِكْرِ ٱلرَّحْمَٰنِ هُمْ كَٰفِرُونَ ٣٦

37. Man is a creature of haste; soon (enough) will I show you My signs; then you will not ask Me to hasten them!

خُلِقَ ٱلْإِنسَٰنُ مِنْ عَجَلٍ ۚ سَأُو۟رِيكُمْ
ءَايَٰتِي فَلَا تَسْتَعْجِلُونِ ٣٧

38. They say: "When will this promise come to pass, if you are telling the truth?"

وَيَقُولُونَ مَتَىٰ هَٰذَا ٱلْوَعْدُ إِن كُنتُمْ
صَٰدِقِينَ ٣٨

39. If only the unbelievers knew (the time) when they will not be able to ward off the

لَوْ يَعْلَمُ ٱلَّذِينَ كَفَرُوا۟ حِينَ لَا يَكُفُّونَ

fire from their faces, nor yet from their backs, and (when) no help can reach them!

عَن وُجُوهِهِمُ ٱلنَّارَ وَلَا عَن ظُهُورِهِمۡ وَلَا هُمۡ
يُنصَرُونَ ٣٩

40. Nay, it may come to them all of a sudden and confound them; no power will they have then to avert it, nor will they (then) get respite.

بَلۡ تَأۡتِيهِم بَغۡتَةٗ فَتَبۡهَتُهُمۡ فَلَا
يَسۡتَطِيعُونَ رَدَّهَا وَلَا هُمۡ يُنظَرُونَ ٤٠

41. Mocked were (many) prophets before you; but their scoffers were hemmed in by the thing that they mocked.

وَلَقَدِ ٱسۡتُهۡزِئَ بِرُسُلٖ مِّن قَبۡلِكَ فَحَاقَ بِٱلَّذِينَ
سَخِرُواْ مِنۡهُم مَّا كَانُواْ بِهِۦ يَسۡتَهۡزِءُونَ ٤١

42. Say: "Who can keep you safe by night and by day from (the wrath of) (Allah) Most Gracious?" Yet they turn away from the mention of their Lord.

قُلۡ مَن يَكۡلَؤُكُم بِٱلَّيۡلِ وَٱلنَّهَارِ مِنَ ٱلرَّحۡمَٰنِۚ
بَلۡ هُمۡ عَن ذِكۡرِ رَبِّهِم مُّعۡرِضُونَ ٤٢

43. Or have they gods that can guard them from Us? They have no power to aid themselves, nor can they be defended from Us.

أَمۡ لَهُمۡ ءَالِهَةٞ تَمۡنَعُهُم مِّن دُونِنَاۚ
لَا يَسۡتَطِيعُونَ نَصۡرَ أَنفُسِهِمۡ وَلَا هُم مِّنَّا
يُصۡحَبُونَ ٤٣

44. Nay, We gave the good things of this life to these men and their fathers until the period grew long for them; see they not that We gradually reduce the land (in their control) from its outlying borders? Is it then they who will win?

بَلۡ مَتَّعۡنَا هَٰٓؤُلَآءِ وَءَابَآءَهُمۡ حَتَّىٰ طَالَ عَلَيۡهِمُ
ٱلۡعُمُرُۗ أَفَلَا يَرَوۡنَ أَنَّا نَأۡتِي ٱلۡأَرۡضَ نَنقُصُهَا
مِنۡ أَطۡرَافِهَآۚ أَفَهُمُ ٱلۡغَٰلِبُونَ ٤٤

45. Say, "I do but warn you according to revelation": but the deaf will not hear the call, (even) when they are warned!

قُلۡ إِنَّمَآ أُنذِرُكُم بِٱلۡوَحۡيِۚ وَلَا يَسۡمَعُ ٱلصُّمُّ
ٱلدُّعَآءَ إِذَا مَا يُنذَرُونَ ٤٥

46. If but a breath of the wrath of your Lord does touch them, they will then say, "Woe to us! We did wrong indeed!"

وَلَئِن مَّسَّتۡهُمۡ نَفۡحَةٞ مِّنۡ عَذَابِ رَبِّكَ لَيَقُولُنَّ
يَٰوَيۡلَنَآ إِنَّا كُنَّا ظَٰلِمِينَ ٤٦

47. We shall set up scales of justice for the day of judgement, so that not a soul will be dealt with unjustly in the least. And if there be (no more than) the weight of a mustard seed, We will bring it (to account); and enough are We to take account.

وَنَضَعُ ٱلْمَوَٰزِينَ ٱلْقِسْطَ لِيَوْمِ ٱلْقِيَٰمَةِ فَلَا
تُظْلَمُ نَفْسٌ شَيْـًٔا ۖ وَإِن كَانَ مِثْقَالَ حَبَّةٍ
مِّنْ خَرْدَلٍ أَتَيْنَا بِهَا ۗ وَكَفَىٰ بِنَا حَٰسِبِينَ ﴿٤٧﴾

48. In the past We granted to Moses and Aaron the criterion (for judgement), and a light and a message for those who would do right

وَلَقَدْ ءَاتَيْنَا مُوسَىٰ وَهَٰرُونَ ٱلْفُرْقَانَ
وَضِيَآءً وَذِكْرًا لِّلْمُتَّقِينَ ﴿٤٨﴾

49. Those who fear their Lord in their most secret thoughts, and who hold the hour (of judgement) in awe.

ٱلَّذِينَ يَخْشَوْنَ رَبَّهُم بِٱلْغَيْبِ وَهُم مِّنَ ٱلسَّاعَةِ
مُشْفِقُونَ ﴿٤٩﴾

50. And this is a blessed Message which We have sent down; will you then reject it?

وَهَٰذَا ذِكْرٌ مُّبَارَكٌ أَنزَلْنَٰهُ ۚ أَفَأَنتُمْ لَهُۥ
مُنكِرُونَ ﴿٥٠﴾

51. We bestowed before on Abraham his rectitude of conduct, and well were We acquainted with him.

نصف الحزب ٣٣ ۞ وَلَقَدْ ءَاتَيْنَآ إِبْرَٰهِيمَ رُشْدَهُۥ مِن قَبْلُ وَكُنَّا بِهِۦ
عَٰلِمِينَ ﴿٥١﴾

52. See! He said to his father and his people :"What are these images, to which you are (so assiduously) devoted?"

إِذْ قَالَ لِأَبِيهِ وَقَوْمِهِۦ مَا هَٰذِهِ ٱلتَّمَاثِيلُ ٱلَّتِىٓ
أَنتُمْ لَهَا عَٰكِفُونَ ﴿٥٢﴾

53. They said, "We found our fathers worshipping them."

قَالُوا۟ وَجَدْنَآ ءَابَآءَنَا لَهَا عَٰبِدِينَ ﴿٥٣﴾

54. He said, "Indeed you have been in manifest error - you and your fathers."

قَالَ لَقَدْ كُنتُمْ أَنتُمْ وَءَابَآؤُكُمْ فِى ضَلَٰلٍ مُّبِينٍ ﴿٥٤﴾

55. They said, "Have you brought us the truth, or are you one of those who jest?"

قَالُوٓا۟ أَجِئْتَنَا بِٱلْحَقِّ أَمْ أَنتَ مِنَ ٱللَّٰعِبِينَ ﴿٥٥﴾

56. He said, "Nay your Lord is the Lord of the heavens and the earth. He Who created them (from nothing): and I am a witness to this (truth).

قَالَ بَل رَّبُّكُمْ رَبُّ ٱلسَّمَٰوَٰتِ وَٱلْأَرْضِ ٱلَّذِى
فَطَرَهُنَّ وَأَنَا۠ عَلَىٰ ذَٰلِكُم مِّنَ ٱلشَّٰهِدِينَ ﴿٥٦﴾

57. And by Allah, I have a plan for your idols after you go away and turn your backs".

وَتَٱللَّهِ لَأَكِيدَنَّ أَصۡنَٰمَكُم بَعۡدَ أَن
تُوَلُّواْ مُدۡبِرِينَ ٥٧

58. So he broke them to pieces, (all) but the biggest of them, that they might turn (and address themselves) to it.

فَجَعَلَهُمۡ جُذَٰذًا إِلَّا كَبِيرًا لَّهُمۡ لَعَلَّهُمۡ إِلَيۡهِ
يَرۡجِعُونَ ٥٨

59. They said, "Who has done this to our gods? He must indeed be some man of impiety!"

قَالُواْ مَن فَعَلَ هَٰذَا بِـَٔالِهَتِنَآ إِنَّهُۥ لَمِنَ
ٱلظَّٰلِمِينَ ٥٩

60. They said, "We heard a youth talk of them: he is called Abraham."

قَالُواْ سَمِعۡنَا فَتٗى يَذۡكُرُهُمۡ يُقَالُ لَهُۥٓ إِبۡرَٰهِيمُ ٦٠

61. They said, "Then bring him before the eyes of the people, that they may bear witness:"

قَالُواْ فَأۡتُواْ بِهِۦ عَلَىٰٓ أَعۡيُنِ ٱلنَّاسِ لَعَلَّهُمۡ
يَشۡهَدُونَ ٦١

62. They said, "Are you the one that did this with our gods, O Abraham?"

قَالُوٓاْ ءَأَنتَ فَعَلۡتَ هَٰذَا بِـَٔالِهَتِنَا يَٰٓإِبۡرَٰهِيمُ ٦٢

63. He said: "Nay, this was done by this biggest one! Ask them, if they can speak intelligently!"

قَالَ بَلۡ فَعَلَهُۥ كَبِيرُهُمۡ هَٰذَا فَسۡـَٔلُوهُمۡ إِن
كَانُواْ يَنطِقُونَ ٦٣

64. So they turned to themselves and said, "Surely you are the ones in the wrong!"

فَرَجَعُوٓاْ إِلَىٰٓ أَنفُسِهِمۡ فَقَالُوٓاْ إِنَّكُمۡ أَنتُمُ
ٱلظَّٰلِمُونَ ٦٤

65. Then were they confounded with shame: (they said) "You know full well that these (idols) do not speak!"

ثُمَّ نُكِسُواْ عَلَىٰ رُءُوسِهِمۡ لَقَدۡ عَلِمۡتَ مَا هَٰٓؤُلَآءِ
يَنطِقُونَ ٦٥

66. (Abraham) said, "Do you then worship, besides Allah, things that can neither be of any good to you nor do you harm?"

قَالَ أَفَتَعۡبُدُونَ مِن دُونِ ٱللَّهِ مَا لَا
يَنفَعُكُمۡ شَيۡـٔٗا وَلَا يَضُرُّكُمۡ ٦٦

67. "Fie upon you, and upon the things that you worship besides Allah! Have you no sense?"...

أُفٍّ لَّكُمْ وَلِمَا تَعْبُدُونَ مِن دُونِ ٱللَّهِ
أَفَلَا تَعْقِلُونَ ﴿٦٧﴾

68. They said, "Burn him and protect your gods, if you do (anything at all)!"

قَالُوا۟ حَرِّقُوهُ وَٱنصُرُوٓا۟ ءَالِهَتَكُمْ إِن كُنتُمْ
فَٰعِلِينَ ﴿٦٨﴾

69. We said, "O fire! Be you cool, and (a means of)) safety for Abraham!"

قُلْنَا يَٰنَارُ كُونِى بَرْدًا وَسَلَٰمًا عَلَىٰٓ إِبْرَٰهِيمَ ﴿٦٩﴾

70. Then they sought a stratagem against him: but We made them the ones that lost most!

وَأَرَادُوا۟ بِهِۦ كَيْدًا فَجَعَلْنَٰهُمُ ٱلْأَخْسَرِينَ ﴿٧٠﴾

71. But We delivered him and (his nephew) Lot (and directed them) to the land which We have blessed for the nations.

وَنَجَّيْنَٰهُ وَلُوطًا إِلَى ٱلْأَرْضِ ٱلَّتِى بَٰرَكْنَا فِيهَا
لِلْعَٰلَمِينَ ﴿٧١﴾

72. And We bestowed on him Isaac and, as an additional gift, (a grandson), Jacob, and We made righteous men of every one (of them).

وَوَهَبْنَا لَهُۥٓ إِسْحَٰقَ وَيَعْقُوبَ نَافِلَةً ۖ وَكُلًّا
جَعَلْنَا صَٰلِحِينَ ﴿٧٢﴾

73. And We made them leaders, guiding (men) by Our command, and We sent them inspiration to do good deeds, to establish regular prayers, and to practice regular charity; and they constantly served Us (and Us only).

وَجَعَلْنَٰهُمْ أَئِمَّةً يَهْدُونَ بِأَمْرِنَا وَأَوْحَيْنَآ
إِلَيْهِمْ فِعْلَ ٱلْخَيْرَٰتِ وَإِقَامَ ٱلصَّلَوٰةِ وَإِيتَآءَ
ٱلزَّكَوٰةِ ۖ وَكَانُوا۟ لَنَا عَٰبِدِينَ ﴿٧٣﴾

74. And to Lot, too, we gave judgement and knowledge, and We saved him from the town which practised abominations: truly they were a people given to evil, a rebellious people.

وَلُوطًا ءَاتَيْنَٰهُ حُكْمًا وَعِلْمًا وَنَجَّيْنَٰهُ مِنَ
ٱلْقَرْيَةِ ٱلَّتِى كَانَت تَّعْمَلُ ٱلْخَبَٰٓئِثَ ۗ إِنَّهُمْ
كَانُوا۟ قَوْمَ سَوْءٍ فَٰسِقِينَ ﴿٧٤﴾

75. And We admitted him to Our mercy: for he was one of the righteous.

وَأَدْخَلْنَٰهُ فِى رَحْمَتِنَآ ۖ إِنَّهُۥ مِنَ ٱلصَّٰلِحِينَ ﴿٧٥﴾

76. (Remember) Noah, when he called (to Us) before: We listened to his (prayer)

وَنُوحًا إِذْ نَادَىٰ مِن قَبْلُ فَٱسْتَجَبْنَا لَهُۥ

and delivered him and his family from great distress.

فَنَجَّيۡنَٰهُ وَأَهۡلَهُۥ مِنَ ٱلۡكَرۡبِ ٱلۡعَظِيمِ ٧٦

77. We helped him against people who rejected Our signs; truly they were a people given to evil: so We drowned them (in the flood) all together.

وَنَصَرۡنَٰهُ مِنَ ٱلۡقَوۡمِ ٱلَّذِينَ كَذَّبُواْ بِـَٔايَٰتِنَآۚ
إِنَّهُمۡ كَانُواْ قَوۡمَ سَوۡءٖ فَأَغۡرَقۡنَٰهُمۡ أَجۡمَعِينَ ٧٧

78. And remember David and Solomon, when they gave judgement in the matter of the field into which the sheep of certain people had strayed by night: We did witness their judgement.

وَدَاوُۥدَ وَسُلَيۡمَٰنَ إِذۡ يَحۡكُمَانِ فِي ٱلۡحَرۡثِ إِذۡ
نَفَشَتۡ فِيهِ غَنَمُ ٱلۡقَوۡمِ وَكُنَّا لِحُكۡمِهِمۡ
شَٰهِدِينَ ٧٨

79. To Solomon We inspired the (right) understanding of the matter; to each (of them) We gave judgement and knowledge; it was Our power that made the hills and the birds celebrate Our praises with David: it was We Who did (these things).

فَفَهَّمۡنَٰهَا سُلَيۡمَٰنَۚ وَكُلًّا ءَاتَيۡنَا حُكۡمٗا وَ
عِلۡمٗاۚ وَسَخَّرۡنَا مَعَ دَاوُۥدَ ٱلۡجِبَالَ يُسَبِّحۡنَ
وَٱلطَّيۡرَۚ وَكُنَّا فَٰعِلِينَ ٧٩

80. It was We Who taught him the making of coats of mail for your benefit, to guard you from each others violence: will you then be grateful?

وَعَلَّمۡنَٰهُ صَنۡعَةَ لَبُوسٖ لَّكُمۡ لِتُحۡصِنَكُم
مِّنۢ بَأۡسِكُمۡۖ فَهَلۡ أَنتُمۡ شَٰكِرُونَ ٨٠

81. (It was Our power that made) the violent (unruly) wind flow (tamely) for Solomon, to his order, to the land which We had blessed: for We do know all things.

وَلِسُلَيۡمَٰنَ ٱلرِّيحَ عَاصِفَةٗ تَجۡرِي بِأَمۡرِهِۦٓ إِلَى ٱلۡأَرۡضِ
ٱلَّتِي بَٰرَكۡنَا فِيهَاۚ وَكُنَّا بِكُلِّ شَيۡءٍ عَٰلِمِينَ ٨١

82. And of the evil ones, were some who dived for him, and did other work besides; and it was We Who guarded them.

وَمِنَ ٱلشَّيَٰطِينِ مَن يَغُوصُونَ لَهُۥ وَيَعۡمَلُونَ
عَمَلٗا دُونَ ذَٰلِكَۖ وَكُنَّا لَهُمۡ حَٰفِظِينَ ٨٢

83. And (remember) Job, when he cried to his Lord, "Truly distress has seized me. But You are the Most Merciful of those that are merciful."

۞ وَأَيُّوبَ إِذۡ نَادَىٰ رَبَّهُۥٓ أَنِّي مَسَّنِيَ ٱلضُّرُّ ثلاثة أرباع الحزب ٣١
وَأَنتَ أَرۡحَمُ ٱلرَّٰحِمِينَ ٨٣

84. So We listened to him: We removed the distress that was on him, and We restored his people to him, and doubled their number as a grace from Ourselves, and a thing for commemoration, for all who serve Us.

فَٱسۡتَجَبۡنَا لَهُۥ فَكَشَفۡنَا مَا بِهِۦ مِن ضُرّٖۖ
وَءَاتَيۡنَٰهُ أَهۡلَهُۥ وَمِثۡلَهُم مَّعَهُمۡ رَحۡمَةٗ مِّنۡ
عِندِنَا وَذِكۡرَىٰ لِلۡعَٰبِدِينَ ٨٤

85. And (remember) Ishmael, Idris, and Dhu'l-Kifl, all (men) of constancy and patience;

وَإِسۡمَٰعِيلَ وَإِدۡرِيسَ وَذَا ٱلۡكِفۡلِۖ كُلّٞ مِّنَ
ٱلصَّٰبِرِينَ ٨٥

86. We admitted them to Our mercy: for they were of the righteous ones.

وَأَدۡخَلۡنَٰهُمۡ فِي رَحۡمَتِنَآۖ إِنَّهُم مِّنَ
ٱلصَّٰلِحِينَ ٨٦

87. And remember Dhu'n-Nun, when he departed in wrath: he imagined that We had no power over him! But he cried through the depths of darkness, "There is no god but You: Glory to You; I was indeed wrong!"

وَذَا ٱلنُّونِ إِذ ذَّهَبَ مُغَٰضِبٗا فَظَنَّ أَن لَّن
نَّقۡدِرَ عَلَيۡهِ فَنَادَىٰ فِي ٱلظُّلُمَٰتِ أَن لَّآ إِلَٰهَ
إِلَّآ أَنتَ سُبۡحَٰنَكَ إِنِّي كُنتُ مِنَ
ٱلظَّٰلِمِينَ ٨٧

88. So We listened to him and delivered him from distress: and thus do We deliver those who have faith.

فَٱسۡتَجَبۡنَا لَهُۥ وَنَجَّيۡنَٰهُ مِنَ ٱلۡغَمِّۚ وَكَذَٰلِكَ
نُـۨجِي ٱلۡمُؤۡمِنِينَ ٨٨

89. And (remember) Zakariya, when he called to his Lord: "O my Lord! Leave me not without offspring, though You are the best of inheritors."

وَزَكَرِيَّآ إِذۡ نَادَىٰ رَبَّهُۥ رَبِّ لَا تَذَرۡنِي فَرۡدٗا
وَأَنتَ خَيۡرُ ٱلۡوَٰرِثِينَ ٨٩

90. So We listened to him; and We granted him Yahya; We cured his wife's (barrenness) for him. These three were ever quick in emulation in good works: they used to call on Us with love and reverence, and humble themselves before Us.

فَٱسۡتَجَبۡنَا لَهُۥ وَوَهَبۡنَا لَهُۥ يَحۡيَىٰ
وَأَصۡلَحۡنَا لَهُۥ زَوۡجَهُۥٓۚ إِنَّهُمۡ كَانُواْ
يُسَٰرِعُونَ فِي ٱلۡخَيۡرَٰتِ وَيَدۡعُونَنَا رَغَبٗا
وَرَهَبٗاۖ وَكَانُواْ لَنَا خَٰشِعِينَ ٩٠

91. And (remember) her who guarded her chastity: We breathed into her of Our Spirit, and We made her and her son a sign for all peoples.

وَٱلَّتِيٓ أَحۡصَنَتۡ فَرۡجَهَا فَنَفَخۡنَا فِيهَا
مِن رُّوحِنَا وَجَعَلۡنَٰهَا وَٱبۡنَهَآ ءَايَةٗ
لِّلۡعَٰلَمِينَ ٩١

92. Verily, this brotherhood of yours is a single brotherhood, and I am your Lord and Cherisher: therefore serve Me (and no other).

إِنَّ هَٰذِهِۦٓ أُمَّتُكُمۡ أُمَّةٗ وَٰحِدَةٗ وَأَنَا۠
رَبُّكُمۡ فَٱعۡبُدُونِ ٩٢

93. But (later generations) cut off their affair (of unity) one from another: (yet) will they all return to Us.

وَتَقَطَّعُوٓاْ أَمۡرَهُم بَيۡنَهُمۡۖ كُلٌّ إِلَيۡنَا
رَٰجِعُونَ ٩٣

94. Whoever works any act of righteousness and has faith, his endeavour will not be rejected; We shall record it in his favour.

فَمَن يَعۡمَلۡ مِنَ ٱلصَّٰلِحَٰتِ وَهُوَ مُؤۡمِنٞ فَلَا
كُفۡرَانَ لِسَعۡيِهِۦ وَإِنَّا لَهُۥ كَٰتِبُونَ ٩٤

95. But there is a ban on any population which We have destroyed: that they shall not return.

وَحَرَٰمٌ عَلَىٰ قَرۡيَةٍ أَهۡلَكۡنَٰهَآ أَنَّهُمۡ
لَا يَرۡجِعُونَ ٩٥

96. Until the Gog and Magog (people) are let through (their barrier), and they swiftly swarm from every hill.

حَتَّىٰٓ إِذَا فُتِحَتۡ يَأۡجُوجُ وَمَأۡجُوجُ وَهُم مِّن
كُلِّ حَدَبٖ يَنسِلُونَ ٩٦

97. Then will the true promise draw near (of fulfilment): then see! The eyes of the unbelievers will fixedly stare in horror: "Ah! Woe to us! We were indeed heedless of this; nay we truly did wrong!"

وَٱقۡتَرَبَ ٱلۡوَعۡدُ ٱلۡحَقُّ فَإِذَا هِيَ شَٰخِصَةٌ
أَبۡصَٰرُ ٱلَّذِينَ كَفَرُواْ يَٰوَيۡلَنَا قَدۡ كُنَّا فِي
غَفۡلَةٖ مِّنۡ هَٰذَا بَلۡ كُنَّا ظَٰلِمِينَ ٩٧

98. Verily you, (unbelievers) and the (false) gods that you worship besides Allah, are (but) fuel for hell! To it will you (surely) come!

إِنَّكُمۡ وَمَا تَعۡبُدُونَ مِن دُونِ ٱللَّهِ
حَصَبُ جَهَنَّمَ أَنتُمۡ لَهَا وَٰرِدُونَ ٩٨

99. If these had been gods, they would not have got there! But each one will remain in it.

لَوۡ كَانَ هَٰٓؤُلَآءِ ءَالِهَةٗ مَّا وَرَدُوهَاۖ
وَكُلّٞ فِيهَا خَٰلِدُونَ ٩٩

100. There, sobbing will be their lot, nor will they there hear (anything else).

لَهُمۡ فِيهَا زَفِيرٞ وَهُمۡ فِيهَا لَا يَسۡمَعُونَ ١٠٠

101. Those for whom the good (record) from Us has gone before, will be removed far from it.

إِنَّ ٱلَّذِينَ سَبَقَتۡ لَهُم مِّنَّا ٱلۡحُسۡنَىٰٓ أُوْلَٰٓئِكَ
عَنۡهَا مُبۡعَدُونَ ١٠١

102. Not the slightest sound will they hear of hell: what their souls desired, in that will they dwell.

لَا يَسۡمَعُونَ حَسِيسَهَاۖ وَهُمۡ فِي مَا ٱشۡتَهَتۡ
أَنفُسُهُمۡ خَٰلِدُونَ ١٠٢

103. The great terror will bring them no grief; but the angels will meet them (with mutual greetings): "This is your day (the day) that you were promised."

لَا يَحۡزُنُهُمُ ٱلۡفَزَعُ ٱلۡأَكۡبَرُ وَتَتَلَقَّىٰهُمُ
ٱلۡمَلَٰٓئِكَةُ هَٰذَا يَوۡمُكُمُ ٱلَّذِي كُنتُمۡ
تُوعَدُونَ ١٠٣

104. The day that We roll up the heavens like a scroll rolled up for books (completed) even as We produced the first creation, so shall We produce a new one: a promise We have undertaken: truly shall We fulfil it.

يَوۡمَ نَطۡوِي ٱلسَّمَآءَ كَطَيِّ ٱلسِّجِلِّ لِلۡكُتُبِۚ
كَمَا بَدَأۡنَآ أَوَّلَ خَلۡقٖ نُّعِيدُهُۥۚ وَعۡدًا عَلَيۡنَآۚ
إِنَّا كُنَّا فَٰعِلِينَ ١٠٤

105. Before this We wrote in the Psalms, after the message (given to Moses): My servants, the righteous, shall inherit the earth."

وَلَقَدۡ كَتَبۡنَا فِي ٱلزَّبُورِ مِنۢ بَعۡدِ ٱلذِّكۡرِ أَنَّ
ٱلۡأَرۡضَ يَرِثُهَا عِبَادِيَ ٱلصَّٰلِحُونَ ١٠٥

106. Verily in the (Qur'an) is a message for people who would (truly) worship Allah.

إِنَّ فِي هَٰذَا لَبَلَٰغٗا لِّقَوۡمٍ عَٰبِدِينَ ١٠٦

107. We sent you not, but as a mercy for all creatures.

وَمَآ أَرۡسَلۡنَٰكَ إِلَّا رَحۡمَةٗ لِّلۡعَٰلَمِينَ ١٠٧

108. Say: "What has come to me by inspiration is that your God is One God: will you therefore bow to His will (in Islam)?"

قُلۡ إِنَّمَا يُوحَىٰٓ إِلَيَّ أَنَّمَآ إِلَٰهُكُمۡ إِلَٰهٞ
وَٰحِدٞۖ فَهَلۡ أَنتُم مُّسۡلِمُونَ ١٠٨

109. But if they turn back, say: "I have proclaimed the message to you all alike and in truth; but I know not whether that which you are promised is near or far."

فَإِن تَوَلَّوْا۟ فَقُلْ ءَاذَنتُكُمْ عَلَىٰ سَوَآءٍ ۖ وَإِنْ أَدْرِىٓ
أَقَرِيبٌ أَم بَعِيدٌ مَّا تُوعَدُونَ ﴿١٠٩﴾

110. "It is He Who knows what is open in speech and what you hide (in your hearts)."

إِنَّهُۥ يَعْلَمُ ٱلْجَهْرَ مِنَ ٱلْقَوْلِ وَيَعْلَمُ
مَا تَكْتُمُونَ ﴿١١٠﴾

111. "I know not but that it may be a trial for you, and a grant of (worldly) livelihood (to you) for a time."

وَإِنْ أَدْرِى لَعَلَّهُۥ فِتْنَةٌ لَّكُمْ وَمَتَٰعٌ إِلَىٰ
حِينٍ ﴿١١١﴾

112. Say: "O my Lord! Judge You in truth!" "Our Lord Most Gracious is the One Whose assistance should be sought against the blasphemies you utter!"

قَٰلَ رَبِّ ٱحْكُم بِٱلْحَقِّ ۗ وَرَبُّنَا ٱلرَّحْمَٰنُ
ٱلْمُسْتَعَانُ عَلَىٰ مَا تَصِفُونَ ﴿١١٢﴾

سُورَةُ الحَجِّ

Surah 22: ***Al-Hajj*** **(The Pilgrimage)**

In the name of Allah,
Most Gracious, Most Merciful.

بِسْمِ ٱللَّهِ ٱلرَّحْمَٰنِ ٱلرَّحِيمِ

1. O mankind! Fear your Lord! For the convulsion of the hour (of judgement) will be a thing terrible!

الحِزْبُ ٣٤ يَٰٓأَيُّهَا ٱلنَّاسُ ٱتَّقُوا۟ رَبَّكُمْ ۚ إِنَّ زَلْزَلَةَ ٱلسَّاعَةِ
شَىْءٌ عَظِيمٌ ﴿١﴾

2. The day you shall see it, every mother giving suck shall forget her suckling-babe, and every pregnant female shall drop her load (unformed): you shall see mankind as in a drunken riot, yet not drunk; but dreadful will be the wrath of Allah.

يَوْمَ تَرَوْنَهَا تَذْهَلُ كُلُّ مُرْضِعَةٍ عَمَّآ أَرْضَعَتْ
وَتَضَعُ كُلُّ ذَاتِ حَمْلٍ حَمْلَهَا وَتَرَى ٱلنَّاسَ
سُكَٰرَىٰ وَمَا هُم بِسُكَٰرَىٰ وَلَٰكِنَّ عَذَابَ
ٱللَّهِ شَدِيدٌ ﴿٢﴾

3. And yet among men there are such as dispute about Allah, without knowledge, and follow every evil one obstinate in rebellion!

وَمِنَ ٱلنَّاسِ مَن يُجَٰدِلُ فِى ٱللَّهِ بِغَيْرِ عِلْمٍ وَيَتَّبِعُ
كُلَّ شَيْطَٰنٍ مَّرِيدٍ ﴿٣﴾

4. About the (evil one) it is decreed that whoever turns to him for friendship, him will he lead astray, and he will guide him to the penalty of the fire.

كُتِبَ عَلَيْهِ أَنَّهُۥ مَن تَوَلَّاهُ فَأَنَّهُۥ يُضِلُّهُۥ
وَيَهْدِيهِ إِلَىٰ عَذَابِ ٱلسَّعِيرِ ٤

5. O mankind! If you have a doubt about the resurrection, (consider) that We created you out of dust, then out of sperm, then out of a leech - like clot, then out a morsel of flesh, partly formed and partly unformed, in order that We may manifest (Our power) to you; and We cause whom We will to rest in the wombs for an appointed term, then do We bring you out as babes, then (foster you) that you may reach your age of full strength; and some of you are called to die, and some are sent back to the feeblest old age, so that they know nothing after having known (much). And (further), you see the earth barren and lifeless, but when We pour down rain on it, it is stirred (to life), it swells, and it puts forth every kind of beautiful growth (in pairs).

يَٰٓأَيُّهَا ٱلنَّاسُ إِن كُنتُمْ فِى رَيْبٍ مِّنَ ٱلْبَعْثِ
فَإِنَّا خَلَقْنَٰكُم مِّن تُرَابٍ ثُمَّ مِن نُّطْفَةٍ
ثُمَّ مِنْ عَلَقَةٍ ثُمَّ مِن مُّضْغَةٍ مُّخَلَّقَةٍ وَغَيْرِ
مُخَلَّقَةٍ لِّنُبَيِّنَ لَكُمْ ۚ وَنُقِرُّ فِى ٱلْأَرْحَامِ مَا نَشَآءُ
إِلَىٰٓ أَجَلٍ مُّسَمًّى ثُمَّ نُخْرِجُكُمْ طِفْلًا ثُمَّ لِتَبْلُغُوٓا۟
أَشُدَّكُمْ ۖ وَمِنكُم مَّن يُتَوَفَّىٰ وَمِنكُم مَّن
يُرَدُّ إِلَىٰٓ أَرْذَلِ ٱلْعُمُرِ لِكَيْلَا يَعْلَمَ مِنۢ بَعْدِ
عِلْمٍ شَيْـًٔا ۚ وَتَرَى ٱلْأَرْضَ هَامِدَةً فَإِذَآ أَنزَلْنَا
عَلَيْهَا ٱلْمَآءَ ٱهْتَزَّتْ وَرَبَتْ وَأَنۢبَتَتْ مِن كُلِّ
زَوْجٍۭ بَهِيجٍ ٥

6. This is so, because Allah is the reality: it is He Who gives life to the dead, and it is He Who has power over all things.

ذَٰلِكَ بِأَنَّ ٱللَّهَ هُوَ ٱلْحَقُّ وَأَنَّهُۥ يُحْىِ ٱلْمَوْتَىٰ وَأَنَّهُۥ عَلَىٰ
كُلِّ شَىْءٍ قَدِيرٌ ٦

7. And verily the hour will come: there can be no doubt about it, or about (the fact) that Allah will raise up all who are in the graves.

وَأَنَّ ٱلسَّاعَةَ ءَاتِيَةٌ لَّا رَيْبَ فِيهَا وَأَنَّ ٱللَّهَ يَبْعَثُ مَن
فِى ٱلْقُبُورِ ٧

8. Yet there is among men such a one as disputes about Allah, without knowledge, without guidance, and without a book of enlightenment-

وَمِنَ ٱلنَّاسِ مَن يُجَٰدِلُ فِى ٱللَّهِ بِغَيْرِ عِلْمٍ وَلَا هُدًى
وَلَا كِتَٰبٍ مُّنِيرٍ ٨

9. (Disdainfully) bending his side, in order to (lead men) astray from the path of Allah;

ثَانِىَ عِطْفِهِۦ لِيُضِلَّ عَن سَبِيلِ ٱللَّهِ ۖ لَهُۥ فِى ٱلدُّنْيَا

for him there is disgrace in this life, and on the day of judgement We shall make him taste the penalty of burning (fire).

خِزۡيٞۖ وَنُذِيقُهُۥ يَوۡمَ ٱلۡقِيَٰمَةِ عَذَابَ ٱلۡحَرِيقِ ٩

10. (It will be said): "This is because of the deeds which your hands sent before, for verily Allah is not unjust to His servants."

ذَٰلِكَ بِمَا قَدَّمَتۡ يَدَاكَ وَأَنَّ ٱللَّهَ لَيۡسَ بِظَلَّٰمٖ
لِّلۡعَبِيدِ ١٠

11. There are among men some who serve Allah, as it were, on the verge: if good befalls them, they are with it well content; but if a trial comes to them, they turn on their faces; they lose both this world and the hereafter: that is loss for all to see!

وَمِنَ ٱلنَّاسِ مَن يَعۡبُدُ ٱللَّهَ عَلَىٰ حَرۡفٖۖ فَإِنۡ أَصَابَهُۥ
خَيۡرٌ ٱطۡمَأَنَّ بِهِۦۖ وَإِنۡ أَصَابَتۡهُ فِتۡنَةٌ ٱنقَلَبَ عَلَىٰ
وَجۡهِهِۦ خَسِرَ ٱلدُّنۡيَا وَٱلۡأٓخِرَةَۚ ذَٰلِكَ هُوَ ٱلۡخُسۡرَانُ
ٱلۡمُبِينُ ١١

12. They call on such deities, besides Allah, as can neither hurt nor profit them: that is straying far indeed (from the way)!

يَدۡعُواْ مِن دُونِ ٱللَّهِ مَا لَا يَضُرُّهُۥ وَمَا لَا يَنفَعُهُۥۚ
ذَٰلِكَ هُوَ ٱلضَّلَٰلُ ٱلۡبَعِيدُ ١٢

13. (Perhaps) they call on one whose hurt is nearer than his profit: evil indeed, is the patron, and evil the companion (for help)!

يَدۡعُواْ لَمَن ضَرُّهُۥٓ أَقۡرَبُ مِن نَّفۡعِهِۦۚ لَبِئۡسَ ٱلۡمَوۡلَىٰ
وَلَبِئۡسَ ٱلۡعَشِيرُ ١٣

14. Verily Allah will admit those who believe and work righteous deeds, to gardens, beneath which rivers flow: for Allah carries out all that He plans.

إِنَّ ٱللَّهَ يُدۡخِلُ ٱلَّذِينَ ءَامَنُواْ وَعَمِلُواْ
ٱلصَّٰلِحَٰتِ جَنَّٰتٖ تَجۡرِي مِن تَحۡتِهَا ٱلۡأَنۡهَٰرُۚ
إِنَّ ٱللَّهَ يَفۡعَلُ مَا يُرِيدُ ١٤

15. If any think that Allah will not help him (His messenger) in this world and the hereafter, let him stretch out a rope to the ceiling and cut (himself) off: then let him see whether his plan will remove that which enrages (him)!

مَن كَانَ يَظُنُّ أَن لَّن يَنصُرَهُ ٱللَّهُ فِي ٱلدُّنۡيَا وَٱلۡأٓخِرَةِ
فَلۡيَمۡدُدۡ بِسَبَبٍ إِلَى ٱلسَّمَآءِ ثُمَّ لۡيَقۡطَعۡ فَلۡيَنظُرۡ هَلۡ
يُذۡهِبَنَّ كَيۡدُهُۥ مَا يَغِيظُ ١٥

16. Thus have We sent down clear signs; and verily Allah does guide whom He will!

وَكَذَٰلِكَ أَنزَلۡنَٰهُ ءَايَٰتِۭ بَيِّنَٰتٖ وَأَنَّ ٱللَّهَ يَهۡدِي
مَن يُرِيدُ ١٦

17. Those who believe (in the Qur'an), those who follow the Jewish (scriptures), and the Sabians, Christians, Magians and Polytheists - Allah will judge between them on the day of judgement: for Allah is witness of all things.

إِنَّ ٱلَّذِينَ ءَامَنُواْ وَٱلَّذِينَ هَادُواْ وَٱلصَّٰبِـِٔينَ
وَٱلنَّصَٰرَىٰ وَٱلْمَجُوسَ وَٱلَّذِينَ أَشْرَكُوٓاْ إِنَّ
ٱللَّهَ يَفْصِلُ بَيْنَهُمْ يَوْمَ ٱلْقِيَٰمَةِ ۚ إِنَّ ٱللَّهَ عَلَىٰ كُلِّ
شَىْءٍ شَهِيدٌ ﴿١٧﴾

18. Do you not see that to Allah bow down in worship all things that are in the heavens and on earth - the sun, the moon, the stars; the hills, the trees, the animals; and a great number among mankind? But a great number are (also) such as are fit for punishment; and such as Allah shall disgrace - none can rise to honour: for Allah carries out all that He wills.

أَلَمْ تَرَ أَنَّ ٱللَّهَ يَسْجُدُ لَهُۥ مَن فِى ٱلسَّمَٰوَٰتِ وَمَن
فِى ٱلْأَرْضِ وَٱلشَّمْسُ وَٱلْقَمَرُ وَٱلنُّجُومُ
وَٱلْجِبَالُ وَٱلشَّجَرُ وَٱلدَّوَآبُّ وَكَثِيرٌ مِّنَ ٱلنَّاسِ ۖ
وَكَثِيرٌ حَقَّ عَلَيْهِ ٱلْعَذَابُ ۗ وَمَن يُهِنِ ٱللَّهُ فَمَا لَهُۥ
مِن مُّكْرِمٍ ۚ إِنَّ ٱللَّهَ يَفْعَلُ مَا يَشَآءُ ۩ ﴿١٨﴾ سجدة

19. These two antagonists dispute with each other about their Lord; but those who deny (their Lord) - for them will be cut out a garment of fire: over their heads will be poured out boiling water.

ربع الحزب ٣٤ ۞ هَٰذَانِ خَصْمَانِ ٱخْتَصَمُواْ فِى رَبِّهِمْ ۖ فَٱلَّذِينَ
كَفَرُواْ قُطِّعَتْ لَهُمْ ثِيَابٌ مِّن نَّارٍ يُصَبُّ
مِن فَوْقِ رُءُوسِهِمُ ٱلْحَمِيمُ ﴿١٩﴾

20. With it will be scalded what is within their bodies, as well as (their) skins.

يُصْهَرُ بِهِۦ مَا فِى بُطُونِهِمْ وَٱلْجُلُودُ ﴿٢٠﴾

21. In addition there will be maces of iron (to punish) them.

وَلَهُم مَّقَٰمِعُ مِنْ حَدِيدٍ ﴿٢١﴾

22. Every time they wish to get away from it, from anguish, they will be forced back in it, and (it will be said), "Taste you the penalty of Burning!"

كُلَّمَآ أَرَادُوٓاْ أَن يَخْرُجُواْ مِنْهَا مِنْ غَمٍّ أُعِيدُواْ
فِيهَا وَذُوقُواْ عَذَابَ ٱلْحَرِيقِ ﴿٢٢﴾

23. Allah will admit those who believe and work righteous deeds. To gardens beneath which rivers flow: they shall be adorned in

إِنَّ ٱللَّهَ يُدْخِلُ ٱلَّذِينَ ءَامَنُواْ وَعَمِلُواْ ٱلصَّٰلِحَٰتِ
جَنَّٰتٍ تَجْرِى مِن تَحْتِهَا ٱلْأَنْهَٰرُ يُحَلَّوْنَ

فِيهَا مِنۡ أَسَاوِرَ مِن ذَهَبٖ وَلُؤۡلُؤٗاۖ
وَلِبَاسُهُمۡ فِيهَا حَرِيرٞ ٢٣

it with bracelets of gold and pearls; and their garments there will be of silk.

وَهُدُوٓاْ إِلَى ٱلطَّيِّبِ مِنَ ٱلۡقَوۡلِ وَهُدُوٓاْ إِلَىٰ
صِرَٰطِ ٱلۡحَمِيدِ ٢٤

24. For they have been guided (in this life) to the purest of speeches; they have been guided to the path of Him Who is worthy of (all) praise.

إِنَّ ٱلَّذِينَ كَفَرُواْ وَيَصُدُّونَ عَن سَبِيلِ ٱللَّهِ
وَٱلۡمَسۡجِدِ ٱلۡحَرَامِ ٱلَّذِي جَعَلۡنَٰهُ لِلنَّاسِ سَوَآءً
ٱلۡعَٰكِفُ فِيهِ وَٱلۡبَادِۚ وَمَن يُرِدۡ فِيهِ بِإِلۡحَادِۭ
بِظُلۡمٖ نُّذِقۡهُ مِنۡ عَذَابٍ أَلِيمٖ ٢٥

25. As to those who have rejected (Allah), and would keep back (men) from the way of Allah, and from the Sacred Mosque, which We have made (open) to (all) men - equal is the dweller there and the visitor from the country - and any whose purpose in it is profanity or wrongdoing - them will We cause to taste of a most grievous penalty.

وَإِذۡ بَوَّأۡنَا لِإِبۡرَٰهِيمَ مَكَانَ ٱلۡبَيۡتِ أَن لَّا
تُشۡرِكۡ بِي شَيۡـٔٗا وَطَهِّرۡ بَيۡتِيَ لِلطَّآئِفِينَ
وَٱلۡقَآئِمِينَ وَٱلرُّكَّعِ ٱلسُّجُودِ ٢٦

26. See! We gave the site to Abraham, of the (Sacred) House (saying): "Associate not any thing (in worship) with Me; and sanctify My House for those who encompass it, or stand up, or bow or prostrate themselves (in it in prayer)."

وَأَذِّن فِي ٱلنَّاسِ بِٱلۡحَجِّ يَأۡتُوكَ رِجَالٗا وَعَلَىٰ
كُلِّ ضَامِرٖ يَأۡتِينَ مِن كُلِّ فَجٍّ عَمِيقٖ ٢٧

27. "And proclaim the Pilgrimage among men: they will come to you on foot and (mounted) on every kind of camel, lean on account of journeys through deep and distant mountain highways;

لِّيَشۡهَدُواْ مَنَٰفِعَ لَهُمۡ وَيَذۡكُرُواْ ٱسۡمَ ٱللَّهِ
فِيٓ أَيَّامٖ مَّعۡلُومَٰتٍ عَلَىٰ مَا رَزَقَهُم مِّنۢ
بَهِيمَةِ ٱلۡأَنۡعَٰمِۖ فَكُلُواْ مِنۡهَا وَأَطۡعِمُواْ
ٱلۡبَآئِسَ ٱلۡفَقِيرَ ٢٨

28. That they may witness the benefits (provided) for them, and celebrate the name of Allah, through the Days appointed, over the cattle which He has provided for them (for sacrifice): then eat you of it and feed the distressed ones in want.

ثُمَّ لۡيَقۡضُواْ تَفَثَهُمۡ وَلۡيُوفُواْ نُذُورَهُمۡ

29. Then let them complete the rites

prescribed for them, perform their vows and (again) circumambulate the Ancient House."

وَلۡيَطَّوَّفُواْ بِٱلۡبَيۡتِ ٱلۡعَتِيقِ ٢٩

30. Such (is the Pilgrimage): whoever honours the sacred rites of Allah, for him it is good in the sight of his Lord. Lawful to you (for food in pilgrimage) are cattle, except those mentioned to you (as exceptions): but shun the abomination of idols, and shun the word that is false -

ذَٰلِكَۖ وَمَن يُعَظِّمۡ حُرُمَٰتِ ٱللَّهِ فَهُوَ
خَيۡرٞ لَّهُۥ عِندَ رَبِّهِۦۗ وَأُحِلَّتۡ لَكُمُ
ٱلۡأَنۡعَٰمُ إِلَّا مَا يُتۡلَىٰ عَلَيۡكُمۡۖ فَٱجۡتَنِبُواْ
ٱلرِّجۡسَ مِنَ ٱلۡأَوۡثَٰنِ وَٱجۡتَنِبُواْ قَوۡلَ ٱلزُّورِ ٣٠

31. Being true in faith to Allah, and never assigning partners to Him: if anyone assigns partners to Allah, he is as if he had fallen from heaven and been snatched up by birds, or the wind had swooped (like a bird on its prey) and thrown him into a far-distant place.

حُنَفَآءَ لِلَّهِ غَيۡرَ مُشۡرِكِينَ بِهِۦۚ وَمَن يُشۡرِكۡ بِٱللَّهِ
فَكَأَنَّمَا خَرَّ مِنَ ٱلسَّمَآءِ فَتَخۡطَفُهُ ٱلطَّيۡرُ أَوۡ تَهۡوِي
بِهِ ٱلرِّيحُ فِي مَكَانٖ سَحِيقٖ ٣١

32. Such (is his state) and whoever holds in honour the symbols of Allah, (in the sacrifice of animals) such (honour) should come truly from piety of heart.

ذَٰلِكَۖ وَمَن يُعَظِّمۡ شَعَٰٓئِرَ ٱللَّهِ فَإِنَّهَا مِن تَقۡوَى
ٱلۡقُلُوبِ ٣٢

33. In them you have benefits for a term appointed: in the end their place of sacrifice is near the Ancient House.

لَكُمۡ فِيهَا مَنَٰفِعُ إِلَىٰٓ أَجَلٖ مُّسَمّٗى ثُمَّ مَحِلُّهَآ إِلَى
ٱلۡبَيۡتِ ٱلۡعَتِيقِ ٣٣

34. To every people did We appoint rites (of sacrifice), that they might celebrate the name of Allah over the sustenance He gave them from animals (fit for food), but your Allah is one Allah: submit then your wills to Him (in Islam) and give you the good news to those who humble themselves -

وَلِكُلِّ أُمَّةٖ جَعَلۡنَا مَنسَكٗا لِّيَذۡكُرُواْ ٱسۡمَ
ٱللَّهِ عَلَىٰ مَا رَزَقَهُم مِّنۢ بَهِيمَةِ ٱلۡأَنۡعَٰمِۗ فَإِلَٰهُكُمۡ
إِلَٰهٞ وَٰحِدٞ فَلَهُۥٓ أَسۡلِمُواْۗ وَبَشِّرِ ٱلۡمُخۡبِتِينَ ٣٤

35. To those whose hearts, when Allah is mentioned, are filled with fear, who show patient perseverance over their afflictions, keep up regular prayer, and spend (in charity) out of what We have bestowed upon them.

ٱلَّذِينَ إِذَا ذُكِرَ ٱللَّهُ وَجِلَتۡ قُلُوبُهُمۡ وَٱلصَّٰبِرِينَ
عَلَىٰ مَآ أَصَابَهُمۡ وَٱلۡمُقِيمِي ٱلصَّلَوٰةِ وَمِمَّا
رَزَقۡنَٰهُمۡ يُنفِقُونَ ٣٥

36. The sacrificial camels We have made for you as among the symbols from Allah: in them is (much) good for you; then pronounce the name of Allah over them as they line up (for sacrifice); when they are down on their sides (after slaughter), eat you of it, and feed such as (beg not but) live in contentment, and such as beg with due humility: thus have We made animals subject to you, that you may be grateful.

وَٱلۡبُدۡنَ جَعَلۡنَٰهَا لَكُم مِّن شَعَٰٓئِرِ ٱللَّهِ لَكُمۡ فِيهَا خَيۡرٞۖ
فَٱذۡكُرُواْ ٱسۡمَ ٱللَّهِ عَلَيۡهَا صَوَآفَّۖ فَإِذَا وَجَبَتۡ جُنُوبُهَا
فَكُلُواْ مِنۡهَا وَأَطۡعِمُواْ ٱلۡقَانِعَ وَٱلۡمُعۡتَرَّۚ كَذَٰلِكَ سَخَّرۡنَٰهَا
لَكُمۡ لَعَلَّكُمۡ تَشۡكُرُونَ ٣٦

37. It is not their meat nor their blood, that reaches Allah; it is your piety that reaches Him; He has thus made them subject to you, that you may glorify Allah for His guidance to you: and proclaim the good news to all who do right.

لَن يَنَالَ ٱللَّهَ لُحُومُهَا وَلَا دِمَآؤُهَا وَلَٰكِن يَنَالُهُ
ٱلتَّقۡوَىٰ مِنكُمۡۚ كَذَٰلِكَ سَخَّرَهَا لَكُمۡ لِتُكَبِّرُواْ
ٱللَّهَ عَلَىٰ مَا هَدَىٰكُمۡۗ وَبَشِّرِ ٱلۡمُحۡسِنِينَ ٣٧

38. Verily Allah will defend (from ill) those who believe: verily Allah loves not any that is a traitor to faith, or shows ingratitude.

۞إِنَّ ٱللَّهَ يُدَٰفِعُ عَنِ ٱلَّذِينَ ءَامَنُوٓاْۗ إِنَّ ٱللَّهَ لَا يُحِبُّ نصف الحزب ٣٤
كُلَّ خَوَّانٖ كَفُورٍ ٣٨

39. To those against whom war is made, permission is given (to fight), because they are wronged and verily - Allah is Most Powerful for their aid -

أُذِنَ لِلَّذِينَ يُقَٰتَلُونَ بِأَنَّهُمۡ ظُلِمُواْۚ وَإِنَّ ٱللَّهَ عَلَىٰ
نَصۡرِهِمۡ لَقَدِيرٌ ٣٩

40. (They are) those who have been expelled from their homes in defiance of right - (for no cause) except that they say, "Our Lord is Allah." Did not Allah check one set of people by means of another, there would surely have been pulled down monasteries, churches, synagogues, and mosques, in which the name of Allah is commemorated in abundant measure. Allah will certainly aid those who aid His (cause) - for verily Allah is Full of Strength, Exalted in Might (Able to enforce His Will).

ٱلَّذِينَ أُخۡرِجُواْ مِن دِيَٰرِهِم بِغَيۡرِ حَقٍّ إِلَّآ أَن
يَقُولُواْ رَبُّنَا ٱللَّهُۗ وَلَوۡلَا دَفۡعُ ٱللَّهِ ٱلنَّاسَ بَعۡضَهُم
بِبَعۡضٖ لَّهُدِّمَتۡ صَوَٰمِعُ وَبِيَعٞ وَصَلَوَٰتٞ
وَمَسَٰجِدُ يُذۡكَرُ فِيهَا ٱسۡمُ ٱللَّهِ كَثِيرٗاۗ
وَلَيَنصُرَنَّ ٱللَّهُ مَن يَنصُرُهُۥٓۚ إِنَّ ٱللَّهَ لَقَوِيٌّ
عَزِيزٌ ٤٠

41. (They are) those who, if We establish them in the land, establish regular prayer and give regular charity, enjoin the right and forbid wrong: with Allah rests the end (and decision) of (all) affairs.

ٱلَّذِينَ إِن مَّكَّنَّٰهُمْ فِى ٱلْأَرْضِ أَقَامُوا۟ ٱلصَّلَوٰةَ
وَءَاتَوُا۟ ٱلزَّكَوٰةَ وَأَمَرُوا۟ بِٱلْمَعْرُوفِ وَنَهَوْا۟ عَنِ
ٱلْمُنكَرِ ۗ وَلِلَّهِ عَٰقِبَةُ ٱلْأُمُورِ ﴿٤١﴾

42. If they treat your (mission) as false, so did the peoples before them (with their prophets) - the people of Noah, and 'Ad and Thamud;

وَإِن يُكَذِّبُوكَ فَقَدْ كَذَّبَتْ قَبْلَهُمْ قَوْمُ
نُوحٍ وَعَادٌ وَثَمُودُ ﴿٤٢﴾

43. Those of Abraham and Lot;

وَقَوْمُ إِبْرَٰهِيمَ وَقَوْمُ لُوطٍ ﴿٤٣﴾

44. And the companions of the Madyan people; and Moses was rejected (in the same way). But I granted respite to the unbelievers and (only) after that did I punish them: but how (terrible) was My rejection (of them)!

وَأَصْحَٰبُ مَدْيَنَ ۖ وَكُذِّبَ مُوسَىٰ ۖ فَأَمْلَيْتُ لِلْكَٰفِرِينَ
ثُمَّ أَخَذْتُهُمْ ۖ فَكَيْفَ كَانَ نَكِيرِ ﴿٤٤﴾

45. How many populations have We destroyed, which were given to wrongdoing? They tumbled down on their roofs. And how many wells are lying idle and neglected, and castles lofty and well-built!

فَكَأَيِّن مِّن قَرْيَةٍ أَهْلَكْنَٰهَا وَهِىَ ظَالِمَةٌ
فَهِىَ خَاوِيَةٌ عَلَىٰ عُرُوشِهَا وَبِئْرٍ مُّعَطَّلَةٍ
وَقَصْرٍ مَّشِيدٍ ﴿٤٥﴾

46. Do they not travel through the land, so that their hearts (and mind) may thus learn wisdom and their ears may thus learn to hear? Truly it is not their eyes that are blind, but their hearts which are in their breasts.

أَفَلَمْ يَسِيرُوا۟ فِى ٱلْأَرْضِ فَتَكُونَ لَهُمْ قُلُوبٌ
يَعْقِلُونَ بِهَآ أَوْ ءَاذَانٌ يَسْمَعُونَ بِهَا ۖ فَإِنَّهَا
لَا تَعْمَى ٱلْأَبْصَٰرُ وَلَٰكِن تَعْمَى ٱلْقُلُوبُ ٱلَّتِى فِى
ٱلصُّدُورِ ﴿٤٦﴾

47. Yet they ask you to hasten on the punishment! But Allah will not fail in His promise. Verily a day in the sight of your Lord is like a thousand years of your reckoning.

وَيَسْتَعْجِلُونَكَ بِٱلْعَذَابِ وَلَن يُخْلِفَ ٱللَّهُ وَعْدَهُۥ ۚ
وَإِنَّ يَوْمًا عِندَ رَبِّكَ كَأَلْفِ سَنَةٍ مِّمَّا
تَعُدُّونَ ﴿٤٧﴾

48. And to how many populations did I give respite which were given to wrongdoing? In the end I punished them. To Me is the destination (of all).

وَكَأَيِّن مِّن قَرْيَةٍ أَمْلَيْتُ لَهَا وَهِيَ ظَالِمَةٌ ثُمَّ
أَخَذْتُهَا وَإِلَيَّ الْمَصِيرُ ﴿٤٨﴾

49. Say: "O men! I am (sent) to you only to give a clear warning;

قُلْ يَا أَيُّهَا النَّاسُ إِنَّمَا أَنَا لَكُمْ نَذِيرٌ مُّبِينٌ ﴿٤٩﴾

50. Those who believe and work righteousness, for them is forgiveness and a sustenance most generous.

فَالَّذِينَ آمَنُوا وَعَمِلُوا الصَّالِحَاتِ لَهُم مَّغْفِرَةٌ
وَرِزْقٌ كَرِيمٌ ﴿٥٠﴾

51. But those who strive against Our signs, to frustrate them - they will be companions of the fire."

وَالَّذِينَ سَعَوْا فِي آيَاتِنَا مُعَاجِزِينَ أُولَٰئِكَ
أَصْحَابُ الْجَحِيمِ ﴿٥١﴾

52. Never did We send a messenger or a prophet before you, but, when he framed a desire, Satan threw some (vanity) into his desire; but Allah will cancel anything (vain) that Satan throws in, and Allah will confirm (and establish) His signs: for Allah is full of knowledge and wisdom:

وَمَا أَرْسَلْنَا مِن قَبْلِكَ مِن رَّسُولٍ وَلَا نَبِيٍّ إِلَّا
إِذَا تَمَنَّىٰ أَلْقَى الشَّيْطَانُ فِي أُمْنِيَّتِهِ فَيَنسَخُ اللَّهُ
مَا يُلْقِي الشَّيْطَانُ ثُمَّ يُحْكِمُ اللَّهُ آيَاتِهِ ۗ وَاللَّهُ
عَلِيمٌ حَكِيمٌ ﴿٥٢﴾

53. That He may make the suggestions thrown in by Satan, but a trial for those in whose hearts is a disease and who are hardened of heart: verily the wrongdoers are in a schism far (from the truth):

لِّيَجْعَلَ مَا يُلْقِي الشَّيْطَانُ فِتْنَةً لِّلَّذِينَ فِي قُلُوبِهِم
مَّرَضٌ وَالْقَاسِيَةِ قُلُوبُهُمْ ۗ وَإِنَّ الظَّالِمِينَ
لَفِي شِقَاقٍ بَعِيدٍ ﴿٥٣﴾

54. And that those on whom knowledge has been bestowed may learn that the (Qur'an) is the truth from your Lord, and that they may believe in it, and their hearts may be made humbly (open) to it: for verily Allah is the Guide of those who believe, to the straight way.

وَلِيَعْلَمَ الَّذِينَ أُوتُوا الْعِلْمَ أَنَّهُ الْحَقُّ مِن
رَّبِّكَ فَيُؤْمِنُوا بِهِ فَتُخْبِتَ لَهُ قُلُوبُهُمْ ۗ وَإِنَّ
اللَّهَ لَهَادِ الَّذِينَ آمَنُوا إِلَىٰ صِرَاطٍ مُّسْتَقِيمٍ ﴿٥٤﴾

55. Those who reject faith will not cease to be in doubt concerning (revelation) until the hour (of judgement) comes suddenly upon them, or there comes to them the penalty of a day of disaster.

وَلَا يَزَالُ ٱلَّذِينَ كَفَرُوا۟ فِى مِرْيَةٍ مِّنْهُ حَتَّىٰ
تَأْتِيَهُمُ ٱلسَّاعَةُ بَغْتَةً أَوْ يَأْتِيَهُمْ عَذَابُ يَوْمٍ
عَقِيمٍ ﴿٥٥﴾

56. On that day the dominion will be that of Allah; He will judge between them; so those who believe and work righteous deeds will be in gardens of delight.

ٱلْمُلْكُ يَوْمَئِذٍ لِّلَّهِ يَحْكُمُ بَيْنَهُمْ ۚ فَٱلَّذِينَ
ءَامَنُوا۟ وَعَمِلُوا۟ ٱلصَّٰلِحَٰتِ فِى جَنَّٰتِ
ٱلنَّعِيمِ ﴿٥٦﴾

57. And for those who reject faith and deny Our signs, there will be a humiliating punishment.

وَٱلَّذِينَ كَفَرُوا۟ وَكَذَّبُوا۟ بِـَٔايَٰتِنَا
فَأُو۟لَٰٓئِكَ لَهُمْ عَذَابٌ مُّهِينٌ ﴿٥٧﴾

58. Those who leave their homes in the cause of Allah, and are then slain or die, on them will Allah bestow verily a goodly provision: truly Allah is He Who bestows the best provision.

وَٱلَّذِينَ هَاجَرُوا۟ فِى سَبِيلِ ٱللَّهِ ثُمَّ قُتِلُوٓا۟
أَوْ مَاتُوا۟ لَيَرْزُقَنَّهُمُ ٱللَّهُ رِزْقًا حَسَنًا ۚ وَإِنَّ
ٱللَّهَ لَهُوَ خَيْرُ ٱلرَّٰزِقِينَ ﴿٥٨﴾

59. Verily He will admit them to a place with which they shall be well pleased: for Allah is All-Knowing Most Forbearing.

لَيُدْخِلَنَّهُم مُّدْخَلًا يَرْضَوْنَهُۥ ۗ وَإِنَّ ٱللَّهَ
لَعَلِيمٌ حَلِيمٌ ﴿٥٩﴾

60. That (is so). And if one has retaliated to no greater extent than the injury he received, and is again set upon inordinately, Allah will help him: for Allah is One that blots out (sins) and forgives (again and again).

۞ ذَٰلِكَ ۖ وَمَنْ عَاقَبَ بِمِثْلِ مَا عُوقِبَ بِهِۦ ثُمَّ ثلاثة أرباع الحزب ٣٤
بُغِىَ عَلَيْهِ لَيَنصُرَنَّهُ ٱللَّهُ ۗ إِنَّ ٱللَّهَ
لَعَفُوٌّ غَفُورٌ ﴿٦٠﴾

61. That is because Allah merges night into day and He merges day into night and verily it is Allah Who hears and sees (all things).

ذَٰلِكَ بِأَنَّ ٱللَّهَ يُولِجُ ٱلَّيْلَ فِى ٱلنَّهَارِ
وَيُولِجُ ٱلنَّهَارَ فِى ٱلَّيْلِ وَأَنَّ ٱللَّهَ سَمِيعٌۢ
بَصِيرٌ ﴿٦١﴾

62. That is because Allah He is the Reality; and those besides Him whom they invoke they are but vain falsehood: verily Allah is He Most High Most Great.

ذَٰلِكَ بِأَنَّ ٱللَّهَ هُوَ ٱلۡحَقُّ وَأَنَّ مَا يَدۡعُونَ
مِن دُونِهِۦ هُوَ ٱلۡبَٰطِلُ وَأَنَّ ٱللَّهَ هُوَ ٱلۡعَلِيُّ
ٱلۡكَبِيرُ ٦٢

63. Do you not see that Allah sends down rain from the sky, and forthwith the earth becomes clothed with green? For Allah is He Who understands the finest mysteries, and is well-acquainted (with them).

أَلَمۡ تَرَ أَنَّ ٱللَّهَ أَنزَلَ مِنَ ٱلسَّمَآءِ مَآءٗ فَتُصۡبِحُ
ٱلۡأَرۡضُ مُخۡضَرَّةًۚ إِنَّ ٱللَّهَ لَطِيفٌ خَبِيرٞ ٦٣

64. To Him belongs all that is in the heavens and on earth: for verily Allah He is Free of all wants, Worthy of all praise.

لَّهُۥ مَا فِي ٱلسَّمَٰوَٰتِ وَمَا فِي ٱلۡأَرۡضِۚ وَإِنَّ
ٱللَّهَ لَهُوَ ٱلۡغَنِيُّ ٱلۡحَمِيدُ ٦٤

65. Do you not see that Allah has made subject to you (men) all that is on the earth, and the ships that sail through the sea by His command? He withholds the sky (rain) from falling on the earth except by His leave: for Allah is Most Kind and Most Merciful to man.

أَلَمۡ تَرَ أَنَّ ٱللَّهَ سَخَّرَ لَكُم مَّا فِي ٱلۡأَرۡضِ
وَٱلۡفُلۡكَ تَجۡرِي فِي ٱلۡبَحۡرِ بِأَمۡرِهِۦ وَيُمۡسِكُ
ٱلسَّمَآءَ أَن تَقَعَ عَلَى ٱلۡأَرۡضِ إِلَّا بِإِذۡنِهِۦٓۚ إِنَّ ٱللَّهَ
بِٱلنَّاسِ لَرَءُوفٞ رَّحِيمٞ ٦٥

66. It is He Who gave you life, will cause you to die, and will again give you life: truly man is a most ungrateful creature!

وَهُوَ ٱلَّذِيٓ أَحۡيَاكُمۡ ثُمَّ يُمِيتُكُمۡ ثُمَّ يُحۡيِيكُمۡۗ
إِنَّ ٱلۡإِنسَٰنَ لَكَفُورٞ ٦٦

67. To every people have We appointed rites and ceremonies which they must follow, let them not then dispute with you on the matter, but do you invite (them) to your Lord: for you are assuredly on the right way.

لِّكُلِّ أُمَّةٖ جَعَلۡنَا مَنسَكًا هُمۡ نَاسِكُوهُۖ
فَلَا يُنَٰزِعُنَّكَ فِي ٱلۡأَمۡرِۚ وَٱدۡعُ إِلَىٰ رَبِّكَۖ إِنَّكَ
لَعَلَىٰ هُدٗى مُّسۡتَقِيمٖ ٦٧

68. If they do wrangle with you, say, "Allah knows best what it is you are doing."

وَإِن جَٰدَلُوكَ فَقُلِ ٱللَّهُ أَعۡلَمُ بِمَا تَعۡمَلُونَ ٦٨

69. "Allah will judge between you on the day of judgement concerning the matters in which you differ."

ٱللَّهُ يَحْكُمُ بَيْنَكُمْ يَوْمَ ٱلْقِيَٰمَةِ فِيمَا كُنتُمْ
فِيهِ تَخْتَلِفُونَ ﴿٦٩﴾

70. Do you not know that Allah knows all that is in heaven and on earth? Indeed it is all in a record, and that is easy for Allah.

أَلَمْ تَعْلَمْ أَنَّ ٱللَّهَ يَعْلَمُ مَا فِى ٱلسَّمَآءِ
وَٱلْأَرْضِ ۗ إِنَّ ذَٰلِكَ فِى كِتَٰبٍ ۚ إِنَّ ذَٰلِكَ
عَلَى ٱللَّهِ يَسِيرٌ ﴿٧٠﴾

71. Yet they worship, besides Allah, things for which no authority has been sent down to them, and of which they have (really) no knowledge: for those that do wrong there is no helper.

وَيَعْبُدُونَ مِن دُونِ ٱللَّهِ مَا لَمْ يُنَزِّلْ بِهِۦ سُلْطَٰنًا
وَمَا لَيْسَ لَهُم بِهِۦ عِلْمٌ ۗ وَمَا لِلظَّٰلِمِينَ مِن
نَّصِيرٍ ﴿٧١﴾

72. When Our clear signs are rehearsed to them, you will notice a denial on the faces of the unbelievers! They nearly attack with violence those who rehearse Our signs to them. Say, "Shall I tell you of something (far) worse than these signs? It is the fire (of hell)! Allah has promised it to the unbelievers! And evil is that destination!"

وَإِذَا تُتْلَىٰ عَلَيْهِمْ ءَايَٰتُنَا بَيِّنَٰتٍ تَعْرِفُ فِى وُجُوهِ
ٱلَّذِينَ كَفَرُوا۟ ٱلْمُنكَرَ ۖ يَكَادُونَ يَسْطُونَ بِٱلَّذِينَ
يَتْلُونَ عَلَيْهِمْ ءَايَٰتِنَا ۗ قُلْ أَفَأُنَبِّئُكُم بِشَرٍّ مِّن ذَٰلِكُمُ ۗ
ٱلنَّارُ وَعَدَهَا ٱللَّهُ ٱلَّذِينَ كَفَرُوا۟ ۖ وَبِئْسَ
ٱلْمَصِيرُ ﴿٧٢﴾

73. O men! Here is a parable set out! Listen to it! Those on whom, besides Allah, you call, cannot create (even) a fly, if they all met together for the purpose! And if the fly should snatch away anything from them they would have no power to release it from the fly: feeble are those who petition and those whom they petition!

يَٰٓأَيُّهَا ٱلنَّاسُ ضُرِبَ مَثَلٌ فَٱسْتَمِعُوا۟ لَهُۥٓ ۚ إِنَّ
ٱلَّذِينَ تَدْعُونَ مِن دُونِ ٱللَّهِ لَن يَخْلُقُوا۟ ذُبَابًا
وَلَوِ ٱجْتَمَعُوا۟ لَهُۥ ۖ وَإِن يَسْلُبْهُمُ ٱلذُّبَابُ شَيْـًٔا
لَّا يَسْتَنقِذُوهُ مِنْهُ ۚ ضَعُفَ ٱلطَّالِبُ
وَٱلْمَطْلُوبُ ﴿٧٣﴾

74. No just estimate have they made of Allah: for Allah is He Who is strong and able to carry out His Will.

مَا قَدَرُوا۟ ٱللَّهَ حَقَّ قَدْرِهِۦٓ ۗ إِنَّ ٱللَّهَ لَقَوِىٌّ عَزِيزٌ ﴿٧٤﴾

75. Allah chooses prophets from angels and from men: for Allah is He Who hears and sees (all things).

ٱللَّهُ يَصْطَفِى مِنَ ٱلْمَلَٰٓئِكَةِ رُسُلًا وَمِنَ
ٱلنَّاسِ ۚ إِنَّ ٱللَّهَ سَمِيعٌۢ بَصِيرٌ ﴿٧٥﴾

76. He knows what is before them and what is behind them: and to Allah go back all questions (for decision).

يَعْلَمُ مَا بَيْنَ أَيْدِيهِمْ وَمَا خَلْفَهُمْ ۗ وَإِلَى ٱللَّهِ
تُرْجَعُ ٱلْأُمُورُ ﴿٧٦﴾

77. O you who believe! Bow down, prostrate yourselves, and adore your Lord; and do good; that you may prosper.

يَٰٓأَيُّهَا ٱلَّذِينَ ءَامَنُوا۟ ٱرْكَعُوا۟ وَٱسْجُدُوا۟
وَٱعْبُدُوا۟ رَبَّكُمْ وَٱفْعَلُوا۟ ٱلْخَيْرَ لَعَلَّكُمْ
سجدة تُفْلِحُونَ ۩ ﴿٧٧﴾

78. And strive in His cause as you ought to strive, (with sincerity and under discipline): He has chosen you, and has imposed no difficulties on you in religion; it is the cult of your father Abraham. It is He Who has named you Muslims, both before and in this (revelation); that the messenger may be a witness for you, and you be witnesses for mankind! So establish regular prayer, give regular charity, and hold fast to Allah! He is your protector, the best to protect and the best to help!

وَجَٰهِدُوا۟ فِى ٱللَّهِ حَقَّ جِهَادِهِۦ ۚ هُوَ ٱجْتَبَىٰكُمْ
وَمَا جَعَلَ عَلَيْكُمْ فِى ٱلدِّينِ مِنْ حَرَجٍ ۚ مِّلَّةَ
أَبِيكُمْ إِبْرَٰهِيمَ ۚ هُوَ سَمَّىٰكُمُ ٱلْمُسْلِمِينَ
مِن قَبْلُ وَفِى هَٰذَا لِيَكُونَ ٱلرَّسُولُ شَهِيدًا عَلَيْكُمْ
وَتَكُونُوا۟ شُهَدَآءَ عَلَى ٱلنَّاسِ ۚ فَأَقِيمُوا۟ ٱلصَّلَوٰةَ
وَءَاتُوا۟ ٱلزَّكَوٰةَ وَٱعْتَصِمُوا۟ بِٱللَّهِ هُوَ مَوْلَىٰكُمْ ۖ
فَنِعْمَ ٱلْمَوْلَىٰ وَنِعْمَ ٱلنَّصِيرُ ﴿٧٨﴾

سُورَةُ ٱلْمُؤْمِنُونَ

Surah 23: ***Al-Mu'minun*** **(The Believers)**

In the name of Allah,
Most Gracious, Most Merciful.

بِسْمِ ٱللَّهِ ٱلرَّحْمَٰنِ ٱلرَّحِيمِ

✻**1.** The Believers must (eventually) win through -

الجزء ١٨ الحزب ٣٥ قَدْ أَفْلَحَ ٱلْمُؤْمِنُونَ ﴿١﴾

2. Those who humble themselves in their prayers;

ٱلَّذِينَ هُمْ فِى صَلَاتِهِمْ خَٰشِعُونَ ﴿٢﴾

✻ Part-18

3. Who avoid vain talk;

وَٱلَّذِينَ هُمۡ عَنِ ٱللَّغۡوِ مُعۡرِضُونَ ٣

4. Who are active in deeds of charity;

وَٱلَّذِينَ هُمۡ لِلزَّكَوٰةِ فَٰعِلُونَ ٤

5. Who abstain from sex,

وَٱلَّذِينَ هُمۡ لِفُرُوجِهِمۡ حَٰفِظُونَ ٥

6. Except with those joined to them in the marriage bond, or (the captives) whom their right hands possess - for (in their case) they are free from blame,

إِلَّا عَلَىٰٓ أَزۡوَٰجِهِمۡ أَوۡ مَا مَلَكَتۡ أَيۡمَٰنُهُمۡ فَإِنَّهُمۡ
غَيۡرُ مَلُومِينَ ٦

7. But those whose desires exceed those limits are transgressors -

فَمَنِ ٱبۡتَغَىٰ وَرَآءَ ذَٰلِكَ فَأُوْلَٰٓئِكَ هُمُ
ٱلۡعَادُونَ ٧

8. Those who faithfully observe their trusts and covenants;

وَٱلَّذِينَ هُمۡ لِأَمَٰنَٰتِهِمۡ وَعَهۡدِهِمۡ رَٰعُونَ ٨

9. And who (strictly) guard their prayers -

وَٱلَّذِينَ هُمۡ عَلَىٰ صَلَوَٰتِهِمۡ يُحَافِظُونَ ٩

10. Those will be the heirs,

أُوْلَٰٓئِكَ هُمُ ٱلۡوَٰرِثُونَ ١٠

11. Who will inherit paradise: they will dwell in it (forever).

ٱلَّذِينَ يَرِثُونَ ٱلۡفِرۡدَوۡسَ هُمۡ فِيهَا خَٰلِدُونَ ١١

12. Man We did create from a quintessence (of clay);

وَلَقَدۡ خَلَقۡنَا ٱلۡإِنسَٰنَ مِن سُلَٰلَةٖ مِّن طِينٖ ١٢

13. Then We placed him as (a drop of) sperm in a place of rest, firmly fixed;

ثُمَّ جَعَلۡنَٰهُ نُطۡفَةٗ فِي قَرَارٖ مَّكِينٖ ١٣

14. Then We made the sperm into a clot of congealed blood; then of that clot We made a (foetus) lump; then We made out of that lump bones and clothed the bones with flesh; then We developed out of it another creature. So blessed be Allah, the Best to create!

ثُمَّ خَلَقۡنَا ٱلنُّطۡفَةَ عَلَقَةٗ فَخَلَقۡنَا ٱلۡعَلَقَةَ مُضۡغَةٗ
فَخَلَقۡنَا ٱلۡمُضۡغَةَ عِظَٰمٗا فَكَسَوۡنَا ٱلۡعِظَٰمَ لَحۡمٗا
ثُمَّ أَنشَأۡنَٰهُ خَلۡقًا ءَاخَرَۚ فَتَبَارَكَ ٱللَّهُ أَحۡسَنُ
ٱلۡخَٰلِقِينَ ١٤

15. After that, at length you will die.

ثُمَّ إِنَّكُم بَعۡدَ ذَٰلِكَ لَمَيِّتُونَ ١٥

16. Again, on the day of judgement, will you be raised up.

ثُمَّ إِنَّكُمۡ يَوۡمَ ٱلۡقِيَٰمَةِ تُبۡعَثُونَ ١٦

17. And We have made, above you, seven tracts; and We are never unmindful of (Our) creation.

وَلَقَدۡ خَلَقۡنَا فَوۡقَكُمۡ سَبۡعَ طَرَآئِقَ وَمَا كُنَّا عَنِ
ٱلۡخَلۡقِ غَٰفِلِينَ ١٧

18. And We send down water from the sky according to (due) measure, and We cause it to soak in the soil; and We certainly are able to drain it off (with ease).

وَأَنزَلۡنَا مِنَ ٱلسَّمَآءِ مَآءَۢ بِقَدَرٖ فَأَسۡكَنَّٰهُ فِي
ٱلۡأَرۡضِۖ وَإِنَّا عَلَىٰ ذَهَابِۭ بِهِۦ لَقَٰدِرُونَ ١٨

19. With it We grow for you gardens of date palms and vines: in them have you abundant fruits: and of them you eat (and have enjoyment) -

فَأَنشَأۡنَا لَكُم بِهِۦ جَنَّٰتٖ مِّن نَّخِيلٖ وَأَعۡنَٰبٖ لَّكُمۡ
فِيهَا فَوَٰكِهُ كَثِيرَةٞ وَمِنۡهَا تَأۡكُلُونَ ١٩

20. Also a tree springing out of mount Sinai, which produces oil, and relish for those who use it for food.

وَشَجَرَةٗ تَخۡرُجُ مِن طُورِ سَيۡنَآءَ تَنۢبُتُ بِٱلدُّهۡنِ
وَصِبۡغٖ لِّلۡأٓكِلِينَ ٢٠

21. And in cattle (too) you have an instructive example: from within their bodies We produce (milk) for you to drink; there are, in them (besides), numerous (other) benefits for you; and of their (meat) you eat;

وَإِنَّ لَكُمۡ فِي ٱلۡأَنۡعَٰمِ لَعِبۡرَةٗۖ نُّسۡقِيكُم مِّمَّا فِي بُطُونِهَا
وَلَكُمۡ فِيهَا مَنَٰفِعُ كَثِيرَةٞ وَمِنۡهَا تَأۡكُلُونَ ٢١

22. And on them, as well as in ships, you ride.

وَعَلَيۡهَا وَعَلَى ٱلۡفُلۡكِ تُحۡمَلُونَ ٢٢

23. (Further, We sent a long line of prophets for your instruction). We sent Noah to his people: he said, "O my people! Worship Allah! You have no other god but Him: will you not fear (Him)?"

وَلَقَدۡ أَرۡسَلۡنَا نُوحًا إِلَىٰ قَوۡمِهِۦ فَقَالَ يَٰقَوۡمِ ٱعۡبُدُواْ
ٱللَّهَ مَا لَكُم مِّنۡ إِلَٰهٍ غَيۡرُهُۥٓۚ أَفَلَا تَتَّقُونَ ٢٣

24. The chiefs of the unbelievers among his people said: "He is no more than a man like yourselves: his wish is to assert his superiority over you: if Allah had wished (to send messengers), He could have sent down angels: never did we hear such a thing (as he says), among our ancestors of old."

فَقَالَ ٱلْمَلَؤُا۟ ٱلَّذِينَ كَفَرُوا۟ مِن قَوْمِهِۦ مَا هَٰذَآ إِلَّا
بَشَرٌ مِّثْلُكُمْ يُرِيدُ أَن يَتَفَضَّلَ عَلَيْكُمْ وَلَوْ شَآءَ ٱللَّهُ
لَأَنزَلَ مَلَٰٓئِكَةً مَّا سَمِعْنَا بِهَٰذَا فِىٓ ءَابَآئِنَا
ٱلْأَوَّلِينَ ﴿٢٤﴾

25. (And some said:) "He is only a man possessed: wait (and have patience) with him for a time."

إِنْ هُوَ إِلَّا رَجُلٌۢ بِهِۦ جِنَّةٌ فَتَرَبَّصُوا۟ بِهِۦ حَتَّىٰ حِينٍ ﴿٢٥﴾

26. (Noah) said: "O my Lord! Help me: for that they accuse me of falsehood!"

قَالَ رَبِّ ٱنصُرْنِى بِمَا كَذَّبُونِ ﴿٢٦﴾

27. So We inspired him (with this message): "Construct the ark within Our sight and under Our guidance: then when comes Our command, and the fountains of the earth gush out, take you on board pairs of every species, male and female, and your family - except those of them against whom the word has already gone forth: and address Me not in favour of the wrongdoers; for they shall be drowned (in the flood).

فَأَوْحَيْنَآ إِلَيْهِ أَنِ ٱصْنَعِ ٱلْفُلْكَ بِأَعْيُنِنَا وَوَحْيِنَا
فَإِذَا جَآءَ أَمْرُنَا وَفَارَ ٱلتَّنُّورُ فَٱسْلُكْ فِيهَا مِن كُلٍّ
زَوْجَيْنِ ٱثْنَيْنِ وَأَهْلَكَ إِلَّا مَن سَبَقَ عَلَيْهِ ٱلْقَوْلُ
مِنْهُمْ ۖ وَلَا تُخَٰطِبْنِى فِى ٱلَّذِينَ ظَلَمُوٓا۟ ۖ إِنَّهُم
مُّغْرَقُونَ ﴿٢٧﴾

28. And when you have embarked on the ark - you and those with you - say: 'Praise be to Allah, Who has saved us from the people who do wrong.'

فَإِذَا ٱسْتَوَيْتَ أَنتَ وَمَن مَّعَكَ عَلَى ٱلْفُلْكِ فَقُلِ ٱلْحَمْدُ
لِلَّهِ ٱلَّذِى نَجَّىٰنَا مِنَ ٱلْقَوْمِ ٱلظَّٰلِمِينَ ﴿٢٨﴾

29. And say: 'O my Lord! Enable me to disembark with Your blessing: for You are the Best to enable (us) to disembark.'"

وَقُل رَّبِّ أَنزِلْنِى مُنزَلًا مُّبَارَكًا وَأَنتَ خَيْرُ ٱلْمُنزِلِينَ ﴿٢٩﴾

30. Verily in this there are signs (for men to understand); (thus) do We try (men).

إِنَّ فِى ذَٰلِكَ لَءَايَٰتٍ وَإِن كُنَّا لَمُبْتَلِينَ ﴿٣٠﴾

31. Then We raised after them another generation.

ثُمَّ أَنشَأْنَا مِنۢ بَعْدِهِمْ قَرْنًا ءَاخَرِينَ ﴿٣١﴾

32. And We sent to them a messenger from among themselves, (saying) "Worship Allah! You have no other god but Him. Will you not fear (Him)?"

فَأَرْسَلْنَا فِيهِمْ رَسُولًا مِّنْهُمْ أَنِ ٱعْبُدُوا۟ ٱللَّهَ مَا لَكُم مِّنْ
إِلَٰهٍ غَيْرُهُۥٓ ۖ أَفَلَا تَتَّقُونَ ﴿٣٢﴾

33. And the chiefs of his people, who disbelieved and denied the meeting in the hereafter, and on whom We had bestowed the good things of this life, said: "He is no more than a man like yourselves; he eats of that of which you eat, and drinks of what you drink.

وَقَالَ ٱلْمَلَأُ مِن قَوْمِهِ ٱلَّذِينَ كَفَرُوا۟ وَكَذَّبُوا۟ بِلِقَآءِ
ٱلْءَاخِرَةِ وَأَتْرَفْنَٰهُمْ فِى ٱلْحَيَوٰةِ ٱلدُّنْيَا مَا هَٰذَآ إِلَّا بَشَرٌ
مِّثْلُكُمْ يَأْكُلُ مِمَّا تَأْكُلُونَ مِنْهُ وَيَشْرَبُ
مِمَّا تَشْرَبُونَ ﴿٣٣﴾

34. If you obey a man like yourselves, see, it is certain you will be lost.

وَلَئِنْ أَطَعْتُم بَشَرًا مِّثْلَكُمْ إِنَّكُمْ إِذًا لَّخَٰسِرُونَ ﴿٣٤﴾

35. Does he promise that when you die and become dust and bones, you shall be brought out (again)?

أَيَعِدُكُمْ أَنَّكُمْ إِذَا مِتُّمْ وَكُنتُمْ تُرَابًا وَعِظَٰمًا أَنَّكُم
مُّخْرَجُونَ ﴿٣٥﴾

36. Far, very far, is that which you are promised!

۞ هَيْهَاتَ هَيْهَاتَ لِمَا تُوعَدُونَ ﴿٣٦﴾

37. There is nothing but our life in this world! We shall die and we live! But we shall never be raised up again!

إِنْ هِىَ إِلَّا حَيَاتُنَا ٱلدُّنْيَا نَمُوتُ وَنَحْيَا وَمَا نَحْنُ
بِمَبْعُوثِينَ ﴿٣٧﴾

38. He is only a man who invents a lie against Allah, but we are not the ones to believe in him!"

إِنْ هُوَ إِلَّا رَجُلٌ ٱفْتَرَىٰ عَلَى ٱللَّهِ كَذِبًا وَمَا نَحْنُ لَهُۥ
بِمُؤْمِنِينَ ﴿٣٨﴾

39. (The prophet) said: "O my Lord! Help me: for that they accuse me of falsehood."

قَالَ رَبِّ ٱنصُرْنِى بِمَا كَذَّبُونِ ﴿٣٩﴾

40. (Allah) said: "In but a little while, they are sure to be sorry!"

قَالَ عَمَّا قَلِيلٍ لَّيُصْبِحُنَّ نَٰدِمِينَ ﴿٤٠﴾

41. Then the blast overtook them with justice, and We made them as rubbish of dead leaves (floating on the stream of time)! So away with the people who do wrong!

فَأَخَذَتْهُمُ ٱلصَّيْحَةُ بِٱلْحَقِّ فَجَعَلْنَٰهُمْ غُثَآءً ۚ
فَبُعْدًا لِّلْقَوْمِ ٱلظَّٰلِمِينَ ﴿٤١﴾

42. Then We raised after them other generations.

ثُمَّ أَنشَأْنَا مِنۢ بَعْدِهِمْ قُرُونًا ءَاخَرِينَ ﴿٤٢﴾

43. No people can hasten their term, nor can they delay (it).

مَا تَسْبِقُ مِنْ أُمَّةٍ أَجَلَهَا وَمَا يَسْتَـْٔخِرُونَ ﴿٤٣﴾

44. Then sent We Our messengers in succession: every time there came to a people their messenger, they accused him of falsehood; so We made them follow each other (in punishment); We made them as a tale (that is told); so away with a people that will not believe!

ثُمَّ أَرْسَلْنَا رُسُلَنَا تَتْرَا ۖ كُلَّ مَا جَآءَ أُمَّةً رَّسُولُهَا كَذَّبُوهُ ۚ
فَأَتْبَعْنَا بَعْضَهُم بَعْضًا وَجَعَلْنَـٰهُمْ أَحَادِيثَ ۚ
فَبُعْدًا لِّقَوْمٍ لَّا يُؤْمِنُونَ ﴿٤٤﴾

45. Then We sent Moses and his brother Aaron, with Our signs and authority manifest,

ثُمَّ أَرْسَلْنَا مُوسَىٰ وَأَخَاهُ هَـٰرُونَ بِـَٔايَـٰتِنَا وَسُلْطَـٰنٍ
مُّبِينٍ ﴿٤٥﴾

46. To Pharaoh and his chiefs: but these behaved insolently: they were arrogant people.

إِلَىٰ فِرْعَوْنَ وَمَلَإِي۟هِۦ فَٱسْتَكْبَرُوا۟ وَكَانُوا۟ قَوْمًا عَالِينَ ﴿٤٦﴾

47. They said: "Shall we believe in two men like ourselves? And their people are subject to us!"

فَقَالُوٓا۟ أَنُؤْمِنُ لِبَشَرَيْنِ مِثْلِنَا وَقَوْمُهُمَا لَنَا
عَـٰبِدُونَ ﴿٤٧﴾

48. So they accused them of falsehood, and they became of those who were destroyed.

فَكَذَّبُوهُمَا فَكَانُوا۟ مِنَ ٱلْمُهْلَكِينَ ﴿٤٨﴾

49. And We gave Moses the book, in order that they might receive guidance.

وَلَقَدْ ءَاتَيْنَا مُوسَى ٱلْكِتَـٰبَ لَعَلَّهُمْ يَهْتَدُونَ ﴿٤٩﴾

50. And We made the son of Mary and his mother as a sign: We gave them both shelter on high ground, affording rest and security and furnished with springs.

وَجَعَلْنَا ٱبْنَ مَرْيَمَ وَأُمَّهُۥٓ ءَايَةً وَءَاوَيْنَـٰهُمَآ إِلَىٰ رَبْوَةٍ
ذَاتِ قَرَارٍ وَمَعِينٍ ﴿٥٠﴾

51. O you messengers! Enjoy (all) things good and pure, and work righteousness: for I am well-acquainted with (all) that you do.

يَـٰٓأَيُّهَا ٱلرُّسُلُ كُلُوا۟ مِنَ ٱلطَّيِّبَـٰتِ وَٱعْمَلُوا۟ صَـٰلِحًا ۖ
إِنِّى بِمَا تَعْمَلُونَ عَلِيمٌ ﴿٥١﴾

52. And verily this brotherhood of yours is a single brotherhood. And I am your Lord and Cherisher: therefore fear Me (and no other).

وَإِنَّ هَٰذِهِۦٓ أُمَّتُكُمْ أُمَّةً وَٰحِدَةً وَأَنَا۠ رَبُّكُمْ
فَٱتَّقُونِ ﴿٥٢﴾

53. But people have cut off their affair (of unity), between them, into sects: each party rejoices in that which is with itself.

فَتَقَطَّعُوٓاْ أَمْرَهُم بَيْنَهُمْ زُبُرًا ۖ كُلُّ حِزْبٍۭ بِمَا لَدَيْهِمْ
فَرِحُونَ ﴿٥٣﴾

54. But leave them in their confused ignorance for a time.

فَذَرْهُمْ فِى غَمْرَتِهِمْ حَتَّىٰ حِينٍ ﴿٥٤﴾

55. Do they think that because We have granted them abundance of wealth and sons,

أَيَحْسَبُونَ أَنَّمَا نُمِدُّهُم بِهِۦ مِن مَّالٍ وَبَنِينَ ﴿٥٥﴾

56. We would hasten them on in every good? Nay, they do not understand.

نُسَارِعُ لَهُمْ فِى ٱلْخَيْرَٰتِ ۚ بَل لَّا يَشْعُرُونَ ﴿٥٦﴾

57. Verily those who live in awe for fear of their Lord;

إِنَّ ٱلَّذِينَ هُم مِّنْ خَشْيَةِ رَبِّهِم مُّشْفِقُونَ ﴿٥٧﴾

58. Those who believe in the signs of their Lord;

وَٱلَّذِينَ هُم بِـَٔايَٰتِ رَبِّهِمْ يُؤْمِنُونَ ﴿٥٨﴾

59. Those who join not (in worship) partners with their Lord;

وَٱلَّذِينَ هُم بِرَبِّهِمْ لَا يُشْرِكُونَ ﴿٥٩﴾

60. And those who dispense their charity with their hearts full of fear, because they will return to their Lord -

وَٱلَّذِينَ يُؤْتُونَ مَآ ءَاتَواْ وَّقُلُوبُهُمْ وَجِلَةٌ أَنَّهُمْ إِلَىٰ رَبِّهِمْ
رَٰجِعُونَ ﴿٦٠﴾

61. It is these who hasten in every good work, and these who are foremost in them.

أُوْلَٰٓئِكَ يُسَٰرِعُونَ فِى ٱلْخَيْرَٰتِ وَهُمْ لَهَا سَٰبِقُونَ ﴿٦١﴾

62. On no soul do We place a burden greater than it can bear: before Us is a record which clearly shows the truth. They will never be wronged.

وَلَا نُكَلِّفُ نَفْسًا إِلَّا وُسْعَهَا ۖ وَلَدَيْنَا كِتَٰبٌ يَنطِقُ
بِٱلْحَقِّ ۚ وَهُمْ لَا يُظْلَمُونَ ﴿٦٢﴾

63. But their hearts are in confused ignorance of this; and there are, besides

بَلْ قُلُوبُهُمْ فِى غَمْرَةٍ مِّنْ هَٰذَا وَلَهُمْ أَعْمَٰلٌ مِّن

that, deeds of theirs, which they will (continue) to do;

دُونِ ذَٰلِكَ هُمْ لَهَا عَٰمِلُونَ ٦٣

64. Until, when We seize in punishment those of them who received the good things of this world, see, they will groan in supplication!

حَتَّىٰٓ إِذَآ أَخَذْنَا مُتْرَفِيهِم بِٱلْعَذَابِ إِذَا هُمْ
يَجْـَٔرُونَ ٦٤

65. It will be said: "Groan not in supplication this day; for you shall certainly not be helped by Us."

لَا تَجْـَٔرُوا۟ ٱلْيَوْمَ ۖ إِنَّكُم مِّنَّا لَا تُنصَرُونَ ٦٥

66. "My signs used to be rehearsed to you, but you used to turn back on your heels -

قَدْ كَانَتْ ءَايَٰتِى تُتْلَىٰ عَلَيْكُمْ فَكُنتُمْ عَلَىٰٓ أَعْقَٰبِكُمْ
تَنكِصُونَ ٦٦

67. In arrogance: talking nonsense about the (Qur'an), like one telling fables by night."

مُسْتَكْبِرِينَ بِهِۦ سَٰمِرًا تَهْجُرُونَ ٦٧

68. Do they not ponder over the word (of Allah), or has anything (new) come to them that did not come to their fathers of old?

أَفَلَمْ يَدَّبَّرُوا۟ ٱلْقَوْلَ أَمْ جَآءَهُم مَّا لَمْ يَأْتِ ءَابَآءَهُمُ
ٱلْأَوَّلِينَ ٦٨

69. Or do they not recognise their messenger, that they deny him?

أَمْ لَمْ يَعْرِفُوا۟ رَسُولَهُمْ فَهُمْ لَهُۥ مُنكِرُونَ ٦٩

70. Or do they say "He is possessed"? Nay, he has brought them the truth, but most of them hate the truth.

أَمْ يَقُولُونَ بِهِۦ جِنَّةٌۢ ۚ بَلْ جَآءَهُم بِٱلْحَقِّ
وَأَكْثَرُهُمْ لِلْحَقِّ كَٰرِهُونَ ٧٠

71. If the truth had been in accord with their desires, truly the heavens and the earth, and all beings in it would have been in confusion and corruption! Nay, We have sent them their admonition, but they turn away from their admonition.

وَلَوِ ٱتَّبَعَ ٱلْحَقُّ أَهْوَآءَهُمْ لَفَسَدَتِ ٱلسَّمَٰوَٰتُ وَٱلْأَرْضُ
وَمَن فِيهِنَّ ۚ بَلْ أَتَيْنَٰهُم بِذِكْرِهِمْ فَهُمْ عَن ذِكْرِهِم
مُّعْرِضُونَ ٧١

72. Or is it that you ask them for some recompense? But the recompense of your

أَمْ تَسْـَٔلُهُمْ خَرْجًا فَخَرَاجُ رَبِّكَ خَيْرٌ ۖ وَهُوَ خَيْرُ

Lord is best: He is the Best of those who give sustenance.

ٱلرَّٰزِقِينَ ٧٢

73. But verily you call them to the straight way;

وَإِنَّكَ لَتَدۡعُوهُمۡ إِلَىٰ صِرَٰطٖ مُّسۡتَقِيمٖ ٧٣

74. And verily those who believe not in the hereafter are deviating from that way.

وَإِنَّ ٱلَّذِينَ لَا يُؤۡمِنُونَ بِٱلۡأٓخِرَةِ عَنِ ٱلصِّرَٰطِ
لَنَٰكِبُونَ ٧٤

75. If We had mercy on them, and removed the distress which is on them they would obstinately persist in their transgression, wandering in distraction to and fro.

۞ وَلَوۡ رَحِمۡنَٰهُمۡ وَكَشَفۡنَا مَا بِهِم مِّن ضُرّٖ لَّلَجُّواْ فِي نصف الحزب ٣٥
طُغۡيَٰنِهِمۡ يَعۡمَهُونَ ٧٥

76. We inflicted punishment on them, but they humbled not themselves to their Lord nor do they submissively entreat (Him)! -

وَلَقَدۡ أَخَذۡنَٰهُم بِٱلۡعَذَابِ فَمَا ٱسۡتَكَانُواْ لِرَبِّهِمۡ
وَمَا يَتَضَرَّعُونَ ٧٦

77. Until We open on them a gate leading to a severe punishment: then They will be plunged in despair in it!

حَتَّىٰٓ إِذَا فَتَحۡنَا عَلَيۡهِم بَابٗا ذَا عَذَابٖ شَدِيدٍ إِذَا هُمۡ
فِيهِ مُبۡلِسُونَ ٧٧

78. It is He Who has created for you (the faculties of) hearing, sight, feeling, and understanding: little thanks it is you give!

وَهُوَ ٱلَّذِيٓ أَنشَأَ لَكُمُ ٱلسَّمۡعَ وَٱلۡأَبۡصَٰرَ وَٱلۡأَفۡـِٔدَةَۚ
قَلِيلٗا مَّا تَشۡكُرُونَ ٧٨

79. And He has multiplied you through the earth, and to Him shall you be gathered back.

وَهُوَ ٱلَّذِي ذَرَأَكُمۡ فِي ٱلۡأَرۡضِ وَإِلَيۡهِ تُحۡشَرُونَ ٧٩

80. It is He Who gives life and death, and to Him (is due) the alternation of night and day: will you not then understand?

وَهُوَ ٱلَّذِي يُحۡيِۦ وَيُمِيتُ وَلَهُ ٱخۡتِلَٰفُ ٱلَّيۡلِ
وَٱلنَّهَارِۚ أَفَلَا تَعۡقِلُونَ ٨٠

81. On the contrary they say things similar to what the ancients said.

بَلۡ قَالُواْ مِثۡلَ مَا قَالَ ٱلۡأَوَّلُونَ ٨١

82. They say: "What! When we die and become dust and bones, could we really be raised up again?

قَالُوٓاْ أَءِذَا مِتۡنَا وَكُنَّا تُرَابٗا وَعِظَٰمًا أَءِنَّا
لَمَبۡعُوثُونَ ٨٢

83. Such things have been promised to us and to our fathers before! They are nothing but tales of the ancients!"

لَقَدۡ وُعِدۡنَا نَحۡنُ وَءَابَآؤُنَا هَٰذَا مِن قَبۡلُ إِنۡ
هَٰذَآ إِلَّآ أَسَٰطِيرُ ٱلۡأَوَّلِينَ ٨٣

84. Say: "To whom belong the earth and all beings in it? (Say) if you know!"

قُل لِّمَنِ ٱلۡأَرۡضُ وَمَن فِيهَآ إِن كُنتُمۡ
تَعۡلَمُونَ ٨٤

85. They will say "To Allah!" Say: "Yet will you not receive admonition?"

سَيَقُولُونَ لِلَّهِۚ قُلۡ أَفَلَا تَذَكَّرُونَ ٨٥

86. Say: "Who is the Lord of the seven heavens, and the Lord of the Throne (of Glory) Supreme?"

قُلۡ مَن رَّبُّ ٱلسَّمَٰوَٰتِ ٱلسَّبۡعِ وَرَبُّ ٱلۡعَرۡشِ
ٱلۡعَظِيمِ ٨٦

87. They will say, "(They belong) to Allah." Say: "Will you not then be filled with awe?"

سَيَقُولُونَ لِلَّهِۚ قُلۡ أَفَلَا تَتَّقُونَ ٨٧

88. Say: "Who is it in whose hands is the governance of all things - who protects (all), but is not protected (of any)? (Say) if you know."

قُلۡ مَنۢ بِيَدِهِۦ مَلَكُوتُ كُلِّ شَيۡءٖ وَهُوَ يُجِيرُ
وَلَا يُجَارُ عَلَيۡهِ إِن كُنتُمۡ تَعۡلَمُونَ ٨٨

89. They will say "(It belongs) to Allah." Say: "Then how are you deluded?"

سَيَقُولُونَ لِلَّهِۚ قُلۡ فَأَنَّىٰ تُسۡحَرُونَ ٨٩

90. We have sent them the truth: but they indeed practice falsehood!

بَلۡ أَتَيۡنَٰهُم بِٱلۡحَقِّ وَإِنَّهُمۡ لَكَٰذِبُونَ ٩٠

91. No son did Allah beget, nor is there any god along with Him: (if there were many gods), behold, each god would have taken away what be had created, and some would have lorded it over others! Glory to Allah! (He is free) from the (sort of) things they attribute to Him!

مَا ٱتَّخَذَ ٱللَّهُ مِن وَلَدٖ وَمَا كَانَ مَعَهُۥ مِنۡ إِلَٰهٍۚ
إِذٗا لَّذَهَبَ كُلُّ إِلَٰهِۭ بِمَا خَلَقَ وَلَعَلَا بَعۡضُهُمۡ
عَلَىٰ بَعۡضٖۚ سُبۡحَٰنَ ٱللَّهِ عَمَّا يَصِفُونَ ٩١

92. He knows what is hidden and what is open: too high is He for the partners they attribute to Him!

عَٰلِمِ ٱلۡغَيۡبِ وَٱلشَّهَٰدَةِ فَتَعَٰلَىٰ عَمَّا يُشۡرِكُونَ ٩٢

93. Say: "O my Lord! If You will show me (in my lifetime) that which they are warned against -

قُل رَّبِّ إِمَّا تُرِيَنِّي مَا يُوعَدُونَ ﴿٩٣﴾

94. Then, O my Lord! Put me not amongst the people who do wrong!"

رَبِّ فَلَا تَجْعَلْنِي فِي ٱلْقَوْمِ ٱلظَّٰلِمِينَ ﴿٩٤﴾

95. And We are certainly able to show you (in fulfilment) that against which they are warned.

وَإِنَّا عَلَىٰٓ أَن نُّرِيَكَ مَا نَعِدُهُمْ لَقَٰدِرُونَ ﴿٩٥﴾

96. Repel evil with that which is best: We are well-acquainted with the things they say.

ٱدْفَعْ بِٱلَّتِي هِيَ أَحْسَنُ ٱلسَّيِّئَةَ ۚ نَحْنُ أَعْلَمُ بِمَا
يَصِفُونَ ﴿٩٦﴾

97. And say: "O my Lord! I seek refuge with You from the suggestions of the evil ones.

وَقُل رَّبِّ أَعُوذُ بِكَ مِنْ هَمَزَٰتِ ٱلشَّيَٰطِينِ ﴿٩٧﴾

98. And I seek refuge with You O my Lord! Lest they should come near me."

وَأَعُوذُ بِكَ رَبِّ أَن يَحْضُرُونِ ﴿٩٨﴾

99. (In falsehood will they be) until, when death comes to one of them, he says: "O my Lord! Send me back (to life) -

حَتَّىٰٓ إِذَا جَآءَ أَحَدَهُمُ ٱلْمَوْتُ قَالَ رَبِّ
ٱرْجِعُونِ ﴿٩٩﴾

100. In order that I may work righteousness in the things I neglected" - "By no means! It is but a word he says" - before them is a partition till the day they are raised up.

لَعَلِّيٓ أَعْمَلُ صَٰلِحًا فِيمَا تَرَكْتُ ۚ كَلَّآ ۚ إِنَّهَا
كَلِمَةٌ هُوَ قَآئِلُهَا ۖ وَمِن وَرَآئِهِم بَرْزَخٌ إِلَىٰ يَوْمِ
يُبْعَثُونَ ﴿١٠٠﴾

101. Then when the trumpet is blown, there will be no more relationships between them that day, nor will one ask after another!

فَإِذَا نُفِخَ فِي ٱلصُّورِ فَلَآ أَنسَابَ بَيْنَهُمْ يَوْمَئِذٍ وَلَا
يَتَسَآءَلُونَ ﴿١٠١﴾

102. Then those whose balance (of good deeds) is heavy - they will attain salvation:

فَمَن ثَقُلَتْ مَوَٰزِينُهُۥ فَأُو۟لَٰٓئِكَ هُمُ
ٱلْمُفْلِحُونَ ﴿١٠٢﴾

103. But those whose balance is light, will be those who have lost their souls; in hell will they remain.

وَمَنْ خَفَّتْ مَوَٰزِينُهُۥ فَأُو۟لَٰٓئِكَ ٱلَّذِينَ خَسِرُوٓا۟
أَنفُسَهُمْ فِى جَهَنَّمَ خَٰلِدُونَ ﴿١٠٣﴾

104. The fire will burn their faces, and they will in it grin, with their lips displaced.

تَلْفَحُ وُجُوهَهُمُ ٱلنَّارُ وَهُمْ فِيهَا كَٰلِحُونَ ﴿١٠٤﴾

105. "Were not My signs rehearsed to you, and you did but treat them as falsehoods?"

أَلَمْ تَكُنْ ءَايَٰتِى تُتْلَىٰ عَلَيْكُمْ فَكُنتُم بِهَا
تُكَذِّبُونَ ﴿١٠٥﴾

106. They will say: "Our Lord! Our misfortune overwhelmed us, and we became a people astray!"

قَالُوا۟ رَبَّنَا غَلَبَتْ عَلَيْنَا شِقْوَتُنَا وَكُنَّا قَوْمًا
ضَآلِّينَ ﴿١٠٦﴾

107. "Our Lord! Bring us out of this: if ever we return (to evil), then shall we be wrongdoers indeed!"

رَبَّنَآ أَخْرِجْنَا مِنْهَا فَإِنْ عُدْنَا فَإِنَّا ظَٰلِمُونَ ﴿١٠٧﴾

108. He will say: "Be you driven into it (with disgrace)! And speak you not to Me!"

قَالَ ٱخْسَـُٔوا۟ فِيهَا وَلَا تُكَلِّمُونِ ﴿١٠٨﴾

109. "A part of My servants there was, who used to pray, 'Our Lord! We believe; then do You forgive us, and have mercy upon us: for You are the best of those Who show mercy!'

إِنَّهُۥ كَانَ فَرِيقٌ مِّنْ عِبَادِى يَقُولُونَ رَبَّنَآ ءَامَنَّا
فَٱغْفِرْ لَنَا وَٱرْحَمْنَا وَأَنتَ خَيْرُ ٱلرَّٰحِمِينَ ﴿١٠٩﴾

110. But you treated them with ridicule, so much so that (ridicule of) them made you forget My message while you were laughing at them!

فَٱتَّخَذْتُمُوهُمْ سِخْرِيًّا حَتَّىٰٓ أَنسَوْكُمْ ذِكْرِى وَكُنتُم
مِّنْهُمْ تَضْحَكُونَ ﴿١١٠﴾

111. I have rewarded them this day for their patience and constancy: they are indeed the ones that have achieved bliss."

إِنِّى جَزَيْتُهُمُ ٱلْيَوْمَ بِمَا صَبَرُوٓا۟ أَنَّهُمْ هُمُ
ٱلْفَآئِزُونَ ﴿١١١﴾

112. He will say: "What number of years did you stay on earth?"

قَٰلَ كَمْ لَبِثْتُمْ فِى ٱلْأَرْضِ عَدَدَ سِنِينَ ﴿١١٢﴾

113. They will say: "We stayed a day or part of a day: but ask those who keep account."

قَالُواْ لَبِثۡنَا يَوۡمًا أَوۡ بَعۡضَ يَوۡمٖ فَسۡـَٔلِ ٱلۡعَآدِّينَ ١١٣

114. He will say: "You stayed not but a little - if you had only known!

قَٰلَ إِن لَّبِثۡتُمۡ إِلَّا قَلِيلٗاۖ لَّوۡ أَنَّكُمۡ كُنتُمۡ تَعۡلَمُونَ ١١٤

115. Did you then think that We had created you in jest, and that you would not be brought back to Us (for account)?"

أَفَحَسِبۡتُمۡ أَنَّمَا خَلَقۡنَٰكُمۡ عَبَثٗا وَأَنَّكُمۡ إِلَيۡنَا لَا تُرۡجَعُونَ ١١٥

116. Therefore, exalted be Allah, the King, the Reality; there is no god but He, the Lord of the Throne of Honour!

فَتَعَٰلَى ٱللَّهُ ٱلۡمَلِكُ ٱلۡحَقُّۖ لَآ إِلَٰهَ إِلَّا هُوَ رَبُّ ٱلۡعَرۡشِ ٱلۡكَرِيمِ ١١٦

117. If anyone invokes, besides Allah, any other god, he has no authority therefore; and his reckoning will be only with his Lord! And verily the unbelievers will fail to win through!

وَمَن يَدۡعُ مَعَ ٱللَّهِ إِلَٰهًا ءَاخَرَ لَا بُرۡهَٰنَ لَهُۥ بِهِۦ فَإِنَّمَا حِسَابُهُۥ عِندَ رَبِّهِۦٓۚ إِنَّهُۥ لَا يُفۡلِحُ ٱلۡكَٰفِرُونَ ١١٧

118. So say: "O my Lord! Grant You forgiveness and mercy! For You are the Best of those who show mercy!"

وَقُل رَّبِّ ٱغۡفِرۡ وَٱرۡحَمۡ وَأَنتَ خَيۡرُ ٱلرَّٰحِمِينَ ١١٨

سُورَةُ النُّورِ

Surah 24: ***An-Nur*** **(Light)**

In the name of Allah,
Most Gracious, Most Merciful.

بِسۡمِ ٱللَّهِ ٱلرَّحۡمَٰنِ ٱلرَّحِيمِ

1. A *Surah* which We have sent down and which We have ordained: in it have We sent down clear signs, in order that you may receive admonition.

سُورَةٌ أَنزَلۡنَٰهَا وَفَرَضۡنَٰهَا وَأَنزَلۡنَا فِيهَآ ءَايَٰتِۭ بَيِّنَٰتٖ لَّعَلَّكُمۡ تَذَكَّرُونَ ١ ثلاثة أرباع حزب ٣٥

2. The woman and the man guilty of adultery or fornication flog each of them with a hundred stripes; let not compassion

ٱلزَّانِيَةُ وَٱلزَّانِي فَٱجۡلِدُواْ كُلَّ وَٰحِدٖ مِّنۡهُمَا مِاْئَةَ جَلۡدَةٖۖ

move you in their case, in a matter prescribed by Allah, if you believe in Allah and the last day; and let a party of the believers witness their punishment.

وَلَا تَأۡخُذۡكُم بِهِمَا رَأۡفَةٞ فِي دِينِ ٱللَّهِ إِن كُنتُمۡ تُؤۡمِنُونَ بِٱللَّهِ
وَٱلۡيَوۡمِ ٱلۡأٓخِرِۖ وَلۡيَشۡهَدۡ عَذَابَهُمَا طَآئِفَةٞ مِّنَ ٱلۡمُؤۡمِنِينَ ٢

3. Let no man guilty of adultery or fornication marry any but a woman similarly guilty, or an Unbeliever; nor let any but such a man or an Unbeliever marry such a woman: to the believers such a thing is forbidden.

ٱلزَّانِي لَا يَنكِحُ إِلَّا زَانِيَةً أَوۡ مُشۡرِكَةٗ وَٱلزَّانِيَةُ لَا يَنكِحُهَآ
إِلَّا زَانٍ أَوۡ مُشۡرِكٞۚ وَحُرِّمَ ذَٰلِكَ عَلَى ٱلۡمُؤۡمِنِينَ ٣

4. And those who launch a charge against chaste women, and produce not four witnesses (to support their allegation) - flog them with eighty stripes; and reject their evidence ever after: for such men are wicked transgressors -

وَٱلَّذِينَ يَرۡمُونَ ٱلۡمُحۡصَنَٰتِ ثُمَّ لَمۡ يَأۡتُواْ بِأَرۡبَعَةِ
شُهَدَآءَ فَٱجۡلِدُوهُمۡ ثَمَٰنِينَ جَلۡدَةٗ وَلَا تَقۡبَلُواْ لَهُمۡ
شَهَٰدَةً أَبَدٗاۚ وَأُوْلَٰٓئِكَ هُمُ ٱلۡفَٰسِقُونَ ٤

5. Unless they repent thereafter and mend (their conduct): for Allah is Oft-Forgiving, Most Merciful.

إِلَّا ٱلَّذِينَ تَابُواْ مِنۢ بَعۡدِ ذَٰلِكَ وَأَصۡلَحُواْ فَإِنَّ ٱللَّهَ
غَفُورٞ رَّحِيمٞ ٥

6. And for those who launch a charge against their spouses, and have (in support) no evidence but their own - their solitary evidence (can be received) if they bear witness four times (with an oath) by Allah that they are solemnly telling the truth;

وَٱلَّذِينَ يَرۡمُونَ أَزۡوَٰجَهُمۡ وَلَمۡ يَكُن لَّهُمۡ شُهَدَآءُ
إِلَّآ أَنفُسُهُمۡ فَشَهَٰدَةُ أَحَدِهِمۡ أَرۡبَعُ شَهَٰدَٰتِۭ بِٱللَّهِ إِنَّهُۥ
لَمِنَ ٱلصَّٰدِقِينَ ٦

7. And the fifth (oath) (should be) that they solemnly invoke the curse of Allah on themselves if they tell a lie.

وَٱلۡخَٰمِسَةُ أَنَّ لَعۡنَتَ ٱللَّهِ عَلَيۡهِ إِن كَانَ مِنَ ٱلۡكَٰذِبِينَ ٧

8. But it would avert the punishment from the wife, if she bears witness four times (with an oath) by Allah, that (her husband) is telling a lie;

وَيَدۡرَؤُاْ عَنۡهَا ٱلۡعَذَابَ أَن تَشۡهَدَ أَرۡبَعَ شَهَٰدَٰتِۭ بِٱللَّهِ
إِنَّهُۥ لَمِنَ ٱلۡكَٰذِبِينَ ٨

9. And the fifth (oath) should be that she solemnly invokes the wrath of Allah on herself if (her accuser) is telling the truth.

وَٱلۡخَٰمِسَةَ أَنَّ غَضَبَ ٱللَّهِ عَلَيۡهَآ إِن كَانَ مِنَ ٱلصَّٰدِقِينَ ٩

10. If it were not for Allah's grace and mercy on you and that Allah is Oft- Returning Full of wisdom (you would be ruined indeed).

وَلَوْلَا فَضْلُ ٱللَّهِ عَلَيْكُمْ وَرَحْمَتُهُۥ وَأَنَّ ٱللَّهَ تَوَّابٌ
حَكِيمٌ ١٠

11. Those who brought forward the lie are a body among yourselves; think it not to be an evil to you; on the contrary it is good for you: to every man among them (will come the punishment) of the sin that he earned, and to him who took on himself the lead among them, will be a penalty grievous.

إِنَّ ٱلَّذِينَ جَآءُو بِٱلْإِفْكِ عُصْبَةٌ مِّنكُمْ ۚ لَا تَحْسَبُوهُ
شَرًّا لَّكُم ۖ بَلْ هُوَ خَيْرٌ لَّكُمْ ۚ لِكُلِّ ٱمْرِئٍ مِّنْهُم مَّا
ٱكْتَسَبَ مِنَ ٱلْإِثْمِ ۚ وَٱلَّذِى تَوَلَّىٰ كِبْرَهُۥ مِنْهُمْ لَهُۥ
عَذَابٌ عَظِيمٌ ١١

12. Why did not believers men and women when you heard of the affair, put the best construction on it in their own minds and say, "This (charge) is an obvious lie"?

لَّوْلَآ إِذْ سَمِعْتُمُوهُ ظَنَّ ٱلْمُؤْمِنُونَ وَٱلْمُؤْمِنَٰتُ بِأَنفُسِهِمْ
خَيْرًا وَقَالُوا۟ هَٰذَآ إِفْكٌ مُّبِينٌ ١٢

13. Why did they not bring four witnesses to prove it? When they have not brought the witnesses, such men, in the sight of Allah (stand forth) themselves as liars!

لَّوْلَا جَآءُو عَلَيْهِ بِأَرْبَعَةِ شُهَدَآءَ ۚ فَإِذْ لَمْ يَأْتُوا۟
بِٱلشُّهَدَآءِ فَأُو۟لَٰٓئِكَ عِندَ ٱللَّهِ هُمُ ٱلْكَٰذِبُونَ ١٣

14. Were it not for the grace and mercy of Allah on you, in this world and the hereafter, a grievous penalty would have seized you in that you rushed glibly into this affair.

وَلَوْلَا فَضْلُ ٱللَّهِ عَلَيْكُمْ وَرَحْمَتُهُۥ فِى ٱلدُّنْيَا وَٱلْءَاخِرَةِ
لَمَسَّكُمْ فِى مَآ أَفَضْتُمْ فِيهِ عَذَابٌ عَظِيمٌ ١٤

15. See, you received it on your tongues and said out of your mouths things of which you had no knowledge; and you thought it to be a light matter, while it was most serious in the sight of Allah.

إِذْ تَلَقَّوْنَهُۥ بِأَلْسِنَتِكُمْ وَتَقُولُونَ بِأَفْوَاهِكُم مَّا لَيْسَ
لَكُم بِهِۦ عِلْمٌ وَتَحْسَبُونَهُۥ هَيِّنًا وَهُوَ عِندَ ٱللَّهِ
عَظِيمٌ ١٥

16. And why did you not when you heard it, say "It is not right of us to speak of this: Glory to Allah! This is a most serious slander!"

وَلَوْلَآ إِذْ سَمِعْتُمُوهُ قُلْتُم مَّا يَكُونُ لَنَآ أَن نَّتَكَلَّمَ
بِهَٰذَا سُبْحَٰنَكَ هَٰذَا بُهْتَٰنٌ عَظِيمٌ ١٦

17. Allah does admonish you, that you may never repeat such (conduct), if you are (true) believers.

يَعِظُكُمُ ٱللَّهُ أَن تَعُودُوا۟ لِمِثْلِهِۦٓ أَبَدًا إِن كُنتُم
مُّؤْمِنِينَ ١٧

18. And Allah makes the signs plain to you: for Allah is full of knowledge and wisdom.

وَيُبَيِّنُ ٱللَّهُ لَكُمُ ٱلْـَٔايَٰتِۚ وَٱللَّهُ عَلِيمٌ حَكِيمٌ ﴿١٨﴾

19. Those who love (to see) scandal published broadcast among the believers, will have a grievous penalty in this life and in the hereafter: Allah knows and you know not.

إِنَّ ٱلَّذِينَ يُحِبُّونَ أَن تَشِيعَ ٱلْفَٰحِشَةُ فِى ٱلَّذِينَ
ءَامَنُوا۟ لَهُمْ عَذَابٌ أَلِيمٌ فِى ٱلدُّنْيَا وَٱلْءَاخِرَةِۚ وَٱللَّهُ
يَعْلَمُ وَأَنتُمْ لَا تَعْلَمُونَ ﴿١٩﴾

20. Were it not for the grace and mercy of Allah on you, and that Allah is full of kindness and mercy, (you would be ruined indeed).

وَلَوْلَا فَضْلُ ٱللَّهِ عَلَيْكُمْ وَرَحْمَتُهُۥ وَأَنَّ ٱللَّهَ
رَءُوفٌ رَّحِيمٌ ﴿٢٠﴾

21. O you who believe! Follow not Satan's footsteps: if any will follow the footsteps of Satan, he will (but) command what is shameful and wrong: and were it not for the grace and mercy of Allah on you, not one of you would ever have been pure; but Allah does purify whom He pleases: and Allah is one Who hears and knows (all things).

الحزب ٣٦ ۞ يَٰٓأَيُّهَا ٱلَّذِينَ ءَامَنُوا۟ لَا تَتَّبِعُوا۟ خُطُوَٰتِ ٱلشَّيْطَٰنِۚ
وَمَن يَتَّبِعْ خُطُوَٰتِ ٱلشَّيْطَٰنِ فَإِنَّهُۥ يَأْمُرُ بِٱلْفَحْشَآءِ
وَٱلْمُنكَرِۚ وَلَوْلَا فَضْلُ ٱللَّهِ عَلَيْكُمْ وَرَحْمَتُهُۥ مَا زَكَىٰ
مِنكُم مِّنْ أَحَدٍ أَبَدًا وَلَٰكِنَّ ٱللَّهَ يُزَكِّى مَن يَشَآءُۗ وَٱللَّهُ
سَمِيعٌ عَلِيمٌ ﴿٢١﴾

22. Let not those among you who are endued with grace and amplitude of means resolve by oath against helping their relatives, those in want, and those who have left their homes in Allah's cause: let them forgive and overlook, do you not wish that Allah should forgive you? For Allah is Oft-Forgiving, Most Merciful.

وَلَا يَأْتَلِ أُو۟لُوا۟ ٱلْفَضْلِ مِنكُمْ وَٱلسَّعَةِ أَن يُؤْتُوٓا۟ أُو۟لِى
ٱلْقُرْبَىٰ وَٱلْمَسَٰكِينَ وَٱلْمُهَٰجِرِينَ فِى سَبِيلِ ٱللَّهِۖ
وَلْيَعْفُوا۟ وَلْيَصْفَحُوٓا۟ۗ أَلَا تُحِبُّونَ أَن يَغْفِرَ ٱللَّهُ
لَكُمْۗ وَٱللَّهُ غَفُورٌ رَّحِيمٌ ﴿٢٢﴾

23. Those who slander chaste women, indiscreet but believing, are cursed in this life and in the hereafter: for them is a grievous penalty -

إِنَّ ٱلَّذِينَ يَرْمُونَ ٱلْمُحْصَنَٰتِ ٱلْغَٰفِلَٰتِ ٱلْمُؤْمِنَٰتِ
لُعِنُوا۟ فِى ٱلدُّنْيَا وَٱلْءَاخِرَةِ وَلَهُمْ عَذَابٌ عَظِيمٌ ﴿٢٣﴾

24. On the day when their tongues, their hands, and their feet will bear witness against them as to their actions.

يَوْمَ تَشْهَدُ عَلَيْهِمْ أَلْسِنَتُهُمْ وَأَيْدِيهِمْ وَأَرْجُلُهُم
بِمَا كَانُوا۟ يَعْمَلُونَ ﴿٢٤﴾

25. On that day Allah will pay them back (all) their just dues, and they will realise that Allah is the (very) truth, that makes all things manifest.

يَوْمَئِذٍ يُوَفِّيهِمُ ٱللَّهُ دِينَهُمُ ٱلْحَقَّ وَيَعْلَمُونَ أَنَّ ٱللَّهَ
هُوَ ٱلْحَقُّ ٱلْمُبِينُ ﴿٢٥﴾

26. Women impure are for men impure, and men impure are for women impure, and women of purity are for men of purity, and men of purity are for women of purity; these are not affected by what people say: for them there is forgiveness and a provision honourable.

ٱلْخَبِيثَٰتُ لِلْخَبِيثِينَ وَٱلْخَبِيثُونَ لِلْخَبِيثَٰتِ ۖ
وَٱلطَّيِّبَٰتُ لِلطَّيِّبِينَ وَٱلطَّيِّبُونَ لِلطَّيِّبَٰتِ ۚ
أُو۟لَٰٓئِكَ مُبَرَّءُونَ مِمَّا يَقُولُونَ ۖ لَهُم مَّغْفِرَةٌ وَرِزْقٌ
كَرِيمٌ ﴿٢٦﴾

27. O you who believe! Enter not houses other than your own, until you have asked permission and saluted those in them: that is best for you, in order that you may heed (what is seemly).

يَٰٓأَيُّهَا ٱلَّذِينَ ءَامَنُوا۟ لَا تَدْخُلُوا۟ بُيُوتًا غَيْرَ بُيُوتِكُمْ
حَتَّىٰ تَسْتَأْنِسُوا۟ وَتُسَلِّمُوا۟ عَلَىٰٓ أَهْلِهَا ۚ ذَٰلِكُمْ خَيْرٌ
لَّكُمْ لَعَلَّكُمْ تَذَكَّرُونَ ﴿٢٧﴾

28. If you find no one in the house, enter not until permission is given to you; if you are asked to go back, go back; that makes for greater purity for yourselves: and Allah knows well all that you do.

فَإِن لَّمْ تَجِدُوا۟ فِيهَآ أَحَدًا فَلَا تَدْخُلُوهَا حَتَّىٰ يُؤْذَنَ
لَكُمْ ۖ وَإِن قِيلَ لَكُمُ ٱرْجِعُوا۟ فَٱرْجِعُوا۟ ۖ هُوَ أَزْكَىٰ
لَكُمْ ۚ وَٱللَّهُ بِمَا تَعْمَلُونَ عَلِيمٌ ﴿٢٨﴾

29. It is no fault on your part to enter houses not used for living in, which serve some (other) use for you: and Allah has knowledge of what you reveal and what you conceal.

لَّيْسَ عَلَيْكُمْ جُنَاحٌ أَن تَدْخُلُوا۟ بُيُوتًا غَيْرَ مَسْكُونَةٍ
فِيهَا مَتَٰعٌ لَّكُمْ ۚ وَٱللَّهُ يَعْلَمُ مَا تُبْدُونَ وَمَا
تَكْتُمُونَ ﴿٢٩﴾

30. Say to the believing men that they should lower their gaze and guard their modesty; that will make for greater purity for them: and Allah is well acquainted with all that they do.

قُل لِّلْمُؤْمِنِينَ يَغُضُّوا۟ مِنْ أَبْصَٰرِهِمْ وَيَحْفَظُوا۟
فُرُوجَهُمْ ۚ ذَٰلِكَ أَزْكَىٰ لَهُمْ ۗ إِنَّ ٱللَّهَ خَبِيرٌۢ بِمَا
يَصْنَعُونَ ﴿٣٠﴾

31. And say to the believing women that they should lower their gaze and guard

وَقُل لِّلْمُؤْمِنَٰتِ يَغْضُضْنَ مِنْ أَبْصَٰرِهِنَّ

their modesty; that they should not display their beauty and ornaments except what (must ordinarily) appear of it; that they should draw their veils over their bosoms and not display their beauty except to their husbands, their fathers, their husbands' fathers, their sons, their husbands' sons, their brothers or their brothers' sons, or their sisters' sons, or their women, or the slaves whom their right hands possess, or male servants free of physical needs, or small children who have no sense of the shame of sex; and that they should not strike their feet in order to draw attention to their hidden ornaments. And O you believers! Turn you all together towards Allah, that you may attain bliss.

وَيَحْفَظْنَ فُرُوجَهُنَّ وَلَا يُبْدِينَ زِينَتَهُنَّ إِلَّا
مَا ظَهَرَ مِنْهَا ۖ وَلْيَضْرِبْنَ بِخُمُرِهِنَّ عَلَىٰ جُيُوبِهِنَّ ۖ
وَلَا يُبْدِينَ زِينَتَهُنَّ إِلَّا لِبُعُولَتِهِنَّ أَوْ ءَابَآئِهِنَّ
أَوْ ءَابَآءِ بُعُولَتِهِنَّ أَوْ أَبْنَآئِهِنَّ أَوْ أَبْنَآءِ بُعُولَتِهِنَّ
أَوْ إِخْوَٰنِهِنَّ أَوْ بَنِىٓ إِخْوَٰنِهِنَّ أَوْ بَنِىٓ أَخَوَٰتِهِنَّ
أَوْ نِسَآئِهِنَّ أَوْ مَا مَلَكَتْ أَيْمَٰنُهُنَّ أَوِ ٱلتَّٰبِعِينَ
غَيْرِ أُو۟لِى ٱلْإِرْبَةِ مِنَ ٱلرِّجَالِ أَوِ ٱلطِّفْلِ ٱلَّذِينَ
لَمْ يَظْهَرُوا۟ عَلَىٰ عَوْرَٰتِ ٱلنِّسَآءِ ۖ وَلَا يَضْرِبْنَ
بِأَرْجُلِهِنَّ لِيُعْلَمَ مَا يُخْفِينَ مِن زِينَتِهِنَّ ۚ وَتُوبُوٓا۟
إِلَى ٱللَّهِ جَمِيعًا أَيُّهَ ٱلْمُؤْمِنُونَ لَعَلَّكُمْ
تُفْلِحُونَ ﴿٣١﴾

32. Marry those among you who are single or the virtuous ones among your slaves, male or female; if they are in poverty, Allah will give them means out of His grace: for Allah encompasses all and He knows all things.

وَأَنكِحُوا۟ ٱلْأَيَٰمَىٰ مِنكُمْ وَٱلصَّٰلِحِينَ مِنْ عِبَادِكُمْ
وَإِمَآئِكُمْ ۚ إِن يَكُونُوا۟ فُقَرَآءَ يُغْنِهِمُ ٱللَّهُ مِن
فَضْلِهِۦ ۗ وَٱللَّهُ وَٰسِعٌ عَلِيمٌ ﴿٣٢﴾

33. Let those who find not the wherewithal for marriage keep themselves chaste, until Allah gives them means out of His grace. And if any of your slaves ask for a deed in writing (to enable them to earn their freedom for a certain sum) give them such a deed if you know any good in them; yea give them something yourselves out of the means which Allah has given to you. But force not your maids to prostitution when they desire chastity in order that you may make a gain in the goods of this life. But if anyone compels them yet, after such compulsion, is Allah Oft-Forgiving, Most Merciful (to them).

وَلْيَسْتَعْفِفِ ٱلَّذِينَ لَا يَجِدُونَ نِكَاحًا حَتَّىٰ يُغْنِيَهُمُ ٱللَّهُ
مِن فَضْلِهِۦ ۗ وَٱلَّذِينَ يَبْتَغُونَ ٱلْكِتَٰبَ مِمَّا مَلَكَتْ
أَيْمَٰنُكُمْ فَكَاتِبُوهُمْ إِنْ عَلِمْتُمْ فِيهِمْ خَيْرًا ۖ وَءَاتُوهُم
مِّن مَّالِ ٱللَّهِ ٱلَّذِىٓ ءَاتَىٰكُمْ ۚ وَلَا تُكْرِهُوا۟ فَتَيَٰتِكُمْ عَلَى
ٱلْبِغَآءِ إِنْ أَرَدْنَ تَحَصُّنًا لِّتَبْتَغُوا۟ عَرَضَ ٱلْحَيَوٰةِ
ٱلدُّنْيَا ۚ وَمَن يُكْرِههُّنَّ فَإِنَّ ٱللَّهَ مِنۢ بَعْدِ إِكْرَٰهِهِنَّ
غَفُورٌ رَّحِيمٌ ﴿٣٣﴾

34. We have already sent down to you verses making things clear, an illustration from (the story of) people who passed away before you and an admonition for those who fear (Allah).

وَلَقَدْ أَنزَلْنَآ إِلَيْكُمْ ءَايَٰتٍ مُّبَيِّنَٰتٍ وَمَثَلًا مِّنَ
ٱلَّذِينَ خَلَوْا۟ مِن قَبْلِكُمْ وَمَوْعِظَةً لِّلْمُتَّقِينَ ﴿٣٤﴾

35. Allah is the light of the heavens and the earth. The parable of His light is as if there were a niche and within it a lamp; the Lamp enclosed in glass; the glass as it were a brilliant star; lit from a blessed tree an olive, neither of the east nor of the west, whose oil is well-near luminous, though fire scarce touched it: Light upon light! Allah does guide whom He will to His light. Allah does set out parables for men; and Allah does know all things.

ربع الحزب ٣٦ ۞ ٱللَّهُ نُورُ ٱلسَّمَٰوَٰتِ وَٱلْأَرْضِ ۚ مَثَلُ نُورِهِۦ كَمِشْكَوٰةٍ
فِيهَا مِصْبَاحٌ ۖ ٱلْمِصْبَاحُ فِى زُجَاجَةٍ ۖ ٱلزُّجَاجَةُ كَأَنَّهَا
كَوْكَبٌ دُرِّىٌّ يُوقَدُ مِن شَجَرَةٍ مُّبَٰرَكَةٍ زَيْتُونَةٍ
لَّا شَرْقِيَّةٍ وَلَا غَرْبِيَّةٍ يَكَادُ زَيْتُهَا يُضِىٓءُ وَلَوْ لَمْ
تَمْسَسْهُ نَارٌ ۚ نُّورٌ عَلَىٰ نُورٍ ۗ يَهْدِى ٱللَّهُ لِنُورِهِۦ مَن
يَشَآءُ ۚ وَيَضْرِبُ ٱللَّهُ ٱلْأَمْثَٰلَ لِلنَّاسِ ۗ وَٱللَّهُ بِكُلِّ شَىْءٍ
عَلِيمٌ ﴿٣٥﴾

36. (Lit is such a light) in houses, which Allah has permitted to be raised to honour; for the celebration, in them of His name: in them, is He glorified in the mornings and in the evenings, (again and again) -

فِى بُيُوتٍ أَذِنَ ٱللَّهُ أَن تُرْفَعَ وَيُذْكَرَ فِيهَا ٱسْمُهُۥ
يُسَبِّحُ لَهُۥ فِيهَا بِٱلْغُدُوِّ وَٱلْءَاصَالِ ﴿٣٦﴾

37. By men whom neither traffic nor merchandise can divert from the remembrance of Allah, nor from regular prayer, nor from the practice of regular charity: their (only) fear is for the day when hearts and eyes will be transformed (in a world wholly new) -

رِجَالٌ لَّا تُلْهِيهِمْ تِجَٰرَةٌ وَلَا بَيْعٌ عَن ذِكْرِ ٱللَّهِ وَإِقَامِ
ٱلصَّلَوٰةِ وَإِيتَآءِ ٱلزَّكَوٰةِ ۙ يَخَافُونَ يَوْمًا تَتَقَلَّبُ فِيهِ
ٱلْقُلُوبُ وَٱلْأَبْصَٰرُ ﴿٣٧﴾

38. That Allah may reward them according to the best of their deeds and add even more for them out of His grace: for Allah does provide for those whom He will without measure.

لِيَجْزِيَهُمُ ٱللَّهُ أَحْسَنَ مَا عَمِلُوا۟ وَيَزِيدَهُم مِّن
فَضْلِهِۦ ۗ وَٱللَّهُ يَرْزُقُ مَن يَشَآءُ بِغَيْرِ حِسَابٍ ﴿٣٨﴾

39. But the unbelievers, their deeds are like a mirage in sandy deserts, which the man

وَٱلَّذِينَ كَفَرُوٓا۟ أَعْمَٰلُهُمْ كَسَرَابٍۭ بِقِيعَةٍ يَحْسَبُهُ

parched with thirst mistakes for water; until when he comes up to it, he finds it to be nothing; but he finds Allah (ever) with him, and Allah will pay him his account: and Allah is swift in taking account.

ٱلظَّمۡـَٔانُ مَآءً حَتَّىٰٓ إِذَا جَآءَهُۥ لَمۡ يَجِدۡهُ شَيۡـٔٗا
وَوَجَدَ ٱللَّهَ عِندَهُۥ فَوَفَّىٰهُ حِسَابَهُۥۗ وَٱللَّهُ سَرِيعُ
ٱلۡحِسَابِ ٣٩

40. Or (the unbelievers' state) is like the depths of darkness in a vast deep ocean, overwhelmed with billow topped by billow, topped by (dark) clouds: depths of darkness, one above another; if a man stretches out his hand, he can hardly see it! For any to whom Allah gives not light, there is no light!

أَوۡ كَظُلُمَٰتٖ فِي بَحۡرٖ لُّجِّيّٖ يَغۡشَىٰهُ مَوۡجٞ مِّن فَوۡقِهِۦ مَوۡجٞ
مِّن فَوۡقِهِۦ سَحَابٞۚ ظُلُمَٰتُۢ بَعۡضُهَا فَوۡقَ بَعۡضٍ إِذَآ
أَخۡرَجَ يَدَهُۥ لَمۡ يَكَدۡ يَرَىٰهَاۗ وَمَن لَّمۡ يَجۡعَلِ ٱللَّهُ لَهُۥ
نُورٗا فَمَا لَهُۥ مِن نُّورٍ ٤٠

41. Do you not see that it is Allah Whose praises all beings in the heavens and on earth do celebrate, and the birds (of the air) with wings outspread? Each one knows its own (mode of) prayer and praise. And Allah knows well all that they do.

أَلَمۡ تَرَ أَنَّ ٱللَّهَ يُسَبِّحُ لَهُۥ مَن فِي ٱلسَّمَٰوَٰتِ وَٱلۡأَرۡضِ
وَٱلطَّيۡرُ صَٰٓفَّٰتٖۖ كُلّٞ قَدۡ عَلِمَ صَلَاتَهُۥ وَتَسۡبِيحَهُۥۗ وَٱللَّهُ
عَلِيمُۢ بِمَا يَفۡعَلُونَ ٤١

42. Yea, to Allah belongs the dominion of the heavens and the earth; and to Allah is the final goal (of all).

وَلِلَّهِ مُلۡكُ ٱلسَّمَٰوَٰتِ وَٱلۡأَرۡضِۖ وَإِلَى ٱللَّهِ ٱلۡمَصِيرُ ٤٢

43. Do you not see that Allah makes the clouds move gently, then joins them together, then makes them into a heap? Then will you see rain issue forth from their midst. And He sends down from the sky mountain masses (of clouds) in which is hail: He strikes with it whom He pleases and He turns it away from whom He pleases. The vivid flash of His lightning well-near blinds the sight.

أَلَمۡ تَرَ أَنَّ ٱللَّهَ يُزۡجِي سَحَابٗا ثُمَّ يُؤَلِّفُ بَيۡنَهُۥ ثُمَّ يَجۡعَلُهُۥ
رُكَامٗا فَتَرَى ٱلۡوَدۡقَ يَخۡرُجُ مِنۡ خِلَٰلِهِۦ وَيُنَزِّلُ مِنَ
ٱلسَّمَآءِ مِن جِبَالٖ فِيهَا مِنۢ بَرَدٖ فَيُصِيبُ بِهِۦ مَن يَشَآءُ
وَيَصۡرِفُهُۥ عَن مَّن يَشَآءُۖ يَكَادُ سَنَا بَرۡقِهِۦ يَذۡهَبُ
بِٱلۡأَبۡصَٰرِ ٤٣

44. It is Allah Who alternates the night and the day: verily in these things is an instructive example for those who have vision!

يُقَلِّبُ ٱللَّهُ ٱلَّيۡلَ وَٱلنَّهَارَۚ إِنَّ فِي ذَٰلِكَ لَعِبۡرَةٗ لِّأُوْلِي
ٱلۡأَبۡصَٰرِ ٤٤

45. And Allah has created every animal from water: of them there are some that creep on their bellies; some that walk on two legs; and some that walk on four. Allah creates what He wills: for verily Allah has power over all things.

وَٱللَّهُ خَلَقَ كُلَّ دَآبَّةٍ مِّن مَّآءٍ فَمِنْهُم مَّن يَمْشِي عَلَىٰ بَطْنِهِۦ
وَمِنْهُم مَّن يَمْشِي عَلَىٰ رِجْلَيْنِ وَمِنْهُم مَّن يَمْشِي عَلَىٰٓ
أَرْبَعٍ يَخْلُقُ ٱللَّهُ مَا يَشَآءُ إِنَّ ٱللَّهَ عَلَىٰ كُلِّ شَيْءٍ
قَدِيرٌ ٤٥

46. We have indeed sent down signs that make things manifest: and Allah guides whom He wills to a way that is straight.

لَّقَدْ أَنزَلْنَآ ءَايَٰتٍ مُّبَيِّنَٰتٍ وَٱللَّهُ يَهْدِي مَن يَشَآءُ
إِلَىٰ صِرَٰطٍ مُّسْتَقِيمٍ ٤٦

47. They say, "We believe in Allah and in the messenger and we obey": but even after that, some of them turn away: they are not (really) believers.

وَيَقُولُونَ ءَامَنَّا بِٱللَّهِ وَبِٱلرَّسُولِ وَأَطَعْنَا ثُمَّ يَتَوَلَّىٰ
فَرِيقٌ مِّنْهُم مِّنۢ بَعْدِ ذَٰلِكَ وَمَآ أُو۟لَٰٓئِكَ بِٱلْمُؤْمِنِينَ ٤٧

48. When they are summoned to Allah and His messenger, in order that He may judge between them, see some of them decline (to come).

وَإِذَا دُعُوٓا۟ إِلَى ٱللَّهِ وَرَسُولِهِۦ لِيَحْكُمَ بَيْنَهُمْ إِذَا فَرِيقٌ
مِّنْهُم مُّعْرِضُونَ ٤٨

49. But if the right is on their side, they come to him with all submission.

وَإِن يَكُن لَّهُمُ ٱلْحَقُّ يَأْتُوٓا۟ إِلَيْهِ مُذْعِنِينَ ٤٩

50. Is it that there is a disease in their hearts? Or do they doubt, or are they in fear, that Allah and His messenger will deal unjustly with them? Nay, it is they themselves who do wrong.

أَفِي قُلُوبِهِم مَّرَضٌ أَمِ ٱرْتَابُوٓا۟ أَمْ يَخَافُونَ أَن يَحِيفَ ٱللَّهُ
عَلَيْهِمْ وَرَسُولُهُۥ بَلْ أُو۟لَٰٓئِكَ هُمُ ٱلظَّٰلِمُونَ ٥٠

51. The answer of the believers, when summoned to Allah and His messenger, in order that He may judge between them, is no other than this: They say, "We hear and we obey"; it is such as these that will attain felicity.

إِنَّمَا كَانَ قَوْلَ ٱلْمُؤْمِنِينَ إِذَا دُعُوٓا۟ إِلَى ٱللَّهِ وَرَسُولِهِۦ
لِيَحْكُمَ بَيْنَهُمْ أَن يَقُولُوا۟ سَمِعْنَا وَأَطَعْنَا وَأُو۟لَٰٓئِكَ
هُمُ ٱلْمُفْلِحُونَ ٥١

52. It is such as obey Allah and His messenger, and fear Allah and do right, that will win (in the end).

وَمَن يُطِعِ ٱللَّهَ وَرَسُولَهُۥ وَيَخْشَ ٱللَّهَ وَيَتَّقْهِ
فَأُو۟لَٰٓئِكَ هُمُ ٱلْفَآئِزُونَ ٥٢

نصف الحزب ٣٦

53. They swear their strongest oaths by Allah that, if only you would command them, they would leave (their homes). Say: "Swear you not; obedience is (more) reasonable: Verily, Allah is well-acquainted with all that you do."

۞ وَأَقۡسَمُواْ بِٱللَّهِ جَهۡدَ أَيۡمَٰنِهِمۡ لَئِنۡ أَمَرۡتَهُمۡ
لَيَخۡرُجُنَّۖ قُل لَّا تُقۡسِمُواْۖ طَاعَةٞ مَّعۡرُوفَةٌۚ إِنَّ
ٱللَّهَ خَبِيرُۢ بِمَا تَعۡمَلُونَ ﴿٥٣﴾

54. Say: "Obey Allah and obey the messenger: but if you turn away, he is only responsible for the duty placed on him and you for that placed on you. If you obey him, you shall be on right guidance. The messenger's duty is only to preach the clear (message)."

قُلۡ أَطِيعُواْ ٱللَّهَ وَأَطِيعُواْ ٱلرَّسُولَۖ فَإِن تَوَلَّوۡاْ فَإِنَّمَا
عَلَيۡهِ مَا حُمِّلَ وَعَلَيۡكُم مَّا حُمِّلۡتُمۡۖ وَإِن تُطِيعُوهُ
تَهۡتَدُواْۚ وَمَا عَلَى ٱلرَّسُولِ إِلَّا ٱلۡبَلَٰغُ ٱلۡمُبِينُ ﴿٥٤﴾

55. Allah has promised, to those among you who believe and work righteous deeds, that He will, of a surety, grant them in the land inheritance (of power), as He granted it to those before them; that He will establish in authority their religion - the one which He has chosen for them; and that He will change (their state), after the fear in which they (lived), to one of security and peace: 'They will worship Me (alone) and not associate anything with Me.' If any do reject faith after this, they are rebellious and wicked.

وَعَدَ ٱللَّهُ ٱلَّذِينَ ءَامَنُواْ مِنكُمۡ وَعَمِلُواْ ٱلصَّٰلِحَٰتِ
لَيَسۡتَخۡلِفَنَّهُمۡ فِي ٱلۡأَرۡضِ كَمَا ٱسۡتَخۡلَفَ
ٱلَّذِينَ مِن قَبۡلِهِمۡ وَلَيُمَكِّنَنَّ لَهُمۡ دِينَهُمُ
ٱلَّذِي ٱرۡتَضَىٰ لَهُمۡ وَلَيُبَدِّلَنَّهُم مِّنۢ بَعۡدِ خَوۡفِهِمۡ
أَمۡنٗاۚ يَعۡبُدُونَنِي لَا يُشۡرِكُونَ بِي شَيۡـٔٗاۚ وَمَن كَفَرَ
بَعۡدَ ذَٰلِكَ فَأُوْلَٰٓئِكَ هُمُ ٱلۡفَٰسِقُونَ ﴿٥٥﴾

56. So establish regular prayer and give regular charity; and obey the messenger; that you may receive mercy.

وَأَقِيمُواْ ٱلصَّلَوٰةَ وَءَاتُواْ ٱلزَّكَوٰةَ وَأَطِيعُواْ ٱلرَّسُولَ
لَعَلَّكُمۡ تُرۡحَمُونَ ﴿٥٦﴾

57. Never think you that the unbelievers are going to frustrate (Allah's Plan) on earth: their abode is the fire and it is indeed an evil refuge!

لَا تَحۡسَبَنَّ ٱلَّذِينَ كَفَرُواْ مُعۡجِزِينَ فِي ٱلۡأَرۡضِۚ
وَمَأۡوَىٰهُمُ ٱلنَّارُۖ وَلَبِئۡسَ ٱلۡمَصِيرُ ﴿٥٧﴾

58. O you who believe! Let those whom your right hands possess, and the (children) among you who have not come of age ask your permission (before they

يَٰٓأَيُّهَا ٱلَّذِينَ ءَامَنُواْ لِيَسۡتَـٔۡذِنكُمُ ٱلَّذِينَ مَلَكَتۡ
أَيۡمَٰنُكُمۡ وَٱلَّذِينَ لَمۡ يَبۡلُغُواْ ٱلۡحُلُمَ مِنكُمۡ ثَلَٰثَ مَرَّٰتٖۚ مِّن قَبۡلِ

come to your presence), on three occasions before morning prayer; the while you take off your clothes for the noonday heat; and after the late-night prayer; these are your three times of undress; outside those times it is not wrong for you or for them to move about attending to each other: thus does Allah make clear the signs to you: for Allah is full of knowledge and wisdom.

صَلَوٰةِ ٱلۡفَجۡرِ وَحِينَ تَضَعُونَ ثِيَابَكُم مِّنَ ٱلظَّهِيرَةِ
وَمِنۢ بَعۡدِ صَلَوٰةِ ٱلۡعِشَآءِۚ ثَلَٰثُ عَوۡرَٰتٖ لَّكُمۡۚ لَيۡسَ عَلَيۡكُمۡ
وَلَا عَلَيۡهِمۡ جُنَاحُۢ بَعۡدَهُنَّۚ طَوَّٰفُونَ عَلَيۡكُم بَعۡضُكُمۡ
عَلَىٰ بَعۡضٖۚ كَذَٰلِكَ يُبَيِّنُ ٱللَّهُ لَكُمُ ٱلۡأٓيَٰتِۗ
وَٱللَّهُ عَلِيمٌ حَكِيمٞ ٥٨

59. But when the children among you come of age, let them (also) ask for permission, as do those senior to them (in age); thus does Allah make clear His signs to you; for Allah is full of knowledge and wisdom.

وَإِذَا بَلَغَ ٱلۡأَطۡفَٰلُ مِنكُمُ ٱلۡحُلُمَ فَلۡيَسۡتَـٔۡذِنُواْ
كَمَا ٱسۡتَـٔۡذَنَ ٱلَّذِينَ مِن قَبۡلِهِمۡۚ كَذَٰلِكَ
يُبَيِّنُ ٱللَّهُ لَكُمۡ ءَايَٰتِهِۦۗ وَٱللَّهُ عَلِيمٌ
حَكِيمٞ ٥٩

60. Such elderly women as are past the prospect of marriage - there is no blame on them if they lay aside their (outer) garments, provided they make not a wanton display of their beauty; but it is best for them to be modest: and Allah is One Who sees and knows all things.

وَٱلۡقَوَٰعِدُ مِنَ ٱلنِّسَآءِ ٱلَّٰتِي لَا يَرۡجُونَ نِكَاحٗا
فَلَيۡسَ عَلَيۡهِنَّ جُنَاحٌ أَن يَضَعۡنَ ثِيَابَهُنَّ غَيۡرَ
مُتَبَرِّجَٰتِۭ بِزِينَةٖۖ وَأَن يَسۡتَعۡفِفۡنَ خَيۡرٞ
لَّهُنَّۗ وَٱللَّهُ سَمِيعٌ عَلِيمٞ ٦٠

61. It is no fault in the blind nor in one born lame, nor in one afflicted with illness, nor in yourselves, that yous hould eat in your own houses, or those of your fathers, or your mothers, or your brothers, or your sisters, or your father's brothers, or your father's sisters, or your mother's brothers, or your mother's sisters, or in houses of which the keys are in your possession, or in the house of a sincere friend of yours: there is no blame on you, whether you eat in company or separately. But if you enter

لَّيۡسَ عَلَى ٱلۡأَعۡمَىٰ حَرَجٞ وَلَا عَلَى ٱلۡأَعۡرَجِ حَرَجٞ
وَلَا عَلَى ٱلۡمَرِيضِ حَرَجٞ وَلَا عَلَىٰٓ أَنفُسِكُمۡ أَن تَأۡكُلُواْ
مِنۢ بُيُوتِكُمۡ أَوۡ بُيُوتِ ءَابَآئِكُمۡ أَوۡ بُيُوتِ
أُمَّهَٰتِكُمۡ أَوۡ بُيُوتِ إِخۡوَٰنِكُمۡ أَوۡ بُيُوتِ
أَخَوَٰتِكُمۡ أَوۡ بُيُوتِ أَعۡمَٰمِكُمۡ أَوۡ بُيُوتِ
عَمَّٰتِكُمۡ أَوۡ بُيُوتِ أَخۡوَٰلِكُمۡ أَوۡ بُيُوتِ
خَٰلَٰتِكُمۡ أَوۡ مَا مَلَكۡتُم مَّفَاتِحَهُۥٓ

houses, salute each other a greeting or blessing and purity as from Allah, thus does Allah make clear the signs to you: that you may understand.

أَوْ صَدِيقِكُمْ لَيْسَ عَلَيْكُمْ جُنَاحٌ أَن
تَأْكُلُوا۟ جَمِيعًا أَوْ أَشْتَاتًا فَإِذَا دَخَلْتُم بُيُوتًا
فَسَلِّمُوا۟ عَلَىٰٓ أَنفُسِكُمْ تَحِيَّةً مِّنْ عِندِ ٱللَّهِ مُبَـٰرَكَةً
طَيِّبَةً كَذَٰلِكَ يُبَيِّنُ ٱللَّهُ لَكُمُ ٱلْـَٔايَـٰتِ
لَعَلَّكُمْ تَعْقِلُونَ ﴿٦١﴾

62. Only those are believers, who believe in Allah and His messenger; when they are with him on a matter requiring collective action, they do not depart until they have asked for his leave; those who ask for your leave are those who believe in Allah and His messenger; so when they ask for your leave, for some business of theirs, give leave to those of them whom you will, and ask Allah for their forgiveness: for Allah is Oft-Forgiving, Most Merciful.

إِنَّمَا ٱلْمُؤْمِنُونَ ٱلَّذِينَ ءَامَنُوا۟ بِٱللَّهِ وَرَسُولِهِۦ وَإِذَا
كَانُوا۟ مَعَهُۥ عَلَىٰٓ أَمْرٍ جَامِعٍ لَّمْ يَذْهَبُوا۟ حَتَّىٰ يَسْتَـْٔذِنُوهُ
إِنَّ ٱلَّذِينَ يَسْتَـْٔذِنُونَكَ أُو۟لَـٰٓئِكَ ٱلَّذِينَ يُؤْمِنُونَ
بِٱللَّهِ وَرَسُولِهِۦ فَإِذَا ٱسْتَـْٔذَنُوكَ لِبَعْضِ شَأْنِهِمْ
فَأْذَن لِّمَن شِئْتَ مِنْهُمْ وَٱسْتَغْفِرْ لَهُمُ ٱللَّهَ
إِنَّ ٱللَّهَ غَفُورٌ رَّحِيمٌ ﴿٦٢﴾

63. Think not the summons of the messenger among yourselves like the summons of one of you to another: Allah does know those of you who slip away under shelter of some excuse: then let those beware who withstand the messenger's order, lest some trial befall them, or a grievous penalty be inflicted on them.

لَّا تَجْعَلُوا۟ دُعَآءَ ٱلرَّسُولِ بَيْنَكُمْ كَدُعَآءِ
بَعْضِكُم بَعْضًا قَدْ يَعْلَمُ ٱللَّهُ ٱلَّذِينَ يَتَسَلَّلُونَ
مِنكُمْ لِوَاذًا فَلْيَحْذَرِ ٱلَّذِينَ يُخَالِفُونَ عَنْ
أَمْرِهِۦٓ أَن تُصِيبَهُمْ فِتْنَةٌ أَوْ يُصِيبَهُمْ عَذَابٌ
أَلِيمٌ ﴿٦٣﴾

64. Be quite sure that to Allah does belong whatever is in the heavens and on earth. Well does He know what you are intent upon; and one day they will be brought back to Him, and He will tell them the truth of what they did: for Allah does know all things.

أَلَآ إِنَّ لِلَّهِ مَا فِى ٱلسَّمَـٰوَٰتِ وَٱلْأَرْضِ قَدْ يَعْلَمُ
مَآ أَنتُمْ عَلَيْهِ وَيَوْمَ يُرْجَعُونَ إِلَيْهِ فَيُنَبِّئُهُم بِمَا
عَمِلُوا۟ وَٱللَّهُ بِكُلِّ شَىْءٍ عَلِيمٌۢ ﴿٦٤﴾

سُورَةُ الفُرْقَانِ

Surah 25: ***Al-Furqan*** **(The Criterion)**

In the name of Allah,
Most Gracious, Most Merciful.

بِسْمِ ٱللَّهِ ٱلرَّحْمَـٰنِ ٱلرَّحِيمِ

1. Blessed is He Who sent down the criterion to His servant, that it may be an admonition to all creatures-

ثلاثة أرباع حزب ٣٦
تَبَارَكَ ٱلَّذِى نَزَّلَ ٱلْفُرْقَانَ عَلَىٰ عَبْدِهِۦ لِيَكُونَ
لِلْعَـٰلَمِينَ نَذِيرًا ﴿١﴾

2. He to Whom belongs the dominion of the heavens and the earth; no son has He begotten, nor has He a partner in His dominion: it is He Who created all things, and ordered them in due proportions.

ٱلَّذِى لَهُۥ مُلْكُ ٱلسَّمَـٰوَٰتِ وَٱلْأَرْضِ وَلَمْ يَتَّخِذْ وَلَدًا
وَلَمْ يَكُن لَّهُۥ شَرِيكٌ فِى ٱلْمُلْكِ وَخَلَقَ كُلَّ شَىْءٍ
فَقَدَّرَهُۥ تَقْدِيرًا ﴿٢﴾

3. Yet have they taken, besides Him, gods that can create nothing but are themselves created; that have no control of hurt or good to themselves; nor can they control death nor life nor resurrection.

وَٱتَّخَذُوا۟ مِن دُونِهِۦٓ ءَالِهَةً لَّا يَخْلُقُونَ شَيْـًٔا
وَهُمْ يُخْلَقُونَ وَلَا يَمْلِكُونَ لِأَنفُسِهِمْ ضَرًّا وَلَا
نَفْعًا وَلَا يَمْلِكُونَ مَوْتًا وَلَا حَيَوٰةً وَلَا نُشُورًا ﴿٣﴾

4. But the unbelievers say: "Nothing is this but a lie which he has forged, and others have helped him at it." In truth it is they who have put forward an iniquity and a falsehood.

وَقَالَ ٱلَّذِينَ كَفَرُوٓا۟ إِنْ هَـٰذَآ إِلَّآ إِفْكٌ ٱفْتَرَىٰهُ
وَأَعَانَهُۥ عَلَيْهِ قَوْمٌ ءَاخَرُونَ ۖ فَقَدْ جَآءُو ظُلْمًا
وَزُورًا ﴿٤﴾

5. And they say: "Tales of the ancients, which he has caused to be written: and they are dictated before him morning and evening."

وَقَالُوٓا۟ أَسَـٰطِيرُ ٱلْأَوَّلِينَ ٱكْتَتَبَهَا فَهِىَ تُمْلَىٰ
عَلَيْهِ بُكْرَةً وَأَصِيلًا ﴿٥﴾

6. Say: "The (Qur'an) was sent down by Him Who knows the mystery (that is) in the heavens and the earth: verily He is Oft-Forgiving, Most Merciful."

قُلْ أَنزَلَهُ ٱلَّذِى يَعْلَمُ ٱلسِّرَّ فِى ٱلسَّمَـٰوَٰتِ
وَٱلْأَرْضِ ۚ إِنَّهُۥ كَانَ غَفُورًا رَّحِيمًا ﴿٦﴾

7. And they say: "What sort of a messenger is this, who eats food, and walks through the streets? Why has not an angel been sent down to him to give admonition with him?

وَقَالُوا۟ مَالِ هَـٰذَا ٱلرَّسُولِ يَأْكُلُ ٱلطَّعَامَ
وَيَمْشِى فِى ٱلْأَسْوَاقِ لَوْلَآ أُنزِلَ إِلَيْهِ مَلَكٌ
فَيَكُونَ مَعَهُۥ نَذِيرًا ﴿٧﴾

8. Or (why) has not a treasure been bestowed on him, or why has he (not) a garden for enjoyment?" The wicked say: "You follow none other than a man bewitched."

أَوْ يُلْقَىٰٓ إِلَيْهِ كَنزٌ أَوْ تَكُونُ لَهُۥ جَنَّةٌ يَأْكُلُ
مِنْهَا ۚ وَقَالَ ٱلظَّـٰلِمُونَ إِن تَتَّبِعُونَ إِلَّا رَجُلًا
مَّسْحُورًا ﴿٨﴾

9. See what kinds of companions they make for you! But they have gone astray, and never a way will they be able to find!

ٱنظُرْ كَيْفَ ضَرَبُوا۟ لَكَ ٱلْأَمْثَـٰلَ فَضَلُّوا۟
فَلَا يَسْتَطِيعُونَ سَبِيلًا ﴿٩﴾

10. Blessed is He Who, if that were His will, could give you better (things) than those gardens beneath which rivers flow; and He could give you palaces (secure to dwell in).

تَبَارَكَ ٱلَّذِىٓ إِن شَآءَ جَعَلَ لَكَ خَيْرًا مِّن ذَٰلِكَ
جَنَّـٰتٍ تَجْرِى مِن تَحْتِهَا ٱلْأَنْهَـٰرُ وَيَجْعَل لَّكَ
قُصُورًا ﴿١٠﴾

11. Nay, they deny the hour (of the judgement to come): but We have prepared a blazing fire for such as deny the hour:

بَلْ كَذَّبُوا۟ بِٱلسَّاعَةِ ۖ وَأَعْتَدْنَا لِمَن كَذَّبَ
بِٱلسَّاعَةِ سَعِيرًا ﴿١١﴾

12. When it sees them from a place far off, they will hear its fury and its raging sigh.

إِذَا رَأَتْهُم مِّن مَّكَانٍۭ بَعِيدٍ سَمِعُوا۟ لَهَا تَغَيُّظًا
وَزَفِيرًا ﴿١٢﴾

13. And when they are cast, bound together, into a constricted place in it, they will plead for destruction there and then!

وَإِذَآ أُلْقُوا۟ مِنْهَا مَكَانًا ضَيِّقًا مُّقَرَّنِينَ دَعَوْا۟
هُنَالِكَ ثُبُورًا ﴿١٣﴾

14. "This day plead not for a single destruction: plead for destruction oft-repeated!"

لَّا تَدْعُوا۟ ٱلْيَوْمَ ثُبُورًا وَٰحِدًا وَٱدْعُوا۟ ثُبُورًا
كَثِيرًا ﴿١٤﴾

15. Say: "Is that best, or the eternal garden, promised to the righteous? For them, that is a reward as well as a goal (of attainment).

قُلۡ أَذَٰلِكَ خَيۡرٌ أَمۡ جَنَّةُ ٱلۡخُلۡدِ ٱلَّتِي وُعِدَ
ٱلۡمُتَّقُونَۚ كَانَتۡ لَهُمۡ جَزَآءٗ وَمَصِيرٗا ﴿١٥﴾

16. For them there will be in it all that they wish for: they will dwell (there) for ever; a promise to be prayed for from your Lord."

لَّهُمۡ فِيهَا مَا يَشَآءُونَ خَٰلِدِينَۚ كَانَ عَلَىٰ
رَبِّكَ وَعۡدٗا مَّسۡـُٔولٗا ﴿١٦﴾

17. The day He will gather them together as well as those whom they worship besides Allah, He will ask: "Was it you who led these My servants astray or did they stray from the path themselves?"

وَيَوۡمَ يَحۡشُرُهُمۡ وَمَا يَعۡبُدُونَ مِن دُونِ ٱللَّهِ
فَيَقُولُ ءَأَنتُمۡ أَضۡلَلۡتُمۡ عِبَادِي هَٰٓؤُلَآءِ أَمۡ هُمۡ
ضَلُّواْ ٱلسَّبِيلَ ﴿١٧﴾

18. They will say: "Glory to You! Not fit was it for us that we should take for protectors others besides You: but You did bestow on them, and their fathers, good things (in life), until they forgot the message: for they were a people (worthless and) lost.

قَالُواْ سُبۡحَٰنَكَ مَا كَانَ يَنۢبَغِي لَنَآ أَن نَّتَّخِذَ مِن
دُونِكَ مِنۡ أَوۡلِيَآءَ وَلَٰكِن مَّتَّعۡتَهُمۡ وَءَابَآءَهُمۡ
حَتَّىٰ نَسُواْ ٱلذِّكۡرَ وَكَانُواْ قَوۡمَۢا بُورٗا ﴿١٨﴾

19. (Allah will say): "Now have they proved you liars in what you say; so you cannot avert (your penalty) nor (get) help." And whoever among you does wrong, him shall We cause to taste of a grievous penalty.

فَقَدۡ كَذَّبُوكُم بِمَا تَقُولُونَ فَمَا تَسۡتَطِيعُونَ
صَرۡفٗا وَلَا نَصۡرٗاۚ وَمَن يَظۡلِم مِّنكُمۡ نُذِقۡهُ
عَذَابٗا كَبِيرٗا ﴿١٩﴾

20. And the prophets whom We sent before you were all (men) who ate food and walked through the streets: We have made some of you as a trial for others: will you have patience? For Allah is One Who sees (all things).

وَمَآ أَرۡسَلۡنَا قَبۡلَكَ مِنَ ٱلۡمُرۡسَلِينَ إِلَّآ إِنَّهُمۡ
لَيَأۡكُلُونَ ٱلطَّعَامَ وَيَمۡشُونَ فِي ٱلۡأَسۡوَاقِۗ
وَجَعَلۡنَا بَعۡضَكُمۡ لِبَعۡضٖ فِتۡنَةً أَتَصۡبِرُونَۗ
وَكَانَ رَبُّكَ بَصِيرٗا ﴿٢٠﴾

※**21.** Such as fear not the meeting with Us (for judgement) say: "Why are not the angels sent down to us, or (why) do we not see our Lord?" Indeed they have an

※ وَقَالَ ٱلَّذِينَ لَا يَرۡجُونَ لِقَآءَنَا لَوۡلَآ أُنزِلَ عَلَيۡنَا
ٱلۡمَلَٰٓئِكَةُ أَوۡ نَرَىٰ رَبَّنَاۗ لَقَدِ ٱسۡتَكۡبَرُواْ فِيٓ

※ Part-19

arrogant conceit of themselves, and mighty is the insolence of their impiety!

أَنفُسِهِمْ وَعَتَوْ عُتُوًّا كَبِيرًا ﴿٢١﴾

22. The day they see the angels no joy will there be to the sinners that day; the (angels) will say: "There is a barrier forbidden (to you) altogether!"

يَوْمَ يَرَوْنَ ٱلْمَلَٰٓئِكَةَ لَا بُشْرَىٰ يَوْمَئِذٍ لِّلْمُجْرِمِينَ
وَيَقُولُونَ حِجْرًا مَّحْجُورًا ﴿٢٢﴾

23. And We shall turn to whatever deeds they did (in this life), and We shall make such deeds as floating dust scattered about.

وَقَدِمْنَآ إِلَىٰ مَا عَمِلُوا۟ مِنْ عَمَلٍ فَجَعَلْنَٰهُ
هَبَآءً مَّنثُورًا ﴿٢٣﴾

24. The companions of the garden will be well, that day, in their abode, and have the fairest of places for repose.

أَصْحَٰبُ ٱلْجَنَّةِ يَوْمَئِذٍ خَيْرٌ مُّسْتَقَرًّا
وَأَحْسَنُ مَقِيلًا ﴿٢٤﴾

25. The day the heaven shall be rent asunder with clouds, and angels shall be sent down descending (in ranks)-

وَيَوْمَ تَشَقَّقُ ٱلسَّمَآءُ بِٱلْغَمَٰمِ وَنُزِّلَ ٱلْمَلَٰٓئِكَةُ تَنزِيلًا ﴿٢٥﴾

26. That day, the dominion as of right and truth, shall be (wholly) for (Allah) Most Merciful: it will be a day of dire difficulty for the unbelievers.

ٱلْمُلْكُ يَوْمَئِذٍ ٱلْحَقُّ لِلرَّحْمَٰنِ ۚ وَكَانَ يَوْمًا عَلَى
ٱلْكَٰفِرِينَ عَسِيرًا ﴿٢٦﴾

27. The day that the wrongdoer will bite at his hands, He will say "Oh! Would that I had taken a (straight) path with the messenger!"

وَيَوْمَ يَعَضُّ ٱلظَّالِمُ عَلَىٰ يَدَيْهِ يَقُولُ يَٰلَيْتَنِى
ٱتَّخَذْتُ مَعَ ٱلرَّسُولِ سَبِيلًا ﴿٢٧﴾

28. "Ah! Woe is me! Would that I had never taken such a one for a friend!

يَٰوَيْلَتَىٰ لَيْتَنِى لَمْ أَتَّخِذْ فُلَانًا خَلِيلًا ﴿٢٨﴾

29. He did lead me astray from the message (of Allah) after it had come to me! Ah! The evil one is but a traitor to man!"

لَّقَدْ أَضَلَّنِى عَنِ ٱلذِّكْرِ بَعْدَ إِذْ جَآءَنِى ۗ وَكَانَ
ٱلشَّيْطَٰنُ لِلْإِنسَٰنِ خَذُولًا ﴿٢٩﴾

30. Then the messenger will say: "O my Lord! Truly my people took this Qur'an for just foolish nonsense."

وَقَالَ ٱلرَّسُولُ يَٰرَبِّ إِنَّ قَوْمِى ٱتَّخَذُوا۟ هَٰذَا
ٱلْقُرْءَانَ مَهْجُورًا ﴿٣٠﴾

31. Thus have We made for every prophet an enemy among the sinners: but enough is your Lord to guide and to help.

وَكَذَٰلِكَ جَعَلْنَا لِكُلِّ نَبِيٍّ عَدُوًّا مِّنَ
ٱلْمُجْرِمِينَ ۗ وَكَفَىٰ بِرَبِّكَ هَادِيًا وَنَصِيرًا ﴿٣١﴾

32. Those who reject faith say: "Why is not the Qur'an revealed to him all at once?" Thus (is it revealed), that We may strengthen your heart by it, and We have rehearsed it to you in slow, well-arranged stages, gradually.

وَقَالَ ٱلَّذِينَ كَفَرُوا۟ لَوْلَا نُزِّلَ عَلَيْهِ ٱلْقُرْءَانُ جُمْلَةً
وَٰحِدَةً ۚ كَذَٰلِكَ لِنُثَبِّتَ بِهِۦ فُؤَادَكَ ۖ وَرَتَّلْنَٰهُ
تَرْتِيلًا ﴿٣٢﴾

33. And no question do they bring to you but We reveal to you the truth and the best explanation (of it).

وَلَا يَأْتُونَكَ بِمَثَلٍ إِلَّا جِئْنَٰكَ بِٱلْحَقِّ
وَأَحْسَنَ تَفْسِيرًا ﴿٣٣﴾

34. Those who will be gathered to hell, (prone) on their faces they will be in an evil plight, and as to path, most astray.

ٱلَّذِينَ يُحْشَرُونَ عَلَىٰ وُجُوهِهِمْ إِلَىٰ جَهَنَّمَ
أُو۟لَٰٓئِكَ شَرٌّ مَّكَانًا وَأَضَلُّ سَبِيلًا ﴿٣٤﴾

35. Before this, We sent Moses the book, and appointed his brother Aaron with him as minister;

وَلَقَدْ ءَاتَيْنَا مُوسَى ٱلْكِتَٰبَ وَجَعَلْنَا مَعَهُۥٓ
أَخَاهُ هَٰرُونَ وَزِيرًا ﴿٣٥﴾

36. And We commanded: "Go you both, to the people who have rejected Our signs": and those (people) We destroyed with utter destruction.

فَقُلْنَا ٱذْهَبَآ إِلَى ٱلْقَوْمِ ٱلَّذِينَ كَذَّبُوا۟ بِـَٔايَٰتِنَا
فَدَمَّرْنَٰهُمْ تَدْمِيرًا ﴿٣٦﴾

37. And the people of Noah when they rejected the messengers, We drowned them, and We made them as a sign for mankind; and We have prepared for (all) wrongdoers a grievous penalty;

وَقَوْمَ نُوحٍ لَّمَّا كَذَّبُوا۟ ٱلرُّسُلَ أَغْرَقْنَٰهُمْ
وَجَعَلْنَٰهُمْ لِلنَّاسِ ءَايَةً ۖ وَأَعْتَدْنَا لِلظَّٰلِمِينَ
عَذَابًا أَلِيمًا ﴿٣٧﴾

38. As also 'Ad and Thamud, and the companions of ar-Rass, and many a generation between them.

وَعَادًا وَثَمُودَا۟ وَأَصْحَٰبَ ٱلرَّسِّ وَقُرُونًۢا
بَيْنَ ذَٰلِكَ كَثِيرًا ﴿٣٨﴾

39. To teach one We set out parables and examples; and each one We broke to utter annihilation (for their sins).

وَكُلًّا ضَرَبْنَا لَهُ ٱلْأَمْثَٰلَ ۖ وَكُلًّا تَبَّرْنَا
تَتْبِيرًا ﴿٣٩﴾

40. And the (unbelievers) must indeed have passed by the town on which was rained a shower of evil: did they not then see it (with their own eyes)? But they fear not the resurrection.

وَلَقَدْ أَتَوْا۟ عَلَى ٱلْقَرْيَةِ ٱلَّتِىٓ أُمْطِرَتْ مَطَرَ ٱلسَّوْءِ ۚ
أَفَلَمْ يَكُونُوا۟ يَرَوْنَهَا ۚ بَلْ كَانُوا۟ لَا يَرْجُونَ
نُشُورًا ﴿٤٠﴾

41. When they see you they treat you, no otherwise than in mockery: "Is this the one whom Allah has sent as a messenger?"

وَإِذَا رَأَوْكَ إِن يَتَّخِذُونَكَ إِلَّا هُزُوًا أَهَٰذَا ٱلَّذِى
بَعَثَ ٱللَّهُ رَسُولًا ﴿٤١﴾

42. "He indeed would well-near have misled us from our gods, had it not been that we were constant to them!" Soon will they know, when they see the penalty, who it is that is most misled in path!

إِن كَادَ لَيُضِلُّنَا عَنْ ءَالِهَتِنَا لَوْلَآ أَن صَبَرْنَا
عَلَيْهَا ۚ وَسَوْفَ يَعْلَمُونَ حِينَ يَرَوْنَ ٱلْعَذَابَ
مَنْ أَضَلُّ سَبِيلًا ﴿٤٢﴾

43. See you such a one as takes for his god his own passion (or impulse)? Could you be a disposer of affairs for him?

أَرَءَيْتَ مَنِ ٱتَّخَذَ إِلَٰهَهُۥ هَوَىٰهُ أَفَأَنتَ تَكُونُ
عَلَيْهِ وَكِيلًا ﴿٤٣﴾

44. Or do you think that most of them listen or understand? They are only like cattle; nay, they are worse astray in path.

أَمْ تَحْسَبُ أَنَّ أَكْثَرَهُمْ يَسْمَعُونَ أَوْ يَعْقِلُونَ ۚ
إِنْ هُمْ إِلَّا كَٱلْأَنْعَٰمِ ۖ بَلْ هُمْ أَضَلُّ سَبِيلًا ﴿٤٤﴾

45. Have you not turned your vision to your Lord? how He does prolong the shadow! If He willed, He could make it stationary! Then do We make the sun its guide;

أَلَمْ تَرَ إِلَىٰ رَبِّكَ كَيْفَ مَدَّ ٱلظِّلَّ وَلَوْ شَآءَ لَجَعَلَهُۥ
سَاكِنًا ثُمَّ جَعَلْنَا ٱلشَّمْسَ عَلَيْهِ دَلِيلًا ﴿٤٥﴾

46. Then We draw it in towards Ourselves - a contraction by easy stages.

ثُمَّ قَبَضْنَٰهُ إِلَيْنَا قَبْضًا يَسِيرًا ﴿٤٦﴾

47. And He it is Who makes the night as a robe for you, and sleep as repose, and makes the day (as it were) a resurrection.

وَهُوَ ٱلَّذِى جَعَلَ لَكُمُ ٱلَّيْلَ لِبَاسًا وَٱلنَّوْمَ سُبَاتًا
وَجَعَلَ ٱلنَّهَارَ نُشُورًا ﴿٤٧﴾

48. And He it is Who sends the winds as heralds of glad tidings, going before His mercy, and We send down purifying water from the sky -

وَهُوَ ٱلَّذِىٓ أَرْسَلَ ٱلرِّيَٰحَ بُشْرًۢا بَيْنَ يَدَىْ
رَحْمَتِهِۦ ۚ وَأَنزَلْنَا مِنَ ٱلسَّمَآءِ مَآءً طَهُورًا ﴿٤٨﴾

49. That with it, We may give life to a dead land, and slake the thirst of things We have created cattle and men in great numbers.

لِّنُحْـِۧىَ بِهِۦ بَلْدَةً مَّيْتًا وَنُسْقِيَهُۥ مِمَّا خَلَقْنَآ
أَنْعَٰمًا وَأَنَاسِىَّ كَثِيرًا ﴿٤٩﴾

50. And We have distributed the (water) amongst them, in order that they may celebrate (Our) praises, but most men are averse (to anything) but (rank) ingratitude.

وَلَقَدْ صَرَّفْنَٰهُ بَيْنَهُمْ لِيَذَّكَّرُوا۟ فَأَبَىٰٓ أَكْثَرُ ٱلنَّاسِ
إِلَّا كُفُورًا ﴿٥٠﴾

51. Had it been Our will, We could have sent a warner to every centre of population,

وَلَوْ شِئْنَا لَبَعَثْنَا فِى كُلِّ قَرْيَةٍ نَّذِيرًا ﴿٥١﴾

52. Therefore, listen not to the unbelievers, but strive against them with the utmost strenuousness, with the (Qur'an).

فَلَا تُطِعِ ٱلْكَٰفِرِينَ وَجَٰهِدْهُم بِهِۦ جِهَادًا
كَبِيرًا ﴿٥٢﴾

53. It is He Who has let free the two bodies of flowing water: one palatable and sweet, and the other salty and bitter; yet has He made a barrier between them, a partition that is forbidden to be passed.

ربع الحزب ٣٧ ۞ وَهُوَ ٱلَّذِى مَرَجَ ٱلْبَحْرَيْنِ هَٰذَا عَذْبٌ فُرَاتٌ
وَهَٰذَا مِلْحٌ أُجَاجٌ وَجَعَلَ بَيْنَهُمَا بَرْزَخًا
وَحِجْرًا مَّحْجُورًا ﴿٥٣﴾

54. It is He Who has created man from water: then has He established relationships of lineage and marriage: for your Lord has power (over all things).

وَهُوَ ٱلَّذِى خَلَقَ مِنَ ٱلْمَآءِ بَشَرًا فَجَعَلَهُۥ نَسَبًا
وَصِهْرًا ۗ وَكَانَ رَبُّكَ قَدِيرًا ﴿٥٤﴾

55. Yet do they worship, besides Allah, things that can neither profit them nor harm them: and the unbeliever is a helper (of evil), against his own Lord!

وَيَعْبُدُونَ مِن دُونِ ٱللَّهِ مَا لَا يَنفَعُهُمْ وَلَا يَضُرُّهُمْ ۗ
وَكَانَ ٱلْكَافِرُ عَلَىٰ رَبِّهِۦ ظَهِيرًا ﴿٥٥﴾

56. But you We only sent to give glad tidings and admonition.

وَمَآ أَرْسَلْنَٰكَ إِلَّا مُبَشِّرًا وَنَذِيرًا ﴿٥٦﴾

57. Say: "No reward do I ask of you for it but this: that each one who will may take a (straight) path to his Lord."

قُلْ مَآ أَسْـَٔلُكُمْ عَلَيْهِ مِنْ أَجْرٍ إِلَّا مَن شَآءَ أَن
يَتَّخِذَ إِلَىٰ رَبِّهِۦ سَبِيلًا ﴿٥٧﴾

58. And put your trust in Him Who lives and dies not; and celebrate His praise; and enough is He to be acquainted with the faults of His servants-

وَتَوَكَّلْ عَلَى ٱلْحَىِّ ٱلَّذِى لَا يَمُوتُ وَسَبِّحْ
بِحَمْدِهِۦ ۚ وَكَفَىٰ بِهِۦ بِذُنُوبِ عِبَادِهِۦ خَبِيرًا ﴿٥٨﴾

59. He Who created the heavens and the earth and all that is between, in six days, and is firmly established on the throne (of authority): Allah, Most Gracious: ask you, then, about Him of any acquainted (with such things).

ٱلَّذِى خَلَقَ ٱلسَّمَٰوَٰتِ وَٱلْأَرْضَ وَمَا بَيْنَهُمَا فِى
سِتَّةِ أَيَّامٍ ثُمَّ ٱسْتَوَىٰ عَلَى ٱلْعَرْشِ ۚ ٱلرَّحْمَٰنُ
فَسْـَٔلْ بِهِۦ خَبِيرًا ﴿٥٩﴾

60. When it is said to them, "Adore you (Allah) Most Gracious!", They say, "And what is (Allah) Most Gracious? Shall we adore that which you command us?" and it increases their flight (from the truth).

وَإِذَا قِيلَ لَهُمُ ٱسْجُدُوا۟ لِلرَّحْمَٰنِ قَالُوا۟ وَمَا ٱلرَّحْمَٰنُ
سَجْدَةٌ أَنَسْجُدُ لِمَا تَأْمُرُنَا وَزَادَهُمْ نُفُورًا ۩ ﴿٦٠﴾

61. Blessed is He Who made constellations in the skies, and placed in it a lamp and a moon giving light;

تَبَارَكَ ٱلَّذِى جَعَلَ فِى ٱلسَّمَآءِ بُرُوجًا وَجَعَلَ
فِيهَا سِرَٰجًا وَقَمَرًا مُّنِيرًا ﴿٦١﴾

62. And it is He Who made the night and the day to follow each other: for such as have the will to celebrate His praises or to show their gratitude.

وَهُوَ ٱلَّذِى جَعَلَ ٱلَّيْلَ وَٱلنَّهَارَ خِلْفَةً لِّمَنْ أَرَادَ
أَن يَذَّكَّرَ أَوْ أَرَادَ شُكُورًا ﴿٦٢﴾

63. And the servants of (Allah) Most Gracious are those who walk on the earth in humility, and when the ignorant address them, they say, "Peace!";

وَعِبَادُ ٱلرَّحْمَٰنِ ٱلَّذِينَ يَمْشُونَ عَلَى ٱلْأَرْضِ هَوْنًا وَإِذَا
خَاطَبَهُمُ ٱلْجَٰهِلُونَ قَالُوا۟ سَلَٰمًا ﴿٦٣﴾

64. Those who spend the night in adoration of their Lord prostrate and standing;

وَٱلَّذِينَ يَبِيتُونَ لِرَبِّهِمْ سُجَّدًا وَقِيَٰمًا ﴿٦٤﴾

65. Those who say: "Our Lord! Avert from us the wrath of hell, for its wrath is indeed an affliction grievous -

وَٱلَّذِينَ يَقُولُونَ رَبَّنَا ٱصۡرِفۡ عَنَّا عَذَابَ جَهَنَّمَۖ
إِنَّ عَذَابَهَا كَانَ غَرَامًا ٦٥

66. Evil indeed is it as an abode, and as a place to rest in";

إِنَّهَا سَآءَتۡ مُسۡتَقَرّٗا وَمُقَامٗا ٦٦

67. Those who, when they spend, are not extravagant and not niggardly, but hold a just (balance) between those (extremes);

وَٱلَّذِينَ إِذَآ أَنفَقُواْ لَمۡ يُسۡرِفُواْ وَلَمۡ يَقۡتُرُواْ
وَكَانَ بَيۡنَ ذَٰلِكَ قَوَامٗا ٦٧

68. Those who invoke not, with Allah, any other god, nor slay such life as Allah has made sacred, except for just cause, nor commit fornication - and any that does this (not only) meets punishment.

وَٱلَّذِينَ لَا يَدۡعُونَ مَعَ ٱللَّهِ إِلَٰهًا ءَاخَرَ وَلَا يَقۡتُلُونَ
ٱلنَّفۡسَ ٱلَّتِي حَرَّمَ ٱللَّهُ إِلَّا بِٱلۡحَقِّ وَلَا يَزۡنُونَۚ
وَمَن يَفۡعَلۡ ذَٰلِكَ يَلۡقَ أَثَامٗا ٦٨

69. (But) the penalty on the day of judgement will be doubled to him, and he will dwell in it in disgrace -

يُضَٰعَفۡ لَهُ ٱلۡعَذَابُ يَوۡمَ ٱلۡقِيَٰمَةِ وَيَخۡلُدۡ فِيهِۦ
مُهَانًا ٦٩

70. Unless he repents, believes and works righteous deeds, for Allah will change the evil of such persons into good, and Allah is Oft-Forgiving, Most Merciful,

إِلَّا مَن تَابَ وَءَامَنَ وَعَمِلَ عَمَلٗا صَٰلِحٗا
فَأُوْلَٰٓئِكَ يُبَدِّلُ ٱللَّهُ سَيِّـَٔاتِهِمۡ حَسَنَٰتٖۗ
وَكَانَ ٱللَّهُ غَفُورٗا رَّحِيمٗا ٧٠

71. And whoever repents and does good has truly turned to Allah with an (acceptable) conversion -

وَمَن تَابَ وَعَمِلَ صَٰلِحٗا فَإِنَّهُۥ يَتُوبُ إِلَى ٱللَّهِ
مَتَابٗا ٧١

72. Those who witness no falsehood and, if they pass by futility, they pass by it with honourable (avoidance);

وَٱلَّذِينَ لَا يَشۡهَدُونَ ٱلزُّورَ وَإِذَا مَرُّواْ
بِٱللَّغۡوِ مَرُّواْ كِرَامٗا ٧٢

73. Those who, when they are admonished with the signs of their Lord, droop not down at them as if they were deaf or blind:

وَٱلَّذِينَ إِذَا ذُكِّرُواْ بِـَٔايَٰتِ رَبِّهِمۡ لَمۡ يَخِرُّواْ
عَلَيۡهَا صُمّٗا وَعُمۡيَانٗا ٧٣

وَٱلَّذِينَ يَقُولُونَ رَبَّنَا هَبْ لَنَا مِنْ أَزْوَٰجِنَا وَذُرِّيَّتِنَا
قُرَّةَ أَعْيُنٍ وَٱجْعَلْنَا لِلْمُتَّقِينَ إِمَامًا ٧٤

74. And those who pray, "Our Lord! Grant to us wives and offspring who will be the comfort of our eyes, and give us (the grace) to lead the righteous."

أُوْلَٰٓئِكَ يُجْزَوْنَ ٱلْغُرْفَةَ بِمَا صَبَرُواْ وَيُلَقَّوْنَ
فِيهَا تَحِيَّةً وَسَلَٰمًا ٧٥

75. Those are the ones who will be rewarded with the highest place in heaven, because of their patient constancy; in it shall they be met with salutations and peace,

خَٰلِدِينَ فِيهَا ۚ حَسُنَتْ مُسْتَقَرًّا
وَمُقَامًا ٧٦

76. Dwelling in it - how beautiful an abode and place of rest!

قُلْ مَا يَعْبَؤُاْ بِكُمْ رَبِّي لَوْلَا دُعَآؤُكُمْ ۖ فَقَدْ
كَذَّبْتُمْ فَسَوْفَ يَكُونُ لِزَامًۢا ٧٧

77. Say (to the rejecters): "My Lord is not uneasy because of you if you call not on Him, but you have indeed rejected (Him), and soon will come the inevitable (punishment)!"

سُورَةُ الشُّعَرَاءِ

Surah 26: **Ash-Shu'ara (The Poets)**

بِسْمِ ٱللَّهِ ٱلرَّحْمَٰنِ ٱلرَّحِيمِ

In the name of Allah,
Most Gracious, Most Merciful.

نصف الحزب ٣٧

طسٓمٓ ١

1. *Ta Sin Mim.*

تِلْكَ ءَايَٰتُ ٱلْكِتَٰبِ ٱلْمُبِينِ ٢

2. These are verses of the book that makes (things) clear.

لَعَلَّكَ بَٰخِعٌ نَّفْسَكَ أَلَّا يَكُونُواْ مُؤْمِنِينَ ٣

3. It may be you torment your soul with grief, that they do not become believers.

إِن نَّشَأْ نُنَزِّلْ عَلَيْهِم مِّنَ ٱلسَّمَآءِ ءَايَةً فَظَلَّتْ أَعْنَٰقُهُمْ
لَهَا خَٰضِعِينَ ٤

4. If (such) were Our will We could send down to them from the sky a sign, to which they would bend their necks in humility.

5. But there comes not to them a newly-revealed message from (Allah) Most Gracious, but they turn away from it.

وَمَا يَأْتِيهِم مِّن ذِكْرٍ مِّنَ ٱلرَّحْمَٰنِ مُحْدَثٍ إِلَّا كَانُوا۟ عَنْهُ مُعْرِضِينَ ٥

6. They have indeed rejected (the message): so they will know soon (enough) the truth of what they mocked at!

فَقَدْ كَذَّبُوا۟ فَسَيَأْتِيهِمْ أَنۢبَٰٓؤُا۟ مَا كَانُوا۟ بِهِۦ يَسْتَهْزِءُونَ ٦

7. Do they not look at the earth how many noble things of all kinds We have produced in it?

أَوَلَمْ يَرَوْا۟ إِلَى ٱلْأَرْضِ كَمْ أَنۢبَتْنَا فِيهَا مِن كُلِّ زَوْجٍ كَرِيمٍ ٧

8. Verily in this is a sign: but most of them do not believe.

إِنَّ فِى ذَٰلِكَ لَءَايَةً ۖ وَمَا كَانَ أَكْثَرُهُم مُّؤْمِنِينَ ٨

9. And verily, your Lord is He, the Exalted in Might, Most Merciful.

وَإِنَّ رَبَّكَ لَهُوَ ٱلْعَزِيزُ ٱلرَّحِيمُ ٩

10. See, your Lord called Moses: "Go to the people of iniquity -

وَإِذْ نَادَىٰ رَبُّكَ مُوسَىٰٓ أَنِ ٱئْتِ ٱلْقَوْمَ ٱلظَّٰلِمِينَ ١٠

11. The people of Pharaoh: will they not fear Allah?"

قَوْمَ فِرْعَوْنَ ۚ أَلَا يَتَّقُونَ ١١

12. He said: "O my Lord! I do fear that they will charge me with falsehood:

قَالَ رَبِّ إِنِّىٓ أَخَافُ أَن يُكَذِّبُونِ ١٢

13. My breast will be straitened. And my speech may not go (smoothly): so send to Aaron.

وَيَضِيقُ صَدْرِى وَلَا يَنطَلِقُ لِسَانِى فَأَرْسِلْ إِلَىٰ هَٰرُونَ ١٣

14. And (further), they have a charge of crime against me; and I fear they may slay me."

وَلَهُمْ عَلَىَّ ذَنۢبٌ فَأَخَافُ أَن يَقْتُلُونِ ١٤

15. Allah said: "By no means! Proceed then, both of you, with Our signs; We are with you, and will listen (to your call).

قَالَ كَلَّا ۖ فَٱذْهَبَا بِـَٔايَٰتِنَآ ۖ إِنَّا مَعَكُم مُّسْتَمِعُونَ ١٥

16. So go ahead, both of you to Pharaoh, and say: 'We have been sent by the Lord and Cherisher of the Worlds;

فَأْتِيَا فِرْعَوْنَ فَقُولَآ إِنَّا رَسُولُ رَبِّ ٱلْعَٰلَمِينَ ١٦

17. Send you with us the Children of Israel.'"

أَنْ أَرْسِلْ مَعَنَا بَنِىٓ إِسْرَٰٓءِيلَ ﴿١٧﴾

18. (Pharaoh) said: "Did we not cherish you as a child among us, and did you not stay in our midst many years of your life?

قَالَ أَلَمْ نُرَبِّكَ فِينَا وَلِيدًا وَلَبِثْتَ فِينَا مِنْ عُمُرِكَ
سِنِينَ ﴿١٨﴾

19. And you did a deed of yours which (you know) you did, and you are an ungrateful (wretch)!"

وَفَعَلْتَ فَعْلَتَكَ ٱلَّتِى فَعَلْتَ وَأَنتَ مِنَ
ٱلْكَٰفِرِينَ ﴿١٩﴾

20. Moses: "I did it then, when I was in error.

قَالَ فَعَلْتُهَآ إِذًا وَأَنَا۠ مِنَ ٱلضَّآلِّينَ ﴿٢٠﴾

21. So I fled from you (all) when I feared you; but my Lord has (since) invested me with judgement (and wisdom) and appointed me as one of the messengers.

فَفَرَرْتُ مِنكُمْ لَمَّا خِفْتُكُمْ فَوَهَبَ لِى رَبِّى حُكْمًا
وَجَعَلَنِى مِنَ ٱلْمُرْسَلِينَ ﴿٢١﴾

22. And this is the favour with which you do reproach me - that you have enslaved the Children of Israel!"

وَتِلْكَ نِعْمَةٌ تَمُنُّهَا عَلَىَّ أَنْ عَبَّدتَّ بَنِىٓ إِسْرَٰٓءِيلَ ﴿٢٢﴾

23. Pharaoh said: "And what is the 'Lord and Cherisher of the Worlds?'"

قَالَ فِرْعَوْنُ وَمَا رَبُّ ٱلْعَٰلَمِينَ ﴿٢٣﴾

24. (Moses) said: "The Lord and Cherisher of the heavens and the earth, and all between - if you want to be quite sure."

قَالَ رَبُّ ٱلسَّمَٰوَٰتِ وَٱلْأَرْضِ وَمَا بَيْنَهُمَآ ۖ إِن كُنتُم
مُّوقِنِينَ ﴿٢٤﴾

25. (Pharaoh) said to those around: "Do you not listen (to what he says)?"

قَالَ لِمَنْ حَوْلَهُۥٓ أَلَا تَسْتَمِعُونَ ﴿٢٥﴾

26. (Moses) said: "Your Lord and the Lord of your fathers from the beginning!"

قَالَ رَبُّكُمْ وَرَبُّ ءَابَآئِكُمُ ٱلْأَوَّلِينَ ﴿٢٦﴾

27. (Pharaoh) said: "Truly your messenger who has been sent to you is a veritable madman!"

قَالَ إِنَّ رَسُولَكُمُ ٱلَّذِىٓ أُرْسِلَ إِلَيْكُمْ لَمَجْنُونٌ ﴿٢٧﴾

28. (Moses) said: "Lord of the east and the west, and all between! If you only had sense!"

قَالَ رَبُّ ٱلْمَشْرِقِ وَٱلْمَغْرِبِ وَمَا بَيْنَهُمَآ ۖ إِن كُنتُمْ
تَعْقِلُونَ ﴿٢٨﴾

29. (Pharaoh) said: "If you do put forward any god other than me, I will certainly put you in prison!"

قَالَ لَئِنِ ٱتَّخَذۡتَ إِلَٰهًا غَيۡرِي لَأَجۡعَلَنَّكَ مِنَ
ٱلۡمَسۡجُونِينَ ٢٩

30. (Moses) said: "Even if I showed you something clear (and) convincing?"

قَالَ أَوَلَوۡ جِئۡتُكَ بِشَيۡءٖ مُّبِينٖ ٣٠

31. (Pharaoh) said: "Show it then if you tell the truth!"

قَالَ فَأۡتِ بِهِۦٓ إِن كُنتَ مِنَ ٱلصَّٰدِقِينَ ٣١

32. So (Moses) threw his rod, and see, it was a serpent, plain (for all to see)!

فَأَلۡقَىٰ عَصَاهُ فَإِذَا هِيَ ثُعۡبَانٞ مُّبِينٞ ٣٢

33. And he drew out his hand, and see, it was white to all onlookers!

وَنَزَعَ يَدَهُۥ فَإِذَا هِيَ بَيۡضَآءُ لِلنَّٰظِرِينَ ٣٣

34. (Pharaoh) said to the chiefs around him: "This is indeed a sorcerer well-versed:

قَالَ لِلۡمَلَإِ حَوۡلَهُۥٓ إِنَّ هَٰذَا لَسَٰحِرٌ عَلِيمٞ ٣٤

35. His plan is to get you out of your land by his sorcery; then what is it you counsel?"

يُرِيدُ أَن يُخۡرِجَكُم مِّنۡ أَرۡضِكُم بِسِحۡرِهِۦ
فَمَاذَا تَأۡمُرُونَ ٣٥

36. They said: "Keep him and his brother in suspense (for a while), and dispatch to the cities heralds to collect -

قَالُوٓاْ أَرۡجِهۡ وَأَخَاهُ وَٱبۡعَثۡ فِي ٱلۡمَدَآئِنِ حَٰشِرِينَ ٣٦

37. And bring up to you all (our) sorcerers well-versed."

يَأۡتُوكَ بِكُلِّ سَحَّارٍ عَلِيمٖ ٣٧

38. So the sorcerers were got together for the appointment of a day well-known,

فَجُمِعَ ٱلسَّحَرَةُ لِمِيقَٰتِ يَوۡمٖ مَّعۡلُومٖ ٣٨

39. And the people were told: "Are you (now) assembled? -

وَقِيلَ لِلنَّاسِ هَلۡ أَنتُم مُّجۡتَمِعُونَ ٣٩

40. That we may follow the sorcerers (in religion) if they win?"

لَعَلَّنَا نَتَّبِعُ ٱلسَّحَرَةَ إِن كَانُواْ هُمُ ٱلۡغَٰلِبِينَ ٤٠

41. So when the sorcerers arrived, they said to Pharaoh: "Of course - shall we have a (suitable) reward if we win?"

فَلَمَّا جَآءَ ٱلسَّحَرَةُ قَالُواْ لِفِرۡعَوۡنَ أَئِنَّ لَنَا لَأَجۡرًا إِن كُنَّا
نَحۡنُ ٱلۡغَٰلِبِينَ ٤١

42. He said: "Yea (and more) - for you shall in that case be (raised to posts) nearest (to my person)."

قَالَ نَعَمۡ وَإِنَّكُمۡ إِذٗا لَّمِنَ ٱلۡمُقَرَّبِينَ ٤٢

43. Moses said to them: "Throw you - that which you are about to throw!"

قَالَ لَهُم مُّوسَىٰٓ أَلۡقُواْ مَآ أَنتُم مُّلۡقُونَ ٤٣

44. So they threw their ropes and their rods, and said: "By the might of Pharaoh it is we who will certainly win!"

فَأَلۡقَوۡاْ حِبَالَهُمۡ وَعِصِيَّهُمۡ وَقَالُواْ بِعِزَّةِ فِرۡعَوۡنَ
إِنَّا لَنَحۡنُ ٱلۡغَٰلِبُونَ ٤٤

45. Then Moses threw his rod, when, see, it straight away swallows up all the falsehoods which they fake!

فَأَلۡقَىٰ مُوسَىٰ عَصَاهُ فَإِذَا هِيَ تَلۡقَفُ مَا يَأۡفِكُونَ ٤٥

46. Then did the sorcerers fall down, prostrate in adoration,

فَأُلۡقِيَ ٱلسَّحَرَةُ سَٰجِدِينَ ٤٦

47. Saying: "We believe in the Lord of the Worlds,

قَالُوٓاْ ءَامَنَّا بِرَبِّ ٱلۡعَٰلَمِينَ ٤٧

48. The Lord of Moses and Aaron."

رَبِّ مُوسَىٰ وَهَٰرُونَ ٤٨

49. Said (Pharaoh): "Do you believe in him before I give you permission? Surely he is your leader, who has taught you sorcery! But soon shall you know! Be sure I will cut off your hands and your feet on opposite sides, and I will cause you all to die on the cross!"

قَالَ ءَامَنتُمۡ لَهُۥ قَبۡلَ أَنۡ ءَاذَنَ لَكُمۡۖ إِنَّهُۥ لَكَبِيرُكُمُ
ٱلَّذِي عَلَّمَكُمُ ٱلسِّحۡرَ فَلَسَوۡفَ تَعۡلَمُونَۚ لَأُقَطِّعَنَّ أَيۡدِيَكُمۡ
وَأَرۡجُلَكُم مِّنۡ خِلَٰفٖ وَلَأُصَلِّبَنَّكُمۡ أَجۡمَعِينَ ٤٩

50. They said: "No matter! For us, we shall but return to our Lord!

قَالُواْ لَا ضَيۡرَۖ إِنَّآ إِلَىٰ رَبِّنَا مُنقَلِبُونَ ٥٠

51. Only, our desire is that our Lord will forgive us our faults, that we may become foremost among the believers!"

إِنَّا نَطۡمَعُ أَن يَغۡفِرَ لَنَا رَبُّنَا خَطَٰيَٰنَآ أَن كُنَّآ أَوَّلَ
ٱلۡمُؤۡمِنِينَ ٥١

52. By inspiration We told Moses: "Travel by night with My servants; for surely you shall be pursued."

۞ وَأَوۡحَيۡنَآ إِلَىٰ مُوسَىٰٓ أَنۡ أَسۡرِ بِعِبَادِيٓ إِنَّكُم ثلاثة أرباع الحزب ٣٧
مُّتَّبَعُونَ ٥٢

53. Then Pharaoh sent heralds to (all) the cities,

فَأَرْسَلَ فِرْعَوْنُ فِى ٱلْمَدَآئِنِ حَٰشِرِينَ ٥٣

54. (Saying): "These (Israelites) are but a small band,

إِنَّ هَٰٓؤُلَآءِ لَشِرْذِمَةٌ قَلِيلُونَ ٥٤

55. And they are raging furiously against us;

وَإِنَّهُمْ لَنَا لَغَآئِظُونَ ٥٥

56. But we are a multitude amply forewarned."

وَإِنَّا لَجَمِيعٌ حَٰذِرُونَ ٥٦

57. So We expelled them from gardens, springs,

فَأَخْرَجْنَٰهُم مِّن جَنَّٰتٍ وَعُيُونٍ ٥٧

58. Treasures, and every kind of honourable position;

وَكُنُوزٍ وَمَقَامٍ كَرِيمٍ ٥٨

59. Thus it was, but We made the Children of Israel inheritors of such things.

كَذَٰلِكَ وَأَوْرَثْنَٰهَا بَنِىٓ إِسْرَٰٓءِيلَ ٥٩

60. So they pursued them at sunrise.

فَأَتْبَعُوهُم مُّشْرِقِينَ ٦٠

61. And when the two bodies saw each other, the people of Moses said: "We are sure to be overtaken."

فَلَمَّا تَرَٰٓءَا ٱلْجَمْعَانِ قَالَ أَصْحَٰبُ مُوسَىٰٓ
إِنَّا لَمُدْرَكُونَ ٦١

62. (Moses) said: "By no means! My Lord is with me! Soon will He guide me!"

قَالَ كَلَّآ إِنَّ مَعِىَ رَبِّى سَيَهْدِينِ ٦٢

63. Then We told Moses by inspiration: "Strike the sea with your rod." So it divided, and each separate part become like the huge, firm mass of a mountain.

فَأَوْحَيْنَآ إِلَىٰ مُوسَىٰٓ أَنِ ٱضْرِب بِّعَصَاكَ ٱلْبَحْرَ
فَٱنفَلَقَ فَكَانَ كُلُّ فِرْقٍ كَٱلطَّوْدِ ٱلْعَظِيمِ ٦٣

64. And We made the other party approach there.

وَأَزْلَفْنَا ثَمَّ ٱلْءَاخَرِينَ ٦٤

65. We delivered Moses and all who were with him;

وَأَنجَيْنَا مُوسَىٰ وَمَن مَّعَهُۥٓ أَجْمَعِينَ ٦٥

66. But We drowned the others.

ثُمَّ أَغْرَقْنَا ٱلْـَٔاخَرِينَ ﴿٦٦﴾

67. Verily in this is a sign: but most of them do not believe.

إِنَّ فِى ذَٰلِكَ لَـَٔايَةً ۖ وَمَا كَانَ أَكْثَرُهُم
مُّؤْمِنِينَ ﴿٦٧﴾

68. And verily your Lord is He, the Exalted in Might, Most Merciful.

وَإِنَّ رَبَّكَ لَهُوَ ٱلْعَزِيزُ ٱلرَّحِيمُ ﴿٦٨﴾

69. And rehearse to them (something of) Abraham's story.

وَٱتْلُ عَلَيْهِمْ نَبَأَ إِبْرَٰهِيمَ ﴿٦٩﴾

70. See, he said to his father and his people: "What do you worship?"

إِذْ قَالَ لِأَبِيهِ وَقَوْمِهِۦ مَا تَعْبُدُونَ ﴿٧٠﴾

71. They said: "We worship idols, and we remain constantly in attendance on them."

قَالُوا۟ نَعْبُدُ أَصْنَامًا فَنَظَلُّ لَهَا عَـٰكِفِينَ ﴿٧١﴾

72. He said: "Do they listen to you when you call (on them),

قَالَ هَلْ يَسْمَعُونَكُمْ إِذْ تَدْعُونَ ﴿٧٢﴾

73. Or do you good or harm?"

أَوْ يَنفَعُونَكُمْ أَوْ يَضُرُّونَ ﴿٧٣﴾

74. They said: "Nay, but we found our fathers doing thus (what we do)."

قَالُوا۟ بَلْ وَجَدْنَآ ءَابَآءَنَا كَذَٰلِكَ يَفْعَلُونَ ﴿٧٤﴾

75. He said: "Do you then see whom you have been worshipping -

قَالَ أَفَرَءَيْتُم مَّا كُنتُمْ تَعْبُدُونَ ﴿٧٥﴾

76. You and your fathers before you? -

أَنتُمْ وَءَابَآؤُكُمُ ٱلْأَقْدَمُونَ ﴿٧٦﴾

77. For they are enemies to me; not so the Lord and Cherisher of the Worlds;

فَإِنَّهُمْ عَدُوٌّ لِّىٓ إِلَّا رَبَّ ٱلْعَـٰلَمِينَ ﴿٧٧﴾

78. Who created me, and it is He Who guides me;

ٱلَّذِى خَلَقَنِى فَهُوَ يَهْدِينِ ﴿٧٨﴾

79. Who gives me food and drink.

وَٱلَّذِى هُوَ يُطْعِمُنِى وَيَسْقِينِ ﴿٧٩﴾

وَإِذَا مَرِضْتُ فَهُوَ يَشْفِينِ ﴿٨٠﴾

80. And when I am ill, it is He Who cures me;

وَالَّذِي يُمِيتُنِي ثُمَّ يُحْيِينِ ﴿٨١﴾

81. Who will cause me to die, and then to live (again);

وَالَّذِي أَطْمَعُ أَن يَغْفِرَ لِي خَطِيئَتِي يَوْمَ الدِّينِ ﴿٨٢﴾

82. And Who, I hope, will forgive me my faults on the day of judgement.

رَبِّ هَبْ لِي حُكْمًا وَأَلْحِقْنِي بِالصَّالِحِينَ ﴿٨٣﴾

83. O my Lord! Bestow wisdom on me, and join me with the righteous;

وَاجْعَل لِّي لِسَانَ صِدْقٍ فِي الْآخِرِينَ ﴿٨٤﴾

84. Grant me honourable mention on the tongue of truth among the latest (generations);

وَاجْعَلْنِي مِن وَرَثَةِ جَنَّةِ النَّعِيمِ ﴿٨٥﴾

85. Make me one of the inheritors of the garden of bliss;

وَاغْفِرْ لِأَبِي إِنَّهُ كَانَ مِنَ الضَّالِّينَ ﴿٨٦﴾

86. Forgive my father, for that he is among those astray;

وَلَا تُخْزِنِي يَوْمَ يُبْعَثُونَ ﴿٨٧﴾

87. And let me not be in disgrace on the day when (men) will be raised up -

يَوْمَ لَا يَنفَعُ مَالٌ وَلَا بَنُونَ ﴿٨٨﴾

88. The day on which neither wealth nor sons will benefit,

إِلَّا مَنْ أَتَى اللَّهَ بِقَلْبٍ سَلِيمٍ ﴿٨٩﴾

89. But only he (will prosper) that brings to Allah a sound heart;

وَأُزْلِفَتِ الْجَنَّةُ لِلْمُتَّقِينَ ﴿٩٠﴾

90. To the righteous the garden will be brought near,

وَبُرِّزَتِ الْجَحِيمُ لِلْغَاوِينَ ﴿٩١﴾

91. And to those straying in evil, the fire will be placed in full view;

وَقِيلَ لَهُمْ أَيْنَ مَا كُنتُمْ تَعْبُدُونَ ﴿٩٢﴾

92. And it shall be said to them: 'Where are the (gods) you worshipped -

مِن دُونِ اللَّهِ هَلْ يَنصُرُونَكُمْ أَوْ يَنتَصِرُونَ ﴿٩٣﴾

93. Besides Allah? Can they help you or help themselves?'

94. Then they will be thrown headlong into the (fire) - they and those straying in evil,

فَكُبْكِبُوا۟ فِيهَا هُمْ وَٱلْغَاوُۥنَ ﴿٩٤﴾

95. And the whole hosts of Iblis together.

وَجُنُودُ إِبْلِيسَ أَجْمَعُونَ ﴿٩٥﴾

96. They will say there in their mutual bickerings:

قَالُوا۟ وَهُمْ فِيهَا يَخْتَصِمُونَ ﴿٩٦﴾

97. 'By Allah, we were truly in an error manifest,

تَٱللَّهِ إِن كُنَّا لَفِى ضَلَـٰلٍ مُّبِينٍ ﴿٩٧﴾

98. When we held you as equals with the Lord of the Worlds;

إِذْ نُسَوِّيكُم بِرَبِّ ٱلْعَـٰلَمِينَ ﴿٩٨﴾

99. And our seducers were only those who were steeped in guilt.

وَمَآ أَضَلَّنَآ إِلَّا ٱلْمُجْرِمُونَ ﴿٩٩﴾

100. Now then, we have none to intercede (for us),

فَمَا لَنَا مِن شَـٰفِعِينَ ﴿١٠٠﴾

101. Nor a single friend to feel (for us).

وَلَا صَدِيقٍ حَمِيمٍ ﴿١٠١﴾

102. Now if we only had a chance of return, we shall truly be of those who believe!'"

فَلَوْ أَنَّ لَنَا كَرَّةً فَنَكُونَ مِنَ ٱلْمُؤْمِنِينَ ﴿١٠٢﴾

103. Verily in this is a sign but most of them do not believe.

إِنَّ فِى ذَٰلِكَ لَـَٔايَةً ۖ وَمَا كَانَ أَكْثَرُهُم مُّؤْمِنِينَ ﴿١٠٣﴾

104. And verily the Lord is He, the Exalted in Might, Most Merciful.

وَإِنَّ رَبَّكَ لَهُوَ ٱلْعَزِيزُ ٱلرَّحِيمُ ﴿١٠٤﴾

105. The people of Noah rejected the messengers.

كَذَّبَتْ قَوْمُ نُوحٍ ٱلْمُرْسَلِينَ ﴿١٠٥﴾

106. See, their brother Noah said to them: "Will you not fear (Allah)?"

إِذْ قَالَ لَهُمْ أَخُوهُمْ نُوحٌ أَلَا تَتَّقُونَ ﴿١٠٦﴾

107. "I am to you a messenger worthy of all trust:

إِنِّى لَكُمْ رَسُولٌ أَمِينٌ ﴿١٠٧﴾

108. So fear Allah, and obey me."

فَٱتَّقُوا۟ ٱللَّهَ وَأَطِيعُونِ ﴿١٠٨﴾

109. "No reward do I ask of you for it: my reward is only from the Lord of the Worlds:

وَمَآ أَسۡـَٔلُكُمۡ عَلَيۡهِ مِنۡ أَجۡرٍۖ إِنۡ أَجۡرِيَ إِلَّا عَلَىٰ رَبِّ ٱلۡعَٰلَمِينَ ١٠٩

110. So fear Allah, and obey me."

فَٱتَّقُواْ ٱللَّهَ وَأَطِيعُونِ ١١٠

111. They said: "Shall we believe in you when it is the meanest that follow you?"

الحزب ٣٨ ۞قَالُوٓاْ أَنُؤۡمِنُ لَكَ وَٱتَّبَعَكَ ٱلۡأَرۡذَلُونَ ١١١

112. He said: "And what do I know as to what they do?

قَالَ وَمَا عِلۡمِي بِمَا كَانُواْ يَعۡمَلُونَ ١١٢

113. Their account is only with my Lord, if you could (but) understand.

إِنۡ حِسَابُهُمۡ إِلَّا عَلَىٰ رَبِّيۖ لَوۡ تَشۡعُرُونَ ١١٣

114. I am not one to drive away those who believe.

وَمَآ أَنَا۠ بِطَارِدِ ٱلۡمُؤۡمِنِينَ ١١٤

115. I am sent only to warn plainly in public."

إِنۡ أَنَا۠ إِلَّا نَذِيرٞ مُّبِينٞ ١١٥

116. They said: "If you desist not, O Noah! You shall be stoned (to death)."

قَالُواْ لَئِن لَّمۡ تَنتَهِ يَٰنُوحُ لَتَكُونَنَّ مِنَ ٱلۡمَرۡجُومِينَ ١١٦

117. He said: "O my Lord! Truly my people have rejected me.

قَالَ رَبِّ إِنَّ قَوۡمِي كَذَّبُونِ ١١٧

118. Judge you, then, between me and them openly, and deliver me and those of the believers who are with me."

فَٱفۡتَحۡ بَيۡنِي وَبَيۡنَهُمۡ فَتۡحٗا وَنَجِّنِي وَمَن مَّعِيَ مِنَ ٱلۡمُؤۡمِنِينَ ١١٨

119. So We delivered him and those with him, in the ark filled (with all creatures).

فَأَنجَيۡنَٰهُ وَمَن مَّعَهُۥ فِي ٱلۡفُلۡكِ ٱلۡمَشۡحُونِ ١١٩

120. Thereafter We drowned those who remained behind.

ثُمَّ أَغۡرَقۡنَا بَعۡدُ ٱلۡبَاقِينَ ١٢٠

121. Verily in this is a sign: but most of them do not believe.

إِنَّ فِي ذَٰلِكَ لَأٓيَةٗۖ وَمَا كَانَ أَكۡثَرُهُم مُّؤۡمِنِينَ ١٢١

122. And verily your Lord is He, the Exalted in Might, Most Merciful.

وَإِنَّ رَبَّكَ لَهُوَ ٱلْعَزِيزُ ٱلرَّحِيمُ ١٢٢

123. The 'Ad (people) rejected the prophets.

كَذَّبَتْ عَادٌ ٱلْمُرْسَلِينَ ١٢٣

124. See, their brother Hud said to them: "Will you not fear (Allah)?

إِذْ قَالَ لَهُمْ أَخُوهُمْ هُودٌ أَلَا تَتَّقُونَ ١٢٤

125. I am to you a messenger worthy of all trust.

إِنِّي لَكُمْ رَسُولٌ أَمِينٌ ١٢٥

126. So fear Allah and obey me."

فَٱتَّقُوا۟ ٱللَّهَ وَأَطِيعُونِ ١٢٦

127. "No reward do I ask of you for it: my reward is only from the Lord of the Worlds."

وَمَآ أَسْـَٔلُكُمْ عَلَيْهِ مِنْ أَجْرٍ ۖ إِنْ أَجْرِيَ إِلَّا عَلَىٰ
رَبِّ ٱلْعَٰلَمِينَ ١٢٧

128. "Do you build a landmark on every high place to amuse yourselves?

أَتَبْنُونَ بِكُلِّ رِيعٍ ءَايَةً تَعْبَثُونَ ١٢٨

129. And do you get for yourselves fine buildings in the hope of living in it (forever)?

وَتَتَّخِذُونَ مَصَانِعَ لَعَلَّكُمْ تَخْلُدُونَ ١٢٩

130. And when you exert your strong hand, do you do it like men of absolute power?

وَإِذَا بَطَشْتُم بَطَشْتُمْ جَبَّارِينَ ١٣٠

131. Now fear Allah, and obey me.

فَٱتَّقُوا۟ ٱللَّهَ وَأَطِيعُونِ ١٣١

132. Yea, fear Him Who has bestowed on you freely all that you know.

وَٱتَّقُوا۟ ٱلَّذِيٓ أَمَدَّكُم بِمَا تَعْلَمُونَ ١٣٢

133. Freely has He bestowed on you cattle and sons -

أَمَدَّكُم بِأَنْعَٰمٍ وَبَنِينَ ١٣٣

134. And gardens and springs.

وَجَنَّٰتٍ وَعُيُونٍ ١٣٤

135. Truly I fear for you the penalty of a great day."

إِنِّيٓ أَخَافُ عَلَيْكُمْ عَذَابَ يَوْمٍ عَظِيمٍ ١٣٥

136. They said: "It is the same to us whether you admonish us or be not among (our) admonishers!

قَالُوا۟ سَوَآءٌ عَلَيْنَآ أَوَعَظْتَ أَمْ لَمْ تَكُن مِّنَ ٱلْوَٰعِظِينَ ١٣٦

137. This is no other than a customary device of the ancients,

إِنْ هَٰذَآ إِلَّا خُلُقُ ٱلْأَوَّلِينَ ١٣٧

138. And we are not the ones to receive pains and penalties!"

وَمَا نَحْنُ بِمُعَذَّبِينَ ١٣٨

139. So they rejected him, and We destroyed them. Verily in this is a sign: but most of them do not believe.

فَكَذَّبُوهُ فَأَهْلَكْنَٰهُمْ ۗ إِنَّ فِى ذَٰلِكَ لَءَايَةً ۖ وَمَا كَانَ أَكْثَرُهُم مُّؤْمِنِينَ ١٣٩

140. And verily your Lord is He, the Exalted in Might, Most Merciful.

وَإِنَّ رَبَّكَ لَهُوَ ٱلْعَزِيزُ ٱلرَّحِيمُ ١٤٠

141. The Thamud (people) rejected the messengers.

كَذَّبَتْ ثَمُودُ ٱلْمُرْسَلِينَ ١٤١

142. See, their brother Salih said to them: "Will you fear (Allah)?

إِذْ قَالَ لَهُمْ أَخُوهُمْ صَٰلِحٌ أَلَا تَتَّقُونَ ١٤٢

143. "I am to you a messenger worthy of all trust.

إِنِّى لَكُمْ رَسُولٌ أَمِينٌ ١٤٣

144. So fear Allah, and obey me.

فَٱتَّقُوا۟ ٱللَّهَ وَأَطِيعُونِ ١٤٤

145. No reward do I ask of you for it: my reward is only from the Lord of the Worlds.

وَمَآ أَسْـَٔلُكُمْ عَلَيْهِ مِنْ أَجْرٍ ۖ إِنْ أَجْرِىَ إِلَّا عَلَىٰ رَبِّ ٱلْعَٰلَمِينَ ١٤٥

146. Will you be left secure, in (the enjoyment of) all that you have here?

أَتُتْرَكُونَ فِى مَا هَٰهُنَآ ءَامِنِينَ ١٤٦

147. Gardens and Springs,

فِى جَنَّٰتٍ وَعُيُونٍ ١٤٧

148. And corn-fields and date-palms with spathes near breaking (with the weight of fruit)?

وَزُرُوعٍ وَنَخْلٍ طَلْعُهَا هَضِيمٌ ١٤٨

149. And you carve houses out of (rocky) mountains with great skill.

وَتَنْحِتُونَ مِنَ ٱلْجِبَالِ بُيُوتًا فَٰرِهِينَ ﴿١٤٩﴾

150. But fear Allah and obey me;

فَٱتَّقُوا۟ ٱللَّهَ وَأَطِيعُونِ ﴿١٥٠﴾

151. And follow not the bidding of those who are extravagant -

وَلَا تُطِيعُوٓا۟ أَمْرَ ٱلْمُسْرِفِينَ ﴿١٥١﴾

152. Who make mischief in the land, and mend not (their ways)."

ٱلَّذِينَ يُفْسِدُونَ فِى ٱلْأَرْضِ وَلَا يُصْلِحُونَ ﴿١٥٢﴾

153. They said: "You are only of those bewitched!

قَالُوٓا۟ إِنَّمَآ أَنتَ مِنَ ٱلْمُسَحَّرِينَ ﴿١٥٣﴾

154. You are no more than a mortal like us: then bring us a sign, if you tell the truth!"

مَآ أَنتَ إِلَّا بَشَرٌ مِّثْلُنَا فَأْتِ بِـَٔايَةٍ إِن كُنتَ مِنَ ٱلصَّٰدِقِينَ ﴿١٥٤﴾

155. He said: "Here is a she-camel: she has a right of watering, and you have a right of watering, (severally) on a day appointed.

قَالَ هَٰذِهِۦ نَاقَةٌ لَّهَا شِرْبٌ وَلَكُمْ شِرْبُ يَوْمٍ مَّعْلُومٍ ﴿١٥٥﴾

156. Touch her not with harm, lest the penalty of a great day seize you."

وَلَا تَمَسُّوهَا بِسُوٓءٍ فَيَأْخُذَكُمْ عَذَابُ يَوْمٍ عَظِيمٍ ﴿١٥٦﴾

157. But they hamstrung her: then did they become full of regrets.

فَعَقَرُوهَا فَأَصْبَحُوا۟ نَٰدِمِينَ ﴿١٥٧﴾

158. But the penalty seized them. Verily in this is a sign: but most of them do not believe.

فَأَخَذَهُمُ ٱلْعَذَابُ ۗ إِنَّ فِى ذَٰلِكَ لَءَايَةً ۖ وَمَا كَانَ أَكْثَرُهُم مُّؤْمِنِينَ ﴿١٥٨﴾

159. And verily your Lord is He, the Exalted in Might, Most Merciful.

وَإِنَّ رَبَّكَ لَهُوَ ٱلْعَزِيزُ ٱلرَّحِيمُ ﴿١٥٩﴾

160. The people of Lot rejected the messengers.

كَذَّبَتْ قَوْمُ لُوطٍ ٱلْمُرْسَلِينَ ﴿١٦٠﴾

161. See, their brother Lot said to them: "Will you not fear (Allah)?

إِذْ قَالَ لَهُمْ أَخُوهُمْ لُوطٌ أَلَا تَتَّقُونَ ﴿١٦١﴾

162. I am to you a messenger worthy of all trust.

إِنِّي لَكُمْ رَسُولٌ أَمِينٌ ﴿١٦٢﴾

163. So fear Allah and obey me.

فَاتَّقُوا اللَّهَ وَأَطِيعُونِ ﴿١٦٣﴾

164. No reward do I ask of you for it: my reward is only from the Lord of the Worlds.

وَمَا أَسْأَلُكُمْ عَلَيْهِ مِنْ أَجْرٍ ۖ إِنْ أَجْرِيَ إِلَّا عَلَىٰ رَبِّ الْعَالَمِينَ ﴿١٦٤﴾

165. Of all the creatures in the world, will you approach males,

أَتَأْتُونَ الذُّكْرَانَ مِنَ الْعَالَمِينَ ﴿١٦٥﴾

166. And leave those whom Allah has created for you to be your mates? Nay, you are a people transgressing (all limits)!"

وَتَذَرُونَ مَا خَلَقَ لَكُمْ رَبُّكُمْ مِنْ أَزْوَاجِكُمْ ۚ بَلْ أَنْتُمْ قَوْمٌ عَادُونَ ﴿١٦٦﴾

167. They said: "If you desist not O Lot! You will assuredly be cast out!"

قَالُوا لَئِنْ لَمْ تَنْتَهِ يَا لُوطُ لَتَكُونَنَّ مِنَ الْمُخْرَجِينَ ﴿١٦٧﴾

168. He said: "I do detest your doings:"

قَالَ إِنِّي لِعَمَلِكُمْ مِنَ الْقَالِينَ ﴿١٦٨﴾

169. "O my Lord! Deliver me and my family from such things as they do!"

رَبِّ نَجِّنِي وَأَهْلِي مِمَّا يَعْمَلُونَ ﴿١٦٩﴾

170. So We delivered him and his family - all

فَنَجَّيْنَاهُ وَأَهْلَهُ أَجْمَعِينَ ﴿١٧٠﴾

171. Except an old woman who lingered behind.

إِلَّا عَجُوزًا فِي الْغَابِرِينَ ﴿١٧١﴾

172. But the rest We destroyed utterly.

ثُمَّ دَمَّرْنَا الْآخَرِينَ ﴿١٧٢﴾

173. We rained down on them a shower (of brimstone): and evil was the shower on those who were admonished (but heeded not)!

وَأَمْطَرْنَا عَلَيْهِمْ مَطَرًا ۖ فَسَاءَ مَطَرُ الْمُنْذَرِينَ ﴿١٧٣﴾

174. Verily in this is a sign: but most of them do not believe.

إِنَّ فِي ذَٰلِكَ لَآيَةً ۖ وَمَا كَانَ أَكْثَرُهُمْ مُؤْمِنِينَ ﴿١٧٤﴾

175. And verily your Lord is He, the Exalted in Might, Most Merciful.

وَإِنَّ رَبَّكَ لَهُوَ ٱلْعَزِيزُ ٱلرَّحِيمُ ١٧٥

176. The Companions of the Wood rejected the prophets.

كَذَّبَ أَصْحَٰبُ لْـَٔيْكَةِ ٱلْمُرْسَلِينَ ١٧٦

177. See, Shu'ayb said to them: "Will you not fear (Allah)?

إِذْ قَالَ لَهُمْ شُعَيْبٌ أَلَا تَتَّقُونَ ١٧٧

178. I am to you a messenger worthy of all trust.

إِنِّى لَكُمْ رَسُولٌ أَمِينٌ ١٧٨

179. So fear Allah and obey me.

فَٱتَّقُوا۟ ٱللَّهَ وَأَطِيعُونِ ١٧٩

180. No reward do I ask of you for it: my reward is only from the Lord of the Worlds.

وَمَآ أَسْـَٔلُكُمْ عَلَيْهِ مِنْ أَجْرٍ ۖ إِنْ أَجْرِىَ إِلَّا عَلَىٰ
رَبِّ ٱلْعَٰلَمِينَ ١٨٠

181. Give just measure, and cause no loss (to others by fraud).

ربع الحزب ٣٨ ۞ أَوْفُوا۟ ٱلْكَيْلَ وَلَا تَكُونُوا۟ مِنَ ٱلْمُخْسِرِينَ ١٨١

182. And weigh with scales true and upright.

وَزِنُوا۟ بِٱلْقِسْطَاسِ ٱلْمُسْتَقِيمِ ١٨٢

183. And withhold not things justly due to men, nor do evil in the land, working mischief.

وَلَا تَبْخَسُوا۟ ٱلنَّاسَ أَشْيَآءَهُمْ وَلَا تَعْثَوْا۟ فِى ٱلْأَرْضِ
مُفْسِدِينَ ١٨٣

184. And fear Him Who created you and (Who created) the generations before (you)."

وَٱتَّقُوا۟ ٱلَّذِى خَلَقَكُمْ وَٱلْجِبِلَّةَ ٱلْأَوَّلِينَ ١٨٤

185. They said: "You are only one of those bewitched!

قَالُوٓا۟ إِنَّمَآ أَنتَ مِنَ ٱلْمُسَحَّرِينَ ١٨٥

186. You are no more than a mortal like us, and indeed we think you are a liar!

وَمَآ أَنتَ إِلَّا بَشَرٌ مِّثْلُنَا وَإِن نَّظُنُّكَ لَمِنَ
ٱلْكَٰذِبِينَ ١٨٦

187. Now cause a piece of the sky to fall on us, if you are truthful!"

فَأَسْقِطْ عَلَيْنَا كِسَفًا مِّنَ ٱلسَّمَآءِ إِن كُنتَ
مِنَ ٱلصَّٰدِقِينَ ١٨٧

188. He said: "My Lord knows best what you do."

قَالَ رَبِّيٓ أَعۡلَمُ بِمَا تَعۡمَلُونَ ١٨٨

189. But they rejected him. Then the punishment of a day of overshadowing gloom seized them and that was the penalty of a great day.

فَكَذَّبُوهُ فَأَخَذَهُمۡ عَذَابُ يَوۡمِ ٱلظُّلَّةِۚ إِنَّهُۥ كَانَ
عَذَابَ يَوۡمٍ عَظِيمٍ ١٨٩

190. Verily in that is a sign: but most of them do not believe.

إِنَّ فِي ذَٰلِكَ لَأٓيَةٗۖ وَمَا كَانَ أَكۡثَرُهُم مُّؤۡمِنِينَ ١٩٠

191. And verily your Lord is He, the Exalted in Might, Most Merciful.

وَإِنَّ رَبَّكَ لَهُوَ ٱلۡعَزِيزُ ٱلرَّحِيمُ ١٩١

192. Verily this is a revelation from the Lord of the Worlds:

وَإِنَّهُۥ لَتَنزِيلُ رَبِّ ٱلۡعَٰلَمِينَ ١٩٢

193. With it came down the spirit of faith and truth -

نَزَلَ بِهِ ٱلرُّوحُ ٱلۡأَمِينُ ١٩٣

194. To your heart and mind, that you may admonish -

عَلَىٰ قَلۡبِكَ لِتَكُونَ مِنَ ٱلۡمُنذِرِينَ ١٩٤

195. In the perspicuous Arabic tongue.

بِلِسَانٍ عَرَبِيّٖ مُّبِينٖ ١٩٥

196. Without doubt it is (announced) in the revealed books of former peoples.

وَإِنَّهُۥ لَفِي زُبُرِ ٱلۡأَوَّلِينَ ١٩٦

197. Is it not a sign to them that the learned of the Children of Israel knew it (as true)?

أَوَلَمۡ يَكُن لَّهُمۡ ءَايَةً أَن يَعۡلَمَهُۥ عُلَمَٰٓؤُاْ بَنِيٓ إِسۡرَٰٓءِيلَ ١٩٧

198. Had We revealed it to any of the non-Arabs,

وَلَوۡ نَزَّلۡنَٰهُ عَلَىٰ بَعۡضِ ٱلۡأَعۡجَمِينَ ١٩٨

199. And had he recited it to them, they would not have believed in it.

فَقَرَأَهُۥ عَلَيۡهِم مَّا كَانُواْ بِهِۦ مُؤۡمِنِينَ ١٩٩

200. Thus have We caused it to enter the hearts of the sinners.

كَذَٰلِكَ سَلَكۡنَٰهُ فِي قُلُوبِ ٱلۡمُجۡرِمِينَ ٢٠٠

201. They will not believe in it until they see the grievous penalty;

لَا يُؤْمِنُونَ بِهِۦ حَتَّىٰ يَرَوُا۟ ٱلْعَذَابَ ٱلْأَلِيمَ ﴿٢٠١﴾

202. But the (penalty) will come to them of a sudden, while they perceive it not;

فَيَأْتِيَهُم بَغْتَةً وَهُمْ لَا يَشْعُرُونَ ﴿٢٠٢﴾

203. Then they will say: "Shall we be respited?"

فَيَقُولُوا۟ هَلْ نَحْنُ مُنظَرُونَ ﴿٢٠٣﴾

204. Do they then ask for Our penalty to be hastened on?

أَفَبِعَذَابِنَا يَسْتَعْجِلُونَ ﴿٢٠٤﴾

205. Do you see? If We do let them enjoy (this life) for a few years,

أَفَرَءَيْتَ إِن مَّتَّعْنَٰهُمْ سِنِينَ ﴿٢٠٥﴾

206. Yet there comes to them at length the (punishment) which they were promised!

ثُمَّ جَآءَهُم مَّا كَانُوا۟ يُوعَدُونَ ﴿٢٠٦﴾

207. It will profit them not that they enjoyed (this life)!

مَآ أَغْنَىٰ عَنْهُم مَّا كَانُوا۟ يُمَتَّعُونَ ﴿٢٠٧﴾

208. Never did We destroy a population, but had its warners -

وَمَآ أَهْلَكْنَا مِن قَرْيَةٍ إِلَّا لَهَا مُنذِرُونَ ﴿٢٠٨﴾

209. By way of reminder; and We never are unjust.

ذِكْرَىٰ وَمَا كُنَّا ظَٰلِمِينَ ﴿٢٠٩﴾

210. No evil ones have brought down this (revelation):

وَمَا تَنَزَّلَتْ بِهِ ٱلشَّيَٰطِينُ ﴿٢١٠﴾

211. It would neither suit them nor would they be able (to produce it).

وَمَا يَنۢبَغِى لَهُمْ وَمَا يَسْتَطِيعُونَ ﴿٢١١﴾

212. Indeed they have been removed far from even (a chance of) hearing it.

إِنَّهُمْ عَنِ ٱلسَّمْعِ لَمَعْزُولُونَ ﴿٢١٢﴾

213. So call not on any other god with Allah, or you will be among those under the penalty.

فَلَا تَدْعُ مَعَ ٱللَّهِ إِلَٰهًا ءَاخَرَ فَتَكُونَ
مِنَ ٱلْمُعَذَّبِينَ ﴿٢١٣﴾

214. And admonish your nearest relatives,

وَأَنذِرۡ عَشِيرَتَكَ ٱلۡأَقۡرَبِينَ ٢١٤

215. And lower your wing to the believers who follow you.

وَٱخۡفِضۡ جَنَاحَكَ لِمَنِ ٱتَّبَعَكَ مِنَ ٱلۡمُؤۡمِنِينَ ٢١٥

216. Then if they disobey you say: "I am free (of responsibility) for what you do!"

فَإِنۡ عَصَوۡكَ فَقُلۡ إِنِّي بَرِيٓءٞ مِّمَّا تَعۡمَلُونَ ٢١٦

217. And put your trust on the Exalted in Might, the Merciful -

وَتَوَكَّلۡ عَلَى ٱلۡعَزِيزِ ٱلرَّحِيمِ ٢١٧

218. Who sees you standing up (in prayer),

ٱلَّذِي يَرَىٰكَ حِينَ تَقُومُ ٢١٨

219. And your movements among those who prostrate themselves.

وَتَقَلُّبَكَ فِي ٱلسَّٰجِدِينَ ٢١٩

220. For it is He Who hears and knows all things.

إِنَّهُۥ هُوَ ٱلسَّمِيعُ ٱلۡعَلِيمُ ٢٢٠

221. Shall I inform you (O people!), on whom it is that the evil ones descend?

هَلۡ أُنَبِّئُكُمۡ عَلَىٰ مَن تَنَزَّلُ ٱلشَّيَٰطِينُ ٢٢١

222. They descend on every lying wicked person,

تَنَزَّلُ عَلَىٰ كُلِّ أَفَّاكٍ أَثِيمٖ ٢٢٢

223. (Into whose ears) they pour hearsay vanities, and most of them are liars.

يُلۡقُونَ ٱلسَّمۡعَ وَأَكۡثَرُهُمۡ كَٰذِبُونَ ٢٢٣

224. And the poets - it is those straying in evil who follow them:

وَٱلشُّعَرَآءُ يَتَّبِعُهُمُ ٱلۡغَاوُۥنَ ٢٢٤

225. Do you not see that they wander distracted in every valley? -

أَلَمۡ تَرَ أَنَّهُمۡ فِي كُلِّ وَادٖ يَهِيمُونَ ٢٢٥

226. And that they say what they practice not? -

وَأَنَّهُمۡ يَقُولُونَ مَا لَا يَفۡعَلُونَ ٢٢٦

227. Except those who believe, work righteousness, engage much in the

إِلَّا ٱلَّذِينَ ءَامَنُواْ وَعَمِلُواْ ٱلصَّٰلِحَٰتِ وَذَكَرُواْ

remembrance of Allah, and defend themselves only after they are unjustly attacked. And soon will the unjust assailants know what vicissitudes their affairs will take!

ٱللَّهَ كَثِيرًا وَٱنتَصَرُوا۟ مِنۢ بَعْدِ مَا ظُلِمُوا۟ ۗ وَسَيَعْلَمُ
ٱلَّذِينَ ظَلَمُوٓا۟ أَىَّ مُنقَلَبٍ يَنقَلِبُونَ ﴿٢٢٧﴾

سُورَةُ النَّمْلِ

Surah 27: ***An-Naml*** **(The Ant)**

In the name of Allah,
Most Gracious, Most Merciful.

بِسْمِ ٱللَّهِ ٱلرَّحْمَـٰنِ ٱلرَّحِيمِ

1. *Ta Sin*. These are verses of the Qur'an - a book that makes (things) clear;

نصف الحزب ٣٨ طسٓ ۚ تِلْكَ ءَايَـٰتُ ٱلْقُرْءَانِ وَكِتَابٍ مُّبِينٍ ﴿١﴾

2. A guide; and glad tidings for the believers -

هُدًى وَبُشْرَىٰ لِلْمُؤْمِنِينَ ﴿٢﴾

3. Those who establish regular prayers and give in regular charity, and also have (full) assurance of the hereafter.

ٱلَّذِينَ يُقِيمُونَ ٱلصَّلَوٰةَ وَيُؤْتُونَ ٱلزَّكَوٰةَ وَهُم
بِٱلْـَٔاخِرَةِ هُمْ يُوقِنُونَ ﴿٣﴾

4. As to those who believe not in the hereafter, We have made their deeds pleasing in their eyes; and so they wander about in distraction.

إِنَّ ٱلَّذِينَ لَا يُؤْمِنُونَ بِٱلْـَٔاخِرَةِ زَيَّنَّا لَهُمْ أَعْمَـٰلَهُمْ
فَهُمْ يَعْمَهُونَ ﴿٤﴾

5. Such are they for whom a grievous penalty is (waiting): and in the hereafter theirs will be the greatest loss.

أُو۟لَـٰٓئِكَ ٱلَّذِينَ لَهُمْ سُوٓءُ ٱلْعَذَابِ وَهُمْ فِى ٱلْـَٔاخِرَةِ
هُمُ ٱلْأَخْسَرُونَ ﴿٥﴾

6. As to you, the Qur'an is bestowed upon you from the presence of One Who is Wise and All-Knowing.

وَإِنَّكَ لَتُلَقَّى ٱلْقُرْءَانَ مِن لَّدُنْ حَكِيمٍ عَلِيمٍ ﴿٦﴾

7. See! Moses said to his family: "I perceive a fire; soon will I bring you from there some information, or I will bring you a burning brand to light our fuel, that you may warm yourselves."

إِذْ قَالَ مُوسَىٰ لِأَهْلِهِۦٓ إِنِّىٓ ءَانَسْتُ نَارًا سَـَٔاتِيكُم مِّنْهَا
بِخَبَرٍ أَوْ ءَاتِيكُم بِشِهَابٍ قَبَسٍ لَّعَلَّكُمْ تَصْطَلُونَ ﴿٧﴾

8. But when he came to the (fire), a voice was heard: "Blessed are those in the fire and those around: and Glory to Allah, the Lord of the Worlds.

فَلَمَّا جَآءَهَا نُودِيَ أَنۢ بُورِكَ مَن فِي ٱلنَّارِ وَمَنْ حَوْلَهَا
وَسُبْحَٰنَ ٱللَّهِ رَبِّ ٱلْعَٰلَمِينَ ٨

9. O Moses! Verily, I am Allah, the Exalted in Might, the Wise!...

يَٰمُوسَىٰٓ إِنَّهُۥٓ أَنَا ٱللَّهُ ٱلْعَزِيزُ ٱلْحَكِيمُ ٩

10. Now do you throw your rod!" But when he saw it moving (of its own accord) as if it had been a snake, he turned back in retreat, and retraced not his steps: "O Moses!" (it was said) "Fear not: truly, in My presence, those called as messengers have no fear -

وَأَلْقِ عَصَاكَۚ فَلَمَّا رَءَاهَا تَهْتَزُّ كَأَنَّهَا جَآنٌّ وَلَّىٰ مُدْبِرًا
وَلَمْ يُعَقِّبْۚ يَٰمُوسَىٰ لَا تَخَفْ إِنِّي لَا يَخَافُ لَدَيَّ ٱلْمُرْسَلُونَ ١٠

11. But if any have done wrong and have thereafter substituted good to take the place of evil, truly I am Oft-Forgiving, Most Merciful.

إِلَّا مَن ظَلَمَ ثُمَّ بَدَّلَ حُسْنًۢا بَعْدَ سُوٓءٍ فَإِنِّي غَفُورٌ رَّحِيمٌ ١١

12. Now put your hand into your chest, and it will come out white without stain (or harm): (these are) among the nine signs (you will take) to Pharaoh and his people: for they are a people rebellious in transgression."

وَأَدْخِلْ يَدَكَ فِي جَيْبِكَ تَخْرُجْ بَيْضَآءَ مِنْ غَيْرِ سُوٓءٍۖ فِي
تِسْعِ ءَايَٰتٍ إِلَىٰ فِرْعَوْنَ وَقَوْمِهِۦٓۚ إِنَّهُمْ كَانُواْ قَوْمًا فَٰسِقِينَ ١٢

13. But when our signs came to them, that should have opened their eyes, they said: "This is sorcery manifest!"

فَلَمَّا جَآءَتْهُمْ ءَايَٰتُنَا مُبْصِرَةً قَالُواْ هَٰذَا
سِحْرٌ مُّبِينٌ ١٣

14. And they rejected those signs in iniquity and arrogance, though their souls were convinced of it: so see what was the end of those who acted corruptly!

وَجَحَدُواْ بِهَا وَٱسْتَيْقَنَتْهَآ أَنفُسُهُمْ ظُلْمًا وَعُلُوًّاۚ
فَٱنظُرْ كَيْفَ كَانَ عَٰقِبَةُ ٱلْمُفْسِدِينَ ١٤

15. We gave (in the past) knowledge to David and Solomon; and they both said: "Praise be to Allah, Who has favoured us above many of His servants who believe!"

وَلَقَدْ ءَاتَيْنَا دَاوُۥدَ وَسُلَيْمَٰنَ عِلْمًاۖ وَقَالَا ٱلْحَمْدُ
لِلَّهِ ٱلَّذِي فَضَّلَنَا عَلَىٰ كَثِيرٍ مِّنْ عِبَادِهِ ٱلْمُؤْمِنِينَ ١٥

16. And Solomon was David's heir. He said: "O you people! We have been taught

وَوَرِثَ سُلَيْمَٰنُ دَاوُۥدَۖ وَقَالَ يَٰٓأَيُّهَا ٱلنَّاسُ عُلِّمْنَا

the speech of birds, and on us has been bestowed (a little) of all things: this is indeed grace manifest (from Allah)."

مَنطِقَ ٱلطَّيۡرِ وَأُوتِينَا مِن كُلِّ شَيۡءٍۖ إِنَّ هَٰذَا
لَهُوَ ٱلۡفَضۡلُ ٱلۡمُبِينُ ١٦

17. And before Solomon were marshalled his forces - of Jinns and men and birds, and they were all kept in order and ranks.

وَحُشِرَ لِسُلَيۡمَٰنَ جُنُودُهُۥ مِنَ ٱلۡجِنِّ وَٱلۡإِنسِ
وَٱلطَّيۡرِ فَهُمۡ يُوزَعُونَ ١٧

18. At length, when they came to a (lowly) valley of ants, one of the ants said: "O you ants, get into your habitations, lest Solomon and his forces crush you (under foot) without knowing it."

حَتَّىٰٓ إِذَآ أَتَوۡاْ عَلَىٰ وَادِ ٱلنَّمۡلِ قَالَتۡ نَمۡلَةٞ يَٰٓأَيُّهَا
ٱلنَّمۡلُ ٱدۡخُلُواْ مَسَٰكِنَكُمۡ لَا يَحۡطِمَنَّكُمۡ سُلَيۡمَٰنُ
وَجُنُودُهُۥ وَهُمۡ لَا يَشۡعُرُونَ ١٨

19. So he smiled, amused at her speech; and he said: "O my Lord! So order me that I may be grateful for Your favours, which You have bestowed on me and on my parents, and that I may work the righteousness that will please You; and admit me, by Your grace, to the ranks of Your righteous servants."

فَتَبَسَّمَ ضَاحِكٗا مِّن قَوۡلِهَا وَقَالَ رَبِّ أَوۡزِعۡنِيٓ أَنۡ
أَشۡكُرَ نِعۡمَتَكَ ٱلَّتِيٓ أَنۡعَمۡتَ عَلَيَّ وَعَلَىٰ وَٰلِدَيَّ وَأَنۡ
أَعۡمَلَ صَٰلِحٗا تَرۡضَىٰهُ وَأَدۡخِلۡنِي بِرَحۡمَتِكَ فِي
عِبَادِكَ ٱلصَّٰلِحِينَ ١٩

20. And he took a muster of the birds; and he said: "Why is it I see not the Hoopoe? Or is he among thc absentees?

وَتَفَقَّدَ ٱلطَّيۡرَ فَقَالَ مَالِيَ لَآ أَرَى ٱلۡهُدۡهُدَ أَمۡ
كَانَ مِنَ ٱلۡغَآئِبِينَ ٢٠

21. I will certainly punish him with a severe penalty, or execute him, unless he bring me a clear reason (for absence)."

لَأُعَذِّبَنَّهُۥ عَذَابٗا شَدِيدًا أَوۡ لَأَاْذۡبَحَنَّهُۥٓ
أَوۡ لَيَأۡتِيَنِّي بِسُلۡطَٰنٖ مُّبِينٖ ٢١

22. But the Hoopoe tarried not far: I encompassed (territory) which you have not encompassed, and I have come to you from Saba with tidings true.

فَمَكَثَ غَيۡرَ بَعِيدٖ فَقَالَ أَحَطتُ بِمَا لَمۡ تُحِطۡ بِهِۦ
وَجِئۡتُكَ مِن سَبَإِۭ بِنَبَإٖ يَقِينٍ ٢٢

23. "I found (there) a woman ruling over them and provided with every requisite; and she has a magnificent throne."

إِنِّي وَجَدتُّ ٱمۡرَأَةٗ تَمۡلِكُهُمۡ وَأُوتِيَتۡ مِن كُلِّ
شَيۡءٖ وَلَهَا عَرۡشٌ عَظِيمٞ ٢٣

24. "I found her and her people worshipping the sun besides Allah: Satan has made their deeds seem pleasing in their eyes, and has kept them away from the path - so they receive no guidance -

وَجَدتُّهَا وَقَوْمَهَا يَسْجُدُونَ لِلشَّمْسِ مِن
دُونِ ٱللَّهِ وَزَيَّنَ لَهُمُ ٱلشَّيْطَٰنُ أَعْمَٰلَهُمْ فَصَدَّهُمْ عَنِ
ٱلسَّبِيلِ فَهُمْ لَا يَهْتَدُونَ ﴿٢٤﴾

25. (Kept them away from the path), that they should not worship Allah, Who brings to light what is hidden in the heavens and the earth, and knows what you hide and what you reveal.

أَلَّا يَسْجُدُوا۟ لِلَّهِ ٱلَّذِى يُخْرِجُ ٱلْخَبْءَ فِى ٱلسَّمَٰوَٰتِ
وَٱلْأَرْضِ وَيَعْلَمُ مَا تُخْفُونَ وَمَا تُعْلِنُونَ ﴿٢٥﴾

26. Allah! There is no god but He! Lord of the Throne Supreme!"

ٱللَّهُ لَآ إِلَٰهَ إِلَّا هُوَ رَبُّ ٱلْعَرْشِ ٱلْعَظِيمِ ۩ ﴿٢٦﴾ سَجْدَة

27. (Solomon) said: "Soon shall we see whether you have told the truth or lied!"

ثلاثة أرباع الحزب ٣٨ ۞ قَالَ سَنَنظُرُ أَصَدَقْتَ أَمْ كُنتَ مِنَ
ٱلْكَٰذِبِينَ ﴿٢٧﴾

28. "Go you, with this letter of mine, and deliver it to them: then draw back from them, and (wait to) see what answer they return".

ٱذْهَب بِّكِتَٰبِى هَٰذَا فَأَلْقِهْ إِلَيْهِمْ ثُمَّ تَوَلَّ عَنْهُمْ
فَٱنظُرْ مَاذَا يَرْجِعُونَ ﴿٢٨﴾

29. (The Queen) said: "You chiefs! Here is - delivered to me - a letter worthy of respect.

قَالَتْ يَٰٓأَيُّهَا ٱلْمَلَؤُا۟ إِنِّىٓ أُلْقِىَ إِلَىَّ كِتَٰبٌ كَرِيمٌ ﴿٢٩﴾

30. It is from Solomon, and is (as follows): 'In the name of Allah, Most Gracious, Most Merciful:

إِنَّهُۥ مِن سُلَيْمَٰنَ وَإِنَّهُۥ بِسْمِ ٱللَّهِ ٱلرَّحْمَٰنِ ٱلرَّحِيمِ ﴿٣٠﴾

31. Be you not arrogant against me, but come to me in submission to the true religion.'"

أَلَّا تَعْلُوا۟ عَلَىَّ وَأْتُونِى مُسْلِمِينَ ﴿٣١﴾

32. She said: "You chiefs! Advise me in (this) my affair: no affair have I decided except in your presence."

قَالَتْ يَٰٓأَيُّهَا ٱلْمَلَؤُا۟ أَفْتُونِى فِىٓ أَمْرِى مَا كُنتُ قَاطِعَةً
أَمْرًا حَتَّىٰ تَشْهَدُونِ ﴿٣٢﴾

33. They said: "We are endued with strength, and given to vehement war: but the command is with you; so consider what you will command."

قَالُوا۟ نَحْنُ أُو۟لُوا۟ قُوَّةٍ وَأُو۟لُوا۟ بَأْسٍ شَدِيدٍ وَٱلْأَمْرُ
إِلَيْكِ فَٱنظُرِى مَاذَا تَأْمُرِينَ ﴿٣٣﴾

34. She said: "Kings, when they enter a country, despoil it, and make the noblest of its people its meanest: thus do they behave.

قَالَتۡ إِنَّ ٱلۡمُلُوكَ إِذَا دَخَلُواْ قَرۡيَةً أَفۡسَدُوهَا وَجَعَلُوٓاْ
أَعِزَّةَ أَهۡلِهَآ أَذِلَّةٗۚ وَكَذَٰلِكَ يَفۡعَلُونَ ٣٤

35. But I am going to send him a present, and (wait) to see with what (answer) return (my) ambassadors."

وَإِنِّي مُرۡسِلَةٌ إِلَيۡهِم بِهَدِيَّةٖ فَنَاظِرَةُۢ بِمَ يَرۡجِعُ
ٱلۡمُرۡسَلُونَ ٣٥

36. How when (the embassy) came to Solomon, he said: "Will you give me abundance in wealth? But that which Allah has given me is better than that which He has given you! Nay, it is you who rejoice in your gift!

فَلَمَّا جَآءَ سُلَيۡمَٰنَ قَالَ أَتُمِدُّونَنِ بِمَالٖ فَمَآ ءَاتَىٰنِۦَ ٱللَّهُ
خَيۡرٞ مِّمَّآ ءَاتَىٰكُمۚ بَلۡ أَنتُم بِهَدِيَّتِكُمۡ تَفۡرَحُونَ ٣٦

37. Go back to them, and be sure we shall come to them with such hosts as they will never be able to meet: we shall expel them from there in disgrace, and they will feel humbled (indeed)."

ٱرۡجِعۡ إِلَيۡهِمۡ فَلَنَأۡتِيَنَّهُم بِجُنُودٖ لَّا قِبَلَ لَهُم بِهَا
وَلَنُخۡرِجَنَّهُم مِّنۡهَآ أَذِلَّةٗ وَهُمۡ صَٰغِرُونَ ٣٧

38. He said (to his own men): "You chiefs! Which of you can bring me her throne before they come to me in submission?"

قَالَ يَٰٓأَيُّهَا ٱلۡمَلَؤُاْ أَيُّكُمۡ يَأۡتِينِي بِعَرۡشِهَا قَبۡلَ أَن
يَأۡتُونِي مُسۡلِمِينَ ٣٨

39. Said an Ifrit, of the Jinns: "I will bring it to you before you rise from your council: indeed I have full strength for the purpose, and may be trusted."

قَالَ عِفۡرِيتٞ مِّنَ ٱلۡجِنِّ أَنَا۠ ءَاتِيكَ بِهِۦ قَبۡلَ أَن تَقُومَ مِن
مَّقَامِكَۖ وَإِنِّي عَلَيۡهِ لَقَوِيٌّ أَمِينٞ ٣٩

40. Said one who had knowledge of the book: "I will bring it to you within the twinkling of an eye!" Then when (Solomon) saw it placed firmly before him, he said: "This is by the grace of my Lord! To test me whether I am grateful or ungrateful! And if any is grateful, truly his gratitude is (a gain) for his own soul; but if any is ungrateful, truly my Lord is Free of All Needs, Supreme in Honour!"

قَالَ ٱلَّذِي عِندَهُۥ عِلۡمٞ مِّنَ ٱلۡكِتَٰبِ أَنَا۠ ءَاتِيكَ بِهِۦ قَبۡلَ
أَن يَرۡتَدَّ إِلَيۡكَ طَرۡفُكَۚ فَلَمَّا رَءَاهُ مُسۡتَقِرًّا عِندَهُۥ قَالَ
هَٰذَا مِن فَضۡلِ رَبِّي لِيَبۡلُوَنِيٓ ءَأَشۡكُرُ أَمۡ أَكۡفُرُۖ وَمَن
شَكَرَ فَإِنَّمَا يَشۡكُرُ لِنَفۡسِهِۦۖ وَمَن كَفَرَ فَإِنَّ رَبِّي
غَنِيّٞ كَرِيمٞ ٤٠

41. He said: "Transform her throne out of all recognition by her: let us see whether she is guided (to the truth) or is one of those who receive no guidance."

قَالَ نَكِّرُوا۟ لَهَا عَرْشَهَا نَنظُرْ أَتَهْتَدِىٓ أَمْ تَكُونُ مِنَ
ٱلَّذِينَ لَا يَهْتَدُونَ ﴿٤١﴾

42. So when she arrived, she was asked, "Is this your throne?" She said, "It was just like this" and knowledge was bestowed on us in advance of this, and we have submitted to Allah (in Islam).

فَلَمَّا جَآءَتْ قِيلَ أَهَٰكَذَا عَرْشُكِ ۖ قَالَتْ كَأَنَّهُۥ هُوَ ۚ
وَأُوتِينَا ٱلْعِلْمَ مِن قَبْلِهَا وَكُنَّا مُسْلِمِينَ ﴿٤٢﴾

43. And he diverted her from the worship of others besides Allah: for she was (sprung) of a people that had no faith.

وَصَدَّهَا مَا كَانَت تَّعْبُدُ مِن دُونِ ٱللَّهِ ۖ إِنَّهَا كَانَتْ مِن
قَوْمٍ كَٰفِرِينَ ﴿٤٣﴾

44. She was asked to enter that lofty palace; but when she saw it, she thought it was a lake of water, and she (tucked up her skirts), uncovering her legs. He said. "This is but a palace paved smooth with slabs of glass." She said: "My Lord! I have indeed wronged my soul: I do (now) submit (in Islam) with Solomon to the Lord of the Worlds."

قِيلَ لَهَا ٱدْخُلِى ٱلصَّرْحَ ۖ فَلَمَّا رَأَتْهُ حَسِبَتْهُ لُجَّةً
وَكَشَفَتْ عَن سَاقَيْهَا ۚ قَالَ إِنَّهُۥ صَرْحٌ مُّمَرَّدٌ مِّن قَوَارِيرَ ۗ
قَالَتْ رَبِّ إِنِّى ظَلَمْتُ نَفْسِى وَأَسْلَمْتُ مَعَ سُلَيْمَٰنَ
لِلَّهِ رَبِّ ٱلْعَٰلَمِينَ ﴿٤٤﴾

45. We sent (before), to the Thamud, their brother Salih, saying: "Serve Allah": but see, they became two factions quarrelling with each other.

وَلَقَدْ أَرْسَلْنَآ إِلَىٰ ثَمُودَ أَخَاهُمْ صَٰلِحًا أَنِ
ٱعْبُدُوا۟ ٱللَّهَ فَإِذَا هُمْ فَرِيقَانِ يَخْتَصِمُونَ ﴿٤٥﴾

46. He said: "O my people! Why do you ask to hasten on the evil in preference to the good? If only you ask Allah for forgiveness, you may hope to receive mercy."

قَالَ يَٰقَوْمِ لِمَ تَسْتَعْجِلُونَ بِٱلسَّيِّئَةِ قَبْلَ ٱلْحَسَنَةِ ۖ
لَوْلَا تَسْتَغْفِرُونَ ٱللَّهَ لَعَلَّكُمْ تُرْحَمُونَ ﴿٤٦﴾

47. They said: "Ill omen do we augur from you and those that are with you." He said: "Your ill omen is with Allah, yea, you are a people under trial."

قَالُوا۟ ٱطَّيَّرْنَا بِكَ وَبِمَن مَّعَكَ ۚ قَالَ طَٰٓئِرُكُمْ
عِندَ ٱللَّهِ ۖ بَلْ أَنتُمْ قَوْمٌ تُفْتَنُونَ ﴿٤٧﴾

48. There were in the city nine men of a family who made mischief in the land, and would not reform.

وَكَانَ فِى ٱلْمَدِينَةِ تِسْعَةُ رَهْطٍ يُفْسِدُونَ
فِى ٱلْأَرْضِ وَلَا يُصْلِحُونَ ﴿٤٨﴾

49. They said: "Swear a mutual oath by Allah that we shall make a secret night attack on him and his people, and that we shall then say to his heir (when he seeks vengeance): 'We were not present at the slaughter of his people and we are positively telling the truth.'"

قَالُوا۟ تَقَاسَمُوا۟ بِٱللَّهِ لَنُبَيِّتَنَّهُۥ وَأَهْلَهُۥ ثُمَّ
لَنَقُولَنَّ لِوَلِيِّهِۦ مَا شَهِدْنَا مَهْلِكَ أَهْلِهِۦ
وَإِنَّا لَصَـٰدِقُونَ ﴿٤٩﴾

50. They plotted and planned, but We too planned, even while they perceived it not.

وَمَكَرُوا۟ مَكْرًا وَمَكَرْنَا مَكْرًا وَهُمْ
لَا يَشْعُرُونَ ﴿٥٠﴾

51. Then see what was the end of their plot! - This, that We destroyed them and their people, all (of them).

فَٱنظُرْ كَيْفَ كَانَ عَـٰقِبَةُ مَكْرِهِمْ
أَنَّا دَمَّرْنَـٰهُمْ وَقَوْمَهُمْ أَجْمَعِينَ ﴿٥١﴾

52. Now such were their houses - in utter ruin - because they practised wrongdoing. Verily in this is a sign for people of knowledge.

فَتِلْكَ بُيُوتُهُمْ خَاوِيَةًۢ بِمَا ظَلَمُوٓا۟ ۗ إِنَّ فِى
ذَٰلِكَ لَـَٔايَةً لِّقَوْمٍ يَعْلَمُونَ ﴿٥٢﴾

53. And We saved those who believed and practised righteousness.

وَأَنجَيْنَا ٱلَّذِينَ ءَامَنُوا۟ وَكَانُوا۟ يَتَّقُونَ ﴿٥٣﴾

54. We also sent Lot (as a messenger): behold, he said to his people, "Do you do what is shameful though you see (its iniquity)?

وَلُوطًا إِذْ قَالَ لِقَوْمِهِۦٓ أَتَأْتُونَ ٱلْفَـٰحِشَةَ
وَأَنتُمْ تُبْصِرُونَ ﴿٥٤﴾

55. Would you really approach men in your lusts rather than women? Nay, you are a people (grossly) ignorant!"

أَئِنَّكُمْ لَتَأْتُونَ ٱلرِّجَالَ شَهْوَةً مِّن دُونِ
ٱلنِّسَآءِ ۚ بَلْ أَنتُمْ قَوْمٌ تَجْهَلُونَ ﴿٥٥﴾

✻**56.** But his people gave no other answer but this: they said, "Drive out the followers of Lot from your city: these are indeed men who want to be clean and pure!"

الجزء ٢٠ الحزب ٣٩ ✻ فَمَا كَانَ جَوَابَ قَوْمِهِۦٓ إِلَّآ أَن قَالُوٓا۟
أَخْرِجُوٓا۟ ءَالَ لُوطٍ مِّن قَرْيَتِكُمْ ۖ إِنَّهُمْ أُنَاسٌ
يَتَطَهَّرُونَ ﴿٥٦﴾

57. But We saved him and his family, except his wife: her We destined to be of those who lagged behind.

فَأَنجَيْنَـٰهُ وَأَهْلَهُۥٓ إِلَّا ٱمْرَأَتَهُۥ قَدَّرْنَـٰهَا مِنَ
ٱلْغَـٰبِرِينَ ﴿٥٧﴾

✻ Part-20

58. And We rained down on them a shower (of brimstone): and evil was the shower on those who were admonished (but heeded not)!

وَأَمْطَرْنَا عَلَيْهِم مَّطَرًا ۖ فَسَآءَ مَطَرُ ٱلْمُنذَرِينَ ﴿٥٨﴾

59. Say: Praise be to Allah, and peace on His servants whom He has chosen (for his message). (Who) is better? - Allah or the false gods they associate with Him?

قُلِ ٱلْحَمْدُ لِلَّهِ وَسَلَٰمٌ عَلَىٰ عِبَادِهِ ٱلَّذِينَ
ٱصْطَفَىٰٓ ۗ ءَآللَّهُ خَيْرٌ أَمَّا يُشْرِكُونَ ﴿٥٩﴾

60. Or, who has created the heaven and the earth, and who sends you down rain from the sky? Yea, with it We cause to grow well-planted orchards full of beauty and delight: it is not in your power to cause the growth of the trees in them. (Can there be another) god besides Allah? Nay, they are a people who swerve from justice.

أَمَّنْ خَلَقَ ٱلسَّمَٰوَٰتِ وَٱلْأَرْضَ وَأَنزَلَ لَكُم مِّنَ
ٱلسَّمَآءِ مَآءً فَأَنۢبَتْنَا بِهِۦ حَدَآئِقَ ذَاتَ بَهْجَةٍ
مَّا كَانَ لَكُمْ أَن تُنۢبِتُوا۟ شَجَرَهَآ ۗ أَءِلَٰهٌ
مَّعَ ٱللَّهِ ۚ بَلْ هُمْ قَوْمٌ يَعْدِلُونَ ﴿٦٠﴾

61. Or, who has made the earth firm to live in; made rivers in its midst; set thereon mountains immovable, and made a separating bar between the two bodies of flowing water? (Can there be another) god besides Allah? Nay, most of them know not.

أَمَّن جَعَلَ ٱلْأَرْضَ قَرَارًا وَجَعَلَ خِلَٰلَهَآ أَنْهَٰرًا
وَجَعَلَ لَهَا رَوَٰسِىَ وَجَعَلَ بَيْنَ ٱلْبَحْرَيْنِ
حَاجِزًا ۗ أَءِلَٰهٌ مَّعَ ٱللَّهِ ۚ بَلْ أَكْثَرُهُمْ
لَا يَعْلَمُونَ ﴿٦١﴾

62. Or, who listens to the (soul) distressed when it calls on Him, and who relieves its suffering, and makes you (mankind) inheritors of the earth? (Can there be another) god besides Allah? Little it is that you heed!

أَمَّن يُجِيبُ ٱلْمُضْطَرَّ إِذَا دَعَاهُ وَيَكْشِفُ ٱلسُّوٓءَ
وَيَجْعَلُكُمْ خُلَفَآءَ ٱلْأَرْضِ ۗ أَءِلَٰهٌ مَّعَ ٱللَّهِ ۚ
قَلِيلًا مَّا تَذَكَّرُونَ ﴿٦٢﴾

63. Or, who guides you through the depths of darkness on land and sea, and who sends the winds as heralds of glad tidings, going before his mercy? (Can there be another) god besides Allah? - High is Allah above what they associate with Him!

أَمَّن يَهْدِيكُمْ فِى ظُلُمَٰتِ ٱلْبَرِّ وَٱلْبَحْرِ وَمَن
يُرْسِلُ ٱلرِّيَٰحَ بُشْرًۢا بَيْنَ يَدَىْ رَحْمَتِهِۦٓ ۗ أَءِلَٰهٌ
مَّعَ ٱللَّهِ ۚ تَعَٰلَى ٱللَّهُ عَمَّا يُشْرِكُونَ ﴿٦٣﴾

64. Or, who originates creation, then repeats it, and who gives you sustenance from heaven and earth? (Can there be another) god besides Allah? Say, "Bring forward your argument, if you are telling the truth!"

أَمَّن يَبۡدَؤُاْ ٱلۡخَلۡقَ ثُمَّ يُعِيدُهُۥ وَمَن يَرۡزُقُكُم مِّنَ ٱلسَّمَآءِ
وَٱلۡأَرۡضِۗ أَءِلَٰهٞ مَّعَ ٱللَّهِۚ قُلۡ هَاتُواْ بُرۡهَٰنَكُمۡ إِن
كُنتُمۡ صَٰدِقِينَ ٦٤

65. Say: None in the heavens or on earth, except Allah, knows what is hidden: nor can they perceive when they shall be raised up (for judgement).

قُل لَّا يَعۡلَمُ مَن فِي ٱلسَّمَٰوَٰتِ وَٱلۡأَرۡضِ ٱلۡغَيۡبَ إِلَّا ٱللَّهُۚ
وَمَا يَشۡعُرُونَ أَيَّانَ يُبۡعَثُونَ ٦٥

66. Still less can their knowledge comprehend the hereafter: nay, they are in doubt and uncertainty of it; nay, they are blind to it!

بَلِ ٱدَّٰرَكَ عِلۡمُهُمۡ فِي ٱلۡأٓخِرَةِۚ بَلۡ هُمۡ فِي شَكّٖ مِّنۡهَاۖ
بَلۡ هُم مِّنۡهَا عَمُونَ ٦٦

67. The unbelievers say: "What! When we become dust - we and our fathers - shall we really be raised (from the dead)?

وَقَالَ ٱلَّذِينَ كَفَرُوٓاْ أَءِذَا كُنَّا تُرَٰبٗا وَءَابَآؤُنَآ
أَئِنَّا لَمُخۡرَجُونَ ٦٧

68. It is true we were promised this - we and our fathers before (us): these are nothing but tales of the ancients."

لَقَدۡ وُعِدۡنَا هَٰذَا نَحۡنُ وَءَابَآؤُنَا مِن قَبۡلُ إِنۡ هَٰذَآ
إِلَّآ أَسَٰطِيرُ ٱلۡأَوَّلِينَ ٦٨

69. Say: "Go you through the earth and see what has been the end of those guilty (of sin)."

قُلۡ سِيرُواْ فِي ٱلۡأَرۡضِ فَٱنظُرُواْ كَيۡفَ كَانَ عَٰقِبَةُ
ٱلۡمُجۡرِمِينَ ٦٩

70. But grieve not over them, nor distress yourself because of their plots.

وَلَا تَحۡزَنۡ عَلَيۡهِمۡ وَلَا تَكُن فِي ضَيۡقٖ مِّمَّا
يَمۡكُرُونَ ٧٠

71. They also say: "When will this promise (come to pass)? (Say) if you are truthful."

وَيَقُولُونَ مَتَىٰ هَٰذَا ٱلۡوَعۡدُ إِن كُنتُمۡ صَٰدِقِينَ ٧١

72. Say: "It may be that some of the events which you wish to hasten on may be (close) in your pursuit!"

قُلۡ عَسَىٰٓ أَن يَكُونَ رَدِفَ لَكُم بَعۡضُ ٱلَّذِي
تَسۡتَعۡجِلُونَ ٧٢

73. But verily your Lord is full of grace to mankind: yet most of them are ungrateful.

وَإِنَّ رَبَّكَ لَذُو فَضْلٍ عَلَى ٱلنَّاسِ وَلَٰكِنَّ أَكْثَرَهُمْ
لَا يَشْكُرُونَ ﴿٧٣﴾

74. And verily your Lord knows all that their hearts do hide, as well as all that they reveal.

وَإِنَّ رَبَّكَ لَيَعْلَمُ مَا تُكِنُّ صُدُورُهُمْ وَمَا يُعْلِنُونَ ﴿٧٤﴾

75. Nor is there anything of the unseen, in heaven or earth, but is (recorded) in a clear record.

وَمَا مِنْ غَآئِبَةٍ فِى ٱلسَّمَآءِ وَٱلْأَرْضِ إِلَّا فِى
كِتَٰبٍ مُّبِينٍ ﴿٧٥﴾

76. Verily this Qur'an does explain to the Children of Israel most of the matters in which they disagree.

إِنَّ هَٰذَا ٱلْقُرْءَانَ يَقُصُّ عَلَىٰ بَنِىٓ إِسْرَٰٓءِيلَ أَكْثَرَ
ٱلَّذِى هُمْ فِيهِ يَخْتَلِفُونَ ﴿٧٦﴾

77. And it certainly is a guide and mercy to those who believe.

وَإِنَّهُۥ لَهُدًى وَرَحْمَةٌ لِّلْمُؤْمِنِينَ ﴿٧٧﴾

78. Verily, your Lord will decide between them by His decree: and He is Exalted in Might, All-Knowing.

إِنَّ رَبَّكَ يَقْضِى بَيْنَهُم بِحُكْمِهِۦ ۚ وَهُوَ
ٱلْعَزِيزُ ٱلْعَلِيمُ ﴿٧٨﴾

79. So put your trust in Allah: for you are on (the path of) manifest truth.

فَتَوَكَّلْ عَلَى ٱللَّهِ ۖ إِنَّكَ عَلَى ٱلْحَقِّ ٱلْمُبِينِ ﴿٧٩﴾

80. Truly you can not cause the dead to listen, nor can you cause the deaf to hear the call, (especially) when they turn back in retreat.

إِنَّكَ لَا تُسْمِعُ ٱلْمَوْتَىٰ وَلَا تُسْمِعُ ٱلصُّمَّ ٱلدُّعَآءَ إِذَا
وَلَّوْا۟ مُدْبِرِينَ ﴿٨٠﴾

81. Nor can you be a guide to the blind, (to prevent them) from straying; only those will you get to listen who believe in Our signs, and they will bow in Islam.

وَمَآ أَنتَ بِهَٰدِى ٱلْعُمْىِ عَن ضَلَٰلَتِهِمْ ۖ إِن تُسْمِعُ
إِلَّا مَن يُؤْمِنُ بِـَٔايَٰتِنَا فَهُم مُّسْلِمُونَ ﴿٨١﴾

82. And when the word is fulfilled against them (the unjust) We shall produce from the earth a beast to (face) them: he will speak to them, for that mankind did not believe with assurance in our signs.

۞ وَإِذَا وَقَعَ ٱلْقَوْلُ عَلَيْهِمْ أَخْرَجْنَا لَهُمْ دَآبَّةً مِّنَ
ٱلْأَرْضِ تُكَلِّمُهُمْ أَنَّ ٱلنَّاسَ كَانُوا۟ بِـَٔايَٰتِنَا لَا يُوقِنُونَ ﴿٨٢﴾

83. One day We shall gather together from every people a troop of those who reject Our signs, and they shall be kept in ranks -

وَيَوۡمَ نَحۡشُرُ مِن كُلِّ أُمَّةٖ فَوۡجٗا مِّمَّن يُكَذِّبُ
بِـَٔايَٰتِنَا فَهُمۡ يُوزَعُونَ ﴿٨٣﴾

84. Until, when they come (before the judgement-seat), Allah will say: "Did you reject My signs, though you comprehended them not in knowledge, or what was it you did?"

حَتَّىٰٓ إِذَا جَآءُو قَالَ أَكَذَّبۡتُم بِـَٔايَٰتِي وَلَمۡ تُحِيطُواْ بِهَا
عِلۡمًا أَمَّاذَا كُنتُمۡ تَعۡمَلُونَ ﴿٨٤﴾

85. And the word will be fulfilled against them, because of their wrongdoing, and they will be unable to speak (in plea).

وَوَقَعَ ٱلۡقَوۡلُ عَلَيۡهِم بِمَا ظَلَمُواْ فَهُمۡ لَا يَنطِقُونَ ﴿٨٥﴾

86. Do they not see that We have made the night for them to rest in and the day to give them light? Verily in this are signs for any people that believe!

أَلَمۡ يَرَوۡاْ أَنَّا جَعَلۡنَا ٱلَّيۡلَ لِيَسۡكُنُواْ فِيهِ وَٱلنَّهَارَ
مُبۡصِرًاۚ إِنَّ فِي ذَٰلِكَ لَأٓيَٰتٖ لِّقَوۡمٖ يُؤۡمِنُونَ ﴿٨٦﴾

87. And the day that the trumpet will be sounded - then will be smitten with terror those who are in the heavens, and those who are on earth, except such as Allah will please (to exempt): and all shall come to His (presence) as beings conscious of their lowliness.

وَيَوۡمَ يُنفَخُ فِي ٱلصُّورِ فَفَزِعَ مَن فِي ٱلسَّمَٰوَٰتِ وَمَن
فِي ٱلۡأَرۡضِ إِلَّا مَن شَآءَ ٱللَّهُۚ وَكُلٌّ أَتَوۡهُ دَٰخِرِينَ ﴿٨٧﴾

88. You see the mountains and think them firmly fixed: but they shall pass away as the clouds pass away: (such is) the artistry of Allah, Who disposes of all things in perfect order: for He is well-acquainted with all that you do.

وَتَرَى ٱلۡجِبَالَ تَحۡسَبُهَا جَامِدَةٗ وَهِيَ تَمُرُّ مَرَّ ٱلسَّحَابِۚ
صُنۡعَ ٱللَّهِ ٱلَّذِيٓ أَتۡقَنَ كُلَّ شَيۡءٍۚ إِنَّهُۥ خَبِيرُۢ
بِمَا تَفۡعَلُونَ ﴿٨٨﴾

89. If any do good, good will (accrue) to them from it; and they will be secure from terror that day.

مَن جَآءَ بِٱلۡحَسَنَةِ فَلَهُۥ خَيۡرٞ مِّنۡهَا وَهُم مِّن فَزَعٖ يَوۡمَئِذٍ
ءَامِنُونَ ﴿٨٩﴾

90. And if any do evil, their faces will be thrown headlong into the fire: "Do you receive a reward other than that which you have earned by your deeds?"

وَمَن جَآءَ بِٱلسَّيِّئَةِ فَكُبَّتۡ وُجُوهُهُمۡ فِي ٱلنَّارِ هَلۡ
تُجۡزَوۡنَ إِلَّا مَا كُنتُمۡ تَعۡمَلُونَ ﴿٩٠﴾

91. For me, I have been commanded to serve the Lord of this city, Him Who has sanctified it and to Whom (belong) all things: and I am commanded to be of those who bow in Islam to Allah's Will -

إِنَّمَآ أُمِرۡتُ أَنۡ أَعۡبُدَ رَبَّ هَٰذِهِ ٱلۡبَلۡدَةِ ٱلَّذِي
حَرَّمَهَا وَلَهُۥ كُلُّ شَيۡءٖۖ وَأُمِرۡتُ أَنۡ أَكُونَ
مِنَ ٱلۡمُسۡلِمِينَ ٩١

92. And to rehearse the Qur'an: and if any accept guidance, they do it for the good of their own souls, and if any stray, say: "I am a warner."

وَأَنۡ أَتۡلُوَاْ ٱلۡقُرۡءَانَۖ فَمَنِ ٱهۡتَدَىٰ فَإِنَّمَا يَهۡتَدِي
لِنَفۡسِهِۦۖ وَمَن ضَلَّ فَقُلۡ إِنَّمَآ أَنَا۠ مِنَ ٱلۡمُنذِرِينَ ٩٢

93. And say: "Praise be to Allah, Who will soon show you His signs, so that you shall know them"; and your Lord is not unmindful of all that you do.

وَقُلِ ٱلۡحَمۡدُ لِلَّهِ سَيُرِيكُمۡ ءَايَٰتِهِۦ فَتَعۡرِفُونَهَاۚ
وَمَا رَبُّكَ بِغَٰفِلٍ عَمَّا تَعۡمَلُونَ ٩٣

سُورَةُ ٱلۡقَصَصِ

Surah 28: ***Al-Qasas*** **(The Story)**

In the name of Allah,
Most Gracious, Most Merciful.

بِسۡمِ ٱللَّهِ ٱلرَّحۡمَٰنِ ٱلرَّحِيمِ

1. *Ta Sin Mim.*

طسٓمٓ ١

2. These are verses of the book that makes (things) clear.

تِلۡكَ ءَايَٰتُ ٱلۡكِتَٰبِ ٱلۡمُبِينِ ٢

3. We rehearse to you some of the story of Moses and Pharaoh in truth, for people who believe.

نَتۡلُواْ عَلَيۡكَ مِن نَّبَإِ مُوسَىٰ وَفِرۡعَوۡنَ بِٱلۡحَقِّ
لِقَوۡمٖ يُؤۡمِنُونَ ٣

4. Truly Pharaoh elated himself in the land and broke up its people into sections, depressing a small group among them: their sons he slew, but he kept alive their females: for he was indeed a maker of mischief.

إِنَّ فِرۡعَوۡنَ عَلَا فِي ٱلۡأَرۡضِ وَجَعَلَ أَهۡلَهَا شِيَعٗا
يَسۡتَضۡعِفُ طَآئِفَةٗ مِّنۡهُمۡ يُذَبِّحُ أَبۡنَآءَهُمۡ
وَيَسۡتَحۡيِۦ نِسَآءَهُمۡۚ إِنَّهُۥ كَانَ مِنَ ٱلۡمُفۡسِدِينَ ٤

5. And We wished to be gracious to those who were being depressed on the land. To

وَنُرِيدُ أَن نَّمُنَّ عَلَى ٱلَّذِينَ ٱسۡتُضۡعِفُواْ فِي ٱلۡأَرۡضِ

make them leaders (in faith) and make them heirs,

وَنَجْعَلَهُمْ أَئِمَّةً وَنَجْعَلَهُمُ ٱلْوَٰرِثِينَ ٥

6. To establish a firm place for them in the land, and to show Pharaoh, Haman, and their hosts, at their hands, the very things against which they were taking precautions.

وَنُمَكِّنَ لَهُمْ فِى ٱلْأَرْضِ وَنُرِىَ فِرْعَوْنَ وَهَٰمَٰنَ
وَجُنُودَهُمَا مِنْهُم مَّا كَانُوا۟ يَحْذَرُونَ ٦

7. So We sent this inspiration to the mother of Moses: "Suckle (your child), but when you have fears about him, cast him into the river, but fear not nor grieve: for We shall restore him to you, and We shall make him one of Our prophets."

وَأَوْحَيْنَآ إِلَىٰٓ أُمِّ مُوسَىٰٓ أَنْ أَرْضِعِيهِ ۖ فَإِذَا خِفْتِ
عَلَيْهِ فَأَلْقِيهِ فِى ٱلْيَمِّ وَلَا تَخَافِى وَلَا تَحْزَنِىٓ ۖ
إِنَّا رَآدُّوهُ إِلَيْكِ وَجَاعِلُوهُ مِنَ ٱلْمُرْسَلِينَ ٧

8. Then the people of Pharaoh picked him up (from the river): (it was intended) that (Moses) should be to them an adversary and a cause of sorrow: for Pharaoh and Haman and (all) their forces were men of sin.

فَٱلْتَقَطَهُۥٓ ءَالُ فِرْعَوْنَ لِيَكُونَ لَهُمْ عَدُوًّا
وَحَزَنًا ۗ إِنَّ فِرْعَوْنَ وَهَٰمَٰنَ وَجُنُودَهُمَا
كَانُوا۟ خَٰطِـِٔينَ ٨

9. The wife of Pharaoh said: "(Here is) a joy of the eye, for me and for you: slay him not. It may be that he will be of use to us, or we may adopt him as a son." And they perceived not (what they were doing)!

وَقَالَتِ ٱمْرَأَتُ فِرْعَوْنَ قُرَّتُ عَيْنٍ لِّى وَلَكَ ۖ
لَا تَقْتُلُوهُ عَسَىٰٓ أَن يَنفَعَنَآ أَوْ نَتَّخِذَهُۥ وَلَدًا
وَهُمْ لَا يَشْعُرُونَ ٩

10. But there came to be a void in the heart of the mother of Moses: she was going almost to disclose his (case), had We not strengthened her heart (with faith), so that she might remain a (firm) believer.

وَأَصْبَحَ فُؤَادُ أُمِّ مُوسَىٰ فَٰرِغًا ۖ إِن كَادَتْ لَتُبْدِى
بِهِۦ لَوْلَآ أَن رَّبَطْنَا عَلَىٰ قَلْبِهَا لِتَكُونَ مِنَ
ٱلْمُؤْمِنِينَ ١٠

11. And she said to the sister of (Moses), "Follow him." So she (the sister) watched him in the character of a stranger. And they knew not.

وَقَالَتْ لِأُخْتِهِۦ قُصِّيهِ ۖ فَبَصُرَتْ بِهِۦ عَن جُنُبٍ
وَهُمْ لَا يَشْعُرُونَ ١١

12. And We ordained that he refused suck at first, until (his sister came up and) said:

نصف الحزب ٣٩
۞ وَحَرَّمْنَا عَلَيْهِ ٱلْمَرَاضِعَ مِن قَبْلُ فَقَالَتْ هَلْ

"Shall I point out to you the people of a house that will nourish and bring him up for you and be sincerely attached to him?"

أَدُلُّكُمْ عَلَىٰٓ أَهْلِ بَيْتٍ يَكْفُلُونَهُۥ لَكُمْ وَهُمْ
لَهُۥ نَٰصِحُونَ ١٢

13. Thus did We restore him to his mother, that her eye might be comforted, that she might not grieve and that she might know that the promise of Allah is true; but most of them do not understand.

فَرَدَدْنَٰهُ إِلَىٰٓ أُمِّهِۦ كَىْ تَقَرَّ عَيْنُهَا وَلَا تَحْزَنَ
وَلِتَعْلَمَ أَنَّ وَعْدَ ٱللَّهِ حَقٌّ وَلَٰكِنَّ أَكْثَرَهُمْ
لَا يَعْلَمُونَ ١٣

14. When he reached full age, and was firmly established (in life), We bestowed on him wisdom and knowledge: for thus do We reward those who do good.

وَلَمَّا بَلَغَ أَشُدَّهُۥ وَٱسْتَوَىٰٓ ءَاتَيْنَٰهُ حُكْمًا وَعِلْمًا ۚ
وَكَذَٰلِكَ نَجْزِى ٱلْمُحْسِنِينَ ١٤

15. And he entered the city at a time when its people were not watching: and he found there two men fighting - one of his own people and the other, of his foes. Now the man of his own people appealed to him against his foe, and Moses struck him with his fist and made an end of him. He said: "This is a work of evil (Satan): for he is an enemy that manifestly misleads!"

وَدَخَلَ ٱلْمَدِينَةَ عَلَىٰ حِينِ غَفْلَةٍ مِّنْ أَهْلِهَا فَوَجَدَ
فِيهَا رَجُلَيْنِ يَقْتَتِلَانِ هَٰذَا مِن شِيعَتِهِۦ وَهَٰذَا مِنْ
عَدُوِّهِۦ ۖ فَٱسْتَغَٰثَهُ ٱلَّذِى مِن شِيعَتِهِۦ عَلَى ٱلَّذِى مِنْ
عَدُوِّهِۦ فَوَكَزَهُۥ مُوسَىٰ فَقَضَىٰ عَلَيْهِ ۖ قَالَ هَٰذَا مِنْ
عَمَلِ ٱلشَّيْطَٰنِ ۖ إِنَّهُۥ عَدُوٌّ مُّضِلٌّ مُّبِينٌ ١٥

16. He prayed: "O my Lord! I have indeed wronged my soul! Do You then forgive me!" So (Allah) forgave him: for He is the Oft-Forgiving, Most Merciful.

قَالَ رَبِّ إِنِّى ظَلَمْتُ نَفْسِى فَٱغْفِرْ لِى فَغَفَرَ لَهُۥٓ ۚ إِنَّهُۥ
هُوَ ٱلْغَفُورُ ٱلرَّحِيمُ ١٦

17. He said: "O my Lord! For that You have bestowed Your grace on me, never shall I be a help to those who sin!"

قَالَ رَبِّ بِمَآ أَنْعَمْتَ عَلَىَّ فَلَنْ أَكُونَ
ظَهِيرًا لِّلْمُجْرِمِينَ ١٧

18. So he saw the morning in the city, looking about, in a state of fear, when behold, the man who had, the day before, sought his help called aloud for his help (again). Moses said to him: "You are truly, it is clear, a quarrelsome fellow!"

فَأَصْبَحَ فِى ٱلْمَدِينَةِ خَآئِفًا يَتَرَقَّبُ فَإِذَا ٱلَّذِى
ٱسْتَنصَرَهُۥ بِٱلْأَمْسِ يَسْتَصْرِخُهُۥ ۚ قَالَ لَهُۥ مُوسَىٰٓ إِنَّكَ
لَغَوِىٌّ مُّبِينٌ ١٨

19. Then, when he decided to lay hold of the man who was an enemy to both of them, that man said: "O Moses! Is it your intention to slay me as you slew a man yesterday? Your intention is none other than to become a powerful violent man in the land, and not to be one who sets things right!"

فَلَمَّآ أَنۡ أَرَادَ أَن يَبۡطِشَ بِٱلَّذِي هُوَ عَدُوّٞ لَّهُمَا قَالَ
يَٰمُوسَىٰٓ أَتُرِيدُ أَن تَقۡتُلَنِي كَمَا قَتَلۡتَ نَفۡسَۢا بِٱلۡأَمۡسِۖ
إِن تُرِيدُ إِلَّآ أَن تَكُونَ جَبَّارٗا فِي ٱلۡأَرۡضِ وَمَا تُرِيدُ أَن
تَكُونَ مِنَ ٱلۡمُصۡلِحِينَ ١٩

20. And there came a man, running, from the furthest end of the city. He said: "O Moses! The chiefs are taking counsel together about you, to slay you: so get you away, for I do give you sincere advice."

وَجَآءَ رَجُلٞ مِّنۡ أَقۡصَا ٱلۡمَدِينَةِ يَسۡعَىٰ قَالَ يَٰمُوسَىٰٓ
إِنَّ ٱلۡمَلَأَ يَأۡتَمِرُونَ بِكَ لِيَقۡتُلُوكَ فَٱخۡرُجۡ إِنِّي
لَكَ مِنَ ٱلنَّٰصِحِينَ ٢٠

21. He therefore got away from it, looking about, in a state of fear. He prayed: "O my Lord! Save me from people given to wrongdoing."

فَخَرَجَ مِنۡهَا خَآئِفٗا يَتَرَقَّبُۖ قَالَ رَبِّ نَجِّنِي مِنَ
ٱلۡقَوۡمِ ٱلظَّٰلِمِينَ ٢١

22. Then, when he turned his face towards (the land of) Madyan, he said: "I do hope that my Lord will show me the smooth and straight path."

وَلَمَّا تَوَجَّهَ تِلۡقَآءَ مَدۡيَنَ قَالَ عَسَىٰ رَبِّيٓ أَن
يَهۡدِيَنِي سَوَآءَ ٱلسَّبِيلِ ٢٢

23. And when he arrived at the watering (place) in Madyan, he found there a group of men watering (their flocks), and besides them he found two women who were keeping back (their flocks). He said: "What is the matter with you?" They said: "We cannot water (our flocks) until the shepherds take back (their flocks): and our father is a very old man."

وَلَمَّا وَرَدَ مَآءَ مَدۡيَنَ وَجَدَ عَلَيۡهِ أُمَّةٗ مِّنَ
ٱلنَّاسِ يَسۡقُونَ وَوَجَدَ مِن دُونِهِمُ ٱمۡرَأَتَيۡنِ
تَذُودَانِۖ قَالَ مَا خَطۡبُكُمَاۖ قَالَتَا لَا نَسۡقِي حَتَّىٰ
يُصۡدِرَ ٱلرِّعَآءُۖ وَأَبُونَا شَيۡخٞ كَبِيرٞ ٢٣

24. So he watered (their flocks) for them; then he turned back to the shade, and said: "O my Lord! Truly am I in (desperate) need of any good that You do send me!"

فَسَقَىٰ لَهُمَا ثُمَّ تَوَلَّىٰٓ إِلَى ٱلظِّلِّ فَقَالَ رَبِّ إِنِّي
لِمَآ أَنزَلۡتَ إِلَيَّ مِنۡ خَيۡرٖ فَقِيرٞ ٢٤

25. Afterwards one of the (girls) came (back) to him, walking bashfully. She said:

فَجَآءَتۡهُ إِحۡدَىٰهُمَا تَمۡشِي عَلَى ٱسۡتِحۡيَآءٖ قَالَتۡ

"My father invites you that he may reward you for having watered (our flocks) for us." So when he came to him and narrated the story, he said: "Fear you not: (well) have you escaped from unjust people."

إِنَّ أَبِي يَدْعُوكَ لِيَجْزِيَكَ أَجْرَ مَا سَقَيْتَ لَنَا ۚ
فَلَمَّا جَاءَهُ وَقَصَّ عَلَيْهِ الْقَصَصَ قَالَ لَا تَخَفْ ۖ
نَجَوْتَ مِنَ الْقَوْمِ الظَّالِمِينَ ﴿٢٥﴾

26. Said one of the (girls): "O my (dear) father! Engage him on wages: truly the best of men for you to employ is the (man) who is strong and trusty".

قَالَتْ إِحْدَاهُمَا يَا أَبَتِ اسْتَأْجِرْهُ ۖ إِنَّ خَيْرَ مَنِ
اسْتَأْجَرْتَ الْقَوِيُّ الْأَمِينُ ﴿٢٦﴾

27. He said: "I intended to wed one of these my daughters to you, on condition that you serve me for eight years; but if you complete ten years, it will be (grace) from you. But I intend not to place you under a difficulty: you will find me, indeed, if Allah wills, one of the righteous."

قَالَ إِنِّي أُرِيدُ أَنْ أُنْكِحَكَ إِحْدَى ابْنَتَيَّ هَاتَيْنِ
عَلَىٰ أَنْ تَأْجُرَنِي ثَمَانِيَ حِجَجٍ ۖ فَإِنْ أَتْمَمْتَ
عَشْرًا فَمِنْ عِنْدِكَ ۖ وَمَا أُرِيدُ أَنْ أَشُقَّ عَلَيْكَ ۚ
سَتَجِدُنِي إِنْ شَاءَ اللَّهُ مِنَ الصَّالِحِينَ ﴿٢٧﴾

28. He said: "Be that (the agreement) between me and you: whichever of the two terms I fulfil, let there be no ill-will to me. Be Allah a witness to what we say."

قَالَ ذَٰلِكَ بَيْنِي وَبَيْنَكَ ۖ أَيَّمَا الْأَجَلَيْنِ قَضَيْتُ
فَلَا عُدْوَانَ عَلَيَّ ۖ وَاللَّهُ عَلَىٰ مَا نَقُولُ وَكِيلٌ ﴿٢٨﴾

29. Now when Moses had fulfilled the term, and was travelling with his family, he perceived a fire in the direction of mount Tur. He said to his family: "Stay you; I perceive a fire; I hope to bring you from there some information, or a burning firebrand, that you may warm yourselves."

۞ فَلَمَّا قَضَىٰ مُوسَى الْأَجَلَ وَسَارَ بِأَهْلِهِ آنَسَ ثلاثة أرباع الحزب ٣٩
مِنْ جَانِبِ الطُّورِ نَارًا ۖ قَالَ لِأَهْلِهِ امْكُثُوا إِنِّي
آنَسْتُ نَارًا لَعَلِّي آتِيكُمْ مِنْهَا بِخَبَرٍ أَوْ جَذْوَةٍ
مِنَ النَّارِ لَعَلَّكُمْ تَصْطَلُونَ ﴿٢٩﴾

30. But when he came to the (fire), a voice was heard from the right bank of the valley, from a tree in sacred ground: "O Moses! Verily I am Allah, the Lord of the Worlds."

فَلَمَّا أَتَاهَا نُودِيَ مِنْ شَاطِئِ الْوَادِ الْأَيْمَنِ فِي
الْبُقْعَةِ الْمُبَارَكَةِ مِنَ الشَّجَرَةِ أَنْ يَا مُوسَىٰ
إِنِّي أَنَا اللَّهُ رَبُّ الْعَالَمِينَ ﴿٣٠﴾

31. "Now do you throw your rod!" But when he saw it moving (of its own accord)

وَأَنْ أَلْقِ عَصَاكَ ۖ فَلَمَّا رَآهَا تَهْتَزُّ كَأَنَّهَا جَانٌّ

as if it had been a snake, He turned back in retreat, and retraced not his steps: "O Moses!" (It was said) "Draw near, and fear not: for you are of those who are secure.

وَلَّىٰ مُدْبِرًا وَلَمْ يُعَقِّبْ ۚ يَٰمُوسَىٰٓ أَقْبِلْ وَلَا
تَخَفْ ۖ إِنَّكَ مِنَ ٱلْءَامِنِينَ ٣١

32. Move your hand into your chest, and it will come out white without stain (or harm), and draw your hand close to your side (to guard) against fear. Those are the two credentials from your Lord to Pharaoh and his chiefs: for truly they are a people rebellious and wicked."

ٱسْلُكْ يَدَكَ فِى جَيْبِكَ تَخْرُجْ بَيْضَآءَ مِنْ غَيْرِ
سُوٓءٍ وَٱضْمُمْ إِلَيْكَ جَنَاحَكَ مِنَ ٱلرَّهْبِ ۖ
فَذَٰنِكَ بُرْهَٰنَانِ مِن رَّبِّكَ إِلَىٰ فِرْعَوْنَ
وَمَلَإِي۟هِۦٓ ۚ إِنَّهُمْ كَانُوا۟ قَوْمًا فَٰسِقِينَ ٣٢

33. He said: "O my Lord! I have slain a man among them, and I fear lest they slay me.

قَالَ رَبِّ إِنِّى قَتَلْتُ مِنْهُمْ نَفْسًا فَأَخَافُ أَن يَقْتُلُونِ ٣٣

34. And my brother Aaron - he is more eloquent in speech than I: so send him with me as a helper, to confirm (and strengthen) me; for I fear that they may accuse me of falsehood."

وَأَخِى هَٰرُونُ هُوَ أَفْصَحُ مِنِّى لِسَانًا فَأَرْسِلْهُ مَعِىَ
رِدْءًا يُصَدِّقُنِىٓ ۖ إِنِّىٓ أَخَافُ أَن يُكَذِّبُونِ ٣٤

35. He said: "We will certainly strengthen your arm through your brother, and invest you both with authority, so they shall not be able to touch you: with Our signs shall you triumph, you two as well as those who follow you."

قَالَ سَنَشُدُّ عَضُدَكَ بِأَخِيكَ وَنَجْعَلُ لَكُمَا
سُلْطَٰنًا فَلَا يَصِلُونَ إِلَيْكُمَا ۚ بِـَٔايَٰتِنَآ أَنتُمَا وَمَنِ
ٱتَّبَعَكُمَا ٱلْغَٰلِبُونَ ٣٥

36. When Moses came to them with Our clear signs, they said: "This is nothing but sorcery faked up: never did we hear the like among our fathers of old!"

فَلَمَّا جَآءَهُم مُّوسَىٰ بِـَٔايَٰتِنَا بَيِّنَٰتٍ قَالُوا۟ مَا هَٰذَآ
إِلَّا سِحْرٌ مُّفْتَرًى وَمَا سَمِعْنَا بِهَٰذَا فِىٓ
ءَابَآئِنَا ٱلْأَوَّلِينَ ٣٦

37. Moses said: "My Lord knows best who it is that comes with guidance from Him and whose end will be best in the hereafter: certain it is that the wrongdoers will not prosper."

وَقَالَ مُوسَىٰ رَبِّىٓ أَعْلَمُ بِمَن جَآءَ بِٱلْهُدَىٰ مِنْ
عِندِهِۦ وَمَن تَكُونُ لَهُۥ عَٰقِبَةُ ٱلدَّارِ ۖ إِنَّهُۥ لَا
يُفْلِحُ ٱلظَّٰلِمُونَ ٣٧

38. Pharaoh said: "O chiefs! No god do I know for you but myself: therefore, "O Haman! Light me a (kiln to bake bricks) out of clay, and build me a lofty palace, that I may mount up to the god of Moses; but as far as I am concerned, I think (Moses) is a liar!"

وَقَالَ فِرْعَوْنُ يَٰٓأَيُّهَا ٱلْمَلَأُ مَا عَلِمْتُ لَكُم
مِّنْ إِلَٰهٍ غَيْرِى فَأَوْقِدْ لِى يَٰهَٰمَٰنُ عَلَى ٱلطِّينِ
فَٱجْعَل لِّى صَرْحًا لَّعَلِّىٓ أَطَّلِعُ إِلَىٰٓ إِلَٰهِ مُوسَىٰ
وَإِنِّى لَأَظُنُّهُۥ مِنَ ٱلْكَٰذِبِينَ ٣٨

39. And he was arrogant and insolent in the land, beyond reason he and his hosts: they thought that they would not have to return to Us!

وَٱسْتَكْبَرَ هُوَ وَجُنُودُهُۥ فِى ٱلْأَرْضِ بِغَيْرِ
ٱلْحَقِّ وَظَنُّوٓا۟ أَنَّهُمْ إِلَيْنَا لَا يُرْجَعُونَ ٣٩

40. So We seized him and his hosts, and We flung them into the sea: now see what was the end of those who did wrong!

فَأَخَذْنَٰهُ وَجُنُودَهُۥ فَنَبَذْنَٰهُمْ فِى ٱلْيَمِّ ۖ فَٱنظُرْ كَيْفَ
كَانَ عَٰقِبَةُ ٱلظَّٰلِمِينَ ٤٠

41. And We made them (but) leaders inviting to the fire; and on the day of judgement no help shall they find.

وَجَعَلْنَٰهُمْ أَئِمَّةً يَدْعُونَ إِلَى ٱلنَّارِ ۖ
وَيَوْمَ ٱلْقِيَٰمَةِ لَا يُنصَرُونَ ٤١

42. In this world We made a curse to follow them: and on the day of judgement they will be among the loathed (and despised).

وَأَتْبَعْنَٰهُمْ فِى هَٰذِهِ ٱلدُّنْيَا لَعْنَةً ۖ
وَيَوْمَ ٱلْقِيَٰمَةِ هُم مِّنَ ٱلْمَقْبُوحِينَ ٤٢

43. We did reveal to Moses the book after We had destroyed the earlier generations, (to give) insight to men, and guidance and mercy, that they might receive admonition.

وَلَقَدْ ءَاتَيْنَا مُوسَى ٱلْكِتَٰبَ مِنۢ بَعْدِ مَآ
أَهْلَكْنَا ٱلْقُرُونَ ٱلْأُولَىٰ بَصَآئِرَ لِلنَّاسِ
وَهُدًى وَرَحْمَةً لَّعَلَّهُمْ يَتَذَكَّرُونَ ٤٣

44. You were not on the western side when We decreed the commission to Moses, nor were you a witness (of those events).

وَمَا كُنتَ بِجَانِبِ ٱلْغَرْبِىِّ إِذْ قَضَيْنَآ إِلَىٰ مُوسَى
ٱلْأَمْرَ وَمَا كُنتَ مِنَ ٱلشَّٰهِدِينَ ٤٤

45. But We raised up (new) generations, and long were the ages that passed over them; but you were not a dweller among the people of Madyan, rehearsing Our signs to

وَلَٰكِنَّآ أَنشَأْنَا قُرُونًا فَتَطَاوَلَ عَلَيْهِمُ ٱلْعُمُرُ ۚ
وَمَا كُنتَ ثَاوِيًا فِىٓ أَهْلِ مَدْيَنَ تَتْلُوا۟ عَلَيْهِمْ

ءَايَٰتِنَا وَلَٰكِنَّا كُنَّا مُرْسِلِينَ ﴿٤٥﴾

them; but it is We Who send prophets (with inspiration).

وَمَا كُنتَ بِجَانِبِ ٱلطُّورِ إِذْ نَادَيْنَا وَلَٰكِن
رَّحْمَةً مِّن رَّبِّكَ لِتُنذِرَ قَوْمًا مَّآ أَتَىٰهُم مِّن نَّذِيرٍ
مِّن قَبْلِكَ لَعَلَّهُمْ يَتَذَكَّرُونَ ﴿٤٦﴾

46. Nor were you at the side of (the mountain of) Tur when We called (to Moses). Yet (are you sent) as a mercy from your Lord, to give warning to a people to whom no warner had come before you; in order that they may receive admonition.

وَلَوْلَآ أَن تُصِيبَهُم مُّصِيبَةٌۢ بِمَا قَدَّمَتْ أَيْدِيهِمْ
فَيَقُولُوا۟ رَبَّنَا لَوْلَآ أَرْسَلْتَ إِلَيْنَا رَسُولًا فَنَتَّبِعَ
ءَايَٰتِكَ وَنَكُونَ مِنَ ٱلْمُؤْمِنِينَ ﴿٤٧﴾

47. If (We had) not (sent you to the Quraysh) - in case a calamity should seize them for (the deeds) that their hands have sent before they might say: "Our Lord! Why did You not send us a messenger? We should then have followed the signs and been amongst those who believe!"

فَلَمَّا جَآءَهُمُ ٱلْحَقُّ مِنْ عِندِنَا قَالُوا۟ لَوْلَآ أُوتِىَ
مِثْلَ مَآ أُوتِىَ مُوسَىٰٓ ۚ أَوَلَمْ يَكْفُرُوا۟ بِمَآ أُوتِىَ
مُوسَىٰ مِن قَبْلُ ۖ قَالُوا۟ سِحْرَانِ تَظَٰهَرَا وَقَالُوٓا۟ إِنَّا
بِكُلٍّ كَٰفِرُونَ ﴿٤٨﴾

48. But (now), when the truth has come to them from Ourselves, They say "Why are not (signs) sent to him, like those which were sent to Moses?" Do they not then reject (the signs) which were formerly sent to Moses? They say: "Two kinds of sorcery, each assisting the other!" And they say: "For us we reject all (such things)!"

قُلْ فَأْتُوا۟ بِكِتَٰبٍ مِّنْ عِندِ ٱللَّهِ هُوَ أَهْدَىٰ مِنْهُمَآ
أَتَّبِعْهُ إِن كُنتُمْ صَٰدِقِينَ ﴿٤٩﴾

49. Say: "Then bring you a book from Allah, which is a better guide than either of them, that I may follow it! (Do) if you are truthful!"

فَإِن لَّمْ يَسْتَجِيبُوا۟ لَكَ فَٱعْلَمْ أَنَّمَا يَتَّبِعُونَ
أَهْوَآءَهُمْ ۚ وَمَنْ أَضَلُّ مِمَّنِ ٱتَّبَعَ هَوَىٰهُ بِغَيْرِ هُدًى
مِّنَ ٱللَّهِ ۚ إِنَّ ٱللَّهَ لَا يَهْدِى ٱلْقَوْمَ ٱلظَّٰلِمِينَ ﴿٥٠﴾

50. But if they do not listen to you, know that they only follow their own lusts: and who is more astray than one who follows his own lusts, devoid of guidance from Allah? For Allah guides not people given to wrongdoing.

الحِزْبُ ٤٠ ۞ وَلَقَدْ وَصَّلْنَا لَهُمُ ٱلْقَوْلَ لَعَلَّهُمْ يَتَذَكَّرُونَ ﴿٥١﴾

51. Now have We caused the word to reach them themselves, in order that they may receive admonition.

52. Those to whom We sent the book before this - they do believe in this (revelation);

ٱلَّذِينَ ءَاتَيْنَٰهُمُ ٱلْكِتَٰبَ مِن قَبْلِهِۦ هُم بِهِۦ يُؤْمِنُونَ ٥٢

53. And when it is recited to them they say: "We believe in it, for it is the truth from our Lord: indeed we have been Muslims (bowing to Allah's Will) from before this."

وَإِذَا يُتْلَىٰ عَلَيْهِمْ قَالُوٓا۟ ءَامَنَّا بِهِۦٓ إِنَّهُ ٱلْحَقُّ مِن رَّبِّنَآ
إِنَّا كُنَّا مِن قَبْلِهِۦ مُسْلِمِينَ ٥٣

54. Twice will they be given their reward, for that they have persevered, that they avert evil with good, and that they spend (in charity) out of what We have given them.

أُو۟لَٰٓئِكَ يُؤْتَوْنَ أَجْرَهُم مَّرَّتَيْنِ بِمَا صَبَرُوا۟ وَيَدْرَءُونَ
بِٱلْحَسَنَةِ ٱلسَّيِّئَةَ وَمِمَّا رَزَقْنَٰهُمْ يُنفِقُونَ ٥٤

55. And when they hear vain talk, they turn away from it and say: "To us our deeds, and to you yours; peace be to you: we seek not the ignorant."

وَإِذَا سَمِعُوا۟ ٱللَّغْوَ أَعْرَضُوا۟ عَنْهُ وَقَالُوا۟ لَنَآ أَعْمَٰلُنَا
وَلَكُمْ أَعْمَٰلُكُمْ سَلَٰمٌ عَلَيْكُمْ لَا نَبْتَغِى
ٱلْجَٰهِلِينَ ٥٥

56. It is true you will not be able to guide everyone whom you love: but Allah guides those whom He will and He knows best those who receive guidance.

إِنَّكَ لَا تَهْدِى مَنْ أَحْبَبْتَ وَلَٰكِنَّ ٱللَّهَ يَهْدِى
مَن يَشَآءُ ۚ وَهُوَ أَعْلَمُ بِٱلْمُهْتَدِينَ ٥٦

57. They say: "If we were to follow the guidance with you we should be snatched away from our land." Have We not established for them a secure sanctuary, to which are brought as tribute fruits of all kinds - a provision from Ourselves? But most of them understand not.

وَقَالُوٓا۟ إِن نَّتَّبِعِ ٱلْهُدَىٰ مَعَكَ نُتَخَطَّفْ مِنْ
أَرْضِنَآ ۚ أَوَلَمْ نُمَكِّن لَّهُمْ حَرَمًا ءَامِنًا يُجْبَىٰٓ إِلَيْهِ
ثَمَرَٰتُ كُلِّ شَىْءٍ رِّزْقًا مِّن لَّدُنَّا وَلَٰكِنَّ أَكْثَرَهُمْ
لَا يَعْلَمُونَ ٥٧

58. And how many populations We destroyed, which exulted in their life (of ease and plenty)! Now those habitations of theirs, after them are deserted - all but a (miserable) few! And We are their heirs!

وَكَمْ أَهْلَكْنَا مِن قَرْيَةٍۭ بَطِرَتْ مَعِيشَتَهَا ۖ فَتِلْكَ
مَسَٰكِنُهُمْ لَمْ تُسْكَن مِّنۢ بَعْدِهِمْ إِلَّا قَلِيلًا ۖ
وَكُنَّا نَحْنُ ٱلْوَٰرِثِينَ ٥٨

59. Nor was your Lord the one to destroy a population until He had sent to its centre a

وَمَا كَانَ رَبُّكَ مُهْلِكَ ٱلْقُرَىٰ حَتَّىٰ يَبْعَثَ فِىٓ

messenger, rehearsing to them Our signs: nor are We going to destroy a population except when its members practice iniquity.

أُمِّهَا رَسُولًا يَتْلُوا۟ عَلَيْهِمْ ءَايَٰتِنَا ۚ وَمَا كُنَّا
مُهْلِكِى ٱلْقُرَىٰٓ إِلَّا وَأَهْلُهَا ظَٰلِمُونَ ٥٩

60. The (material) things which you are given are but the conveniences of this life and the glitter of it; but that which is with Allah is better and more enduring: will you not then be wise?

وَمَآ أُوتِيتُم مِّن شَىْءٍ فَمَتَٰعُ ٱلْحَيَوٰةِ ٱلدُّنْيَا وَزِينَتُهَا ۚ
وَمَا عِندَ ٱللَّهِ خَيْرٌ وَأَبْقَىٰٓ ۚ أَفَلَا تَعْقِلُونَ ٦٠

61. Are (these two) alike? One to whom We have made a goodly promise and who is going to reach its (fulfilment). And one to whom We have given the good things of this life, but who, on the day of judgement, is to be among those brought up (for punishment)?

أَفَمَن وَعَدْنَٰهُ وَعْدًا حَسَنًا فَهُوَ لَٰقِيهِ كَمَن مَّتَّعْنَٰهُ
مَتَٰعَ ٱلْحَيَوٰةِ ٱلدُّنْيَا ثُمَّ هُوَ يَوْمَ ٱلْقِيَٰمَةِ مِنَ
ٱلْمُحْضَرِينَ ٦١

62. That day Allah will call to them, and say: "Where are my 'partners'? whom you imagined (to be such)?"

وَيَوْمَ يُنَادِيهِمْ فَيَقُولُ أَيْنَ شُرَكَآءِىَ ٱلَّذِينَ
كُنتُمْ تَزْعُمُونَ ٦٢

63. Those against whom the charge will be proved, will say: "Our Lord! These are the ones whom we led astray; we led them astray, as we were astray ourselves; we free ourselves (from them) in Your presence! It was not us they worshipped."

قَالَ ٱلَّذِينَ حَقَّ عَلَيْهِمُ ٱلْقَوْلُ رَبَّنَا هَٰٓؤُلَآءِ ٱلَّذِينَ
أَغْوَيْنَآ أَغْوَيْنَٰهُمْ كَمَا غَوَيْنَا ۖ تَبَرَّأْنَآ إِلَيْكَ ۖ
مَا كَانُوٓا۟ إِيَّانَا يَعْبُدُونَ ٦٣

64. It will be said (to them): "Call upon your 'partners' (for help)"; they will call upon them but they will not listen to them; and they will see the penalty (before them); (how they will wish) 'If only they had been open to guidance!'

وَقِيلَ ٱدْعُوا۟ شُرَكَآءَكُمْ فَدَعَوْهُمْ فَلَمْ يَسْتَجِيبُوا۟ لَهُمْ
وَرَأَوُا۟ ٱلْعَذَابَ ۚ لَوْ أَنَّهُمْ كَانُوا۟ يَهْتَدُونَ ٦٤

65. That day (Allah) will call to them, and say: "What was the answer you gave to the messengers?"

وَيَوْمَ يُنَادِيهِمْ فَيَقُولُ مَاذَآ أَجَبْتُمُ
ٱلْمُرْسَلِينَ ٦٥

66. Then the (whole) story that day will seem obscure to them (like light to the

فَعَمِيَتْ عَلَيْهِمُ ٱلْأَنۢبَآءُ يَوْمَئِذٍ فَهُمْ

blind), and they will not be able (even) to question each other.

لَا يَتَسَآءَلُونَ ٦٦

67. But any that (in this life) had repented, believed, and worked righteousness, will have hopes to be among those who achieve salvation.

فَأَمَّا مَن تَابَ وَءَامَنَ وَعَمِلَ صَٰلِحًا فَعَسَىٰٓ أَن يَكُونَ
مِنَ ٱلْمُفْلِحِينَ ٦٧

68. Your Lord does create and choose as He pleases: no choice have they (in the matter): Glory to Allah! And far is He above the partners they ascribe (to Him)!

وَرَبُّكَ يَخْلُقُ مَا يَشَآءُ وَيَخْتَارُ ۗ مَا كَانَ لَهُمُ ٱلْخِيَرَةُ ۚ
سُبْحَٰنَ ٱللَّهِ وَتَعَٰلَىٰ عَمَّا يُشْرِكُونَ ٦٨

69. And your Lord knows all that their hearts conceal and all that they reveal.

وَرَبُّكَ يَعْلَمُ مَا تُكِنُّ صُدُورُهُمْ وَمَا
يُعْلِنُونَ ٦٩

70. And He is Allah: there is no god but He. To Him be praise, at the first and at the last; for Him is the command and to Him shall you (all) be brought back.

وَهُوَ ٱللَّهُ لَآ إِلَٰهَ إِلَّا هُوَ ۖ لَهُ ٱلْحَمْدُ فِى ٱلْأُولَىٰ
وَٱلْءَاخِرَةِ ۖ وَلَهُ ٱلْحُكْمُ وَإِلَيْهِ تُرْجَعُونَ ٧٠

71. Say: Do you see? If Allah were to make the night perpetual over you to the day of judgement, what god is there other than Allah, who can give you enlightenment? Will you not then listen?

قُلْ أَرَءَيْتُمْ إِن جَعَلَ ٱللَّهُ عَلَيْكُمُ ٱلَّيْلَ سَرْمَدًا
إِلَىٰ يَوْمِ ٱلْقِيَٰمَةِ مَنْ إِلَٰهٌ غَيْرُ ٱللَّهِ يَأْتِيكُم
بِضِيَآءٍ ۖ أَفَلَا تَسْمَعُونَ ٧١

72. Say: Do you see? If Allah were to make the day perpetual over you to the day of judgement, what god is there other than Allah, who can give you a night in which you can rest? Will you not then see?

قُلْ أَرَءَيْتُمْ إِن جَعَلَ ٱللَّهُ عَلَيْكُمُ ٱلنَّهَارَ سَرْمَدًا
إِلَىٰ يَوْمِ ٱلْقِيَٰمَةِ مَنْ إِلَٰهٌ غَيْرُ ٱللَّهِ يَأْتِيكُم
بِلَيْلٍ تَسْكُنُونَ فِيهِ ۖ أَفَلَا تُبْصِرُونَ ٧٢

73. It is out of His mercy that He has made for you night and day - that you may rest in it, and that you may seek of His grace - and in order that you may be grateful.

وَمِن رَّحْمَتِهِۦ جَعَلَ لَكُمُ ٱلَّيْلَ وَٱلنَّهَارَ
لِتَسْكُنُوا۟ فِيهِ وَلِتَبْتَغُوا۟ مِن فَضْلِهِۦ وَلَعَلَّكُمْ
تَشْكُرُونَ ٧٣

74. The day that He will call on them, He will say: "Where are My 'partners' whom you imagined (to be such)?"

وَيَوۡمَ يُنَادِيهِمۡ فَيَقُولُ أَيۡنَ شُرَكَآءِيَ ٱلَّذِينَ
كُنتُمۡ تَزۡعُمُونَ ٧٤

75. And from each people shall We draw a witness, and We shall say: "Produce your proof"; then shall they know that the truth is in Allah (alone), and the (lies) which they invented will leave them in the lurch.

وَنَزَعۡنَا مِن كُلِّ أُمَّةٖ شَهِيدٗا فَقُلۡنَا هَاتُواْ
بُرۡهَٰنَكُمۡ فَعَلِمُوٓاْ أَنَّ ٱلۡحَقَّ لِلَّهِ وَضَلَّ
عَنۡهُم مَّا كَانُواْ يَفۡتَرُونَ ٧٥

76. Qarun was doubtless of the people of Moses; but he acted insolently towards them: such were the treasures We had bestowed on him, that their very keys would have been a burden to a body of strong men: See, his people said to him: "Exult not, for Allah loves not those who exult (in riches).

ربع الحزب ٤٠ ۞إِنَّ قَٰرُونَ كَانَ مِن قَوۡمِ مُوسَىٰ فَبَغَىٰ عَلَيۡهِمۡۖ
وَءَاتَيۡنَٰهُ مِنَ ٱلۡكُنُوزِ مَآ إِنَّ مَفَاتِحَهُۥ لَتَنُوٓأُ
بِٱلۡعُصۡبَةِ أُوْلِي ٱلۡقُوَّةِ إِذۡ قَالَ لَهُۥ قَوۡمُهُۥ لَا تَفۡرَحۡۖ
إِنَّ ٱللَّهَ لَا يُحِبُّ ٱلۡفَرِحِينَ ٧٦

77. But seek, with the (wealth) which Allah has bestowed on you, the home of the hereafter, nor forget your portion in this world; but do you good, as Allah has been good to you, and seek not (occasions for) mischief in the land: for Allah loves not those who do mischief."

وَٱبۡتَغِ فِيمَآ ءَاتَىٰكَ ٱللَّهُ ٱلدَّارَ ٱلۡأٓخِرَةَۖ وَلَا تَنسَ
نَصِيبَكَ مِنَ ٱلدُّنۡيَاۖ وَأَحۡسِن كَمَآ أَحۡسَنَ ٱللَّهُ إِلَيۡكَۖ
وَلَا تَبۡغِ ٱلۡفَسَادَ فِي ٱلۡأَرۡضِۖ إِنَّ ٱللَّهَ لَا يُحِبُّ
ٱلۡمُفۡسِدِينَ ٧٧

78. He said: "This has been given to me because of a certain knowledge which I have." Did he not know that Allah had destroyed, before him (whole) generations - which were superior to him in strength and greater in amount (of riches) they had collected? But the wicked are not called (immediately) to account for their sins.

قَالَ إِنَّمَآ أُوتِيتُهُۥ عَلَىٰ عِلۡمٍ عِندِيٓۚ أَوَلَمۡ يَعۡلَمۡ أَنَّ ٱللَّهَ
قَدۡ أَهۡلَكَ مِن قَبۡلِهِۦ مِنَ ٱلۡقُرُونِ مَنۡ هُوَ أَشَدُّ مِنۡهُ
قُوَّةٗ وَأَكۡثَرُ جَمۡعٗاۚ وَلَا يُسۡـَٔلُ عَن ذُنُوبِهِمُ
ٱلۡمُجۡرِمُونَ ٧٨

79. So he went forth among his people in the (pride of his worldly) glitter. Said those whose aim is the life of this world: "Oh that

فَخَرَجَ عَلَىٰ قَوۡمِهِۦ فِي زِينَتِهِۦۖ قَالَ ٱلَّذِينَ يُرِيدُونَ
ٱلۡحَيَوٰةَ ٱلدُّنۡيَا يَٰلَيۡتَ لَنَا مِثۡلَ مَآ أُوتِيَ قَٰرُونُ

we had the like of what Qarun has got! For he is truly a lord of mighty good fortune."

إِنَّهُۥ لَذُو حَظٍّ عَظِيمٖ ٧٩

80. But those who had been granted (true) knowledge said: "Alas for you! The reward of Allah (in the hereafter) is best for those who believe and work righteousness: but this none shall attain, save those who steadfastly persevere (in good)."

وَقَالَ ٱلَّذِينَ أُوتُواْ ٱلۡعِلۡمَ وَيۡلَكُمۡ ثَوَابُ ٱللَّهِ
خَيۡرٞ لِّمَنۡ ءَامَنَ وَعَمِلَ صَٰلِحٗاۚ وَلَا يُلَقَّىٰهَآ
إِلَّا ٱلصَّٰبِرُونَ ٨٠

81. Then We caused the earth to swallow him up and his house; and he had not (the least little) party to help him against Allah nor could he defend himself.

فَخَسَفۡنَا بِهِۦ وَبِدَارِهِ ٱلۡأَرۡضَ فَمَا كَانَ لَهُۥ
مِن فِئَةٖ يَنصُرُونَهُۥ مِن دُونِ ٱللَّهِ وَمَا كَانَ مِنَ
ٱلۡمُنتَصِرِينَ ٨١

82. And those who had envied his position the day before began to say in the morning: "Ah! It is indeed Allah Who enlarges the provision or restricts it, to any of His servants He pleases! Had it not been that Allah was gracious to us, He could have caused the earth to swallow us up! Ah! Those who reject Allah will assuredly never prosper."

وَأَصۡبَحَ ٱلَّذِينَ تَمَنَّوۡاْ مَكَانَهُۥ بِٱلۡأَمۡسِ يَقُولُونَ
وَيۡكَأَنَّ ٱللَّهَ يَبۡسُطُ ٱلرِّزۡقَ لِمَن يَشَآءُ مِنۡ عِبَادِهِۦ
وَيَقۡدِرُۖ لَوۡلَآ أَن مَّنَّ ٱللَّهُ عَلَيۡنَا لَخَسَفَ بِنَاۖ
وَيۡكَأَنَّهُۥ لَا يُفۡلِحُ ٱلۡكَٰفِرُونَ ٨٢

83. That House of the hereafter We shall give to those who intend not high-handedness or mischief on earth: and the end is (best) for the righteous.

تِلۡكَ ٱلدَّارُ ٱلۡأٓخِرَةُ نَجۡعَلُهَا لِلَّذِينَ لَا يُرِيدُونَ عُلُوّٗا
فِي ٱلۡأَرۡضِ وَلَا فَسَادٗاۚ وَٱلۡعَٰقِبَةُ لِلۡمُتَّقِينَ ٨٣

84. If any does good, the reward to him is better than his deed; but if any does evil, the doers of evil are only punished (to the extent) of their deeds.

مَن جَآءَ بِٱلۡحَسَنَةِ فَلَهُۥ خَيۡرٞ مِّنۡهَاۖ وَمَن جَآءَ
بِٱلسَّيِّئَةِ فَلَا يُجۡزَى ٱلَّذِينَ عَمِلُواْ ٱلسَّيِّـَٔاتِ إِلَّا
مَا كَانُواْ يَعۡمَلُونَ ٨٤

85. Verily He Who ordained the Qur'an for you will bring you back to the place of return. Say: "My Lord knows best who it is that brings true guidance and who is in manifest error."

إِنَّ ٱلَّذِي فَرَضَ عَلَيۡكَ ٱلۡقُرۡءَانَ لَرَآدُّكَ إِلَىٰ
مَعَادٖۚ قُل رَّبِّيٓ أَعۡلَمُ مَن جَآءَ بِٱلۡهُدَىٰ وَمَنۡ هُوَ
فِي ضَلَٰلٖ مُّبِينٖ ٨٥

86. And you had not expected that the book would be sent to you except as a mercy from your Lord: therefore lend not your support in any way to those who reject (Allah's message).

وَمَا كُنتَ تَرْجُوٓاْ أَن يُلْقَىٰٓ إِلَيْكَ ٱلْكِتَٰبُ إِلَّا
رَحْمَةً مِّن رَّبِّكَ ۖ فَلَا تَكُونَنَّ ظَهِيرًا لِّلْكَٰفِرِينَ ﴿٨٦﴾

87. And let nothing keep you back from the signs of Allah after they have been revealed to you: and invite (men) to your Lord and be not of the company of those who join gods with Allah.

وَلَا يَصُدُّنَّكَ عَنْ ءَايَٰتِ ٱللَّهِ بَعْدَ إِذْ أُنزِلَتْ إِلَيْكَ ۖ
وَٱدْعُ إِلَىٰ رَبِّكَ ۖ وَلَا تَكُونَنَّ مِنَ ٱلْمُشْرِكِينَ ﴿٨٧﴾

88. And call not besides Allah on another god. There is no god but He. Everything (that exists) will perish except His own Face. To Him belongs the command and to Him will you (all) be brought back.

وَلَا تَدْعُ مَعَ ٱللَّهِ إِلَٰهًا ءَاخَرَ ۘ لَآ إِلَٰهَ إِلَّا هُوَ ۚ كُلُّ شَىْءٍ
هَالِكٌ إِلَّا وَجْهَهُۥ ۚ لَهُ ٱلْحُكْمُ وَإِلَيْهِ تُرْجَعُونَ ﴿٨٨﴾

سُورَةُ ٱلْعَنكَبُوتِ

Surah 29: **Al-`Ankabut (The Spider)**

In the name of Allah,
Most Gracious, Most Merciful.

بِسْمِ ٱللَّهِ ٱلرَّحْمَٰنِ ٱلرَّحِيمِ

1. *Alif Lam Mim.*

نصف الحزب ٤٠

الٓمٓ ﴿١﴾

2. Do men think that they will be left alone on saying, "We believe," and that they will not be tested?

أَحَسِبَ ٱلنَّاسُ أَن يُتْرَكُوٓاْ أَن يَقُولُوٓاْ ءَامَنَّا
وَهُمْ لَا يُفْتَنُونَ ﴿٢﴾

3. We did test those before them, and Allah will certainly know those who are true from those who are false.

وَلَقَدْ فَتَنَّا ٱلَّذِينَ مِن قَبْلِهِمْ ۖ فَلَيَعْلَمَنَّ ٱللَّهُ ٱلَّذِينَ
صَدَقُواْ وَلَيَعْلَمَنَّ ٱلْكَٰذِبِينَ ﴿٣﴾

4. Do those who practice evil think that they will get the better of Us? Evil is their judgement!

أَمْ حَسِبَ ٱلَّذِينَ يَعْمَلُونَ ٱلسَّيِّـَٔاتِ أَن يَسْبِقُونَا ۚ
سَآءَ مَا يَحْكُمُونَ ﴿٤﴾

5. For those whose hopes are in the meeting with Allah (in the hereafter, let them strive); for the term (appointed) by Allah is surely coming: and He hears and knows (all things).

مَن كَانَ يَرۡجُواْ لِقَآءَ ٱللَّهِ فَإِنَّ أَجَلَ ٱللَّهِ لَأٓتٖۚ
وَهُوَ ٱلسَّمِيعُ ٱلۡعَلِيمُ ٥

6. And if any strive (with might and main), they do so for their own souls: for Allah is free of all needs from all creation.

وَمَن جَٰهَدَ فَإِنَّمَا يُجَٰهِدُ لِنَفۡسِهِۦٓۚ إِنَّ ٱللَّهَ لَغَنِيٌّ
عَنِ ٱلۡعَٰلَمِينَ ٦

7. Those who believe and work righteous deeds - from them shall We blot out all evil (that may be) in them, and We shall reward them according to the best of their deeds.

وَٱلَّذِينَ ءَامَنُواْ وَعَمِلُواْ ٱلصَّٰلِحَٰتِ لَنُكَفِّرَنَّ عَنۡهُمۡ
سَيِّـَٔاتِهِمۡ وَلَنَجۡزِيَنَّهُمۡ أَحۡسَنَ ٱلَّذِي كَانُواْ يَعۡمَلُونَ ٧

8. We have enjoined on man kindness to parents: but if they (either of them) strive (to force) you to join with Me (in worship) anything of which you have no knowledge, obey them not. You have (all) to return to Me, and I will tell you (the truth) of all that you did.

وَوَصَّيۡنَا ٱلۡإِنسَٰنَ بِوَٰلِدَيۡهِ حُسۡنٗاۖ وَإِن جَٰهَدَاكَ
لِتُشۡرِكَ بِي مَا لَيۡسَ لَكَ بِهِۦ عِلۡمٞ فَلَا تُطِعۡهُمَآۚ إِلَيَّ
مَرۡجِعُكُمۡ فَأُنَبِّئُكُم بِمَا كُنتُمۡ تَعۡمَلُونَ ٨

9. And those who believe and work righteous deeds - them shall We admit to the company of the righteous.

وَٱلَّذِينَ ءَامَنُواْ وَعَمِلُواْ ٱلصَّٰلِحَٰتِ لَنُدۡخِلَنَّهُمۡ فِي
ٱلصَّٰلِحِينَ ٩

10. Then there are among men such as say: "We believe in Allah"; but when they suffer affliction in (the cause of) Allah, they treat men's oppression as if it were the wrath of Allah! And if help comes (to you) from your Lord, they are sure to say, "We have (always) been with you!" Does not Allah know best all that is in the hearts of all creation?

وَمِنَ ٱلنَّاسِ مَن يَقُولُ ءَامَنَّا بِٱللَّهِ فَإِذَآ أُوذِيَ فِي ٱللَّهِ
جَعَلَ فِتۡنَةَ ٱلنَّاسِ كَعَذَابِ ٱللَّهِۖ وَلَئِن جَآءَ نَصۡرٞ
مِّن رَّبِّكَ لَيَقُولُنَّ إِنَّا كُنَّا مَعَكُمۡۚ أَوَلَيۡسَ ٱللَّهُ
بِأَعۡلَمَ بِمَا فِي صُدُورِ ٱلۡعَٰلَمِينَ ١٠

11. And Allah most certainly knows those who believe, and as certainly those who are hypocrites.

وَلَيَعۡلَمَنَّ ٱللَّهُ ٱلَّذِينَ ءَامَنُواْ وَلَيَعۡلَمَنَّ
ٱلۡمُنَٰفِقِينَ ١١

12. And the unbelievers say to those who believe: "Follow our path, and we will bear

وَقَالَ ٱلَّذِينَ كَفَرُواْ لِلَّذِينَ ءَامَنُواْ ٱتَّبِعُواْ

(the consequences) of your faults." Never in the least will they bear their faults: in fact they are liars!

سَبِيلَنَا وَلْنَحْمِلْ خَطَـٰيَـٰكُمْ وَمَا هُم بِحَـٰمِلِينَ
مِنْ خَطَـٰيَـٰهُم مِّن شَىْءٍ ۖ إِنَّهُمْ لَكَـٰذِبُونَ ﴿١٢﴾

13. They will bear their own burdens, and (other) burdens along with their own, and on the day of judgement they will be called to account for their falsehoods.

وَلَيَحْمِلُنَّ أَثْقَالَهُمْ وَأَثْقَالًا مَّعَ أَثْقَالِهِمْ ۖ وَلَيُسْـَٔلُنَّ
يَوْمَ ٱلْقِيَـٰمَةِ عَمَّا كَانُوا۟ يَفْتَرُونَ ﴿١٣﴾

14. We (once) sent Noah to his people, and he stayed among them a thousand years less fifty: but the deluge overwhelmed them while they (persisted in) sin.

وَلَقَدْ أَرْسَلْنَا نُوحًا إِلَىٰ قَوْمِهِۦ فَلَبِثَ فِيهِمْ أَلْفَ
سَنَةٍ إِلَّا خَمْسِينَ عَامًا فَأَخَذَهُمُ ٱلطُّوفَانُ
وَهُمْ ظَـٰلِمُونَ ﴿١٤﴾

15. But We saved him and the companions of the ark, and We made the (ark) a sign for all peoples!

فَأَنجَيْنَـٰهُ وَأَصْحَـٰبَ ٱلسَّفِينَةِ وَجَعَلْنَـٰهَآ ءَايَةً
لِّلْعَـٰلَمِينَ ﴿١٥﴾

16. And (We also saved) Abraham: See, he said to his people: "Serve Allah and fear Him: that will be best for you - if you understand!

وَإِبْرَٰهِيمَ إِذْ قَالَ لِقَوْمِهِ ٱعْبُدُوا۟ ٱللَّهَ وَٱتَّقُوهُ ۖ
ذَٰلِكُمْ خَيْرٌ لَّكُمْ إِن كُنتُمْ تَعْلَمُونَ ﴿١٦﴾

17. For you do worship idols besides Allah, and you invent falsehood. The things that you worship besides Allah have no power to give you sustenance; then seek you sustenance from Allah, serve Him, and be grateful to Him: to Him will be your return.

إِنَّمَا تَعْبُدُونَ مِن دُونِ ٱللَّهِ أَوْثَـٰنًا وَتَخْلُقُونَ
إِفْكًا ۚ إِنَّ ٱلَّذِينَ تَعْبُدُونَ مِن دُونِ ٱللَّهِ
لَا يَمْلِكُونَ لَكُمْ رِزْقًا فَٱبْتَغُوا۟ عِندَ ٱللَّهِ ٱلرِّزْقَ
وَٱعْبُدُوهُ وَٱشْكُرُوا۟ لَهُۥٓ ۖ إِلَيْهِ تُرْجَعُونَ ﴿١٧﴾

18. And if you reject (the message) so did generations before you; and the duty of the messenger is only to preach publicly (and clearly)."

وَإِن تُكَذِّبُوا۟ فَقَدْ كَذَّبَ أُمَمٌ مِّن قَبْلِكُمْ ۖ
وَمَا عَلَى ٱلرَّسُولِ إِلَّا ٱلْبَلَـٰغُ ٱلْمُبِينُ ﴿١٨﴾

19. Do they not see how Allah originates creation, then repeats it: truly that is easy for Allah.

أَوَلَمْ يَرَوْا۟ كَيْفَ يُبْدِئُ ٱللَّهُ ٱلْخَلْقَ ثُمَّ
يُعِيدُهُۥٓ ۚ إِنَّ ذَٰلِكَ عَلَى ٱللَّهِ يَسِيرٌ ﴿١٩﴾

20. Say: "Travel through the earth and see how Allah did originate creation: so will Allah produce a later creation: for Allah has power over all things."

قُلْ سِيرُوا۟ فِى ٱلْأَرْضِ فَٱنظُرُوا۟ كَيْفَ بَدَأَ ٱلْخَلْقَ ۚ
ثُمَّ ٱللَّهُ يُنشِئُ ٱلنَّشْأَةَ ٱلْـَٔاخِرَةَ ۚ إِنَّ ٱللَّهَ عَلَىٰ كُلِّ
شَىْءٍ قَدِيرٌ ٢٠

21. "He punishes whom He pleases, and He grants mercy to whom He pleases, and towards Him are you turned."

يُعَذِّبُ مَن يَشَآءُ وَيَرْحَمُ مَن يَشَآءُ ۖ وَإِلَيْهِ
تُقْلَبُونَ ٢١

22. "Not on earth nor in heaven will you be able (fleeing) to frustrate (His plan), nor have you besides Allah, any protector or helper."

وَمَآ أَنتُم بِمُعْجِزِينَ فِى ٱلْأَرْضِ وَلَا فِى
ٱلسَّمَآءِ ۖ وَمَا لَكُم مِّن دُونِ ٱللَّهِ مِن وَلِىٍّ
وَلَا نَصِيرٍ ٢٢

23. Those who reject the signs of Allah and the meeting with Him (in the hereafter) - it is they who shall despair of My mercy: it is they who will (suffer) a most grievous penalty.

وَٱلَّذِينَ كَفَرُوا۟ بِـَٔايَٰتِ ٱللَّهِ وَلِقَآئِهِۦٓ أُو۟لَٰٓئِكَ
يَئِسُوا۟ مِن رَّحْمَتِى وَأُو۟لَٰٓئِكَ لَهُمْ عَذَابٌ أَلِيمٌ ٢٣

24. So nothing was the answer of (Abraham's) people except that they said: "Slay him or burn him." But Allah did save him from the fire: verily in this are signs for people who believe.

فَمَا كَانَ جَوَابَ قَوْمِهِۦٓ إِلَّآ أَن قَالُوا۟ ٱقْتُلُوهُ
أَوْ حَرِّقُوهُ فَأَنجَىٰهُ ٱللَّهُ مِنَ ٱلنَّارِ ۚ إِنَّ فِى ذَٰلِكَ
لَءَايَٰتٍ لِّقَوْمٍ يُؤْمِنُونَ ٢٤

25. And he said: "For you, you have taken (for worship) idols besides Allah, out of mutual love and regard between yourselves in this life; but on the day of judgement you shall disown each other and curse each other: and your abode will be the fire, and you shall have none to help.

وَقَالَ إِنَّمَا ٱتَّخَذْتُم مِّن دُونِ ٱللَّهِ أَوْثَٰنًا مَّوَدَّةَ
بَيْنِكُمْ فِى ٱلْحَيَوٰةِ ٱلدُّنْيَا ۖ ثُمَّ يَوْمَ ٱلْقِيَٰمَةِ
يَكْفُرُ بَعْضُكُم بِبَعْضٍ وَيَلْعَنُ بَعْضُكُم
بَعْضًا وَمَأْوَىٰكُمُ ٱلنَّارُ وَمَا لَكُم
مِّن نَّٰصِرِينَ ٢٥

26. But Lot had faith in him; he said: "I will leave home for the sake of my Lord: for He

۞ فَـَٔامَنَ لَهُۥ لُوطٌ ۘ وَقَالَ إِنِّى مُهَاجِرٌ إِلَىٰ

ة أرباع
زب
٤

is Exalted in Might, and Wise."

رَبِّيٓۖ إِنَّهُۥ هُوَ ٱلۡعَزِيزُ ٱلۡحَكِيمُ ٢٦

27. And We gave (Abraham) Isaac and Jacob, and ordained among his progeny prophethood and revelation, and We granted him his reward in this life; and he was in the hereafter (of the company) of the righteous.

وَوَهَبۡنَا لَهُۥٓ إِسۡحَٰقَ وَيَعۡقُوبَ وَجَعَلۡنَا
فِي ذُرِّيَّتِهِ ٱلنُّبُوَّةَ وَٱلۡكِتَٰبَ وَءَاتَيۡنَٰهُ
أَجۡرَهُۥ فِي ٱلدُّنۡيَاۖ وَإِنَّهُۥ فِي ٱلۡأٓخِرَةِ لَمِنَ
ٱلصَّٰلِحِينَ ٢٧

28. And (remember) Lot: see, he said to his people: "You do commit lewdness, such as no people in creation (ever) committed before you."

وَلُوطًا إِذۡ قَالَ لِقَوۡمِهِۦٓ إِنَّكُمۡ لَتَأۡتُونَ
ٱلۡفَٰحِشَةَ مَا سَبَقَكُم بِهَا مِنۡ أَحَدٖ
مِّنَ ٱلۡعَٰلَمِينَ ٢٨

29. "Do you indeed approach men and cut off the highway? - And practice wickedness (even) in your councils?" But his people gave no answer but this: they said: "Bring us the wrath of Allah if you tell the truth."

أَئِنَّكُمۡ لَتَأۡتُونَ ٱلرِّجَالَ وَتَقۡطَعُونَ ٱلسَّبِيلَ
وَتَأۡتُونَ فِي نَادِيكُمُ ٱلۡمُنكَرَۖ فَمَا كَانَ جَوَابَ
قَوۡمِهِۦٓ إِلَّآ أَن قَالُواْ ٱئۡتِنَا بِعَذَابِ ٱللَّهِ إِن
كُنتَ مِنَ ٱلصَّٰدِقِينَ ٢٩

30. He said: "O my Lord! Help You me against people who do mischief!"

قَالَ رَبِّ ٱنصُرۡنِي عَلَى ٱلۡقَوۡمِ ٱلۡمُفۡسِدِينَ ٣٠

31. When Our messengers came to Abraham with the good news, they said: "We are indeed going to destroy the people of this township: for truly they are (addicted to) crime."

وَلَمَّا جَآءَتۡ رُسُلُنَآ إِبۡرَٰهِيمَ بِٱلۡبُشۡرَىٰ قَالُوٓاْ إِنَّا
مُهۡلِكُوٓاْ أَهۡلِ هَٰذِهِ ٱلۡقَرۡيَةِۖ إِنَّ أَهۡلَهَا
كَانُواْ ظَٰلِمِينَ ٣١

32. He said: "But there is Lot there." They said: "Well do we know who is there; we will certainly save him and his following - except his wife; she is of those who lag behind!"

قَالَ إِنَّ فِيهَا لُوطٗاۚ قَالُواْ نَحۡنُ أَعۡلَمُ بِمَن فِيهَاۖ
لَنُنَجِّيَنَّهُۥ وَأَهۡلَهُۥٓ إِلَّا ٱمۡرَأَتَهُۥ كَانَتۡ مِنَ
ٱلۡغَٰبِرِينَ ٣٢

33. And when Our messengers came to Lot,

وَلَمَّآ أَن جَآءَتۡ رُسُلُنَا لُوطٗا سِيٓءَ بِهِمۡ

he was grieved on their account, and felt himself powerless (to protect) them: but they said "Fear you not, nor grieve: we are (here) to save you and your following, except your wife: she is of those who lag behind.

وَضَاقَ بِهِمْ ذَرْعًا ۖ وَقَالُوا۟ لَا تَخَفْ وَلَا
تَحْزَنْ إِنَّا مُنَجُّوكَ وَأَهْلَكَ إِلَّا ٱمْرَأَتَكَ
كَانَتْ مِنَ ٱلْغَٰبِرِينَ ﴿٣٣﴾

34. For we are going to bring down on the people of this township a punishment from heaven, because they have been wickedly rebellious."

إِنَّا مُنزِلُونَ عَلَىٰٓ أَهْلِ هَٰذِهِ ٱلْقَرْيَةِ رِجْزًا مِّنَ
ٱلسَّمَآءِ بِمَا كَانُوا۟ يَفْسُقُونَ ﴿٣٤﴾

35. And We have left of it an evident sign, for any people who (care to) understand.

وَلَقَد تَّرَكْنَا مِنْهَآ ءَايَةًۢ بَيِّنَةً لِّقَوْمٍ
يَعْقِلُونَ ﴿٣٥﴾

36. To the Madyan (people) (We sent) their brother Shu'ayb. Then he said: "O my people! Serve Allah, and fear the last day: nor commit evil on the earth with intent to do mischief."

وَإِلَىٰ مَدْيَنَ أَخَاهُمْ شُعَيْبًا فَقَالَ يَٰقَوْمِ ٱعْبُدُوا۟
ٱللَّهَ وَٱرْجُوا۟ ٱلْيَوْمَ ٱلْءَاخِرَ وَلَا تَعْثَوْا۟ فِى
ٱلْأَرْضِ مُفْسِدِينَ ﴿٣٦﴾

37. But they rejected him: then the mighty blast seized them, and they lay prostrate in their homes by the morning.

فَكَذَّبُوهُ فَأَخَذَتْهُمُ ٱلرَّجْفَةُ فَأَصْبَحُوا۟ فِى
دَارِهِمْ جَٰثِمِينَ ﴿٣٧﴾

38. Remember also the 'Ad and the Thamud (people): clearly will appear to you from (the traces) of their buildings (their fate): the evil one made their deeds alluring to them, and kept them back from the path, though they were gifted with intelligence and skill.

وَعَادًا وَثَمُودَا۟ وَقَد تَّبَيَّنَ لَكُم مِّن
مَّسَٰكِنِهِمْ ۖ وَزَيَّنَ لَهُمُ ٱلشَّيْطَٰنُ
أَعْمَٰلَهُمْ فَصَدَّهُمْ عَنِ ٱلسَّبِيلِ وَكَانُوا۟
مُسْتَبْصِرِينَ ﴿٣٨﴾

39. (Remember also) Qarun, Pharaoh, and Haman: there came to them Moses with clear signs, but they behaved with insolence on the earth; yet they could not overreach (Us).

وَقَٰرُونَ وَفِرْعَوْنَ وَهَٰمَٰنَ ۖ وَلَقَدْ جَآءَهُم مُّوسَىٰ
بِٱلْبَيِّنَٰتِ فَٱسْتَكْبَرُوا۟ فِى ٱلْأَرْضِ وَمَا
كَانُوا۟ سَٰبِقِينَ ﴿٣٩﴾

40. Each one of them We seized for his crime: of them, against some We sent a violent tornado (with showers of stones); some were caught by a (mighty) blast; some We caused the earth to swallow up; and some We drowned (in the waters); it was not Allah Who injured (or oppressed) them; they injured (and oppressed) their own souls.

فَكُلًّا أَخَذْنَا بِذَنۢبِهِۦ ۖ فَمِنْهُم مَّنْ أَرْسَلْنَا
عَلَيْهِ حَاصِبًا وَمِنْهُم مَّنْ أَخَذَتْهُ ٱلصَّيْحَةُ
وَمِنْهُم مَّنْ خَسَفْنَا بِهِ ٱلْأَرْضَ وَمِنْهُم مَّنْ
أَغْرَقْنَا ۚ وَمَا كَانَ ٱللَّهُ لِيَظْلِمَهُمْ وَلَٰكِن
كَانُوٓا۟ أَنفُسَهُمْ يَظْلِمُونَ ٤٠

41. The parable of those who take protectors other than Allah is that of the spider who builds (to itself) a house; but truly the flimsiest of houses is the spider's house - if they but knew.

مَثَلُ ٱلَّذِينَ ٱتَّخَذُوا۟ مِن دُونِ ٱللَّهِ أَوْلِيَآءَ
كَمَثَلِ ٱلْعَنكَبُوتِ ٱتَّخَذَتْ بَيْتًا ۖ وَإِنَّ
أَوْهَنَ ٱلْبُيُوتِ لَبَيْتُ ٱلْعَنكَبُوتِ ۖ لَوْ كَانُوا۟
يَعْلَمُونَ ٤١

42. Verily Allah does know of (everything) whatever that they call upon besides Him: and He is Exalted (in Power), Wise.

إِنَّ ٱللَّهَ يَعْلَمُ مَا يَدْعُونَ مِن دُونِهِۦ مِن شَىْءٍ ۚ
وَهُوَ ٱلْعَزِيزُ ٱلْحَكِيمُ ٤٢

43. And such are the parables We set for mankind, but only those understand them who have knowledge.

وَتِلْكَ ٱلْأَمْثَٰلُ نَضْرِبُهَا لِلنَّاسِ ۖ وَمَا يَعْقِلُهَآ
إِلَّا ٱلْعَٰلِمُونَ ٤٣

44. Allah created the heavens and the earth in true (proportions): verily in that is a sign for those who believe.

خَلَقَ ٱللَّهُ ٱلسَّمَٰوَٰتِ وَٱلْأَرْضَ بِٱلْحَقِّ ۚ إِنَّ فِى
ذَٰلِكَ لَءَايَةً لِّلْمُؤْمِنِينَ ٤٤

45. Recite what is sent of the book by inspiration to you, and establish regular prayer: for prayer restrains from shameful and unjust deeds; and remembrance of Allah is the greatest (thing in life) without doubt. And Allah knows the (deeds) that you do.

ٱتْلُ مَآ أُوحِىَ إِلَيْكَ مِنَ ٱلْكِتَٰبِ وَأَقِمِ ٱلصَّلَوٰةَ ۖ
إِنَّ ٱلصَّلَوٰةَ تَنْهَىٰ عَنِ ٱلْفَحْشَآءِ
وَٱلْمُنكَرِ ۗ وَلَذِكْرُ ٱللَّهِ أَكْبَرُ ۗ وَٱللَّهُ يَعْلَمُ
مَا تَصْنَعُونَ ٤٥

✻ **46.** And do not dispute with the People of the Book, except with means better (than

الجزء ٢١ الحزب ٤١ ✻ وَلَا تُجَٰدِلُوٓا۟ أَهْلَ ٱلْكِتَٰبِ إِلَّا بِٱلَّتِى هِىَ

✻ Part-21

mere disputation), unless it be with those of them who inflict wrong (and injury); but say "We believe in the revelation which has come down to us and in that which came down to you; our God and your God is one; and it is to Him we bow (in Islam)."

أَحۡسَنُ إِلَّا ٱلَّذِينَ ظَلَمُواْ مِنۡهُمۡۖ وَقُولُوٓاْ ءَامَنَّا
بِٱلَّذِيٓ أُنزِلَ إِلَيۡنَا وَأُنزِلَ إِلَيۡكُمۡ وَإِلَٰهُنَا
وَإِلَٰهُكُمۡ وَٰحِدٞ وَنَحۡنُ لَهُۥ مُسۡلِمُونَ ٤٦

47. And thus (it is) that We have sent down the book to you. So the People of the Book believe in it, as also do some of these (pagan Arabs); and none but unbelievers reject Our signs.

وَكَذَٰلِكَ أَنزَلۡنَآ إِلَيۡكَ ٱلۡكِتَٰبَۚ فَٱلَّذِينَ
ءَاتَيۡنَٰهُمُ ٱلۡكِتَٰبَ يُؤۡمِنُونَ بِهِۦۖ وَمِنۡ
هَٰٓؤُلَآءِ مَن يُؤۡمِنُ بِهِۦۚ وَمَا يَجۡحَدُ بِـَٔايَٰتِنَآ
إِلَّا ٱلۡكَٰفِرُونَ ٤٧

48. And you were not (able) to recite a book before this (book came), nor are you (able) to transcribe it with your right hand; in that case, indeed, would the talkers of vanities have doubted.

وَمَا كُنتَ تَتۡلُواْ مِن قَبۡلِهِۦ مِن كِتَٰبٖ وَلَا
تَخُطُّهُۥ بِيَمِينِكَۖ إِذٗا لَّٱرۡتَابَ ٱلۡمُبۡطِلُونَ ٤٨

49. Nay, here are signs self-evident in the hearts of those endowed with knowledge; and none but the unjust rejects Our signs.

بَلۡ هُوَ ءَايَٰتُۢ بَيِّنَٰتٞ فِي صُدُورِ ٱلَّذِينَ أُوتُواْ
ٱلۡعِلۡمَۚ وَمَا يَجۡحَدُ بِـَٔايَٰتِنَآ إِلَّا ٱلظَّٰلِمُونَ ٤٩

50. Yet they say: "Why are not signs sent down to him from his Lord?" Say: "The signs are indeed with Allah; and I am indeed a clear warner."

وَقَالُواْ لَوۡلَآ أُنزِلَ عَلَيۡهِ ءَايَٰتٞ مِّن رَّبِّهِۦۖ قُلۡ إِنَّمَا
ٱلۡأٓيَٰتُ عِندَ ٱللَّهِ وَإِنَّمَآ أَنَا۠ نَذِيرٞ مُّبِينٌ ٥٠

51. And is it not enough for them that We have sent down to you the book which is rehearsed to them? Verily, in it is mercy and a reminder to those who believe.

أَوَلَمۡ يَكۡفِهِمۡ أَنَّآ أَنزَلۡنَا عَلَيۡكَ ٱلۡكِتَٰبَ يُتۡلَىٰ
عَلَيۡهِمۡۚ إِنَّ فِي ذَٰلِكَ لَرَحۡمَةٗ وَذِكۡرَىٰ
لِقَوۡمٖ يُؤۡمِنُونَ ٥١

52. Say: "Enough is Allah for a witness between me and you: He knows what is in the heavens and on earth. And it is those who believe in vanities and reject Allah, that will perish (in the end)."

قُلۡ كَفَىٰ بِٱللَّهِ بَيۡنِي وَبَيۡنَكُمۡ شَهِيدٗاۖ يَعۡلَمُ
مَا فِي ٱلسَّمَٰوَٰتِ وَٱلۡأَرۡضِۗ وَٱلَّذِينَ ءَامَنُواْ بِٱلۡبَٰطِلِ
وَكَفَرُواْ بِٱللَّهِ أُوْلَٰٓئِكَ هُمُ ٱلۡخَٰسِرُونَ ٥٢

53. They ask you to hasten on the punishment (for them): had it not been for a term (of respite) appointed, the punishment would certainly have come to them: and it will certainly reach them - of a sudden while they perceive not!

وَيَسْتَعْجِلُونَكَ بِٱلْعَذَابِ وَلَوْلَآ أَجَلٌ مُّسَمًّى لَّجَآءَهُمُ
ٱلْعَذَابُ وَلَيَأْتِيَنَّهُم بَغْتَةً وَهُمْ لَا يَشْعُرُونَ ﴿٥٣﴾

54. They ask you to hasten on the punishment: but certainly, hell will encompass the rejecters of faith! -

يَسْتَعْجِلُونَكَ بِٱلْعَذَابِ وَإِنَّ جَهَنَّمَ لَمُحِيطَةٌۢ
بِٱلْكَٰفِرِينَ ﴿٥٤﴾

55. On the day that the punishment shall cover them from above them and from below them, and (a voice) shall say: "Taste you (the fruits) of your deeds!"

يَوْمَ يَغْشَىٰهُمُ ٱلْعَذَابُ مِن فَوْقِهِمْ وَمِن تَحْتِ
أَرْجُلِهِمْ وَيَقُولُ ذُوقُوا۟ مَا كُنتُمْ تَعْمَلُونَ ﴿٥٥﴾

56. O My servants who believe! Truly spacious is My earth: therefore serve you Me - (and Me alone)!

يَٰعِبَادِىَ ٱلَّذِينَ ءَامَنُوٓا۟ إِنَّ أَرْضِى وَٰسِعَةٌ فَإِيَّٰىَ
فَٱعْبُدُونِ ﴿٥٦﴾

57. Every soul shall have a taste of death: in the end to Us shall you be brought back.

كُلُّ نَفْسٍ ذَآئِقَةُ ٱلْمَوْتِ ثُمَّ إِلَيْنَا تُرْجَعُونَ ﴿٥٧﴾

58. But those who believe and work deeds of righteousness - to them shall We give a home in heaven - lofty mansions beneath which flow rivers - to dwell in it for ever - an excellent reward for those who do (good)! -

وَٱلَّذِينَ ءَامَنُوا۟ وَعَمِلُوا۟ ٱلصَّٰلِحَٰتِ لَنُبَوِّئَنَّهُم مِّنَ
ٱلْجَنَّةِ غُرَفًا تَجْرِى مِن تَحْتِهَا ٱلْأَنْهَٰرُ خَٰلِدِينَ فِيهَا
نِعْمَ أَجْرُ ٱلْعَٰمِلِينَ ﴿٥٨﴾

59. Those who persevere in patience, and put their trust in their Lord and Cherisher.

ٱلَّذِينَ صَبَرُوا۟ وَعَلَىٰ رَبِّهِمْ يَتَوَكَّلُونَ ﴿٥٩﴾

60. How many are the creatures that carry not their own sustenance? It is Allah Who feeds (both) them and you, for He hears and knows (all things).

وَكَأَيِّن مِّن دَآبَّةٍ لَّا تَحْمِلُ رِزْقَهَا ٱللَّهُ يَرْزُقُهَا
وَإِيَّاكُمْ وَهُوَ ٱلسَّمِيعُ ٱلْعَلِيمُ ﴿٦٠﴾

61. If indeed you ask them who has created the heavens and the earth, and subjected the

وَلَئِن سَأَلْتَهُم مَّنْ خَلَقَ ٱلسَّمَٰوَٰتِ وَٱلْأَرْضَ

sun and the moon (to His law); they will certainly reply "Allah." How are they then deluded away (from the truth)?

وَسَخَّرَ ٱلشَّمْسَ وَٱلْقَمَرَ لَيَقُولُنَّ ٱللَّهُ ۖ فَأَنَّىٰ يُؤْفَكُونَ ٦١

62. Allah enlarges the sustenance (which He gives) to whichever of His servants He pleases; and He (similarly) grants by (strict) measure, (as He pleases): for Allah has full knowledge of all things.

ٱللَّهُ يَبْسُطُ ٱلرِّزْقَ لِمَن يَشَآءُ مِنْ عِبَادِهِۦ وَيَقْدِرُ لَهُۥٓ ۚ
إِنَّ ٱللَّهَ بِكُلِّ شَىْءٍ عَلِيمٌ ٦٢

63. And if indeed you ask them who it is that sends down rain from the sky, and gives life with it to the earth after its death, they will certainly reply, "Allah!" Say, "Praise be to Allah!" But most of them understand not.

وَلَئِن سَأَلْتَهُم مَّن نَّزَّلَ مِنَ ٱلسَّمَآءِ مَآءً فَأَحْيَا
بِهِ ٱلْأَرْضَ مِنۢ بَعْدِ مَوْتِهَا لَيَقُولُنَّ ٱللَّهُ ۚ قُلِ ٱلْحَمْدُ
لِلَّهِ ۚ بَلْ أَكْثَرُهُمْ لَا يَعْقِلُونَ ٦٣

64. What is the life of this world but amusement and play? But verily the home in the hereafter - that is life indeed if they but knew.

وَمَا هَٰذِهِ ٱلْحَيَوٰةُ ٱلدُّنْيَآ إِلَّا لَهْوٌ وَلَعِبٌ ۚ وَإِنَّ
ٱلدَّارَ ٱلْءَاخِرَةَ لَهِىَ ٱلْحَيَوَانُ ۚ لَوْ كَانُوا۟ يَعْلَمُونَ ٦٤

65. Now, if they embark on a boat, they call on Allah making their devotion sincerely (and exclusively) to Him; but when He had delivered them safely to (dry) land, See, they give a share (of their worship to others)! -

فَإِذَا رَكِبُوا۟ فِى ٱلْفُلْكِ دَعَوُا۟ ٱللَّهَ مُخْلِصِينَ لَهُ ٱلدِّينَ
فَلَمَّا نَجَّىٰهُمْ إِلَى ٱلْبَرِّ إِذَا هُمْ يُشْرِكُونَ ٦٥

66. Disdaining ungratefully Our gifts, and giving themselves up to (worldly) enjoyment! But soon will they know.

لِيَكْفُرُوا۟ بِمَآ ءَاتَيْنَٰهُمْ وَلِيَتَمَتَّعُوا۟ ۖ فَسَوْفَ
يَعْلَمُونَ ٦٦

67. Do they not then see that We have made a sanctuary secure, and that men are being snatched away from all around them? Then, do they believe in that which is vain, and reject the grace of Allah!

أَوَلَمْ يَرَوْا۟ أَنَّا جَعَلْنَا حَرَمًا ءَامِنًا وَيُتَخَطَّفُ
ٱلنَّاسُ مِنْ حَوْلِهِمْ ۚ أَفَبِٱلْبَٰطِلِ يُؤْمِنُونَ وَبِنِعْمَةِ
ٱللَّهِ يَكْفُرُونَ ٦٧

68. And who does more wrong than he who invents a lie against Allah or rejects the truth when it reaches Him? Is there not a home in hell for those who reject faith?

وَمَنْ أَظْلَمُ مِمَّنِ ٱفْتَرَىٰ عَلَى ٱللَّهِ كَذِبًا أَوْ كَذَّبَ بِٱلْحَقِّ
لَمَّا جَآءَهُۥٓ ۚ أَلَيْسَ فِى جَهَنَّمَ مَثْوًى لِّلْكَٰفِرِينَ ٦٨

69. And those who strive in Our (cause) - We will certainly guide them to Our paths: for verily Allah is with those who do right.

وَٱلَّذِينَ جَٰهَدُوا۟ فِينَا لَنَهْدِيَنَّهُمْ سُبُلَنَا ۚ وَإِنَّ
ٱللَّهَ لَمَعَ ٱلْمُحْسِنِينَ ﴿٦٩﴾

سُورَةُ الرُّومِ

Surah 30: ***Ar-Rum*** **(The Romans)**

In the name of Allah,
Most Gracious, Most Merciful.

بِسْمِ ٱللَّهِ ٱلرَّحْمَٰنِ ٱلرَّحِيمِ

1. *Alif Lam Mim.*

ربع الحزب ٤١ الٓمٓ ﴿١﴾

2. The Roman empire has been defeated -

غُلِبَتِ ٱلرُّومُ ﴿٢﴾

3. In a land close by: but they, (even) after (this) defeat of theirs, will soon be victorious -

فِىٓ أَدْنَى ٱلْأَرْضِ وَهُم مِّنۢ بَعْدِ غَلَبِهِمْ
سَيَغْلِبُونَ ﴿٣﴾

4. Within a few years. With Allah is the decision, in the past and in the future: on that day shall the believers rejoice -

فِى بِضْعِ سِنِينَ ۗ لِلَّهِ ٱلْأَمْرُ مِن قَبْلُ وَمِنۢ بَعْدُ ۚ
وَيَوْمَئِذٍ يَفْرَحُ ٱلْمُؤْمِنُونَ ﴿٤﴾

5. With the help of Allah. He helps whom He will, and He is Exalted in Might, Most Merciful.

بِنَصْرِ ٱللَّهِ ۚ يَنصُرُ مَن يَشَآءُ ۖ وَهُوَ ٱلْعَزِيزُ
ٱلرَّحِيمُ ﴿٥﴾

6. (It is) the promise of Allah. Never does Allah depart from His promise: but most men understand not.

وَعْدَ ٱللَّهِ ۖ لَا يُخْلِفُ ٱللَّهُ وَعْدَهُۥ وَلَٰكِنَّ أَكْثَرَ ٱلنَّاسِ
لَا يَعْلَمُونَ ﴿٦﴾

7. They know but the outer (things) in the life of this world: but of the end of things they are heedless.

يَعْلَمُونَ ظَٰهِرًا مِّنَ ٱلْحَيَوٰةِ ٱلدُّنْيَا وَهُمْ عَنِ
ٱلْءَاخِرَةِ هُمْ غَٰفِلُونَ ﴿٧﴾

8. Do they not reflect in their own minds? Not but for just ends and for a term appointed

أَوَلَمْ يَتَفَكَّرُوا۟ فِىٓ أَنفُسِهِم ۗ مَّا خَلَقَ ٱللَّهُ ٱلسَّمَٰوَٰتِ

did Allah create the heavens and the earth, and all between them: yet are there truly many among men who deny the meeting with their Lord (at the resurrection)!

وَٱلۡأَرۡضَ وَمَا بَيۡنَهُمَآ إِلَّا بِٱلۡحَقِّ وَأَجَلٖ مُّسَمّٗىۗ
وَإِنَّ كَثِيرٗا مِّنَ ٱلنَّاسِ بِلِقَآيِٕ رَبِّهِمۡ لَكَٰفِرُونَ ٨

9. Do they not travel through the earth, and see what was the end of those before them? They were superior to them in strength; they tilled the soil and populated it in greater numbers than these have done; there came to them their messengers with clear (signs) (which they rejected to their own destruction): it was not Allah Who wronged them, but they wronged their own souls.

أَوَلَمۡ يَسِيرُواْ فِي ٱلۡأَرۡضِ فَيَنظُرُواْ كَيۡفَ كَانَ
عَٰقِبَةُ ٱلَّذِينَ مِن قَبۡلِهِمۡۚ كَانُوٓاْ أَشَدَّ مِنۡهُمۡ قُوَّةٗ
وَأَثَارُواْ ٱلۡأَرۡضَ وَعَمَرُوهَآ أَكۡثَرَ مِمَّا
عَمَرُوهَا وَجَآءَتۡهُمۡ رُسُلُهُم بِٱلۡبَيِّنَٰتِۖ فَمَا
كَانَ ٱللَّهُ لِيَظۡلِمَهُمۡ وَلَٰكِن كَانُوٓاْ أَنفُسَهُمۡ
يَظۡلِمُونَ ٩

10. In the long run, evil in the extreme will be the end of those who do evil; for that they rejected the signs of Allah, and held them up to ridicule.

ثُمَّ كَانَ عَٰقِبَةَ ٱلَّذِينَ أَسَٰٓـُٔواْ ٱلسُّوٓأَىٰٓ أَن كَذَّبُواْ
بِـَٔايَٰتِ ٱللَّهِ وَكَانُواْ بِهَا يَسۡتَهۡزِءُونَ ١٠

11. It is Allah Who begins (the process of) creation; then repeats it; then shall you be brought back to Him.

ٱللَّهُ يَبۡدَؤُاْ ٱلۡخَلۡقَ ثُمَّ يُعِيدُهُۥ ثُمَّ إِلَيۡهِ تُرۡجَعُونَ ١١

12. On the day that the hour will be established, the guilty will be struck dumb with despair.

وَيَوۡمَ تَقُومُ ٱلسَّاعَةُ يُبۡلِسُ ٱلۡمُجۡرِمُونَ ١٢

13. No intercessor will they have among their "partners," and they will (themselves) reject their "partners."

وَلَمۡ يَكُن لَّهُم مِّن شُرَكَآئِهِمۡ شُفَعَٰٓؤُاْ وَكَانُواْ
بِشُرَكَآئِهِمۡ كَٰفِرِينَ ١٣

14. On the day that the hour will be established that day shall (all men) be sorted out.

وَيَوۡمَ تَقُومُ ٱلسَّاعَةُ يَوۡمَئِذٖ يَتَفَرَّقُونَ ١٤

15. Then those who have believed and worked righteous deeds, shall be made happy in a mead of delight.

فَأَمَّا ٱلَّذِينَ ءَامَنُواْ وَعَمِلُواْ ٱلصَّٰلِحَٰتِ فَهُمۡ فِي
رَوۡضَةٖ يُحۡبَرُونَ ١٥

16. And those who have rejected faith and falsely denied Our signs and the meeting of the hereafter - such shall be brought out to punishment.

وَأَمَّا ٱلَّذِينَ كَفَرُواْ وَكَذَّبُواْ بِـَٔايَٰتِنَا وَلِقَآيِٕ
ٱلۡأٓخِرَةِ فَأُوْلَٰٓئِكَ فِي ٱلۡعَذَابِ مُحۡضَرُونَ ١٦

17. So (give) glory to Allah, when you reach evening and when you rise in the morning;

فَسُبۡحَٰنَ ٱللَّهِ حِينَ تُمۡسُونَ وَحِينَ تُصۡبِحُونَ ١٧

18. Yea, to Him be praise in the heavens and on earth; and in the late afternoon and when the day begins to decline.

وَلَهُ ٱلۡحَمۡدُ فِي ٱلسَّمَٰوَٰتِ وَٱلۡأَرۡضِ وَعَشِيّٗا
وَحِينَ تُظۡهِرُونَ ١٨

19. It is He Who brings out the living from the dead, and brings out the dead from the living, and Who gives life to the earth after it is dead: and thus shall you be brought out (from the dead).

يُخۡرِجُ ٱلۡحَيَّ مِنَ ٱلۡمَيِّتِ وَيُخۡرِجُ ٱلۡمَيِّتَ مِنَ ٱلۡحَيِّ
وَيُحۡيِ ٱلۡأَرۡضَ بَعۡدَ مَوۡتِهَاۚ وَكَذَٰلِكَ تُخۡرَجُونَ ١٩

20. Among His signs is this, that He created you from dust; and then - See, you are men scattered (far and wide)!

وَمِنۡ ءَايَٰتِهِۦٓ أَنۡ خَلَقَكُم مِّن تُرَابٖ ثُمَّ إِذَآ
أَنتُم بَشَرٞ تَنتَشِرُونَ ٢٠

21. And among His signs is this, that He created for you mates from among yourselves, that you may dwell in tranquillity with them, and He has put love and mercy between your (hearts): verily in that are signs for those who reflect.

وَمِنۡ ءَايَٰتِهِۦٓ أَنۡ خَلَقَ لَكُم مِّنۡ أَنفُسِكُمۡ أَزۡوَٰجٗا
لِّتَسۡكُنُوٓاْ إِلَيۡهَا وَجَعَلَ بَيۡنَكُم مَّوَدَّةٗ وَرَحۡمَةًۚ
إِنَّ فِي ذَٰلِكَ لَأٓيَٰتٖ لِّقَوۡمٖ يَتَفَكَّرُونَ ٢١

22. And among His signs is the creation of the heavens and the earth, and the variations in your languages and your colours: verily in that are signs for those who know.

وَمِنۡ ءَايَٰتِهِۦ خَلۡقُ ٱلسَّمَٰوَٰتِ وَٱلۡأَرۡضِ وَٱخۡتِلَٰفُ
أَلۡسِنَتِكُمۡ وَأَلۡوَٰنِكُمۡۚ إِنَّ فِي ذَٰلِكَ لَأٓيَٰتٖ
لِّلۡعَٰلِمِينَ ٢٢

23. And among His signs is the sleep that you take by night and by day, and the quest that you (make for livelihood) out of His bounty: verily in that are signs for those who listen.

وَمِنۡ ءَايَٰتِهِۦ مَنَامُكُم بِٱلَّيۡلِ وَٱلنَّهَارِ وَٱبۡتِغَآؤُكُم
مِّن فَضۡلِهِۦٓۚ إِنَّ فِي ذَٰلِكَ لَأٓيَٰتٖ لِّقَوۡمٖ
يَسۡمَعُونَ ٢٣

24. And among His signs, He shows you the lightning, by way both of fear and of hope, and He sends down rain from the sky and with it gives life to the earth after it is dead: verily in that are signs for those who are wise.

وَمِنْ ءَايَٰتِهِۦ يُرِيكُمُ ٱلْبَرْقَ خَوْفًا وَطَمَعًا وَيُنَزِّلُ
مِنَ ٱلسَّمَآءِ مَآءً فَيُحْىِۦ بِهِ ٱلْأَرْضَ بَعْدَ مَوْتِهَآ ۚ
إِنَّ فِى ذَٰلِكَ لَءَايَٰتٍ لِّقَوْمٍ يَعْقِلُونَ ٢٤

25. And among His signs is this, that heaven and earth stand by His command: then when He calls you, by a single call, from the earth, see, you (straight away) come out.

وَمِنْ ءَايَٰتِهِۦٓ أَن تَقُومَ ٱلسَّمَآءُ وَٱلْأَرْضُ بِأَمْرِهِۦ ۚ ثُمَّ
إِذَا دَعَاكُمْ دَعْوَةً مِّنَ ٱلْأَرْضِ إِذَآ أَنتُمْ تَخْرُجُونَ ٢٥

26. To Him belongs every being that is in the heavens and on earth: all are devoutly obedient to Him.

وَلَهُۥ مَن فِى ٱلسَّمَٰوَٰتِ وَٱلْأَرْضِ ۖ كُلٌّ لَّهُۥ قَٰنِتُونَ ٢٦

27. It is He Who begins (the process of) creation; then repeats it; and for Him it is most easy. To Him belongs the loftiest similitude (we can think of) in the heavens and the earth: for He is Exalted in Might, Full of wisdom.

وَهُوَ ٱلَّذِى يَبْدَؤُا۟ ٱلْخَلْقَ ثُمَّ يُعِيدُهُۥ وَهُوَ أَهْوَنُ
عَلَيْهِ ۚ وَلَهُ ٱلْمَثَلُ ٱلْأَعْلَىٰ فِى ٱلسَّمَٰوَٰتِ وَٱلْأَرْضِ ۚ
وَهُوَ ٱلْعَزِيزُ ٱلْحَكِيمُ ٢٧

28. He does present to you a similitude from your own (experience): do you have partners among those whom your right hands possess, to share as equals in the wealth We have bestowed on you? Do you fear them as you fear each other? Thus do We explain the signs in detail to a people that understand.

ضَرَبَ لَكُم مَّثَلًا مِّنْ أَنفُسِكُمْ ۖ هَل لَّكُم
مِّن مَّا مَلَكَتْ أَيْمَٰنُكُم مِّن شُرَكَآءَ فِى
مَا رَزَقْنَٰكُمْ فَأَنتُمْ فِيهِ سَوَآءٌ تَخَافُونَهُمْ
كَخِيفَتِكُمْ أَنفُسَكُمْ ۚ كَذَٰلِكَ نُفَصِّلُ
ٱلْءَايَٰتِ لِقَوْمٍ يَعْقِلُونَ ٢٨

29. Nay, the wrongdoers (merely) follow their own lusts, being devoid of knowledge. But who will guide those whom Allah leaves astray? To them there will be no helpers.

بَلِ ٱتَّبَعَ ٱلَّذِينَ ظَلَمُوٓا۟ أَهْوَآءَهُم بِغَيْرِ عِلْمٍ ۖ فَمَن
يَهْدِى مَنْ أَضَلَّ ٱللَّهُ ۖ وَمَا لَهُم مِّن نَّٰصِرِينَ ٢٩

30. So set you your face steadily and truly to the faith: (establish) Allah's handiwork according to the pattern on which He has

فَأَقِمْ وَجْهَكَ لِلدِّينِ حَنِيفًا ۚ فِطْرَتَ ٱللَّهِ ٱلَّتِى

made mankind: no change (let there be) in the work (wrought) by Allah: that is the standard religion: but most among mankind understand not.

فَطَرَ ٱلنَّاسَ عَلَيْهَا ۚ لَا تَبْدِيلَ لِخَلْقِ ٱللَّهِ ۚ ذَٰلِكَ
ٱلدِّينُ ٱلْقَيِّمُ وَلَٰكِنَّ أَكْثَرَ ٱلنَّاسِ لَا يَعْلَمُونَ ﴿٣٠﴾

31. Turn you back in repentance to Him, and fear Him: establish regular prayers, and be not you among those who join gods with Allah -

نصف الحزب ٤١
۞ مُنِيبِينَ إِلَيْهِ وَٱتَّقُوهُ وَأَقِيمُوا۟ ٱلصَّلَوٰةَ وَلَا
تَكُونُوا۟ مِنَ ٱلْمُشْرِكِينَ ﴿٣١﴾

32. Those who split up their religion, and become (mere) sects - each party rejoicing in that which is with itself!

مِنَ ٱلَّذِينَ فَرَّقُوا۟ دِينَهُمْ وَكَانُوا۟ شِيَعًا ۖ كُلُّ
حِزْبٍۭ بِمَا لَدَيْهِمْ فَرِحُونَ ﴿٣٢﴾

33. When trouble touches men, they cry to their Lord, turning back to Him in repentance: but when He gives them a taste of mercy as from Himself, see, some of them pay part-worship to other gods besides their Lord -

وَإِذَا مَسَّ ٱلنَّاسَ ضُرٌّ دَعَوْا۟ رَبَّهُم مُّنِيبِينَ إِلَيْهِ ثُمَّ
إِذَآ أَذَاقَهُم مِّنْهُ رَحْمَةً إِذَا فَرِيقٌ مِّنْهُم بِرَبِّهِمْ
يُشْرِكُونَ ﴿٣٣﴾

34. (As if) to show their ingratitude for the (favours) We have bestowed on them! Then enjoy (your brief day); but soon will you know (your folly).

لِيَكْفُرُوا۟ بِمَآ ءَاتَيْنَٰهُمْ ۚ فَتَمَتَّعُوا۟ فَسَوْفَ
تَعْلَمُونَ ﴿٣٤﴾

35. Or have We sent down authority to them, which points out to them the things to which they pay part-worship?

أَمْ أَنزَلْنَا عَلَيْهِمْ سُلْطَٰنًا فَهُوَ يَتَكَلَّمُ بِمَا كَانُوا۟
بِهِۦ يُشْرِكُونَ ﴿٣٥﴾

36. When We give men a taste of mercy, they exult at it: and when some evil afflicts them because of what their (own) hands have sent before, see, they are in despair!

وَإِذَآ أَذَقْنَا ٱلنَّاسَ رَحْمَةً فَرِحُوا۟ بِهَا ۖ وَإِن تُصِبْهُمْ
سَيِّئَةٌۢ بِمَا قَدَّمَتْ أَيْدِيهِمْ إِذَا هُمْ يَقْنَطُونَ ﴿٣٦﴾

37. Do they not see that Allah enlarges the provision and restricts it, to whomsoever He pleases? Verily in that are signs for those who believe.

أَوَلَمْ يَرَوْا۟ أَنَّ ٱللَّهَ يَبْسُطُ ٱلرِّزْقَ لِمَن يَشَآءُ وَيَقْدِرُ ۚ
إِنَّ فِى ذَٰلِكَ لَءَايَٰتٍ لِّقَوْمٍ يُؤْمِنُونَ ﴿٣٧﴾

38. So give what is due to relations, the needy, and the wayfarer. That is best for those who seek the countenance of Allah, and it is they who will prosper.

فَـَٔاتِ ذَا ٱلْقُرْبَىٰ حَقَّهُۥ وَٱلْمِسْكِينَ وَٱبْنَ ٱلسَّبِيلِ ۚ
ذَٰلِكَ خَيْرٌ لِّلَّذِينَ يُرِيدُونَ وَجْهَ ٱللَّهِ ۖ وَأُو۟لَـٰٓئِكَ
هُمُ ٱلْمُفْلِحُونَ ٣٨

39. That which you lay out for increase through the property of (other) people, will have no increase with Allah: but that which you lay out for charity, seeking the countenance of Allah, (will increase): it is these who will get a recompense multiplied.

وَمَآ ءَاتَيْتُم مِّن رِّبًا لِّيَرْبُوَا۟ فِىٓ أَمْوَٰلِ ٱلنَّاسِ فَلَا يَرْبُوا۟
عِندَ ٱللَّهِ ۖ وَمَآ ءَاتَيْتُم مِّن زَكَوٰةٍ تُرِيدُونَ وَجْهَ
ٱللَّهِ فَأُو۟لَـٰٓئِكَ هُمُ ٱلْمُضْعِفُونَ ٣٩

40. It is Allah Who has created you: further, He has provided for your sustenance; then He will cause you to die; and again He will give you life. Are there any of your (false) "partners" who can do any single one of these things? Glory to Him! And High is He above the partners they attribute (to Him)!

ٱللَّهُ ٱلَّذِى خَلَقَكُمْ ثُمَّ رَزَقَكُمْ ثُمَّ يُمِيتُكُمْ ثُمَّ
يُحْيِيكُمْ ۖ هَلْ مِن شُرَكَآئِكُم مَّن يَفْعَلُ مِن
ذَٰلِكُم مِّن شَىْءٍ ۚ سُبْحَـٰنَهُۥ وَتَعَـٰلَىٰ عَمَّا يُشْرِكُونَ ٤٠

41. Mischief has appeared on land and sea because of (the dues) that the hands of men have earned, that (Allah) may give them a taste of some of their deeds: in order that they may turn back (from evil).

ظَهَرَ ٱلْفَسَادُ فِى ٱلْبَرِّ وَٱلْبَحْرِ بِمَا كَسَبَتْ أَيْدِى
ٱلنَّاسِ لِيُذِيقَهُم بَعْضَ ٱلَّذِى عَمِلُوا۟ لَعَلَّهُمْ
يَرْجِعُونَ ٤١

42. Say: "Travel through the earth and see what was the end of those before (you): most of them worshipped others besides Allah."

قُلْ سِيرُوا۟ فِى ٱلْأَرْضِ فَٱنظُرُوا۟ كَيْفَ كَانَ عَـٰقِبَةُ ٱلَّذِينَ
مِن قَبْلُ ۚ كَانَ أَكْثَرُهُم مُّشْرِكِينَ ٤٢

43. But set you your face to the right religion, before there come from Allah the day which there is no chance of averting: on that day shall men be divided (in two).

فَأَقِمْ وَجْهَكَ لِلدِّينِ ٱلْقَيِّمِ مِن قَبْلِ أَن يَأْتِىَ يَوْمٌ
لَّا مَرَدَّ لَهُۥ مِنَ ٱللَّهِ ۖ يَوْمَئِذٍ يَصَّدَّعُونَ ٤٣

44. Those who reject faith will suffer from that rejection; and those who work righteousness will spread their couch (of repose) for themselves (in heaven);

مَن كَفَرَ فَعَلَيْهِ كُفْرُهُۥ ۖ وَمَنْ عَمِلَ صَـٰلِحًا
فَلِأَنفُسِهِمْ يَمْهَدُونَ ٤٤

45. That He may reward those who believe and work righteous deeds, out of His bounty. For He loves not those who reject faith.

لِيَجْزِيَ ٱلَّذِينَ ءَامَنُوا۟ وَعَمِلُوا۟ ٱلصَّٰلِحَٰتِ مِن فَضْلِهِۦٓ ۚ
إِنَّهُۥ لَا يُحِبُّ ٱلْكَٰفِرِينَ ﴿٤٥﴾

46. Among His signs is this, that He sends the winds, as heralds of glad tidings, giving you a taste of His (grace and) mercy - that the ships may sail (majestically) by His command and that you may seek of His bounty; in order that you may be grateful.

وَمِنْ ءَايَٰتِهِۦٓ أَن يُرْسِلَ ٱلرِّيَاحَ مُبَشِّرَٰتٍ وَلِيُذِيقَكُم
مِّن رَّحْمَتِهِۦ وَلِتَجْرِيَ ٱلْفُلْكُ بِأَمْرِهِۦ وَلِتَبْتَغُوا۟ مِن
فَضْلِهِۦ وَلَعَلَّكُمْ تَشْكُرُونَ ﴿٤٦﴾

47. We did indeed send, before you messengers to their (respective) peoples, and they came to them with clear signs; then, to those who transgressed, We meted out Retribution; and it was due from Us to aid those who believed.

وَلَقَدْ أَرْسَلْنَا مِن قَبْلِكَ رُسُلًا إِلَىٰ قَوْمِهِمْ فَجَآءُوهُم
بِٱلْبَيِّنَٰتِ فَٱنتَقَمْنَا مِنَ ٱلَّذِينَ أَجْرَمُوا۟ ۖ وَكَانَ حَقًّا
عَلَيْنَا نَصْرُ ٱلْمُؤْمِنِينَ ﴿٤٧﴾

48. It is Allah Who sends the winds, and they raise the clouds: then does He spread them in the sky as He wills, and break them into fragments, until you see raindrops issue from the midst of it; then when He has made them reach such of His servants as He wills, see they do rejoice! -

ٱللَّهُ ٱلَّذِى يُرْسِلُ ٱلرِّيَٰحَ فَتُثِيرُ سَحَابًا فَيَبْسُطُهُۥ فِى
ٱلسَّمَآءِ كَيْفَ يَشَآءُ وَيَجْعَلُهُۥ كِسَفًا فَتَرَى ٱلْوَدْقَ
يَخْرُجُ مِنْ خِلَٰلِهِۦ ۖ فَإِذَآ أَصَابَ بِهِۦ مَن يَشَآءُ مِنْ
عِبَادِهِۦٓ إِذَا هُمْ يَسْتَبْشِرُونَ ﴿٤٨﴾

49. Even though, before they received (the rain) - just before this - they were dumb with despair!

وَإِن كَانُوا۟ مِن قَبْلِ أَن يُنَزَّلَ عَلَيْهِم مِّن قَبْلِهِۦ
لَمُبْلِسِينَ ﴿٤٩﴾

50. Then contemplate (O man!) the memorials of Allah's mercy! - How He gives life to the earth after its death: verily the Same will give life to the men who are dead: for He has power over all things.

فَٱنظُرْ إِلَىٰٓ ءَاثَٰرِ رَحْمَتِ ٱللَّهِ كَيْفَ يُحْىِ ٱلْأَرْضَ بَعْدَ
مَوْتِهَآ ۚ إِنَّ ذَٰلِكَ لَمُحْىِ ٱلْمَوْتَىٰ ۖ وَهُوَ عَلَىٰ
كُلِّ شَىْءٍ قَدِيرٌ ﴿٥٠﴾

51. And if We (but) send a wind from which they see (their tilth) turn yellow - behold, they become thereafter ungrateful (unbelievers)!

وَلَئِنْ أَرْسَلْنَا رِيحًا فَرَأَوْهُ مُصْفَرًّا لَّظَلُّوا۟ مِنۢ بَعْدِهِۦ
يَكْفُرُونَ ﴿٥١﴾

52. So verily you can not make the dead to hear; nor can you make the deaf to hear the call, when they show their backs and turn away.

فَإِنَّكَ لَا تُسْمِعُ ٱلْمَوْتَىٰ وَلَا تُسْمِعُ ٱلصُّمَّ ٱلدُّعَآءَ
إِذَا وَلَّوْا۟ مُدْبِرِينَ ﴿٥٢﴾

53. Nor can you lead back the blind from their straying: only those will you make to hear, who believe in Our signs and submit (their wills in Islam).

وَمَآ أَنتَ بِهَٰدِ ٱلْعُمْىِ عَن ضَلَٰلَتِهِمْ ۖ إِن تُسْمِعُ إِلَّا
مَن يُؤْمِنُ بِـَٔايَٰتِنَا فَهُم مُّسْلِمُونَ ﴿٥٣﴾

ثلاثة أرباع الحزب ٤١

54. It is Allah Who created you in a state of (helpless) weakness, then gave (you) strength after weakness, then, after strength, gave (you) weakness and a hoary head: He creates as He wills, and it is He Who has all knowledge and power.

۞ ٱللَّهُ ٱلَّذِى خَلَقَكُم مِّن ضَعْفٍ ثُمَّ جَعَلَ مِنۢ
بَعْدِ ضَعْفٍ قُوَّةً ثُمَّ جَعَلَ مِنۢ بَعْدِ قُوَّةٍ ضَعْفًا
وَشَيْبَةً ۚ يَخْلُقُ مَا يَشَآءُ ۖ وَهُوَ ٱلْعَلِيمُ ٱلْقَدِيرُ ﴿٥٤﴾

55. On the day that the hour (of reckoning) will be established, the transgressors will swear that they stayed not but an hour: thus were they used to being deluded!

وَيَوْمَ تَقُومُ ٱلسَّاعَةُ يُقْسِمُ ٱلْمُجْرِمُونَ
مَا لَبِثُوا۟ غَيْرَ سَاعَةٍ ۚ كَذَٰلِكَ كَانُوا۟ يُؤْفَكُونَ ﴿٥٥﴾

56. But those endued with knowledge and faith will say: "Indeed you did stay, within Allah's decree to the day of resurrection and this is the day of resurrection: but you - you were not aware!"

وَقَالَ ٱلَّذِينَ أُوتُوا۟ ٱلْعِلْمَ وَٱلْإِيمَٰنَ لَقَدْ لَبِثْتُمْ
فِى كِتَٰبِ ٱللَّهِ إِلَىٰ يَوْمِ ٱلْبَعْثِ ۖ فَهَٰذَا يَوْمُ ٱلْبَعْثِ
وَلَٰكِنَّكُمْ كُنتُمْ لَا تَعْلَمُونَ ﴿٥٦﴾

57. So on that day no excuse of theirs will benefit the transgressors, nor will they be invited (then) to seek grace (by repentance).

فَيَوْمَئِذٍ لَّا يَنفَعُ ٱلَّذِينَ ظَلَمُوا۟ مَعْذِرَتُهُمْ
وَلَا هُمْ يُسْتَعْتَبُونَ ﴿٥٧﴾

58. Verily We have presented for men in this Qur'an, every kind of parable: but if you bring to them any sign, the unbelievers are sure to say, "You do nothing but talk vanities."

وَلَقَدْ ضَرَبْنَا لِلنَّاسِ فِى هَٰذَا ٱلْقُرْءَانِ مِن كُلِّ
مَثَلٍ ۚ وَلَئِن جِئْتَهُم بِـَٔايَةٍ لَّيَقُولَنَّ ٱلَّذِينَ
كَفَرُوٓا۟ إِنْ أَنتُمْ إِلَّا مُبْطِلُونَ ﴿٥٨﴾

59. Thus does Allah seal up the hearts of those who understand not.

كَذَٰلِكَ يَطْبَعُ ٱللَّهُ عَلَىٰ قُلُوبِ ٱلَّذِينَ لَا يَعْلَمُونَ ﴿٥٩﴾

60. So patiently persevere: for verily the promise of Allah is true: nor let those shake your firmness, who have (themselves) no certainty of faith.

فَٱصۡبِرۡ إِنَّ وَعۡدَ ٱللَّهِ حَقّٞۖ وَلَا يَسۡتَخِفَّنَّكَ ٱلَّذِينَ
لَا يُوقِنُونَ ٦٠

سُورَةُ لُقۡمَانَ

Surah 31: **Luqman**

In the name of Allah,
Most Gracious, Most Merciful.

بِسۡمِ ٱللَّهِ ٱلرَّحۡمَٰنِ ٱلرَّحِيمِ

1. *Alif Lam Mim.*

الٓمٓ ١

2. These are verses of the wise book -

تِلۡكَ ءَايَٰتُ ٱلۡكِتَٰبِ ٱلۡحَكِيمِ ٢

3. A guide and a mercy to the doers of good -

هُدٗى وَرَحۡمَةٗ لِّلۡمُحۡسِنِينَ ٣

4. Those who establish regular prayer, and give regular charity, and have (in their hearts) the assurance of the hereafter.

ٱلَّذِينَ يُقِيمُونَ ٱلصَّلَوٰةَ وَيُؤۡتُونَ ٱلزَّكَوٰةَ وَهُم
بِٱلۡأٓخِرَةِ هُمۡ يُوقِنُونَ ٤

5. These are on (true) guidance from their Lord; and these are the ones who will prosper.

أُوْلَٰٓئِكَ عَلَىٰ هُدٗى مِّن رَّبِّهِمۡۖ وَأُوْلَٰٓئِكَ
هُمُ ٱلۡمُفۡلِحُونَ ٥

6. But there are, among men, those who purchase idle tales, without knowledge (or meaning), to mislead (men) from the path of Allah and throw ridicule (on the path): for such there will be a humiliating penalty.

وَمِنَ ٱلنَّاسِ مَن يَشۡتَرِي لَهۡوَ ٱلۡحَدِيثِ لِيُضِلَّ عَن
سَبِيلِ ٱللَّهِ بِغَيۡرِ عِلۡمٖ وَيَتَّخِذَهَا هُزُوًاۚ أُوْلَٰٓئِكَ لَهُمۡ
عَذَابٞ مُّهِينٞ ٦

7. When Our signs are rehearsed to such a one, he turns away in arrogance, as if he heard them not, as if there were deafness in both his ears: announce to him a grievous penalty.

وَإِذَا تُتۡلَىٰ عَلَيۡهِ ءَايَٰتُنَا وَلَّىٰ مُسۡتَكۡبِرٗا كَأَن لَّمۡ
يَسۡمَعۡهَا كَأَنَّ فِيٓ أُذُنَيۡهِ وَقۡرٗاۖ فَبَشِّرۡهُ بِعَذَابٍ
أَلِيمٍ ٧

8. For those who believe and work righteous deeds, there will be gardens of bliss -

إِنَّ ٱلَّذِينَ ءَامَنُواْ وَعَمِلُواْ ٱلصَّٰلِحَٰتِ لَهُمۡ جَنَّٰتُ
ٱلنَّعِيمِ ٨

9. To dwell in it. The promise of Allah is true: and He is Exalted in Power, Wise.

خَٰلِدِينَ فِيهَاۖ وَعۡدَ ٱللَّهِ حَقّٗاۚ وَهُوَ ٱلۡعَزِيزُ
ٱلۡحَكِيمُ ٩

10. He created the heavens without any pillars that you can see; He set on the earth mountains standing firm, lest it should shake with you; and He scattered through it beasts of all kinds. We send down rain from the sky, and produce on the earth every kind of noble creature, in pairs.

خَلَقَ ٱلسَّمَٰوَٰتِ بِغَيۡرِ عَمَدٖ تَرَوۡنَهَاۖ وَأَلۡقَىٰ فِي ٱلۡأَرۡضِ
رَوَٰسِيَ أَن تَمِيدَ بِكُمۡ وَبَثَّ فِيهَا مِن كُلِّ دَآبَّةٖۚ
وَأَنزَلۡنَا مِنَ ٱلسَّمَآءِ مَآءٗ فَأَنۢبَتۡنَا فِيهَا مِن كُلِّ زَوۡجٖ
كَرِيمٍ ١٠

11. Such is the creation of Allah; now show Me what is there that others besides Him have created: nay, but the transgressors are in manifest error.

هَٰذَا خَلۡقُ ٱللَّهِ فَأَرُونِي مَاذَا خَلَقَ ٱلَّذِينَ مِن
دُونِهِۦۚ بَلِ ٱلظَّٰلِمُونَ فِي ضَلَٰلٖ مُّبِينٖ ١١

12. We bestowed (in the past) wisdom on Luqman: "Show (your) gratitude to Allah." Any who is (so) grateful does so to the profit of his own soul: but if any is ungrateful, verily Allah is Free of all Wants, worthy of all praise.

وَلَقَدۡ ءَاتَيۡنَا لُقۡمَٰنَ ٱلۡحِكۡمَةَ أَنِ ٱشۡكُرۡ لِلَّهِۚ وَمَن
يَشۡكُرۡ فَإِنَّمَا يَشۡكُرُ لِنَفۡسِهِۦۖ وَمَن كَفَرَ فَإِنَّ ٱللَّهَ
غَنِيٌّ حَمِيدٞ ١٢

13. See, Luqman said to his son by way of instruction: "O my son! Join not in worship (others) with Allah: for false worship is indeed the highest wrongdoing."

وَإِذۡ قَالَ لُقۡمَٰنُ لِٱبۡنِهِۦ وَهُوَ يَعِظُهُۥ يَٰبُنَيَّ لَا تُشۡرِكۡ
بِٱللَّهِۖ إِنَّ ٱلشِّرۡكَ لَظُلۡمٌ عَظِيمٞ ١٣

14. And We have enjoined on man (to be good) to his parents: in travail upon travail did his mother bear him, and in two years was his weaning: (hear the command), "Show gratitude to Me and to your parents: to Me is (your final) goal."

وَوَصَّيۡنَا ٱلۡإِنسَٰنَ بِوَٰلِدَيۡهِ حَمَلَتۡهُ أُمُّهُۥ وَهۡنًا
عَلَىٰ وَهۡنٖ وَفِصَٰلُهُۥ فِي عَامَيۡنِ أَنِ ٱشۡكُرۡ لِي
وَلِوَٰلِدَيۡكَ إِلَيَّ ٱلۡمَصِيرُ ١٤

15. "But if they strive to make you join in worship with Me things of which you have no knowledge, obey them not; yet bear them company in this life with justice (and consideration), and follow the way of those who turn to Me (in love): in the end the return of you all is to Me, and I will tell you the truth (and meaning) of all that you did."

وَإِن جَٰهَدَاكَ عَلَىٰٓ أَن تُشۡرِكَ بِي مَا لَيۡسَ لَكَ بِهِۦ
عِلۡمٞ فَلَا تُطِعۡهُمَاۖ وَصَاحِبۡهُمَا فِي ٱلدُّنۡيَا مَعۡرُوفٗاۖ
وَٱتَّبِعۡ سَبِيلَ مَنۡ أَنَابَ إِلَيَّۚ ثُمَّ إِلَيَّ مَرۡجِعُكُمۡ
فَأُنَبِّئُكُم بِمَا كُنتُمۡ تَعۡمَلُونَ ١٥

16. "O my son," (said Luqman), "if there be (but) the weight of a mustard seed and it were (hidden) in a rock, or (anywhere) in the heavens or on earth, Allah will bring it out: for Allah understands the finest mysteries, (and) is well-acquainted (with them).

يَٰبُنَيَّ إِنَّهَآ إِن تَكُ مِثۡقَالَ حَبَّةٖ مِّنۡ خَرۡدَلٖ فَتَكُن فِي
صَخۡرَةٍ أَوۡ فِي ٱلسَّمَٰوَٰتِ أَوۡ فِي ٱلۡأَرۡضِ يَأۡتِ بِهَا
ٱللَّهُۚ إِنَّ ٱللَّهَ لَطِيفٌ خَبِيرٞ ١٦

17. "O my son! Establish regular prayer, enjoin what is just, and forbid what is wrong: and bear with patient constancy whatever befall you; for this is firmness (of purpose) in (the conduct of) affairs."

يَٰبُنَيَّ أَقِمِ ٱلصَّلَوٰةَ وَأۡمُرۡ بِٱلۡمَعۡرُوفِ وَٱنۡهَ عَنِ
ٱلۡمُنكَرِ وَٱصۡبِرۡ عَلَىٰ مَآ أَصَابَكَۖ إِنَّ ذَٰلِكَ مِنۡ
عَزۡمِ ٱلۡأُمُورِ ١٧

18. "And swell not your cheek (for pride) at men, nor walk in insolence through the earth; for Allah loves not any arrogant boaster."

وَلَا تُصَعِّرۡ خَدَّكَ لِلنَّاسِ وَلَا تَمۡشِ فِي ٱلۡأَرۡضِ مَرَحًاۖ
إِنَّ ٱللَّهَ لَا يُحِبُّ كُلَّ مُخۡتَالٖ فَخُورٖ ١٨

19. "And be moderate in your pace, and lower your voice; for the harshest of sounds without doubt is the braying of the ass."

وَٱقۡصِدۡ فِي مَشۡيِكَ وَٱغۡضُضۡ مِن صَوۡتِكَۚ إِنَّ أَنكَرَ
ٱلۡأَصۡوَٰتِ لَصَوۡتُ ٱلۡحَمِيرِ ١٩

20. Do you not see that Allah has subjected to your (use) all things in the heavens and on earth, and has made His bounties flow to you in exceeding measure, (both) seen and unseen? Yet there are among men those who dispute about Allah, without knowledge and without guidance, and without a book to enlighten them!

أَلَمۡ تَرَوۡاْ أَنَّ ٱللَّهَ سَخَّرَ لَكُم مَّا فِي ٱلسَّمَٰوَٰتِ وَمَا فِي ٱلۡأَرۡضِ
وَأَسۡبَغَ عَلَيۡكُمۡ نِعَمَهُۥ ظَٰهِرَةٗ وَبَاطِنَةٗۗ وَمِنَ ٱلنَّاسِ
مَن يُجَٰدِلُ فِي ٱللَّهِ بِغَيۡرِ عِلۡمٖ وَلَا هُدٗى وَلَا كِتَٰبٖ
مُّنِيرٖ ٢٠

21. When they are told to follow the (revelation) that Allah has sent down, they say: "Nay, we shall follow the ways that we found our fathers (following)." What! Even if it is Satan beckoning them to the penalty of the (blazing) fire!

وَإِذَا قِيلَ لَهُمُ ٱتَّبِعُوا۟ مَآ أَنزَلَ ٱللَّهُ قَالُوا۟ بَلْ نَتَّبِعُ مَا
وَجَدْنَا عَلَيْهِ ءَابَآءَنَآ ۚ أَوَلَوْ كَانَ ٱلشَّيْطَٰنُ
يَدْعُوهُمْ إِلَىٰ عَذَابِ ٱلسَّعِيرِ ﴿٢١﴾

22. Whoever submits his whole self to Allah, and is a doer of good, has grasped indeed the most trustworthy handhold: and with Allah rests the end and decision of (all) affairs.

حزب ٤٢ ۞ وَمَن يُسْلِمْ وَجْهَهُۥٓ إِلَى ٱللَّهِ وَهُوَ مُحْسِنٌ فَقَدِ
ٱسْتَمْسَكَ بِٱلْعُرْوَةِ ٱلْوُثْقَىٰ ۗ وَإِلَى ٱللَّهِ عَٰقِبَةُ ٱلْأُمُورِ ﴿٢٢﴾

23. But if any reject faith, let not his rejection grieve you; to Us is their return, and We shall tell them the truth of their deeds: for Allah knows well all that is in (men's) hearts.

وَمَن كَفَرَ فَلَا يَحْزُنكَ كُفْرُهُۥٓ ۚ إِلَيْنَا مَرْجِعُهُمْ
فَنُنَبِّئُهُم بِمَا عَمِلُوٓا۟ ۚ إِنَّ ٱللَّهَ عَلِيمٌۢ بِذَاتِ ٱلصُّدُورِ ﴿٢٣﴾

24. We grant them their pleasure for a little while: in the end shall We drive them to a chastisement unrelenting.

نُمَتِّعُهُمْ قَلِيلًا ثُمَّ نَضْطَرُّهُمْ إِلَىٰ عَذَابٍ غَلِيظٍ ﴿٢٤﴾

25. If you ask them, who it is that created the heavens and the earth, they will certainly say "Allah." Say: "Praise be to Allah!" But most of them understand not.

وَلَئِن سَأَلْتَهُم مَّنْ خَلَقَ ٱلسَّمَٰوَٰتِ وَٱلْأَرْضَ لَيَقُولُنَّ
ٱللَّهُ ۚ قُلِ ٱلْحَمْدُ لِلَّهِ ۚ بَلْ أَكْثَرُهُمْ لَا يَعْلَمُونَ ﴿٢٥﴾

26. To Allah belong all things in heaven and earth: verily Allah is He (that is) Free of all Wants, Worthy of all Praise.

لِلَّهِ مَا فِى ٱلسَّمَٰوَٰتِ وَٱلْأَرْضِ ۚ إِنَّ ٱللَّهَ هُوَ ٱلْغَنِىُّ
ٱلْحَمِيدُ ﴿٢٦﴾

27. And if all the trees on earth were pens and the ocean (were ink), with seven oceans behind it to add to its (supply), yet would not the words of Allah be exhausted (in the writing): for Allah is Exalted in Power, Full of wisdom.

وَلَوْ أَنَّمَا فِى ٱلْأَرْضِ مِن شَجَرَةٍ أَقْلَٰمٌ وَٱلْبَحْرُ
يَمُدُّهُۥ مِنۢ بَعْدِهِۦ سَبْعَةُ أَبْحُرٍ مَّا نَفِدَتْ كَلِمَٰتُ
ٱللَّهِ ۗ إِنَّ ٱللَّهَ عَزِيزٌ حَكِيمٌ ﴿٢٧﴾

28. And your creation or your resurrection is in no way but as an individual soul: for Allah is He Who hears and sees (all things).

مَّا خَلْقُكُمْ وَلَا بَعْثُكُمْ إِلَّا كَنَفْسٍ وَٰحِدَةٍ ۗ إِنَّ ٱللَّهَ
سَمِيعٌۢ بَصِيرٌ ﴿٢٨﴾

29. Do you not see that Allah merges night into day and He merges day into night; that He has subjected the sun and the moon (to His law), each running its course for a term appointed: and that Allah is well acquainted with all that you do?

أَلَمْ تَرَ أَنَّ ٱللَّهَ يُولِجُ ٱلَّيْلَ فِى ٱلنَّهَارِ وَيُولِجُ ٱلنَّهَارَ
فِى ٱلَّيْلِ وَسَخَّرَ ٱلشَّمْسَ وَٱلْقَمَرَ ۖ كُلٌّ يَجْرِىٓ إِلَىٰٓ
أَجَلٍ مُّسَمًّى وَأَنَّ ٱللَّهَ بِمَا تَعْمَلُونَ خَبِيرٌ ﴿٢٩﴾

30. That is because Allah is the (only) Reality, and because whatever else they invoke besides Him is falsehood; and because Allah - He is the Most High, Most Great.

ذَٰلِكَ بِأَنَّ ٱللَّهَ هُوَ ٱلْحَقُّ وَأَنَّ مَا يَدْعُونَ مِن دُونِهِ
ٱلْبَٰطِلُ وَأَنَّ ٱللَّهَ هُوَ ٱلْعَلِىُّ ٱلْكَبِيرُ ﴿٣٠﴾

31. Do you not see that the ships sail through the ocean by the grace of Allah? - That He may show you of His signs? Verily in this are signs for all who constantly persevere and give thanks.

أَلَمْ تَرَ أَنَّ ٱلْفُلْكَ تَجْرِى فِى ٱلْبَحْرِ بِنِعْمَتِ ٱللَّهِ
لِيُرِيَكُم مِّنْ ءَايَٰتِهِۦٓ ۚ إِنَّ فِى ذَٰلِكَ لَءَايَٰتٍ لِّكُلِّ
صَبَّارٍ شَكُورٍ ﴿٣١﴾

32. When a wave covers them like the canopy (of clouds) they call to Allah, offering Him sincere devotion, but when He has delivered them safely to land, there are among them those that halt between (right and wrong). But none reject Our signs except only a perfidious ungrateful (wretch)!

وَإِذَا غَشِيَهُم مَّوْجٌ كَٱلظُّلَلِ دَعَوُا۟ ٱللَّهَ مُخْلِصِينَ
لَهُ ٱلدِّينَ فَلَمَّا نَجَّىٰهُمْ إِلَى ٱلْبَرِّ فَمِنْهُم مُّقْتَصِدٌ ۚ وَمَا
يَجْحَدُ بِـَٔايَٰتِنَآ إِلَّا كُلُّ خَتَّارٍ كَفُورٍ ﴿٣٢﴾

33. O mankind! Do your duty to your Lord, and fear (the coming of) a day when no father can benefit anything for his son, nor a son benefit anything for his father. Verily, the promise of Allah is true: let not then this present life deceive you, nor let the chief deceiver deceive you about Allah.

يَٰٓأَيُّهَا ٱلنَّاسُ ٱتَّقُوا۟ رَبَّكُمْ وَٱخْشَوْا۟ يَوْمًا لَّا يَجْزِى
وَالِدٌ عَن وَلَدِهِۦ وَلَا مَوْلُودٌ هُوَ جَازٍ عَن وَالِدِهِۦ
شَيْـًٔا ۚ إِنَّ وَعْدَ ٱللَّهِ حَقٌّ ۖ فَلَا تَغُرَّنَّكُمُ ٱلْحَيَوٰةُ
ٱلدُّنْيَا وَلَا يَغُرَّنَّكُم بِٱللَّهِ ٱلْغَرُورُ ﴿٣٣﴾

34. Verily the knowledge of the hour is with Allah (alone). It is He Who sends down rain, and He Who knows what is in the wombs. Nor does anyone know what it is that he will earn the next day; nor does anyone know in what land he is to die.

إِنَّ ٱللَّهَ عِندَهُۥ عِلْمُ ٱلسَّاعَةِ وَيُنَزِّلُ ٱلْغَيْثَ
وَيَعْلَمُ مَا فِى ٱلْأَرْحَامِ ۖ وَمَا تَدْرِى نَفْسٌ مَّاذَا
تَكْسِبُ غَدًا ۖ وَمَا تَدْرِى نَفْسٌۢ بِأَىِّ أَرْضٍ تَمُوتُ ۚ

Verily with Allah is full knowledge and He is acquainted (with all things).

إِنَّ ٱللَّهَ عَلِيمٌ خَبِيرٌۢ ٣٤

سُورَةُ السَّجْدَةِ

Surah 32: **As-Sajdah (The Prostration)**

In the name of Allah,
Most Gracious, Most Merciful.

بِسْمِ ٱللَّهِ ٱلرَّحْمَٰنِ ٱلرَّحِيمِ

1. *Alif Lam Mim.*

الٓمٓ ١

2. (This is) the revelation of the book in which there is no doubt - from the Lord of the Worlds.

تَنزِيلُ ٱلْكِتَٰبِ لَا رَيْبَ فِيهِ مِن رَّبِّ
ٱلْعَٰلَمِينَ ٢

3. Or do they say, "He has forged it"? Nay, it is the truth from your Lord, that you may admonish a people to whom no warner has come before you: in order that they may receive guidance.

أَمْ يَقُولُونَ ٱفْتَرَىٰهُ ۚ بَلْ هُوَ ٱلْحَقُّ مِن رَّبِّكَ
لِتُنذِرَ قَوْمًا مَّآ أَتَىٰهُم مِّن نَّذِيرٍ مِّن قَبْلِكَ
لَعَلَّهُمْ يَهْتَدُونَ ٣

4. It is Allah Who has created the heavens and the earth, and all between them, in six days, then He established Himself on the throne (of authority); you have none, besides Him, to protect or intercede (for you): will you not then receive admonition?

ٱللَّهُ ٱلَّذِى خَلَقَ ٱلسَّمَٰوَٰتِ وَٱلْأَرْضَ وَمَا بَيْنَهُمَا
فِى سِتَّةِ أَيَّامٍ ثُمَّ ٱسْتَوَىٰ عَلَى ٱلْعَرْشِ ۖ مَا لَكُم مِّن
دُونِهِۦ مِن وَلِىٍّ وَلَا شَفِيعٍ ۚ أَفَلَا تَتَذَكَّرُونَ ٤

5. He rules (all) affairs from the heavens to the earth: in the end will (all affairs) go up to Him, on a day, the space of which will be (as) a thousand years of your reckoning.

يُدَبِّرُ ٱلْأَمْرَ مِنَ ٱلسَّمَآءِ إِلَى ٱلْأَرْضِ ثُمَّ يَعْرُجُ إِلَيْهِ فِى
يَوْمٍ كَانَ مِقْدَارُهُۥٓ أَلْفَ سَنَةٍ مِّمَّا تَعُدُّونَ ٥

6. Such is He, the Knower of all things, hidden and open, the Exalted (in power), the Merciful -

ذَٰلِكَ عَٰلِمُ ٱلْغَيْبِ وَٱلشَّهَٰدَةِ ٱلْعَزِيزُ ٱلرَّحِيمُ ٦

7. He Who has made everything which He has created most good: He began the creation

ٱلَّذِىٓ أَحْسَنَ كُلَّ شَىْءٍ خَلَقَهُۥ ۖ وَبَدَأَ خَلْقَ ٱلْإِنسَٰنِ

of man with (nothing more than) clay,

مِن طِينٍ ٧

8. And made his progeny from a quintessence of the nature of a fluid despised:

ثُمَّ جَعَلَ نَسْلَهُۥ مِن سُلَٰلَةٍ مِّن مَّآءٍ مَّهِينٍ ٨

9. But He fashioned him in due proportion, and breathed into him something of His spirit. And He gave you (the faculties of) hearing and sight and feeling (and understanding): little thanks do you give!

ثُمَّ سَوَّىٰهُ وَنَفَخَ فِيهِ مِن رُّوحِهِۦ ۖ وَجَعَلَ لَكُمُ ٱلسَّمْعَ
وَٱلْأَبْصَٰرَ وَٱلْأَفْـِٔدَةَ ۚ قَلِيلًا مَّا تَشْكُرُونَ ٩

10. And they say: "What! When we lie, hidden and lost, in the earth, shall we indeed be in a creation renewed?" Nay, they deny the meeting with their Lord!

وَقَالُوٓا۟ أَءِذَا ضَلَلْنَا فِى ٱلْأَرْضِ أَءِنَّا لَفِى خَلْقٍ جَدِيدٍۭ ۚ
بَلْ هُم بِلِقَآءِ رَبِّهِمْ كَٰفِرُونَ ١٠

11. Say: "The angel of death, put in charge of you, will (duly) take your souls: then shall you be brought back to your Lord."

ربع الحزب ٤٢

۞ قُلْ يَتَوَفَّىٰكُم مَّلَكُ ٱلْمَوْتِ ٱلَّذِى وُكِّلَ بِكُمْ
ثُمَّ إِلَىٰ رَبِّكُمْ تُرْجَعُونَ ١١

12. If only you could see when the guilty ones will bend low their heads before their Lord, (saying:) "Our Lord! We have seen and we have heard; now then send us back (to the world); we will work righteousness: for we do indeed (now) believe."

وَلَوْ تَرَىٰٓ إِذِ ٱلْمُجْرِمُونَ نَاكِسُوا۟ رُءُوسِهِمْ
عِندَ رَبِّهِمْ رَبَّنَآ أَبْصَرْنَا وَسَمِعْنَا فَٱرْجِعْنَا نَعْمَلْ
صَٰلِحًا إِنَّا مُوقِنُونَ ١٢

13. If We had so willed, We could certainly have brought every soul its true guidance: but the word from Me will come true. "I will fill hell with Jinns and men all together."

وَلَوْ شِئْنَا لَءَاتَيْنَا كُلَّ نَفْسٍ هُدَىٰهَا وَلَٰكِنْ
حَقَّ ٱلْقَوْلُ مِنِّى لَأَمْلَأَنَّ جَهَنَّمَ مِنَ ٱلْجِنَّةِ
وَٱلنَّاسِ أَجْمَعِينَ ١٣

14. "Taste you then - for you forgot the meeting of this day of yours. And We too will forget you - taste you the penalty of eternity for your (evil) deeds!"

فَذُوقُوا۟ بِمَا نَسِيتُمْ لِقَآءَ يَوْمِكُمْ هَٰذَآ إِنَّا
نَسِينَٰكُمْ ۖ وَذُوقُوا۟ عَذَابَ ٱلْخُلْدِ بِمَا
كُنتُمْ تَعْمَلُونَ ١٤

15. Only those believe in Our signs, who, when they are recited to them fall down in adoration, and celebrate the praises of their Lord, nor are they (ever) puffed up with pride.

إِنَّمَا يُؤْمِنُ بِـَٔايَٰتِنَا ٱلَّذِينَ إِذَا ذُكِّرُوا۟ بِهَا
خَرُّوا۟ سُجَّدًا وَسَبَّحُوا۟ بِحَمْدِ رَبِّهِمْ وَهُمْ
سجدة لَا يَسْتَكْبِرُونَ ۩ ﴿١٥﴾

16. Their limbs do forsake their beds of sleep, the while they call on their Lord, in fear and hope: and they spend (in charity) out of the sustenance which We have bestowed on them.

تَتَجَافَىٰ جُنُوبُهُمْ عَنِ ٱلْمَضَاجِعِ يَدْعُونَ رَبَّهُمْ
خَوْفًا وَطَمَعًا وَمِمَّا رَزَقْنَٰهُمْ يُنفِقُونَ ﴿١٦﴾

17. Now no person knows what delights of the eye are kept hidden (in reserve) for them - as a reward for their (good) deeds.

فَلَا تَعْلَمُ نَفْسٌ مَّآ أُخْفِىَ لَهُم مِّن قُرَّةِ أَعْيُنٍ جَزَآءًۢ
بِمَا كَانُوا۟ يَعْمَلُونَ ﴿١٧﴾

18. Is then the man who believes no better than the man who is rebellious and wicked? Not equal are they.

أَفَمَن كَانَ مُؤْمِنًا كَمَن كَانَ فَاسِقًا ۚ لَّا يَسْتَوُۥنَ ﴿١٨﴾

19. For those who believe and do righteous deeds, are gardens as hospitable homes, for their (good) deeds.

أَمَّا ٱلَّذِينَ ءَامَنُوا۟ وَعَمِلُوا۟ ٱلصَّٰلِحَٰتِ فَلَهُمْ
جَنَّٰتُ ٱلْمَأْوَىٰ نُزُلًۢا بِمَا كَانُوا۟ يَعْمَلُونَ ﴿١٩﴾

20. As to those who are rebellious and wicked, their abode will be the fire: every time they wish to get away from it, they will be forced in it, and it will be said to them: "Taste you the penalty of the fire, which you used to reject as false."

وَأَمَّا ٱلَّذِينَ فَسَقُوا۟ فَمَأْوَىٰهُمُ ٱلنَّارُ ۖ كُلَّمَآ أَرَادُوٓا۟
أَن يَخْرُجُوا۟ مِنْهَآ أُعِيدُوا۟ فِيهَا وَقِيلَ لَهُمْ ذُوقُوا۟ عَذَابَ
ٱلنَّارِ ٱلَّذِى كُنتُم بِهِۦ تُكَذِّبُونَ ﴿٢٠﴾

21. And indeed We will make them taste of the penalty of this (life) prior to the supreme penalty, in order that they may (repent and) return.

وَلَنُذِيقَنَّهُم مِّنَ ٱلْعَذَابِ ٱلْأَدْنَىٰ دُونَ ٱلْعَذَابِ
ٱلْأَكْبَرِ لَعَلَّهُمْ يَرْجِعُونَ ﴿٢١﴾

22. And who does more wrong than one to whom are recited the signs of his Lord and who then turns away from it? Verily from those who transgress We shall exact (due) retribution.

وَمَنْ أَظْلَمُ مِمَّن ذُكِّرَ بِـَٔايَٰتِ رَبِّهِۦ ثُمَّ أَعْرَضَ
عَنْهَآ ۚ إِنَّا مِنَ ٱلْمُجْرِمِينَ مُنتَقِمُونَ ﴿٢٢﴾

23. We did indeed before give the book to Moses: be not then in doubt of its reaching (you): and We made it a guide to the Children of Israel.

وَلَقَدْ ءَاتَيْنَا مُوسَى ٱلْكِتَٰبَ فَلَا تَكُن فِى مِرْيَةٍ
مِّن لِّقَآئِهِۦ ۖ وَجَعَلْنَٰهُ هُدًى لِّبَنِىٓ إِسْرَٰٓءِيلَ ﴿٢٣﴾

24. And We appointed, from among them, leaders, giving guidance under Our command, so long as they persevered with patience and continued to have faith in Our signs.

وَجَعَلْنَا مِنْهُمْ أَئِمَّةً يَهْدُونَ بِأَمْرِنَا لَمَّا صَبَرُوا۟ ۖ
وَكَانُوا۟ بِـَٔايَٰتِنَا يُوقِنُونَ ﴿٢٤﴾

25. Verily your Lord will judge between them on the day of judgement, in the matters in which they differ (among themselves).

إِنَّ رَبَّكَ هُوَ يَفْصِلُ بَيْنَهُمْ يَوْمَ ٱلْقِيَٰمَةِ فِيمَا
كَانُوا۟ فِيهِ يَخْتَلِفُونَ ﴿٢٥﴾

26. Does it not teach them a lesson, how many generations We destroyed before them, in whose dwellings they (now) go to and fro? Verily in that are signs: do they not then listen?

أَوَلَمْ يَهْدِ لَهُمْ كَمْ أَهْلَكْنَا مِن قَبْلِهِم مِّنَ
ٱلْقُرُونِ يَمْشُونَ فِى مَسَٰكِنِهِمْ ۚ إِنَّ فِى ذَٰلِكَ
لَءَايَٰتٍ ۚ أَفَلَا يَسْمَعُونَ ﴿٢٦﴾

27. And do they not see that We do drive rain to parched soil (bare of herbage), and produce with it crops, providing food for their cattle and themselves? Have they not the vision?

أَوَلَمْ يَرَوْا۟ أَنَّا نَسُوقُ ٱلْمَآءَ إِلَى ٱلْأَرْضِ ٱلْجُرُزِ
فَنُخْرِجُ بِهِۦ زَرْعًا تَأْكُلُ مِنْهُ أَنْعَٰمُهُمْ
وَأَنفُسُهُمْ ۚ أَفَلَا يُبْصِرُونَ ﴿٢٧﴾

28. They say: "When will this decision be if you are telling the truth?"

وَيَقُولُونَ مَتَىٰ هَٰذَا ٱلْفَتْحُ إِن كُنتُمْ
صَٰدِقِينَ ﴿٢٨﴾

29. Say: "On the day of decision, no profit will it be to unbelievers if they (then) believe! Nor will they be granted a respite."

قُلْ يَوْمَ ٱلْفَتْحِ لَا يَنفَعُ ٱلَّذِينَ كَفَرُوٓا۟
إِيمَٰنُهُمْ وَلَا هُمْ يُنظَرُونَ ﴿٢٩﴾

30. So turn away from them, and wait: they too are waiting.

فَأَعْرِضْ عَنْهُمْ وَٱنتَظِرْ إِنَّهُم مُّنتَظِرُونَ ﴿٣٠﴾

سُورَةُ الأَحْزَابِ

Surah 33: ***Al-Ahzab*** **(The Clans)**

In the name of Allah,
Most Gracious, Most Merciful.

بِسْمِ ٱللَّهِ ٱلرَّحْمَٰنِ ٱلرَّحِيمِ

1. O Prophet! Fear Allah, and listen not to the unbelievers and the hypocrites: verily Allah is Full of knowledge and wisdom.

يَٰٓأَيُّهَا ٱلنَّبِيُّ ٱتَّقِ ٱللَّهَ وَلَا تُطِعِ ٱلْكَٰفِرِينَ
وَٱلْمُنَٰفِقِينَۗ إِنَّ ٱللَّهَ كَانَ عَلِيمًا حَكِيمًا ١

2. But follow that which comes to you by inspiration from your Lord: for Allah is well acquainted with (all) that you do.

وَٱتَّبِعْ مَا يُوحَىٰٓ إِلَيْكَ مِن رَّبِّكَۚ إِنَّ ٱللَّهَ كَانَ
بِمَا تَعْمَلُونَ خَبِيرًا ٢

3. And put your trust in Allah, and enough is Allah as a Disposer of affairs.

وَتَوَكَّلْ عَلَى ٱللَّهِۚ وَكَفَىٰ بِٱللَّهِ وَكِيلًا ٣

4. Allah has not made for any man two hearts in his (one) body: nor has He made your wives whom you divorce by *zihar* your mothers: nor has He made your adopted sons your sons. Such is (only) your (manner of) speech by your mouths. But Allah tells (you) the truth, and He shows the (right) way.

مَّا جَعَلَ ٱللَّهُ لِرَجُلٍ مِّن قَلْبَيْنِ فِي جَوْفِهِۦۚ وَمَا
جَعَلَ أَزْوَٰجَكُمُ ٱلَّٰٓـِٔي تُظَٰهِرُونَ مِنْهُنَّ
أُمَّهَٰتِكُمْۚ وَمَا جَعَلَ أَدْعِيَآءَكُمْ أَبْنَآءَكُمْۚ ذَٰلِكُمْ
قَوْلُكُم بِأَفْوَٰهِكُمْۖ وَٱللَّهُ يَقُولُ ٱلْحَقَّ وَهُوَ
يَهْدِي ٱلسَّبِيلَ ٤

5. Call them by (the names) of their fathers: that is more just in the sight of Allah. But if you do not know their father's (names, call them) your brothers in faith, or your *Mawlas.* But there is no blame on you if you make a mistake in it; (what counts is) the intention of your hearts: and Allah is Oft-Forgiving, Most Merciful.

ٱدْعُوهُمْ لِءَابَآئِهِمْ هُوَ أَقْسَطُ عِندَ ٱللَّهِۚ فَإِن لَّمْ تَعْلَمُوٓا۟
ءَابَآءَهُمْ فَإِخْوَٰنُكُمْ فِي ٱلدِّينِ وَمَوَٰلِيكُمْۚ وَلَيْسَ
عَلَيْكُمْ جُنَاحٌ فِيمَآ أَخْطَأْتُم بِهِۦ وَلَٰكِن مَّا
تَعَمَّدَتْ قُلُوبُكُمْۚ وَكَانَ ٱللَّهُ غَفُورًا رَّحِيمًا ٥

6. The Prophet is closer to the believers than their own selves, and his wives are their mothers. Blood-relations among each other have closer personal ties, in the decree of Allah, than (the brotherhood of) believers and Muhajirs; nevertheless do you what is just to your closest friends; such is the writing in the decree (of Allah).

ٱلنَّبِىُّ أَوْلَىٰ بِٱلْمُؤْمِنِينَ مِنْ أَنفُسِهِمْ ۖ وَأَزْوَٰجُهُۥٓ
أُمَّهَٰتُهُمْ ۗ وَأُو۟لُوا۟ ٱلْأَرْحَامِ بَعْضُهُمْ أَوْلَىٰ بِبَعْضٍ
فِى كِتَٰبِ ٱللَّهِ مِنَ ٱلْمُؤْمِنِينَ وَٱلْمُهَٰجِرِينَ إِلَّآ أَن
تَفْعَلُوٓا۟ إِلَىٰٓ أَوْلِيَآئِكُم مَّعْرُوفًا ۚ كَانَ ذَٰلِكَ فِى
ٱلْكِتَٰبِ مَسْطُورًا ﴿٦﴾

7. And remember We took from the prophets their covenant as (We did) from you; from Noah, Abraham, Moses, and Jesus the son of Mary; We took from them a solemn covenant:

وَإِذْ أَخَذْنَا مِنَ ٱلنَّبِيِّـۧنَ مِيثَٰقَهُمْ وَمِنكَ وَمِن نُّوحٍ
وَإِبْرَٰهِيمَ وَمُوسَىٰ وَعِيسَى ٱبْنِ مَرْيَمَ ۖ وَأَخَذْنَا مِنْهُم
مِّيثَٰقًا غَلِيظًا ﴿٧﴾

8. That (Allah) may question the (custodians) of truth concerning the truth they (were charged with): and He has prepared for the unbelievers a grievous penalty.

لِّيَسْـَٔلَ ٱلصَّٰدِقِينَ عَن صِدْقِهِمْ ۚ وَأَعَدَّ لِلْكَٰفِرِينَ
عَذَابًا أَلِيمًا ﴿٨﴾

9. O you who believe! Remember the grace of Allah (bestowed) on you, when there came down on you forces (to overwhelm you): but We sent against them a hurricane and force that you saw not. But Allah sees (clearly) all that you do.

يَٰٓأَيُّهَا ٱلَّذِينَ ءَامَنُوا۟ ٱذْكُرُوا۟ نِعْمَةَ ٱللَّهِ عَلَيْكُمْ إِذْ
جَآءَتْكُمْ جُنُودٌ فَأَرْسَلْنَا عَلَيْهِمْ رِيحًا وَجُنُودًا
لَّمْ تَرَوْهَا ۚ وَكَانَ ٱللَّهُ بِمَا تَعْمَلُونَ بَصِيرًا ﴿٩﴾

10. See! They came on you from above you and from below you, and behold, the eyes became dim and the hearts gaped up to the throats, and you imagined various (vain) thoughts about Allah!

إِذْ جَآءُوكُم مِّن فَوْقِكُمْ وَمِنْ أَسْفَلَ مِنكُمْ وَإِذْ
زَاغَتِ ٱلْأَبْصَٰرُ وَبَلَغَتِ ٱلْقُلُوبُ ٱلْحَنَاجِرَ
وَتَظُنُّونَ بِٱللَّهِ ٱلظُّنُونَا۠ ﴿١٠﴾

11. In that situation were the believers tried: they were shaken as by a tremendous shaking.

هُنَالِكَ ٱبْتُلِىَ ٱلْمُؤْمِنُونَ وَزُلْزِلُوا۟ زِلْزَالًا شَدِيدًا ﴿١١﴾

12. And behold! The hypocrites and those in whose hearts is a disease (even) say:

وَإِذْ يَقُولُ ٱلْمُنَٰفِقُونَ وَٱلَّذِينَ فِى قُلُوبِهِم مَّرَضٌ مَّا

"Allah and His messenger promised us nothing but delusions!"

وَعَدَنَا ٱللَّهُ وَرَسُولُهُۥٓ إِلَّا غُرُورًا ﴿١٢﴾

13. See! A party among them said: "You men of Yathrib! You cannot stand (the attack)! Therefore, go back!" And a band of them ask for permission of the prophet saying, "Truly our houses are bare and exposed;" though they were not exposed: they intended nothing but to run away.

وَإِذْ قَالَت طَّآئِفَةٌ مِّنْهُمْ يَٰٓأَهْلَ يَثْرِبَ لَا مُقَامَ لَكُمْ
فَٱرْجِعُوا۟ ۚ وَيَسْتَـْٔذِنُ فَرِيقٌ مِّنْهُمُ ٱلنَّبِىَّ يَقُولُونَ إِنَّ
بُيُوتَنَا عَوْرَةٌ وَمَا هِىَ بِعَوْرَةٍ ۖ إِن يُرِيدُونَ إِلَّا فِرَارًا ﴿١٣﴾

14. And if an entry had been effected to them from the sides of the (city), and they had been incited to sedition, they would certainly have brought it to pass, with none but a brief delay!

وَلَوْ دُخِلَتْ عَلَيْهِم مِّنْ أَقْطَارِهَا ثُمَّ سُئِلُوا۟ ٱلْفِتْنَةَ
لَءَاتَوْهَا وَمَا تَلَبَّثُوا۟ بِهَآ إِلَّا يَسِيرًا ﴿١٤﴾

15. And yet they had already covenanted with Allah not to turn their backs, and a covenant with Allah must (surely) be answered for.

وَلَقَدْ كَانُوا۟ عَٰهَدُوا۟ ٱللَّهَ مِن قَبْلُ لَا يُوَلُّونَ
ٱلْأَدْبَٰرَ ۚ وَكَانَ عَهْدُ ٱللَّهِ مَسْـُٔولًا ﴿١٥﴾

16. Say: "Running away will not profit you if you are running away from death or slaughter; and even if (you do escape) no more than a brief (respite) will you be allowed to enjoy!"

قُل لَّن يَنفَعَكُمُ ٱلْفِرَارُ إِن فَرَرْتُم مِّنَ ٱلْمَوْتِ
أَوِ ٱلْقَتْلِ وَإِذًا لَّا تُمَتَّعُونَ إِلَّا قَلِيلًا ﴿١٦﴾

17. Say: "Who is it that can screen you from Allah if it be His wish to give you punishment or to give you mercy?" Nor will they find for themselves, besides Allah, any protector or helper.

قُلْ مَن ذَا ٱلَّذِى يَعْصِمُكُم مِّنَ ٱللَّهِ إِنْ أَرَادَ بِكُمْ
سُوٓءًا أَوْ أَرَادَ بِكُمْ رَحْمَةً ۚ وَلَا يَجِدُونَ لَهُم مِّن دُونِ
ٱللَّهِ وَلِيًّا وَلَا نَصِيرًا ﴿١٧﴾

18. Verily Allah knows those among you who keep back (men) and those who say to their brothers, "Come along to us," but come not to the fight except for just a little while,

۞ قَدْ يَعْلَمُ ٱللَّهُ ٱلْمُعَوِّقِينَ مِنكُمْ وَٱلْقَآئِلِينَ لِإِخْوَٰنِهِمْ ثلاثة أرباع الحزب ٤٢
هَلُمَّ إِلَيْنَا ۖ وَلَا يَأْتُونَ ٱلْبَأْسَ إِلَّا قَلِيلًا ﴿١٨﴾

19. Covetous over you (believers). Then when fear comes, you will see them looking

أَشِحَّةً عَلَيْكُمْ ۖ فَإِذَا جَآءَ ٱلْخَوْفُ رَأَيْتَهُمْ يَنظُرُونَ

to you, their eyes revolving, like (those of) one over whom hovers death; but when the fear is past, they will strike you with sharp tongues, covetous of goods. Such men have no faith, and so Allah has made their deeds of no effect; and that is easy for Allah.

إِلَيْكَ تَدُورُ أَعْيُنُهُمْ كَالَّذِي يُغْشَىٰ عَلَيْهِ مِنَ الْمَوْتِ ۖ
فَإِذَا ذَهَبَ الْخَوْفُ سَلَقُوكُم بِأَلْسِنَةٍ حِدَادٍ أَشِحَّةً
عَلَى الْخَيْرِ ۚ أُولَٰئِكَ لَمْ يُؤْمِنُوا فَأَحْبَطَ اللَّهُ أَعْمَالَهُمْ ۚ
وَكَانَ ذَٰلِكَ عَلَى اللَّهِ يَسِيرًا ﴿١٩﴾

20. They think that the confederates have not withdrawn; and if the confederates should come (again), they would wish they were in the deserts (wandering) among the Bedouins, and seeking news about you (from a safe distance); and if they were in your midst, they would fight but little.

يَحْسَبُونَ الْأَحْزَابَ لَمْ يَذْهَبُوا ۖ وَإِن يَأْتِ
الْأَحْزَابُ يَوَدُّوا لَوْ أَنَّهُم بَادُونَ فِي الْأَعْرَابِ
يَسْأَلُونَ عَنْ أَنبَائِكُمْ ۖ وَلَوْ كَانُوا فِيكُم مَّا قَاتَلُوا
إِلَّا قَلِيلًا ﴿٢٠﴾

21. You have indeed in the messenger of Allah a beautiful pattern of (conduct) for anyone whose hope is in Allah and the final day, and who engages much in the praise of Allah.

لَّقَدْ كَانَ لَكُمْ فِي رَسُولِ اللَّهِ أُسْوَةٌ حَسَنَةٌ لِّمَن كَانَ
يَرْجُو اللَّهَ وَالْيَوْمَ الْآخِرَ وَذَكَرَ اللَّهَ كَثِيرًا ﴿٢١﴾

22. When the believers saw the confederate forces they said: "This is what Allah and His messenger had promised us and Allah and His messenger told us what was true." And it only added to their faith and their zeal in obedience.

وَلَمَّا رَأَى الْمُؤْمِنُونَ الْأَحْزَابَ قَالُوا هَٰذَا مَا وَعَدَنَا
اللَّهُ وَرَسُولُهُ وَصَدَقَ اللَّهُ وَرَسُولُهُ ۚ وَمَا زَادَهُمْ
إِلَّا إِيمَانًا وَتَسْلِيمًا ﴿٢٢﴾

23. Among the believers are men who have been true to their covenant with Allah; of them, some have completed their vow to (the extreme) and some (still) wait; but they have never changed (their determination) in the least;

مِّنَ الْمُؤْمِنِينَ رِجَالٌ صَدَقُوا مَا عَاهَدُوا اللَّهَ عَلَيْهِ ۖ
فَمِنْهُم مَّن قَضَىٰ نَحْبَهُ وَمِنْهُم مَّن يَنتَظِرُ ۖ وَمَا بَدَّلُوا
تَبْدِيلًا ﴿٢٣﴾

24. That Allah may reward the men of truth for their truth and punish the hypocrites if that be His will or turn to them in mercy: for Allah is Oft-Forgiving, Most Merciful.

لِّيَجْزِيَ اللَّهُ الصَّادِقِينَ بِصِدْقِهِمْ وَيُعَذِّبَ
الْمُنَافِقِينَ إِن شَاءَ أَوْ يَتُوبَ عَلَيْهِمْ ۚ إِنَّ اللَّهَ كَانَ
غَفُورًا رَّحِيمًا ﴿٢٤﴾

25. And Allah turned back the unbelievers for (all) their fury; no advantage did they gain and enough is Allah for the believers in their fight. And Allah is full of strength, Able to enforce His Will.

وَرَدَّ ٱللَّهُ ٱلَّذِينَ كَفَرُوا۟ بِغَيْظِهِمْ لَمْ يَنَالُوا۟ خَيْرًا ۚ
وَكَفَى ٱللَّهُ ٱلْمُؤْمِنِينَ ٱلْقِتَالَ ۚ وَكَانَ ٱللَّهُ قَوِيًّا
عَزِيزًا ﴿٢٥﴾

26. And those of the people of the Book who aided them - Allah did take them down from their strongholds and cast terror into their hearts, (so that) some you slew, and some you made prisoners.

وَأَنزَلَ ٱلَّذِينَ ظَٰهَرُوهُم مِّنْ أَهْلِ ٱلْكِتَٰبِ مِن
صَيَاصِيهِمْ وَقَذَفَ فِى قُلُوبِهِمُ ٱلرُّعْبَ فَرِيقًا
تَقْتُلُونَ وَتَأْسِرُونَ فَرِيقًا ﴿٢٦﴾

27. And He made you heirs of their lands, their houses, and their goods, and of a land which you had not frequented (before). And Allah has power over all things.

وَأَوْرَثَكُمْ أَرْضَهُمْ وَدِيَٰرَهُمْ وَأَمْوَٰلَهُمْ وَأَرْضًا
لَّمْ تَطَـُٔوهَا ۚ وَكَانَ ٱللَّهُ عَلَىٰ كُلِّ شَىْءٍ قَدِيرًا ﴿٢٧﴾

28. O Prophet! Say to your consorts: "If it be that you desire the life of this world, and its glitter, - then come! I will provide for your enjoyment and set you free in a handsome manner."

يَٰٓأَيُّهَا ٱلنَّبِىُّ قُل لِّأَزْوَٰجِكَ إِن كُنتُنَّ تُرِدْنَ
ٱلْحَيَوٰةَ ٱلدُّنْيَا وَزِينَتَهَا فَتَعَالَيْنَ أُمَتِّعْكُنَّ
وَأُسَرِّحْكُنَّ سَرَاحًا جَمِيلًا ﴿٢٨﴾

29. But if you seek Allah and His messenger, and the home of the hereafter, verily Allah has prepared for the well-doers amongst you a great reward.

وَإِن كُنتُنَّ تُرِدْنَ ٱللَّهَ وَرَسُولَهُۥ وَٱلدَّارَ ٱلْـَٔاخِرَةَ
فَإِنَّ ٱللَّهَ أَعَدَّ لِلْمُحْسِنَٰتِ مِنكُنَّ أَجْرًا عَظِيمًا ﴿٢٩﴾

30. O consorts of the prophet! If any of you were guilty of evident unseemly conduct, the punishment would be doubled to her, and that is easy for Allah.

يَٰنِسَآءَ ٱلنَّبِىِّ مَن يَأْتِ مِنكُنَّ بِفَٰحِشَةٍ مُّبَيِّنَةٍ
يُضَٰعَفْ لَهَا ٱلْعَذَابُ ضِعْفَيْنِ ۚ وَكَانَ ذَٰلِكَ
عَلَى ٱللَّهِ يَسِيرًا ﴿٣٠﴾

* **31.** But any of you that is devout in the service of Allah and His messenger, and works righteousness - to her shall We grant her reward twice: and We have prepared for her a generous sustenance.

۞ وَمَن يَقْنُتْ مِنكُنَّ لِلَّهِ وَرَسُولِهِۦ وَتَعْمَلْ صَٰلِحًا الجزء ٢٢ الحزب ٤٣
نُّؤْتِهَآ أَجْرَهَا مَرَّتَيْنِ وَأَعْتَدْنَا لَهَا رِزْقًا
كَرِيمًا ﴿٣١﴾

* Part-22

32. O consorts of the prophet! You are not like any of the (other) women: if you do fear (Allah), be not too complaisant of speech, lest one in whose heart is a disease should be moved with desire: but speak you a speech (that is) just.

يَـٰنِسَآءَ ٱلنَّبِىِّ لَسْتُنَّ كَأَحَدٍ مِّنَ ٱلنِّسَآءِ ۚ إِنِ ٱتَّقَيْتُنَّ
فَلَا تَخْضَعْنَ بِٱلْقَوْلِ فَيَطْمَعَ ٱلَّذِى فِى قَلْبِهِۦ مَرَضٌ
وَقُلْنَ قَوْلًا مَّعْرُوفًا ٣٢

33. And stay quietly in your houses, and make not a dazzling display, like that of the former times of ignorance; and establish regular prayer, and give regular charity; and obey Allah and His messenger. And Allah only wishes to remove all abomination from you, you members of the family, and to make you pure and spotless.

وَقَرْنَ فِى بُيُوتِكُنَّ وَلَا تَبَرَّجْنَ تَبَرُّجَ ٱلْجَـٰهِلِيَّةِ
ٱلْأُولَىٰ ۖ وَأَقِمْنَ ٱلصَّلَوٰةَ وَءَاتِينَ ٱلزَّكَوٰةَ
وَأَطِعْنَ ٱللَّهَ وَرَسُولَهُۥٓ ۚ إِنَّمَا يُرِيدُ ٱللَّهُ لِيُذْهِبَ
عَنكُمُ ٱلرِّجْسَ أَهْلَ ٱلْبَيْتِ وَيُطَهِّرَكُمْ
تَطْهِيرًا ٣٣

34. And recite what is rehearsed to you in your homes of the signs of Allah and His wisdom: for Allah understands the finest mysteries and is well-acquainted (with them).

وَٱذْكُرْنَ مَا يُتْلَىٰ فِى بُيُوتِكُنَّ مِنْ
ءَايَـٰتِ ٱللَّهِ وَٱلْحِكْمَةِ ۚ إِنَّ ٱللَّهَ كَانَ
لَطِيفًا خَبِيرًا ٣٤

35. For Muslim men and women - for believing men and women, for devout men and women, for true men and women, for men and women who are patient and constant, for men and women who humble themselves, for men and women who give in charity, for men and women who fast (and deny themselves), for men and women who guard their chastity, and for men and women who engage much in Allah's praise - for them has Allah prepared forgiveness and great reward.

إِنَّ ٱلْمُسْلِمِينَ وَٱلْمُسْلِمَـٰتِ وَٱلْمُؤْمِنِينَ
وَٱلْمُؤْمِنَـٰتِ وَٱلْقَـٰنِتِينَ وَٱلْقَـٰنِتَـٰتِ وَٱلصَّـٰدِقِينَ
وَٱلصَّـٰدِقَـٰتِ وَٱلصَّـٰبِرِينَ وَٱلصَّـٰبِرَٰتِ وَٱلْخَـٰشِعِينَ
وَٱلْخَـٰشِعَـٰتِ وَٱلْمُتَصَدِّقِينَ وَٱلْمُتَصَدِّقَـٰتِ
وَٱلصَّـٰٓئِمِينَ وَٱلصَّـٰٓئِمَـٰتِ وَٱلْحَـٰفِظِينَ
فُرُوجَهُمْ وَٱلْحَـٰفِظَـٰتِ وَٱلذَّٰكِرِينَ ٱللَّهَ
كَثِيرًا وَٱلذَّٰكِرَٰتِ أَعَدَّ ٱللَّهُ لَهُم مَّغْفِرَةً
وَأَجْرًا عَظِيمًا ٣٥

36. It is not fitting for a believer, man or woman, when a matter has been decided

وَمَا كَانَ لِمُؤْمِنٍ وَلَا مُؤْمِنَةٍ إِذَا قَضَى ٱللَّهُ وَرَسُولُهُۥٓ

by Allah and His messenger, to have any option about their decision: if anyone disobeys Allah and His messenger, he is indeed on a clearly wrong path.

أَمْرًا أَن يَكُونَ لَهُمُ ٱلْخِيَرَةُ مِنْ أَمْرِهِمْ ۗ وَمَن يَعْصِ ٱللَّهَ
وَرَسُولَهُۥ فَقَدْ ضَلَّ ضَلَٰلًا مُّبِينًا ﴿٣٦﴾

37. See! You did say to one who had received the grace of Allah and your favour: "Retain you (in wedlock) your wife, and fear Allah." But you did hide in your heart that which Allah was about to make manifest: you did fear the people, but it is more fitting that you should fear Allah. Then when Zayd had dissolved (his marriage) with her, with the necessary (formality), We joined her in marriage to you: in order that (in future) there may be no difficulty to the believers in (the matter of) marriage with the wives of their adopted sons, when the latter have dissolved with the necessary (formality) (their marriage) with them. And Allah's command must be fulfilled.

وَإِذْ تَقُولُ لِلَّذِىٓ أَنْعَمَ ٱللَّهُ عَلَيْهِ وَأَنْعَمْتَ عَلَيْهِ
أَمْسِكْ عَلَيْكَ زَوْجَكَ وَٱتَّقِ ٱللَّهَ وَتُخْفِى فِى
نَفْسِكَ مَا ٱللَّهُ مُبْدِيهِ وَتَخْشَى ٱلنَّاسَ وَٱللَّهُ أَحَقُّ أَن
تَخْشَىٰهُ ۖ فَلَمَّا قَضَىٰ زَيْدٌ مِّنْهَا وَطَرًا زَوَّجْنَٰكَهَا لِكَىْ
لَا يَكُونَ عَلَى ٱلْمُؤْمِنِينَ حَرَجٌ فِىٓ أَزْوَٰجِ أَدْعِيَآئِهِمْ
إِذَا قَضَوْا۟ مِنْهُنَّ وَطَرًا ۚ وَكَانَ أَمْرُ ٱللَّهِ مَفْعُولًا ﴿٣٧﴾

38. There can be no difficulty to the prophet in what Allah has indicated to him as a duty. It was the practice (approved) of Allah amongst those of old that have passed away, and the command of Allah is a decree determined.

مَّا كَانَ عَلَى ٱلنَّبِىِّ مِنْ حَرَجٍ فِيمَا فَرَضَ ٱللَّهُ لَهُۥ ۖ سُنَّةَ
ٱللَّهِ فِى ٱلَّذِينَ خَلَوْا۟ مِن قَبْلُ ۚ وَكَانَ أَمْرُ ٱللَّهِ قَدَرًا
مَّقْدُورًا ﴿٣٨﴾

39. (It is the practice of those) who preach the messages of Allah, and fear Him, and fear none but Allah. And enough is Allah to call (men) to account.

ٱلَّذِينَ يُبَلِّغُونَ رِسَٰلَٰتِ ٱللَّهِ وَيَخْشَوْنَهُۥ وَلَا يَخْشَوْنَ
أَحَدًا إِلَّا ٱللَّهَ ۗ وَكَفَىٰ بِٱللَّهِ حَسِيبًا ﴿٣٩﴾

40. Muhammad is not the father of any of your men, but (he is) the messenger of Allah, and the seal of the prophets: and Allah has full knowledge of all things.

مَّا كَانَ مُحَمَّدٌ أَبَآ أَحَدٍ مِّن رِّجَالِكُمْ وَلَٰكِن
رَّسُولَ ٱللَّهِ وَخَاتَمَ ٱلنَّبِيِّۦنَ ۗ وَكَانَ ٱللَّهُ بِكُلِّ
شَىْءٍ عَلِيمًا ﴿٤٠﴾

41. O you who believe! Celebrate the praises of Allah, and do this often;

يَٰٓأَيُّهَا ٱلَّذِينَ ءَامَنُوا۟ ٱذْكُرُوا۟ ٱللَّهَ ذِكْرًا كَثِيرًا ﴿٤١﴾

42. And glorify Him morning and evening.

وَسَبِّحُوهُ بُكْرَةً وَأَصِيلًا ﴿٤٢﴾

43. He it is Who sends blessings on you, as do His angels, that He may bring you out from the depths of darkness into light: and He is Full of mercy to the believers.

هُوَ ٱلَّذِى يُصَلِّى عَلَيْكُمْ وَمَلَٰٓئِكَتُهُۥ لِيُخْرِجَكُم
مِّنَ ٱلظُّلُمَٰتِ إِلَى ٱلنُّورِ ۚ وَكَانَ بِٱلْمُؤْمِنِينَ رَحِيمًا ﴿٤٣﴾

44. Their salutation on the day they meet Him will be "peace!": and He has prepared for them a generous reward.

تَحِيَّتُهُمْ يَوْمَ يَلْقَوْنَهُۥ سَلَٰمٌ ۚ وَأَعَدَّ لَهُمْ أَجْرًا
كَرِيمًا ﴿٤٤﴾

45. O prophet! Truly We have sent you as a witness, a bearer of glad tidings, and a warner -

يَٰٓأَيُّهَا ٱلنَّبِىُّ إِنَّآ أَرْسَلْنَٰكَ شَٰهِدًا وَمُبَشِّرًا
وَنَذِيرًا ﴿٤٥﴾

46. And as one who invites to Allah's (grace) by His permission, and as a lamp spreading light.

وَدَاعِيًا إِلَى ٱللَّهِ بِإِذْنِهِۦ وَسِرَاجًا مُّنِيرًا ﴿٤٦﴾

47. Then give the glad tidings to the believers, that they shall have from Allah a very great bounty.

وَبَشِّرِ ٱلْمُؤْمِنِينَ بِأَنَّ لَهُم مِّنَ ٱللَّهِ فَضْلًا كَبِيرًا ﴿٤٧﴾

48. And obey not (the behests) of the unbelievers and the hypocrites, and heed not their annoyances, but put your trust in Allah. For enough is Allah as a Disposer of affairs.

وَلَا تُطِعِ ٱلْكَٰفِرِينَ وَٱلْمُنَٰفِقِينَ وَدَعْ أَذَىٰهُمْ
وَتَوَكَّلْ عَلَى ٱللَّهِ ۚ وَكَفَىٰ بِٱللَّهِ وَكِيلًا ﴿٤٨﴾

49. O you who believe! When you marry believing women, and then divorce them before you have touched them, no period of *Iddah* have you to count in respect of them: so give them a present, and set them free in a handsome manner.

يَٰٓأَيُّهَا ٱلَّذِينَ ءَامَنُوٓا۟ إِذَا نَكَحْتُمُ ٱلْمُؤْمِنَٰتِ ثُمَّ
طَلَّقْتُمُوهُنَّ مِن قَبْلِ أَن تَمَسُّوهُنَّ فَمَا لَكُمْ
عَلَيْهِنَّ مِنْ عِدَّةٍ تَعْتَدُّونَهَا ۖ فَمَتِّعُوهُنَّ وَسَرِّحُوهُنَّ
سَرَاحًا جَمِيلًا ﴿٤٩﴾

50. O prophet! We have made lawful to you your wives to whom you have paid their dowers; and those whom your right hand possesses out of the prisoners of war whom

يَٰٓأَيُّهَا ٱلنَّبِىُّ إِنَّآ أَحْلَلْنَا لَكَ أَزْوَٰجَكَ ٱلَّٰتِىٓ
ءَاتَيْتَ أُجُورَهُنَّ وَمَا مَلَكَتْ يَمِينُكَ مِمَّآ أَفَآءَ

Allah has assigned to you; and daughters of your paternal uncles and aunts, and daughters of your maternal uncles and aunts, who migrated (from Makkah) with you; and any believing woman who dedicates her soul to the prophet if the prophet wishes to wed her - this only for you, and not for the believers (at large); We know what We have appointed for them as to their wives and the captives whom their right hands possess - in order that there should be no difficulty for you. And Allah is Oft-Forgiving, Most Merciful.

ٱللَّهُ عَلَيْكَ وَبَنَاتِ عَمِّكَ وَبَنَاتِ عَمَّٰتِكَ وَبَنَاتِ
خَالِكَ وَبَنَاتِ خَٰلَٰتِكَ ٱلَّٰتِي هَاجَرْنَ مَعَكَ
وَٱمْرَأَةً مُّؤْمِنَةً إِن وَهَبَتْ نَفْسَهَا لِلنَّبِيِّ إِنْ أَرَادَ
ٱلنَّبِيُّ أَن يَسْتَنكِحَهَا خَالِصَةً لَّكَ مِن دُونِ
ٱلْمُؤْمِنِينَ ۗ قَدْ عَلِمْنَا مَا فَرَضْنَا عَلَيْهِمْ فِيٓ
أَزْوَٰجِهِمْ وَمَا مَلَكَتْ أَيْمَٰنُهُمْ لِكَيْلَا
يَكُونَ عَلَيْكَ حَرَجٌ ۗ وَكَانَ ٱللَّهُ غَفُورًا
رَّحِيمًا ﴿٥٠﴾

51. You may defer (the turn of) any of them that you please, and you may receive any you please: and there is no blame on you if you invite one whose (turn) you had set aside. This were nearer to the cooling of their eyes, the prevention of their grief, and their satisfaction - that of all of them - with that which you have to give them: and Allah knows (all) that is in your hearts: and Allah is All-Knowing, Most Forbearing.

ربع الحزب ٤٣
۞ تُرْجِي مَن تَشَآءُ مِنْهُنَّ وَتُـْٔوِيٓ إِلَيْكَ مَن تَشَآءُ ۖ
وَمَنِ ٱبْتَغَيْتَ مِمَّنْ عَزَلْتَ فَلَا جُنَاحَ عَلَيْكَ ۚ
ذَٰلِكَ أَدْنَىٰٓ أَن تَقَرَّ أَعْيُنُهُنَّ وَلَا يَحْزَنَّ وَيَرْضَيْنَ
بِمَآ ءَاتَيْتَهُنَّ كُلُّهُنَّ ۚ وَٱللَّهُ يَعْلَمُ مَا فِي قُلُوبِكُمْ ۚ
وَكَانَ ٱللَّهُ عَلِيمًا حَلِيمًا ﴿٥١﴾

52. It is not lawful for you (to marry more) women after this, nor to change them for (other) wives, even though their beauty attract you, except any your right hand should possess (as hand maidens): and Allah does watch over all things.

لَّا يَحِلُّ لَكَ ٱلنِّسَآءُ مِنۢ بَعْدُ وَلَآ أَن تَبَدَّلَ بِهِنَّ
مِنْ أَزْوَٰجٍ وَلَوْ أَعْجَبَكَ حُسْنُهُنَّ إِلَّا مَا مَلَكَتْ
يَمِينُكَ ۗ وَكَانَ ٱللَّهُ عَلَىٰ كُلِّ شَيْءٍ رَّقِيبًا ﴿٥٢﴾

53. O you who believe! Enter not the prophet's houses - until permission is given you - for a meal, (and then) not (so early as) to wait for its preparation; but when you are invited, enter; and when you have taken your meal, disperse, without seeking familiar talk. Such (behaviour)

يَٰٓأَيُّهَا ٱلَّذِينَ ءَامَنُوا۟ لَا تَدْخُلُوا۟ بُيُوتَ ٱلنَّبِيِّ إِلَّآ أَن
يُؤْذَنَ لَكُمْ إِلَىٰ طَعَامٍ غَيْرَ نَٰظِرِينَ إِنَىٰهُ وَلَٰكِنْ
إِذَا دُعِيتُمْ فَٱدْخُلُوا۟ فَإِذَا طَعِمْتُمْ فَٱنتَشِرُوا۟ وَلَا
مُسْتَـْٔنِسِينَ لِحَدِيثٍ ۚ إِنَّ ذَٰلِكُمْ كَانَ يُؤْذِي ٱلنَّبِيَّ

annoys the prophet: he is ashamed to dismiss you but Allah is not ashamed (to tell you) the truth. And when you ask (his ladies) for anything you want, ask them from before a screen: that makes for greater purity for your hearts and for theirs. Nor is it right for you that you should annoy Allah's messenger, or that you should marry his widows after him at any time. Truly such a thing is in Allah's sight an enormity.

فَيَسْتَحْيِۦ مِنكُمْۖ وَٱللَّهُ لَا يَسْتَحْيِۦ مِنَ ٱلْحَقِّۚ
وَإِذَا سَأَلْتُمُوهُنَّ مَتَٰعًا فَسْـَٔلُوهُنَّ مِن وَرَآءِ حِجَابٍۚ
ذَٰلِكُمْ أَطْهَرُ لِقُلُوبِكُمْ وَقُلُوبِهِنَّۚ وَمَا كَانَ
لَكُمْ أَن تُؤْذُوا۟ رَسُولَ ٱللَّهِ وَلَآ أَن تَنكِحُوٓا۟ أَزْوَٰجَهُۥ
مِنۢ بَعْدِهِۦٓ أَبَدًاۚ إِنَّ ذَٰلِكُمْ كَانَ عِندَ ٱللَّهِ
عَظِيمًا ﴿٥٣﴾

54. Whether you reveal anything or conceal it, verily Allah has full knowledge of all things.

إِن تُبْدُوا۟ شَيْـًٔا أَوْ تُخْفُوهُ فَإِنَّ ٱللَّهَ كَانَ بِكُلِّ
شَىْءٍ عَلِيمًا ﴿٥٤﴾

55. There is no blame (on these ladies if they appear) before their fathers or their sons, their brothers, or their brothers' sons, or their sisters' sons, or their women, or the (slaves) whom their right hands possess. And, (ladies), fear Allah: for Allah is Witness to all things.

لَّا جُنَاحَ عَلَيْهِنَّ فِىٓ ءَابَآئِهِنَّ وَلَآ أَبْنَآئِهِنَّ وَلَآ
إِخْوَٰنِهِنَّ وَلَآ أَبْنَآءِ إِخْوَٰنِهِنَّ وَلَآ أَبْنَآءِ أَخَوَٰتِهِنَّ
وَلَا نِسَآئِهِنَّ وَلَا مَا مَلَكَتْ أَيْمَٰنُهُنَّۗ وَٱتَّقِينَ ٱللَّهَۚ
إِنَّ ٱللَّهَ كَانَ عَلَىٰ كُلِّ شَىْءٍ شَهِيدًا ﴿٥٥﴾

56. Allah and His angels send blessings on the prophet: O you that believe! Send you blessings on him, and salute him with all respect.

إِنَّ ٱللَّهَ وَمَلَٰٓئِكَتَهُۥ يُصَلُّونَ عَلَى ٱلنَّبِىِّۚ
يَٰٓأَيُّهَا ٱلَّذِينَ ءَامَنُوا۟ صَلُّوا۟ عَلَيْهِ وَسَلِّمُوا۟
تَسْلِيمًا ﴿٥٦﴾

57. Those who annoy Allah and His messenger - Allah has cursed them in this world and in the hereafter, and has prepared for them a humiliating punishment.

إِنَّ ٱلَّذِينَ يُؤْذُونَ ٱللَّهَ وَرَسُولَهُۥ لَعَنَهُمُ ٱللَّهُ فِى ٱلدُّنْيَا
وَٱلْءَاخِرَةِ وَأَعَدَّ لَهُمْ عَذَابًا مُّهِينًا ﴿٥٧﴾

58. And those who annoy believing men and women undeservedly, bear (on themselves) a calumny and a glaring sin.

وَٱلَّذِينَ يُؤْذُونَ ٱلْمُؤْمِنِينَ وَٱلْمُؤْمِنَٰتِ بِغَيْرِ
مَا ٱكْتَسَبُوا۟ فَقَدِ ٱحْتَمَلُوا۟ بُهْتَٰنًا وَإِثْمًا
مُّبِينًا ﴿٥٨﴾

59. O prophet! Tell your wives and daughters, and the believing women, that they should cast their outer garments over their persons (when abroad); that is most convenient, that they should be known (as such) and not molested; and Allah is Oft-Forgiving, Most Merciful.

يَٰٓأَيُّهَا ٱلنَّبِيُّ قُل لِّأَزۡوَٰجِكَ وَبَنَاتِكَ وَنِسَآءِ
ٱلۡمُؤۡمِنِينَ يُدۡنِينَ عَلَيۡهِنَّ مِن جَلَٰبِيبِهِنَّۚ ذَٰلِكَ
أَدۡنَىٰٓ أَن يُعۡرَفۡنَ فَلَا يُؤۡذَيۡنَۗ وَكَانَ ٱللَّهُ
غَفُورٗا رَّحِيمٗا ٥٩

60. Truly, if the hypocrites and those in whose hearts is a disease, and those who stir up sedition in the city, desist not, We shall certainly stir you up against them: then will they not be able to stay in it as your neighbours for any length of time;

۞لَّئِن لَّمۡ يَنتَهِ ٱلۡمُنَٰفِقُونَ وَٱلَّذِينَ فِي قُلُوبِهِم مَّرَضٞ
وَٱلۡمُرۡجِفُونَ فِي ٱلۡمَدِينَةِ لَنُغۡرِيَنَّكَ بِهِمۡ ثُمَّ
لَا يُجَاوِرُونَكَ فِيهَآ إِلَّا قَلِيلٗا ٦٠

61. They shall have a curse on them; wherever they are found, they shall be seized and slain (without mercy).

مَّلۡعُونِينَۖ أَيۡنَمَا ثُقِفُوٓاْ أُخِذُواْ وَقُتِّلُواْ تَقۡتِيلٗا ٦١

62. (Such was) the practice (approved) of Allah among those who lived before: no change will you find in the practice (approved) of Allah.

سُنَّةَ ٱللَّهِ فِي ٱلَّذِينَ خَلَوۡاْ مِن قَبۡلُۖ وَلَن
تَجِدَ لِسُنَّةِ ٱللَّهِ تَبۡدِيلٗا ٦٢

63. Men ask you concerning the hour: say, "The knowledge thereof is with Allah (alone)": and what will make you understand? - Perhaps the hour is near!

يَسۡـَٔلُكَ ٱلنَّاسُ عَنِ ٱلسَّاعَةِۖ قُلۡ إِنَّمَا عِلۡمُهَا عِندَ ٱللَّهِۚ
وَمَا يُدۡرِيكَ لَعَلَّ ٱلسَّاعَةَ تَكُونُ قَرِيبًا ٦٣

64. Verily Allah has cursed the unbelievers and prepared for them a blazing fire -

إِنَّ ٱللَّهَ لَعَنَ ٱلۡكَٰفِرِينَ وَأَعَدَّ لَهُمۡ سَعِيرًا ٦٤

65. To dwell in it forever: no protector will they find, nor helper.

خَٰلِدِينَ فِيهَآ أَبَدٗاۖ لَّا يَجِدُونَ وَلِيّٗا وَلَا نَصِيرٗا ٦٥

66. The day that their faces will be turned upside down in the fire they will say: "Woe to us! Would that we had obeyed Allah and obeyed the messenger!"

يَوۡمَ تُقَلَّبُ وُجُوهُهُمۡ فِي ٱلنَّارِ يَقُولُونَ يَٰلَيۡتَنَآ
أَطَعۡنَا ٱللَّهَ وَأَطَعۡنَا ٱلرَّسُولَا۠ ٦٦

وَقَالُواْ رَبَّنَآ إِنَّآ أَطَعۡنَا سَادَتَنَا وَكُبَرَآءَنَا فَأَضَلُّونَا
ٱلسَّبِيلَا۠ ٦٧

67. And they would say: "Our Lord! We obeyed our chiefs and our great ones, and they misled us as to the (right) path.

رَبَّنَآ ءَاتِهِمۡ ضِعۡفَيۡنِ مِنَ ٱلۡعَذَابِ وَٱلۡعَنۡهُمۡ لَعۡنٗا
كَبِيرٗا ٦٨

68. "Our Lord! Give them double penalty and curse them with a very great curse!"

يَٰٓأَيُّهَا ٱلَّذِينَ ءَامَنُواْ لَا تَكُونُواْ كَٱلَّذِينَ ءَاذَوۡاْ مُوسَىٰ
فَبَرَّأَهُ ٱللَّهُ مِمَّا قَالُواْۚ وَكَانَ عِندَ ٱللَّهِ وَجِيهٗا ٦٩

69. O you who believe! Be you not like those who vexed and insulted Moses, but Allah cleared him of the (calumnies) they had uttered: and he was honourable in Allah's sight.

يَٰٓأَيُّهَا ٱلَّذِينَ ءَامَنُواْ ٱتَّقُواْ ٱللَّهَ وَقُولُواْ قَوۡلٗا سَدِيدٗا ٧٠

70. O you who believe! Fear Allah, and (always) say a word directed to the right:

يُصۡلِحۡ لَكُمۡ أَعۡمَٰلَكُمۡ وَيَغۡفِرۡ لَكُمۡ ذُنُوبَكُمۡۗ وَمَن
يُطِعِ ٱللَّهَ وَرَسُولَهُۥ فَقَدۡ فَازَ فَوۡزًا عَظِيمًا ٧١

71. That He may make your conduct whole and sound and forgive you your sins: he that obeys Allah and His messenger, has already attained the highest achievement.

إِنَّا عَرَضۡنَا ٱلۡأَمَانَةَ عَلَى ٱلسَّمَٰوَٰتِ وَٱلۡأَرۡضِ
وَٱلۡجِبَالِ فَأَبَيۡنَ أَن يَحۡمِلۡنَهَا وَأَشۡفَقۡنَ مِنۡهَا وَحَمَلَهَا
ٱلۡإِنسَٰنُۖ إِنَّهُۥ كَانَ ظَلُومٗا جَهُولٗا ٧٢

72. We did indeed offer the trust to the heavens and the earth and the mountains: but they refused to undertake it, being afraid of it: but man undertook it - he was indeed unjust and foolish -

لِّيُعَذِّبَ ٱللَّهُ ٱلۡمُنَٰفِقِينَ وَٱلۡمُنَٰفِقَٰتِ وَٱلۡمُشۡرِكِينَ
وَٱلۡمُشۡرِكَٰتِ وَيَتُوبَ ٱللَّهُ عَلَى ٱلۡمُؤۡمِنِينَ
وَٱلۡمُؤۡمِنَٰتِۗ وَكَانَ ٱللَّهُ غَفُورٗا رَّحِيمَۢا ٧٣

73. (With the result) that Allah has to punish the hypocrites, men and women, and the unbelievers, men and women, and Allah turns in mercy to the believers, men and women: for Allah is Oft-Forgiving, Most Merciful.

سُورَةُ سَبَإٍ

Surah 34: **Saba** (Sheba)

In the name of Allah,
Most Gracious, Most Merciful.

بِسْمِ ٱللَّهِ ٱلرَّحْمَٰنِ ٱلرَّحِيمِ

1. Praise be to Allah, to Whom belong all things in the heavens and on earth: to Him be Praise in the hereafter: and He is Full of wisdom, acquainted with all things.

ٱلْحَمْدُ لِلَّهِ ٱلَّذِى لَهُۥ مَا فِى ٱلسَّمَٰوَٰتِ وَمَا فِى ٱلْأَرْضِ
وَلَهُ ٱلْحَمْدُ فِى ٱلْءَاخِرَةِ ۚ وَهُوَ ٱلْحَكِيمُ ٱلْخَبِيرُ ١

2. He knows all that goes into the earth, and all that comes out of it: all that comes down from the sky and all that ascends to it: and He is the Most Merciful, the Oft-Forgiving.

يَعْلَمُ مَا يَلِجُ فِى ٱلْأَرْضِ وَمَا يَخْرُجُ مِنْهَا وَمَا
يَنزِلُ مِنَ ٱلسَّمَآءِ وَمَا يَعْرُجُ فِيهَا ۚ وَهُوَ
ٱلرَّحِيمُ ٱلْغَفُورُ ٢

3. The unbelievers say, "Never to us will come the hour": say, "Nay! But most surely, by my Lord, it will come upon you - by Him Who knows the unseen - from Whom is not hidden the least little atom in the heavens or on earth: nor is there anything less than that, or greater, but is in the record perspicuous:

وَقَالَ ٱلَّذِينَ كَفَرُوا۟ لَا تَأْتِينَا ٱلسَّاعَةُ ۖ قُلْ بَلَىٰ
وَرَبِّى لَتَأْتِيَنَّكُمْ عَٰلِمِ ٱلْغَيْبِ ۖ لَا يَعْزُبُ عَنْهُ مِثْقَالُ
ذَرَّةٍ فِى ٱلسَّمَٰوَٰتِ وَلَا فِى ٱلْأَرْضِ وَلَآ أَصْغَرُ
مِن ذَٰلِكَ وَلَآ أَكْبَرُ إِلَّا فِى كِتَٰبٍ مُّبِينٍ ٣

4. That He may reward those who believe and work deeds of righteousness: for such is forgiveness and a sustenance Most Generous."

لِّيَجْزِىَ ٱلَّذِينَ ءَامَنُوا۟ وَعَمِلُوا۟ ٱلصَّٰلِحَٰتِ ۚ
أُو۟لَٰٓئِكَ لَهُم مَّغْفِرَةٌ وَرِزْقٌ كَرِيمٌ ٤

5. But those who strive against Our signs, to frustrate them - for such will be a punishment most humiliating.

وَٱلَّذِينَ سَعَوْ فِىٓ ءَايَٰتِنَا مُعَٰجِزِينَ أُو۟لَٰٓئِكَ
لَهُمْ عَذَابٌ مِّن رِّجْزٍ أَلِيمٌ ٥

6. And those to whom knowledge has come see that the (revelation) sent down to you from your Lord - that is the truth, and that it guides to the path of the Exalted (in

وَيَرَى ٱلَّذِينَ أُوتُوا۟ ٱلْعِلْمَ ٱلَّذِىٓ أُنزِلَ إِلَيْكَ
مِن رَّبِّكَ هُوَ ٱلْحَقَّ وَيَهْدِىٓ إِلَىٰ صِرَٰطِ

Might), Worthy of all praise.

ٱلْعَزِيزِ ٱلْحَمِيدِ ٦

7. The unbelievers say (in ridicule): "Shall we point out to you a man that will tell you, when you are all scattered to pieces in disintegration, that you shall (then be raised) in a new creation?"

وَقَالَ ٱلَّذِينَ كَفَرُوا۟ هَلْ نَدُلُّكُمْ عَلَىٰ رَجُلٍ يُنَبِّئُكُمْ
إِذَا مُزِّقْتُمْ كُلَّ مُمَزَّقٍ إِنَّكُمْ لَفِى خَلْقٍ جَدِيدٍ ٧

8. "Has he invented a falsehood against Allah or has a spirit (seized) him?" - Nay, it is those who believe not in the hereafter, that are in (real) penalty, and in farthest error.

أَفْتَرَىٰ عَلَى ٱللَّهِ كَذِبًا أَم بِهِۦ جِنَّةٌۢ ۗ بَلِ ٱلَّذِينَ لَا يُؤْمِنُونَ
بِٱلْـَٔاخِرَةِ فِى ٱلْعَذَابِ وَٱلضَّلَـٰلِ ٱلْبَعِيدِ ٨

9. Do they not see what is before them and behind them, of the sky and the earth? If We wished, We could cause the earth to swallow them up, or cause a piece of the sky to fall upon them. Verily in this is a sign for every devotee that turns to Allah (in repentance).

أَفَلَمْ يَرَوْا۟ إِلَىٰ مَا بَيْنَ أَيْدِيهِمْ وَمَا خَلْفَهُم مِّنَ ٱلسَّمَآءِ
وَٱلْأَرْضِ ۚ إِن نَّشَأْ نَخْسِفْ بِهِمُ ٱلْأَرْضَ أَوْ نُسْقِطْ
عَلَيْهِمْ كِسَفًا مِّنَ ٱلسَّمَآءِ ۚ إِنَّ فِى ذَٰلِكَ لَـَٔايَةً
لِّكُلِّ عَبْدٍ مُّنِيبٍ ٩

10. We bestowed grace before on David from Ourselves: "O you mountains! Sing you back the praises of Allah with him! And you birds (also)! And We made the iron soft for him -

ثلاثة أرباع الحزب ٤٣

۞ وَلَقَدْ ءَاتَيْنَا دَاوُۥدَ مِنَّا فَضْلًا ۖ يَـٰجِبَالُ أَوِّبِى
مَعَهُۥ وَٱلطَّيْرَ ۖ وَأَلَنَّا لَهُ ٱلْحَدِيدَ ١٠

11. (Commanding), "Make you coats of mail, balancing well the rings of chain armour, and work you righteousness; for be sure I see (clearly) all that you do."

أَنِ ٱعْمَلْ سَـٰبِغَـٰتٍ وَقَدِّرْ فِى ٱلسَّرْدِ ۖ وَٱعْمَلُوا۟
صَـٰلِحًا ۖ إِنِّى بِمَا تَعْمَلُونَ بَصِيرٌ ١١

12. And to Solomon (We made) the wind (obedient): its early morning (stride) was a month's (journey), and its evening (stride) was a month's (journey); and We made a font of molten brass to flow for him; and there were Jinns that worked in front of him, by the leave of his Lord, and if any of them turned aside from Our command, We made Him taste of the penalty of the blazing fire.

وَلِسُلَيْمَـٰنَ ٱلرِّيحَ غُدُوُّهَا شَهْرٌ وَرَوَاحُهَا شَهْرٌ ۖ
وَأَسَلْنَا لَهُۥ عَيْنَ ٱلْقِطْرِ ۖ وَمِنَ ٱلْجِنِّ مَن يَعْمَلُ بَيْنَ
يَدَيْهِ بِإِذْنِ رَبِّهِۦ ۖ وَمَن يَزِغْ مِنْهُمْ عَنْ أَمْرِنَا نُذِقْهُ
مِنْ عَذَابِ ٱلسَّعِيرِ ١٢

13. They worked for him as he desired, (making) arches, images, basins, as large as reservoirs, and (cooking) cauldrons fixed (in their places): "Work you, sons of David with thanks! But few of My servants are grateful!"

يَعۡمَلُونَ لَهُۥ مَا يَشَآءُ مِن مَّحَٰرِيبَ وَتَمَٰثِيلَ وَجِفَانٖ
كَٱلۡجَوَابِ وَقُدُورٖ رَّاسِيَٰتٍۚ ٱعۡمَلُوٓاْ ءَالَ دَاوُۥدَ
شُكۡرٗاۚ وَقَلِيلٞ مِّنۡ عِبَادِيَ ٱلشَّكُورُ ١٣

14. Then, when We decreed (Solomon's) death, nothing showed them his death except a little worm of the earth, which kept (slowly) gnawing away at his staff: so when he fell down the Jinns saw plainly that if they had known the unseen, they would not have stayed in the humiliating penalty (of their task).

فَلَمَّا قَضَيۡنَا عَلَيۡهِ ٱلۡمَوۡتَ مَا دَلَّهُمۡ عَلَىٰ مَوۡتِهِۦٓ إِلَّا
دَآبَّةُ ٱلۡأَرۡضِ تَأۡكُلُ مِنسَأَتَهُۥۖ فَلَمَّا خَرَّ تَبَيَّنَتِ
ٱلۡجِنُّ أَن لَّوۡ كَانُواْ يَعۡلَمُونَ ٱلۡغَيۡبَ مَا لَبِثُواْ فِي
ٱلۡعَذَابِ ٱلۡمُهِينِ ١٤

15. There was for Saba before, a sign in their homeland - two gardens to the right and to the left. Eat of the sustenance (provided) by your Lord, and be grateful to Him: a territory fair and happy, and a Lord Oft-Forgiving!

لَقَدۡ كَانَ لِسَبَإٖ فِي مَسۡكَنِهِمۡ ءَايَةٞۖ جَنَّتَانِ عَن يَمِينٖ
وَشِمَالٖۖ كُلُواْ مِن رِّزۡقِ رَبِّكُمۡ وَٱشۡكُرُواْ لَهُۥۚ بَلۡدَةٞ
طَيِّبَةٞ وَرَبٌّ غَفُورٞ ١٥

16. But they turned away (from Allah) and We sent against them the flood (released) from the dams, and We converted their two garden (rows) into "gardens" producing bitter fruit, and tamarisks, and some few (stunted) lote trees.

فَأَعۡرَضُواْ فَأَرۡسَلۡنَا عَلَيۡهِمۡ سَيۡلَ ٱلۡعَرِمِ وَبَدَّلۡنَٰهُم
بِجَنَّتَيۡهِمۡ جَنَّتَيۡنِ ذَوَاتَيۡ أُكُلٍ خَمۡطٖ وَأَثۡلٖ
وَشَيۡءٖ مِّن سِدۡرٖ قَلِيلٖ ١٦

17. That was the requital We gave them because they ungratefully rejected faith: and never do We give (such) requital except to such as are ungrateful rejecters.

ذَٰلِكَ جَزَيۡنَٰهُم بِمَا كَفَرُواْۖ وَهَلۡ نُجَٰزِيٓ إِلَّا
ٱلۡكَفُورَ ١٧

18. Between them and the cities on which We had poured Our blessings, We had placed cities in prominent positions, and between them We had appointed stages of journey in due proportion: "Travel in it, secure by night and by day."

وَجَعَلۡنَا بَيۡنَهُمۡ وَبَيۡنَ ٱلۡقُرَى ٱلَّتِي بَٰرَكۡنَا فِيهَا
قُرٗى ظَٰهِرَةٗ وَقَدَّرۡنَا فِيهَا ٱلسَّيۡرَۖ سِيرُواْ فِيهَا لَيَالِيَ
وَأَيَّامًا ءَامِنِينَ ١٨

19. But they said: "Our Lord! Place longer distances between our journey-stages." But they wronged themselves (in it). At length We made them as a tale (that is told), and We dispersed them all in scattered fragments. Verily in this are signs for every (soul that is) patiently constant and grateful.

فَقَالُوا۟ رَبَّنَا بَـٰعِدْ بَيْنَ أَسْفَارِنَا وَظَلَمُوٓا۟ أَنفُسَهُمْ
فَجَعَلْنَـٰهُمْ أَحَادِيثَ وَمَزَّقْنَـٰهُمْ كُلَّ مُمَزَّقٍ ۚ إِنَّ فِى
ذَٰلِكَ لَـَٔايَـٰتٍ لِّكُلِّ صَبَّارٍ شَكُورٍ ١٩

20. And on them did Satan prove true his idea, and they followed him, all but a party that believed.

وَلَقَدْ صَدَّقَ عَلَيْهِمْ إِبْلِيسُ ظَنَّهُۥ فَٱتَّبَعُوهُ إِلَّا
فَرِيقًا مِّنَ ٱلْمُؤْمِنِينَ ٢٠

21. But he had no authority over them - except that We might test the man who believes in the hereafter from him who is in doubt concerning it: and your Lord does watch over all things.

وَمَا كَانَ لَهُۥ عَلَيْهِم مِّن سُلْطَـٰنٍ إِلَّا لِنَعْلَمَ مَن
يُؤْمِنُ بِٱلْـَٔاخِرَةِ مِمَّنْ هُوَ مِنْهَا فِى شَكٍّ ۗ
وَرَبُّكَ عَلَىٰ كُلِّ شَىْءٍ حَفِيظٌ ٢١

22. Say: "Call upon other (gods) whom you fancy, besides Allah: they have no power - not the weight of an atom - in the heavens or on earth; no (sort of) share have they in it, nor is any of them a helper to Allah."

قُلِ ٱدْعُوا۟ ٱلَّذِينَ زَعَمْتُم مِّن دُونِ ٱللَّهِ لَا يَمْلِكُونَ
مِثْقَالَ ذَرَّةٍ فِى ٱلسَّمَـٰوَٰتِ وَلَا فِى ٱلْأَرْضِ وَمَا لَهُمْ
فِيهِمَا مِن شِرْكٍ وَمَا لَهُۥ مِنْهُم مِّن ظَهِيرٍ ٢٢

23. "No intercession can benefit in His presence, except for those for whom He has granted permission. So far (is this the case) that when terror is removed from their hearts (at the day of judgement, then) will they say, 'What is it that your Lord commanded?' They will say: 'That which is true and just; and He is the Most High, Most Great.'"

وَلَا تَنفَعُ ٱلشَّفَـٰعَةُ عِندَهُۥٓ إِلَّا لِمَنْ أَذِنَ لَهُۥ ۚ حَتَّىٰٓ
إِذَا فُزِّعَ عَن قُلُوبِهِمْ قَالُوا۟ مَاذَا قَالَ رَبُّكُمْ ۖ قَالُوا۟
ٱلْحَقَّ ۖ وَهُوَ ٱلْعَلِىُّ ٱلْكَبِيرُ ٢٣

24. Say: "Who gives you sustenance, from the heavens and the earth?" Say: "It is Allah; and certain it is that either we or you are on right guidance or in manifest error!"

۞ قُلْ مَن يَرْزُقُكُم مِّنَ ٱلسَّمَـٰوَٰتِ وَٱلْأَرْضِ ۖ الحزب ٤٤
قُلِ ٱللَّهُ ۖ وَإِنَّآ أَوْ إِيَّاكُمْ لَعَلَىٰ هُدًى أَوْ فِى
ضَلَـٰلٍ مُّبِينٍ ٢٤

25. Say: "You shall not be questioned as to

قُل لَّا تُسْـَٔلُونَ عَمَّآ أَجْرَمْنَا وَلَا نُسْـَٔلُ

our sins, nor shall we be questioned as to what you do."

عَمَّا تَعْمَلُونَ ﴿٢٥﴾

26. Say: "Our Lord will gather us together and will in the end decide the matter between us (and you) in truth and justice: and He is the One to decide, the One Who knows all."

قُلْ يَجْمَعُ بَيْنَنَا رَبُّنَا ثُمَّ يَفْتَحُ بَيْنَنَا بِالْحَقِّ
وَهُوَ الْفَتَّاحُ الْعَلِيمُ ﴿٢٦﴾

27. Say: "Show me those whom you have joined with Him as partners: by no means (can you). Nay, He is Allah, the Exalted in Power, the Wise."

قُلْ أَرُونِيَ الَّذِينَ أَلْحَقْتُم بِهِ شُرَكَاءَ ۖ كَلَّا ۚ بَلْ
هُوَ اللَّهُ الْعَزِيزُ الْحَكِيمُ ﴿٢٧﴾

28. We have not sent you but as a universal (messenger) to men, giving them glad tidings, and warning them (against sin), but most men understand not.

وَمَا أَرْسَلْنَاكَ إِلَّا كَافَّةً لِّلنَّاسِ بَشِيرًا وَنَذِيرًا
وَلَٰكِنَّ أَكْثَرَ النَّاسِ لَا يَعْلَمُونَ ﴿٢٨﴾

29. They say: "When will this promise (come to pass) if you are telling the truth?"

وَيَقُولُونَ مَتَىٰ هَٰذَا الْوَعْدُ إِن كُنتُمْ
صَادِقِينَ ﴿٢٩﴾

30. Say: "The appointment to you is for a day, which you cannot put back for an hour nor put forward."

قُل لَّكُم مِّيعَادُ يَوْمٍ لَّا تَسْتَأْخِرُونَ عَنْهُ سَاعَةً وَلَا
تَسْتَقْدِمُونَ ﴿٣٠﴾

31. The unbelievers say: "We shall neither believe in this scripture nor in (any) that (came) before it." Could you but see when the wrongdoers will be made to stand before their Lord, throwing back the word (of blame) on one another! Those who had been despised will say to the arrogant ones: "Had it not been for you, we should certainly have been believers!"

وَقَالَ الَّذِينَ كَفَرُوا لَن نُّؤْمِنَ بِهَٰذَا الْقُرْآنِ
وَلَا بِالَّذِي بَيْنَ يَدَيْهِ ۗ وَلَوْ تَرَىٰ إِذِ الظَّالِمُونَ
مَوْقُوفُونَ عِندَ رَبِّهِمْ يَرْجِعُ بَعْضُهُمْ إِلَىٰ
بَعْضٍ الْقَوْلَ يَقُولُ الَّذِينَ اسْتُضْعِفُوا لِلَّذِينَ
اسْتَكْبَرُوا لَوْلَا أَنتُمْ لَكُنَّا مُؤْمِنِينَ ﴿٣١﴾

32. The arrogant ones will say to those who had been despised: "Was it we who kept you back from guidance after it reached you? Nay, rather it was you who transgressed."

قَالَ الَّذِينَ اسْتَكْبَرُوا لِلَّذِينَ اسْتُضْعِفُوا أَنَحْنُ
صَدَدْنَاكُمْ عَنِ الْهُدَىٰ بَعْدَ إِذْ جَاءَكُم ۖ بَلْ كُنتُم
مُّجْرِمِينَ ﴿٣٢﴾

33. Those who had been despised will say to the arrogant ones: "Nay! It was a plot (of yours) by day and by night: See! You (constantly) ordered us to be ungrateful to Allah and to attribute equals to Him!" They will declare (their) repentance when they see the penalty: We shall put yokes on the necks of the unbelievers: it would only be a requital for their (ill) deeds.

وَقَالَ ٱلَّذِينَ ٱسْتُضْعِفُوا۟ لِلَّذِينَ ٱسْتَكْبَرُوا۟ بَلْ
مَكْرُ ٱلَّيْلِ وَٱلنَّهَارِ إِذْ تَأْمُرُونَنَآ أَن نَّكْفُرَ بِٱللَّهِ
وَنَجْعَلَ لَهُۥٓ أَندَادًا ۚ وَأَسَرُّوا۟ ٱلنَّدَامَةَ لَمَّا رَأَوُا۟
ٱلْعَذَابَ ۚ وَجَعَلْنَا ٱلْأَغْلَٰلَ فِىٓ أَعْنَاقِ ٱلَّذِينَ
كَفَرُوا۟ ۖ هَلْ يُجْزَوْنَ إِلَّا مَا كَانُوا۟ يَعْمَلُونَ ﴿٣٣﴾

34. Never did We send a warner to a population, but the wealthy ones among them said: "We believe not in the (message) with which you have been sent."

وَمَآ أَرْسَلْنَا فِى قَرْيَةٍ مِّن نَّذِيرٍ إِلَّا قَالَ مُتْرَفُوهَآ
إِنَّا بِمَآ أُرْسِلْتُم بِهِۦ كَٰفِرُونَ ﴿٣٤﴾

35. They said: "We have more in wealth and in sons, and we cannot be punished."

وَقَالُوا۟ نَحْنُ أَكْثَرُ أَمْوَٰلًا وَأَوْلَٰدًا وَمَا نَحْنُ
بِمُعَذَّبِينَ ﴿٣٥﴾

36. Say: "Verily my Lord enlarges and restricts the provision to whom He pleases, but most men understand not."

قُلْ إِنَّ رَبِّى يَبْسُطُ ٱلرِّزْقَ لِمَن يَشَآءُ وَيَقْدِرُ وَلَٰكِنَّ
أَكْثَرَ ٱلنَّاسِ لَا يَعْلَمُونَ ﴿٣٦﴾

37. It is not your wealth nor your sons, that will bring you nearer to Us in degree; but only those who believe and work righteousness - these are the ones for whom there is a multiplied reward for their deeds, while secure they (reside) in the dwellings on high!

وَمَآ أَمْوَٰلُكُمْ وَلَآ أَوْلَٰدُكُم بِٱلَّتِى تُقَرِّبُكُمْ عِندَنَا زُلْفَىٰٓ
إِلَّا مَنْ ءَامَنَ وَعَمِلَ صَٰلِحًا فَأُو۟لَٰٓئِكَ لَهُمْ جَزَآءُ
ٱلضِّعْفِ بِمَا عَمِلُوا۟ وَهُمْ فِى ٱلْغُرُفَٰتِ ءَامِنُونَ ﴿٣٧﴾

38. Those who strive against Our signs, to frustrate them, will be given over into punishment.

وَٱلَّذِينَ يَسْعَوْنَ فِىٓ ءَايَٰتِنَا مُعَٰجِزِينَ أُو۟لَٰٓئِكَ فِى
ٱلْعَذَابِ مُحْضَرُونَ ﴿٣٨﴾

39. Say: "Verily my Lord enlarges and restricts the sustenance to such of His servants as He pleases: and nothing do you spend in the least (in His cause) but He replaces it: for He is the best of those Who grant sustenance.

قُلْ إِنَّ رَبِّى يَبْسُطُ ٱلرِّزْقَ لِمَن يَشَآءُ مِنْ عِبَادِهِۦ
وَيَقْدِرُ لَهُۥ ۚ وَمَآ أَنفَقْتُم مِّن شَىْءٍ فَهُوَ يُخْلِفُهُۥ ۖ
وَهُوَ خَيْرُ ٱلرَّٰزِقِينَ ﴿٣٩﴾

40. One day, He will gather them all together and say to the angels, "Was it you that these men used to worship?"

وَيَوْمَ يَحْشُرُهُمْ جَمِيعًا ثُمَّ يَقُولُ لِلْمَلَٰٓئِكَةِ أَهَٰٓؤُلَآءِ
إِيَّاكُمْ كَانُوا۟ يَعْبُدُونَ ﴿٤٠﴾

41. They will say "Glory to You! Our (tie) is with You - as protector - not with them. Nay, but they worshipped the Jinns: most of them believed in them."

قَالُوا۟ سُبْحَٰنَكَ أَنتَ وَلِيُّنَا مِن دُونِهِم ۖ بَلْ كَانُوا۟
يَعْبُدُونَ ٱلْجِنَّ ۖ أَكْثَرُهُم بِهِم مُّؤْمِنُونَ ﴿٤١﴾

42. So on that day no power shall they have over each other, for profit or harm: and We shall say to the wrongdoers, "Taste you the penalty of the fire - which you used to deny!"

فَٱلْيَوْمَ لَا يَمْلِكُ بَعْضُكُمْ لِبَعْضٍ نَّفْعًا وَلَا ضَرًّا
وَنَقُولُ لِلَّذِينَ ظَلَمُوا۟ ذُوقُوا۟ عَذَابَ ٱلنَّارِ ٱلَّتِى كُنتُم
بِهَا تُكَذِّبُونَ ﴿٤٢﴾

43. When Our clear signs are rehearsed to them, they say, "This is only a man who wishes to hinder you from the (worship) which your fathers practised." And they say, "This is only a falsehood invented!" And the unbelievers say of the truth when it comes to them: "This is nothing but evident magic!"

وَإِذَا تُتْلَىٰ عَلَيْهِمْ ءَايَٰتُنَا بَيِّنَٰتٍ قَالُوا۟ مَا هَٰذَآ إِلَّا رَجُلٌ
يُرِيدُ أَن يَصُدَّكُمْ عَمَّا كَانَ يَعْبُدُ ءَابَآؤُكُمْ وَقَالُوا۟
مَا هَٰذَآ إِلَّآ إِفْكٌ مُّفْتَرًى ۚ وَقَالَ ٱلَّذِينَ كَفَرُوا۟ لِلْحَقِّ
لَمَّا جَآءَهُمْ إِنْ هَٰذَآ إِلَّا سِحْرٌ مُّبِينٌ ﴿٤٣﴾

44. But We had not given them books which they could study, nor sent messengers to them before you as warners.

وَمَآ ءَاتَيْنَٰهُم مِّن كُتُبٍ يَدْرُسُونَهَا ۖ وَمَآ أَرْسَلْنَآ
إِلَيْهِمْ قَبْلَكَ مِن نَّذِيرٍ ﴿٤٤﴾

45. And their predecessors rejected (the truth); these have not received a tenth of what We had granted to those: yet when they rejected My messengers, how (terrible) was My rejection (of them)!

وَكَذَّبَ ٱلَّذِينَ مِن قَبْلِهِمْ وَمَا بَلَغُوا۟ مِعْشَارَ
مَآ ءَاتَيْنَٰهُمْ فَكَذَّبُوا۟ رُسُلِى ۖ فَكَيْفَ كَانَ نَكِيرِ ﴿٤٥﴾

46. Say: "I do admonish you on one point: that you do stand up before Allah - (it may be) in pairs, or (it may be) singly, and reflect (within yourselves): your companion is not possessed: he is no less than a warner to you, in face of a terrible penalty."

۞ قُلْ إِنَّمَآ أَعِظُكُم بِوَٰحِدَةٍ ۖ أَن تَقُومُوا۟ لِلَّهِ مَثْنَىٰ وَفُرَٰدَىٰ ربع الحزب ٤٤
وَفُرَٰدَىٰ ثُمَّ تَتَفَكَّرُوا۟ ۚ مَا بِصَاحِبِكُم مِّن جِنَّةٍ ۚ إِنْ
هُوَ إِلَّا نَذِيرٌ لَّكُم بَيْنَ يَدَىْ عَذَابٍ شَدِيدٍ ﴿٤٦﴾

47. Say: "No reward do I ask of you: it is (all) in your interest: my reward is only due from Allah: and He is Witness to all things."

قُلْ مَا سَأَلْتُكُم مِّنْ أَجْرٍ فَهُوَ لَكُمْ ۖ إِنْ أَجْرِيَ إِلَّا
عَلَى ٱللَّهِ ۖ وَهُوَ عَلَىٰ كُلِّ شَيْءٍ شَهِيدٌ ﴿٤٧﴾

48. Say: "Verily my Lord does cast the (mantle of) truth (over His servants) - He that has full knowledge of (all) that is hidden."

قُلْ إِنَّ رَبِّي يَقْذِفُ بِٱلْحَقِّ عَلَّٰمُ ٱلْغُيُوبِ ﴿٤٨﴾

49. Say: "The truth has arrived and falsehood neither creates anything new, nor restores anything."

قُلْ جَآءَ ٱلْحَقُّ وَمَا يُبْدِئُ ٱلْبَٰطِلُ وَمَا يُعِيدُ ﴿٤٩﴾

50. Say: "If I am astray, I only stray to the loss of my own soul; but if I receive guidance, it is because of the inspiration of my Lord to me: it is He Who hears all things and is (ever) near."

قُلْ إِن ضَلَلْتُ فَإِنَّمَآ أَضِلُّ عَلَىٰ نَفْسِي ۖ وَإِنِ ٱهْتَدَيْتُ
فَبِمَا يُوحِيٓ إِلَيَّ رَبِّيٓ ۚ إِنَّهُۥ سَمِيعٌ قَرِيبٌ ﴿٥٠﴾

51. If you could but see when they will quake with terror: but then there will be no escape (for them), and they will be seized from a position (quite) near.

وَلَوْ تَرَىٰٓ إِذْ فَزِعُوا۟ فَلَا فَوْتَ وَأُخِذُوا۟ مِن
مَّكَانٍ قَرِيبٍ ﴿٥١﴾

52. And they will say, "We do believe (now) in the (truth)"; but how could they receive (faith) from a position (so) far off -

وَقَالُوٓا۟ ءَامَنَّا بِهِۦ وَأَنَّىٰ لَهُمُ ٱلتَّنَاوُشُ مِن
مَّكَانٍۭ بَعِيدٍ ﴿٥٢﴾

53. Seeing that they did reject faith (entirely) before, and that they (continually) cast (slanders) on the unseen from a position far off?

وَقَدْ كَفَرُوا۟ بِهِۦ مِن قَبْلُ ۖ وَيَقْذِفُونَ بِٱلْغَيْبِ
مِن مَّكَانٍۭ بَعِيدٍ ﴿٥٣﴾

54. And between them and their desires, is placed a barrier, as was done in the past with their partisans: for they were indeed in suspicious (disquieting) doubt.

وَحِيلَ بَيْنَهُمْ وَبَيْنَ مَا يَشْتَهُونَ كَمَا فُعِلَ
بِأَشْيَاعِهِم مِّن قَبْلُ ۚ إِنَّهُمْ كَانُوا۟ فِي شَكٍّ مُّرِيبٍۭ ﴿٥٤﴾

سُورَةُ فَاطِرٍ

Surah 35: ***Fatir*** **(The Originator of Creation)**

In the name of Allah,
Most Gracious, Most Merciful.

بِسْمِ ٱللَّهِ ٱلرَّحْمَٰنِ ٱلرَّحِيمِ

1. Praise be to Allah, Who created (out of nothing) the heavens and the earth, Who made the angels messengers with wings - two, or three, or four (pairs): He adds to creation as He pleases: for Allah has power over all things.

ٱلْحَمْدُ لِلَّهِ فَاطِرِ ٱلسَّمَٰوَٰتِ وَٱلْأَرْضِ جَاعِلِ ٱلْمَلَٰٓئِكَةِ
رُسُلًا أُو۟لِىٓ أَجْنِحَةٍ مَّثْنَىٰ وَثُلَٰثَ وَرُبَٰعَ ۚ يَزِيدُ فِى ٱلْخَلْقِ
مَا يَشَآءُ ۚ إِنَّ ٱللَّهَ عَلَىٰ كُلِّ شَىْءٍ قَدِيرٌ ١

2. What Allah out of His mercy does bestow on mankind there is none that can withhold: what He does withhold there is none that can grant apart from Him: and He is the Exalted in power, Full of wisdom.

مَّا يَفْتَحِ ٱللَّهُ لِلنَّاسِ مِن رَّحْمَةٍ فَلَا مُمْسِكَ لَهَا ۖ وَمَا
يُمْسِكْ فَلَا مُرْسِلَ لَهُۥ مِنۢ بَعْدِهِۦ ۚ وَهُوَ ٱلْعَزِيزُ
ٱلْحَكِيمُ ٢

3. O men! Call to mind the grace of Allah to you! Is there a creator, other than Allah, to give you sustenance from heaven or earth? There is no god but He: how then are you deluded away from the truth?

يَٰٓأَيُّهَا ٱلنَّاسُ ٱذْكُرُوا۟ نِعْمَتَ ٱللَّهِ عَلَيْكُمْ ۚ هَلْ مِنْ
خَٰلِقٍ غَيْرُ ٱللَّهِ يَرْزُقُكُم مِّنَ ٱلسَّمَآءِ وَٱلْأَرْضِ ۚ لَآ إِلَٰهَ
إِلَّا هُوَ ۖ فَأَنَّىٰ تُؤْفَكُونَ ٣

4. And if hey reject you, so were messengers rejected before you: to Allah go back for decision all affairs.

وَإِن يُكَذِّبُوكَ فَقَدْ كُذِّبَتْ رُسُلٌ مِّن قَبْلِكَ ۚ وَإِلَى ٱللَّهِ
تُرْجَعُ ٱلْأُمُورُ ٤

5. O men! Certainly the promise of Allah is true. Let not then this present life deceive you, nor let the chief deceiver deceive you about Allah.

يَٰٓأَيُّهَا ٱلنَّاسُ إِنَّ وَعْدَ ٱللَّهِ حَقٌّ ۖ فَلَا تَغُرَّنَّكُمُ
ٱلْحَيَوٰةُ ٱلدُّنْيَا ۖ وَلَا يَغُرَّنَّكُم بِٱللَّهِ ٱلْغَرُورُ ٥

6. Verily Satan is an enemy to you: so treat him as an enemy. He only invites his adherents, that they may become companions of the blazing fire.

إِنَّ ٱلشَّيْطَٰنَ لَكُمْ عَدُوٌّ فَٱتَّخِذُوهُ عَدُوًّا ۚ إِنَّمَا يَدْعُوا۟
حِزْبَهُۥ لِيَكُونُوا۟ مِنْ أَصْحَٰبِ ٱلسَّعِيرِ ٦

7. For those who reject Allah, is a terrible penalty: but for those who believe and work righteous deeds, is forgiveness, and a magnificent reward.

ٱلَّذِينَ كَفَرُوا۟ لَهُمْ عَذَابٌ شَدِيدٌ ۖ وَٱلَّذِينَ ءَامَنُوا۟ وَعَمِلُوا۟
ٱلصَّٰلِحَٰتِ لَهُم مَّغْفِرَةٌ وَأَجْرٌ كَبِيرٌ ٧

8. Is he, then, to whom the evil of his conduct is made alluring, so that he looks upon it as good, (equal to one who is rightly guided)? For Allah leaves to stray whom He wills, and guides whom He wills. So let not your soul go out in (vainly) sighing after them: for Allah knows well all that they do!

أَفَمَن زُيِّنَ لَهُۥ سُوٓءُ عَمَلِهِۦ فَرَءَاهُ حَسَنًا ۖ فَإِنَّ ٱللَّهَ يُضِلُّ
مَن يَشَآءُ وَيَهْدِى مَن يَشَآءُ ۖ فَلَا تَذْهَبْ نَفْسُكَ عَلَيْهِمْ
حَسَرَٰتٍ ۚ إِنَّ ٱللَّهَ عَلِيمٌۢ بِمَا يَصْنَعُونَ ٨

9. It is Allah Who sends ahead the winds, so that they raise up the clouds, and We drive them to a land that is dead, and revive the earth with it after its death: even so (will be) the resurrection!

وَٱللَّهُ ٱلَّذِىٓ أَرْسَلَ ٱلرِّيَٰحَ فَتُثِيرُ سَحَابًا فَسُقْنَٰهُ إِلَىٰ
بَلَدٍ مَّيِّتٍ فَأَحْيَيْنَا بِهِ ٱلْأَرْضَ بَعْدَ مَوْتِهَا ۚ كَذَٰلِكَ
ٱلنُّشُورُ ٩

10. If any do seek for glory and power - to Allah belong all glory and power. To Him mount up (all) words of purity: it is He Who exalts each deed of righteousness. Those that lay plots of evil - for them is a penalty terrible; and the plotting of such will be void (of result).

مَن كَانَ يُرِيدُ ٱلْعِزَّةَ فَلِلَّهِ ٱلْعِزَّةُ جَمِيعًا ۚ إِلَيْهِ يَصْعَدُ
ٱلْكَلِمُ ٱلطَّيِّبُ وَٱلْعَمَلُ ٱلصَّٰلِحُ يَرْفَعُهُۥ ۚ وَٱلَّذِينَ
يَمْكُرُونَ ٱلسَّيِّـَٔاتِ لَهُمْ عَذَابٌ شَدِيدٌ ۖ وَمَكْرُ
أُو۟لَٰٓئِكَ هُوَ يَبُورُ ١٠

11. And Allah did create you from dust; then from a sperm-drop; then He made you in pairs. And no female conceives, or lays down (her load), but with His knowledge. Nor is a man long-lived granted length of days, nor is a part cut off from his life, but it is in a decree (ordained). All this is easy for Allah.

وَٱللَّهُ خَلَقَكُم مِّن تُرَابٍ ثُمَّ مِن نُّطْفَةٍ ثُمَّ جَعَلَكُمْ
أَزْوَٰجًا ۚ وَمَا تَحْمِلُ مِنْ أُنثَىٰ وَلَا تَضَعُ إِلَّا بِعِلْمِهِۦ ۚ
وَمَا يُعَمَّرُ مِن مُّعَمَّرٍ وَلَا يُنقَصُ مِنْ عُمُرِهِۦٓ إِلَّا فِى
كِتَٰبٍ ۚ إِنَّ ذَٰلِكَ عَلَى ٱللَّهِ يَسِيرٌ ١١

12. Nor are the two bodies of flowing water alike - the one palatable, sweet, and pleasant to drink, and the other, salty and bitter. Yet from each (kind of water) do you

وَمَا يَسْتَوِى ٱلْبَحْرَانِ هَٰذَا عَذْبٌ فُرَاتٌ سَآئِغٌ
شَرَابُهُۥ وَهَٰذَا مِلْحٌ أُجَاجٌ ۖ وَمِن كُلٍّ تَأْكُلُونَ

eat flesh fresh and tender, and you extract ornaments to wear; and you see the ships in it that plough the waves, that you may seek (thus) of the bounty of Allah that you may be grateful.

لَحْمًا طَرِيًّا وَتَسْتَخْرِجُونَ حِلْيَةً تَلْبَسُونَهَا ۖ وَتَرَى الْفُلْكَ فِيهِ مَوَاخِرَ لِتَبْتَغُوا مِنْ فَضْلِهِ وَلَعَلَّكُمْ تَشْكُرُونَ ﴿١٢﴾

13. He merges night into day and He merges day into night, and He has subjected the sun and the moon (to His law): each one runs its course for a term appointed. Such is Allah your Lord: to Him belongs all dominion. And those whom you invoke besides Him have not the least power.

يُولِجُ اللَّيْلَ فِي النَّهَارِ وَيُولِجُ النَّهَارَ فِي اللَّيْلِ وَسَخَّرَ الشَّمْسَ وَالْقَمَرَ ۖ كُلٌّ يَجْرِي لِأَجَلٍ مُسَمًّى ۚ ذَٰلِكُمُ اللَّهُ رَبُّكُمْ لَهُ الْمُلْكُ ۚ وَالَّذِينَ تَدْعُونَ مِنْ دُونِهِ مَا يَمْلِكُونَ مِنْ قِطْمِيرٍ ﴿١٣﴾

14. If you invoke them, they will not listen to your call, and if they were to listen, they cannot answer your (prayer). On the day of judgement they will reject your "partnership." And none, (O man!) can tell you (the truth) like the One Who is acquainted with all things.

إِنْ تَدْعُوهُمْ لَا يَسْمَعُوا دُعَاءَكُمْ وَلَوْ سَمِعُوا مَا اسْتَجَابُوا لَكُمْ ۖ وَيَوْمَ الْقِيَامَةِ يَكْفُرُونَ بِشِرْكِكُمْ ۚ وَلَا يُنَبِّئُكَ مِثْلُ خَبِيرٍ ﴿١٤﴾

15. O you men! It is you that have need of Allah: but Allah is the One Free of all wants, Worthy of all praise.

۞ يَا أَيُّهَا النَّاسُ أَنْتُمُ الْفُقَرَاءُ إِلَى اللَّهِ ۖ وَاللَّهُ هُوَ الْغَنِيُّ الْحَمِيدُ ﴿١٥﴾

نصف حزب ٤٤

16. If He so pleased, He could blot you out and bring in a new creation.

إِنْ يَشَأْ يُذْهِبْكُمْ وَيَأْتِ بِخَلْقٍ جَدِيدٍ ﴿١٦﴾

17. Nor is that (at all) difficult for Allah.

وَمَا ذَٰلِكَ عَلَى اللَّهِ بِعَزِيزٍ ﴿١٧﴾

18. Nor can a bearer of burdens bear another's burden. If one heavily laden should call another to (bear) his load not the least portion of it can be carried (by the other) even though he be nearly related. You can but admonish such as fear their Lord unseen and establish regular prayer. And whoever purifies himself does so for

وَلَا تَزِرُ وَازِرَةٌ وِزْرَ أُخْرَىٰ ۚ وَإِنْ تَدْعُ مُثْقَلَةٌ إِلَىٰ حِمْلِهَا لَا يُحْمَلْ مِنْهُ شَيْءٌ وَلَوْ كَانَ ذَا قُرْبَىٰ ۗ إِنَّمَا تُنْذِرُ الَّذِينَ يَخْشَوْنَ رَبَّهُمْ بِالْغَيْبِ وَأَقَامُوا الصَّلَاةَ ۚ وَمَنْ تَزَكَّىٰ فَإِنَّمَا يَتَزَكَّىٰ لِنَفْسِهِ ۚ وَإِلَى

the benefit of his own soul; and the destination (of all) is to Allah.

ٱللَّهِ ٱلۡمَصِيرُ ١٨

19. The blind and the seeing are not alike;

وَمَا يَسۡتَوِي ٱلۡأَعۡمَىٰ وَٱلۡبَصِيرُ ١٩

20. Nor are the depths of darkness and the light;

وَلَا ٱلظُّلُمَٰتُ وَلَا ٱلنُّورُ ٢٠

21. Nor are the (chilly) shade and the (genial) heat of the sun:

وَلَا ٱلظِّلُّ وَلَا ٱلۡحَرُورُ ٢١

22. Nor are alike those that are living and those that are dead. Allah can make any that He wills to hear; but you can not make those to hear who are (buried) in graves.

وَمَا يَسۡتَوِي ٱلۡأَحۡيَآءُ وَلَا ٱلۡأَمۡوَٰتُۚ إِنَّ ٱللَّهَ يُسۡمِعُ
مَن يَشَآءُۖ وَمَآ أَنتَ بِمُسۡمِعٖ مَّن فِي ٱلۡقُبُورِ ٢٢

23. You are no other than a warner.

إِنۡ أَنتَ إِلَّا نَذِيرٌ ٢٣

24. Verily We have sent you in truth, as a bearer of glad tidings, and as a warner: and there never was a people, without a warner having lived among them (in the past).

إِنَّآ أَرۡسَلۡنَٰكَ بِٱلۡحَقِّ بَشِيرٗا وَنَذِيرٗاۚ وَإِن مِّنۡ أُمَّةٍ
إِلَّا خَلَا فِيهَا نَذِيرٞ ٢٤

25. And if they reject you, so did their predecessors to whom came their messengers with clear signs, scriptures and the book of enlightenment.

وَإِن يُكَذِّبُوكَ فَقَدۡ كَذَّبَ ٱلَّذِينَ مِن قَبۡلِهِمۡ
جَآءَتۡهُمۡ رُسُلُهُم بِٱلۡبَيِّنَٰتِ وَبِٱلزُّبُرِ
وَبِٱلۡكِتَٰبِ ٱلۡمُنِيرِ ٢٥

26. In the end did I punish those who rejected faith: and how (terrible) was My rejection (of them)!

ثُمَّ أَخَذۡتُ ٱلَّذِينَ كَفَرُواْۖ فَكَيۡفَ كَانَ نَكِيرِ ٢٦

27. Do you not see that Allah sends down rain from the sky? With it We then bring out produce of various colours. And in the mountains are tracts white and red, of various shades of colour, and black intense in hue.

أَلَمۡ تَرَ أَنَّ ٱللَّهَ أَنزَلَ مِنَ ٱلسَّمَآءِ مَآءٗ فَأَخۡرَجۡنَا
بِهِۦ ثَمَرَٰتٖ مُّخۡتَلِفًا أَلۡوَٰنُهَاۚ وَمِنَ ٱلۡجِبَالِ
جُدَدُۢ بِيضٞ وَحُمۡرٞ مُّخۡتَلِفٌ أَلۡوَٰنُهَا وَغَرَابِيبُ
سُودٞ ٢٧

28. And so amongst men and crawling creatures and cattle, are they of various colours. Those truly fear Allah, among His servants, who have knowledge: for Allah is Exalted in Might, Oft-Forgiving.

وَمِنَ ٱلنَّاسِ وَٱلدَّوَآبِّ وَٱلْأَنْعَٰمِ مُخْتَلِفٌ
أَلْوَٰنُهُۥ كَذَٰلِكَ ۗ إِنَّمَا يَخْشَى ٱللَّهَ مِنْ عِبَادِهِ ٱلْعُلَمَٰٓؤُا۟ ۗ
إِنَّ ٱللَّهَ عَزِيزٌ غَفُورٌ ﴿٢٨﴾

29. Those who rehearse the book of Allah, establish regular prayer, and spend (in charity) out of what We have provided for them, secretly and openly, hope for a commerce that will never fail:

إِنَّ ٱلَّذِينَ يَتْلُونَ كِتَٰبَ ٱللَّهِ وَأَقَامُوا۟ ٱلصَّلَوٰةَ
وَأَنفَقُوا۟ مِمَّا رَزَقْنَٰهُمْ سِرًّا وَعَلَانِيَةً يَرْجُونَ
تِجَٰرَةً لَّن تَبُورَ ﴿٢٩﴾

30. For He will pay them their reward, nay, He will give them (even) more out of His bounty: for He is Oft-Forgiving, Most Ready to appreciate (service).

لِيُوَفِّيَهُمْ أُجُورَهُمْ وَيَزِيدَهُم مِّن فَضْلِهِۦٓ ۚ إِنَّهُۥ
غَفُورٌ شَكُورٌ ﴿٣٠﴾

31. That which We have revealed to you of the book is the truth - confirming what was (revealed) before it: for Allah is assuredly - with respect to His servants Well Acquainted and Fully-Observant.

وَٱلَّذِىٓ أَوْحَيْنَآ إِلَيْكَ مِنَ ٱلْكِتَٰبِ هُوَ ٱلْحَقُّ
مُصَدِّقًا لِّمَا بَيْنَ يَدَيْهِ ۗ إِنَّ ٱللَّهَ بِعِبَادِهِۦ
لَخَبِيرٌۢ بَصِيرٌ ﴿٣١﴾

32. Then We have given the book for inheritance to such of Our servants as We have chosen: but there are among them some who wrong their own souls; some who follow a middle course; and some who are by Allah's leave, foremost in good deeds; that is the highest grace.

ثُمَّ أَوْرَثْنَا ٱلْكِتَٰبَ ٱلَّذِينَ ٱصْطَفَيْنَا مِنْ عِبَادِنَا ۖ
فَمِنْهُمْ ظَالِمٌ لِّنَفْسِهِۦ وَمِنْهُم مُّقْتَصِدٌ وَمِنْهُمْ
سَابِقٌۢ بِٱلْخَيْرَٰتِ بِإِذْنِ ٱللَّهِ ۚ ذَٰلِكَ هُوَ
ٱلْفَضْلُ ٱلْكَبِيرُ ﴿٣٢﴾

33. Gardens of eternity will they enter: in it will they be adorned with bracelets of gold and pearls; and their garments there will be of silk.

جَنَّٰتُ عَدْنٍ يَدْخُلُونَهَا يُحَلَّوْنَ فِيهَا مِنْ أَسَاوِرَ
مِن ذَهَبٍ وَلُؤْلُؤًا ۖ وَلِبَاسُهُمْ فِيهَا حَرِيرٌ ﴿٣٣﴾

34. And they will say: "Praise be to Allah, Who has removed from us (all) sorrow: for Our Lord is indeed Oft-Forgiving, Ready to appreciate (service).

وَقَالُوا۟ ٱلْحَمْدُ لِلَّهِ ٱلَّذِىٓ أَذْهَبَ عَنَّا ٱلْحَزَنَ ۖ إِنَّ
رَبَّنَا لَغَفُورٌ شَكُورٌ ﴿٣٤﴾

35. Who has, out of His bounty, settled us in a home that will last: no toil nor sense of weariness shall touch us in it."

ٱلَّذِىٓ أَحَلَّنَا دَارَ ٱلْمُقَامَةِ مِن فَضْلِهِۦ لَا يَمَسُّنَا
فِيهَا نَصَبٌ وَلَا يَمَسُّنَا فِيهَا لُغُوبٌ ٣٥

36. But those who reject (Allah) for them will be the fire of hell: no term shall be determined for them, so they should die, nor shall its penalty be lightened for them. Thus do We reward every ungrateful one!

وَٱلَّذِينَ كَفَرُوا۟ لَهُمْ نَارُ جَهَنَّمَ لَا يُقْضَىٰ عَلَيْهِمْ
فَيَمُوتُوا۟ وَلَا يُخَفَّفُ عَنْهُم مِّنْ عَذَابِهَا ۚ كَذَٰلِكَ
نَجْزِى كُلَّ كَفُورٍ ٣٦

37. In it will they call aloud (for assistance): "Our Lord! Bring us out: we shall work righteousness, not the (deeds) we used to do!" - Did We not give you long enough life so that he that would, should receive admonition? And (moreover) the warner came to you. So taste you (the fruits of your deeds): For the wrongdoers there is no helper."

وَهُمْ يَصْطَرِخُونَ فِيهَا رَبَّنَآ أَخْرِجْنَا نَعْمَلْ
صَٰلِحًا غَيْرَ ٱلَّذِى كُنَّا نَعْمَلُ ۚ أَوَلَمْ نُعَمِّرْكُم
مَّا يَتَذَكَّرُ فِيهِ مَن تَذَكَّرَ وَجَآءَكُمُ ٱلنَّذِيرُ ۖ
فَذُوقُوا۟ فَمَا لِلظَّٰلِمِينَ مِن نَّصِيرٍ ٣٧

38. Verily Allah knows (all) the hidden things of the heavens and the earth; verily He has full knowledge of all that is in (men's) hearts.

إِنَّ ٱللَّهَ عَٰلِمُ غَيْبِ ٱلسَّمَٰوَٰتِ وَٱلْأَرْضِ ۚ
إِنَّهُۥ عَلِيمٌۢ بِذَاتِ ٱلصُّدُورِ ٣٨

39. He it is that has made you inheritors in the earth; if, then, any do reject (Allah), their rejection (works) against themselves; their rejection but adds to the odium for the unbelievers in the sight of their Lord; their rejection but adds to (their own) undoing.

هُوَ ٱلَّذِى جَعَلَكُمْ خَلَٰٓئِفَ فِى ٱلْأَرْضِ ۚ فَمَن كَفَرَ فَعَلَيْهِ
كُفْرُهُۥ ۖ وَلَا يَزِيدُ ٱلْكَٰفِرِينَ كُفْرُهُمْ عِندَ رَبِّهِمْ إِلَّا
مَقْتًا ۖ وَلَا يَزِيدُ ٱلْكَٰفِرِينَ كُفْرُهُمْ إِلَّا خَسَارًا ٣٩

40. Say: "Have you seen (these) 'partners' of yours whom you call upon besides Allah?" Show me what it is they have created in the (wide) earth. Or have they a share in the heavens? Or have We given them a book from which they (can derive) clear (evidence)? - Nay, the wrongdoers promise each other nothing but delusions.

قُلْ أَرَءَيْتُمْ شُرَكَآءَكُمُ ٱلَّذِينَ تَدْعُونَ مِن دُونِ ٱللَّهِ
أَرُونِى مَاذَا خَلَقُوا۟ مِنَ ٱلْأَرْضِ أَمْ لَهُمْ شِرْكٌ فِى ٱلسَّمَٰوَٰتِ
أَمْ ءَاتَيْنَٰهُمْ كِتَٰبًا فَهُمْ عَلَىٰ بَيِّنَتٍ مِّنْهُ ۚ بَلْ إِن يَعِدُ
ٱلظَّٰلِمُونَ بَعْضُهُم بَعْضًا إِلَّا غُرُورًا ٤٠

ثلاثة أرباع الحزب ٤٤

41. It is Allah Who sustains the heavens and the earth, lest they cease (to function): and if they should fail, there is none - not one - can sustain them thereafter: verily He is Most Forbearing, Oft-Forgiving.

۞ إِنَّ ٱللَّهَ يُمۡسِكُ ٱلسَّمَٰوَٰتِ وَٱلۡأَرۡضَ أَن تَزُولَاۚ
وَلَئِن زَالَتَآ إِنۡ أَمۡسَكَهُمَا مِنۡ أَحَدٖ مِّنۢ بَعۡدِهِۦٓۚ إِنَّهُۥ كَانَ
حَلِيمًا غَفُورٗا ﴿٤١﴾

42. They swore their strongest oaths by Allah that if a warner came to them, they would follow his guidance better than any (other) of the peoples: but when a warner came to them, it has only increased their flight (from righteousness) -

وَأَقۡسَمُواْ بِٱللَّهِ جَهۡدَ أَيۡمَٰنِهِمۡ لَئِن جَآءَهُمۡ نَذِيرٞ لَّيَكُونُنَّ
أَهۡدَىٰ مِنۡ إِحۡدَى ٱلۡأُمَمِۖ فَلَمَّا جَآءَهُمۡ نَذِيرٞ
مَّا زَادَهُمۡ إِلَّا نُفُورًا ﴿٤٢﴾

43. On account of their arrogance in the land and their plotting of evil. But the plotting of evil will hem in only the authors of it. Now are they but looking for the way the ancients were dealt with? But no change will you find in Allah's way (of dealing): no turning off will you find in Allah's way (of dealing).

ٱسۡتِكۡبَارٗا فِي ٱلۡأَرۡضِ وَمَكۡرَ ٱلسَّيِّيِٕۚ وَلَا يَحِيقُ
ٱلۡمَكۡرُ ٱلسَّيِّئُ إِلَّا بِأَهۡلِهِۦۚ فَهَلۡ يَنظُرُونَ إِلَّا سُنَّتَ
ٱلۡأَوَّلِينَۚ فَلَن تَجِدَ لِسُنَّتِ ٱللَّهِ تَبۡدِيلٗاۖ وَلَن تَجِدَ لِسُنَّتِ
ٱللَّهِ تَحۡوِيلًا ﴿٤٣﴾

44. Do they not travel through the earth, and see what was the end of those before them - though they were superior to them in strength? Nor is Allah to be frustrated by anything whatever in the heavens or on earth: for He is All-Knowing, All-Powerful.

أَوَلَمۡ يَسِيرُواْ فِي ٱلۡأَرۡضِ فَيَنظُرُواْ كَيۡفَ كَانَ عَٰقِبَةُ
ٱلَّذِينَ مِن قَبۡلِهِمۡ وَكَانُوٓاْ أَشَدَّ مِنۡهُمۡ قُوَّةٗۚ وَمَا كَانَ
ٱللَّهُ لِيُعۡجِزَهُۥ مِن شَيۡءٖ فِي ٱلسَّمَٰوَٰتِ وَلَا فِي ٱلۡأَرۡضِۚ
إِنَّهُۥ كَانَ عَلِيمٗا قَدِيرٗا ﴿٤٤﴾

45. If Allah were to punish men according to what they deserve, He would not leave on the back of the (earth) a single living creature; but He gives them respite for a stated term: when their term expires, verily Allah has in His sight all His servants.

وَلَوۡ يُؤَاخِذُ ٱللَّهُ ٱلنَّاسَ بِمَا كَسَبُواْ مَا تَرَكَ
عَلَىٰ ظَهۡرِهَا مِن دَآبَّةٖ وَلَٰكِن يُؤَخِّرُهُمۡ
إِلَىٰٓ أَجَلٖ مُّسَمّٗىۖ فَإِذَا جَآءَ أَجَلُهُمۡ فَإِنَّ ٱللَّهَ
كَانَ بِعِبَادِهِۦ بَصِيرَۢا ﴿٤٥﴾

سُورَةُ يسٓ

Surah 36: ***Ya Sin***

In the name of Allah,
Most Gracious, Most Merciful.

بِسۡمِ ٱللَّهِ ٱلرَّحۡمَٰنِ ٱلرَّحِيمِ

1. *Ya-Sin.*

يسٓ ١

2. By the Qur'an, full of wisdom -

وَٱلۡقُرۡءَانِ ٱلۡحَكِيمِ ٢

3. You are indeed one of the messengers.

إِنَّكَ لَمِنَ ٱلۡمُرۡسَلِينَ ٣

4. On a straight way.

عَلَىٰ صِرَٰطٖ مُّسۡتَقِيمٖ ٤

5. It is a revelation sent down by (Him), the Exalted in Might, Most Merciful,

تَنزِيلَ ٱلۡعَزِيزِ ٱلرَّحِيمِ ٥

6. In order that you may admonish a people, whose fathers had received no admonition, and who therefore remain heedless (of the signs of Allah).

لِتُنذِرَ قَوۡمٗا مَّآ أُنذِرَ ءَابَآؤُهُمۡ فَهُمۡ غَٰفِلُونَ ٦

7. The word is proved true against the greater part of them; for they do not believe.

لَقَدۡ حَقَّ ٱلۡقَوۡلُ عَلَىٰٓ أَكۡثَرِهِمۡ فَهُمۡ لَا يُؤۡمِنُونَ ٧

8. We have put yokes round their necks right up to their chins, so that their heads are forced up (and they cannot see).

إِنَّا جَعَلۡنَا فِيٓ أَعۡنَٰقِهِمۡ أَغۡلَٰلٗا فَهِيَ إِلَى ٱلۡأَذۡقَانِ
فَهُم مُّقۡمَحُونَ ٨

9. And We have put a bar in front of them and a bar behind them, and further, We have covered them up; so that they cannot see.

وَجَعَلۡنَا مِنۢ بَيۡنِ أَيۡدِيهِمۡ سَدّٗا وَمِنۡ خَلۡفِهِمۡ سَدّٗا
فَأَغۡشَيۡنَٰهُمۡ فَهُمۡ لَا يُبۡصِرُونَ ٩

10. The same is it to them whether you admonish them or you do not admonish them: they will not believe.

وَسَوَآءٌ عَلَيۡهِمۡ ءَأَنذَرۡتَهُمۡ أَمۡ لَمۡ تُنذِرۡهُمۡ لَا يُؤۡمِنُونَ ١٠

11. You can but admonish such a one as follows the message and fears the (Lord) Most Gracious, unseen: give such a one, therefore, good tidings of forgiveness and a reward most generous.

إِنَّمَا تُنذِرُ مَنِ ٱتَّبَعَ ٱلذِّكۡرَ وَخَشِيَ ٱلرَّحۡمَٰنَ
بِٱلۡغَيۡبِۖ فَبَشِّرۡهُ بِمَغۡفِرَةٖ وَأَجۡرٖ كَرِيمٍ ١١

12. Verily We shall give life to the dead, and We record that which they sent before and that which they leave behind, and of all things have We taken account in a clear book (of evidence).

إِنَّا نَحۡنُ نُحۡيِ ٱلۡمَوۡتَىٰ وَنَكۡتُبُ مَا قَدَّمُواْ وَءَاثَٰرَهُمۡۚ
وَكُلَّ شَيۡءٍ أَحۡصَيۡنَٰهُ فِيٓ إِمَامٖ مُّبِينٖ ١٢

13. Set out to them, by way of a parable, the (story of) the companions of the city. See, there came messengers to it.

وَٱضۡرِبۡ لَهُم مَّثَلًا أَصۡحَٰبَ ٱلۡقَرۡيَةِ إِذۡ جَآءَهَا
ٱلۡمُرۡسَلُونَ ١٣

14. When We (first) sent to them two messengers, they rejected them: but We strengthened them with a third: they said, "Truly, we have been sent on a mission to you."

إِذۡ أَرۡسَلۡنَآ إِلَيۡهِمُ ٱثۡنَيۡنِ فَكَذَّبُوهُمَا فَعَزَّزۡنَا بِثَالِثٖ
فَقَالُوٓاْ إِنَّآ إِلَيۡكُم مُّرۡسَلُونَ ١٤

15. The (people) said: "You are only men like ourselves; and (Allah) Most Gracious sends no sort of revelation: you do nothing but lie."

قَالُواْ مَآ أَنتُمۡ إِلَّا بَشَرٞ مِّثۡلُنَا وَمَآ أَنزَلَ ٱلرَّحۡمَٰنُ
مِن شَيۡءٍ إِنۡ أَنتُمۡ إِلَّا تَكۡذِبُونَ ١٥

16. They said: "Our Lord does know that we have been sent on a mission to you:

قَالُواْ رَبُّنَا يَعۡلَمُ إِنَّآ إِلَيۡكُمۡ لَمُرۡسَلُونَ ١٦

17. And our duty is only to proclaim the clear message."

وَمَا عَلَيۡنَآ إِلَّا ٱلۡبَلَٰغُ ٱلۡمُبِينُ ١٧

18. The (people) said: "For us, we augur an evil omen from you: if you desist not, we will certainly stone you, and a grievous punishment indeed will be inflicted on you by us."

قَالُوٓاْ إِنَّا تَطَيَّرۡنَا بِكُمۡۖ لَئِن لَّمۡ تَنتَهُواْ لَنَرۡجُمَنَّكُمۡ
وَلَيَمَسَّنَّكُم مِّنَّا عَذَابٌ أَلِيمٞ ١٨

19. They said: "Your evil omens are with yourselves: (think you this an evil omen),

قَالُواْ طَٰٓئِرُكُم مَّعَكُمۡۚ أَيِن ذُكِّرۡتُمۚ بَلۡ أَنتُمۡ

if you are admonished? Nay, but you are a people transgressing all bounds!"

قَوْمٌ مُّسْرِفُونَ ١٩

20. Then there came running from the farthest part of the city, a man saying, "O my people! Obey the messengers:

وَجَآءَ مِنْ أَقْصَا ٱلْمَدِينَةِ رَجُلٌ يَسْعَىٰ قَالَ يَٰقَوْمِ
ٱتَّبِعُوا۟ ٱلْمُرْسَلِينَ ٢٠

21. Obey those who ask no reward of you (for themselves), and who have themselves received guidance.

ٱتَّبِعُوا۟ مَن لَّا يَسْـَٔلُكُمْ أَجْرًا وَهُم مُّهْتَدُونَ ٢١

22. It would not be reasonable in me if I did not serve Him Who created me, and to Whom you shall (all) be brought back.

وَمَا لِىَ لَآ أَعْبُدُ ٱلَّذِى فَطَرَنِى وَإِلَيْهِ تُرْجَعُونَ ٢٢

23. Shall I take (other) gods besides Him? If (Allah) Most Gracious should intend some adversity for me, of no use whatever will be their intercession for me, nor can they deliver me.

ءَأَتَّخِذُ مِن دُونِهِۦٓ ءَالِهَةً إِن يُرِدْنِ ٱلرَّحْمَٰنُ
بِضُرٍّ لَّا تُغْنِ عَنِّى شَفَٰعَتُهُمْ شَيْـًٔا وَلَا
يُنقِذُونِ ٢٣

24. I would indeed if I were to do so, be in manifest error.

إِنِّىٓ إِذًا لَّفِى ضَلَٰلٍ مُّبِينٍ ٢٤

25. For me, I have faith in the Lord of you (all): listen then, to me!"

إِنِّىٓ ءَامَنتُ بِرَبِّكُمْ فَٱسْمَعُونِ ٢٥

26. It was said: "Enter you the garden." He said: "Ah me! Would that my people knew (what I know)! -

قِيلَ ٱدْخُلِ ٱلْجَنَّةَ ۖ قَالَ يَٰلَيْتَ قَوْمِى يَعْلَمُونَ ٢٦

27. For that my Lord has granted me forgiveness and has enrolled me among those held in honour!"

بِمَا غَفَرَ لِى رَبِّى وَجَعَلَنِى مِنَ ٱلْمُكْرَمِينَ ٢٧

✻ **28.** And We sent not down against his people, after him, any forces from heaven, nor was it needful for Us so to do.

الجزء ٢٣ الحزب ٤٥

✻ وَمَآ أَنزَلْنَا عَلَىٰ قَوْمِهِۦ مِنۢ بَعْدِهِۦ مِن جُندٍ مِّنَ
ٱلسَّمَآءِ وَمَا كُنَّا مُنزِلِينَ ٢٨

✻ Part-23

29. It was no more than a single mighty blast, and see! They were (like ashes) quenched and silent.

إِن كَانَتۡ إِلَّا صَيۡحَةٗ وَٰحِدَةٗ فَإِذَا هُمۡ خَٰمِدُونَ ٢٩

30. Ah! Alas for (My) servants! There comes not a messenger to them but they mock him!

يَٰحَسۡرَةً عَلَى ٱلۡعِبَادِۚ مَا يَأۡتِيهِم مِّن رَّسُولٍ إِلَّا
كَانُواْ بِهِۦ يَسۡتَهۡزِءُونَ ٣٠

31. Do they not see how many generations before them We destroyed? Not to them will they return:

أَلَمۡ يَرَوۡاْ كَمۡ أَهۡلَكۡنَا قَبۡلَهُم مِّنَ ٱلۡقُرُونِ أَنَّهُمۡ
إِلَيۡهِمۡ لَا يَرۡجِعُونَ ٣١

32. But each one of them all will be brought before Us (for judgement).

وَإِن كُلّٞ لَّمَّا جَمِيعٞ لَّدَيۡنَا مُحۡضَرُونَ ٣٢

33. A sign for them is the earth that is dead: We do give it life and produce grain from it, of which you do eat.

وَءَايَةٞ لَّهُمُ ٱلۡأَرۡضُ ٱلۡمَيۡتَةُ أَحۡيَيۡنَٰهَا وَأَخۡرَجۡنَا
مِنۡهَا حَبّٗا فَمِنۡهُ يَأۡكُلُونَ ٣٣

34. And We produce in it orchards with date-palms and vines, and We cause springs to gush out in it;

وَجَعَلۡنَا فِيهَا جَنَّٰتٖ مِّن نَّخِيلٖ وَأَعۡنَٰبٖ
وَفَجَّرۡنَا فِيهَا مِنَ ٱلۡعُيُونِ ٣٤

35. That they may enjoy the fruits of this (artistry); it was not their hands that made this: will they not then give thanks?

لِيَأۡكُلُواْ مِن ثَمَرِهِۦ وَمَا عَمِلَتۡهُ أَيۡدِيهِمۡۚ أَفَلَا
يَشۡكُرُونَ ٣٥

36. Glory to Allah, Who created in pairs all things that the earth produces, as well as their own (human) kind and (other) things of which they have no knowledge.

سُبۡحَٰنَ ٱلَّذِي خَلَقَ ٱلۡأَزۡوَٰجَ كُلَّهَا مِمَّا
تُنۢبِتُ ٱلۡأَرۡضُ وَمِنۡ أَنفُسِهِمۡ وَمِمَّا لَا يَعۡلَمُونَ ٣٦

37. And a sign for them is the night: We withdraw from it the day, and behold they are plunged in darkness;

وَءَايَةٞ لَّهُمُ ٱلَّيۡلُ نَسۡلَخُ مِنۡهُ ٱلنَّهَارَ فَإِذَا هُم
مُّظۡلِمُونَ ٣٧

38. And the sun runs its course for a period determined for it: that is the

وَٱلشَّمۡسُ تَجۡرِي لِمُسۡتَقَرّٖ لَّهَاۚ ذَٰلِكَ تَقۡدِيرُ

decree of (Him), the Exalted in Might, the All-Knowing.

ٱلْعَزِيزِ ٱلْعَلِيمِ ٣٨

39. And the moon - We have measured for it mansions (to traverse) till it returns like the old (and withered) lower part of a date stalk.

وَٱلْقَمَرَ قَدَّرْنَٰهُ مَنَازِلَ حَتَّىٰ عَادَ كَٱلْعُرْجُونِ
ٱلْقَدِيمِ ٣٩

40. It is not permitted to the sun to catch up the moon, nor can the night outstrip the day: each (just) swims along in (its own) orbit (according to law).

لَا ٱلشَّمْسُ يَنۢبَغِي لَهَآ أَن تُدْرِكَ ٱلْقَمَرَ وَلَا ٱلَّيْلُ
سَابِقُ ٱلنَّهَارِ ۚ وَكُلٌّ فِي فَلَكٍ يَسْبَحُونَ ٤٠

41. And a sign for them is that We bore their race (through the flood) in the loaded ark;

وَءَايَةٌ لَّهُمْ أَنَّا حَمَلْنَا ذُرِّيَّتَهُمْ فِي ٱلْفُلْكِ ٱلْمَشْحُونِ ٤١

42. And We have created for them similar (vessels) on which they ride.

وَخَلَقْنَا لَهُم مِّن مِّثْلِهِۦ مَا يَرْكَبُونَ ٤٢

43. If it were Our will, We could drown them: then would there be no helper (to hear their call), nor could they be delivered.

وَإِن نَّشَأْ نُغْرِقْهُمْ فَلَا صَرِيخَ لَهُمْ وَلَا هُمْ يُنقَذُونَ ٤٣

44. Except by way of mercy from Us, and by way of (worldly) convenience (to serve them) for a time.

إِلَّا رَحْمَةً مِّنَّا وَمَتَٰعًا إِلَىٰ حِينٍ ٤٤

45. When they are told, "Fear you that which is before you and that which will be after you, in order that you may receive mercy," (they turn back).

وَإِذَا قِيلَ لَهُمُ ٱتَّقُوا۟ مَا بَيْنَ أَيْدِيكُمْ وَمَا خَلْفَكُمْ
لَعَلَّكُمْ تُرْحَمُونَ ٤٥

46. Not a sign comes to them from among the signs of their Lord, but they turn away from it.

وَمَا تَأْتِيهِم مِّنْ ءَايَةٍ مِّنْ ءَايَٰتِ رَبِّهِمْ إِلَّا كَانُوا۟
عَنْهَا مُعْرِضِينَ ٤٦

47. And when they are told, "Spend you of (the bounties) with which Allah has provided you," the unbelievers say to those who believe: "Shall we then feed those whom, if Allah had so willed, He would have fed, (Himself)? - You are in nothing but manifest error."

وَإِذَا قِيلَ لَهُمْ أَنفِقُوا۟ مِمَّا رَزَقَكُمُ ٱللَّهُ قَالَ ٱلَّذِينَ
كَفَرُوا۟ لِلَّذِينَ ءَامَنُوٓا۟ أَنُطْعِمُ مَن لَّوْ يَشَآءُ ٱللَّهُ
أَطْعَمَهُۥٓ إِنْ أَنتُمْ إِلَّا فِي ضَلَٰلٍ مُّبِينٍ ٤٧

48. Further, they say, "When will this promise (come to pass), if what you say is true?"

وَيَقُولُونَ مَتَىٰ هَٰذَا ٱلْوَعْدُ إِن كُنتُمْ صَٰدِقِينَ ﴿٤٨﴾

49. They will not (have to) wait for anything but a single blast: it will seize them while they are yet disputing among themselves!

مَا يَنظُرُونَ إِلَّا صَيْحَةً وَٰحِدَةً تَأْخُذُهُمْ وَهُمْ
يَخِصِّمُونَ ﴿٤٩﴾

50. No (chance) will they then have, by will, to dispose (of their affairs), nor to return to their own people!

فَلَا يَسْتَطِيعُونَ تَوْصِيَةً وَلَآ إِلَىٰٓ أَهْلِهِمْ
يَرْجِعُونَ ﴿٥٠﴾

51. The trumpet shall be sounded, when see, from the graves (men) will rush forward to their Lord!

وَنُفِخَ فِى ٱلصُّورِ فَإِذَا هُم مِّنَ ٱلْأَجْدَاثِ إِلَىٰ رَبِّهِمْ
يَنسِلُونَ ﴿٥١﴾

52. They will say: "Ah! Woe to us! Who has raised us up from our beds of rest? (A voice will say:) "This is what (Allah) Most Gracious had promised, and true was the word of the messengers!"

قَالُوا۟ يَٰوَيْلَنَا مَنۢ بَعَثَنَا مِن مَّرْقَدِنَا ۜ هَٰذَا مَا وَعَدَ
ٱلرَّحْمَٰنُ وَصَدَقَ ٱلْمُرْسَلُونَ ﴿٥٢﴾

كتة يفة لا ألف

53. It will be no more than a single blast, when lo, they will all be brought up before Us!

إِن كَانَتْ إِلَّا صَيْحَةً وَٰحِدَةً فَإِذَا هُمْ جَمِيعٌ
لَّدَيْنَا مُحْضَرُونَ ﴿٥٣﴾

54. Then, on that day, not a soul will be wronged in the least, and you shall but be repaid the dues of your past deeds.

فَٱلْيَوْمَ لَا تُظْلَمُ نَفْسٌ شَيْـًٔا وَلَا تُجْزَوْنَ إِلَّا
مَا كُنتُمْ تَعْمَلُونَ ﴿٥٤﴾

55. Verily the companions of the garden shall that day have joy in all that they do;

إِنَّ أَصْحَٰبَ ٱلْجَنَّةِ ٱلْيَوْمَ فِى شُغُلٍ فَٰكِهُونَ ﴿٥٥﴾

56. They and their associates will be in groves of (cool) shade, reclining on thrones (of dignity);

هُمْ وَأَزْوَٰجُهُمْ فِى ظِلَٰلٍ عَلَى ٱلْأَرَآئِكِ مُتَّكِـُٔونَ ﴿٥٦﴾

57. (Every) fruit (enjoyment) will be there for them; they shall have whatever they call for;

لَهُمْ فِيهَا فَٰكِهَةٌ وَلَهُم مَّا يَدَّعُونَ ﴿٥٧﴾

58. "Peace! - A word (of salutation) from a Lord Most Merciful!

سَلَٰمٞ قَوۡلٗا مِّن رَّبّٖ رَّحِيمٖ ٥٨

59. And O you in sin! Get you apart this day!

وَٱمۡتَٰزُواْ ٱلۡيَوۡمَ أَيُّهَا ٱلۡمُجۡرِمُونَ ٥٩

60. Did I not enjoin on you, O you children of Adam, that you should not worship Satan; for that he was to you an enemy avowed?-

ربع الحزب ٤٥

۞أَلَمۡ أَعۡهَدۡ إِلَيۡكُمۡ يَٰبَنِيٓ ءَادَمَ أَن لَّا تَعۡبُدُواْ
ٱلشَّيۡطَٰنَۖ إِنَّهُۥ لَكُمۡ عَدُوّٞ مُّبِينٞ ٦٠

61. And that you should worship Me, (for that) this was the straight way?

وَأَنِ ٱعۡبُدُونِيۚ هَٰذَا صِرَٰطٞ مُّسۡتَقِيمٞ ٦١

62. But he did lead astray a great multitude of you. Did you not, then, understand?

وَلَقَدۡ أَضَلَّ مِنكُمۡ جِبِلّٗا كَثِيرًاۖ أَفَلَمۡ تَكُونُواْ
تَعۡقِلُونَ ٦٢

63. This is the hell of which you were (repeatedly) warned!

هَٰذِهِۦ جَهَنَّمُ ٱلَّتِي كُنتُمۡ تُوعَدُونَ ٦٣

64. Embrace you the (fire) this day, for that you (persistently) rejected (truth)."

ٱصۡلَوۡهَا ٱلۡيَوۡمَ بِمَا كُنتُمۡ تَكۡفُرُونَ ٦٤

65. That day shall We set a seal on their mouths. But their hands will speak to Us, and their feet bear witness, to all that they did.

ٱلۡيَوۡمَ نَخۡتِمُ عَلَىٰٓ أَفۡوَٰهِهِمۡ وَتُكَلِّمُنَآ أَيۡدِيهِمۡ
وَتَشۡهَدُ أَرۡجُلُهُم بِمَا كَانُواْ يَكۡسِبُونَ ٦٥

66. If it had been Our will, We could surely have blotted out their eyes; then should they have run about groping for the path, but how could they have seen?

وَلَوۡ نَشَآءُ لَطَمَسۡنَا عَلَىٰٓ أَعۡيُنِهِمۡ فَٱسۡتَبَقُواْ
ٱلصِّرَٰطَ فَأَنَّىٰ يُبۡصِرُونَ ٦٦

67. And if it had been Our will, We could have transformed them (to remain) in their places; then should they have been unable to move about, nor could they have returned (after error).

وَلَوۡ نَشَآءُ لَمَسَخۡنَٰهُمۡ عَلَىٰ مَكَانَتِهِمۡ فَمَا
ٱسۡتَطَٰعُواْ مُضِيّٗا وَلَا يَرۡجِعُونَ ٦٧

68. If We grant long life to any, We cause

وَمَن نُّعَمِّرۡهُ نُنَكِّسۡهُ فِي ٱلۡخَلۡقِۚ أَفَلَا

him to be reversed in nature: will they not then understand?

يَعْقِلُونَ ﴿٦٨﴾

69. We have not instructed the (prophet) in poetry nor is it befitting for Him: this is no less than a message and a Qur'an making things clear:

وَمَا عَلَّمْنَٰهُ ٱلشِّعْرَ وَمَا يَنۢبَغِى لَهُۥٓ ۚ إِنْ هُوَ إِلَّا ذِكْرٌ
وَقُرْءَانٌ مُّبِينٌ ﴿٦٩﴾

70. That it may give admonition to any (who are) alive, and that the charge may be proved against those who reject (truth).

لِّيُنذِرَ مَن كَانَ حَيًّا وَيَحِقَّ ٱلْقَوْلُ عَلَى
ٱلْكَٰفِرِينَ ﴿٧٠﴾

71. Do they not see that it is We Who have created for them - among the things which Our hands have fashioned - cattle, which are under their dominion?-

أَوَلَمْ يَرَوْا۟ أَنَّا خَلَقْنَا لَهُم مِّمَّا عَمِلَتْ أَيْدِينَآ أَنْعَٰمًا
فَهُمْ لَهَا مَٰلِكُونَ ﴿٧١﴾

72. And that We have subjected them to their (use)? Of them some do carry them and some they eat:

وَذَلَّلْنَٰهَا لَهُمْ فَمِنْهَا رَكُوبُهُمْ وَمِنْهَا يَأْكُلُونَ ﴿٧٢﴾

73. And they have (other) profits from them (besides), and they get (milk) to drink. Will they not then be grateful?

وَلَهُمْ فِيهَا مَنَٰفِعُ وَمَشَارِبُ ۖ أَفَلَا يَشْكُرُونَ ﴿٧٣﴾

74. Yet they take (for worship) gods other than Allah, (hoping) that they might be helped!

وَٱتَّخَذُوا۟ مِن دُونِ ٱللَّهِ ءَالِهَةً لَّعَلَّهُمْ يُنصَرُونَ ﴿٧٤﴾

75. They have not the power to help them: but they will be brought up (before Our judgement seat) as a troop (to be condemned).

لَا يَسْتَطِيعُونَ نَصْرَهُمْ وَهُمْ لَهُمْ جُندٌ
مُّحْضَرُونَ ﴿٧٥﴾

76. Let not their speech then grieve you. Verily We know what they hide as well as what they disclose.

فَلَا يَحْزُنكَ قَوْلُهُمْ ۘ إِنَّا نَعْلَمُ مَا يُسِرُّونَ وَمَا
يُعْلِنُونَ ﴿٧٦﴾

77. Does not man see that it is We Who created Him from sperm? Yet see! He (stands up) as an open adversary!

أَوَلَمْ يَرَ ٱلْإِنسَٰنُ أَنَّا خَلَقْنَٰهُ مِن نُّطْفَةٍ فَإِذَا
هُوَ خَصِيمٌ مُّبِينٌ ﴿٧٧﴾

78. And he makes comparisons for Us, and forgets his own (origin and) creation: He says, "Who can give life to (dry) bones and decomposed ones (at that)?"

وَضَرَبَ لَنَا مَثَلًا وَنَسِىَ خَلْقَهُۥ ۖ قَالَ مَن يُحْىِ
ٱلْعِظَٰمَ وَهِىَ رَمِيمٌ ﴿٧٨﴾

79. Say, "He will give them life Who created them for the first time! For He is well-versed in every kind of creation!-

قُلْ يُحْيِيهَا ٱلَّذِىٓ أَنشَأَهَآ أَوَّلَ مَرَّةٍ ۖ وَهُوَ بِكُلِّ
خَلْقٍ عَلِيمٌ ﴿٧٩﴾

80. The same Who produces for you fire out of the green tree, when behold, you kindle with it (your own fires)!

ٱلَّذِى جَعَلَ لَكُم مِّنَ ٱلشَّجَرِ ٱلْأَخْضَرِ نَارًا فَإِذَآ
أَنتُم مِّنْهُ تُوقِدُونَ ﴿٨٠﴾

81. Is not He Who created the heavens and the earth able to create the like of it?" Yea, indeed! For He is the Creator Supreme of skill and knowledge (infinite)!

أَوَلَيْسَ ٱلَّذِى خَلَقَ ٱلسَّمَٰوَٰتِ وَٱلْأَرْضَ بِقَٰدِرٍ
عَلَىٰٓ أَن يَخْلُقَ مِثْلَهُم ۚ بَلَىٰ وَهُوَ ٱلْخَلَّٰقُ ٱلْعَلِيمُ ﴿٨١﴾

82. Verily, when He intends a thing, His command is, "Be", and it is!

إِنَّمَآ أَمْرُهُۥٓ إِذَآ أَرَادَ شَيْـًٔا أَن يَقُولَ لَهُۥ
كُن فَيَكُونُ ﴿٨٢﴾

83. So glory to Him in Whose hands is the dominion of all things; and to Him will you be all brought back.

فَسُبْحَٰنَ ٱلَّذِى بِيَدِهِۦ مَلَكُوتُ كُلِّ شَىْءٍ وَإِلَيْهِ
تُرْجَعُونَ ﴿٨٣﴾

سُورَةُ ٱلصَّافَّاتِ

Surah 37: ***As-Saffat*** **(Those Ranged In Ranks)**

In the name of Allah,
Most Gracious, Most Merciful.

بِسْمِ ٱللَّهِ ٱلرَّحْمَٰنِ ٱلرَّحِيمِ

1. By those who range themselves in ranks,

وَٱلصَّٰٓفَّٰتِ صَفًّا ﴿١﴾

2. And so are strong in repelling (evil),

فَٱلزَّٰجِرَٰتِ زَجْرًا ﴿٢﴾

3. And thus proclaim the message (of Allah)!

فَٱلتَّٰلِيَٰتِ ذِكْرًا ﴿٣﴾

4. Verily, your God is One!-

إِنَّ إِلَٰهَكُمْ لَوَاحِدٌ ٤

5. Lord of the heavens and of the earth, and all between them, and Lord of every point at the rising of the sun!

رَّبُّ ٱلسَّمَٰوَٰتِ وَٱلْأَرْضِ وَمَا بَيْنَهُمَا وَرَبُّ ٱلْمَشَٰرِقِ ٥

6. We have indeed decked the lower heaven with beauty (in) the stars -

إِنَّا زَيَّنَّا ٱلسَّمَآءَ ٱلدُّنْيَا بِزِينَةٍ ٱلْكَوَاكِبِ ٦

7. (For beauty) and for guard against all obstinate rebellious evil spirits.

وَحِفْظًا مِّن كُلِّ شَيْطَٰنٍ مَّارِدٍ ٧

8. (So) they should not strain their ears in the direction of the exalted assembly but be cast away from every side,

لَّا يَسَّمَّعُونَ إِلَى ٱلْمَلَإِ ٱلْأَعْلَىٰ وَيُقْذَفُونَ مِن كُلِّ جَانِبٍ ٨

9. Repulsed for they are under a perpetual penalty,

دُحُورًا ۖ وَلَهُمْ عَذَابٌ وَاصِبٌ ٩

10. Except such as snatch away something by stealth, and they are pursued by a flaming fire, of piercing brightness.

إِلَّا مَنْ خَطِفَ ٱلْخَطْفَةَ فَأَتْبَعَهُۥ شِهَابٌ ثَاقِبٌ ١٠

11. Just ask their opinion: are they the more difficult to create, or the (other) beings We have created? Them have We created out of a sticky clay!

فَٱسْتَفْتِهِمْ أَهُمْ أَشَدُّ خَلْقًا أَم مَّنْ خَلَقْنَآ ۚ إِنَّا خَلَقْنَٰهُم مِّن طِينٍ لَّازِبٍ ١١

12. Truly do you marvel, while they ridicule,

بَلْ عَجِبْتَ وَيَسْخَرُونَ ١٢

13. And, when they are admonished, pay no heed -

وَإِذَا ذُكِّرُوا۟ لَا يَذْكُرُونَ ١٣

14. And, when they see a sign, turn it to mockery,

وَإِذَا رَأَوْا۟ ءَايَةً يَسْتَسْخِرُونَ ١٤

15. And say, "This is nothing but evident sorcery!

وَقَالُوٓا۟ إِنْ هَٰذَآ إِلَّا سِحْرٌ مُّبِينٌ ١٥

16. What! When we die, and become dust and bones, shall we (then) be raised up (again)?

أَءِذَا مِتْنَا وَكُنَّا تُرَابًا وَعِظَٰمًا أَءِنَّا لَمَبْعُوثُونَ ١٦

17. And also our fathers of old?"

أَوَءَابَآؤُنَا ٱلْأَوَّلُونَ ١٧

18. Say you: "Yea, and you shall then be humiliated (on account of your evil)."

قُلْ نَعَمْ وَأَنتُمْ دَٰخِرُونَ ١٨

19. Then it will be a single (compelling) call; and see, they will begin to see!

فَإِنَّمَا هِىَ زَجْرَةٌ وَٰحِدَةٌ فَإِذَا هُمْ يَنظُرُونَ ١٩

20. They will say, "Ah! Woe to us! This is the day of judgement!"

وَقَالُوا۟ يَٰوَيْلَنَا هَٰذَا يَوْمُ ٱلدِّينِ ٢٠

21. (A voice will say,) "This is the day of sorting out, whose truth you (once) denied!"

هَٰذَا يَوْمُ ٱلْفَصْلِ ٱلَّذِى كُنتُم بِهِۦ تُكَذِّبُونَ ٢١

22. "Bring you up", it shall be said, "The wrongdoers and their wives, and the things they worshipped-

نصف الحزب ٤٥
۞ ٱحْشُرُوا۟ ٱلَّذِينَ ظَلَمُوا۟ وَأَزْوَٰجَهُمْ وَمَا كَانُوا۟ يَعْبُدُونَ ٢٢

23. Besides Allah, and lead them to the way to the (fierce) fire!

مِن دُونِ ٱللَّهِ فَٱهْدُوهُمْ إِلَىٰ صِرَٰطِ ٱلْجَحِيمِ ٢٣

24. But stop them, for they must be asked:

وَقِفُوهُمْ ۖ إِنَّهُم مَّسْـُٔولُونَ ٢٤

25. 'What is the matter with you that you help not each other?'"

مَا لَكُمْ لَا تَنَاصَرُونَ ٢٥

26. Nay, but that day they shall submit (to judgement);

بَلْ هُمُ ٱلْيَوْمَ مُسْتَسْلِمُونَ ٢٦

27. And they will turn to one another, and question one another.

وَأَقْبَلَ بَعْضُهُمْ عَلَىٰ بَعْضٍ يَتَسَآءَلُونَ ٢٧

28. They will say: "It was you who used to come to us from the right hand (of power and authority)!"

قَالُوٓا۟ إِنَّكُمْ كُنتُمْ تَأْتُونَنَا عَنِ ٱلْيَمِينِ ٢٨

29. They will reply: "Nay, you yourselves had no faith!

قَالُوا۟ بَلْ لَّمْ تَكُونُوا۟ مُؤْمِنِينَ ٢٩

30. Nor had we any authority over you. Nay, it was you who were a people in obstinate rebellion!

وَمَا كَانَ لَنَا عَلَيْكُم مِّن سُلْطَٰنٍۭ ۖ بَلْ كُنتُمْ قَوْمًا
طَٰغِينَ ٣٠

31. So now has been proved true, against us, the word of our Lord that we shall indeed (have to) taste (the punishment of our sins):

فَحَقَّ عَلَيْنَا قَوْلُ رَبِّنَآ ۖ إِنَّا لَذَآئِقُونَ ٣١

32. We led you astray: for truly, we were ourselves astray."

فَأَغْوَيْنَٰكُمْ إِنَّا كُنَّا غَٰوِينَ ٣٢

33. Truly, that day, they will (all) share in the penalty.

فَإِنَّهُمْ يَوْمَئِذٍ فِى ٱلْعَذَابِ مُشْتَرِكُونَ ٣٣

34. Verily that is how We shall deal with sinners.

إِنَّا كَذَٰلِكَ نَفْعَلُ بِٱلْمُجْرِمِينَ ٣٤

35. For they, when they were told that there is no god except Allah, would puff themselves up with pride,

إِنَّهُمْ كَانُوٓا۟ إِذَا قِيلَ لَهُمْ لَآ إِلَٰهَ إِلَّا ٱللَّهُ
يَسْتَكْبِرُونَ ٣٥

36. And say: "What! Shall we give up our gods for the sake of a poet possessed?"

وَيَقُولُونَ أَئِنَّا لَتَارِكُوٓا۟ ءَالِهَتِنَا لِشَاعِرٍ مَّجْنُونٍۭ ٣٦

37. Nay! He has come with the (very) truth, and he confirms (the message of) the messengers (before Him).

بَلْ جَآءَ بِٱلْحَقِّ وَصَدَّقَ ٱلْمُرْسَلِينَ ٣٧

38. You shall indeed taste of the grievous penalty -

إِنَّكُمْ لَذَآئِقُوا۟ ٱلْعَذَابِ ٱلْأَلِيمِ ٣٨

39. But it will be no more than the retribution of (the evil) that you have wrought -

وَمَا تُجْزَوْنَ إِلَّا مَا كُنتُمْ تَعْمَلُونَ ٣٩

40. But the sincere (and devoted) servants of Allah -

إِلَّا عِبَادَ ٱللَّهِ ٱلْمُخْلَصِينَ ٤٠

41. For them is a sustenance determined,

أُو۟لَٰٓئِكَ لَهُمْ رِزْقٌ مَّعْلُومٌ ٤١

42. Fruits (delights); and they (shall enjoy) honour and dignity,

فَوَٰكِهُ وَهُم مُّكۡرَمُونَ ﴿٤٢﴾

43. In gardens of felicity,

فِي جَنَّٰتِ ٱلنَّعِيمِ ﴿٤٣﴾

44. Facing each other on thrones (of dignity):

عَلَىٰ سُرُرٖ مُّتَقَٰبِلِينَ ﴿٤٤﴾

45. Round will be passed to them a cup from a clear-flowing fountain,

يُطَافُ عَلَيۡهِم بِكَأۡسٖ مِّن مَّعِينِۭ ﴿٤٥﴾

46. Crystal-white, of a taste delicious to those who drink (of it),

بَيۡضَآءَ لَذَّةٖ لِّلشَّٰرِبِينَ ﴿٤٦﴾

47. Free from headiness; nor will they suffer intoxication from it.

لَا فِيهَا غَوۡلٞ وَلَا هُمۡ عَنۡهَا يُنزَفُونَ ﴿٤٧﴾

48. And beside them will be chaste women; restraining their glances, with big eyes (of wonder and beauty).

وَعِندَهُمۡ قَٰصِرَٰتُ ٱلطَّرۡفِ عِينٞ ﴿٤٨﴾

49. As if they were (delicate) eggs closely guarded.

كَأَنَّهُنَّ بَيۡضٞ مَّكۡنُونٞ ﴿٤٩﴾

50. Then they will turn to one another and question one another.

فَأَقۡبَلَ بَعۡضُهُمۡ عَلَىٰ بَعۡضٖ يَتَسَآءَلُونَ ﴿٥٠﴾

51. One of them will start the talk and say: "I had an intimate companion (on the earth),

قَالَ قَآئِلٞ مِّنۡهُمۡ إِنِّي كَانَ لِي قَرِينٞ ﴿٥١﴾

52. Who used to say, 'What! Are you amongst those who bear witness to the truth (of the message)?

يَقُولُ أَءِنَّكَ لَمِنَ ٱلۡمُصَدِّقِينَ ﴿٥٢﴾

53. When we die and become dust and bones, shall we indeed receive rewards and punishments?'"

أَءِذَا مِتۡنَا وَكُنَّا تُرَابٗا وَعِظَٰمًا أَءِنَّا لَمَدِينُونَ ﴿٥٣﴾

54. (A voice) said: "Would you like to look down?"

قَالَ هَلۡ أَنتُم مُّطَّلِعُونَ ﴿٥٤﴾

55. He looked down and saw him in the midst of the fire.

فَٱطَّلَعَ فَرَءَاهُ فِي سَوَآءِ ٱلۡجَحِيمِ ٥٥

56. He said: "By Allah! You were little short of bringing me to perdition!

قَالَ تَٱللَّهِ إِن كِدتَّ لَتُرۡدِينِ ٥٦

57. Had it not been for the grace of my Lord, I should certainly have been among those brought (there)!

وَلَوۡلَا نِعۡمَةُ رَبِّي لَكُنتُ مِنَ ٱلۡمُحۡضَرِينَ ٥٧

58. Is it (the case) that we shall not die,

أَفَمَا نَحۡنُ بِمَيِّتِينَ ٥٨

59. Except our first death, and that we shall not be punished?"

إِلَّا مَوۡتَتَنَا ٱلۡأُولَىٰ وَمَا نَحۡنُ بِمُعَذَّبِينَ ٥٩

60. Verily this is the supreme achievement!

إِنَّ هَٰذَا لَهُوَ ٱلۡفَوۡزُ ٱلۡعَظِيمُ ٦٠

61. For the like of this let all strive, who wish to strive.

لِمِثۡلِ هَٰذَا فَلۡيَعۡمَلِ ٱلۡعَٰمِلُونَ ٦١

62. Is that the better entertainment or the tree of Zaqqum?

أَذَٰلِكَ خَيۡرٞ نُّزُلًا أَمۡ شَجَرَةُ ٱلزَّقُّومِ ٦٢

63. For We have truly made it (as) a trial for the wrongdoers.

إِنَّا جَعَلۡنَٰهَا فِتۡنَةٗ لِّلظَّٰلِمِينَ ٦٣

64. For it is a tree that springs out of the bottom of hellfire;

إِنَّهَا شَجَرَةٞ تَخۡرُجُ فِيٓ أَصۡلِ ٱلۡجَحِيمِ ٦٤

65. The shoots of its fruit-stalks are like the heads of devils;

طَلۡعُهَا كَأَنَّهُۥ رُءُوسُ ٱلشَّيَٰطِينِ ٦٥

66. Truly they will eat of it and fill their bellies with it.

فَإِنَّهُمۡ لَأٓكِلُونَ مِنۡهَا فَمَالِـُٔونَ مِنۡهَا ٱلۡبُطُونَ ٦٦

67. Then on top of that they will be given a mixture made of boiling water.

ثُمَّ إِنَّ لَهُمۡ عَلَيۡهَا لَشَوۡبٗا مِّنۡ حَمِيمٖ ٦٧

68. Then shall their return be to the (blazing) fire.

ثُمَّ إِنَّ مَرۡجِعَهُمۡ لَإِلَى ٱلۡجَحِيمِ ٦٨

69. Truly they found their fathers on the wrong path;

إِنَّهُمۡ أَلۡفَوۡاْ ءَابَآءَهُمۡ ضَآلِّينَ ﴿٦٩﴾

70. So they (too) were rushed down on their footsteps!

فَهُمۡ عَلَىٰٓ ءَاثَٰرِهِمۡ يُهۡرَعُونَ ﴿٧٠﴾

71. And truly before them, many of the ancients went astray -

وَلَقَدۡ ضَلَّ قَبۡلَهُمۡ أَكۡثَرُ ٱلۡأَوَّلِينَ ﴿٧١﴾

72. But We sent before, among them, (messengers) to admonish them -

وَلَقَدۡ أَرۡسَلۡنَا فِيهِم مُّنذِرِينَ ﴿٧٢﴾

73. Then see what was the end of those who were admonished (but heeded not) -

فَٱنظُرۡ كَيۡفَ كَانَ عَٰقِبَةُ ٱلۡمُنذَرِينَ ﴿٧٣﴾

74. Except the sincere (and devoted) servants of Allah.

إِلَّا عِبَادَ ٱللَّهِ ٱلۡمُخۡلَصِينَ ﴿٧٤﴾

75. (In the days of old), Noah called to Us, and We are the Best to hear prayer.

وَلَقَدۡ نَادَىٰنَا نُوحٞ فَلَنِعۡمَ ٱلۡمُجِيبُونَ ﴿٧٥﴾

76. And We delivered him and his people from the great calamity,

وَنَجَّيۡنَٰهُ وَأَهۡلَهُۥ مِنَ ٱلۡكَرۡبِ ٱلۡعَظِيمِ ﴿٧٦﴾

77. And made his progeny to endure (on this earth);

وَجَعَلۡنَا ذُرِّيَّتَهُۥ هُمُ ٱلۡبَاقِينَ ﴿٧٧﴾

78. And We left (this blessing) for him among generations to come in later times:

وَتَرَكۡنَا عَلَيۡهِ فِي ٱلۡأٓخِرِينَ ﴿٧٨﴾

79. "Peace and salutation to Noah among the nations!"

سَلَٰمٌ عَلَىٰ نُوحٖ فِي ٱلۡعَٰلَمِينَ ﴿٧٩﴾

80. Thus indeed do We reward those who do right.

إِنَّا كَذَٰلِكَ نَجۡزِي ٱلۡمُحۡسِنِينَ ﴿٨٠﴾

81. For he was one of Our believing servants.

إِنَّهُۥ مِنۡ عِبَادِنَا ٱلۡمُؤۡمِنِينَ ﴿٨١﴾

82. Then the rest We overwhelmed in the flood.

ثُمَّ أَغۡرَقۡنَا ٱلۡأٓخَرِينَ ﴿٨٢﴾

ثلاثة أرباع الحزب ٤٥

83. Verily among those who followed his way was Abraham.

۞ وَإِنَّ مِن شِيعَتِهِۦ لَإِبْرَٰهِيمَ ﴿٨٣﴾

84. See, He approached his Lord with a sound heart.

إِذْ جَآءَ رَبَّهُۥ بِقَلْبٍ سَلِيمٍ ﴿٨٤﴾

85. See, he said to his father and to his people, "What is that which you worship?

إِذْ قَالَ لِأَبِيهِ وَقَوْمِهِۦ مَاذَا تَعْبُدُونَ ﴿٨٥﴾

86. Is it a falsehood - gods other than Allah that you desire?

أَئِفْكًا ءَالِهَةً دُونَ ٱللَّهِ تُرِيدُونَ ﴿٨٦﴾

87. Then what is your idea about the Lord of the Worlds?"

فَمَا ظَنُّكُم بِرَبِّ ٱلْعَٰلَمِينَ ﴿٨٧﴾

88. Then did he cast a glance at the stars.

فَنَظَرَ نَظْرَةً فِى ٱلنُّجُومِ ﴿٨٨﴾

89. And he said, "I am indeed sick (at heart)!"

فَقَالَ إِنِّى سَقِيمٌ ﴿٨٩﴾

90. So they turned away from him, and departed.

فَتَوَلَّوْا۟ عَنْهُ مُدْبِرِينَ ﴿٩٠﴾

91. Then did he turn to their gods and said, "Will you not eat (of the offerings before you)?

فَرَاغَ إِلَىٰٓ ءَالِهَتِهِمْ فَقَالَ أَلَا تَأْكُلُونَ ﴿٩١﴾

92. What is the matter with you that you speak not (intelligently)?"

مَا لَكُمْ لَا تَنطِقُونَ ﴿٩٢﴾

93. Then did he turn upon them striking (them) with the right hand.

فَرَاغَ عَلَيْهِمْ ضَرْبًۢا بِٱلْيَمِينِ ﴿٩٣﴾

94. Then came (the worshippers) with hurried steps, and faced (him).

فَأَقْبَلُوٓا۟ إِلَيْهِ يَزِفُّونَ ﴿٩٤﴾

95. He said: "Worship you that which you have (yourselves) carved?

قَالَ أَتَعْبُدُونَ مَا تَنْحِتُونَ ﴿٩٥﴾

96. But Allah has created you and your handiwork!"

وَٱللَّهُ خَلَقَكُمْ وَمَا تَعْمَلُونَ ﴿٩٦﴾

قَالُوا۟ ٱبْنُوا۟ لَهُۥ بُنْيَـٰنًا فَأَلْقُوهُ فِى ٱلْجَحِيمِ ﴿٩٧﴾

97. They said, "Build him a furnace, and throw him into the blazing fire!"

فَأَرَادُوا۟ بِهِۦ كَيْدًا فَجَعَلْنَـٰهُمُ ٱلْأَسْفَلِينَ ﴿٩٨﴾

98. (This failing) they then sought a stratagem against him, but We made them the ones most humiliated!

وَقَالَ إِنِّى ذَاهِبٌ إِلَىٰ رَبِّى سَيَهْدِينِ ﴿٩٩﴾

99. He said: "I will go to my Lord! He will surely guide me!

رَبِّ هَبْ لِى مِنَ ٱلصَّـٰلِحِينَ ﴿١٠٠﴾

100. O my Lord! Grant me a righteous (son)!"

فَبَشَّرْنَـٰهُ بِغُلَـٰمٍ حَلِيمٍ ﴿١٠١﴾

101. So We gave him the good news of a boy ready to suffer and forbear.

فَلَمَّا بَلَغَ مَعَهُ ٱلسَّعْىَ قَالَ يَـٰبُنَىَّ إِنِّىٓ أَرَىٰ فِى ٱلْمَنَامِ
أَنِّىٓ أَذْبَحُكَ فَٱنظُرْ مَاذَا تَرَىٰ ۚ قَالَ يَـٰٓأَبَتِ ٱفْعَلْ
مَا تُؤْمَرُ ۖ سَتَجِدُنِىٓ إِن شَآءَ ٱللَّهُ مِنَ
ٱلصَّـٰبِرِينَ ﴿١٠٢﴾

102. Then, when (the son) reached (the age of) (serious) work with him, he said: "O my son! I see in vision that I offer you in sacrifice: now see what is your view!" (The son) said: "O my father! Do as you are commanded: you will find me, if Allah so wills, one practising patience and constancy!"

فَلَمَّآ أَسْلَمَا وَتَلَّهُۥ لِلْجَبِينِ ﴿١٠٣﴾

103. So when they had both submitted their wills (to Allah), and He had laid Him prostrate on his forehead (for sacrifice),

وَنَـٰدَيْنَـٰهُ أَن يَـٰٓإِبْرَٰهِيمُ ﴿١٠٤﴾

104. We called out to him, "O Abraham!

قَدْ صَدَّقْتَ ٱلرُّءْيَآ ۚ إِنَّا كَذَٰلِكَ نَجْزِى
ٱلْمُحْسِنِينَ ﴿١٠٥﴾

105. "You have already fulfilled the vision!" - thus indeed do We reward those who do right.

إِنَّ هَـٰذَا لَهُوَ ٱلْبَلَـٰٓؤُا۟ ٱلْمُبِينُ ﴿١٠٦﴾

106. For this was obviously a trial -

وَفَدَيْنَـٰهُ بِذِبْحٍ عَظِيمٍ ﴿١٠٧﴾

107. And We ransomed him with a momentous sacrifice:

وَتَرَكْنَا عَلَيْهِ فِى ٱلْـَٔاخِرِينَ ﴿١٠٨﴾

108. And We left (this blessing) for him among generations (to come) in later times:

109. "Peace and salutation to Abraham!"

سَلَٰمٌ عَلَىٰٓ إِبۡرَٰهِيمَ ١٠٩

110. Thus indeed do We reward those who do right.

كَذَٰلِكَ نَجۡزِي ٱلۡمُحۡسِنِينَ ١١٠

111. For he was one of Our believing servants.

إِنَّهُۥ مِنۡ عِبَادِنَا ٱلۡمُؤۡمِنِينَ ١١١

112. And We gave him the good news of Isaac - a prophet - one of the righteous.

وَبَشَّرۡنَٰهُ بِإِسۡحَٰقَ نَبِيّٗا مِّنَ ٱلصَّٰلِحِينَ ١١٢

113. We blessed him and Isaac: but of their progeny are (some) that do right, and (some) that obviously do wrong, to their own souls.

وَبَٰرَكۡنَا عَلَيۡهِ وَعَلَىٰٓ إِسۡحَٰقَۚ وَمِن ذُرِّيَّتِهِمَا مُحۡسِنٞ
وَظَالِمٞ لِّنَفۡسِهِۦ مُبِينٞ ١١٣

114. Again, (of old), We bestowed Our favour on Moses and Aaron,

وَلَقَدۡ مَنَنَّا عَلَىٰ مُوسَىٰ وَهَٰرُونَ ١١٤

115. And We delivered them and their people from (their) great calamity;

وَنَجَّيۡنَٰهُمَا وَقَوۡمَهُمَا مِنَ ٱلۡكَرۡبِ ٱلۡعَظِيمِ ١١٥

116. And We helped them, so they overcame (their troubles);

وَنَصَرۡنَٰهُمۡ فَكَانُواْ هُمُ ٱلۡغَٰلِبِينَ ١١٦

117. And We gave them the book which helps to make things clear;

وَءَاتَيۡنَٰهُمَا ٱلۡكِتَٰبَ ٱلۡمُسۡتَبِينَ ١١٧

118. And We guided them to the straight way.

وَهَدَيۡنَٰهُمَا ٱلصِّرَٰطَ ٱلۡمُسۡتَقِيمَ ١١٨

119. And We left (this blessing) for them among generations (to come) in later times:

وَتَرَكۡنَا عَلَيۡهِمَا فِي ٱلۡأٓخِرِينَ ١١٩

120. "Peace and salutation to Moses and Aaron!"

سَلَٰمٌ عَلَىٰ مُوسَىٰ وَهَٰرُونَ ١٢٠

121. Thus indeed do We reward those who do right.

إِنَّا كَذَٰلِكَ نَجۡزِي ٱلۡمُحۡسِنِينَ ١٢١

122. For they were two of Our believing servants.

إِنَّهُمَا مِنۡ عِبَادِنَا ٱلۡمُؤۡمِنِينَ ١٢٢

123. So also was Elias among those sent (by Us).

وَإِنَّ إِلۡيَاسَ لَمِنَ ٱلۡمُرۡسَلِينَ ١٢٣

124. See, he said to his people, "Will you not fear (Allah)?

إِذۡ قَالَ لِقَوۡمِهِۦٓ أَلَا تَتَّقُونَ ١٢٤

125. Will you call upon Baal and forsake the Best of Creators -

أَتَدۡعُونَ بَعۡلٗا وَتَذَرُونَ أَحۡسَنَ ٱلۡخَٰلِقِينَ ١٢٥

126. Allah, your Lord and Cherisher and the Lord and Cherisher of your fathers of old?"

ٱللَّهَ رَبَّكُمۡ وَرَبَّ ءَابَآئِكُمُ ٱلۡأَوَّلِينَ ١٢٦

127. But they rejected him, and they will certainly be called up (for punishment) -

فَكَذَّبُوهُ فَإِنَّهُمۡ لَمُحۡضَرُونَ ١٢٧

128. Except the sincere and devoted servants of Allah (among them).

إِلَّا عِبَادَ ٱللَّهِ ٱلۡمُخۡلَصِينَ ١٢٨

129. And We left (this blessing) for him among generations (to come) in later times:

وَتَرَكۡنَا عَلَيۡهِ فِي ٱلۡأٓخِرِينَ ١٢٩

130. "Peace and salutation to such as Elias!"

سَلَٰمٌ عَلَىٰٓ إِلۡ يَاسِينَ ١٣٠

131. Thus indeed do We reward those who do right.

إِنَّا كَذَٰلِكَ نَجۡزِي ٱلۡمُحۡسِنِينَ ١٣١

132. For He was one of Our believing servants.

إِنَّهُۥ مِنۡ عِبَادِنَا ٱلۡمُؤۡمِنِينَ ١٣٢

133. So also was Lot among those sent (by Us).

وَإِنَّ لُوطٗا لَّمِنَ ٱلۡمُرۡسَلِينَ ١٣٣

134. See, We delivered him and his adherents, all

إِذۡ نَجَّيۡنَٰهُ وَأَهۡلَهُۥٓ أَجۡمَعِينَ ١٣٤

135. Except an old woman who was among those who lagged behind:

إِلَّا عَجُوزٗا فِي ٱلۡغَٰبِرِينَ ١٣٥

136. Then We destroyed the rest.

ثُمَّ دَمَّرۡنَا ٱلۡأٓخَرِينَ ١٣٦

137. Verily, you pass by their (sites), by day -	وَإِنَّكُمْ لَتَمُرُّونَ عَلَيْهِم مُّصْبِحِينَ ﴿١٣٧﴾
138. And by night: will you not understand?	وَبِالَّيْلِ أَفَلَا تَعْقِلُونَ ﴿١٣٨﴾
139. So also was Jonah among those sent (by Us).	وَإِنَّ يُونُسَ لَمِنَ الْمُرْسَلِينَ ﴿١٣٩﴾
140. When he ran away (like a slave from captivity) to the ship (fully) laden,	إِذْ أَبَقَ إِلَى الْفُلْكِ الْمَشْحُونِ ﴿١٤٠﴾
141. He (agreed to) cast lots, and he was condemned:	فَسَاهَمَ فَكَانَ مِنَ الْمُدْحَضِينَ ﴿١٤١﴾
142. Then the big fish did swallow him, and he had done acts worthy of blame.	فَالْتَقَمَهُ الْحُوتُ وَهُوَ مُلِيمٌ ﴿١٤٢﴾
143. Had it not been that he (repented and) glorified Allah,	فَلَوْلَا أَنَّهُ كَانَ مِنَ الْمُسَبِّحِينَ ﴿١٤٣﴾
144. He would certainly have remained inside the fish till the day of resurrection.	لَلَبِثَ فِي بَطْنِهِ إِلَى يَوْمِ يُبْعَثُونَ ﴿١٤٤﴾
145. But We cast him out on the naked shore in a state of sickness,	۞ فَنَبَذْنَاهُ بِالْعَرَاءِ وَهُوَ سَقِيمٌ ﴿١٤٥﴾ الحزب ٤٦
146. And We caused to grow over him, a spreading plant of the gourd kind,	وَأَنبَتْنَا عَلَيْهِ شَجَرَةً مِّن يَقْطِينٍ ﴿١٤٦﴾
147. And We sent him (on a mission) to a hundred thousand (men) or more.	وَأَرْسَلْنَاهُ إِلَىٰ مِائَةِ أَلْفٍ أَوْ يَزِيدُونَ ﴿١٤٧﴾
148. And they believed; so We permitted them to enjoy (their life) for a while.	فَآمَنُوا فَمَتَّعْنَاهُمْ إِلَىٰ حِينٍ ﴿١٤٨﴾
149. Now ask them their opinion: Is it that your Lord has (only) daughters, and they have sons? -	فَاسْتَفْتِهِمْ أَلِرَبِّكَ الْبَنَاتُ وَلَهُمُ الْبَنُونَ ﴿١٤٩﴾
150. Or that We created the angels female, and they are witnesses (to it)?	أَمْ خَلَقْنَا الْمَلَائِكَةَ إِنَاثًا وَهُمْ شَاهِدُونَ ﴿١٥٠﴾

151. Is it not that they say, from their own invention,

أَلَآ إِنَّهُم مِّنْ إِفْكِهِمْ لَيَقُولُونَ ﴿١٥١﴾

152. "Allah has begotten children"? But they are liars!

وَلَدَ ٱللَّهُ وَإِنَّهُمْ لَكَـٰذِبُونَ ﴿١٥٢﴾

153. Did He (then) choose daughters rather than sons?

أَصْطَفَى ٱلْبَنَاتِ عَلَى ٱلْبَنِينَ ﴿١٥٣﴾

154. What is the matter with you? How judge you?

مَا لَكُمْ كَيْفَ تَحْكُمُونَ ﴿١٥٤﴾

155. Will you not then receive admonition?

أَفَلَا تَذَكَّرُونَ ﴿١٥٥﴾

156. Or have you an authority manifest?

أَمْ لَكُمْ سُلْطَـٰنٌ مُّبِينٌ ﴿١٥٦﴾

157. Then bring you your book (of authority) if you be truthful!

فَأْتُوا۟ بِكِتَـٰبِكُمْ إِن كُنتُمْ صَـٰدِقِينَ ﴿١٥٧﴾

158. And they have invented a blood-relationship between Him and the Jinns: but the Jinns know (quite well) that they have indeed to appear (before His judgement seat)!

وَجَعَلُوا۟ بَيْنَهُۥ وَبَيْنَ ٱلْجِنَّةِ نَسَبًا ۚ وَلَقَدْ عَلِمَتِ ٱلْجِنَّةُ
إِنَّهُمْ لَمُحْضَرُونَ ﴿١٥٨﴾

159. Glory to Allah! (He is free) from the things they ascribe (to Him)!

سُبْحَـٰنَ ٱللَّهِ عَمَّا يَصِفُونَ ﴿١٥٩﴾

160. Not (so do) the servants of Allah, sincere and devoted.

إِلَّا عِبَادَ ٱللَّهِ ٱلْمُخْلَصِينَ ﴿١٦٠﴾

161. For, verily, neither you nor those you worship -

فَإِنَّكُمْ وَمَا تَعْبُدُونَ ﴿١٦١﴾

162. Can lead (any) into temptation concerning Allah,

مَآ أَنتُمْ عَلَيْهِ بِفَـٰتِنِينَ ﴿١٦٢﴾

163. Except such as are (themselves) going to the blazing fire!

إِلَّا مَنْ هُوَ صَالِ ٱلْجَحِيمِ ﴿١٦٣﴾

164. (Those ranged in ranks say): "Not one of us but has a place appointed

وَمَا مِنَّآ إِلَّا لَهُۥ مَقَامٞ مَّعۡلُومٞ ١٦٤

165. And we are verily ranged in ranks (for service);

وَإِنَّا لَنَحۡنُ ٱلصَّآفُّونَ ١٦٥

166. And we are verily those who declare (Allah's) glory!"

وَإِنَّا لَنَحۡنُ ٱلۡمُسَبِّحُونَ ١٦٦

167. And there were those who said,

وَإِن كَانُواْ لَيَقُولُونَ ١٦٧

168. "If only we had had before us a message from those of old,

لَوۡ أَنَّ عِندَنَا ذِكۡرٗا مِّنَ ٱلۡأَوَّلِينَ ١٦٨

169. We should certainly have been servants of Allah, sincere (and devoted)!"

لَكُنَّا عِبَادَ ٱللَّهِ ٱلۡمُخۡلَصِينَ ١٦٩

170. But (now that the Qur'an has come), they reject it: but soon will they know!

فَكَفَرُواْ بِهِۦۖ فَسَوۡفَ يَعۡلَمُونَ ١٧٠

171. Already has Our word been passed before (this) to Our servants sent (by Us),

وَلَقَدۡ سَبَقَتۡ كَلِمَتُنَا لِعِبَادِنَا ٱلۡمُرۡسَلِينَ ١٧١

172. That they would certainly be assisted,

إِنَّهُمۡ لَهُمُ ٱلۡمَنصُورُونَ ١٧٢

173. And that Our forces - they surely must conquer.

وَإِنَّ جُندَنَا لَهُمُ ٱلۡغَٰلِبُونَ ١٧٣

174. So turn you away from them for a little while,

فَتَوَلَّ عَنۡهُمۡ حَتَّىٰ حِينٖ ١٧٤

175. And watch them (how they fare), and they soon shall see (how you fare)!

وَأَبۡصِرۡهُمۡ فَسَوۡفَ يُبۡصِرُونَ ١٧٥

176. Do they wish (indeed) to hurry on Our punishment?

أَفَبِعَذَابِنَا يَسۡتَعۡجِلُونَ ١٧٦

177. But when it descends into the open space before them, evil will be the morning for those who were warned (and heeded not)!

فَإِذَا نَزَلَ بِسَاحَتِهِمۡ فَسَآءَ صَبَاحُ ٱلۡمُنذَرِينَ ١٧٧

178. So turn you away from them for a little while,

وَتَوَلَّ عَنْهُمْ حَتَّىٰ حِينٍ ﴿١٧٨﴾

179. And watch (how they fare) and they soon shall see (how you fare)!

وَأَبْصِرْ فَسَوْفَ يُبْصِرُونَ ﴿١٧٩﴾

180. Glory to your Lord, the Lord of Honour and Power! (He is free) from what they ascribe (to him)!

سُبْحَٰنَ رَبِّكَ رَبِّ ٱلْعِزَّةِ عَمَّا يَصِفُونَ ﴿١٨٠﴾

181. And peace on the messengers!

وَسَلَٰمٌ عَلَى ٱلْمُرْسَلِينَ ﴿١٨١﴾

182. And praise to Allah, the Lord and Cherisher of the Worlds.

وَٱلْحَمْدُ لِلَّهِ رَبِّ ٱلْعَٰلَمِينَ ﴿١٨٢﴾

سُورَةُ صٓ

Surah 38: ***Sad*** **(The Letter 'Sad')**

In the name of Allah,
Most Gracious, Most Merciful.

بِسْمِ ٱللَّهِ ٱلرَّحْمَٰنِ ٱلرَّحِيمِ

1. *Sad.* By the Qur'an full of admonition: (This is the truth).

صٓ ۚ وَٱلْقُرْءَانِ ذِى ٱلذِّكْرِ ﴿١﴾

2. But the unbelievers (are steeped) in self-glory and separatism.

بَلِ ٱلَّذِينَ كَفَرُوا۟ فِى عِزَّةٍ وَشِقَاقٍ ﴿٢﴾

3. How many generations before them did We destroy? In the end they cried (for mercy) - when there was no longer time for being saved!

كَمْ أَهْلَكْنَا مِن قَبْلِهِم مِّن قَرْنٍ فَنَادَوا۟ وَّلَاتَ حِينَ
مَنَاصٍ ﴿٣﴾

4. So they wonder that a warner has come to them from among themselves! And the unbelievers say, "This is a sorcerer telling lies!

وَعَجِبُوٓا۟ أَن جَآءَهُم مُّنذِرٌ مِّنْهُمْ ۖ وَقَالَ ٱلْكَٰفِرُونَ هَٰذَا
سَٰحِرٌ كَذَّابٌ ﴿٤﴾

5. Has he made the gods (all) into one God? Truly this is a wonderful thing!"

أَجَعَلَ ٱلْءَالِهَةَ إِلَٰهًا وَٰحِدًا ۖ إِنَّ هَٰذَا لَشَىْءٌ عُجَابٌ ﴿٥﴾

6. And the leaders among them go away (impatiently) (saying), "Walk you away, and remain constant to your gods! For this is truly a thing designed (against you)!

وَٱنطَلَقَ ٱلۡمَلَأُ مِنۡهُمۡ أَنِ ٱمۡشُواْ وَٱصۡبِرُواْ عَلَىٰٓ ءَالِهَتِكُمۡۖ
إِنَّ هَٰذَا لَشَيۡءٞ يُرَادُ ٦

7. We never heard (the like) of this among the people of these latter days: this is nothing but a made-up tale!"

مَا سَمِعۡنَا بِهَٰذَا فِي ٱلۡمِلَّةِ ٱلۡأٓخِرَةِ إِنۡ هَٰذَآ إِلَّا ٱخۡتِلَٰقٌ ٧

8. "What! Has the message been sent to him - (of all persons) among us?" But they are in doubt concerning My (own) message! Nay, they have not yet tasted My punishment!

أَءُنزِلَ عَلَيۡهِ ٱلذِّكۡرُ مِنۢ بَيۡنِنَاۚ بَلۡ هُمۡ فِي شَكّٖ مِّن ذِكۡرِيۚ
بَل لَّمَّا يَذُوقُواْ عَذَابِ ٨

9. Or do they have the treasures of the mercy of your Lord - the Exalted in Power, the Grantor of Bounties without measure!

أَمۡ عِندَهُمۡ خَزَآئِنُ رَحۡمَةِ رَبِّكَ ٱلۡعَزِيزِ ٱلۡوَهَّابِ ٩

10. Or do they have the dominion of the heavens and the earth and all between? If so, let them mount up with the ropes and means (to reach that end)!

أَمۡ لَهُم مُّلۡكُ ٱلسَّمَٰوَٰتِ وَٱلۡأَرۡضِ وَمَا بَيۡنَهُمَاۖ
فَلۡيَرۡتَقُواْ فِي ٱلۡأَسۡبَٰبِ ١٠

11. But they will be put to flight even a host of confederates.

جُندٞ مَّا هُنَالِكَ مَهۡزُومٞ مِّنَ ٱلۡأَحۡزَابِ ١١

12. Before them (were many who) rejected messengers - the people of Noah, and 'Ad, and Pharaoh the Lord of stakes,

كَذَّبَتۡ قَبۡلَهُمۡ قَوۡمُ نُوحٖ وَعَادٞ وَفِرۡعَوۡنُ ذُو ٱلۡأَوۡتَادِ ١٢

13. And Thamud, and the people of Lot, and the Companions of the Wood - such were the confederates.

وَثَمُودُ وَقَوۡمُ لُوطٖ وَأَصۡحَٰبُ لۡـَٔيۡكَةِۚ أُوْلَٰٓئِكَ
ٱلۡأَحۡزَابُ ١٣

14. Not one (of them) but rejected the messengers, but My punishment came justly and inevitably (on them).

إِن كُلٌّ إِلَّا كَذَّبَ ٱلرُّسُلَ فَحَقَّ عِقَابِ ١٤

15. These (today) only wait for a single mighty blast, which (when it comes) will tolerate no delay.

وَمَا يَنظُرُ هَٰٓؤُلَآءِ إِلَّا صَيۡحَةٗ وَٰحِدَةٗ مَّا لَهَا
مِن فَوَاقٖ ١٥

16. They say: "Our Lord! Hasten to us our sentence (even) before the day of account!"

وَقَالُوا۟ رَبَّنَا عَجِّل لَّنَا قِطَّنَا قَبْلَ يَوْمِ ٱلْحِسَابِ ﴿١٦﴾

17. Have patience at what they say, and remember Our servant David, the man of strength: for he ever turned (to Allah).

ٱصْبِرْ عَلَىٰ مَا يَقُولُونَ وَٱذْكُرْ عَبْدَنَا دَاوُۥدَ ذَا ٱلْأَيْدِ ۖ
إِنَّهُۥٓ أَوَّابٌ ﴿١٧﴾

18. It was We that made the hills declare, in unison with him, Our praises, at eventide and at break of day,

إِنَّا سَخَّرْنَا ٱلْجِبَالَ مَعَهُۥ يُسَبِّحْنَ بِٱلْعَشِىِّ
وَٱلْإِشْرَاقِ ﴿١٨﴾

19. And the birds gathered (in assemblies): all with him did turn (to Allah).

وَٱلطَّيْرَ مَحْشُورَةً ۖ كُلٌّ لَّهُۥٓ أَوَّابٌ ﴿١٩﴾

20. We strengthened his kingdom, and gave him wisdom and sound judgement in speech and decision.

وَشَدَدْنَا مُلْكَهُۥ وَءَاتَيْنَٰهُ ٱلْحِكْمَةَ وَفَصْلَ
ٱلْخِطَابِ ﴿٢٠﴾

21. Has the story of the disputants reached you? See, they climbed over the wall of the private chamber;

ربع الحزب ٤٦ ۞ وَهَلْ أَتَىٰكَ نَبَؤُا۟ ٱلْخَصْمِ إِذْ تَسَوَّرُوا۟ ٱلْمِحْرَابَ ﴿٢١﴾

22. When they entered the presence of David, and he was terrified of them, they said: "Fear not; we are two disputants, one of whom has wronged the other; decide now between us with truth, and treat us not with injustice, but guide us to the even path.

إِذْ دَخَلُوا۟ عَلَىٰ دَاوُۥدَ فَفَزِعَ مِنْهُمْ ۖ قَالُوا۟ لَا تَخَفْ ۖ
خَصْمَانِ بَغَىٰ بَعْضُنَا عَلَىٰ بَعْضٍ فَٱحْكُم بَيْنَنَا بِٱلْحَقِّ
وَلَا تُشْطِطْ وَٱهْدِنَآ إِلَىٰ سَوَآءِ ٱلصِّرَٰطِ ﴿٢٢﴾

23. This man is my brother: he has nine and ninety ewes, and I have (but) one: Yet he says, 'Commit her to my care,' and is (moreover) harsh to me in speech."

إِنَّ هَٰذَآ أَخِى لَهُۥ تِسْعٌ وَتِسْعُونَ نَعْجَةً وَلِىَ نَعْجَةٌ وَٰحِدَةٌ
فَقَالَ أَكْفِلْنِيهَا وَعَزَّنِى فِى ٱلْخِطَابِ ﴿٢٣﴾

24. (David) said: "He has undoubtedly wronged you in demanding your (single) ewe to be added to his (flock of) ewes; truly many are the partners (in business) who wrong each other: not so do those who believe and work deeds of righteousness, and

قَالَ لَقَدْ ظَلَمَكَ بِسُؤَالِ نَعْجَتِكَ إِلَىٰ نِعَاجِهِۦ ۖ وَإِنَّ كَثِيرًا
مِّنَ ٱلْخُلَطَآءِ لَيَبْغِى بَعْضُهُمْ عَلَىٰ بَعْضٍ إِلَّا ٱلَّذِينَ ءَامَنُوا۟
وَعَمِلُوا۟ ٱلصَّٰلِحَٰتِ وَقَلِيلٌ مَّا هُمْ ۗ وَظَنَّ دَاوُۥدُ أَنَّمَا

how few are they?" And David gathered that We had tried him: he asked forgiveness of his Lord, fell down, bowing (in prostration), and turned (to Allah in repentance).

سجدة
فَتَنَّٰهُ فَٱسۡتَغۡفَرَ رَبَّهُۥ وَخَرَّۤ رَاكِعٗا وَأَنَابَ ۩ ﴿٢٤﴾

25. So We forgave him this (lapse): he enjoyed, indeed, a near approach to Us, and a beautiful place of (final) return.

فَغَفَرۡنَا لَهُۥ ذَٰلِكَۖ وَإِنَّ لَهُۥ عِندَنَا لَزُلۡفَىٰ وَحُسۡنَ
مَـَٔابٖ ﴿٢٥﴾

26. O David! We did indeed make you a vicegerent on earth: so judge you between men in truth (and justice): nor follow you the lusts (of your heart), for they will mislead you from the path of Allah: for those who wander astray from the path of Allah, is a penalty grievous, for that they forget the day of account.

يَٰدَاوُۥدُ إِنَّا جَعَلۡنَٰكَ خَلِيفَةٗ فِي ٱلۡأَرۡضِ فَٱحۡكُم بَيۡنَ
ٱلنَّاسِ بِٱلۡحَقِّ وَلَا تَتَّبِعِ ٱلۡهَوَىٰ فَيُضِلَّكَ عَن سَبِيلِ
ٱللَّهِۚ إِنَّ ٱلَّذِينَ يَضِلُّونَ عَن سَبِيلِ ٱللَّهِ لَهُمۡ عَذَابٞ
شَدِيدُۢ بِمَا نَسُواْ يَوۡمَ ٱلۡحِسَابِ ﴿٢٦﴾

27. Not without purpose did We create heaven and earth and all between! That were the thought of unbelievers! But woe to the unbelievers because of the fire (of hell)!

وَمَا خَلَقۡنَا ٱلسَّمَآءَ وَٱلۡأَرۡضَ وَمَا بَيۡنَهُمَا بَٰطِلٗاۚ ذَٰلِكَ
ظَنُّ ٱلَّذِينَ كَفَرُواْۚ فَوَيۡلٞ لِّلَّذِينَ كَفَرُواْ مِنَ ٱلنَّارِ ﴿٢٧﴾

28. Shall We treat those who believe and work deeds of righteousness, the same as those who do mischief on earth? Shall We treat those who guard against evil, the same as those who turn aside from the right?

أَمۡ نَجۡعَلُ ٱلَّذِينَ ءَامَنُواْ وَعَمِلُواْ ٱلصَّٰلِحَٰتِ كَٱلۡمُفۡسِدِينَ
فِي ٱلۡأَرۡضِ أَمۡ نَجۡعَلُ ٱلۡمُتَّقِينَ كَٱلۡفُجَّارِ ﴿٢٨﴾

29. (Here is) a book which We have sent down to you, full of blessings, that they may meditate on its signs, and that men of understanding may receive admonition.

كِتَٰبٌ أَنزَلۡنَٰهُ إِلَيۡكَ مُبَٰرَكٞ لِّيَدَّبَّرُوٓاْ ءَايَٰتِهِۦ
وَلِيَتَذَكَّرَ أُوْلُواْ ٱلۡأَلۡبَٰبِ ﴿٢٩﴾

30. To David We gave Solomon (for a son) - how excellent in Our service! Ever did he turn (to Us)!

وَوَهَبۡنَا لِدَاوُۥدَ سُلَيۡمَٰنَۚ نِعۡمَ ٱلۡعَبۡدُ إِنَّهُۥٓ أَوَّابٌ ﴿٣٠﴾

31. See, there were brought before him, at eventide, coursers of the highest breeding, and swift of foot;

إِذۡ عُرِضَ عَلَيۡهِ بِٱلۡعَشِيِّ ٱلصَّٰفِنَٰتُ ٱلۡجِيَادُ ﴿٣١﴾

32. And he said, "Truly do I love the love of good, with a view to the glory of my Lord" - until (the sun) was hidden in the veil (of night):

فَقَالَ إِنِّيٓ أَحۡبَبۡتُ حُبَّ ٱلۡخَيۡرِ عَن ذِكۡرِ رَبِّي حَتَّىٰ تَوَارَتۡ
بِٱلۡحِجَابِ ﴿٣٢﴾

33. "Bring them back to me." Then began he to pass his hand over (their) legs and their necks.

رُدُّوهَا عَلَيَّۖ فَطَفِقَ مَسۡحَۢا بِٱلسُّوقِ وَٱلۡأَعۡنَاقِ ﴿٣٣﴾

34. And We did try Solomon: We placed on his throne a body (without life): but he did turn (to Us in true devotion):

وَلَقَدۡ فَتَنَّا سُلَيۡمَٰنَ وَأَلۡقَيۡنَا عَلَىٰ كُرۡسِيِّهِۦ جَسَدٗا
ثُمَّ أَنَابَ ﴿٣٤﴾

35. He said: "O my Lord! Forgive me, and grant me a kingdom which, (it may be), suits not another after me: for You are the Grantor of Bounties (without measure)."

قَالَ رَبِّ ٱغۡفِرۡ لِي وَهَبۡ لِي مُلۡكٗا لَّا يَنۢبَغِي لِأَحَدٖ مِّنۢ
بَعۡدِيٓۖ إِنَّكَ أَنتَ ٱلۡوَهَّابُ ﴿٣٥﴾

36. Then We subjected the wind to his power, to flow gently to his order, which ever way he willed -

فَسَخَّرۡنَا لَهُ ٱلرِّيحَ تَجۡرِي بِأَمۡرِهِۦ رُخَآءً حَيۡثُ أَصَابَ ﴿٣٦﴾

37. As also the evil ones, (including) every kind of builder and diver -

وَٱلشَّيَٰطِينَ كُلَّ بَنَّآءٖ وَغَوَّاصٖ ﴿٣٧﴾

38. As also others bound together in fetters.

وَءَاخَرِينَ مُقَرَّنِينَ فِي ٱلۡأَصۡفَادِ ﴿٣٨﴾

39. "Such are Our bounties: whether you bestow them (on others) or withhold them, no account will be asked."

هَٰذَا عَطَآؤُنَا فَٱمۡنُنۡ أَوۡ أَمۡسِكۡ بِغَيۡرِ حِسَابٖ ﴿٣٩﴾

40. And he enjoyed, indeed, a near approach to Us, and a beautiful place of (final) return.

وَإِنَّ لَهُۥ عِندَنَا لَزُلۡفَىٰ وَحُسۡنَ مَـَٔابٖ ﴿٤٠﴾

41. Commemorate Our servant Job. See, he called to his Lord: "The evil one has afflicted me with distress and suffering!"

وَٱذۡكُرۡ عَبۡدَنَآ أَيُّوبَ إِذۡ نَادَىٰ رَبَّهُۥٓ أَنِّي مَسَّنِيَ ٱلشَّيۡطَٰنُ
بِنُصۡبٖ وَعَذَابٍ ﴿٤١﴾

42. (The command was given:) "Strike with your foot: here is (water) in which to wash, cool and refreshing and (water) to drink."

ٱرۡكُضۡ بِرِجۡلِكَۖ هَٰذَا مُغۡتَسَلُۢ بَارِدٞ وَشَرَابٞ ﴿٤٢﴾

43. And We gave him (back) his people and doubled their number - as a grace from Ourselves, and a thing for commemoration, for all who have understanding.

وَوَهَبْنَا لَهُۥٓ أَهْلَهُۥ وَمِثْلَهُم مَّعَهُمْ رَحْمَةً مِّنَّا وَذِكْرَىٰ لِأُو۟لِى ٱلْأَلْبَٰبِ ﴿٤٣﴾

44. "And take in your hand a little grass, and strike with it: and break not (your oath)." Truly We found him full of patience and constancy, how excellent in Our service! Ever did he turn (to Us)!

وَخُذْ بِيَدِكَ ضِغْثًا فَٱضْرِب بِّهِۦ وَلَا تَحْنَثْ ۗ إِنَّا وَجَدْنَٰهُ صَابِرًا ۚ نِّعْمَ ٱلْعَبْدُ ۖ إِنَّهُۥٓ أَوَّابٌ ﴿٤٤﴾

45. And commemorate Our servants Abraham, Isaac, and Jacob, possessors of power and vision.

وَٱذْكُرْ عِبَٰدَنَآ إِبْرَٰهِيمَ وَإِسْحَٰقَ وَيَعْقُوبَ أُو۟لِى ٱلْأَيْدِى وَٱلْأَبْصَٰرِ ﴿٤٥﴾

46. Verily, We did choose them for a special (purpose) - proclaiming the message of the hereafter.

إِنَّآ أَخْلَصْنَٰهُم بِخَالِصَةٍ ذِكْرَى ٱلدَّارِ ﴿٤٦﴾

47. They were, in Our sight, truly, of the company of the elect and the good.

وَإِنَّهُمْ عِندَنَا لَمِنَ ٱلْمُصْطَفَيْنَ ٱلْأَخْيَارِ ﴿٤٧﴾

48. And commemorate Ishmael, al-Yasa, and Dhu al-Kifl: each of them was of the company of the good.

وَٱذْكُرْ إِسْمَٰعِيلَ وَٱلْيَسَعَ وَذَا ٱلْكِفْلِ ۖ وَكُلٌّ مِّنَ ٱلْأَخْيَارِ ﴿٤٨﴾

49. This is a message (of admonition): and verily, for the righteous is a beautiful place of (final) return -

هَٰذَا ذِكْرٌ ۚ وَإِنَّ لِلْمُتَّقِينَ لَحُسْنَ مَـَٔابٍ ﴿٤٩﴾

50. Gardens of Eternity, whose doors will (ever) be open to them;

جَنَّٰتِ عَدْنٍ مُّفَتَّحَةً لَّهُمُ ٱلْأَبْوَٰبُ ﴿٥٠﴾

51. In it will they recline (at ease); in it can they call (at pleasure) for fruit in abundance, and (delicious) drink;

مُتَّكِـِٔينَ فِيهَا يَدْعُونَ فِيهَا بِفَٰكِهَةٍ كَثِيرَةٍ وَشَرَابٍ ﴿٥١﴾

52. And beside them will be chaste women restraining their glances, (companions) of equal age.

نصف حزب ٤٦ * وَعِندَهُمْ قَٰصِرَٰتُ ٱلطَّرْفِ أَتْرَابٌ ﴿٥٢﴾

53. Such is the promise made to you for the day of account!

هَٰذَا مَا تُوعَدُونَ لِيَوْمِ ٱلْحِسَابِ ﴿٥٣﴾

54. Truly such will be Our bounty (to you); it will never fail -

إِنَّ هَٰذَا لَرِزْقُنَا مَا لَهُۥ مِن نَّفَادٍ ﴿٥٤﴾

55. Yea, such! But - for the wrongdoers will be an evil place of (final) return!

هَٰذَا ۚ وَإِنَّ لِلطَّٰغِينَ لَشَرَّ مَـَٔابٍ ﴿٥٥﴾

56. Hell! - They will burn in it - an evil bed (indeed to lie on)! -

جَهَنَّمَ يَصْلَوْنَهَا فَبِئْسَ ٱلْمِهَادُ ﴿٥٦﴾

57. Yea, such! - Then shall they taste it - a boiling fluid, and a fluid dark, murky, intensely cold! -

هَٰذَا فَلْيَذُوقُوهُ حَمِيمٌ وَغَسَّاقٌ ﴿٥٧﴾

58. And other penalties of a similar kind, to match them!

وَءَاخَرُ مِن شَكْلِهِۦٓ أَزْوَٰجٌ ﴿٥٨﴾

59. Here is a troop rushing headlong with you! No welcome for them! Truly they shall burn in the fire!

هَٰذَا فَوْجٌ مُّقْتَحِمٌ مَّعَكُمْ ۖ لَا مَرْحَبًۢا بِهِمْ ۚ
إِنَّهُمْ صَالُوا۟ ٱلنَّارِ ﴿٥٩﴾

60. (The followers shall call to the misleaders:) "Nay, you (too)! No welcome for you! It is you who have brought this upon us! Now evil is (this) place to stay in!"

قَالُوا۟ بَلْ أَنتُمْ لَا مَرْحَبًۢا بِكُمْ ۖ أَنتُمْ قَدَّمْتُمُوهُ لَنَا ۖ
فَبِئْسَ ٱلْقَرَارُ ﴿٦٠﴾

61. They will say: "Our Lord! Whoever brought this upon us - add to him a double penalty in the fire!"

قَالُوا۟ رَبَّنَا مَن قَدَّمَ لَنَا هَٰذَا فَزِدْهُ عَذَابًا ضِعْفًا
فِى ٱلنَّارِ ﴿٦١﴾

62. And they will say: "What has happened to us that we do not see men whom we used to number among the bad ones?

وَقَالُوا۟ مَا لَنَا لَا نَرَىٰ رِجَالًا كُنَّا نَعُدُّهُم مِّنَ ٱلْأَشْرَارِ ﴿٦٢﴾

63. Did we treat them (as such) in ridicule or have (our) eyes failed to perceive them?"

أَتَّخَذْنَٰهُمْ سِخْرِيًّا أَمْ زَاغَتْ عَنْهُمُ ٱلْأَبْصَٰرُ ﴿٦٣﴾

64. Truly that is just and fitting - the mutual recriminations of the people of the fire!

إِنَّ ذَٰلِكَ لَحَقٌّ تَخَاصُمُ أَهْلِ ٱلنَّارِ ﴿٦٤﴾

65. Say: "Truly am I a warner: no god is there but the One God, Supreme and Irresistible -

قُلْ إِنَّمَآ أَنَا۠ مُنذِرٌ ۖ وَمَا مِنْ إِلَٰهٍ إِلَّا ٱللَّهُ ٱلْوَٰحِدُ ٱلْقَهَّارُ ﴿٦٥﴾

66. The Lord of the heavens and the earth, and all between - Exalted in Might, Able to enforce His will, Forgiving again and again."

رَبُّ ٱلسَّمَٰوَٰتِ وَٱلْأَرْضِ وَمَا بَيْنَهُمَا ٱلْعَزِيزُ ٱلْغَفَّٰرُ ﴿٦٦﴾

67. Say: "That is a message supreme (above all) -

قُلْ هُوَ نَبَؤٌا۟ عَظِيمٌ ﴿٦٧﴾

68. From which you do turn away!

أَنتُمْ عَنْهُ مُعْرِضُونَ ﴿٦٨﴾

69. No knowledge have I of the chiefs on high, when they discuss (matters) among themselves.

مَا كَانَ لِىَ مِنْ عِلْمٍۭ بِٱلْمَلَإِ ٱلْأَعْلَىٰٓ إِذْ يَخْتَصِمُونَ ﴿٦٩﴾

70. Only this has been revealed to me: that I am to give warning plainly and publicly."

إِن يُوحَىٰٓ إِلَىَّ إِلَّآ أَنَّمَآ أَنَا۠ نَذِيرٌ مُّبِينٌ ﴿٧٠﴾

71. See, your Lord said to the angels: "I am about to create man from clay:

إِذْ قَالَ رَبُّكَ لِلْمَلَٰٓئِكَةِ إِنِّى خَٰلِقٌۢ بَشَرًا مِّن طِينٍ ﴿٧١﴾

72. When I have fashioned him (in due proportion) and breathed into him of My spirit, fall you down in obeisance to him."

فَإِذَا سَوَّيْتُهُۥ وَنَفَخْتُ فِيهِ مِن رُّوحِى فَقَعُوا۟ لَهُۥ
سَٰجِدِينَ ﴿٧٢﴾

73. So the angels prostrated themselves, all of them together;

فَسَجَدَ ٱلْمَلَٰٓئِكَةُ كُلُّهُمْ أَجْمَعُونَ ﴿٧٣﴾

74. Not so Iblis: he was haughty, and became one of those who reject faith.

إِلَّآ إِبْلِيسَ ٱسْتَكْبَرَ وَكَانَ مِنَ ٱلْكَٰفِرِينَ ﴿٧٤﴾

75. (Allah) said: "O Iblis! What prevents you from prostrating yourself to one whom I have created with My hands? Are you haughty? Or are you one of the high (and mighty) ones?"

قَالَ يَٰٓإِبْلِيسُ مَا مَنَعَكَ أَن تَسْجُدَ لِمَا خَلَقْتُ بِيَدَىَّ ۖ
أَسْتَكْبَرْتَ أَمْ كُنتَ مِنَ ٱلْعَالِينَ ﴿٧٥﴾

76. (Iblis) said: "I am better than he: You created me from fire, and him You created from clay."

قَالَ أَنَا۠ خَيْرٌ مِّنْهُ خَلَقْتَنِى مِن نَّارٍ وَخَلَقْتَهُۥ مِن طِينٍ ٧٦

77. (Allah) said: "Then get you out from here: for you are rejected, accursed.

قَالَ فَٱخْرُجْ مِنْهَا فَإِنَّكَ رَجِيمٌ ٧٧

78. And My curse shall be on you till the day of judgement."

وَإِنَّ عَلَيْكَ لَعْنَتِىٓ إِلَىٰ يَوْمِ ٱلدِّينِ ٧٨

79. (Iblis) said: "O my Lord! Give me then respite till the day the (dead) are raised."

قَالَ رَبِّ فَأَنظِرْنِىٓ إِلَىٰ يَوْمِ يُبْعَثُونَ ٧٩

80. (Allah) said: "Respite then is granted you -

قَالَ فَإِنَّكَ مِنَ ٱلْمُنظَرِينَ ٨٠

81. Till the day of the time appointed."

إِلَىٰ يَوْمِ ٱلْوَقْتِ ٱلْمَعْلُومِ ٨١

82. (Iblis) said: "Then, by Your power, I will put them all in the wrong -

قَالَ فَبِعِزَّتِكَ لَأُغْوِيَنَّهُمْ أَجْمَعِينَ ٨٢

83. Except Your servants amongst them, sincere and purified (by Your grace)."

إِلَّا عِبَادَكَ مِنْهُمُ ٱلْمُخْلَصِينَ ٨٣

84. (Allah) said: "Then it is just and fitting - and I say what is just and fitting -

قَالَ فَٱلْحَقُّ وَٱلْحَقَّ أَقُولُ ٨٤

85. That I will certainly fill hell with you and those that follow you - everyone."

لَأَمْلَأَنَّ جَهَنَّمَ مِنكَ وَمِمَّن تَبِعَكَ مِنْهُمْ أَجْمَعِينَ ٨٥

86. Say: "No reward do I ask of you for this (Qur'an), nor am I a pretender.

قُلْ مَآ أَسْـَٔلُكُمْ عَلَيْهِ مِنْ أَجْرٍ وَمَآ أَنَا۠ مِنَ ٱلْمُتَكَلِّفِينَ ٨٦

87. This is no less than a message to (all) the worlds.

إِنْ هُوَ إِلَّا ذِكْرٌ لِّلْعَٰلَمِينَ ٨٧

88. And you shall certainly know the truth of it (all) after a while."

وَلَتَعْلَمُنَّ نَبَأَهُۥ بَعْدَ حِينٍۭ ٨٨

سُورَةُ الزُّمَرِ

Surah 39: **Az-Zumar (Crowds)**

In the name of Allah,
Most Gracious, Most Merciful.

بِسۡمِ ٱللَّهِ ٱلرَّحۡمَٰنِ ٱلرَّحِيمِ

1. The revelation of this book is from Allah, the Exalted in power, Full of wisdom.

تَنزِيلُ ٱلۡكِتَٰبِ مِنَ ٱللَّهِ ٱلۡعَزِيزِ ٱلۡحَكِيمِ ١

2. Verily it is We Who have revealed the book to you in truth: so serve Allah, offering Him sincere devotion.

إِنَّآ أَنزَلۡنَآ إِلَيۡكَ ٱلۡكِتَٰبَ بِٱلۡحَقِّ فَٱعۡبُدِ ٱللَّهَ
مُخۡلِصٗا لَّهُ ٱلدِّينَ ٢

3. Is it not to Allah that sincere devotion is due? But those who take for protectors other than Allah (say): "We only serve them in order that they may bring us nearer to Allah." Truly Allah will judge between them in that in which they differ. But Allah guides not such as are false and ungrateful.

أَلَا لِلَّهِ ٱلدِّينُ ٱلۡخَالِصُۚ وَٱلَّذِينَ ٱتَّخَذُواْ مِن
دُونِهِۦٓ أَوۡلِيَآءَ مَا نَعۡبُدُهُمۡ إِلَّا لِيُقَرِّبُونَآ إِلَى
ٱللَّهِ زُلۡفَىٰٓ إِنَّ ٱللَّهَ يَحۡكُمُ بَيۡنَهُمۡ فِي مَا هُمۡ
فِيهِ يَخۡتَلِفُونَۗ إِنَّ ٱللَّهَ لَا يَهۡدِي مَنۡ هُوَ
كَٰذِبٞ كَفَّارٞ ٣

4. Had Allah wished to take to Himself a son, He could have chosen whom He pleased out of those whom He does create: but glory be to Him! (He is above such things.) He is Allah, the One, the Irresistible.

لَّوۡ أَرَادَ ٱللَّهُ أَن يَتَّخِذَ وَلَدٗا لَّٱصۡطَفَىٰ مِمَّا يَخۡلُقُ
مَا يَشَآءُۚ سُبۡحَٰنَهُۥۖ هُوَ ٱللَّهُ ٱلۡوَٰحِدُ ٱلۡقَهَّارُ ٤

5. He created the heavens and the earth in true (proportions): He makes the night overlap the day, and the day overlap the night: He has subjected the sun and the moon (to His law): each one follows a course for a time appointed. Is not He the Exalted in power - He Who forgives again and again?

خَلَقَ ٱلسَّمَٰوَٰتِ وَٱلۡأَرۡضَ بِٱلۡحَقِّۖ يُكَوِّرُ
ٱلَّيۡلَ عَلَى ٱلنَّهَارِ وَيُكَوِّرُ ٱلنَّهَارَ عَلَى ٱلَّيۡلِۖ
وَسَخَّرَ ٱلشَّمۡسَ وَٱلۡقَمَرَۖ كُلّٞ يَجۡرِي لِأَجَلٖ
مُّسَمًّىۗ أَلَا هُوَ ٱلۡعَزِيزُ ٱلۡغَفَّٰرُ ٥

6. He created you (all) from a single person: then created, of like nature, his mate; and He sent down for you eight head of cattle in pairs: He makes you, in the wombs of your mothers, in stages, one after another, in three veils of darkness. Such is Allah, your Lord and Cherisher: to Him belongs (all) dominion. There is no god but He: then how are you turned away (from your true centre)?

خَلَقَكُم مِّن نَّفْسٍ وَٰحِدَةٍ ثُمَّ جَعَلَ مِنْهَا زَوْجَهَا
وَأَنزَلَ لَكُم مِّنَ ٱلْأَنْعَٰمِ ثَمَٰنِيَةَ أَزْوَٰجٍ ۚ يَخْلُقُكُمْ
فِى بُطُونِ أُمَّهَٰتِكُمْ خَلْقًا مِّنۢ بَعْدِ خَلْقٍ فِى ظُلُمَٰتٍ
ثَلَٰثٍ ۚ ذَٰلِكُمُ ٱللَّهُ رَبُّكُمْ لَهُ ٱلْمُلْكُ ۖ لَآ إِلَٰهَ إِلَّا هُوَ ۖ
فَأَنَّىٰ تُصْرَفُونَ ٦

7. It you reject (Allah), truly Allah has no need of you; but He likes not ingratitude from His servants: if you are grateful, He is pleased with you. No bearer of burdens can bear the burden of another. In the end, to your Lord is your return, when He will tell you the truth of all that you did (in this life). For He knows well all that is in (men's) hearts.

إِن تَكْفُرُوا۟ فَإِنَّ ٱللَّهَ غَنِىٌّ عَنكُمْ ۖ وَلَا يَرْضَىٰ
لِعِبَادِهِ ٱلْكُفْرَ ۖ وَإِن تَشْكُرُوا۟ يَرْضَهُ لَكُمْ ۗ وَلَا تَزِرُ
وَازِرَةٌ وِزْرَ أُخْرَىٰ ۗ ثُمَّ إِلَىٰ رَبِّكُم مَّرْجِعُكُمْ
فَيُنَبِّئُكُم بِمَا كُنتُمْ تَعْمَلُونَ ۚ إِنَّهُۥ عَلِيمٌۢ بِذَاتِ
ٱلصُّدُورِ ٧

8. When some trouble touches man, he cries to his Lord, turning to Him in repentance: but when He bestows a favour upon him, as from Himself, (man) does forget what he cried and prayed for before, and he does set up rivals to Allah, thus misleading others from Allah's path. Say, "Enjoy your blasphemy for a little while: verily you are (one) of the companions of the fire!"

ثلاثة أرباع الحزب ٤٦
۞ وَإِذَا مَسَّ ٱلْإِنسَٰنَ ضُرٌّ دَعَا رَبَّهُۥ مُنِيبًا إِلَيْهِ ثُمَّ إِذَا
خَوَّلَهُۥ نِعْمَةً مِّنْهُ نَسِىَ مَا كَانَ يَدْعُوٓا۟ إِلَيْهِ مِن قَبْلُ
وَجَعَلَ لِلَّهِ أَندَادًا لِّيُضِلَّ عَن سَبِيلِهِۦ ۚ قُلْ تَمَتَّعْ
بِكُفْرِكَ قَلِيلًا ۖ إِنَّكَ مِنْ أَصْحَٰبِ ٱلنَّارِ ٨

9. Is one who worships devoutly during the hours of the night prostrating himself or standing (in adoration), who takes heed of the hereafter, and who places his hope in the mercy of his Lord - (like one who does not)? Say: "Are those equal, those who know and those who do not know? It is those who are endued with understanding that receive admonition."

أَمَّنْ هُوَ قَٰنِتٌ ءَانَآءَ ٱلَّيْلِ سَاجِدًا وَقَآئِمًا يَحْذَرُ
ٱلْءَاخِرَةَ وَيَرْجُوا۟ رَحْمَةَ رَبِّهِۦ ۗ قُلْ هَلْ يَسْتَوِى ٱلَّذِينَ
يَعْلَمُونَ وَٱلَّذِينَ لَا يَعْلَمُونَ ۗ إِنَّمَا يَتَذَكَّرُ أُو۟لُوا۟
ٱلْأَلْبَٰبِ ٩

10. Say: "(Thus speaks God:) O you My servants who believe! Fear your Lord. Good is (the reward) for those who do good in this world. Spacious is Allah's earth! Those who patiently persevere will truly receive a reward without measure!"

قُلْ يَٰعِبَادِ ٱلَّذِينَ ءَامَنُوا۟ ٱتَّقُوا۟ رَبَّكُمْ ۚ لِلَّذِينَ
أَحْسَنُوا۟ فِى هَٰذِهِ ٱلدُّنْيَا حَسَنَةٌ ۗ وَأَرْضُ ٱللَّهِ
وَٰسِعَةٌ ۗ إِنَّمَا يُوَفَّى ٱلصَّٰبِرُونَ أَجْرَهُم بِغَيْرِ حِسَابٍ ١٠

11. Say: "Verily, I am commanded to serve Allah with sincere devotion;

قُلْ إِنِّىٓ أُمِرْتُ أَنْ أَعْبُدَ ٱللَّهَ مُخْلِصًا لَّهُ ٱلدِّينَ ١١

12. And I am commanded to be the first of those who bow to Allah in Islam."

وَأُمِرْتُ لِأَنْ أَكُونَ أَوَّلَ ٱلْمُسْلِمِينَ ١٢

13. Say: "I would, if I disobeyed my Lord, indeed have fear of the penalty of a mighty day."

قُلْ إِنِّىٓ أَخَافُ إِنْ عَصَيْتُ رَبِّى عَذَابَ يَوْمٍ عَظِيمٍ ١٣

14. Say: "It is Allah I serve, with my sincere (and exclusive) devotion:

قُلِ ٱللَّهَ أَعْبُدُ مُخْلِصًا لَّهُۥ دِينِى ١٤

15. Serve you what you will besides Him." Say: "Truly, those in loss are those who lose their own souls and their people on the day of judgement: Ah! That is indeed the (real and) evident loss!"

فَٱعْبُدُوا۟ مَا شِئْتُم مِّن دُونِهِۦ ۗ قُلْ إِنَّ ٱلْخَٰسِرِينَ ٱلَّذِينَ
خَسِرُوٓا۟ أَنفُسَهُمْ وَأَهْلِيهِمْ يَوْمَ ٱلْقِيَٰمَةِ ۗ أَلَا ذَٰلِكَ
هُوَ ٱلْخُسْرَانُ ٱلْمُبِينُ ١٥

16. They shall have layers of fire above them, and layers (of fire) below them: with this does Allah warn off His servants: "O My servants! Then fear you Me!"

لَهُم مِّن فَوْقِهِمْ ظُلَلٌ مِّنَ ٱلنَّارِ وَمِن تَحْتِهِمْ ظُلَلٌ ۚ ذَٰلِكَ
يُخَوِّفُ ٱللَّهُ بِهِۦ عِبَادَهُۥ ۚ يَٰعِبَادِ فَٱتَّقُونِ ١٦

17. Those who eschew evil - and fall not into its worship - and turn to Allah (in repentance) - for them is good news: so announce the good news to My servants -

وَٱلَّذِينَ ٱجْتَنَبُوا۟ ٱلطَّٰغُوتَ أَن يَعْبُدُوهَا وَأَنَابُوٓا۟ إِلَى ٱللَّهِ
لَهُمُ ٱلْبُشْرَىٰ ۚ فَبَشِّرْ عِبَادِ ١٧

18. Those who listen to the word, and follow the best (meaning) in it: those are the ones whom Allah has guided, and those are the ones endued with understanding.

ٱلَّذِينَ يَسْتَمِعُونَ ٱلْقَوْلَ فَيَتَّبِعُونَ أَحْسَنَهُۥٓ ۚ
أُو۟لَٰٓئِكَ ٱلَّذِينَ هَدَىٰهُمُ ٱللَّهُ ۖ وَأُو۟لَٰٓئِكَ هُمْ أُو۟لُوا۟
ٱلْأَلْبَٰبِ ١٨

19. Is then, one against whom the decree of punishment is justly due (equal to one who eschews evil)? Would you, then, deliver one (who is) in the fire?

أَفَمَنْ حَقَّ عَلَيْهِ كَلِمَةُ ٱلْعَذَابِ أَفَأَنتَ تُنقِذُ مَن
فِى ٱلنَّارِ ١٩

20. But it is for those who fear their Lord, that lofty mansions, one above another, have been built; beneath them flow rivers (of delight); (such is) the promise of Allah: never does Allah fail in (His) promise.

لَٰكِنِ ٱلَّذِينَ ٱتَّقَوْا۟ رَبَّهُمْ لَهُمْ غُرَفٌ مِّن فَوْقِهَا غُرَفٌ
مَّبْنِيَّةٌ تَجْرِى مِن تَحْتِهَا ٱلْأَنْهَٰرُ ۖ وَعْدَ ٱللَّهِ ۖ لَا يُخْلِفُ
ٱللَّهُ ٱلْمِيعَادَ ٢٠

21. Do you not see that Allah sends down rain from the sky, and leads it through springs in the earth? Then He causes to grow, with it, produce of various colours; then it withers; you will see it grow yellow; then He makes it dry up and crumble away. Truly, in this, is a message of remembrance to men of understanding.

أَلَمْ تَرَ أَنَّ ٱللَّهَ أَنزَلَ مِنَ ٱلسَّمَآءِ مَآءً فَسَلَكَهُۥ
يَنَٰبِيعَ فِى ٱلْأَرْضِ ثُمَّ يُخْرِجُ بِهِۦ زَرْعًا مُّخْتَلِفًا أَلْوَٰنُهُۥ
ثُمَّ يَهِيجُ فَتَرَىٰهُ مُصْفَرًّا ثُمَّ يَجْعَلُهُۥ حُطَٰمًا ۚ
إِنَّ فِى ذَٰلِكَ لَذِكْرَىٰ لِأُو۟لِى ٱلْأَلْبَٰبِ ٢١

22. Is one whose heart Allah has opened to Islam, so that he has received enlightenment from Allah, (no better than one hardhearted)? Woe to those whose hearts are hardened against celebrating the praises of Allah! They are manifestly wandering (in error)!

أَفَمَن شَرَحَ ٱللَّهُ صَدْرَهُۥ لِلْإِسْلَٰمِ فَهُوَ عَلَىٰ نُورٍ مِّن
رَّبِّهِۦ ۚ فَوَيْلٌ لِّلْقَٰسِيَةِ قُلُوبُهُم مِّن ذِكْرِ ٱللَّهِ ۚ أُو۟لَٰٓئِكَ
فِى ضَلَٰلٍ مُّبِينٍ ٢٢

23. Allah has revealed (from time to time) the most beautiful message in the form of a book, consistent with itself, (yet) repeating (its teaching in various aspects); the skins of those who fear their Lord tremble at it; then their skins and their hearts do soften to the celebration of Allah's praises. Such is the guidance of Allah: He guides with it whom He pleases, but such as Allah leaves to stray, can have none to guide.

ٱللَّهُ نَزَّلَ أَحْسَنَ ٱلْحَدِيثِ كِتَٰبًا مُّتَشَٰبِهًا مَّثَانِىَ
تَقْشَعِرُّ مِنْهُ جُلُودُ ٱلَّذِينَ يَخْشَوْنَ رَبَّهُمْ ثُمَّ
تَلِينُ جُلُودُهُمْ وَقُلُوبُهُمْ إِلَىٰ ذِكْرِ ٱللَّهِ ۚ ذَٰلِكَ
هُدَى ٱللَّهِ يَهْدِى بِهِۦ مَن يَشَآءُ ۚ وَمَن يُضْلِلِ ٱللَّهُ
فَمَا لَهُۥ مِنْ هَادٍ ٢٣

24. Is, then, one who has to fear the brunt of the penalty on the day of judgement (and

أَفَمَن يَتَّقِى بِوَجْهِهِۦ سُوٓءَ ٱلْعَذَابِ يَوْمَ ٱلْقِيَٰمَةِ ۚ

receive it) on his face, (like one guarded from it)? It will be said to the wrongdoers: "Taste you (the fruits of) what you earned!"

وَقِيلَ لِلظَّٰلِمِينَ ذُوقُواْ مَا كُنتُمۡ تَكۡسِبُونَ ٢٤

25. Those before them (also) rejected (revelation) and so the punishment came to them from directions they did not perceive.

كَذَّبَ ٱلَّذِينَ مِن قَبۡلِهِمۡ فَأَتَىٰهُمُ ٱلۡعَذَابُ مِنۡ
حَيۡثُ لَا يَشۡعُرُونَ ٢٥

26. So Allah gave them a taste of humiliation in the present life, but greater is the punishment of the hereafter, if they only knew!

فَأَذَاقَهُمُ ٱللَّهُ ٱلۡخِزۡيَ فِي ٱلۡحَيَوٰةِ ٱلدُّنۡيَاۖ وَلَعَذَابُ
ٱلۡأٓخِرَةِ أَكۡبَرُۚ لَوۡ كَانُواْ يَعۡلَمُونَ ٢٦

27. We have put out for men, in this Qur'an every kind of parable, in order that they may receive admonition.

وَلَقَدۡ ضَرَبۡنَا لِلنَّاسِ فِي هَٰذَا ٱلۡقُرۡءَانِ مِن كُلِّ مَثَلٖ
لَّعَلَّهُمۡ يَتَذَكَّرُونَ ٢٧

28. (It is) a Qur'an in Arabic, without any crookedness (in it): in order that they may guard against evil.

قُرۡءَانًا عَرَبِيًّا غَيۡرَ ذِي عِوَجٖ لَّعَلَّهُمۡ يَتَّقُونَ ٢٨

29. Allah puts out a parable - a man belonging to many partners at variance with each other, and a man belonging entirely to one master: are those two equal in comparison? Praise be to Allah! But most of them have no knowledge.

ضَرَبَ ٱللَّهُ مَثَلٗا رَّجُلٗا فِيهِ شُرَكَآءُ مُتَشَٰكِسُونَ
وَرَجُلٗا سَلَمٗا لِّرَجُلٍ هَلۡ يَسۡتَوِيَانِ مَثَلًاۚ ٱلۡحَمۡدُ لِلَّهِۚ
بَلۡ أَكۡثَرُهُمۡ لَا يَعۡلَمُونَ ٢٩

30. (O prophet!) Truly you will die (one day), and truly they (too) will die (one day).

إِنَّكَ مَيِّتٞ وَإِنَّهُم مَّيِّتُونَ ٣٠

31. In the end will you (all), on the day of judgement, settle your disputes in the presence of your Lord.

ثُمَّ إِنَّكُمۡ يَوۡمَ ٱلۡقِيَٰمَةِ عِندَ رَبِّكُمۡ تَخۡتَصِمُونَ ٣١

✻**32.** Who, then, does more wrong than one who utters a lie concerning Allah, and rejects the truth when it comes to him! Is there not in hell an abode for blasphemers?

الجزء ٢٤ الحزب ٤٧

✻ فَمَنۡ أَظۡلَمُ مِمَّن كَذَبَ عَلَى ٱللَّهِ وَكَذَّبَ
بِٱلصِّدۡقِ إِذۡ جَآءَهُۥٓۚ أَلَيۡسَ فِي جَهَنَّمَ مَثۡوٗى
لِّلۡكَٰفِرِينَ ٣٢

✻ Part-24

33. And he who brings the truth and he who confirms (and supports) it - such are the men who do right.

وَٱلَّذِى جَآءَ بِٱلصِّدْقِ وَصَدَّقَ بِهِۦٓ أُو۟لَـٰٓئِكَ
هُمُ ٱلْمُتَّقُونَ ﴿٣٣﴾

34. They shall have all that they wish for, in the presence of their Lord: such is the reward of those who do good:

لَهُم مَّا يَشَآءُونَ عِندَ رَبِّهِمْ ۚ ذَٰلِكَ جَزَآءُ
ٱلْمُحْسِنِينَ ﴿٣٤﴾

35. So that Allah will turn off from them (even) the worst in their deeds and give them their reward according to the best of what they have done.

لِيُكَفِّرَ ٱللَّهُ عَنْهُمْ أَسْوَأَ ٱلَّذِى عَمِلُوا۟ وَيَجْزِيَهُمْ
أَجْرَهُم بِأَحْسَنِ ٱلَّذِى كَانُوا۟ يَعْمَلُونَ ﴿٣٥﴾

36. Is not Allah enough for His servant? But they try to frighten you with other (gods) besides Him! For such as Allah leaves to stray, there can be no guide.

أَلَيْسَ ٱللَّهُ بِكَافٍ عَبْدَهُۥ ۖ وَيُخَوِّفُونَكَ بِٱلَّذِينَ
مِن دُونِهِۦ ۚ وَمَن يُضْلِلِ ٱللَّهُ فَمَا لَهُۥ مِنْ هَادٍ ﴿٣٦﴾

37. And such as Allah does guide there can be none to lead astray. Is not Allah Exalted in power, (able to enforce His will), Lord of retribution?

وَمَن يَهْدِ ٱللَّهُ فَمَا لَهُۥ مِن مُّضِلٍّ ۗ أَلَيْسَ ٱللَّهُ
بِعَزِيزٍ ذِى ٱنتِقَامٍ ﴿٣٧﴾

38. If indeed you ask them who it is that created the heavens and the earth, they would be sure to say, "Allah." Say: "See you then? The things that you invoke besides Allah - can they, if Allah wills some penalty for me, remove His penalty? - Or if He wills some grace for me, can they keep back His grace?" Say: "Sufficient is Allah for me! In Him trust those who put their trust."

وَلَئِن سَأَلْتَهُم مَّنْ خَلَقَ ٱلسَّمَـٰوَٰتِ وَٱلْأَرْضَ
لَيَقُولُنَّ ٱللَّهُ ۚ قُلْ أَفَرَءَيْتُم مَّا تَدْعُونَ مِن دُونِ ٱللَّهِ
إِنْ أَرَادَنِىَ ٱللَّهُ بِضُرٍّ هَلْ هُنَّ كَـٰشِفَـٰتُ
ضُرِّهِۦٓ أَوْ أَرَادَنِى بِرَحْمَةٍ هَلْ هُنَّ مُمْسِكَـٰتُ
رَحْمَتِهِۦ ۚ قُلْ حَسْبِىَ ٱللَّهُ ۖ عَلَيْهِ يَتَوَكَّلُ
ٱلْمُتَوَكِّلُونَ ﴿٣٨﴾

39. Say: "O my people! Do whatever you can: I will do (my part): but soon will you know -

قُلْ يَـٰقَوْمِ ٱعْمَلُوا۟ عَلَىٰ مَكَانَتِكُمْ إِنِّى عَـٰمِلٌ ۖ
فَسَوْفَ تَعْلَمُونَ ﴿٣٩﴾

40. Who it is to whom comes a penalty of

مَن يَأْتِيهِ عَذَابٌ يُخْزِيهِ وَيَحِلُّ عَلَيْهِ عَذَابٌ

disgrace, and on whom descends a penalty that lasts."

مُّقِيمٌ ﴿٤٠﴾

41. Verily We have revealed the book to you in truth, for (instructing) mankind. He, then, that receives guidance benefits his own soul: but he that strays injures his own soul. Nor are you set over them to dispose of their affairs.

إِنَّآ أَنزَلۡنَا عَلَيۡكَ ٱلۡكِتَٰبَ لِلنَّاسِ بِٱلۡحَقِّۖ فَمَنِ
ٱهۡتَدَىٰ فَلِنَفۡسِهِۦۖ وَمَن ضَلَّ فَإِنَّمَا يَضِلُّ عَلَيۡهَاۖ
وَمَآ أَنتَ عَلَيۡهِم بِوَكِيلٍ ﴿٤١﴾

42. It is Allah that takes the souls (of men) at death; and those that die not (He takes) during their sleep: those on whom He has passed the decree of death, He keeps back (from returning to life), but the rest He sends (to their bodies) for a term appointed. Verily in this are signs for those who reflect.

ٱللَّهُ يَتَوَفَّى ٱلۡأَنفُسَ حِينَ مَوۡتِهَا وَٱلَّتِي
لَمۡ تَمُتۡ فِي مَنَامِهَاۖ فَيُمۡسِكُ ٱلَّتِي قَضَىٰ عَلَيۡهَا
ٱلۡمَوۡتَ وَيُرۡسِلُ ٱلۡأُخۡرَىٰٓ إِلَىٰٓ أَجَلٖ مُّسَمًّىۚ إِنَّ
فِي ذَٰلِكَ لَأٓيَٰتٖ لِّقَوۡمٖ يَتَفَكَّرُونَ ﴿٤٢﴾

43. What! Do they take for intercessors others besides Allah? Say: "Even if they have no power whatever and no intelligence?"

أَمِ ٱتَّخَذُواْ مِن دُونِ ٱللَّهِ شُفَعَآءَۚ قُلۡ أَوَلَوۡ
كَانُواْ لَا يَمۡلِكُونَ شَيۡـٔٗا وَلَا يَعۡقِلُونَ ﴿٤٣﴾

44. Say: "To Allah belongs exclusively (the right to grant) intercession: to Him belongs the dominion of the heavens and the earth: in the end it is to Him that you shall be brought back."

قُل لِّلَّهِ ٱلشَّفَٰعَةُ جَمِيعٗاۖ لَّهُۥ مُلۡكُ ٱلسَّمَٰوَٰتِ
وَٱلۡأَرۡضِۖ ثُمَّ إِلَيۡهِ تُرۡجَعُونَ ﴿٤٤﴾

45. When Allah, the One and Only, is mentioned, the hearts of those who believe not in the hereafter are filled with disgust and horror; but when (gods) other than He are mentioned, behold they are filled with joy!

وَإِذَا ذُكِرَ ٱللَّهُ وَحۡدَهُ ٱشۡمَأَزَّتۡ قُلُوبُ
ٱلَّذِينَ لَا يُؤۡمِنُونَ بِٱلۡأٓخِرَةِۖ وَإِذَا ذُكِرَ ٱلَّذِينَ
مِن دُونِهِۦٓ إِذَا هُمۡ يَسۡتَبۡشِرُونَ ﴿٤٥﴾

46. Say: "O Allah! Creator of the heavens and the earth! Knower of all that is hidden and open! It is You that will judge between Your servants in those matters about which they have differed."

قُلِ ٱللَّهُمَّ فَاطِرَ ٱلسَّمَٰوَٰتِ وَٱلۡأَرۡضِ عَٰلِمَ ٱلۡغَيۡبِ
وَٱلشَّهَٰدَةِ أَنتَ تَحۡكُمُ بَيۡنَ عِبَادِكَ فِي مَا كَانُواْ
فِيهِ يَخۡتَلِفُونَ ﴿٤٦﴾

47. Even if the wrongdoers had all that there is on earth, and as much more, (in vain) would they offer it for ransom from the pain of the penalty on the day of judgement: but something will confront them from Allah, which they could never have counted upon!

وَلَوۡ أَنَّ لِلَّذِينَ ظَلَمُواْ مَا فِي ٱلۡأَرۡضِ جَمِيعٗا وَمِثۡلَهُۥ
مَعَهُۥ لَٱفۡتَدَوۡاْ بِهِۦ مِن سُوٓءِ ٱلۡعَذَابِ يَوۡمَ ٱلۡقِيَٰمَةِۚ
وَبَدَا لَهُم مِّنَ ٱللَّهِ مَا لَمۡ يَكُونُواْ يَحۡتَسِبُونَ ٤٧

48. For the evils of their deeds will confront them, and they will be (completely) encircled by that which they used to mock at!

وَبَدَا لَهُمۡ سَيِّـَٔاتُ مَا كَسَبُواْ وَحَاقَ بِهِم مَّا
كَانُواْ بِهِۦ يَسۡتَهۡزِءُونَ ٤٨

49. Now, when trouble touches man, he cries to Us; but when We bestow a favour upon him as from Ourselves, he says, "This has been given to me because of a certain knowledge (I have)!" Nay, but this is but a trial, but most of them understand not!

فَإِذَا مَسَّ ٱلۡإِنسَٰنَ ضُرّٞ دَعَانَا ثُمَّ إِذَا خَوَّلۡنَٰهُ نِعۡمَةٗ
مِّنَّا قَالَ إِنَّمَآ أُوتِيتُهُۥ عَلَىٰ عِلۡمِۭۚ بَلۡ هِيَ فِتۡنَةٞ
وَلَٰكِنَّ أَكۡثَرَهُمۡ لَا يَعۡلَمُونَ ٤٩

50. Thus did the (generations) before them say! But all that they did was of no profit to them.

قَدۡ قَالَهَا ٱلَّذِينَ مِن قَبۡلِهِمۡ فَمَآ أَغۡنَىٰ عَنۡهُم
مَّا كَانُواْ يَكۡسِبُونَ ٥٠

51. Nay, the evil results of their deeds overtook them. And the wrongdoers of this (generation) - the evil results of their deeds will soon overtake them (too), and they will never be able to frustrate (Our plan)!

فَأَصَابَهُمۡ سَيِّـَٔاتُ مَا كَسَبُواْۚ وَٱلَّذِينَ ظَلَمُواْ مِنۡ
هَٰٓؤُلَآءِ سَيُصِيبُهُمۡ سَيِّـَٔاتُ مَا كَسَبُواْ وَمَا هُم
بِمُعۡجِزِينَ ٥١

52. Do they not know that Allah enlarges the provision or restricts it, for any He pleases? Verily, in this are signs for those who believe!

أَوَلَمۡ يَعۡلَمُوٓاْ أَنَّ ٱللَّهَ يَبۡسُطُ ٱلرِّزۡقَ لِمَن يَشَآءُ
وَيَقۡدِرُۚ إِنَّ فِي ذَٰلِكَ لَأٓيَٰتٖ لِّقَوۡمٖ يُؤۡمِنُونَ ٥٢

53. Say: "O My servants who have transgressed against their souls! Despair not of the mercy of Allah: for Allah forgives all sins: for He is Oft-Forgiving, Most Merciful.

ربع الحزب ٤٧ ۞ قُلۡ يَٰعِبَادِيَ ٱلَّذِينَ أَسۡرَفُواْ عَلَىٰٓ أَنفُسِهِمۡ لَا
تَقۡنَطُواْ مِن رَّحۡمَةِ ٱللَّهِۚ إِنَّ ٱللَّهَ يَغۡفِرُ ٱلذُّنُوبَ
جَمِيعًاۚ إِنَّهُۥ هُوَ ٱلۡغَفُورُ ٱلرَّحِيمُ ٥٣

54. Turn you to your Lord (in repentance) and bow to His (Will), before the penalty comes on you: after that you shall not be helped.

وَأَنِيبُوٓا۟ إِلَىٰ رَبِّكُمْ وَأَسْلِمُوا۟ لَهُۥ مِن قَبْلِ أَن
يَأْتِيَكُمُ ٱلْعَذَابُ ثُمَّ لَا تُنصَرُونَ ٥٤

55. And follow the Best of (the courses) revealed to you from your Lord, before the penalty comes on you - of a sudden, while you perceive not! -

وَٱتَّبِعُوٓا۟ أَحْسَنَ مَآ أُنزِلَ إِلَيْكُم مِّن رَّبِّكُم مِّن
قَبْلِ أَن يَأْتِيَكُمُ ٱلْعَذَابُ بَغْتَةً وَأَنتُمْ لَا تَشْعُرُونَ ٥٥

56. Lest the soul should (then) say: 'Ah! Woe is me! - In that I neglected (my duty) towards Allah, and was but among those who mocked!' -

أَن تَقُولَ نَفْسٌ يَٰحَسْرَتَىٰ عَلَىٰ مَا فَرَّطتُ فِى
جَنۢبِ ٱللَّهِ وَإِن كُنتُ لَمِنَ ٱلسَّٰخِرِينَ ٥٦

57. Or (lest) it should say: 'If only Allah had guided me, I should certainly have been among the righteous!' -

أَوْ تَقُولَ لَوْ أَنَّ ٱللَّهَ هَدَىٰنِى لَكُنتُ مِنَ ٱلْمُتَّقِينَ ٥٧

58. Or (lest) it should say when it (actually) sees the penalty: 'If only I had another chance, I should certainly be among those who do good!'"

أَوْ تَقُولَ حِينَ تَرَى ٱلْعَذَابَ لَوْ أَنَّ لِى كَرَّةً فَأَكُونَ
مِنَ ٱلْمُحْسِنِينَ ٥٨

59. "(The reply will be) Nay, but there came to you My signs, and you did reject them: you were haughty, and became one of those who reject faith!"

بَلَىٰ قَدْ جَآءَتْكَ ءَايَٰتِى فَكَذَّبْتَ بِهَا وَٱسْتَكْبَرْتَ
وَكُنتَ مِنَ ٱلْكَٰفِرِينَ ٥٩

60. On the day of judgement will you see those who told lies against Allah - their faces will be turned black; is there not in hell an abode for the haughty?

وَيَوْمَ ٱلْقِيَٰمَةِ تَرَى ٱلَّذِينَ كَذَبُوا۟ عَلَى ٱللَّهِ
وُجُوهُهُم مُّسْوَدَّةٌ ۚ أَلَيْسَ فِى جَهَنَّمَ مَثْوًى
لِّلْمُتَكَبِّرِينَ ٦٠

61. But Allah will deliver the righteous to their place of salvation: no evil shall touch them, nor shall they grieve.

وَيُنَجِّى ٱللَّهُ ٱلَّذِينَ ٱتَّقَوْا۟ بِمَفَازَتِهِمْ لَا يَمَسُّهُمُ
ٱلسُّوٓءُ وَلَا هُمْ يَحْزَنُونَ ٦١

62. Allah is the Creator of all things, and He is the Guardian and Disposer of all affairs.

ٱللَّهُ خَٰلِقُ كُلِّ شَيۡءٖۖ وَهُوَ عَلَىٰ كُلِّ شَيۡءٖ
وَكِيلٞ ٦٢

63. To Him belong the keys of the heavens and the earth: and those who reject the signs of Allah it is they who will be in loss.

لَّهُۥ مَقَالِيدُ ٱلسَّمَٰوَٰتِ وَٱلۡأَرۡضِۗ وَٱلَّذِينَ كَفَرُواْ
بِـَٔايَٰتِ ٱللَّهِ أُوْلَٰٓئِكَ هُمُ ٱلۡخَٰسِرُونَ ٦٣

64. Say: "Is it someone other than Allah that you order me to worship, O you ignorant ones?"

قُلۡ أَفَغَيۡرَ ٱللَّهِ تَأۡمُرُوٓنِّيٓ أَعۡبُدُ أَيُّهَا ٱلۡجَٰهِلُونَ ٦٤

65. But it has already been revealed to you - as it was to those before you - "If you were to join (gods with Allah) truly fruitless will be your work (in life), and you will surely be in the ranks of those who lose (all spiritual good)."

وَلَقَدۡ أُوحِيَ إِلَيۡكَ وَإِلَى ٱلَّذِينَ مِن قَبۡلِكَ
لَئِنۡ أَشۡرَكۡتَ لَيَحۡبَطَنَّ عَمَلُكَ
وَلَتَكُونَنَّ مِنَ ٱلۡخَٰسِرِينَ ٦٥

66. Nay, but worship Allah, and be of those who give thanks.

بَلِ ٱللَّهَ فَٱعۡبُدۡ وَكُن مِّنَ ٱلشَّٰكِرِينَ ٦٦

67. No just estimate have they made of Allah, such as is due to Him: on the day of judgement the whole of the earth will be but His handful and the heavens will be rolled up in His right hand: Glory to Him! High is He above the partners they attribute to Him!

وَمَا قَدَرُواْ ٱللَّهَ حَقَّ قَدۡرِهِۦ وَٱلۡأَرۡضُ جَمِيعٗا
قَبۡضَتُهُۥ يَوۡمَ ٱلۡقِيَٰمَةِ وَٱلسَّمَٰوَٰتُ مَطۡوِيَّٰتُۢ
بِيَمِينِهِۦۚ سُبۡحَٰنَهُۥ وَتَعَٰلَىٰ عَمَّا يُشۡرِكُونَ ٦٧

68. The trumpet will (just) be sounded, when all that are in the heavens and on earth will swoon, except such as it will please Allah (to exempt). Then will a second one be sounded, when, see, they will be standing and looking on!

وَنُفِخَ فِي ٱلصُّورِ فَصَعِقَ مَن فِي ٱلسَّمَٰوَٰتِ وَمَن
فِي ٱلۡأَرۡضِ إِلَّا مَن شَآءَ ٱللَّهُۖ ثُمَّ نُفِخَ فِيهِ أُخۡرَىٰ
فَإِذَا هُمۡ قِيَامٞ يَنظُرُونَ ٦٨

69. And the earth will shine with the glory of its Lord: the record (of deeds) will be placed (open); the prophets and the witnesses will be brought forward: and a

وَأَشۡرَقَتِ ٱلۡأَرۡضُ بِنُورِ رَبِّهَا وَوُضِعَ ٱلۡكِتَٰبُ
وَجِاْيٓءَ بِٱلنَّبِيِّـۧنَ وَٱلشُّهَدَآءِ وَقُضِيَ بَيۡنَهُم بِٱلۡحَقِّ

just decision pronounced between them; and they will not be wronged (in the least).

وَهُمْ لَا يُظْلَمُونَ ٦٩

70. And to every soul will be paid in full (the fruit) of its deeds; and (Allah) knows best all that they do.

وَوُفِّيَتْ كُلُّ نَفْسٍ مَّا عَمِلَتْ وَهُوَ أَعْلَمُ بِمَا
يَفْعَلُونَ ٧٠

71. The unbelievers will be led to hell in crowds: until, when they arrive there, its gates will be opened, and its keepers will say, "Did not messengers come to you from among yourselves, rehearsing to you the signs of your Lord, and warning you of the meeting of this day of yours?" The answer will be: "True: but the decree of punishment has been proved true against the unbelievers!"

وَسِيقَ ٱلَّذِينَ كَفَرُوٓا۟ إِلَىٰ جَهَنَّمَ زُمَرًا ۖ حَتَّىٰٓ إِذَا
جَآءُوهَا فُتِحَتْ أَبْوَٰبُهَا وَقَالَ لَهُمْ خَزَنَتُهَآ أَلَمْ
يَأْتِكُمْ رُسُلٌ مِّنكُمْ يَتْلُونَ عَلَيْكُمْ ءَايَـٰتِ رَبِّكُمْ
وَيُنذِرُونَكُمْ لِقَآءَ يَوْمِكُمْ هَـٰذَا ۚ قَالُوا۟ بَلَىٰ
وَلَـٰكِنْ حَقَّتْ كَلِمَةُ ٱلْعَذَابِ عَلَى ٱلْكَـٰفِرِينَ ٧١

72. (To them) will be said: "Enter you the gates of hell, to dwell in it: and evil is (this) abode of the arrogant!"

قِيلَ ٱدْخُلُوٓا۟ أَبْوَٰبَ جَهَنَّمَ خَـٰلِدِينَ فِيهَا ۖ فَبِئْسَ
مَثْوَى ٱلْمُتَكَبِّرِينَ ٧٢

73. And those who feared their Lord will be led to the garden in crowds: until behold they arrive there; its gates will be opened; and its keepers will say: "Peace be upon you! Well have you done! Enter you here, to dwell in it."

وَسِيقَ ٱلَّذِينَ ٱتَّقَوْا۟ رَبَّهُمْ إِلَى ٱلْجَنَّةِ زُمَرًا ۖ
حَتَّىٰٓ إِذَا جَآءُوهَا وَفُتِحَتْ أَبْوَٰبُهَا وَقَالَ لَهُمْ
خَزَنَتُهَا سَلَـٰمٌ عَلَيْكُمْ طِبْتُمْ فَٱدْخُلُوهَا
خَـٰلِدِينَ ٧٣

74. They will say: "Praise be to Allah, Who has truly fulfilled His promise to us, and has given us (this) land in heritage; we can dwell in the garden as we will; how excellent a reward for those who work (righteousness)!"

وَقَالُوا۟ ٱلْحَمْدُ لِلَّهِ ٱلَّذِى صَدَقَنَا وَعْدَهُۥ وَ
أَوْرَثَنَا ٱلْأَرْضَ نَتَبَوَّأُ مِنَ ٱلْجَنَّةِ حَيْثُ
نَشَآءُ ۖ فَنِعْمَ أَجْرُ ٱلْعَـٰمِلِينَ ٧٤

75. And you will see the angels surrounding the throne (divine) on all sides, singing glory

وَتَرَى ٱلْمَلَـٰٓئِكَةَ حَآفِّينَ مِنْ حَوْلِ ٱلْعَرْشِ

and praise to their Lord. The decision between them (at judgement) will be in (perfect) justice, and the call (on all sides) will be, "Praise be to Allah, the Lord of the Worlds!"

يُسَبِّحُونَ بِحَمْدِ رَبِّهِمْ ۖ وَقُضِيَ بَيْنَهُم بِالْحَقِّ وَقِيلَ
الْحَمْدُ لِلَّهِ رَبِّ الْعَالَمِينَ ﴿٧٥﴾

سُورَةُ غَافِرٍ

Surah 40: ***Ghafir*** **(The Forgiver) or** ***Al-Mu'min*** **(The Believer)**

In the name of Allah,
Most Gracious, Most Merciful.

بِسْمِ اللَّهِ الرَّحْمَٰنِ الرَّحِيمِ

1. *Ha Mim.*

نصف الحزب ٤٧ حمٓ ﴿١﴾

2. The revelation of this book is from Allah, Exalted in power, Full of knowledge -

تَنزِيلُ الْكِتَابِ مِنَ اللَّهِ الْعَزِيزِ الْعَلِيمِ ﴿٢﴾

3. Who forgives sin, accepts repentance, is strict in punishment, and has a long reach (in all things). There is no god but He: to Him is the final goal.

غَافِرِ الذَّنبِ وَقَابِلِ التَّوْبِ شَدِيدِ الْعِقَابِ ذِي
الطَّوْلِ ۖ لَا إِلَٰهَ إِلَّا هُوَ ۖ إِلَيْهِ الْمَصِيرُ ﴿٣﴾

4. None can dispute about the signs of Allah but the unbelievers. Let not, then, their strutting about through the land deceive you!

مَا يُجَادِلُ فِي آيَاتِ اللَّهِ إِلَّا الَّذِينَ كَفَرُوا فَلَا يَغْرُرْكَ
تَقَلُّبُهُمْ فِي الْبِلَادِ ﴿٤﴾

5. But (there were people) before them, who denied (the signs) - the people of Noah, and the confederates (of evil) after them; and every people plotted against their prophet, to seize him, and disputed by means of vanities, with it to condemn the truth: but it was I that seized them! And how (terrible) was My requital!

كَذَّبَتْ قَبْلَهُمْ قَوْمُ نُوحٍ وَالْأَحْزَابُ مِن بَعْدِهِمْ ۖ
وَهَمَّتْ كُلُّ أُمَّةٍ بِرَسُولِهِمْ لِيَأْخُذُوهُ ۖ
وَجَادَلُوا بِالْبَاطِلِ لِيُدْحِضُوا بِهِ الْحَقَّ فَأَخَذْتُهُمْ ۖ
فَكَيْفَ كَانَ عِقَابِ ﴿٥﴾

6. Thus was the decree of your Lord proved true against the unbelievers; that truly they are companions of fire!

وَكَذَٰلِكَ حَقَّتْ كَلِمَتُ رَبِّكَ عَلَى الَّذِينَ كَفَرُوا
أَنَّهُمْ أَصْحَابُ النَّارِ ﴿٦﴾

7. Those who sustain the throne (of Allah) and those around it sing glory and praise to their Lord; believe in Him; and implore forgiveness for those who believe: "Our Lord! Your reach is over all things, in mercy and knowledge. Forgive, then, those who turn in repentance, and follow Your path: and preserve them from the penalty of the blazing fire!

ٱلَّذِينَ يَحۡمِلُونَ ٱلۡعَرۡشَ وَمَنۡ حَوۡلَهُۥ يُسَبِّحُونَ بِحَمۡدِ
رَبِّهِمۡ وَيُؤۡمِنُونَ بِهِۦ وَيَسۡتَغۡفِرُونَ لِلَّذِينَ ءَامَنُواْۖ
رَبَّنَا وَسِعۡتَ كُلَّ شَيۡءٖ رَّحۡمَةٗ وَعِلۡمٗا فَٱغۡفِرۡ
لِلَّذِينَ تَابُواْ وَٱتَّبَعُواْ سَبِيلَكَ وَقِهِمۡ عَذَابَ
ٱلۡجَحِيمِ ٧

8. And grant, our Lord! That they enter the gardens of eternity, which You have promised to them, and to the righteous among their fathers, their wives, and their posterity! For You are (He), the Exalted in Might, Full of wisdom.

رَبَّنَا وَأَدۡخِلۡهُمۡ جَنَّٰتِ عَدۡنٍ ٱلَّتِي وَعَدتَّهُمۡ وَمَن
صَلَحَ مِنۡ ءَابَآئِهِمۡ وَأَزۡوَٰجِهِمۡ وَذُرِّيَّٰتِهِمۡۚ
إِنَّكَ أَنتَ ٱلۡعَزِيزُ ٱلۡحَكِيمُ ٨

9. And preserve them from (all) ills; and any whom You do preserve from ills that day - on them will You have bestowed mercy indeed: and that will be truly (for them) the highest achievement."

وَقِهِمُ ٱلسَّيِّـَٔاتِۚ وَمَن تَقِ ٱلسَّيِّـَٔاتِ يَوۡمَئِذٖ
فَقَدۡ رَحِمۡتَهُۥۚ وَذَٰلِكَ هُوَ ٱلۡفَوۡزُ ٱلۡعَظِيمُ ٩

10. The unbelievers will be addressed: "Greater was the aversion of Allah to you than (is) your aversion to yourselves, seeing that you were called to the faith and you used to refuse."

إِنَّ ٱلَّذِينَ كَفَرُواْ يُنَادَوۡنَ لَمَقۡتُ ٱللَّهِ أَكۡبَرُ
مِن مَّقۡتِكُمۡ أَنفُسَكُمۡ إِذۡ تُدۡعَوۡنَ إِلَى ٱلۡإِيمَٰنِ
فَتَكۡفُرُونَ ١٠

11. They will say: "Our Lord! Twice have You made us without life, and twice have You given us life! Now have we recognised our sins: is there any way out (of this)?"

قَالُواْ رَبَّنَآ أَمَتَّنَا ٱثۡنَتَيۡنِ وَأَحۡيَيۡتَنَا ٱثۡنَتَيۡنِ فَٱعۡتَرَفۡنَا
بِذُنُوبِنَا فَهَلۡ إِلَىٰ خُرُوجٖ مِّن سَبِيلٖ ١١

12. (The answer will be:) "This is because, when Allah was invoked as the only (object of worship), you did reject faith, but when partners were joined to Him, you believed! The command is with Allah, Most High, Most Great!"

ذَٰلِكُم بِأَنَّهُۥٓ إِذَا دُعِيَ ٱللَّهُ وَحۡدَهُۥ
كَفَرۡتُمۡ وَإِن يُشۡرَكۡ بِهِۦ تُؤۡمِنُواْۚ فَٱلۡحُكۡمُ
لِلَّهِ ٱلۡعَلِيِّ ٱلۡكَبِيرِ ١٢

13. He it is Who shows you His signs, and sends down sustenance for you from the sky: but only those receive admonition who turn (to Allah).

هُوَ ٱلَّذِى يُرِيكُمْ ءَايَٰتِهِۦ وَيُنَزِّلُ لَكُم مِّنَ ٱلسَّمَآءِ
رِزْقًا ۚ وَمَا يَتَذَكَّرُ إِلَّا مَن يُنِيبُ ﴿١٣﴾

14. Call you, then, upon Allah with sincere devotion to Him, even though the unbelievers may detest it.

فَٱدْعُوا۟ ٱللَّهَ مُخْلِصِينَ لَهُ ٱلدِّينَ وَلَوْ كَرِهَ
ٱلْكَٰفِرُونَ ﴿١٤﴾

15. Raised high above ranks (or degrees), (He is) the Lord of the Throne (of authority): by His command does He send the spirit (of inspiration) to any of His servants He pleases, that it may warn (men) of the day of mutual meeting -

رَفِيعُ ٱلدَّرَجَٰتِ ذُو ٱلْعَرْشِ يُلْقِى ٱلرُّوحَ مِنْ
أَمْرِهِۦ عَلَىٰ مَن يَشَآءُ مِنْ عِبَادِهِۦ لِيُنذِرَ يَوْمَ
ٱلتَّلَاقِ ﴿١٥﴾

16. The day on which they will (all) come out: Not a single thing concerning them is hidden from Allah. Whose will be the dominion that day? That of Allah, the One, the Irresistible!

يَوْمَ هُم بَٰرِزُونَ ۖ لَا يَخْفَىٰ عَلَى ٱللَّهِ مِنْهُمْ شَىْءٌ ۚ لِّمَنِ
ٱلْمُلْكُ ٱلْيَوْمَ ۖ لِلَّهِ ٱلْوَٰحِدِ ٱلْقَهَّارِ ﴿١٦﴾

17. That day will every soul be requited for what it earned; no injustice will there be that day, for Allah is swift in taking account.

ٱلْيَوْمَ تُجْزَىٰ كُلُّ نَفْسٍۭ بِمَا كَسَبَتْ ۚ لَا ظُلْمَ
ٱلْيَوْمَ ۚ إِنَّ ٱللَّهَ سَرِيعُ ٱلْحِسَابِ ﴿١٧﴾

18. Warn them of the day that is (ever) drawing near, when the hearts will (come) right up to the throats to choke (them); no intimate friend nor intercessor will the wrongdoers have, who could be listened to.

وَأَنذِرْهُمْ يَوْمَ ٱلْءَازِفَةِ إِذِ ٱلْقُلُوبُ لَدَى ٱلْحَنَاجِرِ
كَٰظِمِينَ ۚ مَا لِلظَّٰلِمِينَ مِنْ حَمِيمٍ وَلَا شَفِيعٍ
يُطَاعُ ﴿١٨﴾

19. (Allah) knows of (the tricks) that deceive with the eyes, and all that hearts (of men) conceal.

يَعْلَمُ خَآئِنَةَ ٱلْأَعْيُنِ وَمَا تُخْفِى ٱلصُّدُورُ ﴿١٩﴾

20. And Allah will judge with (justice and) truth: but those whom (men) invoke besides Him, will not (be in a position) to judge at all. Verily it is Allah (alone) Who hears and sees (all things).

وَٱللَّهُ يَقْضِى بِٱلْحَقِّ ۖ وَٱلَّذِينَ يَدْعُونَ مِن
دُونِهِۦ لَا يَقْضُونَ بِشَىْءٍ ۗ إِنَّ ٱللَّهَ هُوَ ٱلسَّمِيعُ
ٱلْبَصِيرُ ﴿٢٠﴾

ثلاثة أرباع الحزب ٤٧

21. Do they not travel through the earth and see what was the end of those before them? They were even superior to them in strength, and in the traces (they have left) in the land: but Allah did call them to account for their sins, and none had they to defend them against Allah.

۞ أَوَلَمْ يَسِيرُوا۟ فِى ٱلْأَرْضِ فَيَنظُرُوا۟ كَيْفَ كَانَ
عَٰقِبَةُ ٱلَّذِينَ كَانُوا۟ مِن قَبْلِهِمْ ۚ كَانُوا۟ هُمْ أَشَدَّ
مِنْهُمْ قُوَّةً وَءَاثَارًا فِى ٱلْأَرْضِ فَأَخَذَهُمُ ٱللَّهُ
بِذُنُوبِهِمْ وَمَا كَانَ لَهُم مِّنَ ٱللَّهِ مِن وَاقٍ ﴿٢١﴾

22. That was because there came to them their messengers with clear (signs) but they rejected them: So Allah called them to account: for He is Full of Strength, Strict in punishment.

ذَٰلِكَ بِأَنَّهُمْ كَانَت تَّأْتِيهِمْ رُسُلُهُم بِٱلْبَيِّنَٰتِ
فَكَفَرُوا۟ فَأَخَذَهُمُ ٱللَّهُ ۚ إِنَّهُۥ قَوِىٌّ شَدِيدُ ٱلْعِقَابِ ﴿٢٢﴾

23. Of old We sent Moses, with Our signs and an authority manifest,

وَلَقَدْ أَرْسَلْنَا مُوسَىٰ بِـَٔايَٰتِنَا وَسُلْطَٰنٍ مُّبِينٍ ﴿٢٣﴾

24. To Pharaoh, Haman, and Qarun; but they called (him) "A sorcerer telling lies!"

إِلَىٰ فِرْعَوْنَ وَهَٰمَٰنَ وَقَٰرُونَ فَقَالُوا۟
سَٰحِرٌ كَذَّابٌ ﴿٢٤﴾

25. Now, when he came to them in truth, from Us, they said, "Slay the sons of those who believe with him, and keep alive their females," but the plots of unbelievers (end) in nothing but errors (and delusions)!

فَلَمَّا جَآءَهُم بِٱلْحَقِّ مِنْ عِندِنَا قَالُوا۟ ٱقْتُلُوٓا۟
أَبْنَآءَ ٱلَّذِينَ ءَامَنُوا۟ مَعَهُۥ وَٱسْتَحْيُوا۟ نِسَآءَهُمْ ۚ
وَمَا كَيْدُ ٱلْكَٰفِرِينَ إِلَّا فِى ضَلَٰلٍ ﴿٢٥﴾

26. Said Pharaoh: "Leave me to slay Moses; and let him call on his Lord! What I fear is lest he should change your religion, or lest he should cause mischief to appear in the land!"

وَقَالَ فِرْعَوْنُ ذَرُونِىٓ أَقْتُلْ مُوسَىٰ وَلْيَدْعُ رَبَّهُۥٓ ۖ
إِنِّىٓ أَخَافُ أَن يُبَدِّلَ دِينَكُمْ أَوْ أَن يُظْهِرَ
فِى ٱلْأَرْضِ ٱلْفَسَادَ ﴿٢٦﴾

27. Moses said: "I have indeed called upon my Lord and your Lord (for protection) from every arrogant one who believes not in the day of account!"

وَقَالَ مُوسَىٰٓ إِنِّى عُذْتُ بِرَبِّى وَرَبِّكُم مِّن كُلِّ
مُتَكَبِّرٍ لَّا يُؤْمِنُ بِيَوْمِ ٱلْحِسَابِ ﴿٢٧﴾

28. A believer, a man from among the people of Pharaoh, who had concealed his faith, said: "Will you slay a man because he says 'My Lord is Allah'? - When he has indeed come to you with clear (signs) from your Lord? And if he be a liar, on him is (the sin of) his lie; but, if he is telling the truth, then will fall on you something of the (calamity) of which he warns you: truly Allah guides not one who transgresses and lies!"

وَقَالَ رَجُلٌ مُّؤْمِنٌ مِّنْ ءَالِ فِرْعَوْنَ يَكْتُمُ
إِيمَٰنَهُۥٓ أَتَقْتُلُونَ رَجُلًا أَن يَقُولَ رَبِّيَ ٱللَّهُ
وَقَدْ جَآءَكُم بِٱلْبَيِّنَٰتِ مِن رَّبِّكُمْ ۖ وَإِن
يَكُ كَٰذِبًا فَعَلَيْهِ كَذِبُهُۥ ۖ وَإِن يَكُ صَادِقًا
يُصِبْكُم بَعْضُ ٱلَّذِى يَعِدُكُمْ ۖ إِنَّ ٱللَّهَ
لَا يَهْدِى مَنْ هُوَ مُسْرِفٌ كَذَّابٌ ﴿٢٨﴾

29. "O my people! Yours is the dominion this day; you have the upper hand in the land; but who will help us from the punishment of Allah, should it befall us?" Pharaoh said: "I but point out to you that which I see (myself); nor do I guide you but to the path of right!"

يَٰقَوْمِ لَكُمُ ٱلْمُلْكُ ٱلْيَوْمَ ظَٰهِرِينَ فِى ٱلْأَرْضِ
فَمَن يَنصُرُنَا مِنۢ بَأْسِ ٱللَّهِ إِن جَآءَنَا ۚ قَالَ فِرْعَوْنُ
مَآ أُرِيكُمْ إِلَّا مَآ أَرَىٰ وَمَآ أَهْدِيكُمْ إِلَّا سَبِيلَ
ٱلرَّشَادِ ﴿٢٩﴾

30. Then said the man who believed: "O my people! Truly I do fear for you something like the day (of disaster) of the confederates (in sin)! -

وَقَالَ ٱلَّذِىٓ ءَامَنَ يَٰقَوْمِ إِنِّىٓ أَخَافُ عَلَيْكُم مِّثْلَ
يَوْمِ ٱلْأَحْزَابِ ﴿٣٠﴾

31. Something like the fate of the people of Noah, the 'Ad, and the Thamud, and those who came after them: but Allah never wishes injustice to His servants.

مِثْلَ دَأْبِ قَوْمِ نُوحٍ وَعَادٍ وَثَمُودَ وَٱلَّذِينَ مِنۢ
بَعْدِهِمْ ۚ وَمَا ٱللَّهُ يُرِيدُ ظُلْمًا لِّلْعِبَادِ ﴿٣١﴾

32. And O my people! I fear for you a day when there will be mutual calling (and wailing) -

وَيَٰقَوْمِ إِنِّىٓ أَخَافُ عَلَيْكُمْ يَوْمَ ٱلتَّنَادِ ﴿٣٢﴾

33. A day when you shall turn your backs and flee: no defender shall you have from Allah: any whom Allah leaves to stray there is none to guide.

يَوْمَ تُوَلُّونَ مُدْبِرِينَ مَا لَكُم مِّنَ ٱللَّهِ مِنْ عَاصِمٍ ۗ وَمَن
يُضْلِلِ ٱللَّهُ فَمَا لَهُۥ مِنْ هَادٍ ﴿٣٣﴾

34. And to you there came Joseph in times gone by, with clear signs, but you ceased not to doubt of the (mission) for which he had come: at length, when he died, you said: 'No messenger will Allah send after him.' Thus does Allah leave to stray such as transgress and live in doubt -

وَلَقَدْ جَآءَكُمْ يُوسُفُ مِن قَبْلُ بِٱلْبَيِّنَٰتِ فَمَا
زِلْتُمْ فِى شَكٍّ مِّمَّا جَآءَكُم بِهِۦ ۖ حَتَّىٰٓ إِذَا هَلَكَ
قُلْتُمْ لَن يَبْعَثَ ٱللَّهُ مِنۢ بَعْدِهِۦ رَسُولًا ۚ كَذَٰلِكَ
يُضِلُّ ٱللَّهُ مَنْ هُوَ مُسْرِفٌ مُّرْتَابٌ ﴿٣٤﴾

35. (Such) as dispute about the signs of Allah, without any authority that has reached them. Grievous and odious (is such conduct) in the sight of Allah and of the believers. Thus does Allah seal up every heart - of arrogant and obstinate transgressors."

ٱلَّذِينَ يُجَٰدِلُونَ فِىٓ ءَايَٰتِ ٱللَّهِ بِغَيْرِ سُلْطَٰنٍ
أَتَىٰهُمْ ۖ كَبُرَ مَقْتًا عِندَ ٱللَّهِ وَعِندَ ٱلَّذِينَ
ءَامَنُوا۟ ۚ كَذَٰلِكَ يَطْبَعُ ٱللَّهُ عَلَىٰ كُلِّ قَلْبِ
مُتَكَبِّرٍ جَبَّارٍ ﴿٣٥﴾

36. Pharaoh said: "O Haman! Build me a lofty palace, that I may attain the ways and means -

وَقَالَ فِرْعَوْنُ يَٰهَٰمَٰنُ ٱبْنِ لِى صَرْحًا لَّعَلِّىٓ أَبْلُغُ
ٱلْأَسْبَٰبَ ﴿٣٦﴾

37. "The ways and means of (reaching) the heavens, and that I may mount up to the God of Moses; but as far as I am concerned, I think (Moses) is a liar!" Thus was made alluring in Pharaoh's eyes, the evil of his deeds, and he was hindered from the path; and the plot of Pharaoh led to nothing but perdition (for him).

أَسْبَٰبَ ٱلسَّمَٰوَٰتِ فَأَطَّلِعَ إِلَىٰٓ إِلَٰهِ مُوسَىٰ وَإِنِّى
لَأَظُنُّهُۥ كَٰذِبًا ۚ وَكَذَٰلِكَ زُيِّنَ لِفِرْعَوْنَ
سُوٓءُ عَمَلِهِۦ وَصُدَّ عَنِ ٱلسَّبِيلِ ۚ وَمَا كَيْدُ
فِرْعَوْنَ إِلَّا فِى تَبَابٍ ﴿٣٧﴾

38. The man who believed said further: "O my people! Follow me; I will lead you to the path of right.

وَقَالَ ٱلَّذِىٓ ءَامَنَ يَٰقَوْمِ ٱتَّبِعُونِ أَهْدِكُمْ
سَبِيلَ ٱلرَّشَادِ ﴿٣٨﴾

39. O my people! This life of the present is nothing but (temporary) convenience: it is the hereafter that is the home that will last.

يَٰقَوْمِ إِنَّمَا هَٰذِهِ ٱلْحَيَوٰةُ ٱلدُّنْيَا مَتَٰعٌ وَإِنَّ
ٱلْءَاخِرَةَ هِىَ دَارُ ٱلْقَرَارِ ﴿٣٩﴾

40. He that works evil will not be requited but by the like of it; and he that works a

مَنْ عَمِلَ سَيِّئَةً فَلَا يُجْزَىٰٓ إِلَّا مِثْلَهَا ۖ وَمَنْ

righteous deed - whether man or woman - and is a believer - such will enter the garden (of bliss): in it will they have abundance without measure.

عَمِلَ صَٰلِحًا مِّن ذَكَرٍ أَوْ أُنثَىٰ وَهُوَ مُؤْمِنٌ
فَأُوْلَٰٓئِكَ يَدْخُلُونَ ٱلْجَنَّةَ يُرْزَقُونَ فِيهَا
بِغَيْرِ حِسَابٍ ﴿٤٠﴾

41. And O my people! How (strange) it is for me to call you to salvation while you call me to the fire!

الحزب ٤٨ ۞ وَيَٰقَوْمِ مَا لِيٓ أَدْعُوكُمْ إِلَى ٱلنَّجَوٰةِ وَتَدْعُونَنِيٓ
إِلَى ٱلنَّارِ ﴿٤١﴾

42. You do call upon me to blaspheme against Allah, and to join with Him partners of whom I have no knowledge; and I call you to the Exalted in Power, Who forgives again and again!"

تَدْعُونَنِي لِأَكْفُرَ بِٱللَّهِ وَأُشْرِكَ بِهِۦ مَا لَيْسَ
لِي بِهِۦ عِلْمٌ وَأَنَا۠ أَدْعُوكُمْ إِلَى ٱلْعَزِيزِ ٱلْغَفَّٰرِ ﴿٤٢﴾

43. Without doubt you do call me to one who is not fit to be called to, whether in this world or in the hereafter; our return will be to Allah; and the transgressors will be companions of the fire!

لَا جَرَمَ أَنَّمَا تَدْعُونَنِيٓ إِلَيْهِ لَيْسَ لَهُۥ دَعْوَةٌ
فِي ٱلدُّنْيَا وَلَا فِي ٱلْـَٔاخِرَةِ وَأَنَّ مَرَدَّنَآ إِلَى ٱللَّهِ
وَأَنَّ ٱلْمُسْرِفِينَ هُمْ أَصْحَٰبُ ٱلنَّارِ ﴿٤٣﴾

44. Soon will you remember what I say to you (now). My (own) affair I commit to Allah: for Allah (ever) watches over His servants."

فَسَتَذْكُرُونَ مَآ أَقُولُ لَكُمْ ۚ وَأُفَوِّضُ أَمْرِيٓ
إِلَى ٱللَّهِ ۚ إِنَّ ٱللَّهَ بَصِيرٌۢ بِٱلْعِبَادِ ﴿٤٤﴾

45. Then Allah saved him from (every) ill that they plotted (against him), but the brunt of the penalty encompassed on all sides the people of Pharaoh.

فَوَقَىٰهُ ٱللَّهُ سَيِّـَٔاتِ مَا مَكَرُوا۟ ۖ وَحَاقَ بِـَٔالِ
فِرْعَوْنَ سُوٓءُ ٱلْعَذَابِ ﴿٤٥﴾

46. In front of the fire will they be brought, morning and evening: and (the sentence will be) on the day that judgement will be established: "Cast you the people of Pharaoh into the severest penalty!"

ٱلنَّارُ يُعْرَضُونَ عَلَيْهَا غُدُوًّا وَعَشِيًّا ۖ وَيَوْمَ تَقُومُ
ٱلسَّاعَةُ أَدْخِلُوٓا۟ ءَالَ فِرْعَوْنَ أَشَدَّ ٱلْعَذَابِ ﴿٤٦﴾

47. See, they will dispute with each other in the fire! The weak ones (who followed) will

وَإِذْ يَتَحَآجُّونَ فِي ٱلنَّارِ فَيَقُولُ ٱلضُّعَفَٰٓؤُا۟

say to those who had been arrogant, "We but followed you: can you then take (on yourselves) from us some share of the fire?"

لِلَّذِينَ ٱسْتَكْبَرُوٓا۟ إِنَّا كُنَّا لَكُمْ تَبَعًا فَهَلْ
أَنتُم مُّغْنُونَ عَنَّا نَصِيبًا مِّنَ ٱلنَّارِ ﴿٤٧﴾

48. Those who had been arrogant will say: "We are all in this (fire)! Truly Allah has judged between (His) servants!"

قَالَ ٱلَّذِينَ ٱسْتَكْبَرُوٓا۟ إِنَّا كُلٌّ فِيهَآ إِنَّ
ٱللَّهَ قَدْ حَكَمَ بَيْنَ ٱلْعِبَادِ ﴿٤٨﴾

49. Those in the fire will say to the keepers of hell: "Pray to your Lord to lighten us the penalty for a day (at least)!"

وَقَالَ ٱلَّذِينَ فِى ٱلنَّارِ لِخَزَنَةِ جَهَنَّمَ ٱدْعُوا۟
رَبَّكُمْ يُخَفِّفْ عَنَّا يَوْمًا مِّنَ ٱلْعَذَابِ ﴿٤٩﴾

50. They will say: "Did there not come to you your messengers with clear signs?" They will say "Yes." They will reply, "Then pray (as you like)! But the prayer of those without faith is nothing but (futile wandering) in (mazes of) error!"

قَالُوٓا۟ أَوَلَمْ تَكُ تَأْتِيكُمْ رُسُلُكُم بِٱلْبَيِّنَٰتِ ۖ
قَالُوا۟ بَلَىٰ ۚ قَالُوا۟ فَٱدْعُوا۟ ۗ وَمَا دُعَٰٓؤُا۟ ٱلْكَٰفِرِينَ
إِلَّا فِى ضَلَٰلٍ ﴿٥٠﴾

51. We will, without doubt, help Our messengers, and those who believe, (both) in this world's life and on the day when the witnesses will stand up -

إِنَّا لَنَنصُرُ رُسُلَنَا وَٱلَّذِينَ ءَامَنُوا۟ فِى ٱلْحَيَوٰةِ
ٱلدُّنْيَا وَيَوْمَ يَقُومُ ٱلْأَشْهَٰدُ ﴿٥١﴾

52. The day when no profit will it be to wrongdoers to present their excuses, but they will (only) have the curse and the home of misery.

يَوْمَ لَا يَنفَعُ ٱلظَّٰلِمِينَ مَعْذِرَتُهُمْ ۖ وَلَهُمُ ٱللَّعْنَةُ
وَلَهُمْ سُوٓءُ ٱلدَّارِ ﴿٥٢﴾

53. We did before give Moses the (book of) guidance, and We gave the book in inheritance to the Children of Israel -

وَلَقَدْ ءَاتَيْنَا مُوسَى ٱلْهُدَىٰ وَأَوْرَثْنَا بَنِىٓ
إِسْرَٰٓءِيلَ ٱلْكِتَٰبَ ﴿٥٣﴾

54. A guide and a message to men of understanding.

هُدًى وَذِكْرَىٰ لِأُو۟لِى ٱلْأَلْبَٰبِ ﴿٥٤﴾

55. Patiently, then, persevere: for the promise of Allah is true: and ask forgiveness for your fault, and celebrate the praises of your Lord in the evening and in the morning.

فَٱصْبِرْ إِنَّ وَعْدَ ٱللَّهِ حَقٌّ وَٱسْتَغْفِرْ لِذَنۢبِكَ
وَسَبِّحْ بِحَمْدِ رَبِّكَ بِٱلْعَشِىِّ وَٱلْإِبْكَٰرِ ﴿٥٥﴾

56. Those who dispute about the signs of Allah without any authority bestowed on them - there is nothing in their breasts but (the quest of) greatness which they shall never attain to: seek refuge, then, in Allah: it is He Who hears and sees (all things).

إِنَّ ٱلَّذِينَ يُجَٰدِلُونَ فِىٓ ءَايَٰتِ ٱللَّهِ بِغَيْرِ
سُلْطَٰنٍ أَتَىٰهُمْ إِن فِى صُدُورِهِمْ إِلَّا كِبْرٌ
مَّا هُم بِبَٰلِغِيهِ ۚ فَٱسْتَعِذْ بِٱللَّهِ ۖ إِنَّهُۥ
هُوَ ٱلسَّمِيعُ ٱلْبَصِيرُ ٥٦

57. Assuredly the creation of the heavens and the earth is a greater (matter) than the creation of men: Yet most men do not understand.

لَخَلْقُ ٱلسَّمَٰوَٰتِ وَٱلْأَرْضِ أَكْبَرُ مِنْ خَلْقِ
ٱلنَّاسِ وَلَٰكِنَّ أَكْثَرَ ٱلنَّاسِ لَا يَعْلَمُونَ ٥٧

58. Not equal are the blind and those who (clearly) see: nor are (equal) those who believe and work deeds of righteousness, and those who do evil. Little do you learn by admonition!

وَمَا يَسْتَوِى ٱلْأَعْمَىٰ وَٱلْبَصِيرُ وَٱلَّذِينَ ءَامَنُوا۟
وَعَمِلُوا۟ ٱلصَّٰلِحَٰتِ وَلَا ٱلْمُسِىٓءُ ۚ قَلِيلًا
مَّا تَتَذَكَّرُونَ ٥٨

59. The hour will certainly come: in it is no doubt: yet most men do not believe.

إِنَّ ٱلسَّاعَةَ لَءَاتِيَةٌ لَّا رَيْبَ فِيهَا وَلَٰكِنَّ أَكْثَرَ
ٱلنَّاسِ لَا يُؤْمِنُونَ ٥٩

60. And your Lord says: "Call on Me; I will answer your (prayer): but those who are too arrogant to serve Me will surely find themselves in hell - in humiliation!"

وَقَالَ رَبُّكُمُ ٱدْعُونِىٓ أَسْتَجِبْ لَكُمْ ۚ إِنَّ ٱلَّذِينَ
يَسْتَكْبِرُونَ عَنْ عِبَادَتِى سَيَدْخُلُونَ جَهَنَّمَ
دَاخِرِينَ ٦٠

61. It is Allah Who has made the night for you, that you may rest in it, and the day, as that which helps (you) to see. Verily Allah is Full of grace and bounty to men: yet most men give no thanks.

ٱللَّهُ ٱلَّذِى جَعَلَ لَكُمُ ٱلَّيْلَ لِتَسْكُنُوا۟ فِيهِ
وَٱلنَّهَارَ مُبْصِرًا ۚ إِنَّ ٱللَّهَ لَذُو فَضْلٍ عَلَى ٱلنَّاسِ
وَلَٰكِنَّ أَكْثَرَ ٱلنَّاسِ لَا يَشْكُرُونَ ٦١

62. Such is Allah, your Lord, the Creator of all things. There is no god but He: then how you are deluded away from the truth!

ذَٰلِكُمُ ٱللَّهُ رَبُّكُمْ خَٰلِقُ كُلِّ شَىْءٍ لَّآ إِلَٰهَ
إِلَّا هُوَ ۖ فَأَنَّىٰ تُؤْفَكُونَ ٦٢

63. Thus are deluded those who used to reject the signs of Allah.

كَذَٰلِكَ يُؤْفَكُ ٱلَّذِينَ كَانُوا۟ بِـَٔايَٰتِ ٱللَّهِ
يَجْحَدُونَ ﴿٦٣﴾

64. It is Allah Who has made for you the earth as a resting place, and the sky as a canopy, and has given you shape - and made your shapes beautiful - and has provided for you sustenance of things pure and good - such is Allah your Lord. So glory to Allah, the Lord of the Worlds!

ٱللَّهُ ٱلَّذِى جَعَلَ لَكُمُ ٱلْأَرْضَ قَرَارًا وَٱلسَّمَآءَ
بِنَآءً وَصَوَّرَكُمْ فَأَحْسَنَ صُوَرَكُمْ
وَرَزَقَكُم مِّنَ ٱلطَّيِّبَٰتِ ۚ ذَٰلِكُمُ ٱللَّهُ
رَبُّكُمْ ۖ فَتَبَارَكَ ٱللَّهُ رَبُّ ٱلْعَٰلَمِينَ ﴿٦٤﴾

65. He is the Living (One). There is no god but He: call upon Him, giving Him sincere devotion. praise be to Allah, Lord of the Worlds!

هُوَ ٱلْحَىُّ لَآ إِلَٰهَ إِلَّا هُوَ فَٱدْعُوهُ مُخْلِصِينَ لَهُ
ٱلدِّينَ ۗ ٱلْحَمْدُ لِلَّهِ رَبِّ ٱلْعَٰلَمِينَ ﴿٦٥﴾

66. Say: "I have been forbidden to invoke those whom you invoke besides Allah - seeing that the clear signs have come to me from my Lord: and I have been commanded to bow (in Islam) to the Lord of the Worlds."

ربع الحزب ٤٨ ۞ قُلْ إِنِّى نُهِيتُ أَنْ أَعْبُدَ ٱلَّذِينَ تَدْعُونَ
مِن دُونِ ٱللَّهِ لَمَّا جَآءَنِىَ ٱلْبَيِّنَٰتُ مِن رَّبِّى وَأُمِرْتُ
أَنْ أُسْلِمَ لِرَبِّ ٱلْعَٰلَمِينَ ﴿٦٦﴾

67. It is He Who has created you from dust, then from a sperm-drop, then from a leech-like clot; then does He get you out (into the light) as a child; then lets you (grow and) reach your age of full strength; then lets you become old - though of you there are some who die before - and lets you reach a term appointed; in order that you may learn wisdom.

هُوَ ٱلَّذِى خَلَقَكُم مِّن تُرَابٍ ثُمَّ مِن نُّطْفَةٍ ثُمَّ مِنْ
عَلَقَةٍ ثُمَّ يُخْرِجُكُمْ طِفْلًا ثُمَّ لِتَبْلُغُوٓا۟ أَشُدَّكُمْ
ثُمَّ لِتَكُونُوا۟ شُيُوخًا ۚ وَمِنكُم مَّن يُتَوَفَّىٰ مِن قَبْلُ ۖ
وَلِتَبْلُغُوٓا۟ أَجَلًا مُّسَمًّى وَلَعَلَّكُمْ تَعْقِلُونَ ﴿٦٧﴾

68. It is He Who gives life and death; and when He decides upon an affair, He says to it, "Be," and it is.

هُوَ ٱلَّذِى يُحْىِۦ وَيُمِيتُ ۖ فَإِذَا قَضَىٰٓ أَمْرًا فَإِنَّمَا
يَقُولُ لَهُۥ كُن فَيَكُونُ ﴿٦٨﴾

69. Do you not see those that dispute concerning the signs of Allah? How are they turned away (from reality)? -

أَلَمْ تَرَ إِلَى ٱلَّذِينَ يُجَٰدِلُونَ فِىٓ ءَايَٰتِ ٱللَّهِ أَنَّىٰ
يُصْرَفُونَ ﴿٦٩﴾

70. Those who reject the book and the (revelations) with which We sent Our messengers: but soon shall they know-

ٱلَّذِينَ كَذَّبُوا۟ بِٱلْكِتَـٰبِ وَبِمَآ أَرْسَلْنَا بِهِۦ رُسُلَنَا ۖ
فَسَوْفَ يَعْلَمُونَ ٧٠

71. When the yokes (shall be) round their necks, and the chains; they shall be dragged along -

إِذِ ٱلْأَغْلَـٰلُ فِىٓ أَعْنَـٰقِهِمْ وَٱلسَّلَـٰسِلُ يُسْحَبُونَ ٧١

72. In the boiling fetid fluid; then in the fire shall they be burned;

فِى ٱلْحَمِيمِ ثُمَّ فِى ٱلنَّارِ يُسْجَرُونَ ٧٢

73. Then shall it be said to them: "Where are the (deities) to which you gave part-worship -

ثُمَّ قِيلَ لَهُمْ أَيْنَ مَا كُنتُمْ تُشْرِكُونَ ٧٣

74. In derogation of Allah?" They will reply: "They have left us in the lurch: nay, we invoked not, of old, anything (that had real existence)." Thus does Allah leave the unbelievers to stray.

مِن دُونِ ٱللَّهِ ۖ قَالُوا۟ ضَلُّوا۟ عَنَّا بَل لَّمْ نَكُن نَّدْعُوا۟
مِن قَبْلُ شَيْـًٔا ۚ كَذَٰلِكَ يُضِلُّ ٱللَّهُ ٱلْكَـٰفِرِينَ ٧٤

75. "That was because you used to rejoice on the earth in things other than the truth, and that you used to be insolent.

ذَٰلِكُم بِمَا كُنتُمْ تَفْرَحُونَ فِى ٱلْأَرْضِ بِغَيْرِ ٱلْحَقِّ
وَبِمَا كُنتُمْ تَمْرَحُونَ ٧٥

76. Enter you the gates of hell, to dwell in it: and evil is (this) abode of the arrogant!"

ٱدْخُلُوٓا۟ أَبْوَٰبَ جَهَنَّمَ خَـٰلِدِينَ فِيهَا ۖ فَبِئْسَ مَثْوَى
ٱلْمُتَكَبِّرِينَ ٧٦

77. So persevere in patience; for the promise of Allah is true: and whether We show you (in this life) some part of what We promise them - or We take your soul (to Our mercy) (before that) - (in any case) it is to Us that they shall (all) return.

فَٱصْبِرْ إِنَّ وَعْدَ ٱللَّهِ حَقٌّ ۚ فَإِمَّا نُرِيَنَّكَ بَعْضَ
ٱلَّذِى نَعِدُهُمْ أَوْ نَتَوَفَّيَنَّكَ فَإِلَيْنَا يُرْجَعُونَ ٧٧

78. We did before send messengers before you: of them there are some whose story We have related to you, and some whose story We have not related to you. It was not (possible) for any messenger to bring a sign except by the leave of Allah: but when

وَلَقَدْ أَرْسَلْنَا رُسُلًا مِّن قَبْلِكَ مِنْهُم مَّن قَصَصْنَا
عَلَيْكَ وَمِنْهُم مَّن لَّمْ نَقْصُصْ عَلَيْكَ ۗ وَمَا كَانَ
لِرَسُولٍ أَن يَأْتِىَ بِـَٔايَةٍ إِلَّا بِإِذْنِ ٱللَّهِ ۚ فَإِذَا جَآءَ

the command of Allah issued, the matter was decided in truth and justice, and there perished, there and then, those who stood on falsehoods.

أَمْرُ ٱللَّهِ قُضِىَ بِٱلْحَقِّ وَخَسِرَ هُنَالِكَ ٱلْمُبْطِلُونَ ﴿٧٨﴾

79. It is Allah Who made cattle for you, that you may use some for riding and some for food;

ٱللَّهُ ٱلَّذِى جَعَلَ لَكُمُ ٱلْأَنْعَـٰمَ لِتَرْكَبُوا۟
مِنْهَا وَمِنْهَا تَأْكُلُونَ ﴿٧٩﴾

80. And there are (other) advantages in them for you (besides); that you may through them attain to any need (there may be) in your hearts; and on them and on ships you are carried.

وَلَكُمْ فِيهَا مَنَـٰفِعُ وَلِتَبْلُغُوا۟ عَلَيْهَا حَاجَةً فِى
صُدُورِكُمْ وَعَلَيْهَا وَعَلَى ٱلْفُلْكِ تُحْمَلُونَ ﴿٨٠﴾

81. And He shows you always His signs; then which of the signs of Allah will you deny?

وَيُرِيكُمْ ءَايَـٰتِهِۦ فَأَىَّ ءَايَـٰتِ ٱللَّهِ تُنكِرُونَ ﴿٨١﴾

82. Do they not travel through the earth and see what was the end of those before them? They were more numerous than these and superior in strength and in the traces (they have left) in the land: yet all that they accomplished was of no profit to them.

أَفَلَمْ يَسِيرُوا۟ فِى ٱلْأَرْضِ فَيَنظُرُوا۟ كَيْفَ كَانَ
عَـٰقِبَةُ ٱلَّذِينَ مِن قَبْلِهِمْ ۚ كَانُوٓا۟ أَكْثَرَ مِنْهُمْ
وَأَشَدَّ قُوَّةً وَءَاثَارًا فِى ٱلْأَرْضِ فَمَآ أَغْنَىٰ عَنْهُم
مَّا كَانُوا۟ يَكْسِبُونَ ﴿٨٢﴾

83. For when their messengers came to them with clear signs, they exulted in such knowledge (and skill) as they had; but that very (wrath) at which they used to scoff hemmed them in.

فَلَمَّا جَآءَتْهُمْ رُسُلُهُم بِٱلْبَيِّنَـٰتِ فَرِحُوا۟ بِمَا
عِندَهُم مِّنَ ٱلْعِلْمِ وَحَاقَ بِهِم مَّا كَانُوا۟ بِهِۦ
يَسْتَهْزِءُونَ ﴿٨٣﴾

84. But when they saw Our punishment, they said: "We believe in Allah - the One God - and we reject the partners we used to join with Him."

فَلَمَّا رَأَوْا۟ بَأْسَنَا قَالُوٓا۟ ءَامَنَّا بِٱللَّهِ وَحْدَهُۥ وَكَفَرْنَا
بِمَا كُنَّا بِهِۦ مُشْرِكِينَ ﴿٨٤﴾

85. But their professing the faith when they (actually) saw Our punishment was not going to profit them. (Such has been) Allah's

فَلَمْ يَكُ يَنفَعُهُمْ إِيمَـٰنُهُمْ لَمَّا رَأَوْا۟ بَأْسَنَا ۖ سُنَّتَ

way of dealing with His servants (from the most ancient times). And even thus did the rejecters of Allah perish (utterly)!

ٱللَّهِ ٱلَّتِي قَدْ خَلَتْ فِي عِبَادِهِۦ ۖ وَخَسِرَ هُنَالِكَ
ٱلْكَٰفِرُونَ ٨٥

سُورَةُ فُصِّلَتْ

Surah 41: ***Fussilat*** **(Explained)**

In the name of Allah,
Most Gracious, Most Merciful.

بِسْمِ ٱللَّهِ ٱلرَّحْمَٰنِ ٱلرَّحِيمِ

1. *Ha Mim.*

حمٓ ١

2. A revelation from (Allah), Most Gracious, Most Merciful -

تَنزِيلٌ مِّنَ ٱلرَّحْمَٰنِ ٱلرَّحِيمِ ٢

3. A book, of which the verses are explained in detail - a Qur'an in Arabic, for people who understand -

كِتَٰبٌ فُصِّلَتْ ءَايَٰتُهُۥ قُرْءَانًا عَرَبِيًّا لِّقَوْمٍ يَعْلَمُونَ ٣

4. Giving good news and admonition: yet most of them turn away, and so they hear not.

بَشِيرًا وَنَذِيرًا فَأَعْرَضَ أَكْثَرُهُمْ فَهُمْ لَا يَسْمَعُونَ ٤

5. They say: "Our hearts are under veils, (concealed) from that to which you do invite us, and in our ears is a deafness and between us and you is a screen: so do you (what you will); for us, we shall do (what we will!)."

وَقَالُوا۟ قُلُوبُنَا فِىٓ أَكِنَّةٍ مِّمَّا تَدْعُونَآ إِلَيْهِ وَفِىٓ ءَاذَانِنَا
وَقْرٌ وَمِنۢ بَيْنِنَا وَبَيْنِكَ حِجَابٌ فَٱعْمَلْ إِنَّنَا
عَٰمِلُونَ ٥

6. (O prophet!) Say you: "I am but a man like you: it is revealed to me by inspiration, that your God is One God: so stand true to Him and ask for His forgiveness." And woe to those who join gods with Allah -

قُلْ إِنَّمَآ أَنَا۠ بَشَرٌ مِّثْلُكُمْ يُوحَىٰٓ إِلَىَّ أَنَّمَآ إِلَٰهُكُمْ إِلَٰهٌ
وَٰحِدٌ فَٱسْتَقِيمُوٓا۟ إِلَيْهِ وَٱسْتَغْفِرُوهُ ۗ وَوَيْلٌ
لِّلْمُشْرِكِينَ ٦

7. Those who practice not regular charity, and who even deny the hereafter.

ٱلَّذِينَ لَا يُؤْتُونَ ٱلزَّكَوٰةَ وَهُم بِٱلْءَاخِرَةِ هُمْ
كَٰفِرُونَ ٧

8. For those who believe and work deeds of righteousness is a reward that will never fail.

إِنَّ ٱلَّذِينَ ءَامَنُواْ وَعَمِلُواْ ٱلصَّٰلِحَٰتِ لَهُمۡ أَجۡرٌ
غَيۡرُ مَمۡنُونٖ ٨

9. Say: "Is it that you deny Him Who created the earth in two Days? And do you join equals with Him? He is the Lord of (all) the Worlds."

نصف الحزب ٤٨
۞قُلۡ أَئِنَّكُمۡ لَتَكۡفُرُونَ بِٱلَّذِي خَلَقَ ٱلۡأَرۡضَ فِي
يَوۡمَيۡنِ وَتَجۡعَلُونَ لَهُۥٓ أَندَادٗاۚ ذَٰلِكَ رَبُّ ٱلۡعَٰلَمِينَ ٩

10. He set on the (earth) mountains standing firm, high above it, and bestowed blessings on the earth, and measured in it all things to give them nourishment in due proportion, in four days in accordance with (the needs of) those who seek (sustenance).

وَجَعَلَ فِيهَا رَوَٰسِيَ مِن فَوۡقِهَا وَبَٰرَكَ فِيهَا
وَقَدَّرَ فِيهَآ أَقۡوَٰتَهَا فِيٓ أَرۡبَعَةِ أَيَّامٖ سَوَآءٗ
لِّلسَّآئِلِينَ ١٠

11. Moreover, He comprehended in His design the sky, and it had been (as) smoke: He said to it and to the earth: "Come you together, willingly or unwillingly." They said: "We do come (together), in willing obedience."

ثُمَّ ٱسۡتَوَىٰٓ إِلَى ٱلسَّمَآءِ وَهِيَ دُخَانٞ فَقَالَ لَهَا
وَلِلۡأَرۡضِ ٱئۡتِيَا طَوۡعًا أَوۡ كَرۡهٗا قَالَتَآ أَتَيۡنَا
طَآئِعِينَ ١١

12. So He completed them as seven firmaments in two days and He assigned to each heaven its duty and command. And We adorned the lower heaven with lights, and (provided it) with guard. Such is the decree of (Him) the Exalted in Might, Full of knowledge.

فَقَضَىٰهُنَّ سَبۡعَ سَمَٰوَاتٖ فِي يَوۡمَيۡنِ وَأَوۡحَىٰ فِي كُلِّ
سَمَآءٍ أَمۡرَهَاۚ وَزَيَّنَّا ٱلسَّمَآءَ ٱلدُّنۡيَا بِمَصَٰبِيحَ
وَحِفۡظٗاۚ ذَٰلِكَ تَقۡدِيرُ ٱلۡعَزِيزِ ٱلۡعَلِيمِ ١٢

13. But if they turn away, say you: "I have warned you of a stunning punishment (as of thunder and lightning) like that which (overtook) the 'Ad and the Thamud!"

فَإِنۡ أَعۡرَضُواْ فَقُلۡ أَنذَرۡتُكُمۡ صَٰعِقَةٗ مِّثۡلَ صَٰعِقَةِ
عَادٖ وَثَمُودَ ١٣

14. See, the messengers came to them, from before them and behind them, (preaching): "Serve none but Allah." They said, "If our Lord had so pleased He would certainly have sent down angels (to preach): now we reject your mission (altogether)."

إِذۡ جَآءَتۡهُمُ ٱلرُّسُلُ مِنۢ بَيۡنِ أَيۡدِيهِمۡ وَمِنۡ
خَلۡفِهِمۡ أَلَّا تَعۡبُدُوٓاْ إِلَّا ٱللَّهَۖ قَالُواْ لَوۡ شَآءَ رَبُّنَا لَأَنزَلَ
مَلَٰٓئِكَةٗ فَإِنَّا بِمَآ أُرۡسِلۡتُم بِهِۦ كَٰفِرُونَ ١٤

15. Now the 'Ad behaved arrogantly through the land, against (all) truth and reason, and said: "Who is superior to us in strength?" What! Did they not see that Allah, Who created them, was superior to them in strength? But they continued to reject Our signs!

فَأَمَّا عَادٌ فَٱسْتَكْبَرُوا۟ فِى ٱلْأَرْضِ بِغَيْرِ ٱلْحَقِّ وَقَالُوا۟
مَنْ أَشَدُّ مِنَّا قُوَّةً ۖ أَوَلَمْ يَرَوْا۟ أَنَّ ٱللَّهَ ٱلَّذِى خَلَقَهُمْ
هُوَ أَشَدُّ مِنْهُمْ قُوَّةً ۖ وَكَانُوا۟ بِـَٔايَٰتِنَا يَجْحَدُونَ ﴿١٥﴾

16. So We sent against them a furious wind through days of disaster, that We might give them a taste of a penalty of humiliation in this life; but the penalty of the hereafter will be more humiliating still: and they will find no help.

فَأَرْسَلْنَا عَلَيْهِمْ رِيحًا صَرْصَرًا فِىٓ أَيَّامٍ نَّحِسَاتٍ
لِّنُذِيقَهُمْ عَذَابَ ٱلْخِزْىِ فِى ٱلْحَيَوٰةِ ٱلدُّنْيَا ۖ
وَلَعَذَابُ ٱلْـَٔاخِرَةِ أَخْزَىٰ ۖ وَهُمْ لَا يُنصَرُونَ ﴿١٦﴾

17. As to the Thamud, We gave them guidance, but they preferred blindness (of heart) to guidance; so the stunning punishment of humiliation seized them, because of what they had earned.

وَأَمَّا ثَمُودُ فَهَدَيْنَٰهُمْ فَٱسْتَحَبُّوا۟ ٱلْعَمَىٰ عَلَى
ٱلْهُدَىٰ فَأَخَذَتْهُمْ صَٰعِقَةُ ٱلْعَذَابِ ٱلْهُونِ بِمَا كَانُوا۟
يَكْسِبُونَ ﴿١٧﴾

18. But We delivered those who believed and practised righteousness.

وَنَجَّيْنَا ٱلَّذِينَ ءَامَنُوا۟ وَكَانُوا۟ يَتَّقُونَ ﴿١٨﴾

19. On the day that the enemies of Allah will be gathered together to the fire, they will be marched in ranks.

وَيَوْمَ يُحْشَرُ أَعْدَآءُ ٱللَّهِ إِلَى ٱلنَّارِ فَهُمْ يُوزَعُونَ ﴿١٩﴾

20. At length, when they reach the (fire), their hearing, their sight, and their skins will bear witness against them, as to (all) their deeds.

حَتَّىٰٓ إِذَا مَا جَآءُوهَا شَهِدَ عَلَيْهِمْ سَمْعُهُمْ
وَأَبْصَٰرُهُمْ وَجُلُودُهُم بِمَا كَانُوا۟ يَعْمَلُونَ ﴿٢٠﴾

21. They will say to their skins: "Why bear you witness against us?" They will say: "Allah has given us speech - (He) Who gives speech to everything: He created you for the first time, and to Him were you to return.

وَقَالُوا۟ لِجُلُودِهِمْ لِمَ شَهِدتُّمْ عَلَيْنَا ۖ قَالُوٓا۟ أَنطَقَنَا
ٱللَّهُ ٱلَّذِىٓ أَنطَقَ كُلَّ شَىْءٍ وَهُوَ خَلَقَكُمْ أَوَّلَ مَرَّةٍ
وَإِلَيْهِ تُرْجَعُونَ ﴿٢١﴾

22. You did not seek to hide yourselves,

وَمَا كُنتُمْ تَسْتَتِرُونَ أَن يَشْهَدَ عَلَيْكُمْ سَمْعُكُمْ وَلَآ

أَبْصَٰرُكُمْ وَلَا جُلُودُكُمْ وَلَٰكِن ظَنَنتُمْ أَنَّ ٱللَّهَ لَا يَعْلَمُ
كَثِيرًا مِّمَّا تَعْمَلُونَ ﴿٢٢﴾

lest your hearing, your sight, and your skins should bear witness against you! But you did think that Allah knew not many of the things that you used to do!

وَذَٰلِكُمْ ظَنُّكُمُ ٱلَّذِى ظَنَنتُم بِرَبِّكُمْ أَرْدَىٰكُمْ
فَأَصْبَحْتُم مِّنَ ٱلْخَٰسِرِينَ ﴿٢٣﴾

23. But this thought of yours which you did entertain concerning your Lord, has brought you to destruction, and (now) have you become of those utterly lost!"

فَإِن يَصْبِرُوا۟ فَٱلنَّارُ مَثْوًى لَّهُمْ ۖ وَإِن يَسْتَعْتِبُوا۟ فَمَا هُم
مِّنَ ٱلْمُعْتَبِينَ ﴿٢٤﴾

24. If, then, they have patience, the fire will be a home for them! And if they beg to be received into favour, into favour will they not (then) be received.

ثلاثة أرباع الحزب ٤٨

۞ وَقَيَّضْنَا لَهُمْ قُرَنَآءَ فَزَيَّنُوا۟ لَهُم مَّا بَيْنَ أَيْدِيهِمْ
وَمَا خَلْفَهُمْ وَحَقَّ عَلَيْهِمُ ٱلْقَوْلُ فِىٓ أُمَمٍ قَدْ خَلَتْ
مِن قَبْلِهِم مِّنَ ٱلْجِنِّ وَٱلْإِنسِ ۖ إِنَّهُمْ كَانُوا۟ خَٰسِرِينَ ﴿٢٥﴾

25. And We have destined for them intimate companions (of like nature), who made alluring to them what was before them and behind them; and the sentence among the previous generations of Jinns and men, who have passed away, is proved against them; for they are utterly lost.

وَقَالَ ٱلَّذِينَ كَفَرُوا۟ لَا تَسْمَعُوا۟ لِهَٰذَا ٱلْقُرْءَانِ
وَٱلْغَوْا۟ فِيهِ لَعَلَّكُمْ تَغْلِبُونَ ﴿٢٦﴾

26. The unbelievers say: "Listen not to this Qur'an, but talk at random in the midst of its (reading), that you may gain the upper hand!"

فَلَنُذِيقَنَّ ٱلَّذِينَ كَفَرُوا۟ عَذَابًا شَدِيدًا
وَلَنَجْزِيَنَّهُمْ أَسْوَأَ ٱلَّذِى كَانُوا۟ يَعْمَلُونَ ﴿٢٧﴾

27. But We will certainly give the unbelievers a taste of a severe penalty, and We will repay them for the worst of their deeds.

ذَٰلِكَ جَزَآءُ أَعْدَآءِ ٱللَّهِ ٱلنَّارُ ۖ لَهُمْ فِيهَا دَارُ ٱلْخُلْدِ ۖ جَزَآءًۢ
بِمَا كَانُوا۟ بِـَٔايَٰتِنَا يَجْحَدُونَ ﴿٢٨﴾

28. Such is the requital of the enemies of Allah - the fire: in it will be for them the eternal home: a (fit) requital for that they used to reject Our signs.

وَقَالَ ٱلَّذِينَ كَفَرُوا۟ رَبَّنَآ أَرِنَا ٱلَّذَيْنِ أَضَلَّانَا مِنَ
ٱلْجِنِّ وَٱلْإِنسِ نَجْعَلْهُمَا تَحْتَ أَقْدَامِنَا لِيَكُونَا

29. And the unbelievers will say: "Our Lord! Show us those among Jinns and men who misled us: we shall crush them

مِنَ ٱلۡأَسۡفَلِينَ ٢٩

beneath our feet, so that they become the vilest (before all)."

إِنَّ ٱلَّذِينَ قَالُواْ رَبُّنَا ٱللَّهُ ثُمَّ ٱسۡتَقَٰمُواْ تَتَنَزَّلُ
عَلَيۡهِمُ ٱلۡمَلَٰٓئِكَةُ أَلَّا تَخَافُواْ وَلَا تَحۡزَنُواْ
وَأَبۡشِرُواْ بِٱلۡجَنَّةِ ٱلَّتِي كُنتُمۡ تُوعَدُونَ ٣٠

30. In the case of those who say, "Our Lord is Allah," and, further, stand straight and steadfast, the angels descend on them (from time to time): "Fear you not!" (they suggest), "Nor grieve! But receive the glad tidings of the garden (of bliss), that which you were promised!

نَحۡنُ أَوۡلِيَآؤُكُمۡ فِي ٱلۡحَيَوٰةِ ٱلدُّنۡيَا وَفِي ٱلۡأٓخِرَةِۖ
وَلَكُمۡ فِيهَا مَا تَشۡتَهِيٓ أَنفُسُكُمۡ وَلَكُمۡ
فِيهَا مَا تَدَّعُونَ ٣١

31. We are your protectors in this life and in the hereafter: in it shall you have all that your souls shall desire; in it shall you have all that you ask for! -

نُزُلٗا مِّنۡ غَفُورٖ رَّحِيمٖ ٣٢

32. A hospitable gift from One Oft-Forgiving, Most Merciful!"

وَمَنۡ أَحۡسَنُ قَوۡلٗا مِّمَّن دَعَآ إِلَى ٱللَّهِ وَعَمِلَ
صَٰلِحٗا وَقَالَ إِنَّنِي مِنَ ٱلۡمُسۡلِمِينَ ٣٣

33. Who is better in speech than one who calls (men) to Allah, works righteousness, and says, "I am of those who bow in Islam"?

وَلَا تَسۡتَوِي ٱلۡحَسَنَةُ وَلَا ٱلسَّيِّئَةُۚ ٱدۡفَعۡ بِٱلَّتِي
هِيَ أَحۡسَنُ فَإِذَا ٱلَّذِي بَيۡنَكَ وَبَيۡنَهُۥ عَدَٰوَةٞ
كَأَنَّهُۥ وَلِيٌّ حَمِيمٞ ٣٤

34. Nor can goodness and evil be equal. Repel (evil) with what is better: then will he between whom and you was hatred become as it were your friend and intimate!

وَمَا يُلَقَّىٰهَآ إِلَّا ٱلَّذِينَ صَبَرُواْ وَمَا يُلَقَّىٰهَآ إِلَّا
ذُو حَظٍّ عَظِيمٖ ٣٥

35. And no one will be granted such goodness except those who exercise patience, and self-restraint - none but persons of the greatest good fortune.

وَإِمَّا يَنزَغَنَّكَ مِنَ ٱلشَّيۡطَٰنِ نَزۡغٞ فَٱسۡتَعِذۡ
بِٱللَّهِۖ إِنَّهُۥ هُوَ ٱلسَّمِيعُ ٱلۡعَلِيمُ ٣٦

36. And if (at any time) an incitement to discord is made to you by the evil one, seek refuge in Allah. He is the One Who hears and knows all things.

37. Among His signs are the night and the day, and the sun and moon. Adore not the sun and the moon but adore Allah, Who created them, if it is Him you wish to serve.

وَمِنۡ ءَايَٰتِهِ ٱلَّيۡلُ وَٱلنَّهَارُ وَٱلشَّمۡسُ وَٱلۡقَمَرُۚ
لَا تَسۡجُدُواْ لِلشَّمۡسِ وَلَا لِلۡقَمَرِ وَٱسۡجُدُواْۤ لِلَّهِۤ
ٱلَّذِي خَلَقَهُنَّ إِن كُنتُمۡ إِيَّاهُ تَعۡبُدُونَ ٣٧

38. But if they (unbelievers) are arrogant, (no matter): for in the presence of your Lord are those who celebrate His praises by night and by day. And they never flag (nor feel themselves above it).

فَإِنِ ٱسۡتَكۡبَرُواْ فَٱلَّذِينَ عِندَ رَبِّكَ
يُسَبِّحُونَ لَهُۥ بِٱلَّيۡلِ وَٱلنَّهَارِ وَهُمۡ لَا يَسۡـَٔمُونَ۩ ٣٨ سَجۡدَة

39. And among His signs is this: you see the earth barren and desolate; but when We send down rain to it, it is stirred to life and yields increase. Truly, He Who gives life to the (dead) earth can surely give life to (men) who are dead. For He has power over all things.

وَمِنۡ ءَايَٰتِهِۦٓ أَنَّكَ تَرَى ٱلۡأَرۡضَ خَٰشِعَةٗ فَإِذَآ أَنزَلۡنَا
عَلَيۡهَا ٱلۡمَآءَ ٱهۡتَزَّتۡ وَرَبَتۡۚ إِنَّ ٱلَّذِيٓ أَحۡيَاهَا لَمُحۡيِ
ٱلۡمَوۡتَىٰٓۚ إِنَّهُۥ عَلَىٰ كُلِّ شَيۡءٖ قَدِيرٌ ٣٩

40. Those who pervert the truth in Our signs are not hidden from Us. Which is better? - he that is cast into the fire, or he that comes safe through, on the day of judgement? Do what you will: verily He sees (clearly) all that you do.

إِنَّ ٱلَّذِينَ يُلۡحِدُونَ فِيٓ ءَايَٰتِنَا لَا يَخۡفَوۡنَ عَلَيۡنَآۗ
أَفَمَن يُلۡقَىٰ فِي ٱلنَّارِ خَيۡرٌ أَم مَّن يَأۡتِيٓ ءَامِنٗا يَوۡمَ ٱلۡقِيَٰمَةِۚ
ٱعۡمَلُواْ مَا شِئۡتُمۡ إِنَّهُۥ بِمَا تَعۡمَلُونَ بَصِيرٌ ٤٠

41. Those who reject the message when it comes to them (are not hidden from Us); and indeed it is a book of exalted power.

إِنَّ ٱلَّذِينَ كَفَرُواْ بِٱلذِّكۡرِ لَمَّا جَآءَهُمۡۖ وَإِنَّهُۥ لَكِتَٰبٌ
عَزِيزٞ ٤١

42. No falsehood can approach it from before or behind it: it is sent down by One Full of wisdom, worthy of all praise.

لَّا يَأۡتِيهِ ٱلۡبَٰطِلُ مِنۢ بَيۡنِ يَدَيۡهِ وَلَا مِنۡ خَلۡفِهِۦۖ تَنزِيلٞ
مِّنۡ حَكِيمٍ حَمِيدٖ ٤٢

43. Nothing is said to you that was not said to the messengers before you: that your Lord has at His command (all) forgiveness as well as a most grievous penalty.

مَّا يُقَالُ لَكَ إِلَّا مَا قَدۡ قِيلَ لِلرُّسُلِ مِن قَبۡلِكَۚ إِنَّ
رَبَّكَ لَذُو مَغۡفِرَةٖ وَذُو عِقَابٍ أَلِيمٖ ٤٣

44. Had We sent this as a Qur'an (in a language) other than Arabic they would have said: "Why are not its verses explained in detail? What! (a book) not in Arabic and (a prophet) an Arab?" Say: "It is a guide and a healing to those who believe; and for those who believe not, there is a deafness in their ears, and it is blindness in their (eyes); they are (as it were) being called from a place far distant!"

وَلَوْ جَعَلْنَٰهُ قُرْءَانًا أَعْجَمِيًّا لَّقَالُوا۟ لَوْلَا فُصِّلَتْ
ءَايَٰتُهُۥٓ ۖ ءَا۬عْجَمِىٌّ وَعَرَبِىٌّ ۗ قُلْ هُوَ لِلَّذِينَ ءَامَنُوا۟
هُدًى وَشِفَآءٌ ۖ وَٱلَّذِينَ لَا يُؤْمِنُونَ فِىٓ ءَاذَانِهِمْ وَقْرٌ
وَهُوَ عَلَيْهِمْ عَمًى ۚ أُو۟لَٰٓئِكَ يُنَادَوْنَ مِن
مَّكَانٍۭ بَعِيدٍ ﴿٤٤﴾

45. We certainly gave Moses the book before: but dispute arose in this. Had it not been for a word that went forth before from your Lord, (their differences) would have been settled between them: but they remained in suspicious disquieting doubt about it.

وَلَقَدْ ءَاتَيْنَا مُوسَى ٱلْكِتَٰبَ فَٱخْتُلِفَ فِيهِ ۗ وَلَوْلَا
كَلِمَةٌ سَبَقَتْ مِن رَّبِّكَ لَقُضِىَ بَيْنَهُمْ ۚ
وَإِنَّهُمْ لَفِى شَكٍّ مِّنْهُ مُرِيبٍ ﴿٤٥﴾

46. Whoever works righteousness benefits his own soul; whoever works evil, it is against his own soul: nor is your Lord ever unjust (in the least) to His servants.

مَّنْ عَمِلَ صَٰلِحًا فَلِنَفْسِهِۦ ۖ وَمَنْ أَسَآءَ فَعَلَيْهَا ۗ
وَمَا رَبُّكَ بِظَلَّٰمٍ لِّلْعَبِيدِ ﴿٤٦﴾

✻ **47.** To Him is referred the knowledge of the hour (of judgement: He knows all): no date-fruit comes out of its sheath, nor does a female conceive (within her womb) nor bring out (young), but by His knowledge. The day that (Allah) will propound to them the (question), "Where are the partners (you attributed) to Me?" They will say, "We do assure You not one of us can bear witness!"

الجزء ٢٥ الحزب ٤٩
✻ إِلَيْهِ يُرَدُّ عِلْمُ ٱلسَّاعَةِ ۚ وَمَا تَخْرُجُ مِن ثَمَرَٰتٍ مِّنْ
أَكْمَامِهَا وَمَا تَحْمِلُ مِنْ أُنثَىٰ وَلَا تَضَعُ إِلَّا بِعِلْمِهِۦ ۚ
وَيَوْمَ يُنَادِيهِمْ أَيْنَ شُرَكَآءِى قَالُوٓا۟ ءَاذَنَّٰكَ مَا
مِنَّا مِن شَهِيدٍ ﴿٤٧﴾

48. The (deities) they used to invoke before will leave them in the lurch, and they will perceive that they have no way of escape.

وَضَلَّ عَنْهُم مَّا كَانُوا۟ يَدْعُونَ مِن قَبْلُ ۖ وَظَنُّوا۟
مَا لَهُم مِّن مَّحِيصٍ ﴿٤٨﴾

49. Man does not weary of asking for good (things), but if ill touches him, he gives up all hope (and) is lost in despair.

لَّا يَسْـَٔمُ ٱلْإِنسَٰنُ مِن دُعَآءِ ٱلْخَيْرِ وَإِن مَّسَّهُ
ٱلشَّرُّ فَيَـُٔوسٌ قَنُوطٌ ﴿٤٩﴾

✻ Part-25

50. When We give him a taste of some mercy from Ourselves after some adversity has touched him, he is sure to say, "This is due to my (merit): I think not that the hour (of judgement) will (ever) be established; but if I am brought back to my Lord, I have (much) good (stored) in His sight!" But We will show the unbelievers the truth of all that they did, and We shall give them the taste of a severe penalty.

وَلَئِنْ أَذَقْنَٰهُ رَحْمَةً مِّنَّا مِنۢ بَعْدِ ضَرَّآءَ مَسَّتْهُ
لَيَقُولَنَّ هَٰذَا لِى وَمَآ أَظُنُّ ٱلسَّاعَةَ قَآئِمَةً وَلَئِن
رُّجِعْتُ إِلَىٰ رَبِّىٓ إِنَّ لِى عِندَهُۥ لَلْحُسْنَىٰ ۚ فَلَنُنَبِّئَنَّ
ٱلَّذِينَ كَفَرُوا۟ بِمَا عَمِلُوا۟ وَلَنُذِيقَنَّهُم مِّنْ عَذَابٍ
غَلِيظٍ ﴿٥٠﴾

51. When We bestow favours on man, he turns away, and gets himself remote on his side (instead of coming to Us); and when evil seizes him (he comes) full of prolonged prayer!

وَإِذَآ أَنْعَمْنَا عَلَى ٱلْإِنسَٰنِ أَعْرَضَ وَنَـَٔا بِجَانِبِهِۦ
وَإِذَا مَسَّهُ ٱلشَّرُّ فَذُو دُعَآءٍ عَرِيضٍ ﴿٥١﴾

52. Say: "See you if the (revelation) is (really) from Allah and yet do you reject it? Who is more astray than one who is in a schism far (from any purpose)?"

قُلْ أَرَءَيْتُمْ إِن كَانَ مِنْ عِندِ ٱللَّهِ ثُمَّ كَفَرْتُم
بِهِۦ مَنْ أَضَلُّ مِمَّنْ هُوَ فِى شِقَاقٍۭ بَعِيدٍ ﴿٥٢﴾

53. Soon will We show them Our signs in the (furthest) regions (of the earth), and in their own souls, until it becomes manifest to them that this is the truth. Is it not enough that your Lord does witness all things?

سَنُرِيهِمْ ءَايَٰتِنَا فِى ٱلْءَافَاقِ وَفِىٓ أَنفُسِهِمْ حَتَّىٰ
يَتَبَيَّنَ لَهُمْ أَنَّهُ ٱلْحَقُّ ۗ أَوَلَمْ يَكْفِ بِرَبِّكَ أَنَّهُۥ
عَلَىٰ كُلِّ شَىْءٍ شَهِيدٌ ﴿٥٣﴾

54. Ah indeed! Are they in doubt concerning the meeting with their Lord? Ah indeed! It is He that does encompass all things!

أَلَآ إِنَّهُمْ فِى مِرْيَةٍ مِّن لِّقَآءِ رَبِّهِمْ ۗ أَلَآ إِنَّهُۥ
بِكُلِّ شَىْءٍ مُّحِيطٌۢ ﴿٥٤﴾

سُورَةُ الشُّورَىٰ

Surah 42: **Ash-Shura** **(Counsultation)**

In the name of Allah,
Most Gracious, Most Merciful.

بِسۡمِ ٱللَّهِ ٱلرَّحۡمَٰنِ ٱلرَّحِيمِ

1. *Ha Mim;*

حمٓ ﴿١﴾

2. *Ayn. Sin. Qaf.*

عٓسٓقٓ ﴿٢﴾

3. Thus does (He) send inspiration to you as (He did) to those before you - Allah, Exalted in Power, full of wisdom.

كَذَٰلِكَ يُوحِيٓ إِلَيۡكَ وَإِلَى ٱلَّذِينَ مِن قَبۡلِكَ ٱللَّهُ
ٱلۡعَزِيزُ ٱلۡحَكِيمُ ﴿٣﴾

4. To Him belongs all that is in the heavens and on earth: and He is Most High, Most Great.

لَهُۥ مَا فِي ٱلسَّمَٰوَٰتِ وَمَا فِي ٱلۡأَرۡضِۖ وَهُوَ
ٱلۡعَلِيُّ ٱلۡعَظِيمُ ﴿٤﴾

5. The heavens are almost split apart from above them (by His glory): and the angels celebrate the praises of their Lord, and pray for forgiveness for all beings on earth: see! Verily Allah is He, the Oft-Forgiving, Most Merciful.

تَكَادُ ٱلسَّمَٰوَٰتُ يَتَفَطَّرۡنَ مِن فَوۡقِهِنَّۚ وَٱلۡمَلَٰٓئِكَةُ
يُسَبِّحُونَ بِحَمۡدِ رَبِّهِمۡ وَيَسۡتَغۡفِرُونَ لِمَن فِي
ٱلۡأَرۡضِۗ أَلَآ إِنَّ ٱللَّهَ هُوَ ٱلۡغَفُورُ ٱلرَّحِيمُ ﴿٥﴾

6. And those who take as protectors others besides Him - Allah does watch over them; and you are not the disposer of their affairs.

وَٱلَّذِينَ ٱتَّخَذُواْ مِن دُونِهِۦٓ أَوۡلِيَآءَ ٱللَّهُ حَفِيظٌ
عَلَيۡهِمۡ وَمَآ أَنتَ عَلَيۡهِم بِوَكِيلٖ ﴿٦﴾

7. Thus have We sent by inspiration to you an Arabic Qur'an: that you may warn the mother of cities and all around her - and warn (them) of the day of assembly, of which there is no doubt: (when) some will be in the garden, and some in the blazing fire.

وَكَذَٰلِكَ أَوۡحَيۡنَآ إِلَيۡكَ قُرۡءَانًا عَرَبِيّٗا لِّتُنذِرَ أُمَّ ٱلۡقُرَىٰ
وَمَنۡ حَوۡلَهَا وَتُنذِرَ يَوۡمَ ٱلۡجَمۡعِ لَا رَيۡبَ فِيهِۚ فَرِيقٞ
فِي ٱلۡجَنَّةِ وَفَرِيقٞ فِي ٱلسَّعِيرِ ﴿٧﴾

8. If Allah had so willed, He could have made them a single people; but He admits whom He will to His mercy; and the wrongdoers will have no protector nor helper.

وَلَوْ شَآءَ ٱللَّهُ لَجَعَلَهُمْ أُمَّةً وَٰحِدَةً وَلَٰكِن يُدْخِلُ مَن
يَشَآءُ فِى رَحْمَتِهِۦ ۚ وَٱلظَّٰلِمُونَ مَا لَهُم مِّن وَلِىٍّ
وَلَا نَصِيرٍ ﴿٨﴾

9. What! Have they taken (for worship) protectors besides Him? But it is Allah - He is the protector, and it is He Who gives life to the dead: it is He Who has power over all things.

أَمِ ٱتَّخَذُوا۟ مِن دُونِهِۦٓ أَوْلِيَآءَ ۖ فَٱللَّهُ هُوَ ٱلْوَلِىُّ وَهُوَ يُحْىِ
ٱلْمَوْتَىٰ وَهُوَ عَلَىٰ كُلِّ شَىْءٍ قَدِيرٌ ﴿٩﴾

10. Whatever it be in which you differ, the decision of it is with Allah; such is Allah my Lord: in Him I trust, and to Him I turn.

وَمَا ٱخْتَلَفْتُمْ فِيهِ مِن شَىْءٍ فَحُكْمُهُۥٓ إِلَى ٱللَّهِ ۚ
ذَٰلِكُمُ ٱللَّهُ رَبِّى عَلَيْهِ تَوَكَّلْتُ وَإِلَيْهِ أُنِيبُ ﴿١٠﴾

11. (He is) the Creator of the heavens and the earth; He has made for you pairs from among yourselves, and pairs among cattle; by this means does He multiply you: there is nothing whatever like to Him, and He is the One that hears and sees (all things).

فَاطِرُ ٱلسَّمَٰوَٰتِ وَٱلْأَرْضِ ۚ جَعَلَ لَكُم مِّنْ أَنفُسِكُمْ
أَزْوَٰجًا وَمِنَ ٱلْأَنْعَٰمِ أَزْوَٰجًا ۖ يَذْرَؤُكُمْ فِيهِ ۚ
لَيْسَ كَمِثْلِهِۦ شَىْءٌ ۖ وَهُوَ ٱلسَّمِيعُ ٱلْبَصِيرُ ﴿١١﴾

12. To Him belong the keys of the heavens and the earth; He enlarges and restricts the sustenance to whom He will; for He knows full well all things.

لَهُۥ مَقَالِيدُ ٱلسَّمَٰوَٰتِ وَٱلْأَرْضِ ۖ يَبْسُطُ ٱلرِّزْقَ لِمَن
يَشَآءُ وَيَقْدِرُ ۚ إِنَّهُۥ بِكُلِّ شَىْءٍ عَلِيمٌ ﴿١٢﴾

13. The same religion has He established for you as that which He enjoined on Noah - that which We have sent by inspiration to you - and that which We enjoined on Abraham, Moses, and Jesus: namely, that you should remain steadfast in religion, and make no divisions in it: to those who worship other things than Allah, hard is the (way) to which you call them. Allah chooses to Himself those whom He pleases and guides to Himself those who turn (to Him).

۞ شَرَعَ لَكُم مِّنَ ٱلدِّينِ مَا وَصَّىٰ بِهِۦ نُوحًا وَٱلَّذِىٓ ربع الحزب ٤٩
أَوْحَيْنَآ إِلَيْكَ وَمَا وَصَّيْنَا بِهِۦٓ إِبْرَٰهِيمَ وَمُوسَىٰ
وَعِيسَىٰٓ ۖ أَنْ أَقِيمُوا۟ ٱلدِّينَ وَلَا تَتَفَرَّقُوا۟ فِيهِ ۚ كَبُرَ
عَلَى ٱلْمُشْرِكِينَ مَا تَدْعُوهُمْ إِلَيْهِ ۚ ٱللَّهُ يَجْتَبِىٓ
إِلَيْهِ مَن يَشَآءُ وَيَهْدِىٓ إِلَيْهِ مَن يُنِيبُ ﴿١٣﴾

14. And they became divided only after knowledge reached them - through selfish

وَمَا تَفَرَّقُوٓا۟ إِلَّا مِنۢ بَعْدِ مَا جَآءَهُمُ ٱلْعِلْمُ بَغْيًۢا

envy as between themselves. Had it not been for a word that went before from your Lord, (tending) to a term appointed, the matter would have been settled between them: but truly those who have inherited the book after them are in suspicious (disquieting) doubt concerning it.

بَيْنَهُمْۚ وَلَوْلَا كَلِمَةٌ سَبَقَتْ مِن رَّبِّكَ إِلَىٰٓ أَجَلٍ
مُّسَمًّى لَّقُضِىَ بَيْنَهُمْۚ وَإِنَّ ٱلَّذِينَ أُورِثُوا۟ ٱلْكِتَٰبَ
مِنۢ بَعْدِهِمْ لَفِى شَكٍّ مِّنْهُ مُرِيبٍ ﴿١٤﴾

15. Now then, for that (reason) call (them to the faith), and stand steadfast as you are commanded, nor follow you their vain desires; but say: "I believe in the book which Allah has sent down; and I am commanded to judge justly between you. Allah is Our Lord and your Lord. For us (is the responsibility for) our deeds and for you for your deeds. There is no contention between us and you. Allah will bring us together, and to Him is (Our) final goal."

فَلِذَٰلِكَ فَٱدْعُۖ وَٱسْتَقِمْ كَمَآ أُمِرْتَۖ وَلَا
تَتَّبِعْ أَهْوَآءَهُمْۖ وَقُلْ ءَامَنتُ بِمَآ أَنزَلَ ٱللَّهُ مِن
كِتَٰبٍۖ وَأُمِرْتُ لِأَعْدِلَ بَيْنَكُمُۖ ٱللَّهُ رَبُّنَا
وَرَبُّكُمْۖ لَنَآ أَعْمَٰلُنَا وَلَكُمْ أَعْمَٰلُكُمْۖ لَا حُجَّةَ
بَيْنَنَا وَبَيْنَكُمُۖ ٱللَّهُ يَجْمَعُ بَيْنَنَاۖ وَإِلَيْهِ
ٱلْمَصِيرُ ﴿١٥﴾

16. But those who dispute concerning Allah after He has been accepted - futile is their dispute in the sight of their Lord: on them is wrath, and for them will be a penalty terrible.

وَٱلَّذِينَ يُحَآجُّونَ فِى ٱللَّهِ مِنۢ بَعْدِ مَا ٱسْتُجِيبَ
لَهُۥ حُجَّتُهُمْ دَاحِضَةٌ عِندَ رَبِّهِمْ وَعَلَيْهِمْ
غَضَبٌ وَلَهُمْ عَذَابٌ شَدِيدٌ ﴿١٦﴾

17. It is Allah Who has sent down the book in truth, and the balance (by which to weigh conduct). And what will make you realise that perhaps the hour is close at hand?

ٱللَّهُ ٱلَّذِىٓ أَنزَلَ ٱلْكِتَٰبَ بِٱلْحَقِّ وَٱلْمِيزَانَۗ
وَمَا يُدْرِيكَ لَعَلَّ ٱلسَّاعَةَ قَرِيبٌ ﴿١٧﴾

18. Only those wish to hasten it who believe not in it: those who believe hold it in awe, and know that it is the truth. See, verily those that dispute concerning the hour are far astray.

يَسْتَعْجِلُ بِهَا ٱلَّذِينَ لَا يُؤْمِنُونَ بِهَاۖ وَٱلَّذِينَ
ءَامَنُوا۟ مُشْفِقُونَ مِنْهَا وَيَعْلَمُونَ أَنَّهَا ٱلْحَقُّۗ
أَلَآ إِنَّ ٱلَّذِينَ يُمَارُونَ فِى ٱلسَّاعَةِ لَفِى ضَلَٰلٍۭ
بَعِيدٍ ﴿١٨﴾

19. Gracious is Allah to His servants: He gives sustenance to whom He pleases: and

ٱللَّهُ لَطِيفٌۢ بِعِبَادِهِۦ يَرْزُقُ مَن يَشَآءُۖ وَهُوَ ٱلْقَوِىُّ

He has power and can carry out His will.

ٱلْعَزِيزُ ١٩

20. To any that desires the tilth of the hereafter, We give increase in his tilth; and to any that desires the tilth of this world, We grant somewhat of it, but he has no share or lot in the hereafter.

مَن كَانَ يُرِيدُ حَرْثَ ٱلْـَٔاخِرَةِ نَزِدْ لَهُۥ فِى حَرْثِهِۦ ۖ وَمَن كَانَ يُرِيدُ حَرْثَ ٱلدُّنْيَا نُؤْتِهِۦ مِنْهَا وَمَا لَهُۥ فِى ٱلْـَٔاخِرَةِ مِن نَّصِيبٍ ٢٠

21. What! Have they partners (in godhead), who have established for them some religion without the permission of Allah? Had it not been for the decree of judgement, the matter would have been decided between them (at once). But verily the wrongdoers will have a grievous penalty.

أَمْ لَهُمْ شُرَكَـٰٓؤُا۟ شَرَعُوا۟ لَهُم مِّنَ ٱلدِّينِ مَا لَمْ يَأْذَنۢ بِهِ ٱللَّهُ ۚ وَلَوْلَا كَلِمَةُ ٱلْفَصْلِ لَقُضِىَ بَيْنَهُمْ ۗ وَإِنَّ ٱلظَّـٰلِمِينَ لَهُمْ عَذَابٌ أَلِيمٌ ٢١

22. You will see the wrongdoers in fear on account of what they have earned, and (the burden of) that must (necessarily) fall on them. But those who believe and work righteous deeds will be in the luxuriant meads of the gardens: they shall have, before their Lord, all that they wish for: that will indeed be the magnificent bounty (of Allah).

تَرَى ٱلظَّـٰلِمِينَ مُشْفِقِينَ مِمَّا كَسَبُوا۟ وَهُوَ وَاقِعٌۢ بِهِمْ ۗ وَٱلَّذِينَ ءَامَنُوا۟ وَعَمِلُوا۟ ٱلصَّـٰلِحَـٰتِ فِى رَوْضَاتِ ٱلْجَنَّاتِ ۖ لَهُم مَّا يَشَآءُونَ عِندَ رَبِّهِمْ ۚ ذَٰلِكَ هُوَ ٱلْفَضْلُ ٱلْكَبِيرُ ٢٢

23. That is (the bounty) of which Allah gives glad tidings to His servants who believe and do righteous deeds. Say: "No reward do I ask of you for this except the love of those near of kin." And if anyone earns any good, We shall give Him an increase of good in respect of it: for Allah is Oft-Forgiving, Most ready to appreciate (service).

ذَٰلِكَ ٱلَّذِى يُبَشِّرُ ٱللَّهُ عِبَادَهُ ٱلَّذِينَ ءَامَنُوا۟ وَعَمِلُوا۟ ٱلصَّـٰلِحَـٰتِ ۗ قُل لَّآ أَسْـَٔلُكُمْ عَلَيْهِ أَجْرًا إِلَّا ٱلْمَوَدَّةَ فِى ٱلْقُرْبَىٰ ۗ وَمَن يَقْتَرِفْ حَسَنَةً نَّزِدْ لَهُۥ فِيهَا حُسْنًا ۚ إِنَّ ٱللَّهَ غَفُورٌ شَكُورٌ ٢٣

24. What! Do they say, "He has forged a falsehood against Allah"? But if Allah willed He could seal up your heart. And Allah blots out vanity, and proves the truth by His words. For He knows well the secrets of all hearts.

أَمْ يَقُولُونَ ٱفْتَرَىٰ عَلَى ٱللَّهِ كَذِبًا ۖ فَإِن يَشَإِ ٱللَّهُ يَخْتِمْ عَلَىٰ قَلْبِكَ ۗ وَيَمْحُ ٱللَّهُ ٱلْبَـٰطِلَ وَيُحِقُّ ٱلْحَقَّ بِكَلِمَـٰتِهِۦٓ ۚ إِنَّهُۥ عَلِيمٌۢ بِذَاتِ ٱلصُّدُورِ ٢٤

25. He is the One that accepts repentance from His servants and forgives sins: and He knows all that you do.

وَهُوَ ٱلَّذِي يَقۡبَلُ ٱلتَّوۡبَةَ عَنۡ عِبَادِهِۦ وَيَعۡفُواْ عَنِ
ٱلسَّيِّـَٔاتِ وَيَعۡلَمُ مَا تَفۡعَلُونَ ٢٥

26. And He listens to those who believe and do deeds of righteousness, and gives them increase of His bounty: but for the unbelievers there is a terrible penalty.

وَيَسۡتَجِيبُ ٱلَّذِينَ ءَامَنُواْ وَعَمِلُواْ ٱلصَّٰلِحَٰتِ
وَيَزِيدُهُم مِّن فَضۡلِهِۦۚ وَٱلۡكَٰفِرُونَ لَهُمۡ عَذَابٞ
شَدِيدٞ ٢٦

27. If Allah were to enlarge the provision for His servants, they would indeed transgress beyond all bounds through the earth; but He sends (it) down in due measure as He pleases: for He is with His servants Well-Acquainted, Watchful.

نصف الحزب ٤٩ ۞وَلَوۡ بَسَطَ ٱللَّهُ ٱلرِّزۡقَ لِعِبَادِهِۦ لَبَغَوۡاْ فِي ٱلۡأَرۡضِ
وَلَٰكِن يُنَزِّلُ بِقَدَرٖ مَّا يَشَآءُۚ إِنَّهُۥ بِعِبَادِهِۦ خَبِيرُۢ
بَصِيرٞ ٢٧

28. He is the One that sends down rain (even) after (men) have given up all hope, and scatters His mercy (far and wide). And He is the Protector, worthy of all praise.

وَهُوَ ٱلَّذِي يُنَزِّلُ ٱلۡغَيۡثَ مِنۢ بَعۡدِ مَا قَنَطُواْ وَيَنشُرُ رَحۡمَتَهُۥۚ
وَهُوَ ٱلۡوَلِيُّ ٱلۡحَمِيدُ ٢٨

29. And among His signs is the creation of the heavens and the earth, and the living creatures that He has scattered through them: and He has power to gather them together when He wills.

وَمِنۡ ءَايَٰتِهِۦ خَلۡقُ ٱلسَّمَٰوَٰتِ وَٱلۡأَرۡضِ وَمَا بَثَّ فِيهِمَا
مِن دَآبَّةٖۚ وَهُوَ عَلَىٰ جَمۡعِهِمۡ إِذَا يَشَآءُ قَدِيرٞ ٢٩

30. Whatever misfortune happens to you, is because of the things your hands have wrought, and for many (of them) He grants forgiveness.

وَمَآ أَصَٰبَكُم مِّن مُّصِيبَةٖ فَبِمَا كَسَبَتۡ أَيۡدِيكُمۡ وَيَعۡفُواْ
عَن كَثِيرٖ ٣٠

31. Nor can you frustrate (anything) (fleeing) through the earth; nor have you, besides Allah, anyone to protect or to help.

وَمَآ أَنتُم بِمُعۡجِزِينَ فِي ٱلۡأَرۡضِۖ وَمَا لَكُم مِّن دُونِ
ٱللَّهِ مِن وَلِيّٖ وَلَا نَصِيرٖ ٣١

32. And among His signs are the ships, smooth-running through the ocean, (tall) as mountains.

وَمِنۡ ءَايَٰتِهِ ٱلۡجَوَارِ فِي ٱلۡبَحۡرِ كَٱلۡأَعۡلَٰمِ ٣٢

33. If it be His will, He can still the wind: then would they become motionless on the back of the (ocean). Verily in this are signs for everyone who patiently perseveres and is grateful.

إِن يَشَأْ يُسْكِنِ ٱلرِّيحَ فَيَظْلَلْنَ رَوَاكِدَ عَلَىٰ ظَهْرِهِۦٓ ۚ
إِنَّ فِى ذَٰلِكَ لَءَايَٰتٍ لِّكُلِّ صَبَّارٍ شَكُورٍ ٣٣

34. Or He can cause them to perish because of the (evil) which (the men) have earned: but much does He forgive.

أَوْ يُوبِقْهُنَّ بِمَا كَسَبُوا۟ وَيَعْفُ عَن كَثِيرٍ ٣٤

35. But let those know, who dispute about Our signs, that there is for them no way of escape.

وَيَعْلَمَ ٱلَّذِينَ يُجَٰدِلُونَ فِىٓ ءَايَٰتِنَا مَا لَهُم مِّن مَّحِيصٍ ٣٥

36. Whatever you are given (here) is (but) a convenience of this life; but that which is with Allah is better and more lasting: (it is) for those who believe and put their trust in their Lord;

فَمَآ أُوتِيتُم مِّن شَىْءٍ فَمَتَٰعُ ٱلْحَيَوٰةِ ٱلدُّنْيَا ۖ وَمَا عِندَ ٱللَّهِ
خَيْرٌ وَأَبْقَىٰ لِلَّذِينَ ءَامَنُوا۟ وَعَلَىٰ رَبِّهِمْ يَتَوَكَّلُونَ ٣٦

37. Those who avoid the greater crimes and shameful deeds, and when they are angry even then forgive;

وَٱلَّذِينَ يَجْتَنِبُونَ كَبَٰٓئِرَ ٱلْإِثْمِ وَٱلْفَوَٰحِشَ وَإِذَا مَا
غَضِبُوا۟ هُمْ يَغْفِرُونَ ٣٧

38. Those who listen to their Lord, and establish regular prayer; who (conduct) their affairs by mutual consultation; who spend out of what We bestow on them for sustenance;

وَٱلَّذِينَ ٱسْتَجَابُوا۟ لِرَبِّهِمْ وَأَقَامُوا۟ ٱلصَّلَوٰةَ وَأَمْرُهُمْ شُورَىٰ
بَيْنَهُمْ وَمِمَّا رَزَقْنَٰهُمْ يُنفِقُونَ ٣٨

39. And those who when an oppressive wrong is inflicted on them, (are not cowed but) help and defend themselves.

وَٱلَّذِينَ إِذَآ أَصَابَهُمُ ٱلْبَغْىُ هُمْ يَنتَصِرُونَ ٣٩

40. The recompense for an injury is an injury equal to it (in degree); but if a person forgives and makes reconciliation, His reward is due from Allah: for (Allah) loves not those who do wrong.

وَجَزَٰٓؤُا۟ سَيِّئَةٍ سَيِّئَةٌ مِّثْلُهَا ۖ فَمَنْ عَفَا وَأَصْلَحَ
فَأَجْرُهُۥ عَلَى ٱللَّهِ ۚ إِنَّهُۥ لَا يُحِبُّ ٱلظَّٰلِمِينَ ٤٠

41. But indeed if any do help and defend themselves after a wrong (done) to them,

وَلَمَنِ ٱنتَصَرَ بَعْدَ ظُلْمِهِۦ فَأُو۟لَٰٓئِكَ مَا عَلَيْهِم مِّن

against such there is no cause of blame.

سَبِيلٍ ﴿٤١﴾

42. The blame is only against those who oppress men with wrongdoing and insolently transgress beyond bounds through the land, defying right and justice: for such there will be a penalty grievous.

إِنَّمَا ٱلسَّبِيلُ عَلَى ٱلَّذِينَ يَظْلِمُونَ ٱلنَّاسَ وَيَبْغُونَ فِي
ٱلْأَرْضِ بِغَيْرِ ٱلْحَقِّ أُوْلَٰٓئِكَ لَهُمْ عَذَابٌ أَلِيمٌ ﴿٤٢﴾

43. But indeed if any show patience and forgive, that would truly be an exercise of courageous will and resolution in the conduct of affairs.

وَلَمَن صَبَرَ وَغَفَرَ إِنَّ ذَٰلِكَ لَمِنْ عَزْمِ ٱلْأُمُورِ ﴿٤٣﴾

44. For any whom Allah leaves astray, there is no protector after that. And you will see the wrongdoers, when in sight of the penalty, say: "Is there any way (to effect) a return?"

وَمَن يُضْلِلِ ٱللَّهُ فَمَا لَهُۥ مِن وَلِيٍّ مِّنۢ بَعْدِهِۦ وَتَرَى
ٱلظَّٰلِمِينَ لَمَّا رَأَوُاْ ٱلْعَذَابَ يَقُولُونَ هَلْ إِلَىٰ مَرَدٍّ مِّن
سَبِيلٍ ﴿٤٤﴾

45. And you will see them brought forward to the (penalty), in a humble frame of mind because of (their) disgrace, (and) looking with a stealthy glance. And the believers will say: "Those are indeed in loss who have given to perdition their own selves and those belonging to them on the day of judgement. See! Truly the wrongdoers are in a lasting penalty!"

وَتَرَىٰهُمْ يُعْرَضُونَ عَلَيْهَا خَٰشِعِينَ مِنَ ٱلذُّلِّ
يَنظُرُونَ مِن طَرْفٍ خَفِيٍّ وَقَالَ ٱلَّذِينَ ءَامَنُوٓاْ
إِنَّ ٱلْخَٰسِرِينَ ٱلَّذِينَ خَسِرُوٓاْ أَنفُسَهُمْ وَأَهْلِيهِمْ
يَوْمَ ٱلْقِيَٰمَةِ أَلَآ إِنَّ ٱلظَّٰلِمِينَ فِي عَذَابٍ مُّقِيمٍ ﴿٤٥﴾

46. And no protectors have they to help them, other than Allah: and for any whom Allah leaves to stray, there is no way (to the goal).

وَمَا كَانَ لَهُم مِّنْ أَوْلِيَآءَ يَنصُرُونَهُم مِّن دُونِ
ٱللَّهِ وَمَن يُضْلِلِ ٱللَّهُ فَمَا لَهُۥ مِن سَبِيلٍ ﴿٤٦﴾

47. Listen you to your Lord, before there come a day which there will be no putting back, because of (the ordainment of) Allah! That day there will be for you no place of refuge nor will there be for you any room for denial (of your sins)!

ٱسْتَجِيبُواْ لِرَبِّكُم مِّن قَبْلِ أَن يَأْتِيَ يَوْمٌ لَّا مَرَدَّ لَهُۥ
مِنَ ٱللَّهِ مَا لَكُم مِّن مَّلْجَإٍ يَوْمَئِذٍ وَمَا لَكُم
مِّن نَّكِيرٍ ﴿٤٧﴾

48. If then they turn away, We have not sent you as a guard over them. Your duty is but to convey (the message). And truly, when We give man a taste of a mercy from Ourselves, he does exult at it, but when some ill happens to him, on account of the deeds which his hands have sent before, truly then is man ungrateful!

فَإِنۡ أَعۡرَضُواْ فَمَآ أَرۡسَلۡنَٰكَ عَلَيۡهِمۡ حَفِيظًاۖ إِنۡ
عَلَيۡكَ إِلَّا ٱلۡبَلَٰغُۗ وَإِنَّآ إِذَآ أَذَقۡنَا ٱلۡإِنسَٰنَ مِنَّا
رَحۡمَةٗ فَرِحَ بِهَاۖ وَإِن تُصِبۡهُمۡ سَيِّئَةُۢ بِمَا
قَدَّمَتۡ أَيۡدِيهِمۡ فَإِنَّ ٱلۡإِنسَٰنَ كَفُورٞ ﴿٤٨﴾

49. To Allah belongs the dominion of the heavens and the earth. He creates what He wills (and plans). He bestows (children) male or female according to His will (and plan).

لِّلَّهِ مُلۡكُ ٱلسَّمَٰوَٰتِ وَٱلۡأَرۡضِۚ يَخۡلُقُ مَا يَشَآءُۚ
يَهَبُ لِمَن يَشَآءُ إِنَٰثٗا وَيَهَبُ لِمَن يَشَآءُ ٱلذُّكُورَ ﴿٤٩﴾

50. Or He bestows both males and females, and He leaves barren whom He will: for He is full of knowledge and power.

أَوۡ يُزَوِّجُهُمۡ ذُكۡرَانٗا وَإِنَٰثٗاۖ وَيَجۡعَلُ مَن يَشَآءُ
عَقِيمًاۚ إِنَّهُۥ عَلِيمٞ قَدِيرٞ ﴿٥٠﴾

51. It is not fitting for a man that Allah should speak to him except by inspiration, or from behind a veil, or by the sending of a messenger to reveal, with Allah's permission, what Allah wills: for He is Most High, Most Wise.

۞وَمَا كَانَ لِبَشَرٍ أَن يُكَلِّمَهُ ٱللَّهُ إِلَّا وَحۡيًا أَوۡ مِن ثلاثة أرباع الحزب ٤٩
وَرَآيِٕ حِجَابٍ أَوۡ يُرۡسِلَ رَسُولٗا فَيُوحِيَ بِإِذۡنِهِۦ
مَا يَشَآءُۚ إِنَّهُۥ عَلِيٌّ حَكِيمٞ ﴿٥١﴾

52. And thus have We, by Our command, sent inspiration to you; you knew not (before) what was revelation, and what was faith; but We have made the Qur'an) a light, with which We guide such of Our servants as We will; and verily you do guide (men) to the straight way -

وَكَذَٰلِكَ أَوۡحَيۡنَآ إِلَيۡكَ رُوحٗا مِّنۡ أَمۡرِنَاۚ مَا كُنتَ تَدۡرِي
مَا ٱلۡكِتَٰبُ وَلَا ٱلۡإِيمَٰنُ وَلَٰكِن جَعَلۡنَٰهُ نُورٗا نَّهۡدِي
بِهِۦ مَن نَّشَآءُ مِنۡ عِبَادِنَاۚ وَإِنَّكَ لَتَهۡدِيٓ إِلَىٰ
صِرَٰطٖ مُّسۡتَقِيمٖ ﴿٥٢﴾

53. The way of Allah to whom belongs whatever is in the heavens and whatever is on earth: see (how) all affairs tend towards Allah!

صِرَٰطِ ٱللَّهِ ٱلَّذِي لَهُۥ مَا فِي ٱلسَّمَٰوَٰتِ وَمَا فِي ٱلۡأَرۡضِۗ
أَلَآ إِلَى ٱللَّهِ تَصِيرُ ٱلۡأُمُورُ ﴿٥٣﴾

سُورَةُ الزُّخۡرُفِ

Surah 43: ***Az-Zukhruf*** **(The Gold Ornaments)**

In the name of Allah,
Most Gracious, Most Merciful.

بِسۡمِ ٱللَّهِ ٱلرَّحۡمَٰنِ ٱلرَّحِيمِ

1. *Ha Mim.*

حمٓ ١

2. By the book that makes things clear -

وَٱلۡكِتَٰبِ ٱلۡمُبِينِ ٢

3. We have made it a Qur'an in Arabic, that you may be able to understand (and learn wisdom).

إِنَّا جَعَلۡنَٰهُ قُرۡءَٰنًا عَرَبِيّٗا لَّعَلَّكُمۡ تَعۡقِلُونَ ٣

4. And verily, it is in the mother of the book in Our presence, high (in dignity), full of wisdom.

وَإِنَّهُۥ فِيٓ أُمِّ ٱلۡكِتَٰبِ لَدَيۡنَا لَعَلِيٌّ حَكِيمٌ ٤

5. Shall We then take away the message from you and repel (you), for that you are a people transgressing beyond bounds?

أَفَنَضۡرِبُ عَنكُمُ ٱلذِّكۡرَ صَفۡحًا أَن كُنتُمۡ
قَوۡمٗا مُّسۡرِفِينَ ٥

6. But how many were the prophets We sent amongst the peoples of old?

وَكَمۡ أَرۡسَلۡنَا مِن نَّبِيّٖ فِي ٱلۡأَوَّلِينَ ٦

7. And never came there a prophet to them but they mocked him.

وَمَا يَأۡتِيهِم مِّن نَّبِيٍّ إِلَّا كَانُواْ بِهِۦ يَسۡتَهۡزِءُونَ ٧

8. So We destroyed (them) - stronger in power than these - and (thus) has passed on the parable of the peoples of old.

فَأَهۡلَكۡنَآ أَشَدَّ مِنۡهُم بَطۡشٗا وَمَضَىٰ مَثَلُ
ٱلۡأَوَّلِينَ ٨

9. If you were to question them, "Who created the heavens and the earth?" They would be sure to reply, "They were created by (Him) the Exalted in power, Full of knowledge."

وَلَئِن سَأَلۡتَهُم مَّنۡ خَلَقَ ٱلسَّمَٰوَٰتِ وَٱلۡأَرۡضَ
لَيَقُولُنَّ خَلَقَهُنَّ ٱلۡعَزِيزُ ٱلۡعَلِيمُ ٩

10. (Yea, the same that) has made for you the earth (like a carpet) spread out, and has made for you roads (and channels) in it, in order that you may find guidance (on the way);

ٱلَّذِى جَعَلَ لَكُمُ ٱلْأَرْضَ مَهْدًا وَجَعَلَ
لَكُمْ فِيهَا سُبُلًا لَّعَلَّكُمْ تَهْتَدُونَ ١٠

11. That sends down (from time to time) rain from the sky in due measure - and We raise to life with it a land that is dead; even so will you be raised (from the dead) -

وَٱلَّذِى نَزَّلَ مِنَ ٱلسَّمَآءِ مَآءًۢ بِقَدَرٍ فَأَنشَرْنَا بِهِۦ
بَلْدَةً مَّيْتًا ۚ كَذَٰلِكَ تُخْرَجُونَ ١١

12. That has created pairs in all things, and has made for you ships and cattle on which you ride,

وَٱلَّذِى خَلَقَ ٱلْأَزْوَٰجَ كُلَّهَا وَجَعَلَ لَكُم مِّنَ
ٱلْفُلْكِ وَٱلْأَنْعَٰمِ مَا تَرْكَبُونَ ١٢

13. In order that you may sit firm and square on their backs, and when so seated, you may celebrate the (kind) favour of your Lord, and say, "Glory to Him Who has subjected these to our (use), for We could never have accomplished this (by ourselves).

لِتَسْتَوُۥا۟ عَلَىٰ ظُهُورِهِۦ ثُمَّ تَذْكُرُوا۟ نِعْمَةَ رَبِّكُمْ إِذَا
ٱسْتَوَيْتُمْ عَلَيْهِ وَتَقُولُوا۟ سُبْحَٰنَ ٱلَّذِى سَخَّرَ لَنَا
هَٰذَا وَمَا كُنَّا لَهُۥ مُقْرِنِينَ ١٣

14. And to our Lord, surely, must we turn back!"

وَإِنَّآ إِلَىٰ رَبِّنَا لَمُنقَلِبُونَ ١٤

15. Yet they attribute to some of His servants a share with Him (in His godhead)! Truly is man a blasphemous ingrate avowed!

وَجَعَلُوا۟ لَهُۥ مِنْ عِبَادِهِۦ جُزْءًا ۚ إِنَّ ٱلْإِنسَٰنَ
لَكَفُورٌ مُّبِينٌ ١٥

16. What! Has He taken daughters out of what He Himself creates, and granted to you sons for choice?

أَمِ ٱتَّخَذَ مِمَّا يَخْلُقُ بَنَاتٍ وَأَصْفَىٰكُم بِٱلْبَنِينَ ١٦

17. When news is brought to one of them of (the birth of) what he sets up as a likeness to (Allah) Most Gracious, his face darkens, and he is filled with inward grief!

وَإِذَا بُشِّرَ أَحَدُهُم بِمَا ضَرَبَ لِلرَّحْمَٰنِ مَثَلًا
ظَلَّ وَجْهُهُۥ مُسْوَدًّا وَهُوَ كَظِيمٌ ١٧

18. Is then one brought up among trinkets, and unable to give a clear account in a dispute (to be associated with Allah)?

أَوَمَن يُنَشَّؤُا۟ فِى ٱلْحِلْيَةِ وَهُوَ فِى ٱلْخِصَامِ غَيْرُ
مُبِينٍ ١٨

19. And they make into females angels who themselves serve Allah. Did they witness their creation? Their evidence will be recorded, and they will be called to account!

وَجَعَلُوا۟ ٱلْمَلَٰٓئِكَةَ ٱلَّذِينَ هُمْ عِبَٰدُ ٱلرَّحْمَٰنِ إِنَٰثًا ۚ
أَشَهِدُوا۟ خَلْقَهُمْ ۚ سَتُكْتَبُ شَهَٰدَتُهُمْ
وَيُسْـَٔلُونَ ﴿١٩﴾

20. ("Ah!") They say, "If it had been the will of (Allah) Most Gracious, We should not have worshipped such (deities)!" Of that they have no knowledge! They do nothing but lie!

وَقَالُوا۟ لَوْ شَآءَ ٱلرَّحْمَٰنُ مَا عَبَدْنَٰهُم ۗ مَّا لَهُم بِذَٰلِكَ
مِنْ عِلْمٍ ۖ إِنْ هُمْ إِلَّا يَخْرُصُونَ ﴿٢٠﴾

21. What! Have We given them a book before this, to which they are holding fast?

أَمْ ءَاتَيْنَٰهُمْ كِتَٰبًا مِّن قَبْلِهِۦ فَهُم بِهِۦ
مُسْتَمْسِكُونَ ﴿٢١﴾

22. Nay! They say: "We found our fathers following a certain religion, and we do guide ourselves by their footsteps."

بَلْ قَالُوٓا۟ إِنَّا وَجَدْنَآ ءَابَآءَنَا عَلَىٰٓ أُمَّةٍ وَإِنَّا
عَلَىٰٓ ءَاثَٰرِهِم مُّهْتَدُونَ ﴿٢٢﴾

23. Just in the same way, whenever We sent a warner before you to any people, the wealthy ones among them said: "We found our fathers following a certain religion, and we will certainly follow in their footsteps."

وَكَذَٰلِكَ مَآ أَرْسَلْنَا مِن قَبْلِكَ فِى قَرْيَةٍ مِّن نَّذِيرٍ إِلَّا
قَالَ مُتْرَفُوهَآ إِنَّا وَجَدْنَآ ءَابَآءَنَا عَلَىٰٓ أُمَّةٍ وَإِنَّا عَلَىٰٓ
ءَاثَٰرِهِم مُّقْتَدُونَ ﴿٢٣﴾

24. He said: "What! Even if I brought you better guidance than that which you found your fathers following?" They said: "For us, We deny that you (prophets) are sent (on a mission at all)."

الحِزْبُ ٥٠
۞ قَٰلَ أَوَلَوْ جِئْتُكُم بِأَهْدَىٰ مِمَّا وَجَدتُّمْ عَلَيْهِ
ءَابَآءَكُمْ ۖ قَالُوٓا۟ إِنَّا بِمَآ أُرْسِلْتُم بِهِۦ كَٰفِرُونَ ﴿٢٤﴾

25. So We exacted retribution from them: now see what was the end of those who rejected (truth)!

فَٱنتَقَمْنَا مِنْهُمْ ۖ فَٱنظُرْ كَيْفَ كَانَ عَٰقِبَةُ ٱلْمُكَذِّبِينَ ﴿٢٥﴾

26. See! Abraham said to his father and his people: "I do indeed clear myself of what you worship:

وَإِذْ قَالَ إِبْرَٰهِيمُ لِأَبِيهِ وَقَوْمِهِۦٓ إِنَّنِى بَرَآءٌ مِّمَّا
تَعْبُدُونَ ﴿٢٦﴾

27. (I worship) only Him who made me, and He will certainly guide me."

إِلَّا ٱلَّذِى فَطَرَنِى فَإِنَّهُۥ سَيَهْدِينِ ٢٧

28. And he left it as a word to endure among those who came after him, that they may turn back (to Allah).

وَجَعَلَهَا كَلِمَةًۢ بَاقِيَةً فِى عَقِبِهِۦ لَعَلَّهُمْ يَرْجِعُونَ ٢٨

29. Yea, I have given the good things of this life to these (men) and their fathers, until the truth has come to them, and a messenger making things clear.

بَلْ مَتَّعْتُ هَٰٓؤُلَآءِ وَءَابَآءَهُمْ حَتَّىٰ جَآءَهُمُ ٱلْحَقُّ
وَرَسُولٌ مُّبِينٌ ٢٩

30. But when the truth came to them, they said: "This is sorcery, and We do reject it."

وَلَمَّا جَآءَهُمُ ٱلْحَقُّ قَالُوا۟ هَٰذَا سِحْرٌ وَإِنَّا بِهِۦ
كَٰفِرُونَ ٣٠

31. Also, they say: "Why is not this Qur'an sent down to some leading man in either of the two (chief) cities?"

وَقَالُوا۟ لَوْلَا نُزِّلَ هَٰذَا ٱلْقُرْءَانُ عَلَىٰ رَجُلٍ مِّنَ
ٱلْقَرْيَتَيْنِ عَظِيمٍ ٣١

32. Is it they who would portion out the mercy of your Lord? It is We Who portion out between them their livelihood in the life of this world: and We raise some of them above others in ranks, so that some may command work from others. But the mercy of your Lord is better than the (wealth) which they amass.

أَهُمْ يَقْسِمُونَ رَحْمَتَ رَبِّكَ ۚ نَحْنُ قَسَمْنَا بَيْنَهُم
مَّعِيشَتَهُمْ فِى ٱلْحَيَوٰةِ ٱلدُّنْيَا ۚ وَرَفَعْنَا بَعْضَهُمْ فَوْقَ
بَعْضٍ دَرَجَٰتٍ لِّيَتَّخِذَ بَعْضُهُم بَعْضًا سُخْرِيًّا ۗ
وَرَحْمَتُ رَبِّكَ خَيْرٌ مِّمَّا يَجْمَعُونَ ٣٢

33. And were it not that (all) men might become of one (evil) way of life, We would provide, for everyone that blasphemes against (Allah) Most Gracious, silver roofs for their houses, and (silver) stairways on which to go up,

وَلَوْلَآ أَن يَكُونَ ٱلنَّاسُ أُمَّةً وَٰحِدَةً لَّجَعَلْنَا لِمَن
يَكْفُرُ بِٱلرَّحْمَٰنِ لِبُيُوتِهِمْ سُقُفًا مِّن فِضَّةٍ
وَمَعَارِجَ عَلَيْهَا يَظْهَرُونَ ٣٣

34. And (silver) doors to their houses, and thrones (of silver) on which they could recline,

وَلِبُيُوتِهِمْ أَبْوَٰبًا وَسُرُرًا عَلَيْهَا يَتَّكِـُٔونَ ٣٤

35. And also adornments of gold. But all this were nothing but conveniences of the present life: the hereafter, in the sight of your Lord, is for the righteous.

وَزُخۡرُفٗاۚ وَإِن كُلُّ ذَٰلِكَ لَمَّا مَتَٰعُ ٱلۡحَيَوٰةِ ٱلدُّنۡيَاۚ
وَٱلۡأٓخِرَةُ عِندَ رَبِّكَ لِلۡمُتَّقِينَ ٣٥

36. If anyone withdraws himself from remembrance of (Allah) Most Gracious, We appoint for him an evil one, to be an intimate companion to him.

وَمَن يَعۡشُ عَن ذِكۡرِ ٱلرَّحۡمَٰنِ نُقَيِّضۡ لَهُۥ شَيۡطَٰنٗا
فَهُوَ لَهُۥ قَرِينٞ ٣٦

37. Such (evil ones) really hinder them from the path, but they think that they are being guided aright!

وَإِنَّهُمۡ لَيَصُدُّونَهُمۡ عَنِ ٱلسَّبِيلِ وَيَحۡسَبُونَ أَنَّهُم
مُّهۡتَدُونَ ٣٧

38. At length, when (such a one) comes to Us, he says (to his evil-companion): "Would that between me and you were the distance of east and west!" Ah! evil is the companion (indeed)!

حَتَّىٰٓ إِذَا جَآءَنَا قَالَ يَٰلَيۡتَ بَيۡنِي وَبَيۡنَكَ بُعۡدَ
ٱلۡمَشۡرِقَيۡنِ فَبِئۡسَ ٱلۡقَرِينُ ٣٨

39. When you have done wrong, it will benefit you nothing, that day, that you shall be partners in punishment!

وَلَن يَنفَعَكُمُ ٱلۡيَوۡمَ إِذ ظَّلَمۡتُمۡ أَنَّكُمۡ فِي ٱلۡعَذَابِ
مُشۡتَرِكُونَ ٣٩

40. Can you then make the deaf to hear, or give direction to the blind, or to such as (wander) in manifest error?

أَفَأَنتَ تُسۡمِعُ ٱلصُّمَّ أَوۡ تَهۡدِي ٱلۡعُمۡيَ وَمَن كَانَ فِي
ضَلَٰلٖ مُّبِينٖ ٤٠

41. Even if We take you away, We shall be sure to exact retribution from them,

فَإِمَّا نَذۡهَبَنَّ بِكَ فَإِنَّا مِنۡهُم مُّنتَقِمُونَ ٤١

42. Or We shall show you that (accomplished) which We have promised them: for verily We shall prevail over them.

أَوۡ نُرِيَنَّكَ ٱلَّذِي وَعَدۡنَٰهُمۡ فَإِنَّا عَلَيۡهِم مُّقۡتَدِرُونَ ٤٢

43. So hold you fast to the revelation sent down to you: verily you are on a straight way.

فَٱسۡتَمۡسِكۡ بِٱلَّذِيٓ أُوحِيَ إِلَيۡكَۖ إِنَّكَ عَلَىٰ صِرَٰطٖ
مُّسۡتَقِيمٖ ٤٣

44. The (Qur'an) is indeed the message, for you and for your people; and soon shall you (all) be brought to account.

وَإِنَّهُۥ لَذِكْرٌ لَّكَ وَلِقَوْمِكَ ۖ وَسَوْفَ تُسْـَٔلُونَ ﴿٤٤﴾

45. And question you Our messengers whom We sent before you; did We appoint any deities other than (Allah) Most Gracious, to be worshipped?

وَسْـَٔلْ مَنْ أَرْسَلْنَا مِن قَبْلِكَ مِن رُّسُلِنَآ أَجَعَلْنَا
مِن دُونِ ٱلرَّحْمَٰنِ ءَالِهَةً يُعْبَدُونَ ﴿٤٥﴾

46. We did send Moses before, with Our signs, to Pharaoh and his chiefs: he said, "I am a messenger of the Lord of the Worlds."

وَلَقَدْ أَرْسَلْنَا مُوسَىٰ بِـَٔايَٰتِنَآ إِلَىٰ فِرْعَوْنَ وَمَلَإِي۟هِۦ
فَقَالَ إِنِّى رَسُولُ رَبِّ ٱلْعَٰلَمِينَ ﴿٤٦﴾

47. But when he came to them with Our signs, behold, they ridiculed them.

فَلَمَّا جَآءَهُم بِـَٔايَٰتِنَآ إِذَا هُم مِّنْهَا يَضْحَكُونَ ﴿٤٧﴾

48. We showed them sign after sign, each greater then its fellow, and We seized them with punishment, in order that they might turn (to Us).

وَمَا نُرِيهِم مِّنْ ءَايَةٍ إِلَّا هِىَ أَكْبَرُ مِنْ أُخْتِهَا ۖ
وَأَخَذْنَٰهُم بِٱلْعَذَابِ لَعَلَّهُمْ يَرْجِعُونَ ﴿٤٨﴾

49. And they said, "O you sorcerer! Invoke your Lord for us according to His covenant with you; for We shall truly accept guidance."

وَقَالُوا۟ يَٰٓأَيُّهَ ٱلسَّاحِرُ ٱدْعُ لَنَا رَبَّكَ بِمَا عَهِدَ
عِندَكَ إِنَّنَا لَمُهْتَدُونَ ﴿٤٩﴾

50. But when We removed the penalty from them, see, they broke their word.

فَلَمَّا كَشَفْنَا عَنْهُمُ ٱلْعَذَابَ إِذَا هُمْ يَنكُثُونَ ﴿٥٠﴾

51. And Pharaoh proclaimed among his people, saying: "O my people! Does not the dominion of Egypt belong to me, (witness) these streams flowing underneath my (palace)? What! Do you not see then?

وَنَادَىٰ فِرْعَوْنُ فِى قَوْمِهِۦ قَالَ يَٰقَوْمِ أَلَيْسَ لِى مُلْكُ
مِصْرَ وَهَٰذِهِ ٱلْأَنْهَٰرُ تَجْرِى مِن تَحْتِىٓ ۚ أَفَلَا
تُبْصِرُونَ ﴿٥١﴾

52. Am I not better than this (Moses), who is a contemptible wretch and can scarcely express himself clearly?

أَمْ أَنَا۠ خَيْرٌ مِّنْ هَٰذَا ٱلَّذِى هُوَ مَهِينٌ وَلَا
يَكَادُ يُبِينُ ﴿٥٢﴾

53. Then why are not gold bracelets bestowed on him, or (why) come (not)

فَلَوْلَآ أُلْقِىَ عَلَيْهِ أَسْوِرَةٌ مِّن ذَهَبٍ أَوْ جَآءَ مَعَهُ

with him angels accompanying him in procession?"

ٱلْمَلَٰٓئِكَةُ مُقْتَرِنِينَ ﴿٥٣﴾

54. Thus did he make fools of his people, and they obeyed him: Truly were they a people rebellious (against Allah).

فَٱسْتَخَفَّ قَوْمَهُۥ فَأَطَاعُوهُ ۚ إِنَّهُمْ كَانُوا۟
قَوْمًا فَٰسِقِينَ ﴿٥٤﴾

55. When at length they provoked Us, We exacted retribution from them, and We drowned them all.

فَلَمَّآ ءَاسَفُونَا ٱنتَقَمْنَا مِنْهُمْ فَأَغْرَقْنَٰهُمْ
أَجْمَعِينَ ﴿٥٥﴾

56. And We made them (a people) of the past and an example to later ages.

فَجَعَلْنَٰهُمْ سَلَفًا وَمَثَلًا لِّلْءَاخِرِينَ ﴿٥٦﴾

57. When (Jesus) the son of Mary is held up as an example, behold your people raise a clamour at it (in ridicule)!

ربع الحزب ٥٠ ۞ وَلَمَّا ضُرِبَ ٱبْنُ مَرْيَمَ مَثَلًا إِذَا قَوْمُكَ مِنْهُ
يَصِدُّونَ ﴿٥٧﴾

58. And they say, "Are our gods best or He?" This they set out to you, only by way of disputation: yea, they are a contentious people.

وَقَالُوٓا۟ ءَأَٰلِهَتُنَا خَيْرٌ أَمْ هُوَ ۚ مَا ضَرَبُوهُ لَكَ إِلَّا
جَدَلًۢا ۚ بَلْ هُمْ قَوْمٌ خَصِمُونَ ﴿٥٨﴾

59. He was no more than a servant: We granted Our favour to him, and We made him an example to the Children of Israel.

إِنْ هُوَ إِلَّا عَبْدٌ أَنْعَمْنَا عَلَيْهِ وَجَعَلْنَٰهُ مَثَلًا
لِّبَنِىٓ إِسْرَٰٓءِيلَ ﴿٥٩﴾

60. And if it were Our will, We could make angels from amongst you succeeding each other on the earth.

وَلَوْ نَشَآءُ لَجَعَلْنَا مِنكُم مَّلَٰٓئِكَةً فِى ٱلْأَرْضِ
يَخْلُفُونَ ﴿٦٠﴾

61. And (Jesus) shall be a sign (for the coming of) the hour (of judgement): therefore have no doubt about the (hour) but follow you Me: this is a straight way.

وَإِنَّهُۥ لَعِلْمٌ لِّلسَّاعَةِ فَلَا تَمْتَرُنَّ بِهَا وَٱتَّبِعُونِ ۚ
هَٰذَا صِرَٰطٌ مُّسْتَقِيمٌ ﴿٦١﴾

62. Let not the evil one hinder you: for he is to you an enemy avowed.

وَلَا يَصُدَّنَّكُمُ ٱلشَّيْطَٰنُ ۖ إِنَّهُۥ لَكُمْ عَدُوٌّ مُّبِينٌ ﴿٦٢﴾

63. When Jesus came with clear signs he said: "Now have I come to you with wisdom and in order to make clear to you some of the (points) on which you dispute: therefore fear Allah and obey me.

وَلَمَّا جَآءَ عِيسَىٰ بِٱلۡبَيِّنَٰتِ قَالَ قَدۡ جِئۡتُكُم
بِٱلۡحِكۡمَةِ وَلِأُبَيِّنَ لَكُم بَعۡضَ ٱلَّذِي تَخۡتَلِفُونَ فِيهِۖ
فَٱتَّقُواْ ٱللَّهَ وَأَطِيعُونِ ٦٣

64. For Allah; He is my Lord and your Lord: so worship you Him: this is a straight way."

إِنَّ ٱللَّهَ هُوَ رَبِّي وَرَبُّكُمۡ فَٱعۡبُدُوهُۚ هَٰذَا صِرَٰطٞ
مُّسۡتَقِيمٞ ٦٤

65. But sects from among themselves fell into disagreement: then woe to the wrongdoers from the penalty of a grievous day!

فَٱخۡتَلَفَ ٱلۡأَحۡزَابُ مِنۢ بَيۡنِهِمۡۖ فَوَيۡلٞ لِّلَّذِينَ
ظَلَمُواْ مِنۡ عَذَابِ يَوۡمٍ أَلِيمٍ ٦٥

66. Do they only wait for the hour - that it should come on them all of a sudden, while they perceive not?

هَلۡ يَنظُرُونَ إِلَّا ٱلسَّاعَةَ أَن تَأۡتِيَهُم بَغۡتَةٗ
وَهُمۡ لَا يَشۡعُرُونَ ٦٦

67. Friends on that day will be foes, one to another - except the righteous.

ٱلۡأَخِلَّآءُ يَوۡمَئِذِۢ بَعۡضُهُمۡ لِبَعۡضٍ عَدُوٌّ إِلَّا
ٱلۡمُتَّقِينَ ٦٧

68. My devotees! No fear shall be on you that day, nor shall you grieve -

يَٰعِبَادِ لَا خَوۡفٌ عَلَيۡكُمُ ٱلۡيَوۡمَ وَلَآ أَنتُمۡ تَحۡزَنُونَ ٦٨

69. (Being) those who have believed in Our signs and bowed (their wills to Ours) in Islam.

ٱلَّذِينَ ءَامَنُواْ بِـَٔايَٰتِنَا وَكَانُواْ مُسۡلِمِينَ ٦٩

70. Enter you the garden, you and your wives, in (beauty and) rejoicing.

ٱدۡخُلُواْ ٱلۡجَنَّةَ أَنتُمۡ وَأَزۡوَٰجُكُمۡ تُحۡبَرُونَ ٧٠

71. To them will be passed round, dishes and goblets of gold: there will be there all that the souls could desire, all that the eyes could delight in: and you shall remain in it (for ever).

يُطَافُ عَلَيۡهِم بِصِحَافٖ مِّن ذَهَبٖ وَأَكۡوَابٖۖ
وَفِيهَا مَا تَشۡتَهِيهِ ٱلۡأَنفُسُ وَتَلَذُّ ٱلۡأَعۡيُنُۖ
وَأَنتُمۡ فِيهَا خَٰلِدُونَ ٧١

72. Such will be the garden of which you are made heirs for your (good) deeds (in life).

وَتِلْكَ ٱلْجَنَّةُ ٱلَّتِىٓ أُورِثْتُمُوهَا بِمَا كُنتُمْ
تَعْمَلُونَ ﴿٧٢﴾

73. You shall have in it abundance of fruit, from which you shall have satisfaction.

لَكُمْ فِيهَا فَٰكِهَةٌ كَثِيرَةٌ مِّنْهَا تَأْكُلُونَ ﴿٧٣﴾

74. The sinners will be in the punishment of hell, to dwell in it (for ever):

إِنَّ ٱلْمُجْرِمِينَ فِى عَذَابِ جَهَنَّمَ خَٰلِدُونَ ﴿٧٤﴾

75. In no way will the (punishment) be lightened for them, and in despair will they be there overwhelmed.

لَا يُفَتَّرُ عَنْهُمْ وَهُمْ فِيهِ مُبْلِسُونَ ﴿٧٥﴾

76. In no way shall We be unjust to them: but it is they who have been unjust themselves.

وَمَا ظَلَمْنَٰهُمْ وَلَٰكِن كَانُوا۟ هُمُ ٱلظَّٰلِمِينَ ﴿٧٦﴾

77. They will call: "O Malik! Would that your Lord put and end to us!" He will say, "Nay, but you shall remain!"

وَنَادَوْا۟ يَٰمَٰلِكُ لِيَقْضِ عَلَيْنَا رَبُّكَ ۖ قَالَ إِنَّكُم
مَّٰكِثُونَ ﴿٧٧﴾

78. Verily We have brought the truth to you: but most of you have a hatred for truth.

لَقَدْ جِئْنَٰكُم بِٱلْحَقِّ وَلَٰكِنَّ أَكْثَرَكُمْ لِلْحَقِّ كَٰرِهُونَ ﴿٧٨﴾

79. What! Have they settled some plan (among themselves)? But it is We Who settle things.

أَمْ أَبْرَمُوٓا۟ أَمْرًا فَإِنَّا مُبْرِمُونَ ﴿٧٩﴾

80. Or do they think that We hear not their secrets and their private counsels? Indeed (We do) and Our messengers are by them, to record.

أَمْ يَحْسَبُونَ أَنَّا لَا نَسْمَعُ سِرَّهُمْ وَنَجْوَىٰهُم ۚ بَلَىٰ
وَرُسُلُنَا لَدَيْهِمْ يَكْتُبُونَ ﴿٨٠﴾

81. Say: "If (Allah) Most Gracious had a son, I would be the first to worship."

قُلْ إِن كَانَ لِلرَّحْمَٰنِ وَلَدٌ فَأَنَا۠ أَوَّلُ ٱلْعَٰبِدِينَ ﴿٨١﴾

82. Glory to the Lord of the heavens and the earth, the Lord of the throne (of authority)! (He is free) from the things they attribute (to Him)!

سُبْحَٰنَ رَبِّ ٱلسَّمَٰوَٰتِ وَٱلْأَرْضِ رَبِّ ٱلْعَرْشِ
عَمَّا يَصِفُونَ ﴿٨٢﴾

فَذَرْهُمْ يَخُوضُوا۟ وَيَلْعَبُوا۟ حَتَّىٰ يُلَٰقُوا۟ يَوْمَهُمُ ٱلَّذِى يُوعَدُونَ ﴿٨٣﴾

83. So leave them to babble and play (with vanities) until they meet that day of theirs, which they have been promised.

وَهُوَ ٱلَّذِى فِى ٱلسَّمَآءِ إِلَٰهٌ وَفِى ٱلْأَرْضِ إِلَٰهٌ ۚ وَهُوَ ٱلْحَكِيمُ ٱلْعَلِيمُ ﴿٨٤﴾

84. It is He Who is God in heaven and God on earth; and He is full of wisdom and knowledge.

وَتَبَارَكَ ٱلَّذِى لَهُۥ مُلْكُ ٱلسَّمَٰوَٰتِ وَٱلْأَرْضِ وَمَا بَيْنَهُمَا وَعِندَهُۥ عِلْمُ ٱلسَّاعَةِ وَإِلَيْهِ تُرْجَعُونَ ﴿٨٥﴾

85. And blessed is He to Whom belongs the dominion of the heavens and the earth, and all between them: with Him is the knowledge of the hour (of judgement): And to Him shall you be brought back.

وَلَا يَمْلِكُ ٱلَّذِينَ يَدْعُونَ مِن دُونِهِ ٱلشَّفَٰعَةَ إِلَّا مَن شَهِدَ بِٱلْحَقِّ وَهُمْ يَعْلَمُونَ ﴿٨٦﴾

86. And those whom they invoke besides Allah have no power of intercession - only he who bears witness to the truth, and they know (him).

وَلَئِن سَأَلْتَهُم مَّنْ خَلَقَهُمْ لَيَقُولُنَّ ٱللَّهُ ۖ فَأَنَّىٰ يُؤْفَكُونَ ﴿٨٧﴾

87. If you ask them, Who created them, they will certainly say, Allah: how then are they deluded away (from the truth)?

وَقِيلِهِۦ يَٰرَبِّ إِنَّ هَٰٓؤُلَآءِ قَوْمٌ لَّا يُؤْمِنُونَ ﴿٨٨﴾

88. (Allah has knowledge) of the (prophet's) call, "O my Lord! Truly these are a people who will not believe!"

فَٱصْفَحْ عَنْهُمْ وَقُلْ سَلَٰمٌ ۚ فَسَوْفَ يَعْلَمُونَ ﴿٨٩﴾

89. But turn away from them and say, "Peace!" But soon shall they know!

سُورَةُ الدُّخَانِ

Surah 44: **Ad-Dukhan** **(The Smoke)**

بِسْمِ ٱللَّهِ ٱلرَّحْمَٰنِ ٱلرَّحِيمِ

In the name of Allah,
Most Gracious, Most Merciful.

حمٓ ﴿١﴾

1. *Ha Mim.*

2. By the book that makes things clear -

وَٱلۡكِتَٰبِ ٱلۡمُبِينِ ٢

3. We sent it down during a blessed night: for We (ever) wish to warn (against evil).

إِنَّآ أَنزَلۡنَٰهُ فِي لَيۡلَةٖ مُّبَٰرَكَةٍۚ إِنَّا كُنَّا مُنذِرِينَ ٣

4. In that (night) is made distinct every affair of wisdom,

فِيهَا يُفۡرَقُ كُلُّ أَمۡرٍ حَكِيمٍ ٤

5. By command, from Our presence. For We (ever) send (revelations),

أَمۡرٗا مِّنۡ عِندِنَآۚ إِنَّا كُنَّا مُرۡسِلِينَ ٥

6. As a mercy from your Lord: for He hears and knows (all things);

رَحۡمَةٗ مِّن رَّبِّكَۚ إِنَّهُۥ هُوَ ٱلسَّمِيعُ ٱلۡعَلِيمُ ٦

7. The Lord of the heavens and the earth and all between them, if you (but) have an assured faith.

رَبِّ ٱلسَّمَٰوَٰتِ وَٱلۡأَرۡضِ وَمَا بَيۡنَهُمَآۖ إِن كُنتُم مُّوقِنِينَ ٧

8. There is no god but He: it is He Who gives life and gives death - the Lord and Cherisher to you and your earliest ancestors.

لَآ إِلَٰهَ إِلَّا هُوَ يُحۡيِۦ وَيُمِيتُۖ رَبُّكُمۡ وَرَبُّ ءَابَآئِكُمُ ٱلۡأَوَّلِينَ ٨

9. Yet they play about in doubt.

بَلۡ هُمۡ فِي شَكّٖ يَلۡعَبُونَ ٩

10. Then watch you for the day that the sky will bring forth a kind of smoke (or mist) plainly visible,

فَٱرۡتَقِبۡ يَوۡمَ تَأۡتِي ٱلسَّمَآءُ بِدُخَانٖ مُّبِينٖ ١٠

11. Enveloping the people: this will be a penalty grievous.

يَغۡشَى ٱلنَّاسَۖ هَٰذَا عَذَابٌ أَلِيمٞ ١١

12. (They will say:) "Our Lord! Remove the penalty from us, for We do really believe!"

رَّبَّنَا ٱكۡشِفۡ عَنَّا ٱلۡعَذَابَ إِنَّا مُؤۡمِنُونَ ١٢

13. How shall the message be (effectual) for them, seeing that a messenger explaining things clearly has (already) come to them -

أَنَّىٰ لَهُمُ ٱلذِّكۡرَىٰ وَقَدۡ جَآءَهُمۡ رَسُولٞ مُّبِينٞ ١٣

ثُمَّ تَوَلَّوْا۟ عَنْهُ وَقَالُوا۟ مُعَلَّمٌ مَّجْنُونٌ ﴿١٤﴾

14. Yet they turn away from him and say: "Tutored (by others), a man possessed!"

إِنَّا كَاشِفُوا۟ ٱلْعَذَابِ قَلِيلًا ۚ إِنَّكُمْ عَآئِدُونَ ﴿١٥﴾

15. We shall indeed remove the penalty for a while, (but) truly you will revert (to your ways).

يَوْمَ نَبْطِشُ ٱلْبَطْشَةَ ٱلْكُبْرَىٰٓ إِنَّا مُنتَقِمُونَ ﴿١٦﴾

16. One day We shall seize you with a mighty onslaught: We will indeed (then) exact retribution!

نصف الحزب ٥٠

۞ وَلَقَدْ فَتَنَّا قَبْلَهُمْ قَوْمَ فِرْعَوْنَ وَجَآءَهُمْ
رَسُولٌ كَرِيمٌ ﴿١٧﴾

17. We did, before them, try the people of Pharaoh: there came to them a messenger most honourable,

أَنْ أَدُّوٓا۟ إِلَىَّ عِبَادَ ٱللَّهِ ۖ إِنِّى لَكُمْ رَسُولٌ
أَمِينٌ ﴿١٨﴾

18. Saying: "Restore to me the servants of Allah: I am to you a messenger worthy of all trust;

وَأَن لَّا تَعْلُوا۟ عَلَى ٱللَّهِ ۖ إِنِّىٓ ءَاتِيكُم بِسُلْطَٰنٍ مُّبِينٍ ﴿١٩﴾

19. And be not arrogant as against Allah: for I come to you with authority manifest.

وَإِنِّى عُذْتُ بِرَبِّى وَرَبِّكُمْ أَن تَرْجُمُونِ ﴿٢٠﴾

20. For me, I have sought safety with my Lord and your Lord, against your injuring me.

وَإِن لَّمْ تُؤْمِنُوا۟ لِى فَٱعْتَزِلُونِ ﴿٢١﴾

21. If you believe me not, at least keep yourselves away from me."

فَدَعَا رَبَّهُۥٓ أَنَّ هَٰٓؤُلَآءِ قَوْمٌ مُّجْرِمُونَ ﴿٢٢﴾

22. (But they were aggressive): then he cried to his Lord: "These are indeed a people given to sin."

فَأَسْرِ بِعِبَادِى لَيْلًا إِنَّكُم مُّتَّبَعُونَ ﴿٢٣﴾

23. (The reply came): "March out with My servants by night: for you are sure to be pursued.

وَٱتْرُكِ ٱلْبَحْرَ رَهْوًا ۖ إِنَّهُمْ جُندٌ مُّغْرَقُونَ ﴿٢٤﴾

24. And leave the sea as a furrow (divided). For they are a host (destined) to be drowned."

25. How many were the gardens and springs they left behind,

كَمْ تَرَكُوا۟ مِن جَنَّـٰتٍ وَعُيُونٍ ﴿٢٥﴾

26. And cornfields and noble buildings,

وَزُرُوعٍ وَمَقَامٍ كَرِيمٍ ﴿٢٦﴾

27. And wealth (and conveniences of life) in which they had taken such delight!

وَنَعْمَةٍ كَانُوا۟ فِيهَا فَـٰكِهِينَ ﴿٢٧﴾

28. Thus (was their end)! And We made other people inherit (those things)!

كَذَٰلِكَ ۖ وَأَوْرَثْنَـٰهَا قَوْمًا ءَاخَرِينَ ﴿٢٨﴾

29. And neither heaven nor earth shed a tear over them: nor were they given a respite (again).

فَمَا بَكَتْ عَلَيْهِمُ ٱلسَّمَآءُ وَٱلْأَرْضُ وَمَا كَانُوا۟
مُنظَرِينَ ﴿٢٩﴾

30. We did deliver before the Children of Israel from humiliating punishment,

وَلَقَدْ نَجَّيْنَا بَنِىٓ إِسْرَٰٓءِيلَ مِنَ ٱلْعَذَابِ ٱلْمُهِينِ ﴿٣٠﴾

31. Inflicted by Pharaoh, for he was arrogant (even) among inordinate transgressors.

مِن فِرْعَوْنَ ۚ إِنَّهُۥ كَانَ عَالِيًا مِّنَ ٱلْمُسْرِفِينَ ﴿٣١﴾

32. And We chose them before above the nations knowingly,

وَلَقَدِ ٱخْتَرْنَـٰهُمْ عَلَىٰ عِلْمٍ عَلَى ٱلْعَـٰلَمِينَ ﴿٣٢﴾

33. And granted them signs in which there was a manifest trial.

وَءَاتَيْنَـٰهُم مِّنَ ٱلْـَٔايَـٰتِ مَا فِيهِ بَلَـٰٓؤٌا۟ مُّبِينٌ ﴿٣٣﴾

34. As to these (Quraysh) they say:

إِنَّ هَـٰٓؤُلَآءِ لَيَقُولُونَ ﴿٣٤﴾

35. "There is nothing beyond our first death and we shall not be raised again.

إِنْ هِىَ إِلَّا مَوْتَتُنَا ٱلْأُولَىٰ وَمَا نَحْنُ بِمُنشَرِينَ ﴿٣٥﴾

36. Then bring (back) our forefathers, if what you say is true!"

فَأْتُوا۟ بِـَٔابَآئِنَآ إِن كُنتُمْ صَـٰدِقِينَ ﴿٣٦﴾

37. What! Are they better than the people of Tubba and those who were before them? We destroyed them because they were guilty of sin.

أَهُمْ خَيْرٌ أَمْ قَوْمُ تُبَّعٍ وَٱلَّذِينَ مِن قَبْلِهِمْ أَهْلَكْنَـٰهُمْ ۖ
إِنَّهُمْ كَانُوا۟ مُجْرِمِينَ ﴿٣٧﴾

38. We created not the heavens, the earth, and all between them merely in (idle) sport:

وَمَا خَلَقْنَا ٱلسَّمَٰوَٰتِ وَٱلْأَرْضَ وَمَا بَيْنَهُمَا لَٰعِبِينَ ﴿٣٨﴾

39. We created them not except for just ends: but most of them do not understand.

مَا خَلَقْنَٰهُمَآ إِلَّا بِٱلْحَقِّ وَلَٰكِنَّ أَكْثَرَهُمْ لَا
يَعْلَمُونَ ﴿٣٩﴾

40. Verily the day of sorting out is the time appointed for all of them -

إِنَّ يَوْمَ ٱلْفَصْلِ مِيقَٰتُهُمْ أَجْمَعِينَ ﴿٤٠﴾

41. The day when no protector can benefit his client in anything, and no help can they receive.

يَوْمَ لَا يُغْنِى مَوْلًى عَن مَّوْلًى شَيْـًٔا وَلَا هُمْ
يُنصَرُونَ ﴿٤١﴾

42. Except such as receive Allah's mercy: for He is Exalted in Might, Most Merciful.

إِلَّا مَن رَّحِمَ ٱللَّهُ ۚ إِنَّهُۥ هُوَ ٱلْعَزِيزُ ٱلرَّحِيمُ ﴿٤٢﴾

43. Verily the tree of Zaqqum

إِنَّ شَجَرَتَ ٱلزَّقُّومِ ﴿٤٣﴾

44. Will be the food of the sinful -

طَعَامُ ٱلْأَثِيمِ ﴿٤٤﴾

45. Like molten brass; it will boil in their insides,

كَٱلْمُهْلِ يَغْلِى فِى ٱلْبُطُونِ ﴿٤٥﴾

46. Like the boiling of scalding water.

كَغَلْىِ ٱلْحَمِيمِ ﴿٤٦﴾

47. (A voice will call:) "Seize you him and drag him into the midst of the blazing fire!

خُذُوهُ فَٱعْتِلُوهُ إِلَىٰ سَوَآءِ ٱلْجَحِيمِ ﴿٤٧﴾

48. Then pour over his head the penalty of boiling water;

ثُمَّ صُبُّوا۟ فَوْقَ رَأْسِهِۦ مِنْ عَذَابِ ٱلْحَمِيمِ ﴿٤٨﴾

49. Taste you (this)! Truly were you mighty, full of honour!

ذُقْ إِنَّكَ أَنتَ ٱلْعَزِيزُ ٱلْكَرِيمُ ﴿٤٩﴾

50. Truly this is what you used to doubt!"

إِنَّ هَٰذَا مَا كُنتُم بِهِۦ تَمْتَرُونَ ﴿٥٠﴾

51. As to the righteous (they will be) in a position of security,

إِنَّ ٱلْمُتَّقِينَ فِى مَقَامٍ أَمِينٍ ﴿٥١﴾

52. Among gardens and springs;

فِي جَنَّٰتٖ وَعُيُونٖ ٥٢

53. Dressed in fine silk and in rich brocade, they will face each other;

يَلۡبَسُونَ مِن سُندُسٖ وَإِسۡتَبۡرَقٖ
مُّتَقَٰبِلِينَ ٥٣

54. Moreover, We shall join them to companions with beautiful, big, and lustrous eyes.

كَذَٰلِكَ وَزَوَّجۡنَٰهُم بِحُورٍ عِينٖ ٥٤

55. There can they call for every kind of fruit in peace and security;

يَدۡعُونَ فِيهَا بِكُلِّ فَٰكِهَةٍ ءَامِنِينَ ٥٥

56. Nor will they there taste death, except the first death; and He will preserve them from the penalty of the blazing fire -

لَا يَذُوقُونَ فِيهَا ٱلۡمَوۡتَ إِلَّا ٱلۡمَوۡتَةَ ٱلۡأُولَىٰۖ
وَوَقَىٰهُمۡ عَذَابَ ٱلۡجَحِيمِ ٥٦

57. As a bounty from your Lord! That will be the supreme achievement!

فَضۡلٗا مِّن رَّبِّكَۚ ذَٰلِكَ هُوَ ٱلۡفَوۡزُ ٱلۡعَظِيمُ ٥٧

58. Verily, We have made this (Qur'an) easy, in your tongue, in order that they may give heed.

فَإِنَّمَا يَسَّرۡنَٰهُ بِلِسَانِكَ لَعَلَّهُمۡ يَتَذَكَّرُونَ ٥٨

59. So wait you and watch; for they (too) are waiting.

فَٱرۡتَقِبۡ إِنَّهُم مُّرۡتَقِبُونَ ٥٩

سُورَةُ الجَاثِيَة

Surah 45: ***Al-Jathiyah*** **(The Kneeling Down)**

In the name of Allah,
Most Gracious, Most Merciful.

بِسۡمِ ٱللَّهِ ٱلرَّحۡمَٰنِ ٱلرَّحِيمِ

1. *Ha Mim.*

حمٓ ١

2. The revelation of the book is from Allah the Exalted in power, Full of wisdom.

تَنزِيلُ ٱلۡكِتَٰبِ مِنَ ٱللَّهِ ٱلۡعَزِيزِ ٱلۡحَكِيمِ ٢

3. Verily in the heavens and the earth, are signs for those who believe.

إِنَّ فِي ٱلسَّمَٰوَٰتِ وَٱلۡأَرۡضِ لَأٓيَٰتٖ لِّلۡمُؤۡمِنِينَ ٣

4. And in the creation of yourselves and the fact that animals are scattered (through the earth), are signs for those of assured faith.

وَفِي خَلۡقِكُمۡ وَمَا يَبُثُّ مِن دَآبَّةٍ ءَايَٰتٞ لِّقَوۡمٖ يُوقِنُونَ ٤

5. And in the alternation of night and day, and the fact that Allah sends down sustenance from the sky, and revives with it the earth after its death, and the change of the winds - are signs for those that are wise.

وَٱخۡتِلَٰفِ ٱلَّيۡلِ وَٱلنَّهَارِ وَمَآ أَنزَلَ ٱللَّهُ مِنَ ٱلسَّمَآءِ مِن
رِّزۡقٖ فَأَحۡيَا بِهِ ٱلۡأَرۡضَ بَعۡدَ مَوۡتِهَا وَتَصۡرِيفِ ٱلرِّيَٰحِ
ءَايَٰتٞ لِّقَوۡمٖ يَعۡقِلُونَ ٥

6. Such are the signs of Allah, which We rehearse to you in truth: then in what exposition will they believe after (rejecting) Allah and His signs?

تِلۡكَ ءَايَٰتُ ٱللَّهِ نَتۡلُوهَا عَلَيۡكَ بِٱلۡحَقِّۖ فَبِأَيِّ حَدِيثِۭ بَعۡدَ
ٱللَّهِ وَءَايَٰتِهِۦ يُؤۡمِنُونَ ٦

7. Woe to each sinful dealer in falsehoods:

وَيۡلٞ لِّكُلِّ أَفَّاكٍ أَثِيمٖ ٧

8. He hears the signs of Allah rehearsed to him, yet is obstinate and lofty, as if he had not heard them: then announce to him a penalty grievous!

يَسۡمَعُ ءَايَٰتِ ٱللَّهِ تُتۡلَىٰ عَلَيۡهِ ثُمَّ يُصِرُّ مُسۡتَكۡبِرٗا كَأَن لَّمۡ
يَسۡمَعۡهَاۖ فَبَشِّرۡهُ بِعَذَابٍ أَلِيمٖ ٨

9. And when he learns something of Our signs, he takes them in jest: for such there will be a humiliating penalty.

وَإِذَا عَلِمَ مِنۡ ءَايَٰتِنَا شَيۡـًٔا ٱتَّخَذَهَا هُزُوًاۚ أُوْلَٰٓئِكَ لَهُمۡ
عَذَابٞ مُّهِينٞ ٩

10. In front of them is hell; and of no profit to them is anything they may have earned, nor any protectors they may have taken to themselves besides Allah; for them is a tremendous penalty.

مِّن وَرَآئِهِمۡ جَهَنَّمُۖ وَلَا يُغۡنِي عَنۡهُم مَّا كَسَبُواْ
شَيۡـٔٗا وَلَا مَا ٱتَّخَذُواْ مِن دُونِ ٱللَّهِ أَوۡلِيَآءَۖ
وَلَهُمۡ عَذَابٌ عَظِيمٌ ١٠

11. This is (true) guidance: and for those who reject the signs of their Lord, is a grievous penalty of abomination.

هَٰذَا هُدٗىۖ وَٱلَّذِينَ كَفَرُواْ بِـَٔايَٰتِ رَبِّهِمۡ لَهُمۡ عَذَابٞ
مِّن رِّجۡزٍ أَلِيمٌ ١١

ثلاثة أرباع الحزب ٥٠

12. It is Allah Who has subjected the sea to you, that ships may sail through it by His command, that you may seek of His bounty, and that you may be grateful.

۞ ٱللَّهُ ٱلَّذِى سَخَّرَ لَكُمُ ٱلْبَحْرَ لِتَجْرِىَ ٱلْفُلْكُ فِيهِ بِأَمْرِهِۦ
وَلِتَبْتَغُوا۟ مِن فَضْلِهِۦ وَلَعَلَّكُمْ تَشْكُرُونَ ١٢

13. And He has subjected to you, as from Him, all that is in the heavens and on earth: see in that are signs indeed for those who reflect.

وَسَخَّرَ لَكُم مَّا فِى ٱلسَّمَٰوَٰتِ وَمَا فِى ٱلْأَرْضِ جَمِيعًا مِّنْهُ ۚ
إِنَّ فِى ذَٰلِكَ لَءَايَٰتٍ لِّقَوْمٍ يَتَفَكَّرُونَ ١٣

14. Tell those who believe to forgive those who do not look forward to the days of Allah: it is for Him to recompense (for good or ill) each people according to what they have earned.

قُل لِّلَّذِينَ ءَامَنُوا۟ يَغْفِرُوا۟ لِلَّذِينَ لَا يَرْجُونَ أَيَّامَ
ٱللَّهِ لِيَجْزِىَ قَوْمًۢا بِمَا كَانُوا۟ يَكْسِبُونَ ١٤

15. If anyone does a righteous deed, it enures to the benefit of his own soul; if he does evil, it works against (His own soul). In the end will you (all) be brought back to your Lord.

مَنْ عَمِلَ صَٰلِحًا فَلِنَفْسِهِۦ ۖ وَمَنْ أَسَآءَ فَعَلَيْهَا ۖ
ثُمَّ إِلَىٰ رَبِّكُمْ تُرْجَعُونَ ١٥

16. We did before grant to the Children of Israel the book, the power of command and prophethood; We gave them, for sustenance, things good and pure; and We favoured them above the nations.

وَلَقَدْ ءَاتَيْنَا بَنِىٓ إِسْرَٰٓءِيلَ ٱلْكِتَٰبَ وَٱلْحُكْمَ وَٱلنُّبُوَّةَ
وَرَزَقْنَٰهُم مِّنَ ٱلطَّيِّبَٰتِ وَفَضَّلْنَٰهُمْ عَلَى ٱلْعَٰلَمِينَ ١٦

17. And We granted them clear signs in affairs (of religion); it was only after knowledge had been granted to them that they fell into schisms, through insolent envy among themselves. Verily your Lord will judge between them on the day of judgement as to those matters in which they set up differences.

وَءَاتَيْنَٰهُم بَيِّنَٰتٍ مِّنَ ٱلْأَمْرِ ۖ فَمَا ٱخْتَلَفُوٓا۟ إِلَّا مِنۢ
بَعْدِ مَا جَآءَهُمُ ٱلْعِلْمُ بَغْيًۢا بَيْنَهُمْ ۚ إِنَّ رَبَّكَ يَقْضِى
بَيْنَهُمْ يَوْمَ ٱلْقِيَٰمَةِ فِيمَا كَانُوا۟ فِيهِ يَخْتَلِفُونَ ١٧

18. Then We put you on the (right) way of religion: so follow you that (way), and follow not the desires of those who know not.

ثُمَّ جَعَلْنَٰكَ عَلَىٰ شَرِيعَةٍ مِّنَ ٱلْأَمْرِ فَٱتَّبِعْهَا
وَلَا تَتَّبِعْ أَهْوَآءَ ٱلَّذِينَ لَا يَعْلَمُونَ ١٨

19. They will be of no use to you in the sight of Allah; it is only wrongdoers (that stand as) protectors, one to another; but Allah is the protector of the righteous.

إِنَّهُمْ لَن يُغْنُوا۟ عَنكَ مِنَ ٱللَّهِ شَيْـًٔا ۚ وَإِنَّ ٱلظَّـٰلِمِينَ
بَعْضُهُمْ أَوْلِيَآءُ بَعْضٍ ۖ وَٱللَّهُ وَلِىُّ ٱلْمُتَّقِينَ ﴿١٩﴾

20. These are clear evidences to men, and a guidance and mercy to those of assured faith.

هَـٰذَا بَصَـٰٓئِرُ لِلنَّاسِ وَهُدًى وَرَحْمَةٌ لِّقَوْمٍ
يُوقِنُونَ ﴿٢٠﴾

21. What! Do those who seek after evil ways think that We shall hold them equal with those who believe and do righteous deeds - that equal will be their life and their death? Ill is the judgement that they make.

أَمْ حَسِبَ ٱلَّذِينَ ٱجْتَرَحُوا۟ ٱلسَّيِّـَٔاتِ أَن نَّجْعَلَهُمْ
كَٱلَّذِينَ ءَامَنُوا۟ وَعَمِلُوا۟ ٱلصَّـٰلِحَـٰتِ سَوَآءً
مَّحْيَاهُمْ وَمَمَاتُهُمْ ۚ سَآءَ مَا يَحْكُمُونَ ﴿٢١﴾

22. Allah created the heavens and the earth for just ends and in order that each soul may find the recompense of what it has earned, and none of them be wronged.

وَخَلَقَ ٱللَّهُ ٱلسَّمَـٰوَٰتِ وَٱلْأَرْضَ بِٱلْحَقِّ وَلِتُجْزَىٰ
كُلُّ نَفْسٍۭ بِمَا كَسَبَتْ وَهُمْ لَا يُظْلَمُونَ ﴿٢٢﴾

23. Then do you see such a one as takes, as his god, his own vain desire? Allah has, knowing (him as such), left him astray, and sealed his hearing and his heart (and understanding) and put a cover on his sight. Who, then, will guide him after Allah (has withdrawn guidance)? ill you not then receive admonition?

أَفَرَءَيْتَ مَنِ ٱتَّخَذَ إِلَـٰهَهُۥ هَوَىٰهُ وَأَضَلَّهُ ٱللَّهُ عَلَىٰ عِلْمٍ وَخَتَمَ
عَلَىٰ سَمْعِهِۦ وَقَلْبِهِۦ وَجَعَلَ عَلَىٰ بَصَرِهِۦ غِشَـٰوَةً فَمَن
يَهْدِيهِ مِنۢ بَعْدِ ٱللَّهِ ۚ أَفَلَا تَذَكَّرُونَ ﴿٢٣﴾

24. And they say: "What is there but our life in this world? We shall die and we live, and nothing but time can destroy us." But of that they have no knowledge: they merely conjecture:

وَقَالُوا۟ مَا هِىَ إِلَّا حَيَاتُنَا ٱلدُّنْيَا نَمُوتُ وَنَحْيَا وَمَا يُهْلِكُنَآ
إِلَّا ٱلدَّهْرُ ۚ وَمَا لَهُم بِذَٰلِكَ مِنْ عِلْمٍ ۖ إِنْ هُمْ إِلَّا يَظُنُّونَ ﴿٢٤﴾

25. And when Our clear signs are rehearsed to them, their argument is nothing but this: they say, "Bring (back) our forefathers, if what you say is true!"

وَإِذَا تُتْلَىٰ عَلَيْهِمْ ءَايَـٰتُنَا بَيِّنَـٰتٍ مَّا كَانَ حُجَّتَهُمْ إِلَّآ أَن
قَالُوا۟ ٱئْتُوا۟ بِـَٔابَآئِنَآ إِن كُنتُمْ صَـٰدِقِينَ ﴿٢٥﴾

26. Say: "It is Allah Who gives you life, then gives you death; then He will gather you together for the day of judgement about which there is no doubt": but most men do not understand.

قُلِ ٱللَّهُ يُحْيِيكُمْ ثُمَّ يُمِيتُكُمْ ثُمَّ يَجْمَعُكُمْ إِلَىٰ يَوْمِ ٱلْقِيَٰمَةِ
لَا رَيْبَ فِيهِ وَلَٰكِنَّ أَكْثَرَ ٱلنَّاسِ لَا يَعْلَمُونَ ﴿٢٦﴾

27. To Allah belongs the dominion of the heavens and the earth, and the day that the hour of judgement is established - that day will the dealers in falsehood perish!

وَلِلَّهِ مُلْكُ ٱلسَّمَٰوَٰتِ وَٱلْأَرْضِ ۚ وَيَوْمَ تَقُومُ ٱلسَّاعَةُ
يَوْمَئِذٍ يَخْسَرُ ٱلْمُبْطِلُونَ ﴿٢٧﴾

28. And you will see every sect bowing the knee: every sect will be called to its record: "This day shall you be recompensed for all that you did!

وَتَرَىٰ كُلَّ أُمَّةٍ جَاثِيَةً ۚ كُلُّ أُمَّةٍ تُدْعَىٰٓ إِلَىٰ كِتَٰبِهَا ٱلْيَوْمَ
تُجْزَوْنَ مَا كُنتُمْ تَعْمَلُونَ ﴿٢٨﴾

29. "This Our record speaks about you with truth: for We used to put on record all that you did."

هَٰذَا كِتَٰبُنَا يَنطِقُ عَلَيْكُم بِٱلْحَقِّ ۚ إِنَّا كُنَّا نَسْتَنسِخُ
مَا كُنتُمْ تَعْمَلُونَ ﴿٢٩﴾

30. Then, as to those who believed and did righteous deeds, their Lord will admit them to His mercy: that will be the achievement for all to see.

فَأَمَّا ٱلَّذِينَ ءَامَنُوا۟ وَعَمِلُوا۟ ٱلصَّٰلِحَٰتِ فَيُدْخِلُهُمْ
رَبُّهُمْ فِى رَحْمَتِهِۦ ۚ ذَٰلِكَ هُوَ ٱلْفَوْزُ ٱلْمُبِينُ ﴿٣٠﴾

31. But as to those who reject Allah, (to them will be said): "Were not Our signs rehearsed to you? But you were arrogant, and were a people given to sin!

وَأَمَّا ٱلَّذِينَ كَفَرُوٓا۟ أَفَلَمْ تَكُنْ ءَايَٰتِى تُتْلَىٰ عَلَيْكُمْ فَٱسْتَكْبَرْتُمْ
وَكُنتُمْ قَوْمًا مُّجْرِمِينَ ﴿٣١﴾

32. And when it was said that the promise of Allah was true, and that the hour - there was no doubt about its (coming), you used to say, 'We know not what is the hour: we only think it is an idea, and we have no firm assurance.'"

وَإِذَا قِيلَ إِنَّ وَعْدَ ٱللَّهِ حَقٌّ وَٱلسَّاعَةُ لَا رَيْبَ فِيهَا
قُلْتُم مَّا نَدْرِى مَا ٱلسَّاعَةُ إِن نَّظُنُّ إِلَّا ظَنًّا وَمَا نَحْنُ
بِمُسْتَيْقِنِينَ ﴿٣٢﴾

33. Then will appear to them the evil (fruits) of what they did, and they will be completely encircled by that which they used to mock at!

وَبَدَا لَهُمْ سَيِّـَٔاتُ مَا عَمِلُوا۟ وَحَاقَ بِهِم مَّا كَانُوا۟ بِهِۦ
يَسْتَهْزِءُونَ ﴿٣٣﴾

34. It will also be said: "This day We will forget you as you forgot the meeting of this day of yours! And your abode is the fire, and no helpers have you!

وَقِيلَ ٱلْيَوْمَ نَنسَىٰكُمْ كَمَا نَسِيتُمْ لِقَآءَ يَوْمِكُمْ هَٰذَا وَ
مَأْوَىٰكُمُ ٱلنَّارُ وَمَا لَكُم مِّن نَّٰصِرِينَ ٣٤

35. This, because you used to take the signs of Allah in jest, and the life of the world deceived you." (From) the day, therefore, they shall not be taken out from there, nor shall they be received into grace.

ذَٰلِكُم بِأَنَّكُمُ ٱتَّخَذْتُمْ ءَايَٰتِ ٱللَّهِ هُزُوًا وَغَرَّتْكُمُ
ٱلْحَيَوٰةُ ٱلدُّنْيَا ۚ فَٱلْيَوْمَ لَا يُخْرَجُونَ مِنْهَا وَلَا هُمْ
يُسْتَعْتَبُونَ ٣٥

36. Then praise be to Allah Lord of the heavens and Lord of the earth - Lord and Cherisher of all the Worlds!

فَلِلَّهِ ٱلْحَمْدُ رَبِّ ٱلسَّمَٰوَٰتِ وَرَبِّ ٱلْأَرْضِ
رَبِّ ٱلْعَٰلَمِينَ ٣٦

37. To Him be glory throughout the heavens and the earth: and He is Exalted in Power, Full of Wisdom!

وَلَهُ ٱلْكِبْرِيَآءُ فِى ٱلسَّمَٰوَٰتِ وَٱلْأَرْضِ ۖ وَهُوَ
ٱلْعَزِيزُ ٱلْحَكِيمُ ٣٧

سُورَةُ الأَحْقَافِ

Surah 46: ***Al-Ahqaf*** **(The Winding Sand-Tracts)**

In the name of Allah,
Most Gracious, Most Merciful.

بِسْمِ ٱللَّهِ ٱلرَّحْمَٰنِ ٱلرَّحِيمِ

✼ **1.** *Ha Mim.*

حمٓ ١

الجزء ٢٦ الحزب ٥١

2. The revelation of the book is from Allah the Exalted in Power, Full of Wisdom.

تَنزِيلُ ٱلْكِتَٰبِ مِنَ ٱللَّهِ ٱلْعَزِيزِ ٱلْحَكِيمِ ٢

3. We created not the heavens and the earth and all between them but for just ends, and for a term appointed: but those who reject faith turn away from that of which they are warned.

مَا خَلَقْنَا ٱلسَّمَٰوَٰتِ وَٱلْأَرْضَ وَمَا بَيْنَهُمَآ إِلَّا بِٱلْحَقِّ
وَأَجَلٍ مُّسَمًّى ۚ وَٱلَّذِينَ كَفَرُوا۟ عَمَّآ أُنذِرُوا۟ مُعْرِضُونَ ٣

4. Say: "Do you see what it is you invoke besides Allah? Show me what it is they have

قُلْ أَرَءَيْتُم مَّا تَدْعُونَ مِن دُونِ ٱللَّهِ أَرُونِى مَاذَا

✼ Part-26

created on earth, or have they a share in the heavens? Bring me a book (revealed) before this, or any remnant of knowledge (you may have), if you are telling the truth!"

خَلَقُوا۟ مِنَ ٱلْأَرْضِ أَمْ لَهُمْ شِرْكٌ فِى ٱلسَّمَٰوَٰتِ ۖ
ٱئْتُونِى بِكِتَٰبٍ مِّن قَبْلِ هَٰذَآ أَوْ أَثَٰرَةٍ مِّنْ عِلْمٍ إِن كُنتُمْ
صَٰدِقِينَ ﴿٤﴾

5. And who is more astray than one who invokes, besides Allah, such as will not answer him to the day of judgement, and who (in fact) are unconscious of their call (to them)?

وَمَنْ أَضَلُّ مِمَّن يَدْعُوا۟ مِن دُونِ ٱللَّهِ مَن
لَّا يَسْتَجِيبُ لَهُۥٓ إِلَىٰ يَوْمِ ٱلْقِيَٰمَةِ وَهُمْ عَن دُعَآئِهِمْ
غَٰفِلُونَ ﴿٥﴾

6. And when mankind are gathered together (at the resurrection), they will be hostile to them and reject their worship (altogether)!

وَإِذَا حُشِرَ ٱلنَّاسُ كَانُوا۟ لَهُمْ أَعْدَآءً وَكَانُوا۟ بِعِبَادَتِهِمْ
كَٰفِرِينَ ﴿٦﴾

7. When Our clear signs are rehearsed to them, the unbelievers say, of the truth when it comes to them: "This is evident sorcery!"

وَإِذَا تُتْلَىٰ عَلَيْهِمْ ءَايَٰتُنَا بَيِّنَٰتٍ قَالَ ٱلَّذِينَ كَفَرُوا۟ لِلْحَقِّ
لَمَّا جَآءَهُمْ هَٰذَا سِحْرٌ مُّبِينٌ ﴿٧﴾

8. Or do they say, "He has forged it"? Say: "Had I forged it, then can you obtain no single (blessing) for me from Allah. He knows best of that of which you talk (so glibly)! Enough is He for a witness between me and you! And He is Oft-Forgiving, Most Merciful."

أَمْ يَقُولُونَ ٱفْتَرَىٰهُ ۖ قُلْ إِنِ ٱفْتَرَيْتُهُۥ فَلَا تَمْلِكُونَ لِى مِنَ
ٱللَّهِ شَيْـًٔا ۖ هُوَ أَعْلَمُ بِمَا تُفِيضُونَ فِيهِ ۖ كَفَىٰ بِهِۦ شَهِيدًۢا
بَيْنِى وَبَيْنَكُمْ ۖ وَهُوَ ٱلْغَفُورُ ٱلرَّحِيمُ ﴿٨﴾

9. Say: "I am no bringer of new-fangled doctrine among the messengers, nor do I know what will be done with me or with you. I follow but that which is revealed to me by inspiration: I am but a warner, open and clear."

قُلْ مَا كُنتُ بِدْعًا مِّنَ ٱلرُّسُلِ وَمَآ أَدْرِى مَا يُفْعَلُ بِى
وَلَا بِكُمْ ۖ إِنْ أَتَّبِعُ إِلَّا مَا يُوحَىٰٓ إِلَىَّ وَمَآ أَنَا۠ إِلَّا
نَذِيرٌ مُّبِينٌ ﴿٩﴾

10. Say: "Do you see? If (this teaching) be from Allah, and you reject it and a witness from among the Children of Israel testifies to its similarity (with earlier scriptures),

قُلْ أَرَءَيْتُمْ إِن كَانَ مِنْ عِندِ ٱللَّهِ وَكَفَرْتُم بِهِۦ وَشَهِدَ
شَاهِدٌ مِّنۢ بَنِىٓ إِسْرَٰٓءِيلَ عَلَىٰ مِثْلِهِۦ فَـَٔامَنَ وَٱسْتَكْبَرْتُمْ

إِنَّ ٱللَّهَ لَا يَهۡدِي ٱلۡقَوۡمَ ٱلظَّٰلِمِينَ ١٠

and has believed while you are arrogant, (how unjust you are!) Truly Allah guides not a people unjust."

وَقَالَ ٱلَّذِينَ كَفَرُواْ لِلَّذِينَ ءَامَنُواْ لَوۡ كَانَ خَيۡرٗا
مَّا سَبَقُونَآ إِلَيۡهِۚ وَإِذۡ لَمۡ يَهۡتَدُواْ بِهِۦ فَسَيَقُولُونَ هَٰذَآ
إِفۡكٞ قَدِيمٞ ١١

11. The unbelievers say of those who believe: "If (this message) were a good thing, (such men) would not have gone to it first, before us!" And seeing that they guide not themselves thereby, they will say, "This is an (old) old falsehood!"

وَمِن قَبۡلِهِۦ كِتَٰبُ مُوسَىٰٓ إِمَامٗا وَرَحۡمَةٗۚ وَهَٰذَا
كِتَٰبٞ مُّصَدِّقٞ لِّسَانًا عَرَبِيّٗا لِّيُنذِرَ ٱلَّذِينَ ظَلَمُواْ
وَبُشۡرَىٰ لِلۡمُحۡسِنِينَ ١٢

12. And before this, was the book of Moses as a guide and a mercy; and this book confirms (it) in the Arabic tongue; to admonish the unjust, and as glad tidings to those who do right.

إِنَّ ٱلَّذِينَ قَالُواْ رَبُّنَا ٱللَّهُ ثُمَّ ٱسۡتَقَٰمُواْ فَلَا خَوۡفٌ
عَلَيۡهِمۡ وَلَا هُمۡ يَحۡزَنُونَ ١٣

13. Verily those who say, "Our Lord is Allah," and remain firm (on that path) - on them shall be no fear, nor shall they grieve.

أُوْلَٰٓئِكَ أَصۡحَٰبُ ٱلۡجَنَّةِ خَٰلِدِينَ فِيهَا جَزَآءَۢ بِمَا كَانُواْ
يَعۡمَلُونَ ١٤

14. Such shall be companions of the garden, dwelling in it (for ever): a recompense for their (good) deeds.

وَوَصَّيۡنَا ٱلۡإِنسَٰنَ بِوَٰلِدَيۡهِ إِحۡسَٰنًاۖ حَمَلَتۡهُ أُمُّهُۥ
كُرۡهٗا وَوَضَعَتۡهُ كُرۡهٗاۖ وَحَمۡلُهُۥ وَفِصَٰلُهُۥ ثَلَٰثُونَ شَهۡرًاۚ
حَتَّىٰٓ إِذَا بَلَغَ أَشُدَّهُۥ وَبَلَغَ أَرۡبَعِينَ سَنَةٗ قَالَ رَبِّ
أَوۡزِعۡنِيٓ أَنۡ أَشۡكُرَ نِعۡمَتَكَ ٱلَّتِيٓ أَنۡعَمۡتَ عَلَيَّ وَعَلَىٰ
وَٰلِدَيَّ وَأَنۡ أَعۡمَلَ صَٰلِحٗا تَرۡضَىٰهُ وَأَصۡلِحۡ لِي فِي ذُرِّيَّتِيٓۖ
إِنِّي تُبۡتُ إِلَيۡكَ وَإِنِّي مِنَ ٱلۡمُسۡلِمِينَ ١٥

15. We have enjoined on man kindness to his parents: in pain did his mother bear him, and in pain did she give him birth. The carrying of the (child) to his weaning is (a period of) thirty months. At length when he reaches the age of full strength and attains forty years, he says, "O my Lord! Grant me that I may be grateful for Your favour which You have bestowed upon me, and upon both my parents, and that I may work righteousness such as You may approve; and be gracious to me in my issue. Truly have I turned to You and truly do I bow (to You) in Islam."

16. Such are they from whom We shall accept the best of their deeds and pass by their ill deeds; (they shall be) among the companions of the garden: a promise of truth, which was made to them (in this life).

أُوْلَٰٓئِكَ ٱلَّذِينَ نَتَقَبَّلُ عَنْهُمْ أَحْسَنَ مَا عَمِلُواْ
وَنَتَجَاوَزُ عَن سَيِّـَٔاتِهِمْ فِيٓ أَصْحَٰبِ ٱلْجَنَّةِۖ وَعْدَ
ٱلصِّدْقِ ٱلَّذِي كَانُواْ يُوعَدُونَ ١٦

17. But (there is one) who says to his parents, "Fie on you! Do you hold out the promise to me that I shall be raised up, even though generations have passed before me (without rising again)?" And they two seek Allah's aid (and rebuke the son): "Woe to you! Have faith! For the promise of Allah is true." But he says, "This is nothing but tales of the ancients!"

وَٱلَّذِي قَالَ لِوَٰلِدَيْهِ أُفّٖ لَّكُمَآ أَتَعِدَانِنِيٓ أَنْ أُخْرَجَ
وَقَدْ خَلَتِ ٱلْقُرُونُ مِن قَبْلِي وَهُمَا يَسْتَغِيثَانِ ٱللَّهَ
وَيْلَكَ ءَامِنْ إِنَّ وَعْدَ ٱللَّهِ حَقّٞ فَيَقُولُ مَا هَٰذَآ إِلَّآ
أَسَٰطِيرُ ٱلْأَوَّلِينَ ١٧

18. Such are they against whom is proved the sentence among the previous generations of Jinns and men, that have passed away; for they will be (utterly) lost.

أُوْلَٰٓئِكَ ٱلَّذِينَ حَقَّ عَلَيْهِمُ ٱلْقَوْلُ فِيٓ أُمَمٖ قَدْ خَلَتْ مِن
قَبْلِهِم مِّنَ ٱلْجِنِّ وَٱلْإِنسِۖ إِنَّهُمْ كَانُواْ خَٰسِرِينَ ١٨

19. And to all are (assigned) degrees according to the deeds which they (have done), and in order that (Allah) may recompense their deeds, and no injustice be done to them.

وَلِكُلّٖ دَرَجَٰتٞ مِّمَّا عَمِلُواْۖ وَلِيُوَفِّيَهُمْ أَعْمَٰلَهُمْ وَهُمْ
لَا يُظْلَمُونَ ١٩

20. And on the day that the unbelievers will be placed before the fire, (it will be said to them): "You received your good things in the life of the world, and you took your pleasure out of them; but today shall you be recompensed with a penalty of humiliation; for that you were arrogant on earth without just cause, and that you (ever) transgressed."

وَيَوْمَ يُعْرَضُ ٱلَّذِينَ كَفَرُواْ عَلَى ٱلنَّارِ أَذْهَبْتُمْ طَيِّبَٰتِكُمْ فِي
حَيَاتِكُمُ ٱلدُّنْيَا وَٱسْتَمْتَعْتُم بِهَا فَٱلْيَوْمَ تُجْزَوْنَ عَذَابَ
ٱلْهُونِ بِمَا كُنتُمْ تَسْتَكْبِرُونَ فِي ٱلْأَرْضِ بِغَيْرِ ٱلْحَقِّ
وَبِمَا كُنتُمْ تَفْسُقُونَ ٢٠

21. Mention (Hud) one of 'Ad's (own) brothers: behold, he warned his people about the winding sand-tracts; but there have been warners before him and after him: "Worship you none other than Allah; truly I fear for you the penalty of a mighty day."

۞ وَٱذْكُرْ أَخَا عَادٍ إِذْ أَنذَرَ قَوْمَهُۥ بِٱلْأَحْقَافِ وَقَدْ ربع الحزب ٥١
خَلَتِ ٱلنُّذُرُ مِنۢ بَيْنِ يَدَيْهِ وَمِنْ خَلْفِهِۦٓ أَلَّا تَعْبُدُوٓاْ
إِلَّا ٱللَّهَ إِنِّيٓ أَخَافُ عَلَيْكُمْ عَذَابَ يَوْمٍ عَظِيمٖ ٢١

22. They said: "Have you come in order to turn us aside from our gods? Then bring upon us the (calamity) with which you do threaten us, if you are telling the truth!"

قَالُوٓا۟ أَجِئْتَنَا لِتَأْفِكَنَا عَنْ ءَالِهَتِنَا فَأْتِنَا بِمَا تَعِدُنَآ
إِن كُنتَ مِنَ ٱلصَّـٰدِقِينَ ﴿٢٢﴾

23. He said: "The knowledge (of when it will come) is only with Allah: I proclaim to you the mission on which I have been sent: but I see that you are a people in ignorance!"

قَالَ إِنَّمَا ٱلْعِلْمُ عِندَ ٱللَّهِ وَأُبَلِّغُكُم مَّآ أُرْسِلْتُ بِهِۦ
وَلَـٰكِنِّىٓ أَرَىٰكُمْ قَوْمًا تَجْهَلُونَ ﴿٢٣﴾

24. Then when they saw the (penalty in the shape of) a cloud traversing the sky coming to meet their valleys, they said, "This cloud will give us rain!" "Nay, it is the (calamity) you were asking to be hastened! - A wind in which is a grievous penalty!

فَلَمَّا رَأَوْهُ عَارِضًا مُّسْتَقْبِلَ أَوْدِيَتِهِمْ قَالُوا۟ هَـٰذَا
عَارِضٌ مُّمْطِرُنَا ۚ بَلْ هُوَ مَا ٱسْتَعْجَلْتُم بِهِۦ ۖ رِيحٌ فِيهَا
عَذَابٌ أَلِيمٌ ﴿٢٤﴾

25. Everything will it destroy by the command of its Lord!" Then by the morning they - nothing was to be seen but (the ruins of) their houses! Thus do We recompense those given to sin!

تُدَمِّرُ كُلَّ شَىْءٍۭ بِأَمْرِ رَبِّهَا فَأَصْبَحُوا۟ لَا يُرَىٰٓ إِلَّا
مَسَـٰكِنُهُمْ ۚ كَذَٰلِكَ نَجْزِى ٱلْقَوْمَ ٱلْمُجْرِمِينَ ﴿٢٥﴾

26. And We had firmly established them in a (prosperity and) power which We have not given to you (you Quraysh!) and We had endowed them with (faculties of) hearing, seeing, heart and intellect; but of no profit to them were their (faculties of) hearing, sight, and heart and intellect, when they went on rejecting the signs of Allah; and they were (completely) encircled by that which they used to mock at!

وَلَقَدْ مَكَّنَّـٰهُمْ فِيمَآ إِن مَّكَّنَّـٰكُمْ فِيهِ وَجَعَلْنَا
لَهُمْ سَمْعًا وَأَبْصَـٰرًا وَأَفْـِٔدَةً فَمَآ أَغْنَىٰ عَنْهُمْ سَمْعُهُمْ
وَلَآ أَبْصَـٰرُهُمْ وَلَآ أَفْـِٔدَتُهُم مِّن شَىْءٍ إِذْ كَانُوا۟ يَجْحَدُونَ
بِـَٔايَـٰتِ ٱللَّهِ وَحَاقَ بِهِم مَّا كَانُوا۟ بِهِۦ يَسْتَهْزِءُونَ ﴿٢٦﴾

27. We destroyed before populations round about you; and We have shown the signs in various ways that they may turn (to Us).

وَلَقَدْ أَهْلَكْنَا مَا حَوْلَكُم مِّنَ ٱلْقُرَىٰ وَصَرَّفْنَا
ٱلْـَٔايَـٰتِ لَعَلَّهُمْ يَرْجِعُونَ ﴿٢٧﴾

28. Why then was no help forthcoming to them from those whom they worshipped as gods, besides Allah, as a means of access

فَلَوْلَا نَصَرَهُمُ ٱلَّذِينَ ٱتَّخَذُوا۟ مِن دُونِ ٱللَّهِ
قُرْبَانًا ءَالِهَةًۢ ۖ بَلْ ضَلُّوا۟ عَنْهُمْ ۚ وَذَٰلِكَ إِفْكُهُمْ

وَمَا كَانُوا۟ يَفْتَرُونَ ﴿٢٨﴾

(to Allah)? Nay, they left them in the lurch: but that was their falsehood and their invention.

وَإِذْ صَرَفْنَآ إِلَيْكَ نَفَرًا مِّنَ ٱلْجِنِّ يَسْتَمِعُونَ
ٱلْقُرْءَانَ فَلَمَّا حَضَرُوهُ قَالُوٓا۟ أَنصِتُوا۟ ۖ فَلَمَّا قُضِىَ
وَلَّوْا۟ إِلَىٰ قَوْمِهِم مُّنذِرِينَ ﴿٢٩﴾

29. See, We turned towards you a company of Jinns (quietly) listening to the Qur'an: when they stood in the presence of it, they said, "Listen in silence!" When the (reading) was finished, they returned to their people, to warn (them of their sins).

قَالُوا۟ يَٰقَوْمَنَآ إِنَّا سَمِعْنَا كِتَٰبًا أُنزِلَ مِنۢ بَعْدِ
مُوسَىٰ مُصَدِّقًا لِّمَا بَيْنَ يَدَيْهِ يَهْدِىٓ إِلَى ٱلْحَقِّ
وَإِلَىٰ طَرِيقٍ مُّسْتَقِيمٍ ﴿٣٠﴾

30. They said, "O our people! We have heard a book revealed after Moses, confirming what came before it: it guides (men) to the truth and to a straight path.

يَٰقَوْمَنَآ أَجِيبُوا۟ دَاعِىَ ٱللَّهِ وَءَامِنُوا۟ بِهِۦ يَغْفِرْ لَكُم
مِّن ذُنُوبِكُمْ وَيُجِرْكُم مِّنْ عَذَابٍ أَلِيمٍ ﴿٣١﴾

31. O our people, listen to the one who invites (you) to Allah, and believe in him: He will forgive you your faults, and deliver you from a penalty grievous.

وَمَن لَّا يُجِبْ دَاعِىَ ٱللَّهِ فَلَيْسَ بِمُعْجِزٍ فِى ٱلْأَرْضِ
وَلَيْسَ لَهُۥ مِن دُونِهِۦٓ أَوْلِيَآءُ ۚ أُو۟لَٰٓئِكَ فِى ضَلَٰلٍ مُّبِينٍ ﴿٣٢﴾

32. If any does not listen to the one who invites (us) to Allah, he cannot frustrate (Allah's plan) on earth, and no protectors can he have besides Allah: such men (wander) in manifest error."

أَوَلَمْ يَرَوْا۟ أَنَّ ٱللَّهَ ٱلَّذِى خَلَقَ ٱلسَّمَٰوَٰتِ وَٱلْأَرْضَ
وَلَمْ يَعْىَ بِخَلْقِهِنَّ بِقَٰدِرٍ عَلَىٰٓ أَن يُحْۦِىَ ٱلْمَوْتَىٰ ۚ بَلَىٰٓ
إِنَّهُۥ عَلَىٰ كُلِّ شَىْءٍ قَدِيرٌ ﴿٣٣﴾

33. Do they not see that Allah Who created the heavens and the earth, and never wearied with their creation, is able to give life to the dead? Yea, verily He has power over all things.

وَيَوْمَ يُعْرَضُ ٱلَّذِينَ كَفَرُوا۟ عَلَى ٱلنَّارِ أَلَيْسَ هَٰذَا بِٱلْحَقِّ ۖ
قَالُوا۟ بَلَىٰ وَرَبِّنَا ۚ قَالَ فَذُوقُوا۟ ٱلْعَذَابَ بِمَا كُنتُمْ
تَكْفُرُونَ ﴿٣٤﴾

34. And on the day that the unbelievers will be placed before the fire, (they will be asked,) "Is this not the truth? " They will say, "Yea, by our Lord!" (One will say:) "Then taste you the penalty, for that you used to deny (truth)!"

35. Therefore, patiently persevere as did (all) messengers of inflexible purpose; and be in no haste about the (unbelievers). On the day that they see the (punishment) promised them, (it will be) as if they had not stayed more than an hour in a single day. (Yours is but) to proclaim the message; but shall any be destroyed except those who transgress?

فَٱصۡبِرۡ كَمَا صَبَرَ أُوْلُواْ ٱلۡعَزۡمِ مِنَ ٱلرُّسُلِ وَلَا
تَسۡتَعۡجِل لَّهُمۡۚ كَأَنَّهُمۡ يَوۡمَ يَرَوۡنَ مَا يُوعَدُونَ لَمۡ
يَلۡبَثُوٓاْ إِلَّا سَاعَةٗ مِّن نَّهَارِۭۚ بَلَٰغٞۚ فَهَلۡ يُهۡلَكُ إِلَّا
ٱلۡقَوۡمُ ٱلۡفَٰسِقُونَ ٣٥

سُورَةُ مُحَمَّدٍ

Surah 47: **Muhammad**

In the name of Allah,
Most Gracious, Most Merciful.

بِسۡمِ ٱللَّهِ ٱلرَّحۡمَٰنِ ٱلرَّحِيمِ

1. Those who reject Allah and hinder (men) from the path of Allah - their deeds will Allah render astray (from their mark).

ٱلَّذِينَ كَفَرُواْ وَصَدُّواْ عَن سَبِيلِ ٱللَّهِ أَضَلَّ أَعۡمَٰلَهُمۡ ١

2. But those who believe and work deeds of righteousness, and believe in the (revelation) sent down to Muhammad - for it is the truth from their Lord - He will remove from them their ills and improve their condition.

وَٱلَّذِينَ ءَامَنُواْ وَعَمِلُواْ ٱلصَّٰلِحَٰتِ وَءَامَنُواْ بِمَا نُزِّلَ
عَلَىٰ مُحَمَّدٖ وَهُوَ ٱلۡحَقُّ مِن رَّبِّهِمۡ كَفَّرَ عَنۡهُمۡ سَيِّـَٔاتِهِمۡ
وَأَصۡلَحَ بَالَهُمۡ ٢

3. This because those who reject Allah follow vanities, while those who believe follow the truth from their Lord: thus does Allah set out for men their lessons by similitudes.

ذَٰلِكَ بِأَنَّ ٱلَّذِينَ كَفَرُواْ ٱتَّبَعُواْ ٱلۡبَٰطِلَ وَأَنَّ ٱلَّذِينَ ءَامَنُواْ
ٱتَّبَعُواْ ٱلۡحَقَّ مِن رَّبِّهِمۡۚ كَذَٰلِكَ يَضۡرِبُ ٱللَّهُ لِلنَّاسِ
أَمۡثَٰلَهُمۡ ٣

4. Therefore, when you meet the unbelievers (in fight), strike at their necks; at length, when you have thoroughly subdued them, bind a bond firmly (on them); thereafter (is the time for) either generosity or ransom; until the war lays down its burdens. Thus (are

فَإِذَا لَقِيتُمُ ٱلَّذِينَ كَفَرُواْ فَضَرۡبَ ٱلرِّقَابِ حَتَّىٰٓ إِذَآ أَثۡخَنتُمُوهُمۡ
فَشُدُّواْ ٱلۡوَثَاقَ فَإِمَّا مَنَّۢا بَعۡدُ وَإِمَّا فِدَآءً حَتَّىٰ تَضَعَ ٱلۡحَرۡبُ
أَوۡزَارَهَاۚ ذَٰلِكَۖ وَلَوۡ يَشَآءُ ٱللَّهُ لَٱنتَصَرَ مِنۡهُمۡ وَلَٰكِن

you commanded); but if it had been Allah's Will He could certainly have exacted retribution from them (Himself); but (He lets you fight) in order to test you, some with others. But those who are slain in the way of Allah - He will never let their deeds be lost.

لِّيَبْلُوَا۟ بَعْضَكُم بِبَعْضٍ ۗ وَٱلَّذِينَ قُتِلُوا۟ فِى سَبِيلِ ٱللَّهِ فَلَن
يُضِلَّ أَعْمَٰلَهُمْ ٤

5. Soon will He guide them and improve their condition,

سَيَهْدِيهِمْ وَيُصْلِحُ بَالَهُمْ ٥

6. And admit them to the garden which He has announced for them.

وَيُدْخِلُهُمُ ٱلْجَنَّةَ عَرَّفَهَا لَهُمْ ٦

7. O you who believe! If you will aid (the cause of) Allah, He will aid you, and plant your feet firmly.

يَٰٓأَيُّهَا ٱلَّذِينَ ءَامَنُوٓا۟ إِن تَنصُرُوا۟ ٱللَّهَ يَنصُرْكُمْ وَيُثَبِّتْ
أَقْدَامَكُمْ ٧

8. But those who reject (Allah) for them is destruction, and (Allah) will render their deeds astray (from their mark).

وَٱلَّذِينَ كَفَرُوا۟ فَتَعْسًا لَّهُمْ وَأَضَلَّ أَعْمَٰلَهُمْ ٨

9. That is because they hate the revelation of Allah; so He has made their deeds fruitless.

ذَٰلِكَ بِأَنَّهُمْ كَرِهُوا۟ مَآ أَنزَلَ ٱللَّهُ فَأَحْبَطَ أَعْمَٰلَهُمْ ٩

10. Do they not travel through the earth, and see what was the end of those before them (who did evil)? Allah brought utter destruction on them, and similar (fates await) those who reject Allah.

نصف الحزب ٥١ ۞ أَفَلَمْ يَسِيرُوا۟ فِى ٱلْأَرْضِ فَيَنظُرُوا۟ كَيْفَ كَانَ عَٰقِبَةُ
ٱلَّذِينَ مِن قَبْلِهِمْ ۖ دَمَّرَ ٱللَّهُ عَلَيْهِمْ ۖ وَلِلْكَٰفِرِينَ أَمْثَٰلُهَا ١٠

11. That is because Allah is the protector of those who believe, but those who reject Allah have no protector.

ذَٰلِكَ بِأَنَّ ٱللَّهَ مَوْلَى ٱلَّذِينَ ءَامَنُوا۟ وَأَنَّ ٱلْكَٰفِرِينَ
لَا مَوْلَىٰ لَهُمْ ١١

12. Verily Allah will admit those who believe and do righteous deeds, to gardens beneath which rivers flow; while those who reject Allah will enjoy (this world) and eat as cattle eat; and the fire will be their abode.

إِنَّ ٱللَّهَ يُدْخِلُ ٱلَّذِينَ ءَامَنُوا۟ وَعَمِلُوا۟ ٱلصَّٰلِحَٰتِ
جَنَّٰتٍ تَجْرِى مِن تَحْتِهَا ٱلْأَنْهَٰرُ ۖ وَٱلَّذِينَ كَفَرُوا۟ يَتَمَتَّعُونَ
وَيَأْكُلُونَ كَمَا تَأْكُلُ ٱلْأَنْعَٰمُ وَٱلنَّارُ مَثْوًى لَّهُمْ ١٢

13. And how many cities, with more power than your city which has driven you out, have We destroyed (for their sins)? And there was none to aid them.

وَكَأَيِّن مِّن قَرۡيَةٍ هِيَ أَشَدُّ قُوَّةٗ مِّن قَرۡيَتِكَ ٱلَّتِيٓ
أَخۡرَجَتۡكَ أَهۡلَكۡنَٰهُمۡ فَلَا نَاصِرَ لَهُمۡ ١٣

14. Is then one who is on a clear (path) from his Lord, no better than one to whom the evil of his conduct seems pleasing, and such as follow their own lusts?

أَفَمَن كَانَ عَلَىٰ بَيِّنَةٖ مِّن رَّبِّهِۦ كَمَن زُيِّنَ لَهُۥ سُوٓءُ عَمَلِهِۦ
وَٱتَّبَعُوٓاْ أَهۡوَآءَهُم ١٤

15. (Here is) a parable of the garden which the righteous are promised: in it are rivers of water incorruptible; rivers of milk of which the taste never changes; rivers of wine, a joy to those who drink; and rivers of honey pure and clear. In it there are for them all kinds of fruits, and grace from their Lord. (Can those in such bliss) be compared to such as shall dwell forever in the fire, and be given to drink boiling water, so that it cuts up their bowels (to pieces)?

مَّثَلُ ٱلۡجَنَّةِ ٱلَّتِي وُعِدَ ٱلۡمُتَّقُونَۖ فِيهَآ أَنۡهَٰرٞ مِّن مَّآءٍ غَيۡرِ
ءَاسِنٖ وَأَنۡهَٰرٞ مِّن لَّبَنٖ لَّمۡ يَتَغَيَّرۡ طَعۡمُهُۥ وَأَنۡهَٰرٞ مِّنۡ خَمۡرٖ لَّذَّةٖ
لِّلشَّٰرِبِينَ وَأَنۡهَٰرٞ مِّنۡ عَسَلٖ مُّصَفّٗىۖ وَلَهُمۡ فِيهَا مِن كُلِّ
ٱلثَّمَرَٰتِ وَمَغۡفِرَةٞ مِّن رَّبِّهِمۡۖ كَمَنۡ هُوَ خَٰلِدٞ فِي ٱلنَّارِ وَسُقُواْ
مَآءً حَمِيمٗا فَقَطَّعَ أَمۡعَآءَهُمۡ ١٥

16. And among them are men who listen to you, but in the end, when they go out from you, they say to those who have received knowledge, "What is it he said just then?" Such are men whose hearts Allah has sealed, and who follow their own lusts.

وَمِنۡهُم مَّن يَسۡتَمِعُ إِلَيۡكَ حَتَّىٰٓ إِذَا خَرَجُواْ مِنۡ عِندِكَ
قَالُواْ لِلَّذِينَ أُوتُواْ ٱلۡعِلۡمَ مَاذَا قَالَ ءَانِفًاۚ أُوْلَٰٓئِكَ ٱلَّذِينَ
طَبَعَ ٱللَّهُ عَلَىٰ قُلُوبِهِمۡ وَٱتَّبَعُوٓاْ أَهۡوَآءَهُمۡ ١٦

17. But to those who receive guidance, He increases (the light of) guidance, and bestows on them their piety and restraint (from evil).

وَٱلَّذِينَ ٱهۡتَدَوۡاْ زَادَهُمۡ هُدٗى وَءَاتَىٰهُمۡ تَقۡوَىٰهُمۡ ١٧

18. Do they then only wait for the hour - that it should come on them of a sudden? But already have come some signs of it, and when it (actually) is on them, how can they benefit then by their admonition?

فَهَلۡ يَنظُرُونَ إِلَّا ٱلسَّاعَةَ أَن تَأۡتِيَهُم بَغۡتَةٗۖ فَقَدۡ جَآءَ
أَشۡرَاطُهَاۚ فَأَنَّىٰ لَهُمۡ إِذَا جَآءَتۡهُمۡ ذِكۡرَىٰهُمۡ ١٨

19. Know, therefore, that there is no god but Allah, and ask forgiveness for your fault, and for the men and women who believe: for Allah knows how you move about and how you dwell in your homes.

فَٱعْلَمْ أَنَّهُۥ لَآ إِلَٰهَ إِلَّا ٱللَّهُ وَٱسْتَغْفِرْ لِذَنۢبِكَ
وَلِلْمُؤْمِنِينَ وَٱلْمُؤْمِنَٰتِ ۗ وَٱللَّهُ يَعْلَمُ مُتَقَلَّبَكُمْ
وَمَثْوَىٰكُمْ ﴿١٩﴾

20. Those who believe say, "Why is not a Surah sent down (for us)?" But when a Surah of basic or categorical meaning is revealed and fighting is mentioned in it, you will see those in whose hearts is a disease looking at you with a look of one in swoon at the approach of death. But more fitting for them -

وَيَقُولُ ٱلَّذِينَ ءَامَنُوا۟ لَوْلَا نُزِّلَتْ سُورَةٌ ۖ فَإِذَآ أُنزِلَتْ
سُورَةٌ مُّحْكَمَةٌ وَذُكِرَ فِيهَا ٱلْقِتَالُ ۙ رَأَيْتَ ٱلَّذِينَ
فِى قُلُوبِهِم مَّرَضٌ يَنظُرُونَ إِلَيْكَ نَظَرَ ٱلْمَغْشِىِّ
عَلَيْهِ مِنَ ٱلْمَوْتِ ۖ فَأَوْلَىٰ لَهُمْ ﴿٢٠﴾

21. Were it to obey and say what is just and when a matter is resolved on, it were best for them if they were true to Allah.

طَاعَةٌ وَقَوْلٌ مَّعْرُوفٌ ۚ فَإِذَا عَزَمَ ٱلْأَمْرُ فَلَوْ
صَدَقُوا۟ ٱللَّهَ لَكَانَ خَيْرًا لَّهُمْ ﴿٢١﴾

22. Then, is it to be expected of you, if you were put in authority that you will do no mischief in the land, and break your ties of relationship?

فَهَلْ عَسَيْتُمْ إِن تَوَلَّيْتُمْ أَن تُفْسِدُوا۟ فِى ٱلْأَرْضِ
وَتُقَطِّعُوٓا۟ أَرْحَامَكُمْ ﴿٢٢﴾

23. Such are the men whom Allah has cursed for He has made them deaf and blinded their sight.

أُو۟لَٰٓئِكَ ٱلَّذِينَ لَعَنَهُمُ ٱللَّهُ فَأَصَمَّهُمْ وَأَعْمَىٰٓ
أَبْصَٰرَهُمْ ﴿٢٣﴾

24. Do they not then earnestly seek to understand the Qur'an or are their hearts locked up by them?

أَفَلَا يَتَدَبَّرُونَ ٱلْقُرْءَانَ أَمْ عَلَىٰ قُلُوبٍ أَقْفَالُهَآ ﴿٢٤﴾

25. Those who turn back as apostates after guidance was clearly shown to them - the evil one has instigated them and buoyed them up with false hopes.

إِنَّ ٱلَّذِينَ ٱرْتَدُّوا۟ عَلَىٰٓ أَدْبَٰرِهِم مِّنۢ بَعْدِ
مَا تَبَيَّنَ لَهُمُ ٱلْهُدَى ۙ ٱلشَّيْطَٰنُ سَوَّلَ لَهُمْ وَأَمْلَىٰ
لَهُمْ ﴿٢٥﴾

26. This, because they said to those who hate what Allah has revealed, "We will

ذَٰلِكَ بِأَنَّهُمْ قَالُوا۟ لِلَّذِينَ كَرِهُوا۟ مَا نَزَّلَ ٱللَّهُ

obey you in part of (this) matter"; but Allah knows their (inner) secrets.

سَنُطِيعُكُمْ فِي بَعْضِ الْأَمْرِ ۖ وَاللَّهُ يَعْلَمُ
إِسْرَارَهُمْ ٢٦

27. But how (will it be) when the angels take their souls at death, and strike their faces and their backs?

فَكَيْفَ إِذَا تَوَفَّتْهُمُ الْمَلَائِكَةُ يَضْرِبُونَ
وُجُوهَهُمْ وَأَدْبَارَهُمْ ٢٧

28. This because they followed that which called the wrath of Allah, and they hated Allah's good pleasure; so He made their deeds of no effect.

ذَٰلِكَ بِأَنَّهُمُ اتَّبَعُوا مَا أَسْخَطَ اللَّهَ
وَكَرِهُوا رِضْوَانَهُ فَأَحْبَطَ أَعْمَالَهُمْ ٢٨

29. Or do those in whose hearts is a disease, think that Allah will not bring to light all their rancour?

أَمْ حَسِبَ الَّذِينَ فِي قُلُوبِهِمْ مَرَضٌ أَنْ لَنْ
يُخْرِجَ اللَّهُ أَضْغَانَهُمْ ٢٩

30. Had We so willed, We could have shown them up to you, and you should have known them by their marks: but surely you will know them by the tone of their speech! And Allah knows all that you do.

وَلَوْ نَشَاءُ لَأَرَيْنَاكَهُمْ فَلَعَرَفْتَهُمْ بِسِيمَاهُمْ ۚ
وَلَتَعْرِفَنَّهُمْ فِي لَحْنِ الْقَوْلِ ۚ وَاللَّهُ يَعْلَمُ أَعْمَالَكُمْ ٣٠

31. And We shall try you until We test those among you who strive their utmost and persevere in patience; and We shall try your reported (mettle).

وَلَنَبْلُوَنَّكُمْ حَتَّىٰ نَعْلَمَ الْمُجَاهِدِينَ مِنْكُمْ
وَالصَّابِرِينَ وَنَبْلُوَ أَخْبَارَكُمْ ٣١

32. Those who reject Allah, hinder (men) from the path of Allah, and resist the messenger, after guidance has been clearly shown to them, will not injure Allah in the least, but He will make their deeds of no effect.

إِنَّ الَّذِينَ كَفَرُوا وَصَدُّوا عَنْ سَبِيلِ اللَّهِ وَشَاقُّوا
الرَّسُولَ مِنْ بَعْدِ مَا تَبَيَّنَ لَهُمُ الْهُدَىٰ لَنْ يَضُرُّوا
اللَّهَ شَيْئًا وَسَيُحْبِطُ أَعْمَالَهُمْ ٣٢

33. O you who believe! Obey Allah, and obey the messenger, and make not vain your deeds!

* يَا أَيُّهَا الَّذِينَ آمَنُوا أَطِيعُوا اللَّهَ وَأَطِيعُوا أرباع الحزب ٥١
الرَّسُولَ وَلَا تُبْطِلُوا أَعْمَالَكُمْ ٣٣

34. Those who reject Allah, and hinder (men) from the path of Allah, then die rejecting Allah - Allah will not forgive them.

إِنَّ ٱلَّذِينَ كَفَرُواْ وَصَدُّواْ عَن سَبِيلِ ٱللَّهِ ثُمَّ مَاتُواْ
وَهُمۡ كُفَّارٞ فَلَن يَغۡفِرَ ٱللَّهُ لَهُمۡ ٣٤

35. Be not weary and faint-hearted, crying for peace, when you should be uppermost: for Allah is with you, and will never put you in loss for your (good) deeds.

فَلَا تَهِنُواْ وَتَدۡعُوٓاْ إِلَى ٱلسَّلۡمِ وَأَنتُمُ ٱلۡأَعۡلَوۡنَ وَٱللَّهُ
مَعَكُمۡ وَلَن يَتِرَكُمۡ أَعۡمَٰلَكُمۡ ٣٥

36. The life of this world is but play and amusement: and if you believe and guard against evil, He will grant you your recompense, and will not ask you (to give up) your possessions.

إِنَّمَا ٱلۡحَيَوٰةُ ٱلدُّنۡيَا لَعِبٞ وَلَهۡوٞۚ وَإِن تُؤۡمِنُواْ وَتَتَّقُواْ
يُؤۡتِكُمۡ أُجُورَكُمۡ وَلَا يَسۡـَٔلۡكُمۡ أَمۡوَٰلَكُمۡ ٣٦

37. If He were to ask you for all of them, and press you, you would covetously withhold, and He would bring out all your ill-feeling.

إِن يَسۡـَٔلۡكُمُوهَا فَيُحۡفِكُمۡ تَبۡخَلُواْ وَيُخۡرِجۡ
أَضۡغَٰنَكُمۡ ٣٧

38. See, you are those invited to spend (of your substance) in the way of Allah; but among you are some that are niggardly. But any who are niggardly are so at the expense of their own souls. But Allah is free of all wants, and it is you that are needy. If you turn back (from the path), He will substitute in your stead another people; then they would not be like you!

هَٰٓأَنتُمۡ هَٰٓؤُلَآءِ تُدۡعَوۡنَ لِتُنفِقُواْ فِي سَبِيلِ ٱللَّهِ
فَمِنكُم مَّن يَبۡخَلُۖ وَمَن يَبۡخَلۡ فَإِنَّمَا يَبۡخَلُ عَن
نَّفۡسِهِۦۚ وَٱللَّهُ ٱلۡغَنِيُّ وَأَنتُمُ ٱلۡفُقَرَآءُۚ وَإِن تَتَوَلَّوۡاْ
يَسۡتَبۡدِلۡ قَوۡمًا غَيۡرَكُمۡ ثُمَّ لَا يَكُونُوٓاْ أَمۡثَٰلَكُم ٣٨

سُورَةُ الفَتۡحِ

Surah 48: **Al-Fath (Victory)**

In the name of Allah,
Most Gracious, Most Merciful.

بِسۡمِ ٱللَّهِ ٱلرَّحۡمَٰنِ ٱلرَّحِيمِ

1. Verily We have granted you a manifest victory:

إِنَّا فَتَحۡنَا لَكَ فَتۡحٗا مُّبِينٗا ١

2. That Allah may forgive you your faults of the past and those to follow; fulfil His favour to you; and guide you on the straight way;

لِّيَغْفِرَ لَكَ ٱللَّهُ مَا تَقَدَّمَ مِن ذَنۢبِكَ وَمَا تَأَخَّرَ وَيُتِمَّ
نِعْمَتَهُۥ عَلَيْكَ وَيَهْدِيَكَ صِرَٰطًا مُّسْتَقِيمًا ﴿٢﴾

3. And that Allah may help you with powerful help.

وَيَنصُرَكَ ٱللَّهُ نَصْرًا عَزِيزًا ﴿٣﴾

4. It is He Who sent down tranquillity into the hearts of the believers, that they may add faith to their faith - for to Allah belong the forces of the heavens and the earth; and Allah is full of knowledge and wisdom -

هُوَ ٱلَّذِىٓ أَنزَلَ ٱلسَّكِينَةَ فِى قُلُوبِ ٱلْمُؤْمِنِينَ لِيَزْدَادُوٓا۟
إِيمَٰنًا مَّعَ إِيمَٰنِهِمْ ۗ وَلِلَّهِ جُنُودُ ٱلسَّمَٰوَٰتِ وَٱلْأَرْضِ ۚ
وَكَانَ ٱللَّهُ عَلِيمًا حَكِيمًا ﴿٤﴾

5. That He may admit the men and women who believe, to gardens beneath which rivers flow, to dwell in it for ever, and remove their ills from them - and that is, in the sight of Allah, the highest achievement (for man) -

لِّيُدْخِلَ ٱلْمُؤْمِنِينَ وَٱلْمُؤْمِنَٰتِ جَنَّٰتٍ تَجْرِى مِن تَحْتِهَا
ٱلْأَنْهَٰرُ خَٰلِدِينَ فِيهَا وَيُكَفِّرَ عَنْهُمْ سَيِّـَٔاتِهِمْ ۚ
وَكَانَ ذَٰلِكَ عِندَ ٱللَّهِ فَوْزًا عَظِيمًا ﴿٥﴾

6. And that He may punish the hypocrites, men and women, and the polytheists, men and women, who imagine an evil opinion of Allah. On them is a round of evil; the wrath of Allah is on them; He has cursed them and got hell ready for them; and evil is it for a destination.

وَيُعَذِّبَ ٱلْمُنَٰفِقِينَ وَٱلْمُنَٰفِقَٰتِ وَٱلْمُشْرِكِينَ
وَٱلْمُشْرِكَٰتِ ٱلظَّآنِّينَ بِٱللَّهِ ظَنَّ ٱلسَّوْءِ ۚ عَلَيْهِمْ
دَآئِرَةُ ٱلسَّوْءِ ۖ وَغَضِبَ ٱللَّهُ عَلَيْهِمْ وَلَعَنَهُمْ وَأَعَدَّ
لَهُمْ جَهَنَّمَ ۖ وَسَآءَتْ مَصِيرًا ﴿٦﴾

7. For to Allah belong the forces of the heavens and the earth; and Allah is Exalted in Power, Full of Wisdom.

وَلِلَّهِ جُنُودُ ٱلسَّمَٰوَٰتِ وَٱلْأَرْضِ ۚ وَكَانَ ٱللَّهُ
عَزِيزًا حَكِيمًا ﴿٧﴾

8. We have truly sent you as a witness, as a bringer of glad tidings, and as a warner:

إِنَّآ أَرْسَلْنَٰكَ شَٰهِدًا وَمُبَشِّرًا وَنَذِيرًا ﴿٨﴾

9. In order that you (O men) may believe in Allah and His messenger, that you may assist and honour Him, and celebrate His praises morning and evening.

لِّتُؤْمِنُوا۟ بِٱللَّهِ وَرَسُولِهِۦ وَتُعَزِّرُوهُ وَتُوَقِّرُوهُ ۚ
وَتُسَبِّحُوهُ بُكْرَةً وَأَصِيلًا ﴿٩﴾

10. Verily those who pledge their fealty to you do no less than pledge their fealty to Allah: the Hand of Allah is over their hands: then anyone who violates his oath, does so to the harm of his own soul, and anyone who fulfils what he has covenanted with Allah - Allah will soon grant him a great reward.

إِنَّ ٱلَّذِينَ يُبَايِعُونَكَ إِنَّمَا يُبَايِعُونَ ٱللَّهَ يَدُ ٱللَّهِ
فَوْقَ أَيْدِيهِمْ ۚ فَمَن نَّكَثَ فَإِنَّمَا يَنكُثُ عَلَىٰ
نَفْسِهِۦ ۖ وَمَنْ أَوْفَىٰ بِمَا عَٰهَدَ عَلَيْهُ ٱللَّهَ فَسَيُؤْتِيهِ
أَجْرًا عَظِيمًا ﴿١٠﴾

11. The desert Arabs who lagged behind will say to you: "We were engaged in (looking after) our flocks and herds, and our families; do you then ask forgiveness for us." They say with their tongues what is not in their hearts. Say: "Who then has any power at all (to intervene) on your behalf with Allah, if His will is to give you some loss or to give you some profit? But Allah is well acquainted with all that you do.

سَيَقُولُ لَكَ ٱلْمُخَلَّفُونَ مِنَ ٱلْأَعْرَابِ شَغَلَتْنَآ
أَمْوَٰلُنَا وَأَهْلُونَا فَٱسْتَغْفِرْ لَنَا ۚ يَقُولُونَ بِأَلْسِنَتِهِم
مَّا لَيْسَ فِى قُلُوبِهِمْ ۚ قُلْ فَمَن يَمْلِكُ لَكُم مِّنَ ٱللَّهِ
شَيْـًٔا إِنْ أَرَادَ بِكُمْ ضَرًّا أَوْ أَرَادَ بِكُمْ نَفْعًۢا ۚ بَلْ كَانَ
ٱللَّهُ بِمَا تَعْمَلُونَ خَبِيرًۢا ﴿١١﴾

12. Nay, you thought that the messenger and the believers would never return to their families; this seemed pleasing in your hearts, and you conceived an evil thought, for you are a people lost (in wickedness)."

بَلْ ظَنَنتُمْ أَن لَّن يَنقَلِبَ ٱلرَّسُولُ وَٱلْمُؤْمِنُونَ
إِلَىٰٓ أَهْلِيهِمْ أَبَدًا وَزُيِّنَ ذَٰلِكَ فِى قُلُوبِكُمْ وَظَنَنتُمْ
ظَنَّ ٱلسَّوْءِ وَكُنتُمْ قَوْمًۢا بُورًا ﴿١٢﴾

13. And if any believe not in Allah and His messenger, We have prepared for those who reject Allah, a blazing fire!

وَمَن لَّمْ يُؤْمِنۢ بِٱللَّهِ وَرَسُولِهِۦ فَإِنَّآ أَعْتَدْنَا لِلْكَٰفِرِينَ
سَعِيرًا ﴿١٣﴾

14. To Allah belongs the dominion of the heavens and the earth: He forgives whom He wills, and He punishes whom He wills; but Allah is Oft-Forgiving, Most Merciful.

وَلِلَّهِ مُلْكُ ٱلسَّمَٰوَٰتِ وَٱلْأَرْضِ ۚ يَغْفِرُ لِمَن يَشَآءُ
وَيُعَذِّبُ مَن يَشَآءُ ۚ وَكَانَ ٱللَّهُ غَفُورًا رَّحِيمًا ﴿١٤﴾

15. Those who lagged behind (will say), when you (are free to) march and take booty (in war): "Permit us to follow you." They wish to change Allah's decree; say: "Not thus

سَيَقُولُ ٱلْمُخَلَّفُونَ إِذَا ٱنطَلَقْتُمْ إِلَىٰ مَغَانِمَ
لِتَأْخُذُوهَا ذَرُونَا نَتَّبِعْكُمْ ۖ يُرِيدُونَ أَن يُبَدِّلُوا۟

will you follow us; Allah has already declared (this) beforehand"; then they will say, "But you are jealous of us." Nay, but little do they understand (such things).

كَلَٰمَ ٱللَّهِۚ قُل لَّن تَتَّبِعُونَا كَذَٰلِكُمۡ قَالَ ٱللَّهُ مِن قَبۡلُۖ
فَسَيَقُولُونَ بَلۡ تَحۡسُدُونَنَاۚ بَلۡ كَانُواْ لَا يَفۡقَهُونَ
إِلَّا قَلِيلٗا ١٥

16. Say to the desert Arabs who lagged behind: "You shall be summoned (to fight) against a people given to vehement war: then shall you fight or they shall submit. Then if you show obedience, Allah will grant you a goodly reward, but if you turn back as you did before, He will punish you with a grievous penalty."

قُل لِّلۡمُخَلَّفِينَ مِنَ ٱلۡأَعۡرَابِ سَتُدۡعَوۡنَ إِلَىٰ قَوۡمٍ أُوْلِي
بَأۡسٖ شَدِيدٖ تُقَٰتِلُونَهُمۡ أَوۡ يُسۡلِمُونَۖ فَإِن تُطِيعُواْ
يُؤۡتِكُمُ ٱللَّهُ أَجۡرًا حَسَنٗاۖ وَإِن تَتَوَلَّوۡاْ كَمَا تَوَلَّيۡتُم
مِّن قَبۡلُ يُعَذِّبۡكُمۡ عَذَابًا أَلِيمٗا ١٦

17. No blame is there on the blind, nor is there blame on the lame, nor on one ill (if he joins not the war); but he that obeys Allah and His messenger - (Allah) will admit him to gardens beneath which rivers flow; and he who turns back, (Allah) will punish him with a grievous penalty.

لَّيۡسَ عَلَى ٱلۡأَعۡمَىٰ حَرَجٞ وَلَا عَلَى ٱلۡأَعۡرَجِ حَرَجٞ وَلَا
عَلَى ٱلۡمَرِيضِ حَرَجٞۗ وَمَن يُطِعِ ٱللَّهَ وَرَسُولَهُۥ يُدۡخِلۡهُ
جَنَّٰتٖ تَجۡرِي مِن تَحۡتِهَا ٱلۡأَنۡهَٰرُۖ وَمَن يَتَوَلَّ
يُعَذِّبۡهُ عَذَابًا أَلِيمٗا ١٧

18. Allah's good pleasure was on the believers when they swore allegiance to you under the tree: He knew what was in their hearts and He sent down tranquillity to them and He rewarded them with a speedy victory;

حزب ٥٢ ۞لَّقَدۡ رَضِيَ ٱللَّهُ عَنِ ٱلۡمُؤۡمِنِينَ إِذۡ يُبَايِعُونَكَ
تَحۡتَ ٱلشَّجَرَةِ فَعَلِمَ مَا فِي قُلُوبِهِمۡ فَأَنزَلَ
ٱلسَّكِينَةَ عَلَيۡهِمۡ وَأَثَٰبَهُمۡ فَتۡحٗا قَرِيبٗا ١٨

19. And many gains will they acquire (besides): and Allah is Exalted in Power, Full of Wisdom.

وَمَغَانِمَ كَثِيرَةٗ يَأۡخُذُونَهَاۗ وَكَانَ ٱللَّهُ عَزِيزًا
حَكِيمٗا ١٩

20. Allah has promised you many gains that you shall acquire, and He has given you these beforehand; and He has restrained the hands of men from you; that

وَعَدَكُمُ ٱللَّهُ مَغَانِمَ كَثِيرَةٗ تَأۡخُذُونَهَا فَعَجَّلَ
لَكُمۡ هَٰذِهِۦ وَكَفَّ أَيۡدِيَ ٱلنَّاسِ عَنكُمۡ وَلِتَكُونَ

it may be a sign for the believers, and that He may guide you to a straight path;

ءَايَةً لِّلْمُؤْمِنِينَ وَيَهْدِيَكُمْ صِرَٰطًا مُّسْتَقِيمًا ﴿٢٠﴾

21. And other gains (there are) which are not within your power, but which Allah has encompassed: and Allah has power over all things.

وَأُخْرَىٰ لَمْ تَقْدِرُوا۟ عَلَيْهَا قَدْ أَحَاطَ ٱللَّهُ بِهَا ۚ وَكَانَ
ٱللَّهُ عَلَىٰ كُلِّ شَىْءٍ قَدِيرًا ﴿٢١﴾

22. If the unbelievers should fight you, they would certainly turn their backs; then would they find neither protector nor helper.

وَلَوْ قَٰتَلَكُمُ ٱلَّذِينَ كَفَرُوا۟ لَوَلَّوُا۟ ٱلْأَدْبَٰرَ ثُمَّ
لَا يَجِدُونَ وَلِيًّا وَلَا نَصِيرًا ﴿٢٢﴾

23. (Such has been) the practice (approved) of Allah already in the past: no change will you find in the practice (approved) of Allah.

سُنَّةَ ٱللَّهِ ٱلَّتِى قَدْ خَلَتْ مِن قَبْلُ ۖ وَلَن تَجِدَ لِسُنَّةِ
ٱللَّهِ تَبْدِيلًا ﴿٢٣﴾

24. And it is He Who has restrained their hands from you and your hand from them in the midst of Makkah, after that He gave you the victory over them. And Allah sees well all that you do.

وَهُوَ ٱلَّذِى كَفَّ أَيْدِيَهُمْ عَنكُمْ وَأَيْدِيَكُمْ عَنْهُم بِبَطْنِ
مَكَّةَ مِنۢ بَعْدِ أَنْ أَظْفَرَكُمْ عَلَيْهِمْ ۚ وَكَانَ ٱللَّهُ بِمَا
تَعْمَلُونَ بَصِيرًا ﴿٢٤﴾

25. They are the ones who denied revelation and hindered you from the Sacred Mosque and the sacrificial animals, detained from reaching their place of sacrifice. Had there not been believing men and believing women whom you did not know that you were trampling down and on whose account a crime would have accrued to you without (your) knowledge, (Allah would have allowed you to force your way, but He held back your hands) that He may admit to His mercy whom He will. If they had been apart, We should certainly have punished the unbelievers among them with a grievous punishment.

هُمُ ٱلَّذِينَ كَفَرُوا۟ وَصَدُّوكُمْ عَنِ ٱلْمَسْجِدِ
ٱلْحَرَامِ وَٱلْهَدْىَ مَعْكُوفًا أَن يَبْلُغَ مَحِلَّهُۥ ۚ وَلَوْلَا
رِجَالٌ مُّؤْمِنُونَ وَنِسَآءٌ مُّؤْمِنَٰتٌ لَّمْ تَعْلَمُوهُمْ أَن تَطَـُٔوهُمْ
فَتُصِيبَكُم مِّنْهُم مَّعَرَّةٌۢ بِغَيْرِ عِلْمٍ ۖ لِّيُدْخِلَ ٱللَّهُ
فِى رَحْمَتِهِۦ مَن يَشَآءُ ۚ لَوْ تَزَيَّلُوا۟ لَعَذَّبْنَا ٱلَّذِينَ كَفَرُوا۟
مِنْهُمْ عَذَابًا أَلِيمًا ﴿٢٥﴾

26. While the unbelievers got up in their hearts heat and zeal - the heat and zeal of ignorance - Allah sent down His tranquillity to His messenger and to the believers, and made them stick close to the command of self-restraint; and well were they entitled to it and worthy of it. And Allah has full knowledge of all things.

إِذْ جَعَلَ ٱلَّذِينَ كَفَرُوا۟ فِى قُلُوبِهِمُ ٱلْحَمِيَّةَ حَمِيَّةَ
ٱلْجَٰهِلِيَّةِ فَأَنزَلَ ٱللَّهُ سَكِينَتَهُۥ عَلَىٰ رَسُولِهِۦ وَعَلَى
ٱلْمُؤْمِنِينَ وَأَلْزَمَهُمْ كَلِمَةَ ٱلتَّقْوَىٰ وَكَانُوٓا۟
أَحَقَّ بِهَا وَأَهْلَهَا ۚ وَكَانَ ٱللَّهُ بِكُلِّ شَىْءٍ عَلِيمًا ﴿٢٦﴾

27. Truly did Allah fulfil the vision for His messenger: you shall enter the Sacred Mosque, if Allah wills with minds secure, heads shaved, hair cut short, and without fear. For He knew what you knew not and He granted, besides this, a speedy victory.

لَّقَدْ صَدَقَ ٱللَّهُ رَسُولَهُ ٱلرُّءْيَا بِٱلْحَقِّ ۖ لَتَدْخُلُنَّ
ٱلْمَسْجِدَ ٱلْحَرَامَ إِن شَآءَ ٱللَّهُ ءَامِنِينَ مُحَلِّقِينَ
رُءُوسَكُمْ وَمُقَصِّرِينَ لَا تَخَافُونَ ۖ فَعَلِمَ مَا لَمْ
تَعْلَمُوا۟ فَجَعَلَ مِن دُونِ ذَٰلِكَ فَتْحًا قَرِيبًا ﴿٢٧﴾

28. It is He Who has sent His messenger with guidance and the religion of truth, to proclaim it over all religion: and enough is Allah for a witness.

هُوَ ٱلَّذِىٓ أَرْسَلَ رَسُولَهُۥ بِٱلْهُدَىٰ وَدِينِ ٱلْحَقِّ
لِيُظْهِرَهُۥ عَلَى ٱلدِّينِ كُلِّهِۦ ۚ وَكَفَىٰ بِٱللَّهِ شَهِيدًا ﴿٢٨﴾

29. Muhammad is the messenger of Allah; and those who are with him are strong against unbelievers, (but) compassionate amongst each other. You will see them bow and prostrate themselves (in prayer), seeking grace from Allah and (His) good pleasure. On their faces are their marks, (being) the traces of their prostration. This is their similitude in the Tawrah; and their similitude in the Gospel is like a seed which sends out its blade, then makes it strong; it then becomes thick, and it stands on its own stem, (filling) the sowers with wonder and delight. As a result, it fills the unbelievers with rage at him. Allah has promised those among them who believe and do righteous deeds forgiveness and a great reward.

مُّحَمَّدٌ رَّسُولُ ٱللَّهِ ۚ وَٱلَّذِينَ مَعَهُۥٓ أَشِدَّآءُ عَلَى ٱلْكُفَّارِ
رُحَمَآءُ بَيْنَهُمْ ۖ تَرَىٰهُمْ رُكَّعًا سُجَّدًا يَبْتَغُونَ فَضْلًا مِّنَ
ٱللَّهِ وَرِضْوَٰنًا ۖ سِيمَاهُمْ فِى وُجُوهِهِم مِّنْ أَثَرِ ٱلسُّجُودِ ۚ
ذَٰلِكَ مَثَلُهُمْ فِى ٱلتَّوْرَىٰةِ ۚ وَمَثَلُهُمْ فِى ٱلْإِنجِيلِ كَزَرْعٍ
أَخْرَجَ شَطْـَٔهُۥ فَـَٔازَرَهُۥ فَٱسْتَغْلَظَ فَٱسْتَوَىٰ عَلَىٰ
سُوقِهِۦ يُعْجِبُ ٱلزُّرَّاعَ لِيَغِيظَ بِهِمُ ٱلْكُفَّارَ ۗ وَعَدَ ٱللَّهُ
ٱلَّذِينَ ءَامَنُوا۟ وَعَمِلُوا۟ ٱلصَّٰلِحَٰتِ مِنْهُم مَّغْفِرَةً
وَأَجْرًا عَظِيمًۢا ﴿٢٩﴾

سُورَةُ الحُجُرَات

Surah 49: **Al-Hujurat** (The Chambers)

***In the name of Allah,
Most Gracious, Most Merciful.***

بِسۡمِ ٱللَّهِ ٱلرَّحۡمَٰنِ ٱلرَّحِيمِ

1. O you who believe! Put not yourselves forward before Allah and His messenger: but fear Allah: for Allah is He Who hears and knows all things.

ربع الحزب ٥٢ يَٰٓأَيُّهَا ٱلَّذِينَ ءَامَنُواْ لَا تُقَدِّمُواْ بَيۡنَ يَدَيِ ٱللَّهِ
وَرَسُولِهِۦۖ وَٱتَّقُواْ ٱللَّهَۚ إِنَّ ٱللَّهَ سَمِيعٌ عَلِيمٞ ١

2. O you who believe! Raise not your voices above the voice of the messenger, nor speak aloud to him in talk, as you may speak aloud to one another, lest your deeds become vain and you perceive not.

يَٰٓأَيُّهَا ٱلَّذِينَ ءَامَنُواْ لَا تَرۡفَعُوٓاْ أَصۡوَٰتَكُمۡ فَوۡقَ صَوۡتِ
ٱلنَّبِيِّ وَلَا تَجۡهَرُواْ لَهُۥ بِٱلۡقَوۡلِ كَجَهۡرِ بَعۡضِكُمۡ لِبَعۡضٍ
أَن تَحۡبَطَ أَعۡمَٰلُكُمۡ وَأَنتُمۡ لَا تَشۡعُرُونَ ٢

3. Those that lower their voice in the presence of Allah's messenger - their hearts has Allah tested for piety: for them is forgiveness and a great reward.

إِنَّ ٱلَّذِينَ يَغُضُّونَ أَصۡوَٰتَهُمۡ عِندَ رَسُولِ ٱللَّهِ
أُوْلَٰٓئِكَ ٱلَّذِينَ ٱمۡتَحَنَ ٱللَّهُ قُلُوبَهُمۡ لِلتَّقۡوَىٰۚ لَهُم
مَّغۡفِرَةٞ وَأَجۡرٌ عَظِيمٌ ٣

4. Those who shout out to you from without the inner apartments - most of them lack understanding.

إِنَّ ٱلَّذِينَ يُنَادُونَكَ مِن وَرَآءِ ٱلۡحُجُرَٰتِ
أَكۡثَرُهُمۡ لَا يَعۡقِلُونَ ٤

5. If only they had patience until you could come out to them, it would be best for them: but Allah is Oft-Forgiving, Most Merciful.

وَلَوۡ أَنَّهُمۡ صَبَرُواْ حَتَّىٰ تَخۡرُجَ إِلَيۡهِمۡ لَكَانَ خَيۡرٗا لَّهُمۡۚ
وَٱللَّهُ غَفُورٞ رَّحِيمٞ ٥

6. O you who believe! If a wicked person comes to you with any news, ascertain the truth, lest you harm people unwittingly, and afterwards become full of repentance for what you have done.

يَٰٓأَيُّهَا ٱلَّذِينَ ءَامَنُوٓاْ إِن جَآءَكُمۡ فَاسِقُۢ بِنَبَإٖ فَتَبَيَّنُوٓاْ أَن
تُصِيبُواْ قَوۡمَۢا بِجَهَٰلَةٖ فَتُصۡبِحُواْ عَلَىٰ مَا فَعَلۡتُمۡ
نَٰدِمِينَ ٦

7. And know that among you is Allah's messenger: were he, in many matters, to follow your (wishes), you would certainly fall into misfortune; but Allah has endeared the faith to you, and has made it beautiful in your hearts, and He has made hateful to you unbelief, wickedness, and rebellion: such indeed are those who walk in righteousness -

وَٱعۡلَمُوٓاْ أَنَّ فِيكُمۡ رَسُولَ ٱللَّهِۚ لَوۡ يُطِيعُكُمۡ فِي كَثِيرٖ مِّنَ
ٱلۡأَمۡرِ لَعَنِتُّمۡ وَلَٰكِنَّ ٱللَّهَ حَبَّبَ إِلَيۡكُمُ ٱلۡإِيمَٰنَ
وَزَيَّنَهُۥ فِي قُلُوبِكُمۡ وَكَرَّهَ إِلَيۡكُمُ ٱلۡكُفۡرَ
وَٱلۡفُسُوقَ وَٱلۡعِصۡيَانَۚ أُوْلَٰٓئِكَ هُمُ ٱلرَّٰشِدُونَ ٧

8. A grace and favour from Allah; and Allah is full of Knowledge and Wisdom.

فَضۡلٗا مِّنَ ٱللَّهِ وَنِعۡمَةٗۚ وَٱللَّهُ عَلِيمٌ حَكِيمٞ ٨

9. If two parties among the believers fall into a quarrel, make you peace between them; but if one of them transgresses beyond bounds against the other, then fight you (all) against the one that transgresses until it complies with the command of Allah; but if it complies, then make peace between them with justice, and be fair: for Allah loves those who are fair (and just).

وَإِن طَآئِفَتَانِ مِنَ ٱلۡمُؤۡمِنِينَ ٱقۡتَتَلُواْ فَأَصۡلِحُواْ
بَيۡنَهُمَاۖ فَإِنۢ بَغَتۡ إِحۡدَىٰهُمَا عَلَى ٱلۡأُخۡرَىٰ فَقَٰتِلُواْ
ٱلَّتِي تَبۡغِي حَتَّىٰ تَفِيٓءَ إِلَىٰٓ أَمۡرِ ٱللَّهِۚ فَإِن فَآءَتۡ
فَأَصۡلِحُواْ بَيۡنَهُمَا بِٱلۡعَدۡلِ وَأَقۡسِطُوٓاْۖ إِنَّ ٱللَّهَ يُحِبُّ
ٱلۡمُقۡسِطِينَ ٩

10. The believers are but a single brotherhood; so make peace and reconciliation between your two (contending) brothers: and fear Allah that you may receive mercy.

إِنَّمَا ٱلۡمُؤۡمِنُونَ إِخۡوَةٞ فَأَصۡلِحُواْ بَيۡنَ أَخَوَيۡكُمۡۚ
وَٱتَّقُواْ ٱللَّهَ لَعَلَّكُمۡ تُرۡحَمُونَ ١٠

11. O you who believe! Let not some men among you laugh at others; it may be that the (latter) are better than the (former); nor let some women laugh at others; it may be that the (latter) are better than the (former); nor defame, nor be sarcastic to each other, nor call each other by (offensive) nicknames: ill-seeming is a name connoting wickedness, (to be used of one) after he has believed; and those who do not desist are (indeed) doing wrong.

يَٰٓأَيُّهَا ٱلَّذِينَ ءَامَنُواْ لَا يَسۡخَرۡ قَوۡمٞ مِّن قَوۡمٍ عَسَىٰٓ أَن
يَكُونُواْ خَيۡرٗا مِّنۡهُمۡ وَلَا نِسَآءٞ مِّن نِّسَآءٍ عَسَىٰٓ أَن يَكُنَّ
خَيۡرٗا مِّنۡهُنَّۖ وَلَا تَلۡمِزُوٓاْ أَنفُسَكُمۡ وَلَا تَنَابَزُواْ
بِٱلۡأَلۡقَٰبِۖ بِئۡسَ ٱلِٱسۡمُ ٱلۡفُسُوقُ بَعۡدَ ٱلۡإِيمَٰنِۚ وَمَن
لَّمۡ يَتُبۡ فَأُوْلَٰٓئِكَ هُمُ ٱلظَّٰلِمُونَ ١١

12. O you who believe! Avoid suspicion as much (as possible); for suspicion in some cases is a sin; and spy not on each other, nor speak ill of each other behind their backs. Would any of you like to eat the flesh of his dead brother? Nay you would abhor it, but fear Allah: for Allah is Oft-Returning, Most Merciful.

يَٰٓأَيُّهَا ٱلَّذِينَ ءَامَنُوا۟ ٱجْتَنِبُوا۟ كَثِيرًا مِّنَ ٱلظَّنِّ إِنَّ
بَعْضَ ٱلظَّنِّ إِثْمٌ ۖ وَلَا تَجَسَّسُوا۟ وَلَا يَغْتَب بَّعْضُكُم
بَعْضًا ۚ أَيُحِبُّ أَحَدُكُمْ أَن يَأْكُلَ لَحْمَ أَخِيهِ مَيْتًا
فَكَرِهْتُمُوهُ ۚ وَٱتَّقُوا۟ ٱللَّهَ ۚ إِنَّ ٱللَّهَ تَوَّابٌ رَّحِيمٌ ﴿١٢﴾

13. O mankind! We created you from a single (pair) of a male and a female and made you into nations and tribes, that you may know each other (not that you may despise each other). Verily the most honoured of you in the sight of Allah is (he who is) the most righteous of you. And Allah has full knowledge and is well acquainted (with all things).

يَٰٓأَيُّهَا ٱلنَّاسُ إِنَّا خَلَقْنَٰكُم مِّن ذَكَرٍ وَأُنثَىٰ وَجَعَلْنَٰكُمْ شُعُوبًا
وَقَبَآئِلَ لِتَعَارَفُوٓا۟ ۚ إِنَّ أَكْرَمَكُمْ عِندَ ٱللَّهِ أَتْقَىٰكُمْ ۚ
إِنَّ ٱللَّهَ عَلِيمٌ خَبِيرٌ ﴿١٣﴾

14. The desert Arabs say, "We believe." Say, "You have no faith; but you (should) say, 'We have submitted our wills to Allah,' for not yet has faith entered your hearts. But if you obey Allah and His messenger, He will not belittle anything of your deeds: for Allah is Oft-Forgiving, Most Merciful."

۞ قَالَتِ ٱلْأَعْرَابُ ءَامَنَّا ۖ قُل لَّمْ تُؤْمِنُوا۟ وَلَٰكِن قُولُوٓا۟ نصف الحزب ٥٢
أَسْلَمْنَا وَلَمَّا يَدْخُلِ ٱلْإِيمَٰنُ فِى قُلُوبِكُمْ ۖ وَإِن تُطِيعُوا۟
ٱللَّهَ وَرَسُولَهُۥ لَا يَلِتْكُم مِّنْ أَعْمَٰلِكُمْ شَيْـًٔا ۚ إِنَّ
ٱللَّهَ غَفُورٌ رَّحِيمٌ ﴿١٤﴾

15. Only those are believers who have believed in Allah and His messenger, and have never since doubted, but have striven with their belongings and their persons in the cause of Allah: such are the sincere ones.

إِنَّمَا ٱلْمُؤْمِنُونَ ٱلَّذِينَ ءَامَنُوا۟ بِٱللَّهِ وَرَسُولِهِۦ
ثُمَّ لَمْ يَرْتَابُوا۟ وَجَٰهَدُوا۟ بِأَمْوَٰلِهِمْ وَأَنفُسِهِمْ
فِى سَبِيلِ ٱللَّهِ ۚ أُو۟لَٰٓئِكَ هُمُ ٱلصَّٰدِقُونَ ﴿١٥﴾

16. Say: "What! Will you instruct Allah about your religion?" But Allah knows all that is in the heavens and on earth: He has full knowledge of all things.

قُلْ أَتُعَلِّمُونَ ٱللَّهَ بِدِينِكُمْ وَٱللَّهُ يَعْلَمُ مَا فِى
ٱلسَّمَٰوَٰتِ وَمَا فِى ٱلْأَرْضِ ۚ وَٱللَّهُ بِكُلِّ شَىْءٍ عَلِيمٌ ﴿١٦﴾

17. They impress on you as a favour that they have embraced Islam. Say, "Count

يَمُنُّونَ عَلَيْكَ أَنْ أَسْلَمُوا۟ ۖ قُل لَّا تَمُنُّوا۟ عَلَىَّ

إِسْلَٰمَكُم ۖ بَلِ ٱللَّهُ يَمُنُّ عَلَيْكُمْ أَنْ هَدَىٰكُمْ
لِلْإِيمَٰنِ إِن كُنتُمْ صَٰدِقِينَ ١٧

not your Islam as a favour upon me: nay, Allah has conferred a favour upon you that He has guided you to the faith, if you be true and sincere.

إِنَّ ٱللَّهَ يَعْلَمُ غَيْبَ ٱلسَّمَٰوَٰتِ وَٱلْأَرْضِ ۚ وَٱللَّهُ
بَصِيرٌۢ بِمَا تَعْمَلُونَ ١٨

18. Verily Allah knows the secrets of the heavens and the earth: and Allah sees well all that you do."

سُورَةُ قٓ

Surah 50: ***Qaf*** **(The Letter 'Qaf')**

بِسْمِ ٱللَّهِ ٱلرَّحْمَٰنِ ٱلرَّحِيمِ

In the name of Allah,
Most Gracious, Most Merciful.

قٓ ۚ وَٱلْقُرْءَانِ ٱلْمَجِيدِ ١

1. *Qaf.* By the Glorious Qur'an (You are Allah's messenger).

بَلْ عَجِبُوٓا۟ أَن جَآءَهُم مُّنذِرٌ مِّنْهُمْ فَقَالَ ٱلْكَٰفِرُونَ
هَٰذَا شَىْءٌ عَجِيبٌ ٢

2. But they wonder that there has come to them a warner from among themselves. So the unbelievers say: "This is a wonderful thing!

أَءِذَا مِتْنَا وَكُنَّا تُرَابًا ۖ ذَٰلِكَ رَجْعٌۢ بَعِيدٌ ٣

3. What! When we die and become dust, (shall we live again?). That is a (sort of) return far (from our understanding)."

قَدْ عَلِمْنَا مَا تَنقُصُ ٱلْأَرْضُ مِنْهُمْ ۖ وَعِندَنَا كِتَٰبٌ
حَفِيظٌۢ ٤

4. We already know how much of them the earth takes away: with Us is a record guarding (the full account).

بَلْ كَذَّبُوا۟ بِٱلْحَقِّ لَمَّا جَآءَهُمْ فَهُمْ فِىٓ أَمْرٍ مَّرِيجٍ ٥

5. But they deny the truth when it comes to them: so they are in a confused state.

أَفَلَمْ يَنظُرُوٓا۟ إِلَى ٱلسَّمَآءِ فَوْقَهُمْ كَيْفَ بَنَيْنَٰهَا
وَزَيَّنَّٰهَا وَمَا لَهَا مِن فُرُوجٍ ٦

6. Do they not look at the sky above them? - How We have made it and adorned it, and there are no flaws in it?

7. And the earth - We have spread it out, and set on it mountains standing firm, and produced in it every kind of beautiful growth (in pairs) -

وَٱلۡأَرۡضَ مَدَدۡنَٰهَا وَأَلۡقَيۡنَا فِيهَا رَوَٰسِيَ وَأَنۢبَتۡنَا فِيهَا
مِن كُلِّ زَوۡجِۭ بَهِيجٖ ٧

8. To be observed and commemorated by every devotee turning (to Allah).

تَبۡصِرَةٗ وَذِكۡرَىٰ لِكُلِّ عَبۡدٖ مُّنِيبٖ ٨

9. And We send down from the sky rain charged with blessing, and We produce with it gardens and grain for harvests;

وَنَزَّلۡنَا مِنَ ٱلسَّمَآءِ مَآءٗ مُّبَٰرَكٗا فَأَنۢبَتۡنَا بِهِۦ جَنَّٰتٖ
وَحَبَّ ٱلۡحَصِيدِ ٩

10. And tall (and stately) palm trees, with shoots of fruit-stalks, piled one over another -

وَٱلنَّخۡلَ بَاسِقَٰتٖ لَّهَا طَلۡعٞ نَّضِيدٞ ١٠

11. As sustenance for (Allah's) servants - and We give (new) life therewith to land that is dead: thus will be the resurrection.

رِّزۡقٗا لِّلۡعِبَادِۖ وَأَحۡيَيۡنَا بِهِۦ بَلۡدَةٗ مَّيۡتٗاۚ كَذَٰلِكَ ٱلۡخُرُوجُ ١١

12. Before them was denied (the hereafter) by the people of Noah, the companions of ar-Rass, the Thamud,

كَذَّبَتۡ قَبۡلَهُمۡ قَوۡمُ نُوحٖ وَأَصۡحَٰبُ ٱلرَّسِّ وَثَمُودُ ١٢

13. The 'Ad, Pharaoh, the brothers of Lot,

وَعَادٞ وَفِرۡعَوۡنُ وَإِخۡوَٰنُ لُوطٖ ١٣

14. The companions of the wood, and the people of Tubba; each one (of them) rejected the messengers, and My warning was duly fulfilled (in them).

وَأَصۡحَٰبُ ٱلۡأَيۡكَةِ وَقَوۡمُ تُبَّعٖۚ كُلّٞ كَذَّبَ ٱلرُّسُلَ فَحَقَّ
وَعِيدِ ١٤

15. Were We then weary with the first creation, that they should be in confused doubt about a new creation?

أَفَعَيِينَا بِٱلۡخَلۡقِ ٱلۡأَوَّلِۚ بَلۡ هُمۡ فِي لَبۡسٖ مِّنۡ خَلۡقٖ
جَدِيدٖ ١٥

16. It was We Who created man and We know what dark suggestions his soul makes to him: for We are nearer to him than (his) jugular vein.

وَلَقَدۡ خَلَقۡنَا ٱلۡإِنسَٰنَ وَنَعۡلَمُ مَا تُوَسۡوِسُ بِهِۦ نَفۡسُهُۥۖ
وَنَحۡنُ أَقۡرَبُ إِلَيۡهِ مِنۡ حَبۡلِ ٱلۡوَرِيدِ ١٦

17. See, two (guardian angels) appointed to learn (his doings) learn (and note them), one sitting on the right and one on the left.

إِذۡ يَتَلَقَّى ٱلۡمُتَلَقِّيَانِ عَنِ ٱلۡيَمِينِ وَعَنِ ٱلشِّمَالِ قَعِيدٞ ١٧

18. Not a word does he utter but there is a sentinel by him ready (to note it).

مَّا يَلۡفِظُ مِن قَوۡلٍ إِلَّا لَدَيۡهِ رَقِيبٌ عَتِيدٞ ١٨

19. And the stupor of death will bring truth (before his eyes): "This was the thing which you were trying to escape!"

وَجَآءَتۡ سَكۡرَةُ ٱلۡمَوۡتِ بِٱلۡحَقِّۖ ذَٰلِكَ مَا كُنتَ مِنۡهُ
تَحِيدُ ١٩

20. And the trumpet shall be blown: that will be the day of which warning (had been given).

وَنُفِخَ فِي ٱلصُّورِۚ ذَٰلِكَ يَوۡمُ ٱلۡوَعِيدِ ٢٠

21. And there will come out every soul: with each will be an (angel) to drive, and an (angel) to bear witness.

وَجَآءَتۡ كُلُّ نَفۡسٖ مَّعَهَا سَآئِقٞ وَشَهِيدٞ ٢١

22. (It will be said:) "You were heedless of this; now have We removed your veil and sharp is your sight this day!"

لَّقَدۡ كُنتَ فِي غَفۡلَةٖ مِّنۡ هَٰذَا فَكَشَفۡنَا عَنكَ غِطَآءَكَ
فَبَصَرُكَ ٱلۡيَوۡمَ حَدِيدٞ ٢٢

23. And his companion will say: "Here is (his record) ready with me!"

وَقَالَ قَرِينُهُۥ هَٰذَا مَا لَدَيَّ عَتِيدٌ ٢٣

24. (The sentence will be:) "Throw, throw into hell every contumacious rejecter, (of Allah)! -

أَلۡقِيَا فِي جَهَنَّمَ كُلَّ كَفَّارٍ عَنِيدٖ ٢٤

25. Who forbade what was good, transgressed all bounds, cast doubts and suspicions;

مَّنَّاعٖ لِّلۡخَيۡرِ مُعۡتَدٖ مُّرِيبٍ ٢٥

26. Who set up another god besides Allah: throw him into a severe penalty."

ٱلَّذِي جَعَلَ مَعَ ٱللَّهِ إِلَٰهًا ءَاخَرَ فَأَلۡقِيَاهُ فِي ٱلۡعَذَابِ
ٱلشَّدِيدِ ٢٦

27. His companion will say: "Our Lord! I did not make him transgress, but he was (himself) far astray."

۞قَالَ قَرِينُهُۥ رَبَّنَا مَآ أَطۡغَيۡتُهُۥ وَلَٰكِن كَانَ فِي ضَلَٰلِۭ ثة أرباع حزب ٥٢
بَعِيدٖ ٢٧

28. He will say: "Dispute not with each other in My presence: I had already in advance sent you warning.

قَالَ لَا تَخْتَصِمُوا۟ لَدَىَّ وَقَدْ قَدَّمْتُ إِلَيْكُم بِٱلْوَعِيدِ ﴿٢٨﴾

29. The word changes not before Me, and I do not the least injustice to My servants."

مَا يُبَدَّلُ ٱلْقَوْلُ لَدَىَّ وَمَآ أَنَا۠ بِظَلَّٰمٍ لِّلْعَبِيدِ ﴿٢٩﴾

30. One day We will ask hell, "Are you filled to the full?" It will say, "Are there any more (to come)?"

يَوْمَ نَقُولُ لِجَهَنَّمَ هَلِ ٱمْتَلَأْتِ وَتَقُولُ هَلْ مِن
مَّزِيدٍ ﴿٣٠﴾

31. And the garden will be brought near to the righteous - no more a thing distant.

وَأُزْلِفَتِ ٱلْجَنَّةُ لِلْمُتَّقِينَ غَيْرَ بَعِيدٍ ﴿٣١﴾

32. (A voice will say:) "This is what was promised for you - for everyone who turned (to Allah) in sincere repentance, who kept (His law).

هَٰذَا مَا تُوعَدُونَ لِكُلِّ أَوَّابٍ حَفِيظٍ ﴿٣٢﴾

33. Who feared (Allah) Most Gracious unseen, and brought a heart turned in devotion (to Him):

مَّنْ خَشِىَ ٱلرَّحْمَٰنَ بِٱلْغَيْبِ وَجَآءَ بِقَلْبٍ مُّنِيبٍ ﴿٣٣﴾

34. Enter you in it in peace and security; this is a day of eternal life!"

ٱدْخُلُوهَا بِسَلَٰمٍ ۖ ذَٰلِكَ يَوْمُ ٱلْخُلُودِ ﴿٣٤﴾

35. There will be for them in it all that they wish and more besides in Our presence.

لَهُم مَّا يَشَآءُونَ فِيهَا وَلَدَيْنَا مَزِيدٌ ﴿٣٥﴾

36. But how many generations before them did We destroy (for their sins) - stronger in power than they? Then did they wander through the land: was there any place of escape (for them)?

وَكَمْ أَهْلَكْنَا قَبْلَهُم مِّن قَرْنٍ هُمْ أَشَدُّ مِنْهُم
بَطْشًا فَنَقَّبُوا۟ فِى ٱلْبِلَٰدِ هَلْ مِن مَّحِيصٍ ﴿٣٦﴾

37. Verily in this is a message for any that has a heart and understanding or who gives ear and earnestly witnesses (the truth).

إِنَّ فِى ذَٰلِكَ لَذِكْرَىٰ لِمَن كَانَ لَهُۥ قَلْبٌ
أَوْ أَلْقَى ٱلسَّمْعَ وَهُوَ شَهِيدٌ ﴿٣٧﴾

38. We created the heavens and the earth

وَلَقَدْ خَلَقْنَا ٱلسَّمَٰوَٰتِ وَٱلْأَرْضَ وَمَا بَيْنَهُمَا فِى

سِتَّةِ أَيَّامٖ وَمَا مَسَّنَا مِن لُّغُوبٖ ٣٨

and all between them in six days, nor did any sense of weariness touch Us.

فَٱصۡبِرۡ عَلَىٰ مَا يَقُولُونَ وَسَبِّحۡ بِحَمۡدِ رَبِّكَ قَبۡلَ
طُلُوعِ ٱلشَّمۡسِ وَقَبۡلَ ٱلۡغُرُوبِ ٣٩

39. Bear, then, with patience, all that they say, and celebrate the praises of your Lord, before the rising of the sun and before (its) setting,

وَمِنَ ٱلَّيۡلِ فَسَبِّحۡهُ وَأَدۡبَٰرَ ٱلسُّجُودِ ٤٠

40. And during part of the night, (also,) celebrate His praises and (so likewise) after the postures of adoration.

وَٱسۡتَمِعۡ يَوۡمَ يُنَادِ ٱلۡمُنَادِ مِن مَّكَانٖ قَرِيبٖ ٤١

41. And listen for the day when the caller will call out from a place quite near -

يَوۡمَ يَسۡمَعُونَ ٱلصَّيۡحَةَ بِٱلۡحَقِّۚ ذَٰلِكَ يَوۡمُ ٱلۡخُرُوجِ ٤٢

42. The day when they will hear a (mighty) blast in (very) truth: that will be the day of resurrection.

إِنَّا نَحۡنُ نُحۡيِۦ وَنُمِيتُ وَإِلَيۡنَا ٱلۡمَصِيرُ ٤٣

43. Verily it is We Who give life and death; and to Us is the final goal -

يَوۡمَ تَشَقَّقُ ٱلۡأَرۡضُ عَنۡهُمۡ سِرَاعٗاۚ ذَٰلِكَ حَشۡرٌ عَلَيۡنَا
يَسِيرٞ ٤٤

44. The day when the earth will be split apart, from (men) hurrying out: that will be a gathering together - quite easy for Us.

نَّحۡنُ أَعۡلَمُ بِمَا يَقُولُونَۖ وَمَآ أَنتَ عَلَيۡهِم بِجَبَّارٖۖ فَذَكِّرۡ
بِٱلۡقُرۡءَانِ مَن يَخَافُ وَعِيدِ ٤٥

45. We know best what they say; and you are not one to overawe them by force. So admonish with the Qur'an such as fear My warning!

سُورَةُ الذَّارِيَاتِ

Surah 51: ***Adh-Dhariyat*** **(The Winds That Scatter)**

بِسۡمِ ٱللَّهِ ٱلرَّحۡمَٰنِ ٱلرَّحِيمِ

In the name of Allah,
Most Gracious, Most Merciful.

وَٱلذَّٰرِيَٰتِ ذَرۡوٗا ١

1. By the (winds) that scatter broadcast;

2. And those that lift and bear away heavy weights;

فَٱلْحَٰمِلَٰتِ وِقْرًا ﴿٢﴾

3. And those that flow with ease and gentleness;

فَٱلْجَٰرِيَٰتِ يُسْرًا ﴿٣﴾

4. And those that distribute and apportion by command -

فَٱلْمُقَسِّمَٰتِ أَمْرًا ﴿٤﴾

5. Verily that which you are promised is true;

إِنَّمَا تُوعَدُونَ لَصَادِقٌ ﴿٥﴾

6. And verily judgement and justice must indeed come to pass.

وَإِنَّ ٱلدِّينَ لَوَٰقِعٌ ﴿٦﴾

7. By the sky with (its) numerous paths,

وَٱلسَّمَآءِ ذَاتِ ٱلْحُبُكِ ﴿٧﴾

8. Truly you are in a doctrine discordant,

إِنَّكُمْ لَفِى قَوْلٍ مُّخْتَلِفٍ ﴿٨﴾

9. Through which are deluded (away from the truth) such as would be deluded.

يُؤْفَكُ عَنْهُ مَنْ أُفِكَ ﴿٩﴾

10. Woe to the falsehood-mongers -

قُتِلَ ٱلْخَرَّٰصُونَ ﴿١٠﴾

11. Those who (flounder) heedless in a flood of confusion:

ٱلَّذِينَ هُمْ فِى غَمْرَةٍ سَاهُونَ ﴿١١﴾

12. They ask, "When will be the day of judgement and justice?"

يَسْـَٔلُونَ أَيَّانَ يَوْمُ ٱلدِّينِ ﴿١٢﴾

13. (It will be) a day when they will be tried (and tested) over the fire!

يَوْمَ هُمْ عَلَى ٱلنَّارِ يُفْتَنُونَ ﴿١٣﴾

14. "Taste you your trial! This is what you used to ask to be hastened!"

ذُوقُوا۟ فِتْنَتَكُمْ هَٰذَا ٱلَّذِى كُنتُم بِهِۦ تَسْتَعْجِلُونَ ﴿١٤﴾

15. As to the righteous, they will be in the midst of gardens and springs,

إِنَّ ٱلْمُتَّقِينَ فِى جَنَّٰتٍ وَعُيُونٍ ﴿١٥﴾

16. Taking joy in the things which their

ءَاخِذِينَ مَآ ءَاتَىٰهُمْ رَبُّهُمْ ۚ إِنَّهُمْ كَانُوا۟ قَبْلَ ذَٰلِكَ

مُحْسِنِينَ ﴿١٦﴾

Lord gives them, because, before then they lived a good life.

كَانُوا۟ قَلِيلًا مِّنَ ٱلَّيْلِ مَا يَهْجَعُونَ ﴿١٧﴾

17. They were in the habit of sleeping but little by night,

وَبِٱلْأَسْحَارِ هُمْ يَسْتَغْفِرُونَ ﴿١٨﴾

18. And in the hours of early dawn, they (were found) praying for forgiveness;

وَفِىٓ أَمْوَٰلِهِمْ حَقٌّ لِّلسَّآئِلِ وَٱلْمَحْرُومِ ﴿١٩﴾

19. And in their wealth and possessions (was remembered) the right of the (needy), him who asked, and him who (for some reason) was prevented (from asking).

وَفِى ٱلْأَرْضِ ءَايَٰتٌ لِّلْمُوقِنِينَ ﴿٢٠﴾

20. On the earth are signs for those of assured faith,

وَفِىٓ أَنفُسِكُمْ ۚ أَفَلَا تُبْصِرُونَ ﴿٢١﴾

21. As also in your own selves: will you not then see?

وَفِى ٱلسَّمَآءِ رِزْقُكُمْ وَمَا تُوعَدُونَ ﴿٢٢﴾

22. And in heaven is your sustenance, as (also) that which you are promised.

فَوَرَبِّ ٱلسَّمَآءِ وَٱلْأَرْضِ إِنَّهُۥ لَحَقٌّ مِّثْلَ مَآ أَنَّكُمْ
تَنطِقُونَ ﴿٢٣﴾

23. Then, by the Lord of heaven and earth, this is the very truth, as much as the fact that you can speak intelligently to each other.

هَلْ أَتَىٰكَ حَدِيثُ ضَيْفِ إِبْرَٰهِيمَ ٱلْمُكْرَمِينَ ﴿٢٤﴾

24. Has the story reached you, of the honoured guests of Abraham?

إِذْ دَخَلُوا۟ عَلَيْهِ فَقَالُوا۟ سَلَٰمًا ۖ قَالَ سَلَٰمٌ قَوْمٌ
مُّنكَرُونَ ﴿٢٥﴾

25. See, they entered his presence, and said: "Peace!" He said: "Peace!" (And thought,) "These seem unusual people."

فَرَاغَ إِلَىٰٓ أَهْلِهِۦ فَجَآءَ بِعِجْلٍ سَمِينٍ ﴿٢٦﴾

26. Then he turned quickly to his household, brought out a fatted calf.

فَقَرَّبَهُۥٓ إِلَيْهِمْ قَالَ أَلَا تَأْكُلُونَ ﴿٢٧﴾

27. And placed it before them. He said, "Will you not eat?"

فَأَوْجَسَ مِنْهُمْ خِيفَةً ۖ قَالُوا لَا تَخَفْ ۖ وَبَشَّرُوهُ بِغُلَامٍ
عَلِيمٍ ﴿٢٨﴾

28. (When they did not eat) he conceived a fear of them. They said, "Fear not," and they gave him glad tidings of a son endowed with knowledge.

فَأَقْبَلَتِ امْرَأَتُهُ فِي صَرَّةٍ فَصَكَّتْ وَجْهَهَا وَقَالَتْ
عَجُوزٌ عَقِيمٌ ﴿٢٩﴾

29. But his wife came forward (laughing) aloud: she struck her forehead and said: "A barren old woman!"

قَالُوا كَذَٰلِكِ قَالَ رَبُّكِ ۖ إِنَّهُ هُوَ الْحَكِيمُ
الْعَلِيمُ ﴿٣٠﴾

30. They said, "Even so has your Lord spoken: and He is full of Wisdom and Knowledge."

الجزء ٢٧ الحزب ٥٣

۞ قَالَ فَمَا خَطْبُكُمْ أَيُّهَا الْمُرْسَلُونَ ﴿٣١﴾

✻**31.** (Abraham) said: "And what, O you messengers, is your errand (now)?"

قَالُوا إِنَّا أُرْسِلْنَا إِلَىٰ قَوْمٍ مُجْرِمِينَ ﴿٣٢﴾

32. They said, "We have been sent to a people (deep) in sin -

لِنُرْسِلَ عَلَيْهِمْ حِجَارَةً مِنْ طِينٍ ﴿٣٣﴾

33. To bring on, on them, (a shower of) stones of clay (brimstone),

مُسَوَّمَةً عِنْدَ رَبِّكَ لِلْمُسْرِفِينَ ﴿٣٤﴾

34. Marked as from your Lord for those who trespass beyond bounds."

فَأَخْرَجْنَا مَنْ كَانَ فِيهَا مِنَ الْمُؤْمِنِينَ ﴿٣٥﴾

35. Then We evacuated those of the believers who were there,

فَمَا وَجَدْنَا فِيهَا غَيْرَ بَيْتٍ مِنَ الْمُسْلِمِينَ ﴿٣٦﴾

36. But We found not there any just (Muslim) persons except in one house:

وَتَرَكْنَا فِيهَا آيَةً لِلَّذِينَ يَخَافُونَ الْعَذَابَ الْأَلِيمَ ﴿٣٧﴾

37. And We left there a sign for such as fear the grievous penalty.

وَفِي مُوسَىٰ إِذْ أَرْسَلْنَاهُ إِلَىٰ فِرْعَوْنَ بِسُلْطَانٍ مُبِينٍ ﴿٣٨﴾

38. And in Moses (was another sign): behold, We sent him to Pharaoh, with authority manifest.

فَتَوَلَّىٰ بِرُكْنِهِ وَقَالَ سَاحِرٌ أَوْ مَجْنُونٌ ﴿٣٩﴾

39. But (Pharaoh) turned back with his chiefs, and said, "A sorcerer, or one possessed!"

✻ Part-27

40. So We took him and his forces, and threw them into the sea: and his was the blame.

فَأَخَذۡنَٰهُ وَجُنُودَهُۥ فَنَبَذۡنَٰهُمۡ فِي ٱلۡيَمِّ وَهُوَ مُلِيمٞ ٤٠

41. And in the 'Ad (people) (was another sign): see, We sent against them the devastating wind:

وَفِي عَادٍ إِذۡ أَرۡسَلۡنَا عَلَيۡهِمُ ٱلرِّيحَ ٱلۡعَقِيمَ ٤١

42. It left nothing whatever that it came up against, but reduced it to ruin and rottenness.

مَا تَذَرُ مِن شَيۡءٍ أَتَتۡ عَلَيۡهِ إِلَّا جَعَلَتۡهُ كَٱلرَّمِيمِ ٤٢

43. And in the Thamud (was another sign): see they were told, "Enjoy (your brief day) for a little while!"

وَفِي ثَمُودَ إِذۡ قِيلَ لَهُمۡ تَمَتَّعُواْ حَتَّىٰ حِينٖ ٤٣

44. But they insolently defied the command of their Lord: so the stunning noise (of an earthquake) seized them, even while they were looking on.

فَعَتَوۡاْ عَنۡ أَمۡرِ رَبِّهِمۡ فَأَخَذَتۡهُمُ ٱلصَّٰعِقَةُ وَهُمۡ
يَنظُرُونَ ٤٤

45. Then they could not even stand (on their feet), nor could they help themselves.

فَمَا ٱسۡتَطَٰعُواْ مِن قِيَامٖ وَمَا كَانُواْ مُنتَصِرِينَ ٤٥

46. So were the people of Noah before them: for they wickedly transgressed.

وَقَوۡمَ نُوحٖ مِّن قَبۡلُۖ إِنَّهُمۡ كَانُواْ قَوۡمٗا فَٰسِقِينَ ٤٦

47. With the power and skill did We construct the firmament: for it is We Who create the vastness of space.

وَٱلسَّمَآءَ بَنَيۡنَٰهَا بِأَيۡيْدٖ وَإِنَّا لَمُوسِعُونَ ٤٧

48. And We have spread out the (spacious) earth: how excellently We do spread out!

وَٱلۡأَرۡضَ فَرَشۡنَٰهَا فَنِعۡمَ ٱلۡمَٰهِدُونَ ٤٨

49. And of everything We have created pairs: that you may receive instruction.

وَمِن كُلِّ شَيۡءٍ خَلَقۡنَا زَوۡجَيۡنِ لَعَلَّكُمۡ تَذَكَّرُونَ ٤٩

50. Hasten you then (at once) to Allah: I am from Him a warner to you clear and open!

فَفِرُّوٓاْ إِلَى ٱللَّهِۖ إِنِّي لَكُم مِّنۡهُ نَذِيرٞ مُّبِينٞ ٥٠

51. And make not another an object of worship with Allah: I am from Him a warner to you, clear and open!

وَلَا تَجۡعَلُواْ مَعَ ٱللَّهِ إِلَٰهًا ءَاخَرَۖ إِنِّي لَكُم مِّنۡهُ
نَذِيرٞ مُّبِينٞ ٥١

52. Similarly, no messenger came to the peoples before them, but they said (of him) in like manner, "A sorcerer, or one possessed!"

كَذَٰلِكَ مَآ أَتَى ٱلَّذِينَ مِن قَبۡلِهِم مِّن رَّسُولٍ إِلَّا قَالُواْ سَاحِرٌ
أَوۡ مَجۡنُونٌ ٥٢

53. Is this the legacy they have transmitted, one to another? Nay, they are themselves a people transgressing beyond bounds!

أَتَوَاصَوۡاْ بِهِۦۚ بَلۡ هُمۡ قَوۡمٞ طَاغُونَ ٥٣

54. So turn away from them: not yours is the blame.

فَتَوَلَّ عَنۡهُمۡ فَمَآ أَنتَ بِمَلُومٖ ٥٤

55. But teach (your message): for teaching benefits the believers.

وَذَكِّرۡ فَإِنَّ ٱلذِّكۡرَىٰ تَنفَعُ ٱلۡمُؤۡمِنِينَ ٥٥

56. I have only created jinns and men, that they may serve Me.

وَمَا خَلَقۡتُ ٱلۡجِنَّ وَٱلۡإِنسَ إِلَّا لِيَعۡبُدُونِ ٥٦

57. No sustenance do I require of them, nor do I require that they should feed Me.

مَآ أُرِيدُ مِنۡهُم مِّن رِّزۡقٖ وَمَآ أُرِيدُ أَن يُطۡعِمُونِ ٥٧

58. For Allah is He Who gives (all) sustenance - Lord of Power - steadfast (forever).

إِنَّ ٱللَّهَ هُوَ ٱلرَّزَّاقُ ذُو ٱلۡقُوَّةِ ٱلۡمَتِينُ ٥٨

59. For the wrongdoers, their portion is like to the portion of their fellows (of earlier generations): then let them not ask Me to hasten (that portion)!

فَإِنَّ لِلَّذِينَ ظَلَمُواْ ذَنُوبٗا مِّثۡلَ ذَنُوبِ أَصۡحَٰبِهِمۡ فَلَا
يَسۡتَعۡجِلُونِ ٥٩

60. Woe, then, to the unbelievers, on account of that day of theirs which they have been promised!

فَوَيۡلٞ لِّلَّذِينَ كَفَرُواْ مِن يَوۡمِهِمُ ٱلَّذِي
يُوعَدُونَ ٦٠

سُورَةُ الطُّورِ

Surah 52: ***At-Tur*** **(The Mount)**

In the name of Allah,
Most Gracious, Most Merciful.

بِسۡمِ ٱللَّهِ ٱلرَّحۡمَٰنِ ٱلرَّحِيمِ

1. By the mount (of revelation);	وَٱلطُّورِ ١
2. By a decree inscribed,	وَكِتَٰبٖ مَّسۡطُورٖ ٢
3. In a scroll unfolded;	فِي رَقّٖ مَّنشُورٖ ٣
4. By the much-frequented fane;	وَٱلۡبَيۡتِ ٱلۡمَعۡمُورِ ٤
5. By the canopy raised high;	وَٱلسَّقۡفِ ٱلۡمَرۡفُوعِ ٥
6. And by the ocean filled with swell -	وَٱلۡبَحۡرِ ٱلۡمَسۡجُورِ ٦
7. Verily, the doom of your Lord will indeed come to pass -	إِنَّ عَذَابَ رَبِّكَ لَوَٰقِعٞ ٧
8. There is none that can avert it -	مَّا لَهُۥ مِن دَافِعٖ ٨
9. On the day when the firmament will be in dreadful commotion.	يَوۡمَ تَمُورُ ٱلسَّمَآءُ مَوۡرٗا ٩
10. And the mountains will fly here and there.	وَتَسِيرُ ٱلۡجِبَالُ سَيۡرٗا ١٠
11. Then woe that day to those that treat (truth) as falsehood -	فَوَيۡلٞ يَوۡمَئِذٖ لِّلۡمُكَذِّبِينَ ١١
12. That play (and paddle) in shallow trifles.	ٱلَّذِينَ هُمۡ فِي خَوۡضٖ يَلۡعَبُونَ ١٢
13. That day shall they be thrust down to the fire of hell, irresistibly.	يَوۡمَ يُدَعُّونَ إِلَىٰ نَارِ جَهَنَّمَ دَعًّا ١٣
14. "This," it will be said, "Is the fire - which you used to deny!	هَٰذِهِ ٱلنَّارُ ٱلَّتِي كُنتُم بِهَا تُكَذِّبُونَ ١٤
15. Is this then a fake, or is it you that do not see?	أَفَسِحۡرٌ هَٰذَآ أَمۡ أَنتُمۡ لَا تُبۡصِرُونَ ١٥

16. Burn you in it: the same is it to you whether you bear it with patience, or not: you but receive the recompense of your (own) deeds."

ٱصۡلَوۡهَا فَٱصۡبِرُوٓاْ أَوۡ لَا تَصۡبِرُواْ سَوَآءٌ عَلَيۡكُمۡۖ
إِنَّمَا تُجۡزَوۡنَ مَا كُنتُمۡ تَعۡمَلُونَ ١٦

17. As to the righteous, they will be in gardens, and in happiness -

إِنَّ ٱلۡمُتَّقِينَ فِي جَنَّٰتٖ وَنَعِيمٖ ١٧

18. Enjoying the (bliss) which their Lord has bestowed on them, and their Lord shall deliver them from the penalty of the fire.

فَٰكِهِينَ بِمَآ ءَاتَىٰهُمۡ رَبُّهُمۡ وَوَقَىٰهُمۡ رَبُّهُمۡ عَذَابَ
ٱلۡجَحِيمِ ١٨

19. (To them will be said:) "Eat and drink you, with profit and health, because of your (good) deeds."

كُلُواْ وَٱشۡرَبُواْ هَنِيٓـَٔۢا بِمَا كُنتُمۡ تَعۡمَلُونَ ١٩

20. They will recline (with ease) on thrones (of dignity) arranged in ranks; and We shall join them to companions, with beautiful big and lustrous eyes.

مُتَّكِـِٔينَ عَلَىٰ سُرُرٖ مَّصۡفُوفَةٖۖ وَزَوَّجۡنَٰهُم
بِحُورٍ عِينٖ ٢٠

21. And those who believe and whose families follow them in faith - to them shall We join their families: nor shall We deprive them (of the fruit) of anything of their works: (yet) is each individual in pledge for his deeds.

وَٱلَّذِينَ ءَامَنُواْ وَٱتَّبَعَتۡهُمۡ ذُرِّيَّتُهُم بِإِيمَٰنٍ أَلۡحَقۡنَا
بِهِمۡ ذُرِّيَّتَهُمۡ وَمَآ أَلَتۡنَٰهُم مِّنۡ عَمَلِهِم مِّن شَيۡءٖۚ كُلُّ
ٱمۡرِيِٕۭ بِمَا كَسَبَ رَهِينٞ ٢١

22. And We shall bestow on them, of fruit and meat, anything they shall desire.

وَأَمۡدَدۡنَٰهُم بِفَٰكِهَةٖ وَلَحۡمٖ مِّمَّا يَشۡتَهُونَ ٢٢

23. They shall there exchange one with another, a (loving) cup free of frivolity, free of all taint of ill.

يَتَنَٰزَعُونَ فِيهَا كَأۡسٗا لَّا لَغۡوٞ فِيهَا وَلَا تَأۡثِيمٞ ٢٣

24. Round about them will serve, (devoted) to them, youths (handsome) as pearls well-guarded.

۞ وَيَطُوفُ عَلَيۡهِمۡ غِلۡمَانٞ لَّهُمۡ كَأَنَّهُمۡ ربع الحزب ٥٣
لُؤۡلُؤٞ مَّكۡنُونٞ ٢٤

25. They will advance to each other, engaging in mutual enquiry.

وَأَقۡبَلَ بَعۡضُهُمۡ عَلَىٰ بَعۡضٖ يَتَسَآءَلُونَ ٢٥

26. They will say: "Before, we were not without fear for the sake of our people.

قَالُوٓاْ إِنَّا كُنَّا قَبۡلُ فِيٓ أَهۡلِنَا مُشۡفِقِينَ ٢٦

27. But Allah has been good to us, and has delivered us from the penalty of the scorching wind.

فَمَنَّ ٱللَّهُ عَلَيۡنَا وَوَقَىٰنَا عَذَابَ ٱلسَّمُومِ ٢٧

28. Truly, we did call to Him from of old: truly it is He, the Beneficent, the Merciful."

إِنَّا كُنَّا مِن قَبۡلُ نَدۡعُوهُۖ إِنَّهُۥ هُوَ ٱلۡبَرُّ ٱلرَّحِيمُ ٢٨

29. Therefore, proclaim you the praises (of your Lord): for by the grace of your Lord, you are no (vulgar) soothsayer, nor are you one possessed,

فَذَكِّرۡ فَمَآ أَنتَ بِنِعۡمَتِ رَبِّكَ بِكَاهِنٖ وَلَا مَجۡنُونٍ ٢٩

30. Or do they say - "A poet! We await for him some calamity (hatched) by time!"

أَمۡ يَقُولُونَ شَاعِرٞ نَّتَرَبَّصُ بِهِۦ رَيۡبَ ٱلۡمَنُونِ ٣٠

31. Say you: "Await you! - I too will wait along with you!"

قُلۡ تَرَبَّصُواْ فَإِنِّي مَعَكُم مِّنَ ٱلۡمُتَرَبِّصِينَ ٣١

32. Is it that their faculties of understanding urge them to this, or are they but a people transgressing beyond bounds?

أَمۡ تَأۡمُرُهُمۡ أَحۡلَٰمُهُم بِهَٰذَآۚ أَمۡ هُمۡ قَوۡمٞ طَاغُونَ ٣٢

33. Or do they say, "He fabricated the (message)?" Nay, they have no faith!

أَمۡ يَقُولُونَ تَقَوَّلَهُۥۚ بَل لَّا يُؤۡمِنُونَ ٣٣

34. Let them then produce a recital like it - if (it be) they speak the truth!

فَلۡيَأۡتُواْ بِحَدِيثٖ مِّثۡلِهِۦٓ إِن كَانُواْ صَٰدِقِينَ ٣٤

35. Were they created of nothing, or were they themselves the creators?

أَمۡ خُلِقُواْ مِنۡ غَيۡرِ شَيۡءٍ أَمۡ هُمُ ٱلۡخَٰلِقُونَ ٣٥

36. Or did they create the heavens and the earth? Nay, they have no firm belief.

أَمۡ خَلَقُواْ ٱلسَّمَٰوَٰتِ وَٱلۡأَرۡضَۚ بَل لَّا يُوقِنُونَ ٣٦

37. Or are the treasures of your Lord with them, or are they the managers (of affairs)?

أَمۡ عِندَهُمۡ خَزَآئِنُ رَبِّكَ أَمۡ هُمُ ٱلۡمُصَۜيۡطِرُونَ ٣٧

38. Or have they a ladder by which they can (climb up to heaven and) listen (to its secrets)? Then let (such a) listener of theirs produce a manifest proof.

أَمْ لَهُمْ سُلَّمٌ يَسْتَمِعُونَ فِيهِ ۖ فَلْيَأْتِ مُسْتَمِعُهُم
بِسُلْطَٰنٍ مُّبِينٍ ﴿٣٨﴾

39. Or has He only daughters and you have sons?

أَمْ لَهُ ٱلْبَنَٰتُ وَلَكُمُ ٱلْبَنُونَ ﴿٣٩﴾

40. Or is it that you do ask for a reward, so that they are burdened with a load of debt? -

أَمْ تَسْـَٔلُهُمْ أَجْرًا فَهُم مِّن مَّغْرَمٍ مُّثْقَلُونَ ﴿٤٠﴾

41. Or that the unseen is in their hands, and they write it down?

أَمْ عِندَهُمُ ٱلْغَيْبُ فَهُمْ يَكْتُبُونَ ﴿٤١﴾

42. Or do they intend a plot (against you)? But those who defy Allah are themselves involved in a plot!

أَمْ يُرِيدُونَ كَيْدًا ۖ فَٱلَّذِينَ كَفَرُوا۟ هُمُ ٱلْمَكِيدُونَ ﴿٤٢﴾

43. Or have they a god other than Allah? Exalted is Allah far above the things they associate with Him!

أَمْ لَهُمْ إِلَٰهٌ غَيْرُ ٱللَّهِ ۚ سُبْحَٰنَ ٱللَّهِ عَمَّا يُشْرِكُونَ ﴿٤٣﴾

44. Were they to see a piece of the sky falling (on them), they would (only) say: "Clouds gathered in heaps!"

وَإِن يَرَوْا۟ كِسْفًا مِّنَ ٱلسَّمَآءِ سَاقِطًا يَقُولُوا۟ سَحَابٌ
مَّرْكُومٌ ﴿٤٤﴾

45. So leave them alone until they encounter that day of theirs, in which they shall (involuntarily) swoon (with terror) -

فَذَرْهُمْ حَتَّىٰ يُلَٰقُوا۟ يَوْمَهُمُ ٱلَّذِى فِيهِ يُصْعَقُونَ ﴿٤٥﴾

46. The day when their plotting will benefit them nothing and no help shall be given them.

يَوْمَ لَا يُغْنِى عَنْهُمْ كَيْدُهُمْ شَيْـًٔا وَلَا هُمْ يُنصَرُونَ ﴿٤٦﴾

47. And verily, for those who do wrong, there is another punishment besides this: but most of them understand not.

وَإِنَّ لِلَّذِينَ ظَلَمُوا۟ عَذَابًا دُونَ ذَٰلِكَ وَلَٰكِنَّ أَكْثَرَهُمْ
لَا يَعْلَمُونَ ﴿٤٧﴾

48. Now await in patience the command of your Lord: for verily you are in Our eyes:

وَٱصْبِرْ لِحُكْمِ رَبِّكَ فَإِنَّكَ بِأَعْيُنِنَا ۖ وَسَبِّحْ بِحَمْدِ رَبِّكَ

حِينَ تَقُومُ ٤٨

and celebrate the praises of your Lord the while you stand up.

وَمِنَ ٱلَّيۡلِ فَسَبِّحۡهُ وَإِدۡبَٰرَ ٱلنُّجُومِ ٤٩

49. And for part of the night also praise you Him and at the retreat of the stars!

سُورَةُ النَّجۡمِ

Surah 53: ***An-Najm*** **(The Star)**

بِسۡمِ ٱللَّهِ ٱلرَّحۡمَٰنِ ٱلرَّحِيمِ

In the name of Allah,
Most Gracious, Most Merciful.

وَٱلنَّجۡمِ إِذَا هَوَىٰ ١

1. By the star when it goes down -

مَا ضَلَّ صَاحِبُكُمۡ وَمَا غَوَىٰ ٢

2. Your companion is neither astray nor being misled,

وَمَا يَنطِقُ عَنِ ٱلۡهَوَىٰٓ ٣

3. Nor does he say (anything) of (his own) desire.

إِنۡ هُوَ إِلَّا وَحۡيٞ يُوحَىٰ ٤

4. It is no less than inspiration sent down to him:

عَلَّمَهُۥ شَدِيدُ ٱلۡقُوَىٰ ٥

5. He was taught by one Mighty in power,

ذُو مِرَّةٖ فَٱسۡتَوَىٰ ٦

6. Endued with wisdom: for he appeared (in stately form),

وَهُوَ بِٱلۡأُفُقِ ٱلۡأَعۡلَىٰ ٧

7. While he was in the highest part of the horizon:

ثُمَّ دَنَا فَتَدَلَّىٰ ٨

8. Then he approached and came closer,

فَكَانَ قَابَ قَوۡسَيۡنِ أَوۡ أَدۡنَىٰ ٩

9. And was at a distance of but two bow-lengths or (even) nearer;

فَأَوۡحَىٰٓ إِلَىٰ عَبۡدِهِۦ مَآ أَوۡحَىٰ ١٠

10. So did (Allah) convey the inspiration to His servant - (conveyed) what He (meant) to convey.

11. The (prophet's) (mind and) heart in no way falsified that which he saw.

مَا كَذَبَ ٱلْفُؤَادُ مَا رَأَىٰٓ ﴿١١﴾

12. Will you then dispute with him concerning what he saw?

أَفَتُمَٰرُونَهُۥ عَلَىٰ مَا يَرَىٰ ﴿١٢﴾

13. For indeed he saw him at a second descent,

وَلَقَدْ رَءَاهُ نَزْلَةً أُخْرَىٰ ﴿١٣﴾

14. Near the lote-tree beyond which none may pass:

عِندَ سِدْرَةِ ٱلْمُنتَهَىٰ ﴿١٤﴾

15. Near it is the garden of abode.

عِندَهَا جَنَّةُ ٱلْمَأْوَىٰٓ ﴿١٥﴾

16. See, the lote-tree was shrouded (in mystery unspeakable!)

إِذْ يَغْشَى ٱلسِّدْرَةَ مَا يَغْشَىٰ ﴿١٦﴾

17. (His) sight never swerved, nor did it go wrong!

مَا زَاغَ ٱلْبَصَرُ وَمَا طَغَىٰ ﴿١٧﴾

18. For truly did he see, of the signs of his Lord, the Greatest!

لَقَدْ رَأَىٰ مِنْ ءَايَٰتِ رَبِّهِ ٱلْكُبْرَىٰٓ ﴿١٨﴾

19. Have you seen Lat, and Uzza,

أَفَرَءَيْتُمُ ٱللَّٰتَ وَٱلْعُزَّىٰ ﴿١٩﴾

20. And another, the third (goddess), Manat?

وَمَنَوٰةَ ٱلثَّالِثَةَ ٱلْأُخْرَىٰٓ ﴿٢٠﴾

21. What! For you the male sex, and for Him, the female?

أَلَكُمُ ٱلذَّكَرُ وَلَهُ ٱلْأُنثَىٰ ﴿٢١﴾

22. See, such would be indeed a division most unfair!

تِلْكَ إِذًا قِسْمَةٌ ضِيزَىٰٓ ﴿٢٢﴾

23. These are nothing but names which you have devised - you and your fathers - for which Allah has sent down no authority (whatever). They follow nothing but conjecture and what their own souls desire! - Even though there has already come to them guidance from their Lord!

إِنْ هِىَ إِلَّآ أَسْمَآءٌ سَمَّيْتُمُوهَآ أَنتُمْ وَءَابَآؤُكُم مَّآ أَنزَلَ
ٱللَّهُ بِهَا مِن سُلْطَٰنٍ ۚ إِن يَتَّبِعُونَ إِلَّا ٱلظَّنَّ وَمَا تَهْوَى
ٱلْأَنفُسُ ۖ وَلَقَدْ جَآءَهُم مِّن رَّبِّهِمُ ٱلْهُدَىٰٓ ﴿٢٣﴾

24. Nay, shall man have (just) anything he hankers after?

أَمۡ لِلۡإِنسَٰنِ مَا تَمَنَّىٰ ٢٤

25. But it is to Allah that the end and the beginning (of all things) belong.

فَلِلَّهِ ٱلۡأٓخِرَةُ وَٱلۡأُولَىٰ ٢٥

26. How many so ever be the angels in the heavens, their intercession will benefit nothing except after Allah has given leave for whom He pleases and that he is acceptable to Him.

نصف الحزب ٥٣ ۞وَكَم مِّن مَّلَكٖ فِي ٱلسَّمَٰوَٰتِ لَا تُغۡنِي شَفَٰعَتُهُمۡ
شَيۡـًٔا إِلَّا مِنۢ بَعۡدِ أَن يَأۡذَنَ ٱللَّهُ لِمَن يَشَآءُ وَيَرۡضَىٰٓ ٢٦

27. Those who believe not in the hereafter, name the angels with female names.

إِنَّ ٱلَّذِينَ لَا يُؤۡمِنُونَ بِٱلۡأٓخِرَةِ لَيُسَمُّونَ ٱلۡمَلَٰٓئِكَةَ
تَسۡمِيَةَ ٱلۡأُنثَىٰ ٢٧

28. But they have no knowledge in it. They follow nothing but conjecture; and conjecture avails nothing against truth.

وَمَا لَهُم بِهِۦ مِنۡ عِلۡمٍۖ إِن يَتَّبِعُونَ إِلَّا ٱلظَّنَّۖ وَإِنَّ ٱلظَّنَّ
لَا يُغۡنِي مِنَ ٱلۡحَقِّ شَيۡـٔٗا ٢٨

29. Therefore, shun those who turn away from Our message and desire nothing but the life of this world.

فَأَعۡرِضۡ عَن مَّن تَوَلَّىٰ عَن ذِكۡرِنَا وَلَمۡ يُرِدۡ إِلَّا ٱلۡحَيَوٰةَ
ٱلدُّنۡيَا ٢٩

30. That is as far as knowledge will reach them. Verily your Lord knows best those who stray from His path and He knows best those who receive guidance.

ذَٰلِكَ مَبۡلَغُهُم مِّنَ ٱلۡعِلۡمِۚ إِنَّ رَبَّكَ هُوَ أَعۡلَمُ بِمَن ضَلَّ عَن
سَبِيلِهِۦ وَهُوَ أَعۡلَمُ بِمَنِ ٱهۡتَدَىٰ ٣٠

31. Yea, to Allah belongs all that is in the heavens and on earth; so that He rewards those who do evil, according to their deeds, and He rewards those who do good, with what is best.

وَلِلَّهِ مَا فِي ٱلسَّمَٰوَٰتِ وَمَا فِي ٱلۡأَرۡضِ لِيَجۡزِيَ ٱلَّذِينَ
أَسَٰٓـُٔواْ بِمَا عَمِلُواْ وَيَجۡزِيَ ٱلَّذِينَ أَحۡسَنُواْ بِٱلۡحُسۡنَى ٣١

32. Those who avoid great sins and shameful deeds, only (falling into) small faults - verily your Lord is ample in forgiveness. He knows you well when He brings you out of the earth and when you

ٱلَّذِينَ يَجۡتَنِبُونَ كَبَٰٓئِرَ ٱلۡإِثۡمِ وَٱلۡفَوَٰحِشَ إِلَّا ٱللَّمَمَۚ
إِنَّ رَبَّكَ وَٰسِعُ ٱلۡمَغۡفِرَةِۚ هُوَ أَعۡلَمُ بِكُمۡ إِذۡ أَنشَأَكُم

are hidden in your mothers' wombs. Therefore, justify not yourselves: He knows best who it is that guards against evil.

مِّنَ ٱلۡأَرۡضِ وَإِذۡ أَنتُمۡ أَجِنَّةٞ فِي بُطُونِ أُمَّهَٰتِكُمۡۖ فَلَا
تُزَكُّوٓاْ أَنفُسَكُمۡۖ هُوَ أَعۡلَمُ بِمَنِ ٱتَّقَىٰٓ ٣٢

33. See you one who turns back,

أَفَرَءَيۡتَ ٱلَّذِي تَوَلَّىٰ ٣٣

34. Gives a little, then hardens (his heart)?

وَأَعۡطَىٰ قَلِيلٗا وَأَكۡدَىٰٓ ٣٤

35. What! Has he knowledge of the unseen so that he can see?

أَعِندَهُۥ عِلۡمُ ٱلۡغَيۡبِ فَهُوَ يَرَىٰٓ ٣٥

36. Nay, is he not acquainted with what is in the books of Moses -

أَمۡ لَمۡ يُنَبَّأۡ بِمَا فِي صُحُفِ مُوسَىٰ ٣٦

37. And of Abraham who fulfilled his engagements -

وَإِبۡرَٰهِيمَ ٱلَّذِي وَفَّىٰٓ ٣٧

38. Namely, that no bearer of burdens can bear the burden of another;

أَلَّا تَزِرُ وَازِرَةٞ وِزۡرَ أُخۡرَىٰ ٣٨

39. That man can have nothing but what he strives for;

وَأَن لَّيۡسَ لِلۡإِنسَٰنِ إِلَّا مَا سَعَىٰ ٣٩

40. That (the fruit of) his striving will soon come in sight;

وَأَنَّ سَعۡيَهُۥ سَوۡفَ يُرَىٰ ٤٠

41. Then will he be rewarded with a reward complete;

ثُمَّ يُجۡزَىٰهُ ٱلۡجَزَآءَ ٱلۡأَوۡفَىٰ ٤١

42. That to your Lord is the final goal;

وَأَنَّ إِلَىٰ رَبِّكَ ٱلۡمُنتَهَىٰ ٤٢

43. That it is He Who grants laughter and tears;

وَأَنَّهُۥ هُوَ أَضۡحَكَ وَأَبۡكَىٰ ٤٣

44. That it is He Who grants death and life;

وَأَنَّهُۥ هُوَ أَمَاتَ وَأَحۡيَا ٤٤

45. That He did create in pairs - male and female,

وَأَنَّهُۥ خَلَقَ ٱلزَّوۡجَيۡنِ ٱلذَّكَرَ وَٱلۡأُنثَىٰ ٤٥

46. From a seed when lodged (in its place);

مِن نُّطۡفَةٍ إِذَا تُمۡنَىٰ ٤٦

47. That He has promised a second creation (raising of the dead);

وَأَنَّ عَلَيۡهِ ٱلنَّشۡأَةَ ٱلۡأُخۡرَىٰ ٤٧

48. That it is He Who gives wealth and satisfaction;

وَأَنَّهُۥ هُوَ أَغۡنَىٰ وَأَقۡنَىٰ ٤٨

49. That He is the Lord of Sirius (the mighty star);

وَأَنَّهُۥ هُوَ رَبُّ ٱلشِّعۡرَىٰ ٤٩

50. And that it is He Who destroyed the (powerful) ancient 'Ad (people),

وَأَنَّهُۥٓ أَهۡلَكَ عَادًا ٱلۡأُولَىٰ ٥٠

51. And the Thamud, nor gave them a lease of perpetual life.

وَثَمُودَاْ فَمَآ أَبۡقَىٰ ٥١

52. And before them, the people of Noah, for that they were (all) most unjust and most insolent transgressors,

وَقَوۡمَ نُوحٖ مِّن قَبۡلُۖ إِنَّهُمۡ كَانُواْ هُمۡ أَظۡلَمَ
وَأَطۡغَىٰ ٥٢

53. And He destroyed the overthrown cities (of Sodom and Gomorrah),

وَٱلۡمُؤۡتَفِكَةَ أَهۡوَىٰ ٥٣

54. So that (ruins unknown) have covered them up.

فَغَشَّىٰهَا مَا غَشَّىٰ ٥٤

55. Then which of the gifts of your Lord (O man,) will you dispute about?

فَبِأَيِّ ءَالَآءِ رَبِّكَ تَتَمَارَىٰ ٥٥

56. This is a warner, of the (series of) warners of old!

هَٰذَا نَذِيرٞ مِّنَ ٱلنُّذُرِ ٱلۡأُولَىٰٓ ٥٦

57. The (judgement) ever approaching draws near:

أَزِفَتِ ٱلۡأٓزِفَةُ ٥٧

58. No (soul) but Allah can lay it bare.

لَيۡسَ لَهَا مِن دُونِ ٱللَّهِ كَاشِفَةٌ ٥٨

59. Do you then wonder at this recital?

أَفَمِنۡ هَٰذَا ٱلۡحَدِيثِ تَعۡجَبُونَ ٥٩

60. And will you laugh and not weep, -

وَتَضْحَكُونَ وَلَا تَبْكُونَ ﴿٦٠﴾

61. Wasting your time in vanities?

وَأَنتُمْ سَٰمِدُونَ ﴿٦١﴾

62. But fall you down in prostration to Allah and adore (Him)!

سجدة فَٱسْجُدُوا۟ لِلَّهِ وَٱعْبُدُوا۟ ۩ ﴿٦٢﴾

سُورَةُ القَمَرِ

Surah 54: **Al-Qamar (The Moon)**

In the name of Allah,
Most Gracious, Most Merciful.

بِسْمِ ٱللَّهِ ٱلرَّحْمَٰنِ ٱلرَّحِيمِ

1. The hour (of judgement) is near, and the moon is cleft asunder.

ٱقْتَرَبَتِ ٱلسَّاعَةُ وَٱنشَقَّ ٱلْقَمَرُ ﴿١﴾

2. But if they see a sign, they turn away, and say, "This is (but) transient magic."

وَإِن يَرَوْا۟ ءَايَةً يُعْرِضُوا۟ وَيَقُولُوا۟ سِحْرٌ مُّسْتَمِرٌّ ﴿٢﴾

3. They reject (the warning) and follow their (own) lusts, but every matter has its appointed time.

وَكَذَّبُوا۟ وَٱتَّبَعُوٓا۟ أَهْوَآءَهُمْ ۚ وَكُلُّ أَمْرٍ مُّسْتَقِرٌّ ﴿٣﴾

4. There have already come to them recitals in which there is (enough) to check (them),

وَلَقَدْ جَآءَهُم مِّنَ ٱلْأَنۢبَآءِ مَا فِيهِ مُزْدَجَرٌ ﴿٤﴾

5. Mature wisdom - but (the preaching of) warners profits them not.

حِكْمَةٌۢ بَٰلِغَةٌ ۖ فَمَا تُغْنِ ٱلنُّذُرُ ﴿٥﴾

6. Therefore, (O prophet), turn away from them. The day that the caller will call (them) to a terrible affair,

فَتَوَلَّ عَنْهُمْ يَوْمَ يَدْعُ ٱلدَّاعِ إِلَىٰ شَىْءٍ نُّكُرٍ ﴿٦﴾

7. They will come forth - their eyes humbled - from (their) graves, (torpid) like locusts scattered abroad,

خُشَّعًا أَبْصَٰرُهُمْ يَخْرُجُونَ مِنَ ٱلْأَجْدَاثِ كَأَنَّهُمْ جَرَادٌ
مُّنتَشِرٌ ﴿٧﴾

8. Hastening, with eyes transfixed, towards the caller! "Hard is this day!" - The unbelievers will say.

مُّهْطِعِينَ إِلَى ٱلدَّاعِ ۖ يَقُولُ ٱلْكَٰفِرُونَ هَٰذَا يَوْمٌ عَسِرٌ ﴿٨﴾

ثلاثة أرباع الحزب ٥٣

9. Before them the people of Noah rejected (their messenger): they rejected Our servant, and said, "Here is one possessed!" And he was driven out.

۞ كَذَّبَتْ قَبْلَهُمْ قَوْمُ نُوحٍ فَكَذَّبُوا عَبْدَنَا وَقَالُوا مَجْنُونٌ
وَازْدُجِرَ ﴿٩﴾

10. Then he called on his Lord: "I am one overcome: do You then help (me)!"

فَدَعَا رَبَّهُ أَنِّي مَغْلُوبٌ فَانْتَصِرْ ﴿١٠﴾

11. So We opened the gates of heaven, with water pouring out.

فَفَتَحْنَا أَبْوَابَ السَّمَاءِ بِمَاءٍ مُنْهَمِرٍ ﴿١١﴾

12. And We caused the earth to gush out with springs. So the waters met (and rose) to the extent decreed.

وَفَجَّرْنَا الْأَرْضَ عُيُونًا فَالْتَقَى الْمَاءُ عَلَىٰ أَمْرٍ
قَدْ قُدِرَ ﴿١٢﴾

13. But We bore him on an (ark) made of broad planks and caulked with palm-fibre:

وَحَمَلْنَاهُ عَلَىٰ ذَاتِ أَلْوَاحٍ وَدُسُرٍ ﴿١٣﴾

14. She floated under Our eyes (and care): a recompense to one who had been rejected (with scorn)!

تَجْرِي بِأَعْيُنِنَا جَزَاءً لِمَنْ كَانَ كُفِرَ ﴿١٤﴾

15. And We have left this as a sign (for all time): then is there any that will receive admonition?

وَلَقَدْ تَرَكْنَاهَا آيَةً فَهَلْ مِنْ مُدَّكِرٍ ﴿١٥﴾

16. But how (terrible) was My penalty and My warning?

فَكَيْفَ كَانَ عَذَابِي وَنُذُرِ ﴿١٦﴾

17. And We have indeed made the Qur'an easy to understand and remember: then is there any that will receive admonition?

وَلَقَدْ يَسَّرْنَا الْقُرْآنَ لِلذِّكْرِ فَهَلْ مِنْ مُدَّكِرٍ ﴿١٧﴾

18. The 'Ad (people) (too) rejected (truth): then how terrible was my penalty and my warning!

كَذَّبَتْ عَادٌ فَكَيْفَ كَانَ عَذَابِي وَنُذُرِ ﴿١٨﴾

19. For We sent against them a furious wind, on a day of violent disaster,

إِنَّا أَرْسَلْنَا عَلَيْهِمْ رِيحًا صَرْصَرًا فِي يَوْمِ نَحْسٍ
مُسْتَمِرٍّ ﴿١٩﴾

20. Plucking out men as if they were roots of palm-trees torn up (from the ground).

تَنزِعُ ٱلنَّاسَ كَأَنَّهُمْ أَعْجَازُ نَخْلٍ مُّنقَعِرٍ ﴿٢٠﴾

21. Yea, how (terrible) was My penalty and My warning!

فَكَيْفَ كَانَ عَذَابِى وَنُذُرِ ﴿٢١﴾

22. But We have indeed made the Qur'an easy to understand and remember: then is there any that will receive admonition?

وَلَقَدْ يَسَّرْنَا ٱلْقُرْءَانَ لِلذِّكْرِ فَهَلْ مِن مُّدَّكِرٍ ﴿٢٢﴾

23. The Thamud (also) rejected (their) warners.

كَذَّبَتْ ثَمُودُ بِٱلنُّذُرِ ﴿٢٣﴾

24. For they said: "What! A man! A solitary one from among ourselves! Shall we follow such a one? Truly should we then be straying in mind, and mad!

فَقَالُوٓا۟ أَبَشَرًا مِّنَّا وَٰحِدًا نَّتَّبِعُهُۥٓ إِنَّآ إِذًا لَّفِى ضَلَٰلٍ
وَسُعُرٍ ﴿٢٤﴾

25. Is it that the message is sent to him, of all people amongst us? Nay, he is a liar, an insolent one!"

أَءُلْقِىَ ٱلذِّكْرُ عَلَيْهِ مِنۢ بَيْنِنَا بَلْ هُوَ كَذَّابٌ أَشِرٌ ﴿٢٥﴾

26. Ah! They will know on the morrow which is the liar, the insolent one!

سَيَعْلَمُونَ غَدًا مَّنِ ٱلْكَذَّابُ ٱلْأَشِرُ ﴿٢٦﴾

27. For We will send the she-camel by way of trial for them. So watch them, (O Salih) and possess yourself in patience!

إِنَّا مُرْسِلُوا۟ ٱلنَّاقَةِ فِتْنَةً لَّهُمْ فَٱرْتَقِبْهُمْ
وَٱصْطَبِرْ ﴿٢٧﴾

28. And tell them that the water is to be divided between them: each one's right to drink being brought forward (by suitable turns).

وَنَبِّئْهُمْ أَنَّ ٱلْمَآءَ قِسْمَةٌۢ بَيْنَهُمْ ۖ كُلُّ شِرْبٍ مُّحْتَضَرٌ ﴿٢٨﴾

29. But they called to their companion, and he took a sword in hand, and hamstrung (her).

فَنَادَوْا۟ صَاحِبَهُمْ فَتَعَاطَىٰ فَعَقَرَ ﴿٢٩﴾

30. Ah! How (terrible) was My penalty and My warning!

فَكَيْفَ كَانَ عَذَابِى وَنُذُرِ ﴿٣٠﴾

31. For We sent against them a single mighty blast, and they became like the dry stubble used by one who pens cattle.

إِنَّآ أَرۡسَلۡنَا عَلَيۡهِمۡ صَيۡحَةٗ وَٰحِدَةٗ فَكَانُواْ كَهَشِيمِ
ٱلۡمُحۡتَظِرِ ٣١

32. And We have indeed made the Qur'an easy to understand and remember: then is there any that will receive admonition?

وَلَقَدۡ يَسَّرۡنَا ٱلۡقُرۡءَانَ لِلذِّكۡرِ فَهَلۡ مِن مُّدَّكِرٖ ٣٢

33. The people of Lot rejected (his) warning.

كَذَّبَتۡ قَوۡمُ لُوطِۭ بِٱلنُّذُرِ ٣٣

34. We sent against them a violent tornado with showers of stones (which destroyed them), except Lot's household: them We delivered by early dawn -

إِنَّآ أَرۡسَلۡنَا عَلَيۡهِمۡ حَاصِبًا إِلَّآ ءَالَ لُوطٖۖ نَّجَّيۡنَٰهُم
بِسَحَرٖ ٣٤

35. As a grace from Us: thus do We reward those who give thanks.

نِّعۡمَةٗ مِّنۡ عِندِنَاۚ كَذَٰلِكَ نَجۡزِي مَن شَكَرَ ٣٥

36. And (Lot) did warn them of Our punishment, but they disputed about the warning.

وَلَقَدۡ أَنذَرَهُم بَطۡشَتَنَا فَتَمَارَوۡاْ بِٱلنُّذُرِ ٣٦

37. And they even sought to snatch away his guests from him, but We blinded their eyes. (They heard:) "Now taste you My wrath and My warning."

وَلَقَدۡ رَٰوَدُوهُ عَن ضَيۡفِهِۦ فَطَمَسۡنَآ أَعۡيُنَهُمۡ
فَذُوقُواْ عَذَابِي وَنُذُرِ ٣٧

38. Early on the morrow a lasting punishment seized them:

وَلَقَدۡ صَبَّحَهُم بُكۡرَةً عَذَابٞ مُّسۡتَقِرّٞ ٣٨

39. "So taste you My wrath and My warning."

فَذُوقُواْ عَذَابِي وَنُذُرِ ٣٩

40. And We have indeed made the Qur'an easy to understand and remember: then is there any that will receive admonition?

وَلَقَدۡ يَسَّرۡنَا ٱلۡقُرۡءَانَ لِلذِّكۡرِ فَهَلۡ مِن مُّدَّكِرٖ ٤٠

41. To the people of Pharaoh, too, before came warners (from Allah).

وَلَقَدۡ جَآءَ ءَالَ فِرۡعَوۡنَ ٱلنُّذُرُ ٤١

42. The (people) rejected all Our signs; but We seized them with such penalty (as comes) from One Exalted in Power, able to carry out His will.

كَذَّبُوا۟ بِـَٔايَـٰتِنَا كُلِّهَا فَأَخَذْنَـٰهُمْ أَخْذَ عَزِيزٍ مُّقْتَدِرٍ ﴿٤٢﴾

43. Are your unbelievers, (O Quraysh), better than they? Or have you an immunity in the sacred books?

أَكُفَّارُكُمْ خَيْرٌ مِّنْ أُو۟لَـٰٓئِكُمْ أَمْ لَكُم بَرَآءَةٌ فِى ٱلزُّبُرِ ﴿٤٣﴾

44. Or do they say: "We acting together can defend ourselves"?

أَمْ يَقُولُونَ نَحْنُ جَمِيعٌ مُّنتَصِرٌ ﴿٤٤﴾

45. Soon will their multitude be put to flight, and they will show their backs.

سَيُهْزَمُ ٱلْجَمْعُ وَيُوَلُّونَ ٱلدُّبُرَ ﴿٤٥﴾

46. Nay, the hour (of judgement) is the time promised them (for their full recompense): and that hour will be most grievous and most bitter.

بَلِ ٱلسَّاعَةُ مَوْعِدُهُمْ وَٱلسَّاعَةُ أَدْهَىٰ وَأَمَرُّ ﴿٤٦﴾

47. Truly those in sin are the ones straying in mind, and mad.

إِنَّ ٱلْمُجْرِمِينَ فِى ضَلَـٰلٍ وَسُعُرٍ ﴿٤٧﴾

48. The day they will be dragged through the fire on their faces, (they will hear:) "Taste you the touch of hell!"

يَوْمَ يُسْحَبُونَ فِى ٱلنَّارِ عَلَىٰ وُجُوهِهِمْ ذُوقُوا۟ مَسَّ
سَقَرَ ﴿٤٨﴾

49. Verily, all things have We created in proportion and measure.

إِنَّا كُلَّ شَىْءٍ خَلَقْنَـٰهُ بِقَدَرٍ ﴿٤٩﴾

50. And Our command is but a single (Act) - like the twinkling of an eye.

وَمَآ أَمْرُنَآ إِلَّا وَٰحِدَةٌ كَلَمْحٍۭ بِٱلْبَصَرِ ﴿٥٠﴾

51. And (oft) in the past, have We destroyed gangs like you: then is there any that will receive admonition?

وَلَقَدْ أَهْلَكْنَآ أَشْيَاعَكُمْ فَهَلْ مِن مُّدَّكِرٍ ﴿٥١﴾

52. All that they do is noted in (their) books (of deeds):

وَكُلُّ شَىْءٍ فَعَلُوهُ فِى ٱلزُّبُرِ ﴿٥٢﴾

53. Every matter, small and great, is on record.

وَكُلُّ صَغِيرٍ وَكَبِيرٍ مُّسْتَطَرٌ ﴿٥٣﴾

54. As to the righteous, they will be in the midst of gardens and rivers.

إِنَّ ٱلْمُتَّقِينَ فِى جَنَّٰتٍ وَنَهَرٍ ٥٤

55. In an assembly to truth, in the presence of a sovereign omnipotent.

فِى مَقْعَدِ صِدْقٍ عِندَ مَلِيكٍ مُّقْتَدِرٍۭ ٥٥

سُورَةُ الرَّحْمَٰن

Surah 55: **Ar-Rahman (The Most Gracious)**

In the name of Allah,
Most Gracious, Most Merciful.

بِسْمِ ٱللَّهِ ٱلرَّحْمَٰنِ ٱلرَّحِيمِ

1. (Allah) Most Gracious!

ٱلرَّحْمَٰنُ ١

الحزب ٥٤

2. It is He Who has taught the Qur'an.

عَلَّمَ ٱلْقُرْءَانَ ٢

3. He has created man:

خَلَقَ ٱلْإِنسَٰنَ ٣

4. He has taught him speech (and Intelligence).

عَلَّمَهُ ٱلْبَيَانَ ٤

5. The sun and the moon follow courses (exactly) computed;

ٱلشَّمْسُ وَٱلْقَمَرُ بِحُسْبَانٍ ٥

6. And the herbs and the trees - both (alike) bow in adoration.

وَٱلنَّجْمُ وَٱلشَّجَرُ يَسْجُدَانِ ٦

7. And the firmament has He raised high, and He has set up the balance (of justice),

وَٱلسَّمَآءَ رَفَعَهَا وَوَضَعَ ٱلْمِيزَانَ ٧

8. In order that you may not transgress (due) balance.

أَلَّا تَطْغَوْا۟ فِى ٱلْمِيزَانِ ٨

9. So establish weight with justice and fall not short in the balance.

وَأَقِيمُوا۟ ٱلْوَزْنَ بِٱلْقِسْطِ وَلَا تُخْسِرُوا۟ ٱلْمِيزَانَ ٩

10. It is He Who has spread out the earth for (His) creatures:

وَٱلْأَرْضَ وَضَعَهَا لِلْأَنَامِ ١٠

11. In it is fruit and date-palms, producing spathes (enclosing dates):

فِيهَا فَٰكِهَةٞ وَٱلنَّخۡلُ ذَاتُ ٱلۡأَكۡمَامِ ١١

12. Also corn, with (its) leaves and stalk for fodder, and sweet-smelling plants.

وَٱلۡحَبُّ ذُو ٱلۡعَصۡفِ وَٱلرَّيۡحَانُ ١٢

13. Then which of the favours of your Lord will you deny?

فَبِأَيِّ ءَالَآءِ رَبِّكُمَا تُكَذِّبَانِ ١٣

14. He created man from sounding clay like pottery.

خَلَقَ ٱلۡإِنسَٰنَ مِن صَلۡصَٰلٖ كَٱلۡفَخَّارِ ١٤

15. And He created Jinns from fire free of smoke:

وَخَلَقَ ٱلۡجَآنَّ مِن مَّارِجٖ مِّن نَّارٖ ١٥

16. Then which of the favours of your Lord will you deny?

فَبِأَيِّ ءَالَآءِ رَبِّكُمَا تُكَذِّبَانِ ١٦

17. (He is) Lord of the two easts and Lord of the two wests:

رَبُّ ٱلۡمَشۡرِقَيۡنِ وَرَبُّ ٱلۡمَغۡرِبَيۡنِ ١٧

18. Then which of the favours of your Lord will you deny?

فَبِأَيِّ ءَالَآءِ رَبِّكُمَا تُكَذِّبَانِ ١٨

19. He has let free the two bodies of flowing water meeting together:

مَرَجَ ٱلۡبَحۡرَيۡنِ يَلۡتَقِيَانِ ١٩

20. Between them is a barrier which they do not transgress:

بَيۡنَهُمَا بَرۡزَخٞ لَّا يَبۡغِيَانِ ٢٠

21. Then which of the favours of your Lord will you deny?

فَبِأَيِّ ءَالَآءِ رَبِّكُمَا تُكَذِّبَانِ ٢١

22. Out of them come pearls and coral:

يَخۡرُجُ مِنۡهُمَا ٱللُّؤۡلُؤُ وَٱلۡمَرۡجَانُ ٢٢

23. Then which of the favours of your Lord will you deny?

فَبِأَيِّ ءَالَآءِ رَبِّكُمَا تُكَذِّبَانِ ٢٣

24. And His are the ships sailing smoothly through the seas, lofty as mountains:

وَلَهُ ٱلۡجَوَارِ ٱلۡمُنشَـَٔاتُ فِي ٱلۡبَحۡرِ كَٱلۡأَعۡلَٰمِ ٢٤

25. Then which of the favours of your Lord will you deny?

فَبِأَيِّ ءَالَآءِ رَبِّكُمَا تُكَذِّبَانِ ٢٥

26. All that is on earth will perish:

كُلُّ مَنْ عَلَيْهَا فَانٍ ٢٦

27. But will remain (forever) the face of your Lord - Full of majesty, bounty and honour.

وَيَبْقَىٰ وَجْهُ رَبِّكَ ذُو ٱلْجَلَٰلِ وَٱلْإِكْرَامِ ٢٧

28. Then which of the favours of your Lord will you deny?

فَبِأَيِّ ءَالَآءِ رَبِّكُمَا تُكَذِّبَانِ ٢٨

29. Of Him seeks (its needs) every creature in the heavens and on earth: every day in (new) splendour does He (shine)!

يَسْـَٔلُهُۥ مَن فِى ٱلسَّمَٰوَٰتِ وَٱلْأَرْضِ ۚ كُلَّ يَوْمٍ هُوَ فِى شَأْنٍ ٢٩

30. Then which of the favours of your Lord will you deny?

فَبِأَيِّ ءَالَآءِ رَبِّكُمَا تُكَذِّبَانِ ٣٠

31. Soon shall We settle your affairs, O both you worlds!

سَنَفْرُغُ لَكُمْ أَيُّهَ ٱلثَّقَلَانِ ٣١

32. Then which of the favours of your Lord will you deny?

فَبِأَيِّ ءَالَآءِ رَبِّكُمَا تُكَذِّبَانِ ٣٢

33. O you assembly of Jinns and men! If it be you can pass beyond the zones of the heavens and the earth, pass you! Not without authority shall you be able to pass!

يَٰمَعْشَرَ ٱلْجِنِّ وَٱلْإِنسِ إِنِ ٱسْتَطَعْتُمْ أَن تَنفُذُوا۟
مِنْ أَقْطَارِ ٱلسَّمَٰوَٰتِ وَٱلْأَرْضِ فَٱنفُذُوا۟ ۚ لَا تَنفُذُونَ
إِلَّا بِسُلْطَٰنٍ ٣٣

34. Then which of the favours of your Lord will you deny?

فَبِأَيِّ ءَالَآءِ رَبِّكُمَا تُكَذِّبَانِ ٣٤

35. On you will be sent (O you evil ones twain!) a flame of fire (to burn) and a smoke (to choke): no defence will you have:

يُرْسَلُ عَلَيْكُمَا شُوَاظٌ مِّن نَّارٍ وَنُحَاسٌ فَلَا
تَنتَصِرَانِ ٣٥

36. Then which of the favours of your Lord will you deny?

فَبِأَيِّ ءَالَآءِ رَبِّكُمَا تُكَذِّبَانِ ٣٦

37. When the sky is rent asunder, and it becomes red like ointment:

فَإِذَا ٱنشَقَّتِ ٱلسَّمَآءُ فَكَانَتْ وَرْدَةً كَٱلدِّهَانِ ﴿٣٧﴾

38. Then which of the favours of your Lord will you deny?

فَبِأَيِّ ءَالَآءِ رَبِّكُمَا تُكَذِّبَانِ ﴿٣٨﴾

39. On that day, no question will be asked of man or Jinn as to his sin,

فَيَوْمَئِذٍ لَّا يُسْـَٔلُ عَن ذَنۢبِهِۦٓ إِنسٌ وَلَا جَآنٌّ ﴿٣٩﴾

40. Then which of the favours of your Lord will you deny?

فَبِأَيِّ ءَالَآءِ رَبِّكُمَا تُكَذِّبَانِ ﴿٤٠﴾

41. (For) the sinners will be known by their marks: and they will be seized by their forelocks and their feet.

يُعْرَفُ ٱلْمُجْرِمُونَ بِسِيمَٰهُمْ فَيُؤْخَذُ بِٱلنَّوَٰصِى وَٱلْأَقْدَامِ ﴿٤١﴾

42. Then which of the favours of your Lord will you deny?

فَبِأَيِّ ءَالَآءِ رَبِّكُمَا تُكَذِّبَانِ ﴿٤٢﴾

43. This is the hell which the sinners deny.

هَٰذِهِۦ جَهَنَّمُ ٱلَّتِى يُكَذِّبُ بِهَا ٱلْمُجْرِمُونَ ﴿٤٣﴾

44. In its midst and in the midst of boiling hot water will they wander round!

يَطُوفُونَ بَيْنَهَا وَبَيْنَ حَمِيمٍ ءَانٍ ﴿٤٤﴾

45. Then which of the favours of your Lord will you deny?

فَبِأَيِّ ءَالَآءِ رَبِّكُمَا تُكَذِّبَانِ ﴿٤٥﴾

46. But for such as fear the time when they will stand before (the judgement seat of) their Lord, there will be two gardens -

وَلِمَنْ خَافَ مَقَامَ رَبِّهِۦ جَنَّتَانِ ﴿٤٦﴾

47. Then which of the favours of your Lord will you deny?

فَبِأَيِّ ءَالَآءِ رَبِّكُمَا تُكَذِّبَانِ ﴿٤٧﴾

48. Containing all kinds (of trees and delights) -

ذَوَاتَآ أَفْنَانٍ ﴿٤٨﴾

49. Then which of the favours of your Lord will you deny?

فَبِأَيِّ ءَالَآءِ رَبِّكُمَا تُكَذِّبَانِ ﴿٤٩﴾

50. In them (each) will be two springs flowing (free);

فِيهِمَا عَيْنَانِ تَجْرِيَانِ ٥٠

51. Then which of the favours of your Lord will you deny?

فَبِأَيِّ ءَالَآءِ رَبِّكُمَا تُكَذِّبَانِ ٥١

52. In them will be fruits of every kind, two and two.

فِيهِمَا مِن كُلِّ فَٰكِهَةٍ زَوْجَانِ ٥٢

53. Then which of the favours of your Lord will you deny?

فَبِأَيِّ ءَالَآءِ رَبِّكُمَا تُكَذِّبَانِ ٥٣

54. They will recline on carpets, whose inner linings will be of rich brocade: the fruit of the gardens will be near (and easy of reach).

مُتَّكِـِٔينَ عَلَىٰ فُرُشٍۭ بَطَآئِنُهَا مِنْ إِسْتَبْرَقٍ ۚ
وَجَنَى ٱلْجَنَّتَيْنِ دَانٍ ٥٤

55. Then which of the favours of your Lord will you deny?

فَبِأَيِّ ءَالَآءِ رَبِّكُمَا تُكَذِّبَانِ ٥٥

56. In them will be (maidens), chaste, restraining their glances, whom no man or Jinn before them has touched -

فِيهِنَّ قَٰصِرَٰتُ ٱلطَّرْفِ لَمْ يَطْمِثْهُنَّ إِنسٌ قَبْلَهُمْ
وَلَا جَآنٌّ ٥٦

57. Then which of the favours of your Lord will you deny?

فَبِأَيِّ ءَالَآءِ رَبِّكُمَا تُكَذِّبَانِ ٥٧

58. Like rubies and coral.

كَأَنَّهُنَّ ٱلْيَاقُوتُ وَٱلْمَرْجَانُ ٥٨

59. Then which of the favours of your lord will you deny?

فَبِأَيِّ ءَالَآءِ رَبِّكُمَا تُكَذِّبَانِ ٥٩

60. Is there any reward for good - other than good?

هَلْ جَزَآءُ ٱلْإِحْسَٰنِ إِلَّا ٱلْإِحْسَٰنُ ٦٠

61. Then which of the favours of your Lord will you deny?

فَبِأَيِّ ءَالَآءِ رَبِّكُمَا تُكَذِّبَانِ ٦١

62. And besides these two, there are two other gardens -

وَمِن دُونِهِمَا جَنَّتَانِ ٦٢

63. Then which of the favours of your Lord will you deny?

فَبِأَيِّ ءَالَآءِ رَبِّكُمَا تُكَذِّبَانِ ٦٣

64. Dark green in colour (from plentiful watering).

مُدْهَآمَّتَانِ ٦٤

65. Then which of the favours of your Lord will you deny?

فَبِأَيِّ ءَالَآءِ رَبِّكُمَا تُكَذِّبَانِ ٦٥

66. In them (each) will be two springs pouring forth water in continuous abundance:

فِيهِمَا عَيْنَانِ نَضَّاخَتَانِ ٦٦

67. Then which of the favours of your Lord will you deny?

فَبِأَيِّ ءَالَآءِ رَبِّكُمَا تُكَذِّبَانِ ٦٧

68. In them will be fruits, and dates and pomegranates:

فِيهِمَا فَٰكِهَةٌ وَنَخْلٌ وَرُمَّانٌ ٦٨

69. Then which of the favours of your Lord will you deny?

فَبِأَيِّ ءَالَآءِ رَبِّكُمَا تُكَذِّبَانِ ٦٩

70. In them will be fair (companions), good, beautiful -

فِيهِنَّ خَيْرَٰتٌ حِسَانٌ ٧٠

71. Then which of the favours of your Lord will you deny?

فَبِأَيِّ ءَالَآءِ رَبِّكُمَا تُكَذِّبَانِ ٧١

72. companions restrained (as to their glances), in (goodly) pavilions -

حُورٌ مَّقْصُورَٰتٌ فِى ٱلْخِيَامِ ٧٢

73. Then which of the favour of your Lord will you deny?

فَبِأَيِّ ءَالَآءِ رَبِّكُمَا تُكَذِّبَانِ ٧٣

74. Whom no man or Jinn before them has touched -

لَمْ يَطْمِثْهُنَّ إِنسٌ قَبْلَهُمْ وَلَا جَآنٌّ ٧٤

75. Then which of the favours of your Lord will you deny?

فَبِأَيِّ ءَالَآءِ رَبِّكُمَا تُكَذِّبَانِ ﴿٧٥﴾

76. Reclining on green cushions and rich carpets of beauty.

مُتَّكِـِٔينَ عَلَىٰ رَفْرَفٍ خُضْرٍ وَعَبْقَرِيٍّ حِسَانٍ ﴿٧٦﴾

77. Then which of the favours of your Lord will you deny?

فَبِأَيِّ ءَالَآءِ رَبِّكُمَا تُكَذِّبَانِ ﴿٧٧﴾

78. Blessed be the name of your Lord, full of Majesty, bounty and Honour.

تَبَٰرَكَ ٱسْمُ رَبِّكَ ذِى ٱلْجَلَٰلِ وَٱلْإِكْرَامِ ﴿٧٨﴾

سُورَةُ الوَاقِعَةِ

Surah 56: ***Al-Waqi'ah*** **(The Inevitable)**

In the name of Allah,
Most Gracious, Most Merciful.

بِسْمِ ٱللَّهِ ٱلرَّحْمَٰنِ ٱلرَّحِيمِ

1. When the event inevitable comes to pass,

إِذَا وَقَعَتِ ٱلْوَاقِعَةُ ﴿١﴾ ربع الحزب ٥٤

2. Then will no (soul) entertain falsehood concerning its coming.

لَيْسَ لِوَقْعَتِهَا كَاذِبَةٌ ﴿٢﴾

3. (Many) will it bring low, (many) will it exalt;

خَافِضَةٌ رَّافِعَةٌ ﴿٣﴾

4. When the earth shall be shaken to its depths,

إِذَا رُجَّتِ ٱلْأَرْضُ رَجًّا ﴿٤﴾

5. And the mountains shall be crumbled to atoms,

وَبُسَّتِ ٱلْجِبَالُ بَسًّا ﴿٥﴾

6. Becoming dust scattered abroad,

فَكَانَتْ هَبَآءً مُّنۢبَثًّا ﴿٦﴾

7. And you shall be sorted out into three classes.

وَكُنتُمْ أَزْوَٰجًا ثَلَٰثَةً ﴿٧﴾

8. Then (there will be) the companions of the right hand - what will be the companions of the right hand?

فَأَصْحَٰبُ ٱلْمَيْمَنَةِ مَآ أَصْحَٰبُ ٱلْمَيْمَنَةِ ﴿٨﴾

9. And the companions of the left hand - what will be the companions of the left hand?	وَأَصْحَٰبُ ٱلْمَشْـَٔمَةِ مَآ أَصْحَٰبُ ٱلْمَشْـَٔمَةِ ﴿٩﴾
10. And those foremost (in faith) will be foremost (in the hereafter).	وَٱلسَّٰبِقُونَ ٱلسَّٰبِقُونَ ﴿١٠﴾
11. These will be those nearest to Allah:	أُو۟لَٰٓئِكَ ٱلْمُقَرَّبُونَ ﴿١١﴾
12. In gardens of bliss:	فِى جَنَّٰتِ ٱلنَّعِيمِ ﴿١٢﴾
13. A number of people from those of old,	ثُلَّةٌ مِّنَ ٱلْأَوَّلِينَ ﴿١٣﴾
14. And a few from those of later times.	وَقَلِيلٌ مِّنَ ٱلْـَٔاخِرِينَ ﴿١٤﴾
15. (They will be) on thrones encrusted (with gold and precious stones),	عَلَىٰ سُرُرٍ مَّوْضُونَةٍ ﴿١٥﴾
16. Reclining on them facing each other.	مُّتَّكِـِٔينَ عَلَيْهَا مُتَقَٰبِلِينَ ﴿١٦﴾
17. Round about them will (serve) youths of perpetual (freshness),	يَطُوفُ عَلَيْهِمْ وِلْدَٰنٌ مُّخَلَّدُونَ ﴿١٧﴾
18. With goblets, (shining) beakers, and cups (filled) out of clear-flowing fountains:	بِأَكْوَابٍ وَأَبَارِيقَ وَكَأْسٍ مِّن مَّعِينٍ ﴿١٨﴾
19. No after-ache will they receive from it, nor will they suffer intoxication:	لَّا يُصَدَّعُونَ عَنْهَا وَلَا يُنزِفُونَ ﴿١٩﴾
20. And with fruits, any that they may select;	وَفَٰكِهَةٍ مِّمَّا يَتَخَيَّرُونَ ﴿٢٠﴾
21. And the flesh of fowls, any that they may desire.	وَلَحْمِ طَيْرٍ مِّمَّا يَشْتَهُونَ ﴿٢١﴾
22. And (there will be) companions with beautiful, big, and lustrous eyes -	وَحُورٌ عِينٌ ﴿٢٢﴾
23. Like to pearls well-guarded.	كَأَمْثَٰلِ ٱللُّؤْلُؤِ ٱلْمَكْنُونِ ﴿٢٣﴾

24. A reward for the deeds of their past (life).

جَزَآءَۢ بِمَا كَانُواْ يَعۡمَلُونَ ٢٤

25. No frivolity will they hear in it nor any taint of ill -

لَا يَسۡمَعُونَ فِيهَا لَغۡوٗا وَلَا تَأۡثِيمًا ٢٥

26. Only the saying, "Peace! Peace."

إِلَّا قِيلٗا سَلَٰمٗا سَلَٰمٗا ٢٦

27. The companions of the right hand - what will be the companions of the right hand?

وَأَصۡحَٰبُ ٱلۡيَمِينِ مَآ أَصۡحَٰبُ ٱلۡيَمِينِ ٢٧

28. (They will be) among lote trees without thorns,

فِي سِدۡرٖ مَّخۡضُودٖ ٢٨

29. Among Talh trees with flowers (or fruits) piled one above another -

وَطَلۡحٖ مَّنضُودٖ ٢٩

30. In shade long-extended,

وَظِلّٖ مَّمۡدُودٖ ٣٠

31. By water flowing constantly,

وَمَآءٖ مَّسۡكُوبٖ ٣١

32. And fruit in abundance,

وَفَٰكِهَةٖ كَثِيرَةٖ ٣٢

33. Whose season is not limited nor (supply) forbidden,

لَّا مَقۡطُوعَةٖ وَلَا مَمۡنُوعَةٖ ٣٣

34. And on thrones (of dignity), raised high.

وَفُرُشٖ مَّرۡفُوعَةٍ ٣٤

35. We have created (their companions) of special creation,

إِنَّآ أَنشَأۡنَٰهُنَّ إِنشَآءٗ ٣٥

36. And made them virgin-pure (and undefiled) -

فَجَعَلۡنَٰهُنَّ أَبۡكَارًا ٣٦

37. Beloved (by nature), equal in age -

عُرُبًا أَتۡرَابٗا ٣٧

38. For the companions of the right hand.

لِّأَصۡحَٰبِ ٱلۡيَمِينِ ٣٨

39. A (goodly) number from those of old,

ثُلَّةٞ مِّنَ ٱلۡأَوَّلِينَ ٣٩

40. And a (goodly) number from those of later times.

وَثُلَّةٞ مِّنَ ٱلۡأٓخِرِينَ ٤٠

41. The companions of the left hand - what will be the companions of the left hand?

وَأَصۡحَٰبُ ٱلشِّمَالِ مَآ أَصۡحَٰبُ ٱلشِّمَالِ ٤١

42. (They will be) in the midst of a fierce blast of fire and in boiling water,

فِي سَمُومٖ وَحَمِيمٖ ٤٢

43. And in the shades of black smoke:

وَظِلّٖ مِّن يَحۡمُومٖ ٤٣

44. Nothing (will there be) to refresh, nor to please:

لَّا بَارِدٖ وَلَا كَرِيمٍ ٤٤

45. For that they used to be indulged, before that, in wealth (and luxury),

إِنَّهُمۡ كَانُواْ قَبۡلَ ذَٰلِكَ مُتۡرَفِينَ ٤٥

46. And persisted obstinately in wickedness supreme!

وَكَانُواْ يُصِرُّونَ عَلَى ٱلۡحِنثِ ٱلۡعَظِيمِ ٤٦

47. And they used to say, "What! When we die and become dust and bones, shall we then indeed be raised up again? -

وَكَانُواْ يَقُولُونَ أَئِذَا مِتۡنَا وَكُنَّا تُرَابٗا وَعِظَٰمًا
أَءِنَّا لَمَبۡعُوثُونَ ٤٧

48. "(We) and our fathers of old?"

أَوَ ءَابَآؤُنَا ٱلۡأَوَّلُونَ ٤٨

49. Say: "Yea, those of old and those of later times,

قُلۡ إِنَّ ٱلۡأَوَّلِينَ وَٱلۡأٓخِرِينَ ٤٩

50. All will certainly be gathered together for the meeting appointed for a day well-known.

لَمَجۡمُوعُونَ إِلَىٰ مِيقَٰتِ يَوۡمٖ مَّعۡلُومٖ ٥٠

51. Then will you truly - O you that go wrong, and treat (truth) as falsehood!

ثُمَّ إِنَّكُمۡ أَيُّهَا ٱلضَّآلُّونَ ٱلۡمُكَذِّبُونَ ٥١

52. You will surely taste of the tree of Zaqqum.

لَأٓكِلُونَ مِن شَجَرٖ مِّن زَقُّومٖ ٥٢

53. Then will you fill your insides therewith.

فَمَالِـُٔونَ مِنْهَا ٱلْبُطُونَ ٥٣

54. And drink boiling Water on top of it:

فَشَٰرِبُونَ عَلَيْهِ مِنَ ٱلْحَمِيمِ ٥٤

55. Indeed you shall drink like diseased camels raging with thirst!"

فَشَٰرِبُونَ شُرْبَ ٱلْهِيمِ ٥٥

56. Such will be their entertainment on the day of requital!

هَٰذَا نُزُلُهُمْ يَوْمَ ٱلدِّينِ ٥٦

57. It is We Who have created you: why will you not witness the truth?

نَحْنُ خَلَقْنَٰكُمْ فَلَوْلَا تُصَدِّقُونَ ٥٧

58. Do you then see? - the (human seed) that you throw out, -

أَفَرَءَيْتُم مَّا تُمْنُونَ ٥٨

59. Is it you who create it, or are We the Creators?

ءَأَنتُمْ تَخْلُقُونَهُۥٓ أَمْ نَحْنُ ٱلْخَٰلِقُونَ ٥٩

60. We have decreed death to be your common lot, and We are not to be frustrated -

نَحْنُ قَدَّرْنَا بَيْنَكُمُ ٱلْمَوْتَ وَمَا نَحْنُ بِمَسْبُوقِينَ ٦٠

61. From changing your forms and creating you (again) in (forms) that you know not.

عَلَىٰٓ أَن نُّبَدِّلَ أَمْثَٰلَكُمْ وَنُنشِئَكُمْ فِى مَا لَا تَعْلَمُونَ ٦١

62. And you certainly know already the first form of creation: why then do you not celebrate His praises?

وَلَقَدْ عَلِمْتُمُ ٱلنَّشْأَةَ ٱلْأُولَىٰ فَلَوْلَا تَذَكَّرُونَ ٦٢

63. See you the seed that you sow in the ground?

أَفَرَءَيْتُم مَّا تَحْرُثُونَ ٦٣

64. Is it you that cause it to grow, or are We the cause?

ءَأَنتُمْ تَزْرَعُونَهُۥٓ أَمْ نَحْنُ ٱلزَّٰرِعُونَ ٦٤

65. Were it Our will, We could crumble it to dry powder, and you would be left in wonderment,

لَوْ نَشَآءُ لَجَعَلْنَٰهُ حُطَٰمًا فَظَلْتُمْ تَفَكَّهُونَ ٦٥

66. (Saying), "We are indeed left with debts (for nothing):

إِنَّا لَمُغْرَمُونَ ٦٦

67. Indeed are we shut out (of the fruits of our labour)."

بَلْ نَحْنُ مَحْرُومُونَ ٦٧

68. See you the water which you drink?

أَفَرَءَيْتُمُ ٱلْمَآءَ ٱلَّذِى تَشْرَبُونَ ٦٨

69. Do you bring it down (in rain) from the cloud or do We?

ءَأَنتُمْ أَنزَلْتُمُوهُ مِنَ ٱلْمُزْنِ أَمْ نَحْنُ ٱلْمُنزِلُونَ ٦٩

70. Were it Our will, We could make it salt (and unpalatable): then why do you not give thanks?

لَوْ نَشَآءُ جَعَلْنَٰهُ أُجَاجًا فَلَوْلَا تَشْكُرُونَ ٧٠

71. See you the fire which you kindle?

أَفَرَءَيْتُمُ ٱلنَّارَ ٱلَّتِى تُورُونَ ٧١

72. Is it you who grow the tree which feeds the fire, or do We grow it?

ءَأَنتُمْ أَنشَأْتُمْ شَجَرَتَهَآ أَمْ نَحْنُ ٱلْمُنشِـُٔونَ ٧٢

73. We have made it a memorial (of our handiwork), and an article of comfort and convenience for the denizens of deserts.

نَحْنُ جَعَلْنَٰهَا تَذْكِرَةً وَمَتَٰعًا لِّلْمُقْوِينَ ٧٣

74. Then celebrate with praises the name of your Lord, the Supreme!

فَسَبِّحْ بِٱسْمِ رَبِّكَ ٱلْعَظِيمِ ٧٤

75. Furthermore, I call to witness the setting of the stars -

۞ فَلَآ أُقْسِمُ بِمَوَٰقِعِ ٱلنُّجُومِ ٧٥ نصف الحزب ٥٤

76. And that is indeed a mighty adjuration if you but knew -

وَإِنَّهُۥ لَقَسَمٌ لَّوْ تَعْلَمُونَ عَظِيمٌ ٧٦

77. That this is indeed a Qur'an most honourable,

إِنَّهُۥ لَقُرْءَانٌ كَرِيمٌ ٧٧

78. In a book well-guarded,

فِى كِتَٰبٍ مَّكْنُونٍ ٧٨

79. Which none shall touch but those who are clean:

لَّا يَمَسُّهُۥٓ إِلَّا ٱلْمُطَهَّرُونَ ٧٩

80. A revelation from the Lord of the Worlds.

تَنزِيلٌ مِّن رَّبِّ ٱلْعَٰلَمِينَ ٨٠

81. Is it such a message that you would hold in light esteem?

أَفَبِهَٰذَا ٱلْحَدِيثِ أَنتُم مُّدْهِنُونَ ٨١

82. And have you made it your livelihood that you should declare it false?

وَتَجْعَلُونَ رِزْقَكُمْ أَنَّكُمْ تُكَذِّبُونَ ٨٢

83. Then why do you not (intervene) when (the soul of the dying man) reaches the throat -

فَلَوْلَآ إِذَا بَلَغَتِ ٱلْحُلْقُومَ ٨٣

84. And you the while (sit) looking on-

وَأَنتُمْ حِينَئِذٍ تَنظُرُونَ ٨٤

85. But We are nearer to him than you, and yet see not -

وَنَحْنُ أَقْرَبُ إِلَيْهِ مِنكُمْ وَلَٰكِن لَّا تُبْصِرُونَ ٨٥

86. Then why do you not - if you are exempt from (future) account -

فَلَوْلَآ إِن كُنتُمْ غَيْرَ مَدِينِينَ ٨٦

87. Call back the soul, if you are true (in your claim of independence)?

تَرْجِعُونَهَآ إِن كُنتُمْ صَٰدِقِينَ ٨٧

88. Thus, then, if he be of those nearest to Allah,

فَأَمَّآ إِن كَانَ مِنَ ٱلْمُقَرَّبِينَ ٨٨

89. (There is for him) rest and satisfaction, and a garden of delights.

فَرَوْحٌ وَرَيْحَانٌ وَجَنَّتُ نَعِيمٍ ٨٩

90. And if he be of the companions of the right hand,

وَأَمَّآ إِن كَانَ مِنْ أَصْحَٰبِ ٱلْيَمِينِ ٩٠

91. (For him is the salutation), "Peace be to you," from the companions of the right hand.

فَسَلَٰمٌ لَّكَ مِنْ أَصْحَٰبِ ٱلْيَمِينِ ٩١

92. And if he be of those who treat (truth) as falsehood, who go wrong.

وَأَمَّآ إِن كَانَ مِنَ ٱلْمُكَذِّبِينَ ٱلضَّآلِّينَ ٩٢

93. For him is entertainment with boiling water,

فَنُزُلٌ مِّنْ حَمِيمٍ ٩٣

94. And burning in hellfire.

وَتَصۡلِيَةُ جَحِيمٍ ٩٤

95. Verily, this is the very truth and certainty.

إِنَّ هَٰذَا لَهُوَ حَقُّ ٱلۡيَقِينِ ٩٥

96. So celebrate with praises the name of your Lord, the Supreme.

فَسَبِّحۡ بِٱسۡمِ رَبِّكَ ٱلۡعَظِيمِ ٩٦

سُورَةُ الحَدِيدِ

Surah 57: ***Al-Hadid*** **(Iron)**

In the name of Allah,
Most Gracious, Most Merciful.

بِسۡمِ ٱللَّهِ ٱلرَّحۡمَٰنِ ٱلرَّحِيمِ

1. Whatever is in the heavens and on earth - let it declare the praises and glory of Allah: for He is the Exalted in Might, the Wise.

سَبَّحَ لِلَّهِ مَا فِي ٱلسَّمَٰوَٰتِ وَٱلۡأَرۡضِۖ وَهُوَ ٱلۡعَزِيزُ ٱلۡحَكِيمُ ١

2. To Him belongs the dominion of the heavens and the earth; it is He Who gives life and death; and He has power over all things.

لَهُۥ مُلۡكُ ٱلسَّمَٰوَٰتِ وَٱلۡأَرۡضِۖ يُحۡيِۦ وَيُمِيتُۖ وَهُوَ عَلَىٰ
كُلِّ شَيۡءٖ قَدِيرٌ ٢

3. He is the first and the last, the evident and the hidden: and He has full knowledge of all things.

هُوَ ٱلۡأَوَّلُ وَٱلۡأٓخِرُ وَٱلظَّٰهِرُ وَٱلۡبَاطِنُۖ وَهُوَ بِكُلِّ
شَيۡءٍ عَلِيمٌ ٣

4. He it is Who created the heavens and the earth in six days, and is moreover firmly established on the throne (of authority). He knows what enters within the earth and what comes out of it, what comes down from heaven and what mounts up to it. And He is with you wheresoever you may be. And Allah sees well all that you do.

هُوَ ٱلَّذِي خَلَقَ ٱلسَّمَٰوَٰتِ وَٱلۡأَرۡضَ فِي سِتَّةِ أَيَّامٖ
ثُمَّ ٱسۡتَوَىٰ عَلَى ٱلۡعَرۡشِۖ يَعۡلَمُ مَا يَلِجُ فِي ٱلۡأَرۡضِ وَمَا
يَخۡرُجُ مِنۡهَا وَمَا يَنزِلُ مِنَ ٱلسَّمَآءِ وَمَا يَعۡرُجُ فِيهَاۖ
وَهُوَ مَعَكُمۡ أَيۡنَ مَا كُنتُمۡۚ وَٱللَّهُ بِمَا تَعۡمَلُونَ بَصِيرٞ ٤

5. To Him belongs the dominion of the heavens and the earth: and all affairs are referred back to Allah.

لَّهُۥ مُلۡكُ ٱلسَّمَٰوَٰتِ وَٱلۡأَرۡضِۚ وَإِلَى ٱللَّهِ تُرۡجَعُ ٱلۡأُمُورُ ٥

6. He merges night into day, and He merges day into night; and He has full knowledge of the secrets of (all) hearts.

يُولِجُ ٱلَّيْلَ فِى ٱلنَّهَارِ وَيُولِجُ ٱلنَّهَارَ فِى ٱلَّيْلِ ۚ وَهُوَ عَلِيمٌۢ
بِذَاتِ ٱلصُّدُورِ ٦

7. Believe in Allah and His messenger, and spend (in charity) out of the (substance) of which He has made you heirs. For those of you who believe and spend (in charity) - for them is a great reward.

ءَامِنُوا۟ بِٱللَّهِ وَرَسُولِهِۦ وَأَنفِقُوا۟ مِمَّا جَعَلَكُم
مُّسْتَخْلَفِينَ فِيهِ ۖ فَٱلَّذِينَ ءَامَنُوا۟ مِنكُمْ وَأَنفَقُوا۟ لَهُمْ
أَجْرٌ كَبِيرٌ ٧

8. What cause have you why you should not believe in Allah? - And the messenger invites you to believe in your Lord, and has indeed taken your covenant, if you are men of faith.

وَمَا لَكُمْ لَا تُؤْمِنُونَ بِٱللَّهِ ۙ وَٱلرَّسُولُ يَدْعُوكُمْ لِتُؤْمِنُوا۟
بِرَبِّكُمْ وَقَدْ أَخَذَ مِيثَـٰقَكُمْ إِن كُنتُم مُّؤْمِنِينَ ٨

9. He is the One Who sends to His servants manifest signs, that He may lead you from the depths of darkness into the light. And verily, Allah is to you Most Kind and Merciful.

هُوَ ٱلَّذِى يُنَزِّلُ عَلَىٰ عَبْدِهِۦٓ ءَايَـٰتٍۭ بَيِّنَـٰتٍ لِّيُخْرِجَكُم مِّنَ
ٱلظُّلُمَـٰتِ إِلَى ٱلنُّورِ ۚ وَإِنَّ ٱللَّهَ بِكُمْ لَرَءُوفٌ رَّحِيمٌ ٩

10. And what cause have you why you should not spend in the cause of Allah? - For to Allah belongs the heritage of the heavens and the earth. Not equal among you are those who spent (freely) and fought, before the victory (with those who did so later). Those are higher in rank than those who spent (freely) and fought afterwards. But to all has Allah promised a goodly (reward) and Allah is well-acquainted with all that you do.

وَمَا لَكُمْ أَلَّا تُنفِقُوا۟ فِى سَبِيلِ ٱللَّهِ وَلِلَّهِ مِيرَٰثُ
ٱلسَّمَـٰوَٰتِ وَٱلْأَرْضِ ۚ لَا يَسْتَوِى مِنكُم مَّنْ أَنفَقَ مِن
قَبْلِ ٱلْفَتْحِ وَقَـٰتَلَ ۚ أُو۟لَـٰٓئِكَ أَعْظَمُ دَرَجَةً مِّنَ ٱلَّذِينَ
أَنفَقُوا۟ مِنۢ بَعْدُ وَقَـٰتَلُوا۟ ۚ وَكُلًّا وَعَدَ ٱللَّهُ ٱلْحُسْنَىٰ ۚ
وَٱللَّهُ بِمَا تَعْمَلُونَ خَبِيرٌ ١٠

11. Who is he that will loan to Allah a beautiful loan? For (Allah) will increase it manifold to his credit, and he will have (besides) a liberal reward.

مَّن ذَا ٱلَّذِى يُقْرِضُ ٱللَّهَ قَرْضًا حَسَنًا فَيُضَـٰعِفَهُۥ
لَهُۥ وَلَهُۥٓ أَجْرٌ كَرِيمٌ ١١

12. One day shall you see the believing men and the believing women - how their light runs forward before them and by their right hands: (their greeting will be): "Good news

يَوْمَ تَرَى ٱلْمُؤْمِنِينَ وَٱلْمُؤْمِنَـٰتِ يَسْعَىٰ نُورُهُم
بَيْنَ أَيْدِيهِمْ وَبِأَيْمَـٰنِهِم بُشْرَىٰكُمُ ٱلْيَوْمَ جَنَّـٰتٌ تَجْرِى

مِن تَحْتِهَا الْأَنْهَارُ خَالِدِينَ فِيهَا ۚ ذَٰلِكَ هُوَ الْفَوْزُ الْعَظِيمُ ﴿١٢﴾

for you this day! Gardens beneath which flow rivers! To dwell in it for ever! This is indeed the highest achievement!"

يَوْمَ يَقُولُ الْمُنَافِقُونَ وَالْمُنَافِقَاتُ لِلَّذِينَ آمَنُوا
انظُرُونَا نَقْتَبِسْ مِن نُّورِكُمْ قِيلَ ارْجِعُوا وَرَاءَكُمْ
فَالْتَمِسُوا نُورًا فَضُرِبَ بَيْنَهُم بِسُورٍ لَّهُ بَابٌ بَاطِنُهُ
فِيهِ الرَّحْمَةُ وَظَاهِرُهُ مِن قِبَلِهِ الْعَذَابُ ﴿١٣﴾

13. One day will the hypocrites - men and women - say to the believers: "Wait for us! Let us borrow (a light) from your light!" It will be said: "Turn you back to your rear! Then seek a light (where you can)!" So a wall will be put up between them, with a gate in it. Within it will be mercy throughout, and without it, all alongside will be (wrath and) punishment!

يُنَادُونَهُمْ أَلَمْ نَكُن مَّعَكُمْ ۖ قَالُوا بَلَىٰ وَلَٰكِنَّكُمْ فَتَنتُمْ
أَنفُسَكُمْ وَتَرَبَّصْتُمْ وَارْتَبْتُمْ وَغَرَّتْكُمُ الْأَمَانِيُّ حَتَّىٰ
جَاءَ أَمْرُ اللَّهِ وَغَرَّكُم بِاللَّهِ الْغَرُورُ ﴿١٤﴾

14. (Those without) will call out, "Were we not with you?" (The others) will reply, "True! But you led yourselves into temptation; you looked forward (to our ruin); you doubted (Allah's promise); and (your false) desires deceived you; until there issued the command of Allah. And the deceiver deceived you in respect of Allah.

فَالْيَوْمَ لَا يُؤْخَذُ مِنكُمْ فِدْيَةٌ وَلَا مِنَ الَّذِينَ كَفَرُوا ۚ
مَأْوَاكُمُ النَّارُ ۖ هِيَ مَوْلَاكُمْ ۖ وَبِئْسَ الْمَصِيرُ ﴿١٥﴾

15. This day shall no ransom be accepted of you, nor of those who rejected Allah. Your abode is the fire: that is the proper place to claim you: and an evil refuge it is!"

ثلاثة أرباع الحزب ٥٤

۞ أَلَمْ يَأْنِ لِلَّذِينَ آمَنُوا أَن تَخْشَعَ قُلُوبُهُمْ
لِذِكْرِ اللَّهِ وَمَا نَزَلَ مِنَ الْحَقِّ وَلَا يَكُونُوا كَالَّذِينَ
أُوتُوا الْكِتَابَ مِن قَبْلُ فَطَالَ عَلَيْهِمُ الْأَمَدُ فَقَسَتْ
قُلُوبُهُمْ ۖ وَكَثِيرٌ مِّنْهُمْ فَاسِقُونَ ﴿١٦﴾

16. Has not the time arrived for the believers that their hearts in all humility should engage in the remembrance of Allah and of the truth which has been revealed (to them), and that they should not become like those to whom was given revelation before, but long ages passed over them and their hearts grew hard? For many among them are rebellious transgressors.

اعْلَمُوا أَنَّ اللَّهَ يُحْيِي الْأَرْضَ بَعْدَ مَوْتِهَا ۚ قَدْ بَيَّنَّا لَكُمُ

17. Know you (all) that Allah gives life to the earth after its death! Already have We shown the signs plainly to you, that you may learn wisdom.

ٱلْـَٔايَٰتِ لَعَلَّكُمْ تَعْقِلُونَ ﴿١٧﴾

18. For those who give in charity, men and women, and loan to Allah a beautiful loan, it shall be increased manifold (to their credit), and they shall have (besides) a liberal reward.

إِنَّ ٱلْمُصَّدِّقِينَ وَٱلْمُصَّدِّقَٰتِ وَأَقْرَضُوا۟ ٱللَّهَ قَرْضًا
حَسَنًا يُضَٰعَفُ لَهُمْ وَلَهُمْ أَجْرٌ كَرِيمٌ ﴿١٨﴾

19. And those who believe in Allah and His messengers - they are the sincere (lovers of truth), and the witnesses (who testify), in the eyes of their Lord: they shall have their reward and their light. But those who reject Allah and deny Our signs - they are the companions of hellfire.

وَٱلَّذِينَ ءَامَنُوا۟ بِٱللَّهِ وَرُسُلِهِۦٓ أُو۟لَٰٓئِكَ هُمُ ٱلصِّدِّيقُونَ ۖ
وَٱلشُّهَدَآءُ عِندَ رَبِّهِمْ لَهُمْ أَجْرُهُمْ وَنُورُهُمْ ۖ وَٱلَّذِينَ
كَفَرُوا۟ وَكَذَّبُوا۟ بِـَٔايَٰتِنَآ أُو۟لَٰٓئِكَ أَصْحَٰبُ
ٱلْجَحِيمِ ﴿١٩﴾

20. Know you (all), that the life of this world is but play and amusement, pomp and mutual boasting and multiplying, (in rivalry) among yourselves, riches and children. Here is a similitude: how rain and the growth which it brings out delight (the hearts of) the tillers; soon it withers; you will see it grow yellow; then it becomes dry and crumbles away. But in the hereafter is a penalty severe (for the devotees of wrong). And forgiveness from Allah and (His) good pleasure (for the devotees of Allah). And what is the life of this world, but goods and chattels of deception?

ٱعْلَمُوٓا۟ أَنَّمَا ٱلْحَيَوٰةُ ٱلدُّنْيَا لَعِبٌ وَلَهْوٌ وَزِينَةٌ
وَتَفَاخُرٌۢ بَيْنَكُمْ وَتَكَاثُرٌ فِى ٱلْأَمْوَٰلِ وَٱلْأَوْلَٰدِ ۖ كَمَثَلِ
غَيْثٍ أَعْجَبَ ٱلْكُفَّارَ نَبَاتُهُۥ ثُمَّ يَهِيجُ فَتَرَىٰهُ مُصْفَرًّا
ثُمَّ يَكُونُ حُطَٰمًا ۖ وَفِى ٱلْـَٔاخِرَةِ عَذَابٌ شَدِيدٌ وَمَغْفِرَةٌ
مِّنَ ٱللَّهِ وَرِضْوَٰنٌ ۚ وَمَا ٱلْحَيَوٰةُ ٱلدُّنْيَآ إِلَّا مَتَٰعُ
ٱلْغُرُورِ ﴿٢٠﴾

21. Be you foremost (in seeking) forgiveness from your Lord, and a garden (of bliss), the width of which is as the width of heaven and earth, prepared for those who believe in Allah and His messengers; that is the grace of Allah, which He bestows on whom He pleases: and Allah is the Lord of grace abounding.

سَابِقُوٓا۟ إِلَىٰ مَغْفِرَةٍ مِّن رَّبِّكُمْ وَجَنَّةٍ عَرْضُهَا كَعَرْضِ
ٱلسَّمَآءِ وَٱلْأَرْضِ أُعِدَّتْ لِلَّذِينَ ءَامَنُوا۟ بِٱللَّهِ
وَرُسُلِهِۦ ۚ ذَٰلِكَ فَضْلُ ٱللَّهِ يُؤْتِيهِ مَن يَشَآءُ ۚ وَٱللَّهُ
ذُو ٱلْفَضْلِ ٱلْعَظِيمِ ﴿٢١﴾

22. No misfortune can happen on earth or in your souls but is recorded in a decree before We bring it into existence: that is truly easy for Allah:

مَآ أَصَابَ مِن مُّصِيبَةٖ فِي ٱلۡأَرۡضِ وَلَا فِيٓ أَنفُسِكُمۡ
إِلَّا فِي كِتَٰبٖ مِّن قَبۡلِ أَن نَّبۡرَأَهَآۚ إِنَّ ذَٰلِكَ عَلَى
ٱللَّهِ يَسِيرٞ ٢٢

23. In order that you may not despair over matters that pass you by, nor exult over favours bestowed upon you. For Allah loves not any vainglorious boaster -

لِّكَيۡلَا تَأۡسَوۡاْ عَلَىٰ مَا فَاتَكُمۡ وَلَا تَفۡرَحُواْ
بِمَآ ءَاتَىٰكُمۡۗ وَٱللَّهُ لَا يُحِبُّ كُلَّ مُخۡتَالٖ فَخُورٍ ٢٣

24. Such persons as are covetous and commend covetousness to men, and if any turn back (from Allah's way), verily Allah is free of all needs, worthy of all praise.

ٱلَّذِينَ يَبۡخَلُونَ وَيَأۡمُرُونَ ٱلنَّاسَ بِٱلۡبُخۡلِۗ وَمَن
يَتَوَلَّ فَإِنَّ ٱللَّهَ هُوَ ٱلۡغَنِيُّ ٱلۡحَمِيدُ ٢٤

25. We sent before our messengers with clear signs and sent down with them the book and the balance (of right and wrong), that men may stand forth in justice; and We sent down Iron, in which is (material for) mighty war, as well as many benefits for mankind, that Allah may test who it is that will help, unseen, Him and His messengers; for Allah is Full of Strength, Exalted in Might (and able to enforce His will).

لَقَدۡ أَرۡسَلۡنَا رُسُلَنَا بِٱلۡبَيِّنَٰتِ وَأَنزَلۡنَا مَعَهُمُ
ٱلۡكِتَٰبَ وَٱلۡمِيزَانَ لِيَقُومَ ٱلنَّاسُ بِٱلۡقِسۡطِۖ
وَأَنزَلۡنَا ٱلۡحَدِيدَ فِيهِ بَأۡسٞ شَدِيدٞ وَمَنَٰفِعُ لِلنَّاسِ
وَلِيَعۡلَمَ ٱللَّهُ مَن يَنصُرُهُۥ وَرُسُلَهُۥ بِٱلۡغَيۡبِۚ إِنَّ ٱللَّهَ
قَوِيٌّ عَزِيزٞ ٢٥

26. And We sent Noah and Abraham, and established in their line prophethood and revelation: and some of them were on right guidance, but many of them became rebellious transgressors.

وَلَقَدۡ أَرۡسَلۡنَا نُوحٗا وَإِبۡرَٰهِيمَ وَجَعَلۡنَا فِي ذُرِّيَّتِهِمَا
ٱلنُّبُوَّةَ وَٱلۡكِتَٰبَۖ فَمِنۡهُم مُّهۡتَدٖۖ وَكَثِيرٞ
مِّنۡهُمۡ فَٰسِقُونَ ٢٦

27. Then, in their wake, We followed them up with (others of) Our messengers: We sent after them Jesus the son of Mary, and bestowed on him the gospel; and We ordained in the hearts of those who followed him compassion and mercy. But the monasticism which they invented for

ثُمَّ قَفَّيۡنَا عَلَىٰٓ ءَاثَٰرِهِم بِرُسُلِنَا وَقَفَّيۡنَا بِعِيسَى
ٱبۡنِ مَرۡيَمَ وَءَاتَيۡنَٰهُ ٱلۡإِنجِيلَۖ وَجَعَلۡنَا فِي قُلُوبِ
ٱلَّذِينَ ٱتَّبَعُوهُ رَأۡفَةٗ وَرَحۡمَةٗۚ وَرَهۡبَانِيَّةً

themselves, We did not prescribe for them: (We commanded) only the seeking for the good pleasure of Allah; but that they did not foster as they should have done. Yet We bestowed, on those among them who believed, their (due) reward, but many of them are rebellious transgressors.

ٱبْتَدَعُوهَا مَا كَتَبْنَٰهَا عَلَيْهِمْ إِلَّا ٱبْتِغَآءَ
رِضْوَٰنِ ٱللَّهِ فَمَا رَعَوْهَا حَقَّ رِعَايَتِهَا ۖ فَـَٔاتَيْنَا ٱلَّذِينَ
ءَامَنُوا۟ مِنْهُمْ أَجْرَهُمْ ۖ وَكَثِيرٌ مِّنْهُمْ فَٰسِقُونَ ٢٧

28. O you that believe! Fear Allah and believe in His messenger, and He will bestow on you a double portion of His mercy: He will provide for you a light by which you shall walk (straight in your path), and He will forgive you (your past); for Allah is Oft-Forgiving, Most Merciful:

يَٰٓأَيُّهَا ٱلَّذِينَ ءَامَنُوا۟ ٱتَّقُوا۟ ٱللَّهَ وَءَامِنُوا۟ بِرَسُولِهِۦ
يُؤْتِكُمْ كِفْلَيْنِ مِن رَّحْمَتِهِۦ وَيَجْعَل لَّكُمْ نُورًا تَمْشُونَ
بِهِۦ وَيَغْفِرْ لَكُمْ ۚ وَٱللَّهُ غَفُورٌ رَّحِيمٌ ٢٨

29. That the People of the Book may know that they have no power whatever over the grace of Allah, that (His) grace is (entirely) in His Hand, to bestow it on whomsoever He wills. For Allah is the Lord of grace abounding.

لِّئَلَّا يَعْلَمَ أَهْلُ ٱلْكِتَٰبِ أَلَّا يَقْدِرُونَ عَلَىٰ شَىْءٍ
مِّن فَضْلِ ٱللَّهِ ۙ وَأَنَّ ٱلْفَضْلَ بِيَدِ ٱللَّهِ يُؤْتِيهِ
مَن يَشَآءُ ۚ وَٱللَّهُ ذُو ٱلْفَضْلِ ٱلْعَظِيمِ ٢٩

سُورَةُ المُجَادِلَةِ

Surah 58: *Al-Mujadilah* (The Woman Who Pleads)

In the name of Allah,
Most Gracious, Most Merciful.

بِسْمِ ٱللَّهِ ٱلرَّحْمَٰنِ ٱلرَّحِيمِ

✻**1.** Allah has indeed heard (and accepted) the statement of the woman who pleads with you concerning her husband and carries her complaint (in prayer) to Allah: and Allah (always) hears the arguments between both sides among you: for Allah hears and sees (all things).

الجزء ٢٨ الحزب ٥٥ قَدْ سَمِعَ ٱللَّهُ قَوْلَ ٱلَّتِى تُجَٰدِلُكَ فِى زَوْجِهَا وَتَشْتَكِىٓ
إِلَى ٱللَّهِ وَٱللَّهُ يَسْمَعُ تَحَاوُرَكُمَآ ۚ إِنَّ ٱللَّهَ سَمِيعٌۢ
بَصِيرٌ ١

2. If any men among you divorce their wives by *zihar* (calling them mothers), they cannot

ٱلَّذِينَ يُظَٰهِرُونَ مِنكُم مِّن نِّسَآئِهِم مَّا هُنَّ أُمَّهَٰتِهِمْ ۖ

✻ Part-28

be their mothers: none can be their mothers except those who gave them birth. And in fact they use words (both) iniquitous and false: but truly Allah is One that blots out (sins), and forgives (again and again).

إِنْ أُمَّهَٰتُهُمْ إِلَّا ٱلَّٰٓـِٔى وَلَدْنَهُمْ ۚ وَإِنَّهُمْ لَيَقُولُونَ
مُنكَرًا مِّنَ ٱلْقَوْلِ وَزُورًا ۚ وَإِنَّ ٱللَّهَ لَعَفُوٌّ غَفُورٌ ٢

3. But those who divorce their wives by *zihar,* then wish to go back on the words they uttered - (it is ordained that such a one) should free a slave before they touch each other; this are you admonished to perform: and Allah is well-acquainted with (all) that you do.

وَٱلَّذِينَ يُظَٰهِرُونَ مِن نِّسَآئِهِمْ ثُمَّ يَعُودُونَ لِمَا قَالُوا۟
فَتَحْرِيرُ رَقَبَةٍ مِّن قَبْلِ أَن يَتَمَآسَّا ۚ ذَٰلِكُمْ تُوعَظُونَ
بِهِۦ ۚ وَٱللَّهُ بِمَا تَعْمَلُونَ خَبِيرٌ ٣

4. And if any has not (the means), he should fast for two months consecutively before they touch each other. But if any is unable to do so, he should feed sixty needy ones. This, that you may show your faith in Allah and His messenger. Those are limits (set by) Allah. For those who reject (Him), there is a grievous penalty.

فَمَن لَّمْ يَجِدْ فَصِيَامُ شَهْرَيْنِ مُتَتَابِعَيْنِ مِن قَبْلِ أَن
يَتَمَآسَّا ۖ فَمَن لَّمْ يَسْتَطِعْ فَإِطْعَامُ سِتِّينَ مِسْكِينًا ۚ
ذَٰلِكَ لِتُؤْمِنُوا۟ بِٱللَّهِ وَرَسُولِهِۦ ۚ وَتِلْكَ حُدُودُ ٱللَّهِ ۗ
وَلِلْكَٰفِرِينَ عَذَابٌ أَلِيمٌ ٤

5. Those who resist Allah and His messenger will be humbled to dust, as were those before them: for We have already sent down clear signs. And the unbelievers (will have) a humiliating penalty.

إِنَّ ٱلَّذِينَ يُحَآدُّونَ ٱللَّهَ وَرَسُولَهُۥ كُبِتُوا۟ كَمَا كُبِتَ
ٱلَّذِينَ مِن قَبْلِهِمْ ۚ وَقَدْ أَنزَلْنَآ ءَايَٰتٍۭ بَيِّنَٰتٍ ۚ
وَلِلْكَٰفِرِينَ عَذَابٌ مُّهِينٌ ٥

6. On the day that Allah will raise them all up (again) and show them the truth (and meaning) of their conduct. Allah has reckoned its (value), though they may have forgotten it: for Allah is witness to all things.

يَوْمَ يَبْعَثُهُمُ ٱللَّهُ جَمِيعًا فَيُنَبِّئُهُم بِمَا عَمِلُوٓا۟ ۚ
أَحْصَىٰهُ ٱللَّهُ وَنَسُوهُ ۚ وَٱللَّهُ عَلَىٰ كُلِّ شَىْءٍ شَهِيدٌ ٦

7. Do you not see that Allah does know (all) that is in the heavens and on earth? There is not a secret consultation between three but He makes the fourth among them nor between five but He makes the sixth - nor

أَلَمْ تَرَ أَنَّ ٱللَّهَ يَعْلَمُ مَا فِى ٱلسَّمَٰوَٰتِ وَمَا فِى ٱلْأَرْضِ ۖ
مَا يَكُونُ مِن نَّجْوَىٰ ثَلَٰثَةٍ إِلَّا هُوَ رَابِعُهُمْ وَلَا خَمْسَةٍ
إِلَّا هُوَ سَادِسُهُمْ وَلَآ أَدْنَىٰ مِن ذَٰلِكَ وَلَآ أَكْثَرَ إِلَّا هُوَ

between fewer nor more, but He is in their midst wheresoever they be: in the end will He tell them the truth of their conduct, on the day of judgement, for Allah has full knowledge of all things.

مَعَهُمْ أَيْنَ مَا كَانُوا ۖ ثُمَّ يُنَبِّئُهُم بِمَا عَمِلُوا يَوْمَ الْقِيَامَةِ ۚ
إِنَّ اللَّهَ بِكُلِّ شَيْءٍ عَلِيمٌ (٧)

8. Do not turn your sight towards those who were forbidden secret counsels yet revert to that which they were forbidden (to do)? And they hold secret counsels among themselves for iniquity and hostility, and disobedience to the messenger. And when they come to you, they salute you, not as Allah salutes you, (but in crooked ways): and they say to themselves, "Why does not Allah punish us for our words?" Enough for them is hell: in it will they burn, and evil is that destination!

أَلَمْ تَرَ إِلَى الَّذِينَ نُهُوا عَنِ النَّجْوَىٰ ثُمَّ يَعُودُونَ
لِمَا نُهُوا عَنْهُ وَيَتَنَاجَوْنَ بِالْإِثْمِ وَالْعُدْوَانِ وَمَعْصِيَتِ
الرَّسُولِ وَإِذَا جَاءُوكَ حَيَّوْكَ بِمَا لَمْ يُحَيِّكَ بِهِ اللَّهُ
وَيَقُولُونَ فِي أَنفُسِهِمْ لَوْلَا يُعَذِّبُنَا اللَّهُ بِمَا نَقُولُ ۚ
حَسْبُهُمْ جَهَنَّمُ يَصْلَوْنَهَا ۖ فَبِئْسَ الْمَصِيرُ (٨)

9. O you who believe! When you hold secret counsel, do it not for iniquity and hostility, and disobedience to the messenger; but do it for righteousness and self-restraint; and fear Allah, to Whom you shall be brought back.

يَا أَيُّهَا الَّذِينَ آمَنُوا إِذَا تَنَاجَيْتُمْ فَلَا تَتَنَاجَوْا بِالْإِثْمِ
وَالْعُدْوَانِ وَمَعْصِيَتِ الرَّسُولِ وَتَنَاجَوْا بِالْبِرِّ
وَالتَّقْوَىٰ ۖ وَاتَّقُوا اللَّهَ الَّذِي إِلَيْهِ تُحْشَرُونَ (٩)

10. Secret counsels are only (inspired) by the evil one, in order that he may cause grief to the believers; but he cannot harm them in the least, except as Allah permits; and on Allah let the believers put their trust.

إِنَّمَا النَّجْوَىٰ مِنَ الشَّيْطَانِ لِيَحْزُنَ الَّذِينَ آمَنُوا
وَلَيْسَ بِضَارِّهِمْ شَيْئًا إِلَّا بِإِذْنِ اللَّهِ ۚ وَعَلَى اللَّهِ
فَلْيَتَوَكَّلِ الْمُؤْمِنُونَ (١٠)

11. O you who believe! When you are told to make room in the assemblies (spread out and) make room: (ample) room will Allah provide for you. And when you are told to rise up, rise up: Allah will raise up, to (suitable) ranks (and degrees), those of you who believe and who have been granted knowledge. And Allah is well-acquainted with all you do.

يَا أَيُّهَا الَّذِينَ آمَنُوا إِذَا قِيلَ لَكُمْ تَفَسَّحُوا فِي الْمَجَالِسِ
فَافْسَحُوا يَفْسَحِ اللَّهُ لَكُمْ ۖ وَإِذَا قِيلَ انشُزُوا فَانشُزُوا
يَرْفَعِ اللَّهُ الَّذِينَ آمَنُوا مِنكُمْ وَالَّذِينَ أُوتُوا الْعِلْمَ
دَرَجَاتٍ ۚ وَاللَّهُ بِمَا تَعْمَلُونَ خَبِيرٌ (١١)

12. O you who believe! When you consult the messenger in private, spend something in charity before your private consultation. That will be best for you, and most conducive to purity (of conduct). But if you find not (the means), Allah is Oft-Forgiving, Most Merciful.

يَـٰٓأَيُّهَا ٱلَّذِينَ ءَامَنُوٓا۟ إِذَا نَـٰجَيْتُمُ ٱلرَّسُولَ فَقَدِّمُوا۟ بَيْنَ
يَدَىْ نَجْوَىٰكُمْ صَدَقَةً ۚ ذَٰلِكَ خَيْرٌ لَّكُمْ وَأَطْهَرُ ۚ فَإِن لَّمْ
تَجِدُوا۟ فَإِنَّ ٱللَّهَ غَفُورٌ رَّحِيمٌ ﴿١٢﴾

13. Is it that you are afraid of spending sums in charity before your private consultation (with him)? If, then, you do not so and Allah forgives you, then (at least) establish regular prayer; practice regular charity; and obey Allah and His messenger: and Allah is well-acquainted will all that you do.

ءَأَشْفَقْتُمْ أَن تُقَدِّمُوا۟ بَيْنَ يَدَىْ نَجْوَىٰكُمْ صَدَقَـٰتٍ ۚ
فَإِذْ لَمْ تَفْعَلُوا۟ وَتَابَ ٱللَّهُ عَلَيْكُمْ فَأَقِيمُوا۟ ٱلصَّلَوٰةَ وَءَاتُوا۟
ٱلزَّكَوٰةَ وَأَطِيعُوا۟ ٱللَّهَ وَرَسُولَهُۥ ۚ وَٱللَّهُ خَبِيرٌۢ بِمَا
تَعْمَلُونَ ﴿١٣﴾

14. Do you not turn your attention to those who turn (in friendship) to such as have the wrath of Allah upon them? They are neither of you nor of them, and they swear to falsehood knowingly.

ربع الحزب ٥٥ ۞ أَلَمْ تَرَ إِلَى ٱلَّذِينَ تَوَلَّوْا۟ قَوْمًا غَضِبَ ٱللَّهُ عَلَيْهِم مَّا هُم
مِّنكُمْ وَلَا مِنْهُمْ وَيَحْلِفُونَ عَلَى ٱلْكَذِبِ وَهُمْ يَعْلَمُونَ ﴿١٤﴾

15. Allah has prepared for them a severe penalty: evil indeed are their deeds.

أَعَدَّ ٱللَّهُ لَهُمْ عَذَابًا شَدِيدًا ۖ إِنَّهُمْ سَآءَ مَا كَانُوا۟
يَعْمَلُونَ ﴿١٥﴾

16. They have made their oaths a screen (for their misdeeds): thus they obstruct (men) from the path of Allah: therefore shall they have a humiliating penalty.

ٱتَّخَذُوٓا۟ أَيْمَـٰنَهُمْ جُنَّةً فَصَدُّوا۟ عَن سَبِيلِ ٱللَّهِ فَلَهُمْ
عَذَابٌ مُّهِينٌ ﴿١٦﴾

17. Of no profit whatever to them, against Allah, will be their riches nor their sons: they will be companions of the fire to dwell in it (for ever)!

لَّن تُغْنِىَ عَنْهُمْ أَمْوَٰلُهُمْ وَلَآ أَوْلَـٰدُهُم مِّنَ ٱللَّهِ شَيْـًٔا ۚ
أُو۟لَـٰٓئِكَ أَصْحَـٰبُ ٱلنَّارِ ۖ هُمْ فِيهَا خَـٰلِدُونَ ﴿١٧﴾

18. One day will Allah raise them all up (for judgement): then will they swear to Him as they swear to you: and they think that they have something (to stand upon). No, indeed! They are but liars!

يَوْمَ يَبْعَثُهُمُ ٱللَّهُ جَمِيعًا فَيَحْلِفُونَ لَهُۥ كَمَا يَحْلِفُونَ
لَكُمْ ۖ وَيَحْسَبُونَ أَنَّهُمْ عَلَىٰ شَىْءٍ ۚ أَلَآ إِنَّهُمْ هُمُ
ٱلْكَـٰذِبُونَ ﴿١٨﴾

19. The evil one has got the better of them: so he has made them lose the remembrance of Allah. They are the party of the evil one. Truly, it is the party of the evil one that will perish!

ٱسْتَحْوَذَ عَلَيْهِمُ ٱلشَّيْطَـٰنُ فَأَنسَىٰهُمْ ذِكْرَ ٱللَّهِ ۚ أُو۟لَـٰٓئِكَ
حِزْبُ ٱلشَّيْطَـٰنِ ۚ أَلَآ إِنَّ حِزْبَ ٱلشَّيْطَـٰنِ هُمُ ٱلْخَـٰسِرُونَ ﴿١٩﴾

20. Those who resist Allah and His messenger will be among those most humiliated.

إِنَّ ٱلَّذِينَ يُحَآدُّونَ ٱللَّهَ وَرَسُولَهُۥٓ أُو۟لَـٰٓئِكَ فِى ٱلْأَذَلِّينَ ﴿٢٠﴾

21. Allah has decreed: "It is I and My messengers who must prevail": for Allah is One full of strength, able to enforce His will.

كَتَبَ ٱللَّهُ لَأَغْلِبَنَّ أَنَا۠ وَرُسُلِىٓ ۚ إِنَّ ٱللَّهَ قَوِىٌّ
عَزِيزٌ ﴿٢١﴾

22. You will not find any people who believe in Allah and the last day, loving those who resist Allah and His messenger, even though they were their fathers or their sons, or their brothers, or their relations. For such, He has written faith in their hearts, and strengthened them with a spirit from Himself. And He will admit them to gardens beneath which rivers flow, to dwell in it (forever). Allah will be well pleased with them, and they with Him. They are the party of Allah. Truly it is the party of Allah that will achieve felicity.

لَّا تَجِدُ قَوْمًا يُؤْمِنُونَ بِٱللَّهِ وَٱلْيَوْمِ ٱلْـَٔاخِرِ يُوَآدُّونَ
مَنْ حَآدَّ ٱللَّهَ وَرَسُولَهُۥ وَلَوْ كَانُوٓا۟ ءَابَآءَهُمْ
أَوْ أَبْنَآءَهُمْ أَوْ إِخْوَٰنَهُمْ أَوْ عَشِيرَتَهُمْ ۚ أُو۟لَـٰٓئِكَ
كَتَبَ فِى قُلُوبِهِمُ ٱلْإِيمَـٰنَ وَأَيَّدَهُم بِرُوحٍ مِّنْهُ ۖ
وَيُدْخِلُهُمْ جَنَّـٰتٍ تَجْرِى مِن تَحْتِهَا ٱلْأَنْهَـٰرُ
خَـٰلِدِينَ فِيهَا ۚ رَضِىَ ٱللَّهُ عَنْهُمْ وَرَضُوا۟ عَنْهُ ۚ
أُو۟لَـٰٓئِكَ حِزْبُ ٱللَّهِ ۚ أَلَآ إِنَّ حِزْبَ ٱللَّهِ هُمُ
ٱلْمُفْلِحُونَ ﴿٢٢﴾

سُورَةُ الحَشْرِ

Surah 59: **Al-Hashr** (The Mustering)

In the name of Allah,
Most Gracious, Most Merciful.

بِسْمِ ٱللَّهِ ٱلرَّحْمَـٰنِ ٱلرَّحِيمِ

1. Whatever is in the heavens and on earth, let it declare the praises and glory of Allah: for He is the Exalted in Might, the Wise.

سَبَّحَ لِلَّهِ مَا فِى ٱلسَّمَـٰوَٰتِ وَمَا فِى ٱلْأَرْضِ ۖ وَهُوَ
ٱلْعَزِيزُ ٱلْحَكِيمُ ﴿١﴾

2. It is He Who got out the unbelievers among the People of the Book from their homes at the first gathering (of the forces). Little did you think that they would get out: and they thought that their fortresses would defend them from Allah! But the (wrath of) Allah came to them from quarters from which they little expected (it), and cast terror into their hearts, so that they destroyed their dwellings by their own hands and the hands of the believers. Take warning, then O you with eyes (to see)!

هُوَ ٱلَّذِيٓ أَخۡرَجَ ٱلَّذِينَ كَفَرُواْ مِنۡ أَهۡلِ ٱلۡكِتَٰبِ مِن
دِيَٰرِهِمۡ لِأَوَّلِ ٱلۡحَشۡرِۚ مَا ظَنَنتُمۡ أَن يَخۡرُجُواْۖ وَظَنُّوٓاْ
أَنَّهُم مَّانِعَتُهُمۡ حُصُونُهُم مِّنَ ٱللَّهِ فَأَتَىٰهُمُ ٱللَّهُ
مِنۡ حَيۡثُ لَمۡ يَحۡتَسِبُواْۖ وَقَذَفَ فِي قُلُوبِهِمُ ٱلرُّعۡبَۚ
يُخۡرِبُونَ بُيُوتَهُم بِأَيۡدِيهِمۡ وَأَيۡدِي ٱلۡمُؤۡمِنِينَ فَٱعۡتَبِرُواْ
يَٰٓأُوْلِي ٱلۡأَبۡصَٰرِ ٢

3. And had it not been that Allah has decreed banishment for them, He would certainly have punished them in this world: and in the hereafter they shall (certainly) have the punishment of the fire.

وَلَوۡلَآ أَن كَتَبَ ٱللَّهُ عَلَيۡهِمُ ٱلۡجَلَآءَ لَعَذَّبَهُمۡ فِي
ٱلدُّنۡيَاۖ وَلَهُمۡ فِي ٱلۡأٓخِرَةِ عَذَابُ ٱلنَّارِ ٣

4. That is because they resisted Allah and His messenger: and if anyone resists Allah, verily Allah is severe in punishment.

ذَٰلِكَ بِأَنَّهُمۡ شَآقُّواْ ٱللَّهَ وَرَسُولَهُۥۖ وَمَن يُشَآقِّ ٱللَّهَ
فَإِنَّ ٱللَّهَ شَدِيدُ ٱلۡعِقَابِ ٤

5. Whether you cut down (O you Muslims!) the tender palm-trees, or you left them standing on their roots, it was by leave of Allah, and in order that He might cover with shame the rebellious transgressors.

مَا قَطَعۡتُم مِّن لِّينَةٍ أَوۡ تَرَكۡتُمُوهَا قَآئِمَةً عَلَىٰٓ
أُصُولِهَا فَبِإِذۡنِ ٱللَّهِ وَلِيُخۡزِيَ ٱلۡفَٰسِقِينَ ٥

6. What Allah has bestowed on His messenger (and taken away) from them - for this you made no expedition with either cavalry or camelry: but Allah gives power to His messengers over any He pleases: and Allah has power over all things.

وَمَآ أَفَآءَ ٱللَّهُ عَلَىٰ رَسُولِهِۦ مِنۡهُمۡ فَمَآ أَوۡجَفۡتُمۡ
عَلَيۡهِ مِنۡ خَيۡلٖ وَلَا رِكَابٖ وَلَٰكِنَّ ٱللَّهَ يُسَلِّطُ
رُسُلَهُۥ عَلَىٰ مَن يَشَآءُۚ وَٱللَّهُ عَلَىٰ كُلِّ شَيۡءٖ قَدِيرٞ ٦

7. What Allah has bestowed on His messenger (and taken away) from the people of the townships - belongs to Allah

مَّآ أَفَآءَ ٱللَّهُ عَلَىٰ رَسُولِهِۦ مِنۡ أَهۡلِ ٱلۡقُرَىٰ فَلِلَّهِ وَلِلرَّسُولِ
وَلِذِي ٱلۡقُرۡبَىٰ وَٱلۡيَتَٰمَىٰ وَٱلۡمَسَٰكِينِ وَٱبۡنِ ٱلسَّبِيلِ

- to His messenger and to relations and orphans, the needy and the wayfarer; in order that it may not (merely) make a circuit between the wealthy among you. So take what the messenger assigns to you, and deny yourselves that which he withholds from you. And fear Allah; for Allah is strict in punishment.

كَيۡ لَا يَكُونَ دُولَةَۢ بَيۡنَ ٱلۡأَغۡنِيَآءِ مِنكُمۡۚ وَمَآ
ءَاتَىٰكُمُ ٱلرَّسُولُ فَخُذُوهُ وَمَا نَهَىٰكُمۡ عَنۡهُ
فَٱنتَهُواْۚ وَٱتَّقُواْ ٱللَّهَۖ إِنَّ ٱللَّهَ شَدِيدُ ٱلۡعِقَابِ ٧

8. (Some part is due) to the needy *Muhajirs,* those who were expelled from their homes and their property, while seeking grace from Allah and (His) good pleasure, and aiding Allah and His messenger: such are indeed the sincere ones -

لِلۡفُقَرَآءِ ٱلۡمُهَٰجِرِينَ ٱلَّذِينَ أُخۡرِجُواْ مِن دِيَٰرِهِمۡ
وَأَمۡوَٰلِهِمۡ يَبۡتَغُونَ فَضۡلٗا مِّنَ ٱللَّهِ وَرِضۡوَٰنٗا
وَيَنصُرُونَ ٱللَّهَ وَرَسُولَهُۥٓۚ أُوْلَٰٓئِكَ هُمُ ٱلصَّٰدِقُونَ ٨

9. But those who before them, had homes (in Madinah) and had adopted the faith - show their affection to such as came to them for refuge, and entertain no desire in their hearts for things given to the (latter), but give them preference over themselves, even though poverty was their (own lot). And those saved from the covetousness of their own souls - they are the ones that achieve prosperity.

وَٱلَّذِينَ تَبَوَّءُو ٱلدَّارَ وَٱلۡإِيمَٰنَ مِن قَبۡلِهِمۡ يُحِبُّونَ
مَنۡ هَاجَرَ إِلَيۡهِمۡ وَلَا يَجِدُونَ فِي صُدُورِهِمۡ
حَاجَةٗ مِّمَّآ أُوتُواْ وَيُؤۡثِرُونَ عَلَىٰٓ أَنفُسِهِمۡ وَلَوۡ كَانَ بِهِمۡ
خَصَاصَةٞۚ وَمَن يُوقَ شُحَّ نَفۡسِهِۦ فَأُوْلَٰٓئِكَ
هُمُ ٱلۡمُفۡلِحُونَ ٩

10. And those who came after them say: "Our Lord! Forgive us and our brothers who came before us into the faith, and leave not, in our hearts, rancour (or sense of injury) against those who have believed. Our Lord! You are indeed Full of Kindness, Most Merciful."

وَٱلَّذِينَ جَآءُو مِنۢ بَعۡدِهِمۡ يَقُولُونَ رَبَّنَا ٱغۡفِرۡ لَنَا
وَلِإِخۡوَٰنِنَا ٱلَّذِينَ سَبَقُونَا بِٱلۡإِيمَٰنِ وَلَا تَجۡعَلۡ
فِي قُلُوبِنَا غِلّٗا لِّلَّذِينَ ءَامَنُواْ رَبَّنَآ إِنَّكَ رَءُوفٞ
رَّحِيمٌ ١٠

11. Have you not observed the hypocrites say to their misbelieving brothers among the People of the Book? - "If you are expelled, we too will go out with you, and we will never listen to anyone in your affair; and if you are attacked (in fight) we

نصف الحزب ٥٥
۞ أَلَمۡ تَرَ إِلَى ٱلَّذِينَ نَافَقُواْ يَقُولُونَ لِإِخۡوَٰنِهِمُ
ٱلَّذِينَ كَفَرُواْ مِنۡ أَهۡلِ ٱلۡكِتَٰبِ لَئِنۡ أُخۡرِجۡتُمۡ
لَنَخۡرُجَنَّ مَعَكُمۡ وَلَا نُطِيعُ فِيكُمۡ أَحَدًا أَبَدٗا وَإِن

will help you." But Allah is witness that they are indeed liars.

قُوتِلْتُمْ لَنَنصُرَنَّكُمْ وَٱللَّهُ يَشْهَدُ إِنَّهُمْ
لَكَٰذِبُونَ ﴿١١﴾

12. If they are expelled, never will they go out with them; and if they are attacked (in fight), they will never help them; and if they do help them, they will turn their backs; so they will receive no help.

لَئِنْ أُخْرِجُوا۟ لَا يَخْرُجُونَ مَعَهُمْ وَلَئِن قُوتِلُوا۟
لَا يَنصُرُونَهُمْ وَلَئِن نَّصَرُوهُمْ لَيُوَلُّنَّ ٱلْأَدْبَٰرَ ثُمَّ
لَا يُنصَرُونَ ﴿١٢﴾

13. Of a truth you are stronger (than they) because of the terror in their hearts, (sent) by Allah. This is because they are men devoid of understanding.

لَأَنتُمْ أَشَدُّ رَهْبَةً فِى صُدُورِهِم مِّنَ ٱللَّهِ ۚ
ذَٰلِكَ بِأَنَّهُمْ قَوْمٌ لَّا يَفْقَهُونَ ﴿١٣﴾

14. They will not fight you (even) together, except in fortified townships or from behind walls. Strong is their fighting (spirit) amongst themselves; you would think they were united, but their hearts are divided: that is because they are a people devoid of wisdom.

لَا يُقَٰتِلُونَكُمْ جَمِيعًا إِلَّا فِى قُرًى مُّحَصَّنَةٍ أَوْ مِن
وَرَآءِ جُدُرٍۭ ۚ بَأْسُهُم بَيْنَهُمْ شَدِيدٌ ۚ تَحْسَبُهُمْ
جَمِيعًا وَقُلُوبُهُمْ شَتَّىٰ ۚ ذَٰلِكَ بِأَنَّهُمْ قَوْمٌ
لَّا يَعْقِلُونَ ﴿١٤﴾

15. Like those who lately preceded them, they have tasted the evil result of their conduct; and (in the hereafter there is) for them a grievous penalty -

كَمَثَلِ ٱلَّذِينَ مِن قَبْلِهِمْ قَرِيبًا ۖ ذَاقُوا۟ وَبَالَ
أَمْرِهِمْ وَلَهُمْ عَذَابٌ أَلِيمٌ ﴿١٥﴾

16. (Their allies deceived them), like the evil one, when he says to man, "Deny Allah": but when (man) denies Allah, (the evil one) says, "I am free of you: I do fear Allah, the Lord of the Worlds!"

كَمَثَلِ ٱلشَّيْطَٰنِ إِذْ قَالَ لِلْإِنسَٰنِ ٱكْفُرْ فَلَمَّا
كَفَرَ قَالَ إِنِّى بَرِىٓءٌ مِّنكَ إِنِّىٓ أَخَافُ ٱللَّهَ
رَبَّ ٱلْعَٰلَمِينَ ﴿١٦﴾

17. The end of both will be that they will go into the fire, dwelling in it forever. Such is the reward of wrongdoers.

فَكَانَ عَٰقِبَتَهُمَآ أَنَّهُمَا فِى ٱلنَّارِ خَٰلِدَيْنِ فِيهَا ۚ
وَذَٰلِكَ جَزَٰٓؤُا۟ ٱلظَّٰلِمِينَ ﴿١٧﴾

18. O you who believe! Fear Allah, and let every soul look to what (provision)

يَٰٓأَيُّهَا ٱلَّذِينَ ءَامَنُوا۟ ٱتَّقُوا۟ ٱللَّهَ وَلْتَنظُرْ نَفْسٌ

he has sent forth for the morrow. Yea, fear Allah: for Allah is well-acquainted with (all) they you do.

مَّا قَدَّمَتۡ لِغَدٖۖ وَٱتَّقُواْ ٱللَّهَۚ إِنَّ ٱللَّهَ خَبِيرُۢ بِمَا
تَعۡمَلُونَ ١٨

19. And be you not like those who forgot Allah; and He made them forget their own souls! Such are the rebellious transgressors!

وَلَا تَكُونُواْ كَٱلَّذِينَ نَسُواْ ٱللَّهَ فَأَنسَىٰهُمۡ أَنفُسَهُمۡۚ
أُوْلَٰٓئِكَ هُمُ ٱلۡفَٰسِقُونَ ١٩

20. Not equal are the companions of the fire and the companions of the garden: it is the companions of the garden, that will achieve felicity.

لَا يَسۡتَوِيٓ أَصۡحَٰبُ ٱلنَّارِ وَأَصۡحَٰبُ ٱلۡجَنَّةِۚ
أَصۡحَٰبُ ٱلۡجَنَّةِ هُمُ ٱلۡفَآئِزُونَ ٢٠

21. Had We sent down this Qur'an on a mountain, verily, you would have seen it humble itself and cleave asunder for fear of Allah. Such are the similitudes which We propound to men, that they may reflect.

لَوۡ أَنزَلۡنَا هَٰذَا ٱلۡقُرۡءَانَ عَلَىٰ جَبَلٖ لَّرَأَيۡتَهُۥ خَٰشِعٗا
مُّتَصَدِّعٗا مِّنۡ خَشۡيَةِ ٱللَّهِۚ وَتِلۡكَ ٱلۡأَمۡثَٰلُ نَضۡرِبُهَا
لِلنَّاسِ لَعَلَّهُمۡ يَتَفَكَّرُونَ ٢١

22. Allah is He, than Whom there is no other god - Who knows (all things) both secret and open; He, Most Gracious, Most Merciful.

هُوَ ٱللَّهُ ٱلَّذِي لَآ إِلَٰهَ إِلَّا هُوَۖ عَٰلِمُ ٱلۡغَيۡبِ
وَٱلشَّهَٰدَةِۖ هُوَ ٱلرَّحۡمَٰنُ ٱلرَّحِيمُ ٢٢

23. Allah is He, than Whom there is no other god - the Sovereign, the Holy One, the Source of Peace (and Perfection), the Guardian of faith, the Preserver of Safety, the Exalted in Might, the Irresistible, the Supreme: Glory to Allah! (High is He) above the partners they attribute to Him.

هُوَ ٱللَّهُ ٱلَّذِي لَآ إِلَٰهَ إِلَّا هُوَ ٱلۡمَلِكُ ٱلۡقُدُّوسُ
ٱلسَّلَٰمُ ٱلۡمُؤۡمِنُ ٱلۡمُهَيۡمِنُ ٱلۡعَزِيزُ ٱلۡجَبَّارُ
ٱلۡمُتَكَبِّرُۚ سُبۡحَٰنَ ٱللَّهِ عَمَّا يُشۡرِكُونَ ٢٣

24. He is Allah, the Creator, the Evolver, the Bestower of forms (or colours). To Him belong the Most beautiful names: whatever is in the heavens and on earth, does declare His praises and glory: and He is the Exalted in Might, the Wise.

هُوَ ٱللَّهُ ٱلۡخَٰلِقُ ٱلۡبَارِئُ ٱلۡمُصَوِّرُۖ لَهُ ٱلۡأَسۡمَآءُ
ٱلۡحُسۡنَىٰۚ يُسَبِّحُ لَهُۥ مَا فِي ٱلسَّمَٰوَٰتِ وَٱلۡأَرۡضِۖ
وَهُوَ ٱلۡعَزِيزُ ٱلۡحَكِيمُ ٢٤

سُورَةُ المُمتَحنَة

Surah 60: ***Al-Mumtahanah*** **(That Which Examines)**

In the name of Allah,
Most Gracious, Most Merciful.

بِسْمِ ٱللَّهِ ٱلرَّحْمَٰنِ ٱلرَّحِيمِ

1. O you who believe! Take not My enemies and yours as friends (or protectors) - offering them (your) love, even though they have rejected the truth that has come to you, and have (on the contrary) driven out the messenger and yourselves (from your homes), (simply) because you believe in Allah your Lord! If you have come out to strive in My way and to seek My good pleasure, (take them not as friends), holding secret converse of love (and friendship) with them: for I know full well all that you conceal and all that you reveal. And any of you that does this has strayed from the straight path.

يَٰٓأَيُّهَا ٱلَّذِينَ ءَامَنُوا۟ لَا تَتَّخِذُوا۟ عَدُوِّى وَعَدُوَّكُمْ أَوْلِيَآءَ
تُلْقُونَ إِلَيْهِم بِٱلْمَوَدَّةِ وَقَدْ كَفَرُوا۟ بِمَا جَآءَكُم مِّنَ ٱلْحَقِّ
يُخْرِجُونَ ٱلرَّسُولَ وَإِيَّاكُمْ أَن تُؤْمِنُوا۟ بِٱللَّهِ رَبِّكُمْ إِن
كُنتُمْ خَرَجْتُمْ جِهَٰدًا فِى سَبِيلِى وَٱبْتِغَآءَ مَرْضَاتِى ۚ
تُسِرُّونَ إِلَيْهِم بِٱلْمَوَدَّةِ وَأَنَا۠ أَعْلَمُ بِمَآ أَخْفَيْتُمْ وَمَآ
أَعْلَنتُمْ ۚ وَمَن يَفْعَلْهُ مِنكُمْ فَقَدْ ضَلَّ سَوَآءَ ٱلسَّبِيلِ ﴿١﴾

2. If they were to get the better of you, they would behave to you as enemies, and stretch forth their hands and their tongues against you for evil; and they desire that you should reject the truth.

إِن يَثْقَفُوكُمْ يَكُونُوا۟ لَكُمْ أَعْدَآءً وَيَبْسُطُوٓا۟ إِلَيْكُمْ أَيْدِيَهُمْ
وَأَلْسِنَتَهُم بِٱلسُّوٓءِ وَوَدُّوا۟ لَوْ تَكْفُرُونَ ﴿٢﴾

3. Of no profit to you will be your relatives and your children on the day of judgement: He will judge between you: for Allah sees well all that you do.

لَن تَنفَعَكُمْ أَرْحَامُكُمْ وَلَآ أَوْلَٰدُكُمْ ۚ يَوْمَ ٱلْقِيَٰمَةِ يَفْصِلُ
بَيْنَكُمْ ۚ وَٱللَّهُ بِمَا تَعْمَلُونَ بَصِيرٌ ﴿٣﴾

4. There is for you an excellent example (to follow) in Abraham and those with him, when they said to their people: "We are clear of you and of whatever you worship besides Allah: we have rejected you, and there has arisen between us and you, enmity and hatred forever - unless you believe in Allah and Him alone"; But not

قَدْ كَانَتْ لَكُمْ أُسْوَةٌ حَسَنَةٌ فِىٓ إِبْرَٰهِيمَ وَٱلَّذِينَ مَعَهُۥٓ
إِذْ قَالُوا۟ لِقَوْمِهِمْ إِنَّا بُرَءَٰٓؤُا۟ مِنكُمْ وَمِمَّا تَعْبُدُونَ مِن
دُونِ ٱللَّهِ كَفَرْنَا بِكُمْ وَبَدَا بَيْنَنَا وَبَيْنَكُمُ ٱلْعَدَٰوَةُ
وَٱلْبَغْضَآءُ أَبَدًا حَتَّىٰ تُؤْمِنُوا۟ بِٱللَّهِ وَحْدَهُۥٓ إِلَّا قَوْلَ

when Abraham said to his father: "I will pray for forgiveness for you, though I have no power (to get) anything on your behalf from Allah." (They prayed): "Our Lord! In You do we trust, and to You do we turn in repentance: to You is (our) final goal.

إِبْرَٰهِيمَ لِأَبِيهِ لَأَسْتَغْفِرَنَّ لَكَ وَمَآ أَمْلِكُ لَكَ مِنَ ٱللَّهِ
مِن شَيْءٍ ۖ رَّبَّنَا عَلَيْكَ تَوَكَّلْنَا وَإِلَيْكَ أَنَبْنَا وَإِلَيْكَ
ٱلْمَصِيرُ ﴿٤﴾

5. Our Lord! Make us not a (test and) trial for the unbelievers, but forgive us, our Lord! For You are the Exalted in Might, the Wise."

رَبَّنَا لَا تَجْعَلْنَا فِتْنَةً لِّلَّذِينَ كَفَرُوا۟ وَٱغْفِرْ لَنَا رَبَّنَآ ۖ
إِنَّكَ أَنتَ ٱلْعَزِيزُ ٱلْحَكِيمُ ﴿٥﴾

6. There was indeed in them an excellent example for you to follow - for those whose hope is in Allah and in the last day. But if any turn away, truly Allah is Free of all wants, Worthy of all praise.

لَقَدْ كَانَ لَكُمْ فِيهِمْ أُسْوَةٌ حَسَنَةٌ لِّمَن كَانَ يَرْجُوا۟ ٱللَّهَ
وَٱلْيَوْمَ ٱلْءَاخِرَ ۚ وَمَن يَتَوَلَّ فَإِنَّ ٱللَّهَ هُوَ ٱلْغَنِىُّ ٱلْحَمِيدُ ﴿٦﴾

7. It may be that Allah will grant love (and friendship) between you and those whom you (now) hold as enemies. For Allah has power (over all things); and Allah is Oft-Forgiving, Most Merciful.

۞ عَسَى ٱللَّهُ أَن يَجْعَلَ بَيْنَكُمْ وَبَيْنَ ٱلَّذِينَ عَادَيْتُم مِّنْهُم ثلاثة أرباع الحزب ٥٥
مَّوَدَّةً ۚ وَٱللَّهُ قَدِيرٌ ۚ وَٱللَّهُ غَفُورٌ رَّحِيمٌ ﴿٧﴾

8. Allah forbids you not, with regard to those who fight you not for (your) faith nor drive you out of your homes, from dealing kindly and justly with them: for Allah loves those who are just.

لَّا يَنْهَىٰكُمُ ٱللَّهُ عَنِ ٱلَّذِينَ لَمْ يُقَٰتِلُوكُمْ فِى ٱلدِّينِ وَلَمْ
يُخْرِجُوكُم مِّن دِيَٰرِكُمْ أَن تَبَرُّوهُمْ وَتُقْسِطُوٓا۟ إِلَيْهِمْ ۚ
إِنَّ ٱللَّهَ يُحِبُّ ٱلْمُقْسِطِينَ ﴿٨﴾

9. Allah only forbids you, with regard to those who fight you for (your) faith, and drive you out, of your homes, and support (others) in driving you out, from turning to them (for friendship and protection). It is such as turn to them (in these circumstances), that do wrong.

إِنَّمَا يَنْهَىٰكُمُ ٱللَّهُ عَنِ ٱلَّذِينَ قَٰتَلُوكُمْ فِى ٱلدِّينِ
وَأَخْرَجُوكُم مِّن دِيَٰرِكُمْ وَظَٰهَرُوا۟ عَلَىٰٓ إِخْرَاجِكُمْ أَن
تَوَلَّوْهُمْ ۚ وَمَن يَتَوَلَّهُمْ فَأُو۟لَٰٓئِكَ هُمُ ٱلظَّٰلِمُونَ ﴿٩﴾

10. O you who believe! When there come to you believing women refugees, examine

يَٰٓأَيُّهَا ٱلَّذِينَ ءَامَنُوٓا۟ إِذَا جَآءَكُمُ ٱلْمُؤْمِنَٰتُ مُهَٰجِرَٰتٍ

فَٱمۡتَحِنُوهُنَّۖ ٱللَّهُ أَعۡلَمُ بِإِيمَٰنِهِنَّۖ فَإِنۡ عَلِمۡتُمُوهُنَّ
مُؤۡمِنَٰتٖ فَلَا تَرۡجِعُوهُنَّ إِلَى ٱلۡكُفَّارِۖ لَا هُنَّ حِلّٞ لَّهُمۡ
وَلَا هُمۡ يَحِلُّونَ لَهُنَّۖ وَءَاتُوهُم مَّآ أَنفَقُواْۚ وَلَا جُنَاحَ عَلَيۡكُمۡ
أَن تَنكِحُوهُنَّ إِذَآ ءَاتَيۡتُمُوهُنَّ أُجُورَهُنَّۚ وَلَا تُمۡسِكُواْ
بِعِصَمِ ٱلۡكَوَافِرِ وَسۡـَٔلُواْ مَآ أَنفَقۡتُمۡ وَلۡيَسۡـَٔلُواْ مَآ أَنفَقُواْۚ
ذَٰلِكُمۡ حُكۡمُ ٱللَّهِ يَحۡكُمُ بَيۡنَكُمۡۖ وَٱللَّهُ عَلِيمٌ حَكِيمٞ ١٠

(and test) them: Allah knows best as to their faith: if you ascertain that they are believers, then send them not back to the unbelievers. They are not lawful (wives) for the unbelievers, nor are the (unbelievers) lawful (husbands) for them. But pay the unbelievers what they have spent (on their dower). And there will be no blame on you if you marry them on payment of their dower to them. But hold not to the guardianship of unbelieving women: ask for what you have spent on their dowers, and let the (unbelievers) ask for what they have spent (on the dowers of women who come over to you). Such is the command of Allah. He judges (with justice) between you. And Allah is Full of Knowledge and Wisdom.

وَإِن فَاتَكُمۡ شَيۡءٞ مِّنۡ أَزۡوَٰجِكُمۡ إِلَى ٱلۡكُفَّارِ فَعَاقَبۡتُمۡ
فَـَٔاتُواْ ٱلَّذِينَ ذَهَبَتۡ أَزۡوَٰجُهُم مِّثۡلَ مَآ أَنفَقُواْۚ
وَٱتَّقُواْ ٱللَّهَ ٱلَّذِيٓ أَنتُم بِهِۦ مُؤۡمِنُونَ ١١

11. And if any of your wives deserts you to the unbelievers, and you have an accession (by the coming over of a woman from the other side), then pay to those whose wives have deserted the equivalent of what they had spent (on their (dower). And fear Allah, in Whom you believe.

يَٰٓأَيُّهَا ٱلنَّبِيُّ إِذَا جَآءَكَ ٱلۡمُؤۡمِنَٰتُ يُبَايِعۡنَكَ عَلَىٰٓ أَن
لَّا يُشۡرِكۡنَ بِٱللَّهِ شَيۡـٔٗا وَلَا يَسۡرِقۡنَ وَلَا يَزۡنِينَ وَلَا
يَقۡتُلۡنَ أَوۡلَٰدَهُنَّ وَلَا يَأۡتِينَ بِبُهۡتَٰنٖ يَفۡتَرِينَهُۥ بَيۡنَ
أَيۡدِيهِنَّ وَأَرۡجُلِهِنَّ وَلَا يَعۡصِينَكَ فِي مَعۡرُوفٖ
فَبَايِعۡهُنَّ وَٱسۡتَغۡفِرۡ لَهُنَّ ٱللَّهَۖ إِنَّ ٱللَّهَ غَفُورٞ
رَّحِيمٞ ١٢

12. O prophet! When believing women come to you to take the oath of fealty to you, that they will not associate in worship any other thing whatever with Allah, that they will not steal, that they will not commit adultery (or fornication), that they will not kill their children, that they will not utter slander, intentionally forging falsehood, and that they will not disobey you in any just matter - then do you receive their fealty, and pray to Allah for the forgiveness (of their sins): for Allah is Oft-Forgiving, Most Merciful.

13. O you who believe! Turn not (for friendship) to people on whom is the wrath of Allah. Of the hereafter they are already in despair, just as the unbelievers are in despair about those (buried) in graves.

يَا أَيُّهَا الَّذِينَ آمَنُوا لَا تَتَوَلَّوْا قَوْمًا غَضِبَ اللَّهُ
عَلَيْهِمْ قَدْ يَئِسُوا مِنَ الْآخِرَةِ كَمَا يَئِسَ الْكُفَّارُ
مِنْ أَصْحَابِ الْقُبُورِ ﴿١٣﴾

سُورَةُ الصَّفِّ

Surah 61: ***As-Saff*** **(The Battle Array)**

In the name of Allah,
Most Gracious, Most Merciful.

بِسْمِ اللَّهِ الرَّحْمَٰنِ الرَّحِيمِ

1. Whatever is in the heavens and on earth, let it declare the praises and glory of Allah: for He is the Exalted in Might, the Wise.

سَبَّحَ لِلَّهِ مَا فِي السَّمَاوَاتِ وَمَا فِي الْأَرْضِ ۖ وَهُوَ
الْعَزِيزُ الْحَكِيمُ ﴿١﴾

2. O you who believe! Why do you say that which you do not?

يَا أَيُّهَا الَّذِينَ آمَنُوا لِمَ تَقُولُونَ مَا لَا تَفْعَلُونَ ﴿٢﴾

3. Grievously odious is it in the sight of Allah that you say that which you do not.

كَبُرَ مَقْتًا عِنْدَ اللَّهِ أَنْ تَقُولُوا مَا لَا تَفْعَلُونَ ﴿٣﴾

4. Truly Allah loves those who fight in His cause in battle array, as if they were a solid cemented structure.

إِنَّ اللَّهَ يُحِبُّ الَّذِينَ يُقَاتِلُونَ فِي سَبِيلِهِ صَفًّا
كَأَنَّهُمْ بُنْيَانٌ مَرْصُوصٌ ﴿٤﴾

5. And remember, Moses said to his people: "O my people! Why do you vex and insult me, though you know that I am the messenger of Allah (sent) to you?" Then when they went wrong, Allah let their hearts go wrong. For Allah guides not those who are rebellious transgressors.

وَإِذْ قَالَ مُوسَىٰ لِقَوْمِهِ يَا قَوْمِ لِمَ تُؤْذُونَنِي
وَقَدْ تَعْلَمُونَ أَنِّي رَسُولُ اللَّهِ إِلَيْكُمْ ۖ فَلَمَّا زَاغُوا
أَزَاغَ اللَّهُ قُلُوبَهُمْ ۚ وَاللَّهُ لَا يَهْدِي الْقَوْمَ
الْفَاسِقِينَ ﴿٥﴾

6. And remember, Jesus, the son of Mary, said: "O Children of Israel! I am the

وَإِذْ قَالَ عِيسَى ابْنُ مَرْيَمَ يَا بَنِي إِسْرَائِيلَ إِنِّي رَسُولُ اللَّهِ إِلَيْكُمْ

مُصَدِّقًا لِّمَا بَيْنَ يَدَيَّ مِنَ ٱلتَّوْرَىٰةِ وَمُبَشِّرًۢا بِرَسُولٍ يَأْتِى
مِنۢ بَعْدِى ٱسْمُهُۥٓ أَحْمَدُ ۖ فَلَمَّا جَآءَهُم بِٱلْبَيِّنَـٰتِ قَالُوا۟ هَـٰذَا
سِحْرٌ مُّبِينٌ ﴿٦﴾

messenger of Allah (sent) to you, confirming the law (which came) before me, and giving glad tidings of a messenger to come after me, whose name shall be Ahmad." But when he came to them with clear signs, they said, "This is evident sorcery!"

وَمَنْ أَظْلَمُ مِمَّنِ ٱفْتَرَىٰ عَلَى ٱللَّهِ ٱلْكَذِبَ وَهُوَ يُدْعَىٰٓ إِلَى
ٱلْإِسْلَـٰمِ ۚ وَٱللَّهُ لَا يَهْدِى ٱلْقَوْمَ ٱلظَّـٰلِمِينَ ﴿٧﴾

7. Who does greater wrong than one who invents falsehood against Allah, even as he is being invited to Islam? And Allah guides not those who do wrong.

يُرِيدُونَ لِيُطْفِـُٔوا۟ نُورَ ٱللَّهِ بِأَفْوَٰهِهِمْ وَٱللَّهُ مُتِمُّ نُورِهِۦ
وَلَوْ كَرِهَ ٱلْكَـٰفِرُونَ ﴿٨﴾

8. Their intention is to extinguish Allah's light (by blowing) with their mouths: but Allah will complete (the revelation of) His light even though the unbelievers may detest (it).

هُوَ ٱلَّذِىٓ أَرْسَلَ رَسُولَهُۥ بِٱلْهُدَىٰ وَدِينِ ٱلْحَقِّ لِيُظْهِرَهُۥ
عَلَى ٱلدِّينِ كُلِّهِۦ وَلَوْ كَرِهَ ٱلْمُشْرِكُونَ ﴿٩﴾

9. It is He Who has sent His messenger with guidance and the religion of truth, that he may proclaim it over all religion, even though the pagans may detest (it).

يَـٰٓأَيُّهَا ٱلَّذِينَ ءَامَنُوا۟ هَلْ أَدُلُّكُمْ عَلَىٰ تِجَـٰرَةٍ تُنجِيكُم مِّنْ
عَذَابٍ أَلِيمٍ ﴿١٠﴾

10. O you who believe! Shall I lead you to a bargain that will save you from a grievous penalty? -

تُؤْمِنُونَ بِٱللَّهِ وَرَسُولِهِۦ وَتُجَـٰهِدُونَ فِى سَبِيلِ ٱللَّهِ
بِأَمْوَٰلِكُمْ وَأَنفُسِكُمْ ۚ ذَٰلِكُمْ خَيْرٌ لَّكُمْ إِن كُنتُمْ تَعْلَمُونَ ﴿١١﴾

11. That you believe in Allah and His messenger, and that you strive (your utmost) in the cause of Allah, with your property and your persons: that will be best for you, if you but knew!

يَغْفِرْ لَكُمْ ذُنُوبَكُمْ وَيُدْخِلْكُمْ جَنَّـٰتٍ تَجْرِى مِن تَحْتِهَا
ٱلْأَنْهَـٰرُ وَمَسَـٰكِنَ طَيِّبَةً فِى جَنَّـٰتِ عَدْنٍ ۚ ذَٰلِكَ ٱلْفَوْزُ
ٱلْعَظِيمُ ﴿١٢﴾

12. He will forgive you your sins, and admit you to gardens beneath which rivers flow, and to beautiful mansions in gardens of eternity: that is indeed the supreme achievement.

13. And another (favour will He bestow), which you do love - help from Allah and a speedy victory. So give the glad tidings to the believers.

وَأُخْرَىٰ تُحِبُّونَهَا ۖ نَصْرٌ مِّنَ ٱللَّهِ وَفَتْحٌ قَرِيبٌ ۗ وَبَشِّرِ
ٱلْمُؤْمِنِينَ ﴿١٣﴾

14. O you who believe! Be you helpers of Allah: as said Jesus, the son of Mary, to the disciples, "Who will be my helpers to (the work of) Allah?" Said the disciples, "We are Allah's helpers!" Then a portion of the Children of Israel believed, and a portion disbelieved: but We gave power to those who believed against their enemies and they became the ones that prevailed.

يَٰٓأَيُّهَا ٱلَّذِينَ ءَامَنُوا۟ كُونُوٓا۟ أَنصَارَ ٱللَّهِ كَمَا قَالَ عِيسَى
ٱبْنُ مَرْيَمَ لِلْحَوَارِيِّـۧنَ مَنْ أَنصَارِىٓ إِلَى ٱللَّهِ ۖ قَالَ ٱلْحَوَارِيُّونَ
نَحْنُ أَنصَارُ ٱللَّهِ ۖ فَـَٔامَنَت طَّآئِفَةٌ مِّنۢ بَنِىٓ إِسْرَٰٓءِيلَ
وَكَفَرَت طَّآئِفَةٌ ۖ فَأَيَّدْنَا ٱلَّذِينَ ءَامَنُوا۟ عَلَىٰ عَدُوِّهِمْ
فَأَصْبَحُوا۟ ظَٰهِرِينَ ﴿١٤﴾

سُورَةُ الجُمُعَةِ

Surah 62: **Al-Jummu'ah (The Congregation)**

In the name of Allah,
Most Gracious, Most Merciful.

بِسْمِ ٱللَّهِ ٱلرَّحْمَٰنِ ٱلرَّحِيمِ

1. Whatever is in the heavens and on earth, does declare the praises and glory of Allah - the Sovereign, the Holy One, the Exalted in Might, the Wise.

الحزب ٥٦ يُسَبِّحُ لِلَّهِ مَا فِى ٱلسَّمَٰوَٰتِ وَمَا فِى ٱلْأَرْضِ ٱلْمَلِكِ
ٱلْقُدُّوسِ ٱلْعَزِيزِ ٱلْحَكِيمِ ﴿١﴾

2. It is He Who has sent amongst the unlettered a messenger from among themselves, to rehearse to them His signs, to sanctify them, and to instruct them in scripture and wisdom - although they had been, before, in manifest error -

هُوَ ٱلَّذِى بَعَثَ فِى ٱلْأُمِّيِّـۧنَ رَسُولًا مِّنْهُمْ يَتْلُوا۟ عَلَيْهِمْ
ءَايَٰتِهِۦ وَيُزَكِّيهِمْ وَيُعَلِّمُهُمُ ٱلْكِتَٰبَ وَٱلْحِكْمَةَ
وَإِن كَانُوا۟ مِن قَبْلُ لَفِى ضَلَٰلٍ مُّبِينٍ ﴿٢﴾

3. As well as (to confer all these benefits upon) others of them, who have not already joined them: and He is Exalted in Might, Wise.

وَءَاخَرِينَ مِنْهُمْ لَمَّا يَلْحَقُوا۟ بِهِمْ ۚ وَهُوَ ٱلْعَزِيزُ ٱلْحَكِيمُ ﴿٣﴾

4. Such is the bounty of Allah, which He bestows on whom He will: and Allah is the Lord of the highest bounty.

ذَٰلِكَ فَضْلُ ٱللَّهِ يُؤْتِيهِ مَن يَشَآءُ ۚ وَٱللَّهُ ذُو ٱلْفَضْلِ
ٱلْعَظِيمِ ﴿٤﴾

5. The similitude of those who were charged with the (obligations of the) Mosaic law, but who subsequently failed in those (obligations), is that of a donkey which carries huge tomes (but understands them not). Evil is the similitude of people who falsify the signs of Allah: and Allah guides not people who do wrong.

مَثَلُ ٱلَّذِينَ حُمِّلُوا۟ ٱلتَّوْرَىٰةَ ثُمَّ لَمْ يَحْمِلُوهَا
كَمَثَلِ ٱلْحِمَارِ يَحْمِلُ أَسْفَارًۢا ۚ بِئْسَ مَثَلُ ٱلْقَوْمِ
ٱلَّذِينَ كَذَّبُوا۟ بِـَٔايَـٰتِ ٱللَّهِ ۚ وَٱللَّهُ لَا يَهْدِى ٱلْقَوْمَ
ٱلظَّـٰلِمِينَ ﴿٥﴾

6. Say: "O you that stand on Judaism! If you think that you are friends to Allah, to the exclusion of (other) men, then express your desire for death, if you are truthful!"

قُلْ يَـٰٓأَيُّهَا ٱلَّذِينَ هَادُوٓا۟ إِن زَعَمْتُمْ أَنَّكُمْ أَوْلِيَآءُ
لِلَّهِ مِن دُونِ ٱلنَّاسِ فَتَمَنَّوُا۟ ٱلْمَوْتَ إِن كُنتُمْ
صَـٰدِقِينَ ﴿٦﴾

7. But never will they express their desire (for death), because of the (deeds) their hands have sent on before them! And Allah knows well those that do wrong!

وَلَا يَتَمَنَّوْنَهُۥٓ أَبَدًۢا بِمَا قَدَّمَتْ أَيْدِيهِمْ ۚ وَٱللَّهُ عَلِيمٌۢ
بِٱلظَّـٰلِمِينَ ﴿٧﴾

8. Say: "The death from which you flee will truly overtake you: then will you be sent back to the Knower of things secret and open: and He will tell you (the truth of) the things that you did!"

قُلْ إِنَّ ٱلْمَوْتَ ٱلَّذِى تَفِرُّونَ مِنْهُ فَإِنَّهُۥ
مُلَـٰقِيكُمْ ۖ ثُمَّ تُرَدُّونَ إِلَىٰ عَـٰلِمِ ٱلْغَيْبِ وَٱلشَّهَـٰدَةِ
فَيُنَبِّئُكُم بِمَا كُنتُمْ تَعْمَلُونَ ﴿٨﴾

9. O you who believe! When the call is proclaimed to prayer on Friday (the day of assembly), hasten earnestly to the remembrance of Allah, and leave off business (and traffic): that is best for you if you but knew!

يَـٰٓأَيُّهَا ٱلَّذِينَ ءَامَنُوٓا۟ إِذَا نُودِىَ لِلصَّلَوٰةِ مِن يَوْمِ
ٱلْجُمُعَةِ فَٱسْعَوْا۟ إِلَىٰ ذِكْرِ ٱللَّهِ وَذَرُوا۟ ٱلْبَيْعَ ۚ ذَٰلِكُمْ
خَيْرٌ لَّكُمْ إِن كُنتُمْ تَعْلَمُونَ ﴿٩﴾

10. And when the prayer is finished, then may you disperse through the land, and

فَإِذَا قُضِيَتِ ٱلصَّلَوٰةُ فَٱنتَشِرُوا۟ فِى ٱلْأَرْضِ

seek of the bounty of Allah: and celebrate the praises of Allah often (and without neglect): that you may prosper.

وَٱبْتَغُوا۟ مِن فَضْلِ ٱللَّهِ وَٱذْكُرُوا۟ ٱللَّهَ كَثِيرًا
لَّعَلَّكُمْ تُفْلِحُونَ ١٠

11. But when they see some bargain or some amusement, they disperse headlong to it, and leave you standing. Say: "The (blessing) from the presence of Allah is better than any amusement or bargain! And Allah is the Best to provide (for all needs)."

وَإِذَا رَأَوْا۟ تِجَٰرَةً أَوْ لَهْوًا ٱنفَضُّوٓا۟ إِلَيْهَا وَتَرَكُوكَ قَآئِمًا ۚ
قُلْ مَا عِندَ ٱللَّهِ خَيْرٌ مِّنَ ٱللَّهْوِ وَمِنَ ٱلتِّجَٰرَةِ ۚ وَٱللَّهُ
خَيْرُ ٱلرَّٰزِقِينَ ١١

سُورَةُ المُنَافِقُونَ

Surah 63: ***Al-Munafiqun*** **(The Hypocrites)**

In the name of Allah,
Most Gracious, Most Merciful.

بِسْمِ ٱللَّهِ ٱلرَّحْمَٰنِ ٱلرَّحِيمِ

1. When the hypocrites come to you, they say, "We bear witness that you are indeed the messenger of Allah." Yea, Allah knows that you are indeed His messenger, and Allah bears witness that the hypocrites are indeed liars.

إِذَا جَآءَكَ ٱلْمُنَٰفِقُونَ قَالُوا۟ نَشْهَدُ إِنَّكَ لَرَسُولُ ٱللَّهِ ۗ
وَٱللَّهُ يَعْلَمُ إِنَّكَ لَرَسُولُهُۥ وَٱللَّهُ يَشْهَدُ إِنَّ ٱلْمُنَٰفِقِينَ
لَكَٰذِبُونَ ١

2. They have made their oaths a screen (for their misdeeds): thus they obstruct (men) from the path of Allah: truly evil are their deeds.

ٱتَّخَذُوٓا۟ أَيْمَٰنَهُمْ جُنَّةً فَصَدُّوا۟ عَن سَبِيلِ ٱللَّهِ ۚ
إِنَّهُمْ سَآءَ مَا كَانُوا۟ يَعْمَلُونَ ٢

3. That is because they believed, then they rejected faith: so a seal was set on their hearts: therefore they understand not.

ذَٰلِكَ بِأَنَّهُمْ ءَامَنُوا۟ ثُمَّ كَفَرُوا۟ فَطُبِعَ عَلَىٰ قُلُوبِهِمْ فَهُمْ
لَا يَفْقَهُونَ ٣

4. When you look at them, their exteriors please you; and when they speak, you listen to their words. They are as (worthless as hollow) pieces of timber propped up, (unable to stand on their

ربع الحزب ٥٦ ۞ وَإِذَا رَأَيْتَهُمْ تُعْجِبُكَ أَجْسَامُهُمْ ۖ وَإِن يَقُولُوا۟
تَسْمَعْ لِقَوْلِهِمْ ۖ كَأَنَّهُمْ خُشُبٌ مُّسَنَّدَةٌ ۖ يَحْسَبُونَ

own). They think that every call is against them. They are the enemies; so beware of them. The curse of Allah be on them! How are they deluded (away from the truth)!

كُلَّ صَيْحَةٍ عَلَيْهِمْ ۚ هُمُ ٱلْعَدُوُّ فَٱحْذَرْهُمْ ۚ قَٰتَلَهُمُ
ٱللَّهُ ۖ أَنَّىٰ يُؤْفَكُونَ ﴿٤﴾

5. And when it is said to them, "Come, the messenger of Allah will pray for your forgiveness," they turn aside their heads, and you would see them turning away their faces in arrogance.

وَإِذَا قِيلَ لَهُمْ تَعَالَوْا۟ يَسْتَغْفِرْ لَكُمْ رَسُولُ ٱللَّهِ لَوَّوْا۟
رُءُوسَهُمْ وَرَأَيْتَهُمْ يَصُدُّونَ وَهُم مُّسْتَكْبِرُونَ ﴿٥﴾

6. It is equal to them whether you pray for their forgiveness or not. Allah will not forgive them. Truly Allah guides not rebellious transgressors.

سَوَآءٌ عَلَيْهِمْ أَسْتَغْفَرْتَ لَهُمْ أَمْ لَمْ تَسْتَغْفِرْ لَهُمْ
لَن يَغْفِرَ ٱللَّهُ لَهُمْ ۚ إِنَّ ٱللَّهَ لَا يَهْدِى ٱلْقَوْمَ
ٱلْفَٰسِقِينَ ﴿٦﴾

7. They are the ones who say, "Spend nothing on those who are with Allah's messenger, to the end that they may disperse (and quit Madinah). But to Allah belong the treasures of the heavens and the earth; but the hypocrites understand not.

هُمُ ٱلَّذِينَ يَقُولُونَ لَا تُنفِقُوا۟ عَلَىٰ مَنْ عِندَ رَسُولِ
ٱللَّهِ حَتَّىٰ يَنفَضُّوا۟ ۗ وَلِلَّهِ خَزَآئِنُ ٱلسَّمَٰوَٰتِ
وَٱلْأَرْضِ وَلَٰكِنَّ ٱلْمُنَٰفِقِينَ لَا يَفْقَهُونَ ﴿٧﴾

8. They say, "If we return to Madinah surely the more honourable (element) will expel therefrom the meaner." But honour belongs to Allah and His messenger, and to the believers; but the hypocrites know not.

يَقُولُونَ لَئِن رَّجَعْنَآ إِلَى ٱلْمَدِينَةِ لَيُخْرِجَنَّ
ٱلْأَعَزُّ مِنْهَا ٱلْأَذَلَّ ۚ وَلِلَّهِ ٱلْعِزَّةُ وَلِرَسُولِهِۦ
وَلِلْمُؤْمِنِينَ وَلَٰكِنَّ ٱلْمُنَٰفِقِينَ لَا يَعْلَمُونَ ﴿٨﴾

9. O you who believe! Let not your riches or your children divert you from the remembrance of Allah. If any act thus, the loss is their own.

يَٰٓأَيُّهَا ٱلَّذِينَ ءَامَنُوا۟ لَا تُلْهِكُمْ أَمْوَٰلُكُمْ وَلَآ
أَوْلَٰدُكُمْ عَن ذِكْرِ ٱللَّهِ ۚ وَمَن يَفْعَلْ ذَٰلِكَ
فَأُو۟لَٰٓئِكَ هُمُ ٱلْخَٰسِرُونَ ﴿٩﴾

10. And spend something (in charity) out of the substance which We have bestowed on you, before death should

وَأَنفِقُوا۟ مِن مَّا رَزَقْنَٰكُم مِّن قَبْلِ أَن يَأْتِىَ أَحَدَكُمُ

come to any of you and he should say, "O my Lord! Why did you not give me respite for a little while? I should then have given (largely) in charity, and I should have been one of the doers of good."

ٱلْمَوْتُ فَيَقُولَ رَبِّ لَوْلَآ أَخَّرْتَنِىٓ إِلَىٰٓ أَجَلٍ قَرِيبٍ
فَأَصَّدَّقَ وَأَكُن مِّنَ ٱلصَّٰلِحِينَ ١٠

11. But to no soul will Allah grant respite when the time appointed (for it) has come: and Allah is well-acquainted with (all) that you do.

وَلَن يُؤَخِّرَ ٱللَّهُ نَفْسًا إِذَا جَآءَ أَجَلُهَا ۚ وَٱللَّهُ خَبِيرٌۢ
بِمَا تَعْمَلُونَ ١١

سُورَةُ ٱلتَّغَابُنِ

Surah 64: ***At-Taghabun*** **(The Mutual Loss and Gain)**

In the name of Allah,
Most Gracious, Most Merciful.

بِسْمِ ٱللَّهِ ٱلرَّحْمَٰنِ ٱلرَّحِيمِ

1. Whatever is in the heavens and on earth, does declare the praises and glory of Allah: to Him belongs dominion and to Him belongs praise: and He has power over all things.

يُسَبِّحُ لِلَّهِ مَا فِى ٱلسَّمَٰوَٰتِ وَمَا فِى ٱلْأَرْضِ ۖ لَهُ ٱلْمُلْكُ
وَلَهُ ٱلْحَمْدُ ۖ وَهُوَ عَلَىٰ كُلِّ شَىْءٍ قَدِيرٌ ١

2. It is He Who has created you; and of you are some that are unbelievers and some that are believers: and Allah sees well all that you do.

هُوَ ٱلَّذِى خَلَقَكُمْ فَمِنكُمْ كَافِرٌ وَمِنكُم مُّؤْمِنٌ ۚ وَٱللَّهُ
بِمَا تَعْمَلُونَ بَصِيرٌ ٢

3. He has created the heavens and the earth in just proportions and has given you shape, and made your shapes beautiful: and to Him is the final goal.

خَلَقَ ٱلسَّمَٰوَٰتِ وَٱلْأَرْضَ بِٱلْحَقِّ وَصَوَّرَكُمْ فَأَحْسَنَ
صُوَرَكُمْ ۖ وَإِلَيْهِ ٱلْمَصِيرُ ٣

4. He knows what is in the heavens and on earth: and He knows what you conceal and what you reveal: yea, Allah knows well the (secrets) of (all) hearts.

يَعْلَمُ مَا فِى ٱلسَّمَٰوَٰتِ وَٱلْأَرْضِ وَيَعْلَمُ مَا تُسِرُّونَ
وَمَا تُعْلِنُونَ ۚ وَٱللَّهُ عَلِيمٌۢ بِذَاتِ ٱلصُّدُورِ ٤

5. Has not the story reached you of those who rejected faith before? So they tasted

أَلَمْ يَأْتِكُمْ نَبَؤُا۟ ٱلَّذِينَ كَفَرُوا۟ مِن قَبْلُ فَذَاقُوا۟ وَبَالَ

the evil result of their conduct; and they had a grievous penalty.

أَمْرِهِمْ وَلَهُمْ عَذَابٌ أَلِيمٌ ٥

6. That was because there came to them messengers with clear signs, but they said: "Shall (mere) human beings direct us?" So they rejected (the message) and turned away. But Allah can do without (them): and Allah is free of all needs, worthy of all praise.

ذَٰلِكَ بِأَنَّهُۥ كَانَت تَّأْتِيهِمْ رُسُلُهُم بِٱلْبَيِّنَٰتِ فَقَالُوٓا۟
أَبَشَرٌ يَهْدُونَنَا فَكَفَرُوا۟ وَتَوَلَّوا۟ ۚ وَّٱسْتَغْنَى ٱللَّهُ ۚ وَٱللَّهُ
غَنِىٌّ حَمِيدٌ ٦

7. The unbelievers think that they will not be raised up (for judgement). Say: "Yea, by my Lord, you shall surely be raised up: then shall you be told (the truth) of all that you did. And that is easy for Allah."

زَعَمَ ٱلَّذِينَ كَفَرُوٓا۟ أَن لَّن يُبْعَثُوا۟ ۚ قُلْ بَلَىٰ وَرَبِّى لَتُبْعَثُنَّ
ثُمَّ لَتُنَبَّؤُنَّ بِمَا عَمِلْتُمْ ۚ وَذَٰلِكَ عَلَى ٱللَّهِ يَسِيرٌ ٧

8. Believe, therefore, in Allah and His messenger, and in the light which We have sent down. And Allah is well-acquainted with all that you do.

فَـَٔامِنُوا۟ بِٱللَّهِ وَرَسُولِهِۦ وَٱلنُّورِ ٱلَّذِىٓ أَنزَلْنَا ۚ وَٱللَّهُ
بِمَا تَعْمَلُونَ خَبِيرٌ ٨

9. The day that He assembles you (all) for a day of assembly - that will be a day of mutual loss and gain (among you). And those who believe in Allah and work righteousness - He will remove from them their ills, and He will admit them to gardens beneath which rivers flow, to dwell in it forever: that will be the supreme achievement.

يَوْمَ يَجْمَعُكُمْ لِيَوْمِ ٱلْجَمْعِ ۖ ذَٰلِكَ يَوْمُ ٱلتَّغَابُنِ ۗ وَمَن يُؤْمِنۢ
بِٱللَّهِ وَيَعْمَلْ صَٰلِحًا يُكَفِّرْ عَنْهُ سَيِّـَٔاتِهِۦ وَيُدْخِلْهُ
جَنَّٰتٍ تَجْرِى مِن تَحْتِهَا ٱلْأَنْهَٰرُ خَٰلِدِينَ فِيهَآ
أَبَدًا ۚ ذَٰلِكَ ٱلْفَوْزُ ٱلْعَظِيمُ ٩

10. But those who reject faith and treat Our signs as falsehoods, they will be companions of the fire, to dwell in it for ever: and evil is that goal.

وَٱلَّذِينَ كَفَرُوا۟ وَكَذَّبُوا۟ بِـَٔايَٰتِنَآ أُو۟لَٰٓئِكَ أَصْحَٰبُ
ٱلنَّارِ خَٰلِدِينَ فِيهَا ۖ وَبِئْسَ ٱلْمَصِيرُ ١٠

11. No kind of calamity can occur, except by the leave of Allah: and if anyone believes in Allah, (Allah) guides his heart (aright): for Allah knows all things.

مَآ أَصَابَ مِن مُّصِيبَةٍ إِلَّا بِإِذْنِ ٱللَّهِ ۗ وَمَن يُؤْمِنۢ
بِٱللَّهِ يَهْدِ قَلْبَهُۥ ۚ وَٱللَّهُ بِكُلِّ شَىْءٍ عَلِيمٌ ١١

12. So obey Allah, and obey His messenger; but if you turn back, the duty of Our messenger is but to proclaim (the message) clearly and openly.

وَأَطِيعُواْ ٱللَّهَ وَأَطِيعُواْ ٱلرَّسُولَۚ فَإِن تَوَلَّيۡتُمۡ
فَإِنَّمَا عَلَىٰ رَسُولِنَا ٱلۡبَلَٰغُ ٱلۡمُبِينُ ١٢

13. Allah! There is no god but He: and on Allah therefore let the believers put their trust.

ٱللَّهُ لَآ إِلَٰهَ إِلَّا هُوَۚ وَعَلَى ٱللَّهِ فَلۡيَتَوَكَّلِ
ٱلۡمُؤۡمِنُونَ ١٣

14. O you who believe! Truly, among your wives and your children are (some that are) enemies to yourselves: so beware of them! But if you forgive and overlook, and cover up (their faults), verily Allah is Oft-Forgiving, Most Merciful.

يَٰٓأَيُّهَا ٱلَّذِينَ ءَامَنُوٓاْ إِنَّ مِنۡ أَزۡوَٰجِكُمۡ
وَأَوۡلَٰدِكُمۡ عَدُوّٗا لَّكُمۡ فَٱحۡذَرُوهُمۡۚ
وَإِن تَعۡفُواْ وَتَصۡفَحُواْ وَتَغۡفِرُواْ فَإِنَّ ٱللَّهَ
غَفُورٞ رَّحِيمٌ ١٤

15. Your riches and your children may be but a trial: but in the presence of Allah is the highest reward.

إِنَّمَآ أَمۡوَٰلُكُمۡ وَأَوۡلَٰدُكُمۡ فِتۡنَةٞۚ وَٱللَّهُ
عِندَهُۥٓ أَجۡرٌ عَظِيمٞ ١٥

16. So fear Allah as much as you can; listen and obey; and spend in charity for the benefit of your own souls. And those saved from the covetousness of their own souls - they are the ones that achieve prosperity.

فَٱتَّقُواْ ٱللَّهَ مَا ٱسۡتَطَعۡتُمۡ وَٱسۡمَعُواْ وَأَطِيعُواْ
وَأَنفِقُواْ خَيۡرٗا لِّأَنفُسِكُمۡۗ وَمَن يُوقَ شُحَّ نَفۡسِهِۦ
فَأُوْلَٰٓئِكَ هُمُ ٱلۡمُفۡلِحُونَ ١٦

17. If you loan to Allah a beautiful loan, He will double it to your (credit), and He will grant you forgiveness: for Allah is most Ready to appreciate (service), Most Forbearing -

إِن تُقۡرِضُواْ ٱللَّهَ قَرۡضًا حَسَنٗا يُضَٰعِفۡهُ لَكُمۡ
وَيَغۡفِرۡ لَكُمۡۚ وَٱللَّهُ شَكُورٌ حَلِيمٌ ١٧

18. Knower of what is hidden and what is open, Exalted in Might, Full of Wisdom.

عَٰلِمُ ٱلۡغَيۡبِ وَٱلشَّهَٰدَةِ ٱلۡعَزِيزُ ٱلۡحَكِيمُ ١٨

سُورَةُ الطَّلَاقِ

Surah 65: **At-Talaq** **(Divorce)**

In the name of Allah,
Most Gracious, Most Merciful.

بِسْمِ ٱللَّهِ ٱلرَّحْمَٰنِ ٱلرَّحِيمِ

1. O prophet! When you do divorce women, divorce them at their prescribed periods, and count (accurately) their prescribed periods; and fear Allah your Lord; and turn them not out of their houses, nor shall they (themselves) leave, except in case they are guilty of some open lewdness. Those are limits set by Allah: and any who transgresses the limits of Allah, does verily wrong his (own) soul: you know not if perhaps Allah will bring about after that some new situation.

نصف الحزب ٥٦ يَٰٓأَيُّهَا ٱلنَّبِيُّ إِذَا طَلَّقْتُمُ ٱلنِّسَآءَ فَطَلِّقُوهُنَّ لِعِدَّتِهِنَّ
وَأَحْصُوا۟ ٱلْعِدَّةَ ۖ وَٱتَّقُوا۟ ٱللَّهَ رَبَّكُمْ ۖ لَا تُخْرِجُوهُنَّ مِنۢ
بُيُوتِهِنَّ وَلَا يَخْرُجْنَ إِلَّآ أَن يَأْتِينَ بِفَٰحِشَةٍ مُّبَيِّنَةٍ ۚ
وَتِلْكَ حُدُودُ ٱللَّهِ ۚ وَمَن يَتَعَدَّ حُدُودَ ٱللَّهِ فَقَدْ ظَلَمَ
نَفْسَهُۥ ۚ لَا تَدْرِى لَعَلَّ ٱللَّهَ يُحْدِثُ بَعْدَ ذَٰلِكَ أَمْرًا ١

2. Thus when they fulfil their term appointed, either take them back on equitable terms or part with them on equitable terms; and take for witness two persons from among you, endued with justice, and establish the evidence (as) before Allah. Such is the admonition given to him who believes in Allah and the last day. And for those who fear Allah, He (ever) prepares a way out,

فَإِذَا بَلَغْنَ أَجَلَهُنَّ فَأَمْسِكُوهُنَّ بِمَعْرُوفٍ أَوْ فَارِقُوهُنَّ
بِمَعْرُوفٍ وَأَشْهِدُوا۟ ذَوَىْ عَدْلٍ مِّنكُمْ وَأَقِيمُوا۟
ٱلشَّهَٰدَةَ لِلَّهِ ۚ ذَٰلِكُمْ يُوعَظُ بِهِۦ مَن كَانَ يُؤْمِنُ بِٱللَّهِ
وَٱلْيَوْمِ ٱلْءَاخِرِ ۚ وَمَن يَتَّقِ ٱللَّهَ يَجْعَل لَّهُۥ مَخْرَجًا ٢

3. And He provides for him from (sources) he never could imagine. And if anyone puts his trust in Allah, sufficient is (Allah) for him. For Allah will surely accomplish His purpose: verily, for all things has Allah appointed a due proportion.

وَيَرْزُقْهُ مِنْ حَيْثُ لَا يَحْتَسِبُ ۚ وَمَن يَتَوَكَّلْ عَلَى ٱللَّهِ
فَهُوَ حَسْبُهُۥٓ ۚ إِنَّ ٱللَّهَ بَٰلِغُ أَمْرِهِۦ ۚ قَدْ جَعَلَ ٱللَّهُ
لِكُلِّ شَىْءٍ قَدْرًا ٣

4. Such of your women as have passed the age of monthly courses, for them the prescribed

وَٱلَّٰٓـِٔى يَئِسْنَ مِنَ ٱلْمَحِيضِ مِن نِّسَآئِكُمْ إِنِ

period, if you have any doubts, is three months, and for those who have no courses (it is the same): for those who carry (life within their wombs), their period is until they deliver their burdens: and for those who fear Allah, He will make their path easy.

ٱرۡتَبۡتُمۡ فَعِدَّتُهُنَّ ثَلَٰثَةُ أَشۡهُرٖ وَٱلَّٰٓـِٔي لَمۡ يَحِضۡنَۚ
وَأُوْلَٰتُ ٱلۡأَحۡمَالِ أَجَلُهُنَّ أَن يَضَعۡنَ حَمۡلَهُنَّۚ
وَمَن يَتَّقِ ٱللَّهَ يَجۡعَل لَّهُۥ مِنۡ أَمۡرِهِۦ يُسۡرٗا ﴿٤﴾

5. That is the command of Allah, which He has sent down to you: and if anyone fears Allah, He will remove his ills from him, and will enlarge his reward.

ذَٰلِكَ أَمۡرُ ٱللَّهِ أَنزَلَهُۥٓ إِلَيۡكُمۡۚ وَمَن يَتَّقِ ٱللَّهَ
يُكَفِّرۡ عَنۡهُ سَيِّـَٔاتِهِۦ وَيُعۡظِمۡ لَهُۥٓ أَجۡرًا ﴿٥﴾

6. Let the women live (in Iddah) in the same style as you live, according to your means: annoy them not, so as to restrict them. And if they carry (life in their wombs), then spend (your substance) on them until they deliver their burden; and if they suckle your (offspring), give them their recompense; and take mutual counsel together, according to what is just and reasonable. And if you find yourselves in difficulties, let another woman suckle (the child) on the (father's) behalf.

أَسۡكِنُوهُنَّ مِنۡ حَيۡثُ سَكَنتُم مِّن وُجۡدِكُمۡ وَلَا تُضَآرُّوهُنَّ
لِتُضَيِّقُواْ عَلَيۡهِنَّۚ وَإِن كُنَّ أُوْلَٰتِ حَمۡلٖ فَأَنفِقُواْ عَلَيۡهِنَّ
حَتَّىٰ يَضَعۡنَ حَمۡلَهُنَّۚ فَإِنۡ أَرۡضَعۡنَ لَكُمۡ فَـَٔاتُوهُنَّ أُجُورَهُنَّ
وَأۡتَمِرُواْ بَيۡنَكُم بِمَعۡرُوفٖۖ وَإِن تَعَاسَرۡتُمۡ فَسَتُرۡضِعُ
لَهُۥٓ أُخۡرَىٰ ﴿٦﴾

7. Let the man of means spend according to his means; and the man whose resources are restricted, let him spend according to what Allah has given him. Allah puts no burden on any person beyond what He has given him. After a difficulty, Allah will soon grant relief.

لِيُنفِقۡ ذُو سَعَةٖ مِّن سَعَتِهِۦۖ وَمَن قُدِرَ عَلَيۡهِ رِزۡقُهُۥ فَلۡيُنفِقۡ
مِمَّآ ءَاتَىٰهُ ٱللَّهُۚ لَا يُكَلِّفُ ٱللَّهُ نَفۡسًا إِلَّا مَآ ءَاتَىٰهَاۚ
سَيَجۡعَلُ ٱللَّهُ بَعۡدَ عُسۡرٖ يُسۡرٗا ﴿٧﴾

8. How many populations that insolently opposed the command of their Lord and of His messengers, did We call to account - to severe account? - And We imposed on them an exemplary punishment.

وَكَأَيِّن مِّن قَرۡيَةٍ عَتَتۡ عَنۡ أَمۡرِ رَبِّهَا وَرُسُلِهِۦ فَحَاسَبۡنَٰهَا
حِسَابٗا شَدِيدٗا وَعَذَّبۡنَٰهَا عَذَابٗا نُّكۡرٗا ﴿٨﴾

9. Then did they taste the evil result of their conduct, and the end of their conduct was perdition.

فَذَاقَتۡ وَبَالَ أَمۡرِهَا وَكَانَ عَٰقِبَةُ أَمۡرِهَا خُسۡرًا ﴿٩﴾

10. Allah has prepared for them a severe punishment (in the hereafter). Therefore, fear Allah, O you men of understanding - who have believed! - For Allah has indeed sent down to you a message -

أَعَدَّ ٱللَّهُ لَهُمْ عَذَابًا شَدِيدًا ۖ فَٱتَّقُوا۟ ٱللَّهَ يَـٰٓأُو۟لِى ٱلْأَلْبَـٰبِ
ٱلَّذِينَ ءَامَنُوا۟ ۚ قَدْ أَنزَلَ ٱللَّهُ إِلَيْكُمْ ذِكْرًا ﴿١٠﴾

11. A messenger, who rehearses to you the signs of Allah containing clear explanations, that he may lead forth those who believe and do righteous deeds from the depths of darkness into light. And those who believe in Allah and work righteousness, He will admit to gardens beneath which rivers flow to dwell in it forever: Allah has indeed granted for them a most excellent provision.

رَّسُولًا يَتْلُوا۟ عَلَيْكُمْ ءَايَـٰتِ ٱللَّهِ مُبَيِّنَـٰتٍ لِّيُخْرِجَ ٱلَّذِينَ
ءَامَنُوا۟ وَعَمِلُوا۟ ٱلصَّـٰلِحَـٰتِ مِنَ ٱلظُّلُمَـٰتِ إِلَى ٱلنُّورِ ۚ وَمَن
يُؤْمِنۢ بِٱللَّهِ وَيَعْمَلْ صَـٰلِحًا يُدْخِلْهُ جَنَّـٰتٍ تَجْرِى مِن تَحْتِهَا
ٱلْأَنْهَـٰرُ خَـٰلِدِينَ فِيهَآ أَبَدًا ۖ قَدْ أَحْسَنَ ٱللَّهُ لَهُۥ رِزْقًا ﴿١١﴾

12. Allah is He Who created seven firmaments and of the earth a similar number. Through the midst of them (all) descends His command: that you may know that Allah has power over all things, and that Allah comprehends all things in (His) knowledge.

ٱللَّهُ ٱلَّذِى خَلَقَ سَبْعَ سَمَـٰوَٰتٍ وَمِنَ ٱلْأَرْضِ مِثْلَهُنَّ ۖ
يَتَنَزَّلُ ٱلْأَمْرُ بَيْنَهُنَّ لِتَعْلَمُوٓا۟ أَنَّ ٱللَّهَ عَلَىٰ كُلِّ شَىْءٍ
قَدِيرٌ وَأَنَّ ٱللَّهَ قَدْ أَحَاطَ بِكُلِّ شَىْءٍ عِلْمًۢا ﴿١٢﴾

سُورَةُ التَّحْرِيمِ

Surah 66: ***At-Tahrim*** **(Prohibition)**

In the name of Allah,
Most Gracious, Most Merciful.

بِسْمِ ٱللَّهِ ٱلرَّحْمَـٰنِ ٱلرَّحِيمِ

ثلاثة أرباع الحزب ٥٦

1. O Prophet! Why do you hold to be forbidden that which Allah has made lawful to you? You seek to please your consorts. But Allah is Oft-Forgiving, Most Merciful.

يَـٰٓأَيُّهَا ٱلنَّبِىُّ لِمَ تُحَرِّمُ مَآ أَحَلَّ ٱللَّهُ لَكَ ۖ تَبْتَغِى مَرْضَاتَ
أَزْوَٰجِكَ ۚ وَٱللَّهُ غَفُورٌ رَّحِيمٌ ﴿١﴾

2. Allah has already ordained for you, (O men), the dissolution of your oaths (in some cases): and Allah is your protector, and He is Full of Knowledge and Wisdom.

قَدْ فَرَضَ ٱللَّهُ لَكُمْ تَحِلَّةَ أَيْمَـٰنِكُمْ ۚ وَٱللَّهُ مَوْلَىٰكُمْ ۖ وَهُوَ
ٱلْعَلِيمُ ٱلْحَكِيمُ ﴿٢﴾

3. When the prophet disclosed a matter in confidence to one of his consorts, and she then divulged it (to another), and Allah made it known to him, he confirmed part of it and repudiated a part. Then when he told her of it, she said, "Who told you this?" He said, "He told me Who knows and is well-acquainted (with all things)."

وَإِذْ أَسَرَّ ٱلنَّبِىُّ إِلَىٰ بَعْضِ أَزْوَٰجِهِۦ حَدِيثًا فَلَمَّا نَبَّأَتْ بِهِۦ
وَأَظْهَرَهُ ٱللَّهُ عَلَيْهِ عَرَّفَ بَعْضَهُۥ وَأَعْرَضَ عَنۢ بَعْضٍ ۖ فَلَمَّا
نَبَّأَهَا بِهِۦ قَالَتْ مَنْ أَنۢبَأَكَ هَٰذَا ۖ قَالَ نَبَّأَنِىَ ٱلْعَلِيمُ
ٱلْخَبِيرُ ٣

4. If you two turn in repentance to Him, your hearts are indeed so inclined; but if you back up each other against him, truly Allah is his protector, and Gabriel, and (every) righteous one among those who believe - and furthermore, the angels - will back (him) up.

إِن تَتُوبَآ إِلَى ٱللَّهِ فَقَدْ صَغَتْ قُلُوبُكُمَا ۖ وَإِن تَظَٰهَرَا
عَلَيْهِ فَإِنَّ ٱللَّهَ هُوَ مَوْلَىٰهُ وَجِبْرِيلُ وَصَٰلِحُ
ٱلْمُؤْمِنِينَ ۖ وَٱلْمَلَٰٓئِكَةُ بَعْدَ ذَٰلِكَ ظَهِيرٌ ٤

5. It may be, if he divorced you (all), that Allah will give him in exchange consorts better than you - who submit (their wills), who believe, who are devout, who turn to Allah in repentance, who worship (in humility), who travel (for faith) and fast - previously married or virgins.

عَسَىٰ رَبُّهُۥٓ إِن طَلَّقَكُنَّ أَن يُبْدِلَهُۥٓ أَزْوَٰجًا خَيْرًا مِّنكُنَّ
مُسْلِمَٰتٍ مُّؤْمِنَٰتٍ قَٰنِتَٰتٍ تَٰٓئِبَٰتٍ عَٰبِدَٰتٍ سَٰٓئِحَٰتٍ
ثَيِّبَٰتٍ وَأَبْكَارًا ٥

6. O you who believe! Save yourselves and your families from a fire whose fuel is men and stones, over which are (appointed) angels stern (and) severe, who flinch not (from executing) the commands they receive from Allah, but do (precisely) what they are commanded.

يَٰٓأَيُّهَا ٱلَّذِينَ ءَامَنُوا۟ قُوٓا۟ أَنفُسَكُمْ وَأَهْلِيكُمْ نَارًا
وَقُودُهَا ٱلنَّاسُ وَٱلْحِجَارَةُ عَلَيْهَا مَلَٰٓئِكَةٌ غِلَاظٌ
شِدَادٌ لَّا يَعْصُونَ ٱللَّهَ مَآ أَمَرَهُمْ وَيَفْعَلُونَ مَا يُؤْمَرُونَ ٦

7. (They will say), "O you unbelievers! Make no excuses this day! You are being but repaid for all that you did!"

يَٰٓأَيُّهَا ٱلَّذِينَ كَفَرُوا۟ لَا تَعْتَذِرُوا۟ ٱلْيَوْمَ ۖ إِنَّمَا تُجْزَوْنَ
مَا كُنتُمْ تَعْمَلُونَ ٧

8. O you who believe! Turn to Allah with sincere repentance: in the hope that your Lord will remove from you your ills and admit you to gardens beneath which rivers

يَٰٓأَيُّهَا ٱلَّذِينَ ءَامَنُوا۟ تُوبُوٓا۟ إِلَى ٱللَّهِ تَوْبَةً نَّصُوحًا
عَسَىٰ رَبُّكُمْ أَن يُكَفِّرَ عَنكُمْ سَيِّـَٔاتِكُمْ

flow - the day that Allah will not permit to be humiliated the prophet and those who believe with him. Their light will run forward before them and by their right hands, while they say, "Our Lord! Perfect our light for us and grant us forgiveness; for You have power over all things."

وَيُدْخِلَكُمْ جَنَّٰتٍ تَجْرِى مِن تَحْتِهَا ٱلْأَنْهَٰرُ
يَوْمَ لَا يُخْزِى ٱللَّهُ ٱلنَّبِىَّ وَٱلَّذِينَ ءَامَنُوا۟ مَعَهُۥ ۖ
نُورُهُمْ يَسْعَىٰ بَيْنَ أَيْدِيهِمْ وَبِأَيْمَٰنِهِمْ يَقُولُونَ
رَبَّنَآ أَتْمِمْ لَنَا نُورَنَا وَٱغْفِرْ لَنَآ ۖ إِنَّكَ عَلَىٰ كُلِّ
شَىْءٍ قَدِيرٌ ﴿٨﴾

9. O Prophet! Strive hard against the unbelievers and the hypocrites, and be firm against them. Their abode is hell - an evil refuge (indeed).

يَٰٓأَيُّهَا ٱلنَّبِىُّ جَٰهِدِ ٱلْكُفَّارَ وَٱلْمُنَٰفِقِينَ وَٱغْلُظْ
عَلَيْهِمْ ۚ وَمَأْوَىٰهُمْ جَهَنَّمُ ۖ وَبِئْسَ ٱلْمَصِيرُ ﴿٩﴾

10. Allah sets out for an example to the unbelievers, the wife of Noah and the wife of Lot: they were (respectively) under two of Our righteous servants but they were false to their (husbands) and they profited nothing before Allah on their account, but were told: "Enter you the fire along with (others) that enter!"

ضَرَبَ ٱللَّهُ مَثَلًا لِّلَّذِينَ كَفَرُوا۟ ٱمْرَأَتَ نُوحٍ
وَٱمْرَأَتَ لُوطٍ ۖ كَانَتَا تَحْتَ عَبْدَيْنِ مِنْ عِبَادِنَا
صَٰلِحَيْنِ فَخَانَتَاهُمَا فَلَمْ يُغْنِيَا عَنْهُمَا مِنَ ٱللَّهِ
شَيْـًٔا وَقِيلَ ٱدْخُلَا ٱلنَّارَ مَعَ ٱلدَّٰخِلِينَ ﴿١٠﴾

11. And Allah sets out, as an example to those who believe, the wife of Pharaoh: See, she said: "O my Lord! Build for me, in nearness to You, a mansion in the garden, and save me from Pharaoh and his doings, and save me from those that do wrong";

وَضَرَبَ ٱللَّهُ مَثَلًا لِّلَّذِينَ ءَامَنُوا۟ ٱمْرَأَتَ
فِرْعَوْنَ إِذْ قَالَتْ رَبِّ ٱبْنِ لِى عِندَكَ بَيْتًا فِى
ٱلْجَنَّةِ وَنَجِّنِى مِن فِرْعَوْنَ وَعَمَلِهِۦ وَنَجِّنِى مِنَ
ٱلْقَوْمِ ٱلظَّٰلِمِينَ ﴿١١﴾

12. And Mary the daughter of 'Imran, who guarded her chastity; and We breathed into her (body) of Our spirit; and she testified to the truth of the words of her Lord and of His revelations, and was one of the devout (servants).

وَمَرْيَمَ ٱبْنَتَ عِمْرَٰنَ ٱلَّتِىٓ أَحْصَنَتْ فَرْجَهَا
فَنَفَخْنَا فِيهِ مِن رُّوحِنَا وَصَدَّقَتْ بِكَلِمَٰتِ رَبِّهَا
وَكُتُبِهِۦ وَكَانَتْ مِنَ ٱلْقَٰنِتِينَ ﴿١٢﴾

سُورَةُ المُلْكِ

Surah 67: ***Al-Mulk*** **(The Dominion)**

In the name of Allah,
Most Gracious, Most Merciful.

بِسْمِ ٱللَّهِ ٱلرَّحْمَٰنِ ٱلرَّحِيمِ

*1. Blessed be He in Whose hands is dominion: and He over all things has power -

الجزء ٢٩ الحزب ٥٧

تَبَٰرَكَ ٱلَّذِى بِيَدِهِ ٱلْمُلْكُ وَهُوَ عَلَىٰ كُلِّ شَىْءٍ قَدِيرٌ ١

2. He Who created death and life, that He may try which of you is best in deed; and He is the Exalted in Might, Oft-Forgiving -

ٱلَّذِى خَلَقَ ٱلْمَوْتَ وَٱلْحَيَوٰةَ لِيَبْلُوَكُمْ أَيُّكُمْ أَحْسَنُ
عَمَلًا ۚ وَهُوَ ٱلْعَزِيزُ ٱلْغَفُورُ ٢

3. He Who created the seven heavens one above another: no want of proportion will you see in the creation of (Allah) Most Gracious. So turn your vision again: do you see any flaw?

ٱلَّذِى خَلَقَ سَبْعَ سَمَٰوَٰتٍ طِبَاقًا ۖ مَّا تَرَىٰ فِى خَلْقِ
ٱلرَّحْمَٰنِ مِن تَفَٰوُتٍ ۖ فَٱرْجِعِ ٱلْبَصَرَ هَلْ تَرَىٰ مِن فُطُورٍ ٣

4. Again turn your vision a second time: (your) vision will come back to you dull and discomfited, in a state worn out.

ثُمَّ ٱرْجِعِ ٱلْبَصَرَ كَرَّتَيْنِ يَنقَلِبْ إِلَيْكَ ٱلْبَصَرُ خَاسِئًا وَهُوَ
حَسِيرٌ ٤

5. And We have, (from of old) adorned the lowest heaven with lamps, and We have made such lamps) (as) missiles to drive away the Evil Ones, and have prepared for them the penalty of the blazing fire.

وَلَقَدْ زَيَّنَّا ٱلسَّمَآءَ ٱلدُّنْيَا بِمَصَٰبِيحَ وَجَعَلْنَٰهَا رُجُومًا
لِّلشَّيَٰطِينِ ۖ وَأَعْتَدْنَا لَهُمْ عَذَابَ ٱلسَّعِيرِ ٥

6. For those who reject their Lord (and Cherisher) is the penalty of hell: and evil is (such) destination.

وَلِلَّذِينَ كَفَرُوا۟ بِرَبِّهِمْ عَذَابُ جَهَنَّمَ ۖ وَبِئْسَ
ٱلْمَصِيرُ ٦

7. When they are cast in it, they will hear the (terrible) drawing in of its breath even as it blazes,

إِذَآ أُلْقُوا۟ فِيهَا سَمِعُوا۟ لَهَا شَهِيقًا وَهِىَ تَفُورُ ٧

---

* Part-29

8. Almost bursting with fury: every time a group is cast in it, its keepers will ask, "Did no warner come to you?"

تَكَادُ تَمَيَّزُ مِنَ ٱلْغَيْظِ ۖ كُلَّمَآ أُلْقِىَ فِيهَا فَوْجٌ سَأَلَهُمْ
خَزَنَتُهَآ أَلَمْ يَأْتِكُمْ نَذِيرٌ ٨

9. They will say: "Yes indeed; a warner did come to us, but we rejected him and said, 'Allah never sent down any (message): you are in nothing but an egregious delusion!'"

قَالُوا۟ بَلَىٰ قَدْ جَآءَنَا نَذِيرٌ فَكَذَّبْنَا وَقُلْنَا مَا نَزَّلَ ٱللَّهُ مِن
شَىْءٍ إِنْ أَنتُمْ إِلَّا فِى ضَلَٰلٍ كَبِيرٍ ٩

10. They will further say: "Had we but listened or used our intelligence, we should not (now) be among the companions of the blazing fire!"

وَقَالُوا۟ لَوْ كُنَّا نَسْمَعُ أَوْ نَعْقِلُ مَا كُنَّا فِىٓ أَصْحَٰبِ ٱلسَّعِيرِ ١٠

11. They will then confess their sins: but far will be (forgiveness) from the companions of the blazing fire!

فَٱعْتَرَفُوا۟ بِذَنۢبِهِمْ فَسُحْقًا لِّأَصْحَٰبِ ٱلسَّعِيرِ ١١

12. As for those who fear their Lord unseen, for them is forgiveness and a great reward.

إِنَّ ٱلَّذِينَ يَخْشَوْنَ رَبَّهُم بِٱلْغَيْبِ لَهُم مَّغْفِرَةٌ
وَأَجْرٌ كَبِيرٌ ١٢

13. And whether you hide your word or publish it, He certainly has (full) knowledge of the secrets of (all) hearts.

وَأَسِرُّوا۟ قَوْلَكُمْ أَوِ ٱجْهَرُوا۟ بِهِۦٓ ۖ إِنَّهُۥ عَلِيمٌۢ بِذَاتِ
ٱلصُّدُورِ ١٣

14. Should He not know - He that created? And He is the One that understands the finest mysteries (and) is well-acquainted (with them).

أَلَا يَعْلَمُ مَنْ خَلَقَ وَهُوَ ٱللَّطِيفُ ٱلْخَبِيرُ ١٤

15. It is He Who has made the earth manageable for you, so traverse you through its tracts and enjoy of the sustenance which He furnishes: but to Him is the resurrection.

هُوَ ٱلَّذِى جَعَلَ لَكُمُ ٱلْأَرْضَ ذَلُولًا فَٱمْشُوا۟ فِى مَنَاكِبِهَا
وَكُلُوا۟ مِن رِّزْقِهِۦ ۖ وَإِلَيْهِ ٱلنُّشُورُ ١٥

16. Do you feel secure that He Who is in heaven will not cause you to be swallowed up by the earth when it shakes (as in an earthquake)?

ءَأَمِنتُم مَّن فِى ٱلسَّمَآءِ أَن يَخْسِفَ بِكُمُ ٱلْأَرْضَ فَإِذَا هِىَ
تَمُورُ ١٦

17. Or do you feel secure that He Who is in heaven will not send against you a violent tornado (with showers of stones) so that you shall know how (terrible) was My warning?

أَمْ أَمِنتُم مَّن فِى ٱلسَّمَآءِ أَن يُرْسِلَ عَلَيْكُمْ حَاصِبًا ۖ
فَسَتَعْلَمُونَ كَيْفَ نَذِيرِ ﴿١٧﴾

18. But indeed men before them rejected (My warning): then how (terrible) was My rejection (of them)?

وَلَقَدْ كَذَّبَ ٱلَّذِينَ مِن قَبْلِهِمْ فَكَيْفَ كَانَ نَكِيرِ ﴿١٨﴾

19. Do they not observe the birds above them, spreading their wings and folding them in? None can uphold them except (Allah) Most Gracious: truly it is He that watches over all things.

أَوَلَمْ يَرَوْا۟ إِلَى ٱلطَّيْرِ فَوْقَهُمْ صَٰٓفَّٰتٍ وَيَقْبِضْنَ ۚ
مَا يُمْسِكُهُنَّ إِلَّا ٱلرَّحْمَٰنُ ۚ إِنَّهُۥ بِكُلِّ شَىْءٍۭ بَصِيرٌ ﴿١٩﴾

20. Nay, who is there that can help you, (even as) an army, besides (Allah) Most Merciful? In nothing but delusion are the unbelievers.

أَمَّنْ هَٰذَا ٱلَّذِى هُوَ جُندٌ لَّكُمْ يَنصُرُكُم مِّن دُونِ ٱلرَّحْمَٰنِ ۚ
إِنِ ٱلْكَٰفِرُونَ إِلَّا فِى غُرُورٍ ﴿٢٠﴾

21. Or who is there that can provide you with sustenance if He were to withhold His provision? Nay, they obstinately persist in insolent impiety and flight (from the truth).

أَمَّنْ هَٰذَا ٱلَّذِى يَرْزُقُكُمْ إِنْ أَمْسَكَ رِزْقَهُۥ ۚ بَل لَّجُّوا۟
فِى عُتُوٍّ وَنُفُورٍ ﴿٢١﴾

22. Is then one who walks headlong, with his face grovelling, better guided - or one who walks evenly on a straight way?

أَفَمَن يَمْشِى مُكِبًّا عَلَىٰ وَجْهِهِۦٓ أَهْدَىٰٓ أَمَّن يَمْشِى
سَوِيًّا عَلَىٰ صِرَٰطٍ مُّسْتَقِيمٍ ﴿٢٢﴾

23. Say: "It is He Who has created you (and made you grow), and made for you the faculties of hearing, seeing, feeling and understanding: little thanks it is you give."

قُلْ هُوَ ٱلَّذِىٓ أَنشَأَكُمْ وَجَعَلَ لَكُمُ ٱلسَّمْعَ وَٱلْأَبْصَٰرَ
وَٱلْأَفْـِٔدَةَ ۖ قَلِيلًا مَّا تَشْكُرُونَ ﴿٢٣﴾

24. Say: "It is He Who has multiplied you through the earth, and to Him shall you be gathered together."

قُلْ هُوَ ٱلَّذِى ذَرَأَكُمْ فِى ٱلْأَرْضِ وَإِلَيْهِ تُحْشَرُونَ ﴿٢٤﴾

25. They ask: when will this promise be (fulfilled)? If you are telling the truth.

وَيَقُولُونَ مَتَىٰ هَٰذَا ٱلْوَعْدُ إِن كُنتُمْ صَٰدِقِينَ ﴿٢٥﴾

قُلْ إِنَّمَا ٱلْعِلْمُ عِندَ ٱللَّهِ وَإِنَّمَآ أَنَا۠ نَذِيرٌ مُّبِينٌ ٢٦

26. Say: "As to the knowledge of the time, it is with Allah alone: I am (sent) only to warn plainly in public."

فَلَمَّا رَأَوْهُ زُلْفَةً سِيٓـَٔتْ وُجُوهُ ٱلَّذِينَ كَفَرُوا۟ وَقِيلَ هَٰذَا
ٱلَّذِى كُنتُم بِهِۦ تَدَّعُونَ ٢٧

27. At length when they see it close at hand, grieved will be the faces of the unbelievers, and it will be said (to them): "This is (the promise fulfilled) which you were calling for!"

قُلْ أَرَءَيْتُمْ إِنْ أَهْلَكَنِىَ ٱللَّهُ وَمَن مَّعِىَ أَوْ رَحِمَنَا فَمَن
يُجِيرُ ٱلْكَٰفِرِينَ مِنْ عَذَابٍ أَلِيمٍ ٢٨

28. Say: "Do you see? - If Allah were to destroy me and those with me, or if He bestows His mercy on us - yet who can deliver the unbelievers from a grievous penalty?"

قُلْ هُوَ ٱلرَّحْمَٰنُ ءَامَنَّا بِهِۦ وَعَلَيْهِ تَوَكَّلْنَا ۖ
فَسَتَعْلَمُونَ مَنْ هُوَ فِى ضَلَٰلٍ مُّبِينٍ ٢٩

29. Say: "He is (Allah) Most Gracious: we have believed in Him, and on Him have we put our trust: so, soon will you know which (of us) it is that is in manifest error."

قُلْ أَرَءَيْتُمْ إِنْ أَصْبَحَ مَآؤُكُمْ غَوْرًا فَمَن يَأْتِيكُم بِمَآءٍ
مَّعِينٍۭ ٣٠

30. Say: "Do you see? - If your stream be some morning lost (in the underground earth), who then can supply you with clear-flowing water?"

سُورَةُ ٱلْقَلَمِ

Surah 68: **Al-Qalam (The Pen)**

بِسْمِ ٱللَّهِ ٱلرَّحْمَٰنِ ٱلرَّحِيمِ

In the name of Allah,
Most Gracious, Most Merciful.

ربع الحزب ٥٧

نٓ ۚ وَٱلْقَلَمِ وَمَا يَسْطُرُونَ ١

1. Nun. By the pen and by the (record) which (men) write -

مَآ أَنتَ بِنِعْمَةِ رَبِّكَ بِمَجْنُونٍ ٢

2. You are not by the grace of your Lord mad or possessed.

وَإِنَّ لَكَ لَأَجْرًا غَيْرَ مَمْنُونٍ ٣

3. Nay, verily for you is a reward unfailing:

4. And you (stand) on an exalted standard of character.

وَإِنَّكَ لَعَلَىٰ خُلُقٍ عَظِيمٍ ٤

5. Soon will you see, and they will see,

فَسَتُبْصِرُ وَيُبْصِرُونَ ٥

6. Which of you is afflicted with madness.

بِأَييِّكُمُ ٱلْمَفْتُونُ ٦

7. Verily it is your Lord that knows best, which (among men) has strayed from His path: and He knows best those who receive (true) guidance.

إِنَّ رَبَّكَ هُوَ أَعْلَمُ بِمَن ضَلَّ عَن سَبِيلِهِۦ وَهُوَ أَعْلَمُ
بِٱلْمُهْتَدِينَ ٧

8. So listen not to those who deny (the truth).

فَلَا تُطِعِ ٱلْمُكَذِّبِينَ ٨

9. Their desire is that you should be accommodating; so would they be accommodating.

وَدُّواْ لَوْ تُدْهِنُ فَيُدْهِنُونَ ٩

10. Heed not the type of despicable man - ready with oaths,

وَلَا تُطِعْ كُلَّ حَلَّافٍ مَّهِينٍ ١٠

11. A slanderer, going about with calumnies,

هَمَّازٍ مَّشَّآءِۭ بِنَمِيمٍ ١١

12. (Habitually) hindering (all) good, transgressing beyond bounds, deep in sin,

مَّنَّاعٍ لِّلْخَيْرِ مُعْتَدٍ أَثِيمٍ ١٢

13. Violent (and cruel) with all that base-born -

عُتُلٍّۭ بَعْدَ ذَٰلِكَ زَنِيمٍ ١٣

14. Because he possesses wealth and (numerous) sons.

أَن كَانَ ذَا مَالٍ وَبَنِينَ ١٤

15. When to him are rehearsed Our signs, "Tales of the ancients," he cries!

إِذَا تُتْلَىٰ عَلَيْهِ ءَايَٰتُنَا قَالَ أَسَٰطِيرُ ٱلْأَوَّلِينَ ١٥

16. Soon shall We brand (the beast) on the snout!

سَنَسِمُهُۥ عَلَى ٱلْخُرْطُومِ ١٦

17. Verily We have tried them as We tried the people of the garden, when they resolved to gather the fruits of the (garden) in the morning.

إِنَّا بَلَوْنَٰهُمْ كَمَا بَلَوْنَآ أَصْحَٰبَ ٱلْجَنَّةِ إِذْ أَقْسَمُوا۟ لَيَصْرِمُنَّهَا
مُصْبِحِينَ ﴿١٧﴾

18. But made no reservation, ("If it be Allah's will").

وَلَا يَسْتَثْنُونَ ﴿١٨﴾

19. So there came on the (garden) a visitation from your Lord, (which swept away) all around, while they were asleep.

فَطَافَ عَلَيْهَا طَآئِفٌ مِّن رَّبِّكَ وَهُمْ نَآئِمُونَ ﴿١٩﴾

20. So the (garden) became, by the morning, like a dark and desolate spot, (whose fruit had been gathered).

فَأَصْبَحَتْ كَٱلصَّرِيمِ ﴿٢٠﴾

21. As the morning broke, they called out, one to another -

فَتَنَادَوْا۟ مُصْبِحِينَ ﴿٢١﴾

22. "Go you to your tilth (early) in morning, if you would gather the fruits."

أَنِ ٱغْدُوا۟ عَلَىٰ حَرْثِكُمْ إِن كُنتُمْ صَٰرِمِينَ ﴿٢٢﴾

23. So they departed, conversing in secret low tones, (saying) -

فَٱنطَلَقُوا۟ وَهُمْ يَتَخَٰفَتُونَ ﴿٢٣﴾

24. "Let not a single needy person break in upon you into the (garden) this day."

أَن لَّا يَدْخُلَنَّهَا ٱلْيَوْمَ عَلَيْكُم مِّسْكِينٌ ﴿٢٤﴾

25. And they opened the morning, strong in an (unjust) resolve.

وَغَدَوْا۟ عَلَىٰ حَرْدٍ قَٰدِرِينَ ﴿٢٥﴾

26. But when they saw the (garden), they said: "We have surely lost our way:

فَلَمَّا رَأَوْهَا قَالُوٓا۟ إِنَّا لَضَآلُّونَ ﴿٢٦﴾

27. Indeed we are shut out (of the fruits of our labour)!"

بَلْ نَحْنُ مَحْرُومُونَ ﴿٢٧﴾

28. Said one of them, more just (than the rest): "Did I not say to you, 'Why not glorify (Allah)?'"

قَالَ أَوْسَطُهُمْ أَلَمْ أَقُل لَّكُمْ لَوْلَا تُسَبِّحُونَ ﴿٢٨﴾

29. They said: "glory to our Lord! Verily we have been doing wrong!"

قَالُواْ سُبۡحَٰنَ رَبِّنَآ إِنَّا كُنَّا ظَٰلِمِينَ ٢٩

30. Then they turned, one against another, in reproach.

فَأَقۡبَلَ بَعۡضُهُمۡ عَلَىٰ بَعۡضٖ يَتَلَٰوَمُونَ ٣٠

31. They said: "Alas for us! We have indeed transgressed!

قَالُواْ يَٰوَيۡلَنَآ إِنَّا كُنَّا طَٰغِينَ ٣١

32. It may be that our Lord will give us in exchange a better (garden) than this: for we do turn to Him (in repentance)!"

عَسَىٰ رَبُّنَآ أَن يُبۡدِلَنَا خَيۡرٗا مِّنۡهَآ إِنَّآ إِلَىٰ رَبِّنَا رَٰغِبُونَ ٣٢

33. Such is the punishment (in this life); but greater is the punishment in the hereafter - if only they knew!

كَذَٰلِكَ ٱلۡعَذَابُۖ وَلَعَذَابُ ٱلۡأٓخِرَةِ أَكۡبَرُۚ لَوۡ كَانُواْ يَعۡلَمُونَ ٣٣

34. Verily, for the righteous are gardens of delight, in the presence of their Lord.

إِنَّ لِلۡمُتَّقِينَ عِندَ رَبِّهِمۡ جَنَّٰتِ ٱلنَّعِيمِ ٣٤

35. Shall We then treat the people of faith like the people of sin?

أَفَنَجۡعَلُ ٱلۡمُسۡلِمِينَ كَٱلۡمُجۡرِمِينَ ٣٥

36. What is the matter with you? How do you judge?

مَا لَكُمۡ كَيۡفَ تَحۡكُمُونَ ٣٦

37. Or do you have a book through which you learn -

أَمۡ لَكُمۡ كِتَٰبٞ فِيهِ تَدۡرُسُونَ ٣٧

38. That you shall have, through it whatever you choose?

إِنَّ لَكُمۡ فِيهِ لَمَا تَخَيَّرُونَ ٣٨

39. Or do you have covenants with Us on oath, reaching to the day of judgement, (providing) that you shall have whatever you shall demand?

أَمۡ لَكُمۡ أَيۡمَٰنٌ عَلَيۡنَا بَٰلِغَةٌ إِلَىٰ يَوۡمِ ٱلۡقِيَٰمَةِ إِنَّ لَكُمۡ لَمَا تَحۡكُمُونَ ٣٩

40. Do you ask of them which of them will stand surety for that!

سَلۡهُمۡ أَيُّهُم بِذَٰلِكَ زَعِيمٌ ٤٠

41. Or do they have some "partners" (in Allah)? Then let them produce their "partners" if they are truthful!

أَمۡ لَهُمۡ شُرَكَآءُ فَلۡيَأۡتُواْ بِشُرَكَآئِهِمۡ إِن كَانُواْ صَٰدِقِينَ ٤١

42. The day that the shin shall be laid bare, and they shall be summoned to bow in adoration, but they shall not be able -

يَوۡمَ يُكۡشَفُ عَن سَاقٖ وَيُدۡعَوۡنَ إِلَى ٱلسُّجُودِ فَلَا
يَسۡتَطِيعُونَ ٤٢

43. Their eyes will be cast down - disgrace will cover them; seeing that they had been summoned before to bow in adoration, while they were whole (and had refused).

خَٰشِعَةً أَبۡصَٰرُهُمۡ تَرۡهَقُهُمۡ ذِلَّةٞۖ وَقَدۡ كَانُواْ يُدۡعَوۡنَ إِلَى
ٱلسُّجُودِ وَهُمۡ سَٰلِمُونَ ٤٣

44. Then leave Me alone with such as reject this message: by degrees shall We punish them from directions they perceive not.

فَذَرۡنِي وَمَن يُكَذِّبُ بِهَٰذَا ٱلۡحَدِيثِۖ سَنَسۡتَدۡرِجُهُم
مِّنۡ حَيۡثُ لَا يَعۡلَمُونَ ٤٤

45. A (long) respite will I grant them: truly powerful is My plan.

وَأُمۡلِي لَهُمۡۚ إِنَّ كَيۡدِي مَتِينٌ ٤٥

46. Or is it that you do ask them for a reward, so that they are burdened with a load of debt? -

أَمۡ تَسۡـَٔلُهُمۡ أَجۡرٗا فَهُم مِّن مَّغۡرَمٖ مُّثۡقَلُونَ ٤٦

47. Or that the unseen is in their hands, so that they can write it down?

أَمۡ عِندَهُمُ ٱلۡغَيۡبُ فَهُمۡ يَكۡتُبُونَ ٤٧

48. So wait with patience for the command of your Lord, and be not like the companion of the fish - when he cried out in agony.

فَٱصۡبِرۡ لِحُكۡمِ رَبِّكَ وَلَا تَكُن كَصَاحِبِ ٱلۡحُوتِ إِذۡ
نَادَىٰ وَهُوَ مَكۡظُومٞ ٤٨

49. Had not grace from His Lord reached him, he would indeed have been cast off on the naked shore, in disgrace.

لَّوۡلَآ أَن تَدَٰرَكَهُۥ نِعۡمَةٞ مِّن رَّبِّهِۦ لَنُبِذَ بِٱلۡعَرَآءِ وَهُوَ
مَذۡمُومٞ ٤٩

50. Thus did his Lord choose him and make him of the company of the righteous.

فَٱجۡتَبَٰهُ رَبُّهُۥ فَجَعَلَهُۥ مِنَ ٱلصَّٰلِحِينَ ٥٠

51. And the unbelievers would almost trip you up with their eyes when they

وَإِن يَكَادُ ٱلَّذِينَ كَفَرُواْ لَيُزۡلِقُونَكَ بِأَبۡصَٰرِهِمۡ

لَمَّا سَمِعُوا۟ ٱلذِّكْرَ وَيَقُولُونَ إِنَّهُۥ لَمَجْنُونٌ ﴿٥١﴾

hear the message; and they say: "Surely he is possessed!"

وَمَا هُوَ إِلَّا ذِكْرٌ لِّلْعَٰلَمِينَ ﴿٥٢﴾

52. But it is nothing less than a message to all the worlds.

سُورَةُ الحَاقَّةِ

Surah 69: ***Al-Haqqah*** **(The Sure Reality)**

بِسْمِ ٱللَّهِ ٱلرَّحْمَٰنِ ٱلرَّحِيمِ

In the name of Allah,
Most Gracious, Most Merciful.

نصف الحزب ٥٧

ٱلْحَآقَّةُ ﴿١﴾

1. The sure reality!

مَا ٱلْحَآقَّةُ ﴿٢﴾

2. What is the sure reality?

وَمَآ أَدْرَىٰكَ مَا ٱلْحَآقَّةُ ﴿٣﴾

3. And what will make you realise what the sure reality is?

كَذَّبَتْ ثَمُودُ وَعَادٌۢ بِٱلْقَارِعَةِ ﴿٤﴾

4. The Thamud and the 'Ad people (branded) as false the stunning calamity!

فَأَمَّا ثَمُودُ فَأُهْلِكُوا۟ بِٱلطَّاغِيَةِ ﴿٥﴾

5. But the Thamud - they were destroyed by a terrible storm of thunder and lightning!

وَأَمَّا عَادٌ فَأُهْلِكُوا۟ بِرِيحٍ صَرْصَرٍ عَاتِيَةٍ ﴿٦﴾

6. And the 'Ad - they were destroyed by a furious wind, exceedingly violent;

سَخَّرَهَا عَلَيْهِمْ سَبْعَ لَيَالٍ وَثَمَٰنِيَةَ أَيَّامٍ حُسُومًا فَتَرَى
ٱلْقَوْمَ فِيهَا صَرْعَىٰ كَأَنَّهُمْ أَعْجَازُ نَخْلٍ خَاوِيَةٍ ﴿٧﴾

7. He made it rage against them seven nights and eight days in succession: so that you could see the (whole) people lying prostrate in its (path), as if they had been roots of hollow palm-trees tumbled down!

فَهَلْ تَرَىٰ لَهُم مِّنۢ بَاقِيَةٍ ﴿٨﴾

8. Then do you see any of them left surviving?

وَجَآءَ فِرْعَوْنُ وَمَن قَبْلَهُۥ وَٱلْمُؤْتَفِكَٰتُ بِٱلْخَاطِئَةِ ﴿٩﴾

9. And Pharaoh and those before him, and the cities overthrown, committed habitual sin,

فَعَصَوۡاْ رَسُولَ رَبِّهِمۡ فَأَخَذَهُمۡ أَخۡذَةٗ رَّابِيَةً ١٠

10. And disobeyed (each) the messenger of their Lord; so He punished them with an abundant penalty.

إِنَّا لَمَّا طَغَا ٱلۡمَآءُ حَمَلۡنَٰكُمۡ فِي ٱلۡجَارِيَةِ ١١

11. We, when the water (of Noah's flood) overflowed beyond its limits, carried you (mankind) in the floating (ark).

لِنَجۡعَلَهَا لَكُمۡ تَذۡكِرَةٗ وَتَعِيَهَآ أُذُنٞ وَٰعِيَةٞ ١٢

12. That We might make it a message to you, and that ears (that should hear the tale and) retain its memory should bear its (lessons) in remembrance.

فَإِذَا نُفِخَ فِي ٱلصُّورِ نَفۡخَةٞ وَٰحِدَةٞ ١٣

13. Then, when one blast is sounded on the trumpet,

وَحُمِلَتِ ٱلۡأَرۡضُ وَٱلۡجِبَالُ فَدُكَّتَا دَكَّةٗ وَٰحِدَةٗ ١٤

14. And the earth is moved, and its mountains, and they are crushed to powder at one stroke -

فَيَوۡمَئِذٖ وَقَعَتِ ٱلۡوَاقِعَةُ ١٥

15. On that day shall the (great) event come to pass,

وَٱنشَقَّتِ ٱلسَّمَآءُ فَهِيَ يَوۡمَئِذٖ وَاهِيَةٞ ١٦

16. And the sky will be rent asunder, for it will that day be flimsy,

وَٱلۡمَلَكُ عَلَىٰٓ أَرۡجَآئِهَاۚ وَيَحۡمِلُ عَرۡشَ رَبِّكَ فَوۡقَهُمۡ
يَوۡمَئِذٖ ثَمَٰنِيَةٞ ١٧

17. And the angels will be on its sides, and eight will, that day bear the throne of your Lord above them.

يَوۡمَئِذٖ تُعۡرَضُونَ لَا تَخۡفَىٰ مِنكُمۡ خَافِيَةٞ ١٨

18. That day shall you be brought to judgement: not an act of yours that you hide will be hidden.

فَأَمَّا مَنۡ أُوتِيَ كِتَٰبَهُۥ بِيَمِينِهِۦ فَيَقُولُ هَآؤُمُ ٱقۡرَءُواْ
كِتَٰبِيَهۡ ١٩

19. Then he that will be given his record in his right hand will say: "Ah here! Read you my record!

إِنِّي ظَنَنتُ أَنِّي مُلَٰقٍ حِسَابِيَهۡ ٢٠

20. I did really understand that my account would (one day) reach me!"

21. And he will be in a life of bliss,	فَهُوَ فِي عِيشَةٖ رَّاضِيَةٖ ٢١
22. In a garden on high,	فِي جَنَّةٍ عَالِيَةٖ ٢٢
23. The fruits of which (will hang in bunches) low and near.	قُطُوفُهَا دَانِيَةٞ ٢٣
24. "Eat you and drink you, with full satisfaction; because of the (good) that you sent before you, in the days that are gone!"	كُلُواْ وَٱشۡرَبُواْ هَنِيٓـَٔۢا بِمَآ أَسۡلَفۡتُمۡ فِي ٱلۡأَيَّامِ ٱلۡخَالِيَةِ ٢٤
25. And he that will be given his record in his left hand, will say: "Ah! Would that my record had not been given to me!	وَأَمَّا مَنۡ أُوتِيَ كِتَٰبَهُۥ بِشِمَالِهِۦ فَيَقُولُ يَٰلَيۡتَنِي لَمۡ أُوتَ كِتَٰبِيَهۡ ٢٥
26. And that I had never realised how my account (stood)!	وَلَمۡ أَدۡرِ مَا حِسَابِيَهۡ ٢٦
27. Ah! Would that (death) had made an end of me!	يَٰلَيۡتَهَا كَانَتِ ٱلۡقَاضِيَةَ ٢٧
28. Of no profit to me has been my wealth!	مَآ أَغۡنَىٰ عَنِّي مَالِيَهۡۜ ٢٨ (سكتة لطيفة من هاء ماليه)
29. My power has perished from me!"	هَلَكَ عَنِّي سُلۡطَٰنِيَهۡ ٢٩
30. (The stern command will say): "Seize you him, and bind you him,	خُذُوهُ فَغُلُّوهُ ٣٠
31. And burn you him in the blazing fire.	ثُمَّ ٱلۡجَحِيمَ صَلُّوهُ ٣١
32. Further, make him march in a chain, of which the length is seventy cubits!	ثُمَّ فِي سِلۡسِلَةٖ ذَرۡعُهَا سَبۡعُونَ ذِرَاعٗا فَٱسۡلُكُوهُ ٣٢
33. This was he that would not believe in Allah Most High,	إِنَّهُۥ كَانَ لَا يُؤۡمِنُ بِٱللَّهِ ٱلۡعَظِيمِ ٣٣
34. And would not encourage the feeding of the needy!	وَلَا يَحُضُّ عَلَىٰ طَعَامِ ٱلۡمِسۡكِينِ ٣٤
35. So no friend has he here this day.	فَلَيۡسَ لَهُ ٱلۡيَوۡمَ هَٰهُنَا حَمِيمٞ ٣٥

36. Nor has he any food except the corruption from the washing of wounds,

وَلَا طَعَامٌ إِلَّا مِنْ غِسْلِينٍ ٣٦

37. Which none do eat but those in sin."

لَّا يَأْكُلُهُۥٓ إِلَّا ٱلْخَٰطِـُٔونَ ٣٧

38. So I do call to witness what you see,

فَلَآ أُقْسِمُ بِمَا تُبْصِرُونَ ٣٨

39. And what you do not see,

وَمَا لَا تُبْصِرُونَ ٣٩

40. That this is verily the word of an honoured messenger;

إِنَّهُۥ لَقَوْلُ رَسُولٍ كَرِيمٍ ٤٠

41. It is not the word of a poet: little it is you believe!

وَمَا هُوَ بِقَوْلِ شَاعِرٍ ۚ قَلِيلًا مَّا تُؤْمِنُونَ ٤١

42. Nor is it the word of a soothsayer: little admonition it is you receive.

وَلَا بِقَوْلِ كَاهِنٍ ۚ قَلِيلًا مَّا تَذَكَّرُونَ ٤٢

43. (This is) a message sent down from the Lord of the worlds.

تَنزِيلٌ مِّن رَّبِّ ٱلْعَٰلَمِينَ ٤٣

44. And if (the messenger) were to invent any sayings in Our name,

وَلَوْ تَقَوَّلَ عَلَيْنَا بَعْضَ ٱلْأَقَاوِيلِ ٤٤

45. We should certainly seize him by his right hand,

لَأَخَذْنَا مِنْهُ بِٱلْيَمِينِ ٤٥

46. And We should certainly then cut off the artery of his heart:

ثُمَّ لَقَطَعْنَا مِنْهُ ٱلْوَتِينَ ٤٦

47. Nor could any of you withhold him (from Our wrath).

فَمَا مِنكُم مِّنْ أَحَدٍ عَنْهُ حَٰجِزِينَ ٤٧

48. But verily this is a message for the God-fearing.

وَإِنَّهُۥ لَتَذْكِرَةٌ لِّلْمُتَّقِينَ ٤٨

49. And We certainly know that there are amongst you those that reject (it).

وَإِنَّا لَنَعْلَمُ أَنَّ مِنكُم مُّكَذِّبِينَ ٤٩

50. But truly (revelation) is a cause of sorrow for the unbelievers.

وَإِنَّهُۥ لَحَسْرَةٌ عَلَى ٱلْكَٰفِرِينَ ٥٠

51. But verily it is truth of assured certainty.

وَإِنَّهُۥ لَحَقُّ ٱلْيَقِينِ ﴿٥١﴾

52. So glorify the name of your Lord Most High.

فَسَبِّحْ بِٱسْمِ رَبِّكَ ٱلْعَظِيمِ ﴿٥٢﴾

سُورَةُ المَعَارِجِ

Surah 70: ***Al-Ma'arij*** **(The Ways Of Ascent)**

In the name of Allah,
Most Gracious, Most Merciful.

بِسْمِ ٱللَّهِ ٱلرَّحْمَٰنِ ٱلرَّحِيمِ

1. A questioner asked about a penalty to befall -

سَأَلَ سَآئِلٌۢ بِعَذَابٍ وَاقِعٍ ﴿١﴾

2. The unbelievers, the which there is none to ward off -

لِّلْكَٰفِرِينَ لَيْسَ لَهُۥ دَافِعٌ ﴿٢﴾

3. (A penalty) from Allah, Lord of the ways of ascent.

مِّنَ ٱللَّهِ ذِى ٱلْمَعَارِجِ ﴿٣﴾

4. The angels and the spirit ascend to Him in a day the measure of which is (as) fifty thousand years:

تَعْرُجُ ٱلْمَلَٰٓئِكَةُ وَٱلرُّوحُ إِلَيْهِ فِى يَوْمٍ كَانَ
مِقْدَارُهُۥ خَمْسِينَ أَلْفَ سَنَةٍ ﴿٤﴾

5. Therefore, do you hold patience - a patience of beautiful (contentment).

فَٱصْبِرْ صَبْرًا جَمِيلًا ﴿٥﴾

6. They see the (day) indeed as a far-off (event):

إِنَّهُمْ يَرَوْنَهُۥ بَعِيدًا ﴿٦﴾

7. But We see it (quite) near.

وَنَرَىٰهُ قَرِيبًا ﴿٧﴾

8. The day that the sky will be like molten brass,

يَوْمَ تَكُونُ ٱلسَّمَآءُ كَٱلْمُهْلِ ﴿٨﴾

9. And the mountains will be like wool,

وَتَكُونُ ٱلْجِبَالُ كَٱلْعِهْنِ ﴿٩﴾

10. And no friend will ask after a friend,

وَلَا يَسْـَٔلُ حَمِيمٌ حَمِيمًا ﴿١٠﴾

11. Though they will be put in sight of each other - the sinner's desire will be: would that he could redeem himself from the penalty of that day by (sacrificing) his children,

يُبَصَّرُونَهُمْ ۚ يَوَدُّ ٱلْمُجْرِمُ لَوْ يَفْتَدِى مِنْ عَذَابِ
يَوْمِئِذٍۭ بِبَنِيهِ ﴿١١﴾

12. His wife and his brother,

وَصَـٰحِبَتِهِۦ وَأَخِيهِ ﴿١٢﴾

13. His relations who sheltered him.

وَفَصِيلَتِهِ ٱلَّتِى تُـْٔوِيهِ ﴿١٣﴾

14. And all, all that is on earth - so it could deliver him:

وَمَن فِى ٱلْأَرْضِ جَمِيعًا ثُمَّ يُنجِيهِ ﴿١٤﴾

15. By no means! For it would be the fire of hell! -

كَلَّآ ۖ إِنَّهَا لَظَىٰ ﴿١٥﴾

16. Plucking out (his being) right to the skull! -

نَزَّاعَةً لِّلشَّوَىٰ ﴿١٦﴾

17. Inviting (all) such as turn their backs and turn away their faces (from the right),

تَدْعُوا۟ مَنْ أَدْبَرَ وَتَوَلَّىٰ ﴿١٧﴾

18. And collect (wealth) and hide it (from use)!

وَجَمَعَ فَأَوْعَىٰٓ ﴿١٨﴾

19. Truly man was created very impatient-

۞ إِنَّ ٱلْإِنسَـٰنَ خُلِقَ هَلُوعًا ﴿١٩﴾ ثلاثة أرباع الحزب ٥٧

20. Fretful when evil touches him;

إِذَا مَسَّهُ ٱلشَّرُّ جَزُوعًا ﴿٢٠﴾

21. And niggardly when good reaches him-

وَإِذَا مَسَّهُ ٱلْخَيْرُ مَنُوعًا ﴿٢١﴾

22. Not so those devoted to prayer -

إِلَّا ٱلْمُصَلِّينَ ﴿٢٢﴾

23. Those who remain steadfast to their prayer;

ٱلَّذِينَ هُمْ عَلَىٰ صَلَاتِهِمْ دَآئِمُونَ ﴿٢٣﴾

24. And those in whose wealth is a recognised right -

وَٱلَّذِينَ فِىٓ أَمْوَٰلِهِمْ حَقٌّ مَّعْلُومٌ ﴿٢٤﴾

25. For the (needy) who asks and him who is prevented (for some reason from asking);

لِّلسَّآئِلِ وَٱلْمَحْرُومِ ﴿٢٥﴾

26. And those who hold to the truth of the day of judgement;

وَٱلَّذِينَ يُصَدِّقُونَ بِيَوْمِ ٱلدِّينِ ﴿٢٦﴾

27. And those who fear the displeasure of their Lord -

وَٱلَّذِينَ هُم مِّنْ عَذَابِ رَبِّهِم مُّشْفِقُونَ ﴿٢٧﴾

28. For their Lord's displeasure is the opposite of peace and tranquillity -

إِنَّ عَذَابَ رَبِّهِمْ غَيْرُ مَأْمُونٍ ﴿٢٨﴾

29. And those who guard their chastity,

وَٱلَّذِينَ هُمْ لِفُرُوجِهِمْ حَٰفِظُونَ ﴿٢٩﴾

30. Except with their wives and the (captives) whom their right hands possess - for (then) they are not to be blamed,

إِلَّا عَلَىٰٓ أَزْوَٰجِهِمْ أَوْ مَا مَلَكَتْ أَيْمَٰنُهُمْ فَإِنَّهُمْ
غَيْرُ مَلُومِينَ ﴿٣٠﴾

31. But those who trespass beyond this are transgressors -

فَمَنِ ٱبْتَغَىٰ وَرَآءَ ذَٰلِكَ فَأُو۟لَٰٓئِكَ هُمُ ٱلْعَادُونَ ﴿٣١﴾

32. And those who respect their trusts and covenants;

وَٱلَّذِينَ هُمْ لِأَمَٰنَٰتِهِمْ وَعَهْدِهِمْ رَٰعُونَ ﴿٣٢﴾

33. And those who stand firm in their testimonies;

وَٱلَّذِينَ هُم بِشَهَٰدَٰتِهِمْ قَآئِمُونَ ﴿٣٣﴾

34. And those who guard (the sacredness) of their worship -

وَٱلَّذِينَ هُمْ عَلَىٰ صَلَاتِهِمْ يُحَافِظُونَ ﴿٣٤﴾

35. Such will be the honoured ones in the gardens (of bliss).

أُو۟لَٰٓئِكَ فِى جَنَّٰتٍ مُّكْرَمُونَ ﴿٣٥﴾

36. Now what is the matter with the unbelievers that they rush madly before you -

فَمَالِ ٱلَّذِينَ كَفَرُوا۟ قِبَلَكَ مُهْطِعِينَ ﴿٣٦﴾

37. From the right and from the left, in crowds?

عَنِ ٱلْيَمِينِ وَعَنِ ٱلشِّمَالِ عِزِينَ ﴿٣٧﴾

38. Does every man of them long to enter the garden of bliss?

أَيَطْمَعُ كُلُّ ٱمْرِيٍٕ مِّنْهُمْ أَن يُدْخَلَ جَنَّةَ نَعِيمٍ ٣٨

39. By no means! For We have created them out of the (base matter) they know!

كَلَّآ إِنَّا خَلَقْنَٰهُم مِّمَّا يَعْلَمُونَ ٣٩

40. Now I do call to witness the Lord of all points in the east and the west that We can certainly -

فَلَآ أُقْسِمُ بِرَبِّ ٱلْمَشَٰرِقِ وَٱلْمَغَٰرِبِ إِنَّا لَقَٰدِرُونَ ٤٠

41. Substitute for them better (men) than they; and We are not to be defeated (in Our plan).

عَلَىٰٓ أَن نُّبَدِّلَ خَيْرًا مِّنْهُمْ وَمَا نَحْنُ بِمَسْبُوقِينَ ٤١

42. So leave them to plunge in vain talk and play about, until they encounter that day of theirs which they have been promised! -

فَذَرْهُمْ يَخُوضُوا۟ وَيَلْعَبُوا۟ حَتَّىٰ يُلَٰقُوا۟ يَوْمَهُمُ ٱلَّذِى
يُوعَدُونَ ٤٢

43. The day whereon they will issue from their sepulchres in sudden haste as if they were rushing to a goalpost (fixed for them) -

يَوْمَ يَخْرُجُونَ مِنَ ٱلْأَجْدَاثِ سِرَاعًا كَأَنَّهُمْ إِلَىٰ نُصُبٍ
يُوفِضُونَ ٤٣

44. Their eyes lowered in dejection - disgrace covering them (all over)! Such is the day the which they are promised!

خَٰشِعَةً أَبْصَٰرُهُمْ تَرْهَقُهُمْ ذِلَّةٌ ذَٰلِكَ ٱلْيَوْمُ ٱلَّذِى كَانُوا۟
يُوعَدُونَ ٤٤

سُورَةُ نُوحٍ

Surah 71: **Nuh (Noah)**

In the name of Allah,
Most Gracious, Most Merciful.

بِسْمِ ٱللَّهِ ٱلرَّحْمَٰنِ ٱلرَّحِيمِ

1. We sent Noah to his people (with the command): "Do you warn your people before there comes to them a grievous penalty."

إِنَّآ أَرْسَلْنَا نُوحًا إِلَىٰ قَوْمِهِۦٓ أَنْ أَنذِرْ قَوْمَكَ مِن قَبْلِ
أَن يَأْتِيَهُمْ عَذَابٌ أَلِيمٌ ١

2. He said: "O my people! I am to you a warner, clear and open:

قَالَ يَٰقَوۡمِ إِنِّي لَكُمۡ نَذِيرٞ مُّبِينٌ ٢

3. That you should worship Allah, fear Him and obey me:

أَنِ ٱعۡبُدُواْ ٱللَّهَ وَٱتَّقُوهُ وَأَطِيعُونِ ٣

4. So He may forgive you your sins and give you respite for a stated term: for when the term given by Allah is accomplished, it cannot be put forward: if you only knew."

يَغۡفِرۡ لَكُم مِّن ذُنُوبِكُمۡ وَيُؤَخِّرۡكُمۡ إِلَىٰٓ أَجَلٖ مُّسَمًّىۚ
إِنَّ أَجَلَ ٱللَّهِ إِذَا جَآءَ لَا يُؤَخَّرُۚ لَوۡ كُنتُمۡ تَعۡلَمُونَ ٤

5. He said: "O my Lord! I have called to my people night and day:

قَالَ رَبِّ إِنِّي دَعَوۡتُ قَوۡمِي لَيۡلٗا وَنَهَارٗا ٥

6. But my call only increases (their) flight (from the right)."

فَلَمۡ يَزِدۡهُمۡ دُعَآءِيٓ إِلَّا فِرَارٗا ٦

7. And every time I have called to them, that you might forgive them, they have (only) thrust their fingers into their ears, covered themselves up with their garments, grown obstinate, and given themselves up to arrogance.

وَإِنِّي كُلَّمَا دَعَوۡتُهُمۡ لِتَغۡفِرَ لَهُمۡ جَعَلُوٓاْ أَصَٰبِعَهُمۡ فِيٓ
ءَاذَانِهِمۡ وَٱسۡتَغۡشَوۡاْ ثِيَابَهُمۡ وَأَصَرُّواْ وَٱسۡتَكۡبَرُواْ
ٱسۡتِكۡبَارٗا ٧

8. So I have called to them aloud;

ثُمَّ إِنِّي دَعَوۡتُهُمۡ جِهَارٗا ٨

9. Further, I have spoken to them in public and secretly in private,

ثُمَّ إِنِّيٓ أَعۡلَنتُ لَهُمۡ وَأَسۡرَرۡتُ لَهُمۡ إِسۡرَارٗا ٩

10. Saying: "Ask forgiveness from your Lord; for He is Oft-Forgiving;

فَقُلۡتُ ٱسۡتَغۡفِرُواْ رَبَّكُمۡ إِنَّهُۥ كَانَ غَفَّارٗا ١٠

11. He will send rain to you in abundance;"

يُرۡسِلِ ٱلسَّمَآءَ عَلَيۡكُم مِّدۡرَارٗا ١١

12. Give you increase in wealth and sons; and bestow on you gardens and bestow on you rivers (of flowing water).

وَيُمۡدِدۡكُم بِأَمۡوَٰلٖ وَبَنِينَ وَيَجۡعَل لَّكُمۡ جَنَّٰتٖ وَيَجۡعَل
لَّكُمۡ أَنۡهَٰرٗا ١٢

13. What is the matter with you, that you place not your hope for kindness and long-suffering in Allah -

مَّا لَكُمۡ لَا تَرۡجُونَ لِلَّهِ وَقَارٗا ١٣

14. Seeing that it is He that has created you in diverse stages?

وَقَدْ خَلَقَكُمْ أَطْوَارًا ﴿١٤﴾

15. Do you not see how Allah has created the seven heavens one above another,

أَلَمْ تَرَوْا۟ كَيْفَ خَلَقَ ٱللَّهُ سَبْعَ سَمَٰوَٰتٍ طِبَاقًا ﴿١٥﴾

16. And made the moon a light in their midst, and made the sun as a (glorious) lamp?

وَجَعَلَ ٱلْقَمَرَ فِيهِنَّ نُورًا وَجَعَلَ ٱلشَّمْسَ سِرَاجًا ﴿١٦﴾

17. And Allah has produced you from the earth growing (gradually),

وَٱللَّهُ أَنۢبَتَكُم مِّنَ ٱلْأَرْضِ نَبَاتًا ﴿١٧﴾

18. And in the end He will return you into the (earth), and raise you forth (again at the resurrection)?

ثُمَّ يُعِيدُكُمْ فِيهَا وَيُخْرِجُكُمْ إِخْرَاجًا ﴿١٨﴾

19. And Allah has made the earth for you as a carpet (spread out),

وَٱللَّهُ جَعَلَ لَكُمُ ٱلْأَرْضَ بِسَاطًا ﴿١٩﴾

20. That you may go about in it in spacious roads.'"

لِّتَسْلُكُوا۟ مِنْهَا سُبُلًا فِجَاجًا ﴿٢٠﴾

21. Noah said: "O my Lord! They have disobeyed me, but they follow (men) whose wealth and children give them no increase but only loss.

قَالَ نُوحٌ رَّبِّ إِنَّهُمْ عَصَوْنِى وَٱتَّبَعُوا۟ مَن لَّمْ يَزِدْهُ مَالُهُۥ
وَوَلَدُهُۥٓ إِلَّا خَسَارًا ﴿٢١﴾

22. And they have devised a tremendous plot.

وَمَكَرُوا۟ مَكْرًا كُبَّارًا ﴿٢٢﴾

23. And they have said (to each other), 'abandon not your gods; abandon neither *Wadd* nor *Suwwa*, neither *Yaguth* nor *Ya'uq*, nor *Nasr'* -

وَقَالُوا۟ لَا تَذَرُنَّ ءَالِهَتَكُمْ وَلَا تَذَرُنَّ وَدًّا وَلَا سُوَاعًا
وَلَا يَغُوثَ وَيَعُوقَ وَنَسْرًا ﴿٢٣﴾

24. They have already misled many; and grant You no increase to the wrongdoers but in straying (from their mark)."

وَقَدْ أَضَلُّوا۟ كَثِيرًا ۖ وَلَا تَزِدِ ٱلظَّٰلِمِينَ إِلَّا ضَلَٰلًا ﴿٢٤﴾

25. Because of their sins they were drowned (in the flood), and were made to enter the

مِّمَّا خَطِيٓـَٰٔتِهِمْ أُغْرِقُوا۟ فَأُدْخِلُوا۟ نَارًا فَلَمْ يَجِدُوا۟ لَهُم

fire (of punishment): and they found - in lieu of Allah - none to help them.

مِّن دُونِ ٱللَّهِ أَنصَارًا ﴿٢٥﴾

26. And Noah said: "O my Lord! Leave not of the unbelievers, a single one on earth!

وَقَالَ نُوحٌ رَّبِّ لَا تَذَرْ عَلَى ٱلْأَرْضِ مِنَ ٱلْكَٰفِرِينَ
دَيَّارًا ﴿٢٦﴾

27. For, if You do leave (any of) them, they will but mislead your devotees, and they will breed none but wicked ungrateful ones.

إِنَّكَ إِن تَذَرْهُمْ يُضِلُّوا۟ عِبَادَكَ وَلَا يَلِدُوٓا۟ إِلَّا
فَاجِرًا كَفَّارًا ﴿٢٧﴾

28. O my Lord! Forgive me, my parents, all who enter my house in faith and (all) believing men and believing women: and to the wrongdoers grant You no increase but in perdition!"

رَّبِّ ٱغْفِرْ لِى وَلِوَٰلِدَىَّ وَلِمَن دَخَلَ بَيْتِىَ مُؤْمِنًا
وَلِلْمُؤْمِنِينَ وَٱلْمُؤْمِنَٰتِ ۖ وَلَا تَزِدِ ٱلظَّٰلِمِينَ
إِلَّا تَبَارًۢا ﴿٢٨﴾

سُورَةُ الجِنِّ

Surah 72: ***Al-Jinn*** **(The Spirits)**

In the name of Allah,
Most Gracious, Most Merciful.

بِسْمِ ٱللَّهِ ٱلرَّحْمَٰنِ ٱلرَّحِيمِ

1. Say: It has been revealed to me that a company of Jinns listened (to the Qur'an). They said, "We have really heard a wonderful recital!

قُلْ أُوحِىَ إِلَىَّ أَنَّهُ ٱسْتَمَعَ نَفَرٌ مِّنَ ٱلْجِنِّ فَقَالُوٓا۟ إِنَّا الحزب ٥٨
سَمِعْنَا قُرْءَانًا عَجَبًا ﴿١﴾

2. It gives guidance to the right, and we have believed in it: we shall not join (in worship) any (gods) with our Lord.

يَهْدِىٓ إِلَى ٱلرُّشْدِ فَـَٔامَنَّا بِهِۦ ۖ وَلَن نُّشْرِكَ بِرَبِّنَآ
أَحَدًا ﴿٢﴾

3. And exalted is the Majesty of our Lord: He has taken neither a wife nor a son.

وَأَنَّهُۥ تَعَٰلَىٰ جَدُّ رَبِّنَا مَا ٱتَّخَذَ صَٰحِبَةً وَلَا وَلَدًا ﴿٣﴾

4. There were some foolish ones among us, who used to utter extravagant lies against Allah;

وَأَنَّهُۥ كَانَ يَقُولُ سَفِيهُنَا عَلَى ٱللَّهِ شَطَطًا ﴿٤﴾

5. But we do think that no man or spirit should say anything that is untrue against Allah.

وَأَنَّا ظَنَنَّآ أَن لَّن تَقُولَ ٱلْإِنسُ وَٱلْجِنُّ عَلَى ٱللَّهِ كَذِبًا ٥

6. True, there were persons among mankind who took shelter with persons among the Jinns, but they increased them in folly.

وَأَنَّهُۥ كَانَ رِجَالٌ مِّنَ ٱلْإِنسِ يَعُوذُونَ بِرِجَالٍ مِّنَ ٱلْجِنِّ
فَزَادُوهُمْ رَهَقًا ٦

7. And they (came to) think as you thought, that Allah would not raise up anyone (to judgement).

وَأَنَّهُمْ ظَنُّوا۟ كَمَا ظَنَنتُمْ أَن لَّن يَبْعَثَ ٱللَّهُ أَحَدًا ٧

8. And we pried into the secrets of heaven; but we found it filled with stern guards and flaming fires.

وَأَنَّا لَمَسْنَا ٱلسَّمَآءَ فَوَجَدْنَٰهَا مُلِئَتْ حَرَسًا
شَدِيدًا وَشُهُبًا ٨

9. We used indeed, to sit there in (hidden) stations, to (steal) a hearing; but any who listens now will find a flaming fire watching him in ambush.

وَأَنَّا كُنَّا نَقْعُدُ مِنْهَا مَقَٰعِدَ لِلسَّمْعِ ۖ فَمَن يَسْتَمِعِ
ٱلْـَٔانَ يَجِدْ لَهُۥ شِهَابًا رَّصَدًا ٩

10. And we understand not whether ill is intended to those on earth, or whether their Lord (really) intends to guide them to right conduct.

وَأَنَّا لَا نَدْرِىٓ أَشَرٌّ أُرِيدَ بِمَن فِى ٱلْأَرْضِ أَمْ أَرَادَ بِهِمْ
رَبُّهُمْ رَشَدًا ١٠

11. There are among us some that are righteous, and some the contrary: we follow divergent paths.

وَأَنَّا مِنَّا ٱلصَّٰلِحُونَ وَمِنَّا دُونَ ذَٰلِكَ ۖ كُنَّا طَرَآئِقَ
قِدَدًا ١١

12. But we think that we can by no means frustrate Allah throughout the earth, nor can we frustrate Him by flight.

وَأَنَّا ظَنَنَّآ أَن لَّن نُّعْجِزَ ٱللَّهَ فِى ٱلْأَرْضِ وَلَن
نُّعْجِزَهُۥ هَرَبًا ١٢

13. And as for us, since we have listened to the guidance, we have accepted it: and any who believes in his Lord has no fear, either of a short (account) or of any injustice.

وَأَنَّا لَمَّا سَمِعْنَا ٱلْهُدَىٰٓ ءَامَنَّا بِهِۦ ۖ فَمَن يُؤْمِنۢ
بِرَبِّهِۦ فَلَا يَخَافُ بَخْسًا وَلَا رَهَقًا ١٣

14. Amongst us are some that submit their wills (to Allah), and some that swerve from justice. Now those who submit their wills - they have sought out (the path) of right conduct:

وَأَنَّا مِنَّا ٱلْمُسْلِمُونَ وَمِنَّا ٱلْقَٰسِطُونَ ۖ فَمَنْ أَسْلَمَ
فَأُو۟لَٰٓئِكَ تَحَرَّوْا۟ رَشَدًا ﴿١٤﴾

15. But those who swerve - they are (but) fuel for hellfire" -

وَأَمَّا ٱلْقَٰسِطُونَ فَكَانُوا۟ لِجَهَنَّمَ حَطَبًا ﴿١٥﴾

16. (And Allah's message is): "If they (the pagans) had (only) remained on the (right) way, We should certainly have bestowed on them rain in abundance.

وَأَلَّوِ ٱسْتَقَٰمُوا۟ عَلَى ٱلطَّرِيقَةِ لَأَسْقَيْنَٰهُم مَّآءً غَدَقًا ﴿١٦﴾

17. That We might try them by that (means). But if any turns away from the remembrance of his Lord, He will cause him to undergo a severe penalty.

لِّنَفْتِنَهُمْ فِيهِ ۚ وَمَن يُعْرِضْ عَن ذِكْرِ رَبِّهِۦ يَسْلُكْهُ
عَذَابًا صَعَدًا ﴿١٧﴾

18. And the places of worship are for Allah (alone): so invoke not anyone along with Allah;

وَأَنَّ ٱلْمَسَٰجِدَ لِلَّهِ فَلَا تَدْعُوا۟ مَعَ ٱللَّهِ أَحَدًا ﴿١٨﴾

19. Yet when the devotee of Allah stands up to invoke Him, they just make round him a dense crowd."

وَأَنَّهُۥ لَمَّا قَامَ عَبْدُ ٱللَّهِ يَدْعُوهُ كَادُوا۟ يَكُونُونَ عَلَيْهِ
لِبَدًا ﴿١٩﴾

20. Say: "I do no more than invoke my Lord, and I join not with Him any (false god)."

قُلْ إِنَّمَآ أَدْعُوا۟ رَبِّى وَلَآ أُشْرِكُ بِهِۦٓ أَحَدًا ﴿٢٠﴾

21. Say: "It is not in my power to cause you harm, or to bring you to right conduct."

قُلْ إِنِّى لَآ أَمْلِكُ لَكُمْ ضَرًّا وَلَا رَشَدًا ﴿٢١﴾

22. Say: "No one can deliver me from Allah (if I were to disobey Him), nor should I find refuge except in Him.

قُلْ إِنِّى لَن يُجِيرَنِى مِنَ ٱللَّهِ أَحَدٌ وَلَنْ أَجِدَ مِن دُونِهِۦ
مُلْتَحَدًا ﴿٢٢﴾

23. Unless I proclaim what I receive from Allah and His messages: for any that disobey Allah and His messenger for them is hell: they shall dwell in it forever."

إِلَّا بَلَٰغًا مِّنَ ٱللَّهِ وَرِسَٰلَٰتِهِۦ ۚ وَمَن يَعْصِ ٱللَّهَ وَرَسُولَهُۥ
فَإِنَّ لَهُۥ نَارَ جَهَنَّمَ خَٰلِدِينَ فِيهَآ أَبَدًا ﴿٢٣﴾

24. At length, when they see (with their own eyes) that which they are promised - then will they know who it is that is weakest in (his) helper and least important in point of numbers.

حَتَّىٰٓ إِذَا رَأَوۡاْ مَا يُوعَدُونَ فَسَيَعۡلَمُونَ مَنۡ أَضۡعَفُ
نَاصِرٗا وَأَقَلُّ عَدَدٗا ٢٤

25. Say: "I know not whether the (punishment) which you are promised is near, or whether my Lord will appoint for it a distant term.

قُلۡ إِنۡ أَدۡرِيٓ أَقَرِيبٞ مَّا تُوعَدُونَ أَمۡ يَجۡعَلُ لَهُۥ رَبِّيٓ
أَمَدًا ٢٥

26. He (alone) knows the unseen, nor does He make any one acquainted with His mysteries -

عَٰلِمُ ٱلۡغَيۡبِ فَلَا يُظۡهِرُ عَلَىٰ غَيۡبِهِۦٓ أَحَدًا ٢٦

27. Except a messenger whom He has chosen: and then He makes a band of watchers march before him and behind him,

إِلَّا مَنِ ٱرۡتَضَىٰ مِن رَّسُولٖ فَإِنَّهُۥ يَسۡلُكُ مِنۢ بَيۡنِ
يَدَيۡهِ وَمِنۡ خَلۡفِهِۦ رَصَدٗا ٢٧

28. That he may know that they have (truly) brought and delivered the messages of their Lord: and He surrounds (all the mysteries) that are with them, and takes account of every single thing."

لِّيَعۡلَمَ أَن قَدۡ أَبۡلَغُواْ رِسَٰلَٰتِ رَبِّهِمۡ وَأَحَاطَ بِمَا
لَدَيۡهِمۡ وَأَحۡصَىٰ كُلَّ شَيۡءٍ عَدَدَۢا ٢٨

سُورَةُ المُزَّمِّلِ

Surah 73: ***Al-Muzzammil*** **(The Enfolded One)**

In the name of Allah,
Most Gracious, Most Merciful.

بِسۡمِ ٱللَّهِ ٱلرَّحۡمَٰنِ ٱلرَّحِيمِ

1. O you (Muhammad) folded in garments!

يَٰٓأَيُّهَا ٱلۡمُزَّمِّلُ ١

2. Stand (to pray) by night, but not all night-

قُمِ ٱلَّيۡلَ إِلَّا قَلِيلٗا ٢

3. Half of it - or a little less,

نِّصۡفَهُۥٓ أَوِ ٱنقُصۡ مِنۡهُ قَلِيلًا ٣

4. Or a little more; and recite the Qur'an in slow, measured rhythmic tones.

أَوۡ زِدۡ عَلَيۡهِ وَرَتِّلِ ٱلۡقُرۡءَانَ تَرۡتِيلًا ٤

5. Soon shall We send down to you a weighty message.

إِنَّا سَنُلۡقِي عَلَيۡكَ قَوۡلٗا ثَقِيلًا ٥

6. Truly the rising by night is most potent for governing (the soul), and most suitable for (framing) the word (of prayer and praise).

إِنَّ نَاشِئَةَ ٱلَّيۡلِ هِيَ أَشَدُّ وَطۡـٔٗا وَأَقۡوَمُ قِيلًا ٦

7. True, there is for you by day prolonged occupation with ordinary duties:

إِنَّ لَكَ فِي ٱلنَّهَارِ سَبۡحٗا طَوِيلٗا ٧

8. But keep in remembrance the name of the Lord and devote yourself to Him wholeheartedly.

وَٱذۡكُرِ ٱسۡمَ رَبِّكَ وَتَبَتَّلۡ إِلَيۡهِ تَبۡتِيلٗا ٨

9. (He is) Lord of the east and the west: there is no god but He: take Him therefore for (your) disposer of affairs.

رَّبُّ ٱلۡمَشۡرِقِ وَٱلۡمَغۡرِبِ لَآ إِلَٰهَ إِلَّا هُوَ فَٱتَّخِذۡهُ وَكِيلٗا ٩

10. And have patience with what they say, and leave them with noble (dignity).

وَٱصۡبِرۡ عَلَىٰ مَا يَقُولُونَ وَٱهۡجُرۡهُمۡ هَجۡرٗا جَمِيلٗا ١٠

11. And leave Me (alone to deal with) those in possession of the good things of life, who (yet) deny the truth; and bear with them for a little while.

وَذَرۡنِي وَٱلۡمُكَذِّبِينَ أُوْلِي ٱلنَّعۡمَةِ وَمَهِّلۡهُمۡ قَلِيلًا ١١

12. With Us are fetters (to bind them), and a fire (to burn them),

إِنَّ لَدَيۡنَآ أَنكَالٗا وَجَحِيمٗا ١٢

13. And a food that chokes, and a penalty grievous.

وَطَعَامٗا ذَا غُصَّةٖ وَعَذَابًا أَلِيمٗا ١٣

14. One day the earth and the mountains will be in violent commotion. And the mountains will be as a heap of sand poured out and flowing down.

يَوۡمَ تَرۡجُفُ ٱلۡأَرۡضُ وَٱلۡجِبَالُ وَكَانَتِ ٱلۡجِبَالُ كَثِيبٗا
مَّهِيلًا ١٤

15. We have sent to you (O men!) a

إِنَّآ أَرۡسَلۡنَآ إِلَيۡكُمۡ رَسُولٗا شَٰهِدًا عَلَيۡكُمۡ كَمَآ أَرۡسَلۡنَآ

إِلَىٰ فِرۡعَوۡنَ رَسُولٗا ١٥

messenger, to be a witness concerning you, even as We sent a messenger to Pharaoh.

فَعَصَىٰ فِرۡعَوۡنُ ٱلرَّسُولَ فَأَخَذۡنَٰهُ أَخۡذٗا وَبِيلٗا ١٦

16. But Pharaoh disobeyed the messenger; so We seized him with a heavy punishment.

فَكَيۡفَ تَتَّقُونَ إِن كَفَرۡتُمۡ يَوۡمٗا يَجۡعَلُ ٱلۡوِلۡدَٰنَ
شِيبًا ١٧

17. Then how shall you, if you deny (Allah) guard yourselves against a day that will make children hoary-headed?-

ٱلسَّمَآءُ مُنفَطِرُۢ بِهِۦۚ كَانَ وَعۡدُهُۥ مَفۡعُولًا ١٨

18. On which the sky will be cleft asunder? His promise needs must be accomplished.

إِنَّ هَٰذِهِۦ تَذۡكِرَةٞۖ فَمَن شَآءَ ٱتَّخَذَ إِلَىٰ رَبِّهِۦ
سَبِيلًا ١٩

19. Verily this is an admonition: therefore, whoso will let him take a (straight) path to his Lord!

ربع الحزب ٥٨

۞إِنَّ رَبَّكَ يَعۡلَمُ أَنَّكَ تَقُومُ أَدۡنَىٰ مِن ثُلُثَيِ ٱلَّيۡلِ وَنِصۡفَهُۥ
وَثُلُثَهُۥ وَطَآئِفَةٞ مِّنَ ٱلَّذِينَ مَعَكَۚ وَٱللَّهُ يُقَدِّرُ ٱلَّيۡلَ
وَٱلنَّهَارَۚ عَلِمَ أَن لَّن تُحۡصُوهُ فَتَابَ عَلَيۡكُمۡۖ فَٱقۡرَءُواْ
مَا تَيَسَّرَ مِنَ ٱلۡقُرۡءَانِۚ عَلِمَ أَن سَيَكُونُ مِنكُم مَّرۡضَىٰ
وَءَاخَرُونَ يَضۡرِبُونَ فِي ٱلۡأَرۡضِ يَبۡتَغُونَ مِن فَضۡلِ ٱللَّهِ
وَءَاخَرُونَ يُقَٰتِلُونَ فِي سَبِيلِ ٱللَّهِۖ فَٱقۡرَءُواْ مَا تَيَسَّرَ مِنۡهُۚ
وَأَقِيمُواْ ٱلصَّلَوٰةَ وَءَاتُواْ ٱلزَّكَوٰةَ وَأَقۡرِضُواْ ٱللَّهَ قَرۡضًا حَسَنٗاۚ
وَمَا تُقَدِّمُواْ لِأَنفُسِكُم مِّنۡ خَيۡرٖ تَجِدُوهُ عِندَ ٱللَّهِ هُوَ خَيۡرٗا
وَأَعۡظَمَ أَجۡرٗاۚ وَٱسۡتَغۡفِرُواْ ٱللَّهَۖ إِنَّ ٱللَّهَ غَفُورٞ رَّحِيمُۢ ٢٠

20. Your Lord does know that you stand up (to prayer) near two-thirds of the night, or half the night, or a third of the night, and so does a party of those with you. But Allah does appoint night and day in due measure. He knows that you are unable to keep count of it. So He has turned to you (in mercy): read you, therefore, of the Qur'an as much as may be easy for you. He knows that there may be (some) among you in ill-health; others travelling through the land, seeking of Allah's bounty; yet others fighting in Allah's cause. Read you, therefore, as much of the Qur'an as may be easy (for you); and establish regular prayer and give regular charity; and loan to Allah a beautiful loan. And whatever good you send ahead for your souls, You shall find it in Allah's presence - Yea, better and greater in reward, and seek you the grace of Allah: for Allah is Oft-Forgiving, Most Merciful.

سُورَةُ المُدَّثِّرِ

Surah 74: ***Al-Muddaththir*** **(The Wrapped Up One)**

In the name of Allah,
Most Gracious, Most Merciful.

بِسۡمِ ٱللَّهِ ٱلرَّحۡمَٰنِ ٱلرَّحِيمِ

1. O you (Muhammad) wrapped up (in a mantle)!

يَٰٓأَيُّهَا ٱلۡمُدَّثِّرُ ١

2. Arise and deliver your warning!

قُمۡ فَأَنذِرۡ ٢

3. And your Lord do you magnify!

وَرَبَّكَ فَكَبِّرۡ ٣

4. And your garments keep free from stain!

وَثِيَابَكَ فَطَهِّرۡ ٤

5. And all abomination shun!

وَٱلرُّجۡزَ فَٱهۡجُرۡ ٥

6. Nor expect, in giving, any increase (for yourself)!

وَلَا تَمۡنُن تَسۡتَكۡثِرُ ٦

7. But, for your Lord's (cause) be patient and constant!

وَلِرَبِّكَ فَٱصۡبِرۡ ٧

8. Finally, when the trumpet is sounded,

فَإِذَا نُقِرَ فِي ٱلنَّاقُورِ ٨

9. That will be - that day - a day of distress-

فَذَٰلِكَ يَوۡمَئِذٖ يَوۡمٌ عَسِيرٌ ٩

10. Far from easy for those without faith.

عَلَى ٱلۡكَٰفِرِينَ غَيۡرُ يَسِيرٖ ١٠

11. Leave Me alone, (to deal) with the (creature) whom I created (bare and) alone! -

ذَرۡنِي وَمَنۡ خَلَقۡتُ وَحِيدٗا ١١

12. To whom I granted resources in abundance.

وَجَعَلۡتُ لَهُۥ مَالٗا مَّمۡدُودٗا ١٢

13. And sons to be by his side! -

وَبَنِينَ شُهُودٗا ١٣

14. To whom I made (life) smooth and comfortable!

وَمَهَّدتُّ لَهُۥ تَمۡهِيدٗا ١٤

15. Yet is he greedy - that I should add (yet more) -

ثُمَّ يَطۡمَعُ أَنۡ أَزِيدَ ١٥

16. By no means! For to Our signs he has been refractory!

كَلَّآۖ إِنَّهُۥ كَانَ لِأٓيَٰتِنَا عَنِيدٗا ١٦

17. Soon will I visit him with a mount of calamities!

سَأُرۡهِقُهُۥ صَعُودًا ١٧

18. For he thought and he plotted -

إِنَّهُۥ فَكَّرَ وَقَدَّرَ ١٨

19. And woe to him! How he plotted! -

فَقُتِلَ كَيۡفَ قَدَّرَ ١٩

20. Yea, woe to him; how he plotted! -

ثُمَّ قُتِلَ كَيۡفَ قَدَّرَ ٢٠

21. Then he looked round;

ثُمَّ نَظَرَ ٢١

22. Then he frowned and he scowled;

ثُمَّ عَبَسَ وَبَسَرَ ٢٢

23. Then he turned back and was haughty;

ثُمَّ أَدۡبَرَ وَٱسۡتَكۡبَرَ ٢٣

24. Then said he: "This is nothing but magic, derived from of old";

فَقَالَ إِنۡ هَٰذَآ إِلَّا سِحۡرٞ يُؤۡثَرُ ٢٤

25. "This is nothing but the word of a mortal!"

إِنۡ هَٰذَآ إِلَّا قَوۡلُ ٱلۡبَشَرِ ٢٥

26. Soon will I cast him into hellfire!

سَأُصۡلِيهِ سَقَرَ ٢٦

27. And what will explain to you what hellfire is?

وَمَآ أَدۡرَىٰكَ مَا سَقَرُ ٢٧

28. Nothing does it permit to endure, and nothing does it leave alone! -

لَا تُبۡقِي وَلَا تَذَرُ ٢٨

29. Darkening and changing the colour of man!

لَوَّاحَةٌ لِّلۡبَشَرِ ٢٩

30. Over it are nineteen.

عَلَيۡهَا تِسۡعَةَ عَشَرَ ٣٠

31. And We have set none but angels as guardians of the fire; and We have fixed their number only as a trial for unbelievers - in order that the People of the Book may arrive at certainty, and the believers may increase in faith - and that no doubts may be left for the People of the Book and the believers, and that those in whose hearts is a disease and the unbelievers may say, "What symbol does Allah intend by this?" Thus does Allah leave to stray whom He pleases, and guide whom He pleases; and none can know the forces of the Lord, except He. And this is no other than a warning to mankind.

وَمَا جَعَلۡنَآ أَصۡحَٰبَ ٱلنَّارِ إِلَّا مَلَٰٓئِكَةٗۖ وَمَا جَعَلۡنَا عِدَّتَهُمۡ
إِلَّا فِتۡنَةٗ لِّلَّذِينَ كَفَرُواْ لِيَسۡتَيۡقِنَ ٱلَّذِينَ أُوتُواْ ٱلۡكِتَٰبَ
وَيَزۡدَادَ ٱلَّذِينَ ءَامَنُوٓاْ إِيمَٰنٗا وَلَا يَرۡتَابَ ٱلَّذِينَ أُوتُواْ ٱلۡكِتَٰبَ
وَٱلۡمُؤۡمِنُونَ وَلِيَقُولَ ٱلَّذِينَ فِي قُلُوبِهِم مَّرَضٞ
وَٱلۡكَٰفِرُونَ مَاذَآ أَرَادَ ٱللَّهُ بِهَٰذَا مَثَلٗاۚ كَذَٰلِكَ يُضِلُّ ٱللَّهُ
مَن يَشَآءُ وَيَهۡدِي مَن يَشَآءُۚ وَمَا يَعۡلَمُ جُنُودَ رَبِّكَ إِلَّا
هُوَۚ وَمَا هِيَ إِلَّا ذِكۡرَىٰ لِلۡبَشَرِ ٣١

32. Nay, verily: by the moon,

كَلَّا وَٱلۡقَمَرِ ٣٢

33. And by the night as it retreats,

وَٱلَّيۡلِ إِذۡ أَدۡبَرَ ٣٣

34. And by the dawn as it shines -

وَٱلصُّبۡحِ إِذَآ أَسۡفَرَ ٣٤

35. This is but one of the mighty (signs),

إِنَّهَا لَإِحۡدَى ٱلۡكُبَرِ ٣٥

36. A warning to mankind -

نَذِيرٗا لِّلۡبَشَرِ ٣٦

37. To any of you that chooses to press forward, or to follow behind -

لِمَن شَآءَ مِنكُمۡ أَن يَتَقَدَّمَ أَوۡ يَتَأَخَّرَ ٣٧

38. Every soul will be (held) in pledge for its deeds.

كُلُّ نَفۡسِۭ بِمَا كَسَبَتۡ رَهِينَةٌ ٣٨

39. Except the companions of the right hand.

إِلَّآ أَصۡحَٰبَ ٱلۡيَمِينِ ٣٩

40. (They will be) in gardens (of delight); they will question each other,

فِي جَنَّٰتٖ يَتَسَآءَلُونَ ٤٠

41. And (ask) of the sinners:

عَنِ ٱلۡمُجۡرِمِينَ ٤١

42. "What led you into hellfire?"

مَا سَلَكَكُمۡ فِي سَقَرَ ٤٢

43. They will say: "We were not of those who prayed;

قَالُواْ لَمۡ نَكُ مِنَ ٱلۡمُصَلِّينَ ٤٣

44. Nor were we of those who fed the needy;

وَلَمۡ نَكُ نُطۡعِمُ ٱلۡمِسۡكِينَ ٤٤

45. But we used to talk vanities with vain talkers;

وَكُنَّا نَخُوضُ مَعَ ٱلۡخَآئِضِينَ ٤٥

46. And we used to deny the day of judgement,

وَكُنَّا نُكَذِّبُ بِيَوۡمِ ٱلدِّينِ ٤٦

47. Until there came to us (the hour) that is certain."

حَتَّىٰٓ أَتَىٰنَا ٱلۡيَقِينُ ٤٧

48. Then will no intercession of (any) intercessors profit them.

فَمَا تَنفَعُهُمۡ شَفَٰعَةُ ٱلشَّٰفِعِينَ ٤٨

49. Then what is the matter with them that they turn away from admonition? -

فَمَا لَهُمۡ عَنِ ٱلتَّذۡكِرَةِ مُعۡرِضِينَ ٤٩

50. As if they were affrighted asses,

كَأَنَّهُمۡ حُمُرٞ مُّسۡتَنفِرَةٞ ٥٠

51. Fleeing from a lion!

فَرَّتۡ مِن قَسۡوَرَةِۭ ٥١

52. Each one of them wants to be given scrolls (of revelation) spread out!

بَلۡ يُرِيدُ كُلُّ ٱمۡرِيٕٖ مِّنۡهُمۡ أَن يُؤۡتَىٰ صُحُفٗا مُّنَشَّرَةٗ ٥٢

53. By no means! But they fear not the hereafter.

كَلَّاۖ بَل لَّا يَخَافُونَ ٱلۡأٓخِرَةَ ٥٣

54. Nay, this surely is an admonition:

كَلَّآ إِنَّهُۥ تَذۡكِرَةٞ ٥٤

55. Let any who will, keep it in remembrance!

فَمَن شَآءَ ذَكَرَهُۥ ﴿٥٥﴾

56. But none will keep it in remembrance except as Allah wills: He is the Lord of Righteousness and the Lord of forgiveness.

وَمَا يَذْكُرُونَ إِلَّآ أَن يَشَآءَ ٱللَّهُ ۚ هُوَ أَهْلُ ٱلتَّقْوَىٰ
وَأَهْلُ ٱلْمَغْفِرَةِ ﴿٥٦﴾

سُورَةُ الْقِيَامَةِ

Surah 75: ***Al-Qiyamah*** **(The Resurrection)**

In the name of Allah,
Most Gracious, Most Merciful.

بِسْمِ ٱللَّهِ ٱلرَّحْمَٰنِ ٱلرَّحِيمِ

1. I do call to witness the resurrection day;

لَآ أُقْسِمُ بِيَوْمِ ٱلْقِيَٰمَةِ ﴿١﴾ نصف الحزب ٥٨

2. And I do call to witness the self-reproaching spirit; (eschew evil).

وَلَآ أُقْسِمُ بِٱلنَّفْسِ ٱللَّوَّامَةِ ﴿٢﴾

3. Does man think that We cannot assemble his bones?

أَيَحْسَبُ ٱلْإِنسَٰنُ أَلَّن نَّجْمَعَ عِظَامَهُۥ ﴿٣﴾

4. Nay, We are able to put together in perfect order the very tips of his fingers.

بَلَىٰ قَٰدِرِينَ عَلَىٰٓ أَن نُّسَوِّىَ بَنَانَهُۥ ﴿٤﴾

5. But man wishes to do wrong (even) in the time in front of him.

بَلْ يُرِيدُ ٱلْإِنسَٰنُ لِيَفْجُرَ أَمَامَهُۥ ﴿٥﴾

6. He questions: "When is the day of resurrection?"

يَسْـَٔلُ أَيَّانَ يَوْمُ ٱلْقِيَٰمَةِ ﴿٦﴾

7. At length, when the sight is dazed,

فَإِذَا بَرِقَ ٱلْبَصَرُ ﴿٧﴾

8. And the moon is buried in darkness.

وَخَسَفَ ٱلْقَمَرُ ﴿٨﴾

9. And the sun and moon are joined together -

وَجُمِعَ ٱلشَّمْسُ وَٱلْقَمَرُ ﴿٩﴾

10. That day will man say: "Where is the refuge?"

يَقُولُ ٱلۡإِنسَٰنُ يَوۡمَئِذٍ أَيۡنَ ٱلۡمَفَرُّ ١٠

11. By no means! No place of safety!

كَلَّا لَا وَزَرَ ١١

12. Before your Lord (alone), that day will be the place of rest.

إِلَىٰ رَبِّكَ يَوۡمَئِذٍ ٱلۡمُسۡتَقَرُّ ١٢

13. That day will man be told (all) that he put forward, and all that he put back.

يُنَبَّؤُاْ ٱلۡإِنسَٰنُ يَوۡمَئِذِۭ بِمَا قَدَّمَ وَأَخَّرَ ١٣

14. Nay, man will be evidence against himself,

بَلِ ٱلۡإِنسَٰنُ عَلَىٰ نَفۡسِهِۦ بَصِيرَةٞ ١٤

15. Even though he were to put up his excuses.

وَلَوۡ أَلۡقَىٰ مَعَاذِيرَهُۥ ١٥

16. Move not your tongue concerning the (Qur'an) to make haste with it.

لَا تُحَرِّكۡ بِهِۦ لِسَانَكَ لِتَعۡجَلَ بِهِۦٓ ١٦

17. It is for Us to collect it and to promulgate it:

إِنَّ عَلَيۡنَا جَمۡعَهُۥ وَقُرۡءَانَهُۥ ١٧

18. But when We have promulgated it, follow you its recital (as promulgated):

فَإِذَا قَرَأۡنَٰهُ فَٱتَّبِعۡ قُرۡءَانَهُۥ ١٨

19. Nay more, it is for Us to explain it (and make it clear):

ثُمَّ إِنَّ عَلَيۡنَا بَيَانَهُۥ ١٩

20. Nay, (you men!) but you love the fleeting life,

كَلَّا بَلۡ تُحِبُّونَ ٱلۡعَاجِلَةَ ٢٠

21. And leave alone the hereafter.

وَتَذَرُونَ ٱلۡأٓخِرَةَ ٢١

22. Some faces, that day, will beam (in brightness and beauty) -

وُجُوهٞ يَوۡمَئِذٖ نَّاضِرَةٌ ٢٢

23. Looking towards their Lord;

إِلَىٰ رَبِّهَا نَاظِرَةٞ ٢٣

24. And some faces, that day, will be sad and dismal,

وَوُجُوهٞ يَوۡمَئِذِۭ بَاسِرَةٞ ٢٤

25. In the thought that some back-breaking calamity was about to be inflicted on them;

تَظُنُّ أَن يُفْعَلَ بِهَا فَاقِرَةٌ ٢٥

26. Yea, when (the soul) reaches to the collarbone (in its exit),

كَلَّآ إِذَا بَلَغَتِ ٱلتَّرَاقِىَ ٢٦

27. And there will be a call, "Who is a magician (to restore him)?"

وَقِيلَ مَنْۜ رَاقٍ ٢٧ سكتة لطيفة على النون

28. And he will conclude that it was (the time) of parting;

وَظَنَّ أَنَّهُ ٱلْفِرَاقُ ٢٨

29. And one leg will be joined with another:

وَٱلْتَفَّتِ ٱلسَّاقُ بِٱلسَّاقِ ٢٩

30. That day the drive will be (all) to your Lord!

إِلَىٰ رَبِّكَ يَوْمَئِذٍ ٱلْمَسَاقُ ٣٠

31. So he gave nothing in charity, nor did he pray! -

فَلَا صَدَّقَ وَلَا صَلَّىٰ ٣١

32. But on the contrary, He rejected truth and turned away!

وَلَٰكِن كَذَّبَ وَتَوَلَّىٰ ٣٢

33. Then did he stalk to his family in full conceit!

ثُمَّ ذَهَبَ إِلَىٰٓ أَهْلِهِۦ يَتَمَطَّىٰٓ ٣٣

34. Woe to you, (O man!) yea, woe!

أَوْلَىٰ لَكَ فَأَوْلَىٰ ٣٤

35. Again, woe to you (O man!) yea, woe!

ثُمَّ أَوْلَىٰ لَكَ فَأَوْلَىٰٓ ٣٥

36. Does man think that he will be left uncontrolled, (without purpose)?

أَيَحْسَبُ ٱلْإِنسَٰنُ أَن يُتْرَكَ سُدًى ٣٦

37. Was he not a drop of sperm emitted (in lowly form)?

أَلَمْ يَكُ نُطْفَةً مِّن مَّنِىٍّ يُمْنَىٰ ٣٧

38. Then did he become a clinging clot; then did (Allah) make and fashion (him) in due proportion.

ثُمَّ كَانَ عَلَقَةً فَخَلَقَ فَسَوَّىٰ ٣٨

39. And of him He made two sexes, male and female.

فَجَعَلَ مِنْهُ ٱلزَّوْجَيْنِ ٱلذَّكَرَ وَٱلْأُنثَىٰٓ ٣٩

40. Has not He, (the same), the power to give life to the dead?

أَلَيْسَ ذَٰلِكَ بِقَٰدِرٍ عَلَىٰٓ أَن يُحْـِۧىَ ٱلْمَوْتَىٰ ٤٠

سُورَةُ الإِنسَانِ

Surah 76: ***Al-Insan*** **(Man) or** ***Ad-Dahr*** **(The Time)**

In the name of Allah,
Most Gracious, Most Merciful.

بِسْمِ ٱللَّهِ ٱلرَّحْمَٰنِ ٱلرَّحِيمِ

1. Has there not been over man a long period of time, when he was nothing - (not even) mentioned?

هَلْ أَتَىٰ عَلَى ٱلْإِنسَٰنِ حِينٌ مِّنَ ٱلدَّهْرِ لَمْ يَكُن شَيْـًٔا مَّذْكُورًا ١

2. Verily We created man from a drop of mingled sperm, in order to try him: so We gave him (the gifts) of hearing and sight.

إِنَّا خَلَقْنَا ٱلْإِنسَٰنَ مِن نُّطْفَةٍ أَمْشَاجٍ نَّبْتَلِيهِ فَجَعَلْنَٰهُ
سَمِيعًۢا بَصِيرًا ٢

3. We showed him the way: whether he be grateful or ungrateful (rests on his will).

إِنَّا هَدَيْنَٰهُ ٱلسَّبِيلَ إِمَّا شَاكِرًا وَإِمَّا كَفُورًا ٣

4. For the rejecters We have prepared chains, yokes, and a blazing fire.

إِنَّآ أَعْتَدْنَا لِلْكَٰفِرِينَ سَلَٰسِلَا۟ وَأَغْلَٰلًا وَسَعِيرًا ٤

5. As to the righteous. They shall drink of a cup (of wine) mixed with Kafur -

إِنَّ ٱلْأَبْرَارَ يَشْرَبُونَ مِن كَأْسٍ كَانَ مِزَاجُهَا كَافُورًا ٥

6. A fountain where the devotees of Allah do drink, making it flow in unstinted abundance.

عَيْنًا يَشْرَبُ بِهَا عِبَادُ ٱللَّهِ يُفَجِّرُونَهَا تَفْجِيرًا ٦

7. They perform (their) vows, and they fear a day whose evil flies far and wide.

يُوفُونَ بِٱلنَّذْرِ وَيَخَافُونَ يَوْمًا كَانَ شَرُّهُۥ مُسْتَطِيرًا ٧

8. And they feed, for the love of Allah, the needy, the orphan, and the captive -

وَيُطْعِمُونَ ٱلطَّعَامَ عَلَىٰ حُبِّهِۦ مِسْكِينًا وَيَتِيمًا وَأَسِيرًا ٨

9. (Saying) "We feed you for the sake of Allah alone: no reward do we desire from you, nor thanks.

إِنَّمَا نُطْعِمُكُمْ لِوَجْهِ ٱللَّهِ لَا نُرِيدُ مِنكُمْ جَزَآءً وَلَا شُكُورًا ٩

10. We only fear a day of distressful wrath from the side of our Lord."

إِنَّا نَخَافُ مِن رَّبِّنَا يَوْمًا عَبُوسًا قَمْطَرِيرًا ١٠

11. But Allah will deliver them from the evil of that day, and will shed over them a light of beauty and a (blissful) joy.

فَوَقَىٰهُمُ ٱللَّهُ شَرَّ ذَٰلِكَ ٱلْيَوْمِ وَلَقَّىٰهُمْ نَضْرَةً وَسُرُورًا ١١

12. And because they were patient and constant, He will reward them with a garden and (garments of) silk.

وَجَزَىٰهُم بِمَا صَبَرُوا۟ جَنَّةً وَحَرِيرًا ١٢

13. Reclining in the (garden) on raised thrones, they will see there neither the sun's (excessive heat) nor (the moon's) excessive cold.

مُّتَّكِـِٔينَ فِيهَا عَلَى ٱلْأَرَآئِكِ ۖ لَا يَرَوْنَ فِيهَا شَمْسًا وَلَا
زَمْهَرِيرًا ١٣

14. And the shades of the (garden) will come low over them, and the bunches (of fruit), there will hang low in humility.

وَدَانِيَةً عَلَيْهِمْ ظِلَـٰلُهَا وَذُلِّلَتْ قُطُوفُهَا تَذْلِيلًا ١٤

15. And amongst them will be passed round vessels of silver and goblets of crystal -

وَيُطَافُ عَلَيْهِم بِـَٔانِيَةٍ مِّن فِضَّةٍ وَأَكْوَابٍ كَانَتْ قَوَارِيرَا۠ ١٥

16. Crystal-clear made of silver: they will determine the measure of it (according to their wishes).

قَوَارِيرَا۟ مِن فِضَّةٍ قَدَّرُوهَا تَقْدِيرًا ١٦

17. And they will be given to drink there of a cup (of wine) mixed with Zanjabeel -

وَيُسْقَوْنَ فِيهَا كَأْسًا كَانَ مِزَاجُهَا زَنجَبِيلًا ١٧

18. A fountain there, called Salsabeel.

عَيْنًا فِيهَا تُسَمَّىٰ سَلْسَبِيلًا ١٨

19. And round about them will (serve) youths of perpetual (freshness): if you see them, you would think them scattered pearls.

۞ وَيَطُوفُ عَلَيْهِمْ وِلْدَٰنٌ مُّخَلَّدُونَ إِذَا رَأَيْتَهُمْ حَسِبْتَهُمْ ثلاثة أرباع الحزب ٥٨
لُؤْلُؤًا مَّنثُورًا ١٩

20. And when you look, it is there you will see a bliss and a realm magnificent.

وَإِذَا رَأَيْتَ ثَمَّ رَأَيْتَ نَعِيمًا وَمُلْكًا كَبِيرًا ٢٠

21. Upon them will be green garments of fine silk and heavy brocade, and they will be adorned with bracelets of silver; and their Lord will give to them to drink of a wine pure and holy.

عَالِيَهُمْ ثِيَابُ سُندُسٍ خُضْرٌ وَإِسْتَبْرَقٌ ۖ وَحُلُّوٓا۟ أَسَاوِرَ
مِن فِضَّةٍ وَسَقَىٰهُمْ رَبُّهُمْ شَرَابًا طَهُورًا ٢١

22. "Verily this is a reward for you, and your endeavour is accepted and recognised."

إِنَّ هَٰذَا كَانَ لَكُمْ جَزَآءً وَكَانَ سَعْيُكُم مَّشْكُورًا ٢٢

23. It is We Who have sent down the Qur'an to you by stages.

إِنَّا نَحْنُ نَزَّلْنَا عَلَيْكَ ٱلْقُرْءَانَ تَنزِيلًا ٢٣

24. Therefore, be patient, with constancy to the command of your Lord, and listen not to the sinner or the ungrateful among them.

فَٱصْبِرْ لِحُكْمِ رَبِّكَ وَلَا تُطِعْ مِنْهُمْ ءَاثِمًا
أَوْ كَفُورًا ٢٤

25. And celebrate the name of your Lord morning and evening,

وَٱذْكُرِ ٱسْمَ رَبِّكَ بُكْرَةً وَأَصِيلًا ٢٥

26. And part of the night, prostrate yourself to Him; and glorify Him a long night through.

وَمِنَ ٱلَّيْلِ فَٱسْجُدْ لَهُۥ وَسَبِّحْهُ لَيْلًا طَوِيلًا ٢٦

27. As to these, they love the fleeting life, and put away behind them a day (that will be) hard.

إِنَّ هَٰٓؤُلَآءِ يُحِبُّونَ ٱلْعَاجِلَةَ وَيَذَرُونَ وَرَآءَهُمْ يَوْمًا
ثَقِيلًا ٢٧

28. It is We Who created them, and We have made their joints strong; but, when We will We can substitute the like of them by a complete change.

نَّحْنُ خَلَقْنَٰهُمْ وَشَدَدْنَآ أَسْرَهُمْ ۖ وَإِذَا شِئْنَا بَدَّلْنَآ
أَمْثَٰلَهُمْ تَبْدِيلًا ٢٨

29. This is an admonition: whosoever will, let him take a (straight) path to his Lord.

إِنَّ هَٰذِهِۦ تَذْكِرَةٌ ۖ فَمَن شَآءَ ٱتَّخَذَ إِلَىٰ رَبِّهِۦ سَبِيلًا ٢٩

30. But you will not, except as Allah wills; for Allah is full of Knowledge and Wisdom.

وَمَا تَشَآءُونَ إِلَّآ أَن يَشَآءَ ٱللَّهُ ۚ إِنَّ ٱللَّهَ كَانَ
عَلِيمًا حَكِيمًا ٣٠

31. He will admit to His mercy Whom He will; but the wrongdoers - for them has He prepared a grievous penalty.

يُدْخِلُ مَن يَشَآءُ فِى رَحْمَتِهِۦ ۚ وَٱلظَّٰلِمِينَ أَعَدَّ لَهُمْ عَذَابًا أَلِيمًۢا ٣١

سُورَةُ المُرْسَلَاتِ

Surah 77: ***Al-Mursalat*** **(Those Sent)**

In the name of Allah, Most Gracious, Most Merciful.

بِسْمِ ٱللَّهِ ٱلرَّحْمَٰنِ ٱلرَّحِيمِ

1. By the (winds) sent one after another (to man's profit);

وَٱلْمُرْسَلَٰتِ عُرْفًا ١

2. Which then blow violently in tempestuous gusts,

فَٱلْعَٰصِفَٰتِ عَصْفًا ٢

3. And scatter (things) far and wide;

وَٱلنَّٰشِرَٰتِ نَشْرًا ٣

4. Then separate them, one from another,

فَٱلْفَٰرِقَٰتِ فَرْقًا ٤

5. Then spread abroad a message,

فَٱلْمُلْقِيَٰتِ ذِكْرًا ٥

6. Whether of justification or of warning-

عُذْرًا أَوْ نُذْرًا ٦

7. Assuredly, what you are promised must come to pass.

إِنَّمَا تُوعَدُونَ لَوَٰقِعٌ ٧

8. Then when the stars become dim;

فَإِذَا ٱلنُّجُومُ طُمِسَتْ ٨

9. When the heaven is split apart;

وَإِذَا ٱلسَّمَآءُ فُرِجَتْ ٩

10. When the mountains are scattered (to the winds) as dust;

وَإِذَا ٱلْجِبَالُ نُسِفَتْ ١٠

11. And when the messengers are (all) appointed a time (to collect) -

وَإِذَا ٱلرُّسُلُ أُقِّتَتْ ١١

12. For what day are these (signs) deferred?

لِأَيِّ يَوۡمٍ أُجِّلَتۡ ١٢

13. For the day of sorting out.

لِيَوۡمِ ٱلۡفَصۡلِ ١٣

14. And what will explain to you what is the day of sorting out?

وَمَآ أَدۡرَىٰكَ مَا يَوۡمُ ٱلۡفَصۡلِ ١٤

15. Ah woe, that day, to the rejecters of truth!

وَيۡلٞ يَوۡمَئِذٖ لِّلۡمُكَذِّبِينَ ١٥

16. Did We not destroy the men of old (for their evil)?

أَلَمۡ نُهۡلِكِ ٱلۡأَوَّلِينَ ١٦

17. So shall We make later (generations) follow them.

ثُمَّ نُتۡبِعُهُمُ ٱلۡأٓخِرِينَ ١٧

18. Thus do We deal with men of sin.

كَذَٰلِكَ نَفۡعَلُ بِٱلۡمُجۡرِمِينَ ١٨

19. Ah woe, that day to the rejecters of truth!

وَيۡلٞ يَوۡمَئِذٖ لِّلۡمُكَذِّبِينَ ١٩

20. Have We not created you from a fluid (held) despicable? -

أَلَمۡ نَخۡلُقكُّم مِّن مَّآءٖ مَّهِينٖ ٢٠

21. Then We placed it in a place of rest firmly fixed,

فَجَعَلۡنَٰهُ فِي قَرَارٖ مَّكِينٍ ٢١

22. For a period (of gestation), determined (according to need)?

إِلَىٰ قَدَرٖ مَّعۡلُومٖ ٢٢

23. For We do determine (according to need); for We are the best to determine (things).

فَقَدَرۡنَا فَنِعۡمَ ٱلۡقَٰدِرُونَ ٢٣

24. Ah woe, that day! To the rejecters of truth!

وَيۡلٞ يَوۡمَئِذٖ لِّلۡمُكَذِّبِينَ ٢٤

25. Have We not made the earth (as a place) to draw together

أَلَمۡ نَجۡعَلِ ٱلۡأَرۡضَ كِفَاتًا ٢٥

26. The living and the dead,

أَحۡيَآءٗ وَأَمۡوَٰتٗا ٢٦

27. And made in it mountains standing firm, lofty (in stature); and provided for you water sweet (and wholesome)?

وَجَعَلۡنَا فِيهَا رَوَٰسِيَ شَٰمِخَٰتٖ وَأَسۡقَيۡنَٰكُم مَّآءٗ فُرَاتٗا ٢٧

28. Ah woe, that day, to the rejecters of truth!

وَيۡلٞ يَوۡمَئِذٖ لِّلۡمُكَذِّبِينَ ٢٨

29. (It will be said:) "Depart you to that which you used to reject as false!

ٱنطَلِقُوٓاْ إِلَىٰ مَا كُنتُم بِهِۦ تُكَذِّبُونَ ٢٩

30. Depart you to a shadow (of smoke ascending) in three columns,

ٱنطَلِقُوٓاْ إِلَىٰ ظِلّٖ ذِي ثَلَٰثِ شُعَبٖ ٣٠

31. (Which yields) no shade of coolness, and is of no use against the fierce blaze.

لَّا ظَلِيلٖ وَلَا يُغۡنِي مِنَ ٱللَّهَبِ ٣١

32. Indeed it throws about sparks (huge) as forts,

إِنَّهَا تَرۡمِي بِشَرَرٖ كَٱلۡقَصۡرِ ٣٢

33. As if there were (a string of) yellow camels (marching swiftly)."

كَأَنَّهُۥ جِمَٰلَتٞ صُفۡرٞ ٣٣

34. Ah woe, that day, to the rejecters of truth!

وَيۡلٞ يَوۡمَئِذٖ لِّلۡمُكَذِّبِينَ ٣٤

35. That will be a day when they shall not be able to speak,

هَٰذَا يَوۡمُ لَا يَنطِقُونَ ٣٥

36. Nor will it be open to them to put forth pleas.

وَلَا يُؤۡذَنُ لَهُمۡ فَيَعۡتَذِرُونَ ٣٦

37. Ah woe, that day to the rejecters of truth!

وَيۡلٞ يَوۡمَئِذٖ لِّلۡمُكَذِّبِينَ ٣٧

38. That will be a day of sorting out! We shall gather you together and those before (you)!

هَٰذَا يَوۡمُ ٱلۡفَصۡلِۖ جَمَعۡنَٰكُمۡ وَٱلۡأَوَّلِينَ ٣٨

39. Now, if you have a trick (or plot) use it against Me!

فَإِن كَانَ لَكُمۡ كَيۡدٞ فَكِيدُونِ ٣٩

40. Ah woe, that day, to the rejecters of truth!

وَيۡلٞ يَوۡمَئِذٖ لِّلۡمُكَذِّبِينَ ٤٠

41. As to the righteous, they shall be amidst (cool) shades and springs (of water).

إِنَّ ٱلۡمُتَّقِينَ فِي ظِلَٰلٖ وَعُيُونٖ ٤١

42. And (they shall have) fruits - all they desire.

وَفَوَٰكِهَ مِمَّا يَشۡتَهُونَ ٤٢

43. "Eat you and drink you to your heart's content: for that you worked (righteousness)."

كُلُواْ وَٱشۡرَبُواْ هَنِيٓـَٔۢا بِمَا كُنتُمۡ تَعۡمَلُونَ ٤٣

44. Thus do We certainly reward the doers of good.

إِنَّا كَذَٰلِكَ نَجۡزِي ٱلۡمُحۡسِنِينَ ٤٤

45. Ah woe, that day, to the rejecters of truth!

وَيۡلٞ يَوۡمَئِذٖ لِّلۡمُكَذِّبِينَ ٤٥

46. (O you Unjust!) Eat you and enjoy yourselves (but) a little while, for that you are sinners.

كُلُواْ وَتَمَتَّعُواْ قَلِيلًا إِنَّكُم مُّجۡرِمُونَ ٤٦

47. Ah woe, that day, to the rejecters of truth!

وَيۡلٞ يَوۡمَئِذٖ لِّلۡمُكَذِّبِينَ ٤٧

48. And when it is said to them, "Prostrate yourselves!" They do not so.

وَإِذَا قِيلَ لَهُمُ ٱرۡكَعُواْ لَا يَرۡكَعُونَ ٤٨

49. Ah woe, that day, to the rejecters of truth!

وَيۡلٞ يَوۡمَئِذٖ لِّلۡمُكَذِّبِينَ ٤٩

50. Then what message, after that, will they believe in?

فَبِأَيِّ حَدِيثِۭ بَعۡدَهُۥ يُؤۡمِنُونَ ٥٠

سورة النبإ

Surah 78: ***An-Naba*** **(The Great News)**

In the name of Allah, Most Gracious, Most Merciful.	بِسۡمِ ٱللَّهِ ٱلرَّحۡمَٰنِ ٱلرَّحِيمِ
✻**1.** Concerning what are they disputing?	عَمَّ يَتَسَآءَلُونَ ١ (الجزء ٣٠ الحزب ٥٩)
2. Concerning the great news,	عَنِ ٱلنَّبَإِ ٱلۡعَظِيمِ ٢
3. About which they cannot agree.	ٱلَّذِي هُمۡ فِيهِ مُخۡتَلِفُونَ ٣
4. Verily they shall soon (come to) know!	كَلَّا سَيَعۡلَمُونَ ٤
5. Verily, verily they shall soon (come to) know!	ثُمَّ كَلَّا سَيَعۡلَمُونَ ٥
6. Have We not made the earth as a wide expanse,	أَلَمۡ نَجۡعَلِ ٱلۡأَرۡضَ مِهَٰدٗا ٦
7. And the mountains as pegs?	وَٱلۡجِبَالَ أَوۡتَادٗا ٧
8. And (have We not) created you in pairs,	وَخَلَقۡنَٰكُمۡ أَزۡوَٰجٗا ٨
9. And made your sleep for rest,	وَجَعَلۡنَا نَوۡمَكُمۡ سُبَاتٗا ٩
10. And made the night as a covering,	وَجَعَلۡنَا ٱلَّيۡلَ لِبَاسٗا ١٠
11. And made the day as means of subsistence?	وَجَعَلۡنَا ٱلنَّهَارَ مَعَاشٗا ١١
12. And (have We not) built over you the seven firmaments,	وَبَنَيۡنَا فَوۡقَكُمۡ سَبۡعٗا شِدَادٗا ١٢
13. And placed (in it) a light of splendour?	وَجَعَلۡنَا سِرَاجٗا وَهَّاجٗا ١٣

✻ Part-30

14. And do We not send down from the clouds water in abundance,

وَأَنزَلۡنَا مِنَ ٱلۡمُعۡصِرَٰتِ مَآءٗ ثَجَّاجٗا ﴿١٤﴾

15. That We may produce with it corn and vegetables,

لِّنُخۡرِجَ بِهِۦ حَبّٗا وَنَبَاتٗا ﴿١٥﴾

16. And gardens of luxurious growth?

وَجَنَّٰتٍ أَلۡفَافًا ﴿١٦﴾

17. Verily the day of sorting out is a thing appointed -

إِنَّ يَوۡمَ ٱلۡفَصۡلِ كَانَ مِيقَٰتٗا ﴿١٧﴾

18. The day that the trumpet shall be sounded and you shall come out in crowds;

يَوۡمَ يُنفَخُ فِي ٱلصُّورِ فَتَأۡتُونَ أَفۡوَاجٗا ﴿١٨﴾

19. And the heavens shall be opened as if there were doors,

وَفُتِحَتِ ٱلسَّمَآءُ فَكَانَتۡ أَبۡوَٰبٗا ﴿١٩﴾

20. And the mountains shall vanish, as if they were a mirage.

وَسُيِّرَتِ ٱلۡجِبَالُ فَكَانَتۡ سَرَابًا ﴿٢٠﴾

21. Truly hell is as a place of ambush -

إِنَّ جَهَنَّمَ كَانَتۡ مِرۡصَادٗا ﴿٢١﴾

22. For the transgressors a place of destination:

لِّلطَّٰغِينَ مَـَٔابٗا ﴿٢٢﴾

23. They will dwell in it for ages.

لَّٰبِثِينَ فِيهَآ أَحۡقَابٗا ﴿٢٣﴾

24. Nothing cool shall they taste in it, nor any drink,

لَّا يَذُوقُونَ فِيهَا بَرۡدٗا وَلَا شَرَابًا ﴿٢٤﴾

25. Save a boiling fluid and a fluid, dark, murky, intensely cold -

إِلَّا حَمِيمٗا وَغَسَّاقٗا ﴿٢٥﴾

26. A fitting recompense (for them).

جَزَآءٗ وِفَاقًا ﴿٢٦﴾

27. For that they used not to fear any account (for their deeds),

إِنَّهُمۡ كَانُواْ لَا يَرۡجُونَ حِسَابٗا ﴿٢٧﴾

28. But they (impudently) treated Our signs as false.

وَكَذَّبُواْ بِـَٔايَٰتِنَا كِذَّابٗا ﴿٢٨﴾

29. And all things have We preserved on record.

وَكُلَّ شَيۡءٍ أَحۡصَيۡنَٰهُ كِتَٰبٗا ٢٩

30. "So taste you (the fruits of your deeds); for no increase shall We grant you, except in punishment."

فَذُوقُواْ فَلَن نَّزِيدَكُمۡ إِلَّا عَذَابًا ٣٠

31. Verily for the righteous there will be a fulfilment of (the heart's) desires;

إِنَّ لِلۡمُتَّقِينَ مَفَازًا ٣١

32. Gardens enclosed and grapevines;

حَدَآئِقَ وَأَعۡنَٰبٗا ٣٢

33. Companions of equal age;

وَكَوَاعِبَ أَتۡرَابٗا ٣٣

34. And a cup full (to the brim).

وَكَأۡسٗا دِهَاقٗا ٣٤

35. No vanity shall they hear in it, nor untruth -

لَّا يَسۡمَعُونَ فِيهَا لَغۡوٗا وَلَا كِذَّٰبٗا ٣٥

36. Recompense from your Lord, a gift, (amply) sufficient -

جَزَآءٗ مِّن رَّبِّكَ عَطَآءً حِسَابٗا ٣٦

37. (From) the Lord of the heavens and the earth, and all between - (Allah) Most Gracious: none shall have power to argue with Him.

رَّبِّ ٱلسَّمَٰوَٰتِ وَٱلۡأَرۡضِ وَمَا بَيۡنَهُمَا ٱلرَّحۡمَٰنِۖ لَا يَمۡلِكُونَ
مِنۡهُ خِطَابٗا ٣٧

38. The day that the spirit and the angels will stand forth in ranks, none shall speak except any who is permitted by (Allah) Most Gracious, and he will say what is right.

يَوۡمَ يَقُومُ ٱلرُّوحُ وَٱلۡمَلَٰٓئِكَةُ صَفّٗاۖ لَّا يَتَكَلَّمُونَ إِلَّا
مَنۡ أَذِنَ لَهُ ٱلرَّحۡمَٰنُ وَقَالَ صَوَابٗا ٣٨

39. That day will be the sure reality: therefore, whoso will, let him take a (straight) return to his Lord!

ذَٰلِكَ ٱلۡيَوۡمُ ٱلۡحَقُّۖ فَمَن شَآءَ ٱتَّخَذَ إِلَىٰ رَبِّهِۦ مَـَٔابًا ٣٩

40. Verily, We have warned you of a penalty near - the day when man will see (the deeds) which his hands have sent forth and the unbeliever will say, "Woe to me! Would that I were (mere) dust!"

إِنَّآ أَنذَرۡنَٰكُمۡ عَذَابٗا قَرِيبٗا يَوۡمَ يَنظُرُ ٱلۡمَرۡءُ مَا قَدَّمَتۡ
يَدَاهُ وَيَقُولُ ٱلۡكَافِرُ يَٰلَيۡتَنِي كُنتُ تُرَٰبَۢا ٤٠

سُورَةُ النَّازِعَاتِ

Surah 79: ***An-Nazi'at*** **(Those Who Tear Out)**

In the name of Allah,
Most Gracious, Most Merciful.

بِسۡمِ ٱللَّهِ ٱلرَّحۡمَٰنِ ٱلرَّحِيمِ

1. By the (angels) who tear out (the souls of the wicked) with violence;

وَٱلنَّٰزِعَٰتِ غَرۡقٗا ١

2. By those who gently draw out (the souls of the blessed);

وَٱلنَّٰشِطَٰتِ نَشۡطٗا ٢

3. And by those who glide along (on errands of mercy),

وَٱلسَّٰبِحَٰتِ سَبۡحٗا ٣

4. Then press forward as in a race,

فَٱلسَّٰبِقَٰتِ سَبۡقٗا ٤

5. Then arrange to do (the commands of their Lord) -

فَٱلۡمُدَبِّرَٰتِ أَمۡرٗا ٥

6. One day everything that can be in commotion will be in violent commotion,

يَوۡمَ تَرۡجُفُ ٱلرَّاجِفَةُ ٦

7. Followed by oft-repeated (commotions):

تَتۡبَعُهَا ٱلرَّادِفَةُ ٧

8. Hearts that day will be in agitation;

قُلُوبٞ يَوۡمَئِذٖ وَاجِفَةٌ ٨

9. Cast down will be (their owners') eyes.

أَبۡصَٰرُهَا خَٰشِعَةٞ ٩

10. They say (now): "What! Shall we indeed be returned to (our) former state?" -

يَقُولُونَ أَءِنَّا لَمَرۡدُودُونَ فِي ٱلۡحَافِرَةِ ١٠

11. "What! - When we shall have become rotten bones?"

أَءِذَا كُنَّا عِظَٰمٗا نَّخِرَةٗ ١١

12. They say: "It would in that case be a return with loss!"

قَالُواْ تِلۡكَ إِذٗا كَرَّةٌ خَاسِرَةٞ ١٢

13. But verily, it will be but a single (compelling) call,

فَإِنَّمَا هِيَ زَجۡرَةٞ وَٰحِدَةٞ ١٣

14. When, behold, they will be in the (full) awakening (to judgement).

فَإِذَا هُم بِٱلسَّاهِرَةِ ١٤

15. Has the story of Moses reached you?

هَلۡ أَتَىٰكَ حَدِيثُ مُوسَىٰٓ ١٥

16. See, your Lord did call to him in the sacred valley of Tuwa -

إِذۡ نَادَىٰهُ رَبُّهُۥ بِٱلۡوَادِ ٱلۡمُقَدَّسِ طُوًى ١٦

17. "Go you to Pharaoh, for he has indeed transgressed all bounds.

ٱذۡهَبۡ إِلَىٰ فِرۡعَوۡنَ إِنَّهُۥ طَغَىٰ ١٧

18. And say to him, 'Would you that you should be purified (from sin)? -

فَقُلۡ هَل لَّكَ إِلَىٰٓ أَن تَزَكَّىٰ ١٨

19. And that I guide you to your Lord, so you should fear Him?' "

وَأَهۡدِيَكَ إِلَىٰ رَبِّكَ فَتَخۡشَىٰ ١٩

20. Then did (Moses) show him the great sign.

فَأَرَىٰهُ ٱلۡأٓيَةَ ٱلۡكُبۡرَىٰ ٢٠

21. But (Pharaoh) rejected it and disobeyed (guidance);

فَكَذَّبَ وَعَصَىٰ ٢١

22. Further, he turned his back, striving hard (against Allah).

ثُمَّ أَدۡبَرَ يَسۡعَىٰ ٢٢

23. Then he collected (his men) and made a proclamation,

فَحَشَرَ فَنَادَىٰ ٢٣

24. Saying "I am your Lord, Most High."

فَقَالَ أَنَا۠ رَبُّكُمُ ٱلۡأَعۡلَىٰ ٢٤

25. But Allah did punish him (and made an) example of him - in the hereafter as in this life.

فَأَخَذَهُ ٱللَّهُ نَكَالَ ٱلۡأٓخِرَةِ وَٱلۡأُولَىٰٓ ٢٥

26. Verily in this is an instructive warning for whosoever fears (Allah):

إِنَّ فِي ذَٰلِكَ لَعِبۡرَةٗ لِّمَن يَخۡشَىٰٓ ٢٦

27. What! Are you the more difficult to create of the heaven (above)? (Allah) has constructed it:

ءَأَنتُمْ أَشَدُّ خَلْقًا أَمِ ٱلسَّمَآءُ ۚ بَنَىٰهَا ٢٧

28. On high has He raised its canopy, and He has given it order and perfection.

رَفَعَ سَمْكَهَا فَسَوَّىٰهَا ٢٨

29. Its night does He endow with darkness, and its splendour does He bring out (with light).

وَأَغْطَشَ لَيْلَهَا وَأَخْرَجَ ضُحَىٰهَا ٢٩

30. And the earth, moreover, has He extended (to a wide expanse);

وَٱلْأَرْضَ بَعْدَ ذَٰلِكَ دَحَىٰهَآ ٣٠

31. He draws out from it its moisture and its pasture;

أَخْرَجَ مِنْهَا مَآءَهَا وَمَرْعَىٰهَا ٣١

32. And the mountains has He firmly fixed -

وَٱلْجِبَالَ أَرْسَىٰهَا ٣٢

33. For use and convenience to you and your cattle.

مَتَٰعًا لَّكُمْ وَلِأَنْعَٰمِكُمْ ٣٣

34. Therefore, when there comes the great, overwhelming (event) -

فَإِذَا جَآءَتِ ٱلطَّآمَّةُ ٱلْكُبْرَىٰ ٣٤

35. The day when man shall remember (all) that he strove for,

يَوْمَ يَتَذَكَّرُ ٱلْإِنسَٰنُ مَا سَعَىٰ ٣٥

36. And hellfire shall be placed in full view for (all) to see -

وَبُرِّزَتِ ٱلْجَحِيمُ لِمَن يَرَىٰ ٣٦

37. Then, for such as had transgressed all bounds,

فَأَمَّا مَن طَغَىٰ ٣٧

38. And had preferred the life of this world,

وَءَاثَرَ ٱلْحَيَوٰةَ ٱلدُّنْيَا ٣٨

39. The abode will be hellfire;

فَإِنَّ ٱلْجَحِيمَ هِىَ ٱلْمَأْوَىٰ ٣٩

40. And for such as had entertained the fear of standing before their Lord's (tribunal) and had restrained (their) souls from lower desires,

وَأَمَّا مَنْ خَافَ مَقَامَ رَبِّهِۦ وَنَهَى ٱلنَّفْسَ عَنِ ٱلْهَوَىٰ ﴿٤٠﴾

41. Their abode will be the garden.

فَإِنَّ ٱلْجَنَّةَ هِىَ ٱلْمَأْوَىٰ ﴿٤١﴾

42. They ask you about the hour - 'When will be its appointed time?'

يَسْـَٔلُونَكَ عَنِ ٱلسَّاعَةِ أَيَّانَ مُرْسَىٰهَا ﴿٤٢﴾

43. In which are you (concerned) with the declaration of it?

فِيمَ أَنتَ مِن ذِكْرَىٰهَآ ﴿٤٣﴾

44. With your Lord is the limit fixed for it.

إِلَىٰ رَبِّكَ مُنتَهَىٰهَآ ﴿٤٤﴾

45. You are but a warner for such as fear it.

إِنَّمَآ أَنتَ مُنذِرُ مَن يَخْشَىٰهَا ﴿٤٥﴾

46. The day they see it, (it will be) as if they had tarried but a single evening, or (at most 'till) the following morn!

كَأَنَّهُمْ يَوْمَ يَرَوْنَهَا لَمْ يَلْبَثُوٓا۟ إِلَّا عَشِيَّةً
أَوْ ضُحَىٰهَا ﴿٤٦﴾

سُورَةُ عَبَسَ

Surah 80: ***Abasa*** **(He Frowned)**

In the name of Allah,
Most Gracious, Most Merciful.

بِسْمِ ٱللَّهِ ٱلرَّحْمَٰنِ ٱلرَّحِيمِ

1. (The prophet) frowned and turned away,

ربع الحزب ٥٩ عَبَسَ وَتَوَلَّىٰٓ ﴿١﴾

2. Because there came to him the blind man (interrupting).

أَن جَآءَهُ ٱلْأَعْمَىٰ ﴿٢﴾

3. But what could tell you but that perhaps he might grow (in spiritual understanding)?

وَمَا يُدْرِيكَ لَعَلَّهُۥ يَزَّكَّىٰٓ ﴿٣﴾

4. Or that he might receive admonition, and the teaching might profit him?

أَوْ يَذَّكَّرُ فَتَنفَعَهُ ٱلذِّكْرَىٰٓ ﴿٤﴾

5. As to one who regards himself as self-sufficient,

أَمَّا مَنِ ٱسْتَغْنَىٰ ﴿٥﴾

6. To him do you attend;

فَأَنتَ لَهُۥ تَصَدَّىٰ ﴿٦﴾

7. Though it is no blame on you if he grow not (in spiritual understanding).

وَمَا عَلَيْكَ أَلَّا يَزَّكَّىٰ ﴿٧﴾

8. But as to him who came to you striving earnestly,

وَأَمَّا مَن جَآءَكَ يَسْعَىٰ ﴿٨﴾

9. And with fear (in his heart),

وَهُوَ يَخْشَىٰ ﴿٩﴾

10. Of him were you unmindful.

فَأَنتَ عَنْهُ تَلَهَّىٰ ﴿١٠﴾

11. By no means (should it be so)! For it is indeed a message of instruction:

كَلَّآ إِنَّهَا تَذْكِرَةٌ ﴿١١﴾

12. Therefore, let whoso will, keep it in remembrance.

فَمَن شَآءَ ذَكَرَهُۥ ﴿١٢﴾

13. (It is) in books held (greatly) in honour,

فِى صُحُفٍ مُّكَرَّمَةٍ ﴿١٣﴾

14. Exalted (in dignity), kept pure and holy,

مَّرْفُوعَةٍ مُّطَهَّرَةٍۭ ﴿١٤﴾

15. (Written) by the hands of scribes -

بِأَيْدِى سَفَرَةٍ ﴿١٥﴾

16. Honourable and pious and just.

كِرَامٍۭ بَرَرَةٍ ﴿١٦﴾

17. Woe to man! What has made him reject Allah?

قُتِلَ ٱلْإِنسَٰنُ مَآ أَكْفَرَهُۥ ﴿١٧﴾

18. From what stuff Has He created him?

مِنْ أَىِّ شَىْءٍ خَلَقَهُۥ ﴿١٨﴾

19. From a sperm-drop: He has created him, and then moulded him in due proportions;

مِن نُّطْفَةٍ خَلَقَهُۥ فَقَدَّرَهُۥ ﴿١٩﴾

20. Then does He make His path smooth for him;

ثُمَّ ٱلسَّبِيلَ يَسَّرَهُۥ ٢٠

21. Then He causes him to die, and puts him in his grave;

ثُمَّ أَمَاتَهُۥ فَأَقْبَرَهُۥ ٢١

22. Then, when it is His will, He will raise him up (again).

ثُمَّ إِذَا شَآءَ أَنشَرَهُۥ ٢٢

23. By no means has he fulfilled what Allah Has commanded him.

كَلَّا لَمَّا يَقْضِ مَآ أَمَرَهُۥ ٢٣

24. Then let man look at his food, (and how We provide it):

فَلْيَنظُرِ ٱلْإِنسَٰنُ إِلَىٰ طَعَامِهِۦٓ ٢٤

25. For that We pour out water in abundance,

أَنَّا صَبَبْنَا ٱلْمَآءَ صَبًّا ٢٥

26. And We split the earth in fragments,

ثُمَّ شَقَقْنَا ٱلْأَرْضَ شَقًّا ٢٦

27. And produce in it corn,

فَأَنۢبَتْنَا فِيهَا حَبًّا ٢٧

28. And grapes and nutritious plants,

وَعِنَبًا وَقَضْبًا ٢٨

29. And olives and dates,

وَزَيْتُونًا وَنَخْلًا ٢٩

30. And enclosed gardens, dense with lofty trees,

وَحَدَآئِقَ غُلْبًا ٣٠

31. And fruits and fodder -

وَفَٰكِهَةً وَأَبًّا ٣١

32. For use and convenience to you and your cattle.

مَّتَٰعًا لَّكُمْ وَلِأَنْعَٰمِكُمْ ٣٢

33. At length, when there comes the deafening noise -

فَإِذَا جَآءَتِ ٱلصَّآخَّةُ ٣٣

34. That day shall a man flee from his own brother,

يَوْمَ يَفِرُّ ٱلْمَرْءُ مِنْ أَخِيهِ ٣٤

35. And from his mother and his father,

وَأُمِّهِۦ وَأَبِيهِ ٣٥

36. And from his wife and his children.

وَصَٰحِبَتِهِۦ وَبَنِيهِ ٣٦

37. Each one of them, that day, will have enough concern (of his own) to make him indifferent to the others.

لِكُلِّ ٱمْرِئٍ مِّنْهُمْ يَوْمَئِذٍ شَأْنٌ يُغْنِيهِ ٣٧

38. Some faces that day will be beaming,

وُجُوهٌ يَوْمَئِذٍ مُّسْفِرَةٌ ٣٨

39. Laughing, rejoicing.

ضَاحِكَةٌ مُّسْتَبْشِرَةٌ ٣٩

40. And other faces that day will be dust-stained;

وَوُجُوهٌ يَوْمَئِذٍ عَلَيْهَا غَبَرَةٌ ٤٠

41. Blackness will cover them:

تَرْهَقُهَا قَتَرَةٌ ٤١

42. Such will be the rejecters (of Allah), the doers of iniquity.

أُو۟لَٰٓئِكَ هُمُ ٱلْكَفَرَةُ ٱلْفَجَرَةُ ٤٢

سُورَةُ التَّكْوِيرِ

Surah 81: ***At-Takwir*** **(The Folding Up)**

In the name of Allah,
Most Gracious, Most Merciful.

بِسْمِ ٱللَّهِ ٱلرَّحْمَٰنِ ٱلرَّحِيمِ

1. When the sun (with its spacious light) is folded up;

إِذَا ٱلشَّمْسُ كُوِّرَتْ ١

2. When the stars fall, losing their lustre;

وَإِذَا ٱلنُّجُومُ ٱنكَدَرَتْ ٢

3. When the mountains vanish (like a mirage);

وَإِذَا ٱلْجِبَالُ سُيِّرَتْ ٣

4. When the she-camels, ten months with young, are left untended;

وَإِذَا ٱلْعِشَارُ عُطِّلَتْ ٤

5. When the wild beasts are herded together (in human habitations);

وَإِذَا ٱلْوُحُوشُ حُشِرَتْ ٥

6. When the oceans boil over with a swell;

وَإِذَا ٱلْبِحَارُ سُجِّرَتْ ٦

7. When the souls are sorted out, (being joined, like with like);

وَإِذَا ٱلنُّفُوسُ زُوِّجَتْ ٧

8. When the female (infant), buried alive, is questioned -

وَإِذَا ٱلْمَوْءُۥدَةُ سُئِلَتْ ٨

9. For what crime she was killed;

بِأَىِّ ذَنۢبٍ قُتِلَتْ ٩

10. When the scrolls are laid open;

وَإِذَا ٱلصُّحُفُ نُشِرَتْ ١٠

11. When the world on high is unveiled;

وَإِذَا ٱلسَّمَآءُ كُشِطَتْ ١١

12. When the blazing fire is kindled to fierce heat;

وَإِذَا ٱلْجَحِيمُ سُعِّرَتْ ١٢

13. And when the garden is brought near -

وَإِذَا ٱلْجَنَّةُ أُزْلِفَتْ ١٣

14. (Then) shall each soul know what it has put forward.

عَلِمَتْ نَفْسٌ مَّآ أَحْضَرَتْ ١٤

15. So verily I call to witness the planets - that recede,

فَلَآ أُقْسِمُ بِٱلْخُنَّسِ ١٥

16. Go straight, or hide;

ٱلْجَوَارِ ٱلْكُنَّسِ ١٦

17. And the night as it dissipates;

وَٱلَّيْلِ إِذَا عَسْعَسَ ١٧

18. And the dawn as it breathes away the darkness -

وَٱلصُّبْحِ إِذَا تَنَفَّسَ ١٨

19. Verily this is the word of a most honourable messenger,

إِنَّهُۥ لَقَوْلُ رَسُولٍ كَرِيمٍ ١٩

20. Endued with power, with rank before the Lord of the throne,

ذِي قُوَّةٍ عِندَ ذِي ٱلْعَرْشِ مَكِينٍ ٢٠

21. With authority there, (and) faithful to his trust.

مُّطَاعٍ ثَمَّ أَمِينٍ ٢١

22. And (O people!) Your companion is not one possessed;

وَمَا صَاحِبُكُم بِمَجْنُونٍ ٢٢

23. And without doubt he saw him in the clear horizon.

وَلَقَدْ رَءَاهُ بِٱلْأُفُقِ ٱلْمُبِينِ ٢٣

24. Neither does he withhold grudgingly a knowledge of the unseen.

وَمَا هُوَ عَلَى ٱلْغَيْبِ بِضَنِينٍ ٢٤

25. Nor is it the word of an evil spirit accursed.

وَمَا هُوَ بِقَوْلِ شَيْطَٰنٍ رَّجِيمٍ ٢٥

26. Then where do you go?

فَأَيْنَ تَذْهَبُونَ ٢٦

27. Verily this is no less than a message to (all) the worlds:

إِنْ هُوَ إِلَّا ذِكْرٌ لِّلْعَٰلَمِينَ ٢٧

28. (With profit) to whoever among you wills to go straight:

لِمَن شَآءَ مِنكُمْ أَن يَسْتَقِيمَ ٢٨

29. But you shall not will except as Allah wills - the Cherisher of the Worlds.

وَمَا تَشَآءُونَ إِلَّآ أَن يَشَآءَ ٱللَّهُ رَبُّ ٱلْعَٰلَمِينَ ٢٩

سُورَةُ الانفِطَارِ

Surah 82: ***Al-Infitar*** **(The Breaking)**

In the name of Allah,
Most Gracious, Most Merciful.

بِسْمِ ٱللَّهِ ٱلرَّحْمَٰنِ ٱلرَّحِيمِ

1. When the sky is broken;

إِذَا ٱلسَّمَآءُ ٱنفَطَرَتْ ١ نصف الحزب ٥٩

2. When the stars are scattered;

وَإِذَا ٱلْكَوَاكِبُ ٱنتَثَرَتْ ٢

3. When the oceans are suffered to burst;

وَإِذَا ٱلْبِحَارُ فُجِّرَتْ ﴿٣﴾

4. And when the graves are turned upside down -

وَإِذَا ٱلْقُبُورُ بُعْثِرَتْ ﴿٤﴾

5. (Then) shall each soul know what it has sent forward and (what it has) kept back.

عَلِمَتْ نَفْسٌ مَّا قَدَّمَتْ وَأَخَّرَتْ ﴿٥﴾

6. O man! What has seduced you from your Lord Most Beneficent? -

يَٰٓأَيُّهَا ٱلْإِنسَٰنُ مَا غَرَّكَ بِرَبِّكَ ٱلْكَرِيمِ ﴿٦﴾

7. Him Who created you. Fashioned you in due proportion, and gave you a just bias;

ٱلَّذِى خَلَقَكَ فَسَوَّىٰكَ فَعَدَلَكَ ﴿٧﴾

8. In whatever form He wills, does He put you together.

فِىٓ أَىِّ صُورَةٍ مَّا شَآءَ رَكَّبَكَ ﴿٨﴾

9. Nay! But you do reject right and judgement!

كَلَّا بَلْ تُكَذِّبُونَ بِٱلدِّينِ ﴿٩﴾

10. But verily over you (are appointed angels) to protect you -

وَإِنَّ عَلَيْكُمْ لَحَٰفِظِينَ ﴿١٠﴾

11. Kind and honourable - writing down (your deeds):

كِرَامًا كَٰتِبِينَ ﴿١١﴾

12. They know (and understand) all that you do.

يَعْلَمُونَ مَا تَفْعَلُونَ ﴿١٢﴾

13. As for the righteous, they will be in bliss;

إِنَّ ٱلْأَبْرَارَ لَفِى نَعِيمٍ ﴿١٣﴾

14. And the wicked - they will be in the fire,

وَإِنَّ ٱلْفُجَّارَ لَفِى جَحِيمٍ ﴿١٤﴾

15. Which they will enter on the day of judgement,

يَصْلَوْنَهَا يَوْمَ ٱلدِّينِ ﴿١٥﴾

16. And they will not be able to keep away from it.

وَمَا هُمْ عَنْهَا بِغَآئِبِينَ ﴿١٦﴾

17. And what will explain to you what the day of judgement is?

وَمَآ أَدۡرَىٰكَ مَا يَوۡمُ ٱلدِّينِ ١٧

18. Again, what will explain to you what the day of judgement is?

ثُمَّ مَآ أَدۡرَىٰكَ مَا يَوۡمُ ٱلدِّينِ ١٨

19. (It will be) the day when no soul shall have power (to do) anything for another: for the command, that day, will be (wholly) with Allah.

يَوۡمَ لَا تَمۡلِكُ نَفۡسٞ لِّنَفۡسٖ شَيۡـٔٗاۖ وَٱلۡأَمۡرُ يَوۡمَئِذٖ لِّلَّهِ ١٩

سُورَةُ المُطَفِّفِينَ

Surah 83: ***Al-Muttaffifin*** **(The Dealers in Fraud)**

In the name of Allah,
Most Gracious, Most Merciful.

بِسۡمِ ٱللَّهِ ٱلرَّحۡمَٰنِ ٱلرَّحِيمِ

1. Woe to those that deal in fraud -

وَيۡلٞ لِّلۡمُطَفِّفِينَ ١

2. Those who, when they have to receive by measure from men, exact full measure,

ٱلَّذِينَ إِذَا ٱكۡتَالُواْ عَلَى ٱلنَّاسِ يَسۡتَوۡفُونَ ٢

3. But when they have to give by measure or weight to men, give less than due.

وَإِذَا كَالُوهُمۡ أَو وَّزَنُوهُمۡ يُخۡسِرُونَ ٣

4. Do they not think that they will be called to account? -

أَلَا يَظُنُّ أُوْلَٰٓئِكَ أَنَّهُم مَّبۡعُوثُونَ ٤

5. On a mighty day,

لِيَوۡمٍ عَظِيمٖ ٥

6. A day when (all) mankind will stand before the Lord of the Worlds?

يَوۡمَ يَقُومُ ٱلنَّاسُ لِرَبِّ ٱلۡعَٰلَمِينَ ٦

7. Nay! Surely the record of the wicked is (preserved) in Sijjin.

كَلَّآ إِنَّ كِتَٰبَ ٱلۡفُجَّارِ لَفِي سِجِّينٖ ٧

8. And what will explain to you what Sijjin is?

وَمَآ أَدۡرَىٰكَ مَا سِجِّينٞ ٨

9. (There is) a register (fully) inscribed.

كِتَٰبٞ مَّرۡقُومٞ ٩

10. Woe, that day, to those that deny -

وَيۡلٞ يَوۡمَئِذٖ لِّلۡمُكَذِّبِينَ ١٠

11. Those that deny the day of judgement.

ٱلَّذِينَ يُكَذِّبُونَ بِيَوۡمِ ٱلدِّينِ ١١

12. And none can deny it but the transgressor beyond bounds, the sinner!

وَمَا يُكَذِّبُ بِهِۦٓ إِلَّا كُلُّ مُعۡتَدٍ أَثِيمٍ ١٢

13. When Our signs are rehearsed to him, he says, "tales of the ancients!"

إِذَا تُتۡلَىٰ عَلَيۡهِ ءَايَٰتُنَا قَالَ أَسَٰطِيرُ ٱلۡأَوَّلِينَ ١٣

14. By no means! But on their hearts is the stain of the (ill) which they do!

سكتة لطيفة على اللام

كَلَّاۖ بَلۡۜ رَانَ عَلَىٰ قُلُوبِهِم مَّا كَانُواْ يَكۡسِبُونَ ١٤

15. Verily, from (the light of) their Lord, that day, will they be veiled.

كَلَّآ إِنَّهُمۡ عَن رَّبِّهِمۡ يَوۡمَئِذٖ لَّمَحۡجُوبُونَ ١٥

16. Further, they will enter the fire of hell.

ثُمَّ إِنَّهُمۡ لَصَالُواْ ٱلۡجَحِيمِ ١٦

17. Further, it will be said to them: "This is the (reality) which you rejected as false!"

ثُمَّ يُقَالُ هَٰذَا ٱلَّذِي كُنتُم بِهِۦ تُكَذِّبُونَ ١٧

18. Nay, verily the record of the righteous is (preserved) in 'Illiyin.

كَلَّآ إِنَّ كِتَٰبَ ٱلۡأَبۡرَارِ لَفِي عِلِّيِّينَ ١٨

19. And what will explain to you what 'Illiyin is?

وَمَآ أَدۡرَىٰكَ مَا عِلِّيُّونَ ١٩

20. (There is) a register (fully) inscribed,

كِتَٰبٞ مَّرۡقُومٞ ٢٠

21. To which bear witness those nearest (to Allah).

يَشۡهَدُهُ ٱلۡمُقَرَّبُونَ ٢١

22. Truly the righteous will be in bliss:

إِنَّ ٱلۡأَبۡرَارَ لَفِي نَعِيمٍ ٢٢

23. On thrones (of dignity) will they command a sight (of all things):

عَلَى ٱلۡأَرَآئِكِ يَنظُرُونَ ٢٣

24. You will recognise in their faces the beaming brightness of bliss.

تَعۡرِفُ فِي وُجُوهِهِمۡ نَضۡرَةَ ٱلنَّعِيمِ ٢٤

25. Their thirst will be slaked with pure wine sealed:

يُسۡقَوۡنَ مِن رَّحِيقٖ مَّخۡتُومٍ ٢٥

26. The seal of it will be musk: and for this let those aspire, who have aspirations:

خِتَٰمُهُۥ مِسۡكٞۚ وَفِي ذَٰلِكَ فَلۡيَتَنَافَسِ ٱلۡمُتَنَٰفِسُونَ ٢٦

27. With it will be (given) a mixture of Tasnim:

وَمِزَاجُهُۥ مِن تَسۡنِيمٍ ٢٧

28. A spring, from (the waters) of which drink those nearest to Allah.

عَيۡنٗا يَشۡرَبُ بِهَا ٱلۡمُقَرَّبُونَ ٢٨

29. Those in sin used to laugh at those who believed,

إِنَّ ٱلَّذِينَ أَجۡرَمُواْ كَانُواْ مِنَ ٱلَّذِينَ ءَامَنُواْ يَضۡحَكُونَ ٢٩

30. And whenever they passed by them, used to wink at each other (in mockery);

وَإِذَا مَرُّواْ بِهِمۡ يَتَغَامَزُونَ ٣٠

31. And when they returned to their own people, they would return jesting;

وَإِذَا ٱنقَلَبُوٓاْ إِلَىٰٓ أَهۡلِهِمُ ٱنقَلَبُواْ فَكِهِينَ ٣١

32. And whenever they saw them, they would say, "See! These are the people truly astray!"

وَإِذَا رَأَوۡهُمۡ قَالُوٓاْ إِنَّ هَٰٓؤُلَآءِ لَضَآلُّونَ ٣٢

33. But they had not been sent as keepers over them!

وَمَآ أُرۡسِلُواْ عَلَيۡهِمۡ حَٰفِظِينَ ٣٣

34. But on this day the believers will laugh at the unbelievers:

فَٱلۡيَوۡمَ ٱلَّذِينَ ءَامَنُواْ مِنَ ٱلۡكُفَّارِ يَضۡحَكُونَ ٣٤

35. On thrones (of dignity) they will command (a sight) (of all things).

عَلَى ٱلۡأَرَآئِكِ يَنظُرُونَ ٣٥

36. Will not the unbelievers have been paid back for what they did?

هَلۡ ثُوِّبَ ٱلۡكُفَّارُ مَا كَانُواْ يَفۡعَلُونَ ٣٦

سورة الانشقاق

Surah 84: ***Al-Inshiqaq*** **(The Splitting)**

In the name of Allah,
Most Gracious, Most Merciful.

بِسْمِ ٱللَّهِ ٱلرَّحْمَٰنِ ٱلرَّحِيمِ

ثلاثة أرباع الحزب ٥٩

1. When the sky is split apart,

إِذَا ٱلسَّمَآءُ ٱنشَقَّتْ ١

2. And listens to (the command of) its Lord - and it must needs (do so) -

وَأَذِنَتْ لِرَبِّهَا وَحُقَّتْ ٢

3. And when the earth is flattened out,

وَإِذَا ٱلْأَرْضُ مُدَّتْ ٣

4. And casts out what is within it and becomes (clean) empty,

وَأَلْقَتْ مَا فِيهَا وَتَخَلَّتْ ٤

5. And listens to (the command of) its Lord - and it must needs (do so) - (then will come home the full reality).

وَأَذِنَتْ لِرَبِّهَا وَحُقَّتْ ٥

6. O you man! Verily you are ever toiling on towards your Lord - painfully toiling - but you shall meet Him.

يَٰٓأَيُّهَا ٱلْإِنسَٰنُ إِنَّكَ كَادِحٌ إِلَىٰ رَبِّكَ كَدْحًا
فَمُلَٰقِيهِ ٦

7. Then he who is given his record in his right hand,

فَأَمَّا مَنْ أُوتِىَ كِتَٰبَهُۥ بِيَمِينِهِۦ ٧

8. Soon will his account be taken by an easy reckoning,

فَسَوْفَ يُحَاسَبُ حِسَابًا يَسِيرًا ٨

9. And he will turn to his people, rejoicing!

وَيَنقَلِبُ إِلَىٰٓ أَهْلِهِۦ مَسْرُورًا ٩

10. But he who is given his record behind his back -

وَأَمَّا مَنْ أُوتِىَ كِتَٰبَهُۥ وَرَآءَ ظَهْرِهِۦ ١٠

11. Soon will he call for perdition,

فَسَوْفَ يَدْعُوا۟ ثُبُورًا ١١

وَيَصۡلَىٰ سَعِيرًا ١٢

12. And he will enter a blazing fire.

إِنَّهُۥ كَانَ فِيٓ أَهۡلِهِۦ مَسۡرُورًا ١٣

13. Truly, did he go about among his people, rejoicing!

إِنَّهُۥ ظَنَّ أَن لَّن يَحُورَ ١٤

14. Truly, did he think that he would not have to return (to Us)!

بَلَىٰٓۚ إِنَّ رَبَّهُۥ كَانَ بِهِۦ بَصِيرًا ١٥

15. Nay, nay! For his Lord was (ever) watchful of him!

فَلَآ أُقۡسِمُ بِٱلشَّفَقِ ١٦

16. So I do call to witness the ruddy glow of sunset;

وَٱلَّيۡلِ وَمَا وَسَقَ ١٧

17. The night and its homing;

وَٱلۡقَمَرِ إِذَا ٱتَّسَقَ ١٨

18. And the moon in her fullness:

لَتَرۡكَبُنَّ طَبَقًا عَن طَبَقٖ ١٩

19. You shall surely travel from stage to stage.

فَمَا لَهُمۡ لَا يُؤۡمِنُونَ ٢٠

20. What then is the matter with them, that they believe not? -

سَجۡدَة وَإِذَا قُرِئَ عَلَيۡهِمُ ٱلۡقُرۡءَانُ لَا يَسۡجُدُونَ ۩ ٢١

21. And when the Qur'an is read to them, they fall not prostrate,

بَلِ ٱلَّذِينَ كَفَرُواْ يُكَذِّبُونَ ٢٢

22. But on the contrary the unbelievers reject (it).

وَٱللَّهُ أَعۡلَمُ بِمَا يُوعُونَ ٢٣

23. But Allah has full knowledge of what they secrete (in their breasts).

فَبَشِّرۡهُم بِعَذَابٍ أَلِيمٍ ٢٤

24. So announce to them a penalty grievous,

إِلَّا ٱلَّذِينَ ءَامَنُواْ وَعَمِلُواْ ٱلصَّٰلِحَٰتِ لَهُمۡ أَجۡرٌ
غَيۡرُ مَمۡنُونِۭ ٢٥

25. Except to those who believe and work righteous deeds: for them is a reward that will never fail.

سُورَةُ البُرُوجِ

Surah 85: ***Al-Buruj*** **(The Constellations)**

In the name of Allah,
Most Gracious, Most Merciful.

بِسْمِ ٱللَّهِ ٱلرَّحْمَٰنِ ٱلرَّحِيمِ

1. By the sky, (displaying) the zodiacal signs;

وَٱلسَّمَآءِ ذَاتِ ٱلْبُرُوجِ ﴿١﴾

2. By the promised day (of judgement);

وَٱلْيَوْمِ ٱلْمَوْعُودِ ﴿٢﴾

3. By one that witnesses, and the subject of the witness -

وَشَاهِدٍ وَمَشْهُودٍ ﴿٣﴾

4. Woe to the makers of the pit (of fire),

قُتِلَ أَصْحَٰبُ ٱلْأُخْدُودِ ﴿٤﴾

5. Fire supplied (abundantly) with fuel:

ٱلنَّارِ ذَاتِ ٱلْوَقُودِ ﴿٥﴾

6. See! They sat over against the (fire),

إِذْ هُمْ عَلَيْهَا قُعُودٌ ﴿٦﴾

7. And they witnessed (all) that they were doing against the believers.

وَهُمْ عَلَىٰ مَا يَفْعَلُونَ بِٱلْمُؤْمِنِينَ شُهُودٌ ﴿٧﴾

8. And they ill-treated them for no other reason than that they believed in Allah, Exalted in power, worthy of all praise! -

وَمَا نَقَمُوا۟ مِنْهُمْ إِلَّآ أَن يُؤْمِنُوا۟ بِٱللَّهِ
ٱلْعَزِيزِ ٱلْحَمِيدِ ﴿٨﴾

9. Him to Whom belongs the dominion of the heavens and the earth! And Allah is Witness to all things.

ٱلَّذِى لَهُۥ مُلْكُ ٱلسَّمَٰوَٰتِ وَٱلْأَرْضِ ۚ وَٱللَّهُ عَلَىٰ كُلِّ
شَىْءٍ شَهِيدٌ ﴿٩﴾

10. Those who persecute (or draw into temptation) the believers, men and women, and do not turn in repentance, will have the penalty of hell: they will have the penalty of the burning fire.

إِنَّ ٱلَّذِينَ فَتَنُوا۟ ٱلْمُؤْمِنِينَ وَٱلْمُؤْمِنَٰتِ ثُمَّ لَمْ يَتُوبُوا۟
فَلَهُمْ عَذَابُ جَهَنَّمَ وَلَهُمْ عَذَابُ ٱلْحَرِيقِ ﴿١٠﴾

11. For those who believe and do righteous deeds, will be gardens, beneath which rivers flow: that is the great salvation, (the fulfilment of all desires).

إِنَّ ٱلَّذِينَ ءَامَنُوا۟ وَعَمِلُوا۟ ٱلصَّٰلِحَٰتِ لَهُمْ جَنَّٰتٌ
تَجْرِى مِن تَحْتِهَا ٱلْأَنْهَٰرُ ۚ ذَٰلِكَ ٱلْفَوْزُ ٱلْكَبِيرُ ﴿١١﴾

12. Truly strong is the grip (and power) of your Lord.

إِنَّ بَطْشَ رَبِّكَ لَشَدِيدٌ ﴿١٢﴾

13. It is He Who creates from the very beginning, and He can restore (life).

إِنَّهُۥ هُوَ يُبْدِئُ وَيُعِيدُ ﴿١٣﴾

14. And He is the Oft-Forgiving, Full of loving-kindness,

وَهُوَ ٱلْغَفُورُ ٱلْوَدُودُ ﴿١٤﴾

15. Lord of the throne of glory,

ذُو ٱلْعَرْشِ ٱلْمَجِيدُ ﴿١٥﴾

16. Doer (without let) of all that He intends.

فَعَّالٌ لِّمَا يُرِيدُ ﴿١٦﴾

17. Has the story reached you of the Forces-

هَلْ أَتَىٰكَ حَدِيثُ ٱلْجُنُودِ ﴿١٧﴾

18. Of Pharaoh and the Thamud?

فِرْعَوْنَ وَثَمُودَ ﴿١٨﴾

19. And yet the unbelievers (persist) in rejecting (the truth)!

بَلِ ٱلَّذِينَ كَفَرُوا۟ فِى تَكْذِيبٍ ﴿١٩﴾

20. But Allah does encompass them from behind!

وَٱللَّهُ مِن وَرَآئِهِم مُّحِيطٌۢ ﴿٢٠﴾

21. Nay, this is a Glorious Qur'an,

بَلْ هُوَ قُرْءَانٌ مَّجِيدٌ ﴿٢١﴾

22. (Inscribed) in a tablet preserved!

فِى لَوْحٍ مَّحْفُوظٍۭ ﴿٢٢﴾

سُورَةُ الطَّارِقِ

Surah 86: ***At-Tariq*** **(The Night Star)**

In the name of Allah,
Most Gracious, Most Merciful.

بِسْمِ ٱللَّهِ ٱلرَّحْمَٰنِ ٱلرَّحِيمِ

1. By the sky and the night-visitant (in it)-

وَٱلسَّمَآءِ وَٱلطَّارِقِ ١

2. And what will explain to you what the night-visitant is? -

وَمَآ أَدۡرَىٰكَ مَا ٱلطَّارِقُ ٢

3. (It is) the star of piercing brightness -

ٱلنَّجۡمُ ٱلثَّاقِبُ ٣

4. There is no soul but has a protector over it.

إِن كُلُّ نَفۡسٖ لَّمَّا عَلَيۡهَا حَافِظٞ ٤

5. Now let man but think from what he is created!

فَلۡيَنظُرِ ٱلۡإِنسَٰنُ مِمَّ خُلِقَ ٥

6. He is created from a drop emitted -

خُلِقَ مِن مَّآءٖ دَافِقٖ ٦

7. Proceeding from between the backbone and the ribs:

يَخۡرُجُ مِنۢ بَيۡنِ ٱلصُّلۡبِ وَٱلتَّرَآئِبِ ٧

8. Surely (Allah) is able to bring him back (to life)!

إِنَّهُۥ عَلَىٰ رَجۡعِهِۦ لَقَادِرٞ ٨

9. The day that (all) things secret will be tested,

يَوۡمَ تُبۡلَى ٱلسَّرَآئِرُ ٩

10. (Man) will have no power and no helper.

فَمَا لَهُۥ مِن قُوَّةٖ وَلَا نَاصِرٖ ١٠

11. By the firmament which returns (in its round)

وَٱلسَّمَآءِ ذَاتِ ٱلرَّجۡعِ ١١

12. And by the earth which opens out (for the gushing of springs or the sprouting of vegetation) -

وَٱلۡأَرۡضِ ذَاتِ ٱلصَّدۡعِ ١٢

13. See this is the word that distinguishes (good from evil):

إِنَّهُۥ لَقَوۡلٞ فَصۡلٞ ١٣

14. It is not a thing for amusement.

وَمَا هُوَ بِٱلۡهَزۡلِ ١٤

15. As for them, they are but plotting a scheme,

إِنَّهُمۡ يَكِيدُونَ كَيۡدٗا ١٥

16. And I am planning a scheme.

وَأَكِيدُ كَيْدًا ﴿١٦﴾

17. Therefore, grant a delay to the unbelievers: give respite to them gently (for a while).

فَمَهِّلِ ٱلْكَٰفِرِينَ أَمْهِلْهُمْ رُوَيْدًۢا ﴿١٧﴾

سُورَةُ الأَعْلَىٰ

Surah 87: ***Al-A'la*** **(The Most High)**

In the name of Allah,
Most Gracious, Most Merciful.

بِسْمِ ٱللَّهِ ٱلرَّحْمَٰنِ ٱلرَّحِيمِ

1. Glorify the name of your Guardian-Lord Most High,

الحزب ٦٠ سَبِّحِ ٱسْمَ رَبِّكَ ٱلْأَعْلَى ﴿١﴾

2. Who has created, and further, given order and proportion;

ٱلَّذِى خَلَقَ فَسَوَّىٰ ﴿٢﴾

3. Who has ordained laws. And granted guidance;

وَٱلَّذِى قَدَّرَ فَهَدَىٰ ﴿٣﴾

4. And Who brings out the (green and luscious) pasture,

وَٱلَّذِىٓ أَخْرَجَ ٱلْمَرْعَىٰ ﴿٤﴾

5. And then does make it (but) swarthy stubble.

فَجَعَلَهُۥ غُثَآءً أَحْوَىٰ ﴿٥﴾

6. By degrees shall We teach you to declare (the message), so you shall not forget,

سَنُقْرِئُكَ فَلَا تَنسَىٰٓ ﴿٦﴾

7. Except as Allah wills: for He knows what is manifest and what is hidden.

إِلَّا مَا شَآءَ ٱللَّهُ ۚ إِنَّهُۥ يَعْلَمُ ٱلْجَهْرَ وَمَا يَخْفَىٰ ﴿٧﴾

8. And We will make it easy for you (to follow) the simple (path).

وَنُيَسِّرُكَ لِلْيُسْرَىٰ ﴿٨﴾

9. Therefore, give admonition in case the admonition profits (the hearer).

فَذَكِّرْ إِن نَّفَعَتِ ٱلذِّكْرَىٰ ﴿٩﴾

10. The admonition will be received by those who fear (Allah):

سَيَذَّكَّرُ مَن يَخْشَىٰ ﴿١٠﴾

11. But it will be avoided by those most unfortunate ones,

وَيَتَجَنَّبُهَا ٱلْأَشْقَى ﴿١١﴾

12. Who will enter the great fire,

ٱلَّذِى يَصْلَى ٱلنَّارَ ٱلْكُبْرَىٰ ﴿١٢﴾

13. In which they will then neither die nor live.

ثُمَّ لَا يَمُوتُ فِيهَا وَلَا يَحْيَىٰ ﴿١٣﴾

14. But those will prosper who purify themselves,

قَدْ أَفْلَحَ مَن تَزَكَّىٰ ﴿١٤﴾

15. And glorify the name of their Guardian-Lord and (lift their hearts) in prayer.

وَذَكَرَ ٱسْمَ رَبِّهِۦ فَصَلَّىٰ ﴿١٥﴾

16. Nay (see), you prefer the life of this world;

بَلْ تُؤْثِرُونَ ٱلْحَيَوٰةَ ٱلدُّنْيَا ﴿١٦﴾

17. But the hereafter is better and more enduring.

وَٱلْءَاخِرَةُ خَيْرٌ وَأَبْقَىٰٓ ﴿١٧﴾

18. And this is in the books of the earliest (revelations) -

إِنَّ هَـٰذَا لَفِى ٱلصُّحُفِ ٱلْأُولَىٰ ﴿١٨﴾

19. The books of Abraham and Moses.

صُحُفِ إِبْرَٰهِيمَ وَمُوسَىٰ ﴿١٩﴾

سُورَةُ الغَاشِيَةِ

Surah 88: ***Al-Ghashiyah*** **(The Overwhelming Event)**

In the name of Allah, Most Gracious, Most Merciful.

بِسْمِ ٱللَّهِ ٱلرَّحْمَـٰنِ ٱلرَّحِيمِ

1. Has the story reached you, of the overwhelming (event)?

هَلْ أَتَىٰكَ حَدِيثُ ٱلْغَـٰشِيَةِ ﴿١﴾

2. Some faces, that day, will be humiliated,

وُجُوهٌ يَوْمَئِذٍ خَٰشِعَةٌ ٢

3. Labouring (hard), weary -

عَامِلَةٌ نَّاصِبَةٌ ٣

4. The while they enter the blazing fire -

تَصْلَىٰ نَارًا حَامِيَةً ٤

5. The while they are given to drink, of a boiling hot spring.

تُسْقَىٰ مِنْ عَيْنٍ ءَانِيَةٍ ٥

6. No food will there be for them but a bitter Dhari

لَّيْسَ لَهُمْ طَعَامٌ إِلَّا مِن ضَرِيعٍ ٦

7. Which will neither nourish nor satisfy hunger.

لَّا يُسْمِنُ وَلَا يُغْنِي مِن جُوعٍ ٧

8. (Other) faces that day will be joyful,

وُجُوهٌ يَوْمَئِذٍ نَّاعِمَةٌ ٨

9. Pleased with their striving -

لِّسَعْيِهَا رَاضِيَةٌ ٩

10. In a garden on high,

فِي جَنَّةٍ عَالِيَةٍ ١٠

11. Where they shall hear no (word) of vanity:

لَّا تَسْمَعُ فِيهَا لَٰغِيَةً ١١

12. In it will be a bubbling spring:

فِيهَا عَيْنٌ جَارِيَةٌ ١٢

13. In it will be thrones (of dignity), raised on high,

فِيهَا سُرُرٌ مَّرْفُوعَةٌ ١٣

14. Goblets placed (ready),

وَأَكْوَابٌ مَّوْضُوعَةٌ ١٤

15. And cushions set in rows,

وَنَمَارِقُ مَصْفُوفَةٌ ١٥

16. And rich carpets (all) spread out.

وَزَرَابِيُّ مَبْثُوثَةٌ ١٦

17. Do they not look at the camels, how they are made? -

أَفَلَا يَنظُرُونَ إِلَى ٱلْإِبِلِ كَيْفَ خُلِقَتْ ١٧

18. And at the sky, how it is raised high? -

وَإِلَى ٱلسَّمَآءِ كَيْفَ رُفِعَتْ ١٨

19. And at the mountains, how they are fixed firm? -

وَإِلَى ٱلْجِبَالِ كَيْفَ نُصِبَتْ ١٩

20. And at the earth, how it is spread out?

وَإِلَى ٱلْأَرْضِ كَيْفَ سُطِحَتْ ٢٠

21. Therefore, do you give admonition, for you are one to admonish.

فَذَكِّرْ إِنَّمَآ أَنتَ مُذَكِّرٌ ٢١

22. You are not one to manage (men's) affairs.

لَّسْتَ عَلَيْهِم بِمُصَيْطِرٍ ٢٢

23. But if any turn, away and reject Allah -

إِلَّا مَن تَوَلَّىٰ وَكَفَرَ ٢٣

24. Allah will punish him with a mighty punishment.

فَيُعَذِّبُهُ ٱللَّهُ ٱلْعَذَابَ ٱلْأَكْبَرَ ٢٤

25. For to Us will be their return;

إِنَّ إِلَيْنَآ إِيَابَهُمْ ٢٥

26. Then it will be for Us to call them to account.

ثُمَّ إِنَّ عَلَيْنَا حِسَابَهُم ٢٦

سُورَةُ الفَجْرِ

Surah 89: **Al-Fajr (The Dawn)**

In the name of Allah,
Most Gracious, Most Merciful.

بِسْمِ ٱللَّهِ ٱلرَّحْمَٰنِ ٱلرَّحِيمِ

1. By the break of day;

وَٱلْفَجْرِ ١

2. By the ten nights;

وَلَيَالٍ عَشْرٍ ٢

3. By the even and odd (contrasted);

وَٱلشَّفْعِ وَٱلْوَتْرِ ٣

4. And by the night when it passes away -

وَٱلَّيْلِ إِذَا يَسْرِ ٤

5. Is there (not) in these an adjuration (or evidence) for those who understand?

هَلۡ فِي ذَٰلِكَ قَسَمٞ لِّذِي حِجۡرٍ ٥

6. Do you not see how your Lord dealt with the 'Ad (people) -

أَلَمۡ تَرَ كَيۡفَ فَعَلَ رَبُّكَ بِعَادٍ ٦

7. Of the (city of) Iram with lofty pillars,

إِرَمَ ذَاتِ ٱلۡعِمَادِ ٧

8. The like of which were not produced in (all) the land?

ٱلَّتِي لَمۡ يُخۡلَقۡ مِثۡلُهَا فِي ٱلۡبِلَٰدِ ٨

9. And with the Thamud (people), who cut out (huge) rocks in the valley? -

وَثَمُودَ ٱلَّذِينَ جَابُواْ ٱلصَّخۡرَ بِٱلۡوَادِ ٩

10. And with Pharaoh, Lord of stakes?

وَفِرۡعَوۡنَ ذِي ٱلۡأَوۡتَادِ ١٠

11. (All) these transgressed beyond bounds in the lands.

ٱلَّذِينَ طَغَوۡاْ فِي ٱلۡبِلَٰدِ ١١

12. And heaped in it mischief (on mischief).

فَأَكۡثَرُواْ فِيهَا ٱلۡفَسَادَ ١٢

13. Therefore, did your Lord pour on them a scourge of diverse chastisements:

فَصَبَّ عَلَيۡهِمۡ رَبُّكَ سَوۡطَ عَذَابٍ ١٣

14. For your Lord is (as a Guardian) on a watchtower.

إِنَّ رَبَّكَ لَبِٱلۡمِرۡصَادِ ١٤

15. Now, as for man, when his Lord tries him giving him honour and gifts, then says he, (puffed up), "My Lord has honoured me."

فَأَمَّا ٱلۡإِنسَٰنُ إِذَا مَا ٱبۡتَلَىٰهُ رَبُّهُۥ فَأَكۡرَمَهُۥ
وَنَعَّمَهُۥ فَيَقُولُ رَبِّيٓ أَكۡرَمَنِ ١٥

16. But when He tries him, restricting his subsistence for him, then says he (in despair), "My Lord has humiliated me!"

وَأَمَّآ إِذَا مَا ٱبۡتَلَىٰهُ فَقَدَرَ عَلَيۡهِ رِزۡقَهُۥ فَيَقُولُ رَبِّيٓ
أَهَٰنَنِ ١٦

17. Nay, nay! But you do not honour the orphans!

كَلَّاۖ بَل لَّا تُكۡرِمُونَ ٱلۡيَتِيمَ ١٧

18. Nor do you encourage one another to feed the poor! -

وَلَا تَحَٰٓضُّونَ عَلَىٰ طَعَامِ ٱلۡمِسۡكِينِ ١٨

19. And you devour inheritance - all with greed,

وَتَأۡكُلُونَ ٱلتُّرَاثَ أَكۡلٗا لَّمّٗا ١٩

20. And you love wealth with inordinate love!

وَتُحِبُّونَ ٱلۡمَالَ حُبّٗا جَمّٗا ٢٠

21. Nay! When the earth is pounded to powder,

كَلَّآۖ إِذَا دُكَّتِ ٱلۡأَرۡضُ دَكّٗا دَكّٗا ٢١

22. And your Lord comes, and His angels, rank upon rank,

وَجَآءَ رَبُّكَ وَٱلۡمَلَكُ صَفّٗا صَفّٗا ٢٢

23. And hell, that day, is brought (face to face) - on that day will man remember, but how will that remembrance profit him?

وَجِاْيٓءَ يَوۡمَئِذِۭ بِجَهَنَّمَۚ يَوۡمَئِذٖ يَتَذَكَّرُ
ٱلۡإِنسَٰنُ وَأَنَّىٰ لَهُ ٱلذِّكۡرَىٰ ٢٣

24. He will say: "Ah! Would that I had sent forth (good deeds) for (this) my (future) life!"

يَقُولُ يَٰلَيۡتَنِي قَدَّمۡتُ لِحَيَاتِي ٢٤

25. For, that day, His chastisement will be such as none (else) can inflict,

فَيَوۡمَئِذٖ لَّا يُعَذِّبُ عَذَابَهُۥٓ أَحَدٞ ٢٥

26. And His bonds will be such as none (other) can bind.

وَلَا يُوثِقُ وَثَاقَهُۥٓ أَحَدٞ ٢٦

27. (To the righteous soul will be said:) "O (you) soul, in (complete) rest and satisfaction!

يَٰٓأَيَّتُهَا ٱلنَّفۡسُ ٱلۡمُطۡمَئِنَّةُ ٢٧

28. Come back you to your Lord - well pleased (yourself) and well-pleasing to Him!

ٱرۡجِعِيٓ إِلَىٰ رَبِّكِ رَاضِيَةٗ مَّرۡضِيَّةٗ ٢٨

29. Enter you, then among my devotees!

فَٱدۡخُلِي فِي عِبَٰدِي ٢٩

30. Yea, enter you my heaven!"

وَٱدۡخُلِي جَنَّتِي ٣٠

سُورَةُ البَلَدِ

Surah 90: **Al-Balad** (The City)

In the name of Allah, Most Gracious, Most Merciful.

بِسْمِ ٱللَّهِ ٱلرَّحْمَٰنِ ٱلرَّحِيمِ

ربع الحزب ٦٠

1. I do call to witness this city -

لَآ أُقْسِمُ بِهَٰذَا ٱلْبَلَدِ ﴿١﴾

2. And you are a freeman of this city -

وَأَنتَ حِلُّۢ بِهَٰذَا ٱلْبَلَدِ ﴿٢﴾

3. And (the mystic ties of) parent and child -

وَوَالِدٖ وَمَا وَلَدَ ﴿٣﴾

4. Verily We have created man into toil and struggle.

لَقَدْ خَلَقْنَا ٱلْإِنسَٰنَ فِي كَبَدٍ ﴿٤﴾

5. Does he think, that none has power over him?

أَيَحْسَبُ أَن لَّن يَقْدِرَ عَلَيْهِ أَحَدٞ ﴿٥﴾

6. He may say (boastfully): "Wealth have I squandered in abundance!"

يَقُولُ أَهْلَكْتُ مَالٗا لُّبَدًا ﴿٦﴾

7. Does he think that none beholds him?

أَيَحْسَبُ أَن لَّمْ يَرَهُۥٓ أَحَدٌ ﴿٧﴾

8. Have We not made for him a pair of eyes? -

أَلَمْ نَجْعَل لَّهُۥ عَيْنَيْنِ ﴿٨﴾

9. And a tongue, and a pair of lips? -

وَلِسَانٗا وَشَفَتَيْنِ ﴿٩﴾

10. And shown him the two highways?

وَهَدَيْنَٰهُ ٱلنَّجْدَيْنِ ﴿١٠﴾

11. But he has made no haste on the path that is steep.

فَلَا ٱقْتَحَمَ ٱلْعَقَبَةَ ﴿١١﴾

12. And what will explain to you the path that is steep? -

وَمَآ أَدْرَىٰكَ مَا ٱلْعَقَبَةُ ﴿١٢﴾

13. (It is:) freeing the bondman;

فَكُّ رَقَبَةٍ ﴿١٣﴾

14. Or the giving of food in a day of privation,

أَوْ إِطْعَٰمٌ فِى يَوْمٍ ذِى مَسْغَبَةٍ ﴿١٤﴾

15. To the orphan with claims of relationship,

يَتِيمًا ذَا مَقْرَبَةٍ ﴿١٥﴾

16. Or to the needy (down) in the dust.

أَوْ مِسْكِينًا ذَا مَتْرَبَةٍ ﴿١٦﴾

17. Then will he be of those who believe, and enjoin patience, (constancy and self-restraint), and enjoin deeds of kindness and compassion.

ثُمَّ كَانَ مِنَ ٱلَّذِينَ ءَامَنُوا۟ وَتَوَاصَوْا۟ بِٱلصَّبْرِ وَتَوَاصَوْا۟
بِٱلْمَرْحَمَةِ ﴿١٧﴾

18. Such are the companions of the right hand.

أُو۟لَٰٓئِكَ أَصْحَٰبُ ٱلْمَيْمَنَةِ ﴿١٨﴾

19. But those who reject Our signs, they are the (unhappy) companions of the left hand.

وَٱلَّذِينَ كَفَرُوا۟ بِـَٔايَٰتِنَا هُمْ أَصْحَٰبُ ٱلْمَشْـَٔمَةِ ﴿١٩﴾

20. On them will be fire vaulted over (all round).

عَلَيْهِمْ نَارٌ مُّؤْصَدَةٌۢ ﴿٢٠﴾

سُورَةُ الشَّمْسِ

Surah 91: **Ash-Shams (The Sun)**

In the name of Allah,
Most Gracious, Most Merciful.

بِسْمِ ٱللَّهِ ٱلرَّحْمَٰنِ ٱلرَّحِيمِ

1. By the sun and his (glorious) splendour;

وَٱلشَّمْسِ وَضُحَىٰهَا ﴿١﴾

2. By the moon as it follows (the sun);

وَٱلْقَمَرِ إِذَا تَلَىٰهَا ﴿٢﴾

3. By the day as it shows up (the sun's) glory;

وَٱلنَّهَارِ إِذَا جَلَّىٰهَا ﴿٣﴾

4. By the night as it conceals it;

وَٱلَّيْلِ إِذَا يَغْشَىٰهَا ﴿٤﴾

5. By the firmament and its (wonderful) structure;

وَٱلسَّمَآءِ وَمَا بَنَىٰهَا ٥

6. By the earth and its (wide) expanse;

وَٱلۡأَرۡضِ وَمَا طَحَىٰهَا ٦

7. By the soul, and the proportion and order given to it;

وَنَفۡسٖ وَمَا سَوَّىٰهَا ٧

8. And its enlightenment as to its wrong and its right -

فَأَلۡهَمَهَا فُجُورَهَا وَتَقۡوَىٰهَا ٨

9. Truly he succeeds that purifies it,

قَدۡ أَفۡلَحَ مَن زَكَّىٰهَا ٩

10. And he fails that corrupts it!

وَقَدۡ خَابَ مَن دَسَّىٰهَا ١٠

11. The Thamud (people) rejected (their prophet) through their inordinate wrongdoing.

كَذَّبَتۡ ثَمُودُ بِطَغۡوَىٰهَآ ١١

12. See, the most wicked man among them was deputed (for impiety).

إِذِ ٱنۢبَعَثَ أَشۡقَىٰهَا ١٢

13. But the messenger of Allah said to them: "It is a she-camel of Allah! And (bar her not from) having her drink!"

فَقَالَ لَهُمۡ رَسُولُ ٱللَّهِ نَاقَةَ ٱللَّهِ وَسُقۡيَٰهَا ١٣

14. Then they rejected him (as a false prophet), and they hamstrung her. So their Lord, on account of their crime, obliterated their traces and made them equal (in destruction high and low)!

فَكَذَّبُوهُ فَعَقَرُوهَا فَدَمۡدَمَ عَلَيۡهِمۡ رَبُّهُم بِذَنۢبِهِمۡ
فَسَوَّىٰهَا ١٤

15. And for Him is no fear of its consequences.

وَلَا يَخَافُ عُقۡبَٰهَا ١٥

سُورَةُ ٱللَّيۡلِ

Surah 92: ***Al-Lail*** **(The Night)**

In the name of Allah,
Most Gracious, Most Merciful.

بِسۡمِ ٱللَّهِ ٱلرَّحۡمَٰنِ ٱلرَّحِيمِ

1. By the night as it conceals (the light);

وَٱلَّيۡلِ إِذَا يَغۡشَىٰ ١

2. By the day as it appears in glory;

وَٱلنَّهَارِ إِذَا تَجَلَّىٰ ٢

3. By (the mystery of) the creation of male and female -

وَمَا خَلَقَ ٱلذَّكَرَ وَٱلۡأُنثَىٰٓ ٣

4. Verily, (the ends) you strive for are diverse.

إِنَّ سَعۡيَكُمۡ لَشَتَّىٰ ٤

5. So he who gives (in charity) and fears (Allah)

فَأَمَّا مَنۡ أَعۡطَىٰ وَٱتَّقَىٰ ٥

6. And (in all sincerity) testifies to the Best -

وَصَدَّقَ بِٱلۡحُسۡنَىٰ ٦

7. We will indeed make smooth for him the path to bliss.

فَسَنُيَسِّرُهُۥ لِلۡيُسۡرَىٰ ٧

8. But he who is a greedy miser and thinks himself self-sufficient,

وَأَمَّا مَنۢ بَخِلَ وَٱسۡتَغۡنَىٰ ٨

9. And gives the lie to the best -

وَكَذَّبَ بِٱلۡحُسۡنَىٰ ٩

10. We will indeed make smooth for him the path to misery;

فَسَنُيَسِّرُهُۥ لِلۡعُسۡرَىٰ ١٠

11. Nor will his wealth profit him when he falls headlong (into the pit).

وَمَا يُغۡنِي عَنۡهُ مَالُهُۥٓ إِذَا تَرَدَّىٰٓ ١١

12. Verily We take upon Ourselves to guide,

إِنَّ عَلَيۡنَا لَلۡهُدَىٰ ١٢

13. And verily to Us (belong) the end and the beginning.

وَإِنَّ لَنَا لَلْآخِرَةَ وَالْأُولَىٰ ﴿١٣﴾

14. Therefore, do I warn you of a fire blazing fiercely;

فَأَنذَرْتُكُمْ نَارًا تَلَظَّىٰ ﴿١٤﴾

15. None shall reach it but those most unfortunate ones,

لَا يَصْلَاهَا إِلَّا الْأَشْقَى ﴿١٥﴾

16. Who give the lie to truth and turn their backs.

الَّذِي كَذَّبَ وَتَوَلَّىٰ ﴿١٦﴾

17. But those most devoted to Allah shall be removed far from it -

وَسَيُجَنَّبُهَا الْأَتْقَى ﴿١٧﴾

18. Those who spend their wealth for increase in self-purification,

الَّذِي يُؤْتِي مَالَهُ يَتَزَكَّىٰ ﴿١٨﴾

19. And have in their minds no favour from anyone for which a reward is expected in return,

وَمَا لِأَحَدٍ عِندَهُ مِن نِّعْمَةٍ تُجْزَىٰ ﴿١٩﴾

20. But only the desire to seek for the countenance of their Lord Most High;

إِلَّا ابْتِغَاءَ وَجْهِ رَبِّهِ الْأَعْلَىٰ ﴿٢٠﴾

21. And soon will they attain (complete) satisfaction.

وَلَسَوْفَ يَرْضَىٰ ﴿٢١﴾

سُورَةُ الضُّحَىٰ

Surah 93: ***Ad-Duha*** **(The Glorious Morning Light)**

In the name of Allah,
Most Gracious, Most Merciful.

بِسْمِ اللَّهِ الرَّحْمَٰنِ الرَّحِيمِ

1. By the glorious morning light,

وَالضُّحَىٰ ﴿١﴾

2. And by the night when it is still -

وَاللَّيْلِ إِذَا سَجَىٰ ﴿٢﴾

مَا وَدَّعَكَ رَبُّكَ وَمَا قَلَىٰ ٣

3. The Guardian-Lord has not forsaken you, nor is He displeased.

وَلَلْءَاخِرَةُ خَيْرٌ لَّكَ مِنَ ٱلْأُولَىٰ ٤

4. And verily the hereafter will be better for you than the present.

وَلَسَوْفَ يُعْطِيكَ رَبُّكَ فَتَرْضَىٰٓ ٥

5. And soon will your Guardian-Lord give you (that with which) you shall be well-pleased.

أَلَمْ يَجِدْكَ يَتِيمًا فَـَٔاوَىٰ ٦

6. Did He not find you an orphan and give you shelter (and care)?

وَوَجَدَكَ ضَآلًّا فَهَدَىٰ ٧

7. And He found you wandering, and He gave you guidance.

وَوَجَدَكَ عَآئِلًا فَأَغْنَىٰ ٨

8. And He found you in need, and made you independent.

فَأَمَّا ٱلْيَتِيمَ فَلَا تَقْهَرْ ٩

9. Therefore, treat not the orphan with harshness,

وَأَمَّا ٱلسَّآئِلَ فَلَا تَنْهَرْ ١٠

10. Nor repulse the petitioner (unheard);

وَأَمَّا بِنِعْمَةِ رَبِّكَ فَحَدِّثْ ١١

11. But the bounty of your Lord - rehearse and proclaim!

سُورَةُ الشَّرْحِ

Surah 94: ***Ash-Sharh*** **(The Expansion of The Breast)**

بِسْمِ ٱللَّهِ ٱلرَّحْمَٰنِ ٱلرَّحِيمِ

In the name of Allah, Most Gracious, Most Merciful.

نصف الحِزْب ٦٠

أَلَمْ نَشْرَحْ لَكَ صَدْرَكَ ١

1. Have We not expanded you your breast?

وَوَضَعْنَا عَنكَ وِزْرَكَ ٢

2. And removed from you your burden,

ٱلَّذِىٓ أَنقَضَ ظَهْرَكَ ٣

3. Which did break your back? -

4. And raised high the esteem (in which) you (are held)?

وَرَفَعۡنَا لَكَ ذِكۡرَكَ ٤

5. So, verily, with every difficulty, there is relief:

فَإِنَّ مَعَ ٱلۡعُسۡرِ يُسۡرًا ٥

6. Verily, with every difficulty there is relief.

إِنَّ مَعَ ٱلۡعُسۡرِ يُسۡرٗا ٦

7. Therefore, when you are free (from your immediate task), still labour hard,

فَإِذَا فَرَغۡتَ فَٱنصَبۡ ٧

8. And to your Lord turn (all) your attention.

وَإِلَىٰ رَبِّكَ فَٱرۡغَب ٨

سُورَةُ التِّينِ

Surah 95: ***At-Tin*** **(The Fig)**

In the name of Allah,
Most Gracious, Most Merciful.

بِسۡمِ ٱللَّهِ ٱلرَّحۡمَٰنِ ٱلرَّحِيمِ

1. By the fig and the olive,

وَٱلتِّينِ وَٱلزَّيۡتُونِ ١

2. And the mount of Sinai,

وَطُورِ سِينِينَ ٢

3. And this city of security -

وَهَٰذَا ٱلۡبَلَدِ ٱلۡأَمِينِ ٣

4. We have indeed created man in the best of moulds,

لَقَدۡ خَلَقۡنَا ٱلۡإِنسَٰنَ فِيٓ أَحۡسَنِ تَقۡوِيمٖ ٤

5. Then do We abase him (to be) the lowest of the low -

ثُمَّ رَدَدۡنَٰهُ أَسۡفَلَ سَٰفِلِينَ ٥

6. Except such as believe and do righteous deeds: for they shall have a reward unfailing.

إِلَّا ٱلَّذِينَ ءَامَنُواْ وَعَمِلُواْ ٱلصَّٰلِحَٰتِ فَلَهُمۡ أَجۡرٌ
غَيۡرُ مَمۡنُونٖ ٦

7. Then what can, after this contradict you, as to the judgement (to come)?

فَمَا يُكَذِّبُكَ بَعْدُ بِٱلدِّينِ ﴿٧﴾

8. Is not Allah the Wisest of judges?

أَلَيْسَ ٱللَّهُ بِأَحْكَمِ ٱلْحَٰكِمِينَ ﴿٨﴾

سُورَةُ العَلَق

Surah 96: ***Al-'Alaq*** **(The Clinging Clot)**

In the name of Allah,
Most Gracious, Most Merciful.

بِسْمِ ٱللَّهِ ٱلرَّحْمَٰنِ ٱلرَّحِيمِ

1. Proclaim! (or read!) In the name of your Lord and Cherisher, who created

ٱقْرَأْ بِٱسْمِ رَبِّكَ ٱلَّذِى خَلَقَ ﴿١﴾

2. Created man, out of a (mere) clot of congealed blood:

خَلَقَ ٱلْإِنسَٰنَ مِنْ عَلَقٍ ﴿٢﴾

3. Proclaim! And your Lord is Most Bountiful -

ٱقْرَأْ وَرَبُّكَ ٱلْأَكْرَمُ ﴿٣﴾

4. He Who taught (the use of) the pen -

ٱلَّذِى عَلَّمَ بِٱلْقَلَمِ ﴿٤﴾

5. Taught man that which he knew not.

عَلَّمَ ٱلْإِنسَٰنَ مَا لَمْ يَعْلَمْ ﴿٥﴾

6. Nay, but man does transgress all bounds,

كَلَّآ إِنَّ ٱلْإِنسَٰنَ لَيَطْغَىٰٓ ﴿٦﴾

7. In that he looks upon himself as self-sufficient.

أَن رَّءَاهُ ٱسْتَغْنَىٰٓ ﴿٧﴾

8. Verily, to your Lord is the return (of all).

إِنَّ إِلَىٰ رَبِّكَ ٱلرُّجْعَىٰٓ ﴿٨﴾

9. See you one who forbids -

أَرَءَيْتَ ٱلَّذِى يَنْهَىٰ ﴿٩﴾

10. A votary when he (turns) to pray?

عَبْدًا إِذَا صَلَّىٰٓ ﴿١٠﴾

11. See you if he is on (the road of) guidance? -

أَرَءَيْتَ إِن كَانَ عَلَى ٱلْهُدَىٰٓ ﴿١١﴾

12. Or enjoins righteousness?

أَوْ أَمَرَ بِٱلتَّقْوَىٰٓ ١٢

13. See you if he denies (truth) and turns away?

أَرَءَيْتَ إِن كَذَّبَ وَتَوَلَّىٰٓ ١٣

14. Knows he not that Allah does see?

أَلَمْ يَعْلَم بِأَنَّ ٱللَّهَ يَرَىٰ ١٤

15. Let him beware! If he desist not, We will drag him by the forelock -

كَلَّا لَئِن لَّمْ يَنتَهِ لَنَسْفَعًۢا بِٱلنَّاصِيَةِ ١٥

16. A lying, sinful forelock!

نَاصِيَةٍ كَٰذِبَةٍ خَاطِئَةٍ ١٦

17. Then, let him call (for help) to his council (of comrades):

فَلْيَدْعُ نَادِيَهُۥ ١٧

18. We will call on the angels of punishment (to deal with him)!

سَنَدْعُ ٱلزَّبَانِيَةَ ١٨

19. Nay, heed him not: but bow down in adoration and bring yourself the closer (to Allah)!

سَجْدَة — كَلَّا لَا تُطِعْهُ وَٱسْجُدْ وَٱقْتَرِب ۩ ١٩

سُورَةُ الْقَدْرِ

Surah 97: ***Al-Qadr*** **(The Night of Power)**

In the name of Allah,
Most Gracious, Most Merciful.

بِسْمِ ٱللَّهِ ٱلرَّحْمَٰنِ ٱلرَّحِيمِ

1. We have indeed revealed this (message) in the night of power:

إِنَّآ أَنزَلْنَٰهُ فِى لَيْلَةِ ٱلْقَدْرِ ١

2. And what will explain to you what the night of power is?

وَمَآ أَدْرَىٰكَ مَا لَيْلَةُ ٱلْقَدْرِ ٢

3. The night of power is better than a thousand months.

لَيْلَةُ ٱلْقَدْرِ خَيْرٌ مِّنْ أَلْفِ شَهْرٍ ٣

4. In it come down the angels and the spirit by Allah's permission, on every errand:

تَنَزَّلُ ٱلْمَلَـٰٓئِكَةُ وَٱلرُّوحُ فِيهَا بِإِذْنِ رَبِّهِم مِّن كُلِّ
أَمْرٍ ٤

5. Peace! This until the rise of morning!

سَلَـٰمٌ هِىَ حَتَّىٰ مَطْلَعِ ٱلْفَجْرِ ٥

سُورَةُ البَيِّنَةِ

Surah 98: ***Al-Bayyinah*** **(The Clear Evidence)**

In the name of Allah,
Most Gracious, Most Merciful.

بِسْمِ ٱللَّهِ ٱلرَّحْمَـٰنِ ٱلرَّحِيمِ

1. Those who reject (truth) among the People of the Book and among the polytheists, were not going to depart (from their ways) until there should come to them clear evidence -

لَمْ يَكُنِ ٱلَّذِينَ كَفَرُوا۟ مِنْ أَهْلِ ٱلْكِتَـٰبِ وَٱلْمُشْرِكِينَ
مُنفَكِّينَ حَتَّىٰ تَأْتِيَهُمُ ٱلْبَيِّنَةُ ١

2. A messenger from Allah rehearsing scriptures kept pure and holy:

رَسُولٌ مِّنَ ٱللَّهِ يَتْلُوا۟ صُحُفًا مُّطَهَّرَةً ٢

3. In which are laws (or decrees) right and straight.

فِيهَا كُتُبٌ قَيِّمَةٌ ٣

4. Nor did the People of the Book make schisms, until after there came to them clear evidence.

وَمَا تَفَرَّقَ ٱلَّذِينَ أُوتُوا۟ ٱلْكِتَـٰبَ إِلَّا مِنۢ بَعْدِ مَا جَآءَتْهُمُ
ٱلْبَيِّنَةُ ٤

5. And they have been commanded no more than this: to worship Allah, offering Him sincere devotion, being True (in faith); to establish regular prayer; and to practice regular charity; and that is the religion right and straight.

وَمَآ أُمِرُوٓا۟ إِلَّا لِيَعْبُدُوا۟ ٱللَّهَ مُخْلِصِينَ لَهُ ٱلدِّينَ
حُنَفَآءَ وَيُقِيمُوا۟ ٱلصَّلَوٰةَ وَيُؤْتُوا۟ ٱلزَّكَوٰةَ ۚ وَذَٰلِكَ
دِينُ ٱلْقَيِّمَةِ ٥

6. Those who reject (truth), among the People of the Book and among the

إِنَّ ٱلَّذِينَ كَفَرُوا۟ مِنْ أَهْلِ ٱلْكِتَـٰبِ وَٱلْمُشْرِكِينَ

polytheists, will be in hellfire, to dwell in it (for ever). They are the worst of creatures.

فِي نَارِ جَهَنَّمَ خَٰلِدِينَ فِيهَآۚ أُوْلَٰٓئِكَ هُمۡ شَرُّ ٱلۡبَرِيَّةِ ٦

7. Those who have faith and do righteous deeds - they are the best of creatures.

إِنَّ ٱلَّذِينَ ءَامَنُواْ وَعَمِلُواْ ٱلصَّٰلِحَٰتِ أُوْلَٰٓئِكَ
هُمۡ خَيۡرُ ٱلۡبَرِيَّةِ ٧

8. Their reward is with Allah: gardens of eternity, beneath which rivers flow; they will dwell in it for ever; Allah well pleased with them, and they with Him: all this for such as fear their Lord and Cherisher.

جَزَآؤُهُمۡ عِندَ رَبِّهِمۡ جَنَّٰتُ عَدۡنٖ تَجۡرِي مِن
تَحۡتِهَا ٱلۡأَنۡهَٰرُ خَٰلِدِينَ فِيهَآ أَبَدٗاۖ رَّضِيَ ٱللَّهُ عَنۡهُمۡ
وَرَضُواْ عَنۡهُۚ ذَٰلِكَ لِمَنۡ خَشِيَ رَبَّهُۥ ٨

سُورَةُ الزَّلۡزَلَةِ

Surah 99: ***Al-Zalzalah*** **(The Earthquake)**

In the name of Allah,
Most Gracious, Most Merciful.

بِسۡمِ ٱللَّهِ ٱلرَّحۡمَٰنِ ٱلرَّحِيمِ

1. When the earth is shaken to her (utmost) convulsion,

إِذَا زُلۡزِلَتِ ٱلۡأَرۡضُ زِلۡزَالَهَا ١

2. And the earth throws up its burdens (from within),

وَأَخۡرَجَتِ ٱلۡأَرۡضُ أَثۡقَالَهَا ٢

3. And man cries (distressed): 'What is the matter with it?' -

وَقَالَ ٱلۡإِنسَٰنُ مَا لَهَا ٣

4. On that day will it declare its tidings:

يَوۡمَئِذٖ تُحَدِّثُ أَخۡبَارَهَا ٤

5. For that your Lord will have given it inspiration.

بِأَنَّ رَبَّكَ أَوۡحَىٰ لَهَا ٥

6. On that day will men proceed in companies sorted out, to be shown the deeds that they (had done).

يَوۡمَئِذٖ يَصۡدُرُ ٱلنَّاسُ أَشۡتَاتٗا لِّيُرَوۡاْ أَعۡمَٰلَهُمۡ ٦

7. Then shall anyone who has done an atom's weight of good, see it!

فَمَن يَعۡمَلۡ مِثۡقَالَ ذَرَّةٍ خَيۡرٗا يَرَهُۥ ٧

8. And anyone who has done an atom's weight of evil, shall see it.

وَمَن يَعۡمَلۡ مِثۡقَالَ ذَرَّةٖ شَرّٗا يَرَهُۥ ٨

سُورَةُ العَادِيَاتِ

Surah 100: ***Al-'Adiyat*** **(Those that Run)**

In the name of Allah,
Most Gracious, Most Merciful.

بِسۡمِ ٱللَّهِ ٱلرَّحۡمَٰنِ ٱلرَّحِيمِ

1. By the (steeds) that run, with panting (breath),

وَٱلۡعَٰدِيَٰتِ ضَبۡحٗا ١

2. And strike sparks of fire,

فَٱلۡمُورِيَٰتِ قَدۡحٗا ٢

3. And push home the charge in the morning,

فَٱلۡمُغِيرَٰتِ صُبۡحٗا ٣

4. And raise the dust in clouds the while,

فَأَثَرۡنَ بِهِۦ نَقۡعٗا ٤

5. And penetrate forthwith into the midst (of the foe) en masse -

فَوَسَطۡنَ بِهِۦ جَمۡعًا ٥

6. Truly man is, to his Lord, ungrateful;

إِنَّ ٱلۡإِنسَٰنَ لِرَبِّهِۦ لَكَنُودٞ ٦

7. And to that (fact) he bears witness (by his deeds);

وَإِنَّهُۥ عَلَىٰ ذَٰلِكَ لَشَهِيدٞ ٧

8. And violent is he in his love of wealth.

وَإِنَّهُۥ لِحُبِّ ٱلۡخَيۡرِ لَشَدِيدٌ ٨

9. Does he not know - when that which is in the graves is scattered abroad,

۞ أَفَلَا يَعۡلَمُ إِذَا بُعۡثِرَ مَا فِي ٱلۡقُبُورِ ٩ ثلاثة أرباع الحزب ٦٠

10. And that which is (locked up) in (human) breasts is made manifest -

وَحُصِّلَ مَا فِي ٱلصُّدُورِ ١٠

11. That their Lord had been well-acquainted with them, (even to) that day?

إِنَّ رَبَّهُم بِهِمْ يَوْمَئِذٍ لَّخَبِيرٌۢ ﴿١١﴾

سُورَةُ الْقَارِعَةِ

Surah 101: ***Al-Qari'ah*** **(Day of Noise and Clamour)**

In the name of Allah,
Most Gracious, Most Merciful.

بِسْمِ ٱللَّهِ ٱلرَّحْمَٰنِ ٱلرَّحِيمِ

1. The (day) of noise and clamour:

ٱلْقَارِعَةُ ﴿١﴾

2. What is the (day) of noise and clamour?

مَا ٱلْقَارِعَةُ ﴿٢﴾

3. And what will explain to you what the (day) of noise and clamour is?

وَمَآ أَدْرَىٰكَ مَا ٱلْقَارِعَةُ ﴿٣﴾

4. (It is) a day on which men will be like moths scattered about,

يَوْمَ يَكُونُ ٱلنَّاسُ كَٱلْفَرَاشِ ٱلْمَبْثُوثِ ﴿٤﴾

5. And the mountains will be like carded wool.

وَتَكُونُ ٱلْجِبَالُ كَٱلْعِهْنِ ٱلْمَنفُوشِ ﴿٥﴾

6. Then, he whose balance (of good deeds) will be (found) heavy,

فَأَمَّا مَن ثَقُلَتْ مَوَٰزِينُهُۥ ﴿٦﴾

7. Will be in a life of good pleasure and satisfaction.

فَهُوَ فِى عِيشَةٍ رَّاضِيَةٍ ﴿٧﴾

8. But he whose balance (of good deeds) will be (found) light -

وَأَمَّا مَنْ خَفَّتْ مَوَٰزِينُهُۥ ﴿٨﴾

9. Will have his home in a (bottomless) pit.

فَأُمُّهُۥ هَاوِيَةٌ ﴿٩﴾

10. And what will explain to you what this is?

وَمَآ أَدْرَىٰكَ مَا هِيَهْ ﴿١٠﴾

11. (It is) a fire blazing fiercely!

نَارٌ حَامِيَةٌۢ ﴿١١﴾

سُورَةُ التَّكَاثُرِ

*Surah 102: **At-Takathur*** **(The Piling Up)**

***In the name of Allah,
Most Gracious, Most Merciful.***

بِسۡمِ ٱللَّهِ ٱلرَّحۡمَٰنِ ٱلرَّحِيمِ

1. The mutual rivalry for piling up (the good things of this world) diverts you (from the more serious things),

أَلۡهَىٰكُمُ ٱلتَّكَاثُرُ ١

2. Until you visit the graves.

حَتَّىٰ زُرۡتُمُ ٱلۡمَقَابِرَ ٢

3. But nay, you soon shall know (the reality).

كَلَّا سَوۡفَ تَعۡلَمُونَ ٣

4. Again, you soon shall know!

ثُمَّ كَلَّا سَوۡفَ تَعۡلَمُونَ ٤

5. Nay, were you to know with certainty of mind (You would beware!)

كَلَّا لَوۡ تَعۡلَمُونَ عِلۡمَ ٱلۡيَقِينِ ٥

6. You shall certainly see hellfire!

لَتَرَوُنَّ ٱلۡجَحِيمَ ٦

7. Again, you shall see it with certainty of sight!

ثُمَّ لَتَرَوُنَّهَا عَيۡنَ ٱلۡيَقِينِ ٧

8. Then, shall you be questioned that day about the joy (you indulged in!)

ثُمَّ لَتُسۡـَٔلُنَّ يَوۡمَئِذٍ عَنِ ٱلنَّعِيمِ ٨

سُورَةُ العَصۡرِ

*Surah 103: **Al-'Asr*** **(Time Through the Ages)**

***In the name of Allah,
Most Gracious, Most Merciful.***

بِسۡمِ ٱللَّهِ ٱلرَّحۡمَٰنِ ٱلرَّحِيمِ

1. By (the token of) time (through the ages),

وَٱلۡعَصۡرِ ١

2. Verily man is in loss,

إِنَّ ٱلۡإِنسَٰنَ لَفِي خُسۡرٍ ٢

3. Except such as have faith, and do righteous deeds, and (join together) in the mutual teaching of truth, and of patience and constancy.

إِلَّا ٱلَّذِينَ ءَامَنُواْ وَعَمِلُواْ ٱلصَّٰلِحَٰتِ وَتَوَاصَوۡاْ
بِٱلۡحَقِّ وَتَوَاصَوۡاْ بِٱلصَّبۡرِ ٣

سُورَةُ الهُمَزَةِ

Surah 104: **Al-Humazah (The Scandal Mongerer)**

In the name of Allah,
Most Gracious, Most Merciful.

بِسۡمِ ٱللَّهِ ٱلرَّحۡمَٰنِ ٱلرَّحِيمِ

1. Woe to every (kind of) scandalmonger and backbiter,

وَيۡلٞ لِّكُلِّ هُمَزَةٖ لُّمَزَةٍ ١

2. Who piles up wealth and lays it by,

ٱلَّذِي جَمَعَ مَالٗا وَعَدَّدَهُۥ ٢

3. Thinking that his wealth would make him last for ever!

يَحۡسَبُ أَنَّ مَالَهُۥٓ أَخۡلَدَهُۥ ٣

4. By no means! He will be sure to be thrown into that which breaks to pieces.

كَلَّاۖ لَيُنۢبَذَنَّ فِي ٱلۡحُطَمَةِ ٤

5. And what will explain to you that which breaks to pieces?

وَمَآ أَدۡرَىٰكَ مَا ٱلۡحُطَمَةُ ٥

6. (It is) the fire of (the wrath of) Allah kindled (to a blaze),

نَارُ ٱللَّهِ ٱلۡمُوقَدَةُ ٦

7. The which does mount (right) to the hearts:

ٱلَّتِي تَطَّلِعُ عَلَى ٱلۡأَفۡـِٔدَةِ ٧

8. It shall be made into a vault over them,

إِنَّهَا عَلَيۡهِم مُّؤۡصَدَةٞ ٨

9. In columns outstretched.

فِي عَمَدٖ مُّمَدَّدَةِۭ ٩

سُورَةُ الفِيلِ

Surah 105: **Al-Fil (The Elephant)**

***In the name of Allah,
Most Gracious, Most Merciful.***

بِسۡمِ ٱللَّهِ ٱلرَّحۡمَٰنِ ٱلرَّحِيمِ

1. Do you not see how your Lord dealt with the companions of the elephant?

أَلَمۡ تَرَ كَيۡفَ فَعَلَ رَبُّكَ بِأَصۡحَٰبِ ٱلۡفِيلِ ١

2. Did He not make their treacherous plan go astray?

أَلَمۡ يَجۡعَلۡ كَيۡدَهُمۡ فِي تَضۡلِيلٖ ٢

3. And He sent against them flights of birds,

وَأَرۡسَلَ عَلَيۡهِمۡ طَيۡرًا أَبَابِيلَ ٣

4. Striking them with stones of baked clay.

تَرۡمِيهِم بِحِجَارَةٖ مِّن سِجِّيلٖ ٤

5. Then did He make them like an empty field of stalks and straw, (of which the corn) has been eaten up.

فَجَعَلَهُمۡ كَعَصۡفٖ مَّأۡكُولِۭ ٥

سُورَةُ قُرَيۡشٍ

Surah 106: **Quraysh (The Tribe of Quraysh)**

***In the name of Allah,
Most Gracious, Most Merciful.***

بِسۡمِ ٱللَّهِ ٱلرَّحۡمَٰنِ ٱلرَّحِيمِ

1. For the covenants (of security and safeguard enjoyed) by the Quraysh,

لِإِيلَٰفِ قُرَيۡشٍ ١

2. Their covenants (covering) journeys by winter and summer-

إِۦلَٰفِهِمۡ رِحۡلَةَ ٱلشِّتَآءِ وَٱلصَّيۡفِ ٢

3. Let them adore the Lord of this house,

فَلۡيَعۡبُدُواْ رَبَّ هَٰذَا ٱلۡبَيۡتِ ٣

4. Who provides them with food against hunger, and with security against fear (of danger).

ٱلَّذِيٓ أَطۡعَمَهُم مِّن جُوعٖ وَءَامَنَهُم مِّنۡ خَوۡفِۭ ٤

سُورَةُ المَاعُونِ

Surah 107: ***Al-Ma'un*** **(The Neighbourly Assistance)**

In the name of Allah,
Most Gracious, Most Merciful.

بِسْمِ ٱللَّهِ ٱلرَّحْمَٰنِ ٱلرَّحِيمِ

1. Do you see who denies the judgement (to come)?

أَرَءَيْتَ ٱلَّذِى يُكَذِّبُ بِٱلدِّينِ ١

2. Then such is the (man) who repulses the orphan (with harshness),

فَذَٰلِكَ ٱلَّذِى يَدُعُّ ٱلْيَتِيمَ ٢

3. And encourages not the feeding of the needy.

وَلَا يَحُضُّ عَلَىٰ طَعَامِ ٱلْمِسْكِينِ ٣

4. So woe to the worshippers,

فَوَيْلٌ لِّلْمُصَلِّينَ ٤

5. Who are neglectful of their prayers,

ٱلَّذِينَ هُمْ عَن صَلَاتِهِمْ سَاهُونَ ٥

6. Those who (want but) to be seen (of men),

ٱلَّذِينَ هُمْ يُرَآءُونَ ٦

7. But refuse (to supply) (even) neighbourly needs.

وَيَمْنَعُونَ ٱلْمَاعُونَ ٧

سُورَةُ الكَوثَرِ

Surah 108: ***Al-Kauthar*** **(The Abundance)**

In the name of Allah,
Most Gracious, Most Merciful.

بِسْمِ ٱللَّهِ ٱلرَّحْمَٰنِ ٱلرَّحِيمِ

1. To you have We granted the fount (of abundance).

إِنَّآ أَعْطَيْنَٰكَ ٱلْكَوْثَرَ ١

2. Therefore, to your Lord turn in prayer and sacrifice.

فَصَلِّ لِرَبِّكَ وَٱنْحَرْ ٢

3. For he who hates you - he will be cut off (from future hope).

إِنَّ شَانِئَكَ هُوَ ٱلْأَبْتَرُ ٣

سُورَةُ الكَافِرُونَ

Surah 109: ***Al-Kafirun*** **(Those Who Reject Faith)**

In the name of Allah,
Most Gracious, Most Merciful.

بِسْمِ ٱللَّهِ ٱلرَّحْمَٰنِ ٱلرَّحِيمِ

1. Say: O you that reject faith!

قُلْ يَٰٓأَيُّهَا ٱلْكَٰفِرُونَ ١

2. I worship not that which you worship,

لَآ أَعْبُدُ مَا تَعْبُدُونَ ٢

3. Nor will you worship that which I worship.

وَلَآ أَنتُمْ عَٰبِدُونَ مَآ أَعْبُدُ ٣

4. And I will not worship that which you used to worship,

وَلَآ أَنَا۠ عَابِدٌ مَّا عَبَدتُّمْ ٤

5. Nor will you worship that which I worship.

وَلَآ أَنتُمْ عَٰبِدُونَ مَآ أَعْبُدُ ٥

6. To you be your way, and to me mine.

لَكُمْ دِينُكُمْ وَلِىَ دِينِ ٦

سُورَةُ النَّصرِ

Surah 110: ***An-Nasr*** **(The Help)**

In the name of Allah,
Most Gracious, Most Merciful.

بِسْمِ ٱللَّهِ ٱلرَّحْمَٰنِ ٱلرَّحِيمِ

1. When comes the help of Allah, and victory,

إِذَا جَآءَ نَصْرُ ٱللَّهِ وَٱلْفَتْحُ ١

2. And you do see the people enter Allah's religion in crowds,

وَرَأَيْتَ ٱلنَّاسَ يَدْخُلُونَ فِى دِينِ ٱللَّهِ أَفْوَاجًا ٢

3. Celebrate the praises of your Lord, and pray for His forgiveness: for He is Oft-Returning (in grace and mercy).

فَسَبِّحْ بِحَمْدِ رَبِّكَ وَٱسْتَغْفِرْهُ ۚ إِنَّهُۥ كَانَ تَوَّابًۢا ٣

سُورَةُ المَسَد

Surah 111: ***Al-Masad*** **(The Palm Fibre) or** ***Al-Lahab*** **(The Flame)**

In the name of Allah,
Most Gracious, Most Merciful.

بِسْمِ ٱللَّهِ ٱلرَّحْمَٰنِ ٱلرَّحِيمِ

1. Perish the hands of the father of flame! Perish he!

تَبَّتْ يَدَآ أَبِى لَهَبٍ وَتَبَّ ١

2. No profit to him from all his wealth and all his gains!

مَآ أَغْنَىٰ عَنْهُ مَالُهُۥ وَمَا كَسَبَ ٢

3. Burnt soon will he be in a fire of blazing flame!

سَيَصْلَىٰ نَارًا ذَاتَ لَهَبٍ ٣

4. His wife shall carry the (crackling) wood - as fuel! -

وَٱمْرَأَتُهُۥ حَمَّالَةَ ٱلْحَطَبِ ٤

5. A twisted rope of palm-leaf fibre round her (own) neck!

فِى جِيدِهَا حَبْلٌ مِّن مَّسَدٍۭ ٥

سُورَةُ الإخلاص

Surah 112: ***Al-Ikhlas*** **(The Purity of Faith)**

In the name of Allah,
Most Gracious, Most Merciful.

بِسْمِ ٱللَّهِ ٱلرَّحْمَٰنِ ٱلرَّحِيمِ

1. Say: He is Allah, the One and Only;

قُلْ هُوَ ٱللَّهُ أَحَدٌ ١

2. Allah, the Eternal, Absolute;

ٱللَّهُ ٱلصَّمَدُ ٢

3. He begets not, nor is He begotten;

لَمْ يَلِدْ وَلَمْ يُولَدْ ٣

4. And there is none like unto Him.

وَلَمْ يَكُن لَّهُۥ كُفُوًا أَحَدٌۢ ٤

سُورَةُ الفَلَقِ

Surah 113: ***Al-Falaq*** **(The Dawn)**

In the name of Allah,
Most Gracious, Most Merciful.

بِسْمِ ٱللَّهِ ٱلرَّحْمَٰنِ ٱلرَّحِيمِ

1. Say: I seek refuge with the Lord of the dawn,

قُلْ أَعُوذُ بِرَبِّ ٱلْفَلَقِ ١

2. From the mischief of created things;

مِن شَرِّ مَا خَلَقَ ٢

3. From the mischief of darkness as it overspreads;

وَمِن شَرِّ غَاسِقٍ إِذَا وَقَبَ ٣

4. From the mischief of those who practice secret arts;

وَمِن شَرِّ ٱلنَّفَّٰثَٰتِ فِى ٱلْعُقَدِ ٤

5. And from the mischief of the envious one as he practises envy.

وَمِن شَرِّ حَاسِدٍ إِذَا حَسَدَ ٥

سُورَةُ النَّاسِ

Surah 114: ***An-Nas*** **(Mankind)**

In the name of Allah,
Most Gracious, Most Merciful.

بِسْمِ ٱللَّهِ ٱلرَّحْمَٰنِ ٱلرَّحِيمِ

1. Say: I seek refuge with the Lord and Cherisher of mankind,

قُلْ أَعُوذُ بِرَبِّ ٱلنَّاسِ ١

2. The King (or Ruler) of mankind,

مَلِكِ ٱلنَّاسِ ٢

3. The God (or Judge) of mankind,

إِلَٰهِ ٱلنَّاسِ ٣

4. From the mischief of the whisperer (of evil) who withdraws (after his whisper)-

مِن شَرِّ ٱلْوَسْوَاسِ ٱلْخَنَّاسِ ٤

5. (The same) who whispers into the hearts of mankind -

ٱلَّذِى يُوَسْوِسُ فِى صُدُورِ ٱلنَّاسِ ٥

6. Among Jinns and among men.

مِنَ ٱلْجِنَّةِ وَٱلنَّاسِ ٦

دُعَاءُ خَتْمِ الْقُرْآنِ

Dua after Completion of the Qur'an

اَللّٰهُمَّ
آنِسْ وَحْشَتِي فِي
قَبْرِي، اَللّٰهُمَّ ارْحَمْنِي بِالْقُرْآنِ
الْعَظِيمِ وَاجْعَلْهُ لِي إِمَامًا وَّنُورًا وَّهُدًى
وَّرَحْمَةً، اَللّٰهُمَّ ذَكِّرْنِي مِنْهُ مَا نَسِيتُ
وَعَلِّمْنِي مِنْهُ مَا جَهِلْتُ وَارْزُقْنِي
تِلَاوَتَهُ آنَاءَ اللَّيْلِ وَآنَاءَ النَّهَارِ
وَاجْعَلْهُ لِي حُجَّةً يَّا رَبَّ
الْعَالَمِينَ.

O Allah! Grant me peace (with the light of Qur'an) during my frightening loneliness in the grave.

O Allah! Let me receive Your mercy by means of the Noble Qur'an and make it my leader as well as a source of light, guidance and grace for me.

O Allah! Revive my memory of whatever I was made to forget (from the Noble Qur'an), grant me understanding of whatever part I know not, enable me to recite it during hours of day and night and make it the provider of my final testimony (in all matters), O Lord of the worlds!

Brief Index of Subjects

*Due to the recurrence of the mention of the name of Allah throughout the Qur'an, only verses containing specific information on the given subjects have been included for reference.

E

F

Q

R

S

T

U

V

W

Notes

Notes

Notes

Notes